Readings and a Discussion Guide for a Seminar on

LEGAL *and*
POLITICAL PROBLEMS
of WORLD ORDER

Compiled and Edited by

SAUL H. MENDLOVITZ

Professor of Law, Rutgers
University Law School

Published and Distributed by

THE FUND FOR EDUCATION CONCERNING
WORLD PEACE THROUGH WORLD LAW
11 West 42nd Street, New York 36, N.Y.

preliminary edition

This book has been made possible

through the generosity of

the D.S. and R.H. Gottesman Foundation

and the Miriam and Ira D. Wallach Foundation.

Preliminary Edition

This preliminary edition includes all the readings and discussion questions which will be contained in the final edition. The final edition will contain expanded introductory remarks to the various sessions, additional editorial comment, and a more comprehensive bibliography. This preliminary edition is published so that the materials in the book may be available for the many seminar groups and organizations who have been looking forward to studying them.

Foreword

This set of readings is concerned with the most important common problem facing politically organized society: the prevention of war and the establishment of peace. Hopefully the seminar groups for which this book has been designed will find investigation and discussion of its material useful for initiating affirmative solutions to that momentous and imperative task.

There are many ways one could begin to investigate a problem of this broad complexity. The perspective chosen here has been the contribution that law might make to establishing and maintaining peace. The decision to select this particular view is based on three considerations. First, it is now the articulated policy of the United States to work for a disarmed world under law. The implications of this consideration will be discussed more fully below. Secondly, law in domestic society has been used as an instrument of social control to minimize conflict, resolve disputes, redress harm and promote justice and general welfare. It seems useful therefore to inquire to what extent law might be similarly used in the international community to accomplish the same purposes. Finally, as will become readily apparent throughout the seminar, legal processes and institutions are in constant interaction with other major societal processes and institutions and therefore provide a realistic and logical point of departure for looking into the vast range of intricate problems that require understanding if war is to be prevented.

Since 1956 when President Eisenhower declared in a nation-wide radio address that there could be no peace without law, the Government of the United States has been moving steadily toward the development of policy and program to implement that principle. As Arthur Larson has pointed out, President Eisenhower elaborated this theme in two State of the Union Messages, in an address at the University of New Delhi and in a notable speech before the American Bar Association in 1960. Secretary of State Christian Herter, in the closing months of the Eisenhower Administration made a detailed presentation of this point of view before the National Press Conference.

On September 25, 1961, President Kennedy spoke the following words to the Sixteenth Session of the United Nations: "We prefer world law in an age of self-determination to world war in an age of mass-extermination." And again, "To destroy arms, however, is not enough. We must create as we destroy, in creating world-wide law and law enforcement as we outlaw world-wide war and weapons." On the same day the Department of State issued a pamphlet, "Freedom from War — The US Program for a General and Complete Disarmament in a Peaceful World," which reiterated the desire to subject "the use of force to the rule of law." And finally, in May 1962, the United States Government submitted to the Disarmament Conference in Geneva a plan for complete and general disarmament which called for the increased use of the International Court of Justice and the establishment of a United Nations Police Force.

Despite the growing recognition in this country and elsewhere of the part that law might play in establishing the conditions of a more orderly, peaceful world, little progress has been made. It is certainly true that the task of preventing war appears to be overwhelmingly formidable, involving as it does control of behavior patterns rooted deep in human nature and frequently manifested in sophisticated ideological commitments which support massive and complex social organizations. Because of this responsible government officials who must deal with these problems would welcome not only support and criticism of their efforts, but ideas, programs, and suggestions to aid them in working out this magnificent goal of establishing peace through law. These seminars are organized to provide materials for the serious thought and discussion that must precede constructive participation with our government in reaching the defined goal.

Given our perspective of evaluating the use of law to prevent war, we have designed a series of twelve sessions (see Seminar Outline and Reading Assignments, page 1) to examine the following: the concept of law and the part it now plays in regulating the threat of force or the use of force among nations; the effectiveness of present peace-keeping machinery; the problem of disarmament will be explored in some detail; in addition, major political problems which appear to block progress in establishing a peace system will be investigated in a number of contexts.

To explore these problems we have found it very helpful to use *World Peace Through World Law* by Grenville Clark and Louis B. Sohn as a companion text. This book offers comprehensive and detailed proposals for a model of the world legal structure which the authors feel is required to achieve and maintain peace. A carefully written introduction gives the controlling line of the authors' thinking and the basic principles that they see underlying any structure adequate to this task. They have cast their model in the form of an extensive revision of the UN Charter which permits us to compare the present workings and difficulties of the UN as now constituted with a possible revised model. We shall, of course, want to evaluate the proposed revisions, including the series of comments dealing with reasons for each proposed revision which the authors have provided. An essential condition and integral part of their plan is contained in a comprehensive and detailed set of proposals for achieving complete and general disarmament, a subject to which the final third of this course will be devoted. The extensiveness and detail of their proposals in this area provides us with a set of basic materials with which to examine various other approaches and programs that have been suggested. Although their emphasis throughout the entire model is on what is actually needed for an effective, operating world legal structure, they have recognized and attempted to deal with the problem of acceptability of their proposals to relevant governments and peoples of the world. We shall want to explore this matter of acceptability as a general problem.

Two final points should be made about the model offered by Clark and Sohn. It is not presented as an ideal system to be achieved some day in the distant future. It is proposed as a basis for immediate negotiation and implementation, as a viable and realistic solution to the problem of preventing war and establishing world order. In this respect it raises these two general questions: Is it possible to prevent war by a series of small steps, or do we need to take a major step which would entail the creation of an authoritative and powerful world organization in order to accomplish this task? Would it be more difficult to get acceptance of such a major step than of a number of small steps that could realistically be said to be significant in prevention of war and establishment of peace? The final point is that Clark and Sohn present their model as an integrated, unified whole of inter-related parts; in evaluating any single point of their scheme then we must keep the whole in mind, although we shall also investigate its usefulness in a smaller context.

Some omissions. While our perspective of evaluating the use of law to prevent war will provide us with a surprisingly broad view of the subject-matter, we cannot expect to cover all relevant topics adequately; therefore, a bibliography has been included at the end of each session. A few words about the major notions which have been omitted do seem appropriate however.

GRADUALISM. In some sense, all proposals and programs may be said to be gradualist which are based on the premise that whatever the form of world order which emerges in the international community, it will be an order which emanates from an evolutionary and slowly accommodating process of the present international political system. Such diverse ideas as initiating people-to-peoples programs, increasing international competition in sports or placing priority on an agreement to ban testing of nuclear weapons are indicative of the full range of seriously suggested proposals of a limited nature to relieve tensions and thereby produce a climate in which a stable form of world peace might develop. In recent years there has been some attempt to give conceptual organization to these relatively unco-ordinated proposals. We will not be able to cover many of the individual proposals nor the more comprehensive presentations. For our purposes, it is sufficient to note that the perspective of gradualism contrasts with those who would propose the immediate development of significant supranational or world organizational structure. In Session II, however, we will discuss some of the gradualist proposals which are directly related to the potential use of law.

REGIONALISM. From the viewpoint of growing policy, not only in the United States but throughout the world, the most important omisson is a dis-cussion of regionalism. A form of matured gradualism, it assumes or pos-tulates as a goal the development of a relatively small number of politically and economically integrated units each made up of a large number of the present states; it further assumes that the relationships among these new regional units will be the effective source of new world order. We omit an investigation of these matters for two reasons. First, the subject of region-alism and its relationship to establishing the rule of law on the world level is a vast, complicated subject which, if it is to be discussed as fully as it deserves, would require far more space than can be made available in this volume; and secondly, the relationship of regionalism to the development of a world legal structure has just begun to be studied with the same care that has been devoted to the other major subjects included herein. Quite probably material on regionalism will be included in a later edition; in the meantime, it is hoped that a study of the material outlined for our seminar will provide a more solid base for studying the many opportunities and problems associated with regionalism.

POLITICAL SCIENCE THEORY. In some ways it might be said that this approach slights or under-uses political science. This is true only in the sense that systematic theory is not used throughout; the decision to use a broad eclectic framework is based on the conviction that amongst existing theories of political process and law, no single theory is capable of dealing with the range of problems we shall be discussing.

Terminology. For some time now the literature of international relations and international law has made use of the distinction between international and supranational organization. International organization refers to that kind of organization in which member states appear to keep their legal or political capacity to act unilaterally and not be bound by the decisions of the organization. Supranational organization is used for those instances where the organization formed by the states is seen to have been given a grant of authority and powers which makes the individual states bound, legally and politically, to follow the pronouncements of the organization within the area of authority granted. These terms have not been sufficiently clarified conceptually, and there is still some confusion in their use. However, we shall find it convenient to use the distinction as a rough measure of the independent authority, power and influence of an international organization. Wherever the organization has relatively minor authority, power and influence we have used the term international; where the organization can be viewed as having a good deal of independent authority, power and influence we have used the term supranational organization. It should be underscored that our chief focus will be on a particular type of supranational organization, namely that of world organization. For our purposes here, world organization will mean a supranational organization in which there is universal membership and participation of all nation states. The shortcomings and utility of this distinction will be something we shall want to discuss as we proceed through the seminar.

Organizing and running a seminar program. For those who have had little experience in organizing or running a discussion group, the publisher of this book will send you upon request a brochure explaining how this might be done effectively without professional help. It is estimated that careful reading of the assigned materials for the various sessions will require between five and nine hours. If it is necessary to cut the twelve sessions down to some lesser number, you are advised to eliminate sessions in the following order: XII, VI, XI. Suggested discussion questions and additional bibliography (preliminary) will be found after the final reading for each session, except Sessions X and XII. Some of you may find it helpful to read the suggested discussion questions prior to your reading of the materials.

Personal Acknowledgments of the Editor

The publishing of this preliminary edition with its many articles, required the help of many persons. I should like to express my personal appreciation to all of them. Special thanks are due Rita Chartrand and Ann James for marathon typing and stenography. To Philip Chartrand, the traditional award of without-whom-this-book-would-not-have-been-published is gratefully acknowledged; in addition to the many functions which he performed with highest competence and seeming ease, his help on bibliography should also be known. Professor Richard Falk's generous and wise advice on the conceptual organization of the seminar as well as selection of specific articles was a significant contribution to both. To Mr. Harry Hollins, I should like to express my heartfelt appreciation for his steadfast and unstinting support; I should like here to record also my sincere admiration for his willingness and desire to publish a set of materials which could be appreciated by lay people but at the same time did not avoid difficult intellectual problems. Finally, I want to thank my wife and three children for their sacrifices and their combined efforts to make the work on this book as convenient and rewarding as possible.

Saul H. Mendlovitz

Cohasset, Massachusetts
July, 1962

Seminar Outline
and
Reading Assignments*

*Reading assignments are in this book (referred to as Reader) and in *World Peace
Through World Law* by Grenville Clark and Louis B. Sohn (referred to as W.P.T.W.L.).
The items should be read in the order in which they are listed.

2

COPYRIGHT ACKNOWLEDGEMENTS

6

Louis Henkin. " Toward a ' Rule of Law' Community. " Copyright 1961 by the Council on World Tensions and reprinted by permission of the Council from The Promise of World Tensions, ed. Harlan Cleveland (NY: The Macmillan Company, 1961), pp. 17-42.

Stanley Hoffman. " An Evaluation of the United Nations. " Reprinted by permission of the publisher from the Ohio State Law Journal, 22(Summer 1961), pp. 427-494.

Robert M. Hutchins. " Constitutional Foundations for World Order. " Reprinted by special permission of the Social Science Foundation, University of Denver, from Foundation for World Order, ed. The Social Science Foundation (Denver: Denver University Press, 1949), pp. 97-114.

Fred Charles Iklé. " After Detection-What ?" Reprinted by special permission from Foreign Affairs, 39(January 1961), pp. 208-220. Copyright by the Council on Foreign Relations, Inc. , New York.

International Court of Justice. " Conditions of Admission of a State to Membership in the United Nations. " Reprinted by permission of the author and publisher from Cases on United Nations Law, by Louis .B. Sohn (NY: Foundation Press, 1956), pp. 9-20.

Herman Kahn. " The Arms Race and Some of its Hazards. " Reprinted by permission of the publisher from Arms Control, Disarmament and National Security, ed. Donald G. Brennan (NY: George Braziller, 1961) p. 89-121, and by p ermission of the American Academy of Arts and Sciences, in whose journal, Daedalus, this article first appeared.

Morton A. Kaplan and Nicholas de B. Katzenbach. " Law in the International Community, " and " Institutions of International Decision-Making. " R eprinted by permission of the authors and publisher from The Political Foundations of International Order (NY: John Wiley and Sons, 1961), pp. 3-29, 265-283.

Marion H. McVitty. " An Approach to Development of United Nations Peace-Keeping M achinery Based on the Significance of UNEF and ONUC Experience. " Reprinted by permission of the author.

Marion H. McVitty. ." Disarmament Negotiations: 1956-1962. " Reprinted by permission of the author.

Norman J. Padelford. " Politics and the Future of ECOSOC. " Reprinted by permission of the World Peace Foundation from International Organization, 15(Autumn 1961), pp. 564-580.

Gustav F. Papanek. " Criteria for International Programs. " Reprinted by permission of the Carnegie Endowment for International Peace from International Conciliation, No. 527(March 1960), pp. 356-372.

M. S. Rajan. " Defining ' Domestic Jurisdiction' . " Reprinted by permission of the author and the publisher from The Indian Journal of International Law, 1(July 1960), pp. 75-83.

Ruth B. Russell. " The Management of Power and Political Organization: Some Observations on Inis L. Claude' s Conceptual Approach. " Reprinted by permission of The World Peace Foundation from International Organization, 15(Autumn 1961), pp. 630-636.

Harrison Salisbury and Erich Fromm. "The New World of Communism. Reprinted by permission of Dr. Fromm, Mr. Salisbury and NBC Television from the transcribed recording from the program " The Open Mind. " NBC Television, New York City, April 1, 1962.

Thomas C. Schelling. " Reciprocal Measures for Arms Stabilization. " Reprinted by permission of the publisher from Arms Control, Disarmament and National Security, ed. Donald G. Brennan (NY: George Braziller, 1961), pp. 167-186, and by permission of the American Academy of Arts and Sciences in whose journal, Daedalus, the article first appeared.

Thomas C. Schelling. "The Role of Deterrence in Total Disarmament. " Reprinted by special permission from Foreign Affairs, 40 (April 1962),

pp. 392-406. Copyright by the Council on Foreign Relations, Inc.,
New York.

Louis B. Sohn. "The Authority of the United Nations to Establish
and Maintain a Permanent United Nations Force." Reprinted by permission of the author and the American Society of International Law
from the American Journal of International Law, 52 (April 1958),
pp. 229-240.

H. Arthur Steiner. "Attitudes Toward War and Disarmament." Reprinted by permission from the Carnegie Endowment for International
Peace from International Conciliation, No.533 (May 1961), pp. 429-436.

John G. Stoessinger. "Financing the United Nations." Reprinted by
permission of the Carnegie Endowment for International Peace from
International Conciliation, No. 535 (November 1961), pp. 3-72.

U Thant. "The United Nations Development Decade." Reprinted from
the Report of the Secretary-General to the Economic and Social Council in response to General Assembly Resolution 1710(XVI). E/3613,
1962, pp. 1-24 and Annex II.

Edmund Taylor. "How the Russians Wage Political Warfare." Copyright 1962 by The Reporter Magazine Co. Reprinted by permission
of the publisher from The Reporter, 26 (May 10, 1962), pp. 16-20.

Jan F. Triska and Robert M. Slusser. "Treaties and Other Sources of
Order in International Relations: The Soviet View." Reprinted by
permission of the authors and the American Society of International
Law from the American Journal of International Law, 52 (October
1958), pp. 699-700, 720-726.

UN Department of Economic and Social Affairs. "The Economic and
Social Consequences of Disarmament." Reprinted from the Report
of the Secretary-General, E/3593/Rev. 1 (NY, 1962), pp. 1-66.

United Nations General Assembly. "Question of Representation of
China in the United Nations." Reprinted from the Provisional Ver-
batim Record of the 1069th Plenary Meeting of the General Assembly,
A/PV. 1069, December 1, 1961, pp. 2-17; and the 1070th Meeting,
A/PV. 1070, December 4, 1961, pp. 21-24.

U. S. Arms Control and Disarmament Agency. "The Economic and
Social Consequences of Disarmament." Reprinted from the U. S.
Reply to the Inquiry of the Secretary-General of the UN, September 22,
1961. EC 121(13) Washington, D. C., 1962. pp. 1-49.

U. S. Arms Control and Disarmament Agency. "Outline of Basic Provisions of a Treaty on General and Complete Disarmament in a Peaceful World." Reprinted from Blueprint for the Peace Race, Agency
Publication 4 (Washington, D. C., May 1962), pp. 1-35.

U. S. Senate, 79th Congress, First Session, Hearings Before the Committee on Foreign Relations on the Charter of the United Nations.
Reprinted by permission of the author and publisher from Cases on
United Nations Law, by Louis B. Sohn (NY: Foundation Press, 1956).
pp. 588-591.

U. S. S. R. "Treaty on General and Complete Disarmament Under Strict
International Control." Reprinted from Soviet News (London), March
19, 1962, pp. 209-216.

Jerome B. Wiesner. "Comprehensive Arms-Limitation Systems." Reprinted by permission of the publisher from Arms Control, Disarmament and National Security, ed. Donald G. Brennan (NY: George
Braziller, 1961), pp. 207-214, and by permission of the American
Academy of Arts and Sciences in whose journal, Daedalus, this article
first appeared.

SESSION I

THE PROBLEM, THE PLAN, AND SOME PRELIMINARY CONSIDERATIONS

The materials for this session have been selected and organized to provide an introduction to the major issues with which we will be concerned throughout the seminar: the problem of war-prevention will be explored from a number of relevant perspectives, and the broad outline of a solution to that problem based on a scheme for a disarmed world under world law will be articulated and evaluated.

The initial selections from World Peace Through World Law present the basic operational principles of a world legal system which the authors consider essential to the establishment and maintenance of world peace. The details of the scheme are logically consistent and are closely related to these basic principles. You are urged, therefore, to study these principles carefully and to formulate a preliminary appraisal of the scheme keeping in mind the question of what kind of information is needed for a more definitive evaluation.

Secondly, the basic concepts of the disarmament portion of the Clark-Sohn proposal are presented in the introduction to Annex I. The subject of disarmament and arms control raises complicated political-social problems involving intricate security and military questions and the use of advanced technology. You should not, therefore, fix upon a position until you have had an opportunity to discuss the issues within a detailed analysis of the entire scheme for disarmament under world law. As indicated in the Addendum (xiii) and the Introduction (xlii) the authors view the question of whether to use a revised United Nations or set up a new international organization affiliated with the United Nations in order to achieve a disarmed world under law as merely a matter of convenience. (We shall discuss their proposal for this latter approach in Session X .) Their position is that whatever organizational form is used to handle the problem of war-prevention it must be based on the principles of legal structure which they have proposed.

Finally Clark and Sohn raise the question of whether their proposal has any realistic probability of being adopted within the next two decades.

Professor Boulding's article is also directly concerned with the problem of war prevention. He makes the point that international relations may be viewed as a system. System here means that conduct of significant international actors are capable of being discerned and understood as having usual, relatively stable patterns of behavior so that the entire set of patterns as a totality has a strong tendency to persist through many situations. Prediction and perhaps even control in the direction of change from the persistent tendency may therefore be exercised in connection with the system. Boulding states that the present international system faces the probability of "irretrievable disaster" because its most influential actors have failed to realize that modern weapon technology has made anachronistic security notions based on the territorial nation state. His argument on the point is brief but important. (For an analysis of the implications of this argument you will find useful the article "Rise and Demise of the Territorial State" by John H. Herz, Vol. 9 of World Politics, page 473.) Professor Boulding presents a series of five steps which might be taken to avoid major thermonuclear war. The first four points which he suggests need implementation within the near future come close to the solution offered by Clark and Sohn. It would be instructive to compare Boulding's ideas of what should be done now with the guiding principles offered by Clark and Sohn.

Dr. Kahn's essay is perhaps one of the most widely read in the field of disarmament and arms control. Kahn's terminology, while it may be somewhat strange to those less familiar with the literature, has become typical of those who are working with these problems and indicates again the technical complexity of the field. Kahn's demonstration of the proposition that the arms race has become an independent contributing factor to the likelihood of a major thermonuclear holocaust is persuasive, sobering and terrifying. His thesis -- that weapons research produces revolutionary changes in armaments every four or five years thereby rendering obsolete the doctrines that are utilized to maintain the present uneasy stable deterrence system -- is also very compelling. He disagrees with Clark-Sohn in their evaluation that general and complete disarmament is likely to come within this century. His comments on world government (footnote 12) are interesting in this regard.

We shall want to ask the question, is there anything in the Kahn analysis which suggests reason for optimism for the development of world peace through world law?

The excerpt from Richard J. Barnet's book, Who Wants Disarmament?, is intended to place before you a series of important questions about problems that might arise both during the disarmament process itself and in a world "totally" disarmed. He makes the point that we have not given sufficient attention to the problems that would arise in a disarmed world and that this failure may be a formidable obstacle to serious negotiations. Finally he states that serious disarmament negotiations are unlikely to take place until a large number of citizens of the United States become concerned with the problem.

With Robert Maynard Hutchins, the author of the final reading of this session, we return to the idea of law. As Hutchins makes clear, our focus here is constitutional law in the sense of organizational and institutional frameworks ordinarily associated with government. Although this article, written in 1949, is somewhat topical, Hutchins poses clearly the relevant problems which must be solved if we are to achieve world peace through world law.

Readings from World Peace Through World Law:

THE PREVENTION OF WORLD WAR III

By KENNETH E. BOULDING

WHEN we talk about preventing something we imply two things. We imply, first, that there is a dynamic system which is now proceeding that, if allowed to proceed unchanged, will result in an event

11

which is regarded as undesirable and which, therefore, we want to prevent. We imply also that it is possible to change the dynamic system in question and replace it by another dynamic system in which the unwanted event does not occur. Thus, suppose we find ourselves driving towards a railroad crossing and suddenly we see the red lights flashing and a train approaching. Our dynamic system at the moment consists simply of velocity and direction. We are proceeding, say at 50 miles per hour, towards the crossing. The distant early warning system of our eyes informs us the crossing is dangerous. The knowledge which we have of our existing dynamic system informs us that if it continues we will arrive at the crossing at the precise moment when the train is there. The combination of a distant information system coupled with the simple dynamics of automobiles enables us, however, to prevent the disaster. We do this by putting on the brakes long before we get to the crossing. This in effect changes the dynamic system under which we have been operating. It introduces a new variable into it, indeed a new dimension, deceleration. Because of this, we are able to prevent the disaster, as we are able to avoid simultaneous occupancy of the crossing by ourselves and the train.

We must be careful, of course, in applying the analogy of a simple psycho-mechanical system like a man driving a car to the enormous complexities and uncertainties of the international system. However, the international system is still a system, even though it has important random elements in it. Because it is not entirely random, it has elements of predictability. One of the greatest difficulties lies precisely in the stochastic nature of the system. We are driving a car, as it were, that may or may not respond to brakes according to whether dice held by the driver indicate "respond" or "fail." The situation is made all the more difficult by the fact that we face here a stochastic system with a very small universe, that is, a very small number of cases. Stochastic systems with a large number of cases can be treated by the theory of probability. We have a pretty fair idea, for instance, how many people are going to die in automobile accidents next year, although we do not know exactly who they are.

The problem of reducing the total number of automobile accidents is a very different kind of problem from the one that faces the driver of the preceding paragraph. Nevertheless, even with our present knowledge it would not be difficult to design an automobile and a road system which would kill, let us say, 20,000 people a year instead of 40,000. What we would be doing here would be to reduce the probability of disaster on the part of a single individual. It is by no means impossible to think of the international system in a rather similar way, and to talk about the things we can do to reduce the probability of disaster. What we mean by this is that if we had a very large number of planets roughly identical with our own we could postulate changes in the system which would reduce the number of cases in which disaster occurred. This would be the analogue of treating road deaths as a public health problem and seeking to reduce their probability. As far as we know, however, we do not have a large number of planets like ours and for our purposes at least there is only one. Hence, reducing the probability of disaster does us very little good if the disaster actually occurs. The problem of stochastic systems with a small number of cases has received insufficient attention in the theoretical literature. It is precisely this kind of system, however, with which we have to deal in international affairs.

I believe the present international system to be one which has a significant probability built into it of irretrievable disaster for the human race. The longer the number of years we contemplate such a system operating, the larger this probability becomes. I do not know whether in any one year it is one per cent, ten per cent, or even fifty per cent. I feel pretty sure, however, that it is of this order of magnitude, not, shall we say, of the order of magnitude of .01 per cent. The problem of system change, therefore, is urgent and desperate, and we are all in terrible danger. This is largely because of a quantitative change in the parameters of the international system under which we now live. This is still essentially the system of unilateral national defense in spite of the development of the United Nations and certain international organizations. Unilateral national defense is workable only if each nation can be stronger than its potential enemies in its home territory. This is possible under two circumstances. The first is that the nations must be far enough away from each other, and the extent to which their power declines as they operate further away from their own home bases must be sufficiently great. Then each nation can be stronger than the other *at home* with on-the-spot forces because of the fact that in a nation's home territory the enemy operates at a certain disadvantage. There is a second condition, however, which is that each nation must be able to dominate an area around its home base equal in depth to the range of the deadly missile. Because of quantitative changes in these conditions even in the last few years the system of unilateral national defense has become infeasible on a world scale. No nation is now far enough away from potential enemies to be sure that it can dominate even its own territory. Furthermore, the range of the deadly missile is rapidly reaching 12,500 miles, which means that the second condition cannot possibly be fulfilled. The condition which unilateral national defense attempts to establish, therefore, which I call *unconditional viability,* is now no longer possible.

The urgent and desperate nature of the present situation is created by the universality of the disaster with which we are threatened. The system of unilateral national defense has never given permanent security. The rise and fall of nations and empires is a testament to this fact. Indeed, looking with a large historical eye, one may say that unconditional viability has never existed except perhaps for brief periods and the best that unilateral national defense could do for any society was to postpone disaster. The situation of the individual society, that is, is rather analogous to that of the individual, whose life, on this earth at any rate, must also end in irretrievable disaster, that is, in death. Where we have a large number of individuals, however, death for the individual is not death for the race. In fact death for the individual is necessary if the race is to survive. Where the number of individuals becomes smaller and smaller, however, there comes to be a critical point where death for the individual is also death for the race and the irretrievable disaster which the individual suffers is likewise irretrievable disaster for the species. The unilaterally defended national state now seems to me to have got to this state in its development. It is no longer appropriate as a form of organization for the kind of technical society in which we live. Its death throes, however, may destroy the whole human race. The age of civilization out of which we are passing was characterized by a large number of nation-states or independent political organizations practicing unilateral national defense. Because of the large number of these organizations there were always some being born and always some ready to rise into the places of those which suffered disaster. With the number of effectively independent nation-states now reduced to two or perhaps at most three, the possibilities of irretrievable disaster become much greater.

The problem which we face, therefore, is how to effect a system change in the international order, or perhaps we should say the world political order, sufficient to lower the probability of disaster to a tolerable level. The critical problem here might be described as that of "system perception." To revert again to the analogy of the car and the railroad crossing, if the driver of the car does not see that he is approaching the crossing, if the warning lights are not working, and if he cannot see the train approaching, he will naturally not take any steps to avert the disaster. The world problem here is perhaps psychological rather than mechanical. There is a fairly widespread sense abroad of impending doom. The doom, however, is so large that we do not really believe it and we go about our daily actions as if it did not exist. This is the mechanism, as Jerome Frank has pointed out, known to the psychologists as "denial." Up to a point this is actually healthy. We all know that we are going to die sometime and we may die tomorrow; but we act pretty much as if we are going to live forever. We do not spend much time in taking tearful farewells and in writing our last wills and testaments. We plan ahead for months and even for years, in spite of the fact that these plans may never come to fruition. This perfectly legitimate response to uncertainty becomes pathological when it prevents us from taking steps which would postpone disaster or make it less likely. The man who is afraid that he has a cancer but who will not go to a doctor because he might find out that he has one is a good example. Where the prospect of disaster, therefore, is so vague or so uncertain that it merely results in pathological denial, it is necessary to bring the actor to a more realistic appraisal of the system within which he is acting.

If the problem of "denial" is to be overcome, it is necessary to do more than merely scare people with horrendous pictures of the possible future. Indeed, the more horrendous the picture which is drawn, the more it is likely to result in denial and pathological inactivity. The future which faced our driver at the railroad crossing was also horrendous, but instead of denying this and continuing on his way he presumably applied the brakes, that is, initiated a system change. The problem in the international system is that we seem to have no brakes. That is, it is hard for people to visualize the nature of the system change which is necessary for survival. This, then, is one of the major tasks today of the political scientist, the philosopher, the journalist, and the prophet: to give the people an image of changes in the international system which seems small enough to be feasible yet large enough to be successful. It is not useful to picture Utopias which seem utterly unattainable—this perhaps is the main difficulty with the World Federationists—even though the function of Utopias in providing a constant driving force in social dynamics should not be underestimated. The present situation, however, calls not for Utopia, but for political solutions. Indeed, one of our great difficulties today is that we have too many Utopias. We need to think, therefore, in terms of a world social contract: that is, a minimum bargain between the contending parties which will give the world a sufficient system change to relieve it from the intolerable burden which it now bears. This social contract does not even have to be explicit or contractual. It can begin by being tacit; indeed, one can argue that a world social contract already exists in a tacit embryo form. We can visualize perhaps the following five stages of development.

I. The stage of tacit contract. In systems which have an inherent instability, such as duopoly in the relations of firms, or a bipolar system of mutual deterrence in the relations of states, it is often possible to maintain a quasi-stable position for a long time through tacit contract: that is, through mutually consistent unilateral behavior on the part of each party. A quasi-stable position is like that of an egg on a golf-tee—it is stable for small disturbances but not for large. For considerable periods of time, however, the disturbances may be small enough so that Humpty-Dumpty does not fall. Comes a slightly larger disturbance, however, and all the King's horses and men cannot put him together again. The international system under the Eisenhower administration exhibited this kind of quasi-stability. An important element in that stability was a tacit agreement between the United States and the Soviet Union to do nothing effective about civil defense. We agreed, in effect, that our civilian populations should be mutually exchanged as hostages, for we each had the power to destroy large numbers—at least half—of each other's civilians. This meant that the chance of deliberate nuclear war was very small, though the chance of accidental war was appreciable; indeed, the missiles almost went off on at least two occasions. A natural accident, such as a large meteor, or an electronic breakdown, or a social accident, such as a mad pilot, or a political accident, such as an unwise commitment to an irresponsible third party, could under these circumstances easily set off a mutual exchange of nuclear weapons, so that the system could not be regarded as more than a temporary expedient.

Another example of tacit contract was the mutual suspension of nuclear tests, recently broken by the Soviet Union. Here the fear, perhaps, of world opinion, and the fear also of the technical consequences of an uncontrolled race for technical development of weapons, created a temporary tacit agreement. We have had similar tacit agreements in regard to spheres of influence and intervention in third-party quarrels. The United States did not interfere in Hungary, nor the Soviet Union in Egypt during the Suez crisis. The Russians allowed themselves to be thrown out of the Congo, and are not threatening to be more than a nuisance in Cuba. The conflicts in Korea and Viet Nam were temporarily settled by latitudinal partitions. The Arab-Israeli conflict does not become an arena of the cold war. All these represent systems of mutuality of conduct which might be classified as tacit agreement.

II. The fate of the tacit agreement on nuclear testing, and what looks like the impending fate of the tacit agreement on civil defense, is a testimony to the inherent instability of the tacit agreement in the long run. It is something like the gentleman's agreement in economic competition, which suffers from the defect that not all people are gentlemen. The danger is that in the absence of organization between contending parties their only means of communication is by a "threat system." A threat system, which is characteristic of unilateral national defense, is based on the proposition, "If you do something bad to me I will do something bad to you," by contrast with an exchange system, which is based on "If you do something good to me I will do something good to you." Both systems tend to lead to consummation, but whereas the consummation of exchange is an increase of goods, the consummation of threats is an increase of "bads." War is mainly the result of the depreciation in the credibility of threats in the absence of their consummation; and hence a threat system has a basic instability built into it, which tacit contract may postpone but cannot ultimately avoid. The great problem, therefore, is how to get rid of threat systems. This, I suspect, happens historically mainly by their being overlaid with other systems of relationship—trade, communication, organization—until they fall so much to the bottom of the pile that they are no longer significant.

The essential instability of threat systems and the weakness of tacit agreements, therefore, make it highly desirable to pass into the second stage of formalized agreement, and the building of what might be called "peace-defending" organizational structures. The first of these obviously is an arms control organization designed at first perhaps only to limit the present arms race but capable of the ultimate hope of policing genuine disarmament. We could begin, perhaps, with an organization for the prevention of accidental war. This will be a joint organization of the major armed forces of the world. Once this has been accomplished, a major system change is under way. It is the organizational disunity of the armed forces of the world which constitutes the real threat to humanity. If they were united they might threaten us with a great many disagreeable consequences but they would not threaten us with extinction. An arms control organization, therefore, would be the beginning of a very powerful social change. It would constitute the formal recognition of the fact that unilateral national defense is no longer possible. Once this initial break is made, system change may be expected to take place quite rapidly. It may be that we shall have to look forward to a substantial separation of the armed forces organization from the states which they are supposed to defend, and which they can no longer defend. Just as we solved the problem of religious wars by the separation of church and state, so we may be able to solve the problem of nuclear war by the separation of the armed forces from the state. The plain fact is that today the threat which the armed forces of the world present to their own civilian populations is much greater than any conflict among the nations. Arms control will be the beginning of the recognition of this social fact.

III. Arms control must move fairly rapidly into disarmament; otherwise it will be unstable. The organization of the world armed forces will be a loose and unstable one at first, and it will always threaten to break up. It may be, of course, that the major pressure towards disarmament will come from the economic side. Once the threat of war is removed by arms control and by organizational unity of the world armed forces, the economic burden of maintaining these monstrous establishments will seem intolerable, especially in view of the fact that it is the arms burden (equal to the total income of the poorest half of the human race!) which perhaps prevents the world from really tackling the problem of economic development and which condemns hundreds of millions of people and their descendants to live in misery. One looks forward, therefore, to the third stage of rapid and total disarmament, under the arms control organization. There are many difficult problems involved in this which have not been worked out and on which research desperately needs to be done. One research program is on the way at the moment on the broad problems of the economics of disarmament, conducted by Professor Emile Benoit of Columbia University. The United Nations is about to inaugurate a similar study. However, the organizational and social-psychological problems involved are very great and quite unprecedented. Growth is always much easier than decline and the problems of adjustment involved in a rapid decline in the world's armed forces still have to be faced. These problems, however, are difficult rather than insoluble.

IV. Even universal total disarmament, however, is not enough, for this too is likely to be unstable even though disarmament itself will reduce many of the sources of conflict, especially those which arise out of strategic considerations. It will not eliminate all conflicts by any means. In a world as divided as this, ideologically and economically, we may expect serious conflicts continually to arise. These conflicts will constantly present the temptation to the losing side to resort to violence and to redevelop organized armed forces. If disarmament is to be stable, therefore, there must be a system of conflict control. Conflict control is one of the essential functions of government. It is not, however, the only function. In thinking of world government, this is probably where we ought to begin. In the early stages it is more important to establish conflict control than to establish justice or to solve all social problems. Conflict control as a function of government has been inadequately studied and identified. This is perhaps because the study of conflict systems themselves is still in its infancy. However, this is a rapidly developing body of social science and one hopes that it may be possible in the not-too-distant future to develop a substantial body of knowledge on the identification and control of conflict systems. The problem, of course, is the identification of conflict processes in early stages before they become pathological. There are very difficult problems here in the definition of the pathology of conflict, as this, of course, goes very deep into our value systems. Conflict which is regarded as pathological by one person may not be so regarded by another. If, however, we regard violence as generally a sign of pathological conflict, we may be able to identify the processes of social dynamics which lead towards it, and we may therefore be able to interpose counterweights which will correct these processes. We may revert once more to the analogy of the car at the crossing. We need to develop both perception of dangers ahead and also organizations which can act as brakes. These processes have been fairly well worked out in industrial relations, where a whole profession of mediators and conciliators and personnel experts has come to being. There is no reason why these principles should not be applied in other fields of social life and especially to the conflict of states.

V. The last stage, of course, is true world government, capable not only of controlling conflict but of expressing and developing the common concerns and aims of mankind. At the moment this seems to be a long way off. Fortunately, the prevention of war does not depend, I think, on the establishment of full world government. If the stages of development which I have outlined can be pursued rapidly enough, war may be postponed for longer and longer periods until the postponement becomes indefinite by the establishment of a true world government. We must therefore find half-way houses and quarter-way houses which are moderately habitable. We must not allow Utopian longings to deprive us of political bargains. The actual negotiation of the world social contract is going to be a long and arduous business. We need to put many more resources into this than we are now doing. Nevertheless, there is something here which can be done. There is a road which leads somewhere. If we are to break out of the apathy, irrationality, and despair which beset us, we must gain a vision of that road of escape and make at least one step along it. This is the great significance of the growing movement for peace research. Just as we no longer accept depressions as "acts of God," wholly unpredictable and uncontrollable, so we need no longer accept mass violence as unpredictable and uncontrollable. The fact that we cannot yet predict or control it should stir us to a great intellectual effort in this direction, for this way lies hope. The only unforgivable sin in the present crisis of mankind is despair.

21

The Arms Race and Some of Its Hazards

HERMAN KAHN

PREFACE

IT IS EASY TO WRITE GRAPHICALLY AND PERSUASIVELY OF THE DANGERS of the arms race, nuclear and otherwise. Such documents are often well received: the author's heart seems to be in the right place; he is for people and against the abominations science and technology have produced. Yet, this question remains unanswered: Why do nations in general, our own in particular, continue to play such a dangerous and pointless game?

Here we hit on the nub of the matter: the game is indeed dangerous, but not pointless, since not to play it (even to reduce forces or submit to arms control) can also be dangerous: a Pearl Harbor or a Munich is all too possible. If we examine the whole range of possibilities, beginning with unilateral disarmament, surrender, appeasement, or accommodation, and ending with an accelerated arms race, preventive war, Mutual Homicide Pacts, and Doomsday Machines, we discover that there are no pleasant, safe, or even unambiguously moral positions for the individual, for a nation, or for civilization. Unfortunately, the discussions that concentrate on one facet of our dangerous future tend to create a psychological atmosphere conducive to the neglect of the remaining problems of security. This is no reason for not discussing the dangers of the arms race (or any other dangers), but only for emphasizing the ultimate need for a balanced comparison of all the dangers.

I have written elsewhere * on why adequate arms control may be essential if we are to reach 1975 and later years without a major thermonuclear war, while emphasizing that we may also need military establishments of a much higher quality than is usually conceded, even by people who think of themselves as "militarists," and the many difficulties and dangers of arms control. I will not summarize the arguments here. I would only be doing myself a disservice if I did so. This is a difficult, unpleasant, and emotional

---

* This chapter is based in part on my book, *On Thermonuclear War* (Princeton, N.J.: Princeton University Press, December 1960).

subject; the points raised are often irritating or dismaying, and many readers transfer their irritation and dismay to the author. For example, if one presents a balanced account of the risks an attacker might face from a retaliatory blow, it is easy to show that, subject to some chilling uncertainties, there are many circumstances in which the risks the attacker faces are considerably less than is generally believed. As a result, there are plausible situations in which a perfectly sane (but calculating, decisive, or ruthless) attacker might decide that "it is less risky to go to war than to live with the current situation or crisis." At this point, many readers conclude that the analyst is advocating preventive war; in other words, instead of examining the arithmetic, they conclude that anyone who calculates this way wants to act this way.

While the most important problems of the 1960's and 1970's may result from the arms race itself, rather than from the political and military dangers against which the arms race is supposed to protect us, those dangers exist. Today they are manageable only because the arms protect us from them; *ill-advised* measures to control the arms race can still reduce our security.* We are trying to negotiate some very rough and dangerous terrain. While it is by no means clear that there are any "reasonable" routes to wherever we want to go, it is clear that there are precipitous and unscalable heights in all directions. Let us now examine some of this terrain.

VARIOUS WAYS IN WHICH WAR CAN START

The major danger of the arms race lies precisely in the fact that the arms may be used; thermonuclear war may be unthinkable, but it is not impossible. Arms control can reduce the risks that ensue from the ever-present possibility of war by reducing:

1. The number of events, both international (tensions and crises) and technical (false alarms and misunderstandings), that could give rise to war.

2. The probability that an event of the kind that could cause war will actually result in war.

3. The damage of an actual war, not only by abolishing the use of certain weapons and controlling the use of others, but also by facilitating ahead of time the machinery by which wars are ended before they become overwhelmingly destructive.

There is no space here to expand on these possibilities; they are all discussed elsewhere in this book. However, it may be well now to discuss systematically how a war could arise and indicate some of the problems to be considered. I will begin by listing a number of possibilities, in a semi-technical jargon intended to categorize and describe them.

1. *Unpremeditated war* (human or mechanical error, false alarm, self-fulfilling prophecy, unauthorized behavior).

* The possibility implied by the author's use of the word *still* in this sentence is to be noted.—ED.

2. *Miscalculation* (game of "Chicken," rationality of irrationality strategies, escalation, overconfidence).

3. *Calculation* (Type II Deterrence situation; preventive war; pre-emptive war; world domination; solution to a desperate crisis).

4. *Catalytic war* (ambitious third nation; desperate third nation).

The items in these four categories are neither exhaustive nor distinct from one another. They are not exhaustive because our weapon systems are so new, and their impact, both on one another and on international relations, is so little known that it would not be surprising if a war started in some manner not heretofore thought of. However, I have made the list as exhaustive as possible; in doing so it has been convenient to list categories that occasionally overlap. This is probably better than to strain too much to prevent duplication or leave out some important possibility.

Unpremeditated War. The four categories are ordered by the writer's personal estimate of their likelihood of actually being a cause of war in the next decade or two. I have put unpremeditated war at the top of the list, the fearful possibility that a war may occur almost unintentionally. There is a widespread fear that this could occur; that a button may be pressed accidentally, an electrical circuit short, a relay stick, a telephone call or other message be misunderstood, an aurora borealis or meteor or flock of geese be mistaken for an attack, a switch fail, some ICBM's launched through some mechanical or human error, some stockpile weapons accidentally exploded, and so on. Such things have happened in the past and may happen again. However, unless one side or the other is careless enough to install a quick-reacting, nonrecallable strategic system, it is most unlikely that any single one of the above events would trigger off a retaliatory attack. It is just because radars do indeed occasionally give false alarms and accidents do happen that it is essential for both sides to install weapon systems that either have so-called "fail safe" or "positive control" features built into them, or that are large enough and well enough protected that they do not need to be "trigger happy" to survive. If a system can accept the enemy's attack and still strike back effectively, the decision maker has time to evaluate and decide—time to be careful. Such systems may use an ambiguous warning so as to take some temporizing measure that will reduce vulnerability to enemy attack or provide a better posture from which to retaliate. But the commander can then wait for further confirmation before making any irrevocable commitments.

There is a danger that the temporizing measures that are instituted on an ambiguous warning will remove some of the psychological, legal, and physical safeties that normally govern the strategic force, so that there is a greater load thrown on the remaining safeguards. For this reason several accidents in a row or even a simple accident during a period of considerable tension could be dangerous. Actually, the greatest danger is the possibility that a chain of "self-fulfilling prophecies" is set into motion. It is perfectly conceivable for one side's temporizing action to be observed by the other side and to be misinterpreted as being aggressive rather than defensive, thus causing the other side also to make some temporizing defensive move. This second defensive move can in turn be misread by the side originally alerted as confirming his suspicions, so he may make some further moves. It is then possible for reactions and signals to be set into motion which trigger off further reactions and signals by both sides until a point of no return is reached. This is one reason that it is necessary for each side not only to be cautious and responsible, but also to make sure that the other side also understands what is happening. In so far as any temporizing measures depend on doing things which raise apprehensions on the other side, it is important to be prepared to allay those apprehensions. This is possibly a very fruitful area for arms control.

The Soviets are completely aware of the problem. For example, in a Security Council debate of April 21, 1958, Arkady S. Sobolev made the following statement:

American generals refer to the fact that up to the present time the American planes have taken off on their flights and returned to their bases as soon as it became clear that it was a case of false alarm. But what would happen if American military personnel observing their radar screens are not able in time to determine that a flying meteor is not a guided missile and that a flight of geese is not a flight of bombers? Then the American planes will continue their flight and will approach the borders of the Soviet Union.

But in such a case the need to insure the security of the Soviet people would require the USSR to make immediate retaliatory measures to eliminate the oncoming threat. The Soviet Government would like to hope that matters will not go so far.

In order to get a clearer idea of the extremely dangerous character of acts of the United States [that are] dangerous to peace, it is enough to ask the question what would happen if the military Air Force of the Soviet Union began to act in the same way as the American Air Force is now acting? After all, Soviet radar screens also show from time to time blips which are caused by the flight of meteors or electronic interference. If in such cases Soviet aircraft also flew out carrying atom and hydrogen bombs in the direction of the United States and its bases in other states, what situation would arise?

The air fleets of both sides, having observed each other, having discerned each other somewhere over the Arctic wastes or in some other place, apparently would draw the conclusion natural under those circumstances, that a real enemy attack was taking place. Then the world would inevitably be plunged into the hurricane of atomic war.[1]

In spite of their awareness of the problem, the Soviets have tended to emphasize disarmament almost, but not quite, to the exclusion of other aspects of arms control. For example, at the 1958 Surprise Attack Conference, they stressed larger issues and refused to discuss narrow technical issues although our own position may have been excessively narrow. To this writer it seems dangerous to wait for a settlement of the political issues before considering this problem, but in this kind of a problem it takes two to make an agreement. However, even informal implicit agreements or, on some aspects, unilateral concessions can be helpful.

It is also conceivable that some pathological or irresponsible person will deliberately try to start a war or crisis. The Soviets have made much of the possibility that a deranged or irresponsible American pilot on airborne alert would take it into his head to attack Russia alone. Not only are there many safeguards against this, but it is most unlikely that a single-plane attack would touch off a war. A much more ominous possibility is given in the book *Red Alert*,[2] in which a determined SAC general, who, unknown to his superiors, is sick with an incurable ailment (and whose judgment and sense of discipline are thus affected), decides personally to end the Soviet problem once and for all. The most interesting part is the clever way he gets around the rather elaborate system set up to prevent exactly this kind of behavior.

I should make clear that I believe that, currently at least, the probability of unpremeditated war is low. The reason I put it on the top of the list is because I believe (assuming, perhaps optimistically, that both sides are careful, competent, and responsible) the other ways in which a war could occur should have an even lower probability. It is also clear that many of the methods recommended to reduce the probability of war by accident might very well result in increasing the likelihood of war from one of the other causes. After both these points are made, it must also be mentioned that nobody can estimate realistically what the probability of accidental war is. (There seems to be some tendency to underestimate the probability of war. For example, Wheeler-Bennett reports in his book, *Munich: Prologue to Tragedy,* that on January 1, 1939, Lloyds was giving 32 to 1 odds against war in 1939. This was three months after Munich and eight months before the war actually started. While it would be hard to convince me that it is as high as, say, 1 in 10 a year, still, if it were this high, the situation would be entirely unsatisfactory. Even if it were 1 in 100 a year, it would still be unsatisfactory, because the current state of affairs could not be allowed to continue indefinitely. One must eventually introduce a major change in the situation, or expect to get into a war anyway.

The really dangerous intensification in the probability of unpremeditated war is likely to come in the future, partly as a result of increased alertness or dispersal of weapons carriers in the missile age, partly as a result of the increase in the number of buttons that can be pressed accidentally, but mostly as a result of the proliferation of independent nuclear capabilities to other countries, each with its own standards of training, reliability of personnel, and safety practices.

War by Miscalculation. Nearly as worrisome as the possibility of unpremeditated war is the war which is more or less premeditated (perhaps as in the *usually uncalculated* "calculated risk")—but the decision maker doing the premeditating has miscalculated or misunderstood the risks or consequences of his actions. Many believe that the most likely way for this to occur is as a result of the use of a committal strategy. For example, one side may make it clear that it is going to stand firm in some crisis in the belief that "since neither side wants war," the other side will back down. If the other side does not back down, then war can result. A graphic if somewhat oversimplified example of such a situation is given by Bertrand Russell:

> This sport is called "Chicken!" It is played by choosing a long straight road with a white line down the middle and starting two very fast cars towards each other from opposite ends. Each car is expected to keep the wheels of one side on the white line. As they approach each other mutual destruction becomes more and more imminent. If one of them swerves from the white line before the other, the other, as he passes, shouts "Chicken!" and the one who has swerved becomes an object of contempt.[3]

It is clear that if one side really wishes to win this game its best (rational) strategy is to commit itself irrevocably to going ahead. If one can convince the other side that one has done this, then the other side must back down. However, if the other side still refuses to back down after the irrevocable commitment has been made, it would be irrational to carry out the rationally made commitment. Since both sides will be attempting to use this strategy, it is also quite clear that the game may end in a disaster.

According to Bertrand Russell, the game is played by degenerates in America, and by nations everywhere. It is a caricature, because Russell ignores the fact that it is a major purpose of diplomacy to prevent a crisis from arising which can only be settled by the total and humiliating defeat of one side or the other. Most bargaining situations involve gains for both sides, and the major question is on the division of these gains and not the humiliation of the other side. However, the game of Chicken may occur. Barring enforceable adjudication, the less one is willing to play the game, the more likely it may be that one may end up having to play it. Life, liberty, and security may depend on being willing to play this dangerous game. As Russell states:

> Practical politicians may admit all this, but they argue that there is no alternative. If one side is unwilling to risk global war, while the other side is willing to risk it, the side which is willing to run the risk will be victorious in all negotiations and will ultimately reduce the other side to complete impotence. "Perhaps"—so the practical politician will argue—"it might be ideally wise for the sane party to yield to the insane party in view of the dreadful nature of the alternative, but, whether wise or not, no proud nation will long acquiesce in such an ignominious role. We are, therefore, faced, quite inevitably, with the choice between brinkmanship and surrender."

The game of Chicken is an extreme example of the use of "rationality of irrationality" strategies. Because these are so important it may be worthwhile to dwell on them briefly. In any bargaining situation, even the most innocuous, it can make sense to commit oneself irrevocably to do something in a certain eventuality, and at the same time it may not make sense to carry out the commitment if the eventuality occurs; if one could, one would revoke the "irrevocable" commitment. The analogy with the game of Chicken should be clear. It should also be clear that if both sides commit themselves to incompatible positions, there will be no bargain. But if the bargaining is carried on with skill, and if both sides are cautious, then the bargaining will take on the aspects of a normal commercial transaction in which both sides gain, the exact division of the gains depending on their relative skill, but in which neither is driven to the wall.

Unfortunately, in any long period of peace, there is some tendency for governments to become more and more intransigent. The thought of war may become unreal. Even more important, every government is likely to build up a background of experiences in which it did very well by stand-ing firm and very badly when it displayed a flexible, reasonable, or con-ciliatory attitude. It is only when peace fails that the governments are likely to learn that standing firm on incompatible positions is not a feasible symmetrical strategy. One can almost confidently predict that unless ar-rangements are made for adjudication or arbitration, somebody is going to play the international analogue of Chicken once too often.

The rationality-of-irrationality war should be distinguished from one caused by the two sides having incompatible objectives which they are de-termined to achieve, no matter what the risks: in this case war must result. The rationality-of-irrationality war corresponds to a situation in which neither side really believes the issue is big enough to go to war over, but both sides are willing to use some partial or total strategy of commitment to force the other side to back down. As a result, they may end up in a war they would not have gone into, if either side had realized ahead of time that the other side would not back down, even under pressure.

A typical circumstance in which such a situation could arise results from the use of Type II Deterrence.* Imagine, for example, that the Soviets had done some very provocative thing, such as invading Western Europe with conventional armies, on such a large scale that we felt that we could not stop the invasion by any limited actions, and that we would not be able to rescue Europe at a later date. We might still not be willing to strike the Soviets with our SAC, in view of the terrible price we would have to pay to their retaliatory blow, even if we struck them first. However, we could evacuate our cities and place our forces on a super-alert status, and thus

---

* As in my book, I would like to distinguish three kinds of deterrence. Type I is the deterrence of an "all-out" direct attack. Type II is the deterrence of extremely pro-vocative acts, other than an all-out attack on the nation using the deterrence. Type III might be called a graduated or controlled deterrence: it is the deterrence of prov-ocations by making the potential aggressor afraid that the defender or others will then take limited actions, military or nonmilitary, which will make the aggression unprofitable.

put ourselves in a much better position to strike first and accept the retaliatory blow. We might then present the Soviets with an ultimatum. We
would in effect be presenting the Russians with the following three alternatives: to initiate some kind of strike; to prolong the crisis, even though
it would then be very credible that we would strike if they continued to
provoke us; or to back down or compromise the crisis satisfactorily. We
would hope that the Soviets would prefer the third alternative, because our
Type I Deterrence would make the first choice sufficiently unattractive, and
our Type II Deterrence would do the same for the second; but we might
be wrong, and they might take the first alternative. Or they might take the
second alternative in the assumption that we would back down, and we
might not.

Another method of getting into a war by miscalculation would be as a
result of a limited move that appeared safe, but which set into motion a
disastrous sequence that ended in all-out warfare. This increase is called
escalation. One can imagine some sort of crisis which gradually increased
in violence or scope until it triggered one of the reactions already discussed. This could occur either because the limits of a limited war are not
being observed, or because more parties are being drawn into it, or because
the isues themselves become fraught with significances that did not initially exist, or because of some unauthorized or accidental behavior by
subordinates. It is difficult to supply a plausible reason for escalation (except, of course, as a move in the game of Chicken), when it is to everybody's interest to control things, yet almost everyone considers that it can
and perhaps will happen.

Escalation is possible particularly if one of the two contending sides does
not think through the consequences of its actions. To return to the Type II
Deterrence situation discussed above: it is perfectly conceivable that the
Russians, looking at the 60 million hostages we have in our fifty largest
cities, might decide that it was safe to attack Europe, and that we would not
attack them in retaliation. They might also vaguely realize that if they attacked Europe, we would probably evacuate the 60 million hostages; but
they might not understand the full consequences of that evacuation, in
terms of the psychological stiffening of the backbone and the enormous
decrease in the risks this country would be running if it went to war.

The possibility of escalation may actually play a useful role in deterring
certain kinds of crises or limited wars. For example, it is quite clear that
the nuclear-weapon systems we and the British have in Europe are on the
whole fairly vulnerable to Soviet attack, so that they have little second-
strike capability. Yet the Soviets might be afraid to destroy them in a
limited European attack, for fear that the level of by-product destruction
would automatically cause escalation into an all-out World War III. On the
other hand, if the Soviets did not destroy them, the Europeans might use
them, and this in turn would not only be damaging to the Soviets, but
might also cause escalation into World War III. This means that lower than

all-out attacks may be deterred for fear they will escalate. The same mechanism holds, for example, if we decide to open a route to Berlin by force if the Soviets or East Germans try to close it. As of 1961, the Soviets have the capacity to apply all the counterforce they need to stop any such action. The purpose of the action is not to overwhelm Soviet countermeasures, but to make it clear to them that the stakes are large. It is clear that we might be willing to take a small but appreciable risk of an all-out war, even if we were not willing to go immediately into an all-out war. The action might be effective precisely because it was so dangerous. To the extent that various types of arms-control measures reduce the possibility of escalation, then to that extent the deterring effect of escalation on limited actions is decreased. The author finds this no reason for not carrying through such control measures, but he knows many Europeans who are antagonistic to any reliable limits on the use of violence, for the very reason that such limitations may increase the probability of a provocation at that limited level.

Another possibility of a war by miscalculation occurs when one side goes to war in the mistaken belief that it has a sufficient preponderance of force or a clever enough war plan to be able to win satisfactorily. The mistake can occur through some uncertainty being underestimated, some imponderable ignored, or sheer ignorance or recklessness. Given current beliefs in the West, it is almost impossible to imagine this happening to a Western government unless the decision makers have their judgment clouded by desperation or madness. The situation is less certain in the Communist bloc. The Chinese clearly underestimate the effects of nuclear war. Hopefully, it will be some time before they have the power to use nuclear weapons, and time may bring them greater wisdom. The Soviet estimates, as gleaned from their public statements, seem plausible, though whether this comes as a result of more or less sophistication than is prevalent in the West is hard to tell. They talk of the possibility of great destruction and suffering together with the likelihood of the "victor" surviving and recovering. The Soviets do not seem to be trigger-happy or reckless, one judges at this writing, so that it does not seem to be necessary to put much effort into attempts to educate them on the danger of being overconfident about the use of modern weapons. The Soviets may underestimate the need for collaboration in controlling the technological development and dissemination of new weapons and thus be unwilling to make the necessary compromises entailed in getting feasible arms-control programs accepted by both sides. If they go to war, however, it is as likely to be as a result of calculation as of miscalculation. This thought brings us to our next topic.

War by Calculation. War could result from calculation. After due study, a nation might decide that going to war would be the least undesirable of its choices. Common belief, of course, holds just the opposite: that war could arise only as a result of miscalculation—but this is based on the unsophisticated view that all wars result in automatic mutual annihilation.

This could happen, but in all likelihood it would not. One type of war by calculation could occur in the Type II Deterrence situation referred to above. If at that point we attacked the Soviet Union, the damage we received in return would be considerably reduced. We might well decide that our nation was better off to accept this retaliatory blow rather than let Europe be occupied, and also to accept the costs of living in the hostile and dangerous world that would result.

Or, to give another example, the Soviets suffered from 20 to 30 million casualties in World War II, and in addition they lost about one-third of their wealth. It is sometimes pointed out that this did not happen from calculation but was inflicted on a day-by-day basis: no alternatives were ever really put up to them. However, given the nature of the Nazis and their program, I would believe that even the average Soviet citizen (not to mention the government) would have been willing to accept the cost of World War II in order to achieve the position they have since won, as an alternative to Nazi domination.

Another war by calculation would be the so-called preventive war. This does not necessarily mean that one side believes the other is planning eventually to attack the first, which is therefore merely getting in the first blow. One side has only to feel that a war is inevitable—or so likely that it might as well get the disaster over with as soon as it gets a sufficient lead, so that it is safer to seize the opportunity than to wait. Such an edge is most likely to result from a technological change to which the other side has not reacted. The so-called missile gap illustrates how this problem could arise.

The United States SAC (Strategic Air Command) is supposed to be based upon about fifty home bases. If the Soviets happened to acquire, unknown to us, about three hundred missiles, then they could assign about six missiles to the destruction of each base. If the Soviet missiles had, let us say, one chance in two of completing their countdown and otherwise performing reliably, then there would only be 1 chance in 64 that any particular SAC base would survive a Soviet attack. There would be better than an even chance that all the bases would be destroyed, about one chance in three that one base would survive, and a small chance that two or more bases would survive.

A missile gap of the sort described is especially dangerous because missile attacks are so much more calculable than any other kind of attack. They are so calculable that many people feel that even a cautious Soviet planner might be willing to rely on the correctness of his estimates; that Soviet decision makers might find it the path of caution to attack while the opportunity was still available.

Actually the results of missile attacks are not mathematically predictable. There are imponderables and uncertainties with regard to such things as reliability of basic data, field degradation, intelligence leaks, and firing discipline so that the probability of something going wrong cannot be

31

predicted. But so many laymen and professionals persist in regarding the reliable prediction of the results of missile attacks as simple problems in engineering and physics that it would be irresponsible to rely on Soviet caution and sophistication alone as a protection. And if such an attack were successfully carried out, it would truly be a war by calculation.

The need for a quick reaction to even "hypothetical" changes in the enemy's posture is likely to persist indefinitely, in spite of the popular theory that once we get over our current difficulties we will have a so-called minimum nuclear deterrent force that will solve the Type I Deterrence problem. (Some even maintain that it will solve all strategic problems.)

It should be noted that if a serious deterrent gap ever occurred, then, even if the Soviets were not willing, either out of caution or morality, to use their superiority, the situation would still be dangerous. They might well be tempted to a strong (even reckless) foreign policy, if they believed that their military technology entitled them to some gains, or that if they got into trouble they could use their missiles to rescue themselves. This kind of situation could be especially dangerous if the Soviets considered that they could not disclose their superiority, since if they did so, we could take remedial action (e.g., an airborne alert). Still, they might be willing to hint at their superiority, in the belief that this would be just enough to make us weak or uncertain in our response in a crisis, but not move us prior to a crisis to institute the airborne alert in time.

Another possibility for preventive war could occur if an arms-control agreement broke down and one side had a considerable lead, either because of its previous success in evading detection, or its greater ability to rearm. This side might well feel that, rather than see the world subjected again to all the dangers of an arms race, it would be doing a public service to stop the race, once and for all. And this could best be done by stopping the cause of the race—its opponent. It might be especially willing to start the war soon after the arms-control agreement terminated, because the risks, even if things went awry, would not be so great at the existing low level of arms than before the arms-control agreement had lowered the absolute level of the balance of terror. The rather high probability of war breaking out after the arms race had begun again (but before both states were fully armed) is often ignored. Most writers focus attention on the situation existing at the time of the breakdown, when the posture is still determined by the agreement and on the feasible violations of the agreement, rather than on the situation some months or a year or two later.

Then there is the idea of "pre-emption," or as Einstein called it, "anticipatory retaliation." Almost all authorities agree that at present the advantages of striking first are so great that if there seems a high probability that the other side is actually attacking, it may be better to take the certain risk of a relatively small retaliatory strike rather than the high probability of a much more destructive first strike. This calculated pressure for pre-emption is especially likely in one situation very similar to that of "self-fulfillment," previously discussed. Even if only one side suspects that the other may attack, each can easily become convinced that it should attack—not because it wants to, or even because it believes the other side wants to, but only because it believes the other side may attack simply to pre-empt a supposed attack by the first (which is itself being launched as a pre-emptive attack). Schelling has labeled this situation, "the reciprocal fear of surprise attack."[4] As described, it is not a case of miscalculation, but a case of calculating correctly. This is clearly a situation in which each side has nothing to fear but fear, yet the knowledge that the other side is afraid fully justifies that fear.

Many things could touch off a "reciprocal fear of surprise attack" situation. The only reason I have put this possibility low on the list of possible causes of war is because of the belief that as long as decision makers are consciously in control of events, they are very much more likely to draw back from pressing buttons and accept any resulting risks, than to do something which would make war inevitable—particularly, if this war were to occur at a time and under circumstances not of their choosing. However, complicated and dangerous situations can occur. For example, suppose that one of our own Polaris submarines accidentally launched some missiles at our own country. Even if the submarine commander succeeded in informing us of what happened before the missiles landed, the accident could still cause a war. The Soviets might observe these missiles exploding and if they did know where the missiles came from, they might decide that it would be too dangerous to wait. Even if the Soviets knew that the missiles had not accidentally come from a Soviet submarine, they might not believe that we would wait to find out.

We might ourselves be under pressure to attack even if we thought the Soviets knew nothing about the incident because we could not be sure they did not know. It might appear safer to pre-empt than to let precious minutes slip away while we tried to persuade the Soviets that we knew they were innocent. The possibilities for trouble are almost infinite, and it would be wise to reinforce the natural caution of decision makers with explicit measures, both unilateral and multilateral, to facilitate communication and persuasion and to make waiting safe.

The line between preventive and pre-emptive war is sometimes very fine, and it is on this line that some of the most plausible war-making situations can occur. For example, let us imagine the Type II Deterrence situation discussed earlier, in which the Soviets were hypothesized as invading Europe, and we as evacuating our cities as a preliminary to delivering an ultimatum or otherwise exerting pressure. If the Soviets struck us at that time, it would not be a pre-emptive war, because very likely we would not have made up our own minds as to whether we would strike or not; in particular, we would intend to give them the option of backing down or compromising. However, we are so close to making up our minds that this cannot be labeled as a preventive war, either—a war to head off some

33

generalized future threat. Similarly, if after evacuating our cities, we gave the Soviets an ultimatum, and the Soviets chose the alternatives of prolonging the crisis, we might decide to strike, even though we thought there was a big chance that they were going to back down eventually. We would not be sure, and if we had already evacuated our cities, the risks of going to war would have been sharply diminished.

There is also a possibility of going to war simply to achieve world domination. Most people (the author included) believe the risks involved in going to war are so great today that no matter how promising an attack might look on paper, the "imponderables" and other "uncertainties" are large enough so that not even a moderately irresponsible decision maker would go to war for positive gains—though one like Hitler might. However, if we ever disarm, either unilaterally or bilaterally, to the point where the available weapon systems do not present the awful potentialities present today, then, of course, this possibility reappears.

Even if decision makers are unwilling to go to war for positive gains, they may still be willing to go to war, if, in their opinion, "going to war" is less risky than not doing so. There are many situations in which this could occur. One could imagine an internal or external crisis getting out of hand, and one which was being aggravated by the opponent, perhaps merely by his very existence. One may then be tempted to go to war, not because it looks so tempting, but because it looks like the least undesirable alternative.

Catalytic War.[5] The last possibility is the catalytic war. This is the notion that some third party (or country) may deliberately start a war between the two major powers for reasons of its own. As it is usually discussed, the concept holds that some power which is third, fourth, or fifth in the international hierarchy wishes to improve its position by arranging for the top two nations to destroy each other, thus moving itself up two notches. This is one of the major reasons why some people fear the dissemination of nuclear weapons to "ambitious" powers. However, there are several reasons why this particular concept is not considered plausible: (1) risks are so great for the triggering power that it is difficult to believe that one power could make and carry out such a decision, (2) more important, the United States and the Soviets will probably put into effect slow-reacting systems with a lot of stops in them before the decision for all-out war is reached. This means that it will be much harder for a third party to start a war than is often imagined, though if it tries hard enough and has a large enough capability, it is not impossible.

There is another type of catalytic war which I think much more likely and important: a desperate third nation thinks it has a problem that can be solved only by war. Let us imagine a war between India and China which the Indians were losing. The Indians might feel that if they induced the United States to strike at China and Russia, this would solve their problem, and any method they used to achieve this end was as good as any other. Conversely, let us imagine a situation in which the Chinese felt hard pressed (possibly over Formosa) and told the Russians, "We are going to strike the United States tomorrow, and you might as well come along with us, for they will undoubtedly strike you, even if you do not do so."

As stated, the situation may seem somewhat implausible, but one can devise hypothetical situations which make it seem more plausible than I have done here. One may wish to broaden the definition of catalytic war. Any method by which a nation uses military or diplomatic power to embroil larger nations or increase the scope of the conflict could be called catalytic. By this definition, World War I was a catalytic war, set off by Serbia and Austria, which also had some overtones of "reciprocal fear of surprise attack" and "self-fulfilling prophecy," because the side which mobilized first was likely to win. It meant that even a defensive mobilization (by the Russians) touched off a defensive-offensive mobilization (by the Germans), in much the same way some believe that a badly designed, quick-reacting force can be touched off by defensive moves by the other side.

SOME HYPOTHETICAL ULTIMATES

Stability Is Not Enough. Many experts and laymen believe that the best method of preventing any of the four potential causes of war from actually causing a war is to procure what are called "stable deterrent systems." This term implies a military posture which will deter a surprise attack and also not be accident prone or "trigger happy." Even this limited goal is not enough for those strategists who also want stability against provocation (i.e., they also wish to have adequate Type II and Type III Deterrence). However, many strategists, and even some arms controllers, overlook the important requirement that a failure of stability should result in limited and "acceptable" consequences.

In order to illustrate this remark, I would like to discuss the strategic theory of three conceptualized devices, which I shall call respectively the Doomsday Machine, the Doomsday-in-a-Hurry Machine, and the Homicide Pact Machine. To discuss these hypothetical (almost allegorical) devices will not only focus attention on the most spectacular and ominous possibilities of the arms race, but it will also clarify a good deal of our current strategic thinking. In particular the discussion should make clear that:

1. The sole objective of maximizing deterrence is an unacceptable criterion for a weapon system;

2. There is a very difficult fundamental problem in deciding the permissible stakes at risk in the event of failure of deterrence;

3. Although current weapon systems are already quite disturbing, their potentialities could be dwarfed by some of the devices that may be practical in the near future.

The Doomsday Machine. A Doomsday weapon system might hypothetically be described as follows: let us assume that for 10 billion dollars one could build a device whose function is to destroy the world.[6] This device is protected from enemy action (perhaps by being situated thousands of feet underground) and then connected to a computer, in turn connected to thousands of sensory devices all over the United States. The computer would be programmed so that if, say, five nuclear bombs exploded over the United States, the device would be triggered and the world destroyed. Barring such problems as coding errors (an important technical consideration), this machine would seem to be the "ideal" Type I Deterrent. If Khrushchev ordered an attack, both Khrushchev *and* the Soviet population would be automatically and efficiently annihilated. (The emphasis is deliberate: most deterrents are more likely to destroy populations than decision makers.)

Even if this is the ultimate in Type I Deterrence, the Doomsday Machine is an unsatisfactory basis for a weapon system. It is most improbable that either the Soviet Union or the United States would ever authorize procuring such a machine. The project is expensive enough so that it would be subjected to a searching budgetary and operational scrutiny, one which would raise questions the project could never survive.

The Doomsday-in-a-Hurry Machine. Before considering these questions, let us consider how one might adapt the Doomsday Machine to purposes of Type II and Type III Deterrence. For reasons that will become clear, let us call this model the Doomsday-in-a-Hurry Machine. The computer would be given all the facilities it needed to be "well informed" about world affairs. We could then publish a "Soviet Criminal Code." This would list in great detail all the acts which the Soviets were not allowed to commit. The Soviets would then be informed that if the computer detects them in any violations it will blow up the world. The logicians (and some so-called practical men) might then believe that we had solved all our deterrence problems. After all, we would then have drawn a line the Soviets would not dare to cross. We could relax forever our interest in defense and turn our attention to other matters.

Unfortunately, the world is not that simple. First, the Soviets would rush to build their own machine. There would be a race to publish first. This race to publish first involves more than prestige. There is almost a certainty of an incompatibility between the two sets of rules, since Paragraph I of each probably states that the opponent shall not build a Doomsday Machine! To many people, to build a Doomsday Machine would be the greatest provocation short of an attack that the opponent could commit. In fact, because it may destroy so many people, some find it more provocative than an attack. Even if we succeed in publishing first, and even if the Soviets believe our machine will work as advertised, and are deterred from publishing, trouble is still almost certain. It will simply prove impossible to draw a useful, unambiguous line that covers most Type III Deterrence situations—it may even be difficult to cover unambiguously all possible Type I and Type II situations. The first time there is a difference in interpretation the world would be blown up.

The Unacceptability of Doomsday Machines. Let us examine the use of both the Doomsday and Doomsday-in-a-Hurry Machines as deterrents. It is desirable that a deterrent should be: frightening; inexorable; persuasive; cheap; and nonaccident-prone.

As measured by these characteristics, both Doomsday Machines are likely to be better than any current or proposed competitor for deterrence. They are as *frightening* as anything that can be devised. They are more *inexorable,* since they can be made almost invulnerable to direct physical destruction (electromagnetic waves which would set them off go faster than shock waves which might destroy the device); the operation is in principle so simple and reliable that one can really believe it would work (as opposed to a complex weapon system which requires the split-second coordination and almost perfect operation of many complex parts in a strange post-attack environment); and the automatic operation eliminates the human element—including any possible loss of resolve as a result of either humanitarian consideration or threats by the enemy.

The machines are certainly *persuasive.* Even the most simple minded should be able to understand their capabilities. Most likely such machines would be *cheap,* compared to present weapons expenditures.

Finally, they are relatively *foolproof,* in the sense that the probability of an accidental or unauthorized triggering should be low. This means, while the possibility of an unauthorized or accidental use of the machine, in spite of all precautions, would be too high to be acceptable, it would still be lower than the probability of such an action in complicated and dispersed systems such as Polaris, Minuteman, and airborne alert. Not only is the number of buttons very low, but the Doomsday weapon system is so simple that one should be able to see clearly the places where trouble could occur, and then take all possible precautions.

The difficulties lie in the fact that the Doomsday Machine is not sufficiently *controllable.* Even though it maximizes the probability that deterrence will work (including minimizing the probability of accidents or miscalculations), it is totally unsatisfactory, for one must still examine the consequences of a failure. A failure will kill too many people, and kill them too automatically. There is no chance of human intervention, control, and final decision. Even if we give up the computer and make the Doomsday Machine reliably controllable by the decision makers, it is still not controllable enough. Neither NATO nor the United States, possibly not even the Soviet Union, would be willing to spend billions of dollars to give a few individuals this particular kind of life-and-death power over the entire world.

If one were presenting a military briefing advocating some special weapon system as a deterrent and examined only the five qualities on the list, the Doomsday Machine might seem better than any alternative system; nevertheless, it is unacceptable. We thus see that our list of properties should have included a sixth: It is desirable that a deterrent should be *controllable*. The fact that most public discussion ignores this last requirement could imply that either some of the weapon systems currently being proposed are unacceptable, or that the way we talk about these weapon systems is wrong—very likely both.[7] Most decision makers seem to feel very strongly about the unacceptability of Doomsday Machines. If forced to choose among accommodation to the point of surrender, a large risk of surprise attack, or buying a Doomsday Machine, they would choose one of the first two as against the last one.

This last statement may surprise many who feel that irresponsible governments on both sides have already bought the equivalent of Doomsday Machines, almost without a second thought. I used to be wary myself of discussing the concept for fear that some overenthusiastic colonel would issue a General Operating Requirement or Development Planning Objective for the device. For whatever it is worth, my experience in two years of briefings has been exactly the opposite. Except for some intellectuals, especially certain scientists and engineers who have overemphasized the single objective of maximizing the effectiveness of deterrence, the device is universally rejected. Doomsday Machines do not look professional to senior military officers (in a way it threatens them with a fourth service), and they look even worse to senior civilians. The fact that more than a few scientists and engineers do seem attracted to such devices is disquieting, but as long as the development project is expensive, even these dedicated experts are unlikely to get one under way.

A Fundamental Problem. The concept of the Doomsday Machine raises certain awkward questions which must be considered by both policy maker and technician. If it is not acceptable to risk the lives of the *three billion* inhabitants of the earth in order to protect ourselves from surprise attack, *then how many people would we be willing to risk?* It is clear that both the United States and NATO would reluctantly envisage the possibility of one or two hundred million fatalities (i.e., about five times more than those in World War II) from the immediate effects, even if one does not include long-term effects due to radiation, if an all-out thermonuclear war results from a failure of Type I Deterrence. Under somewhat more controversy, similar numbers would apply to Type II Deterrence.* We are willing to live with the possibility partly because we think of it only as a remote possibility. We do not expect either kind of deterrence to fail, and we do not expect the results to be that cataclysmic if deterrence does fail. However, even those who expect deterrence to work might hesitate at introducing a new weapon system that increased the reliability of deterrence, but at the

---

* For example, Brennan would concede the statement for his B Deterrence, but not his C Deterrence. [Primarily because I believe we have the capacity to deal with failures of Type C Deterrence by drastically less expensive methods.—Ed.]

cost of increasing the possible casualties by a factor of ten, so that there would then be one or two billion hostages at risk if their expectations fail.

Neither the 180 million Americans nor the half billion people in the NATO alliance would be willing to procure a security system in which a malfunction could cause the death of one or two billion people. If the choice were made explicit, then the United States or NATO would seriously consider "lower quality" systems, i.e., systems which were less deterring, but whose consequences would be less catastrophic if deterrence failed. They would even consider such possibilities as a dangerous degree of unilateral disarmament, if there were no other acceptable postures. The West might be willing to procure a military system which could cause such damage if used in a totally irrational and unrealistic way, but only if all of the plausible ways of operating the system would not inflict anything like the hypothesized damage. Nor would we knowingly build a strategic system which forced the Soviets to build a Doomsday Machine in self-defense. On the other hand, we would probably be willing ourselves to go to desperate measures rather than give in to a cynical attempt by the Soviets to blackmail us by building or threatening to build a Doomsday Machine.

Possible Future Problems. Aside from moral and political reasons, and aside from the repugnance policy makers and practical men feel for a device that is poised to strike at their own population, the main reason the Soviet Union and the United States would not build a Doomsday Machine is that they are both *status quo* powers; the United States is one because it has so much, and the Soviet Union is one partly because it also has much and partly because it expects to get so much more without running any excessive risks. However, even if we believe that neither the Soviets, nor the Americans, nor other technically competent and wealthy but "satisfied" powers (such as England) would at present deliberately build a Doomsday weapon system, at least three important problems arise. Would a nation build one inadvertently? If not now, will it change its mind in the future? Would a determined non-*status quo* nation build one?

I do not believe that any nation will build a Doomsday Machine inadvertently, partly because it is so hard to build one, but mostly because current discussion is focusing attention on this problem, and decision makers are becoming conscious of its implications. As for a technically advanced *status quo* country's changing its mind, I could easily imagine a crisis in which a nation might desperately wish it had procured such a machine. Fortunately, it seems less likely that a nation would procure a standby capability that could be connected up at the last moment than that it would procure a continuous capability in being. The lead time for designing and constructing such a machine would be so long that the crisis would be settled before the project could get under way. In the long run (one to three decades), the third question, "Would a determined non-*status quo* nation build one?" may turn out to be the most important.

Many scientists believe that Doomsday Machines will inevitably become both clearly feasible and much cheaper than I have suggested, so that the developmental gamble will be much less risky than it is today. In addition, a number of powers which, unlike the United States and the Soviet Union, may not be cautious in outlook, will be getting both richer and more competent technically, yet may retain their non-*status quo* outlook. For example, there may be a nation (like the Germany of 1933) which is wealthy enough and technically competent enough to have an advanced military technology, yet desperate or ambitious enough to gamble all.[8] Or some of the underdeveloped nations may become rich in terms of gross national product, but have such a low per capita income or other social anomaly that they retain attitudes more appropriate to a desperate claimant on the world's resources than a responsible "bourgeois" member of international society.

China presents the outstanding possibility of this last type in the next decade or two. Such a third nation might well decide that an investment in a very high-quality Type I Deterrent would pay dividends. It is unlikely (though not impossible) that the leaders of that nation would plan on threatening the world with annihilation or extreme damage unless given their way. If they can do the damage gradually, they can make the threat clear and demonstrate their resolve, without actually committing suicide. As an example, suppose that the blackmailing nation started a process which it could reverse, but which could not be reversed or negated by others, in which the temperature of the earth was artificially dropped five degrees a year. If they also had a Doomsday Machine to protect themselves from attack (one which might depend on the same mechanism), one could easily imagine that they could demonstrate enough resolve to bring most of the other major nations to terms. A much more likely possibility for the possessor of a Doomsday Machine would be to exploit the sanctuary afforded by his "excellent" Type I Deterrent to be as aggressive as he pleased against his neighbors and to threaten any who interfered with all kinds of punishment—for example, some form of controlled nuclear retaliation, in which he destroyed two or three of the major cities of his interfering opponent. Even if it were feasible to retaliate in kind without setting off the Doomsday Machine, the social and political impact of accepting such losses would raise much more serious internal and external problems in the United States than in China. It seems most likely, for example, that having to accept and explain the rationale of an exchange of two or three major United States cities for an equal number of Chinese cities would result in political suicide for the party in power in the United States, as well as in some instabilities in our alliances, but only in some serious inconvenience to the Chinese government. It should therefore be a major objective of arms control to prevent such hypothetical, but not unimaginable, problems from occurring. (Here is one clear case of joint Soviet–United States interest.)

The Homicide Pact Machine. There is another hypothetical deterrent which, while not a Doomsday Machine, is still an "ultimate" of a sort. This could be called the Homicide Pact Machine, an attempt to make the failure of Type I Deterrence mean automatic *mutual* homicide. The adherents to this somewhat more practical device hope to divide the work of deterrence in a natural way—we poised to destroy the enemy and the enemy poised to destroy us, and neither of us buying any effective active or passive defenses for our respective societies.[9] The Homicide Pact Machine is clearly more satisfactory to both humanitarians and neutrals than the Doomsday Machine, and both should note the distinction. As far as patriots and nationalists are concerned, I believe that the Homicide Pact systems have many of the same drawbacks as the Doomsday Machine, though not in so extreme a form. The major advantage of the Homicide Pact is that one is not in the bizarre situation of being killed with one's own equipment; while intellectuals may not so distinguish, the policy makers and practical men prefer being killed by the other side rather than their own.

It is just because this view no longer strikes some people as bizarre that it is so dangerous. The Homicide Pact used to be, albeit only half-intentionally so, NATO policy and recently has come extremely close to being consciously adopted as official United States policy. It is not known to what extent the Soviets are planning to live up to "their part of the bargain" and move in the same direction. While Khrushchev's speech of January 14, 1960, indicated that Soviet decision makers have begun to accept some of the concepts of deterrence which have so persuasively swept the West since the mid-fifties, there is no indication that this acceptance will lead to a relaxation of current Soviet attempts to attain a capability of fighting and surviving wars as well as of deterring them. The opposite may be true. The main point of the speech was not that the Soviets were disarming, but rather that, by cutting back on conventional capabilities, they would gain in their capability to fight a modern thermonuclear war. Whether this is the somewhat misleading "more bang for the buck" program we once followed or a serious attempt to be prepared for any eventuality, only time or Khrushchev can tell.

THE ARMS RACE ITSELF

In discussing the Doomsday Machine as a weapons system, including computer and sensors, I have ben dealing with a somewhat romanticized and (one hopes) very remote possibility. I have spent so much time on it partly to highlight and satirize some current strategic notions (e.g., some extreme forms of Finite Deterrence). For this reason, much of the section on "hypothetical ultimates" has been cast in a "reassuring" tone; but the mere fact that one feels it necessary to discuss soberly the use and construction of Doomsday Machines indicates in the most dramatic manner that the current arms race has changed in character from previous arms races. The issues are bigger and may eventually come to the stage of Doomsday Machines or close approximations of these devices. While this possibility now seems rather remote, if the event should ever transpire, it would of course constitute *the problem* of the twentieth century. However, one does not have to allude to the Doomsday Machine to be concerned about the arms race and current capabilities. Our normal military forces are frightening enough, and they are improving rapidly (though in some ways the newer systems—Polaris and Minuteman—are less destructive than the old ones).* The most spectacular thing about the arms race is that it *is* a race, and one that is being run with some celerity.

This is also a new thing. There has been some tendency in the past for the military to exploit the products of civilian research and development, but this attempt has been remarkably lackadaisical. There has been even less research and development done specifically for war. (The common belief that the search for improved weapons has been a major source of technological progress seems to be grossly exaggerated, at least for periods of peace, though long wars such as the American Civil War and World Wars I and II did see technological advances spurred on by the requirements of the war.) Previously, really big wars have tended to occur twenty and thirty or more years apart, and there has been a tendency for each war to start where the last one left off or even with more ancient techniques.

Even so, each war has brought startling and unexpected surprises. (For example, the development of the most characteristic feature of World War I, the long line of trenches stretching from the Alps to the English Channel, seems to have been considered by only one writer, Jean de Bloch, and though widely read, he had no impact on military planning.) Now, for the first time in history, we are having a complete technological revolution in the art of war approximately every five years. As a result, we are now three technological revolutions away from World War II. Any attempts to apply the concepts and rules of common sense derived from that experience run the grave risk of being as outmoded as some American Civil War concepts would have been in World War II. In so far as we are trying to plan for the late 'sixties and early 'seventies, we are projecting into an environment which is two or three revolutions ahead of where we are today. An examination of the development of military doctrine in the postwar years, in both the official agencies and the *avant garde,* indicates that the possibility of great success in such planning is not high. While doctrine has evolved with meteoric speed as contrasted with the rates before World War II, it has been hopelessly behind events rather than successful in anticipating the future. I will not try to describe this process in any detail, though I would like to describe the technological revolutions, so as to emphasize the difficulties both we and the Soviets have in understanding and coping with just the military environment in our search for security.

* This is because of weight restrictions on the warheads for these missiles, not because of humanitarian considerations.—ED.

The Technology of 1951. Let us start with the situation in 1951, a convenient date to mark the first peacetime revolution. What follows is a very partial list of the new possibilities (with particular reference to the United States and air warfare) that the military planner (or arms controller) of 1945 would have had to anticipate by 1951: third- or fourth-generation fission bombs; the B-50 and B-36, forming the backbone of the United States SAC; the initial production of the B-47; the first flight of the XB-52; a manual air defense system started; air defense having F-80, F-84, F-86, F-94; production order for Nike A; experimental aerial refueling; a nuclear-powered airplane under development; many organizations, in and out of government, formed to institutionalize innovations in air warfare and to rationalize research, development, procurement, and operation; the Russians possessing TU-4 and MIG-15, and having tested three nuclear weapons.

I will discuss only a few items on the above list and on other lists to be given later, but the whole list will remind us of the complexity and speed of the arms race.

The most pressing questions involve the impact of fission bombs. These devices had had a very vigorous development program, and in 1951 we had third- or fourth-generation models available. Would their use have been decisive or not? The Soviets did not think so: they talked smugly of the "permanently operating factors" and the impracticability of blitz-krieg tactics. Many Americans, particularly the advocates of air power, tended to think that nuclear weapons would be decisive, but we had not bothered to get as many bombs as we could or (from the strictly military point of view) should have. Of course, the Soviets had gone into a vigorous development and procurement program for nuclear weapons. But they did not seem to have made any preparations specifically designed to meet the threats that nuclear weapons pose, though they had done a great deal to meet conventional threats typical of World War II.

In 1951 there was still much talk of the scarcity of uranium, a view which was reinforced by most of the technical people. Few people in or out of government thought of the atom bomb as soon being plentiful; nobody realized that practical and convenient thermonuclear bombs would be available before long. But a few people with high security clearances knew that some work on a rather impractical thermonuclear device was going forward. Though there was some discussion in 1951 about "baby atom bombs" with about the same power as the Hiroshima and Nagasaki bombs but much smaller in both weight and size, not even the experts had any idea of the flexibility, efficiency, and economy soon to be available in the atomic weapons arsenal.

Almost all 1951 discussions of defense against nuclear weapons assumed that the bombs were too precious to be used on anything but important cities or the most valuable production targets, such as Oak Ridge and Hanford. Similarly, NATO planned on the assumption that nuclear weapons would not be generally available for the European theatre except for very special and very high priority targets. However, a few economists were already pointing out that since there was a large disparity between the value of uranium and the marginal cost of production, there was every reason to imagine that much more uranium could and would be produced. There was even some reason to suppose that this large increase in production would be roughly at current prices. Most of the military, the scientists, and the engineers did not think that way.

This overvaluation of bombs as being too precious to use on military targets affected defense planning in our Zone of the Interior. Because of the threat of Soviet attacks, the Air Defense Command and the associated Army Anti-Aircraft Command was set up in Colorado Springs in 1951, but they thought of their highest priority job as the defense of large cities and nuclear facilities; the initial deployment of their facilities (radars and fighters) almost ignored warning and defense for SAC in the event of a surprise attack directed at SAC and not at the cities.

In spite of the emphasis on short wars it was not until 1948 that we seriously started to mold SAC into an ever-ready instrument of war. (The accession of General Curtis LeMay to the command of SAC and the Berlin Blockade apparently played the main roles.) We had not quite finished the process by 1951. Neither had we accepted the implications of the Soviets' testing of an atom bomb. For example, the official point of view (to be reflected soon in the investment of some 11 billion dollars in war reserve tools and raw materials), as opposed to that of the air-power enthusiasts, held that an all-out war of the mid-1950's would be long—from three to five years—even though initiated with atomic weapons.

While it is easy to show that most of these planners had not thought about the problem and were just reacting in a World War II fashion, given the official asumptions as to the scarcity of bombs, they may well have been right about the length of the war. Nobody could show just by physics and engineering that a small number of fission bombs dropped on Russia would in fact have caused them to sue for peace. In fact, one could almost have shown the opposite: that the Russians accepted much more damage in World War II and continued to fight, so that unless such imponderables as the psychological and disorganizing impact of using even a small number of bombs were great, a long war would have been possible.

One thing was almost always completely overlooked in 1951: the possibility that war could have broken out under such circumstances that the United States might not have succeeded in using very many bombs. We had only a small number of SAC bases (18 in 1950,[10] including some strategic fighter bases that did not pose a serious threat to the Soviets) and no organized warning system worthy of the name. (There was not even a Ground Observer Corps, for this organization dates only from July 14, 1952.) Furthermore, under normal conditions, SAC operated unalerted and would have taken some hours before it could get its planes into the air just to evacuate—even longer before the airplanes could have been prepared to go on a mission. Under these circumstances, just a handful of Russian planes carrying a very small number of atom bombs might well have been able to wipe out a large segment, possibly approaching 100 percent, of our strategic military power in a few hours. (I use the term "few hours" deliberately. The Russians needed no superb coordination or piloting to do this task. They simply had to be able to fly from one point to another point, more or less on a Great Circle route.)

In some ways the lack of concern in 1951 for the ground vulnerability of bombers was surprising. Many people had written or lectured about the importance of our having a secure and invulnerable SAC. Furthermore, it was part of both Douhet * and Air Force doctrine that war in the air is decided by the destruction of the enemy air force on the ground. Last, less than a decade had passed since the "bolt out of the blue" at Pearl Harbor. Nevertheless, there was a real doctrinal lag, which by the mid-fifties was just being made up. It is rather interesting that it was the advent of the ICBM, rather than the fact that the Soviets had acquired a strategic bombing force, that persuaded most people to think the vulnerability problem through and learn to distinguish between First Strike (attack) and Second Strike (retaliatory) forces. As long as the problem had any subtlety at all, most people managed to ignore it. One wonders what subtle doctrinal lags exist today.

It was quite true in 1951 that even though the Russians had the basic equipment they needed—the bomb, and a plane which when refueled could reach its target—they probably had neither the tactical knowledge, the operational capability, nor the strategic doctrine which would have enabled them to launch such an attack out of the blue. In fact, given their strange lack of emphasis on aerial refueling (an absolute must for any Soviet war planner devising an attack on the United States), one could have argued that the Soviets were basically planning to refight World War II, and, for example, had built hundreds of submarines to stop convoys of the type of World War II.

In addition, Stalin and his military advisers seem to have been reasonably, if not excessively, cautious. They were willing to fill power vacuums and press relentlessly, but not too aggressively. They were willing to take small but not large risks. There is even evidence that they tried to restrain the Yugoslav, Greek, Indochinese, and Chinese Communists from being too provocative.

However, it also seems likely that Stalin's caution did not stem from fear of the atomic bomb as a decisive weapon. What alarmed him about the United States was Detroit—not SAC. He appears to have been convinced that no sensible government should tangle with a nation that had a gross national product of 350 billion dollars a year. We had both assets, the

---

* Douhet was an Italian strategist who developed in the 1920's much of the air-power strategy later used in World War II. See Bernard Brodie, *Strategy in the Missile Age,* Princeton University Press, 1959.—ED.

bomb and the GNP, so that any difference between the point of view of the United States and the Soviet Union was not crucial.

It should be quite clear, even from the superficial discussion above, that any arms-control system set up in 1951 might easily have been based on some serious misunderstandings of the implications of the technology then current, and on even more serious misunderstandings of the future. In particular, some kinds of inspection schemes might have resulted in making our vulnerabilities both crystal clear and very tempting to Stalin or some of his military advisers. Even to force the Soviets to go through the intellectual exercise of thinking these problems through might have been dangerous. Before we could have safely started discussion of "the control of surprise attack," we would have had to fill in the gaps in our defense posture—that is, engage in a limited rearmament program.

The Technology of 1956. Let us now look at the technology of 1956. It included such factors as: third-generation thermonuclear bombs; three nuclear powers; the last B-47E produced; B-52 and KC-135 being phased into SAC; B-36 being phased out (the last B-36J was produced in August 1954); B-52D in production; B-58, Snark, and XP6M-1 (Martin Seamaster) flying; Regulus I, Nike-Hercules, and Falcon missiles in service; Atlas, Titan, and Thor in crash programs; many other missile programs in progress; Century Series of fighters (F-100 to F-104) being phased into the Air Defense Command; the DEW line being built; MB-1 (nuclear warhead for air-to-air rockets) being tested; production order for Missile Master and SAGE; classified intelligence projects such as the U-2, Turkish Radar, etc.; an atomic-powered plane and rocket under development; an atomic-powered submarine launched; research and development becoming the major business of the aircraft industry, and procurement becoming secondary; the Russians having the Badgers, Bears, Bisons, IRBM's, and their own models of H-bombs.

The most startling change was the development and perfection of thermonuclear bombs. Probably this introduced a more radical change into the technology of war than the introduction of the atom bomb did. The difference between megaton and kiloton is very large, in some ways relatively larger than the difference between kiloton and ton.

The effect of the innovation shows up in the nature of the questions one tends to ask. For kiloton bombs, one asks how much is destroyed—but, barring an extreme course of military events, no one doubts the the nation will continue in some form. With multimegaton weapons, the question of the continuation of the nation (to some, of civilization) is raised even in the shortest of wars. Megaton weapons are comparable to gross forces of nature such as earthquakes, hurricanes, etc. The prospective effects of the use of such weapons are not only extremely widespread, they are also occasionally very subtle and hard to predict. As a result, for the first time in the history of war we have what might be called *the problem of the post-attack environment.* Partly because of one of these environmental effects (fall-out), and partly because we had not thought about or prepared for nonmilitary defense including recuperation, it is most unlikely that the United States really possessed in 1956 and later years much objective Type II Deterrence. But nobody knew it, so we did not suffer any disastrous losses in 1956. However, the instability of such psychological capabilities began to show up even before the next technological revolution in 1961.

Let us look at this notion of post-attack environment in more detail. Multimegaton bombs are so powerful that even if they do not destroy a system, they may damage it by some subtle effects or so change the environment that the system will be temporarily inoperable. The various effects of nuclear weapons include blast, thermal and electromagnetic radiation, ground shock, debris, dust, and ionization—any of which may affect people, equipment, the propagation of electromagnetic signals, etc.

It is quite possible that some of our current systems may have important hidden defects that will only be disclosed by an attack. In the last few years I have worked on several weapon systems in which new weapon effects or new interpretations of old weapon effects were found that had not been thoroughly allowed for and which could have been disastrous. I therefore find it hard to believe that we have uncovered all of the problems from which our systems may suffer. An extreme dependence on such theoretical investigations as a substitute for (unobtainable) experience can be dangerous. For example, imagine that our total posture has ten serious weaknesses in it, but by dint of hard work and much investigation we discover nine out of ten of the weaknesses and correct them. Imagine also that the enemy is trying to find these same weaknesses and succeeds in finding nine of them. Unless the overlap is complete and we have found exactly the same weaknesses, then the enemy has discovered a weakness which he can exploit. If the processes involved were purely random, there would be a 90 percent probability that the enemy had found the one weakness we failed to correct. In practice, the situation should not be that bad: the weakness that was hard for us to find is probably just as hard for the enemy to find. But even if the enemy does not find some weakness that he deliberately exploits, it is not at all clear that we will be able to predict the post-attack environment in enough detail to be able to take into account adequately all of the phenomena that will occur.

Technological Advances by 1961. Let us now glance at some of the technology we shall be facing in 1961: arms control (techniques and capabilities); satellites, such as Tiros, Transit, Notus, Discoverer, Pioneer, Mercury; soft Atlas and soft IRBM's deployed; 25-psi Atlas, 100-psi Titan, and Polaris being phased in; several guidance "breakthroughs"; a crash program on Minuteman and other second-generation missiles; B-47E, B-52H, B-58 forming the bulk of SAC; BMEWS being phased in; Goose, Navajo, Regulus II, Seamaster, etc., canceled; SAC operating alert and dispersed; inexpensive, efficient, and versatile bombs; four nuclear countries; SAGE and Missile Master partially deployed; Bomarc A and Hawk being phased in; Nike-Hercules, F-100, 101, 102, and 104 in service; limited Civil Defense (?); X-15 test vehicle; a nuclear-powered plane and rocket still under development; experimental nuclear explosives; the Russians having . . . ?

The year 1961 will find arms control having some influence on our military posture. On October 31, 1958, the United States suspended the testing of nuclear weapons, and 1961 is likely to be the third year of no weapon-development testing on the part of the United States. Thus, 1961 should be the third year of an uninspected moratorium, and, in addition to all the other uncertainties of a United States military planner, there will be such questions as, "Are the Soviets cheating? If so, to what extent? And what is the military significance?" Even if a treaty were to be signed by the time this book is published it will take a period of from two to five years to install and proof-test whatever inspection network is agreed upon.

The test-suspension negotiations at Geneva illustrate the importance of doing our homework. In July and August of 1958, the Western and Eastern experts at Geneva agreed, after a short hectic conference (at which most of the technical facts were worked out in late evening sessions) that about 180 stations around the world (about 21 in the Soviet Union) would suffice to pick up illegal explosions greater than 5 kilotons in yield. Within months, on the basis of new data and experiments, the Western experts decided they had been off by at least a factor of four. A few months later, several ingenious schemes (testing in big holes or outer space) were worked out to evade the proposed inspection system almost completely, as far as tests of the kiloton type were concerned.

From the viewpoint of arms control, one of the most dangerous innovations of 1961 is the possibility of the experimental use of nuclear explosives in one or more peacetime applications. In May 1959 the Atomic Energy Commission sponsored the Second Plowshare Symposium on the Industrial and Scientific Uses of Nuclear Explosions. At an earlier symposium there had been much interest in the subject, but nobody expected anything to happen very soon. By the second one, many of the ideas had had time to mature. There were about fifty papers presented at the symposium on various aspects of nuclear explosives. The suggestions for peaceful uses of nuclear explosives included: artificial harbors, sea-level ship canals, underground oil storage, power, isotope production, geothermal steam plants, salt water distillation, improvement of underground water supplies, mining, shale oil production, meteorological experiments, and other scientific experiments.

The length of the above list should not surprise the reader. Nuclear explosives are a uniquely concentrated but very simple and relatively cheap source of power, heat, and pressure, as well as of neutrons and other radiation. Once they become even slightly available, many people will look for and find applications for these new devices, which in turn will make them even more available. In fact, the terms on which they are available at this writing were spelled out by the AEC at the Second Plowshare Symposium as follows: roughly a half million dollars will buy explosives in the low kiloton region, and perhaps a million dollars will buy them in the low megaton region. The AEC is careful to note that the above charges are for small quantities.

Very few people at the 1959 symposium would have accepted even odds that a number of the ideas discussed would not be in programs by 1961. In particular, a project to dig an artificial harbor in Alaska is definitely programed at this writing. Since some of the individual projects promised to use hundreds or even thousands of bombs, it is not impossible that even a private international market of buyers and sellers of nuclear explosives could eventually spring up. This last is particularly likely if there is technological progress in the design of very simple bombs made of readily available materials. Once there develops a legitimate market for nuclear explosives, then in the absence of controls many nations will manufacture them for sale or peaceful use, if not by 1970, then by 1980. However, unless one of these nations is very irresponsible, there should be a fair degree of voluntary control over the distribution of these devices.

I will discuss later some of the problems that might arise as a result of the possible dissemination of nuclear weapons. I should point out that at the present writing, however, it is rather unlikely that nuclear explosives will be as successful as I have indicated they might be. As Lewis Bohn has pointed out to me, the above discussion mirrors almost exactly the early (incorrect) postwar expectations on the speed of development of nuclear reactors and the consequent strategic and control problems. Much of the Baruch Plan for the control of nuclear weapons was preoccupied with this much overestimated problem.

I believe that a much better economic and technical case can be made for the use of nuclear explosives than could be made for the early postwar reactors. In addition, there is a much smaller distance between a nuclear explosive and a bomb than between a reactor and a bomb. In the first case, the distinction is often a semantic one; in the second case, one may need a major chemical industry. I therefore believe that if nuclear explosives do not present a problem, it is likely to be because of legal, social, and political obstacles to this development rather than technical and economic ones. This is one place where the pursuit of a higher standard of living for all may result in a drastic reduction.

The Mid-1960's. We have just been looking somewhat superficially at the early 'sixties. I would like to give only a bare listing of the possibilities of the mid-sixties, labeled 1965 for the sake of definiteness. (The reason there are only four years between this technological revolution and the last—I had been using five years between these revolutions—is that technological innovation seems to be even faster today. We are spending more money on research and development, and getting more skillful in its management.) By 1965, then, we would expect to have some of the following:

49

independent nuclear deterrents; Minuteman B and Polaris C; second-generation Atlas and Titan; Dynasoar; BMEWS-B, Midas, and SAMOS; protected B-52G and H, B-47E, B-58A and B; the limits of bomb technology (if testing is continued); commercial nuclear explosives; an airborne ballistic missile; super-guidance; SAGE B, Bomarc B and C, Nike-Zeus A and B, Hawk B, F-108, B-70 technologically possible, but perhaps canceled; antiradiation drugs; protected command and control; exotic fuels and propellants; an inexpensive reliable research missile; inexpensive satellites; a nuclear-powered airplane(?) or rocket (?); experimental climate control; bacteriological and chemical warfare; and astronauts.

The 1970's. Rather than comment on any of the above, I would like to deal with some of the possibilities for the late 'sixties and early 'seventies, which I will label 1969. We now have to take into account more than just the extrapolation of current technology. We have to consider the possibility of "breakthroughs" and other surprises. Although it is not possible to limit or describe in advance what breakthroughs might occur, it is possible to discuss some projects currently being studied which might be called breakthroughs, if successful. This method of trying to estimate the total impact of technological progress is likely to involve some large underestimates of the total change, since one can almost guarantee that many startling and unexpected developments will occur. I will try to make up for this by some judicious exaggeration in the areas to be discussed, for such an exaggeration will give a better "feel" for the over-all possibilities for the late 'sixties or early 'seventies than a more sober discussion of the few items I will consider: cheap, simple bombs; cheap, simple missiles; cheap satellites; controlled thermonuclear reaction; other sources of cheap neutrons; other sources of nuclear fuels; californium bullets; ground-effect machines; reliable sensors; super-calculators; cheap calories; medical progress; advanced materials; cheap, fast transportation (for limited wars); reliable command and control; Doomsday Machines; and disguised warfare.

When we enter the 1970's, the most advanced nations at least will know in theory how to make simple bombs and missiles, and in the absence of explicit or implicit controls will be making them in practice. For this reason, I have put cheap simple bombs and cheap simple missiles at the top of the list because, even with arms control, and certainly without it, these are likely to be the most characteristic features of the late 1960 or the early 1970 period. They may or may not present the most important (and dramatic) problem. This will depend on which nations actually have weapons in their stockpiles, on the explicit and implicit controls, and on the state of international relations.

Under the current programs, 1969 may be a little early for the diffusion of these devices to other than "advanced" nations. It is very difficult to predict the rate at which the technology, materials, and information will be disseminated. Even without explicit controls, it might be the mid-1970's or even a later period before they become cheap and simple for the majority of "developed" nations. But there are many things that could accelerate this dissemination process: the use of nuclear weapons in a limited war; successful programs for the peaceful uses of nuclear explosives in the mid-1960's might at least make nuclear "devices" widely available; the deliberate diffusion of nuclear technology, by either the United States or the Soviet Union, to enough allies so that there will be no more secrets; a breakthrough in technology or materials, etc.

As an example of this last possibility, consider the fusion reactor. It is improbable that this device will be practical by 1969; most experts in this field are somewhat doubtful about any real success before the year 2000. Let us, however, go ahead and outrage the experts by assuming not a qualified, but an outstanding success—such a success that even relatively primitive nations will find it possible either to build or buy a fusion reactor and thereby to acquire a virtually unlimited source of cheap power. This spectacular gift of technology has a significant side effect: it gives off neutrons very copiously, so copiously that it may not be exaggerating to state that the neutrons are for all practical purposes free.

Free neutrons would mean that many kinds of nuclear fuels would be very cheap. With these nuclear fuels and with the kind of technology that is likely to be available in 1969, it may literally turn out that a trained and technically minded person, even one who is a member of a relatively primitive society, would be able to make or obtain bombs. This would raise forcefully the question of the illegal or uncontrolled dissemination of bombs. (One can today buy machine guns, artillery, tanks, and fighter aircraft on the gray market.) Thus the 1969 equivalent of the Malayan guerrillas or the Algerian rebels or the Puerto Rican nationalists, or even less official groups such as gangsters and wealthy dilettantes, might be able to obtain such bombs.

Even if the controlled thermonuclear reaction does not prove to be a success by 1969, there are other possibilities for the cheap production of neutrons. For example, many of the commercial uses of nuclear devices would release neutrons as a by-product. This might lead to either the clandestine or open production of weapon-grade nuclear fuels. There are also possibilities that simple and inexpensive methods for producing weapon-grade nuclear fuels will be developed. It is also possible that we and others will learn how to make bombs using only or mostly materials already widely available, such as deuterium and lithium. (The widely discussed small "clean" bomb would probably use such materials.) In a word, 1969 (though more likely 1979) may see the introduction of the era of the conventional nuclear bomb in which (in the absence of adequate controls) any "legitimate" nation can get some models, and some illegitimate groups or governments may also get access to nuclear weapons, but presumably under more onerous conditions than those to which legitimate purchasers are subject.

Consequences of the Spread of Weapons. We may be too frightened of the possible consequences of the widespread diffusion of weapons. It is quite clear that if one gave the Egyptians and Israelis atomic weapons, one is likely to find both nations acting much more cautiously than they do today, simply because the consequences of "irresponsibility" would be much more disastrous. On the other hand, even a greatly increased sense of responsibility may only mean that, instead of falling upon each other the week after they come into possession of these weapons, the attack may be deferred for a year or two.

In fact, almost any sober analysis indicates that it is somewhat harder for "Nth" countries to cause a cataclysm than is often believed.[11] It is difficult to imagine that China or France, for example, could in the next decade obtain a large enough strategic force to strain United States Type I Deterrence seriously, although the situation in the 1970's and 1980's could become much more difficult. It is even difficult to imagine one of these nations being able to start an accidental war, if the Soviets and the United States have made sensible plans to prevent this eventuality, and it is a little difficult to understand why they would want to start one, unless they were in some kind of a crisis which would be helped by such an action. In this last case, the Soviets and the United States would be likely to be on their guard.

All of the above may be true. Even though it is going to be difficult to get nations to make the necessary concessions until the dangers are both more apparent and more pressing than they are today, nevertheless, I believe that we should still try to make international arrangements *before* the weapons have been distributed, rather than *afterward*. While it is quite possible that many laymen overestimate the immediate impact that the widespread dispersion of weapons will have, I strongly suspect that the "sober" analysts underestimate both the immediate and long-term problems. I will list ten such problems here. It would not be difficult to list many more.

In a nuclear world, the "small" powers, vis-à-vis one another, would have: greater opportunities for blackmail and mischief-making; greater likelihood of an accidental triggering of weapons; an increased possibility of a "local" Munich, a Pearl Harbor, and blitzkriegs; pressures to preemption because of the preceding three items; a tendency to neglect conventional capabilities because of an overreliance on nuclear capabilities; internal (civil war, a *coup d'état,* irresponsibility, etc.) and external (the arms race, fear of fear, etc.) political problems.

Nuclear diffusion to small powers would also: create a situation in which the diffusion of nuclear weapons to irresponsible or criminal organizations and individuals is facilitated; complicate future problems of control by making such control involve the small powers' having to accept an obvious reduction in their sovereignty (that is, they would give up something, rather than abstain); give the Soviet Union or another large power many opportunities to act as agent-provocateur; and create the capability, and therefore the pressure, for many nations to make a crisis serious or to exploit an ongoing crisis (such as by catalytic war or escalation).

In short, the diffusion of nuclear weapons may or may not increase the number of crises, but it will almost undoubtedly tend to increase the seriousness and the grim potentialities of any crisis or even the misunderstandings that do occur, besides increasing enormously the importance of having responsible and competent governments everywhere.

The widespread possession of nuclear weapons and delivery systems strikes many observers as similar to situations in physics that may be described as semi-stable equilibrium. For example, imagine a ball balanced on top of a small cup so that small movements of the ball can be tolerated, but not large ones. If this ball on the cup is isolated, it might sit there on top of its cup forever, but if it is submitted to the vagaries and chances of a sufficiently uncontrolled environment, one can guarantee that sooner or later it will fall. This may be true even though every "reasonable" analysis of the situation that looks at probable or plausible disturbances showed that the forces were in close enough balance so the ball should stay where it is. It takes an improbable or implausible force to topple the ball. But some improbable and implausible events will occur and, barring a major change in the situation, almost certainly the ball will eventually fall. While the analogy may simultaneously be apt and yet misleading, many who have thought about this problem have come to the conclusion that reliable stability can only come through an international agency with an effective monopoly of force.

For many reasons, I do not believe that the twentieth century will see a disarmed world, but it may see a world government or the equivalent.[12] Until that day arrives, it will be of great value to try to keep, indeed *make,* the problem of national security intellectually and diplomatically simple, and the diffusion of nuclear weapons would seem to go exactly the wrong way. The "two-power" case seems both intellectually and practically more controllable than the "N-power" case. The diffusion of nuclear weapons not only complicates the over-all "analytic" problem, but the stakes at risk if events go badly would seem to be less in the "two-power" than in the "N-power" case.

CONCLUSION

In this chapter I have scarcely been able to touch upon the complexities of the technological arms race and the stability of the United States–Soviet balance of terror. I have tried to point out that technological progress is so rapid that there are almost bound to be doctrinal lags. These doctrinal lags will in themselves be dangerous, leading to important gaps in our preparations, the waste of badly needed resources on obsolete concepts, the neglect of possible strengths, the excessive use of especially glamorous tools, and, possibly most important of all, heightened possibilities of serious miscalculations or accidents because we have not had time to understand and make provisions for the requirements of the newly installed systems. To the extent that arms-control measures are supposed to alleviate dangers or costs by allowing the current "balance of power" status and military competition to be conducted, by agreement, at cheaper or safer levels, or to the extent that one hopes to increase each state's objective capability of preventing surprise attack or other disaster, this inability to understand "the military problems" introduces almost intolerable complications. (The reason for the adverb "almost" is that we have these complications, whether or not we have arms control.) I have almost ignored the even more complex problem of the conduct of international relations in a world in which force is becoming both increasingly more available and increasingly less usable, a problem that is complicated by the spectacular increase in the number of sovereign nations, by increased nationalism, militarism, and "ambitions" in these new nations and governments, and by the revolution of rising expectations.

Any attempts to control the arms race must be able to live with all the stresses and strains that the above problems will create. It is most unlikely that all of these problems will be solved in an atmosphere of good will and common fellowship, or by the use of *ad hoc* committees and intuitive judgments derived from experience in almost irrelevant situations. And we may not have much time in which to work.

References

1. The *New York Times,* April 22, 1958.
2. Peter Bryant, *Red Alert* (New York: Ace Books, 1958).
3. Bertrand Russell, *Common Sense and Nuclear Warfare* (New York: Simon and Schuster, 1959).
4. T. C. Schelling, *The Strategy of Conflict* (Cambridge: Harvard University Press, 1960).
5. The term seems to be due to Amrom Katz.
6. While I would not care to guess the exact form an efficient Doomsday Machine would take, I would be willing to conjecture that if the project were started today and were sufficiently supported, one could have such a machine (or close approximation to such a device) by 1970. I would also guess that the cost would be between ten and a hundred billion dollars. Even then it might not be possible to destroy groups of especially well-prepared people. The mechanism one would use would most likely involve, not the breaking up of the earth, but the creation of really large amounts of radioactivity, or the causing of major climatic changes.
7. I should make the point, though, that contrary to many common statements, current (1961) weapon systems are not Doomsday Machines or even close to being such devices.

8. This is actually an extreme view of the German situation. During most of the period 1933–1944 Hitler was restrained by "responsible" elements, and many of his gambles were actually hedged. On many occasions on which he seemed too reckless, military groups prepared a *coup d'état* should he go too far.

9. It is more feasible to survive and recuperate from a war than is generally thought. RAND Report R-322-RC, *Report on a Study of Non-Military Defense,* June 1958, has a description of the possibilities.

10. Testimony of General LeMay before the 1956 Subcommittee on the Air Force, Senate Armed Services Committee, p. 135.

11. See Fred C. Iklé, *Nth Countries and Disarmament* (RAND Corporation Report P-1956), April 1960, for further discussion of this important problem.

12. An international agency with a near-monopoly for force might come from any of the following possibilities, listed in order of apparent probability rather than desirability: (1) a Soviet- or United States-dominated world arising most likely out of war; (2) some other results of a war; (3) a Soviet Union–United States combination which is in effect a world government, though it may not be openly called so; (4) some of the NATO nations and China added to the above combination as influential, if not equal partners; (5) the haves against the have-nots, probably without exploitation, and, perhaps, with aid to underdeveloped nations, but with stringent arms control in which authority and responsibility are roughly proportioned to military and economic development; (6) a sort of world federal state in which power is proportioned to sovereignty and population, as in the United States Congress.

While many of the above possibilities may strike most readers as unpleasant or undesirable, it is quite possible that even a "bad" world government is preferable to an accelerated and uncontrolled arms race. It is to be hoped this last will not be the only choice available.

PREPARATIONS FOR PROGRESS

by

RICHARD J. BARNET

Disarmament has seemed so fundamentally at odds with the hard facts of a divided world that it is widely regarded as a utopian solution. The question is, however, whether disarmament is any more utopian a means of preserving peace than the mechanism of deterrence on which we have put such great reliance. The success of each appears to require a basic change in existing patterns of behavior. Peace through disarmament would demand a willingness to look for security through means other than military power; peace through deterrence, a willingness to accept permanently a threatening status quo. Historical support for each alternative is pessimistic, although perhaps less conclusive in regard to disarmament since so little has been tried. Deterrence by threat of violence—our historical legacy—has never prevented war. Unilateral disarmament and the few cautious steps towards mutual disarmament that have been taken have never prevented war either.

To be "for" or "against" disarmament in our world, therefore, seems a singularly unrealistic approach. Neither the military planner who sees no end to the arms spiral nor the pacifist who calls upon the world to make itself over by a sheer act of will offers any practical basis for progress towards peace. To tell the world to go on making and testing nuclear weapons is like telling a drunk to go on drinking. To say "there has *got* to be progress on disarmament" is as fruitful as telling the drunk to pull himself together.

It is difficult to envisage much progress on disarmament until we stop treating it as a theoretical problem and recognize that it is an approach to salvation that is peculiarly appropriate to our own world. This does not mean that disarmament will necessarily work, but it does mean that it is worth the kind of research we are quite willing to devote to marketing techniques, satellite construction, or refinements of the atomic bomb. Valuable research has already been completed on aspects of inspection, but the mechanics of the disarmament treaty represent only one phase of the problem and by no means the most important or difficult one.

There is, for example, a series of questions waiting to be faced concerning the achievement of security in a disarmed but still divided world. Where can we put our trust in a world where we have abandoned our trust in arms? If an international authority with police power over the major nations is impractical, what alternative stabilizing mechanisms would be available? How much (or, more realistically, how little) would Russia have to change its approach to international relations before the United States should take the risks of substantial disarmament? And what would be the effect of disarmament on our national goals? In a disarmed world would we retain the capacity to guarantee the security of our allies against Communist infiltration? Against spontaneous revolution? Would it be crucial for us to be able to guarantee their security in either such case? Would retention of our system of alliances be desirable? Are we irrevocably committed to the prevention of Communist expansion merely by military means, or must we for our security resist all Communist encroachments by whatever means effected? Would we dare to contend with Russia in a world without arms for the friendship and loyalty of the emerging underdeveloped peoples, or would any competition bound to become so threatening to one side or the other that the use of force would be resumed? In a world disarmed would a revolutionary power be more likely to moderate its ambitions, or would it exploit the physical defenselessness of its neighbors to work their destruction through the treacherous use of force? Would we be willing to see the balance of power shift decisively to the other side as a result of peaceful competition without lifting a hand in anger to stop this course? Would the Soviet Union? What kind of assurance would we want from Russia that it would not try to destroy us whenever it acquired sufficient relative power to justify the attempt? What kind could it give and what would the assurance be worth? What kind of guarantees could we in turn give the Soviet Union?

Then there are questions concerning the conditions under which disarmament might prove acceptable. It has become quite clear by now that neither the Soviet Union nor the United States is willing to make gratuitous contributions to an "atmosphere of mutual trust." Each concession for the relaxation of tensions, quite properly, has a price tag. Arriving at the right price while the arms race continues is particularly difficult because the subjects of possible concessions are themselves intimately involved in the military competition. For example, the reunification of Germany is as much a military as it is a political problem. In a disarmed but still divided world Germany would continue to be the subject of competition, but its overriding importance would be diminished because it would not represent a military threat to either side. Today, however, any solution of the German problem would vitally affect the military balance of power in Europe. In the context of an arms race each side, therefore, has been reluctant to offer real concessions for fear of appearing weak and encouraging the other to make further demands. Concessions have been in such short supply that prices have remained inflationary.

One of the most difficult problems of a disarmament agreement is caused by the natural desire of the signatories to hedge against disaster in case the system should fail. Keeping bombs in reserve for such an eventuality is unsatisfactory because their very existence poses a threat. Is there any other way of providing each signatory an escape in the event of the treachery of its rival without thereby wrecking the treaty? Is there a mechanism for restoring the innocent power to a relative position equivalent to, or at least not much worse than, the relative position he was in with respect to his rival before each of them agreed to disarm? Or must we in order to give disarmament any chance of success burn our bridges behind us?

A related problem involves the integration of arms reduction and arms control. The French delegate to the U.N. Disarmament Commission described the goal in this area in these words: "Neither control without disarmament; neither disarmament without control; but progressively all the disarmament that can be controlled." [1] Implementing this program has proved extraordinarily difficult because the equation in any particular situation is uncertain. To put the question from the Russian viewpoint, how much of a weakening of American military power should be required to offset the disadvantage incurred in exposing such Soviet military secrets as the location of missile launching sites? Or, to put the same question from the American point of view, how much of a guarantee of Soviet compliance should we require before we reduce our strength? Technical studies of the mechanics of control indicate that the more comprehensive the system of inspection the greater the guarantee of compliance.[2] Since comprehensive inspection will only be acceptable in the present world if accompanied by comprehensive disarmament, which involves serious risks in the event of noncompliance, we are in a paradoxical situation in which the disarmament treaty offering the greatest security against evasion also presents the greatest risks if in fact it is evaded. Is there a point at which we would assume those risks short of a millennial change in the Communist world? If so, what is the point and how do we arrive at it?

What about the impact of disarmament on the domestic economy? The Russians are undoubtedly convinced that American business leaders, fulfilling the prophecies of Lenin, are conspiring to keep America armed. Lenin believed that the "crisis of capitalism" could be postponed only by massive military expenditures. Communist propaganda repeats this theme today. And it is undeniable that military expenditures play an important role in our economy. Each year some $25 billion is spent for weapons and military facilities.[3] Conceivably, there might be more general interest in disarmament if the demands of defense production resulted in a shortage of the consumer luxuries to which we are all accustomed. But, unlike the economy of the Soviet Union, where production of consumer goods has been sacrificed in favor of military requirements, the American civilian economy may have benefited from the stimulus of military expenditure.

We have boldly answered the Communists that the American economy can take substantial disarmament in its stride and still produce prosperity. But we have yet to start the necessary planning to make good on our claim. Whatever the ultimate effect of disarmament on the American economy, such a step will require a number of important decisions which must be made well in advance of actual reconversion. Indeed, they ought to be made before serious negotiation begins. We must face such questions as these: How much of the capital presently devoted to weapons production and research should go to support disarmament machinery? What program should be adopted to soften the effects of the unemployment that will result during the transition of the economy from military to nonmilitary production? How should America spend its surplus when disarmament does begin to release resources for other purposes? What kind of additional foreign aid programs would we feel a need to promote for our security in a disarmed world? What domestic projects would deserve our attention?

Answers to these questions are as vital to an approach to disarmament as they are to life in a disarmed world. Yet we do little to answer them.

The investigations of the Senate Subcommittee on Disarmament reveal that as of September 1957, after eleven years of disarmament negotiations, "no agency of the executive branch has made efforts to ascertain the economic consequences of a reduction in armaments." [4] And over a year later, in October 1958, in its Final Report the same Senate subcommittee made this observation:

> There are only some 6 or 7 persons who work full time on disarmament in the State Department. The subcommittee is struck by the disparity in the effort the world is putting into thought and action for controlling and reducing armaments and the effort going into the development, fabrication and build up of armaments.[5]

And outside of the State Department in the other executive agencies there is little sustained and intensive attention to disarmament. From time to time, the Administration has called upon distinguished private citizens to review our policy, make recommendations, and even negotiate agreements with the Russians. The contributions of these individuals have been important, but it is unquestionably true that no one can acquire the background essential to deal with these stubborn problems in a few months of service. There is no more reason to put the responsibility for formulating disarmament policy and negotiating disarmament agreements in the hands of conscientious, but inexperienced, amateurs than there is to put the Pentagon under the control of *ad hoc* committees or part-time generals.

Moreover, the only agencies in the government that do have a continuing interest in disarmament are those which have a primary responsibility for and hence a commitment to military defense. Since bureaucracies are notoriously inefficient at seeking their own dissolution, it is too much to ask those to whom our defense effort and atomic energy program are entrusted to prepare for disarmament as well. This fact has been recognized by a number of prominent political figures, including Senator Kennedy, Governor Rockefeller, and former Governor Stevenson. Clearly what is needed is a permanent agency with responsibility for conducting research in disarmament and advising the President in the formulation of disarmament policy. *

But this is not enough.

Not only the government but the American public must prepare ourselves if there is to be any hope of achieving the breakthrough to peace we are all seeking. While many aspects of disarmament are highly technical and are perhaps completely comprehensible only to experts, the ultimate decisions, whether to take one kind of risk or another, are appropriate to the democratic decision-making process. Indeed, no statesman —of whatever stature—could make the kind of commitment which disarmament requires unless he had the public with him. In the final analysis, the public must sit as a jury to weigh the opinions and recommendations with which we are confronted, as best we can, and then decide. And the decision cannot be delayed. The longer the arms race continues, the more difficult a solution becomes and the greater the risks of war. It is, therefore, more urgent than ever to face the challenge of disarmament and decide whether we *want* disarmament, for upon our decision may well depend the future of civilization on this planet.

Notes

1. U.N. Document DC/SC.1/PV.-69, as quoted in *Final Report, supra,* p. 179.
2. See *Inspection for Disarmament, supra,* p. 8.

3. *Final Report, supra,* p. 66.
4. *Id.,* p. 67.
5. *Id.,* p. 16.

[*Ed. Note: In September 1961 Congress authorized the setting up of the United States Arms Control and Disarmament Agency as a branch of the State Department but with a Director who reported directly to the President as well as to the Secretary of State. Mr. Barnett is presently Deputy Research Director of the Agency. It would be useful for a number of the seminar participants to attempt to find out and evaluate what the Agency is doing.]

CONSTITUTIONAL FOUNDATIONS
FOR WORLD ORDER

by
ROBERT MAYNARD HUTCHINS

We have a mystical notion that all the issues that perplex us are going to be settled by improvements in transportation They will give us one world. A colleague of mine has asked, one world, but whose? We may also inquire, one world, but how long? And one world, but what kind? One world which brings in closer contact the sparks of greed and ambition is sure to be in constant explosion. One world under one tyrant, or one association of tyrants, would be worse than many. In many worlds there is at least the chance of escape from one to the other.

But let us suppose that be one world we mean one good world. Will we stop to ask what one good world involves? It involves, unless we propose to kill them all, such people as the Russians. The proposal to kill them all seems to be gaining in popularity. If we are going to do that we had better do it at once. Now we have a monopoly of the atomic bomb.

There are two propositions about the atomic bomb that are worth remembering. There is no secret. There is no defense. Since there is no secret, other nations will have the bomb almost any day. Since there is no defense, we cannot use the bomb after our monopoly ends to kill other people without being killed ourselves.

In a war in which both sides have atomic bombs the cities of both sides will be destroyed. Since one to ten atomic bombs can reduce any city in the world to ashes, superiority in atomic bombs will not give material advantage to the side possessing it. Superiority in land, sea, and air forces will mean little. The atomic bomb is a weapon directed against civilians. The economy which supports the military can be wiped out before the military can get started. As General Groves has said, "I do not see how it will be possible to supply large armies in the field." When two nations have the atomic bomb, it will be impossible for either of them to win a war. The day of force as the determining factor in world affairs ends with the end of our monopoly of the atomic bomb.

Yet just as the day of force is waning, the official American attitude is to rely on it more than ever. In the greatest moral crisis in history we do not say, "Let us be good." We say, "Let us be powerful - and then we can compel other people to be good." Instead of saying, "Let us use out knowledge and our resources for the benefit of all mankind," we say, "Let us use our knowledge to make more terrifying weapons of destruction; and let us use our resources to usher in the American Century, in which we shall dominate the world." Instead of saying, "Let us feed the starving because all men are brothers," we say, "Let us feed the starving, if we feed them at all, so that they will not vote the Communist ticket." Instead of saying, "Let us have moral education in the United States," we say, "Let us have military training."

Not long ago the Chairman of the Federal Reserve Board said that we had spent twenty-five billions on military forces in the first two post-war fiscal years, compared with sixteen billion spent on foreign aid in that period.

Yet even before the atomic bomb it is possible that General Montgomery was right in saying, as he did recently, that it is not weapons or large armies that win victories, but the character, that is, the education, of the people. A tremendous military establishment can be, and usually is, a Frankenstein; and all history confirms the doctrine that those who rely upon the sword shall perish by it. Power corrupts. A false sense of superiority leads to a false sense of security. Behind an impressive facade the building falls into ruins. The building can be no better than the character of the people who inhabit it.

Force is absolutely amoral, and therefore has no role, except in support of law, in a world that has any title to be called good. Force is almost certain to be immoral. The essence of fascism is pushing other people around; you frighten them into doing what you want them to do. A country composed of people who want to push other people around is a fascist country; a government which pursues a fascist policy will eventually produce a lot of fascist citizens. It will produce a population of immoral individuals who will seek the power to make other individuals serve their ends. Such a country cannot long remain strong; such a population cannot be happy. If the official American attitude is to rely upon force, it follows that the power and the happiness of America have already passed their zenith.

And, if the official policy of America is to rely upon force, it follows that the security of America cannot be guaranteed by force after the day of force is over. The day of force can last only a moment longer. There are only two possibilities: to use the bomb at once, or to create a situation in which nobody can ever use it.

Of these two possibilities, we hear more and more about the first and less and less about the second. The first possibility is a preventive war on Russia. If we seriously entertain this possibility, we ought first to make our

Constitutional

apologies to the Nazis we hanged at Nuremberg.

If we are concerned to create a situation in which the bomb will not be used, we must recognize that international agreements for the control of atomic energy will simply mean that the next war will end with atomic bombs instead of beginning with them. The minute war breaks out, every nation that knows how will start making atomic bombs.

The New York Times, in its editorial on the second anniversary of the bomb, said that the ultimate protection against it can only be the abolition of war itself. The Times suggested that the final success of efforts to abolish war could be realized only in an ultimate world government.

I do not understand the use of the word "ultimate" in this connection. We have now arrived at the ultimate stage in history. We cannot do something intermediate now and ultimately do something ultimate. What is ultimately required of us is required of us now. If what is ultimately required of us is the abolition of war through a world government, then we had better set about trying to get war abolished through world government now.

Any proposal for a world atomic authority is a proposal for world government. Such an authority must have a monopoly of atomic bombs, which means that every nation would be at its mercy, and it must have the right to enter, inspect, and destroy atomic installations anywhere in the world. No nation could call itself sovereign in any usual sense under such conditions.

The major premise of all discussions looking toward agreements for the control of atomic energy has been that the nations retain their sovereignty. Hence, these discussions have not succeeded and cannot succeed. Either we have world federal government and real atomic control, or we have no agreements, or agreements that are meaningless, and eventually atomic war.

It will be said, of course, that if nations will not collaborate in an alliance or debating society or propaganda forum like the United Nations, they cannot be expected to come together or to stay together in a world state. The American states could not or would not collaborate under the Articles of Confederation before 1787, but they did come together, and, with the exception of one period they stayed together under the Constitution.

It may be admitted that there were ties which united them which do not unite the nations today. Moreover, they were remote from the rest of the world. Both their enemies and their friends were too preoccupied to bother them. They had the safety valve of a new country and the western lands. On the other hand, we should not forget that many differences deeply divided the American states, so much so that, three months before the Constitutional Convention, Madison wrote that he "trembled for the issue."

Mr. Hooker has lately shown in the magazine Common Cause how serious the divisions among the states in the confederation were. Virginia had twelve times as many people as Delaware. Georgia claimed a hundred times as many square miles as Rhode Island. There were so many Germans in Pennsylvania that Franklin feared they might make German the language of the state. It was impossible to get along in some sections of New York without knowing Dutch. The trip from Boston to New York, which now takes less than an hour, took four days to a week along the finest road, or longer than it takes now to go round the world.

Gouverneur Morris thought that a federal tax was impossible because of the extent of the country; and one member of the Convention asked, "How can it be supposed that this vast country, including the western territory, will, one hundred and fifty years hence, remain one nation?"

When Washington took charge of the armies surrounding Boston, he wrote that the New Englanders were an exceedingly dirty and nasty people. On the other hand, Ephraim Paine of Vermont complained that the southern members of Congress regarded themselves as a superior order of animals. Tariffs were levied by New York, Pennsylvania, and Maryland on the goods of other states; and New Jersey taxed the New York lighthouse on Sandy Hook. New York, New Hampshire, and Massachusetts quarreled about Vermont, and Pennsylvanians battled Virginians on the Upper Ohio. It is no wonder that when the Constitution was completed by the Convention, the principal attack upon it was that it was utopian, a visionary project, an indigestible panacea.

And it barely was accepted. In the conventions in the critical states it just squeaked through. In Massachusetts it carried by twenty-nine votes, in Virginia by ten; and in New York by only three.

What we are talking about is the relation between world community and world law. Reinhold Niebuhr, whom I greatly admire, takes the view that we cannot discuss world government because we have no world community to support it. The discussion of world government, he thinks, may even retard the development of world community and hence retard world government.

It is true that one good world presupposes a world community. In one good world every man is our neighbor, because every man is our fellow-citizen. The commands of the political community supplement the demands of charity. Three or four years ago the Council of the American

65

Federation of Labor, in response to the suggestion that China was our ally, voted to reaffirm its support of the Chinese Exclusion Act. Mr. William Green took the occasion to announce that "A Chinaman is still a Chinaman." If this is so, the one good world at which Mr. Green doubtless aims is still far off.

Out traditional attitude toward the rest of the world has been expressed in the old question, "Should foreigners be abolished, or should we save some to sell things to?" We have been dedicated to a policy of high tariffs and no immigration. Twenty years ago we regarded national relief of the unemployed as revolutionary socialism. Our system of social security is only twelve years old. We are not yet committed to give national aid to the education of underprivileged American children. And yet, in one good world, we should be called on to support, to educate, to buy from, and to receive as fellow citizens, men of every race, creed, and color, at every economic level, and at every stage of ignorance or enlightenment.

One good world requires more than the sacrifice of ancient prejudices. It requires the formulation and adoption of common principles and common ideals. It requires that this be done on a world-wide basis. A world organization cannot be held together simply by fear. Not transportation but communication lies at the foundation of any durable community. By communication I do not refer to the means of communication, but to a common understanding of what is communicated. The extraordinary development of the telegraph, the telephone, the radio, the motion picture, and airmail in our time has done as much as any single factor to disrupt international relations and exacerbate wounded feelings throughout the world. A vice-president of the General Electric Company has lately commented upon the benefits to civilization from television. He said that, since the principal market for television sets was taverns, what this triumph of technology had meant to society was more booze, less fresh air, and the same old ball-game. It would have been very fortunate if almost every speech made by representatives of great powers since the war, from Mr. Truman's Navy Day address of October, 1945, to Mr. Vishinsky's outpourings, could have been heard or read only by their own people, and a very small fraction of them. Confucius remarked that men cannot work together unless they have common principles. Common principles are essential to communication.

Here it will not do to say that common principles cannot be found. They must be found. And they can be found in the common humanity of all mankind. By patience, tolerence, and good will we can come to understand other human beings, because they

are human beings like ourselves. The most salutary reflection about the Russians in which we can indulge is to
imagine how we would feel about the United States if we
were Russians. And it would do the Russians no harm to
consider how Mr. Vishinsky's speeches would affect them
if they were Americans. By patience, tolerance, and good
will we can come to understand one another; understanding
is essential to communication. Communication is the basis
of community. Transportation hastens consolidation; there
can be no doubt about that. In the last century it has has-
tened consolidation of the most unstable and disagreeable
kind, consolidation by conquest. One good world presupposes that the moral, intellectual, and spiritual foundations
of the community have been laid. Otherwise the improvement of transportation must simply mean more frequent and
terrible wars leading to the despotism of that power which
discovers how best to apply the latest inventions to the destruction of its neighbors.

But I am afraid that Mr. Niebuhr exaggerates the state
of perfection which world community must achieve before
world government can be considered. Before the atomic
bomb we could take world government or leave it. We
could rely on the long process of evolution to bring world
community and world government hand in hand. Any such
program today means another war, and another war means
the end of civilization. The slogan of our faith today must
be, world government is necessary, and therefore possible.

Furthermore, those who oppose discussion of world
government on the ground that a world community must
precede a world government seem to me to overlook the
interaction between the two. This is what the Greeks had
in mind when they said that law was an educational force
and that the city educates the man. The Consitution of the
United States has educated the people of this country to believe in and support the Constitution of the United States.
We are so used to thinking of law as repressive and constitutions as the embodiment of pre-existing agreement that
we neglect the tremendous force which any constitution and
any system of law exerts in behalf of its own acceptance
and perpetuation. Anybody who has studied the relation between the political institutions of a state and its educational
system, for example, must agree with Aristotle that politics is the architectonic science. One of the reasons Aristotle gives for this conclusion is that politics determines
what is studied in the state.

The way to promote world community is to have world
government. But since we, as private citizens, cannot establish a world government, the next best thing we can do
to promote world community is to talk about world govern-

ment. World discussion of world government, far from disrupting the world, may have some chance of uniting it; for the consideration of what is necessary to unite the world, the discussion of a common problem of overwhelming importance, should lead to a growing sense of community among all peoples.

An important reason for talking about world government is that nobody knows what it is. Should a world government aim at limited measures designed to maintain what is called security, or is security itself dependent on the pursuit of broader purposes? Should a world state be federal or unitary, or should it, perhaps, contain the best features of each? What should be the relation of the world government to the citizens of extant states? What taxing powers shall the world state have, and what order of military forces, if any? This list of questions can be prolonged indefinitely, and there are countless possible answers to each of them. Yet people go around saying world government is wonderful or world government is impossible. It may be that many forms of world government would be something less than wonderful; and it may be that some form of world government is possible. The only way to find out whether any form of world government is possible and practicable in our time is to work at it and talk about it.

Such discussion cannot legitimately be interpreted as an attack upon the United Nations. We must support the United Nations; it is all we have. We support it, not because it can guarantee peace, but because it is a highly tentative first step toward world government and world law. To say that the discussion of world government is a criticism of the United Nations is like saying that to talk about buying an automobile is an attack on the baby-carriage industry. The notion that if only we don't say anything about it the United Nations will in some way, while nobody is looking, turn gradually into an effective world government is surely naive. Constitution framing is a highly technical problem. The organization of sentiment for a new constitution is a matter of time, thought, and effort. And when the task must be carried forward on a global scale we must realize that no matter how soon we start we may be too late.

Mr. Molotov defends the United Nations and proposes as a remedy for the ills of the world what he calls the peaceful competition of states and social systems. This is certainly better, if it may be taken at face value, than the stirring calls issued by our statesmen for the largest army, navy, and air force in the world. But Mr. Molotov overlooks or suppresses the fact that between states and social systems there cannot in the long run be peaceful competition unless peace is enforced by law. The history

of our own country from the Gold Rush to the Chicago newspaper wars shows that competition between individuals can
be made peaceful only with some difficulty, and then only
within a framework of law. The competition of sovereign
states is competing anarchy. It is peaceful only so long as
all nations want it to be. When one nation thinks that its
competitive position would be improved if it stopped being
peaceful, it will engage in warlike, instead of peaceful,
competition, and there is no way for other nations to stop
this process except to abandon peaceful competition, too.
The United Nations is composed of independent, sovereign
states. Their competition must be anarchical. Therefore,
in the long run it cannot be peaceful.

Every alteration in the constitution of the United Nations
looking toward making it a world government is to the
good. But any important limitation on the powers of sovereign states means that the whole theory of the United Nations is changed. To allege that anybody who insists on the
basic theory of the United Nations is in some way an enemy
of world peace is unfair. This applies, for example, to
criticism on constitutional grounds of the use of the veto.
Such criticism assumes that the United Nations is a world
government and assails Russia on the ground that it does
not recognize this obvious fact. Actually, the United Nations was not designed to put an end to the competing anarchy of sovereign states, but to perpetuate it.

Does anybody imagine that the United States would consent to any modification of the veto which would endanger
our present majority position? Suppose that we were in a
minority in the United Nations. Would we part with the
veto, which would be the only weapon with which we could
protect ourselves against the majority? Does anybody imagine that we would consent to effective inspection by an
international body of atomic installation in this country?
The United Nations is, and is by its charter declared to be,
an association of independent, sovereign states. How can
we complain if one of the members insists on asserting its
independent sovereignty?

Tinkering with the United Nations will not help us, if we
agree with the New York Times that our only hope is in the
ultimate abolition of war through an ultimate world government. An entirely different constitutional foundation is required. A new set of commitments must be made. Commitments to an alliance can be transformed into allegiance
to a government only by a change of heart which is embodied in a fundamental constitutional reform.

The most futile of all the things we can do is to speculate about the intentions of the Politburo. Even if we were
sure at some given moment that we knew what these gen-

tlemen were planning, we could not be positive that they would adhere to these plans for more than a few minutes. What we should be thinking about is what America should stand for, regardless of what other nations may have in mind. If that policy fails, we shall at least have the satisfaction of knowing that we have done the best we could and that the catastrophe cannot be laid at our door. The policies we have been following - peace by intimidation and peace by purchase - do not seem to be succeeding very well; and, if the catastrophe comes, we shall be unable to evade a large share of the responsibility for it.

The policy of peace by intimidation, otherwise known as "getting tough with Russia," has produced Mr. Vishinsky, who proclaims a policy of peace by vilification, which is the reductio ad absurdum of peace by intimidation. Peace by vilification is that version of peace by intimidation which can be adopted by powerful and remote nations who do not yet have the atomic bomb, but who, since they are powerful and remote, can respond to attempts to intimidate them by showing in as rude and noisy a fashion as possible that two can play at that game. The policy of peace by purchase may succeed temporarily in those portions of the world which are purchasable. In those areas it will last as long as the purchase price is being paid or as long as no other bidder will offer more or until the nations bought come to value their independence more than food, clothing, and houses. But we have really made no attempt to buy peace. We have been attempting to buy allies for the next war. Yet we cannot contemplate another war. Another war will mean the end of civilization. We have reached the point where we cannot have war and civilization, too.

If peace through intimidation and peace through purchase are failing and in the nature of things are bound to fail, we might try peace through justice. Justice means giving every man his due; it means not doing to others what you are unwilling to have them do to you. Justice is suggested to us by a well-known American document which states that all men are created equal. Justice is the cement which holds a political organization together.

If we will grant that what we want is peace, and that justice is the only way to peace, then we may begin dimly to perceive both the outlines of a policy for the present and the constitutional foundations of a future world order. We are required to abandon a policy of power and purchase and pursue a policy of justice at home and abroad.

In order to pursue this policy we have to make certain moral and intellectual commitments, commitments that threaten to take us, in fact, into the realm of metaphysics. We have to admit that men are different from the other

animals and that their moral, rational, and spiritual qualities are the qualities that make them men. These characteristics prevent us from dealing with men as we are free
to deal with other animals. Human dignity forbids us to
apply force to men, except by law. It forbids us to regard
other men as means to our ends, for every man is an end
in himself. The prospects of a human community result
from our common humanity.

To give every man his due, therefore, is to treat every
man as a man, black or white, British or Russian, rich or
poor, ignorant or educated. And we may remember, as
John Stuart Mill pointed out long ago, that we cannot expect
the slave to show the virtues of the free man unless we
first make him free. To say that certain men cannot be
treated as men means simply that they have never had a
chance to be men, and they must be given that chance.

To give every man his due is to give him the Rights of
Man. This means that he must be free from want as long
as he is willing to work. It means that he must be free
from the fear of tyranny, oppression, and exploitation. It
means that his claims to life, liberty, and the dignity of the
human person are inalienable. It means that the necessities of life must be common property of the human race,
and that the management of the necessities of life by individual owners is a trusteeship which such owners hold subject always to the common good. It means that a world
government must be a democracy, because only democracy gives every man his due.

It will be said that a world government which is founded on justice goes further than world government has to go
and that we should limit ourselves to those objects as to
which there can be no debate, the principal one of which is
security. It will be said that nobody wants war and that all
that a world government should do is to try to prevent war.
This it can do by securing a monopoly of arms. Why talk
about justice, the rights of man, and the law of nature when
all we want is peace?

The answer is that men will fight until they get their
rights. The minimum structural requirements of world
government are plain enough. A world government, so as
to preserve the cultural values that now exist in the states
and regions of the world, must be a government which acts
directly on the individual, wherever he may be; for otherwise it is merely a league of sovereign, and hence ultimately warlike, states. But these are minimum structural
requirements. There are minimum moral and spiritual requirements, too; and these may be summed up in the single
word justice. The advancement of man in spiritual excellence and physical welfare is the common goal of mankind.

Universal peace is the prerequisite for the pursuit of that goal. Justice in turn is the prerequisite of peace. Peace and justice stand or fall together. Men will fight until they get their rights.

These are hard sayings; for if we are going to promote justice throughout the world we shall have to rely largely on the power of example. We shall have to start doing justice at home, and shall have to sacrifice many ancient prejudices that are very dear to us. And if we are to have a world government based on justice, we, as the most prosperous and powerful nation of the earth, shall have to give up many economic and political advantages. We shall have to give up also the notion that there are some people in the world who are sub-human and not qualified to participate in any government that will hold sway over us. If we are going to have peace we must pay for it; and the price of peace is justice. If it will cost us a good deal to have world government, it will cost us far more to have war.

We are in no present danger from Russia. We have the atomic bomb. We have the industrial power. We are in no present danger from communism. The people of this country could be made communistic only by conquest, and probably not then. At present we are our own worst enemy. The present danger to us lies in our own hysteria and inertia. Our hysteria means that we will not face the facts of life, and our inertia means that we will not do anything about them. We hysterically build up tremendous military preparations, oblivious to the fact that while we have a monopoly of the atomic bomb we do not need these preparations, and when other nations have the bomb these preparations will do us no good. These preparations are, in fact, a danger to us for they can be used to convince other nations that we are out to dominate the world. Because of our inertia we will not recognize that our first obligation is to make our own system work until it must commend the admiration and imitation of the world. We will not see that the atomic bomb puts all further talk of force out of the question and that the hope of civilization is in world government. The Pax Romana existed before the atomic bomb. The atomic bomb makes a Pax Americana a romantic dream. The attempt to get a Pax Americana will give us not one Rome, but two Carthages.

The task of this generation is to establish peace. Gibbon in a celebrated chapter seeks to relieve the fears of Europe by assuring his contemporaries that there can never be another barbarian conqueror. The reason is simple. War is now so advanced and requires the knowledge of so many arts and sciences that only highly educated men can hope to wage war successfully. The inference is that if men are highly educated they will not be so stupid or so vulgar as to wage war. But the last war was the most barbarous in history precisely because so much knowledge was at the disposal of those who waged it; and the atomic bomb is the final refutation of Gibbon's comforting theory. It can be little consolation to the Japanese who died at Hiroshima and Nagasaki that they were killed by Ph. D.'s.

The crisis of our time may be summed up in the proposition that our knowledge now exceeds our capacity to use it for good. The solution is not to reduce our knowledge, or to halt the progress of science, but to make our moral stamina equal to it. We have now reached the point where the bad character, or even the momentary carelessness, of the human race may lead to its extermination by the tremendous discoveries which the human intellect has achieved. The problem of preserving our civilization is a moral problem. Our difficulty is not to get more knowledge or more goods, but to do the right thing with them when we get them. Today we are confident that every scientific question will in time be answered. We know that every material deficiency of mankind can with good will be supplied. The problem is obtaining the good will. This is a moral problem.

The task of our generation is to establish peace. We cannot establish it by power or by purchase. We can establish it only by justice which begins at home and extends throughout the world. If you ask, what good will it do for us to be just if other nations are unjust, I reply as Plato did 2500 years ago, that the unjust man and the unjust state bear within themselves the seeds of their own destruction; and as General Montgomery did, that the character of a people is its best defense. Character implies moral and intellectual conviction. We must know, understand, and believe in what we are defending. What we are defending is not the American Way of Life, by which we usually seem to mean "all the comforts of home." We are defending the cause of suffering humanity everywhere. This is justice, which is the foundation of any constitutional order and the basis of one good world. *

*Ed. note: The reader is reminded that this article was written in 1949.

What is the likelihood that there will be a major thermo-nuclear war by 1975-80?

If you think that there is only a remote possibility of such a war, what are the facts on which you base this judgment? Assuming that there will be no major war by 1975-80, what do you think the world political structure will look like at that time?

If you feel that the likelihood of war is great, in what way is this war likely to begin? Who will be the participants, and what will be its effects?

What steps would you propose to avoid this war? Do they differ from the principles offered by Clark-Sohn? In what way? Is it that we do not need to implement all the Clark-Sohn principles? Which ones and why? Or is that they have omitted some important ones? Which ones and why?

What is the likelihood that there will be significant implementation of a major disarmament proposal by 1975-80? On what do you base your judgment? Do you agree with Kahn that war can be prevented without general disarmament? Why?

Both Clark-Sohn and Hutchins feel that any system of world order which fails to provide economic and social justice is inherently unstable and will necessarily lead to violence. Is the Clark-Sohn and Hutchins view in this respect true, or are they expressing deeply held preferences? Do you think political leaders and peoples of the more affluent states are willing to program adequately to implement these proposals? On what facts do you base this judgment?

How important do you think the idea of Constitutionalism as practiced in Western societies is and can be made to be in the development and maintenance of world peace? As you understand these practices would any changes have to be introduced in them to achieve world peace? Why?

What are the chances that major portions of the Clark-Sohn proposals will be accepted and implemented by 1975-80? What are the major obstacles blocking their acceptance? What can be done to remove these obstacles?

Do you agree with Clark that leadership to promote the kind of plan he is suggesting is not likely to come from the US or USSR but one of the nations of Western Europe? Why? Can you think of any other nations which might possess a special fitness for this task? What would you say constituted their peculiar qualifications?

Is it fair, feasible or necessary to involve political officials and responsible citizens of the newly independent and developing states in the problems of world order when they

74

are presently faced with establishing viable political and economic structures for their own states? If they did become involved, what ideas and programs do you think they would suggest? Would these tend to be compatible with the Clark-Sohn proposals? How much influence would you expect them to have in these matters?

How much danger of war might still exist if the Clark-Sohn scheme were implemented? Explain your answer.

Are there some values which you cherish more than peace? Would you go to war over them? Is it foreseeable that these values may be so threatened within the next two decades that however reluctantly, you can envision condoning major war?

Do you see any danger that the values which you cherish may be whittled away, even without war, by the exigencies of the present arms race?

BIBLIOGRAPHY

On world order through WORLD STRUCTURE, see:

Carnegie Endowment for International Peace. Perspectives on Peace 1910-1960. NY: Praeger, 1960, 202p. A set of articles by outstanding statesmen who have "framed their contributions around their experiences," reassessing "the premises, assumptions and judgments upon which their approaches have been based."

Claude, Inis L., Jr. Swords Into Plowshares: The Problems and Progress of International Organization. NY: Random House, 1956, 497p. Chapter 17 presents an argument against the kind of scheme Clark and Sohn are presenting.

Millis, Walter, Reinhold Niebuhr, and others. A World Without War. NY: Washington Square Press, 1961, 182p. A series of articles inquiring into the basic factors that underlie possible roads to peace.

Schiffer, Walter, The Legal Community of Mankind: A Critical Analysis of the Modern Concept of World Organization. NY: Columbia U. Press, 1954, 367p. A study of the historic bases of the concept of world organization, and the recurring themes and problems of analysis of such organization.

Slick, Tom. Permanent Peace: A Check and Balance Plan. Englewood Cliffs, N.J.: Prentice-Hall, 1958. A plan for giving the UN power over war, while protecting the nations from their loss of sovereignty by a system of checks and balances.

Thomas, Norman. The Prerequisites for Peace. NY: Norton, 1959, 189p. The author discusses three broad lines of policy for survival: general disarmament, military disengagement in danger zones, and strengthening the powers of the United Nations.

As indicated in the general foreword, the major theoretical alternative to the world structure approach is GRADUALISM. Most of the articles written in the field of international law and international relations are gradualist in that they deal with a particular limited problem and ask for a particular limited solution. (Legal gradualists will be noted in Session II.) There have been a number of books attempting to provide a theoretical underpinning and action program to coordinate the many proposals. The most recent contribution to this effort is:

Etzioni, Amitai. The Hard Way to Peace: A New Strategy. NY: Collier, 1962. The author offers a comprehensive gradualist approach

75

to peace to counter cold-war hysteria and a c h i e v e peace through effective arms reduction combined with accelerated modernization of underdeveloped areas.

While the seminar is unable to discuss that form of g r a d u a l i s m which has matured into a REGIONALISM approach, some of you may find it desirable to look at that material now.

Beloff, Max. "National Government and International Government." Internatl. Org. 13: 538-49 (Autumn 1960).

Bloomfield, Lincoln P. "The United States, The United Nations, and the Creation of Community." Internatl. Org. 14: 503-13 (Autumn 1960).

Burton, J. W. "Regionalism, Functionalism and the United Nations." Australian Outlook 15: 73-87 (Apr. 1961).

Claude, Inis L., Jr. Swords Into Plowshares: The Problems and Progress of International Organization. NY: Random House, 1956, 479p. Especially Chapter 6.

Deutsch, Karl W., and others. Political C o m m u n i t y and the North Atlantic Area. Princeton, N. J.: Princeton U. Press, 1957, 228p. International organization in the light of historical experience.

Fulbright, J. W. "For A Concert of Free Nations." Foreign Affairs 40: 1-18 (Oct. 1961).

Haas, Ernst B. "Regionalism, Functionalism and Universal Organization." World Politics 8: 238-63 (Jan. 1956).

_____. "Regional Integration and N a t i o n a l Policy." Internatl. Concil., No. 513: 381-442 (May 1957).

_____. "The Challenge of Regionalism." Internatl. Org. 12: 440-458 (Autumn 1958).

_____. "International Integration: The European and the Univer-sal Process." Internatl. Org. 15: 336-93 (Summer 1961).

Padelford, Norman J. "A Selected Bibliography on Regionalism and Regional Arrangements." Internatl. Org. 10: 575-603 (Nov. 1956).

Streit, Clarence K. Freedom's Frontiers--Atlantic Union Now. NY: Harpers, 1961, 319p. Includes the basic parts of the 1940 concise edition of the author's "Union Now--A Proposal for an Atlantic Fed-eral Union of the Free," first published in 1939.

The other major theoretical approach suggested in the general fore-word was that of INTERNATIONAL RELATIONS AND POLITICAL SCI-ENCE. There are many general studies and excellent textbooks in this area. The following two are generally considered to be major works, and would be useful both for general understanding and as guides to fur-ther reading:

Morgenthau, Hans J. Politics Among N a t i o n s. 3rd ed. NY: Knopf, 1960, 630p.

Wright, Quincy. The Study of International Relations. NY: Appleton-Century-Crofts, 1955, 642p.

On the SOVIET VIEW, see:

Kennan, George F. "Peaceful Coexistence: A Western View." Foreign Affairs 38: 171-90 (Jan. 1960). A rebuttal to the Soviet coexistence model for international peace.

Khrushchev, Nikita S. "On Peaceful Coexistence." Foreign Affairs 38: 1-18 (Oct. 1959). A definition of the Soviet alternative to greater international authority in the form of national competition with self-imposed restraints.

For materials concerned primarily with disarmament, see the bib-liography to Sessions VIII and IX.

SESSION II

THE PROMISE AND LIMITATION OF INTERNATIONAL LAW AND INTERNATIONAL ORGANIZATION TO ELIMINATE VIOLENCE AMONG NATIONS

Session I introduced us to the problem of war-prevention and the plan by Clark-Sohn for the development of world legal structure to establish and maintain world peace. The present pattern of international relations was usefully viewed as a system in which the armaments race had become a crucial and independent factor moving the system in the direction of a thermo-nuclear war. We recognized that disarmament and arms control would involve sensitive and complicated political, social and military problems. Finally, we explored in general terms the nature and utility of creating world constitutional structures as a method of achieving world peace.

This session will be directed more pointedly to investigation of the entire range of legal methods and techniques which might be appropriate for eliminating the threat or use of force among nations. This will involve inquiry into the nature and function of law within domestic societies, differences and similarities between domestic and international law and the relationship of international law to the international political system. An investigation of these matters will permit us to understand where we are presently in using law to control and prohibit the use of force by states against one another and the gap which exists between our present position and the model for world legal structure proposed by Clark-Sohn.

The chapter "Law in the International Community" by Kaplan and Katzenbach from their book The Political Foundations of International Law is used here to introduce us to general understanding of law. Their discussion points out that our naive conceptions based on observations of the legal structures of relatively well organized societies do not comprehend sufficiently the actual legal processes which take place. In turning then to international law, they make the crucial distinction of horizontal and vertical systems of law indicating that traditional international law was an operative system in the sense that there were a set of rules which guided and controlled the behavior of state officials; these rules grew up slowly by custom and practice and through treaties, but until very recently the international legal system had no central organization either for resolving disputes or keeping the peace. Their emphasis upon the relationship of legal systems to the political context in which they operate will be a major perspective throughout the seminar.

The article by Fisher raises the general question, how

77

come governments obey law at all? In raising the question he is suggesting that p e r h a p s too much emphasis has been placed upon a centralized enforcement agency to enforce law and that it may be u s e f u l to think of other d e v i c e s and mechanisms for achieving our purpose of a peaceful world.

Henkin's piece is a programmatic essay for the exten-sion of the r o l e of law in the i n t e r n a t i o n a l community. Starting with the central notion that a series of issues can be delineated on which there are compelling r e a s o n s for the major a n t a g o n i s t s in the world community to have some resolution, he attempts to indicate the contribution that law might make in the solution of these issues. The theoreti-cal framework is evolutionary and presents the full range of suggestions which legal gradualists have suggested over the past decade.

The first excerpt from Professor Falk's writings pro-vides us with an a n a l y t i c a l yet substantive framework in which international legal order must fit. Starting from the notion that there are three t y p e s of n a t i o n states today, modernizing, r e v o l u t i o n a r y and status quo, he asks the question, how can we regulate, and manipulate the dynamics of their interaction to bring about a warless world. In ad-dition, he recognizes t h e bi-polar nature of the present in-ternational system and the significant and diffuse impact of the increasingly hazardous a r m s race. His discussion of traditional international law, the challenge to it, and how we might meet it, lays bare the fundamental political problems which must be met if we are to d e v e l o p world legal order. You will find his discussion of the development and practice of doctrines of s o v e r e i g n t y especially important for an understanding of traditional international law.

The second excerpt from "The Legal Control of Force in the International Community" deals with the central core of o u r problem. Recognizing again the relationship of law to political structure Professor Falk also makes clear here some of the ethical and moral problems we face in the regu-lation of coercion. Physical force he points out is but one form of c o e r c i o n and it may well be that we shall need to plan to control other forms as well. Nevertheless, he feels that nuclear weapons present such a r a d i c a l and drastic gradation of c o e r c i o n that it may be useful to isolate the problem by controlling t h e s e weapons. Finally, his reci-tation of the attitude of international law towards war makes clear that it is o n l y a little over 40 years that proscription of outlawing of war has been the c o n c e r n of officials of the major politically organized u n i t s in the international com-munity. Though the f r a g i l i t y of this concern is obvious from the events of World War II, it has nevertheless become an a v o w e d world-wide goal the implementation of which is the compelling task of our times.

The articles by Claude and Russell are important con-

ceptual analyses of the relationship of international organization to the regulation of force. The attempt to clarify and
evaluate the three systems--balance of power, collective
security and world government--as a method of achieving
peace is crucial to our understanding and assessment of the
various proposals with which we will deal. Section 3 of
Claude's article in which he analyzes UN attempts to deal
with the threat or use of force should be read carefully as it
presents in somewhat summary manner where the international community stands now in those matters.

The provisions of the Charter which have been assigned
for this session lay out the bare outlines for the permissible
use of force by member states and what response the UN is
willing and capable of taking if it should decide a nation is
threatening or using force illegally. Article 2 (4) pro-
scribes the use of force and is qualified by Article 51 which
permits its use in self-defense. Article 39 provides the
Security Council with authority to deal with any act which is
a "threat to the peace, breach of the peace or act of aggression." There are a number of other provisions which bear
on these problems and all of Chapter Seven of the Charter
provides procedures for the UN to deal with it. There is a
relatively complicated gradation from pacific settlement of
disputes to acts of aggression running through Chapters Six
and Seven of the Charter. In Session V we will become
more familiar with these matters.

All of this is by way of providing a framework for evaluating the Clark-Sohn scheme. Aware as they are of these
matters and in what they consider to be the limited possibilities of evolutionary development, convinced that the stable
deterrence system is inherently unstable, they are proposing
that the next step be a giant one. They believe that the
scheme which they propose provides a rational basis for
acceptability of this step to the public officials and people of
all the states of the world.

For the remainder of this seminar we shall want to
question whether the step they propose is necessary and
whether it can be achieved.

Readings from "World Peace Through World Law":

Present United Nations Charter: Articles 2(4),
1(1), 51, 39, Chapters VI and VII, 89-128.

LAW IN THE INTERNATIONAL COMMUNITY

by
MORTON A. KAPLAN
and
NICHOLAS deB. KATZENBACH

Pᴇʀʜᴀᴘs the purest analytical concept of "law" is that in which an impartial judge objectively applies a pre-established rule to decide a controversy. And perhaps the purest analytical concept of "politics" is that in which the stronger influence or interest regulates the social distribution of values. In the real world, however, judges cannot avoid exercising at least some political discretion in the decision of cases. And in any stable political system, the political process is also subject to normative constraints.

Law exists, and legal institutions operate, only in particular political contexts. Contexts vary through time and space, and are influenced by many social, economic and cultural factors. We can and do legitimately separate "law" from "politics" in particular contexts for particular purposes. In educational institutions, for example, the study of law is largely the study of the judicial process, the application of rules by judges to the resolution of disputes arising from given factual situations. Political scientists, on the other hand, focus primarily on the process through which various policies are transmuted into effective community prescriptions. Yet both lawyers and political scientists are conscious of the fact that judicial institutions are meaningfully related to other processes of law-government which exist in a given community at a given time; that is, to the larger context in which authoritative community decisions are made.

If law is associated with a body of principles, or rules, claimed by someone to be authoritative, then it is relevant to ask who prescribes these principles, who invokes them, in what arenas, and with what results. How, and by whom, are they formulated, applied, and enforced, and what are their effects? If law is associated exclusively with courts composed of impartial judges, then it is important to realize that the impartiality of these courts, the kinds of disputes they can effectively resolve, and their techniques of judicial decision making are closely related to and dependent upon the other institutions of government within the relevant community.

Perhaps the point is most readily illustrated by our domestic institutions of law-government. When we speak of the "rule of law" or of a "government of laws," we clearly do not mean the rule of judges or a government of judges. We are talking about the larger, formal process, through which members of the society pursue and realize values in an orderly way. It scarcely requires argument that "law," viewed as a body of authoritative rules, pervades all the institutions of modern democratic government and is no monopoly of judges. We have a constitutional allocation of functions, supplemented by custom, experience, and ways of doing business within government, which gives to these processes a "legal" character. Legislators, administrators, and judges are all parts of a related process; all are subject to legal rules, and all invoke legal rules in the performance of their official tasks. They play different roles, and the role of each is related in important ways to the existence of, and the role played by, the others. Expectations of the community are generally structured in accordance with going conceptions of role performance.

An examination of the function of legal rules in the Congress would show these rules to be both similar to, yet strikingly different from, those of the Executive or the Judiciary. There are important distinctions between what the Congress does, and how it conceives its role, and what judges do and how they conceive their role. Not all disputes within society will be or should be resolved by judges employing the methods and techniques we associate with the judicial process. These techniques are primarily designed to insure impartiality between litigants and, in modern times, subservience to policies laid down by other governmental organs. It is possible rigorously to insulate our judiciary from partisan politics precisely because there are other institutional means for formulating and prescribing rules which adjust broader disputes as to community policy.

In the international system, the processes of law-government are far less highly developed than comparable processes within nations. Political organization is largely decentralized in the nation states which are the principal participants in the process. Political and legal institutions—institutions for prescribing, applying, and enforcing formal community policies—are not well differentiated. A world court exists, but no world executive or world legislature (at least, none with extensive authority). Their absence quite apparently affects the role which the International Court can successfully play. Similarly, assertions about law in the United Nations General Assembly or in diplomatic correspondence perform important functions contributing to international order, and capable of observation and analysis. But it is clear that these are not the same functions which

81

such assertions would play in the context of impartial adjudication by a court.

No one can observe the international political system without being aware of the fact that order does exist, and that this order is related in important ways to formal and authoritative rules, that is, to a body of law and to a process of law-government. These rules are sustained by the genuine interests which nations have in restraining certain forms of international conduct, even though these constraints must apply to their own conduct as well as to that of other states. To understand the substance and limits of such constraining rules, it is necessary to examine the interests which support them in the international system, the means by which they are made effective, and the functions they perform. Only in this way is it possible to predict the areas in which rules operate, the limits of rules as effective constraints, and the factors which underlie normative change. It is in this sense, then, that we shall be studying the political foundations of international law in this book.

INTERNATIONAL LAW AS "LAW"

Sometimes international law is viewed as a rather strange breed of law to which the term "law" is applied only by courtesy if at all. A number of great legal philosophers—Hobbes, Pufendorf, Bentham, and Austin are examples—have all doubted the legal character of international law, and the charges and counter charges which pervade the international community today seem to provide empirical support for their view. Clearly some definitions of law would exclude international law. Disputes, for example, are not routinely decided by an international judiciary, and there exists no coercive agency of formal international status which can effectively enforce the law. Rules do not emanate from any single "sovereign." Indeed, the legal order is not primarily vertical, or hierarchical, as it normally is in domestic government. Rather it is structured horizontally, composed predominantly of formally equal centers of legal authority called "states." We have only the beginnings of supranational authority in the United Nations and in various regional organizations.

It is possible, of course, to define law in such a way as to require a hierarchical structure. Austin did this in his theory that rules become authoritative and binding because they are sovereign commands. If law is defined in this way, then it is accurate to say that there is little in the international community.

In addition, and perhaps of more importance, is the fact that the present posture of world politics is scarcely favorable to the develop-

82

ment of, or reliance upon, universal legal rules. All systems of law tend to break down in crisis situations. In such situations, there is major provocation to act politically with little deference to pre-existing rules. Revolutionary justice following the collapse of the Vichy Regime in France, and the Gaullist accession to power following the May 13, 1959 uprising in Algeria, even though technically constitutional, are examples. The importance of force in contrast to constitutional procedures is greatly emphasized when the existing institutional structure is endangered—when, for example, a ruling elite finds itself threatened by a counter-elite advocating a coup or a new form of government. Government by decree and the suspension of normal legal processes are common phenomena in such a situation.

Thus emphasis upon force as a means of controlling the decisions of others is usually a function of crisis, often presaging major readjustments in the system of law-government. The nineteenth century saw a series of democratic revolutions. The recurring crises of this century, both in terms of a changing domestic social order and in the international "balance of power," have had noticeable consequences for the international legal order. Violence and the threat of violence mark international politics today.

A realistic study of law must, as has already been noted, see law in relation to its institutional support, examining the larger process through which rules are created, applied, and administered. There is a difference between the institutions which accomplish this within a domestic system and within the international community. This makes it necessary to examine international law within its particular political context. Disputes between states as to what international law requires or permits in a given situation are seldom referred to an international judiciary for decision. In the absence of judicial resolution, controversy may continue as to whether or not a particular act is "lawful." For example, in 1956, President Nasser nationalized the company operating the Suez Canal over the strong protests of the United Kingdom, France, the United States, and others. Those opposed claimed the nationalization was in violation of international law; on the other hand, Nasser, with considerable Afro-Asian support, contended it to be a legitimate exercise of national authority. The latter contention prevailed and effectively disposed of the dispute; the company has remained Egyptian. But those unwilling to accept the rule applied were unwilling to concede the legality of Nasser's decision. To do so would have been to abandon a rule which they hope may be effective as a deterrent to similar acts of nationalization elsewhere. Therefore, they continue to characterize it as "unlawful," and to deplore the lack of effective enforcement of international law.

83

In domestic society, controversy is rarely carried on in these terms because we have in the courts an institution whose judgment we accept as final. Generally, once a case is definitively decided, we, as observers, may criticize the decision as "good" or "bad" according to a variety of relevant criteria ranging from the technical competence of the court to our own ethical and policy preferences; we may castigate the court for overstepping institutional limitations by being guilty of "judicial legislation"; or we may accuse it of being wilfully blind to social consequences, of being either too literal or too liberal in its reasoning, and so forth. We may seek through political channels to reverse or mitigate the rationale of the decision as a norm for similar future situations; and where, as in the American Constitutional system, we find it occasionally beyond the reach of legislative reversal, we may employ a variety of techniques, ranging from scholarly criticism to thinly veiled political pressure (President Franklin Roosevelt's proposal for packing the Supreme Court is the obvious illustration) to limit its future application.

Now, in spite of the differences in terminology and the fact that a critic may get considerable political mileage from invoking the accusation that international law has been flaunted, processes in the international and domestic arenas are in some respects comparable. The particular decision disposes of the case and enters into the body of available precedent, whether that decision is persuasive or not. The focus of critical attention is to undercut its status as a norm to be invoked by others in similar circumstances, and it is to this end that some continue to call it a violation of international law. The more arbitrary it can be made to appear, the more radical the innovation, the more it can be related to selfish objectives of a particular state, and the more it offends widely shared and deeply felt values, the less persuasive it will be as precedent for others.

We cannot ignore the fact that in this process the same official may combine legislative and adjudicative functions, with emphasis, indeed, upon the former. Although national officials talk as if they were concerned only with what the law is, they are in fact equally concerned with promoting rules for the future which support policies they favor. The range of legislative creativity is limited by the interstitial nature of disputes, by the need to state principles that are widely acceptable and that are unobjectionable if invoked by others in like circumstances, and by the political cost of too flagrant a disregard of the expectations of other states based on past practices. In the absence of developed supranational legislative institutions, rules are prescribed, amended, adjusted, and applied by a time-consuming process of agreement or by unilateral state decisions. As a result rules are often quite fluid until formalized in treaties, and are subjected to political strain in their interpretation and application.

Considerations of policy, customarily denominated "political," which would be largely irrelevant in predicting decision by a domestic court because clearly beyond its function, may well be relevant, often controlling, when we examine invocations of law in the international process.

But to say this is not to concede the naive criticisms which plague intelligent discussion about international law. Often it is said that, since a state may decide for itself what constitutes international law, how it should be interpreted, and how it should be applied to a fact situation, it can decide cases arbitrarily. Obviously this argument is but a rephrasing of the thought that an independent judiciary is essential to impartial decision, and, hence, to law. If this argument is meant to imply that states do in fact act without regard to international prescriptions, it is descriptively inaccurate. If it implies that they are "free" to do so, it is wrong on both theoretical and practical grounds. If it implies that upon occasion, and particularly in times of crisis, states act without regard to what is generally accepted as controlling doctrine, it is quite right.

This argument is close cousin to the old saw that the Constitution means what the Supreme Court says it means—a formulation that, without qualification, would imply judicial autocracy. It ignores the institutional framework in which the Supreme Court sits, works, and decides. Similarly, each state has a stake in preserving the general structure of international law—the existence of a system of order effected through compliance with recognized norms—even though particular norms may be distasteful to a particular state. Each state will seek to influence and change those norms which it dislikes, since there is always temptation to evade adverse consequences in particular fact situations. However, the general interest in preserving the system is a force both for self-limitation as a means of inducing others to a similar response, and for the use of a variety of political pressures when others overstep the bounds of what is tolerable. Quite a bit has to be at stake, and a state has to be quite sure of its ability to "get away with it," before it will overtly violate norms which are generally accepted. Radical innovation which offends other decision makers may be worth it, but such innovations have political costs as well as profits.

Another appeal of the enforcement argument relates to the uncertainty, or flexibility, of the legal norms themselves, and to the degree to which different formulations and applications legitimately can be put forward. As we have noted, debate (in the absence of adjudication by an impartial judiciary) tends to be carried on in terms of accusations about non-compliance with the law. If, of course, one accepts as correct one's own formulation, that rule, so interpreted and applied, is not always adhered to by others. This fact creates

85

the illusion of either no law or no enforcement of the law. A limited choice of rules and a limited discretion in their interpretation is, however, a far cry from no rules at all. Most of us would like to have the rule as we interpret and apply it enforced internationally, though we might be more sceptical of a norm formulated and enforced by others. Few of our domestic political leaders are enthusiasts for world government, though they are loud critics of weak international law enforcement.

Doubts about a law-system which lacks judge and sheriff have, we think misleadingly, been frequently expressed as a theory of international law which describes it as a "voluntary" system based on the "consent" of "sovereign" states. It does not require much insight into law-politics to see a parallel between this theory and the consent theory of domestic government. Whatever the moral appeal of the consent theory at both levels (it represents a dislike for coercion), states "consent" to international prescriptions in the same sense that individuals "consent" to existing laws. They recognize the general need for a system of order, they regard the bulk of existing regulation as either desirable or at least tolerable, and they accept what remains because they have to—because they lack the ability to change it. The more intolerable a regulation is, the more pressure there is to seek a change by any means possible.

The point is not, of course, that legal institutions in the international community are adequate to contemporary affairs. Obviously they are not. But these institutions, such as they are, exist and contribute to international order. They will continue until some political combination has the capability to create new institutions more consonant with order and, we can at least hope, with a decent regard for human values. This creative process is presently taking place, on both a universal scale (the United Nations complex) and, perhaps more successfully, in a variety of regional and functional organizations such as NATO and the European Communities.

The authors recognize the merits of criticisms that distinguished observers such as George Kennan have made regarding too great a reliance upon legal processes. American foreign policy has often been formulated without sufficient attention to the role of force and of national interests. We do not wish to encourage naiveté of the sort he describes as "legal idealism," a reliance upon abstract rules that are institutionally unsupported. We concede that nations often do act in partisan ways in support of immediate political objectives. But we contend that much of international conduct is doctrinally consonant with normative standards, even though inconsistent with particular immediate interests, and that long-term self-interest can and does provide political support for internationally lawful conduct.

Furthermore, the terminology employed affects attitudes toward the institution described, and, if it becomes popular terminology, the institution itself. If judges were consistently called "politicians," and their decisions described as political, it would not be surprising if judges eventually behaved in a way appropriate to political or legislative and not to judicial institutions. Similarly, if the process of international decision making is described as wholly political, others are encouraged to focus exclusively upon its political aspects and to develop, in turn, attitudes that legitimize conduct commonly ascribed to political institutions, thus destroying to some degree the moderating influence that legal norms have. Perhaps a brief inquiry into the nature of legal and political processes and the content of law systems will enable us to return to this theme and to stress more clearly toward the end of the chapter the legal aspects of the process of international norm formulation.

The Judicial Role and the Legal Process

The popular conception of the judicial role and of the legal process is dominated by—indeed, abstracted from—the political institutions of modern western government. It takes for granted a separation of legislative and judicial functions and the existence of an independent judiciary with, at most, a limited policy-making role. The focus of legal scholarship has long been upon the judicial process, and the interaction of legislature and courts in their mutual adjustment to social processes has been glossed over, save, perhaps, at the constitutional level. The mythology of impartial adjudication overlooks the political role of judges as well as the impact of existing legal norms upon the legislative process, and seeks an unrealistic dichotomy between judicial and legislative processes. Our purpose here in stressing this interaction is not to obliterate valid analytical distinctions between the adjudicating and policy making roles of officials, considered conceptually, but merely to stress the relationship and interdependence of the legal and political processes—to give emphasis to the political context in which doctrine is operative in helping to shape effective decisions.

It is not necessary to reach far into the political past of England to find functions of policy prescription and adjudication unsegregated. The gradual separation of judicial and legislative functions and the growth of an independent judiciary accompanied the rise of democratic institutions and the fight for parliamentary supremacy on the one hand, and the growing functional inadequacy of rules based purely on custom on the other. In a relatively stable, uncomplicated society it is possible to resolve disputes by reference to customary rules. This is accepted because of the expectations built upon traditional ways of doing things. Although this mode of decision continues to play a role, it becomes far less adequate when a society becomes increasingly complex and interdependent, when government is conceived as a conscious instrument for achieving community policies, and when the society itself is in a process of dynamic change. As democratic industrialism replaced feudal agrarianism, the role of the judiciary changed, as did the role of other governmental institutions, by a process of mutual adjustment to new social and political facts.

In a tradition-oriented society, judges can and do play important legislative roles, for, in the settlement of disputes, they clarify the traditional rules that compose the formal law as they apply them. This was the method of the common law, and it has had its place in other systems as well. But, with the breakdown of tradition, the growth of popular politics and the power of Parliament, this function of the judiciary changed. Judges became independent, thus protecting against autocracy. They could no longer be directly and literally administering the King's justice in a society where the King was to be limited by Parliament; and they, like the King, had to be subservient to whatever rules Parliament formally enacted. Judges could still employ customary rules to decide some cases, but legislation became the dominant source of judicial standards.

A good deal of jurisprudential writing has been concerned with the nature of the judicial process and the extent to which judicial discretion can be limited. It has been popular to conceive the task of judges as the mechanical application of rule to fact. Law is seen as a closed, deductive system, which judges are to apply without any important element of choice. This theory, popularized in the jurisprudence of Austin, reflects a desire for a system of law-government in which judges are given extremely limited and narrow policy-making functions. It is, of course, an overstatement, for it is impossible to remove all discretion and all choice from judicial decision-making. Judges must select from a number of rules urged to be applicable, they must subsume particular facts under general rules, and they must exercise judgment in determining from conflicting evidence what the facts are and what facts are relevant.

In short, extra-doctrinal standards cannot be eliminated from the judicial process if it is to perform its function in society. Thus, there is such a phenomenon as judicial lawmaking. But it is important that judicial lawmaking be firmly constrained within institutionally understood limits. The adjudicating institution—with its prescribed function of impartial application of doctrine to cases—is itself a functionally necessary institution of the social system. Society, therefore, has an interest in maintaining it as a system that, in

88

general, acts according to relatively clear and determinate standards, that is not responsive to local or temporary pressures, and that is insulated from immediate political considerations.

The unique aspect of the judicial process derives from the fact that litigants go to a tribunal that is, in general, unresponsive to them as individuals, a tribunal that treats them anonymously except for the legally relevant facts, hears the matter according to certain established procedures, and decides the case within the constraint of rules that have been established in advance. A legislature may be inhibited from making a radical change in existing law by a desire not to shock existing expectations, by a desire to maintain social peace, or by fear of political reprisal; but that legislature would be acting within its formally limited role in making that kind of radical change. A court may be influenced by any or all of these considerations, but that court is required to relate its decision to existing norms. The technique is different. Some rationales would so clearly violate those norms that a court is very unlikely to use them. The court is limited in its capacity to create new rules; the appeal by both counsel and court is to a justification in terms of rules which already exist, or which can be inferred from pre-existing rules or custom.

The distinction between the legal and political processes is not that matters of political importance lack clear standards for decision, other than counting supporters, and that matters of law are settled according to such standards. The distinction is best made in terms of the different functions and different techniques of separate institutions. The complexity of modern society, and the rapidity of change within it, require an abstract and generalized legal structure permitting judges some freedom in their choice of premises and some freedom in the fitting of premises to facts. What rules are applicable? And what rules determine the subsumption of the factual situations under the rules? These questions require interpretation and leave some freedom of choice to the judge. But the judge must do more than merely justify both determinations in the light of existing standards. He must also recognize that he is establishing a rule for subsequent cases, for even in a system that does not give formal status to decisions as precedent, consistency is a condition of maintaining impartiality among particular disputants.

The range and scope of judicial creativity depend upon the law institutions and traditions of the particular community. Generally, limits are related to a number of variables. Among these may be listed the status (in terms both of official position and, often, of personal reputation) of the particular judge; the considerations, or evidence, he is permitted to evaluate; the existence or non-existence of other forums better equipped to deal with innovations; the extent to which there has been detrimental reliance by a party, or by influential groups generally, upon a rule widely thought to be applicable; the extent to which the new norm will be acceptable to political elites, and therefore has political durability. In particular, the judicial policy maker is limited by the interstitial nature of the judicial process and the consequent haphazard and piecemeal modification of rules pronounced only in relation to particular facts arising in particular dispute contexts. Judicial rule making is always *ex post facto* with respect to the controversy at hand, and, therefore, to be acceptable to the community, it ought not to depart radically from expectations conditioned by norms previously pronounced and by customs widely shared and relied upon. Furthermore, changing one aspect of a rule may require adjusting other relevant doctrine to make it fit into a viable body of law, and judicial ingenuity may be unequal, or the information available to a court inadequate, to so large a task of law revision.

Apart from listing the considerations that must be balanced, no set formula can be offered to determine the limits of judicial law-making. In the final analysis the test is political—the tolerance accorded by the political system and the need to maintain sufficient norm stability to perform the role of impartial adjudication. Laymen are often shocked by the extent to which securing such acceptance is a matter of technique; the skill with which a judge formulates issues, determines relevant facts, and selects applicable norms. But the existence of an informed professional bar makes acceptance more than a matter of mere verbal consistency; the argument must convince on its merits, if not as to its result, at least as to its being within the limits of tolerance.

The role of the judge as impartial arbiter negates open political partisanship. The fact that he is subservient to political officials in matters of policy determination also requires him to be cautious in creating new doctrine which is hotly controversial. He lacks the means to test his proposals in any extensive forum, though, to some extent, he may look to proposals made in the political forum, or by scholars and other influential groups. But both myth and technique make rapid, radical innovation difficult, and the need to be impartial puts a premium upon consistency. For the judge, the past is a safer guide to the future than are orgiastic visions of a new society. But he can exercise choice; some of the possible choices have stabilizing effects on the institutions and values of the society, or may even help to implement values and institutional developments thought to be desirable or just. Even though tempered by a proper caution, the role of the judge can be a creative one in which there is individual intervention and action.

The political lawmaker is more likely than the judge to be identified in a partisan role as the representative of certain interests, which he attempts to promote by establishing rules favorable to them. His influence and his tenure in office depend upon the support of identifiable groups. The political lawmaker may attempt to disguise his partisanship by referring to wider community interests, or he may subordinate the immediate interests of the groups he represents to longer-term interests of the body politic on the basis of values he holds or asserts. But he is under no obligation to derive his decision from prevailing norms.

Like the judge, the lawmaker will use prior experience, or precedent, as a means of legitimizing his proposals. But, unlike the judge, the political law maker is not formally required to relate his position to the past and the range of policy considerations open to him is therefore more extensive. Not being confined to the facts of a particular case or controversy and the need to do justice according to existing norms as well as to formulate prospective norms, he may adjust the scope of his proposals to political considerations.

Part of the political process is a contest to determine what values and what conceptions of the public interest will prevail. Part of the political process involves a contest to determine Constitutional norms, jurisdictional competences, and allocational authorities. Part of the process is a contest to determine who gets what. One of the legitimate functions of the political lawmaker is to influence the distribution of rewards and penalties in the society. For these reasons, the political role is, in part at least, a partisan role. However, other considerations modify and constrain the partisan aspects of the political role. It may be a generally accepted value of a political system that existing values and expectations should not be treated too harshly. Apart from this possible consideration, any political act, whether by vote or force (except under conditions of despotism), establishes a precedent for like situations. Moreover, the political lawmaker will take into account the need to conciliate opponents and to refrain from radical changes that will incite radical reactions should the political pendulum swing. The prudent politician, therefore, in a stable political environment is partisan but moderate. His "fairness" gains assent because it is moderate, not because it is impartial. But the role is conceptually different from the judicial role.

A political leader strong enough to change the structure of government over political opposition is unlikely to tolerate judicial frustration of his political objectives. Even in the American system, where the self-proclaimed Constitutional supremacy of courts is accepted, it is difficult to point to decisions that have thwarted a strong Execu-

91

tive from carrying out popular policies. The Supreme Court is most courageous in its policy role when the storm is past. Indeed, how could it be otherwise?

This conclusion may come hard to many who, with reason, regard the Judiciary as the guardian of the Constitution and particularly of those liberties guaranteed to individuals by the Bill of Rights. The authors do not belittle these functions or the moderating influence imposed on other branches of government by the consciousness of judicial review. But even the Supreme Court exercises its Constitutional prerogative sparingly, and influences policy at the margin only through techniques of interpretation. Courts do play extremely important roles in policing the police, in curbing tendencies toward petty tyranny by minor officials, and, thus, in insuring that in their daily work public officials do not exercise the public power capriciously or beyond the expressed public purpose. It would be dangerous and misleading to underestimate the importance of these functions for the protection of basic human values, or in preserving norms of decency and justice from gradual attrition at the hands of opportunists. But rarely can courts intrude into areas of political importance. Given a genuine political crisis, courts are likely to capitulate or to be bypassed. This may be different in important degree from the situation in the international sphere, but the similarities are nonetheless worthy of attention. Treaties are not the only formal covenants that have been treated as "scraps of paper."

The authors will have more to say about the interdependence of legal and political institutions, and the importance of role and function. For the moment it is sufficient to emphasize that the role customarily ascribed to judges is dependent upon and closely related to contemporaneous political institutions; that the relationship of legal processes to political processes is largely a function of these institutional arrangements; and, finally, that the institutional arrangements themselves can survive only as long as they are politically tolerable. To the extent these institutions can be adapted to orderly change a durable system of law-government exists. To the extent they cannot be so adapted, we may expect change by less orderly means, by the use of violence in varying degrees.

THE CONTENT OF THE LAW

Some observers say that only rules consistent with fundamental principles of justice can properly be regarded as law. They thus posit a "higher" law, the principles of which are universal and eternal, against which one can test so-called positive law. Sometimes this higher law has a divine origin, or at least a religious one, and

92

most of its principles in this secular age are referred to as rules of "natural law." Communists, too, resort occasionally to a somewhat similar technique of criticism of existing law by pointing out that in bourgeois countries law is the instrument by which the bourgeoisie dominates the proletarian masses, an instrument of class warfare, and therefore not true law at all.

In all political systems, formal authority must be legitimized in some way. The rules formally prescribed and enforced constitute the law for all those subject to them. The authors have defined law simply as formal authority coupled with authoritative doctrine. We have sought to distinguish it from pure force by requiring that the exercise of force be subjected to the test of authority, to rules of law known and adhered to.

The authors take no position regarding the substantive contents of the rules other than that these contents exist, can be discovered by observers, and, within unspecified limits of tolerance, are operative as standards governing official action. By putting no limits on the substance of law, we offend all adherents of natural law—although, in terms of personal preferences, we would agree with the values natural law usually embodies, and believe that a good case can be made for the fact that many of these, internationally as well as domestically, are parts of the positive law as it exists. We do not incorporate these rules into our conception simply because it is not necessary to our analysis.

What we do wish to emphasize in this connection is that law is more than a system of order in the sense that any legal system also embodies values other than order. Thus the law prevents *A* from doing something he desires to do; it punishes *B* for something he has done; it transfers *C*'s wealth to *D*, or declares that *E* rather than *F* is the owner of some land or chattels; and so forth. Every decision, every official act, and every norm that authorizes such an act, reflects some system of values, some ethical or moral judgment.

As participants in the political processes of government we all seek to influence official action so that it accords as nearly as possible with our preferences, with the kind of society (local, national, global) that we want, and that supports a distribution of values of which we approve. We seek at every level to persuade, cajole, and coerce the officials who set policy, to make them enact rules that will distribute rewards and penalties in accordance with our desires. We are successful to the extent to which we command political influence, which is variously measured in various societies, and which ranges from rational argument to the threat of violence. Order itself may be high on the scale of values—today violence in the international community may mean annihilation—but history indicates that other values may be more important to various participants.

Thus, in all legal systems, there is a direct connection between the rules prescribed and the prevailing ethics and morality, and throughout the politico-legal process a constant interaction of "ought" and "is." One technique of argument is to identify the two, to persuade the relevant decision maker that the law is so-and-so because that is what it ought to be. To some decision makers, precepts of natural law may be persuasive in this task of convincing. In addition, some values are regarded as more important than others, and often these are, or can be, identified with fundamental natural law doctrine. For example, the American Bill of Rights incorporates what are thought to be fundamental liberties of individuals against constituted authority, and although American judges need go no further than the positive prescription to find these particularly favored rights, others may find these in an "unwritten" constitution.

Through space and time, different polities are likely to give different emphasis to different values—to make different choices when "freedom" of individual action conflicts with the requirements of "order," when "private property" conflicts with some conception of "social welfare." However, the cultural heritage of western civilization has in fact given us a common core of basic human rights which are widely shared, and which, within the limits of judicial creativity, undoubtedly influence the interpretation of legislation and the choice of applicable norms by judges. It is these principles, in various formulations and interpretations, which many natural lawyers, like the authors of the American Declaration of Independence, regard as inviolable and beyond the reach of politics, legislative majorities, charismatic leaders, military juntas, or secular priests. Particular laws that violate these norms are themselves "illegal" because they violate principles of law which are universal, valid for all people, in all times, in all political contexts.

Now it may well be true that nature—human, social, psychological, or physical—does impose some requirements upon individuals and does set constraints upon what can wisely and profitably be regulated through official action. It may be that the true essence of law can only be found in the true nature of man. The authors leave that problem, along with the diversity of standards and their correct application to particular situations, to philosophers. Our task is less ambitious. We are concerned only with the actual practices of states and the norms enacted, promulgated, and enforced by formal governmental institutions. To reflect upon whether or not these practices accord with natural law directs attention to a wholly different question. Even if decision makers decide according to their conception of natural law, its actual existence (save as positive law) is irrelevant to our analysis. For our purposes we can learn more from studying actual decisions, the conceptions which in fact prevail, than we can from attempting to discover what natural law truly is. Of course, a belief in natural law may be operative in decision making, and this belief may be a relevant datum, particularly in the interstices where there is room for judicial creativity. But it is relevant to our analysis because of its influence upon the legal process, not because of its inherent rightness.

This is not to say that there is no connection between law and the prevailing ideas of ethics and morality; or that whatever is, is right; or that legal systems at war with the nature of man are good and will endure. We simply emphasize the role of law as a system of formal authority in effecting a distribution of basic human values, in enforcing social policies, within the relevant society. We are concerned with understanding the norms that are enforced as law within society. Whether these norms accord with a higher or eternal "law" is a different question.

NATURE OF THE INTERNATIONAL LAW SYSTEM

Let us turn to a more specific examination of the international system, its peculiarities and its compass. In the first place, the system lacks any central legislative or judicial authority save that provided by the United Nations and by the International Court of Justice. The present bipolar system of international politics, with its potential instability and tendency toward crisis, makes it difficult for these universal institutions to play a dominant, or even particularly important, role. The most important participants in politico-legal processes continue to be the various states, especially the United States and Soviet Russia, although, in recent years, blocs and loosely organized "uncommitted" nations have become increasingly important. On some matters supranational officials may speak authoritatively and formally for groups of states; but normally law-rules are still formulated, interpreted and administered by state officials. There exists, therefore, a system of law-government in which a large number of decision makers of formally equal authority participate.

The division of the world community along territorial lines among a number of formally equal political entities does not mean that formally equal states are able equally to affect decisions and the distribution of values in that community. The United States, for example, can and does wield considerable influence, directly and indirectly, through its control over a large proportion of the world's productive resources—goods, money, skill, machinery, and so forth. The United States' various foreign-aid programs, its effective control over international lending agencies, its structure of trade and related agreements are instruments that can be used—wisely or unwisely, effectively or ineffectively—in fostering as law in the world community doctrine compatible with its political and social objectives. And, though formal participation is confined to state and supranational officials, we should not underestimate the importance of transnational associations of private interests (business groups, scientists, scholars), who can and do bring their influence to bear on those who have the formal authority to prescribe and administer law.

The peculiar feature of international law-government is its horizontal structure of coequal authority. For reasons to be explained in Chapter 2, states have not until recently been willing or able to create enduring joint institutional arrangements for recommending, prescribing, interpreting and enforcing international law. State officials acknowledge the obligatory character of international law as a body of rules, but reserve to themselves the determination of what the rules are, how they apply to specific facts, and how they are to be administered. Such a decentralized system is not utterly chaotic, and state officials do not have unlimited discretion to act arbitrarily. They are deterred from doing so by many considerations: a consciousness of the general need for order and stability in the conduct of foreign relations and the rules regulating transnational problems; the fact that many rules have reciprocal advantages; the existence of widely shared techniques of legal reasoning and argumentation; the desire not to offend other states for a variety of reasons, including the possibility of incurring various sanctions.

At any given time there is some consensus as to the rules applicable and their interpretation, and considerable good faith in their honest execution. This is not surprising. In domestic societies, too, most groups are satisfied with the bulk of existing legal norms and have no disposition, as well as no political capacity, to change them. By comparison, the area in which change is desired and politically feasible is relatively small. It is here one finds political controversy and the testing of governmental institutions in their capacity to promote orderly change. The test is most rigorous when society is in a process of rapid social and political transition and when there are widely divergent views as to what rules are desirable.

Within a developed system of law-government, such as that of the Western democracies, changes in existing legal rules are accomplished by different institutions performing different roles and employing different techniques. Gradual and moderate change can be and is accomplished by the judiciary in the resolution of specific controversies. Within rather broader limits the executive can formulate rules and orders, as well as recommend various changes to the legislature. Primary formal responsibility for innovation is given to the elected representatives acting by specified majorities in the legislature. In each instance, moreover, there exist both legal (constitutional) and political restraints on legislative decision. A full description of the process would emphasize different roles and functions (separation of powers) and, equally important, institutional interaction.

In international law-government, as already emphasized, there is no comparable separation of function, and legislative devices are primitive and clumsy by comparison. In theory, rules can be prescribed or amended only by formal agreement or by informal consensus based on past practices. Where rules have not been reduced to the form of a treaty, they are created by the more fluid process of claims and concessions. This method is nothing more than unilateral action by a state justified, or justifiable, by reference to a conception of the interests of the international community, and conceding a right of other states to act, or a duty to refrain from acting, in the same way in like circumstances. To the extent that such claims can be related to existing rules or can be reasonably inferred from past experience and past conduct of others in similar situations, the standing of the claims as legitimate and persuasive formulations of principle is enhanced. If, over a period of time, such claims are acknowledged and acquiesced in by other states, they become part of the body of doctrine applicable to all.

This process is similar to the judicial process of gradual modification of rules through interpretation and reformulation in the light of changed factual conditions. The same techniques are employed. Just as the domestic judge rationalizes his decision by verbally identifying it with the law as it "is," rather than acknowledging his choice among doctrinal alternatives as an "ought" or preferential one, so too the international decision maker will identify his view as the correct one required by existing doctrine. Verbally, at least, he will be reluctant to flaunt international law and to rely upon an argument based merely upon his power to do as he prefers. His argument may be accepted by other participants because they accept the statement in justification as being consistent with the existing body of doctrine; because they find it a desirable formulation of law; or because it is moderate and backed by sanctions strong enough to make acquiescence a wise political act. Grounds for conceding the claim are seldom differentiated in practice, and would, indeed, be difficult to differentiate in view of the mixture of motivation, encouraged by the technique, normally present. Only the very abrupt break from the past, unsupported by substantial argument based on accepted norms, is clearly a political act, and even this may be widely accepted by others on its policy merits. The point was made earlier in this chapter that the incentive to act politically is greatly enhanced by crisis. If its basic institutions and values are threatened, a state is likely to act to the full extent of its capacity, whether that capacity is measured in terms of political or of economic capabilities, or even of force; this is true, too, of a domestic government threatened by revolution.

We speak of such unilateral claims as being acknowledged or acquiesced in over a period of time in order to describe one aspect of the process by which authoritative doctrine is created. From the perspective of predicting future conduct, such acquiescence is essential to accurate prediction of how specified officials are likely to act on particular issues. The greater the acquiescence with regard to a rule—the greater the consensus—the more useful it is as a tool to prediction. But even if not acquiesced in—even if protested, rejected, or deplored by other states—an effective act enters into the stream of decisions which make up the total body of law. Like dissenting opinions of the United States Supreme Court, or frustrated legislative proposals in the Congress, such a decision is a potential factor to be reckoned with. It may, like most dissents and unenacted bills, wither away and cease to be operative in future decisions. There is, however, always the possibility that it may be resurrected as the correct and proper statement of the law on some future occasion.

In addition to this process of claims and concessions, or "customary law," rules may be made more explicit in formal agreements, or treaties. Where agreement on a mutually satisfactory basis can be negotiated, treaties have several advantages. In the first place, the explicit language of treaties, even if quite general, tends to limit the discretion of national officials rather more than do several formulations over a period of time by several decision makers. Frequently, treaties are codifications of past practices, and as such perform the useful function of making rules both more certain and more stable. In this respect codification of international rules resembles codification of domestic rules, a practice that has been going on in the United States and England, and elsewhere, for the last century or more. Diversity of interpretation of treaty provisions may still exist in the absence of joint institutions to determine their application, but it tends to be reduced to marginal applications rather than more basic policy—provided that the basic policy continues genuinely to be supported by the signatories.

A treaty, for these reasons, is an effective means for implementing international law nationally; in a modern bureaucracy it is more likely to insure that officials not charged with important policy functions do not, through inadvertence or ignorance, create foreign policy complications. Critics often focus so exclusively upon the crisis situations that they ignore the extent to which international agreements are faithfully executed. This is accomplished through the simple device of giving treaties (either through implementing legislation or regulation, or through a principle which makes them directly effective) the same status as domestic legislation. As a result, national judges and administrators carry out treaty provisions as a matter of course, and it requires a major political decision to vary their terms.

Finally, treaties are a method of securing policy goals in matters previously unrestrained and unregulated by international rules, or of consolidating support for a particular view where conflicting assertions of "customary" law are so numerous as to raise serious questions about what the operative rules may be in any given situation.

Quite often treaties are cast in a general language that permits signatories considerable latitude in their implementation through domestic governmental processes. In the absence of a built-in dispute-resolving mechanism, some differences may arise with respect to the interpretation and application of an agreement in specific situations. In general, such differences are tolerated, or resolved through diplomatic consultation. If serious, however, they may be invoked to suspend or terminate the provisions of the treaty generally. Usually pressures for consonance and toleration exist, and in the absence of major shifts in political power, adjustment is possible. Even agreements which cease to have the reciprocal advantages perceived at the time of signature may be scrupulously adhered to, or, alternatively, voluntarily modified. There are usually enough other objectives requiring cooperation to make either compliance or amendment preferable to treaty violation.

Frequently treaties have provisions for termination on relatively short notice, and such provisions increase the likelihood of continual appraisal and revision. Where this is not the case, and where the period specified is a long one, the necessary job of appraisal and reformation in the light of new conditions is far more difficult to accomplish. In extreme cases, the pressure for strained unilateral interpretation, or even termination, may be irresistible. There is a doctrine occasionally invoked (*rebus sic stantibus*) that holds that treaties do not endure when conditions have so changed as to frustrate their basic purpose. But this may be easier for one party to perceive than the other, and it is never a mutually satisfactory basis for termination; if it were, it would not need to be invoked unilaterally. Often the only conditions which have changed are the political ones; one party has greatly increased its bargaining power.

Unilateral termination is not generally acknowledged as legally proper, but it may be politically feasible if there is support for the contention that the treaty is "unfair" or "unjust." Usually termination is sought to be legitimized by talk of prior violations, implied conditions, or through strained interpretation which makes it less burdensome. It may be tempered, too, by a stated willingness to abide by certain principles in the future. When President Nasser of Egypt nationalized the Suez Canal, he was quick to acknowledge the binding obligations of the Treaty of 1888, which guaranteed free and non-discriminatory passage to foreign ships, and to acknowledge the interests, but not the formal authority or control, of user states in the efficient operation of the canal.

No state is prepared to abandon the principle that agreements must be performed (*pacta sunt servanda*) any more than, in domestic matters, it is willing to abandon the idea that laws must be obeyed. But at the same time it is abundantly clear that whenever the "bargain" concept is projected too far into the future, whenever an agreement is felt to have been unfairly imposed or coerced (as at Versailles), or whenever one of the parties strongly feels that there is no longer any reasonable relationship between benefits and burdens, it runs into difficulty—doctrine to the contrary notwithstanding. The conditions—predispositional as well as environmental—that led to the original agreement do, of course, change, and not necessarily in the same direction and at the same rate among signatories. If changed circumstances lead a party to a treaty to challenge the fairness of applying the treaty's provisions without modification, a refusal by the other party to the treaty to renegotiate may persuade the first nation that it can protect its interests only by violation or abrogation of the treaty.

This problem cannot be solved by doctrine concerning the sanctity of agreements. The difficulties of settling such problems lie not in some doctrinal deficiency but in clumsy political processes for appraisal, recommendation, and modification of treaty provisions. The appropriate analogy for disputes of this kind is not that of contract law but rather that of legislative reform and amendment. Comparison with domestic procedures makes this clear. In domestic law-government, the political organs of government have the responsibility for resolving political disputes by enacting new laws or by changing old laws. For this reason, in domestic law-government there are judicial institutions that can resolve disputes as to the application of legal rules but not differences as to the desirability or direction of major change in the law. Laws must be faithfully observed (with some inevitable latitude in their interpretation), but the possibility of amendment or repeal by the political organs of government is always present.

International disputes that revolve around the interpretation of formal treaty obligations are only partly, and often peripherally, related to genuine disputes as to the meaning or application of the norms. Genuine interpretation problems are soluble through diplomatic discussion, or, indeed, may be voluntarily referred to third-party resolution. The difficult disputes are those in which one of the parties really wants to change the agreement—to amend, repeal, extend, or supplement its provisions—in a way that the other does not support. This desire may be masked as interpretation of existing terms, or reference may be made to "implied conditions," and the issue paraded as a legal question. The dispute could be decided by a court; all disputes can. In domestic law-government, such a dispute would probably be amenable to *both* judicial and legislative resolution. In a sense, this is true internationally because of refusal to submit to adjudication as the exclusive mechanism, thereby looking to resolution through a diplomacy in which judicial and political techniques are intermingled.

What has been said with regard to disputes based on treaties is even more likely to be true in the more fluid process of invocation of "customary" law and general principles of jurisprudence. Here norms are less refined, in a more or less constant process of change, and capable of more broadly divergent application. Nonetheless they do serve as a force for stability, for they act as deterrent to extreme decisions and encourage a moderate approach.

General principles and "customary" rules of international law are said to be universally applicable to state conduct, whereas treaties are viewed as special legal regimes which are obligations of signatories only. However, the distinction is not quite so clear in practice. A great many treaties codify and restate what the signatories believe to be "customary" law adjusted to contemporary conditions. The greater the number of signatories, the more persuasive the codification and the more likely it will be invoked by or against non-signatories, not as a treaty obligation, but as persuasive evidence of a "customary" rule which binds them as well. Indeed, even where there is no contention that a rule is based on past practice and "custom," its incorporation in a number of treaties, or in a single multilateral treaty, may make it the measure of what is "reasonable" or even "lawful" under general standards, and thus arguably binding on non-signatories as well. There is a persistent tendency toward universalizing, or at least projecting as far as possible, rules frequently found in treaties. One reason is simply that it is administratively desirable to have the greatest amount of uniformity with regard to international problems, and it is complicated to administer a number of special legal regimes dealing with substantially the same subject matter.

The other side of the coin is equally interesting. Rules based on "custom" or derived from general principles of law are claimed to be universally applicable, even though it is clear that, in fact, there are often a number of divergent statements as to what the law is and how it should be administered. Some areas approach universality, particularly those where reciprocal advantages and interests are general and obvious; diplomatic immunity would be an example, though even here some rules (for example, asylum in an embassy) are quite variant. In other areas (for example, expropriation of private property owned by foreign nationals) doctrinal divergencies are clear and fundamental. Accurate description would, as in the case of treaties, find in reality a number of legal regimes, rather than a single universal one, among states that share more or less similar views as to what the rule is and how it should be interpreted.

Why are rules that, descriptively, are not universal claimed nonetheless to be so? The answer, of course, is that, in the absence of joint legislative institutions with continuing formal power to prescribe the law, the claim to universality of unilateral formulations is a technique whereby state officials promote rules which serve policies in the international community which these officials support. They wish to make these rules obligatory for others, and the claim that all states are so bound permits them to push their contentions. Reciprocal doctrine to the effect that each state determines international law for itself, and that no state can be bound by a rule unless it consents (but it may consent impliedly), serve the opposite purpose of preserving oneself as a formally coequal legislator.

Conflicting interpretations of treaties and conflicting formulations or applications of "customary" law may lead to disputes. These may be settled by mutual agreement, arrived at through direct diplomatic negotiation, or through third-party intervention in the form of good offices, mediation, conciliation, arbitration, or adjudication. In all these processes legal rules play roles, for they are appealed to by the disputing parties and by third parties seeking to resolve the dispute. Since state officials, unlike private parties in a domestic dispute, do have a legislative role, and have therefore to be prepared in the future to abide by the contentions they urge in particular disputes, the use of legal rules and legal arguments may narrow issues in dispute and assist in promoting moderate approaches. So, too, does the possibility of sanctions of varying degrees of coercive effect. Here the role of legal norms is to justify and legitimize acts of coercion which would otherwise be unlawful.

It is this flow of effective decisions by officials invoking international norms that is the substance of international law. We cannot categorically state its content. Like all legal systems it is in a process of change, and as peoples grow more dependent upon one another for the realization of common values, matters previously unregulated become appropriate subjects for formal regulation. There is a predisposition on the part of national decision makers to be cautious in promulgating norms too detailed and too rigid to permit adjustments to the contingencies of a politically fluid society, or, alternatively, to be cautious in delegating to supranational officials (whether judges or legislators) very much formal authority to prescribe such adjustments. It may be easier to adapt national laws to international facts without attempting to state a binding international standard. After all, an international norm is self-limiting as well as being a potential limitation on others. Political leaders still have great reluctance to limit their own political freedom beyond what is absolutely necessary to secure immediate objectives.

The historian can trace the problems of the last century in the international law-doctrine that grew out of them. Britain's dominant sea power gave her a capacity to "enact," almost by herself, an international law of the sea—a law that, although it undoubtedly served her purposes well, also served those of the larger community. Emigration from Europe led to new problems about the granting of citizenship, as the various national laws failed to mesh in the conflicting interests of new and old. Popular revolutions led to new practices and new doctrine about recognition and interference in internal affairs. Dominant theories of laissez-faire economics, and the pound sterling as an international currency, led European nations to back up their merchants, their businessmen and their money lenders with a series of norms concerning the obligation of debtor states, the sanctity of money, and the protection of commercial property. In addition to colonial governments, the developed countries established a number of regimes in non-European countries for the protection of Europeans from the unfamiliar and harsh requirements of alien legal systems. Technologically backward countries were held accountable for damage to the person or property of foreigners where local law and order was not preserved, and for this purpose, as well as for the collection of debts, doctrine supported creditor self-help. Protests by smaller nations were seldom effective. The Latin American countries, for example, attempted to legislate again the use of force in collecting debts (the so-called Drago doctrine) and against the use of diplomacy in backing up private business. They found, however, that even with the political protection provided by the Monroe Doctrine, they were still unable to make these new laws effective against their European creditors.

In this century we have seen the outbreak of violence on a tremendous scale, and much of our effort has gone into efforts to modernize the laws of war, to prevent, control, limit, and mitigate the consequences of violence. From disarmament, through the punishment of war crimes, to contemporary problems of nuclear energy and space missiles, this problem has dominated the period since the First World War. In addition, we are plagued with the problems of the end of colonialism, of an emergent nationalism which asks for Afro-Asians not merely freedom and independence, but "social justice" as well. The slogans of domestic politics have been internationalized as problems once national in scope have become international. Human problems pass across territorial boundaries with ease and transform themselves into problems for the international community to solve.

Older political solutions became transformed, as political solutions do, into legal norms through treaties, practices, and customs. Many such solutions are not adequate for international problems as they are no longer adequate for comparable domestic ones. The distribution of political influence in the hands of competing national political elites offering competing solutions makes some problems more difficult to resolve. The international community is going through a period of crisis and the preservation of order will depend on the strength, the political ingenuity, and the skill of Western leaders in creating new law and new institutions of law-government if the international community of the future is to reflect the system of values held by the West rather than that held by the Soviet Union. The task of international lawyers and statesmen alike is to weed, to prune, to create—not to cling to outmoded solutions of another era and bemoan the passing of international law as they do so.

BRINGING LAW TO BEAR ON GOVERNMENTS
Roger Fisher *

IT has long been suggested that nations could adjust their conflicts of interest amicably and live in peace forever if they would only conform their conduct to international law. As the world situation has become more explosive, the prospect of a world under law has become more fashionable and there is increasing talk of the "rule of law." But much of the arguments for extending the rule of law to international relations remains "on an inspirational and rhetorical level that does not permit underlying difficulties to come to the surface." [1] While the Senate considers repeal of the Connally amendment,[2] by which the United States reserved the right to decide independently whether a dispute concerning itself was within the jurisdiction of the International Court of Justice, discussion of an international order is pursued with renewed vigor. It is important that this discussion be approached realistically, with an eye to what is now possible, and not lose itself in references to a distant goal. For any decision on the Con-

* Professor of Law, Harvard University. A.B., Harvard, 1943; LL.B., 1948.
This paper is a revised version of a talk given at Boston University Law School on November 17, 1960.

nally amendment must deal with an issue which may well be called *the* problem of international law: why governments comply with law.

Most lawyers hold in common a view of international law which runs somewhat as follows: There is a great difference between positive law — law with a policeman behind it — and so-called international law. International law is a body of vague rules for the attention of the political scientist and the amusement of the law student not much interested in law. It should not be confused with real law, which, as Mr. Justice Holmes pointed out, is "the articulate voice of some sovereign or quasi-sovereign that can be identified," [3] and "does not exist without some definite authority behind it." [4] Law is the command of a sovereign backed by force. And however much it is hoped that nations will abide by acknowledged rules some day, they do not now; nor can they ever be compelled to do so, at least in the absence of world government. Only woolly thinking would confuse positive law enforced by our courts — our Constitution, our civil and criminal laws — with the moral directives which go by the name of international law.

So runs the party line of the profession.[5] But Holmes, who was one of its ardent supporters, also commended to us a "reconsideration of the worth of doctrines which for the most part still are taken for granted without any deliberate, conscious, and systematic questioning of their grounds." [6] He would surely approve the reappraisal of accepted doctrines in the light of a developing understanding. It is time to ask ourselves whether the notion of law as the command of a sovereign is a useful one for the solution of problems of international order.

We are interested in why governments comply with law, why they comply with court decisions. The process by which domestic law is brought to bear upon governments may have general application and be relevant to the international problem. The command theory of law, which was used to distinguish the law that *is* from the law that *ought to be*, was evidently developed out of an examination of the typical private action for a tort or on a contract. If a court declared that Doe must pay Roe a stated amount, the sheriff and the marshall stood ready to enforce the judgment with the full power of the state. This was the situation envisioned by Austin when he spoke of laws as commands. His definition of law did not apply to rules restraining the behavior of the state itself which Austin referred to as rules of "positive morality." [7] The "power of the government," he said, "is incapable of *legal* limitation." [8] It followed that a government had neither legal rights nor legal duties.

> A sovereign government . . . may appear in the character of defendant, or may appear in the character of demandant, before a tribunal of its own appointment, or deriving jurisdiction from itself. But from such an appearance of a sovereign government, we cannot infer that the government lies under legal duties, or has legal rights against its own subjects.[9]

Within such a theory, international law is clearly no more than positive morality. But much of the modern law school curriculum besides international law would have to be similarly characterized. Courses in constitutional law, administrative law, and tax law, to name only a few, deal in large part with limitations on governmental action or involve the Government as a party to a dispute in courts deriving jurisdiction from itself. More than sixty per cent of the cases in which the Supreme Court handed down opinions during its 1959 Term adjudicated rights and duties of the federal government.[10] We can suspect that a definition of law which excludes so much may not be useful today.

But we are not concerned here with a mere matter of definition. Whether or not we are content to call all these areas of law "positive morality," the fact remains that a large part of our courts' work lies in these very areas. Whether or not governments are theoretically capable of legal limitation, they do regularly submit to adverse court decisions. I suggest that we lawyers, in uncritically accepting the command theory and applying it to international law have ourselves been guilty of woolly thinking. I suggest that in denying the status of international law because there is no apparent sovereign issuing the commands, we show a limited understanding of how a court system operates in its relations with a government. In blandly assuming that all law rests on superior force, we have ignored the cases in which the government loses a judgment and honors it.

Is organized force essential to such compliance? Clearly it is not. When a judgment is entered against the United States in the Court of Claims, no superior sovereign compels Congress to vote an appropriation. The judgment is paid because that is the law; but the law is not the articulate voice of a superior sovereign. When, in the *Youngstown* case,[11] the Supreme Court ordered the

Secretary of Commerce to return the steel mills which the President had ordered him to seize, the Court had no regiments at its command. But despite the fact that the Supreme Court sitting in Washington had no greater force at its command vis-à-vis the Government than does the International Court of Justice sitting at the Hague, the steel mills were returned.

The more closely one examines law within this country and within others, the less significant seems the element of force. Even such hard, positive laws as the criminal and tax laws depend ultimately on compliance with them by the Government, and the general pattern is one of compliance. To be sure, Congress, on perhaps a dozen occasions, has failed to honor a judgment of the Court of Claims.[12] But the Government, which is never without funds or absent from the jurisdiction, has a far better record than the private judgment debtor. This record, even if less than perfect, demonstrates that a pattern of governmental compliance can be secured without a supragovernmental police force.

Moreover, even where the organized force of a superior sovereign is available it may be difficult to make a government comply. If a government is not persuaded to obey by other reasons, superior force alone may not be enough. In *Virginia v. West Virginia* [13] the Supreme Court had before it the continuing failure of the West Virginia legislature to raise and appropriate the funds needed to pay Virginia that share of its public debt which West Virginia had undertaken upon becoming a separate state. Assuming that the United States Army was at the Court's disposal, what should the Army do to enforce the judgment? Should it seize the state capitol and sell it at auction? Should it raise funds at the point of a gun? If so, from whom? However effective force or the threat of force may be when applied to an individual, it is difficult to bring force to bear on a political enterprise which offers no obvious point of application.[14] So long as a rule runs only to a political entity rather than to individuals, a superior power must face the problem of trying to apply force to an abstraction.

If it is not the threat of force which induces governmental compliance with domestic law, it is not the absence of force which explains why our Government feels less strongly bound by international law than, for example, by the Constitution. Nor does an explanation lie in the fact that international rules are generically more vague than constitutional rules. They are not. Nor can we look for an answer in our Government's denying the bind-

107

ing nature of international law. It does not. Nor is an answer to be found in the assumption that the Government will comply more readily with rules benefiting citizens than with those benefiting foreigners. The due process clause protects citizen and alien alike.

What is the difference, then, between a judgment of the Court of Claims and a judgment of the International Court? Is it merely that the United States accepted the jurisdiction of the former one hundred years ago and has not yet really accepted the jurisdiction of the latter? The question is worth exploring. An understanding of the factors inducing governmental obedience to domestic law may shed light on the problem of securing obedience to international law. We should not expect to find factors that guarantee obedience. Governments do not always obey rules. In a given case, what are considered vital interests may lead a government to break the law just as they may persuade an individual to steal. The question, rather, is: What are the forces which tend to induce obedience, the elements which impart strength to the law? Knowing that these elements are in fact strong enough to bring about general governmental compliance with domestic law, we will want to appraise their ability to bring about governmental compliance with international law.

In considering whether to respect a rule, one factor which a government takes into account is the danger of external consequences should it not respect the rule. Even where there is no organized superior sovereign power to compel obedience, a government is not free to ignore the conduct and attitudes of those with whom it must deal. The United States Government, considered as an entity, respects the Constitution partly because it fears the retaliatory action which might be taken by the citizens if it did not. A focal point for such retaliation might be the polls. And the Government respects the right to vote, influenced in part, perhaps, by fear of more violent action if it were denied.

Internationally, the most significant forces external to a government are not its own citizens but other nations. Before a government decides to break a rule of international law, it must consider the possible reaction of other states. It is not only the immediate reaction of the states most affected by the breach that is relevant; the effect on what may be called world public opinion must also be considered. Thus, should the United States consider resumption of espionage flights over the Soviet Union in violation of Soviet and international law, an intelligent decision could not ignore three factors external to the government: (1) political criticism within the United States; (2) the possibility of direct retaliation by the Soviet Union; and (3) the likelihood of an adverse reaction among our allies and the uncommitted nations. These considerations are analogous to those which an individual must weigh before deciding to disregard domestic law. Although they do not result from the organized will of a superior sovereign, they are not wholly unpredictable and arbitrary. There are rules about punishing rule-breakers; an injured state cannot engage in excessive retaliation without itself weighing the consequences.

Some rules of international law have long been maintained largely by the pressure of these external forces. If the Soviet Union catches a foreign diplomat photographing military installations in violation of Soviet law, he is not punished, but rather is declared *persona non grata* and politely asked to leave the country. Presumably, a major factor inducing this respect for the international rule of diplomatic immunity is the desire of the Soviet government for similar treatment of its diplomats by other countries. Similarly, in the arms-control field, one force — in many cases, the most important force — causing a country to respect a treaty or other form of restraint is apprehension of the various external consequences of not respecting it. Such apprehension keeps limited wars limited. It is a force that can be used to cause respect for rules limiting preparation for war.

In addition to these pressures from outside, there are internal forces influencing government action. One of these is comparable to that which supports individual respect for law. Man is by and large a moral creature who is usually anxious to believe that what he does is not only practical but right. Individual moral standards may differ, but it is nonetheless true that each of us is influenced by his idea of what he ought to do. An individual will frequently respect a rule simply because he believes that the rule ought to be respected, without appraising his chances of being caught and without a Machiavellian weighing of the pros and cons.

A government is made up of such individuals, and this fact tends to cause governmental respect for law. The strength of this moral force depends on matters of both procedure and substance. It depends on how the rule was established, including such things as the solemnity with which the obligation to respect it was assumed. It depends also on the degree to which the rule coincides with the moral views of the individual officials in the government affected. A rule against assassination of foreign officials might be respected for reasons going beyond a cold calculation of the consequences. On the other hand, rules requiring the officials of one country to inform on their colleagues might be broken because of moral scruples despite a recognized theoretical advantage in compliance.

These pressures from possible external consequences and from internal morality which induce governmental conformity to rules are comparable to those affecting individual behavior. But there are special internal factors which operate on a government which are either not present or are insignificant in the case of an individual. These are at the heart of our problem.

First, a government is an institution which is dedicated to promoting respect for law. In the domestic sphere a government recognizes that rules are necessary for the avoidance of collisions of interest and that it has an affirmative stake in the creation and maintenance of law. But this law-creating and law-maintaining function is less well recognized in the international field. In the United States, the chief legal officer concerned with domestic law, the Attorney General, conceives of his job as the promotion of law and justice. In contrast, the comparable official concerned with international law, the Legal Adviser to the State Department, has rarely considered his job in that light. He has seen himself not as an "Assistant Secretary for International Law," whose job is to promote law in the international area, but rather as a kind of house counsel, whose function is to keep the Department out of trouble.

But whatever views particular officials may have of their offices, it is clear that all governments undertake to create and maintain a legal order. One way to promote such an order is for the government itself to respect laws applicable to it. To the extent (but only to the extent) that a government recognizes that its long-run interests require it to promote a legal order in the international arena, such recognition will tend to create respect for international rules as a means of fulfilling that objective.

A second consideration which is peculiarly applicable to governments is that they have a greater interest in the fair and wise settlement of disputes than in advancing their immediate financial or institutional position. Until 1863, when Congress empowered the Court of Claims to enter judgments against the United States,[15] the Government could "win" every case simply by congressional failure to vote a private bill. But it was perceived, however dimly,[16] that to win any particular case was less important for the Government than to resolve all cases by a demonstrably fair means. Decisions based on executive or legislative discretion must always be justified on the merits; a claim that has been three times rejected may have to be reconsidered. And the possibility of discrimination is great. But if a private claim is determined according to judicial procedure — if it has had its day in court — the Government is protected from political criticism, whether the criticism is that the claim should or should not have been paid. In some respects a judicial decision is like an administrative decision. The government has referred a question of policy to persons qualified to decide it. And having obtained a decision, the government follows it simply because the decision has been made, for reasons not unlike those which cause it to follow a decision of, say, the Secretary of Agriculture.

The political interests of a government may in some cases be particularly well served when the decision is against the government. The judicial process may enable the government to lose an argument gracefully and according to principle. Responsibility for an unpopular but necessary action can often be passed to the courts and immunized from partisan attack. A judicial decision may provide the executive with a good excuse for doing what it would have to do anyway.

These considerations might well apply to decisions of an international court. The international interests of a government may be advanced more by having a matter decided fairly than by refusing to concede the point involved. If the status of China in the United Nations could be submitted to the International Court, a sensible solution might be achieved with far less disadvantage to the United States than would be involved either in abandoning a tenaciously held position under political pressure or in indefinitely prolonging an unsatisfactory situation. Similarly, although the Guantanamo Naval Base may be secure for the present, it is clear that the United States could not insist forever on maintaining a military base against the wishes of the local government. Eventually this country might be better served by abandoning its Cuban base pursuant to an order of an international tribunal, which might provide for the removal of property and payments by the Cuban government, than by lingering on until pushed out by other means. Thus, internationally as well as domestically, situations may arise in which compliance with law is not coerced but proceeds directly from self-interest.

There is a final and signficant way in which a government's reasons for complying with rules of law differ from those of an individual. A government is a complex structure comprising a great many individuals, a structure which depends for its very existence on respect for rules. Every individual in the government has many rules directly applicable to him. Some of these rules demand obedience to superiors. But others, which in the United States include the Constitution and statutes, lay down substantive law. These latter speak not merely to the Government as a whole; they speak also to individual officials and are regarded by each of them as being binding directly upon him. Thus, it is a risky business for a superior to direct his subordinates to disregard a particular rule. Each subordinate will be subjected to conflicting pressures and there is no guaranty of the result. A high official cannot command the breaking of rules without undermining respect for rules generally. And it is upon obedience to rules that his authority to command depends.

This analysis applies to any government. The situation in the Congo vividly attests the weakness of governments whose officials do not respect law. In sharp contrast, the government of the Soviet Union is highly organized and rule-respecting. It is a mistake to think of that government as lawless, and commanding obedience from its officials only at the point of a pistol. No one is holding a pistol to the head of the man who holds the pistol; that man is complying with rules.

Once a rule has become intertwined in the governmental fabric the government is no longer free to ignore it. Once subordinate officials recognize a particular legal rule as being just as binding upon them as is the concept of obedience to the orders of their superior, it will be difficult for the government to ignore that rule. In the United States, rules created by treaty or executive agreement are thought to be binding on officials only through the presidential chain of command. If the President directs disregard of a treaty obligation, subordinate officials tend to think of that as a matter for his decision alone, and, therefore, tend to respect the decision he has reached. If the treaty obligation were incorporated into a statute or constitutional amendment, the President and the Government as a whole would find the treaty far more difficult to ignore. Such action would require a collective decision to break one rule while respecting another.

One can see how such a procedure might operate even in the arms-control field. Should a treaty provide for the abolition of nuclear stockpiles the most complete inspection system that could be devised would be inadequate to guarantee that no weapons remained hidden. But it might be possible to create a structure of rules within each country that would satisfy other countries that there was no evasion of the agreement. The treaty obligation might be incorporated into the national constitutions. The citizens of each country might constantly be reminded by public notices and official speeches that it was their individual duty to notify United Nations officers of any hidden weapons. Rewards might be offered to those who discovered weapons and punishment threatened to those who concealed them. With such a massive effort to develop rules recognized as personally binding by a great number of people, each government would have created significant forces supporting compliance with the international obligation. In addition to the risks of retaliation and adverse world reaction due to the likelihood of detection under such circumstances, it might be difficult to bring about a governmental decision to act against officially declared government policy.

No absolute guaranty can be given that a government will always respect a rule. We have no guaranty that our Government will always respect the Constitution or the decisions of the Supreme Court. But by seeking to understand why governments so generally obey domestic law, we shall be better able to undertake the task of securing respect for international law. Current efforts to deal with pressing international issues, such as the jurisdiction of the International Court and the arms race, are being hamstrung by antiquated dogma about what law is and by an insufficient realization of why governments comply with it. No more in the international than in the domestic sphere should the argument be heard that governments must be lawless because they cannot be coerced.

[1] FULLER, THE FORMS AND LIMITS OF ADJUDICATION 18 (limited publication 1959).

[2] Declaration by the President of the United States of America, August 14, 1946, Respecting Recognition by the United States of America of the Compulsory Jurisdiction of the International Court of Justice, para. 2(b), 61 Stat. 1218, T.I.A.S. No. 1598.

[3] Southern Pac. Co. v. Jensen, 244 U.S. 205, 222 (1917) (dissenting opinion).

[4] Black & White Taxicab & Transfer Co. v. Brown & Yellow Taxicab & Transfer Co., 276 U.S. 518, 533 (1928) (dissenting opinion).

[5] See, e.g., Briggs, The Cloudy Prospects for "Peace Through Law," 46 A.B.A.J. 490 (1960).

[6] Holmes, The Path of the Law, 10 HARV. L. REV. 457, 468 (1897).

[7] 1 AUSTIN, JURISPRUDENCE 267–71 (5th ed. 1885).

[8] *Id.* at 263.

[9] *Id.* at 287–88.

[10] See *The Supreme Court, 1959 Term*, 74 HARV. L. REV. 81, Table III (1960).

[11] Youngstown Sheet & Tube Co. v. Sawyer, 343 U.S. 579 (1952).

[12] See Note, 46 HARV. L. REV. 677, 685–86 n.63 (1933).

[13] 246 U.S. 565 (1918).

[14] The West Virginia controversy was settled by the party states. See W. Va. Acts Ext. Sess. 1919, ch. 10, at 19.

[15] Act of March 3, 1863, ch. 92, 12 Stat. 765 (now 28 U.S.C. §§ 1491–1505 (1958)).

[16] A tie vote in the Senate was broken by the Vice-President. Views uttered by opponents of the Court of Claims are strangely similar to those uttered today by opponents of the International Court of Justice. Senator Hale of New Hampshire prefaced his remarks by declaring:

> I think, sir, when some future Gibbon shall write the history of the decline and fall of the great Republic, and shall give the indications which marked its progress to decay, one of them will be that about the year of grace 1863 the Thirty-Seventh Congress took it into their head that they were wiser than everybody that went before them, and departed from all the precedents established by their fathers, and started out on new, untried, and extravagant theories and notions.

He went on to object:

> But, sir, we are going to give this new Court of Claims power that we have denied and that our fathers have denied always to any and every Court . . . .

CONG. GLOBE, 37th Cong., 3d Sess. 310 (1863).

TOWARD A "RULE OF LAW" COMMUNITY

by
LOUIS HENKIN

Ours is hardly a world at peace. If the principal "war" is a "cold war," yet there is not peace. In the tensions between East and West, aggravated by awesome destructive power on both sides, in equally sharp if less pervasive tensions among smaller nations, lie serious dangers and threats to peace. There are tensions also, and seeds of tension, in the growth of new nationalisms, in the drive of previously non-self-governing people for independence, in the demand of these peoples and other peoples for a greater share of the world's goods and a better life.

To these special sources of tension are added those ever-present in a society of sovereign states with competing economic and political interests. These tensions may lead to the use or threat of force, as recently in Suez. If not force, there may be other retaliation. In any event, there is "injustice." In all events, tension results. The threat of war is pervasive. The sense of order, of justice under law, is largely lacking. There is dis-ease among nations, which, even if it should not in fact erupt into war, poisons relations in the world family.

114

To cure this disease, men of good will turn to "the law," seeking in its concepts, institutions, methods, and mechanics, ways to reduce the threat of war and to enhance international order. And lawyers have responded in different ways. Some have concentrated on ultimate goods, on optimum solutions and programs. They speak almost yearningly of the "rule of law." They respond to a common wish that there shall be a world community with the hallmarks and trappings of law that are known domestically in enlightened Western countries - a community observing accepted rules of conduct between nations; courts applying these rules in cases or controversies not settled amicably by the parties; police to enforce, if necessary, the law as decided by the courts. And so lawyers have formulated, and continue to refine, principles of conduct for nations in a community of nations. They have proposed and developed processes for giving effect to such principles, and programs for applying and administering these processes, and for enforcing the rules of conduct against recalcitrant nations. They concentrate on the development of new rules where none exist, or where present rules are deemed unsatisfactory. They develop and strengthen statutes for international adjudicatory tribunals. They propose new and renewed charters for international organizations and police.

Those who devote their efforts to these goals recognize that wishing for or proclaiming a rule of law does not create in fact a law of nations. They are aware that, in a society of sovereign states, an established order of laws and courts and police - which does not effectively exist even within many domestic societies - is at best a dream to be approximated, and there appears little immediate prospect that nations will agree to give up much of their present sovereignty. But those who labor in this vineyard believe that it is important to keep ultimate goals in sight; that plans and blueprints make it more likely that such a world can be achieved, at least that more progress can be made toward it; that significant educational and even political benefits may derive from reminding nations and peoples how the world might look.

Other lawyers, concerned for the growth and enhancing of international order through law, begin from different positions, give different emphases. They stress that law does not create a World Community; it can only reflect such a community if it exists. In today's world, sharply polarized between East and West, there is not even the foundation for a common society to support a common law. The rule of law, in an ultimate sense, is an ideal state of health, not a prescription for achieving it. The question indeed is how, in a sorely divided world, one can achieve even a small measure of this health. If substantial order is to come without another world holocaust, it must grow from present roots. If it is to be planned, it can only be built on and projected out of the present foundations. Will East and West, with divergent and perhaps inconsistent interests, accept common standards of action, common methods and machinery for enforcing or vindicating these standards? Rules exist, but are they rules which the leading nations, and the new nations, recognize and observe? These are institutions and procedures - judicial, quasi-judicial, or political, multilateral or bilateral - but will nations use them and abide by their outcome?

The East and the West do not agree on many rules; they do not accept courts or other impartial forums to decide disputes; there is no power to compel either side to abide by any rules or decisions, and frequently no voluntary acceptance of them. Although the West has been far more amenable to rules, and more reluctant to incur the onus in world opinion of breaching them, it too may act in disregard of "law" where it feels important interests are at stake. Even the smaller nations find it easier to disregard law as a result of the lack of a strong fabric of a society of nations, or because of the lack of agreed force on behalf of the "law" and the world community, or because there is a big champion who might defend their violations. The nations newly come to independence may have serious question as to the meaning for them of old concepts and institutions; will they agree to accept them? Will they seek changes to which the other nations could agree?

If there is no perfect order and law in today's society of nations, some law, some standards of behavior observed, some machinery for vindicating these standards, do in fact exist. This "law" has strengths and has enjoyed successes. It has serious weaknesses and has suffered defeats. It needs strengthening. It can be strengthened in ways that reflect the world of today, that take account of power and other facts of international life, that reflect the different interests of different nations, as they see their interests.

Law can be achieved to the extent that it is in the common interest of nations, if nations can be made to recognize that it is in their common interests. In a world dominated by two powerful giants, law can be achieved if, and to the extent that, these powers believe that it is in their interests to achieve it. What is required, then, is to persuade nations, particularly the Big Powers, that order and law, at least in some areas, are in their interest. There must be an identification of areas of such coincidence of interest - common interest in having standards of conduct, explicit or tacit, upon given subjects, especially in procedures for implementing or applying these standards, as well as procedures for settling disputes in areas where there are no agreed rules.

There are in fact significant areas of coincidence of interest between East and West within which some "law" exists, and more can be developed. There are wider areas of coincidence of interest between old nations and new, and therefore hope and need for development of legal and political institutions and practices in relations between them. And, finally, there are still larger areas of even deeper coincidence of interest among the Western nations with common values and traditions where law exists and can grow importantly, which would also serve as an example and a focus for extending the rule of law to other countries, other areas and groups. The concepts, methods, and tools of law, we believe, can be invoked to increase the areas of international activity which are subject to law, and therefore contribute to the lessening or arresting of existing tensions, to the prevention of new tensions. The lawyer in close concert with economists and leaders in other disciplines concerned with the cooperation of people and communications among them, can contribute not only in his capacity as outstanding citizen and leader, but through the lawyer's skills and insights - in negotiation and adjustment, in the development and formulation of standards of conduct, in devising procedures for giving effect to such standards, in applying and administering these procedures.

2

The tendency to think of the Rule of Law as denoting a complete system of rules and courts and police has diverted attention from the amount and kind of law that in fact exists. Without stopping to debate what is a proper definition of law, it should be clear that there is a substantial order, and that it gives some promise of continuing.

Rules have existed between nations, perhaps since before the recorded history of nations and of compacts between them. The law of nations of older times, and modern international law, and comity and custom, reflect some rules which have acceptability to this day. There are thousands of treaties, bilateral and multilateral, establishing agreed standards which are very largely observed. Some nations have

116

set themselves standards and live by them. Procedures and machinery too have developed. If international courts are new and still of limited effectiveness, courts are hardly the only or ultimately the best vehicle for maintaining or vindicating order. The exchange of ambassadors and embassies and communications represents an ancient and effective form and forum for negotiation for settlement of disputes in the light of underlying rules or standards of conduct. Mediation or conciliation by others, and arbitration before some acceptable third party, are old forms of giving effect to law. The recent establishment of other tribunals, of political bodies - notably the United Nations - to deal with political disputes, is an important indication and manifestation of law and order. And there is the International Court of Justice, weak though it may be.

Even the most critical area of international relations - the avoidance of war and of the use of force - is not devoid of law. Insofar as there is coincidence of interest, there is some law and order. But such law needs strengthening in important respects.

The Charter of the United Nations outlaws aggressive war. It forbids nations, in effect, to initiate the use of force. All members bind themselves "to refrain in their international relations from the threat or use of force against the territorial integrity or political independence of any state, or in any other manner inconsistent with the purposes of the United Nations." (Article 2, section 4.) They bind themselves "to settle their international disputes by peaceful means in such a manner that international peace and security, and justice, are not endangered." (Article 2, section 3.) Except when it is acting at the behest of the United Nations in support of the purposes of the Charter, a nation may use force only in the exercise of "the inherent right of individual or collective self-defense if an armed attack occurs against a Member of the United Nations...." (Article 51.)

Here are rules of law. These are not vague principles of an old "international law" developed in the West of centuries ago. They are not principles of capitalism or of colonial power. They are new principles adopted after World War II by all nations, East and West, Communist and non-Communist, old and new. The nations just born and those about to be born promptly and eagerly seek membership in the UN, and pledge adherence to the UN Charter and its fundamental purpose of outlawing the use of force in relations between nations.

There is, we believe, a coincidence of interest - between East and West, and with all nations - on this rule against the use of force. Surely there is common interest in avoiding total war and total devastation. And any substantial use of force between nations today can only too readily lead to total war. In the present international context there is a common interest also in being and appearing to be law-observant in this fundamental respect. While there may be some skepticism whether all nations are indeed "true believers," whether they truly desire to observe these rules of "no force," it is yet significant that nations unanimously and for the first time feel obliged to proclaim and preach this "gospel" and maintain their adherence to it. In fact, there has been greater observance of the rule than is sometimes recognized; the exceptions - Palestine, Korea, Suez, Hungary - can be explained, although not, of course, justified. (In Korea and Suez - and in the Palestine area generally - peace was restored, some order established, law largely vindicated.) If it be said that it is fear, not piety, that supports this rule of law, that it is NATO not the UN which is its principal shield, that it is the threat of mutual or self-destruction which alone has saved the world from war, yet it is a fact that to date we have been largely saved. There is observance of the rule; there is some basis for confidence that it will continue to be observed. This too is law. For whatever reasons, by recognized means, machinery, procedures, the law of the UN Charter generally prevails.

This is not to suggest that there is cause for complacence that terrible war will not come. If world tension today is, in a sense, a happy reflection of the fact that the conflicting interests which have created tensions have not erupted into war, yet the existence of these tensions is a continuing reminder of the threat of war, deliberate or accidental. Much must be done to assure that, at least, the situation grows no worse.

The United Nations is essential. The Charter and the machinery which it established must be maintained in full vigor; the voice of the General Assembly against the use of force must remain clear and firm. The presence of the UN should be invoked where it is likely to be effective to prevent or allay crises. The channels of communication between nations through diplomatic missions, through their missions at the UN Headquarters and delegations to UN Assemblies, must be kept open and functioning. They permit continual negotiations which are the basic means for making it possible for nations to settle differences without force, as the UN Charter requires. The conciliatory and mediatory opportunities for governments, for officials of governments, for leading citizens, for officials of the United Nations and particularly for the Secretary-General must be developed and enhanced. In these efforts there is use for the methods of the law and the skills of the lawyers - in negotiating, in developing, expressing and confirming areas of agreement, in evolving the institutional possibilities inherent in a document like the UN Charter; for example, the ascendance of the General Assembly, the establishment of the United Nations Emergency force, the stand-by planning of the Collective Measures Committee. Against a later day, too, particularly as it relates to the possibility of substantial control of armaments, there is a need for additional studies similar to the one conducted by the Carnegie Endowment for International Peace relative to an international police force.

3

If there is now a clear coincidence of interest for all nations to avoid major force, it is also in their interest to make it less likely that force will be used, intentionally or accidentally. The United States, the USSR and other leading countries must themselves refrain from initiating the use of force and exert every influence on all others also to refrain. All nations have an important interest to assure that no single nation anywhere will initiate the use of force against another.

Recognition by both sides in the global conflict that they must avoid force requires also that they recognize that any changes from the status quo must be pursuant to peaceful agreement. In some areas bristling with tension, conflicting interests may not at present permit any substantial changes by peaceful agreement. But force must be avoided, and the incitements and temptations to use force. Thus, for a current example, the Soviet Union must appreciate the circumstances which render it impossible for the West to abandon West Berlin, and which would compel the West to meet forcibly any serious jeopardy to their presence there. Subject to that limitation there may be room for some agreed peaceful change in the status of Berlin, in the presence of Western forces, in access between West Berlin and West Germany. It may be possible - again there will be call on the ingenuity of the law and of lawyers - to substitute a permanent peaceful status for the city for the present occupation status, and the likelihood of agreement may be enhanced by the symbolic, political, administrative role of the UN, or by its presence.

Despite continued failure and frustration, there is also some real coincidence of interest in efforts to control armaments, to give confidence if not assurance that nations which do not yet have them do not acquire weapons of mass destruction, and that nations which do have them will not use them. There must be intensified search, in particular, for agreement on measures to assure that there will be no surprise attack and no accidental war. There is coincidence of interest too in efforts to moderate the frantic race for new weapons of incalculable destructive power. Reliable agreements, however small and preliminary in character, can break the cycle in which tensions lead to more arms and arms increase tensions. If in a world without trust, such agreements require reliability and confidence, both sides may have to pay a price in submitting to essential verifications and inspections. Both sides must earnestly consider that there may be more security for them in known controls on armaments than in the fearful uncertainties of unbridled competition in the armaments of the future.

Areas emerging into international awareness may develop new conflicts of interest and new tensions, but nations may also be persuaded that it would be preferable for all if these areas were isolated from conflict. Agreement by the United States and the Soviet Union on the nonmilitarization of Antarctica is a small example, and an augury of hope.

The development of uses of outer space seems to offer another such opportunity. The potentialities of these uses for mutual destruction are terrifying in their uncertainty; the United States and the USSR might well consider whether it would not be preferable for both to eliminate the risks by agreement that outer space will not be used for launching weapons of destruction. The potentialities, on the other hand, of these uses of outer space for revolutionary benefits to all suggest also a coincidence of interest in cooperation for peaceful development and use. Here again, essential verifications and inspection will be necessary.

Allowing for many differences, there is reminder, if not analogy, in the early state of atomic energy, say in 1945. The tragic failure of attempts to "demilitarize" the atom and to arrange for cooperation in its peaceful exploitation must not be repeated. There is hope that the lessons of that failure, as well as the difference in the two situations, may help avoid a new failure. There is not, as there was in the case of the atom, a monopoly on one side, and a consequent fear that controls would freeze the other in a state of permanent inferiority. There has not yet been sufficient progress on either side to warrant a feeling that controls would involve a sacrifice of advantage. There can be no confidence on either side that, in the long run, a race into use of outer space for weapons would enhance its military superiority or security. It may again be difficult to persuade both sides that exchange of information, "traffic" rules and controls, and joint ventures are indeed in the interest of both nations. There can be new law here - new standards of conduct, new institutions, new procedures. And lawyers can make their contribution here as they did in the Acheson-Lilienthal Report on controlling the atom, and in subsequent, partly successful attempts to achieve cooperation on peaceful uses of atomic energy.

4

After World War II the United States was a leading proponent of further development of international law and institutions. The Soviet Union, by comparison, was recalcitrant and reactionary. Under pressure of the tensions of the East-West conflict, however, the United States too has receded into attitudes far less cooperative, if not isolationist. The barely-escaped Bricker Amendments; the genocide convention buried in the Senate; the indifferent participation in the activities of the International Law Commission and of the Sixth Committee of the General Assembly; the negative attitude of the United States toward adjudication by the International Court of Justice; the abandonment and avoidance of efforts to establish common international standards by multilateral agreement, such as the draft covenant on human rights - these are but examples. Even in established areas of international law, there has been a tendency to deal with issues as problems in American foreign policy, to be determined unilaterally by the United States in the light of immediate United States interests, rather than with a sense of obligation by Congress, the Executive, or the courts to abide by rules of international law or the provisions of a treaty.

If the United States record has not been brilliant, particularly in regard to the further development of international law, the United States has in fact largely abided by international law. The record of the Soviet Union has been deplorable. Although the Soviet Union has not flatly rejected international law as a capitalist invention, it has not given other nations much reason to hope that it would abide by accepted international law even in normal circumstances, or cooperate in the development of further rules in the common interest.

In practice both sides have tacitly observed many of the principles and practices of international law and comity, and even the Soviet Union has, for the most part, avoided overt and flagrant violations. There is also a new, particular hope that both the United States and the Soviet Union may yet recognize an identity of interest in maintaining and promoting international law. For international law may be the bridge between each of the big contenders and the emerging new nations. In the keen competition between East and West for the favor of the neutral, uncommitted and developing nations, both sides may find that the body of international law serves to afford to the new nations a sense of equality, dignity, and sovereign independence. If international law rarely calls for explicit application in regard to issues between the United States and the Soviet Union, each of them may find it advisable to apply international law in relations with Ghana or Morocco. In the bipolar world there is, consequently, a new opportunity for "horizontal" development of international law, for its maintenance and extension to the new nations. If this occurs, international law may be generally strengthened and have greater effect even in its application between the two camps.

The "vertical" growth of international law, the development of new aids to order, is more difficult in a world so sharply divided, but not impossible. If the Soviet Union is not eager to cooperate, other nations can still build law at least for areas which are not the battlefield of the big conflict. And the pressure of the new nations may compel cooperation even from the Soviet Union. As to how to build such law, there are differences of opinion as to whether international law can grow and strengthen better by the process of codification and "legislation," or by a natural, "common law" growth of practice and custom. While the latter may offer more promise, some codification, in selected areas ripe for it, might at least have educational value.

But if the main reliance for growth is to be on practice and custom, it is important that such practice and custom be collected and made available, and perhaps restated from time to time. Today it is difficult if not impossible to learn what nations are in fact doing, what are their customs and practices in international relations. A body like the UN, with special financial assistance from governmental or private sources, should undertake to learn, collect, systematize, and make generally available the practices of the political and judicial organs of governments, as well as those of arbitral and similar bodies dealing with matters of international or transnational concern. Worthy individual contributions to this end have already been initiated: there are Professor E. Lauterpacht's summaries of practice in the United Kingdom; similar materials on the United States have begun to appear in the pages of the American Journal of International Law; efforts of this kind are beginning also in India and promised in Australia. Also, the State Department is engaged in bringing up to date Hackworth's Digest of International Law, and it is reported that similar works have been initiated in the United Kingdom, in France, and in Switzerland.

5

An urgent need, even in a bipolar world, is the development of legal "substitutes for war." The United Nations Charter outlaws the use of force except in defense against armed attack. In fact, with exceptions noted, nationals have abstained from using force in the past when force may have been justified under international law. The result has been to leave areas of international interest unprotected. There have developed no clear agreed standards of conduct, nor any clear, agreed, and effective procedure for handling those situations which in the past were dealt with by force. It is not yet clear what should happen if one nation repeatedly violates the territorial integrity of another, if nations do not meet their financial or other contractual or treaty obligations to other nations, if they mistreat the nationals of other nations, if they endanger important economic interests of other nations or of their nationals, if they defame or deceive them, if they interfere with their communications. Rights of flight over the territory of other nations at various heights are matters in dispute and sources of tension, as is the right to use international waterways which are under national control. And the national treatment of human beings and of their fundamental rights continues to evoke the concern of other nations, while the acting states continue to insist that such matters are entirely domestic and of no international concern.

If, in regard to these and other problems, force continues in fact to be avoided, tensions will remain and fester. (It would not seem desirable to bring every such instance to the General Assembly for ad hoc political consideration, especially since there are really no principles of conduct to guide the Assembly.) Ultimately, then, if the rules against self-help by force are to survive, it is important that standards of conduct and machinery for settling disputes develop quickly - particularly for areas involving important interests which nations might be tempted again to "vindicate" by force. Such developments are more difficult, but some growth appears possible, even in the shadow of the Cold War.

More work is needed to identify the areas and problems to which this concern is particularly applicable, to analyze the competing interests, to set forth or develop equitable standards of conduct, to examine existing procedures, and, if necessary, develop new ones appropriate for the settlement of disputes. It will be necessary to reexamine hitherto accepted ideas of the respective areas of domestic interest and of international concern, and relate them to a world in which many "domestic" matters arouse keen international concern. "Domestic" transactions often have transnational character. Foreign and international acts often have profound impact on the "domestic" life of nations. It will be necessary to achieve - by agreement, or by growth of custom - rules of conduct, as well as procedures for applying them. It is hardly necessary, of course, to develop rules or even identical machinery and procedures for different problems.

In the long run, a strong deterrent to disorder in international affairs lies in the patterns and habits of peaceful intercourse which contribute to order in all nations. Among such institutions in existence are, obviously, the international postal and telecommunications systems. But the daily details of increasing transnational and international relations promise another contribution to order and an important opportunity to law and lawyers. The development, for example, of standard commercial practices, of common "forms" for contracts, bills, and notes, transcends competing ideological and political and security interests, and helps establish a common framework within which tensions recede and order grows. It is desirable to promote uniform or corresponding practices in these and related fields, in direct negotiations through private groups, and through such bodies as the Economic Commission for Europe.

Areas of a different kind also offer some possibilities for increasing order. Meeting of scientists, even in the delicate field of arms control, have proved fruitful. Scientific cooperation in other fields - the International Geophysical Year and the International Committee on Space Research - warrants encouragement for similar endeavors. The artistic and intellectual communities also have proved that they afford opportunities for building up cooperative exchange, and helping create a more open society even behind the Iron Curtain. "Opening up" of the Soviet Union could be a result of, as well as a contribution to, the strengthening of international order.

To some the goal devoutly to be wished is the submission of all disputes and differences between the United States and the Soviet Union to the International Court of Justice. It is common knowledge, however, that the Soviet Union has never used the International Court and that the United States is not overeager to submit to its jurisdiction. Much study and effort have been devoted to developing the Court and other machinery for adjudicating disputes so that they might "work" even between the United States and the Soviet Union. But the weakness is not in existing machinery for adjudication, and it cannot be cured by improving the machinery. There is no agreement between East and West on standards of conduct, and therefore no basis for decisions as to whether any given standards have been observed or violated. There is no agreement between them to submit to a process of adjudication. And the Soviet Union in particular generally rejects the notion basic to adjudication: that any court can be impartial.

It would no doubt be desirable if the United States and the Soviet Union were to submit broadly to the jurisdiction of the Court. The proposal made by a United States spokesman to add a clause to this effect to new treaties which both the United States and the Soviet Union would ratify has something to commend it, in principle; compulsory submission to the jurisdiction of the Court is in fact a common provision in recent treaties. But to be effective there must first be the substantive agreements, and these have been lacking. Indeed the addition of this clause to an agreement might even render it less likely that the Soviet Union would adhere to the agreement. United States insistence upon such a clause in any agreement might be viewed by the Russians, who do not consider the International Court of Justice "impartial," as an effort to load the scales of the agreement against the Russians.

One cannot, then, be optimistic for the future of any adjudicating process for settling disputes or relaxing tensions between East and West. But courts, we have suggested, are not the only "legal" machinery, and in international affairs today may not even be the most promising. In time of tension between big powers, representing a desire for change by at least one of them, courts tend to be an unacceptable preserver of the status quo. They are to be used for important matters; if used they are to be obeyed. If not obeyed, courts may be destroyed. Particularly in situations of tension, other forms of resolution promise better.

There are, of course, the organs of the UN, which may be used at least to confirm a resolution of a dispute if not to bring it about. There are mediatory, conciliatory, "good offices" bodies in the UN and outside it. Most important, there are the lines of direct communication, at embassies, in third countries, in the corridors of the UN - at summit level or working levels - which must be maintained as ultimately the best hope for resolving issues and relaxing tensions. For all "legal" disputes between any nations are also political disputes. Between East and West, where there exist few admitted rules of law and no agreed tribunal to apply them, all disputes are basically political to be resolved through political institutions, primarily by direct contact.

Special machinery, fundamentally political in character, may be created. Some existed and worked when both sides wished it to work, as in Germany and Austria. In Korea an armastice was ultimately negotiated. In each case it was machinery basically bilateral, a body which did not strive for impartial adjudication (which the Soviet Union, we repeat, has not been ready to accept) but a bilateral body for hard, patient negotiation. The creation of such bodies, generally of equal representation, for ad hoc negotiations or perhaps for continuing general contact and discussion, still appears to offer the best hope for relaxing tensions between the East and West. This too is order, and law, and here also the lawyer needs to lend his gifts for planning, building, developing, and administering institutions and procedures.

6

World tensions result not only from the way the big powers glare at each other, but from the quickening explosions of new nationalisms, the demand of dependent peoples for independence and a greater share of the world's wealth. The recent and contemporary history has given new vitality to the "principle of equal rights and self-determination" recognized in the United Nations Charter, although it remains for the lawyers of all nations to consider to what extent this has now become a juridical principle in the law of nations.

Basically, the new nations have set themselves three tremendous tasks: to establish a nation out of heterogeneous groups; to build this nation with meager resources, only a fraction per capita of what developing European nations (for example, Germany, Italy) had in the nineteenth century; to give their people the advantages of a welfare state. The older nations must take account of these gigantic undertakings in their relations with these nations.

The importance of the economic growth of the new nations for the reduction of tensions, and specific programs for assistance to these nations, for cooperative economic development on a bilateral basis or through the UN and other multilateral agencies, are discussed in Chapter 3 of this book.* The machinery and procedures for economic development there suggested are, of course, political and legal institutions also. Ultimately, it is necessary for the lawyer to join the economists and others to fashion arrangements whereby the resources of the older, more developed countries are in fact made available to the newer and poorer countries. There may be need to create, or modify, or develop new international institutions and procedures. There may be need for the lawyer to help accommodate conflicting national legislation, including tax regimes and monetary regulation.

---

* [Chapter 3 has not been included in this reader - Ed.]

123

Here, we would speak also of the relation to the new nations of other aspects of "law." The new nations are, of course, members of the UN and of many specialized agencies, and are already making their voices heard there. They have entered into international relations in accordance with international practice. But there are other areas where law and legal institutions can contribute to the healthy growth of these nations and of their relations to the older nations. To suggest that there may be reexamination is not to urge rejection or to assume even that there will or ought to be important modification. Examination may well show that traditional international law was not a law for the powerful few in a private club of nations, but in fact provides basic accommodations, all generally applicable today in a society of sovereign nations.

In any event, some standards must be agreed upon and accepted. In specific areas the new nations eager for assistance from more developed nations in their struggle to preserve their independence, to develop their resources, to raise their standards of life, will have to recognize and respect the interests of those whose assistance they seek. There will have to be agreement, for example, on the rights of foreign investors, on the status of persons engaged in technical assistance to them, as well as general confidence that the new nations will abide by their agreements and by diplomatic immunities and amenities.

In their integration into an international community with even an imperfect rule of law, the new nations such as those in Africa will need sympathetic assistance. They begin "from scratch" and must come far even to begin to live by the present state of international law. There is need to assist them in their education in international matters, to help them to apply to their own situation the international law and practice of older nations, to train their lawyers and diplomats.

The task is not made easier by the comparatively primitive state of their domestic institutions; by their poverty and large illiterate populations; by differences among the African nations themselves, including differences of language and mores which render difficult even regional grouping and federation. They will have to look to leadership within their own groups. Free nations elsewhere will have to earn leadership by exemplary behavior in accordance with law.

There is urgent need to train young leaders of these new nations in the traditions of democracy and representative government, of individual freedoms and rights under law, modified as need be to meet local needs and mores. The United States and its Western allies, in particular, should invite representatives from these nations to see and to study; they should be prepared also to welcome students to Western institutions, as well as to send teachers and other experts to advise on the establishment and growth of political institutions, the promulgation of constitutions, the training and selection of judges, the creation of a Bar of responsibility and leadership.

7

The nations of the West and other nations with free institutions similar traditions, and generally common political interests undoubtedly have developed, among themselves, the most advanced legal and political institutions and the greatest willingness to submit to the rule of law, even to the adjudicatory process. It is among these nations in particular - or among regionally associated groups of them - that we may look for new international law, new substantive agreements of a bilateral or multilateral character, greater acceptance of mediation, arbitration, and adjudication, and a heartening habit of settling disputes and relaxing tensions by the process of negotiation. If where tensions exist all questions tend to become political, as tensions recede political questions can be rendered "legal," to be decided by tribunals in accordance with agreed standards. Further progress in the rule of law within this group will, of course, minimize tensions among the nations in the group - and also make it less likely that "internecine" differences will be exploited by the Soviet Union.

It will provide, also, a focus and an example for other nations to follow and to join. Immediately, even nations not as close to each other as those of the West may be prepared to accept "rule of law" for particular problems. Consequently, even nations with some hostility between them can better accept the results of an adjudication or some other form of impartial decision or recommendation rather than try to achieve the same result by compromise in negotiations. (In some areas a small group - perhaps the United States, the United Kingdom and Canada - could establish among themselves a near - "perfect" rule of law as an example to the nations. This might be achieved without incurring the dangers of "fragmentation," of new divisions within this rule-of-law bloc, which argue against some other types of regional groupings.)

There is no doubt that within this rule-of-law community there could be more use of the International Court of Justice, at least on issues not of vital moment. Among these nations, it should be possible to establish that using the Court is not a hostile act. The Court would be used and its judgments respected; successful use of the Court contributing to its growth.

In this connection the United States has hardly shown a good example. Current efforts to repeal the Connally Amendment have been unsuccessful to date; this reservation has not even been abolished as between the United States and selected friendly nations.

The Connally Amendment reserves to the United States the right to determine finally that a matter is essentially within the domestic jurisdiction of the United States, and therefore not an international dispute subject to the jurisdiction of the International Court. This raises the most difficult question of all, a question that lies at the root of all efforts to develop law and order: What is essentially a domestic matter which nations are free to decide as they see the right, and what, on the other hand, is a matter of legitimate concern to other nations as to which other nations may properly make representations, seek UN consideration, or even international adjudication?

Article 2(7) of the UN Charter, which provides that the UN is not authorized "to intervene in matters which are essentially within the domestic jurisdiction of any state," has raised as many difficult political and judicial questions as any other provision in the Charter. The United States has generally taken the view that the "domestic jurisdiction" clause does not bar discussion in the General Assembly of matters which concern other nations. Surely nothing can be "essentially domestic" and barred to the United Nations if it becomes a threat to international peace and security.

There are equally great difficulties presented by "domestic jurisdiction" as a bar to the jurisdiction of the International Court of Justice. Presumably the Court will have to take into account developments in international law in determining whether a matter is proper for international adjudication or is the private affair of the acting State. Presumably, the International Court of Justice, a conservative institution as all courts tend to be, will not be the first to see radical growth in international law. Even if there are very few questions, even "domestic" ones, that can be barred from discussion in the UN's General Assembly, it does not follow that the Court will lightly extend the jurisdiction optionally given to it by the nations to areas traditionally "domestic." Surely, the fact that there may be questions about which another nation is in controversy with the United States will not ipso facto render it "nondomestic" to the United States and therefore justiciable by the Court.

In any event whether a matter is justiciable or not is clearly a question about the jurisdiction of the Court which should not be decided by a party to a dispute. The reservation is therefore improper in principle. Because of the applicable rule of reciprocity, it has also hurt the United States by giving the same power to deny the jurisdiction of the Court to any State whom the United States might wish to sue.

What is most unfortunate about the Connally Amendment is the appearance of isolationism, of refusal to submit to the jurisdiction of the Court even vis-a-vis its friends on a reciprocal basis. Even without this reservation there would be few cases in which the United States could be brought to the Court against its will; there are not many causes of action justiciable in the Court, and there have been few cases in which the United States has in fact been sued. Most of the few suits which might arise against the United States would probably arise out of treaties which provide for compulsory Court jurisdiction and to which the Connally Amendment would not apply. On the other hand, even with this reservation, it should be obvious that the United States, through the Executive Branch, cannot properly invoke this reservation in circumstances where the matter at issue is patently not domestic but a legitimate matter of concern to another nation. The reservation then will not properly allow the United States to deny to the Court jurisdiction in the large majority of those disputes which might come to it. Even in the rare instance where invoking the reservation might be proper, the Executive Branch might well and properly decide not to invoke it because of the unfortunate consequences for the United States in world opinion. Finally, where the United States honestly believes that the matter may truly be domestic, it might be better, as has been suggested, to submit that question for a preliminary opinion by the Court.

The reservation then is not of great import to the United States. Withdrawing it would not increase substantially the extent to which the United States is subject to the Court, but would remove a continuous reminder of United States' reluctance to submit to international adjudication. The reservation gives constant lie to our professions of support for the rule of law, and opens to charges of hypocrisy United States criticism of the Soviet Union for its unwillingness to submit to law. Failure to remove the reservation after the recent attempt to do so would only emphasize and aggravate the fault of the United States in the eyes of the world. We may hope that the failure is only a brief delay.

8

In a world of pervasive malaise and disorder the perfect "rule of law" seems remote. Treaties with ideal provisions will not be signed; courts with extensive jurisdiction over all nations and issues will not be used or obeyed, even if created. Efforts directed toward optimum solutions have their principal justification only in hope that they can be soon achieved. Fortunately for mankind, it is in the interest of all, including the Big Powers:

To avoid the use of force themselves and to exert every influence against international use of force by any nation anywhere;

To maintain the United Nations which, among other things, helps preserve the balance between East and West and serves as a bridge to the new nations,

To seek their military security through reliable, reciprocal control of armaments rather than to risk the uncertain consequences and dangers of an unbridled arms race and the ever-present danger of sudden war, accidental or deliberate;

To bar the use of outer space for weapons of destruction and to co-operate in the exploration and use of outer space for beneficial peaceful purposes;

To respect and develop international law, particularly as a common bridge to the new nations;

To develop practices and procedures as "substitutes for war" to deal with situations which in the past may have evoked the use or threat of force;

To promote cooperation and common practices and forms in the daily commerce of nations, among businessmen, scientists, artists, others; and

To keep open and to increase channels of direct communication between all nations, particularly between East and West, as the best forum for settling disputes that may arise as well as for relaxing or preventing tensions.

For the new nations the old must show sympathy and understanding, not only by assisting them in economic ways but by helping to invent useful legal and political institutions. Old and new nations must reason together about maintaining and improving the law of nations. The old must help the new to achieve at least present levels of international law and order, and to establish free institutions and freedom under law for their citizens.

The old free nations of the West with common values and traditions have even greater opportunities. Among them there can be important developments in international law, and substantial growth of international institutions, including the International Court of Justice and other adjudicatory bodies, as an example to the world. The United States must regain its leadership in this group by regaining attitudes of cooperation and submission to law at least vis-a-vis its friends; it can begin clearing its skirts by revoking the Connally Reservation.

Throughout, the responsible role for law and lawyers is clear. They can help develop the possibilities of existing institutions like the UN and help build new institutions and administer them when they are built. Individually, as citizens and leaders, and in their association, they can help meet the challenge presented by the needs of new nations, assist them in developing their domestic institutions, in moving toward regional cooperation, and toward a life under law in the community of nations. Programs for bringing students and sending teachers are an obvious need; an undertaking - say by the American Bar Association - to send books and documents of legal and political import would make an important contribution.

Lawyers have no magic formula for bringing peace and ease among nations. The specific programs suggested - development of legal "substitutes for force," the study of the assumptions of international law, the collection and dissemination of the facts of international practice, and new manifestations of support for the rule of law among the free nations, - are indeed modest. But of such is the kingdom of law in the real world. The hope for relaxing tensions lies in the gradual recognition, especially by the Big Powers, that there are in fact substantial and important areas of common interest among them - and there is consequently a place for law as well as politics.

HISTORICAL TENDENCIES, MODERNIZING AND REVOLUTIONARY NATIONS, AND THE INTERNATIONAL LEGAL ORDER

by

RICHARD A. FALK

I. Towards a Warless World

We approach the historical processes of change that are going on in the world today as a series of transformations of the existing system of international relations. Let us consider the varying perspectives of national actors that now participate in world affairs. It is immediately useful to distinguish between modernizing, revolutionary, and status quo nations for this purpose, although the third category is not fully descriptive of the role played by the leading nations that comprise it. Our concern is with the way in which these classes of national actors respond to the international legal order as adequate for the satisfaction of their major values and interests. Thus the emphasis is upon how the extra-legal unfolding of contemporary events affects the adequacy of international law from the point of view of nations.

We live in a historical period when there is a widespread awareness that survival, prosperity and security depend upon certain basic social and political transformations. The most central transformation involves the endeavor to bring a warless world into being, and from the perspective of liberal democratic values, to achieve this result without increasing the expansive capabilities of totalitarian societies. Putting this slightly differently, we wonder whether the world can eliminate war and the reliance by nations upon their own military defense establishments without increasing vulnerability to oppressive forms of government either introduced by internal processes of revolutionary change or by some form of external coercion?

Thus the transformation that we envision restructures relations, institutions, and values through time--by shifting power, by developing techniques to influence behavior to form new loyalties and new inhibitions, and by acting to create a new world consciousness that accepts the altered distribution of power and loyalty.

One of the central obstacles on the path of transformation is the undesirability of freezing the fundamental political and social status quo as it now exists in several national communities. Although it is desirable to abolish the use of force in international affairs we are not eager to eliminate the possibilities for radical international change. In this connection it must be acknowledged that force has played a central legislative role in world politics, often altering sit-

uations of oppression, injustice and decadence. Therefore, the task of eliminating force includes, but exceeds ,
the problems of controlling processes of national coercion;
it is essential to find alternative ways to legislate changes
in national communities, even in the face of resistance to
these changes by domestic governmental elites. Partly this
broadening of the goal of a warless world to encompass institutions of social change responds to the need for securing the peace in a disarming world. For recourse to force
is an anticipated event when people possessing power lack
alternative means to satisfy aspirations. The job of social
change is to devise alternatives to force, especially when
social objectives accord sufficiently with values that are
widely shared to allow us to assert the presence of an international consensus. Unless peaceful ways exist to make this
consensus operative we anticipate various domestic occasions of civil strife that will elicit sympathy and support
from external sources of power and prestige. Achieving
change through this kind of decentralized coercion would
probably encourage intense conflict between various political competitors. It is important to remember that the
elimination of force from world affairs does not assure or
even make particularly likely the elimination of political and
ideological conflict. In a disarming world the bi-polar conflict we now identify as the cold war would probably increase
in scope and pervasiveness. For the leading antagonists
would find themselves freed from threats to their survival
that now discourage the assumption of risks likely to provoke a major coercive response from their rivals. If the
fear of nuclear war were significantly reduced, one should
suppose that, for instance, Western antipathy to totalitaria n
regimes in East Europe might express itself by intervention
in the event domestic protest movements showed signs of
vitality. Similarly one must assume a Sino-Soviet unwillingness to refrain from extending influence by techniques of
covert domination to Latin America and Africa where inter -
nal conditions favor radical social movements that would
willingly accept, perhaps even solicit, communist support.
One sees therefore that securing peace in a disarming w o rld
is not just a question of weapons control. The indestruc-
tible nature of nuclear technology implies the continuing capacity to restore military uses of this technology; the dangers of nuclear war can never be fully eliminated from the
human situation. If nations possessing this technology begin to suffer unacceptable political defeat in a disarmin g
world, then the goals of a warless world are in serious jeopardy. In such a situation, the domestic pressure to restore nuclear weaponry would probably become overwhelming .
For nuclear weapons give a weaker nation an almost absolute

capacity to inhibit unacceptable provocations, even on the part of stronger nuclear powers.

If one formulates the issues of transformation in this manner, the objectives sought by comprehensive disarmament seem difficult indeed to attain within the framework of existing political tensions and rivalries. But it is hardly possible, given the dangers of mutual catastrophe that now exist, for major states to tolerate a continuation of the existing order of international relations. The dilemma is set then by the need for transformation offset by the difficulties of its attainment. This general awareness is central to a historical understanding of the world as it now exists and acts to inform our inquiries into the adequacy of international law.

* * * * *

III. Aspects of the Traditional System of International Law

We turn now from the statement of the background of our inquiry to a brief depiction of the traditional system of international law and to the contemporary challenges that direct themselves particularly at this system. This leads to an attempt to characterize the present state of international law as one of transitional crisis. Such a transitional crisis in international law is an aspect of the larger crisis described at the outset, and finds itself fully involved in the drive toward transformation and the obstacles to its achievement. The dilemma of transformation stands over and above the perception of transitional crisis which we find describes most accurately the current status of international law.

Several elements of the traditional system of international law convey an understanding of its basic character. First and foremost, the system was constructed on the basis of the interaction of national units. These units were regarded accurately as the repositories of final power and authority in world affairs. As such the attribution of sovereignty to nations was a descriptive generalization. For people could look no further than their national governments for the protection of their economic, military, and spiritual welfare. Of course, the reality of the relations between sovereign nations was often more a function of their varying relative power than an expression of their formal equivalence. Nevertheless, from the perspective of law, the concept of sovereignty provided a suitable foundation upon which to construct rules and processes for the governance of international behavior. In fact, sovereignty underlies several of the additional doctrinal concepts that together form the foundation of the traditional system of international law. Ideas of national independence, territorial jurisdiction, and national independence, are each expressions of the overriding idea that a national center of authority and power is absolute for purposes of international relations and law. This formal concentration upon national sovereignty was ironically offset by internal dispersals of power. A national governments exercised relatively marginal control over the economic activities that took place within its borders. This restricted the capacity of national leaders to mobilize the capabilities of their community for purposes of military conquest or defense. The contrasting intervention of contemporary national governments into all phases of economic life in modern societies, whether those societies be classified as communist, socialist, or capitalist, provides the leadership with the capacity and apparatus to mobilize the power which exists within the society. The national groups most active in world affairs during the period of growth and development between the fifteenth and twentieth centuries were ardently laissez-faire capitalist societies; this suggests the degree to which dispersed domestic power related to concentrated authority in international relations.

A second aspect of the traditional system of international law involves the allocation of authority between national sovereign units. The central endeavor of traditional law was to set limits upon what nations were entitled to do in those situations where their interests overlapped. The development of limiting standards responded to the elemental needs for order that arise whenever men and property cross national frontiers into a different social order. Law routinizes such contacts between sovereign units in a manner that permits actors to plan with security and safety. One can imagine the chaos that would exist in maritime commerce if no rules of the game existed; all nations have a common interest in reducing this kind of international contact to behavior that conforms to prior standards. Legal technique provides a way to express and implement these standards. Where contacts between nations lead individuals and property of one nation into the territory of another, a reciprocal interest may emerge that will lead the territorial state to abandon the full authority that is implied in its sovereignty. Thus international law was very concerned with creating immunities and specifying limits upon territorial authority. This search for areas of immunity and exemption was a consequence of the increasing dependence of powerful states upon international trade and investment. It is obvious that individuals would be less likely to risk their lives and wealth if they felt that they were subject to the arbitrary will of the territorial sovereign whenever they ventured into a foreign country. This led to the exercise of what has been called the diplomatic protection of nationals abroad. A whole body of traditional law seeks to regulate the responsibility of the territorial sovereign toward alien interests and the rights of the non-territorial nations in se-curing compliance with these standards of responsibility on behalf of their nationals. The use of diplomatic protec-tion as a means to impose the external will of richer and more powerful nations inspired a hostile reaction on the part of capital-importing nations that were often the victims of such conduct. Non-colonial forms of imperialism re-lied rather heavily upon rules of international law to retain economic dominance, especially the rules and practices that allowed a nation to protect its nationals. It should be remembered that these rules were usually constructed to satisfy the interests of the capital-exporting nations. These nations were most consistently interested in protecting their aliens abroad. These rules were satisfactory so long as the capital-exporting nations possessed control over the character of international relations. However, it is obvious that insofar as international law developed to promote the interests of capital-exporting nations it will not serve the interests of a world community where capital export is no longer coincident with political power.

The third aspect of the traditional international legal or-der that we examine is the role of war in the achievement of social and political change. As the international legal system gradually liberated itself from the restraining mora-lity and rhetoric of its natural law heritage, there developed an increasing tolerance for the use of force to achieve na-tional purposes. Force was acknowledged to be a crude in-strument of social change, but there was a subtle reconci-liation with progress implicit in events. Especially in the period following the French Revolution widespread confi-dence existed that the expressions of effective power would accord with the progressive realization of justice in human affairs. Theories of social revolution arose to sanction domestic violence whereas notions of the superiority of Western civilization developed to justify many instances of external violence. Thus aggressive uses of power were given a moral basis. In addition to this, there was a grow-ing awareness that nations which possessed the capability to use force successfully could not be restrained by the as-sertion of mere prohibitive rules. Earlier attempts to use legal prohibitions to maintain the peace were abandoned to allow jurists to give a more realistic account of interna-tional behavior. The pretentions of the earlier rules of law, as formulated in the various doctrines of Just War did not seem to influence the behavior of national leaders

132

and hence tended to engender attitudes of disrespect toward the claims of international law, an attitude that lingers on. If law is disobeyed and if no effective methods emerge to compel obedience, one tends to deprecate law's claim to control behavior; legal validity and effectiveness are seen as aspects of a single reality. The growth of international law came to depend upon renouncing claims to regulate recourse to force. This adjustment to the power structure permitted legal rules a modest, but effective, function with regard to the routine matters of commerce, investment, transportation, communication, and travel that served the mutual interests of all members of the world community, thus assuring an automatic effectiveness. The traditional system of international law accommodated itself to a war system of international relations. This war system was stabilized to some extent by techniques of counterforce and alliance that sought to make recourse to war consistently disadvantageous. This meant, however, that war was inhibited, if at all, by considerations of power and not by techniques of law. Furthermore, power was distributed among units of formal equality in the system. It is possible to argue that force is always and only restrained by the presence of superior force elsewhere, but if the elsewhere has superior institutional status it is easier to acknowledge the regime of control as one endowed with attributes of legitimacy. In such a manner we distinguish between the control of force by self-help and governmental technique. We witness today the painful effort to develop in the international system centralized substitutes for self-help. In this context, one should evaluate the peace-keeping ventures of the United Nations, and particularly the more ambitious attempt to establish order in the Congo. We conclude these comments on the role of war in the traditional system of international law by stressing the relation between force and social change on the one hand, and between power and legal effectiveness on the other. In this way we grasp both the legislative function of war and the impotence of attempts by international law to eliminate war from international political experience.

The fourth aspect of the traditional system that appears to be worthy of comment is the common culture that was shared by those nations that took the lead in developing legal rules and procedures that governed all international contacts. Not only did those nations possess a shared cultural experience as result of a common commitment to the values of Christianity, but as well, and perhaps more importantly, they possessed a common set of interests to be protected in international affairs. These interests can be roughly identified with their position as capital-exporting states. This led to the use of law to protect property rights acquired by aliens in foreign societies and generally to preserve the sanctity of economic obligations undertaken in situations of unequal bargaining. For there is no doubt that international law developed at a time when the dominant Western European nations could impose their will upon the rest of the world with the exception, perhaps, of the Western hemisphere where the dominance of the United States produced somewhat equivalent results. This means that international law started the twentieth century with a heavily European bias. Any legal system is slow to change its rules to correspond to changes in its power structure, but the international system is peculiarly ill-adapted to accommodate the pressures of change because it lacks legislative institutions and techniques. In fact, rules, obligations, and doctrines cannot be changed in the traditional system except by the consent of all national actors; this requirement of consent is a further by-product of the formal dominance of the concept of sovereignty. The need for consent hardens old standards of commitment as nations that benefit from earlier obligations are reluctant to give up voluntarily their advantages. This makes the reform of international law exceedingly difficult; it tends to make certain claims of law unacceptable and hence prompts rejection of the whole system in order to avoid the acceptance of legal obligations that are widely perceived as superceded by events taking place in social and political realms. It is this attitude that is often expressed today by newly independent anti-colonialist and anti-capitalist societies that have entered the international scene after the basic network of legal obligations was established.

The final aspect of the traditional legal order that we call attention to is the protection given by international law for the colonial system of domination and exploitation. Colonialism served the interests of the dominant Western actors, subordinating national communities to external direction. This was not a totally malevolent phenomenon, for the most part, as the European nations not unjustly considered that they were bringing a superior way of life to backward and dependent peoples in exchange for certain material advantages. However, colonialism and imperialism are identified with the corpus of traditional international law, and arouse the hostility of anti-colonial groups that have gradually attained ascendancy in the period following the Second World War. Part of the perceived inadequacy of international law arises from this identification which seems, from the perspective of post-colonial nations, to vindicate their attitude of suspicion and hostility toward the claims of international legal order. Since any international legal system must solicit support and respect from all major power centers in the world this basis of distrust cannot be neglected, especially as it coincides with the hostility that accompanies the adoption of an anti-capitalist organization by so many powerful domestic economies. Anti - capitalism, anti - imperialism, and anti - colonialism are three of the most formidable emotional obstacles to the acceptance of international law by the modernizing and revolutionary nations. It is doubtful whether this emotional hostility truly expresses the interests of these nations, as the alternative to a provisional acceptance of traditional international law is a dangerous and self-defeating regime of anarchy. All nations, regardless of their national orientation, have a common interest in certain forms of international stability. There is a shared commitment to economic growth through foreign trade and capital movement and to the discouragement of major recourses to force. However, the perception of this common interest in international legal order may not emerge clearly enough for modernizing and revolutionary nations to moderate their aspirations to accept the existing system of international law.

IV. The Traditional System Challenged

This discussion of the traditional international legal order has sought to emphasize certain characteristics that make it vulnerable to contemporary challenge. We proceed now to consider some leading components of this challenge. First, the development of nuclear weapons makes the outbreak of major war so disadvantageous that it seems desirable to find an alternative to the discretionary uses of national force in the traditional system. Second, the complexity of modern economic development and industrial activity leads to much less sufficiency on the part of the national unit. This coincides with the inability of national societies to organize the defense of their own territory without major reliance upon the protection of a powerful friend or supranational mechanism of collective security. This means that the functional justification of the territorial state is overcome by developments in its economic and military spheres, the two areas within which it had operated most self-sufficiently in earlier periods. The postulate of sovereignty is no longer descriptive for the behavior of nations with respect to matters that affect vital interests. An inevitable degree of functional supranationalism results. This development, however, is not paralleled by supranational assumptions of power and authority. The facts of interdependence have neither been assimilated into the institutional framework of international relations nor into the dominant consciousness of mankind. Third, there is the appearance on the international scene of non-national actors, especially regional organizations and the various organs of the United Nations. These actors, although still impotent when compared to the powerful nations of the world, do play an increasingly important role in the control of international conflict. This partly reflects the stalemated hostility of the two powerful nuclear states, for such a condition permits and encourages the emergence of some alternative to national authority. Fourth, the dominant conflict in the world today represents a clash of nations with rival ideological perspectives that are reluctant to converge upon a common set of legal and political standards of behavior. Ideological rivalry, nuclear weapons, pressures for social change, inadequacies of supranational mechanisms of control and legislation, depict the crisis that besets the international legal order.

V. The Condition of Transitional Crisis

The result of these challenges to the traditional international legal system is to create a situation of transitional crisis. For the inadequacies of the old order have given rise to the beginnings of a new order, but have not yet brought into being a system that adequately responds to the challenges posed by nuclear weapons or by the predispositions of communist and modernizing states. In this period of transition one discerns four categories that appear to be crucial. First, there are problems of conflict management. These can be divided into international and internal conflict. The major objective here is to use the norms and institutions of international law to avoid outbreaks of violence. Especially, there is a widespread attempt to minimize resort to violence within the context of the cold war. For here the capabilities of the antagonists and the stakes of the outcome are such as to aggravate the dangers of nuclear war. Second, the pressures of social change call for significant attention on the part of the legal order. The satisfaction of the pressures for social change relate obviously to the control of conflict. Violence will ensue when certain changes are not brought about. This leads to finding ways in which the international community, acting as a whole or as a region, can take responsibility for coercing certain minimum changes in domestic communities. In this spirit, one should consider the advisability of intervention by regional organizations and the United Nations to achieve limited legislative objectives. Such a consideration contradicts adherence to former images of sovereignty, but it operates as a preferable alternative to the belligerent resolution of conflict in the world as it exists today. Additionally, status quo nations should manifest a willingness to adapt the rules of the international legal order to some of the demands presented on behalf of societies which reject the European heritage as well as the capitalist ethic. This is part of the task of universalizing international law so that it is less genuinely vulnerable to the criticism that it represents the provincial outlook of Western European culture in the period preceding World War I. Third, in response to the transitional crisis, it is very important to discern the areas of consensus and diversity. For the area of consensus discloses potentialities for supranational activity. Obsession with conflict, its dangers and its resolution, has perhaps overly distracted us from the possibilities for supranational cooperation with respect to those problems for which major states in the world agree about the direction and outcome of the solution. Where consensus exists a basis for supranational coercion is present, especially if directed against those isolated instances of rejection of the prevailing consensus. For example, supranational coercion could usefully hasten the solution of the few remaining problems of colonialism. At the same time it is essential that supranational institutions are not used to impose the will of one part of the world community upon another part. This is particularly true when the diversity of practice and belief reflects a disagreement about how to organize the economic life of powerful societies . Here supranational institutions do best by respecting the diversity and concentrating upon those areas where agreement emerges despite ideological, political, and economic conflict. Fourth, there is a need to integrate control over transnational activities in supranational institutions. This will give institutional expression to the functional interdependence that is increasingly characteristic of the modern world. As well, it will provide a depoliticized arena within which to experience international cooperation. Success in this realm may encourage attempts to resolve some of the more controversial difficulties.

VI. Revolutionary and Modernizing Nations and International Law

In this world of radical peril, we give the remainder of our attention to the special problem created by the attitudes of revolutionary and modernizing nations toward the regulatory claims of the traditional system of international law. The Sino-Soviet bloc is the central source of revolutionary animus, seeking fundamental internal reorderings and maximum external expansion of their radical ideology and structures of domination. Non-revolutionary nations resist the external manifestations of revolutionary energy as part of a

struggle to maintain their way of life from outside interference. This encounter of wills has brought us the experience of protracted conflict that we call the Cold War.

Does the conflict underlying the Cold War prohibit the
emergence of a universal legal order capable of controlling
national recourse to nuclear weapons? This problem of conflict resolution dominates all others in the world today, as
well it should.

In addition to revolutionary nations there are a growing
group of states seeking rapid industrialization. These modernizing societies often resort to radical techniques to obtain capital needed for their program. Large holdings of
private property are especially vulnerable to control, even
confiscation. Expropriation, confiscatory taxation, laws
prohibiting repatriation of profits are among the risks assumed by the investor in such a society. Modernizing societies pose their own challenges to the traditional system
of inhibition posited by international law. The challenge of
modernizing societies is far less threatening than that posed
by the revolutionary nations. The modernizing societies
want to cut inherited burdens and find world community support for internal programs designed to improve the economic, social, and cultural wellbeing of their populations;
there is no insistence upon a missionary transformation of
the world, nor is there a rigid domestic imposition of totalitarian control. Peiping China appears to combine most
emphatically the goals of a revolutionary nation with the experience of being a modernizing society.

In 1960 many members of the Legal Committee of the
General Assembly of the United Nations participated in a
discussion of the role of international law in the contemporary world. Most of the non-Western delegates expressed
profound dissatisfaction with the current status of international law. The declining importance of international law
in the practice of the United Nations suggested itself to the
speakers as a result of the dwindling agenda of the Legal
Committee, and even more significantly by the tendency of
the General Assembly to ignore Charter limitations. Also,
the debate revealed widespread support for the view that international law must be modernized to reflect the fundamental changes that had taken place in the world since the
formulation of its basic legal doctrines in the periods between the Protestant Reformation and The First World War.

The Afro-Asian states tended to stress the need to accommodate nations that had achieved independence since
the end of World War II, whereas Soviet bloc members argued in favor of incorporating their notions of peaceful coexistence into the modern structure of international law. It
is perhaps unfortunate that the members of the large West-

ern delegations confined their comments to rather technical matters that arose out of the report made by the preceding session of the International Law Commission. This adds
to the impression that Western leadership refuses to encourage or even to consider, any major revisions of the traditional system of international law. Such refusal appears
to stem partly from a shortsighted identification of Western interests with the status quo as it is expressed by some
of the older doctrines of international law, especially those
dealing with the right of a state to protect its nationals a-
broad against various deprivations charged to the territorial
state. Western defense of its traditional position on matters of state responsibility seems to be unresponsive to the
parallel challenges made by modernizing and revolutionary
nations. It is no longer possible for the more powerful states
to supplement rules with interventionary tactics; in the formative period of international law the capital-exporting states
could use their power to secure their foreign interests. The
use of intervention as a sanction was frequent in the relations between the United States and Latin America in the
century prior to 1933. However, intense hostility to intervention by target states in Latin America combined with the
desire of the United States for hemispheric friendship and
solidarity to discourage coercive enforcement of economic
claims. This meant that the formal rules favorable to capital-exporting states became ineffective because political
realities arose to restrain the use of the primitive sanctions of self-help that were so crucial for consistent enforcement. In the light of this development alone it seems
foolish indeed to hold onto the glories of the past by a refusal to adapt to the needs of the present.

In the Legal Committee discussion Mr. Channas of Lebanon wisely observed that "if the gap between legal structure and political, economic and social realities was permitted to subsist for a long time, the structure would dis-
integrate". He added that this "fact was as certain in international as in the domestic sphere". Such words express
the need to adapt law to changes taking place in the social
environment within which law is expected to function. For
law is a dependent variable that cannot command autonomous
respect if it frustrates the interests and values of those who
possess and understand the various capacities of power within a given community. Law is an instrument for the fulfillment of social policy, not an end-in-itself. Stability arises
partly from the ability of the legal order to develop the kind
of solutions that do not perpetuate old causes of strife and
suffering. Thus our domestic system of law would place
itself in serious peril if it did not reflect the new demands
of the Negro population for effective equality in the United

States. Such a relation between stability and law is even more pronounced in a decentralized legal order, like the international one, where voluntary compliance counts for more than the coercion by the police.

This understanding of the dependence of law upon social conditions suggests the wisdom of a shift in outlook from partisan advantage to community consensus. The national interest of the United States is often served best by encouraging changes in the legal order that acknowledge new interests and demands of the modernizing Afro-Asian and the revolutionary nations. We should want as many nations as possible to have a stake in the legal system as it operates and so discourage disruptive behavior that discloses contempt for orderly processes and institutions. In this light it is well to meditate upon India's choice of solution for its dispute with Portugal about the status of Goa; finding itself buffeted by intense domestic anti-colonial pressures India departed from the Charter commitment to renounce the use of force in international affairs. It is easy to scoff at the peculiarities of Indian morality, especially in view of the oft-proclaimed Gandhian heritage, the rather overbearing self-righteousness of certain prominent Indian diplomats, but this misses the real misfortune of the Goa incident: namely, that India had to choose between a policy of violence and the indefinite toleration of "local" colonialism. Should not the anti-colonial sentiment of the world community find an intermediate solution? Mr. Kechan of Byelorussia asserted in the Sixth Committee that "colonial system should be declared a gross violation of the elementary standards of international law". It is easy, perhaps too easy, to discount such a proposal as Communist propaganda, a cheap tactic to arouse Afro-Asian sympathies. Certainly the Soviet bloc delights in embarrassing the West. And certainly, it is basely hypocritical to condemn the West while using ruthless force to maintain a new colonialism in East Europe. But nevertheless Byelorussia offers a proposal worth taking seriously. For why should not the anti-colonial consensus of world opinion have the opportunity to formalize its sentiments and obtain the active support of existing legal processes to hasten the end of the colonial era? It may still be possible to spare Angola bloody strife by organizing collective support for the independence movement in the United Nations. International law must serve community welfare rather than act to impede the realization of widely shared goals.

But what of Portugal or the Republic of South Africa? What stake can these governmental elites have in encouraging this new international system into being? An oppressive elite will resort to desperate measures to perpetuate its out-moded structure of repression and control. The random murders of innocent and helpless civilians by the Secret Army Organization in Algeria is a grim illustration of the wild frenzy that accompanies the death rattle of those who cannot accept the passing of the old regime of privilege and domination. Exile, ostracism, and finally extinction is the unhappy destiny of those who fail to accept new power relations and value constellations that involve fundamentals in the social order. We must remain prepared to exact this price to achieve social progress. Of course, it remains a prime moral obligation to make the transition to the new order at the lowest attainable human cost. This requires anticipatory changes in the social and legal order to facilitate orderly transitions rather than making it necessary for the progressive movements to gain their ends by violent opposition. President Kennedy said in a domestic address on the Alliance for Progress Program: "Those who make peaceful revolutions impossible will make violent revolutions inevitable".

This aim of peaceful but radical reordering has an urgent relevance for the growth of international legal order . There are no supranational institutions explicitly entrusted with the functions and competences of a legislature . Thus injustices in relations between or within states cannot easily be changed to express changes in the will of the international community. Notions of territorial sovereignty, domestic jurisdiction, and non-intervention further isolate domestic injustice from supranational remedy. If a repressive elite lacks substantial support for its policies beyond its territory then it usually refuses to heed supranational advice, censure, warning or boycott. This leaves domestic victims no alternative but to organize protest movements that circumvent and challenge the domestic legal structure that has institutionalized present injustice. Efforts of the territorial government to repress widespread external sympathy with the protest movement, desires to extend spheres of political influence and ideological impact all provoked insurgents to solicit and receive interventionary support from friendly foreign nations. In Algeria this pattern produced a bloody civil war that was estimated to cost 250, 000 lives and $20, 000, 000 when it was terminated by the Evian truce accords of March 1962. Throughout Southeast Asia the pattern of repression, protest, and intervention leads national struggles to become arenas of conflict for the Cold War. Not only does this increase the intensity and havoc of domestic strife by bringing extensive military equipment into the country, but it draws potential nuclear enemies into a conventional war that jeopardizes the chances for broader settlement and increases the possibility of escalation to nuclear war. These dangerous developments tend to make the superpowers willing "to settle" domestic conflict by compromise or armistice; the intervening Cold War blocs are neither willing to lose limited wars nor to use nuclear weapons to assure victory. Korea and Laos provide prominent illustrations of the insinuation of the Cold War into bitter domestic conflict in a manner that led to unstable solutions by negotiated compromise. The current internal war in South Viet Nam, leading the United States to abandon the standards set by the 1954 Geneva Accords to be able to offset prior North Vietnamese interventions, illustrates the danger of imposing a peaceful "solution" upon a domestic society torn by embittered rivalry.

It is essential to develop collective measures on a supranational level so as to work toward the continuing domestication of civil strife, as well as to encourage supranational interventions to overcome the intolerable injustices that are found today in Angola, Rhodesia, and the Republic of South Africa. The Congo Operation despite all problems, is a salutary attempt to use the United Nations to prevent domestic conflict from commencing escalatory spiral. Analogously, it seems important for the United Nations to increase its role in the various disputes arising out of racial suppression in South Africa. Here the direction of change seems so unmistakable that there is small justification for withholding supranational coercion until the bloody days of reckoning begin in earnest. Besides this, the institutionalized suppression of minority races seems sufficiently contrary to the moral spirit of the times to vindicate the dictation of a supranational solution as a contemporary form of "humanitarian intervention." Thereby the refusal to insulate internal social orders from guidance by supranational organizations promotes stability and peace, changes the status quo in accord with the spirit of the times, and upholds the prevailing moral sensibility. The factual interdependence of the modern world accounts for added pressure to move from a dualist to a monist conception of international relations. Running counter to this are the totalitarian patterns within the Sino-Soviet bloc formation that insist upon a Mid-Victorian distance between internal politics and international law; the socialist states are intensely dualistic in spirit and practice.

The breakdown of international order is constantly threatened by dangers that arise from the nuclear arms race. Here, international law functions to specify certain standards of national behavior that help to keep Cold War conflicts within tolerable (i. e. non-nuclear) bounds. As well, the resources of law provide some hope for stabilizing the military environment by arms control arrangements and for reducing the level and magnitude of hazard by agreements for partial or total disarmament. The non-nuclear nations appear to have a strong incentive to end the arms race and to avoid nuclear war. For one thing, the liberation of resources from military spending would increase the supply of capital available for rapid industrialization of the modernizing states. Furthermore, the indirect economic and physical damage of a nuclear war would hold back, perhaps permanently, the processes of capital accumulation needed to move a national economy to a stage where it produces the surpluses essential for continuing growth.

These comments argue for the spirit adaptive accommodation as the way to keep the international legal order intact. This requires status quo nations to sacrifice their privileged role in exchange for improved stability of the overall system. This presupposes that revolutionary nations will exchange the security of minimum order in a nuclear age for a moderation of their insistence upon "a new order" that incorporates their ideological predisposition. And finally, modernizing nations must try to overcome selfish perspectives and adopt a community perspective that aims at global welfare and order. We need these reorientations of outlook to be in a position to use international law to cut the risks, increase the pace of modernization, and raise the standards of human existence throughout the world.

THE LEGAL CONTROL OF FORCE
IN THE INTERNATIONAL COMMUNITY

by

RICHARD A. FALK

Our foremost aim is the control of force, not the pursuit of force, in a world made safe for mankind.
President John F. Kennedy

I believe the present international system to be one which has a significant probability built into it of irretrievable disaster for the human race.
Kenneth E. Boulding

Among the most profound quests of a moral man is knowledge about the proper use of force in human relations, for

143

force entails a wide range of claims over life and death. As such, it expresses the limiting condition of mortality.

The legal order is given major responsibility for the management of force in domestic society. The progress of centuries has sought to make the legal management of domestic force more rational and humane. Despite this progress fundamental problems remain in civilized societies. Consider, for instance, the current American debates about capital punishment or the use of lethal weapons to keep neighbors and friends out of fallout shelters; arguments for and against the sit-in movement often center upon the moral bases for the use of private coercion in alleged violation of law. And the celebrated dialogue between Camus and Sartre on terrorism in Algeria vividly depicts the search for authoritative limits upon the role of domestic force.

Yet how much more difficult it is to define the proper use of international force. Here the absence of unified institutional control, the diversity of cultural attitudes, the conflict of ideological rivals, and the enormity of destructive potential confront mankind with a variety of tragic prospects. Most quickly we think of nuclear devastation and totalitarian domination. But this quick discernment is also quick deception. For to discern truly we must face the unequal and uncertain risks of various kinds of warfare and the imponderable risks of different forms of totalitarian encroachment. It is the rational selection of risks, not the contemplation of extreme failures of policy, that should engage our creative moral energies. Too often, however, the jurist evades this framework of inquiry, asserting instead the sufficiency or insufficiency of existing legal rules to achieve the control of aggressive force. The relevance of the political environment to the role and function of law is neglected. And yet the nuclear arms race goes on, and crisis situations, especially in Europe, are seen as leading directly to at least limited nuclear warfare if a breakdown of the present fragile balance takes place.

This situation invites the attention of the legal analyst in a variety of ways. This essay reflects upon the bearing of the intertwining perspectives of law, morality, and social policy upon the contemporary use of international force. It inclines more toward the discovery of guidelines, problems, and dilemmas than toward the proposal of solutions.

II. Law and Morality in the Context of Force

> It is naivete, not sophistication, to believe that the conviction statesmen and nations profess and the justifications they urge in defense of their actions have no effect on the policies they pursue.
>
> Robert W. Tucker

144

It may often not be possible to do more than to clarify the factors pointing to the legality and illegality of a particular use of force as guides for those called upon to keep their conduct within "the law." Thus India's attack on Goa might have an indeterminate legal status depending upon whether one considers the enclave as part of Portugal or as an unassimilated part of India. The use of military force by Italy against San Marino would pose a different problem from the use of similar force against France. The norms of international law primarily restrict the use of national force against targets that possess international personality. No one would question for instance, the international right of the United States government to use force to coerce the will of, say, Arkansas. Whether to view Goa as more like Portugal or Arkansas is an act of judgment for which one can provide scientific reasons, but cannot prevision a scientific conclusion.

The assessment of legality which is problematic for any legal order is especially so for the international order. What do we mean by characterizing conduct as "legal" or "illegal"? The possibilities of adversary process and the presence of complementary structures of legal norms suggest that challenged action can simultaneously be described as legal and illegal depending upon the doctrinal line of argument adopted. The frequency of substantial dissents from the judgments of the United States Supreme Court further illustrates how difficult it is for reasonable men to agree upon what the law requires in a specific instance.

A use of force may be described as "aggression," "self-defense," or "reprisal"; internal violence may be described as a matter of "domestic jurisdiction" or an issue of "international concern." The characterization expresses the outcome sought by the actor. Thus the Algerian rebels stressed the international impact of their war against the French Army, whereas the government insisted upon its domestic quality. The difference in characterization controls the status of a use of force in international law, the participation of supranational institutions, the application of the rules of war, and many other things as well. How is an impartial judge to determine which set of norms to apply?

There is a tradition in recent Anglo-American jurisprudence to stress the indeterminacy of legal outcome from the logical point of view. This reacts against the artificial supposition, earlier so dominant in legal thinking, that the certainty and objectivity of law was guaranteed by the logical relationship between the scope of the rule and the controversial facts to which it is said to apply. This logical assurance is undercut if contradictory norms simultaneously

145

apply with equal logical force to identical facts. This has led legal philosophers to emphasize the element of choice that must enter into any determination of legal status. It also puts emphasis upon the decisional situation. This focus highlights the value and policy dimensions that arise in the course of selecting a governing norm. If logic does not supply the criterion of decision, then it seems desirable to use the unavoidable discretion of the judge to reach the decision that most closely accords with community standards of welfare. After all law does not exist for its own sake, but to promote the ends of society. This does not set the judge free to embark on a course of policy that is personally amenable to his sense of public good regardless of past experience. For one thing, the expectations of the community as to outcome should be satisfied if at all possible, as the predictable quality of legal status is one of the things that enables men to plan their lives. This introduces an altogether proper conservative bias into the workings of the legal process. Also there are objective methods available to determine the policies which should govern the legal inquiry. The substitution of policy for logic as a prime criterion for decision-making expands the horizon of relevance rather than personalizes the legal process. It requires a judge to look at the social consequence of alternative decisions, rather than at the logical relations between doctrine and facts.

This view of law as a process of decisions about social policy also leads to a critical distinction between casual observers and authorized decision-makers. We wish to know who the appropriate decision-maker is, as well as content of applicable legal doctrine. Is anyone other than an authoritative decision-maker capable of rendering a legal determination? In a structured domestic society it is easier to identify the authoritative decision-makers than it is in the international order where often there is no assured forum within which to establish conduct as illegal. For example, China and the United States offer contradictory legal interpretations of each other's participation in the internal wars of Southeast Asia. We would not want to identify the legal status of this conduct with the assertions of either partisan; that would be like confusing the differing roles of lawyer and judge in the adversary process. We seek to identify law with the analysis of facts, policies, and doctrine that is made by any impartial observer, regardless of whether this accords with the determinations of an authoritative decision-maker. Thus, for instance, if state A complains about a use of force by B, it is possible to offer a legal appraisal of that use of force even if the appraisal appears to disagree with the judg-

146

ment of the authoritative decision-maker. The participation
of the United States in the invasion of Cuba in 1961 is "illegal" even though the relevant organs of the United Nations
have consistently refused to characterize the United States
conduct as such. Law is not necessarily what the authoritative decision-maker says that it is. An observer's use of
evidence, policy, and norms is independently capable of as-
sessing legal status. Although the decisional situation provides a crucial focus for study and description, the decisions
of the authorized officials do not provide our deepest insights into the application of law to life. The legal order is
not an autonomous undertaking; rather it is subject to reasoned criticism from a variety of meta-legal perspectives.

This argument about "legality" should take note of three
separate aspects of the problem, even though thought and
experience ignores the separation. First, the status of conduct as legal or illegal depending upon the perspective of the
assessor as partisan, authoritative decision-maker, or
scholarly observer. Second, the appraisal of the legal result, however reached, as just or unjust. And third, the
relation between law and justice that is implied by a decision to obey an unjust law or to disobey a just law. This
third point needs elaboration. It is not perhaps the law that
is just or unjust, but its application to a set of circumstances. For instance, to choose a relevant example, rules
against forcible interference in national communities are not
unjust per se, but if their application renders weak states
vulnerable to subversive takeover, then adherence to the
rule may involve the infliction of a net injustice.

There is a need to confront the problem of civil disobed-
ience in international affairs. We are conscious, all too
conscious, of violations of international law, but there is
almost no systematic effort to provide a criterion by which
to distinguish justifiable and unjustifiable illegality in international affairs. The quest for stable limits, made urgent
in this time of nuclear weapons, certainly gives some value
to adherence to law, particularly law dealing with coercion,
for its own sake. But how much value? We do not want to
argue for the absoluteness of law's claim over national or
supra-national discretion. There exists a need for a dis-
ciplined consideration of this matter.

This suggests the linked problem of the relation between
individual and collective behavior with respect to law and
morals. When an official decides, on behalf of the United
States, to violate international law it is different from a decision to violate domestic law and, as well, different from
a decision by an individual to violate the law for private reasons. For a nation is a unit in the international system, not

147

the unit as it is in the domestic system. Furthermore, an individual in his official capacity is an agent restricted to action in accordance with applicable law. Ordinary circumstances, at least in democratic society, give law supremacy within official realms of conduct. Exceptional circumstances, however, seem to authorize official lawlessness as a response to the prior claim to serve the public good. That is, law is subordinate to an extraordinary criterion of welfare mediated through the conscience of the responsible official. There is one other observation: the public good should not be identified exclusively with national welfare when conduct has an international character. A national official acting in international affairs represents the interests of his state, of other states, of international society, and of mankind. The claim of national interest, no matter how well substantiated, does not provide self-sufficient support for conduct that is otherwise illegal. It may not even justify conduct that is legal.

It is useful to distinguish between a legitimation of and a justification for the use of international force. Legitimacy refers to the legal status of a use of force. Justification refers to a demonstration that a given legal status corresponds with relevant moral requirements. For instance, United States military intervention to establish a democratic government in a Latin American country might be justifiable although it would be illegal. In contrast, a nuclear counter strike in retaliation to a nuclear surprise attack would appear to be legal although it might not be justifiable. This analytic distinction seeks to point at two different aspects of a single phenomenon. It should not, then, be read as a separation of levels of explanation. For it is a main contention of this essay that contemporary world affairs tend increasingly to unify the conditions that satisfy the claims of legitimacy and justifications, and that, in fact, the failure to perceive this unity is a serious and dangerous deficiency of most national approaches to international law. Certainly, at least, an essential component of legitimacy is justification and a usual component of justification is legitimacy.

Force is itself a neutral energy. Its value or disvalue arises from the motives, prudence, and consequences of its use. There is no way to banish force from the human condition. John Dewey put this well when he said "not to depend upon and utilize force is simply to be without a foothold in the real world." Major changes in human affairs take place when there is a significant and effective shift in the locus of discretion with regard to the use of force. The formulation of a new rule relocating authority to use force must be accompanied by steps that permit effective imple-

148

mentation. We note that domestic social orders have effectively centralized discretion to use force in political institutions allowing only a narrow exception for self-defense in situations of severe threat from an assailant. Once discretion is centralized the problem becomes the discovery of limits. Procedural due process seeks to achieve this result within a democratic society. Arguments against capital punishment partly seek to confine the discretion of centralized decision-makers by placing a ceiling upon the permissible application of force by the government.

The international society in the form of institutions and rules, now also makes extensive claims over the discretion of a nation to use force. Despite these claims, however, the effective control over the use of force remains on a national level and governs the expectations and behavior of the participating units in world affairs. We should not, however, overlook how far the Charter of the United Nations purports to go in the direction of centralizing discretion over the use of force. But the formulation of rules in the Charter is not enough. For the weakness of central international institutions is such that the rules are neither assured impartial interpretation nor effective application. Effective centralizations of legal control over the use of force involve three basic conditions: formulation of rules and standards for their interpretation, mechanisms to achieve impartial interpretation, and techniques that enable enforcement of impartial interpretations. Legal order is not adequately established until each condition is satisfied.

Force in human affairs is not a crude phenomenon to be identified with physical strength. It is best conceived as a spectrum that ranges from mild forms of intimidation to intense applications of violence. Too often force in international affairs is identified today only with a full-scale nuclear war. Attention must be given to threats to use force and to lesser modes of coercion, and especially, in the world as we find it, to a series of interventionary techniques that usually fall short of direct military action. Considerations of legitimacy and justification must be correlated with the relevent level of force. Analysis is otherwise deceptively crude, generating blanket endorsements or proscriptions of the use of force. The moral subtlety of these problems as they exist in world affairs today casts deep suspicion upon any set of conclusions that achieves a set of assured and forthright recommendations. However, the difficulty of achieving a clear sense of direction should not inhibit attempts to understand and appraise the practical and moral dilemmas posed by the dispersion of nuclear technology. Neither should it lead to bland subservience to the official doctrines of the day. The formulation of reasoned and principled alternatives, no matter how radical, provide officials and citizens with a more illumined context for decision. Uncertainty of conclusion rebukes dogmatism, not radicalism. Our survival and welfare depend upon the capacities of nations and governing groups to have the courage and imagination to transform the world into a different kind of political structure. This is a radical desideratum, and presupposes a willingness to think, feel, and act in a framework that transcends attributes of our present world.

Moral questions arise whenever humans rely upon the use of force. This is the case whether one's concern is the discipline of children, the treatment of crowds and criminals, or the behavior of nations. How does the quality of the weapon used to inflict or threaten violence affect the moral status of a use of force? Does the greater magnitude of destruction that might attend a nuclear war change the moral basis for fighting such a war? It is desirable to avoid a morality that relies upon weights and measures, but the troublesomeness of these questions, at least for those who meditate upon the horror of nuclear war, suggests that we do not understand the moral significance of nuclear weaponry.

Force, we recall, is available as a means to achieve social ends. Its acceptability as a means depends partly upon the value of the end exceeding the cost of getting there. There must be a favorable proportion between the costly consequences of the use of force and the beneficial reasons for its use in order to make its use rational, let alone moral. Magnitude of force, then, bears upon the status of a proposed use of force by increasing commensurately the demands for justification. However, despite the rhetoric of proportionality we have no adequate way to quantify, or rendering otherwise precise, the relation between the cost of and the benefit from the use of force. Therefore, our moral agency leads us to make intuitive distinctions that emphasize the continuing need to justify force by some sense of the cost-benefit relationship. The great damage to persons and property that would arise from a nuclear war imprecisely points, then, to the unprecedented burden of justification that must be made by a moral user of nuclear force. The moral inquiry is thus primarily a matter of rationality in the first instance: a comparison of the relative losses that would most likely follow from such an inquiry in international affairs underscores further the moral ambiguity of the modern situation. It would be impossible to carry through a comparative analysis far enough to know whether force should be used on a particular occasion, and if so, how much.

Such an incapacity wherein it exists, has radical consequences for a moral posture. If we are unable to ascertain whether proposed uses of forces will produce a net benefit then we must consider whether to refrain from the use of force so long as we lack adequate justification. We do claim that adequate justification is the essential quality of a moral policy about the use of force. This leads us to accept, at least, the limited contribution that we can expect reason to make to the development of a moral policy toward the use of force.

IV. International Force and International Law

Paradoxical as it may seem, the fundamental conceptions of international law can best be understood if it is assumed that they maintain and support the rule of force.   ----George W. Keeton
Georg Schwarzenberger

Any presentation of international law is likely to suffer from widespread and contradictory public attitudes of cynicism and utopianism. Many students of world affairs either discount international law altogether or expect everything from it. It is rare indeed to encounter a just appreciation of the limits upon and opportunities for legal order in the world today. In general we have, in Brierly's words, an encounter between "the practical man who imagines that he has shed his illusions, and believes quite simply that international law is a sham" and "the ultra-legalist lawyer who deals in codes and formulas as though they contained a magic of their own, or of the enthusiastic layman who imagines that earnest aspiration after a better international order can take the place of patient study of the problems concerned." Especially with respect to the control of international force there is a tendency on the part of observers to adopt an all-or-nothing attitude towards international law. This introductory remark seeks only to warn cynics and utopians against the text that follows and to reproach them for their refusal to allow the realities of the ongoing system of international law to inform their vision of its shortcomings, achievements, and prospects.

We can begin to understand the relation of law and force in international affairs only if we take the distinctive character of the international legal system into account. This requires an appreciation of the horizontal distribution of authority, the bipolar concentration of power, and the ineffectiveness of vertical institutions and procedures for the development of international legal order. Domestic society relies upon effective vertical concentration of authority and power to compel its members to accept normative restraints. The solidarity of most domestic societies creates

151

spontaneous community support for most legal standards; furthermore, a domestic society possesses adequate mechanisms for change should this support disappear. Prohibition and anti-segregation norms illustrate the difficulties of enforcing law that arouses community hostility and civil strife even in a well-organized democratic society. These difficulties are compounded in international society where nations maintain the dominant tradition that the simultaneous pursuit of national interest by the countries of the world presupposes patterns of conflict more than structures of cooperation. There is an objective basis for this tradition. One must question, however, the tradition in the light of the new prospect of thermonuclear devastation and the claim of one power center to revolutionize the world. There is far less harmony in international society where national units have a tradition of selfish and antagonistic pursuits of wealth and power. Cultural diversity, economic disparity, imperial design are certainly among the basic historical explanations of international violence. Also the international society does not possess effective techniques for the pacific settlement of conflicts and disputes. Especially conflicts that arise from contradictory aspirations for wealth, power, and prestige cannot be adjusted very easily by existing supranational mechanisms. India's invasion of Goa in 1961 and Algerian insurgency from 1954 onwards are recent illustrations of recourse to force as the exclusive means to reach a political result that was in agreement with overwhelming consensus of world opinion.

It is not only a matter of inadequate supranational techniques for the promotion of social change, it is the national possession and retention of the means for violent resolution of conflicts that unsettles international life. In domestic societies there is no normal residuum of private violence available for the pursuit of grievances not satisfied by the institutions of the state. Self-help, except in situations of rebellion and anarchy, is virtually eliminated from the domestic scene. In a sense, the central problem of world order is to achieve a comparable elimination of self-help from the international scene.

But our primary interest is to look at what international law presently contributes to the control of force, not what must be done to make international control as adequate as domestic control. There are special difficulties for international law generated by the distinctive quality of contemporary politics. For instance, one finds the central normative distinction between "war" and "peace" in traditional international law incompatible with the factuality of the Cold War. This dramatizes the need for the development of normative categories that can accommodate the wide range of techniques by which and objectives for which force is used in international affairs. It is obviously a crude system that tends to classify "non-recognition" and "an armed attack" as instances of "intervention" despite the discretionary status of recognition and the forbidden nature of aggressive military operations. This need to particularize inquiry into a contested or proposed use of force is a fundamental aspect of adequate analysis, although it is difficult to achieve because of the poverty of normative resources of traditional international law. This makes it crucial to give a precise description of the facts so that we will not be led to assume the legal equivalence of dissimilar patterns of conduct just because they are put into a single doctrinal category. The entire notion of horizontal legal order is an attempt to expand the normative and institutional resources of the international system.

These problems stem partly from modern developments. The prohibitive costs of general warfare between nuclear blocs puts a premium upon the pursuit of national objectives by lesser modes of coercion. This contrasts with the historical obsession with the regulation of military operations across recognized international frontiers that attain a sufficiently sustained pattern to warrant the characterization "war". This emphasis on war reflected the concern of political actors, as well as provided the focus of inquiry for international jurists. Sophisticated students of international law are skeptical about claiming that law controls coercion that is less than war. The distinguished Danish internationalist, Alf Ross, suggests that "it will be wisest to let the chapter on intervention disappear entirely from International Law, at any rate for the present. For here we have passed the limit of what has a reasonable chance of being respected as law." Ross goes on to say that:

In principle, intervention is violence as part of the policy of states. To stretch expectation too far on this point by pretending that the law can forbid any such thing is merely to undermine the confidence in International Law in a sphere where it really might mean something.

This view has great significance. International law should extend its claims to control on the basis of notions of effectiveness, not wishful thinking. However, in dissent from Ross, it is felt that law can usefully clarify standards pertaining to intervention and thereby reduce the risks of unintended escalation that might otherwise be present when interventionary politics become tainted with Cold War rivalries. It may be helpful to precede a description of the relation between international law and intervention in internal affairs by a short sketch of the main juridical attempts to restrain the use of force in international affairs.

Medieval attempts to restrict the use of force by the specification of moral criteria failed to dissuade nations from conquest. The development of the Just War doctrine, under the sway of Christian moral philosophy, was neither able to discourage violence nor to mobilize the collective force of the community against the unjust breaker of the peace. Gradually jurisprudential concern shifted from efforts to control recourse to belligerency to the development of techniques for the limitation of ensuing hostilities. Therefore, writers emphasized rules governing non-participation (neutrality) and restricting the cruelty of war (law of war). In the nineteenth century, especially, it became clear that political methods were alone able to restrict recourse to force. Thus the balance of power system, in its favorable aspect, sought to confront any potential aggressor with enough defensive force to discourage aggression. There was no serious attempt to condemn the recourse to force as itself illegal or even wrong. In fact, the acceptance of auto-interpretation effectively allowed each belligerent to attribute justice to his own use of force, and this attribution was not subject to revision by the collective judgment of the community of nations or by the impartial judgment of a neutral nation or a panel of experts. The doctrine of sovereignty insulated auto-interpretation from objective review by a secular agency; national decisions were reviewable only in the light of their compatibility with divine ordinance, and then only by the monarcy or the ruling elite within the actor's government. It is hardly necessary to observe that such a regime of auto-interpretation rarely arrives at the conclusion that a use of international force is "illegal" or "unjust." For nations, like individuals, are loathe to make public self-condemning judgments about their conduct, and strive instead to rationalize their behavior by an appeal to some kind of justification, however dubious it may appear to bystanding actors. War, then, operated in the international system as the most intense political technique available to a state for the pursuit of national goals. From a systematic perspective recourse to war had no legal status. More significantly, the fruits of successful conquest were incorporated into a legally valid peace treaty that bound the victim state even if its consent was obtained by duress: "The international law of peace has for three centuries stabilized the equilibrium achieved by force in the fundamental peace treaties concluded since 1648."

This tolerance of war and the ratification of its results does, up to this day, make the claims of international law as law appear problematic to many observers of the international scene. For if a state is entitled to wage war against another state it seems artificial to hold it responsible for all the lesser delinquencies that excite jurists, such as failures to respect the immunity of diplomats. Why should a state worry about its duty to respect the innocent passage of foreign vessels through its territorial waters if it is entitled to wage a war of conquest against any foreign state? Logic misleads here. It is correct to observe the folly of insisting upon the legal control of lesser violations of national rights in contrast to the lawless status of the greatest violations, but it points only to the hazard of the system, not its non-existence. For the normal condition of international relations leads all states to seek a reliable set of standards to govern the wide variety of international transactions. These standards are most conveniently created and sustained within a normative environment that uses the rhetoric and techniques of law. It is to this extent a functioning legal order, despite its inability to exert fully effective control over resort to violence. Up to the present time nations have insisted upon the capacity to use force as a continuing and ultimate alternative to the inhibitions placed upon national freedom by the normative restraints that make up international law.

To gain confidence in international law as law we must identify the distinctive elements and aims of international legal order. International law rests upon a generalized preference for order in all international relationships most of the time and order in some international relationships almost all of the time. Thus considerations of convenience, fairness, and predictability dominate the behavior of those who conduct international relations. These ordering impulses are reenforced by the logic of reciprocity (if X restricts the immunity of diplomats from Y, then Y will do the same or equivalent to X) and by the subservience of bureaucrats to rules that are in existence. Even in wartime the desire to avoid chaos by the maintenance of communication and by refraining from belligerent excess gives law the important task of generating mutually acceptable norms capable of clear discernment and adequate implementation. Furthermore, it is important to achieve clarity of legal rights so as to provide international life with minimum stability. Thus it is essential to have a legal mechanism for absorbing effective changes of legal status achieved on the political level by diplomacy or warfare. The peace treaty that expresses the new distribution of authority constitutes 'the given' at the end of a war. This amounted to a new condition of normalcy that needed the stabilizing control of international law. Victory through force acted in the traditional system of international law as the functional equivalent to legislation and constitutional revision in domestic society. It provided a way for the community to adapt its organic law to new needs and energies that press for fulfillment.

However, the gross disadvantages and the brutalizing consequences of relying upon way to achieve changes in the prevailing order began to make statesmen seek serious alternatives in the late XIXth Century, and especially after the widespread destruction wrought by World War I. The direction of this response led to various attempts to impose rigid restrictions upon the right of a state to use international force. Most nations were persuaded to renounce the use of force in international affairs except for self-defense and to create primitive collective machinery in the League of Nations. The Geneva Protocol of 1924, although abandoned shortly after its adoption, was the first significant attempt of leading nations to prohibit recourse to aggressive war. The Treaty for the Renunciation of War (Briand-Kellogg Pact) in 1928 and the Anti-War Treaty of Rio de Janeiro in 1933 did formally commit a total of 65 nations to accept legal norms proscribing all non-defensive uses of force in international relations.

At the same time that the idea of war was drawn into serious question, the regulation of its conduct was deeply challenged by the developing weapons technology. Submarines and aircraft made their military debut in World War I, threatening to render obsolete the entire corpus of the law of war. This was especially evident in the area of naval and air operations. Traditional notions of contraband, neutral carriage, visit and search seemed obsolete in view of these new weapons. World War II accentuated these trends, climaxing the technological developments by the use of atomic bombs against Hiroshima and Nagasaki and the legal-moral developments by the solemn trials and judgments of Nuremberg and Tokyo that imposed criminal responsibility on many surviving leaders of Germany and Japan for their roles in planning, preparing, and waging aggressive war. The United Nations Charter incorporates the response of the world community in an atmosphere prior to the emergence of the Cold War. Explicit norms oblige members to renounce the use of force in international affairs except for individual or collective self-defense against a prior armed attack. A great part of the Charter seeks to provide a normative framework for a system of collective security in the event that peace is endangered. It is commonplace to note that the Cold War has transformed the Charter, shifting responsibilities from the veto-paralyzed Security Council to the swelling ranks of the General Assembly and the executive discretion of the Secretariat. The financial crisis arising out of the controversial Congo Operation reveals limits just as emerging political stability in the Congo suggests the achievements of the United Nations with respect to the control of force. The future role of the United Nations is highly uncertain, depending heavily upon whether the Soviet Union seeks to keep specific internal wars within or without the ambit of the Cold War. At present, the United Nations provides no direct protection against nuclear warfare, except to provide a forum for disarmament negotiation and world community protest.

The nuclear powers seem to claim and exercise exclusive control over their defense policies including the privilege to engage in unlimited nuclear testing in the atmosphere. Both the Soviet Union and the United States evidently base their decisions to test upon military considerations arising from the arms race: neither state is publicly responsive to the appeals for the end of all nuclear testing made by the overwhelming majority of United Nations membership. However, United States officialdom expresses solicitude for world concern and promise maximum precautions and minimum atmospheric testing. And yet U Thant, Acting Secretary General of the United Nations, seems to speak for the majority of nations when he referred to the anticipated high altitude nuclear testing by the United States as "a manifestation of a very dangerous psychosis which is in evidence today." Here, too, a responsible decision balances the claims of the community against a national responsibility to resist totalitarian encroachment. The United States should not, however, assume that it alone desires to resist or knows best how to resist the totalitarian advance; therefore, responsible participation in an international organization such as the United Nations, usually requires the subordination of national judgment to the collective will or, at least a clear public demonstration of the error or unfairness of the collective judgment. We cannot discharge our moral responsibilities by insisting upon the autonomy of a national version of truth and necessity; such an insistence rejects the postulate of interdependence, as well as underplays the genuineness of the concern about nuclear weaponry felt by the supranational community. It also overlooks the resulting need to legitimate decisions about the use of international force- -including nuclear testing- -by an increasing reliance upon the vertical authorization.

Are nuclear weapons legitimate in warfare? This question concerns the legitimacy of the means of conducting warfare, and it is properly separate from the responsibility for initiating war. If one examines the formal norms of the vertical system then it would appear that a strong case against legality exists. The analogy to poison gas, the inability to confine weapons effects to military targets, the disproportionate ratio between human suffering and military advantage, the analogy to genocide and crimes against humanity are among the grounds urged to support the conclusion of illegality.

The argument for the legality of nuclear weapons rests upon the justice of deterring Communist aggression and the impossibility of doing so (with sufficient reliability) by alternative means. Thus it is an argument which finds its rationale in the logic of collective self-defense and its moral

157

justification in the responsibility of democratic societies to resist totalitarian expansion. This endorsement of legality is quite separate from discussion about the occasions that warrant recourse to nuclear weapons. Here, the argument only asserts the legitimacy of the use of nuclear weapons as a part of the right of self-defense. The duty to avoid an outbreak of nuclear war underscores the correlate need for a narrow and clear definition of self-defense once the legality of nuclear weapons is accepted.

Usually, however, the argument for legality is stated in rather formal terms that stem from the tolerance of the traditional system toward national claims that are not already the subject of an international prohibition. The classical view is that a nation can do whatever it is not explicitly forbidden from doing. This analysis can be used quite easily to support the legality of nuclear weapons. It is succinctly expressed in Article 613 of the United States Naval Instructions of 1955: "There is at present no rule of international law expressly prohibiting states from the use of nuclear weapons in warfare. In the absence of express prohibition, the use of such weapons against enemy combatants and other military objectives is permitted." This claim is consistent with the traditional theory of obligation in international law which rests upon the need for the express or implied consent of the state. Thus the United States is entitled to do whatever is not prohibited by treaty or customary that derive from the formal (positivistic) sources of law--make decisions pertaining to the use of nuclear weapons fully a matter of national discretion.

This presents a basic theoretical problem for contemporary international law: what is the status of unilateral claims to engage in novel action for which there exists no normative experience? The same issue less dramatically underlies the United States claim to orbit espionage satellites over Soviet territory. It is my contention that contemporary facts of interdependence combine with the logic of reciprocity to require a nation to do more than demonstrate the absence of a pre-existing prohibitive norm if it is to validate a controversial unilateral claim. A primary objective of rational policy for a major nation today is the maintenance of minimum international stability. However, once a unilateral claim is made it validates, until a prohibitive norm emerges, equivalent claims by all other states. The use of atomic bombs in World War II, and the initiation of nuclear tests on the high seas illustrate failures to anticipate the destabilizing effects of unilateral claims upon the future prospects for minimum order. We find that here the legal claiming process rests upon inadequate justification. For under present circumstances no claim should be asserted or validated unless it has first been found to cohere with the minimum needs of international stability.

At this stage such a demand has only theoretical relevance to the prospective use of nuclear weapons. For nations are devoting huge resources to the development of nuclear weapons and their delivery systems. There appears to be every reason to expect that these nations would use nuclear weapons in "appropriate circumstances." We shift from the trivial directives of vertical norms that appear to proscribe the use of nuclear weapons in international affairs to the crucial content of horizontal norms. For a horizontal norm is a descriptive proposition about what nations will probably do in light of the interplay of event, interest, conscience, and rule; it is a predictive generalization which acts as a comprehensive ground rule for behavior. Since rules of the game introduce stable limits into the system they function in a normative capacity. Therefore, an adequate description of international law must emphasize the identification of horizontal norms. This is especially true with regard to nuclear weapons as Cold War tensions make it so difficult to achieve stability by the creation of a viable vertical regime of normative control (e. g. comprehensive disarmament). Since agreement seems impossible a lesser form of stability can be had by positing symmetrical sets of unilateral claims. Such a horizontal regime has many defects when applied to the use of nuclear force. First, decisions to retaliate against violations are dangerous. Second, secrecy, threats and bluffs prevent the communication of the actual defense policy to the potential enemy. Third, the ultimate stakes of the struggle provide an incentive to ignore normative restraints in times of heavy stress. Despite these defects horizontal control seems to guard us somewhat against outbreak of nuclear war.

There is a minimum horizontal norm: the initiating use of nuclear weapons must take place in a clear situation of individual or collective self-defense against a prior armed attack that has been carried across an international boundary and threatens the territorial integrity and political independence of an area that possesses sufficient international personality to entitle it to apply for membership as a state in the United Nations. This formulation intends to exclude colonial dependencies--for instance, Angola--from the right of nuclear self-defense by making minimum international personality a condition of use. Beyond this limiting condition, however, is one of greater generality. The use of nuclear weapons is justified only if it is indispensable to an adequate defense; preparations for defense should place maximum reliance upon non-nuclear weapons. Tactical atomic weapons should not be used except when essential to defense, and then only to restore the territory of the state that was a victim of the armed attack. Once fighting is carried on beyond the level of conventional weapons the dangers of escalation seem great, although at each level of use there should be clearly manifest an intention to make no more than a proportional response. All participation in internal wars should be strictly confined to conventional warfare. This means that nuclear weapons are "legal" only if needed as an essential part of self-defense against a sustained armed attack across a significant international boundary. Furthermore, the objective of mass or strategic retaliation appears too costly under existing conditions. All actors should prepare to meet military threats by maximum reliance upon conventional weapons. If the attacking nation is first to use nuclear weapons then the defensive nation is entitled to make a proportionate counter-strike against military targets. An armed attack that consists of a major nuclear attack signifies the collapse of the horizontal system. This permits the target state to choose its own reprisal strategy provided that suffering and destruction is not inflicted capriciously or merely for the sake of revenge. However, the target state must not resort to nuclear weapons until there is an actual attack. The horizontal system becomes very unstable if it provisionally authorizes preventive, anticipatory, or pre-emptive strategies to justify an initial recourse to nuclear weapons. Restoration of the territorial status quo prior to an armed attack should be the maximum legitimate limited war objective. This description of a horizontal legal order governing the use of nuclear weapons combines observed regularities of behavior with a recommendation for policies of self-limitation that seek to reconcile defense needs with maximum security against the outbreak of a major nuclear war. It implies certain adjustments of military planning; for instance, it commends the build-up of a conventional defense system in Western Europe and the Far East where there is great danger of a violent breakdown of the present fragile equilibria. This presentation of a sketch of a horizontal system of legal control for nuclear weapons intends only to illustrate a way of thinking about these problems. It is not meant as a proposal that adequately responds to the many nuances of national defense.

THE MANAGEMENT OF POWER IN THE CHANGING
UNITED NATIONS

INIS L. CLAUDE, JR.

I.

The central problem of our time is to achieve the effective management of the power relations of states. The world is constituted as a system of independent but interdependent states—independent in authority but interdependent in destiny. States are units of power. While power is a complex conception, for present purposes it may be construed in the narrow sense of force. Physical ability to kill, to damage, or to coerce, is the particular aspect of power which serves as the focus of this article. States are characterized by the possession, in varying degrees, of this capacity to damage or destroy each other. This power may be used in competitive struggle, producing destruction on a massive scale. It may be used unilaterally, producing enslavement and degradation of its victims. In short, both survival and freedom, both sheer existence and the higher values that enrich existence, are implicated in the problem of power. The national interest of every state, and the common interest of all men, in the preservation and development of civilization are threatened by the paroxysms of violence which states are capable of unleashing. Hence, the primacy of the task of controlling the use of force by states, of managing the power relations of states, cannot seriously be questioned.

I use the term, *management,* to convey the conviction that the problem of power is here to stay; it is, realistically, not a problem to be eliminated, but one to be managed. At all levels of society, human beings inherently possess and inexorably retain the capacity to do physical violence to each other. The task of socialization is not to abolish power, but to control its exercise. At the level of collectivities, I take it as a basic postulate that there will always be human groups—if no longer national states, then other social sub-divisions—which will be capable of damaging each other. They cannot ultimately be deprived of this capacity. Given brains and brawn, men can contrive instruments of lethal warfare, be they clubs or hydrogen bombs; given human social instincts and skills, men can contrive to organize their violence as the clash of collectivities. The issue will never be whether power exists; it will always be whether power is subjected to effective management.

My emphasis upon the concept of management of power carries with it the specific implication that disarmament is not the key to the problem of international violence. In the literal sense, the notion of disarmament would seem to suggest reliance upon the unattainable ideal of eliminating the potential of states for vio-

INIS L. CLAUDE, JR., is on leave from the University of Michigan to serve as visiting research scholar at the Carnegie Endowment for International Peace. This article is largely drawn from a book-length study, *The Management of Power in International*

Relations, which the author is preparing for publication. The author gratefully acknowledges the financial assistance of the Rockefeller Foundation in enabling him to undertake the study.

lence. Most actual disarmament efforts are, of course, more modestly conceived; they aim at checking the arms race and securing the adoption of systematic programs of arms limitation or reduction. The value of such achievements, if they should prove possible, might be considerable. They might, by restricting the distribution of certain types of weapons and limiting the quantitative levels of power accumulation, prevent the power situation from becoming inherently unmanageable. Thus, that brand of disarmament which is more accurately characterized as arms control may be an essential prologue to, or accompaniment of, any effective scheme for the management of power in the contemporary world. Whether or not disarmament can be attained, however, the basic problem will remain that of establishing and maintaining reliable control over the exercise of power. Even if all existing weapons were destroyed and production of armaments totally suspended, the capacity to devise instruments of terrible power would remain a permanent potentiality; man cannot unlearn what he knows about the means of creating power. My basic criticism of the disarmament motif is that it tends to foster an emphasis upon abolition of power as the key to peace and security, whereas it seems to me that the problem is more realistically defined in terms of the necessity of bringing the exercise of power by states under effective and reliable control.

The theory of international relations, if one may apply that term to a literature which is more a thing of shreds and patches than a seamless garment covering our understanding of the processes of international relations, contains three basic concepts which may be regarded as relevant to the problem of the management of power: balance of power, collective se-

curity, and world government. These concepts have not been defined with care, used with precision, or made to serve as bases for systematically elaborated theoretical structures; at best, they stand as rudimentary snippets of theory which have been used more for polemical than for analytical purposes. Each of them has attracted its quota of advocates and detractors, who have tended to treat the concepts competitively rather than comparatively. In short, balance of power, collective security, and world government are not terms which designate well-developed and generally understood bodies of doctrine. Nevertheless, they do represent the leading ideas regarding the problem of the management of power in international relations, and they figure as the focal points of contemporary discussion and controversy concerning this problem.

It is, of course, hazardous to try to establish definite meanings for terms which have customarily been used so loosely and inconsistently as these. Recognizing that others may exercise the right to invest them with meanings different from mine, I nevertheless venture to suggest that these three concepts can, with considerable justification derived from the literature of the international relations field, be taken as characterizing disparate systems of relationship among states—systems related to each other as successive points along a continuum and differing most fundamentally in the degree of centralization of power and authority which they imply. In this view, balance of power represents the extreme of decentralization, a kind of *laissez-faire* arrangement in the sphere of power politics. It suggests a scheme within which individual states, separate units of power and policy, operate autonomously, without subordination to a central agency for the management of power relations. Singly or in combinations reflecting the coincidence of interests, states seek to influence the pattern of power distribution and to determine their own places within that pattern. In such a balancing system, the constituent states function as coordinate managers of the power situation.

Collective security falls next in line along the scale of centralization, representing an effort to deal with the power problem by superimposing a scheme of partially centralized management upon a situation in which power remains diffused among national units. It involves a centralization of authority over the use of force, to the extent that states are deprived of the legal right to use violence at their own discretion. In its ideal form, it calls for an international organization with authority to determine when a resort to force is illegitimate and to require states to collaborate under its direction in suppressing such use of force.

Finally, world government takes its place at the opposite end of the scale from balance of power, suggesting the creation of an institutional system involving a monopoly of power, comparable to that alleged to exist in a well-ordered national state. In this scheme, both the possession of the instruments of force and the control of policy concerning their use are presumably centralized in an institution superior to the state.

Unfortunately, the differences among these concepts have more often than not been exaggerated and mis-stated. The case for adoption of one or another has often been argued as if a choice had to be made between totally dissimilar systems, one offering hopeful prospects for order and security, and the other leaving the world mired in hopelessness. In fact, the differences among them are far from absolute and are perhaps less interesting and significant than the similarities—to the analyst, if not to the propagandist. Having plotted them along a common scale, I would suggest that they tend to slide into each other, developing points of approximation or overlap, rather than to maintain fixed distances of separation. Both balance of power and collective security are deterrent schemes in that they rely upon countervailing power to frustrate the ambitions of powerful aggressors; moreover, the two systems are heavily dependent upon sets of prerequisite conditions which are similiar in important respects. One can argue, for instance, that the balance system requires the diffusion of power among a number of major states so that no single state will control such a large fraction of the world's power resources as to make the task of counterbalancing it inordinately difficult; the same requirement can be cited for a collective security system, to avoid the possibility that any state will be invulnerable to the pressure of collective sanctions. Thus, a global power configuration marked by bipolarity is equally unfavorable to the operation of a balance system or of a collective security system. One can demonstrate that a successful balance system requires that national policies be adaptable to contingencies that may arise rather than rigidly fixed, so that old friends can be resisted when they endanger the stability of the system and former enemies can be supported when the exigencies of the power situation so require. A similar flexibility of policy, involving the capacity to switch the foci of friendship and enmity, is essential to collective security.

On the other hand, the ideal scheme of collective security is not wholly unlike that of world government. It involves a concentration of authority in a central organ giving that organ a government-like quality that can be ignored only if one dogmatically denies, as many proponents of world government do, that there are many shadings of gray between the "black" of essential anarchy and the "white" of actual government. Moreover, a scheme of world government which undertook to maintain order on a global scale by methods comparable to those used within limited boundaries by national governments would, in fact, involve reliance upon intricate and delicate processes of balancing the power of constituent units of the society. The proposition that government is a matter of exercising a literal or virtual monopoly of power over a society, rather than of presiding over a balancing process, is largely a myth, even though totalitarian dictators have sometimes gained considerable success in translating it into reality. The point is that the typical enthusiast for world government wants a system which has more in common with the balance of power system than he customarily realizes or admits.

Despite these and other points of similarity which might be cited, there are characteristic differences among the implications of the concepts of balance of power, collective security, and world government, sufficiently important to justify the proposition that they designate alternative patterns for the ordering of power relations among states. The balance of power concept allows states to maneuver freely in a competitive world. Its typical institutional expression is a set of flexible alliances within which recurrent shifts of alignment take place; its promise of order lies in the expectation that competing power urges will somehow balance and thereby cancel each other, producing deterrence through equilibration. Collective security looks to a general international

organization, presiding over a collaborative, rather than a competitive, arrangement. It purports to inhibit any aggressor by making virtually all the other states the *ad hoc* allies of any state that suffers attack; thus, it promises deterrence through the mobilization of a preponderance of power against any member of the system which threatens its peace and order. World government relies upon neither the interplay of competitive states nor the collaboration of states organized to uphold the principle of order; it promises to deprive states of their standing as centers of power and policy, where issues of war and peace are concerned, and to superimpose upon them an institution possessed of the authority and capability to maintain, by unchallengeable force so far as may be necessary, the order and stability of a global community.

These are not necessarily the only conceivable patterns for the management of power in international relations. They are, however, the patterns which have become the common currency of intellectual transactions concerning world affairs in the twentieth century. Whether any of these patterns has been, or can be, or should be, fully realized in actuality is not at issue here. They constitute the standard list of theoretical alternatives; they are the intellectual pigeon-holes in constant use.

With this introductory statement of the categories which, however poorly defined, dominate contemporary thinking about the problem of ordering international relations, we can turn to the questions to be considered in parts II and III of this article: 1) what was the nature of the system for management of power in international relations envisaged by the founders of the United Nations; and 2) what is the nature of the system which has in fact taken shape during the period of operation—and alteration—of the United Nations, from 1946 to 1961?

II.

It has been widely assumed and frequently asserted that the United Nations was originally intended and expected to function as the institutional manager of a full-fledged collective security system, capable of bringing collective force to bear against any aggressor. In most instances, this assertion is made in the context of a discussion of the failure of the United Nations to realize that ideal. Sometimes the founders of the Organization are convicted of idealism; they should have known better than to expect the United Nations to be effective as an instrument of collective security. Sometimes an objective analysis of the changes which have occurred in the setting within which the Organization operates is presented as explaining the failure of the collective security scheme; thus:

> The great-power split, together with the admission of large numbers of African, Asian, and European neutralist states, has almost destroyed the collective security functions that were to be the organization's principal reason for existence.[1]

More often, the Soviet Union is pictured as the villain in the piece; by abusing the veto power and obstructing the creation of the enforcement mechanism envisaged in Article 43 of the Charter, it has frustrated the realization of the promise of collective security.[2] Whatever the explanatory argument, the essential point in such statements is that the United Nations was intended to be, but has failed to become, the directing mechanism of a universally effective collective security system.

Why has it been so generally assumed that the establishment of the United Nations represented an effort to institutionalize collective security in the postwar world? An attempt to answer this question must precede an assessment of the validity of the assumption itself.

In the first place, it may be suspected that this interpretation of the United Nations experiment was reached by the processes of elimination and deduction from a preconceived definition of the purposes of general international organization. Was the new world order designed as a balance of power system? Certainly not. Participants in the creation of the United Nations were too emphatic in their criticism of reliance upon balance of power, and too insistent in their assertion that they were creating a system better than balance of power, to permit that interpretation. True, they did not whip the balance of power as vigorously and persistently as their Wilsonian ancestors had done a generation before, but that was presumably because they thought it uneconomical to spend their time in flogging a dead horse. In any case, the United Nations was essentially a new version of the League of Nations, and it was well understood that the latter organization had been conceived by men who repu-

---

[1] Thomas J. Hamilton, "The Changing United Nations: Morale Lowered by Deadlocks," *New York Times*, December 30, 1960.

[2] See Eisenhower's letter to Bulganin, January 12, 1958, reproduced in Paul E. Zinner, ed., *Documents on American Foreign Relations, 1958* (New York: Harper, 1959), p. 89; see also, Sir Leslie Munro, "The Case for a Standing U.N. Army," *New York Times Magazine*, July 27, 1958, p. 27.

diated the balance of power system and aspired to introduce an alternative system. If the projected scheme were not a balance of power system, was it then a world government? No, it was clearly much more modest than that. If proof were needed, one could refer to the Moscow Declaration of October 30, 1943, in which the major powers of the anti-Axis coalition had declared the purpose of "establishing . . . a general international organization, based on the principle of the sovereign equality of all peace-loving states,"[3] or to President Roosevelt's decisive assertion that:

We are not thinking of a superstate with its own police forces and other paraphernalia of coercive power. We are seeking effective agreement and arrangements through which the nations would maintain, according to their capacities, adequate forces to meet the needs of preventing war and of making impossible deliberate preparation for war and to have such forces available for joint action when necessary.[4]

Only one of the standard categories remained. If the United Nations were not designed to implement the concepts of balance of power or world government, then who could doubt that it must be an experiment in collective security? This conclusion must have come easily to men who stressed the resemblance of the new Organization to the defunct League. The original general international organization had been dedicated to the effectuation of collective security. It was natural to assume that the second edition was dedicated to the same purpose.

Secondly, it must be noted that the entire process of planning and formulating the United Nations Charter was dominated by the theme: "We are going to create a collective security system, and this time we are going to make it work." The United States planners were preoccupied with the necessity of providing the new Organization with an enforcement mechanism which would enable it to effectuate the collective security principle by coercive means which had been denied to the League.[5] In the opening sessions of the San Francisco Conference, a long procession of speakers reiterated the proposition that statemen had gathered to create a world organization which could and would maintain the peace, by force if necessary. A typical expression of the prevailing viewpoint was provided by Joseph Bech, speaking for Luxembourg, who declared that the peoples of the world

would not forgive their leaders if they returned to a policy of balance of power, which would inevitably result in a race for armaments heading straight for another war. The protection of peace can only be insured on the basis of collective security.[6]

Moreover, the end of the conference was marked by exultant speeches proclaiming the initiation of a real collective security system. Joseph Paul-Boncour of France declared that "the international organization will no longer be unarmed against violence. . . . That is the great thing, the great historic act accomplished by the San

[3] *A Decade of American Foreign Policy, Basic Documents, 1941–49*, Senate Document No. 123, 81st Congress, 1st Session (Washington, 1950), p. 12.

[4] *Postwar Foreign Policy Preparation 1939–1945*, Department of State Publication 3580, General Foreign Policy Series 15 (Washington, 1949), p. 269.

[5] See Ruth B. Russell and Jeannette E. Muther, *A History of the United Nations Charter* (Washington: Brookings, 1958), p. 3, 4, 206, 209, 227–228, 395, 557.

[6] UN Information Organizations and U. S. Library of Congress, *Documents of the United Nations Conference on International Organization* (New York, 1945), I, p. 502.

Francisco Conference. . . . "[7] The venerable Jan C. Smuts said of the Charter:

> It provides for a peace with teeth; for a united front of peace-loving peoples against future aggressors; for a united front among the great powers backed by the forces of the smaller powers as well. . . . And it provides for central organization and direction of the joint forces for peace.[8]

Thus, the assumption that the creation of the United Nations signaled a new effort to institute a universal collective security system was encouraged. In view of the circumstances, it is hardly surprising that this interpretation gained general acceptance. Nevertheless, it is fundamentally incorrect, as a careful analysis of what the world's statesmen did at San Francisco and a more extensive review of what they said about their handiwork, will indicate.

The crucial element in the analysis is an understanding of the import of the veto rule which enables any of the five permanent members of the Security Council to block decisions on substantive matters in that organ—including the determination that aggression has taken place, the designation of the guilty party, and the decision to resort to sanctions, military or otherwise, against the aggressor. Such decisions, be it noted, are fundamental to the operation of a collective security system. The veto rule clearly gives each of the great powers the capacity to prevent the operation of the United Nations enforcement system against itself, against any state which it chooses to support and protect, or in any other case in which it prefers not to participate or to have others participate in an enforcement venture un-

der United Nations auspices. The veto provision, in short, renders collective security impossible in all the instances most vital to the preservation of world peace and order, and problematical in cases of lesser importance.

It will not do to say that the founding fathers of the United Nations went home from San Francisco with the blissful assurance that they had formulated a beautiful system of collective security, only to be rudely shaken later by the discovery that the system was spoiled by a devilish Soviet Union which insisted upon taking seriously its right to use the veto power. In the first place, logic denies the probability that the veto was regarded as an obstructive capability that would never be used and would therefore never interfere with the operation of collective security. It is difficult to believe that the major powers worked as hard as they did to secure acceptance of the veto provision, in the conviction that it would be superfluous; this grant of a special power to a dissenter reflects the assumption that there will be dissent, not that there will be unity. The veto provision was not inserted in the Charter in a fit of absent-mindedness. It was adopted with full awareness, and deliberate intent, that any of the major powers might use it to block collective action. Its insertion can only be interpreted as a declaration that the United Nations should not and could not be drawn into any attempt to implement the principle of collective security in opposition to a great power.[9]

We need not rely solely upon logical analysis of the provisions of the Charter for evidence that the original United Nations scheme involved a repudiation of the ambition to construct a collective security

[7] *Ibid.*, p. 668.
[8] *Ibid.*, p. 678.
[9] For an early and perceptive statement of this interpretation, see Wellington Koo, Jr., *Voting Procedures in International Political Organizations* (New York: Columbia, 1947), p. 117, 124, 134.

system which would be operative in the type of case most critically relevant to the issue of global war or peace. The records of the San Francisco Conference show that the participants were thoroughly aware of the fact that, in adopting the veto provision, they were renouncing that ambition. The United States declared that the veto rule "meant that if a major power became the aggressor the Council had no power to prevent war."[10] An Indian spokesman warned against the delusion "that the proposed Organization could prevent wars between the great nations or even between small nations, if the great powers were divided in their sympathies."[11] The general understanding of the import of the veto rule was expressed by a delegate from New Zealand, who said that it made collective security impossible.[12] This interpretation of the limits of the system contemplated in the Charter was stated explicitly by Secretary of State Stettinius in the hearings on the Charter.[13]

As I have intimated, a case can be made for the proposition that the founding fathers of the United Nations engaged in some misrepresentation of their product; they did not *always* qualify their praise of the projected Organization with explicit acknowledgment of its deliberately contrived incapacity to function as a collective security agency in cases involving great-power aggression or great-power support of aggressors. Realistically, one should not have expected that they would stress this important limitation of the new Organization. We have, after all, a working understanding that statesmen are not expected or required, any more than adver-

tisers of soap or cigarettes, to put their worst feet forward. However, the accusation that the United Nations was "oversold" by its creators and sponsors has often been made too loosely and without adequate consideration of all the evidence.[14]

The sober truth about the built-in restrictions on the capability of the United Nations as an organ of collective security was frequently and prominently stated. There is, indeed, ample evidence that this limitation was widely understood within the interested United States public. The National League of Women Voters was only one of many groups which revealed this understanding in public statements soon after the San Francisco Conference; in a memorandum inserted in the record of the hearings on the Charter, this organization stated the view that:

If a great power becomes an aggressor, the United Nations Organization will not be able to act, and the situation will have to be handled outside the Organization. This is because we are still in the experimental stage of collective security, and world opinion has not yet developed to the point where nations are willing to delegate sufficient authority to an international organization to make it capable of coercing a great power.[15]

The Senate Committee on Foreign Relations proved itself both cognizant of and eager to encourage public understanding of the inherent limitations of the United Nations when it took care to point out, in its report on the Charter, that:

neither this Charter nor any other docu-

---

[10] UN Information Organizations and U. S. Library of Congress, *Documents of the United Nations Conference on International Organization* (New York, 1945), XI, p. 514.
[11] *Ibid.*, XII, p. 307–308.
[12] *Ibid.*, p. 296.
[13] *The Charter of the United Nations*, Hearings Before the Committee on Foreign Relations, U. S. Senate,

79th Congress, 1st Session (Washington, 1945), p. 215.
[14] See Robert E. Riggs, "Overselling the UN Charter—Fact and Myth," *International Organization*, Spring 1960 (Vol. 14, No. 2), p. 277–290.
[15] *The Charter of the United Nations*, Hearings . . . , p. 422. For other expressions of this viewpoint, see p. 396, 416, 531, 585, 608, 654, 661, 707.

ment or formula that might be devised can prevent war, and the committee would be performing a disservice to the public if its action with respect to the Charter should indicate any such opinion on its part.

The committee held that the creation of the new Organization "will at best be a beginning toward the creation of those conditions of stability throughout the world which will foster peace and security."[16]

The evidence leads me to the conclusion that the formulators of the United Nations Charter deliberately refrained from attempting to create an organization which would undertake to control the use of force by great powers or states supported by them, through the operation of a collective security system. They acted on the assumption that such a venture could not succeed, and ought not to be attempted. In this fundamentally important sense, the establishment of the United Nations represented the repudiation of the idea of collective security, not an unsuccessful effort to institutionalize its application.

What then was the nature of the scheme for management of power in international relations which the Charter set forth? The answer can be found only if we emancipate ourselves from the rigidity of the categories of balance of power, collective security, and world government.

The influence of the collective security orientation is evident in many of the provisions of the Charter. Aggression is prohibited, though left undefined; in principle, states are deprived of the legal right to use force against each other at their own discretion, in pursuit of their uni-

laterally defined interests and purposes. The legitimacy of resort to international violence is made subject to the determination of an international body; an effort is made even to hold states accountable to an international body in their invocation and exercise of the right of defensive action. Moreover, the principle is asserted that any illegitimate use of force in international relations is properly a matter of concern to all Members of the United Nations. The Security Council is expected to be equipped, through agreements to be concluded with Member States, with military forces constantly ready for action at its decision; it bears the responsibility for taking action to uphold peace and security and has a general authority to command the assistance of all member states—except that their obligation to provide military units is limited to the commitments which may be stated in their agreements with the Security Council.[17]

In its restriction of the right of states to resort to force, its espousal of the principle of collective action to repress illegal violence, and its provision for an organ to preside over the arrangements pertaining to the use of force, the UN scheme exhibits some of the essential characteristics of a collective security system. It should be noted that it is incomplete, in that the acceptance by states of an operative obligation to put force at the disposal of the Security Council—and, consequently, the equipping of the Council to perform its enforcement role—is postponed; on this score, the Charter registers merely an agreement to agree. Nevertheless, the scheme clearly reflects the intention to create an international enforcement mechanism capable of functioning in cases

[16] Report of the Senate Committee on Foreign Relations on the United Nations Charter, July 16, 1945, reproduced in *Review of the United Nations Charter: A Collection of Documents*, Senate Document No. 87,

83d Congress, 2d Session (Washington, 1954), p. 68.
[17] This summary of the scheme is based upon Articles 2, 24–25, and 39–51 of the Charter.

which do not involve a conflict of interest and will among the great powers. It might be described as a design for a collective security system applicable only to situations of relatively minor importance as far as maintenance of the general peace is concerned. The framers of the Charter contemplated a system in which the great powers would bear the major responsibility for providing United Nations enforcement potential, with supplementary contributions by lesser states, for the purpose of dealing with aggressors acting without the support or sympathy of any of the major powers. The great powers, it should be recalled, persistently spoke at San Francisco of· the "unanimity rule," not the "veto rule," thereby emphasizing the positive hope that the Security Council would be able to act decisively against aggression insofar as its permanent members could achieve unanimity in supporting such action. There was no middle ground in this arrangement. Either an act of aggression would be committed by a minor state with all the major powers ranged against it, in which case collective suppression of the misdeed would be a relatively simple matter, or it would be committed by a major power or its protégé, in which case the United Nations would be debarred from attempting collective suppression. Although the applicability of the United Nations enforcement scheme to the control of the defeated Axis powers of World War II was excluded, it was provided that this limitation might be removed at the request of the victorious allies.[18]

The key prescription of the Charter for dealing with the potential crises of greatest international importance—those involving antagonism among the great powers or aggressive action undertaken or sponsored by one or more of the great powers

—is to be found in Article 51, with its recognition of "the inherent right of individual or collective self-defense" in response to armed attack. This provision may be interpreted as a declaration that it is incumbent upon states to take the necessary measures, outside the structure of the United Nations, for dealing with the most crucial threats to peace and security which might arise. The framers of the Charter were saying, in effect, that they saw no possibility of implementing collective security safely and effectively against major powers, and that some device other than collective security would have to be improvised if a major power should go on the warpath. They did not, as has often been suggested, assume that no such problem would arise; in this respect, they were hopeful but not smugly confident. Rather, they asserted the conviction that it was impossible to construct a collective security system adequate to deal with such a problem, if it should arise. The advice implicit in Article 51 is that states should establish alliances—combinations for collective self-defense—for dealing with the actuality or threat of attack by powers exempted by the veto rule from the impact of the projected United Nations enforcement mechanism.

In this vitally important respect, the Charter contemplates what is in essence a balance of power system. This was no doubt an unhappy choice for the founding fathers. Their ideological bias clearly ran not toward the balance of power but toward collective security. Their sense of realism, however, impelled them to acknowledge that they could see no way to devise a workable alternative to the balance of power system for dealing with aggressive threats posed directly or indirectly by great powers. It should be noted

[18] See Articles 53 and 107 of the Charter.

that the balance of power system, involving the freedom and responsibility of states to look to their own position within the international configuration of power, does not have to be adopted; it exists, until and unless an alternative arrangement for managing the power relationships of states is put into effect. Failing even to formulate—much less to put into effect—a more centralized scheme for handling conflicts in which major powers might be competitively engaged, the creators of the United Nations left states to "do what comes naturally" in such situations: that is, to develop the power and policy, individually and in alignment with others, for coping with security threats presented by dangerously powerful antagonists.

The original scheme of the United Nations for the management of power on the international scene may thus be described as one which left the balance of power system intact for cases of major importance to global peace and order, and provided for a collective security system to be applicable in cases of relatively minor significance. The Charter endorsed the *ideal* of collective security in unqualified terms, but envisaged its application in severely limited terms. It limited the legal right of states, great or small, to engage in the unfettered maneuvering which has been traditionally associated with the operation of a balance of power system, and reflected the hope that the political processes of the United Nations would inhibit the tendency of states to abuse their strength under the pretext of protecting their relative power positions. In the final analysis, however, the Charter acknowledged that the new Organization could not relieve states of the necessity of attempting on their own to match power with power, as the means of attaining security within the context of great-power rivalry. The scheme of the Charter was a curious amalgam of collective security, dominant in ideological terms, and balance of power, dominant in terms of practical application. The concept of world government, insofar as it figured at all in the consideration of the San Francisco Conference, was viewed as a distant ideal.

III.

The history of the actual operation of the United Nations in the realm of power politics is largely a story of vacillation concerning the degree to which the implementation of collective security should be attempted, and of efforts to find other means by which international organization can be used to modify the working of a balance of power system. The reluctance with which the framers of the Charter viewed the continued dependence of the world, by default, upon the balance of power system has been shared by many of the statesmen who have shaped the subsequent development of the United Nations.

One of the first tasks which confronted the new Organization was that of attempting to create the enforcement mechanism envisaged in Chapter VII—and particularly in Articles 43 and 45—of the Charter. This project, essential to the fulfillment of the promise that the Security Council would function as an agent of collective security in cases not involving discord among the major powers, was fundamentally dependent upon the capacity of the Big Five to agree concerning their contributions to the military force the Council would have at its disposal. Those powers undertook, within the Military Staff Committee and the Security Council, to reach agreement; they failed in 1947, and, despite occasional expressions of interest in trying again, they have not seriously reopened the issue since that time.

These abortive negotiations were marked by a curious refusal on the part of the United States to recognize and adhere to the principle that the United Nations enforcement system was to be operative only against minor aggressors which neither possessed the veto power nor enjoyed the protection of a great power's capacity to block Security Council action. This deviation from the understanding reached at San Francisco was implicitly expressed in a United States position which insisted that a relatively large force should be assigned to the Security Council; the other powers, estimating the requirements of the Council more modestly,[19] evidently based their proposals on the assumption that the force was intended to be used, and therefore needed to be strong enough for effective use, only in coercing states of minor military importance. The United States' deviation was stated explicitly in the argument that the Council should be equipped "to bring to bear, against any breach of the peace anywhere in the world, balanced striking forces drawn from the most powerful and best equipped forces that could be provided by the Members," so that the organization could "enforce peace in all parts of the world."[20] It appeared that the United States had either forgotten or repudiated the consensus, registered in the veto provision of the Charter, that the United Na-

tions should not be constitutionally capable of functioning as an instrument of collective security against, or in opposition to the will of, any of the major powers.

If the United States confused the negotiations with the claim that the task was to create a universally applicable system of collective security, the real lesson of the negotiations was that neither the Soviet Union nor the West seemed sufficiently trustful of the other to contemplate joint action under United Nations auspices for implementing collective security even in a limited range of cases. The various items of disagreement which plagued the discussions all pointed to the same conclusion: each of the major contestants, the Soviet Union and the United States, feared that the other might attempt to dominate any collective action in which it participated, using the pretext of serving the United Nations as a means of exploiting troubled situations to its own ends.[21] One or the other of the great powers may, of course, have been actuated by ulterior motives. What appears from the record of negotiations, however, is that this mutual suspicion operated to force the discarding of the scheme for establishing a limited collective security system under the United Nations. Collective security operations pitting great powers against each other had been excluded in the original design; collective security operations involving collaboration among the great powers were now seen to be politically infeasible.

This initial decline to zero of the modest expectations of collective security entertained by the drafters of the Charter was sharply reversed by the events of 1950. The United Nations response to North

[19] For the provisional estimates submitted by the five permanent members of the Security Council, see *Yearbook of the United Nations, 1947–1948*, p. 495.

[20] Security Council *Official Records*, 138th Meeting, June 4, 1947, p. 954–955, 956.

[21] See my analysis of this point in "The United Nations and the Use of Force," *International Conciliation*, March 1961. Cf. William Reitzel, Morton A. Kaplan, and Constance G. Coblenz, *United States Foreign Policy, 1945–1955* (Washington: Brookings Institution, 1956), p. 239–240.

Korean aggression against South Korea was attributable to a unique complex of circumstances, and it was not by any means a "pure" example of collective security in action. Nevertheless, the early phase of the collective military action in Korea under the banner of the United Nations produced among its participants and supporters an exhilarating sense of involvement in an unprecedented effort to give effect to the principle of collective security. Member States found themselves joined together to suppress an act of aggression which could plausibly be regarded as one sponsored or supported by two major powers, the Soviet Union and Communist China, and they seemed likely to carry off this bold enterprise both successfully and safely. They had, by improvising a reasonable facsimile of collective security action to meet North Korean aggression, cast aside what now seemed the excessive timidity of the framers of the Charter, who had believed it would be neither possible nor prudent for the United Nations to take action in such cases.

The sudden enthusiasm for collective security engendered by the Korean action was translated into support for the Uniting for Peace Resolution, a United States initiative adopted by the General Assembly in the fall of 1950.[22] This scheme involved an assertion by the General Assembly of competence to take over the consideration of threatening situations from a veto-bound Security Council, designate the aggressor, and recommend collective action by Member States. Among other things, it provided for the establishment of a Collective Measures Committee to study the problems of giving effect to the principle of collective security, and called upon states to designate special military units for possible participation in future United Nations enforcement actions. Concretely, this was a plan for enabling the United Nations to react in future situations as it had in Korea. While the Uniting for Peace plan fell short of a full-fledged collective security system, notably in its failure to provide for obligatory participation by states in sanctions, it was clearly put forward as a device for transforming the United Nations into an agency of universal collective security.[23]

Thus, the United Nations moved in 1950 from the expectation that no collective security action would be forthcoming in any case, to the hypothetical possibility of collective security action in every case of aggression. In adopting the Uniting for Peace plan, Members of the United Nations purported to express the determination to develop an international enforcement system applicable even to violations of the peace in which great powers might be directly or indirectly involved. In scope, if not in legal depth, this plan for collective security was far more ambitious than that stated in the Charter.

This was the high-water mark of enthusiasm for turning the United Nations into a collective security system. The flood receded rather quickly and, apparently, irreversibly. The later stages of the Korean conflict engendered second thoughts about the desirability of repeating that experiment. By the time Members of the United Nations had managed to disengage themselves from active fighting in Korea, they had developed a renewed appreciation for the prudence of the founding fathers who had decreed that the Organization ought not to attempt collective action in the face of great-power opposition. Uncommitted states came gradually to recognize that

[22] General Assembly Resolution 377 (V), November 3, 1950.
[23] See General Assembly *Official Records*, Fifth Session, 295th Plenary Meeting, October 24, 1950, p. 246, and 299th Plenary Meeting, November 1, 1950, p. 291–292.

they had a stake in preventing the United Nations from being invoked as an instrumentality of one side against the other in "cold war" conflicts; in these terms, the veto was not so much a special privilege of the great powers as a protection for the minor powers against being pulled, through their membership in the United Nations, into the maelstrom of great-power struggle. The United States, which had conceived the Uniting for Peace plan as a device primarily for legitimizing and mobilizing support for Western action in resistance to Soviet expansionism, gradually lost confidence that the General Assembly could be counted on to put the plan to that use, and began to doubt both the wisdom and the utility of the venture in enhancing the quasi-collective security possibilities of the United Nations which it had sponsored.

The earliest indication of the subsiding of collective security sentiment was provided by the hesitation of Member States to respond positively to the suggestion they had addressed to themselves in the Uniting for Peace Resolution, *i.e.,* that they set aside definite military units for possible use in United Nations enforcement actions. This recommendation produced little more than vague affirmations that armed forces might under certain circumstances be supplied; in effect, this project for developing a military arm of the United Nations was soon relegated to the dead-letter office along with Article 43, which it had been intended to replace.

The Hungarian and Suez crises of 1956 produced further evidence that the aspirations for giving effect to collective security, so fervently expressed in 1950, had been dispelled by sober second thoughts. In these critical cases, both involving coercive action by great powers, the Uniting for

²⁴ *New York Times,* November 6, 1956, p. 10.

Peace plan was invoked and was operative to the point of bringing about condemnation by the General Assembly of the Soviet Union in the one case, and of the United Kingdom, France, and Israel in the other. The latter three states, involved in attacks upon Egypt, were induced to withdraw and thus to spare the Assembly the necessity of deciding whether it should attempt to organize collective compulsion. The Soviet Union, having ruthlessly suppressed the Hungarian Revolution, stood in defiance of an Assembly which gave no evidence of even considering the possibility of attempting to impose military sanctions.

The position of the United States in these two cases reveals the extent to which the urge for collective security had declined since the adoption of the Uniting for Peace Resolution. In the Suez case, the United States exhibited a measure of devotion to the collective security ideology in supporting the condemnation of friends and allies for their attack upon a state whose behavior the United States patently disapproved. United States leaders, however, clearly had no stomach for the possibility of being called upon to participate in coercive measures to enforce the Assembly's demands against the United Kingdom, France, and Israel. Most notably, they were appalled at the thought that the Soviet Union might use "participation in collective security action under the United Nations" as a device for establishing a foothold in the Middle East. When President Eisenhower recoiled at the "unthinkable" suggestion of the Soviet Union that the two giant powers join to enforce the will of the United Nations in that region,²⁴ he was giving new expression to the mistrust which had been apparent in the negotiations, in 1947, for creating a United Nations force to be placed at the disposal of the Security Council. The notion of a collective security action which would bring Soviet Union forces into the Middle East was profoundly unattractive to the United States.

In the Hungarian case, the United States demonstrated that it was equally unattracted by the idea of leading or participating in collective action against the Soviet Union, lest such a move precipitate a general war. In refraining from the initiation of a collective campaign to oust Soviet Union forces from Hungary, the Assembly was supporting, not frustrating, the policy of the United States. This was the sort of case for which the Uniting for Peace plan had ostensibly been designed; the fact that collective measures against the Soviet Union were not seriously contemplated was evidence that the ambition to overcome the veto barrier to the functioning of the United Nations as an agency of collective security had been abandoned.

We have seen that the history of the United Nations has been marked by the fluctuation of sentiment regarding the desirability and feasibility of making the Organization a mechanism to implement the principle of collective security. It seems likely that the ephemeral enthusiasm for collective security engendered by the early phase of the Korean experience and registered in the Uniting for Peace Resolution will prove the last flurry for some time to come. The creators of the United Nations envisaged an extremely modest version of collective security; in the present situation, there is no evidence that Members of the Organization entertain either the expectation or the intention of operating a collective security system, limited or universal in its impact, within the institutional framework of the United Nations. Force may be used for limited purposes under United Nations auspices in particular cases,

as in the Congo, for instance. This, however, does not imply that there is a meaningful possibility of organizing a dependable system of collective military sanctions to repel international aggression. The repudiation of the urge to establish collective security as an operative system for the management of power in international relations appears, for the foreseeable future, definitive.

The Charter's implicit recognition of the necessity for a residual balance of power system to cope with great-power antagonisms has had substantially greater effect than its design for a collective security system to deal with situations of less critical importance. Once it became clear that a struggle between the Soviet Union and the West was to be the dominant motif of postwar international relations, the process of alliance-building and of competitive armament began. On the Western side, the formulation of the North Atlantic Treaty represented an acknowledgment that no alternative to the methods characteristic of the balance of power system could be envisaged for meeting the threat of Soviet Union aggressiveness. It is notable that the United States responded to the lesson of communist aggression in Korea, not simply by sponsoring the Uniting for Peace plan, but also by taking the lead in strengthening the Western alliance, both militarily and institutionally, giving it the form of the North Atlantic Treaty Organization. In the one case, the United States endorsed the ideology of collective security; in the other, it expressed the intent to seek security within the context of a balance of power system. There can be little doubt that the latter was the more significant move, the more reliable indicator of the emphasis which was to characterize United States foreign policy. While the doctrine of collective security has been alternately played up and played down in the United Nations, statesmen have treated the problem of maneuvering successfully within the framework of a balance of power system as the serious business of contemporary diplomacy. This represents the confirmation, not the invalidation, of the assumption expressed in the Charter; if one considers the combination of Articles 27 and 51 of the Charter, one finds the statesmen of San Francisco implying that security problems stemming from discord among the giants call for the application of the concept of balance of power, not the concept of collective security. Great-power antagonisms have dominated the international scene, and they have evoked the type of response which the Charter indicated would be necessary.

In the final analysis, then, the effort to control the use of force in international relations since World War II has been expressed in the form of a balance of power system. What has emerged is a balance system modified by a number of factors including, most significantly for purposes of this analysis, the existence of a general international organization. It would be too much to say that the United Nations "presides over" the operation of the balance of power system, but its functioning does have considerable relevance to the working of that system.

The real question for our time is not whether the United Nations is likely to develop a collective security system—or, more remotely, to institute a scheme for the management of power which would deserve the name of world government— to replace the balance of power system. The real question relates to the manner in which, and the degree to which, the United Nations can and will modify the operation of the balance system and con-

tribute to its success as a device for preventing war. In facilitating diplomatic confrontation, fostering serious and meaningful negotiation, and providing assistance in the pacific settlement of disputes, the Organization plays a role which may be useful in mitigating the dangers of failure. In putting moral and political pressure upon states to conform to the principles of international conduct which the Charter prescribes, the United Nations may help to limit the abusive aspects of state behavior which balance of power operations may otherwise entail. In carrying out its wide-ranging activities within the economic and social sectors, the Organization may contribute to a long-term transformation of the global situation which will create new possibilities for the effective management of the power problem.

Finally, it should be noted that a role for the United Nations, more immediately and directly related to the issue of military violence, has been for some time in the process of development. In a number of instances, the Organization has secured and provided military personnel for supervising truce arrangements, patrolling armistice lines, observing developments in zones of particular instability, and otherwise contributing to the maintenance of precariously peaceful relationships. Against this background, an act of creative political ingenuity occurred in 1956, when the Organization was given the mission of mobilizing a United Nations Emergency Force, composed exclusively of military elements from states other than great powers, to function as a stabilizer of the dangerously tense situation in the Middle East. When a somewhat analogous, albeit infinitely more complex, situation arose in the Congo in 1960, the machinery of the

United Nations was again used to organize and carry out a military operation. There were basic differences in the tasks required of United Nations forces in these two situations, and it may be that those differences will produce different outcomes for the two ventures; at this writing, there seems grave danger that the Congo operation will fail as clearly as the Middle Eastern operation succeeded.

What is important for this analysis, however, is the element of similarity in the two cases. In both instances, the United Nations was used as a device for bringing into a troubled situation military contingents contributed voluntarily by smaller states and placed under the direction of the Secretary-General, for the purpose of preventing the eruption of disorders that might result in the competitive intervention of the rival great-power blocs. This is a far cry from the original notion of a United Nations enforcement system which would depend upon the unanimous participation of the great powers; it expresses the notion of a United Nations stabilization system dependent upon the unanimous abstention of the great powers.[25] Such a system cannot be forced upon unwilling great powers. It can function successfully only with their acquiescence, derived from the recognition that they have a stake in the avoidance of conflicts that might precipitate war. Intervention by the United Nations in the Middle East and in the Congo represents the experimental development of a significant role for the Organization in the balance of power system, that of assisting in its orderly operation by undertaking to insulate particular trouble-spots from the impact of the rivalry which dominates the relationships of the major powers. This experimentation, whatever its outcome, is a hopeful sign, for it points to the general recognition of a basic truth: *i.e.,* that the potential contribution of the United Nations in our time to the management of international power relationships lies not in implementing collective security or instituting world government, but in helping to improve and stabilize the working of the balance of power system which is, for better or for worse, the operative mechanism of contemporary international politics.

[25] Cf. Lincoln P. Bloomfield, *The United Nations and U. S. Foreign Policy* (Boston: Little, Brown, 1960), p. 44–45, 67.

THE MANAGEMENT OF POWER AND POLITICAL ORGANIZATION: SOME OBSERVATIONS ON INIS L. CLAUDE'S CONCEPTUAL APPROACH

Ruth B. Russell

If we consider politics as the organization of social power for political ends, the nature of the political system that organizes such power can be seen as related both to the concrete means of controlling its military and other components and to the abstract standards and objectives of the system itself. The latter form the more important element, since they determine how the material means are used to operate the system. The means are, in short, a function of the ends, in political as in other matters.

This will be true whether the political organization concerned is national or international in scope. There are, however, significant distinctions (as will be noted) among the ways in which power is, and can be, controlled within a single-state governmental unit as compared to its management by an international diplomatic organization of governments. These differences must be kept in mind in analyzing the present organizational scheme by which states seek to govern their power relations and to maintain world peace.

These generalizations were evoked by the recent article by Inis L. Claude, Jr., on "The Management of Power in the Changing United Nations."[1] His thesis was that "balance of power, collective security, and world government" form "the standard list of theoretical alternatives" (as reflected in the literature of the international relations field) pertaining to the problem of "the effective management" of physical power in maintaining peaceful relations among the independent, but interdependent, states of the world. Admitting that the concepts are not clearly and consistently defined, the author nevertheless found that they could be "taken as characterizing disparate systems of relationship among states—systems related to each other as successive points along a continuum and differing most fundamentally in the degree of centralization of power and authority which they imply." He then analyzed the differences among the three concepts and considered them in relation to the United Nations, concluding that the United Nations was not intended to be a full collective security organization; that, in fact, the Charter represents a "curious amalgam" of ideological collective security and applied balance of power; that today, the balance of power is "the operative mechanism of contemporary international politics"; and that the United Nations "potential contribution" in managing power relationships "lies not in implementing collective security . . . but in helping to improve and stabilize the working of the balance of power system."

Claude's concentration on the degree of centralization as the most "fundamental" difference among these concepts I find misleading. Moreover, it results in an inadequate theoretical analysis of the various methods of power management and an oversimplified categorization of the contemporary situation.

Ruth B. Russell is a Senior Staff Member of the Foreign Policy Studies Division of the Brookings Institution, Washington, D. C. The views expressed in this article are the author's and do not necessarily reflect those of other staff members of the Institution.

[1] *International Organization*, Spring 1961 (Vol. 15, No. 2), p. 219–235. Quotations in the following pages, unless otherwise noted, are from this article.

I propose, therefore, to re-examine this problem in terms that relate the degree of centralized control of available force to the standards and objectives of the respective theoretical political organization in question—that relate the means to the ends, in other words.

I.

First, the organization of power should be considered under a single government. When the problem of maintaining international peace is approached by trying to apply to the many extant states of the world a system comparable to that of maintaining the peace within a single state, two incorrect assumptions are often made. One is based on the observable fact that major wars are usually fought between nations, while peaceful conditions are the more general rule within individual states. It is then reasoned that, if the sovereign national units are eliminated (through merger into a world government), war will automatically be eliminated along with them. But this is merely a semantic "solution" that, in effect, transmutes world war into civil war.

The other assumption is that world governmental machinery will be necessary only in the area of politico-military policy as now known in inter-state affairs; thus the proposals for world federation are usually of limited scope, even when authoritative within that scope. But such a restriction ignores the fact that government decisions on the use of force as an instrument of policy directly or indirectly involve most of the other major powers of government. Control of military power is much more than merely the giving of orders to and by generals and admirals. In addition to major political decisions on the purposes for which such power is to be used, military control involves the provision and financing of personnel and matériel, territorial bases for their maintenance, and means of transporting them where needed. Thus, the power to raise taxes, to draft men, to control territory, and to allocate resources will all be involved in any system that seeks only to control foreign and military policy.

A governmental system, moreover, involves complete centralization of authority over the use of physical power in relation to any of its units; that is, the final political decision on such use rests with the central authority, rather than with the component units—whether they be the states of a federation, the provinces of a unitary government, or the units of varying degrees of subordination within an imperial organization. If and when that central power of decision is challenged, the result is civil war or revolution or rebellion, and the challenge must be met effectively by the central authority; else the governing authority will be replaced by a new one or will break up into two or more independent governing authorities—and we are back in the international framework again.

While world government may thus be described (in relation to the control of power) as demanding only a somewhat greater *degree* of centralization than an ideal global collective security system—as the latter would also require a high degree of control through the mechanism of a central international organ— the *kind* of control is quite different in the two cases. A member state of an international agency will turn over control of its forces only in such numbers, on such terms, and for such periods as it sees fit. But if the state agrees to become part of a world government, it will have to relinquish ultimate control completely (save for local police functions), along with at least minimum fiscal, territorial, manpower, and other controls, as mentioned above. This is so vital an act of political decision (some would say, of political abdication) by a state as to constitute a qualitative, as well as quantitative, difference between governmental and intergovernmental organization. In this respect, world government is not a comparable alternative to the two *international* forms of organization.

Most American writers (including Claude) tend to assume that world government, as they use the term, means government by consent rather than by compulsion. This is adequate as an objective, but incomplete as a conceptual analysis. Peace, in the sense of non-war, can just as easily be conceived under a dictatorial world government as under a liberal one. Indeed, under a *pax sovietica* power might well be more "effectively" managed by the central communist authority to prevent any outbreak of violence than it could be under any system requiring consent and, hence, having to permit dissent—which sometimes gets beyond police control.

There seems to be no serious possibility of any form of world state coming into being in the foreseeable future, since—unless history is to be turned topsy-turvy—no such fundamental political revolution as would be required has ever come about both rapidly and peacefully among basically different types of political units. Any sudden transformation of disparate states into constituent parts of larger states or empires has come through conquest. And while the communists might well be willing to try this method, enough of the rest of us are prepared to oppose them so that they are more likely to bring about a nuclear holocaust and a world in ruins than a world state. The voluntary formation of larger states out of smaller ones, so far as I can recall, has occurred only when already similar political units (such as the original thirteen North American states) have joined together. As the precondition of sufficiently like-structured units clearly does not yet exist globally, the most we are likely to see happen voluntarily, for some time to come, is more of the limited steps now being taken toward common markets, economic "communities," and tentative political groupings of a few states.

This was the viewpoint of the planners of the United Nations, both before and at San Francisco, as Claude has noted. It is still valid.

II.

If national governments are not yet ready to turn over to a world government that final power of decision over the use of their respective components of physical force, then the problem of maintaining world peace becomes a question of managing power relations among a large number of independent authorities, each with some degree of power at its command. Any diplomatic form of organization under which those independent states voluntarily attempt to regulate their power relationships will, by definition, be less centralized than any governmental organization.[2]

The various international forms of organizing power relationships may be considered "related to each other as successive points along a continuum" so far as concerns their degree of centralization, and may be described as falling generally under either the balance of power or collective security rubric. These concepts, I concur, while incapable of being defined in firmly agreed terms, do constitute alternative notions of international power relationships that result in significantly different systems. But the significant differences, it seems to me, relate less to their varying degrees of centralization than to the nature of their bases of action and the ends for which their collective power is used.

Thus, the balance of power concept may be described as "a kind of laissez-faire arrangement" by which states "in combinations reflecting the coincidence of interests, . . . seek to influence the pattern of power distribution and to determine their own places within" it.[3] And a collective security system may be represented as one imposing "partially centralized management upon a situation in

---

[2] Without getting involved in fine semantic distinctions, let us simply note that a grouping such as that of the Warsaw Pact countries, while nominally an international organization of independent states, is in actuality nearer a Soviet imperium. For purposes of this paper, it will be so classed. Although its members have separate votes in the United Nations and other international agencies, they are always cast as a unit, which applies to no other so-called "bloc"; there is no nonsense about who controls the power of this group.

[3] I cannot see, however, how the balance of power concept can also cover that "extreme of decentralization," a scheme within which individual states operate *either* "singly or in combinations." Each-state-for-itself is international anarchy—the absence of, rather than a system of, management. Alliance agreements may be very loose, but whatever the understanding entered into, it constitutes a form of joint undertaking, even if the coordinating "agency" of the arrangement is no more than a signed treaty.

which power remains diffused among national units." It would seem to be going too far, however, to describe an "ideal" collective security system as calling for "an international organization with authority to determine when a resort to force is illegitimate and to require states to collaborate under its direction in suppressing such use of force"—as though the international organ were an independent body. Such an agency is not itself a separate authority; it is, rather, the collectivity of its member states—acting on certain principles, by certain methods, within certain limits, and for certain ends, all in accordance with the voluntary undertakings of those members. Claude correctly points out that the member states "function as coordinate managers of the power situation" under a balance of power arrangement; but so do they under a collective security organization, although their management responsibilities may be different in nature.

The important factors that differentiate the two approaches relate to the methods by which each organizes to maintain the peace. A balance of power system will seek to maintain the equilibrium (or restore it) by creating roughly balanced power groups, with neither side able easily to overcome the other. Each group may be organized either defensively or offensively; that is, either to maintain an existing balance as against another group, or to overcome that group's power, which it may consider detrimental potentially or actually. Its members normally will be bound to act together under certain agreed conditions, whether to conquer or to resist conquest. War is accepted as a permissible instrument of national policy, and with it the concept of neutrality.

A collective security system, on the other hand, seeks to *un*balance power so that it is heavily weighted on the side of peaceful states against potential aggressors. The member states foreswear the use of force for national ends; undertake to maintain peaceful relations in their political intercourse; and, abjuring neutrality, agree to combine their joint efforts against any state (including members of the system) which may violate the standard of peaceful conduct. The important element, theoretically, that is "imposed," in Claude's words, is not the "scheme of partially centralized management," but the scheme of generally applicable national obligations (to refrain from the nondefensive use of force), duties (to come to the aid of an injured party when this standard is violated), and rights (to call upon the other members when itself injured) —not in relation to particular states, but, ideally, in relation to any offending state.

A collective security system, moreover, must logically accompany its scheme for controlling force with some positive scheme for peaceful adjustments to changing conditions that alter national interests and power. Such adjustments under a balance of power arrangement can take the form of shifting "collective" arrangements of constituent groups of states; but all states will be included within a single "concert" under a general collective security scheme. The system therefore requires more formal, more centralized organization to carry out these functions than is needed under a balance of power arrangement, which itself changes with changing conditions.

III.

In turning now to the United Nations as a system for managing power relations in the contemporary world, we find that neither of these theoretical concepts really fits the case. Thus, Claude had to "emancipate" himself from the "rigidity" of the standard categories in order to describe what actually happened in setting up the Organization. He is quite right in finding that it was not the original intention to establish "a full-fledged collective security system, capable of bringing collective force to bear against any aggressor," as the veto provisions exempted the Great Powers from enforcement action. It does not follow from this, however, that the original scheme "represented the repudiation of the idea of collective security, not an unsuccessful attempt to institutionalize its application"; nor can it be adequately described as leaving "the balance of power system intact for cases of major importance to global peace and order," while providing "a collective security system to be applicable in cases of relatively minor significance." These are judgments that return to the rigidities of disparate theoretical categories; what actually happened fits less neatly into the pigeonholes.

In considering the problems of establishing the United Nations Organization, the planners of the Charter had to deal, not with theoretical systems, but with a condition of world war. Assuming eventual United Nations victory, there would then exist an overwhelmingly strong concert of power, dominated physically by the major allied powers, with an immediate task of controlling the defeated Axis powers and of deciding what form their own postwar relationships should take in order to maintain the hard-won peace.

There were various American ideas on the best way to do this, including a proposal that there should be one treaty commitment among the major victors to enforce the peace treaties against Germany and Japan, and a completely separate one establishing a general international organization on a purely consultative basis, without military means to enforce peace, but concerned with other aspects of international relations. The higher official view of this approach, set forth in a memorandum to the Secretary of State some months before the Dumbarton Oaks Conversations, clearly explains the evolutionary concept behind the government's ultimate proposals. It contended that the establishment of effective surveillance over disarmed Germany and Japan would not alone suffice to guarantee peace and security:

> What we should strive for is the establishment of an international organization which would, through a series of steps, provide for an effective system of collective security. While it is true that in our present discussion we, too, envisage an international organization which initially would be merely a consultative body, we make definite provision for a general un-

dertaking to use force, if necessary, for the maintenance of peace and security. We also make provision for a procedure through which, by later and supplementary agreement, the general undertaking would be transformed into a specific one, and through which, in the meantime, the major powers and such other states as may be in a position to do so would continue to act in defense of security and peace.[4]

The government experts also agreed that no Great Power would allow its military forces to be ordered into action without its consent, and (an equally important consideration) that the smaller states would not be likely to accept complete Great Power hegemony in the guise of an international organization. They thought, however, that the proposals then being completed by the United States offered a reasonable method of handling these practical difficulties, "even if we fail to find an acceptable way of dealing with controversies in which a major power is invloved." The significant word here is "acceptable."

Granted that any voluntary system for maintaining peace would require the cooperation of the Great Powers, the experts thought such cooperation would more likely develop within a general security system incorporating as broad commitments as possible, than on any narrower base—such as an alliance to control the ex-enemy states—or merely on some *ad hoc* basis, without commitments looking toward a fuller, more effective system. They felt, at the same time, that if one of the great holders of power should resort to aggression in the future, it could be halted only by the combined weight of all the other states, in effect, by all-out war once again. Such a turn of events could not, practically, be prevented by any international organization, despite commitments not to use force for national ends; but without such commitments, there would not even be anything internationally "illegal" in such aggression, immoral though it might be considered.

As the Charter shows, the Great Powers would not accept any enforcement system not

[4] Quoted in Ruth B. Russell, *A History of the United Nations Charter* (Washington, D. C.: Brookings, 1958), p. 396.

dependent on their voluntary accord. But an agreement *was* achieved that: 1) allowed a nascent collective security system to develop as fast as the precondition of Great Power cooperation might develop; 2) provided for a separate form of collective action to be organized outside the global agency, but within the framework of its nonaggressive security commitments, so long as the former was not able to handle matters itself (namely, collective self-defense); and 3) established sufficiently flexible machinery and procedures to permit considerable adaptation on the basis of experience. Rather than a "curious amalgam," the Charter seems to me to represent a rather practical amalgam of the possibilities in the circumstances of 1945.

IV.

In considering what has happened since then, Claude contends that the creators of the United Nations envisaged "an extremely modest version of collective security"; but that, as there is now no "meaningful possibility of organizing a dependable system of collective military sanctions to repel international aggression," collective security as an operative system must be considered repudiated. But the varied array of organized relationships that have developed among the nations to control power internationally in the postwar period is much too complex a reality to be forced into a single theoretical mold. We face here, as always, the conflict between the continuity and complexity of history and the discreteness of theoretical concepts: the evolution of international political forms in life does not occur by clear-cut substitutions of one dominant "operative system" for another. In the long perspective of history, it may be possible to see a single system dominant in certain periods, as historians are wont to do, and then to denominate the intervening periods simply as "transitional" and let them go at that. Living through one of those confused transitional periods, as we are now doing, it would seem more profitable to attempt to sort out its various elements than to try to classify it as dominated by one or the other of two definitely different systems.

Rather than trying to decide, that is, whether we are in a yellow period (with a little blue here and there, it is true) or a blue period (with yellow admixtures, it must be admitted), why not recognize the spectrum of greens in which we actually live? We observe something of the old-fashioned balance of power in the relationships of the nuclear powers. We see a new-model balance of power operation in the collective defense arrangements. We find several "extremely modest versions" of collective security actions under United Nations auspices, none of them, admittedly, of the type specifically foreseen in the Charter; but all of them, be it noted— from Korea, through Suez, to the Congo— representing operations carried out because there existed a sufficient degree of Great Power accord (either through acquiescence or abstinence) to enable them to work within their particular limitations, and because there was enough flexibility in the Charter to adapt to those limitations. We see also a new subversive form of international aggressive force in the Soviet and Chinese use of nationalist-communist groups, that so far has not shown itself very susceptible to either collective-security or balance-of-power forms of resistance.

Where all this may lead, provided we do not blow all our systems into oblivion, is impossible to predict at this stage. Within the United Nations, as Secretary-General Hammarskjöld pointed out in his final testament, "certain members conceive of the organization as a static conference machinery for resolving conflicts of interest and ideology"; while others think of it "primarily as a dynamic instrument of governments through which they jointly . . . should seek . . . also . . . to develop forms of executive action" to resolve and forestall conflicts. The first concept, he added:

is firmly anchored in the time-honored philosophy of sovereign national states in armed competition, of which the most that may be expected in the international field is that they achieve a peaceful coexistence. The second one envisages possibilities of intergovernmental action overriding such a philosophy, and opens the road toward more developed and increasingly effective forms of constructive international cooperation.[5]

The two concepts could as well have been described, in our terms, as balance of power versus collective security. Mr. Hammarskjöld stressed that the direction in which the Organization does move will depend on decisions of the Member States. If they elect to limit its "potential contribution," in Claude's words, to "helping to improve and stabilize the working of the balance of power system," the forward-looking potentials of the Charter will be in danger of atrophy by default. To the extent that its possibilities can be realized through even modest versions of collective security action, the other forms of international political organization may tend less to conflict with, than to supplement, the United Nations in controlling power relationships.

Finally, it might be noted, if all governments behaved as sensibly as those of modern Scandinavia, for example, the effective management of their power relations would present no serious problems; peace would reign under any of the theoretical alternatives discussed above, and under any logical form of organization to control the international use of their national forces. Lacking such general will to peaceful relations, especially among all the Great Powers, the organizational forms used by states in their efforts to control the international power situation will probably continue to be—as they are now—a varied mixture, developed in response to the variety of power problems they seek to solve.

[5] "Introduction to the Annual Report of the Secretary-General on the Work of the Organization 16 June 1960—15 June 1961," General Assembly *Official Records*, Supplement 1A, p. 1.

QUESTIONS FOR SEMINAR DISCUSSION

What do you believe is necessary to create effective operating legal structures for our own society? Are the same elements necessary for creating legal structures in the international community? Are there additional elements necessary for developing legal structure in the international community?

Do you feel that there is such a thing as International Law in the sense of rules which are operative in controlling and guiding behavior of state officials in their dealings with one another? How does it differ from the operation of law in our own society? Do you see any possibility that a progressive development of international law in terms of its present structure and content would be useful to eliminate the use of force among nations?

Does Fisher's suggestion that we study the conditions which make government officials obey their own law seem useful to you as a way to approach the problem of making officials in the international community obey a proscription against the threat or use of force? Specifically, what proposals would you have along these lines?

Do you believe that Henkin's cataloging of issues on which the U.S. and U.S.S.R. are likely to want a settlement is realistic? Which of his many proposals do you think could be agreed upon or put into practice without too much difficulty and relatively soon? Do you think they would be significant steps in the effort to establish peace?

Does Falk's analytical framework of modernizing, revolutionary and status quo nations in relationship to the international political system and the problems in developing an effective international law to eliminate the threat of use of force seem to you to deal with the major problems of world order? Would you delete or add anything to his analysis? Why? Does his analysis suggest any actions that might be taken now to enhance world order? Do you think that the Clark-Sohn principles comprehend such a system and are capable of dealing with it?

Is it sensible to place exclusive emphasis upon the curtailment of physical force (or the threat of it) or do we need to be concerned with other forms of coercion such as economic aggression? Would it be easier to establish a system which dealt only with physical force, or one which took into account the whole range of coercion that one state might use against another?

Though Claude believes that the concepts of balance-of-power, collective security, and world government are not discrete but are positions in a continuum, he does attempt to distinguish among them. However, he is forced to admit that in looking at the United Nations he has to free himself from the "rigidities of the categories." For what purposes, then, are the distinctions useful? In talking about international organization, would it be useful to talk about the "mix" or the extent to which any of the notions was the dominant organizing principle or the extent to which each notion was used within the various activities of the organization? Assuming for the moment that the three concepts can be used to discuss intelligently different forms of world order, what are the strengths and weaknesses of each in establishing and maintaining a peaceful world?

Do you agree with Claude that the balance of power system is "the operative mechanism of contemporary international politics?" Does a balance of power system inherently involve resort to force among the nations? Has the United Nations made any significant difference in the operation of the balance of power system? How viable a system would collective security be for the maintenance of peace? What are the potential instabilities in such a system?

What is the relationship of international law to formally organized international structure? If they are not con-

comitant, can you s p e c i f y their distinguishing characteristics? Are they both n e e d e d for the establishment of a
peaceful world?

On the basis of the readings in the first two sessions do you
believe it is n e c e s s a r y and possible to create world legal
structure or must we move g r a d u a l l y through a series of
accommodative s t e p s over a long period (say one hundred
years) until we have d e v e l o p e d sufficient experience and
trust among leaders and peoples of the states of the world so
that t h e y will be willing to organize the international community along peaceful lines?

BIBLIOGRAPHY

Bloomfield, Lincoln. "Law, Politics and International Disputes." Internatl. Concil. No. 516: 257-316 (Jan. 1958). The author discusses
the relatively peripheral role of international law which he considers
to be the inevitable concomitant of a world in flux. "The world cannot live without law, but law can only o p e r a t e where a consensus
already exists."
Brierly, James L. The Law of Nations; an introduction to the international law of peace. 5th ed. Oxford: C l a r e n d o n Press, 1955,
306p. The best short introduction to the study of international law.
Castaneda, Jorge. "The Underdeveloped Nations and the Development
of International Law." Internatl. Org. 15: 38-48 (Winter 1961).
Commission to Study the Organization of Peace. Organizing Peace in
the Nuclear Age. NY: NY U. Press, 1959, 245p. Two sections:
law and politics in the organization of peace, and the International
Atomic Energy Agency.
Corbett, Percy E. Law and Society in the Relation of States. NY: Har-
court, Brace, 1951, 337p.
Falk, Richard. "International Jurisdiction: Horizontal and Vertical
C o n c e p t i o n s of Legal Order." Temple Law Quarterly 32 (1959),
295-320.
Friedrich, Carl J. Inevitable Peace. Cambridge, Mass.: Harvard U.
Press, 1948, 294p. A philosophical exploration of the concepts of
war, peace, international order, etc.
Hackworth, Green H. Digest of International Law. Washington: Govt.
Printing Office, 1940. 8 vols.
Hahn, H. J. "International and Supranational Public A u t h o r i t i e s."
Law and Contemporary Problems 26: 638-63 (Autumn 1961).
Hoffmann, Stanley. "International S y s t e m s and International Law."
World Politics 14: 205-37 (Oct. 1961).
_____. "The Role of International Organization: Limits and Pos-
sibilities." Internatl. Org. 10: 357-72 (Aug. 1956). A "think
piece" which considers what should and what can i n t e r n a t i o n a l
organizations do to promote the objectives laid out in the UN Charter, given the present structure of world society.
Hyde, Charles C. International Law; Chiefly as Interpreted and Applied
by the United States. 2nd ed. Boston: Little, Brown, 1947. 3 vols.
Jordan, William M. "Concepts and Realities in International Political
Organization." Internatl. Org. 11: 587-96 (A u t u m n 1957). Some
general and rather acute observations on the approach to the problem of maintaining peace, with an historical perspective.

Kelsen, Hans. The Law of the United Nations, A Critical Analysis of its Fundamental Problems. London: Stevens and Co., 1950, 903p.; and a supplement, Recent Trends in the Law of the UN. London: Stevens, 1951, 909p.

_____. Principles of International Law. NY: Rinehart, 1952, 461p. An Austinian view of international law by the best known legal "positivist."

Korowicz, Marek Stanislaw. "Some Present Aspects of Sovereignty in International Law." Recueil des Cours, 1961, No. 1: 1-119. The last several decades, but mainly the period 1945-60, are investigated to see whether the trend in international law is towards a weakening or a strengthening of the doctrine of the sovereignty of states.

Lauterpacht, Hersh. Function of Law in the International Community. Oxford: Clarendon Press, 1933. A short statement of the jurisprudence, hopes, and fears of the best-known contemporary legal scholar.

Levontin, A. V. The Myth of International Security. Jerusalem: Magnus Press, Hebrew U., 1957, 346p.

Lipsky, George Arthur, ed. Law and Politics in the World Community; Essays on Hans Kelsen's Pure Theory and Related Problems in International Law. Berkeley: U. of Calif. Press, 1953, 373p. Excellent series of articles that illustrate a variety of problems confronting international law currently.

McDougal, Myres S. "International Law, Power and Policy: A Contemporary Conception." Recueil des Cours 82(1953, No. 1), p. 137-259. One of the best of many recent studies on the interaction of law and politics.

_____. Studies in World Public Order. New Haven, Yale U. Press, 1960, 1058p.

McDougal, Myres S., and Florentino F. Feliciano. Law and Minimum World Public Order; The Legal Regulation of International Coercion. New Haven: Yale U. Press, 1961, 872p. A sizable compendium "designed as a contribution to the clarification of the common interests of all peoples in the establishment and maintenance of minimum order."

Pound, Roscoe. A World Legal Order--Law and Laws in Relation to World Law. Medford, Mass.: Fletcher School of Law and Diplomacy, 1959, 42p. An address made at Fletcher School, Oct. 27, 1959.

Schiffer, Walter. The Legal Community of Mankind; A Critical Analysis of the Modern Concept of World Organization. NY: Columbia U. Press, 1954, 367p. A study of the historic bases of the concept of world organization, and the recurring themes and problems of analysis of world organization.

Stone, Julius. Agression and World Order; A Critique of United Nations Theories of Agression. Berkeley: U. of Calif. Press., 1958, 226p.

_____. Quest for Survival: The Role of Law and Foreign Policy. Cambridge, Mass.: Harvard U. Press, 1961. An analysis of the relationship between international law and peace.

Tunkin, Grigory I. "Co-existence and International Law." Recueil des Cours, 1958, No. 3: 1-81. Considers, from a Russian viewpoint, the impact of co-existence on the nature of international law and vice versa.

de Visscher, Charles. Theory and Reality in Public International Law. Trans. from the French by P. E. Corbett. Princeton, N. J.: Princeton U. Press, 1957, 381p.

Wright, Quincy. "The Strengthening of International Law." Recueil des Cours, 1959, No. 3: 1-295. A summary of the development of international law up to the present with an analysis of how it can and should be strengthened.

187

SESSION III

STRENGTHENING THE UNITED NATIONS

Our first two sessions have been a rather intensive introduction to the problem of preventing war through the use of law. Initially we tentatively evaluated the basic principles of world legal structure including complete and general disarmament which Clark and Sohn have proposed as a solution to the problem. Then we explored other legal approaches which placed much less emphasis upon centralized formally organized legal structure; these approaches were generally based on the assumption that the strong vertical dimension of legal institutions characteristic of relatively well organized domestic societies would not be acceptable at the level of international community life to relevant political officials of the nation states. Our appraisal of these proposals involved an appreciation of traditional international law and the potentialities for increasing its effectiveness through progressive evolutionary development of international organization. Finally we attempted to clarify and assess various conceptions of international organization relative to the problem of peace-keeping.

This session initiates our study of the possibilities and problems involved in revising and strengthening the United Nations in order to achieve and maintain peace. As indicated in the Foreword, the extended revision of the UN proposed by Clark-Sohn in World Peace Through World Law makes it an ideal focus for our investigation. In evaluating the Clark-Sohn proposals it is important to keep in mind that each revision is offered as a part of the set of interrelated principles discussed in their Introduction (xv-xvii); many of the proposals are closely connected with their detailed plan for general and complete disarmament which we will study later. In addition, the authors state that in proposing revisions they have been guided almost without exception by the criterion of efficient operation of the United Nations in the limited field of war-prevention. A constant question then will be the extent to which a suggested change either fails or has been too zealous for meeting the problem of war-prevention. Finally, we shall be concerned with the underlying political problems which must be resolved if these proposals are to be accepted.

Broadly speaking, the present UN structure places primary responsibility for the maintenance of peace in the Security Council in its granting of power to make decisions binding upon member states. Although the General Assembly has in recent years increased its operations in the peace-keeping area, as a formal Constitutional matter it can only make recommendations to the member states. The single most important change proposed by Clark-Sohn in the materials which we will read for this session is the establishment of the General Assembly as the authoritative legislative body given constitutional capacity to enact legislation binding upon all individuals as well as all the states of the world in order to ensure peace. As we shall see here and in later sessions, this change has far-reaching implications for the internal structure and range of functions of the UN.

In this session we shall look at four major areas: 1) standards and procedures to be used for admission to membership to the United Nations, 2) standards and procedures to be used for determining who shall represent various nations to the UN, 3) the general problem of how much representation especially with regard to voting should be given to each nation state, and 4) an initial exploration of the recurring problem, to what extent may the UN intervene in matters " essentially within the domestic jurisdiction" of any state. (Article 2 (7)).

The Advisory Opinion of the International Court of Justice written at the request of the General Assembly is concerned with standards to be applied to states applying for membership in the UN and provides us with materials to compare present Article 4 dealing with these matters and the sole criterion for admission proposed by Clark and Sohn , namely, is the applicant a legally independent state. The differing procedures for membership application should also be noted. As we approach universal membership the problem of admission standards and procedures will become relatively unimportant (of course it might arise if there were a breakup of a state into two states.) At the moment, however, this matter presents quite formidable transition problems.

The speeches by Ambassador Adlai Stevenson and Dr . G. P. Malalaskera, Head of the Ceylonese Delegation, given at the 16th Session of the General Assembly concern the troublesome question o f what formal affiliation, if any, should the Chinese Communist Government have with the United Nations. Since 1949 there have been demands in almost all the official organs and agencies of the UN that the Chinese Communists be seated as the official representatives of the State of China. General sentiment for bringing Communist China into the UN has increased steadily over the last few years and it is likely that this problem will be a major domestic as well as international issue for the next few years.

Prior to the 16th Session the Chinese "question" has been debated within the context of whether or not the matter should even be placed on the agenda. The Assembly has always answered this in the negative. In this session two items referring to the matter were placed on the agenda. After a debate in which fifty-six members participated, the Assembly voted that the question of Chinese representation was an "important matter" under Article 18 (requiring therefore an affirmative vote of 2/3 of the members present and voting) and then voted in effect to maintain the present Chinese representation. The speeches by Stevenson and Malalaskera are indicative of the major points made in the course of the General Assembly debate.

It should be noted that this question is frequently phrased as one of representation and not admission. You will want to discuss the consequences of phrasing the issue in this fashion. In looking at both the admission and representation problems you will also find it useful to compare the scope of appropriate argument before the International Court of Justice and the General Assembly. In more general terms, what body using what criteria should decide these questions?

Our final two readings revolve around the problem of the extent to which the UN should be permitted to intervene in matters which are essentially within the jurisdiction of member states (See Article 2 (7)). In some ways this is the overriding problem of contemporary international organization and could be expected to be troublesome even under world legal structure. Simply put, the question is what can the international or world organization regulate, control, demand and enforce vis-a-vis the activities that go on within states or are carried on by state officials; what and when is a matter essentially within the domestic jurisdiction and what and when is a matter clearly without? You will want to compare the Clark-Sohn view on the matter with the points made in the exchange between M. Pavosky and the members of the Senate Foreign Relations Committee. The M. Rajan article is useful for its recitation of the underlying legal issues. His attempt to grapple with underlying political problems in a framework of slowly evolving international law and international organization is typical of those legal approaches which do not foresee the establishment of world legal structure in the foreseeable future.

In order to have a better appreciation of some of the changes which are being proposed, you may find it useful to read quickly through the present United Nations Charter. The two diagrams on the final two pages of this book may also be helpful.

Readings from World Peace Through World Law:
Present United Nations Charter; Preliminary Note, Organs, 1-19; The General Assembly, 20-65; Introduction: Membership, The General Assembly, xvii-xix.

CONDITIONS OF ADMISSION OF A STATE TO MEMBERSHIP IN THE UNITED NATIONS

Advisory Opinion of the International Court of Justice, 28 May 1948.
ICJ Reports, 1948, pp. 57–115.

On November 17th, 1947, the General Assembly of the United Nations adopted the following Resolution:

The General Assembly,

"Considering Article 4 of the Charter of the United Nations,

"Considering the exchange of views which has taken place in the Security Council at its Two hundred and fourth, Two hundred and fifth and Two hundred and sixth Meetings, relating to the admission of certain States to membership in the United Nations,

"Considering Article 96 of the Charter,

"Requests the International Court of Justice to give an advisory opinion on the following question:

" 'Is a Member of the United Nations which is called upon, in virtue of Article 4 of the Charter, to pronounce itself by its vote, either in the Security Council or in the General Assembly, on the admission of a State to membership in the United Nations, juridically entitled to make its consent to the admission dependent on conditions not express-

191

ly provided by paragraph 1 of the said Article? In particular, can such a Member, while it recognizes the conditions set forth in that provision to be fulfilled by the State concerned, subject its affirmative vote to the additional condition that other States be admitted to membership in the United Nations together with that State?' . . . "

            *   *   *   *

. . . the Court holds that it is competent, on the basis of Article 96 of the Charter and Article 65 of the Statute, and considers that there are no reasons why it should decline to answer the question put to it.

In framing this answer, it is necessary first to recall the "conditions" required, under paragraph 1 of Article 4, of an applicant for admission. This provision reads as follows:

"Membership in the United Nations is open to all other peace-loving States which accept the obligations contained in the present Charter and, in the judgment of the Organization, are able and willing to carry out these obligations."

The requisite conditions are five in number: to be admitted to membership in the United Nations, an applicant must (1) be a State; (2) be peace-loving; (3) accept the obligations of the Charter; (4) be able to carry out these obligations; and (5) be willing to do so.

All these conditions are subject to the judgment of the Organization. The judgment of the Organization means the judgment of the two organs mentioned in paragraph 2 of Article 4, and, in the last analysis, that of its Members. The question put is concerned with the individual attitude of each Member called upon to pronounce itself on the question of admission.

Having been asked to determine the character, exhaustive or otherwise, of the conditions stated in Article 4, the Court must in the first place consider the text of that Article. The English and French texts of paragraph 1 of Article 4 have the same meaning, and it is impossible to find any conflict between them. The text of this paragraph, by the enumeration which it contains and the choice of its terms, clearly demonstrates the intention of its authors to establish a legal rule which, while it fixes the conditions of admission, determines also the reasons for which admission may be refused; for the text does not differentiate between these two cases and any attempt to restrict it to one of them would be purely arbitrary.

The terms "Membership in the United Nations is open to all other peace-loving States which . . ." and *"Peuvent devenir Membres des Nations unies tous autres États pacifiques"*, indicate that States which fulfil the conditions stated have the qualifications requisite for admission. The natural meaning of the words used leads to the conclusion that these conditions constitute an exhaustive enumeration and are not merely stated by way of guidance or example. The provision would lose its significance and weight, if other conditions, unconnected with those laid down, could be demanded. The conditions stated in paragraph 1 of Article 4 must therefore be regarded not merely as the necessary conditions, but also as the conditions which suffice.

Nor can it be argued that the conditions enumerated represent only an indispensable minimum, in the sense that political considerations could be superimposed upon them, and prevent the admission of an applicant which fulfils them. Such an interpretation would be inconsistent with the terms of paragraph 2 of Article 4, which provide for the admission of *"tout État* remplissant ces conditions"—"any *such* State". It would lead to conferring upon Members an indefinite and practically unlimited power of discretion in the imposition of new conditions. Such a power would be inconsistent with the very character of paragraph 1 of Article 4 which, by reason of the close connexion which it establishes between membership and the observance of the principles and obligations of the Charter, clearly constitutes a legal regulation of the question of the admission of new States. To warrant an interpretation other than that which ensues from the natural meaning of the words, a decisive reason would be required which has not been established.

Moreover, the spirit as well as the terms of the paragraph preclude the idea that considerations extraneous to these principles and obligations can prevent the admission of a State which complies with them. If the authors of the Charter had meant to leave Members free to import into the application of this provision considerations extraneous to the conditions laid down therein, they would undoubtedly have adopted a different wording.

The Court considers that the text is sufficiently clear; consequently, it does not feel that it should deviate from the consistent practice of the Permanent Court of International Justice, according to which there is no occasion to resort to preparatory work if the text of a convention is sufficiently clear in itself.

The Court furthermore observes that Rule 60 of the Provisional Rules of Procedure of the Security Council is based on this interpretation. The first paragraph of this Rule reads as follows:

"The Security Council shall decide whether in its judgment the applicant is a peace-loving State and is able and willing to carry out the obligations contained in the Charter, and accordingly whether to recommend the applicant State for membership."

It does not, however, follow from the exhaustive character of paragraph 1 of Article 4 that an appreciation is precluded of such circumstances of fact as would enable the existence of the requisite conditions to be verified.

Article 4 does not forbid the taking into account of any factor which it is possible reasonably and in good faith to connect with the conditions laid down in that Article. The taking into account of such factors is implied in the very wide and very elastic nature of the prescribed conditions; no relevant political factor—that is to say, none connected with the conditions of admission—is excluded.

It has been sought to deduce either from the second paragraph of Article 4, or from the political character of the organ recommending or deciding upon admission, arguments in favour of an interpretation of paragraph 1 of Article 4, to the effect that the fulfilment of the conditions provided for in that Article is necessary before the admission of a State can be recommended or decided upon, but that it does not preclude the Members of the Organization from advancing considerations of political expediency, extraneous to the conditions of Article 4.

But paragraph 2 is concerned only with the procedure for admission, while the preceding paragraph lays down the substantive law. This procedural character is clearly indicated by the words "will be effected", which, by linking admission to the decision, point clearly to the fact that the paragraph is solely concerned with the manner in which admission is effected, and not with the subject of the judgment of the Organization, nor with the nature of the appreciation involved in that judgment, these two questions being dealt with in the preceding paragraph. Moreover, this paragraph, in referring to the "recommendation" of the Security Council and the "decision" of the General Assembly, is designed only to determine the respective functions of these two organs which consist in pronouncing upon the question whether or not the applicant State shall be admitted to membership after having established whether or not the prescribed conditions are fulfilled.

The political character of an organ cannot release it from the observance of the treaty provisions established by the Charter when they constitute limitations on its powers or criteria for its judgment. To ascertain whether an organ has freedom of choice for its decisions, reference must be made to the terms of its constitution. In this case, the limits of this freedom are fixed by Article 4 and allow for a wide liberty of appreciation. There is therefore no conflict between the functions of the political organs, on the one hand, and the exhaustive character of the prescribed conditions, on the other.

It has been sought to base on the political responsibilities assumed by the Security Council, in virtue of Article 24 of the Charter, an argument justifying the necessity for according to the Security Council as well as to the General Assembly complete freedom of appreciation in connexion with the admission of new Members. But Article 24, owing to the very general nature of its terms, cannot, in the absence of any provision, affect the special rules for admission which emerge from Article 4.

The foregoing considerations establish the exhaustive character of the conditions prescribed in Article 4.

The second part of the question concerns a demand on the part of a Member making its consent to the admission of an applicant dependent on the admission of other applicants.

Judged on the basis of the rule which the Court adopts in its interpretation of Article 4, such a demand clearly constitutes a new condition, since it is entirely unconnected with those prescribed in Article 4. It is also in an entirely different category from those conditions, since it makes admission dependent, not on the conditions required of applicants, qualifications which are supposed to be fulfilled, but on an extraneous consideration concerning States other than the applicant State.

The provisions of Article 4 necessarily imply that every application for admission should be examined and voted on separately and on its own merits; otherwise it would be impossible to determine whether a particular applicant fulfils the necessary conditions. To subject an affirmative vote for the admission of an applicant State to the condition that other States be admitted with that State would prevent Members from exercising their judgment in each case with complete liberty, within the scope of the prescribed conditions. Such a demand is incompatible with the letter and spirit of Article 4 of the Charter.

For these reasons,

THE COURT,

by nine votes to six,

is of opinion that a Member of the United Nations which is called upon, in virtue of Article 4 of the Charter, to pronounce itself by its vote, either in the Security Council or in the General Assembly, on the admission of a State to membership in the United Nations, is not juridically entitled to make its consent to the admission dependent on conditions not expressly provided by paragraph 1 of the said Article;

and that, in particular, a Member of the Organization cannot, while it recognizes the conditions set forth in that provision to be fulfilled by the State concerned, subject its affirmative vote to the additional condition that other States be admitted to membership in the United Nations together with that State. . . .

Judges Alvarez and Azevedo, whilst concurring in the opinion of the Court, have availed themselves of the right conferred on them by Article 57 of the Statute and appended to the opinion a statement of their individual opinion.

Judges Basdevant, Winiarski, McNair, Read, Zoričić and Krylov, declaring that they are unable to concur in the opinion of the Court, have availed themselves of the right conferred on them by Article 57 of the Statute and appended to the opinion a statement of their dissenting opinion. . . .

Individual Opinion by M. ALVAREZ.—I. I do not agree with the method adopted by the Court in giving the opinion for which it has been asked by the General Assembly of the United Nations.

The Court has inferred from the enumeration of the conditions prescribed in Article 4, paragraph 1, of the Charter for the admission of a State to membership in the United Nations, that nothing else can be adduced to justify a negative vote. This question cannot be answered merely by a clarification of the texts, nor by a study of the preparatory work; another method must be adopted and, in particular, recourse must be had to the great principles of the new international law.

More changes have taken place in international life since the last great social cataclysm than would normally occur in a century. Moreover, this life is evolving at a vertiginous speed: inter-State relations are becoming more and more various and complex. The fundamental principles of international law are passing through a serious crisis, and this necessitates its reconstruction. A new international law is developing, which embodies not only this reconstruction, but also some entirely new elements.

For a long time past I have insisted on the rôle which the Court must play in the renewal and development of international law. A recent event supports my opinion. The General Assembly of the United Nations in its Resolution No. 171 of November 14th, 1947, declares that it is of paramount importance, in the first place, that the interpretation of the Charter should be based on recognized principles of international law and, in the second place, that the Court should be utilized, to the greatest practicable extent, in the progressive development of this law, both in regard to legal issues between States and in regard to constitutional interpretation or to questions of a general nature submitted to it for its opinion.

I hold that in this connexion the Court has a free hand to allow scope to the new spirit which is evolving in contact with the new conditions of international life: there must be a renewal of international law corresponding to the renewal of this life.

With regard to the interpretation of legal texts, it is to be observed that, while in some cases preparatory work plays an important part, as a rule this is not the case. The reason lies in the fact that delegates, in discussing a subject, express the most varied views on certain matters and often without a sufficient knowledge of them; sometimes also they change their views without expressly saying so. The preparatory work on the constitution of the United Nations Organization is of but little value. Moreover, the fact should be stressed that an institution, once established, acquires a life of its own, independent of the elements which have given birth to it, and it must develop, not in accordance with the views of those who created it, but in accordance with the requirements of international life.

II.   As the question put to the Court concerns the admission of new States to the United Nations Organization, the character of the international community and the place in it occupied by the Organization must be borne in mind.

As a result of the increasingly closer relations between States, which has led to their ever greater interdependence, the old *community* of nations has been transformed into a veritable international *society,* though it has neither an executive power, nor a legislative power, nor yet a judicial power, which are the characteristics of a national society, but not of international society. This society comprises all States throughout the world, without there being any need for consent on their part or on that of other States; it has aims and interests of its own; States no longer have an absolute sovereignty but are interdependent; they have not only rights, but also *duties* towards each other and towards this society; finally, the latter is organized and governed to an ever increasing extent, by a law of a character quite different from that of customary law.

The foregoing indicates the place occupied by the United Nations Organization in the universal international society. The creation of the League of Nations constituted a great effort to organize this society, particularly from the standpoint of the maintenance of peace. The present United Nations Organization, which is destined to replace it and has the same aims, is therefore merely an institution within the universal international society.

The aims of this Organization are not confined to certain States or to a great number of States, but are of a world-wide nature. They are concerned with the maintenance of peace and the development of co-operation among all States of the world; it will suffice to read the Preamble and Chapter I of the Charter to appreciate this.

But to become a Member of this Organization, a State must apply for admission, must fulfil certain conditions and must be admitted by the Organization. States which are not yet Members of the Organization have not the rights and duties which it has laid down, but they have these conferred or imposed upon them as members of the universal society of nations. Moreover, such States may enter into relations of every kind with those which belong to the United Nations Organization, and these relations are governed by international law.

III.   Before giving the opinion asked of it by the General Assembly of the United Nations, the Court has had to make up its mind as to the legal or political character of the question put.

197

The traditional distinction between what is legal and what is political, and between law and politics, has to-day been profoundly modified. Formerly, everything dependent on precepts of law was regarded as legal and anything left to the free will of States was regarded as political.

Relations between States have become multiple and complex. As a result, they present a variety of aspects: legal, political, economic, social, etc.; there are, therefore, no more strictly legal issues. Moreover, many questions regarded as essentially legal, such as the interpretation of a treaty, may, in certain cases, assume a political character, especially in the case of a peace treaty. Again, many questions have both a legal and a political character, notably those relating to international organization.

A new conception of law in general, and particularly of international law, has also emerged. The traditionally *juridical* and *individualistic* conception of law is being progressively superseded by the following conception: in the first place, international law is not strictly juridical; it is also political, economic, social and psychological; hence, all the fundamental elements of traditional individualistic law are profoundly modified, a fact which necessitates their reconstruction. In the next place, strictly individualistic international law is being more and more superseded by what may be termed the *law of social interdependence*. The latter is the outcome, not of theory, but of the realities of international life and of the juridical conscience of the nations. The Court is the most authoritative organ for the expression of this juridical conscience, which also finds expression in certain treaties, in the most recent national legislative measures and in certain resolutions of associations devoted to the study of international law.

This *law of social interdependence* has certain characteristics of which the following are the most essential: (*a*) it is concerned not only with the delimitation of the rights of States, but also with harmonizing them; (*b*) in every question it takes into account all its various aspects; (*c*) it takes the general interest fully into account; (*d*) it emphasizes the notion of the *duties* of States, not only towards each other but also towards the international society; (*e*) it condemns the abuse of right; (*f*) it adjusts itself to the necessities of international life and evolves together with it; accordingly, it is in harmony with policy; (*g*) to the rights conferred by strictly juridical law it adds that which States possess to belong to the international organization which is being set up.

Far therefore from being in opposition to each other, law and policy are to-day closely linked together. The latter is not always the selfish and arbitrary policy of States; there is also a collective or individual policy inspired by the general interest. This policy now exercises a profound influence on international law; it either confirms it or endows it with new life, or even opposes it if it appears out of date. It is also one of the elements governing the relations between States when no legal precepts exist.

It is however always necessary to differentiate between juridical and political elements, particularly from the standpoint of the Court's jurisdiction.

The United Nations Charter makes the Court one of its organs (Art. 7), and Article 92 lays down that it is its principal judicial organ. The Statute of the present Court, like that of the old, indicates that its task is to hear and determine legal questions, and not political questions. The advisory opinions for which it may be asked must also relate to legal questions (Articles 36, No. 3, and 96 of the Charter; Article 65 of the Statute of the Court).

When a question is referred to the Court, the latter therefore must decide whether its dominant element is legal, and whether it should accordingly deal with it, or whether the political element is dominant and, in that case, it must declare that it has no jurisdiction.

In the questions which it is called upon to consider, the Court must, however, take into account all aspects of the matter, including the political aspect when it is closely bound up with the legal aspect. It would be a manifest mistake to seek to limit the Court to consideration of questions solely from their legal aspect, to the exclusion of other aspects; it would be inconsistent with the realities of international life.

It follows from the foregoing that the constitutional Charter cannot be interpreted according to a strictly legal criterion; another and broader criterion must be employed and room left, if need be, for political considerations.

The Court has decided that the question on which its advisory opinion has been asked is a legal one because it concerns the interpretation of the Charter of the United Nations, which is a treaty.

In reality, this question is both legal and political, but the legal element predominates, not so much because it is a matter of interpreting the Charter but because it is concerned with the problem whether States have a *right* to membership in the United Nations Organization if they fulfil the conditions required by the Statute of the Organization. The question is at the same time a political one, because it is the States comprising the Security Council and those belonging to the General Assembly which determine whether these conditions are, or are not, fulfilled by the applicant.

IV. As regards the essential conditions to be fulfilled by every State desiring to be admitted to membership in the United Nations Organization, these are prescribed in Article 4, paragraph 1, of the

Charter. These conditions are exhaustive because they are the only ones enumerated. If it had been intended to require others, this would have been expressly stated.

Moreover, having regard to the nature of the universal international society, the purposes of the United Nations Organization and its mission of universality, it must be held that all States fulfilling the conditions required by Article 4 of the Charter have a *right* to membership in that Organization. The exercise of this right cannot be blocked by the imposition of other conditions not expressly provided for by the Charter, by international law or by a convention, or on grounds of a political nature.

Nevertheless, it has to be judged in each case whether the conditions of admission required by the Charter are fulfilled. The units which may form this judgment are the States composing the Security Council and the members of the General Assembly. They must be guided solely by considerations of justice and good faith, i. e., they must confine themselves to considering whether the applicant fulfils the conditions required by Article 4, paragraph 1. In actual fact, however, these States are mainly guided by considerations of their own policy and, consequently, if not directly, at all events indirectly, they sometimes require of an applicant conditions other than those provided for in Article 4, since they vote against its admission if such other conditions are not fulfilled. That is an abuse of right which the Court must condemn; but at the present time no sanction attaches to it save the reprobation of public opinion.

Nevertheless, cases may arise in which the admission of a State is liable to disturb the international situation, or at all events the international organization, for instance, if such admission would give a very great influence to certain groups of States, or produce profound divergencies between them. Consequently, even if the conditions of admission are fulfilled by an applicant, admission may be refused. In such cases, the question is no longer a legal one; it becomes a political one and must be regarded as such. In a concrete case of this kind, the Court must declare that it has no jurisdiction.

A claim by a Member of the United Nations Organization, which recognizes the conditions of Article 4 of the Charter to be fulfilled by an applicant State, to subject its affirmative vote to the condition that other States be admitted to membership together with this applicant, would be an act contrary to the letter and spirit of the Charter. Nevertheless, such a claim may be justified in exceptional circumstances, for instance, in the case of applications for admission by two or more States simultaneously brought into existence as the result of the disappearance of the State or colony of which they formed part. It is natural in that case that their admission should be considered simultaneously.

V.   Having regard to the foregoing, I consider that the following replies should be given to the actual questions put in the request for an advisory opinion addressed to the Court:

1°   No State is *juridically* entitled to make its consent to the admission of a new Member to the United Nations Organization dependent on conditions not expressly provided for by Article 4, paragraph 1, of the Charter.

2°   A State may not, while recognizing the conditions required by Article 4, paragraph 1, of the Charter, to be fulfilled by the applicant State, subject its affirmative vote to the condition that other States be admitted to membership in the United Nations together with that State.   Nevertheless, in exceptional cases, such a claim may be justified.

To the above conclusions the following, which ensues from them, should be added:

If there are several simultaneous applications for admission, each must be considered separately, save in exceptional circumstances: there is no ground for establishing a connexion between them not contemplated by the Charter.

The foregoing statement clearly demonstrates the importance of the new method indicated above, and of the rôle which the Court is called upon to play in the development of international life and of international law.   In consequence of Resolution 171 of November 14th, 1947, adopted by the General Assembly of the United Nations, this method and this rôle emerge from the domain of doctrine and become applicable in practice.

SIXTEENTH SESSION GENERAL ASSEMBLY DEBATE ON
AGENDA ITEMS 90 AND 91 DECEMBER 1, 1961
QUESTION OF THE REPRESENTATION OF CHINA IN
THE UNITED NATIONS
RESTORATION OF THE LAWFUL RIGHTS OF THE PEOPLE'S REPUBLIC
OF CHINA IN THE UNITED NATIONS

Mr. STEVENSON (United States of America): The question confronting the Assembly of the representation of China in the United Nations is of world-wide and historical importance.

We live in an age when the ever-expanding family of nations is striving anew to realize the vision of the United Nations Charter: a world community, freed from the overhanging menace of war, acting together in equal dignity and mutual tolerance to create a better life for humanity. This very Assembly, in its majestic diversity, is both the physical symbol and the practical embodiment - however imperfect - of that transcendent vision.

In striving toward that vision, what we decide regarding the representation of China will have momentous consequences. For more is at stake than the status of certain delegations. More is at stake than the registering or reflecting of existing facts of power. Indeed, the underlying question is how the great people of China, who by a tragedy of history have been forcibly cut off from their own traditions and even led into war against the community of nations, can be enabled to achieve their own destinies and live with themselves and with the rest of the world in peace and tolerance.

This question, as we all know, has a long history. For twelve years past, ever since the Communist armies conquered the Chinese mainland and the Republic of China relocated its Government in Taipei, the community of nations has been confronted with a whole set of profoundly vexing problems. Most of them have arisen from aggressive military actions by the Chinese Communists - against Korea, against the Government of the Republic of China on its island refuge, against Tibet, and against South and Southeast Asia.

The problem before us, in its simplest terms, is this. The authorities who have carried out those aggressive actions, who have for twelve years been in continuous and violent defiance of the principles of the United Nations and of the resolutions of the General Assembly and deaf to the restraining pleas of law-abiding Members - these same warlike authorities claim the right to occupy the seat of China here, and demand that we eject from the United Nations the representatives of the Republic of China.

The gravity of this problem is heightened in its world-wide political and moral significance by the fact that the place of the Republic of China in the United Nations, since its founding in 1945, has been filled by its representatives with distinction - filled by representatives of a law-abiding Government which, under most difficult circumstances, has done its duty well and faithfully in the United Nations, and against which there is no ground for serious complaint, let alone expulsion.

The United States believes, as we have believed from the beginning, that the United Nations would make a tragic and perhaps irreparable mistake if it yielded to the claim of an aggressive and unregenerate "People's Republic of China" to replace the Republic of China in the United Nations. I realize that we have sometimes been charged with "unrealism", and even with "ignoring the existence of 600 million people" - to quote familiar phrases.

This seems to us a strange charge indeed. My country's soldiers fought with other soldiers of the United Nations in Korea for nearly three years against a huge invading army from the mainland of China. My country's negotiators have done their best, for nearly ten years, at Panmunjon, at Geneva, at Warsaw, to negotiate with the emissaries of Peking. Almost no country, I dare say, is more aware of the existence of these people than mine.

I think that it could be said with more justice that it would be dangerously unrealistic if this Assembly were to bow to the demands of Peking to expel and replace the Republic of China in the United Nations; it would be ignoring the warlike character and the aggressive behaviour of the rulers who dominate 600 million people and who talk of the inevitability of war as an article of faith and refuse to renounce the use of force.

To consider this subject in its proper light, we must see it against the background of the era in which we live. It is an era of sweeping revolutionary changes. We cannot clearly see the end. With dramatic swiftness the classic age of the empire is drawing to a close. More than one third of the Member States of the United Nations have won their independence since the United Nations itself was founded. Today, together with all other free and aspiring nations, they are working to perfect their independence by developing their economies and training their peoples. Already they play a vital part in the community of nations and in the work of this Organization.

Thus, for the first time on this grand scale, we have seen an imperial system end, not in violent convulsions and the succession of still another empire, but in the largely peaceful rise of new independent states - equal members of a world-wide community.

So diverse is that community in traditions and attitudes, so small and closely knit together is our modern world, so much do we have need of one another - and so frightful are the consequences of war - that all of us whose representatives gather in this General Assembly must more than ever be determined, as the Charter says, "To practice tolerance and live together in peace with one another as good neighbours." For there can be no independence any more except in a community - and there can be no community without tolerance.

Such is one of the great revolutionary changes of our time: a spectacular revolution of emancipation and hope. But this century has also bred more sinister revolutions born out of reaction to old injustices and out of the chaos of world war. These movements have brought into being a plague of warrior States - the scourge of our age. These regimes have been characterized not by democracy but by dictatorship; they have been concerned not with people but with power; not with the consent of the people but with control of the people; not with tolerance and conciliation but with hatred, falsehood and permanent struggle. They have varied in their names and in their ideologies but this has been their essential character.

Nowhere have these qualities been carried to a greater extreme, or on a grander scale, than on the mainland of China under Communist rule. The regime has attempted through intimidation, through hunger, through ceaseless agitation - and through a so-called commune system which even allied Communist States view with distaste - to reduce a brilliant and spirited civilization to a culture of military uniformity and iron discipline. Day and night, by poster, by loudspeaker and by public harangue, the people are reminded of their duty to hate the foreign enemy.

Into the international sphere these leaders have carried the same qualities of arrogance, of regimentation and of aggression. Many persons hoped, after their invasion of Korea ended, that they would thereupon give up the idea of foreign conquest. Instead they sponsored and supplied the communizing of North Vietnam; they resumed their warlike threats against Taiwan; they launched a campaign of armed conquest to end the autonomy of Tibet; and all along their southern borders they have pressed forward into new territory. To this day, in a fashion recalling the earlier authoritarian emperors of China, they pursue all these policies, and in addition seek to use the millions of Chinese residing abroad as agents of their political designs.

In fact, these modern Chinese imperialists have gone further than their imperial ancestors ever dreamed of going. There are at this time in Communist China, in training centres for guerrilla warfare, young men from Asia, from Africa and from Latin America being trained in sabotage and guerrilla tactics for eventual use in their own countries. Thus the strategy of what Mao Tse-tung calls "Protracted Revolutionary War in the Rural Areas," has become one of the principal world exports - and no longer an "Invisible Export" - of Communist China.

We have exact information about some of these activities. For example, we have the testimony of six young men from the Republic of Cameroun who travelled clandestinely from their country to the mainland of China last year. They arrived in China on 9 June; they left on 30 August. During that period they had a ten-week course from French-speaking instructors in a military academy outside Peking. The curriculum of this educational institution, taken from the syllabus that these men brought home, included such items as these - they make interesting reading: The correct use of explosives and grenades; Planning a sabotage operation; How to use explosives against houses, rails, bridges, tanks, guns, trucks, tractors, etc; Manufacture of explosives from easily obtained materials; Manufacture and use of mines and grenades; Use of semi-automatic rifles and carbines; Theory and practice of guerrilla warfare, ambushes, attacks on communications. And then there were political lectures with such titles as "The People's War", "The Party", "The United Front" and, of course, "The Imperialists Are Only Paper Tigers".

This, incidentally, was the fourth in a series of courses to train Camerounians to fight for the overthrow, not of European colonial rulers - for their rule had already ended - but of their own sovereign African Government.

Such an affinity for aggressive violence, and for subversive interference in other countries, is against all the rules of the civilized world; but it accords with the outlook and objective of the rulers in Peking. It was the supreme leader of Chinese Communism, Mao Tsetung, who summed up his world outlook in these words: "Everything can be made to grow out of the barrel of a gun." And again, to quote him: "The central duty and the highest form of revolution is armed seizure of political power and the settling of problems by means of war. This Marxist-Leninist principle is universally correct, whether in China or in foreign countries; it is always true."

President Tito of Yogoslavia knows to what extremes this dogma of violence has been carried. In a speech to his people in 1958, he quoted the "Chinese Leaders" as saying with apparent complacency "that in any possible war. . . there would still be 300 million left; that is to say, 300 million would get killed and 300 million would be left behind. . . ."

In an age when reasonable men throughout the world fear and detest the thought of nuclear war, from the Chinese Communist thinkers there comes the singular boast that, after such a war, "on the debris of a dead imperialism the victorious people would create with extreme rapidity a civilization thousands of times higher than the capitalist system and a truly beautiful future for themselves."

In fact, only three months ago it was the same Chinese Communist leaders who officially acclaimed the resumption of atmospheric nuclear tests by the Soviet Union as, "A powerful inspiration to all peoples striving for world peace." What a queer idea of world peace.

With such a record and with such a philosophy of violence and of fanaticism, no wonder this regime, after twelve years still has no diplomatic relations with almost two-thirds of the Governments of the world. One cannot help wondering what the representatives of such a predatory regime would contribute in our United Nations Councils to the solutions of the many dangerous questions which confront us.

I believe these facts are enough to show how markedly Communist China has deviated from the pattern of progress and peace embodied in our Charter and toward which the community of nations is striving. In its present mood it is a massive and brutal threat to man's very survival. Its gigantic power, its reckless ambition and its unconcern for human values, make it the major world problem.

Now - what is to be done about this problem? And what in particular can the United Nations do?

The problem is, in reality, age-old. How can those who prize tolerance and humility, those whose faith commands them to "love those that hate you", how can they make a just reply to the arrogant, the rapacious and the bitterly intolerant? To answer with equal intolerance would be to betray our humane values. But to answer with meek submission or with a convenient pretense that wrong is not really wrong-- this would betray the institutions on which the future of a peaceful world depend.

There are some who acknowledge the illegal and aggressive conduct of the Chinese Communists, but who believe that the United Nations can somehow accommodate this unbridled power, and bring it in some measure under the control - or at least the influence - of the community of nations. They maintain that this can be accomplished by bringing Communist China unconditionally into participation in the United Nations. By this step - so we are told - the interplay of ideas and interests in the United Nations would sooner or later cause these latter-day empire builders to abandon their warlike ways and accommodate themselves to the rule of law and the comity of nations.

This is a serious view and I intend to discuss it seriously. Certainly we must never abandon hope of winning over even the most stubborn antagonist.

But reason born of sober experience obliges us to restrain our wishful thoughts. There are four principal reasons which I think are of overriding importance, and I most earnestly urge the Assembly to consider them with great care, for the whole future of the United Nations may be at stake.

My first point is that the step advocated, once taken, is irreversible. We cannot try it and then give it up if it fails to work. Given the extraordinary and forbidding difficulty of expulsion under the Charter, we must assume that, once in our midst, the Peking representatives would stay - for better or for worse.

Secondly, there are ample grounds to suspect that a power given to such bitter words and ruthless actions as those of the Peking regime, far from being reformed by its experience in the United Nations, would be encouraged by its success in gaining admission to exert, all the more forcefully, by threats and manoevres, a most disruptive and demoralizing influence on the Organization at this critical moment in its history.

Thirdly, its admission, in circumstances in which it continues to violate and to defy the principles of the Charter, could seriously shake public confidence in the United Nations - I can assure you it would do so among the people of the United States - and this alone would significantly weaken the Organization.

Elementary prudence requires the General Assembly to reflect that there is no sign or record of any intension to pursue a course of action consistent with the Charter. Indeed, the signs all point the other way. The Peking authorities have shown nothing but contempt for the United Nations. They go out of their way to deprecate it and to insult its Members. They refuse to abandon the use of force in the Taiwan Straits. They continue to encroach on the territorial integrity of other States. They apparently do not even get along very well with the Soviet Union.

Fourth, and with particular emphasis, let me recall to the attention of my fellow representatives the explicit conditions which the Chinese Communists themselves demand to be fulfilled before they will deign to accept a seat in the United Nations. I quote here their Prime Minister, Chou En-Lai:

"The United Nations must expel the Chiang Kai-shek clique and restore China's legitimate rights, otherwise it would be impossible for China to have anything to do with the United Nations."

Now in this short sentence are two impossible demands. The first is that we should expel from the United Nations the Republic of China. The second, "to restore China's legitimate rights," in this context and in the light of Peking's persistent demands, can have only one meaning: that the United Nations should acquiesce in Communist China's design to conquer Taiwan and the 11 million people who live there, and thereby contribute to the overthrow and the abolition of the independent Government of the Republic of China.

The effrontery of these demands is shocking. The Republic of China, which we are asked to expel and whose conquest and overthrow we are asked to approve, is one of the founding Members of the United Nations. Its rights in this Organization extend in an unbroken life from 1945, when the Charter was framed and went into effect, to the present.

The Republic of China is a Charter Member of this Organization. The seat of the Republic of China is not empty; it is occupied and should continue to be occupied by the able representatives of the Government of the Republic of China.

The fact that control over the Chinese mainland was wrested from the Government of the Republic of China by force of arms, and its area of actual control was thus greatly reduced, does not in the last justify expulsion, or alter the legitimate rights of that Government.

The de jure authority of the Government of the Republic of China extends throughout the territory of China. Its effective jurisdiction extends over an area of over 14,000 square miles, an area greater than the territory of Albania, Belgium, Cyprus, El Salvador, Haiti, Israel, Lebanon or Luxembourg - all of them Member States of the United Nations. It extends over 11 million people, that is, over more people than exist in the territory of sixty-five United Nations Members. Its effective control, in other words, extends over more people than does the legal jurisdiction of two-thirds of the Governments represented here. The economic and social standard of living of the people under its jurisdiction is one of the highest in all Asia, and is incomparably higher than the standard prevailing on the mainland. The progressive agrarian policy of the Government of the Republic of China and its progress in political, economic and cultural affairs contrast starkly with the policies of the rulers in Peking under whom the unhappy lot of the mainland people has been but little but oppression, communes, famine and cruelty.

All those who have served with the representatives of the Republic of China in the United Nations know their integrity and know their loyalty to the Charter, which we all respect, their high standards of conduct, their unfailing dignity and courtesy, their contributions, and their consistent devotion to the principles and the success of our Organization.

The notion of expelling the Republic of China is thus absurd and unthinkable. But what are we to say of the other condition sought by Peking - that the United Nations stand aside and let them conquer Taiwan and the 11,000,000 people who live there? In effect, Peking is asking the United Nations to set its seal of approval in advance upon what would be as massive a resort to arms as the world has witnessed since the end of World War II. Of course, the United Nations will never stultify itself in such a way.

The issue we face is, among other things, this question - whether it is right for the United Nations to drive the Republic of China from this Organization in order to make room for a regime whose aggressive appetite seems to be insatiable. It is whether we intend to abandon the Charter requirement that all United Nations Members be peace-loving and to give our implicit blessing to an aggressive and bloody war against those Chinese who are still free in Taiwan. What an invitation to aggression the Soviet proposal would be - and what a grievous blow to the good name of the United Nations.

In these circumstances the United States earnestly believes that it is impossible to speak seriously today of "bringing Communist China into the United Nations." No basis exists on which such a step could be taken. We believe that we must first do just the opposite: we must instead find a way to bring the United Nations - its law and its spirit - back into the whole territory of China.

The root of the problem lies, as it has lain from the beginning, in the hostile, callous, and seemingly intractable minds of the rulers of the mainland. Let those members who advocate Peking's admission seek to exert upon its rulers whatever benign influence they can, in the hope of persuading them to accept the standards of the community of nations. Let those rulers respond to these appeals; let them give up trying to impose their demands on this Organization; let them cease their aggression, direct and indirect, and their threats of aggression; let them show respect for the rights of others; let them recognize and accept the independence and diversity of culture and institutions among their neighbors.

Therefore, let the Assembly declare the transcendent importance of this question of the representation of China. Let us reaffirm the position which the General Assembly took ten years ago, that such a question as this "should be considered in the light of the purposes of the Charter."

The issue on which peace and the future of Asia so greatly depend is not simply whether representatives from Peking should take a place in the General Assembly. More profoundly still, it is whether the United Nations, with its universal purposes of peace and tolerance, shall be permitted to take its rightful place in the minds of the people of all of China.

Today the rulers in Peking still repeat the iron maxim of Mao Tsetung: "All political power grows out of the barrel of a gun." If that maxim had been followed, the United Nations would never have been created, and this world would long since have been blanketed with lethal radioactive ashes. It is an obsolete maxim, and the sooner it is abandoned, the sooner the people of all of China are allowed to resume their traditionally peaceful policies, the better for the world.

The United States will vote against the Soviet draft resolution and give its full support to the continued participation of the representatives of the Government of the Republic of China in the United Nations.

No issue remaining before the United Nations this year has such fateful consequences for the future of this Organization. The vital significance which would be attached to any alteration of the current situation needs no explanation. The United States has therefore joined today with the delegations of Australia, Colombia, Italy and Japan in presenting a resolution under which the Assembly would determine that any proposal to change the representation of China would be considered an important question in accordance with the Charter. Indeed, it would be hard to consider such a proposal in any other light, and we trust it will be solidly endorsed by the Assembly.

Mr. Malalasekera (Ceylon): The views of my Government, my people and my delegation on the issue before us are already well known. We hold, as we have always held, that a people m u s t be represented in the United Nations by those who are their effective G o v e r n m e n t. I stress the word "effective," because we thereby want to say that representation which affects the daily lives of the people through the economic, social and political efforts of the United Nations can be carried out only by the day-to-day partnership and hourly collaboration of a people and its Government. This is obviously what the then Secretary-General had in mind when he wrote his letter of 8 March 1950 to the President of the Security Council, contained in document S/1466. H e r e i s part of what he said:

"This Article"--meaning Article 4 of the Charter--"requires that an applicant for membership must be able and willing to carry out the obligations of membership. The obligations of membership can be carried out only by Governments which in fact possess the power to do so. Where a revolutionary Government presents itself as representing a State, in rivalry to an e x i s t i n g Government, the question at issue s h o u l d be which of these two Governments in fact is in a position to employ the resources and and direct the people of the State in fulfilment of the obligations of membership. In essence, this means an inquiry as to whether the new Government exercises effective authority within the t e r r i t o r y of the S t a t e and is habitually obeyed by the bulk of the population.

"If so, it would seem to be appropriate for the United Nations organs, through their collective action, to accord it the right to r e p r e s e n t the State in the Organization, even though individual Members of the Organization refuse, and may continue to refuse, to accord it recognition as the l a w f u l Government for reasons which are valid under their national policies."

These t h i n g s are well known. Equally well known are the arguments for and against which are adduced in this controversy. Indeed we all k n o w them by h e a r t after twelve years of airing them on a procedural level.

But now for the f i r s t time we are discussing this issue on a substantive level. There is the danger that in the next ten days to two weeks we shall expend much time and energy rehashing the old arguments. I s h a l l try my best to avoid this and to deal with the new aspects, whatever new factors can be extracted.

Among these new factors, there is a new American administration and, of c o u r s e, there is its distinguished

Ambassador, Governor Adlai Stevenson for whom, personally, I have great respect and, may I be allowed to add, even affection. I followed him with great attention when in a somewhat formidable manner he presented his case against a positive solution of the China issue.

Mr. Stevenson's statement, I must confess to my regret, I found a little puzzling, because there are apparently not only two Chinas but two streams of thinking in the United States delegation. There seem to be those who supply the brilliant premises and also, alas, others who insist on arriving at the same old conclusions, the wrong conclusions. Take, for instance, these brilliant words, sweeping and majestic in their scope. Speaking of the ever-expanding family of nations, the United States statement said:

"This very Assembly, in its majestic diversity, is both a physical symbol and a practical embodiment--however imperfect--of that transcendent vision."(A/PV. 1069, pp. 2-3.) Further on the United States statement resumes this theme of "majestic diversity" and says:

"So diverse is that community in traditions and attitudes, so small and closely knit together is our modern world, so much do we have need of one another--and so frightful are the consequences of war--that all of us whose representatives gather in this General Assembly must more than ever be determined, as the Charter says, 'To practice tolerance and live together in peace with one another as good neighbours'." (A/PV. 1069, p. 6).

These are noble words and excellent arguments. They are especially good arguments for the universal representation of all people in the United Nations and they are based on an eloquent interpretation of the Charter which the United States statement quotes with such approval.

Now let us imagine to ourselves that some day in an age of Utopia and reason the same delegation is instructed by its Government by some strange and unforeseen development, perhaps by an affiliation against another mighty Communist State, to plead for the seating of mainland China. Could it find words better fitted to speak in favour of the admission of the People's Republic of China? I do not think so.

But then the United States statement embarks on a long journey to nowhere when it sets forth in its discussion of regimes. Where in the Charter, I ask, is the United Nations described as an Organization of regimes? The United Nations Charter in its first three words, "We the peoples," establishes at once the hegemony of peoples. There is no mention here of regimes but only of peoples.

The United Nations programmes also are for peoples. The great revolution of our time, which the United States statement so eloquently described, is the revolution of the common people. The United Nations programme for under-developed areas, the United Nations social programme, the United Nations programme for children, the various agencies for health and food and culture--all these are for people, not for regimes.

Therefore the paramount question we must consider is the question not of regimes but of people. In China there are 650 million people, one-quarter of the human race. These 650 million people are not represented in the United Nations. It is true that somebody in Taiwan claims to represent them. The United States statement claims that that somebody does in fact represent them. We cannot and do not agree with this claim. Let us make it clear that we have no personal quarrel with the representatives from Taiwan. We have no desire at all to refer to them except in terms of great courtesy and correctness. Neither do we approve, therefore, of some of the unfortunate phraseology used in reference to them in the Soviet draft resolution.

But we are forced by the realities of the situation to ask a question: Has the r e g i m e in Taiwan, which makes that claim, implemented any of the programmes that I have men-tioned earlier, for the b e n e f i t of these 650 million people who live on the mainland of China? The answer is an em-phatic no. How then can we morally justify a world Organ-ization which d e n i e s to so many m i l l i o n s of people the ordinary benefits of existence?

I am not s p e a k i n g here of any abstraction alien to the United States Government, a Government which speaks so much of "people-to-people programmes." The United States Government is very intelligently a w a r e of the difference between regimes and peoples.

In this connection the statement I refer to has struck off a clever bit of counterpoint. It says, in so many words, Let us not b r i n g the Chinese People's Republic into the United Nations, but rather let us bring the U n i t e d Nations to the Chinese people. Good. But how does the United States pro-pose to do this? By sending them a United Nations flag? Or shall we send them 650 m i l l i o n copies of the Charter, or perhaps 650 million copies of the United States statement?

I submit, there is only one way to bring the United Nations to the Chinese people or to any other people, and that is by admitting them to membership of this world Organization. Then we shall have a United Nations literature in China. We shall have--as we have in the Soviet Union--a Chinese As-sociation for the United Nations. We shall Have United Nations agencies for China.

Let me cite an illustration. Throughout the life of the

League of Nations the United States Government kept the American people out of the League. Then came World War II. The most intelligent and enlightened Americans--Mr. Stevenson among them--rightly pointed out the danger to the American people of being isolated from a world community. It was even said at the time that this isolationism may have actually contributed to the coming of the Second World War. The problem was how to win over the American people to this great co-operative enterprise after years of isolationism. Well, eventually the United Nations was brought into the United States and that is where we are now. But before this happened it was found necessary for the United States first to become a Member of the United Nations, and through being a Member of the United Nations the American people made this brilliant and historic transition from isolationism to internationalism, one of the most brilliant and constructive evolutions effected by any people anywhere.

Now, the United States, having abandoned American isolationism, preaches the doctrine of enforced isolationism for the Chinese people. If the isolationism of a big Power like America probably contributed to World War II, could it not be deduced, by the same thinking, that a similar isolation of a big Power like China might well become a contributing factor to World War III?

Beyond this, there is really not much more to say. All else--this discussion of how good or how bad certain regimes are; this talk about "dictatorship"; this talk about the system of "communes" in China--seems to my delegation a heap of irrelevancies. Dictatorships indeed! If the United Nations, in 1945 and thereafter, had kept out all the peoples who lived under one dictatorship or another, who but a handful of nations would be here today? The United States has friendly relations with many Governments controlled by dictatorial power, and some of the allies of the United States that started out with parliamentary experiments have later turned to dictatorship, some of them, strangely enough, on the excuse that dictatorial regimes could make better use of American economic aid. Is the "good" Chinese regime in Taiwan a model of democracy? There have been four Presidents in the United States during the reign of Chiang Kai-shek. It is worth recalling that Chiang Kai-shek has been in power much longer than Mao Tse-tung.

No, we shall get nowhere at all if we get lost in the bewildering jungle of passing judgment on political regimes as a qualification for Membership in the United Nations. It would not be difficult at all for my delegation or any other to produce a list of dictators enjoying the friendship and even the aid of the United States. And let me add that in saying this I make no criticism of any Government b e f o r e this Assembly.

Then of course, t h e r e is the very much worn-out and dog-eared catalogue of China's aggressions. The United States statement mentioned Korea, Tibet, South East Asia. Let us take Korea because that is cited as a flagrant case.

The Korean War broke out in 1950. The Chinese People's Republic was set up in 1949. The United States statement cites C h i n e s e intervention in the Korean War as a reason for not admitting the Chinese People's Republic to this Organization. Did the United States express great enthusiasm in support of the Chinese demand for a seat in the United Nations b e f o r e the K o r e a n War broke out? I have no such recollection. The truth is that United States opposition was not due to China's intervention in Korea, but rather to China's socialist system--and that remains true even today. All the other reasons are so much new cellophane wrapping on the same old package.

Speaking of the Korean War, perhaps that war need never have broken out at all if the Chinese People's Republic had been in the United Nations at that time. Some of the older Members here may recall how at Lake Success the United States, aware of China's fears, sought through various United Nations agencies to allay those fears with unofficial assurances that the United Nations armies in Korea would not cross the Yalu River. But China was not at the United Nations to accept those assurances. On the other hand, non-recognition tended to keep China's fears and suspicions alive. Perhaps the United States Government could have saved its people all those terrible casualties if the true representatives of China had been around the Security Council table and in the Assembly hall, where rising tensions leading to the war might have been anticipated, discussed, reduced and blunted, as they frequently are here. It might be pertinent to ask, would the United S t a t e s be more a f r a i d or less afraid if the Soviet Union were not in the United Nations? There are scores of speeches by United States officials to the American people explaining why it is better that the S o v i e t U n i o n is in the United Nations. The American people are told, for instance, that it is better to have the Soviet Union in the Organization here where the United States can keep an eye on it--or, as it is sometimes said, "Better a war of words than a war of bullets"; or as it is also said, at the United Nations the Soviet system could be "exposed"; or, in the U n i t e d Nations this "bad" Soviet Union can be made amenable to benevolent influences; or, at the United Nations, informal consultations could be had such as solved the Berlin crisis in 1949. Mr. Stevenson himself has sometimes used these arguments to explain why it is better for an allegedly warlike nation to be in the United Nations, rather than out of it. Why can we not apply the same arguments to the Chinese People's Republic? The United States statement speaks of the warlike aims of the Peking Government. This argument is based on two things; on China's pronouncements with regard to war and peace in the cold war and on certain directives issued in the training guerilla units.

On this point, I must note that Mr. Kennedy, the President of the United States, recently announced a new training programme for guerillas. I am certain that the manual of arms which is issued to them is not a memo on passive resistance. Mr. Mao Tse-tung allegedly spoke of using nuclear bombs. Can we say in this connection that we have an outright commitment from the nuclear Members of the United Nations that they will never use nuclear bombs? And it is they that have them, while Peking does not have any nuclear bombs. Surely we have more reason to fear Governments who have the bombs and will not say that they will never use them than we have of Governments who say they will use bombs but who, in fact, have no bombs to use.

Reading the United States statement, one gets an impression of a Hollywood script, long out of fashion, in which everybody is good except the villain. At this very moment I see before me here the faces of a number of delegations whose governmental policies and actions in certain parts of the world have been described by other delegations as "warlike". I need not call the roll of the territories, particularly in Africa, where full-scale wars are not being conducted by Western nations, some of them democracies, not against regimes but against people. I refer to Algeria, Angola, Oman, South Africa, Bizerta. Who attacked in the Suez? Does the United States delegation therefore want us to expel all of these warlike Governments? Then there are other Governments which, not I but Mr. Stevenson, would call warlike. Would we expel them? These Governments, in turn, call the Government of the United States warlike. Should they, then, ask for the expulsion of the United States?

Who is going to be the judge? Who is to judge? We do pass judgments on each other on various issues--sometimes much too freely--but we do so because we know that as long as we do it in the United Nations, as Members of the Organization, there is a chance that warlike policies, words and actions can be turned to the ways of peace.

This is not only a house of peace; it is the school of peace where all nations come to learn the lessons of peace. None, therefore, should be kept out of it. The United States statement has expressed fear of making what it calls an "irreversible" decision. As I understand it, the thinking of this Administration on the question of China was not as positive on the issue as the United States statement would seem to convey, according to United States Press reports themselves. The Administration, it was once reported, was inclined to reverse its policy on China and then it was reported that, under great pressure, the reversal was reversed. At what stage in this pondering were the arguments advanced in the United States statement correct?

Let me turn back to the major issue, which is whether a Government can be so judged as to affect either its membership or its desire for membership in the United Nations. It so happens that while Mr. Stevenson was talking in this hall on the China issue, two floors below in the Fourth Committee, at exactly the same time, the American delegate strongly denounced the apartheid policies in the Union of South Africa. The American delegate had some harsh words to say about the policies of the Union Government. Some delegates called the policies genocidal; I think that this is the highest form of destruction and the lowest form of war. But when certain delegates suggested that these policies disqualified the Union of South Africa from continued membership in the Organization, did the United States representative support that stand? He did not even support less drastic sanctions. Yet in the case of the Peking regime, the United States would apply the highest sanction of all--excommunication from this world community. I use the word excommunication in its harshest historic meaning, which amounts to a death sentence.

Let us assume that the United States, as Mr. Stevenson says, abhors the regime but is concerned with the plight of the Chinese people. Then why keep the Chinese People's Republic out of the specialized agencies, most of whose programmes are humanitarian? Much is said about the lack of food in China, a sad plight in which the Food and Agricultural Organization could have been of assistance. The same could be said of the World Health Organization. But the United States fought every attempt to give the People's Republic of China membership even in those agencies.

What the United States is waging is not a war against a regime; it is a war against the Chinese people. This is a blockage, an embargo. It is a Western-imposed iron curtain.

The United States statement cites the failure of Peking to conclude negotiations at Panmunjom, at Geneva, and at Warsaw which, it says proved futile although, Mr. Stevenson says, "My country's negotiators have done their best." This is a strange admission for a country that has a fabulous reputation for doing its best--a best which invariably ends in success. Is it possible that perhaps these negotiations might

have made a little more progress and even ended successfully if both negotiating States had been Members in the United Nations ?

Let me turn for a moment to the four reasons given in the
United States statement for not making a decision now. The
first reason is that the decision would be "irreversible." I
fail to understand this argument, I must confess. I hope, in
the name of the universality which we all desire, that all
membership in the United Nations is irreversible and that,
unlike the League of Nations, the United Nations will never
cease to exist as a result of reversible membership.

The second argument is that the Peking delegation here
might be "a most disruptive and demoralizing influence." In
answer to this argument, we might consider the record of
the United Nations. It seems to me that the question of
China's representation here has been more disruptive and
demoralizing than anything any new State could do. It is a
strange theory and, to me, utterly contradictory to the philosophy of a world organization that representation, rather
than non-representation, could undermine the United Nations.
The United Nations, we would have thought, was by common
acceptance the world's answer and antidote to the disruptive
forces which begot two world wars.

We could go further and state that this cold war between
the United Nations and the Chinese People's Republic, which
the United States statement seeks to promulgate, is today
one of the most dangerous challenges to the peace of the
world--so disruptive, so demoralizing that tomorrow it could
be one thousand times as great as the threat of Berlin.

Let us look at things a little more closely. There are
other disruptive elements in the United Nations. We have
representatives here who refuse to take their seats when
their interests are under discussion. We have many States
which refuse, at least temporarily, to accept Assembly
decisions. Who is disrupting the United Nations in the Congo ?
Shall those who are responsible be expelled ? We heard the

United States representative tell the General Assembly that
his Government could not accept the resolution on the moratorium on test explosions, that it could not accept the resolution on the denuclearization of Africa, that it could not accept
the resolution leading to a ban on the use of terror weapons
in wartime. Is that attitude constructive, or disruptive ?
There have been charges of disruption in the selection of the
Acting Secretary-General, in the assessments on the Congo.
The United States statement bristles with moral judgments
and self-righteousness.

How are we to judge ? Who is to pass judgment ? Obviously, no Government in the world is without sin. Judgment, it seems to me, should be reserved to the world community, and then only with the greatest caution. Unilateral judgments, apart from being unobjective, are too frequently regarded as acts of hostility.

The third reason given in the United States statement is that the seating of the Peiping delegation would seriously shake public confidence in the United Nations. If public confidence in the United Nations were shaken every time some Government offended it in one way or another, the United Nations would have been dead long ago. Fortunately, the moral strength of world public opinion is a hardier plant than the Governments which represent it. It is part of the glorious chapter of modern times and a supreme expression of true faith in the future that world public opinion has stood by the United Nations through thick and thin and in its darkest moments. World opinion, if it is to be defined, means the public opinion of all the peoples of the world, and not of a world divided.

Why do some people wish to perpetuate an indefinitely protracted situation of bitterness, of harsh words, pitting the great people of the United States--175 million of them-- against 650 million people of China, an ancient people of glorious achievements, a people who have seen and lived through many regimes and who do not need the United Nations to give them a lesson in the ways of peace? Experiments in peace were made in China centuries ago, culminating in the doctrines of Lao Tse and Confucius. These are hopeful traditions in the great history of China. These traditions will emerge here in this great laboratory of peace with a new vigour and a rediscovery.

The United States statement wishes the General Assembly of the United Nations to pass a judgment on Peiping's claim to Taiwan. Well, for ten or twelve years we have heard about Taiwan and Korea and other places as reasons for avoiding a positive decision. But let us ask: Have we succeeded in settling these problems with the Chinese People's Republic outside the United Nations?

To complete its lurid picture of an "unregenerate" Government in Peiping--that was the word used--and of a Government which cannot get along with anybody, the United States statement says:"They"--meaning the Chinese People's Republic--"apparently do not even get along very well with the USSR." I should have thought that, given the United States attitude to the USSR, it would welcome that Government into the United Nations if only for that very reason. At any rate, if the USSR is worried about it, if Moscow is afraid of Peiping's future might, the USSR is taking another course--it is the Soviet Union which is leading the campaign to bring Peiping into the United Nations.

I have mentioned the wall of hatred which, it seems to me, its present policy on China is building between the American and the Chinese peoples. It is my delegation's sincere conviction that such a policy cannot add to the security of America. This is the nuclear and missile age. The people who were the first to invest gunpowder will not lose too much time in becoming a nuclear Power--even without outside aid. When that day comes, the United States will be confronted by two mighty nuclear Powers, and that two-front war which was America's nightmare in the Second World War will re-emerge as the double nuclear front of the future.

The General Assembly is now trying desperately to hold the dissemination and spread of these nuclear weapons. If the Chinese People's Republic is seated here now, at this session, there is a good chance that we might head off such a development in one of the world's largest areas. China is building its economy and its social system with national plans which will require decades and which will tax all the national resources which it can muster. Thus engaged, it cannot afford now to divert billions in order to match the existing nuclear Powers. But if China is pushed to the wall or isolated from the forces of peace in the United Nations, it will find itself forced to build for itself a mighty fortress against those who make themselves its enemies. Does anyone doubt that mighty China will meet that challenge? When that day comes, China will be the only nuclear Power outside the United Nations. That, we submit, would be positively dangerous. If the United States Government really believes all it says about the warlike attitude of China, then it seems to me that it should do everything in its power to scotch this cold war and hatred as quickly as possible. Six hundred and fifty million people isolated from the world community of nations and compelled to build themselves into a mighty fortress, soon with nuclear and missile weapons, goaded by harsh words, taunts and insults, can never add to the security of the world. The greatest single reason for seating Peiping now is that it may spare the world another big nuclear Power. And this would be a contribution to world peace worth working for.

But if we miss this opportunity--and next year may be too late in the current high-speed armaments race--the United Nations and world peace itself will be not only disrupted but wrecked and will open the way for one quarter of the world fully armed outside the United Nations. Against this mighty war machine, that puny procedural paper resolution, in which five Powers have joined, will become the comedy of history and the tragedy of mankind. My delegation would like to say, with all respect but with the utmost seriousness, that this procedural obstructionism is unworthy of a delegation representing the wonderful American people, and that we most sincerely hope it will be brought to a halt.

We have talked of what the United Nations can do for China. But this Organization is not a one-way street. There is much that China can do for the United Nations. The Chinese people have much to offer in science, in culture and in industry. Its great strides in these fields have been a loss to the specialized agencies. Economically, China is a mighty laboratory in the way in which a nation can pull itself up by its own bootstraps from under-development. Politically, it is a giant in the rising tide of nationalism which has given birth to many new States and will produce many more as our decolonization programme accelerates. Both in terms of production and consumption, China's mighty population will always be an important factor in world trade.

The important resolutions adopted in the Second Committee of the Assembly, on the promotion of world trade, on industrialization, on the opening of new markets for one-commodity nations and the building of a world planned economy, on the building of the regional autonomy through ECAFE --all these resolutions must remain only partially implemented when the present and potential economic forces of China are left out.

One of these resolutions speaks of making available the benefit of central planning to under-developed countries. Regardless of ideologies, the great experiments and achievements of China in this respect cannot be ignored. They are too valuable a lesson to many new smaller nations desperately hunting for blue-prints in planned economies.

Many nations are now receiving such aid from the Chinese People's Republic bilaterally. China is highly developed medically, socially and scientifically. It is a country whose people and whose leaders are consumed with an unceasing ambition to build a nation from the remnants of colonialist fragmentization into a nationalist unity, seeking a social order based on justice and self-sufficiency.

I could go on indefinitely listing the great benefits which China can make in the fields of technical assistance, engineering, land reform, flood control, the building of dams, irrigation, literacy and education.

When the West says "no" to all these, let us recall the great contribution which China made to the early history of Western Civilization. The caravans moving from the Italian cities to China for its textiles, its art, its culture, is one of the most dramatic chapters in the history of modern civilization.

The nations of the world are being asked to ignore, to bypass, to snub that daring vision and imagination of the Italian and Arab traders who built a golden bridge across oceans, mountains, and deserts to bring China to Europe. In other words, we are being asked to throw progress back by 1,000 years.

Is this the time to move backward in the world which Mr. Stevenson so eloquently described as revolutionary? The United States is the country of the revolution of 1776, and China is the country of the revolution of 1948. In the historic perspective it is the same revolution in different forms. All modern revolutions--the French, the Russian and those of other countries--are a part of that great tidal wave of humanity increasing in vast numbers, marching across the globe and filling every inch of it with hundreds of different cultures.

In this vast and complicated panorama of change, these revolutions have sometimes developed into different and sometimes opposing patterns. The League of Nations was born to resolve the clashes of nations. The United Nations is challenged to resolve the clashes of revolutions. They can be resolved only if they are all represented in this World Organization, and they must be resolved not only in the settling of disputes but even more so in those positive and creative elements which arise from co-operative efforts. Peace in our time can be made not so much by stopping the aggressor as by the organization of a community of peoples in which no nation will find aggression desirable, necessary or even possible.

Therefore, we say that it is essential to bring the United Nations to China and China to the United Nations so that not only their joint economic co-operation but also their joint co-operation can become the epic of peace in our time.

For these reasons the issue under discussion here is not a procedural issue except as a simple matter of credentials. It is an issue which strikes at the deepest roots of the question of war and peace in Asia and in the whole world. We have made a correct decision in abandoning petty procedural tactics in dealing with this great problem and we are now for the first time dealing with it in a substantive manner. Let us have the courage to take the next bold step and dispose of this issue once and for all. Representatives who have an effective and a de facto relationship with the 650 million people of China seated in this House could make one of the greatest contributions to the universality of this Organization by admitting China. Such action could make this Assembly emerge from its present session with splendour. It could make the biggest contribution to peace which the United Nations can make today. Let us, here and now, resolve to make that contribution with vision and unflinching courage.

US Senate, 79th Congress, First Session, Hearings Before the Committee on Foreign Relations, 10 July 1945.

Hearings . . . on the Charter of the United Nations, 10–13 July 1945 [Revised], pp. 309–12.

Senator MILLIKIN.   I notice several reiterations of the thought of the Charter that the Organization shall not interfere with domestic affairs of any country.   How can you get into these social questions and economic questions without conducting investigations and making inquiries in the various countries?

Mr. PASVOLSKY.   Senator, the Charter provides that the Assembly shall have the right to initiate or make studies in all of these economic or social fields.   It is provided that the Economic and Social Council through its commissions and its staff, would be assembling information in the fields that would be necessary for the performance of its duties.   It is provided that the Economic and Social Council would arrange for reports from the specialized agencies, and presumably would arrange for receiving any kind of information that it might need.   The Economic and Social Council is also given the power to make arrangements with the Member States for reports as to steps taken to give effect to recommendations.

Senator MILLIKIN.   Might the activities of the Organization concern themselves with, for example, wage rates and working conditions in different countries?

Mr. PASVOLSKY.   The question of what matters the Organization would be concerned with would depend upon whether or not they had international repercussions.   This Organization is concerned with international problems.   International problems may arise out of all sorts of circumstances.

Senator MILLIKIN.   Could the Organization concern itself with tariff policies of the various countries?

Mr. PASVOLSKY.   The Organization would of course consider questions that arose out of tariff or commercial policies.   But it is very important to note here that the Economic and Social Council can make recommendations to governments generally, rather than to specific governments.

Senator MILLIKIN.   Only to governments generally?

Mr. PASVOLSKY.   Yes.

Senator MILLIKIN.   The reports and recommendations naturally might refer to specific governments?

Mr. PASVOLSKY.   Oh, they might refer to specific conditions, naturally.

Senator MILLIKIN. They would have to be built up out of investigations made of or in specific countries?

Mr. PASVOLSKY. Yes.

Senator MILLIKIN. Could such an Organization concern itself with various forms of discrimination which countries maintain for themselves, bloc currency, subsidies to merchant marine, and things of that kind?

Mr. PASVOLSKY. I should think that the Organization would wish to discuss and consider them. It might even make recommendations on any matters which affect international economic or social relations. The League of Nations did. The International Labor Office has done that. This new Organization being created will be doing a great deal of that.

Senator MILLIKIN. A recommendation along any of those lines, under the basic theory of the whole Organization, would have a powerful effect against an offending nation, would it not?

Mr. PASVOLSKY. The whole document is based on the assumption that recommendations by an agency of this sort would have considerable effect.

Senator MILLIKIN. Let me invite your attention, Doctor, to the fact that we are relatively a "have" nation, in a world of "have not" nations. Might we not find a great number of recommendations focused against us that could finally engender a lot of ill will and might lead to serious difficulties, assuming we did not care to correct them under the recommendations?

Mr. PASVOLSKY. Well, I do not think that there would be any more ill will engendered by the fact that a discussion of that sort takes place. Recommendations would be made to nations in general that certain practices should not be tolerated.

Senator MILLIKIN. Are you not providing means whereby complaints may be focused against ourselves in an official way?

Mr. PASVOLSKY. Complaints can be made at any time and in any way. What is important is that we are providing here a mechanism by means of which maladjustments can be corrected and, therefore, fewer complaints made.

Senator MILLIKIN. Would the investigation of racial discriminations be within the jurisdiction of this body?

Mr. PASVOLSKY. Insofar, I imagine, as the Organization takes over the function of making studies and recommendations on human rights, it may wish to make studies in those fields and make pronouncements.

Senator VANDENBERG. At that point I wish you would reemphasize what you read from the Commission Report specifically applying the exemption of domestic matters to the Social and Economic Council.

Mr. PASVOLSKY. I will read that paragraph again.

Senator VANDENBERG. Yes, please.

Mr. PASVOLSKY. (reading):
"The members of Committee 3 of Commission II are in full agreement that nothing contained in chapter IX can be construed as giving authority to the Organization to intervene in the domestic affairs of Member states."

The CHAIRMAN [Senator Connally]. And, furthermore, whether they do involves no compulsion whatever, but is in the nature of recommendations to the States, and the States are perfectly free to take such recommendations or reject them.

Mr. PASVOLSKY. Quite right.

Senator MILLIKIN. Is there any other international aspect to a labor problem or a racial problem or a religious problem that does not originate domestically?   .   .   .

Mr. PASVOLSKY. Well, Senator, I suppose we can say that there is no such thing as an international problem that is not related to national problems, because the word "international" itself means that there are nations involved. What domestic jurisdiction relates to here, I should say, as it does in all of these matters, is that there are certain matters which are handled internally by nations which do not affect other nations or may not affect other nations. On the other hand, there are certainly many matters handled internally which do affect other nations and which by international law are considered to be of concern to other nations.

Senator MILLIKIN. For example, let me ask you if this would be true. It is conceivable that there are racial questions on the southern shores of the Mediterranean that might have very explosive effects under some circumstances; but they originate locally, do they not, Doctor?

Mr. PASVOLSKY. Yes.

Senator MILLIKIN. And because they might have explosive effects, this Organization might concern itself with them; is that correct?

Mr. PASVOLSKY. It might, if somebody brings them to the attention of the Organization.

Senator MILLIKIN. And by the same token, am I correct in this, that in any racial matter, any of these matters we are talking about, that originates in one country domestically and that has the possibility

223

of making international trouble, might be subject to the investigation and recommendations of the Organization?

Mr. PASVOLSKY. I should think so, because the Organization is created for that. . . .

Senator BARKLEY. Is it not true that almost every problem that concerns international relations must originate somewhere, and that somewhere usually is within the domestic boundaries of one nation and may leap over into another nation and create an international situation?

Mr. PASVOLSKY. Of course.

Senator BARKLEY. Not only economically but from every other standpoint?

Mr. PASVOLSKY. In every respect, of course.

DEFINING 'DOMESTIC JURISDICTION'

Is it Necessary? Is it Feasible? Is it useful?

By M. S. Rajan *

(Formerly Research Secretary, Indian Council of World Affairs)

One of the terms and phrases in the UN Charter, the precise connotation of which has been left undefined, is 'domestic jurisdiction' in Art. 2(7). The term first found its place in Art. 15(8) of the League Covenant. The 26 years League practice did not touch the problem of defining the term. Nor has more than a decade of the working of the UN offered any definition or made the task of definition easier, in spite of the fact that, unlike in League practice, the domestic jurisdiction issue has been raised and debated in the UN organs in a very large number of cases. A curious factor is that even though Members who opposed UN action in those cases expressly relied on Art. 2(7) for their stand, not only have UN resolutions recording action in those cases failed even to mention—except in a single case—the domestic jurisdiction provisions (and there is every reason to believe that the omission was deliberate), but have also failed to specify the reason or reasons for *assuming* competence to act in those cases—for, in no case have UN organs expressly asserted their competence.

What are the reasons for this significant practice? Why has no international organ attempted to define the phrase? Is it necessary to define it at all? Is it feasible to define it? Or is it indefinable, and if so, what are the

---

* Special Fellow, Indian School of International Studies. New Delhi.

reasons therefor? What are the possible consequences of an advance definition? Would a definition really serve any useful purpose? If the term is undefined and undefinable, how are international organs to act on questions in which objections are raised on the strength of claims based on domestic jurisdiction? These are questions which this short paper seeks to explore.

The provisions of Art. 15(8) of the League Covenant which first contained the term 'domestic jurisdiction' did not provide any definition of the term, but laid down the criterion of 'international law' for determining whether or not a certain matter was within the jurisdiction of a member state. But the importance of this criterion need not be exaggerated, for not only has the term nowhere been defined in international law, but also, there are no *specific* rules in general international law enabling one to automatically determine the nature of jurisdiction.

In the 26 years' League practice, only one case provided some illumination on the connotation of the term. In the case concerning Nationality Decrees in Tunis and Morocco, the Permanent Court of International Justice observed in its advisory opinion to the League Council: 'The question whether a certain matter is or is not solely within the jurisdiction of a state is an essentially relative question; it depends upon the development of international relations'. It added that even in the case of a matter which was not in principle regulated by international law, 'the right of a state to use its discretion is nevertheless restricted by obligations which it may have undertaken towards other states. In such a case, jurisdiction which, in principle, belongs solely to the state, is limited by rules of international law'.

This weighty opinion thus established two specific rules: firstly, that the content of domestic jurisdiction is not a rigid quantity and that its precise scope could be determined only when a decision is called for in a concrete case or situation, the nature of the decision depending upon the then prevailing state of international relations; in other words, the scope of domestic jurisdiction cannot be determined generally and once for all. Secondly, the domestic jurisdiction of a state is limited by obligations that it might have expressly undertaken towards other states under a treaty or an agreement.

When the term 'domestic jurisdiction' was taken over into the UN Charter, no definition of the term was laid down in the Charter or otherwise. In fact, at the San Francisco Conference, not one of the fifty participating delegations raised the issue of the definition of the term—though some of the governments did point out the need for a precise definition of the jurisdictional limits of the proposed organization *vis-a-vis* member states. But except for a solitary delegation—viz. Uruguay, which stated that the proposed organization ought not to require of its members any specific form of government, since that would be an indirect form of intervention in the internal affairs of a state—no delegation made any specific proposals towards that end. From this, one might have inferred that the omission was due to a general agreement, or at least understanding, on the connotation of the term. The truth however, was otherwise. According to one view, Art. 2(7) "was deliberately made ambiguous in recognition of the fact that it dealt with an issue so difficult of solution as to be better left unsolved"[1] The main difficulty, one might safely assume, was the definition of the scope and content of the term 'domestic jurisdiction'. Indeed, in the deliberations of the San Francisco Conference, the late Mr. Dulles put up an elaborate defence on behalf of the Sponsoring Powers of the Conference against making Art. 2(7) legally more precise. He also argued in favour of making the provision more a political principle than a legal formula and expressed the hope that it would be capable of evolution in consonance

---

1. Francis O. Wilcox and Carl M. Marcy, Proposals for Changes in the United Nations. 1955, p. 263.

with 'the state of the world, the public opinion of the world, and the factual interdependence of the world'.[2] For these reasons, the preparatory work of the San Francisco Conference which drafted the UN Charter is of little use for the purpose of defining the term 'domestic jurisdiction.'

Unlike in League practice, the domestic jurisdiction issue has been raised in a very large number of cases in UN organs—mostly in the General Assembly and the Security Council. (Among the cases that have so far come up in the International Court of Justice both for advisory opinion and for adjudication in contentious proceedings, the issue of domestic jurisdiction has been raised in very few cases.) But significantly enough, in the numerous resolutions passed in respect of concrete questions both in the General Assembly and the Security Council, not only have UN organs not expressly laid down the grounds of competence for their actions and recommendations, but also they have hesitated in all but one case to refer to Art. 2(7) in their resolutions—even though it was referred to times without number in the course of the debates on these several questions. Since this course was often adopted by the UN organs brushing aside the claims that it had no competence, by virtue of Art. 2(7), the only other course left open to us now is to see if we can make any inferential definition of the term 'domestic jurisdiction' from the numerous actions taken in the more important cases debated and acted upon in UN organs during the last fourteen years.

Under the Charter provision of Art. 2(7), two criteria need to be applied in order to determine whether UN organs have violated or respected the domestic jurisdiction of member states: whether the question, dispute or situation acted upon concerns a matter *essentially* within the domestic jurisdiction of any one of the parties; whether the nature of action taken constitutes 'intervention' within the domestic jurisdiction of any state. Applying the first criterion, it is difficult, if not impossible, to generalise that by acting on many of the questions submitted to them, UN organs sought to assert that the subject categories to which those questions relate (e.g. 'questions concerning non-self-governing territories', 'questions concerning human rights and fundamental freedoms') were *not* essentially within the domestic jurisdiction of states. The questions they have acted upon are of such diverse character, and the circumstances in which they were brought to the forum of the UN and debated upon are so dissimilar, that it would be rash to draw any definite conclusion from those actions as to the connotation of the term 'domestic jurisdiction'. The safest and perhaps the only conclusion that one can draw with some assurance is that in considering and acting upon the numerous questions referred to above, the UN organs only intended to *imply* that just those specific cases were not essentially within the domestic jurisdiction of the states concerned. In other words, these numerous UN decisions lend us little assistance in formulating any precise and comprehensive definition of the term 'domestic jurisdiction'.

As regards the criterion of 'intervention', in the overwhelming majority of cases brought up in the forum of the UN, the General Assembly and the Security Council have discussed them, made recommendations, appointed committees of enquiry or investigation created Good Offices Commissions, appointed subsidiary bodies, individual mediators and taken many similar non-coercive actions. In repeatedly taking this wide variety of non-compulsive actions, the UN organs did not apparently seek to transgress the domestic jurisdiction of any of the states concerned in terms of the provision of Art. 2(7). None of these actions or measures could be considered as 'dictatorial interference' within the domestic jurisdiction of member states and they are therefore altogether different from the intervention of one state in the internal affairs of the other, which customary international law prohibits. To this extent, one might consider that these actions lend us some assistance in defining the

2. Documents of the United Nations Conference on International Organization, San Francisco, 1945, 1945-6, Vol. 6, pp. 507-9.

term 'domestic jurisdiction'.

But then there has not been any general agreement on the correctness of the conclusion drawn above from UN practice—either among members of the UN or writers on UN affairs. Therefore, it would be difficult to prepare a definition of the term based on these fourteen years' of UN practice which would be acceptable to the vast majority of members of the UN or even commentators on the Charter.

In spite of all this—or perhaps because of this—there have been some demands for, and a new effort at defining the term. It is therefore worthwhile considering the pros and cons of defining the term *a priori*.

The case for definition

(i) In favour of defining the term one can argue that there are no legal or constitutional objections or difficulties in the way, and that it could be done in complete conformity with the general rules of international law as well as the terms of the UN Charter. (ii) The desirability of defining the term can also be well-supported. Since the UN is "based on the principle of the sovereign equality of its members", which is a *sine-qua-non* for the continued validity of international law as understood to-day, the definition of the precise limits of the jurisdiction of the members of the Society of Nations with respect to each other as well as of the UN *vis-a-vis* its Members would be highly conducive to smooth relations among states and to the successful working of the UN.

The case against definition

(i) The fundamental objection to the definition of the term 'domestic jurisdiction' (as of similar terms and concepts) is the questionable wisdom of defining jurisdiction in the abstract. (ii) The demand for a definition of the concept presumes that it is not merely a wholly legal concept but that it does not involve some non-legal elements in it. The fact, however, is that the concept has very strong political, military, economic and social elements in it, and concepts relating to these aspects of human affairs are not easily or with any precision definable. (iii) Definition of concepts could be of two kinds: general and enumerative. As regards the first, a general definition would necessarily employ words and phrases which would themselves require further definition, and therefore such a definition would be of little avail in deciding jurisdiction in a concrete case. It would therefore be no improvement on the present situation; on the other hand, it might accentuate existing controversy, if not also confusion. The Institute of International Law in its 1932 and 1954 sessions, and Professors Quincy Wright, C. G. Fenwick and Henri Rolin are among those who have sought to lay down such general definitions. (iv) An enumerative definition would specify either objective criteria of definition or list the subjects which would fall within the field of domestic jurisdiction. In respect of both these methods no two writers seem to agree on the objective criteria to be used or the subjects to be listed. Not infrequently, there is difference of opinion among writers of repute as to whether or not even so typical a subject as the form of a government of a state is a matter entirely left to the discretion of that state. Apart from the subjective elements involved in these methods, there is the difficulty of choosing criteria and subjects that would be uniformly applicable to all the states which in fact widely vary in every condition and circumstance. It would also seem impossible to make an exhaustive listing of the criteria or subjects, and unless they are exhaustive, they would be nearly useless for the purpose of defining jurisdiction in a concrete case. The enumerative approach is based on the misconception that international law is a static and definable quantity and not subject to change as a result of the development of international relations. The approach also presumes that states cannot restrict their own freedom of action by voluntarily entering into treaty obligations even in respect of so-called domestic matters— while in fact the right to enter into such international obligations is a well-

227

recognised attribute of state sovereignty. The demand for a listing of subjects within the domestic jurisdiction of a state is based on the presumption, now generally admitted as erroneous, that there are certain matters naturally, obviously and permanently falling within the jurisdiction of a state. To a third possibility of a combined definition, i.e., a definition which would include a general definition as well as a listing of subjects, much the same criticisms as above would apply. (v) Whatever the nature of definition of the term, the crucial question is who interprets and applies it to a concrete case. It is most unlikely that states would agree in advance to be bound by the decision of any international agency on the application of any definition to a concrete case. The UN Charter does not designate the authority to determine jurisdictional disputes. And it is a well-known fact that relatively few members of the UN have accepted the compulsory jurisdiction of the International Court of Justice and some of those who have ostensibly accepted it, have reserved to themselves the right to determine whether or not a matter out of which a dispute has arisen is within their domestic jurisdiction. (vi) It can be argued that the existence of an advance definition might be dangerous to the maintenance of international peace and security. (vii) The existence of an advance definition might render decisions of international organisations more or less automatic. Automatism would not necessarily and always contribute to the settlement of a dispute or to the remedying of a situation. (viii) One could well argue that in view of the prevailing 'cold war' among two blocs of nations, it would be inopportune to have an advance definition of the term. (ix) One almost insurmountable difficulty in defining the term is that one will be stuck in the quagmire of ancient and theoretical controversies such as the dualistic and monistic theories of international law and the doctrine of the non-justiciability of certain types of international disputes, and its corollary, the doctrine of 'gaps' in international law. In consequence, we have wide disagreement as to the number and nature of the fields of jurisdiction. There are broadly three views on the subject: the first, that there are only two fields, international jurisdiction and domestic jurisdiction, being mutually exclusive of each other; second, that there are three fields, the two above and a third field being a legal 'no man's land' in which neither international law nor municipal laws of states are operative; the third, that there are three fields, the two mentioned above, the third being the field of concurrent jurisdiction in which both international law and the municipal laws of states operate with simultaneous competence. In the circumstances, the demand for a definition of the term 'domestic jurisdiction' is in effect what Prof. Julius Stone has called in another context 'a concealed demand for international legislation on a formidable scale'. It is a demand for laying down with precision and clarity the rights and obligations of states. In the present stage of international relations, this seems to be an impossible demand. (x) One final argument against laying down any definition of the term is that the absence of such a definition during the last fourteen years of the operation of the UN has not wholly inhibited UN organs from acting on numerous questions and situations involving the issue of domestic jurisdictions.

CONCLUSIONS

Thus, the present position is that neither general rules of international law and the preparatory work of the League Covenant and the UN Charter, nor the 26 years' operation of the League and the 14 years' operation of the UN, lend us any assistance in defining the term 'domestic jurisdiction'. Furthermore, attempts at defining the term *a priori* have not also been successful, and the case against defining the term *a priori*, as we have seen, is rather formidable.

Now, in this situation, is there any cause for dissatisfaction?

First of all, there is little reason or evidence to believe that even a small section of members of the UN would want an advance definition of the term:

indeed, at the time the text of Art. 2(7) was drafted at the San Francisco Conference, there was hardly any demand for defining the term. In the course of a little over a decade's operation of the UN, in spite of the strong stand taken by some members against the majority interpretation of the text of Art. 2(7), there have been very few demands for defining the term generally and for all time to come: their efforts were merely directed towards challenging the particular interpretation put forward by those demanding UN action in the concrete case under consideration. In the recent discussions and debates, both in the forum of the UN and outside (concerning revision of the UN Charter as well, there is little desire expressed among Members for any definition of the term. It is noteworthy that in the most ambitious and comprehensive proposals for revising the UN Charter made by Grenville Clark and Louis B. Sohn, the term is left undefined; apparently, it was not considered by them a problem deserving of any attention. Even those Members who recognise the existence of a problem in respect of the provision of Art. 2(7), have not pin-pointed the definition of the term as the core of the problem. Therefore, an intellectual preoccupation and effort at defining the term, such as has been, and is being, devoted to the definition of the term 'aggression', seems hardly called for.

Secondly, it has been pointed out earlier that the absence of a definition of the term has not, on the whole prevented the successful operation of UN organs during the last 14 years in respect of questions and disputes involving the issue of domestic jurisdiction. While in theory it is possible to argue that the availability of an advance definition of the term would make the working of the organization more smooth, it seems even more likely that the very absence of the definition of the term would contribute to the present working and future development of the UN. For, the ambiguity of the term will compel the Organisation — as in fact it has — to take a series of *ad hoc* decisions resulting in the accumulation of a case law on the issue, and this would, in due course, if a general agreement materializes, assist in the definition of the term, or at least render future decisions easier because of precedents. This seems to be a more practical course to adopt than to waste our energies in drafting an *a priori* definition of the term. The point is, the removal of ambiguity in the working of international institutions, whose ambiguity is simply a reflection of the more fundamental ambiguity in the voluntary cooperation and goodwill of nations, might (paradoxical though it may seem) inhibit these institutions from free development which would promote more effectively the purposes for which they are established. This ambiguity is simply a reflection of the more fundamental ambiguity in the relations of sovereign states with international organizations. Until that ambiguity is mitigated, if not wholly removed, it is unreal to expect any precision in the definition of terms such as the one under discussion.

Thirdly, it is a very old and familiar feature of constitutional law that certain terms and phrases in many a constitutional document are left undefined, for a variety of reasons; (a) their meaning might be considered to be self-evident, (b) they might be undefinable in themselves, (c) there might be no general agreement on their definition, (d) it might be considered unwise to define them for all time. If an *a priori* definition of any such term was laid down, it might be either of little practical use or might have the consequence of impeding change and progress. For, any definition would necessarily freeze the ideas prevailing in society at the time, and human society is anything but static. This is especially true in regard to jurisdictional concepts, and the long and fruitless debates on the scope of 'reserved' and 'delegated' powers of the individual states and the federal government under the American Constitution is highly demonstrative and instructive on this point. The general reluctance of Members to seek the opinion of the International Court of Justice, is a clear indication of the lack of faith, *not* in the authority and competence of the Court, but in the desirability, practicability and usefulness of a general and advance definition of the term. After all, this is only one of such terms left undefined in the Charter whose connotation is by no means self-evident, e.g., 'to intervene' (Art. 2: 7) 'peace-loving states' (Art. 4) 'act of aggression' (Art. 39).

Fourthly, this desire for a definition applicable to all members of the international society in all unforeseen situations or cases and at any time, seems to be an instance of the error of what Prof. Julius Stone has termed 'analogical transposition of familiar principles of municipal law to the relations of states', viz., the impersonal and general character of law. However, there is a characteristic difference between the nature of Municipal law and that of international law and the difference arises from the fundamental contrast in the number and nature of *internal* and *international* societies. States, the subjects of international law in the present stage of international relations, are very few as contrasted with the millions of subjects of municipal law, i.e., human beings. Therefore, while in theory it might be desirable to subject all states to a general law, they are so diverse and dissimilar compared to each other that the utility of a general law applicable to all of them is severely limited. As Prof. Brierly has observed, progress towards an international order should not be sought 'from a prolific growth of rules of general application............for that would be to assume a uniformity among states and their interests which often does not exist. It is more likely that the line of progress will be found to lie in the finding of particular solutions for particular problems ....[3] Therefore, it is much wiser to continue to decide *ad hoc* the nature of jurisdiction in which a question, situation or dispute falls, than to strive for an advance definition of the term 'domestic jurisdiction.'

Fifthly, the definition of terms such as 'domestic jurisdiction' is primarily a political function — not a legal one — which is better served by a pragmatic and not a legalistic, *a priori* approach to international problems. Because of the complex, vastly increased and increasing international relationships, international society has reached a stage of development where almost every matter under the category of domestic jurisdiction is today of international concern or has international repercussions. While states still claim, as a matter of form, certain matters as being within their domestic jurisdiction, they are not averse to voluntarily cooperating for mutual benefit with other states in those matters. It is significant that objections of tresspassing on domestic jurisdiction have not been raised with regard to narcotics control, but against atomic energy control. 'The cultivation of poppies is certainly as domestic as is the mining of uranium or the manufacture of atomic bombs. The difference lies not in law but in politics; one is highly controversial, the other is not.[4] In such a situation, the question of where the line that divides domestic and international jurisdictions should be drawn is a matter of politics and not law, and the former, by the very nature of its subject, is much less amenable to automatism than the latter.

Finally, there is need to question the very concept of jurisdiction as a basis for legal classification of international relations. Traditional international law (as it still operates today) was shaped during a period of historical development when nation-states were the *only* subjects of its concern, and consequently, the concept of jurisdiction assumed great importance and meaning. As of today, however, this is hardly the case. It is now widely recognized that states are only the *principal* subjects of international law and that in a realistic modern law of nations individuals as well as international bodies or agencies also have rights and obligations under the law of nations. Thefore it is that many scholars have questioned the appropriateness of the use of the term 'international law' and suggested alternative terminology. Thus Prof. Philip Jessup

---

3. J. L. Brierly. The Outlook for International Law, 1944, p. 45.
4. Wilcox and Marcy, op. cit. p. 264.

has suggested the use of the term 'transnational law' for the law applicable not only to the relations among states, but also those between individuals and non-governmental bodies *vis-a-vis* states. Today where transnational situations, questions or disputes do not involve only states, the concept of jurisdiction is perforce less important and meaningful. What was once a matter of substance needs to be treated today merely as one of procedure.[5]

DISCUSSION

Mr. Narayan Rao: I do not quite like the term 'advance definition' for the simple reason that we draw certain legal consequences. If we have not defined it at the time the Charter was enacted and if we today define it, it is not to say that we are making an advance definition of it. I fully agree that there are difficulties but it is no excuse to say that it is a hopeless task. As you have already suggested, we can adopt an enumerative method. Should we not at least accommodate certain of the situations which we have already experienced in international life in that definition, and later on incorporate a clause on the pattern of the *ejusdem generis* clause in municipal law, so that we can at least guard against problems which we know already?

Mr. Rajan: I have tried to state both the cases. You are simply emphasising one aspect of it. I think that has been fully answered. To say that certain action has been taken is one thing, but to say that to that extent domestic jurisdiction has been defined is quite another. That is precisely the point I am making. Just because the General Assembly has passed a resolution in regard to a particular case, let us say that the treatment of people of Indian origin in South Africa, it does not necessarily follow that all questions concerning the treatment of people in one country have been taken out of the domestic jurisdiction of States.

To take an *ad hoc* decision is one thing and to generalise for the purpose of applying it to another case is quite a different thing. In fact, the problem is that even though the United Nations has passed resolutions and taken action of various kinds in many cases, it is very difficult to generalise on that basis and say that because the United Nations has taken action in a particular case it implies this and we should also apply this in this particular case. No two cases are quite identical really.

Mr. Narayan Rao: But can it not give a general idea? As far as I can recollect, every occasion when the issue of domestic jurisdiction was raised has been fraught with difficulties. We have even had cases which were covered by international agreements, where States claimed exclusive competence under their domestic jurisdiction. So, what I mean to suggest is this: Can there not be certain cases where, for instance, there may be some treaties and one State, say State A, claims that under a treaty State B is obliged to follow a certain code of conduct? Here is a case which does not come under domestic jurisdiction.

Mr. Rajan: I think as the Chairman rightly says, let him try and make one. That is a good challenge. Many people have tried to make a general definition and have failed. In other words, you will be where you are by making a definition. Remember, the purpose of a definition is that it is to enable you to decide jurisdiction in a concrete case. It is no use having it merely to please oneself or purely as a kind of intellectual pleasure. A general definition by its very nature will not necessarily or automatically help you to define jurisdiction in a concrete case. You will more or less be where you were because you have to argue out the case. If you have to argue out the case when there is a general definition, why have one at all?

---

5. See P. C. Jessup, Transnational Law, 1956.

Mr. Govinda Rajan: Article 59 is very precise in saying that the decision of the International Court has no binding force except in respect of the particular case concerned. That shows that the Court itself is not bound by the same definition in other cases. We cannot have a general definition about domestic jurisdiction, nor can the Court lay it down. So, we are like a rudderless ship on the high seas.

Mr. Rajan: After all, the decisions are taken by a very large and representative body of international society the General Assembly. If you cannot trust as representative and universal a body as the UN, I do not see what else you can do. It is just a question whether or not you trust the decision of a vast majority of nations. So, I do not think we are as helpless as you have mentioned.

SUGGESTED QUESTIONS FOR SEMINAR DISCUSSION

Do you agree with Clark-Sohn that the only criterion for membership in the United Nations should be whether or not the political entity involved has "the legal status of an independent state," or do you think that the criteria in Article 4 of the present Charter ought to be retained? What are the facts and value-preferences on which you base your position?

Do you agree with the new procedure for membership application which Clark-Sohn suggest, including ultimate resolution of disputes by the International Court of Justice as to whether a political entity is a legally independent state? Would there be any difference between the way a court would resolve such an issue and, say, the General Assembly?

Is it possible that even if universal membership were achieved, there would still be serious question of who ought to represent various states? For example, within the next three decades there might be civil wars or charges of "stolen elections" in a good number of states and when opposing domestic groups would then ask for seating in the UN as representatives of their state. Do the Clark-Sohn proposals help with these problems? How would you solve such problems?

Assuming for the moment that the problem of Communist China's affiliation with the United Nations is not admission to the organization but representation in the various organs of the UN, which government do you believe ought to represent China? Why? Which of the arguments presented by Ambassador Adali Stevenson and Dr. G. P. Malalasekera, the Ceylonese Delegate, do you find persuasive on this problem? How would you resolve the question of Chinese Communist affiliation with the UN?

232

The authority given to the General Assembly to enact binding legislation to effectuate war-prevention under the Clark-Sohn scheme will make it an extremely important and powerful world organ. Does their scheme of weighted representation from the various nations based on principles in the last full paragraph on page 25 of their book seem sensible to you? Are there other criteria you would introduce? Why or why not?

In a long review of World Peace Through World Law a Soviet author, O. Vahsilyev, in 1961 in the periodical Soviet State and Law, had this to say on the weighted representation portion of the Clark-Sohn scheme:

"In all, the Assembly, according to the author's count, would be composed of approximately 600 representatives with the right to vote. Here the circumstance attracts our attention that in the majority of these six groups the predominant position is assured to the countries of the western military-political bloc. That is the situation in the second (which such countries), the third, the fifth and the sixth groups. In the light of this it is obvious that the criterion put forward by the authors for representation in the General Assembly does not reflect realistically the present alignment of forces in the world area."

Assuming that the principles suggested by Clark-Sohn should be operative in the long run, can you think of some transitional model which would handle the objection made by Vahsilyev and move us towards the use of their suggestions?

What are the arguments for retaining the present single vote for each nation? What are the arguments for a bi-cameral arrangement?

On pages 32 and 33 Clark-Sohn present their reasons for moving by a series of transition steps away from the present system of delegates appointed by the executive branch of member states to election of representatives either from national legislatures or by direct popular vote. Does their proposal seem sound to you? What dangers or problems do you see in it?

Do you think that Britain and France are likely to accept a representation scheme that places them on a par with Brazil, Indonesia and Pakistan, but below China, India, the U.S. and the U.S.S.R.? Will the small powers who now have an equal vote be willing to give up their present strength? Are there any governments who are likely to feel that they are being given insufficient influence? What can be done to satisfy them?

If the problem of overcoming sovereignty is a major obstacle in achieving acceptance of world legal structure, are all the matters proposed by Clark-Sohn in their revised Article 2, paragraph 7, which details the extent to which the United Nations may intervene concerning matters essentially within the domestic jurisdiction of any state, absolutely necessary? Might the authority to make non-binding recommendations, especially as they refer to Articles 13 and 15, be deleted? Why? Would it make sense to enumerate specifically such matters as international trade, immigration, monetary policy, farm programs, etc., as being outside the scope of United Nations' intervention, even by recommendation? Why?

Are there any powers concerning possible UN intervention in matters essentially within the domestic jurisdiction of any state which Clark-Sohn have omitted that you consider necessary to the task of war-prevention?

Is it really possible to set up machinery for effective war-prevention and not become so involved in the tensions caused, for example, by international trade, immigration and monetary policies of individual states that in order to make the scheme work it is necessary to include these matters within the legislative authority of the General Assembly?

Are there any portions of the World Peace Through World Law scheme which you have read for this session which you think might be acceptable to the member states, whether through the Amendment process under Article 108 or through establishment by practice?

Do you have any other questions about these materials which you feel the seminar should discuss?

On the UNITED NATIONS in general, there are available a large number of source materials of which the following are either basic or representative.

Claude, Inis L., Jr. Swords Into Plowshares: The Problems and Progress of International Organization. NY: Random House, 1956, 497p. See especially Chapter 5.

Cohen, B. V. The United Nations; constitutional developments, growth, and possibilities. Cambridge, Mass.: Harvard U. Press, 1961, 106p.

Coyle, David Cushman. The United Nations and How it Works. NY: Columbia U. Press, 1961, 222p. A revised edition of a useful and basic review of the principles and operations of the UN and its related organizations.

Goodrich, Leland M. The United Nations. NY: Crowell, 1959, 419p. A general survey of the organization and its related agencies.

Goodrich, Leland M., and Edvard Hambro. Charter of the UN; Commentary and Documents. 2nd ed. Boston: World Peace Foundation, 1949, 710p. The basic source book on the UN.

Mangone, Gerard J. A Short History of International Organization. NY: McGraw-Hill, 1954, 326p. The author says that he has "attempted to portray the development of international organization along constitutional lines with attention to procedures and law, hoping to indicate a potential, though by no means inevitable, growth toward world order," from 1648 to now.

MacIver, Robert M. The Nations and the United Nations. NY: Manhattan Publishing Co. (for the Carnegie Endowment for International Peace), 1959, 186p. Prof. MacIver summarizes and appraises the findings of the series of volumes prepared under the auspices of the Carnegie Endowment on the experiences and opinions of individual countries regarding the UN.

Detailed reports of the activities of the UN, its related agencies, and other international organizations such as NATO and the Council of Europe are given quarterly in the journal International Organization, along with a detailed bibliography. An annual review of the issues before the current General Assembly appears in International Conciliation, while the organization's activities are summarized in the annual Yearbook of the United Nations.

The question of MEMBERSHIP is considered in:

Boyer, William P., and Neylan Akra. "The United States and the Admission of Communist China." Political Science Q. 86:332-53. (Sept. 1961).

Commission to Study the Organization of Peace. A Unicameral United Nations: 15th Report of the Commission. NY, 1962, 62p.

Gross, Leo. "Progress Towards Universality of Membership in the UN." Am. J. Int. Law 50:791-827 (Oct. 1956).

Hornbeck, Stanley K. "Which Chinese?" Foreign Affairs 34: 24-39 (Oct. 1955). Examines the questions involved in both Chinese recognition and UN representation and membership.

United Nations. "Legal Aspects of Representation in the UN." Internatl. Org. 4:356-362(Mar. 1950).

(Wilcox, Francis O.) U.S. Senate Subcommittee on the UN Charter, Committee on Foreign Relations, 83rd Congress, 2nd Session. "The Problem of Membership in the UN: Staff Study No. 3." Washington, 1954.

Wright, Quincy. "The Chinese Recognition Problem." Am. J. Int. Law 49: 320-38 (July 1955).

On VOTING and REPRESENTATION PROBLEMS in the General Assembly, see:

Liang, Yuen-li. "Recognition by the UN of the Representation of a Member State: Critera and Procedure." Am. J. Int. Law 45: 689-707 (Oct. 1951).

McIntyre, Elizabeth. "Weighted Voting in International Organization." Internatl. Org. 8: 484-97 (Nov. 1954). Examines the past developments of weighted voting and questions whether it meets a genuine need in contemporary international organization.

Rudzinski, Aleksander W. "Election procedures in the UN." Am. J. Int. Law 53: 81-111 (Jan. 1959).

(Wilcox, Francis O.). U.S. Senate, Subcommittee on the UN Charter, Committee on Foreign Relations, 83rd Congress, 2nd Session, "Representation and Voting in the UN General Assembly." Washington: 1954.

For additional information on DOMESTIC JURISDICTION, consult:

Aaronson, Michael. "Some Procedural Aspects of Article 2(7)." Internatl. Relations 2: 80-85 (Oct. 1960).

Abi-Saab, George M. "The Newly Independent States and the Scope of Domestic Jurisdiction." Proc. Am. Soc. Int. Law 54 (1960), 84-90.

Rajan, M. S. United Nations and Domestic Jurisdiction. 2nd ed. Bombay: Asia House, 1961, 539p. A study of the concept of domestic jurisdiction including problems of interpretation, UN practice and jurisdiction.

_____. "United States Attitude Toward Domestic Jurisdiction in the UN." Internatl. Org. 13: 19-37 (Winter 1959).

Wright, Quincy. "Domestic Jurisdiction as a Limit on National and Supra-National Action." Northwestern Law R. 56: 11-40 (Mar.-Apr. 1961).

SESSION IV

STRENGTHENING THE UNITED NATIONS

This session continues our study of how to revise and strengthen the United Nations in order to achieve and maintain world peace; we shall again make extensive use of the Clark-Sohn proposals and their comments.

Our concern here will be primarily with four more of the present major organs of the UN: the Security Council, the Economic and Social Council, the Trusteeship Council and the Secretariat. Each of these organs performs an important function within the existing UN structure and is given increased authority and functions in the Clark-Sohn scheme. With the exception of the Secretariat, Clark and Sohn suggest extensive changes in methods of selection, membership composition and voting procedures of these organs, as they did with the General Assembly. You will note that the relative power among them is changed quite drastically under the Clark-Sohn plan, particularly with respect to the Security Council, which they re-name the Executive Council, and the General Assembly. In the Clark-Sohn scheme, the ultimate power and responsibility with respect to peace-keeping resides in the General Assembly.

Once again it should be stressed that the Clark-Sohn idea of giving increased power to the General Assembly can only be evaluated within the context of their entire scheme which includes not only the delegation of far greater over-all power to the United Nations than it now has, but also drastic revisions in the composition and procedures of the General Assembly itself. Nevertheless it is interesting to note that the portion of the Commission to Study the Organization of Peace report entitled "Development of Political Accommodation" takes the position that under present international conditions there should be a determined effort to resuscitate the Security Council as a primary focus for discussion and negotiation of major international issues; we shall want to compare this with the assumptions underlying the Clark-Sohn proposals.

The selection from Bailey presents a description of the growth of the Secretary General's office and its increasing importance in the UN. Some persons feel that the executive capacity of the world organization would best evolve from this position, and again we shall want to compare the assumptions of that position with those of Clark-Sohn. Bailey is also concerned with the troika proposals of the Soviet Union and presents the argument that the use of this principle in the administration of the office of the Secretary General would frustrate its proper operation.

Fisher's piece indirectly questions that position by suggesting that there are situations where troika administration would be sensible, especially if it is impossible to reach agreement on other ways of proceeding. In addition, he questions whether troika necessarily means veto power and suggests that even if it does governments face constraints (which constraints could be strengthened by appropriate political action) in utilizing that power.

The Padelford article explores some of the political forces focusing on producing an expanded membership of the Economic and Social Council, some political problems that would have to be overcome to achieve such an expansion and some criteria which might be used in bringing about an actual expansion. His position is that more adequate representation is needed for the large number of recently admitted new members, and that if necessary we should try to accomplish this through the use of the amendment procedure provided in Article 108.

Readings from World Peace Through World Law:
The Executive Council, xxii-xxiii, 66-88; Declaration Regarding non-Self-Governing Territories, International Trusteeship System, The Trusteeship Council, xxiii-xxiv, 150-174; The Secretariat, Miscellaneous Provisions, Amendments, etc., xl-xli, 183-205.

DEVELOPMENT OF THE PROCESS OF
POLITICAL ACCOMMODATION

from The Thirteenth Report of

THE COMMISSION TO STUDY
THE ORGANIZATION OF PEACE

We emphasize at the outset that no conceivable transformation of the United Nations will involve making international political adjustment a function performed exclusively by the world organization; whatever structural and procedural changes may be instituted in the United Nations, the importance of improving the methods and manners of diplomacy and of adapting it to the rapid changes in the character of international relations will remain undiminished. Even in the most mature national legislature, diplomacy—in the popular rather than the technical meaning of the term—plays an important part in adjusting the viewpoints of legislators and in preparing the way for acceptance of legislation by the considerable fraction of the citizens whose support or acquiescence is essential to the effectiveness of the legislation. Without such diplomatic preparation, legislation may require so much enforcement as to be ineffective. In short, the process of political accommodation is to some degree decentralized, even in a national state.

In the slow process of developing the international community to the point where it can provide for all its members the means of settling disputes peacefully, sovereign states will for a long time have to bear much of the responsibility. There is a powerful tendency, in a world increasingly complex and interdependent, for matters formerly regarded as falling within domestic jurisdiction to become matters of international concern. This tendency exerts a continual influence favorable to the growth and development of international organization. Yet, sober concern for the safeguarding of national interests and emotional attachment to the symbol of patriotism, among other factors, frequently tend to restrict the development of international competence in areas of importance to the world at large. Hence, much that is in fact international in implication has still to be dealt with as if it were of limited, rather than of broadly international, concern. Thus, it is evident that the traditional methods and manners of diplomacy have a continuing relevance to the conduct of international relations. Negotiation between or among individual nations seems likely to remain an important element in world affairs, even though the scope and authority of the United Nations may develop to become commensurate with the requirements posed by the growth of global interdependence.

Narrowly speaking, the business of diplomacy is to get for a nation what it wants. In the past, the threat or use of military force was regarded as a legitimate and practicable tool of diplomacy, although in many cases military force was regarded primarily as a means of providing defense against coercion by other nations, rather than of directly imposing a policy upon others. But even in past times when war was thinkable as an instrument of policy, it was cheaper to avoid war when practicable, and diplomacy was therefore normally regarded as a means of achieving peaceful compromise among the conflicting interests and purposes of states. Diplomacy had to serve the negative national interest of preventing war, as well as the positive national interest of enabling the state to get what it

239

wanted. In short, the business of diplomacy, broadly speaking, was to get for the nation as much of what it wanted as could be gained without precipitating war. This meant that diplomacy was essentially a process whereby states undertook to reach mutually acceptable agreements. Diplomacy sometimes failed, and it was sometimes deliberately abandoned in favor of coercive techniques for realizing national aims. But the normal role of diplomacy was to promote the peaceful adjustment of disputes and differences among nations.

This function of diplomacy has become infinitely more important in our time, when resort to military force has been largely deprived of both legitimacy and utility. The use of force as an instrument of national policy has lost its standing in international law and in world political opinion, and, perhaps more significantly, it has become too risky to appeal to rational statesmen. This is the essential meaning of the common assertion that "war has become unthinkable." Given this development, it is even more clear now than it was in the past that the proper function of diplomacy is to achieve a reconciliation of the conflicting interests of states so as to prevent disputes from degenerating into armed conflict. Prudent statesmen must recognize that such conflicting interests should be accommodated within the framework of the common interest in preserving peace. The constructive use of diplomacy looks toward the formulation of clear and precise arrangements on contested matters, which are mutually acceptable to the parties concerned. To say that the results of the diplomatic process should be precise is not to deny that changing conditions may eventually render them obsolete and unacceptable to the parties; diplomacy is not exempt from the usual human burden of adjusting to new knowledge and new conditions.

Emphasis upon the conciliatory function of diplomacy suggests the validity of the definition attributed to Count Metternich, that "Diplomacy is the art of avoiding the appearance of victory." In the diplomatic process, a state must aim at promoting its objectives without so seriously hurting the interests or self-esteem of others involved in the negotiations as to make agreement impossible or to cause the general worsening of relations. In an important sense, a diplomatic victory and a diplomatic defeat are both self-contradictory terms. The business of diplomacy is neither to produce pleasant and meaningless generalities nor to score debating points, administer embarrassing disappointments, or deliver edifying lectures on any nation's philosophy, ethics, or manners. These things fall within the field of propaganda, which —however important and useful it may be in certain circumstances—ought not to be confused with diplomacy.

The propagandistic corruption of diplomacy is one of the serious ills of our time. The problem of reestablishing diplomacy as the art of reaching mutually satisfactory agreements expressed in precise terms poses great difficulties, no less for democracies than for dictatorships. The still-prevalent primitive "patriotic" notion that our country must gain at the expense of our rivals makes it difficult for public opinion to understand or accept agreements that may be mutually satisfactory to the United States and the Soviet Union. This attitude leads to the frustrating conclusion that no agreements can be reached, because it suggests that any agreement acceptable to the Soviet Union must be advantageous to that country, and therefore, disadvantageous to us; thus, we become unable to take "Yes" for an answer. Such a public attitude tends to reduce diplomacy to the undiplomatic function of debate aimed at reciprocal disparagement; what passes for diplomacy under these circumstances makes political accommodation less rather than more likely.

Return to the idea and practice of diplomacy as a constructive and reconciling process whose objective is to find mutually satisfactory solutions of international conflicts is an essential requirement for the reduction of tensions and the development of an atmosphere in which the critical problems of this age can be attacked with some hope of success. This task is in large part the responsibility of individual governments and leaders of public opinion within national states, particularly the major powers. The revision of attitudes toward negotiations and the reform of diplomatic manners is essentially a do-it-yourself project for each state.

Nevertheless, this decentralization of responsibility leaves a significant role for the United Nations in promoting a more propitious climate for the effective operation of the diplomatic process. The moral pressures of the international forum should be used to impress upon states that they have a solemn obligation to undertake seriously and genuinely to negotiate their differences. The Secretary-General has already achieved remarkable success in encouraging and facilitating "quiet diplomacy," in which disputants eschew the public confrontations that produce rigidity and bitterness. Continued development of this useful role of the Secretary-General is indispensable, but it must be supplemented by the growth, in the political organs of the United Nations, of a mood inimical to the exploitation of the international public forum as a propaganda platform. It is inherent in the nature of international bodies that they are susceptible to this use; their very existence poses a temptation for states to evade

241

diplomacy. It is doubtful that formal rules and procedures can be devised to eliminate this problem. The task, as we see it, is for the members of the United Nations to develop a political atmosphere conducive to the most effective use of the methods of diplomacy.

In addition to promoting the fullest and most fruitful use of the traditional diplomatic methods, the United Nations itself should develop new mechanisms for political accommodation, suitable for an era of ever-increasing interdependence.

The agenda for the future must give a place of high priority to the improvement of the process of parliamentary diplomacy as practiced, or as it might be practiced, by the Security Council. We are well aware that there is considerable sentiment, among representatives in the United Nations and in other groups, for writing off the Security Council as a lost cause and concentrating on the development of the General Assembly. We are also aware of the fact that preliminary efforts to alter the structure of the Security Council have encountered political difficulties, chiefly the opposition of the Soviet bloc to any change without the prior settlement of the Chinese representation question. This poses a formidable problem, as the politically contentious issue of the representation of the government which rules Mainland China is inexorably tied up with the general problem of making the Security Council reflect the full and varied reality of the world whose political troubles bear upon that body. Neither problem can be solved in isolation from the other. We do not predict easy success in this enterprise, but we do hold to the conviction that the interests of all states, large and small alike, require that every effort be made to revitalize the Security Council so that it can function, along with the Assembly, as an effective organ of the United Nations. We offer our proposals for the reconstruction of the Security Council in the belief that such effort can succeed.

In our Twelfth Report, we urged that "every effort be made to transform the Security Council into the sort of agency which it was originally intended to be—a standing conference of the major powers, accompanied by spokesmen for selected smaller states and by the Secretary-General, within which continuous negotiation of important issues can take place." (p. 31). We contended that the proper reaction to summit conferences and other extra-United Nations negotiations is not to deplore the by-passing of the Security Council, but to inquire *why* the Security Council is not regarded as a valuable center of negotiation. We repeat what we said there in further support of our opinion on this controversial subject:

We suggest that the customary emphasis upon the veto as the primary factor in the failure of the Security Council is misplaced. The tragedy of that body is not so much that *decisions* are not reached there as that serious *negotiations* are not undertaken there. The veto rule adopted at San Francisco symbolized the proposition that, in cases of conflict among great powers, the voting of decisions should be discouraged and the negotiation of agreement should be encouraged. That proposition was, and is, valid. The problem of revitalizing the Security Council is that of making it an attractive arena for the conduct of negotiations among the great powers whose peaceful coexistence is vital to the survival of civilization.

The principal difficulty lies in the fact that the Security Council does not accurately reflect the existing political configuration of the world. The Western bloc has succeeded in dominating its composition so thoroughly that the Council has lost its usefulness to the West as a focal point for negotiation with the Soviet bloc. We recommend that a serious attempt be made to develop an agreed plan for reconstructing the Security Council so that it will always include adequate representation of all those states whose cooperation is essential to solution of problems with which it might deal. The Council might then come to be regarded as a suitable place for doing important diplomatic business, and the uncommitted states might be challenged to develop to the full their mediatorial potential in an organ which could be conceived as the real center of the world's most vital diplomatic activity. The Council can be useful only when it is taken seriously; it will be taken seriously only when its composition is such that the major political groupings are represented in reasonable proportion to their actual importance in world affairs. (p. 32).

This is a problem which our members have long regarded as an important subject of study in planning a better world order. In our Eleventh Report, we recommended that "strenuous efforts be made to revitalize the Security Council as an organ for promoting political accommodation within the framework of law provided by the Charter." (p. 11). To this end we proposed that "the Council be enlarged and effective provision made for assuring a more realistic and equitable distribution of its seats among the significant political groupings." In our Tenth Report, we declared that "advantage should be taken of the growing demand for enlargement of the Security Council to improve its representative character. A moderate expansion of the Council should include provision to ensure implementation of the first criterion for elective members, that is, contribution 'to the maintenance of international peace and security,' as well as of the second, 'equitable geographical distribution.'" (*Strengthening the United Nations,* p. 4).

A larger Security Council is urgently needed. The membership of the United Nations grew from fifty-one at its foundation to ninety-nine, in late 1960, and further enlargement is expected as the liquidation of colonial empires proceeds to its conclusion. Six elective members of the Security Council barely sufficed to represent adequately the states making the largest contributions to the keeping of the peace and to the other purposes of the United Nations, when the Organization was much smaller than it is now. There has always been difficulty in filling the non-permanent seats so as to satisfy the additional requirement of equitable geographical distribution.

If the Security Council of the future is to be a vital political organ, its elective contingent must be sufficiently enlarged to permit adequate representation (1) of the "middle powers" capable of contributing most significantly to the work of the Organization, (2) of the major geographical and cultural regions of the world, and (3) of the leading political groupings. At the very least, provision must be made for giving assured representation in the Security Council to the African states, and to the states of Asia which are uncommitted in the Cold war.

It is no easy matter to divide the members of the United Nations into neat categories for representative purposes. Geographical regions are at best vaguely defined, and regional boundaries do not always coincide with cultural or political dividing lines. It would hardly be valid to assume, for instance, that a "member for the Middle East" could speak for both Israel and the Arab states—or, indeed, for all the states in the region other than Israel. Moreover, there are legitimate objections to bestowing formal recognition upon political blocs. These groupings are, in most instances, relatively informal and fluid, and it would be most unfortunate if they were formalized in such manner as to encourage their rigidification. Khrushchev's proposal for a "triumvirate" at the head of the Secretariat is unacceptable for the reason, among others, that it postulates a clear-cut division among Eastern, Western, and neutralist blocs which is not, and ought not to become, characteristic of the United Nations.

Nevertheless, it is clear that the Member States of the United Nations do fall into a number of roughly-defined groupings, which are significant despite the indistinctness of their dividing lines. Realistically, these must be taken into account; a balance must be found between the extremes of pretending that they do not exist and of recognizing them in such fashion as to promote the hardening of their boundaries.

There is nothing wrong in allowing "politics" to influence elections to the Security Council. On the contrary, political considerations are indispensable, if the composition of the Council is to reflect the realities of world politics. The General Assembly did well to recognize the claim of the British Commonwealth to one of the non-permanent seats, despite the geographical dispersion of its members, since the Commonwealth as a whole made a specially important contribution to the purposes of the Organization. But the same reasoning leads to the conclusion that every important political group should also be equitably represented in an organ which is designed primarily to furnish facilities for parliamentary diplomacy and needs therefore to represent all the major interests in world affairs. In fact, the two standards for the election of non-permanent members of the Security Council which are prescribed in the Charter are flexible enough to permit due allowance for political considerations, if there were a sufficient number of non-permanent seats.

One possible approach to the objective of making the Security Council a more satisfactory representative body would be simply to amend the Charter to provide for a larger Council, thereby making more elective seats available, and to trust in the good sense of members of the Assembly to exercise their choice so as to create a reasonable and politically realistic balance in the composition of the Council. This is certainly the simplest method, and it has the merit of recognizing that states can be only advised, not commanded, as to the use which they make of their voting rights. Its demerit is that it offers no guarantee that additional seats will be distributed in accordance with the essential criterion of representativeness. If this plan were adopted, we would suggest that not more than six elective seats be added to the present six, and that the number of votes required for decision be correspondingly increased.

As a variation on the scheme just described, it might be proposed that an informal "gentlemen's agreement" be worked out among members of the United Nations as to the allocation of an enlarged bloc of elective seats in the Security Council. This would call for a modification and supplementation of the informal understandings which have had considerable influence upon elections to the Council in the past. By this device, a system of precedents might be developed which would provide reasonable assurance that the Assembly's electoral process would regularly produce a realistically proportioned Security Council.

Another variant which might be considered would be to have the Assembly establish a formal set of categories, leaving it to each Member State to opt for inclusion in the group which it desires, and determining the allocation of Council seats among the groups thus formed. This might be accomplished by adopting a new rule of procedure, whereby the Assembly would be, in effect, regulating its own performance of the electoral function. Under such a scheme, it might be desirable to provide that the members of a given group should have effective choice of the state or states to fill that group's Council quota, restricting the full Assembly to ratification of the choices thus made.

Still another possibility would be to reserve the six existing elective seats in the Security Council for the representation of regional groupings, that representation to be worked out by one of the methods suggested above, and to create a number of additional seats to be filled by "election at large." In that case, it might be hoped that Member States, having satisfied their urge for geographical-political distribution in the election of the former group of members, would tend to choose the "members at large" from the ranks of those states which are willing and able to make particularly significant contributions to the work of the United Nations.

It is vitally important to secure adequate representation in the Security Council for states which are "principal contributors," even though it is difficult to define and measure the contributions which are involved, and it probably would be impossible to secure general agreement on a formal scheme for designating the "principal contributors" and giving them a special status in the Security Council. The criteria of importance would include population, economic significance, financial contribution to the United Nations, and capacity to assist the United Nations in military or quasi-military operations. It must be recognized, however, that the smaller, weaker, and poorer states may contribute imponderable political and moral values which in fact outweigh the tangible contributions made by their more impressive fellow members of the United Nations.

Consider, for example, the kind of contribution that may be described as moral. The strength of a Member State's devotion to the purposes of the United Nations and of its faith in the principles on which the Organization is founded may be great or little. A Member State of small population, limited natural resources, and little military power, but strongly devoted to the purposes and principles embodied in the United Nations Charter, may send able and useful representatives to meetings of the General Assembly, supply to that body an occasional president of high distinction and practical capacity for leadership in its affairs, and exert a constructive influence at every crisis in world politics. Thus it may make a more valuable contribution than another Member State of larger population, greater wealth, and superior military power, which drags its feet in every emergency and seems to have little faith in systematic and purposeful efforts to establish a better world order. Moral contributions to the purposes of the United Nations are impossible to measure, but a good reputation for respecting the obligations of membership, regardless of military power or wealth, may be the best of qualifications for election to the Security Council.

The importance of sturdy moral contributors is manifest even in operations designed to deal with threats to the peace and acts of aggression by important military powers. There have been three outstanding tests of the willingness and practical capacity of Member States to give effective aid in connection with such operations: the case of Korea in 1950, that of Suez in 1956, and that of the Congo in 1960. In each case the response of some of the Member States was immediate and impressive, though only token military contributions were accepted from the weaker contributors. But the moral force of the token contributions strengthened the morale of the Organization, enhanced its prestige, and immeasurably added to the impact of the operations in the field. The contributors of contingents to the action in Korea are commemorated by a memorial plaque in the vestibule of the General Assembly building in New York. Included among them are both important and unimportant military powers as well as both large and small financial contributors to the Organization. The same lack of relationship between actual contributions and measurable capacity to contribute appears again in the operations at Suez. In the latter case, indeed, military contributions by the major powers were deliberately excluded in order to prevent conflict between them for control of the situation. The expenses of the operation were defrayed from a special fund, contributions to which bore little relation to the established scale of assessment for the regular expenses of the Organization. It is obvious that the military power and financial capacity of the Member States constitute a very imperfect measure of their contributions to the purposes of the United Nations.

The operations in the Congo demonstrate further how useful the smallest and weakest contributors may be, when men and money are needed to accomplish the purposes of the United Nations. In this case only three states of European population, Canada, Sweden and Ireland, were called upon to furnish military contingents. The main military burden of the peacekeeping operations fell upon African Member States, most of which are both militarily and financially weak. While some of them may have had political axes of their own which they wished to grind, their initial response indicated, for the most part, a strong determination to support the authority of the United Nations with a minimum of aid from outside the Continent. Additional help, when needed, was furnished by Asian Member States, regardless of their distance from the scene of action. The principal test of ability to contribute was political. The basic qualification for a helpful contributor was active sympathy with the main purpose of the United Nations in intervening in the Congo, and practical capacity to give military aid of a kind that would be acceptable to the people of the newly liberated Congo Republic.

Most of the actual contributors to the purposes of the United Nations in these cases were small states, measured by population, wealth, or military power. The greatest potential contributors to the maintenance of international peace and security are doubtless the major powers. It is regrettable that the Charter undertook to specify the states whose importance should entitle them to permanent seats in the Security Council, since the brief history of the United Nations has already confirmed the proposition that such a list becomes outmoded with the passage of time. Ideally, the list of privileged members should be revised and made flexible enough to register future changes in the status of Member States, but this hardly seems politically feasible at the present time. In any event, experience up to now shows the great importance of the military contributions by the lesser powers and ordinary Member States. Still more it shows the great importance of the moral contributions of all those, regardless of size, wealth, or geographical situation, who strongly believe in the purposes of the United Nations and freely contribute according to their means to the actions that may be deemed necessary and proper for dealing with recurrent emergencies and crises.

Moral contributions to the purposes of the United Nations may take the form of furnishing wise councillors and other leaders in the work of the Organization. Outstanding among such contributions have been the successive holders of the office of Secretary-General and the presiding officers of the General Assembly. Scandinavian Member States have supplied spirited and skillful leadership in the former office and all the General Assembly Presidents have come from other Middle Powers or lesser states. The wisest and most useful international statesmen may hail from states of lesser military or economic importance. It is evident that the selection of members of the Security Council on account of their contributions to the purposes of the United Nations involves the weighing of many factors in the making of an international organization that will be equal to its growing responsibilities under the difficult conditions of the nuclear age.

Despite the complexities and difficulties of measurement which we have noted, no one can doubt that there is in fact a group of Member States which make outstanding contributions to the United Nations, and that the liberal representation of this group in the membership of the Security Council would do much to strengthen the political significance of that body. No scheme can guarantee the selection of the best qualified states for membership in the Security Council, but the provision of separate blocks of seats for regional representatives and for "members at large" might enhance the prospect that principal contributors would be given the prominent role in the Security Council to which their importance entitles them.

The alternative schemes which we have described represent more or less elaborately detailed approaches to a common objective: making the Security Council a more broadly representative body and thus, hopefully, a more useful instrument for the adjustment of political differences among states. We put them forward for illustrative purposes. Our aim is not to advocate a particular solution, but to stress our conviction that it is urgently necessary to remodel the Security Council so as to enhance its political usefulness, and to stimulate thought and effort toward that end.

The adoption of a well-considered plan for rehabilitating the Security Council through enlarging and balancing its membership should enable it to reflect in due measure all the important interests in world politics, and ensure that its consent to any controversial proposal would carry with it general international support. Thus, the Council would become an attractive locus for international negotiations looking toward generally acceptable solutions of the bigger problems which nations have heretofore too often sought to settle by the use or threat of armed force.

Good working facilities for the practice of parliamentary diplomacy in the Security Council would go far toward making a more effective United Nations. Segregated summit conferences of the major powers are not enough to compensate for the manifest deficiencies of traditional diplomacy under the strenuous conditions of the nuclear age. The United Nations General Assembly is a kind of permanent summit conference for the middle and minor powers and ordinary states. Let the major

249

powers take their proper places in the Security Council by sending their ablest and most responsible spokesmen to its meetings and thereby make a permanent summit conference for themselves also. Thus the meetings of the Security Council could serve a more constructive purpose than that of providing an arena for cold-war propaganda, and parliamentary diplomacy would come of age.

The improvement of the facilities for parliamentary diplomacy within the framework of the United Nations should help to clear the way for the processes of political accommodation among the major powers. If there is a genuine desire for peaceful coexistence—and our entire hope for the future is premised on the expectation that statesmen will be rational enough to read correctly the nuclear handwriting on the wall of history—the revised Security Council may be the scene of constant efforts to reach negotiated solutions of dangerous political problems and to develop agreement on measures conceived in the general interest of mankind. The outcome of political processes cannot be determined or made predictable by the manipulation of the structure or procedures of international organs; the result depends ultimately upon the rationality and decency, the enlightenment and restraint, the wisdom and vision, of those who make and alter national policies. The most that we can do is to work to establish the conditions and mechanisms conducive to the successful operation of the processes of political accommodation —and we can surely afford to do no less.

We call attention to the fact that, with or without the enlargement and balancing of the Security Council which we have proposed, significant possibilities exist for improving the diplomatic quality of the Council's proceedings. Statesmen who seek the values of diplomacy rather than of propaganda can resist the urge to engage in denunciation and abuse of one another. They can abstain from the public statement of positions which condemn negotiations to failure by giving concessions the flavor of defeat and humiliation.

The Council, even in its present form, might enhance its usefulness by adopting a new procedure for handling disputes: Instead of considering resolutions, to be adopted or rejected, early in its deliberations on an issue, the Council might first undertake a general discussion, for the purpose of gaining information and understanding of the problems. Then, it might seek an agreed solution, drafted by its President, the Secretary-General, a special rapporteur, or an appropriately composed subcommittee, in preference to the consideration of resolutions submitted by parties to the dispute at hand. Such a process, reducing the elements of victory and defeat in Security Council procedure, might go far toward making the Council what it was intended to be: a well-informed body, committed to the maintenance of the peace of the world, able to look ahead and to bring to bear the healing light of awareness and reconciliation on problems before they have become so controversial that hope of solution begins to disappear. An improved Security Council could function as a more valuable companion to the other organs of the United Nations, especially the General Assembly and the International Court of Justice, which provide facilities for promoting the peaceful settlement of international disputes.

The development and maintenance of social order at every level, from the local to the global, requires the utilization of the resources of the process of political accommodation. We have clearly not exhausted those resources in the international community. The imaginative mobilization of those resources is a major item on the agenda of the future.

THE TROIKA AND THE FUTURE OF THE UNITED NATIONS: THE SECRETARY-GENERAL

by

SYDNEY D. BAILEY

IT WAS ALWAYS intended that the Secretary-General should be more than an administrator.[34] This was explicit in the Charter. Indeed, one may classify the responsibilities of the Secretary-General according to constitutional origin as follows:

(a) responsibilities arising from his position as chief administrative officer of the Organization and Secretary-General of the General Assembly and the three Councils;

(b) responsibilities entrusted to him by the above organs;

(c) responsibilities arising from Article 99 of the Charter.

The responsibilities in the first group include those administrative and related duties specified in the Charter and the Rules of Procedure of the principal and subsidiary organs.

When a function is entrusted to the Secretary-General, as the responsibility to appoint staff under regulations established by the General Assembly, the legal authority to exercise it belongs exclusively to him.

Responsibilities entrusted to the Secretary-General by United Nations organs under Article 98, whether in general terms by the rules of procedure or by decisions in particular cases, need not be solely administrative in character. Since 1954, the policy-making organs have increasingly entrusted the Secretary-General with diplomatic and operational functions.

Articles 99 and 98

Article 99 has wide implications for the diplomatic activities of the Secretary-General. Indeed, it was assumed at San Francisco in 1945 that the chief source of the political power of the Secretary-General lay in this Article. The Preparatory Commission considered that Article 99 gives to the Secretary-General "a quite special right which goes beyond any power previously accorded to the head of an international organization"[35]; Lie held that article 99 "confers upon the Secretary-General . . . world political responsibilities which no individual, no representative of a single nation, ever had before."[36] Article 99 is of cardinal importance, and it has been argued that in order to discharge the responsibilities conferred on him by this Article, the Secretary-General must have information which enables him to judge when world peace is threatened.

Dès lors, il a le devoir d'observer l'évolution de la conjoncture internationale, afin de déceler les dangers qu'elle peut recéler et les mesurer. Ce qui implique qu'il en ait aussi les moyens. Ceux-ci n'ayant pas été expressément définis par la Charte, ils semblent se réduire à ce qui ne nécessite pas une habilitation juridique particulière: essentiellement, mise à part l'utilisation des informations publiques, les communications qui lui seront faites par les gouvernements ainsi que les contacts qu'il pourra prendre ou accepter, personnellement ou par ses représentants, avec les personnalités les plus diverses, officielles, officieuses ou simples particuliers. Tout au plus peut-on affirmer que l'article 99 exclut toutes restrictions au cercle de ses entretiens et de ses investigations, sauf celles que pourraient lui imposer éventuellement les règles de la "courtoisie internationale."[37]

Lie was never simply an administrator. He concerned himself with political questions and took up definite positions when he considered that the principles of the Charter were at stake, even if this seemed likely to bring him into conflict with one or other of the great powers. His memorandum on some legal aspects of the problem of Chinese representation annoyed the United States, and his attitude toward the Korean war led to the Soviet decision not to "recognize" him as Secretary-General. His Twenty-Year Programme for achieving peace through the United Nations was an important initiative; it deserved a better reception.

Lie's political and diplomatic activities were broadly in line with the ideas that were current when the United Nations was founded. A group of former officials of the League of Nations had commented in 1944 that little progress in international business was likely unless international officials undertook negotiating functions,[38] and the Preparatory Commission foresaw that the Secretary-General would be called upon from time to time to take decisions which might justly be called political.[39]

That a significant evolution in the Office of Secretary-General took place during Hammarskjold's period of service was due in part to the course of world events, in part to Hammarskjold's own qualities. He took a broad view of his responsibilities under the Charter, but Article 99 did not play as important a part in the evolution of the Office of the Secretary-General as might have been expected. Lie's intervention in the Security Council after the Korean war had broken out reinforced an initiative which had already been taken, and it was only later that he explicitly claimed that his action on that occasion had been taken under Article 99.[40] At the time of the Suez invasion in 1956, Hammarskjold told the Security Council that he would have used his right to call for an immediate meeting of the Council had not the United States government already taken the initiative.[41] In the case of the Laotian appeal to the Secretary-General for a United Nations emergency force to halt aggression in 1959, Hammarskjold requested the President of the Security Council to convene the Council to consider his report on the Laotian request. When the Council met, Hammarskjold asked to be allowed to report, but he made it clear that this request was not "based on the explicit rights granted to the Secretary-General under Article 99 of the Charter." To have invoked Article 99, he said, would necessarily have involved a judgment as to the facts for which, in the prevailing situation, he did not have a sufficient basis.[42] In the Congo case, on the other hand, Hammarskjold was satisfied that there was a threat, or a potential threat, to international peace and security. "I must conclude . . . that the presence of these Belgian troops is a source of internal, and potentially also of international, tension."[43]

But if Article 99 has not been as important as the founders expected, Article 98 has been decisive. It was presumably intended at San Francisco that Article 98 would be used when a policy-making organ wished to entrust the Secretary-General or the Secretariat with a routine administrative function, such as the preparation of a technical report or the collation of the comments of governments. I doubt whether anyone foresaw in 1945 that the Security Council or the General Assembly would one day deal with a grave international crisis by approving a resolution asking the Secretary-General to make such "arrangements as would adequately help in upholding the purposes and principles of the Charter."[44] Yet broad general directives, involving action of a diplomatic or operational nature, have been given to the Secretary-General in connection with imprisoned flyers in China, the problems of the Middle East, the Hungarian revolt, the complaints of Lebanon and Jordan of foreign intervention, race relations in South Africa, and the Congo.

In other cases, policy-making organs have handed awkward problems to the Secretary-General simply by concluding the consideration of a matter with an understanding that the Secretary-General, in the normal course of his duties, would give the matter attention. In 1958, when the General Assembly was considering the future of United Nations assistance to Palestine refugees, a specific request that the Secretary-General should submit proposals on the matter was withdrawn on the understanding that the Secretary-General would, "as part of his regular duties, look into the technical operation of UNRWA in preparation of such proposals as he might consider helpful or necessary to bring forward to the General Assembly. . . ."[45]

Evolution of the Office

Perhaps the most important development in the role of the Secretary-General related to functions exercised without the express authority of a policy-making body. Nobody objected in 1955 when the Secretary-General acted as a "postman" and transmitted to Greece a communication from Albania regarding the restoration of diplomatic relations between the two countries; but no organ had authorized this action.

Hammarskjold, from the beginning, distinguished between those specific responsibilities conferred on him by policy-making organs and those general responsibilities which, explicitly or implicitly, attached to the Office of Secretary-General. When he visited Peking in 1955, following a General Assembly resolution that requested him to seek the release of captured personnel, he was able, in his capacity as Secretary-General of the United Nations and apart from functions entrusted to him by the Assembly, to exchange views with Chinese officials. When in 1956 he was asked by the Security Council to survey various aspects of compliance with the general armistice agreements in the Middle East, he insisted not only that this request did not detract from his authority under the Charter, but also that it did not add to it. On the occasion of his reappointment in 1957, he stated in the General Assembly that the Secretary-General should act if guidance could be found in the Charter or in the decisions of the main organs of the United Nations. He went even further. The Secretary-General, he said, should also act without such guidance "should this appear to him necessary in order to help in filling any vacuum that may appear in the systems which the Charter and traditional diplomacy provide for the safeguarding of peace and security."[46]

This evolution of the concept of the role of the Secretary-General has had far-reaching implications. Hammarskjold was not seeking to usurp the functions of the Security Council or the General Assembly, but he firmly believed that if the policy-making organs, for whatever reason, failed to perform their functions, the responsibilities of the Secretary-General were unimpaired. He was, in a sense, a guardian of the Charter and its principles; governments could abstain from voting, but he could not abstain from acting.

Within a year of his reappointment, his interpretation was put to a severe test. Lebanon had complained to the Security Council of intervention in its internal affairs by the United Arab Republic. The Council, acting on a proposal by Sweden, decided to send an observation group to the area in order to ensure that there was no illegal infiltration across the Lebanese borders. A month later, the Lebanese government requested the United States to send forces to help preserve the country's integrity and independence, and the United States complied with the request.

255

The resulting situation was thereupon considered by the Security Council. A Soviet proposal calling for the immediate withdrawal of United States troops from Lebanon (as well as British troops from Jordan) was defeated, as was a Swedish proposal to suspend the activities of the United Nations Observation Group. The United States proposed that the Secretary-General should make additional arrangements to ensure the independence and integrity of Lebanon but this was blocked by a Soviet veto.

In this confused and grave situation, Japan submitted what was intended to be a compromise proposal, expressed in the most general terms. This asked the Secretary-General to make arrangements forthwith for such measures as he might consider necessary with a view to ensuring the integrity and independence of Lebanon, thus making possible the withdrawal of United States forces from that country. This received ten affirmative votes, but the negative Soviet vote constituted a veto.

Here was a vacuum *par excellence,* and Hammarskjold had no hesitation in acting. His statement to the Security Council conveys most vividly his sense of responsibility.

The Security Council has just failed to take additional action in the grave emergency facing us. However, the responsibility of the United Nations to make all efforts to live up to the purposes and principles of the Charter remains. . . .
In a statement before this Council on 31 October 1956, I said that the discretion and impartiality imposed on the Secretary-General by the character of his immediate task must not degenerate into a policy of expediency. On a later occasion—it was 26 September 1957—I said in a statement before the General Assembly that I believed it to be the duty of the Secretary-General "to use his office and, indeed, the machinery of the Organization to its utmost capacity and to the full extent permitted at each stage by practical circumstances." I added that I believed that it is in keeping with the philosophy of the Charter that the Secretary-General also should be expected to act without any guidance from the Assembly or the Security Council should this appear to him necessary towards helping to fill any vacuum that may appear in the systems which the Charter and traditional diplomacy provide for the safeguarding of peace and security. . . .
I am sure that I will be acting in accordance with the wishes of the members of the Council if I, therefore, use all opportunities offered to the Secretary-General, within the limits set by the Charter and towards developing the United Nations effort, so as to help to prevent a further deterioration of the situation in the Middle East. . . .
First of all . . . this will mean the further development of the Observation Group [in Lebanon]. The Council will excuse me for not being able to spell out at this moment what it may mean beyond that. . . .[47]

Hammarskjold recognized that policy-making organs do not always respond to a crisis smoothly or swiftly; parliamentary diplomacy has its limitations. When tensions arose between Cambodia and Thailand in 1958, the two governments agreed with him that the dispute should not go to a policy-making organ in the first instance. They asked the Secretary-General to designate a representative to help them in finding a solution. This was done without the formal approval of the Security Council, though with the knowledge of its members. "Such actions by the Secretary-General," reported Hammarskjold, "fall within the competence of his Office and are . . . in other respects also in strict accordance with the Charter, when they serve its purpose." The method he had used, he said, avoided public debate in a policy-making organ which might have increased the difficulties. Member states might well have been hesitant to give explicit prior approval to an action without fuller knowledge of the facts. The evolution of the Office of Secretary-General represented "an intensification and a broadening of the interplay" between the policy-making organs and the Secretariat, while maintaining the principle that the activities of the United Nations are "wholly dependent on decisions of the Governments."[48]

In 1959, he again took action on his own responsibility in a difficult situation, even though the matter had come before the Security Council. The Laotian government requested that a United Nations force be sent to Laos to halt aggression. The Security Council met at Hammarskjold's request and decided to appoint a sub-committee to inquire into the situation.[49] The sub-committee reported on 5 November 1959, and three days later Hammarskjold announced that, "taking into account his duties under the Charter, and all the information at present available," he had decided to pay a personal visit to Laos.[50] Later, within the framework of the United Nations technical assistance program, he appointed a special consultant for the coordination of United Nations activities in Laos. The Soviet government took the position that Hammarskjold's visit and his subsequent actions were "designed to cover by the name of the United Nations further interference of the Western powers in Laos. . . ."[51]

In 1960, Hammarskjold interpreted his responsibilities in constitutional terms. His Office, he said, was "a one-man 'executive,' with explicit authority in the administrative field, supplementary to, but not overlapping the authority

257

of either the [Security] Council or the Assembly."[52] And in his speech at Oxford in 1961, he stated that the conception of the Office of Secretary-General originated in the United States.

The United States gave serious consideration to the idea that the Organization should have a President as well as a Secretary-General. Subsequently, it was decided to propose only a single officer, but one in whom there would be combined both the political and executive functions of a President with the internal administrative functions that were previously accorded to a Secretary-General.[53]

There were, then, two parallel and related trends. First, policy-making organs were increasingly entrusting the Secretary-General with broad diplomatic and operational functions; second, the Secretary-General was using all the resources of his Office in the exercise of independent initiatives designed to further the purposes and principles of the Charter. And it cannot be denied that the totality of these developments gave to the Office of Secretary-General a character that had not been foreseen by the founders of the Organization. The Secretary-General had, of course, been appointed by the unanimous will of member states, and his independence was guaranteed by the Charter stipulation that he could neither seek nor receive instructions from any source external to the United Nations. If member states had wished to resist the trends, they could have done so, but they were glad to "leave it to Dag." Sometimes this was wise; sometimes it was an abdication of responsibility.

The fact was that parliamentary diplomacy was becoming more and more parliamentary, and less and less diplomatic. Delegates were often in danger of forgetting the purposes of the United Nations, so admirably set forth in the first Article of the Charter; attention, instead, was increasingly directed, not to purposes, but to methods. Debate was coming to be thought of as an end in itself; a vote was mistaken for action.

The chief purpose of parliamentary diplomacy (though not always the only one) is to cause a reassessment of national interests in the light of the national interests of others. The various elements that together constitute parliamentary diplomacy are occasionally sufficient in themselves to bring the actions of nations into harmony. This seems to have been the case, for example, in the General Assembly's consideration of the Syrian-Turkish tension in 1957 and in the

Security Council's consideration of the Sudan-Egyptian border dispute in 1958. However, parliamentary diplomacy may not always be enough. In a variety of circumstances, it has been found useful to inject the physical presence of the United Nations into situations of difficulty or tension. Such a United Nations presence symbolizes the concern of the international community, but it does more than that. A government may refuse to comply with a decision of a policy-making organ but might think twice before taking action that would bring it into direct, on-the-spot conflict with representatives of the international community. A United Nations presence may create conditions in which it is difficult to assault the principles of the United Nations without at the same time assaulting its representatives.

The presence of the United Nations may consist of the Secretary-General, or one or more representatives appointed by him, or by a policy-making organ; it may consist of an intergovernmental committee; it may consist of persons or contingents, loaned by governments, for observation or police duties; or it may consist of a section of the Secretariat with special regional or functional responsibilities. The form of the presence has to be tailored to the needs of each situation.

In practice there are, naturally, limits to what a United Nations presence can do. It cannot enter territory without the consent of the government concerned. It must have the freedom of movement and the facilities necessary to undertake the tasks committed to it. It must to some extent operate independently of the host government, and yet without becoming a rival authority. It must abstain from actions taken to influence the internal political situation.

The United Nations operations initiated in the Middle East following the crises of 1956 and 1958 created important precedents. In both cases, considerable discretion was given to the Secretary-General in implementing the decisions of policy-making organs. The presences were established in accordance with his proposals, and he was made the agent of the Organization in attempting to secure certain objectives.

The Congo case has been the most intricate and intractable in which the United Nations has been involved. The lack of preparation for independence and the unexpected speed of the transfer of sovereignty resulted in a vacuum that Congolese nationalists were not in a position to fill. The issue before the international community in July 1960 was whether the United Nations could stabilize and insulate the situation for an interim period until adequate and united Congolese leadership had emerged. The Congo operation has been criticized from almost every conceivable point of view, but the critics should bear in mind that the operation had to be conducted in conformity with principles that had been accepted as valid in earlier operations, and that actions taken in the Congo would become precedents for the future. It is easier to complain that this or that political result was not achieved than to lay down an acceptable code for United Nations action, particularly in relation to the internal affairs of a state.

Moreover, the decisions of the Security Council and the General Assembly regarding the Congo did not always give clear guidance to those on the spot. How was the Secretary-General to interpret the mandate to assist the government of the Congo if more than one authority claimed to be that government? How was it possible for the United Nations both to safeguard the unity of the Congo in the face of secessionist activities and at the same time to abstain from any action that would influence any internal conflict? Did the United Nations mandate to prevent civil war extend to resisting by force Central Government troops which might try to enter secessionist areas if their declared purpose was to restore the territorial integrity and unity of the Congo? At what point did the use of force, as a last resort, become necessary? Nor should it be forgotten that a great many member states were content to give instructions to the Secretary-General (and, indeed, to complain in public at the way he carried them out) while denying him the material resources and diplomatic backing he needed.

A "new executive"?

It was the course of events in the Congo that sparked off the Soviet onslaught on Hammarskjold. Until 1959, the Soviet Union appeared to trust and respect him. In spite of his support for the idea of a committee to investigate the situation following the Hungarian revolt in 1956, Khrushchev proposed in 1958 that the Secretary-General should participate in a meeting of heads of government on the Middle East. Although there was some Soviet criticism of Hammarskjold because of his activities in connection with the Laotian appeal for a United Nations force, the attack was relatively muted, and after Hammarskjold had invoked

Article 99 of the Charter in connection with the Congo in July 1960, the Soviet Union supported the first three resolutions asking the Secretary-General to implement the Security Council's decisions. Within a few weeks, however, the Soviet government had launched a bitter personal attack on Hammarskjold. Khrushchev complained, first, that Hammarskjold had disregarded decisions of United Nations organs; second, and more generally, that he had supported the colonialist and capitalist states in the Congo and was biased against the Soviet Union and its allies. Khrushchev said bluntly that the countries of the Soviet bloc no longer trusted Hammarskjold and called on him to resign. Later, the Soviet government went even further and demanded that Hammarskjold be dismissed from his post.[54]

But the Soviet government wanted more than simply the removal of Hammarskjold. Khrushchev considered that there were basic faults in the structure of the Organization. The concrete reality of the present world, he said, is that it comprises three groups of states: the states which he called socialist but which elsewhere are usually called Communist; states which he called neutralist, but which are also called unaligned or uncommitted; and states which he described as belonging to Western military blocs. The post of Secretary-General should be abolished, he said; "the executive organ of the United Nations should reflect the real situation that obtains in the world today." In place of a single Secretary-General there should be a collective executive organ consisting of "persons representing the states belonging to the three basic groups." The crux of the matter, said Khrushchev, is not what should be the name of the new executive body but that this executive organ should "represent" the states belonging to the three groups, thus guaranteeing that the executive work of the United Nations "would not be carried out to the detriment of any one of these groups of states."[55]

What happened between 9 August 1960, when the Soviet government voted for the resolution confirming the authority already given to the Secretary-General in the Congo and entrusting additional responsibilities to him, and 23 September, when Khrushchev publicly attacked Hammarskjold? Was the "troika" proposal a hasty and petulant response to particular United Nations actions in the Congo which had displeased the Soviet government, or did it represent a premeditated demand based on a long-term Soviet interpretation of general trends in world affairs?

It is not in dispute that the Soviet government suffered a setback in the Congo, but it seems to me significant that the "troika" idea was linked closely to possible future developments in relation to disarmament and the peace-keeping functions of the United Nations. The particular form the proposal took was probably based on the following considerations. First, in the light of the growth of the Secretary-General's independent exercise of those functions which the Soviet government regarded as the sole responsibility of the Security Council, the Soviet government wished to have means to prevent action by the Secretariat which it regarded as inimical to its interests. Second, the Soviet government had for some years claimed that the Soviet bloc should have a position of parity with the Western group in United Nations organs. Finally, the Soviet government had considered that the concept of impartiality was merely a mask to conceal the fact that the Secretariat promoted Western policies.[56]

This is not the occasion to attempt to write an objective history of the United Nations operation in the Congo or of Hammarskjold's service as Secretary-General of the United Nations, but I am convinced that no man could have acted with greater independence, integrity, and impartiality than Hammarskjold, that no man could have shown a higher sense of international responsibility. I hope and believe that the day will come when such sentiments will be *comme il faut* in the Soviet Union. Estimates of the character of great men change with the passage of time.

The United Nations responded to the request from the government of the Congo on the basis of complete impartiality and neutrality regarding internal political differences. The United Nations Emergency Force in the Middle East had been based on the same principle that it would never be used to enforce any particular political solution or to influence the political balance in any way.[57] The United Nations Observation Group in Lebanon similarly sought to avoid any partisan act, even during conditions of civil war. The Security Council's resolution of 9 August 1960 regarding the Congo reaffirmed that "the United Nations Force in the Congo will not be a party to or in any way intervene or be used to influence the outcome of any internal conflict, constitutional or otherwise."[58]

It was not possible, at the time the Congo operation was launched by the Security Council, to foresee how difficult it would become to interpret the original mandate. The

United Nations was sending a force to the Congo, not to secure and supervise the cessation of hostilities as had been the task of UNEF in the Middle East, nor to prevent infiltration across borders as had been the case with the Observation Group in Lebanon; the Security Council decided in its first resolution to furnish military assistance to the government of the Congo, and called for the withdrawal of Belgian forces. The United Nations Force was to provide the government of an independent state with military aid. The principle that the United Nations Force would not influence internal conflicts in the Congo was to become increasingly difficult to interpret and implement, particularly when secessionist and other groups in the Congo received encouragement and support from outside.

The crisis leading to the events of which the Soviet Union complained came to a head on 5 September. The Congo was at that time on the verge of economic and political collapse. On the evening of 5 September, President Kasavubu declared over the radio that he had dismissed the government of Patrice Lumumba and had invited Joseph Iléo to form a new government. Lumumba thereupon called a meeting of the Council of Ministers, which decided to depose Kasavubu.

Leopoldville was in an explosive and tense condition, with two rival groups trying to mobilize support among the population. The attempt to insulate the Congo from disruptive external forces was being impeded by the fact that Belgium was openly supporting one faction in the Congo and the Soviet Union another. On the day of Lumumba's dismissal, the Security-General had addressed a blunt communication to the Belgian Delegation in New York on the delay in the evacuation of Belgian troops from the Congo and an equally blunt communication to the Soviet Delegation about the reported arrival in the Congo of Soviet planes, in defiance of the Security Council's resolutions.

United Nations representatives in the Congo had been instructed to avoid any action by which, directly or indirectly, openly or by implication, they might pass judgment on any internal conflict, and they found themselves in a situation in which inaction as well as action was likely to be interpreted by one side or the other as contravening this principle. In an effort to prevent an outbreak of violence in Leopoldville, United Nations representatives temporarily closed the radio station and the airport. It was their intention that the action would be impartial in its consequences; Kasavubu and Lumumba were to be equally affected by it, although in the event the action worked against Lumumba. These emergency measures were taken without consulting the Secretary-General, who was at Headquarters in New York.

Hammarskjold clearly faced a painful dilemma. The action by the men on the spot led to strong protests, not solely from the Communist bloc. While the Secretary-General could hardly disavow a decision taken in good faith by trusted colleagues at a time of acute difficulty, for him to endorse the action would risk bringing him into open conflict with influential member states. Hammarskjold did not hesitate to take that risk and stated plainly that he fully endorsed the action.

After his dismissal, Lumumba sought and was granted United Nations protection in Leopoldville. At the end of November, Lumumba left the residence in which he had been guarded by the United Nations, and some days later he was arrested by the Congolese National Army. In the middle of January 1961, Lumumba was transferred to Elisabethville; on 10 February it was announced by the authorities in Katanga that Lumumba had "escaped," and shortly afterward it became known that he had been killed.

After Lumumba's arrest, United Nations representatives in the Congo had tried to secure all possible legal and humanitarian protection for him. When he was transferred to Elisabethville, the Secretary-General and his representative in the Congo exercised all the influence possible for his return to Leopoldville and for the application of normal legal rules in the protection of his interests. No attempt was made by the United Nations to obtain his release by forcible means, since such action was considered to have been beyond the mandate conferred by the Security Council at that time.

The murder of Lumumba was—to use Hammarskjold's words—a revolting crime; it was also a political tragedy. But when Khrushchev first attacked Hammarskjold, Lumumba was still alive, enjoying the protection of United Nations forces. The launching of the "troika" proposal preceded the assassination of Lumumba by about four months. Indeed, it is doubtful whether the decision of the Soviet government to attack Hammarskjold and propose drastic reforms in the structure of the United Nations was based primarily on one or two incidents in the Congo situation. It seems more likely that what disturbed the Soviet government was the general trend of developments in the United Nations.

It is surely significant that whenever Khrushchev addressed the General Assembly on the subject of tripartite administration in 1960, he immediately proceeded to discuss disarmament and the use of international forces for maintaining peace.

The United Nations Secretariat must therefore be adapted even now to the conditions which will come into being as disarmament decisions are implemented. An identical point of view has emerged . . . regarding the necessity of following up an agreement on disarmament with the establishment of armed forces of all countries, under international control, to be used by the United Nations in accordance with the decision of the Security Council.[59]

It has been said that, after an agreement on disarmament has been reached, international armed forces should be formed. We are, in principle, in agreement with this. But the question arises, who will command these forces? The United Nations Secretary-General? . . . Is it really permissible for the fate of millions to be dependent on the actions of the one man occupying that post? . . . There can be no disarmament, there can be no international armed forces, in the absence of guarantees for all three groups [of States] against the misuse of these armed forces.[60]

"Troika" and Veto

To demand guarantees against misuse is legitimate; the Soviet government is not alone in making this demand. But the proposal for a collective executive body in the form in which it was presented went much further. Each member of the proposed triumvirate would be able, in certain circumstances, to prevent the decisions of policy-making organs from being implemented, either by outright veto or by prevaricating tactics. What other interpretation can there be of the following extract from Khrushchev's first statement on the subject?

We consider it advisable to set up, in the place of a Secretary-General who is at present the interpreter and executor of the decisions of the General Assembly and the Security Council, a collective executive organ of the United Nations consisting of three persons each of whom would represent a certain group of States. That would provide a definite guarantee that the work of the United Nations executive organ would not be carried on to the detriment of any one of these groups of States. The United Nations executive organ would then be a genuinely democratic organ; it would really guard the interests of all States Members of the United Nations. . . .[61]

It is true that the Soviet government has not formally stated that each member of a three-man executive would have the right of veto, but it is a reasonable interpretation of the Soviet position and will no doubt be generally assumed until it is expressly denied. Indeed, in an official elaboration of its views, the Soviet government did not challenge an allegation by the United States that the "troika" proposal would be tantamount to the introduction of the right of veto into the administrative realm.[62]

The veto, even if it is called the rule of unanimity, is essentially negative. Its effect is not to foster cooperation; it is to prevent action. The right of the great powers to exercise the veto in the Security Council may be necessary; it has even been argued that the growing disparity between votes and power in the United Nations makes the veto more necessary now than when the Charter was drafted. But the *de jure* form of veto in the Security Council is by no means the only way of blocking action by the United Nations. A government may, by unilateral act, attempt to nullify the decision of a policy-making organ—for example, by refusing to permit United Nations representatives to enter a territory for which it is responsible. Again, a government may resort to various kinds of harrassing tactics—refusal to pay a share of the cost of United Nations operations, discourteous personal attacks on United Nations officials, pressure to postpone action at times when the only effective action is prompt action, the general disparagement of the United Nations.

The Uniting for Peace procedure was intended to be a means of circumventing the veto in the Security Council, and the states which supported the procedure should not be indignant if the Soviet Union wishes to reintroduce the veto in another form. After all, the Soviet Union is relatively much more powerful than it was fifteen years ago; its rulers are inspired by a dynamic ideology which they believe has universal validity; they believe history is on their side. Yet for all that, the Soviet government finds itself no more able than formerly to block United Nations decisions relating to peace and security which it dislikes.

But the problem is not simply to prevent the United Nations from acting to the detriment of any state or group of states. If it were, one solution would be to extend the veto to all members and all organs of the United Nations. The heart of the matter is whether we will advance toward the goal of a stable international order by limiting or by extending the right of states to act arbitrarily in pursuit of objectives they regard as legitimate.

The veto in the Security Council can prevent the initiation of action, but it cannot ensure its termination. Although a policy-making organ of the United Nations can withdraw a mandate as easily as it can confer it, once a decision has been taken, it is valid until rescinded. An operation authorized by the Security Council cannot be stopped by a veto if one of the permanent members later finds the course of events not to its liking. The return of the Soviet representative to the Security Council after the boycott in 1950 could not lead to the cancellation of the earlier decisions to resist aggression in Korea. In the Lebanon operation of 1958, the Soviet veto of a Japanese proposal that the Secretary-General should make arrangements for such measures as he might consider necessary to ensure the integrity and independence of the Lebanon did not annul the original decision to send an observation group to ensure that there was no illegal infiltration across the Lebanese borders. When the Soviet Union became displeased with events in the Congo, it was unable to use its veto to terminate the United Nations operation.

The situation in the General Assembly is similar. An operation may be launched by a two-thirds majority of those member states present and voting; one-third of the members plus one can prevent a decision. But an operation, once under way, can be halted only by an express decision by a two-thirds majority.

Policy-making and the Secretary-General

Difficulties have undoubtedly arisen when resolutions entrusting the Secretary-General with broad responsibilities have been expressed in vague general terms. It is, of course, impossible to foresee all eventualities; some matters must be left for later interpretation or decision. But there is all the difference in the world between a prudent avoidance of precision when all the circumstances cannot be foreseen and the transfer of total responsibility for decision and action to the Secretary-General because a policy-making organ has failed to agree on what should be done.

Agreement depends on negotiation, and negotiation takes time. The General Assembly, in particular, now has more to do than it can do well. Time can be saved for the more important matters only by the exercise of greater discrimination regarding the agenda and a decrease of what in the British House of Commons is called "irrelevance or tedious repetition." Changes of practice in these matters do not depend primarily on amending the Rules of Procedure—although a review of practice and procedure is desirable for other reasons.

Public debate is an essential part of parliamentary diplomacy, but its limitations must be recognized. After the parties to a dispute have made initial statements in a public session of a policy-making organ, efforts to narrow the differences can usefully be undertaken in private. The use of special rapporteurs, both to elucidate the issues and to make proposals for a solution, was one of the more successful practices of the League of Nations, and it is a pity that United Nations organs have not followed the practice. Individuals can nearly always perform this function more effectively than committees.[63] This is not to say that there is some magic formula for ensuring the sort of agreement that can be embodied in an unambiguous resolution, but there are some methods that tend toward this result and some that do not.

Even when resolutions are fairly precise, later developments may pose problems for the Secretariat which were not foreseen when the resolution was adopted. In some cases, the Secretary-General may be able to consult an advisory committee of member states; in other cases, he may refer the matter to the policy-making organ for clarification or extension of the original mandate. When sharp differences arose between Hammarskjold and Lumumba in August 1960, Hammarskjold called for a meeting of the Security Council to clarify its attitude.[64] At a later stage in the Congo operation, Hammarskjold made it clear that fresh decisions by the Security Council were needed. "It cannot shirk its responsibilities by expecting from the Secretariat action on which it is not prepared to take decisions itself."[65] The Council, after debate, adopted a resolution authorizing the use of force, if necessary, in the last resort, in order to prevent civil war in the Congo.

Hammarskjold was occasionally confronted with issues in which he found it impossible to secure a clear judgment from an advisory committee or a policy-making organ. However, since inaction may have as decisive an effect as action, Hammarskjold was prepared in such circumstances to act "on his own risk but with as faithful an interpretation of the instructions, rights and obligations of the Organisation as possible in view of international law and the decisions already taken."[66] It is no criticism of Hammarskjold to say that no Secretary-General should be expected to decide questions which are so intractable that committees of governments cannot resolve them.

The difficulty of delineating the scope within which a Secretary-General may properly exercise initiative should not be a reason for replacing a single, independent, and impartial officer by a triumvirate of ideological representatives. Although there was a widespread sentiment in 1960 that some organizational changes in the Secretariat were desirable, the Soviet proposal for a tripartite executive evoked virtually no support outside the Soviet bloc. What amounted to a vote of confidence in Hammarskjold took place at the fourth emergency special session of the General Assembly on 19 September 1960 when a resolution requesting the Secretary-General to continue his efforts in the Congo was approved by 70 votes to none, with only the Soviet bloc, France, and South Africa abstaining. An even more vivid expression of confidence was apparent in the General Assembly on 15 April 1961, following a proposal to omit the words "by the Secretary-General" from an operative paragraph in a draft resolution providing that "necessary and effective measures be taken by the Secretary-General" to prevent the introduction of arms and supplies into the Congo by national governments. A roll-call vote was requested by Guinea and the proposal not to refer to the Secretary-General was rejected by 83 votes to 11, with 5 abstentions. The minority comprised the nine Soviet bloc states of Eastern Europe, together with Cuba and Guinea.

When Hammarskjold died, the Soviet Union could have proposed that a three-man executive organ be created, and it could have threatened to veto in the Security Council any attempt to appoint a single successor. One reason why the Soviet Union was prepared to acquiesce in the appointment of U Thant as Acting Secretary-General to fill Hammarskjold's unexpired term was presumably the knowledge that the "troika" idea would have received no more than a dozen or so votes in the General Assembly. It is, I think, significant that Soviet protests about important decisions taken in the Secretariat in the interval between the death of Hammarskjold and the appointment of U Thant were relatively perfunctory.[67]

In the private discussions which preceded the unanimous appointment of U Thant as Acting Secretary-General, much attention was apparently devoted to the distribution of top posts and the responsibilities which should attach to them.

The Charter does not specify how the top level of the Secretariat shall be organized. China suggested at Dumbarton Oaks that six deputy secretaries-general (four being nationals of the major powers) should be elected by the Security Council with approval of the General Assembly, but the suggestion was not pressed. The Soviet Union raised the matter again at San Francisco, and the other Sponsoring Powers agreed to a modification of the Dumbarton Oaks proposals. The medium and smaller states were, however, opposed to anything that might increase the control exercised by the major powers, and the revised proposal of the Big Four was not adopted.[68] The Charter provides simply that the staff shall be appointed by the Secretary-General.

The matter might have rested there, but it was not to be as simple as that—as Lie was soon to find out. The Preparatory Commission of the United Nations devoted a good deal of attention to the organization of the Secretariat, and its proposals were approved by the General Assembly without any amendment of substance.[69] The Secretariat was to be divided into eight principal units, each to be headed by an Assistant Secretary-General. One Assistant Secretary-General was to be designated by the Secretary-General to deputize for him should he be absent or unable to perform his functions. This preparatory work facilitated Lie's task, but it meant that he did not have an entirely free hand. Indeed, the Big Five, he reports, "had agreed among themselves to ask me to appoint a national of each of them as an Assistant Secretary-General."[70] They had also agreed that the top post in the political department should be held by a Soviet national. Shortly after Hammarskjold took office he reorganized the top level of the Secretariat, but the same basic considerations regarding the distribution of top posts to nationals of permanent members of the Security Council still obtained. The deadlock about the appointment of a successor to Hammarskjold was ended when U Thant let it be known that he was prepared to decide the question on his own responsibility in the light of a statement he would make after his appointment.

There has thus been no formal erosion of the provisions of the Charter. The Secretary-General retains the exclusive authority to appoint staff and to determine the organization of the Secretariat. The principle that members of the staff should be international officials, and not regional or ideological representatives, remains unimpaired. The Secretary-General consults his colleagues, at his discretion, in whatever manner seems to him appropriate; and this does not derogate from his responsibilities under the Charter.

In his first months in office, U Thant has shown himself a worthy successor to Lie and Hammarskjold—courteous, fair-minded, and firm. His task is not easy. In addition to the normally heavy responsibilities of the Office he fills, he will have to guide and inspire the Secretariat during a difficult process of reorganization, and at a time when the United Nations as a whole faces grave political and financial problems.

Hammarskjold had never succeeded in creating a satisfactory system of consultation and collaboration at the top level of the Secretariat. He handled much of the political work himself, with the help of a few colleagues on the thirty-eighth floor; the Department of Political and Security Council Affairs tended to lack drive and purpose. The meetings of Under-Secretaries, held on Friday mornings, were primarily occasions for reporting information rather than for resolving issues. Hammarskjold dealt with difficulties by direct discussion with the officials concerned.

A similar problem beset the League of Nations and the idea of constituting an advisory group for the Secretary-General of the League of Nations was frequently mooted. A former League official, after referring to certain "arbitrary measures taken by the second Secretary-General during the critical months of 1940," comments as follows:

It is the almost generally accepted opinion of persons with inside experience that, basically, the head of the international administration must retain the sole and final responsibility but that his relationship to his principal collaborators should be formalized by the creation of an advisory body. . . . Such an advisory body would . . . fulfill an important function without hampering the unity of control and comment.[71]

It is clear from the Charter that it is for the Secretary-General to decide a matter of this kind. Every Secretary-General will take account of both legal and political considerations, and will be influenced by his own temperament and by the personalities of his senior colleagues. Some tasks can be delegated; some responsibilities can be shared; but in the last resort, there are duties that have been expressly conferred on the Secretary-General, who is the only official of the Secretariat appointed by member states.

One problem from which the Acting Secretary-General cannot escape is the Organization's financial crisis. The authorization of the General Assembly to float a $200,000,000 bond issue will no doubt provide at least temporary respite.

The International Court has also been asked to advise whether the expenses of the peace-keeping operations in the Congo and the Middle East constitute "expenses of the Organization" within the meaning of Article 17 (2) of the Charter. If the Court advises affirmatively, resort may be had to the provisions of Article 19 for withdrawing the vote in the General Assembly from member states which are two years or more in arrears. In any case, it may be desirable to include as an integral part of the authorizing resolutions for future peace-keeping operations a specific provision to the effect that the expenses shall be borne by the members as apportioned by the General Assembly.

Relations With Member States

Apart from his varied internal responsibilities of an administrative and related character, the Secretary-General must seek to establish relations of trust with member states. We take it for granted nowadays that this means, in the first place, relations with permanent missions at Headquarters, but this would have been anathema to Sir Eric Drummond. Drummond was very much opposed to permanent diplomatic missions attached to the League of Nations, as he considered it essential that the League Secretariat should have direct access to governments and should not have to go through intermediaries. He also feared that the staff of permanent missions would be used to represent governments on League organs on matters for which they were not technically qualified.[72] The first of Drummond's anxieties has not, in the event, proved to be well founded. Indeed, the institution of permanent missions has, in important respects, facilitated contacts between the Secretariat and member states.

Relations between the Secretary-General and the permanent missions will be largely of an informal kind, but formal institutions of consultation are also needed. Because the General Assembly is so large, select committees of member states have proved useful in connection with some of the functions entrusted to the Secretary-General. Separate advisory committees already exist for the operations in the Middle East and the Congo, and there is also an advisory committee on scientific questions. Certain principles regarding the composition and working of these select committees may be suggested.

1) They should be as representative as possible of the states providing the operation in question with the men, materials, logistical support, finance, or diplomatic backing.

2) In order to facilitate effective working, such committees should be kept small; fifteen should normally be regarded as the maximum size.

3) They should meet in private; there should be no voting; the chairman should sum up the feeling of the meeting, and any member should have the right to place a dissenting opinion on the record or, in the case of acute dissatisfaction, to request a meeting of the appropriate policy-making organ to resolve the issue.

When broad responsibilities are committed to the Secretary-General by the policy-making organs and unforeseen questions of interpretation are possible, it might be useful to have some procedure analogous to that used in a number of national political systems for the scrutiny of delegated legislation. In the United Kingdom, a representative committee of the House of Commons examines each exercise of delegated legislation with a view to determining whether the attention of the House should be drawn to it on any one of a number of grounds.

Such a scrutinizing procedure does not require that the merits of the original decision should be reviewed, but only that the body conferring the mandate should be informed if the authority appears to have been improperly exercised.

The United Nations is an instrument, admittedly imperfect, with which states seek to mitigate the hazards of what would otherwise be international anarchy—if by anarchy is meant the absence of government. No particular form of machinery will ensure that a consensus will emerge among the states of which the Organization is composed; but when a consensus does emerge, when a policy-making organ is able to make a clear decision, it is essential that it be carried out by the Secretary-General and the staff appointed by him in a spirit of independence, impartiality, and integrity.

If it were possible to consider the idea of a three-man

executive apart from the proposal that members of the Secretariat should "represent" groups of states, and with no possibility of the veto being exercised in administrative or executive matters—if, in other words, the three men were to be international officials, responsible only to the United Nations, neither seeking nor receiving instructions from external authorities, and reaching decisions by majority vote, the "troika" idea would not raise major questions of principle, although it might raise major administrative problems. But the plain fact is that the "troika" can be made tolerable for the United Nations only by emasculating it.

The "troika" proposal cannot be regarded, and has not been presented, as being merely a matter of administrative adjustment. To replace a single, independent Secretary- General by a political triumvirate, each armed with a veto on administrative or executive action, would make the United Nations helpless in any situation in which one of the triumvirs considered that, in order to "represent" a group of states, he had to block a particular action, even if in pursuance of a decision of a policy-making organ—and what situation can be conceived in which this possibility would not exist? The "troika" system would confine the Organization to being a forum for conference diplomacy and could bring to a halt a wide range of operational activities, first in the political field and later in the economic and social fields also. It would be the medium and smaller nations whose interests would be most adversely affected.

34 Confusion sometimes arises because the words *administrative* and *executive* are used differently in the United Kingdom and the United States. The top echelon of the Civil Service in Britain is called the Administrative Class and the second echelon is called the Executive Class. To an Englishman administrative duties are more onerous and carry more responsibility than executive duties. In the United States, the meanings are reversed; the President exercises executive power. The Preparatory Commission of the United Nations used both words, though without defining them.

35 *Report of the Preparatory Commission of the United Nations*, PC/20, 23 Dec. 1945, Chap. VIII, Sec. 2, para. 16, pp. 86-87.

36 *Op. cit.*, p. 39.

37 Michel Virally, "Le rôle politique du Secrétaire-Général des Nations Unies," *Annuaire Français de Droit International* (Paris: Centre National de la Recherche Scientifique, 1958), pp. 369-370.

38 *The International Secretariat of the Future, op. cit.*, p. 8.

39 *Report of the Preparatory Commission of the United Nations, loc. cit.*

40 GAOR: 5th Sess., 289th Plenary Mtg., 28 Sept. 1950, para. 40.

41 Security Council, Official Records (SCOR): 11th Year, 751st Mtg., 31 Oct. 1956, para. 1.

42 SCOR: 14th Year, 847th Mtg., 7 Sept. 1959, para. 12.

43 SCOR: 15th Year, 873rd Mtg., 13/14 July 1960, para. 26.

44 General Assembly Res. 1237 (ES-III), 21 Aug. 1958.

45 GAOR: 13th Sess., Special Political Cmtte., 125th Mtg., 10 Dec. 1958, para. 5.

46 GAOR: 12th Sess., 690th Plenary Mtg., 26 Sept. 1957, paras. 72-73.

47 SCOR: 13th Year, 837th Mtg., 22 July 1958, paras. 10-16.

48 GAOR: 14th Sess., 1959, Suppl. No. 1A (A/4132/Add.1), p. 3.

49 The Soviet Union regarded this as a substantive rather than a procedural question, and therefore as subject to the veto. The Council decided by 10 votes to 1 (the Soviet Union) that the decision was only procedural, but the Soviet Union argued that this preliminary question should also be subject to the veto, in accordance with the four-power statement at San Francisco of 7 June 1945. The President of the Council ruled, however, that the resolution had been validly adopted.

50 United Nations Doc. SG/868, 8 Nov. 1959.

51 Soviet Mission to the U.N. Press Release, 16 Nov. 1959.

52 Speech in Chicago. United Nations Doc. SG/910, 1 May 1960, p. 6.

53 Hammarskjold, *The International Civil Servant in Law and in Fact, op. cit.*, p. 11.

54 The main statements of the Soviet position regarding the Secretariat may be found in Khrushchev's speeches in plenary meetings of the General Assembly (GAOR: 15th Sess., 869th, 882nd, and 904th Plenary Mtgs., 23 Sept., 3 and 13 Oct. 1960); in part of a draft resolution on disarmament submitted to the First Committee of the General Assembly (United Nations Doc. A/C.1/L.249, 13 Oct. 1960); in the statement of the Soviet government that it would "not maintain any relations with Hammarskjold and . . . not recognize him as an official of the United Nations" (United Nations Doc. S/4704, 14 Feb. 1961); and in the views of the Soviet member of the Committee of Experts on the Activities and Organization of the Secretariat (United Nations Doc. A/4776, 14 June 1961, Appendix 1, pp. 1-5). Further light on the Soviet position is shed by Soviet statements regarding UNESCO and the administration of a control system in connection with a proposed treaty discontinuing the testing of nuclear weapons.

55 GAOR: 15th Sess., 869th Plenary Mtg., 23 Sept. 1960, paras. 283-285.

56 See, for example, GAOR: 16th Sess., 5th Cmtte., 874th Mtg., 8 Nov. 1961, paras. 27, 29, 32.

57 GAOR: 1st Emergency Special Sess., Annexes, Agenda item 5 (A/3302, 6 Nov. 1956, para. 8) and 13th Sess., Annexes, Agenda item 65 (A/3943, 9 Oct. 1958, paras. 166-167).

58 SCOR: 15th Year, Suppl. for July, August, and September 1960 (S/4426, 9 Aug. 1960, para. 4).

59 GAOR: 15th Sess., 869th Plenary Mtg., 23 Sept. 1960, paras. 278-279.

60 *Ibid.*, 882nd Plenary Mtg., 3 Oct. 1960, paras. 48-49. There seems to have been a change in the Soviet position since 1960. Khrushchev told C. L. Sulzberger that "in setting up disarmament controls there should be no veto and no 'troika'. . . . The 'troika' principle will be necessary only in the event that international forces are set up. The command of these forces should be based on that principle. This would be necessary to guarantee that no state or group of states could use international United Nations forces to the detriment of any other state or group of states." *The New York Times*, 8 Sept. 1961.

61 GAOR: 15th Sess., 869th Plenary Mtg., 23 Sept. 1960, para. 285.

62 United Nations Doc. A/4797, 7 July 1961, p. 8.

63 See the statement by the Rapporteur, in *Report of the Committee of Experts . . ., op. cit.*, Appendix, p. 8.

64 SCOR: 15th Year, 887th Mtg., 21 Aug. 1960.

65 SCOR: 16th Year, 935th Mtg., 15 Feb. 1961, para. 35.

66 Hammarskjold, *The International Civil Servant in Law and in Fact, op. cit.*, p. 23; see also GAOR: 16th Sess., 1961, Suppl. No. 1A (A/4800/Add.1), p. 5.

67 United Nations Doc. S/5003, 27 Nov. 1961.

68 *Documents of the United Nations Conference on International Organization, op. cit.*, Vol. III, p. 627 and Vol. VII, pp. 203-205, 280-281.

69 General Assembly Res. 13 (I), 13 Feb. 1946.   70 Lie, *op. cit.*, p. 45.

71 Egon F. Ranshofen-Wertheimer, *The International Secretariat: A Great Experiment in International Administration* (Washington: Carnegie Endowment for International Peace, 1945), pp. 73-74.

72 *Proceedings of the Exploratory Conference on the Experience of the League of Nations, op. cit.*, pp. 40, 41, 45.

SHOULD WE VETO THE TROIKA?

by
Roger Fisher

Soviet insistence on a tripartite administration -- communist, western and neutral -- for international organizations has been portrayed by journalists, editorialists and cartoonists in extremely simple terms: any organization is unacceptable which allows one country to veto any decision. That is the popular verdict. But as I hope to make clear, troika and the veto cannot be described or dismissed that simply.

Let me say at the outset that what is being discussed in Geneva, Washington and elsewhere is the right, not the power, to veto. For in the case of inspections under the proposed test ban treaty, the Soviet Union would have the actual physical power, whatever agreement is signed, to frustrate any particular inspection within its country. With actual control over roads, railways and airfields within its boundries and with a large army on hand, the Soviet Government could block an inspection by such means as closing a road, putting sugar in the gasoline of the inspection vehicles or detaining the inspectors. Such frustration could be accompanied by plausible excuses which would obscure the question of whether the action was or was not in violation of the agreement. Particularly where speed of inspection is important it would not take great ingenuity to produce a series of "explanations" which would significantly delay inspection without providing a clear-cut breach of the treaty. Whatever a test ban treaty might say about vetoes, a country which had in fact cheated and conducted a secret test without openly repudiating the treaty would hardly permit the international inspectors to come and establish beyond doubt that it had broken its pledge. The evading country might contend that the inspectors had been subverted by the other side and that any further inspecting would have to await agreement on new and satisfactory inspectors. It might charge a violation of some provision by the other side. In brief, whatever a treaty says, any major nation can frustrate international action within its borders and often elsewhere.

There are two basic elements in the Soviet troika proposal which are often confused. The first is that decisions should be made by a group representing different points of view rather than by a single individual. The second is the right of veto. Let us look first at the "group decision" feature.

Roger Fisher is a Professor of Law at the Harvard University Law School.

In the case of the nuclear test ban, the Soviets have proposed that there be "an Administrative Council of three equal representatives, one each from the principal groups of states -- the Socialist states, the countries belonging to Western military blocs and the neutralist states." The theory underlying this proposal was summarized in the Soviet memorandum given President Kennedy in Vienna:

> "The control commission, on which all principal groups of states will be represented, can adopt sound, just decisions, taking into consideration the interests of all states. However, it is not enough to take such decisions. It is imperative to guarantee their impartial implementation. Impartiality cannot be guaranteed if the implementation of the decisions is left to one man alone."

Now, in suggesting that important decisions should be made by a group rather than by an individual Mr. Khrushchev has said nothing new or controversial. Americans are familiar with the device of giving a group rather than an individual responsibility both for formulating policy and for carrying it out. After Congress has decided what policy should be and has adopted appropriate legislation, it is often reluctant to leave its implementation to a single person, as is illustrated by the Atomic Energy Commission, the Federal Trade Commission and other regulatory agencies. Policy decisions in our private corporations are made by boards of directors, and even at the level of execution, the executive committee is common. Military policy in the Defense Department is implemented by the Joint Chiefs of Staff. No clear line can be drawn between the forming of policy, where it is generally recognized that joint wisdom is best, and the carrying out of policy, where the efficiency of a single responsible officer is usually desired. If we, with our common bonds, interests, and law are unwilling to trust a single official we should understand better than we do the concern which the Soviet proposal reflects.

Where the views of different representatives in a group are sharply divided, as might be the case between representatives of East and West, the product of the group will tend to be less a collective judgment and more a collective bargain. But where interests sharply conflict, the group process can nonetheless be a useful means of arriving at an acceptable accommodation.

Having said this, I must add that the particular three-headed monster proposed by Mr. Khrushchev would seem to be ill-designed. There is little value in assuming, and thereby accentuating, a division of the world into three defined camps, each of which can theoretically be represented by one point of view. Moreover, if neutrals are to exert a moderating influence upon representatives of the United States and the Soviet Union, it would be better to have several of them rather than one. There is enormous pressure on a single neutral whatever the merits of particular issues may be. However, Mr. Khruschev is certainly less concerned with giving the neutrals a vote than in getting a veto for himself. The group-decision feature of the troika proposal thus raises a question of degree: how far down toward the details of administration do the benefits of collective judgments and bargaining out weigh the drawbacks? This is a matter which can be discussed and for which any solution, inherently, requires balance and compromise. To repeat, the group-decision feature of the troika proposal is not something to which we should object on principle. But how about the veto?

The Right of Veto

In the light of the physical power which a major nation has to use its army or its police to veto proposed international action against it, the continued existence of an international organization may depend upon there being some legal way of exercising that power. To provide a right of veto at some stage is to recognize the limited power which any international organization has, for example, over the United States and over the Soviet Union. If the Soviet Union had not had the legal right of veto within the Security Council during the last 15 years, it is unlikely that the United Nations would exist today. It is at least probable the Russians would have wrecked a veto-less UN dominated by the West.

The existence of a legal right to exercise a political veto may protect an international administrative machine in another way. If there is no permissible veto, the international civil servants or neutrals who are making decisions must take that into account. They will have to ponder the political resistance to their decisions and whether a particular decision might be "unacceptable" to a major power. One can conceive of a neutral in a veto-less test-ban organization being approached by the Soviet representative with the suggestion that he has been voting too often with the Western members and that the Soviet Union may have to break up the organization unless he will go along with the Soviet Union on a particular vote. Or such an approach might be made by a US representative who thinks that a neutral has been too pro-Soviet. In such a situation, a conscientious neutral may conclude that it is better to preserve the international organization than to conduct an in-spection. ("Both sides have such quantities of nuclear wea-pons that even one test, if it did occur, is not terribly im-portant; far better to vote in a way which will preserve the chances of continued international cooperation and eventual disarmament.") Requiring the administrative staff to take into account the factor of political unacceptability runs the risk of corrupting its integrity.

On the other hand, the existence of a legal right of veto at the political level tends to free the international civil ser-vant from having to modify his judgment to make it politically acceptable. He can give his honest, scientific or impartial views, without having to assume the risk of wrecking the in-stitution by his own action, since if the decision is unac-ceptable to a major power, that country may veto it. ("If you don't like my decision you can veto it, but I must do my duty as I see it.")

Moreover, the veto, like the group decision, is deeply rooted in Anglo-American law. For centuries we have in-sisted that representatives of the people be given a veto power over the enforcement of the criminal laws. Many famous trials, such as that of Peter Zenger in 1735 for printing a libel against the Governor of New York, demon-strate that one of the purposes behind trial by jury is to give people a veto over the enforcement against one of them of laws which the people do not want to see enforced. Not only does the jury as a unit have a veto in every major criminal case; the requirement that the jury's verdict be unanimous gives each of the 12 jurors veto power over a verdict either way. And on the other side the prosecutor is usually given unreviewable descretion to veto the prosecution of any case. There are, of course, differences between the restraints which people impose on a government and those which gov-ernments impose upon international organizations. But if within a community like the US we are so distrustful of authority that we insist upon a system of checks and bal-ances, we should understand that comparable checks and balances may be necessary in a community where there is far less mutual trust.

As a matter of fact, the draft nuclear test ban treaty submitted this spring by the United States and the United Kingdom included a significant number of provisions involv-ing a veto. For example, the major powers are given a right of veto over the appointment of both the Administrator and the Deputy Administrator. The initial location of fixed air inspection routes is subject to veto by the country being inspected, as are the locations of the fixed components of the inspection system. More significantly, perhaps, under the Anglo-American draft treaty "the total amount of each annual budget shall require the concurring votes of the original Parties." The US Government has thus adopted a flexible attitude towards the veto. Not only did we include various veto provisions within our draft treaty but undoubtedly we would have given consideration to additional provisions. We thus recognized the veto as something to be dealt with in practical terms depending upon particular circumstances.

The Soviet position has been represented as being that a veto must apply to everything. With respect to nuclear testing Life magazine reported: "The Soviets say now they will accept only the 'troika' system whereby any of three members could veto any inspection." This is incorrect. The Soviet Union has publicly recognized that the veto is not something to be applied across the board. With respect to nuclear testing its troika proposal involves a veto on matters to be decided by the vote of the Administrative Council. In a section of its June 4th memorandum which was not given wide publicity in the United States, the Soviet Union explained that ". . . On-the-spot inspections within the limits of the agreed quotas must be effected at the request of the side interested in the inspection without any voting in the control commission or any other agency. All that is needed are objective readings of instruments at control posts indicating that a phenomenon took place in some part of the given country which might be suspected as a nuclear explosion. If there is such objective reading, the Soviet proposal envisages that neither the Control Commission nor any other body of the control organization can interfere with the satisfaction of the demand of the side for an inspection. Hence, no obstacles to inspection, to which the United States representatives refer, speaking of the so-called 'veto', can be created by the Administration Council."

Breaking the Rules

How the Soviet Union would actually behave is another question, but one which cannot be answered in advance, regardless of whether a treaty should contain words about a troika or words to the effect that there should be no veto whatever.

But there is another side to the coin -- the disadvantages of a veto. If an international organization is to be effective, it must be able to do or say things which will at least tend to persuade governments to comply. What are the forces that are used by an international organization in seeking to persuade a government to act? And what is the effect on those forces of a veto?

The forces which will tend to cause a government to re-

spect a decision of an international organization can be
roughly divided into three kinds:

Fear of world opinion. Governments which spend vast
sums on propaganda want to look good, not bad, in the eyes
of others. An international organization which can produce
a "binding" decision automatically marshals world public
opinion to some extent in favor of compliance with that decision.

Fear of action by other governments. In considering
whether to comply with the views of an international organization, a government must take into account the possible retaliatory action which other governments might take should it
fail to do what it ought to do. Should the Soviet Union refuse
to allow an international inspection team to inspect in accordance with a test-ban agreement, the Soviet Union would have
to consider how the United Kingdom and the United States
might respond. The more clearly it appeared that the Soviet
Union was defying an obligation the more likely would be the
responsive action by other countries. The ability of other
countries to act and their freedom of action would depend in
turn upon how clear it was that the first government acted
improperly.

Institutional pressures of a government toward respecting
rules. To the extent that officials have been taught that they
ought to do what they are legally obliged to do, they will
tend to cause their government to comply with decisions of
an international organization. A government cannot exist
without rules. Institutional inertia tends to make it easy to
go along with an existing rule. On the other hand, to break
the rule usually requires not only that someone take the initiative to suggest doing so, but also a collective decision
among a group of officials that this particular obligation
should be broken. Freedom to rise above these constraints
is likely to be exercised only at the highest levels where
deterrent political considerations can be most effective.

If these are the principal forces on which an international
organization must rely to cause a government to comply with
its expressed view, one can see how a permissible veto may
undermine the effectiveness of such an organization. An
adverse world public opinion is created when a government
does not do something which it "ought" to do. But if the government in question has the recognized right to veto the
decision of the international organization there is far less
moral stigma in not complying.

Likewise, other states will find it more difficult to take
retaliatory or responsive action if a government is simply
exercising its rights than they would if it were defying a
"binding" decision of an international organization. The
right of veto thus makes it possible to avoid unpleasant

consequences that might follow were a state simply to exercise its physical power of indirectly frustrating a decision.

Internally too, the institutional pressures in support of the decision of an international organization are seriously weakened if the government has a right to veto that decision. Officials will feel little moral obligation not to veto a decision, and no obligation to comply with a decision that has been vetoed.

The existence of a right of veto in an international organization may thus seriously weaken the effectiveness of the organization. But the choice may be between having an organization subject to a right of veto or having no organization at all. The Soviet Union can now veto the creation of any new international organization capable of having binding decisions upon it. If the choice is between having no international organization and having one that is subject to the right of veto, we would probably prefer the latter.

The extent of a multi-national organization's influence will depend largely upon how far it can proceed toward clarifying the rules and the facts before a veto can be exercised. And clarifying the facts requires that factual data be made public. But even this is not usually enough. Data can be disputed or confused by conflicting data. The more that there is an official determination and characterization of the facts the more clear-cut the situation will appear.

Similarly, the effect of a veto is less serious if an international organization is so constructed that the veto can be exercised only after the organization has defined and made public the particular action which, in the absence of veto, it would undertake. Such a process defines the issue sharply. The same forces which deter a government from breaking a legal commitment tend to deter it from exercising a veto if a veto requires the government to stand in the public view and frustrate what a world body thinks ought to be done.

Finally, if the exercise of a veto requires affirmative action at a political level, rather than inaction at the administrative level, the restraints against exercising the veto will be greater.

My point is that the practical effect of the right of veto on a multi-national organization is a matter of degree. Jurors may exercise their veto in secret at the fact-finding level, free from the restraining influence of public opinion. The President, who in the pardon power has comparable authority to let criminals off, must, however, exercise his veto in public after there has been an official determination that the man is guilty and ought to be punished.

Safety Valve?

Suppose, for example, that the proposed nuclear test-ban organization were set up in such a way that there were an administrative determination, below the veto level, that a suspicious disturbance of seismic magnitude 4.75 or above had occurred in a designated locality which would be eligible for inspection. A Soviet veto at such a stage would provide the basis for both an adverse world reaction and responsive action by other countries. Suppose, instead, the test-ban organization were set up in such a way that no release of factual data nor official determination that a seismic event had occurred could be made without the consent of a Soviet representative. Then it would be far easier for the Soviet Union to frustrate an inspection.

The difference between requiring consent at every stage and permitting a "safety valve" veto was demonstrated in the Security Council vote to increase the UN forces in the Congo. The Soviet Union had made clear its position that the UN troops should be withdrawn. If the release of factual reports from the Congo and a decision on what to do had required Soviet consent, such consent would probably not have been forthcoming. But as it was, the Soviet Union was presented with a majority decision of the Council in support of a resolution calling for an increase of UN troops in the Congo in the light of official factual reports. At this stage the Soviet Union found that it chose not to exercise the right of veto which it had.

A veto in an international organization is thus like a safety valve on a steam boiler. If the safety valve is set to go off too quickly it will prevent the machine from accom - plishing much -- although such a machine may still be bet-ter than none. If there is no safety valve at all the machine may blow up. And, as with a safety valve, a veto can be designed in such a way that it will not prevent the machine from doing its job.

POLITICS AND THE FUTURE OF ECOSOC

NORMAN J. PADELFORD

Economic and social cooperation through the United Nations seems destined to face new challenges and alternatives in the coming years as a result of the changed composition of the United Nations membership, the increased bargaining power of the African, Asian, and other states seeking economic and technical assistance, and the precedent of UN operations in the Congo.

Among the issues that must be anticipated in this connection are the enlargement of the Economic and Social Council (ECOSOC), demands by the African and Asian states for a larger voice in determining UN actions in the economic and social field generally, increased requests for economic and technical assistance of many types, and a general upward pressure of costs of running the Organization that will throw added burdens on those states like the United States that contribute the major share of the financial support. Pressures by the underdeveloped states for more "aid without strings" may also necessitate further rethinking of foreign aid programs now being handled largely through bilateral means outside the United Nations.

The new political calculus of the United Nations, stemming from the recently enlarged membership and the energetic activities of the African, the Afro-Asian, and the Latin American caucuses, has given the countries with a vested interest in obtaining assistance for economic development through the United Nations an important leverage in General Assembly proceedings whenever a substantial measure of unity can be mustered among them. The African and Asian states demonstrated, for example, in the convoking of the Special Session of the General Assembly on the Bizerta issue, and in the passing of the resolution there calling upon France to negotiate her withdrawal from the naval base in Tunisia, that under some circumstances, with the support of a relatively few states from Europe, Latin America, or the Soviet bloc, or some combination of these, Assembly action can be taken independently of the Western powers.

The sheer numbers of those who fall within this special-interest category now comprise two-thirds of the UN membership. For if to the 46 countries composing the Afro-Asian caucus (as of September 1, 1961) there are added the twenty Latin American states, each of which also has a vital interest in this matter, and the various European states on both sides of the Iron Curtain that are likewise recipients of UN or foreign economic assistance, there are considerably more than 66 Member States in this grouping. The indications are, moreover, that all, or most, of the entities that may be admitted to the United Nations in the near future will have similar needs and interests. Although there are more often divisions than unity among this group as a whole, bloc politics is a stock-in-trade seldom overlooked by delegates at the UN when it can be employed to self advantage.

With the International Bank for Reconstruction and Development awarding loans

NORMAN J. PADELFORD is Chairman of the Board of Editors of this journal. He is Professor of Political Science at the Massachusetts Institute of Technology and a member of the Senior Staff of the Center for International Studies at MIT.

on the order of a gross expenditure of $600–$700 million a year, the UN's Expanded Program of Technical Assistance and the Special Fund for Economic Development now committed to expending approximately $100–$150 million a year, and with proposals being made for an additional special assistance fund for Africa, the tangible stakes available to nations in need of assistance through the United Nations and the specialized agencies are by no means inconsequential. These nations can hope, furthermore, to gain a good bit of free counsel and help through the deliberations, studies, and recommendations of the regional economic commissions, the specialized agencies, and the various committees and commissions appointed by the Economic and Social Council and the General Assembly.

The United Nations operations in the Congo are relevant in this connection. Notwithstanding the general consensus that the action has been of an exceptional and "temporary" character, to cope with an extraordinary emergency, the fact that the UN has expended something on the order of $100 million in a single year for one country, including support of the military forces sent to the Congo, where previously no nation had received assistance amounting to more than $2 million in one year, will not be overlooked by politicians of other countries wishing assistance. Of course the whole problem of the future of UN financing bears on this. But the mere fact that the Organization is in a crisis of solvency is not likely to deter some governments from demanding added outlays.

In short, the Congo experience, taken in conjunction with the new mathematics of UN bloc politics, the pressures for favor and support inherent in "parliamentary diplomacy," and the maneuverings of international politics in general, may conspire to press many states to reassess the scale on which the United Nations should extend economic, technical, and other assistance to politically emergent or disturbed states that are strategically placed. Economic and social cooperation through the United Nations, in other words, may have to be viewed through a different perspective than heretofore.

II.

As the principal organ of the United Nations responsible for promoting international cooperation in solving a wide range of international problems of an economic, social, cultural, scientific, and humanitarian character, ECOSOC holds the initiative in encouraging and appraising assistance measures by the World Organization. This fact, combined with its power to recommend priorities in their application, quite naturally leads to lively competition, and political maneuvering, for seats on the eighteen-member organ. The fact that the Charter leaves complete discretion to the General Assembly in the selection of the one-third to be named each year enhances the politics associated with this election.

The admission of the large number of new states to the UN since 1955, virtually all of which are heavily preoccupied with economic and social advancement in the shortest possible time and under great popular pressure to "do something" about conditions in their lands, has produced greatly intensified competition for seats upon this Council. The membership change has also placed some groups of states at marked disadvantages in the ratios of seats allocated to them. It is as a result of these circumstances that moves have been made each year since 1956 to obtain the necessary

ELECTIONS TO THE ECONOMIC AND SOCIAL COUNCIL

Year	Session	Common-wealth	Latin American	Western European	Eastern European	Afro-Asian	Others
1946	I—1	U.K. (2) Canada (3)	Colombia (1) Cuba (2) Chile (3) Peru (3)	Greece (1) Norway (2) Belgium (3) France (3)	Yugoslavia (1) Ukraine (1) U.S.S.R. (2) Czechoslo-vakia (2)	Lebanon (1) India (2)*	China (3) U.S. (1)
1946	I—2	New Zealand	Venezuela	Nether-lands (2)**	Byelo-Russia	Lebanon Turkey	U.S.
1947	II	U.K. Australia	Brazil	Denmark	U.S.S.R. Poland		
1948	III		Peru Chile	Belgium France		India*	China
1949	IV	Canada	Mexico		Czechoslo-vakia	Iran Pakistan*	U.S.
1950	V	U.K.	Uruguay	Sweden	U.S.S.R. Poland	Philippines	
1951	VI		Argentina Cuba	Belgium France		Egypt	China
1952	VII	Australia	Venezuela		Yugoslavia	Turkey India*	U.S.
1953	VIII	U.K.	Ecuador	Norway	U.S.S.R. Czechoslo-vakia	Pakistan*	
1954	IX		Argentina	France Netherlands		Egypt	China
1955	X	Canada	Brazil	Greece	Yugoslavia	Indonesia	U.S.
1956	XI	U.K.	Mexico	Finland	U.S.S.R. Poland	Pakistan*	
1957	XII		Chile Costa Rica	France Netherlands		Sudan	China
1958	XIII	New Zealand	Venezuela	Spain	Bulgaria	Afghanistan	U.S.
1959	XIV	U.K.	Brazil	Denmark	U.S.S.R. Poland	Japan	
1960	XV		Uruguay El Salvador	France Italy***		Ethiopia Jordan	
Total Seats Held		13	23	22	19	20	11

*Also member of Commonwealth.
**Elected for 2-year term to fill out seat resigned by Belgium.
***Elected in place of China, which failed of re-election, after Belgium and India withdrew candidacies.

agreement to bring about an enlargement of the Council, or at least to reallocate the seats so that the African and Asian states may have a more equitable representation. As is well known, these moves have been blocked every year up to now by the refusal of the Soviet Union, on one ground or another, to approve amending the Charter to this end. The recurrent frustration has led some delegates to talk of using votes to press through some "crash program" of reallocation if something is not done soon. Although counsels in favor of a more deliberate procedure have carried in the past, the tide of demand for some change in the composition of the Council will not be satisfied with indefinite postponement.

The accompanying tabulation shows the countries that have been elected from year to year and the patterns of distribution that have prevailed in the composition of the Council from 1946 to 1961.

Three features stand out with respect to the composition of ECOSOC during the initial fifteen years of the United Nations.[1] In the first place, the five powers having permanent seats on the Security Council have been continuously re-elected, with the recent exception of China which failed of re-election in 1960. No other states have been similarly privileged. In the second place, there has been a continual mixing of economically advanced and low level income countries and of those favoring private enterprise together with advocates of socialism. The Council has also had a cross section of proponents of strong action on human rights and of those believing the UN should go slowly in this field. In the third place, a considerable number of states not in a position to make substantial contributions to the maintenance of international peace and security, and which have not been elected either frequently or at all to the Security Council, have been elected to ECOSOC. Similarly, a number of states not allied with the Great Powers, such as Afghanistan, Finland, and Indonesia, have been seated on this Council whereas they have not been elected to the Security Council.

There is unavoidably a certain amount of "rough-hewing" in the electoral process of the General Assembly. Current political considerations shape the choices that are made from year to year. But taken by and large the elections over a fifteen-year period have produced a rather remarkable balancing of representation among the principal geographical and political elements in the United Nations, with considerable "give and take" obvious. Thus one finds that the various combinations of states have held the following percentages of seatings as compared with their averaged percentage place in the United Nations membership from 1946 to 1959 (i.e., prior to the large increase in 1960):

	Percent of total ECOSOC seats 1946–1961	Averaged percent of group in UN membership 1946–1959 inclusive
Commonwealth, including United Kingdom	12.0	7.5
Latin America	21.3	30.3
Western European	20.3	16.6
Eastern European, including U.S.S.R.	17.6	11.5
African-Asian, including Commonwealth states in area	18.5	29.4
United States and China	10.1	

[1] The elections under consideration embrace those held to fill places vacant through December 30, 1960, including the voting deferred until April 1961 at the resumed fifteenth session of the Assembly to elect a successor to China.

This is not what some consider an ideal distribution. It is the resultant of applying the initial informal understanding of how the seats would be divided as modified by the "give and take" of the election process. Relatively speaking, the eastern European and the older Commonwealth countries have enjoyed a preferential place upon ECOSOC in terms of their percentage of the UN membership, whereas the African-Asian and Latin American states have been under-represented percentagewise. If the Assembly were seeking to have the Council composed strictly upon a pro rata basis, the eastern European–Soviet bloc states should have fewer seats and the Latin American and African-Asian combinations more. There is no precise definition, however, of what constitutes "under" or "over" representation, and the matter has been handled from year to year as politics has determined.

With the tidal wave of new Member States from Africa in 1960, it is now plain that the former and existent allocations of seats, based upon practice and informal understandings relating to the initial elections, leave the African-Asian countries grossly under-represented relative to their percentage of the UN membership as compared with all others. Readjustment of this situation is a matter of vital and pressing concern to these states in particular, and must be also to all others interested in a just world order. Before we consider what a more equitable adjustment might entail, a word should be said with respect to the 1960–61 election.

The decision of the General Assembly to elect Italy in place of China—which was not able to muster more than 51 out of a necessary 62 votes and quickly dropped to less than 20 votes in the repeated balloting when India and Belgium became serious contenders for the place—was clearly within its prerogative although this decision broke with fourteen years of hitherto unvarying practice. The action of the Assembly was no doubt influenced by the attitudes of many of the Asian and African states, and by those of the Latin American and western European Members who have been disposed to favor the seating of Communist China and who regard the Nationalist government on Taiwan as no longer speaking for the mainland Chinese.

Aside from the regret many will feel over the absence of the Chinese, who have contributed positively to the work of the Council, the action of the General Assembly has one significant aspect. The effect of the decision is to establish beyond question that the allocation of seats, originally determined by the Great Powers in 1946, is subject to alteration by a two-thirds vote of the General Assembly. Although this contingency may have been understood heretofore, the Assembly has not previously seen fit to effect any major departure from the broad outlines of the 1946 formula. Having now breached the pattern, and being the master of how it should execute its mandate with respect to the election of ECOSOC members, the General Assembly may conceivably make other reallocations of the seats. To predict what the new mathematics and politics of the UN may produce in the future elections would be sheer conjecture. But it would perhaps be safe to suppose that the four principal powers will not be by-passed unless one or more of them suffers an unforeseen loss of power and influence or poses by some action or policy such a threat to international peace and security as to lead to an alteration of the fundamental bases of the Organization.

Speculation may occur as to the effect of the Assembly's action upon the future of the seat awarded to Italy in the April 1961 balloting. During the previous balloting considerable effort was exerted to have an Asian or African state elected on the ground that this group does not enjoy a reasonable representation. When the deadlock was finally broken, President Boland stated to the Assembly that an agreement had been reached in conversations whereby

> The Western European group is prepared to agree that if Belgium and India decided not to press their candidatures at this session of the Assembly, and another European candidate is elected now, then the Western European group will be prepared to support two candidates from among the members of the Asian-African group at next autumn's election for the seats now occupied by Afghanistan and Spain.[2]

Such an arrangement was patterned more or less after somewhat similar informal agreements that have been made in the past to break deadlocks in Security Council elections.[3] Beyond this there is no binding commitment with respect to any election. The question is wide open as to what may be done when the three-year term of Italy expires. The Assembly may re-elect Italy one or more times; it may pass the seat around among other European states; it may elect an Asian or an African state to it. The choice is flexible. The Assembly's action may have set up something of a hedge around an assumption that this seat would automatically become the preserve of Communist China should a Peking delegation be seated in the UN. It may be taken to mean that the General Assembly does not recognize that permanent members of the Security Council have permanent claim to seats in ECOSOC.

III.

The major problem relating to the future composition of the Economic and Social Council is how to afford the greatly enlarged circle of Africa and Asian states a more equitable representation than they now have without doing violence to the fair representation of others.

When the original allocations gave these states an alternating two-three seats, which was the same as that accorded the Commonwealth and the eastern European states, there were less than a dozen states from Africa and Asia in the United Nations. The ratio of representation was not quite as favorable as that enjoyed by the members of the Soviet bloc, but it was decidedly more generous than the seating arrangement with which the twenty Latin American states had to contend.

Aside from the Chinese seat, the African-Asian representation has been divided so

that there has regularly been one Middle Eastern state, one Asian Commonwealth power, plus a third party fluctuating between a Far Eastern, a second Middle Eastern or Commonwealth country, or an African nation. This arrangement has corresponded generally with the relative numbers of the various regional elements involved up to 1960. Notwithstanding the intensive caucusing of the African-Asian states, strenuous contests have often developed for the seat or seats available in a given year, reflecting the differences and rivalries within the grouping.

The unprecedented rise of new states in Asia and Africa has brought the representation situation of the states in this megalo-regional area to a pressure point unparalleled among other groupings. As matters stand today, 46 states must share three seats. This is 125 percent more constrictive

---

[2] Document A/PV.987, 987th Plenary Meeting, April 18, 1961.

[3] See Norman J. Padelford, "Politics and Change in the Security Council," *International Organization*, Summer 1960 (Vol. 14, No. 3), p. 381–401.

than the representation situation of the twenty Latin American republics, which have had the tightest ratio heretofore. With the African-Asian states now comprising 44 percent of the over-all membership of the Organization, they have an impressive case—on the assumption that representation should be proportional to numbers of Members—for being accorded a more reasonable basis of representation.

There is perhaps a question as to how long the African-Asian area should be treated as a unit for filling seats on the Economic and Social Council or any other organ. For, in addition to the sheer physical size of the area, the tremendous population inhabiting it, and the number of states involved—enough to encompass six Europes—the differences in culture, in economic and social conditions, and in orientation tend to point in the direction of separate identifications. For the present, nevertheless, these states seem to wish to maintain the concept of an area unity for whatever political advantage this can serve. Under these circumstances, political and regional considerations would make it not unreasonable to think in terms of one seat each being occupied more or less regularly by a Far Eastern country, an Indian Ocean country, a Middle Eastern state, a North and East African state, and a West or Central African Member—provided this could be effected without prejudice to the interests and equitable representation of other groups of states as well.

There are two ways in which an adjustment of this situation may be approached. Both have already been considered and tried, thus far without satisfactory results. The first alternative would be to redistribute the existing seats within the present limits of a Council of eighteen members. Conversations have been conducted at the UN for some years about the feasibility of

such a step. The difficulty that has always arisen and in the end seemed to be insuperable is that no reallocation (except in a very temporary sort of way) can be made save at the expense of some grouping of states, each of which has been accustomed to a certain basis of representation for fifteen years and none of which wishes to see its own opportunity of participating in the Council curtailed. The frustrations felt within the African-Asian grouping were sufficient to tempt some Members at the fifteenth session to utilize their numbers to impose a reallocation. This attempt was resisted by the Latin American group, by some western European states including Britain, and by the United States. As Ambassador Wadsworth pointed out, reallocation is too delicate a matter to be handled on a "crash programme"[4] basis and needs the most careful thought and negotiation.

It is difficult to find a way in which a reallocation within the present eighteen seats can be accomplished without working a hardship on some group or at least arousing opposition. Taking the ratios that presently exist, the group that has the most generous proportionate representation in terms of numbers of states in the UN, and should therefore in principle be prepared to make the first concession, is the eastern European–Soviet bloc. There have been no offers to date by this group, however, to forego one of its places.

A temporary expedient, pending enlargement of the Council and depending upon consent by those involved, might be to make two seats available to the African-Asian combination by a rotating relinquishment involving the present seatings of the eastern European, the western European, and the Commonwealth states. By careful arrangement and goodwill on all sides, this could conceivably be done without requiring either of these groups to curtail its own

[4] See Document A/PV.914, 914th Plenary Meeting, November 11, 1960.

representation by a full place all of the time. To succeed, such an arrangement would demand willingness by the members of each group to forego one place in turn. Refusal by any state within any one of these groups to abide by the rotational plan, and to insist upon pressing its own candidacies out of turn, could throw off the entire scheme. A sufficient consensus to make such a plan work has been lacking up to this time.

The second alternative is to enlarge the membership of 'the Council and in the process to effect a new allocation of seats in such a way as to give the African and Asian states a more generous representation without compelling any other group to forego what it has been accustomed to for fifteen years. This is the procedure favored by an overwhelming majority of the Members of the United Nations.

Formal enlargement of the Economic and Social Council, as of the Security Council, can be constitutionally accomplished only by amending the Charter. To do this requires approval by the General Assembly and ratification by two-thirds of the Member States, including all five of the powers having permanent seats upon the Security Council.

Such a move has been proposed, and discussed, at the General Assembly every year since 1956 in company with corresponding proposals to increase the size of the Security Council and the International Court of Justice.[5]

The proposals along this line have consistently called for an addition of six new seats, to increase the Economic and Social Council to 24 members.

Up to 1960 the Soviet Union categorically opposed every proposal to amend the Charter, regardless of the inequity the current allocation of seats works upon the African

and Asian states. Its delegates, supported by the satellite states, repeatedly asserted that the organization in its existent form met the "essential purposes of the United Nations." It advised the new states to look to the seatings of either the Latin American, the western European, or the Commonwealth groupings for satisfaction. Such a rebuff to the legitimate aspirations of the states of Africa and Asia is quite out of keeping with the professions of support for the former colonial peoples which Soviet delegates have uttered at the United Nations and elsewhere. In addition to its other reasons for opposing proposals to amend the Charter, the Soviet Union has advanced since 1959 the proposition that no move of this kind can be considered until Communist China is admitted to the United Nations and has had a chance to act upon it.

This attempt by the Soviet Union to trade off the aspirations of the underdeveloped nations for support in getting Red China into the UN has met with a sufficient measure of success to lead certain influential delegations to say that they "understand" the Soviet position and, in turn, to favor taking no action on the amendment proposals.

Since the amendment proposals have not been pressed to a vote in the General Assembly up to this time, there is no assurance of what the Soviet Union would do if it were confronted with the fact of an amendment resolution being passed by the General Assembly and being ratified by two-thirds or more of the Member States excepting itself and its satellites. Conceivably the Soviet Union would change its position. It has been known to shift radically on other matters when confronted with inescapable facts. On the other hand, it is equally possible that it would remain

[5] See Document A/3139 for original enlargement proposal introduced by a group of Latin American states and Spain, June 26, 1956. The same or substantially similar proposals have been reintroduced and debated in the Special Political Committee each year since 1956.

adamant, hoping thereby to bargain for higher counters in the game of world politics. It has shown no qualms about adopting such positions heretofore or about raising the ante to the utmost point possible irrespective of frustrations, inconvenience, or even the dangers of precipitating nuclear war.

The United States, the United Kingdom, France, and the overwhelming majority of UN Members from every other area and grouping have stated their belief that something should be done, and done at once, and that their governments are ready to proceed. General Assembly resolutions have recorded this sentiment. The feelings of many were expressed in a statement by the Sudanese delegate at the Fourteenth Assembly to the following effect: the simple fact that the Soviet Union does not like the exclusion of Communist China is no fair ground for refusing to accord Member States in no wise responsible for the Chinese situation equitable representation in the principal organs of the United Nations.[6]

To say, as the delegates from the Soviet Union have done, that the Asian and African countries can attend Council meetings whenever there is a matter of particular concern to any of their number is not a satisfactory answer. This privilege does not give them a vote. Any self-respecting group of Member States would regard indefinite consignment to the sidelines an intolerable indignity. One can imagine what the Soviet delegates would be saying were they to be placed in a similar position.

Some delegates speaking before the General Assembly's Special Political Committee have argued that since there are no permanent seats or built-in veto power in the Economic and Social Council, an amendment to increase the size of this Council may be regarded as "essentially a technical adjustment" to help this organ function more effectively. It is doubtful whether from the viewpoint of constitutional law this argument carries much weight. An amendment to the Charter is an amendment and must meet all of the requirements provided therefor. Every amendment must be adopted by the same process; the Charter makes no distinctions or qualifications so far as subject matter or circumstances go.

How many seats should be added if and when it becomes possible to enlarge the Council? It has customarily been suggested that six elective seats be added to bring the total to 24, leaving the allocation to be worked out through informal arrangements among the Members. This would permit two or three more African-Asian states to be seated on the Council. In terms of the existent composition of the UN membership and the past behavior of the General Assembly, it would be reasonable to expect that one of the states of southern Europe might follow along after the present term of Italy. If one of the additional seats were to be assumed to go to a Latin American state, this would ease the Latin American representation problem. One seat could be left over to general election or to balance off representation wherever this might be needed. Such an arrangement would result in a Council having something like five or six African-Asian members, four or five Latin American, four western and southern European states, three eastern European, and one or two Commonwealth countries (others being represented in the African-Asian quotas), together with the United States, the United Kingdom, France, possibly China, and the Soviet Union.

Some such distribution would bring the representation on ECOSOC more nearly into line with the actualities of today's UN

[6] Special Political Committee, 130th meeting, October 17, 1959.

membership and the problems that must be faced in economic and social cooperation, technical assistance, and human rights in the next few years. It would alleviate one of the principal bottlenecks in UN politics.

It has been suggested in some quarters that the number of seats should be increased by as many as ten, to a total of 28, while the process of enlargement is going on. This, it is said, would allow for even more generous representation and would give a measure of leeway for the years ahead when the membership of the Organization increases further to accommodate the territories that have not yet attained independence. There is some merit in this proposition. On the other hand, it can be argued that it would be wiser to act with moderation, leaving further enlargement beyond 24, or possibly 26, until a later time when the measure of need can again be assessed. The differential is not very great in any case. An addition of either six, eight, or ten seats can be justified. Neither the smaller nor the larger number would be excessively out of line. Of all the principal organs of the United Nations, the Economic and Social Council can most reasonably be enlarged to any one of these figures; for its functions are to review, to study, and to recommend measures of international cooperation, wherein an interchange of information and views can be most helpful to the states Members of the United Nations.

Some comparison might be made with other bodies concerned with similar subject matter. Of the regional economic commissions reporting to ECOSOC, the Economic Commission for Europe has 29 members; the Economic Commission for Latin America, 24; the Economic Commission for Asia and the Far East, 24 plus two associate members; and the Economic Commission for Africa, 31 plus seven associate members. The membership of the ECOSOC func-

tional commissions, which previously stood at either fifteen or eighteen depending on the commission, was increased by three during the 32d (summer 1961) session of the Council, except for the Commission on Narcotics Drugs, the membership of which was increased by six. The Executive Board of the United Nations Educational, Scientific, and Cultural Organization (UNESCO) has 24 members, as does the Council of the Food and Agriculture Organization. The Board of Governors of the International Atomic Energy Agency has 23 members. The Governing Body of the International Labor Organization has 40 members. None of these commissions or bodies is felt to be too large or essentially unwieldy.

Closely relevant to the consideration at hand is the composition of the Council's Technical Assistance Committee. The committee includes the eighteen members of the Council plus six additional members elected by the Council for two-year terms from among other Members of the UN or members of the specialized agencies. Thus, in addition to the eighteen countries currently holding seats on ECOSOC, Haiti, Israel, and Norway were members from January 1960 to December 31, 1961, together with the United Arab Republic, Switzerland, and the Sudan, elected for two years beginning January 1961. Taking the full membership of the committee for the period noted, this arrangement permitted the Latin American states to have one more representative than in the parent organ, the western European states two more, and the African-Asian states two more, together with an additional seat for a nonassociated state. In giving the African-Asian states six seats and the Latin American states five, it came somewhat nearer to affording the larger groupings more equitable representation than they have been holding in ECOSOC in recent years.

All of the bodies mentioned consider matters in the first instance that later come on report or recommendation to the Council. It would not seem unreasonable for the Council to have a membership at least as large when it is remembered that this organ is presented with reports stemming from all of the Specialized Agencies and is encumbered with a very heavy agenda.

IV.

As the debates have developed in recent years, the membership of the UN has tended to polarize around four positions: 1) support for early action on an amendment to enlarge the Council along the lines indicated; 2) opposition to any action until Communist China has been seated; 3) the establishment of a good offices committee to try to conciliate the opposing views, a proposal rebuffed by the Soviet Union; and 4) postponement of action until there is a larger measure of accord among the Great Powers lest a majority move in the absence of Great Power harmony exacerbate present differences—a stance taken by India and others. In effect this latter position—which has carried in the Assembly from year to year—has played into the hands of the Soviet Union.

Two new elements were introduced as the lines were drawn in 1960. The first of these was the insertion of Mr. Khrushchev's troika formula. This added a new hurdle to the already existent one previously imposed by the Soviet Union and in no wise abandoned in the process of raising this angle. Picking up the cue from his chief that the UN structure "was out of date," the Soviet delegate, Mr. Soldatov, told the Assembly's Special Political Committee that account must be taken not only of "the quantitative changes but also of the qualitative which had taken place in the social, economic, and political structure of the world." The states of the world now being divided into "capitalist" (or "West"), "socialist," and "neutralist" categories, it "would therefore only be proper," according to the Soviet delegate, "for the three groups of states . . . to be equitably represented in all the organs of the UN." In the view of his government "the capitalist states" hold a "predominant position" in the Economic and Social Council "in violation of the principle of equality which the two other groups of states should enjoy." Parenthetically, one notes that in talking about the Security Council Soviet delegates have tended to employ the label "imperialist states" in place of "capitalist" when speaking of the Western powers, in keeping with the rigidities of their ideological system.

Soviet delegates in 1960 took the stand that "minor numerical changes" of a "purely quantitative" nature could only divert attention from the need for "a thorough change in the organs of the United Nations," and warned that if only quantitative changes were proposed these were "doomed in advance." There must be, they maintained, a combination of enlargement and redistribution "designed to bring about the equitable participation of the three principal groups with equal rights." This concept presumably takes into account both population and power.

The political sleight of hand implicit in these moves is obvious when it is recalled that up to a few months previously Moscow's delegates had been asserting with equal fervor that the structure of the UN was adequate to the purposes of the Organization and must be scrupulously respected. Clearly, someone in the Kremlin thought he had sighted a clever proposition, one that would gain more time, put off amendment of the Charter longer, divide the unsuspecting African and Asian states from the West while seducing them to the Soviet side by a glamorous vision of equality, and take the Soviet delegations off the hook of standing virtually alone against change in the UN.

Taken in the larger view, the Soviet game has apparently been to introduce such a drastic proposition that others would be compelled to expand vast amounts of time and energy refuting it—hopefully maneuvering them onto the negative side and lining them up against the African-Asian countries in the process—or to force others to negotiate changes on terms of reference of maximum benefit to the Soviet Union. The whole troika proposition, not only with respect to the Economic and Social Council, but also with regard to the office of the Secretary-General and the reorganization of the Security Council, is to be seen in the light of a desperate search by Moscow for means of curbing the freedom of action of organs in which the Soviet Union lacks a veto power, and for simultaneously seizing an initiative in the UN, launching an appeal to the underdeveloped countries, and obtaining a bargaining counter for dealing with the West over review or amendment of the Charter. The delegate of Colombia pinned a value tag on the proposition when he said that the Soviet point of view had changed to the point of becoming "incoherent." And President Kennedy appropriately pointed out in his address to the Sixteenth General Assembly that although the troika may be drawn by three horses it is directed by one driver.

Clever though the Soviet move may have been thought to be from the political and time-gaining points of view, it is hardly compatible with the terms of the Charter or with the objects of economic and social

cooperation which are intended to be served by the Economic and Social Council.

Article 2, paragraph 1, of the Charter explicitly states that the Organization is based on the principle of the sovereign equality of *all* its Members. All other bases— whether ideological, political, economic, military, or social—are left aside. Were the Soviet proposition to be followed, Article 2 would have to be amended as well as the articles relating to the composition of the several organs. There is nothing in Article 61 governing the election of the members of the Economic and Social Council which ordains or warrants selection on the basis of an ideological classification, or any other ground than according to the concept of the equality of states. The Soviet proposition in effect calls for an alteration of one of the most fundamental of the foundations on which the UN rests. It seeks to formalize classifications, to set class against class, and to magnify divisions between states rather than to promote economic and social progress toward unity and the peaceful settlement of disputes. It is alien to the spirit and intent of the San Francisco Charter. It is doubtful that many states, large or small, would choose to belong to an organization that discarded the principle of equality of member states or sought to freeze relationships along an ideological-political cleavage. It is unthinkable that the United States would have any part in such an association.

Taken on the ground of statistics, the Soviet proposition has an air of unreality. If it were applied as Soviet delegates have outlined it, it would work permanent injustice upon the African and Asian states that chose to remain nonaligned. Their representation would be fixed permanently, no matter what their numbers in the UN might become, to the same number of seats as the communist-ruled states. Why should they tie their hands in this way when their numbers already exceed those of the Soviet bloc by more than four-fold? With the Soviet bloc today composing but one-tenth of the UN membership, their demand for one-third of the seats on ECOSOC, and in other organs, is in effect asking the new countries to mortgage their political future and rights in terms of numbers. The world is a much more complex community than the three-fold categorization Moscow suggests. There are many shadings of political outlook, sympathy, and policy. This scheme deserves to be defeated for its crude attempt to employ the united-front concept to gain Kremlin domination of the World Organization.

The second new element introduced into the politics of enlarging ECOSOC at the Fifteenth General Assembly was the appearance of pressure for an immediate reallocation of existing seats if no action was possible on enlargement, or pending such action. This stemmed from the presence of the greatly enlarged circle of states from Africa and Asia facing geographical distributions of elective seats more or less along the lines of the 1946 membership of the Organization. In the words of Mr. Wachuku, the Nigerian delegate:

> The immediate problem was an immediate distribution of the non-permanent seats. No Gentlemen's Agreement could bind countries which had not been party to it . . . No state had a right to any of the non-permanent seats or to bargain away another state's rights without its consent.

In his, and others' views, the seats should all be pooled and candidates openly elected; no regional or other group had a permanent right to any seat or seats; if the Charter could not be amended at once to correct the existing inequity, a reallocation should be made immediately.

The unfortunate effect of the delaying tactic employed by the Soviet Union, and the behind-the-scenes encouragement given to the Africans to demand or to force an immediate reallocation on the basis of their numbers, was to set the Latin Americans and the Africans against one another. For the Latin states quite naturally, and forcefully, announced their determination "never to yield" on the issue of their seats on either the Security Council or the Economic and Social Council, and to warn that attempts to force a redistribution at their expense "might doom that initiative to failure because it created antagonisms between different groups of countries." The old game of fishing in troubled waters was once more being played.

The maneuvering in the General Assembly on the enlargement of the elective membership of the principal organs has skirted one of the major political issues involved in UN elections. This is the question of the right of regional or political groups to designate their representatives under agreed quotas and the obligation of the Assembly to respect these choices and nominations. From an early point in UN proceedings the Soviet Union has insisted on this prerogative and on the duty of the Assembly to confirm bloc selections. Other states have taken issue with this, as well as with the right of the powers to determine the allocations by a gentleman's agreement.

Group selections have not always been accepted by the Assembly either for the Security Council or for ECOSOC. The question of to what extent regional quotas are meaningful if the Members' desires are not respected is a dilemma the Assembly has not resolved. It is obvious that the caucusing and voting blocs are going to continue to press candidacies of their choice and to engage in political bargaining with others. In most instances this will undoubtedly influence the outcome of elections and shape the distributional patterns of representation in the elective bodies. At the same time it is equally clear that the Charter does not obligate the General Assembly to accept these informal group nominations, nor does it bind the Assembly to maintain indefinitely any particular pattern of allocation arrived at by informal agreement of some of the Members.

V.

One of the pertinent questions relating to the future of the Economic and Social Council is what criteria should be applied in determining the size and composition of the Council. The Charter provides no explicit guidance on this point. There are no directives comparable to those embodied in Article 23 concerning the composition of the Security Council. Entire discretion is left to the General Assembly.

It is reasonable to assume that one of the basic criteria to be borne in mind in the choice of members is ability to assist the Council in carrying out the broad sweep of functions assigned to it by Chapters IX and X of the Charter.

To execute its mandate most effectively, the Council should regularly embrace a representative cross-section of the interests, background, experience, knowledge, abilities, and needs found among the UN membership. Only such a cross-section can enable the Council wisely to determine from among the many problems and situations laid before the Organization what matters are most urgent and on what questions recommendations should be made.

The membership of the Council should be such as to enable it to discharge its central functions and duties, that is to say, to contribute to the solution of "international economic, social, health, and related problems," to help promote "higher standards of living, full employment, and conditions of economic and social progress and development," and to further "universal respect for and observance of human rights and fundamental freedoms." The attainment of these objectives, as well as the coordination of the activities of the specialized agencies, calls for a measure of experience and breadth of viewpoint as well as for a sense of immediacy toward situations needing action and assistance. The membership of the Council should, in short, make room for a reasonable, and adequate, cross-section representation of both the older and the newer states, of states in a position to donate economic and technical assistance and states in need of varying forms and degrees of such assistance. The Council should have on it states representing the various economic and social systems. It should have members that have reached mature economic life with a mass production consumer-oriented economy together with states that are at what Walt Rostow has called the "take-off" stage of economic growth, and states that are only at the early stages of transition from a subsistence economy.

Inasmuch as there are widely differing circumstances of need and of economic development in various parts of Latin America, Africa, the Middle East, Asia, and the Pacific, the size and composition of the Council should be such as to permit an optimum representation of these different outlooks, as well as a reasonable balance with the states of the more advanced and diversified economies of Europe, North America, and Japan.

The Charter does not say that the General Assembly should pay special regard to equitable geographical distribution in electing members of ECOSOC as it does in the case of the Security Council. It was perhaps wise that the framers of the Charter did not underscore this, for they wished ECOSOC to have a world-wide viewpoint as well as competence. The realities of Assembly politics being what they are today, it is inescapable that the composition does in fact reflect the strivings of the various regional groupings for representation. This being so, and the entire Organization being based on the premise of the equality of states, there is some justification for saying that the composition should bear some reasonable proportionality to the number of Member States in the different principal geographical areas—provided the other considerations we have mentioned are borne in mind as well.

If this principle is accepted, it then follows that the African and Asian states taken as a whole should have a more generous representation than they have at the present time and that the Council size should permit some adjustment in the balancing of the numbers of states in a position to contribute economic and technical assistance to others and of those in varying stages of economic and political growth that are in need of such help.

To achieve optimum satisfaction and results, the size and composition of ECOSOC should be such that it can be genuinely reflective and representative of the world as it exists in the UN community. Otherwise, it is likely to be out of touch with some of the realities, needs, and forces which shape the actualities of national policies and decisions.

There is no single or simple criterion for determining the future size and composition of ECOSOC. The choices must be rested upon a consideration of all of the elements we have mentioned. The crucial problem of representation for the next few years is, however, the accordance of some more generous seating for the states of Africa and Asia, which happen to be chiefly in widely varying phases of the pre-industrial and pre-take-off stages of economic growth, and at the same time some liberalization of the representation basis for the Latin American states. Neither of these can be accomplished within the bounds of a Council of eighteen without imposing unreasonable and unacceptable sacrifices upon the states with older and more mature economies and without grossly upsetting the balance that should be maintained between states able to provide assistance and those in need of such help. So variable are the economic and social circumstances prevailing in many of the so-called "underdeveloped countries," that no two or three of them, whatever the geographical area involved, can represent the totality of the problems and needs in their part of the world with which the UN must cope.

When the various positions which have been adopted are taken into account, it can be seen that the business of securing more reasonable representation for the newer states from Asia and Africa upon the elective organs of the United Nations has become a complex and difficult matter. A great deal of goodwill, and a spirit of accord and compromise, will be needed to work out this problem that comes so close to the vital interests of all Members of the World Organization. It is not to be dismissed as being of no consequence. It is of large moment to those who feel themselves the objects of discrimination or of what amounts to disenfranchisement. Consummate statesmanship will be needed to find a formula that will save the face of all concerned now that the lines have been drawn as they have and efforts are being made to play upon the susceptibilities of those with little experience but large hopes.

It is of the utmost importance that the United States take a vigorous, unequivocal stand both for the right of the states, like the Latin American and western European and Commonwealth Members, that have been accustomed to a certain measure of representation in the past to retain that position in the Organization, and also for the complementary right of the African-Asian states to a just representation. Only by way of enlarging the membership of the Economic and Social Council, and of effecting at the same time some modification of the 1946 allocation lines, can justice be done to all and the interests of this country served as well.

VI.

Enlargement of the Economic and Social Council poses no dilemma comparable to that which exists with respect to an increase in the membership of the Security Council as it involves no "permanent members" and no question of a veto power. Furthermore, since the Council has no powers regarding the maintenance or enforcement of international peace and security, the election of states pursuing neutralist or pacifist policies causes no difficulties.

Enlargement of the Council might conceivably be followed by more proposals being laid before it for increasing the activities of the Organization in the economic and social sphere. Additional voices would no doubt be heard urging increases in the economic and technical assistance programs of the UN. New pressures might be mounted to put the Council on record in favor of establishing more capital funds for "soft" loans along the lines of the formerly proposed Special United Nations Fund for Economic Development (SUNFED) plan or for long-term capital grants according to less precise criteria than those insisted upon by the International Bank. The appointment of additional study and visitation missions might be sought. And conceivably there would be stepped-up efforts to do more in the sphere of human rights. But it seems likely that all of these moves will come in due course, in one way or another, whether the Council is enlarged or not. Many programs have gone through the General Assembly without waiting for deliberations or action in ECOSOC by reason of the weight of the African-Asian countries in the Assembly.

Whether the Council is increased in size or not, the powerful forces of change that are sweeping through Africa, Asia, Latin America, and other parts of the world are bound to press upon the United Nations for greater assistance in one way or another. What has transpired in the Congo is almost certain to mark a steppingstone toward an era of economic and technical assistance of a much larger scope than heretofore if the struggle between the Great Powers does not so absorb their energies and resources in a vastly magnified arms race or conflict that all else is swept aside.

There can be no doubt that in an enlarged Council the nonaligned countries will poll a larger number of votes for their points of view than in the body as presently constituted. There may be occasions when the positions favored by the United States or the Western powers will not be popular. Nevertheless, weighing all the elements involved, the United States should find sufficient friends upon an enlarged Council composed along the afore-mentioned lines to support on most occasions positions to which it attaches vital importance. Its views will continue to command respect. And barring the unforeseen, its influence will remain strong in view of its experience, its financial and other resources and contributions, and its support for the rights and integrity of the young and small nations. It must expect to have to employ the arts of persuasion and play the game of politics. It will not be any easier in a larger body. But there is no reason to suppose it will be any more difficult than it is now in other bodies of a corresponding membership.

There is nothing to be gained, in the opinion of the writer, from delaying further a full testing of the amendment process in the United Nations. An overwhelming vote in the General Assembly in favor of a formal amendment proposal limited to enlargement of this particular organ, followed by favorable action upon the draft amendment by a large number of states, could conceivably persuade the Soviet Union to modify its previous opposition and follow suit. Conceivably it would not do so. The point made by the Indian delegate on several occasions to the effect that the Organization could not have come into existence save for agreement among the Great Powers and cannot be changed fundamentally without similar agreement among these states is perfectly correct. Nevertheless, only the presentation of an actual test will confront the nations with the need for making a definitive decision. If the Soviet Union or other Member States find that their interests cannot be squared in final analysis with approval and ratification of an amendment, this cannot be helped. It is their right to take such a decision, and none will begrudge or deny them this right. But diplomacy will have been given a full opportunity to exhaust its resources. If there is unmovable opposition when all of the cards are down, this will be unfortunate, but it will stand revealed for what it is.

As the membership of the United Nations has nearly doubled since the Organization was founded, it is time that the elective organ primarily concerned with the advancement of international economic and social cooperation and the promotion of higher standards of living were enlarged to keep step with the configurations of the UN and of world needs more nearly as they exist today. This does not mean that the proposal to reconstitute the entire Organization along utterly different, and unconstitutional lines—with each of the principal organs divided equally along the cleavages of socialism, democracy, and neutralism—advanced by the Soviet premier in 1960, should or must be accepted. That proposal is to be viewed in its own perspective as a political move designed to enhance the Soviet vetoing power within the organs of the UN, to gain bargaining power, and to try to embarrass the Western powers politically. There is room for maneuvers which will protect the basic rights and interests of the Western states and at the same time gain a more reasonable representation for the newer and underdeveloped states of Africa and Asia—whose interests and needs are also vital and pressing to them—within the proposals that have been debated over and again in the General Assembly for enlarging the Economic and Social Council along modest lines in keeping with the basic principles of the Charter. By enabling the newer states to gain more equitable seating through amendment, the representation of other regional groups can be improved also. In the process international collaboration and the sense of community among the Members of the United Nations may be furthered.

300

SUGGESTED QUESTIONS FOR SEMINAR DISCUSSION

The excerpt, "Development of the Process of Political Accommodation," from the thirteenth report of the Commission to Study the Organization of Peace, starts with the assumption that "no conceivable transformation of the United Nations will involve making international political adjustment a function performed exclusively by world organization;" it maintains that diplomacy must play an important part in this adjustment. Do you understand the Clark-Sohn proposals to deny that assumption? If so, which is the sounder judgment and why? If not, precisely how does the Clark-Sohn plan take this point of view into account?

Do you agree with the general thesis of Clark-Sohn that the General Assembly should have ultimate authority in the limited field of war-prevention and that the Security Council should be made into an Executive Council with specific functions to perform under the supervision of the General Assembly in the peace-keeping and disarmament area?

A number of UN delegates, including several from the Afro-Asian nations, have recently called for an expanded Security Council. Assuming no change in the General Assembly, do you think the Clark-Sohn proposal is a reasonable way to expand membership in the Security Council, or would you prefer one of the alternatives given in the Commission's report? On what facts and value preferences do you base your judgment?

Do you think that the Clark-Sohn proposal for voting in the revised Executive Council under Article 27 is reasonable? Would it be sensible to attempt to introduce their system within the present UN structure?

Assuming that some method of national representation in the revised Executive Council has been agreed upon, what is your opinion of the Clark-Sohn proposal (Article 23) regarding the method in which the actual representatives would be elected?

Although the Secretary General would still be able to initiate some action under revised Article 99, and would undoubtedly administer many vital programs of the United Nations, it is clear that Clark-Sohn see major executive formulation coming from the Executive Council and the General Assembly. Do you agree that expansion of the executive capacity of the Secretary General's office would not be warranted? Why?

What do you understand by the notion of troika? Is there anything to be said for the idea as a method of selecting representatives, or in the actual administration of any of the organs and agencies of the United Nations?

What is your opinion of the method proposed by Clark-Sohn for selecting representatives to the Economic and Social Council and the Trusteeship Council? Do you see any problems or potential difficulties that might arise using these methods? What do you consider to be the best features of these proposals? Why? Could the principles on which they are based be used to resolve any pressing problems now.

The Commission's report emphasizes strongly the importance of resuscitating the influence of the Security Council and proposes that it become the locus of serious consultation and negotiation on the important issues of today, Clark-Sohn place their emphasis on a strengthened General Assembly, Sydney Bailey believes that there could be executive development within the Secretary General's office and finally, Roger Fisher suggests that the troika proposal is not altogether as obstreperous and inhibiting as popular discussion would have it. Within the present context of world affairs and without other major modifications in the structure and powers of the UN, which organ of the United Nations do you believe should be given more authority and power in the area of resolving international disputes and peace-keeping?

Are there any portions of World Peace Through World Law discussed in this session that you think might be acceptable to present UN membership, either through the Amendment process under Article 108 or through establishment by practice?

BIBLIOGRAPHY

On the SECURITY COUNCIL, see:

Goodrich, Leland M. "The UN Security Council," Int. Org. 12: 273-287 (Summer 1958). Will the Security Council become an atrophied organ like the appendix?--the author attempts to answer in the negative by reviewing the Council's purpose, its record, the causes of its decline and the likelihood of eliminating these causes.
Kerley, E. L. "Powers of Investigation of the UN Security Council," Am. J. Int. Law 55: 892-915.

McDougal, Myres S. , and G a r d n e r, Richard N. "The Veto and the Charter: An Interpretation for Survival," Yale Law J. 60: 258-292 (Feb. 1951).

Padelford, Norman J. "Politics and Change in the Security Council. " Int. Org. 14: 381-401 (Summer 1960). A consideration of the proposals advanced since 1956 by the g r o w i n g number of Afro-Asian UN members for an increase in Security Council membership.

Vallet, F. A. "The General Assembly and the Security Council of the UN. " Brit. Yearbook of Int. Law 29: 63-104 (1952). Pictures the relations between the two major organs of the UN.

Washington, George Thomas. "Improvement of O r g a n i z a t i o n for Collective Security--Alternatives to the Veto P o w e r, " Proc. Am. Soc. Int. Law 51: 127-134 (1957).

(Wilcox, Francis O.) U. S. Senate, Subcommittee on the UN Charter, Committee on Foreign Relations. "The Problem of the Veto in the UN Security Council." 83rd Congress, 2nd S e s s i o n, Washington, 1954.

On the SECRETARIAT, see:

Jackson, Elmore. "The Developing Role of the Secretary-General. " Int. Org. 15: 431-45 (Summer 1957). The author seeks t h r o u g h a review of the Secretary-General's political actions taken on his own initiative to discover whether too much i n i t i a t i v e is in his hands, what effects his exercise of political initiative has had on his other roles, and a reappraisal of the Secretary-General's role in an expanding UN.

_____ "Constitutional Developments of the UN: the growth of its executive capacity. " Proc. Am. Soc. Int. Law 55: 78-88 (1961). A speech and discussion on the necessity for a devolution of authority to the Secretary-General at a time when there are too many members to effectively direct the organization.

Lengyel, Peter. "Some Trends in the International Civil S e r v i c e. " Int. Org. 13: 520-537 (Autumn 1957). Discusses some of the problems that will face the civil service as it grows older.

Miller, Richard I. Dag Hammarskjold and C r i s i s Diplomacy. NY.: Oceana Publications, Inc. , 1961, 340p. The rise of the Secretary-General is shown t h r o u g h a series of case studies in crisis diplomacy that illuminate some of the significant international events of the past several years.

Schacter, Oscar. "Dag Hammerskjold and the Relation of Law to Politics. " Am. J. Int. Law 56: 1-8 (Jan. 1962).

Schwebel, Stephen M. The Secretary General of the UN; his political powers and practice. Cambridge, Mass.: Harvard U. Press, 1952, 299p.

Sharp, Walter R. "Trends in UN Administration. " Int. Org. 15: 393-407 (Summer 1961). An excellent summary of the more recent development of the UN bureaucracy and its shape and functions.

Siegal, N. "Role of a Proposed Attorney General-Advocate of Peace. " Howard Law J. 7: 145-162 (Spring 1961).

Stein, Eric. "Mr. Hammerskjold, the Charter Law and the Future Role of the UN Secretary-General. " Am. J. Int. Law 56: 9-32 (Jan. 1962).

Swift, Richard N., ed. Annual Review of UN A f f a i r s 1960-61. NY: Oceana Publications, 1960, 207p. Articles and discussion by a distinguished panel on two crucial problems of that year--the authority of the Secretary-General and the activities of the UN in Africa.

Virally, Michel. "Vers une Reforme du Secretariat des Nations Unies?" Int. Org. 15: 236-255 (Spring 1961). (In F r e n c h, but translations available from World Peace Foundation and English abstract at end.) An examination of the current attacks on the UN Secretary-General.

303

SESSION V

MAINTAINING PEACE: PACIFIC SETTLEMENT --A JUDICIAL AND CONCILIATION SYSTEM; COERCIVE SETTLEMENT--A POLICE FORCE

In Session II we explored the use of law and development of international organization to manage and prohibit the use of force among nations. In this session we shall be concerned with the operation and structure of the United Nations directly involved in resolving disputes and keeping the peace. It may be useful to an understanding of this session to read again Professor Falk's article, "The International Control of Force" and section 3 of Professor Claude's article in the reading in Session II.

It is in this area that the core of the Clark-Sohn plan for revising the United Nations is to be found. The essence of their argument is that individual states are unwilling to disarm and to trust their security to the good will of other states unless there is adequate machinery for settlement of disputes among states and prompt police action by the world community to halt the use of force by one state upon another. It is the lack of this machinery, they argue, that accounts for the failure of the UN to establish peace. They propose, then, nothing less than the creation of a comprehensive, international judicial and conciliation system and an effectively organized UN police force. It should be noted here again that general and complete disarmament is an integral part of their plan.

The international judicial and conciliation system which they propose is comprehensive in scope and finely worked out in detail. We shall be interested in the following aspects of it: the extent of compulsory jurisdiction; the relevance of distinguishing matters as issues which are legal, equitable or more suitable for conciliation; and the relatively intricate relationship between the General Assembly and the International Court with regard to these matters.

The establishment of a police force raises perhaps the most controversial and crucial aspect of their scheme. It proposes that all of the nations of the world give up their military might and rely upon an international police force to see to it that their security is maintained. The police force would be gradually built up in a thirteen year period, during which time the general and complete disarmament process would be taking place. The technical aspects of disarmament we shall discuss in the later sections. Here, however, we will want to look at the structure of the force itself to determine whether it is sufficiently strong to do its job or so strong that it may become an instrument for seizure of dictatorial power. This will involve a series of questions such as, what should be the composition of the force, how should they be organized, what will be the relationship of the civilian authorities to the police force.

The article by Kaplan and Katzanbach is intended to provide you with a short description and analysis of the present methods of pacific settlement now in use in the international community. Their emphasis upon diplomacy, good offices, conciliation and arbitration as well as a judicial system accurately describes the present international system and at the same time indicates the extent to which Clark and Sohn are attempting to build upon what presently exists.

A matter which has become an increasingly important domestic issue in the U.S. is the so-called "self-judging" clause in the U.S. submission to jurisdiction of the International Court of Justice. The final paragraphs of the Kaplan and Katzanbach article discuss this as does section 7 of Professor Henkin's article in Session II. For those who are interested in this topic the discussion by Arthur Larson in his book, When Nations Disagree (116-162), is extremely helpful. Among legal gradualists this particular step of submitting to compulsory jurisdiction of the World Court under a set of well defined and well established rules is considered to be in the most important single step we could take at this time in the development of world law.

The article by Professor Sohn discusses the legal problems of establishing a permanent police force within the present framework of the UN. His analysis is persuasive that such a force would be legally permissible and raises in an indirect fashion some of the hard political problems that would have to be solved in order to gain its acceptance.

There have been altogether eight situations (Indonesia, Greece, Palestine, Kashmir, Korea, the Middle East, Lebanon and the Congo) in which it might be said the UN has had a unit operating in a peace-keeping capacity. An analysis of these situations would show that they required different kinds of forces for different kinds of problems. The article by Marion McVitty is an analysis of the experiences of the police force actions in the Israeli-Arab dispute and in the Congo. She provides a real service in specifying at the level of concrete behavior precisely what kinds of problems had arisen under these experiences.

Readings from "World Peace Through World Law":

Pacific Settlement of Disputes, 89-110; the Judicial and Conciliation System, xxxiii-xxxvi, 175-182, 335-344.

Action with Respect to Threat or Use of Force, xxxvi, 111-128; The World Peace Force, xxix-xxxiii, 314-334.

THE INSTITUTIONS
OF INTERNATIONAL
DECISION MAKING

by

MORTON A. KAPLAN
and
NICHOLAS deB. KATZENBACH

In the previous chapter our emphasis was upon the techniques of the international legal process and the limitations upon the discretion of officials imposed by legal methodology—at least whenever the decision maker is concerned with providing a convincing legal justification for action taken or protested. Here we wish to pursue another facet of the process: Who invokes international law, in what arenas, and with what effects? Our points of attention in this chapter are, then, the ways in which the decision-making process is organized and the roles of the various participants.

In general theory and broad outline, the organization of the international legal process is underdeveloped and uncomplicated. As we have seen, international law is viewed as a body of rules binding upon states as entities, or "subjects." States are legally obligated, by whatever means they elect, to insure that state officials comply with international norms, but (at least, up until the Nuernberg trials) the obligation is not conceived as being imposed directly upon the officials themselves. Acts taken by state officials that violate international norms may be protested, through diplomatic channels, by an injured state, the protest being accompanied by a demand that the wrong be righted in some appropriate way. Diplomatic correspondence cast in terms of legal argumentation ordinarily follows such a protest. If disagreement persists at any level—as to the facts, the relevant norms, or the application of the norms to facts—the matter may be settled by the parties, mediated by a disinterested party, referred to an arbitrator or international tribunal, put before an international or supranational body, or simply left unresolved. The offended state may, if other means of resolution are frustrated, resort to appropriate sanctions by way of reprisal if this possibility is technically feasible and politically possible.

Relatively few disputes are resolved by impartial judges. If the states involved desire adjudication, either of existing disputes or

306

prospectively with regard to categories of questions, there is no difficulty in securing the services of objective and impartial observers who can employ the techniques described in the previous chapter to resolve the dispute. The services of the International Court of Justice are, of course, always available to states. The failure of states generally to resort to judicial resolution is attributable not to the lack of a mechanism for handling the dispute, but, rather, to a preference, in most instances, not to use this method of dispute settlement.

Our primary concern here is not with the reasons that underlie this preference, but rather with the fact of its existence. Nonetheless, it may be helpful to suggest at least some of the considerations that lead states to reject a judicial method of dispute resolution.

We must, first, bear in mind that, although all disputes involving normative standards can be decided by impartial reference to authoritative declarations and past practices, even a developed and comprehensive legal system does not attempt to resolve all disputes in this fashion. Although authoritative norms may be and are derived and abstracted from past experience, not all norms are created in this way. We would not ordinarily claim that a disagreement among interest groups as to a desirable general rule could best be resolved by reference to a referee who would determine which proposal more nearly complied with precedent and past practice; yet each group might, as part of its effort to gain political support, invoke precedent from sources analogous to those discussed in the prior chapter.

One factor, then, which influences states to refrain from any comprehensive acquiescence to adjudication is the belief that adjudication is inappropriate, at least until a more satisfactory international legislative system is evolved. The present system of international legislation, whether by multilateral treaty, United Nations vote, or otherwise, requires formal assent by others, and is, to say the least, a tedious process, the more so because the individuals involved operate under limited instructions from the states they represent. The clumsiness of this arrangement is compensated for within the system of international law by a looser technique of doctrinal innovation than exists in a more developed governmental system, by a failure to resolve definitively doctrinal issues, and by legitimizing retroactively, in a variety of ways, a great amount of unilateral policy, including the application of national laws to transnational events and interests. The reliance is upon informal—or political—restraints as well as the doctrine that has existed to enforce moderation. So long as prescribing and adjudicating functions are not embedded in separate institutional structures in the international system, reference to impartial adjudication will be limited.

Not all disputes are best resolved by the judicial process. We may agree that the Constitutional power of the President of the United States to send troops to participate in the UN action in Korea is a legal question. Yet we may doubt that the question would be best resolved by reference to the Supreme Court. Similarly, there are questions of law that courts decline to resolve on the grounds that the issue is "non-justiciable," or "political"; and these are better resolved in other arenas.

Also, disputes that affect the security or continued existence of a state cannot easily be put in the hands of a third party, however impartial, if any alternative is feasible. Even if the risk of unfavorable adjudication is slight, states are understandably reluctant to take any unnecessary risk on fundamental questions.

But basic to these reasons, and to others, is the simple fact that national identification still dominates, and there are no widespread ties of sentiment to the international community, or, though we are in a state of transition, to supranational entities. An important conviction as to the importance of preserving the group and a sense of group solidarity is a necessary condition to the establishment of comprehensive dispute-resolving mechanisms in the present period. Although we can see the growth of this identification in many areas, both geographical and functional, there is no indication that such supranational communities presently exist in any comprehensive way.

As a result of these conditions and of this organizational scheme, the international legal process, unlike its municipal counterpart, is not designed to operate primarily by means of judicial settlement; and international law is typically invoked in arenas other than international judicial arenas. The techniques described in the previous chapter may be employed by an impartial arbiter to decide a dispute, and sometimes are; but they are customarily employed in other contexts by persons who, in various degrees, have partisan political roles. This circumstance is of the utmost importance in understanding the process. It does not by any means defeat the existence of an operative normative order; it does, however, mean that the international process differs importantly from one that includes the operations of an impartial judiciary. State officials may both act differently and conceive their roles differently with respect to international matters from the ways they act or conceive their roles with respect to national matters.

Let us consider the traditional arenas in which international law has been invoked—national courts and diplomatic intercourse—and proceed thereafter to the important institutional modifications resulting from the growth of international procedures and organizations.

National courts. In traditional theory, national courts apply national law—even when they apply international standards. National courts, it is said, apply international law only because the latter has been received into, or incorporated within, national law. There is a reason for this otherwise awkward theory, and that lies in the relationship of the judiciary to other branches of the municipal government. There is international law doctrine which requires a state to adhere to rules of international law, but there is no international requirement that a state take its judiciary's view of what the international norm is or how it applies. The international obligation is that of the state, and it may implement it internally in any way that it sees fit.

Issues of international law arise in national courts indirectly, and not as disputes between states; they are at one remove from diplomatic representation. For example, state officials may attach property and be faced with a claim that the property belongs to another sovereign entitled, under international law, to immunity from local process; a seaman may be apprehended for a minor crime committed on a foreign flagship in a local port and claim that he is immune from prosecution under customary international law; goods may be seized during wartime as contraband and the owner may claim the seizure is in violation of his rights as a neutral; property may be nationalized and the owner may claim that the compensation offered is inadequate under international standards; and so forth.

One primary function of courts, and the *raison d'etre* of an independent judiciary, is to insure that government officials do not exceed their lawful authority. A decision of the executive to take certain action does not automatically establish its lawfulness, and may be tested by impartial judicial review. If international law is a part of the national law, the court is acting on questions raising international standards exactly as it would if only local issues and local law (in a restricted sense) were involved. International law, for a national court, does not assume priority over national law; in fact, the latter almost always supersedes the former if there is unavoidable conflict. A statute in conflict with a prior treaty provision or customary international law will be applied nonetheless in most countries by national courts.

The result of this theory, then, is that the national judiciary must take the views of the political branches as to what international law requires whenever these views are enacted as formal municipal law; otherwise, courts determine independently what the international standard is and what it requires in the case at hand. Thus although national courts, in performing this latter function, develop a good many international standards, they cannot be regarded as independent and faithful custodians of international law doctrine. They may, in this respect, be contrasted rather sharply with state courts in our federal system which do have an independent obligation to uphold the federal Constitution. It hardly requires argument that this difference of role has considerable impact upon the development of the international law process.

The task of developing international law norms on the one hand and deferring to formal national policy on the other can make for awkward situations. A court in State X determines that international law prohibits a certain act, or requires a certain procedure; once this determination is made it is extremely difficult for the state's foreign office, or legislature, to arrive at a different formulation of the international rule without the considerable embarrassment of having its own judiciary cited to the contrary. For this reason, the state may be forced to reverse its judiciary by the tedious process of international agreement, even though, for local purposes, it could do so by simple legislative act.

This same difficulty—in part due to a semantic confusion and failure to clarify issues—often follows from the fact that a number of countries, including the United States, have taken the view that questions of law (what the international standard is) are questions for the judiciary, and that as a result the courts are not bound by foreign office views unless formally a part of municipal law. In the United States, the Constitution specifically describes treaties as "supreme law," and inferentially assigns courts the task of their interpretation. There is, of course, some justification for judicial supremacy where the issue has arisen and the interpretations could retroactively affect private parties in an existing suit. But, at least prospectively, it is difficult to justify anything but the greatest deference of municipal courts to their respective foreign offices.

In practice, courts are extremely sensitive to political involvement, particularly in recent years when it has been increasingly obvious that much traditional doctrine needs modification. Though troubled by the seeming intrusion on independence, courts have been desirous of getting political guidance on policy matters. In the United States, at least, it is not uncommon to see courts and State Department playing Alphonse and Gaston roles, the one saying a question of policy has arisen on which the court should have political guidance, and the other maintaining a discreet silence on the same issue, characterizing it as one of law. In this regard, we are conscious of a change of attitude over time. A century or more ago, courts played far more important roles in law development than they do in the present day. In the early nineteenth century, there was great confidence in a process of law development by the judiciary. As law has come to be thought of more and more in terms of a conscious community policy, initiative has shifted to political bodies. Norms previously conceived as derived from universal reason or practice or custom are now thought of as conscious community policy. With this in mind, courts have lost their confidence to prescribe in the international area, becoming sensitive to both the policy and political issues which may be involved. Often in cases where international law is invoked, American courts, at least, have tended to test the contention as much against foreign policy objectives—the norms the United States would like to see universally established—as against anything that could fairly be said to be derived wholly from any universal practice.

Thus, in the world today, there is relatively little effort by national courts to play what seems to be an overcomplex and difficult task of creating universal norms. This task is left to political officials, whose leads courts are desirous to follow. We might almost say that the theory which led national courts to be subservient to formal national policy has been greatly extended, and that courts are today subservient to even a whisper of national policy. Therefore, rather than playing important creative roles in determining common international standards, national courts have more and more become apologists for national policies determined by political arms of government.

This does not mean that national courts do not continue to play an important moderating role and to invoke international law to assist them in this function. But it suggests that national courts are less important to the performance of this task than in the past, and that the creative use of method and technique to establish new norms has passed to other branches of the government, and to supranational bodies.

Foreign office: diplomatic intercourse. The traditional method of maintaining the integrity of international norms has been through diplomatic protest by the offended state, or states, of action that in its view was incompatible with existing law.

But before a state reaches the point of formal protest, it is subjected to the moderating influence that arises from the self-restraint most states exercise in order to encourage self-restraint on the part of others. As we stated above, the incorporation of international norms into national law permits recourse to legal action by private citizens to insure the compatibility with international law of administrative actions taken by state officials. Municipal officials are thus subjected to judicial restraint in matters litigable in local courts. In addition, all govenments go to considerable lengths to make sure that administrative and military officers respect international norms, at least as set forth by the state involved. In the United States we find manuals prepared for the Armed Services setting forth what is permitted and prohibited in all likely situations, and this is supplemented by a network of competent legal officers whose advice can be sought to clarify close cases. In the Department of State, personnel trained in law check and coordinate policies and programs to insure that they do not violate treaties or customary law. In all aspects of government, and in all governments, there exist similar internal checks on official action to ascertain that it is consistent with international law at least as exposited by the state involved.

The fact that there may be different formulations of rules and different interpretations of doctrine does not invalidate the broad area of agreement thus achieved. Further, many differences are of marginal significance and well within a discretion which other states can tolerate. The important point is that before a state departs consciously and abruptly from norms strongly supported by others, there must be an authorization at a quite high level of government, a policy decision near the top echelon. There is a question of both timing and substance involved and of willingness to take political risks.

A similar judgment must be made by other states in a position to protest, or at least dissent from, the suggested departure. Among friendly nations there is caution. Clarification of the change is often requested, and typically there is an effort to explore and expand points of agreement and narrow as far as possible the area of dispute. Formal protests as to illegality are relatively rare, and are becoming much rarer today among bloc members though perhaps more frequent between blocs. There is, after all, little service to bloc interests in accusing bloc partners of disrespect for international law, although such accusations between blocs may actually help create a politically desired image.

Now, diplomatic negotiation involves techniques which are flexible and range widely in the process of accommodation. Legal doctrine and methods of argumentation may help to clarify issues, but the diplomat is by no means confined, as is the judge, to rendering an opinion based exclusively upon existing doctrine. He employs law more in the fashion of advocate and legislator, with the important qualification that he has to be circumspect in statements which enter into the law process as future sources. He is desirous to preserve certain norms and support them as strongly as he is able. Yet he must weigh the consequences of the immediate controversy in terms of other objectives as well. Finally, of course, he has a domestic public to satisfy.

The diplomat, then, is not using law to decide cases, as is the judge, but to support policies. Although his method may be similar, he is subject to different constraints and has different objectives.

Let us reflect for a minute on the considerations we discussed at the outset. If the decision makers of two states feel that the norm each state espouses involves a really important issue of principle, at least one state, and perhaps both, will refuse adjudication by an impartial tribunal. Each will present its case as strongly as possible and then, almost by an unspoken mutual assent, leave it undecided. If, however, the controversy has to be compromised, each will prefer a non-doctrinal horse-trade to a solution that in any way weakens its doctrinal claim. Yugoslavia and the United States were quite unable to agree on the right of a state to nationalize property of foreigners without compensation, but were able to agree on a lump sum settlement in which neither sacrificed its position. If the controversy is one in which only a doctrinal compromise will suffice because it will apply frequently in like situations affecting both states, then the basic question of whether the doctrine or the relationship is more important must be asked.

INTERNATIONAL PROCEDURES

Good offices, mediation, and conciliation. Good offices, mediation, and conciliation techniques, which make use of "third parties" not directly concerned in the dispute, are, like diplomacy, intended primarily to compose differences. Intervention by a third party, even if not in the form of a court or arbitral tribunal, usually compels the disputing parties, in order to appeal to the third party, to phrase their demands in terms of rules that could be applied universally to all similar cases. It must be added that this fact does not automatically guarantee the success of third-party efforts. Each party to a dispute may enunciate a seemingly reasonable general rule to support its position. The parties to a dispute may differ on the facts, the interpretation of the facts, or the rule to be applied to a particular case.

Nonetheless, the fact that reference to universal standards is facilitated explains in part the usefulness of third-party efforts. Good offices, mediation, and conciliation are variant forms of a common technique. Technically good offices are restricted to interceding with the parties to get them to use diplomacy to settle their quarrel; mediation occurs when the mediator aids in the discussion of the substantive issues; and conciliation occurs when the conciliator proposes for the consideration of the parties either the rules that ought to govern the settlement or the actual terms of the settlement. Despite the seeming distinctions, the lines between good offices, mediation, and conciliation are rather difficult to draw. The use of good offices may founder if completely unresponsive to the substantive issues that led to the quarrel, for the willingness of the parties to accede to the services of those performing the good offices role depends in part upon the relationship of negotiation to an acceptable settlement of the substantive issues.

For instance, in the Franco-Tunisian dispute of 1958, France would have been willing to discuss the question of indemnities for the

313

bombing, but not the question of the right of French troops to remain in Tunisia, and particularly not any aspect of Algerian hostilities. Yet some extension of the discussion was necessary from the Tunisian point of view both for reasons of public demand and because Tunisia believed the issues to be inextricably related. Therefore it was not really possible for the United States to use its good offices to bring about discussions unless it used its influence to affect the agenda of the discussions. Yet it could hardly have done this without some discussion of whether the issues were in fact related. The American representative, Mr. Murphy, was presumably able to discuss whether the issues were related and whether it was advisable to link them in these particular negotiations without prescribing the outcomes of the negotiations on the issues or even the rules that were to govern the settlements. But Mr. Murphy's intervention nonetheless affected the substantive issues. Persuasion of France to discuss Algeria inevitably would have affected the position of France in Algeria.

The use of good offices occurs when the negotiator meets with the contending states separately. The mediator or conciliator may meet with the parties either separately or jointly. In the past, it was generally regarded as a friendly act for a state to offer its services in one of the three roles. Today, it is extremely dubious that such an offer would be regarded as friendly unless the circumstances made it appropriate for that particular state to offer its services. For instance, an offer by the Soviet Union to mediate between France and Tunisia would be regarded—and rightly so—as an effort further to injure relations rather than to ease them. The United States offer of good offices (although made inadvertently) was acceptable to both sides because the United States had a real interest in finding some way to ease the problem. The French could not afford to allow conditions to deteriorate further and therefore welcomed the good offices of a friendly state. The Tunisians desired to remain friendly to the West and hoped that the United States would be forced to link the Algerian and Tunisian situations to prevent the North African position of the NATO states from crumbling.

The peculiarly long-term character of bloc alignment during the loose bipolar period, therefore, specializes the role of negotiator. In the "balance of power" system a state not directly involved in the controversy usually was sufficiently neutral to serve as a mediator. In the loose bipolar system, most conflicts indirectly affect bloc affairs and the blocs have an interest in influencing their course. Finding an appropriate mediator for a dispute becomes enormously difficult under these circumstances. The leading member of a bloc may be the appropriate mediator between two other members of the bloc. But who can mediate between the leading member and another member of the bloc? Even in the first case, less formal diplomacy may be more appropriate than formal good offices or mediation. Who can mediate between the leading members of the two blocs? A single uncommitted state would not have sufficient strength or prestige. Moreover, on any number of issues, many uncommitted states would not genuinely be neutral—for instance, on any issue involving colonialism or thermonuclear tests. If no single uncommitted state is likely to be an acceptable mediator in bloc disputes, large numbers of uncommitted states may have to play such a role through the United Nations or by means of joint political influence exercised informally. Conflicts between uncommitted states can probably be mediated by still other uncommitted states in an effort to keep the dispute from becoming involved in the bloc conflicts. These are not, however, exclusively techniques for law resolution, although their effective use may be responsive to precedent and norms and may, in turn, serve as precedent for future cases.

International arbitration and international courts. International arbitration and judicial settlement are virtually identical procedures. In neither procedure may the judge or arbitrator decide the case with a view primarily to the accommodation or compromise of the conflicting interests, although decisions that fail to take such conflicts of interest into account are unlikely to prove effective. In each case, the settlement must be made according to rules that could be applied with equal validity to all other cases involving the same issues of law and of fact. There is an important difference, however. In arbitration, the arbitration agreement (or special submission to an International Court) may specify the issues that are to be decided and the facts that are to be taken into account. The contending parties may, if they wish, instruct the tribunal to accept an interpretation of the law to which the parties agree or a special rule that is to be applied to the particular case. For these reasons, the norm-creating power of the decision is somewhat limited.

Arbitration may proceed by means of *ad hoc* tribunals or individual arbitrators may be used. Finally, the parties involved may establish a continuing panel to arbitrate specific or general issues between them or recourse may be had to a tribunal open to all parties, such as the Permanent Court of Arbitration created by the Hague Convention of 1899. Arbitration agreements that are general usually exclude the vital interests of the nation, matters of honor, and matters that affect the interests of third parties. Although these limitations are sometimes viewed as defects of the arbitral systems, they actually are necessary if the systems are to be workable. Any system must have political methods for settling important conflicts of interest as well as juridical methods. In the present state of the international society direct negotiations between the disputants, the intervention of third parties, the application of the political machinery of international organizations, or perhaps the use of force constitute political techniques open to the parties.

Ad hoc tribunals, as a general rule, have their members selected by the parties to the dispute. Two disputants, for instance, may each select an arbitrator, and the two arbitrators may then select a third, in order to avoid the possibility of a tie vote. It is usually easier for the two arbitrators to agree upon the third than for the parties to the dispute to select directly an individual whom they can agree will apply the law impartially to the points at issue. The arbitrators selected by the parties usually find for the party who selected them. This somewhat diminishes the impartiality of these arbitrators. But it remains true that the arbitral award must be couched in normative language and not in the language of political negotiations.

The Permanent Court of International Justice, established by the Statute of the Court in 1921, and associated with the League of Nations, has now been replaced by the International Court of Justice as part of the general framework or organization established by the Charter of the United Nations. The judges are appointed to the International Court of Justice by a complicated procedure. Each of the national groups represented on the Permanent Court of Arbitration, and still functioning under the Charter, may nominate up to four judges not more than two of whom may come from their own nation. From this list the General Assembly and the Security Council each choose fifteen persons. Each person receiving a majority vote in both organs is elected, except that if two or more are elected from the same nation, only the elder receives the position. If a deadlock occurs, the sitting judges are empowered, as a last resort, to elect the remaining members of the bench. Five judges are elected every three years for nine-year terms. Judges cannot be dismissed unless their colleagues unanimously agree that they have ceased to satisfy the requirements of the position. Nine judges constitute a quorum, although a smaller bench is provided for when the parties desire a summary decision. If no judge of the nationality of one of the disputing parties is sitting, that party may nominate a judge for the case.

The judges of the International Court of Justice occupy a role of greater impartiality than do the judges of arbitral tribunals despite the provision in the Statute of the International Court of Justice for judges who are nationals of the parties to the dispute. Disputes may be submitted to the Court by all states which have signed its statute and to other states under conditions established by the Security Council. The Court may hear any matter submitted to it by states party to a dispute, and may hear all matters arising from the

316

provisions of treaties or conventions that provide for compulsory jurisdiction. Whether the Court has jurisdiction is determined by the Court. Theoretically, therefore, in the areas where the parties have accepted compulsory jurisdiction, either by acceding to the Court Statute under the "Optional Clause," or by entering into bilateral or multilateral agreements to this effect, one party to the dispute may bring the matter before the Court without the agreement of the other party.

The "Optional Clause" of the Statute of the International Court of Justice provides for compulsory jurisdiction between states that have accepted the clause in all legal disputes over the interpretation of a treaty, questions of international law, the existence of facts that, if established, would constitute a breach of an international obligation, or the kind or extent of reparation to be made for a breach of an international obligation. Although most signers of the Court Statute have also accepted the "Optional Clause," most of these have made reservations that diminish the significance of that action. The United States has excluded from the jurisdiction of the Court matters essentially with its domestic jurisdiction, as determined by the United States rather than by the Court, and disputes arising under a multilateral treaty unless either all the parties to the agreement affected by the dispute are parties to the action or the United States agrees to jurisdiction.

The idea of expanding the jurisdiction of the World Court is currently a very popular one in the United States. As a first step, the highest political circles have come to support a broader form of United States submission, although considerable Senate opposition appears to remain. To date, the Court has been very little used by Members, and there are few submissions to compulsory jurisdiction that are not qualified heavily. The reasons for this refusal to make use of the Court are worth examination.

It has already been noted that disputes about treaty interpretation or the application of rules of customary law are often a means of asserting what is really a desire for legislative reform; that is, for changing the content of the rules. To the extent that this is true disputes about the law are not *bona fide* legal disputes, but rather an aspect of political maneuver. In such cases at least one party does not want resolution by any third party institution, and particularly one employing the relatively narrow legal procedures of a court. A basic precondition to any voluntary submission to judicial resolution would seem to be agreement about the rules that will be applied. This is particularly true when there is no ready alternative to modify the rules except diplomatic negotiation. The unresolved dispute has a legislative impact, for the contentions of both parties enter into the stream of available precedent for others in like situations and for future decision makers to draw upon. This potential legislative power is important to states, and they are hesitant to entrust it to third parties, particularly if they believe, as do the smaller states, that their voice in world affairs is becoming more powerful.

Related to the foregoing is the fact that many disputes which appear to be disputes about the correct interpretation of a treaty or customary law have hidden motivation. Judicial resolution in terms of the legal issues presented would not touch the real source of difficulty, the real problems and policies that are involved. The recent dispute between Iceland and the United Kingdom as to the permissible breadth of the territorial sea is an example in point. Iceland wished to extend her sea to a breadth of twelve miles in order to protect her local fishing industry from foreign, particularly British, competition. Fishing is one of Iceland's most important industries, and the greater efficiency of British trawlers resulted in great loss of income to Icelandic fisherman. The government was under heavy pressure to protect the industry against more efficient foreign competition.

Great Britain wanted to protect its fishing industry from exclusion from Icelandic fishing grounds merely because it was more efficient. But, in addition, the three-mile limit to territorial waters was (and is) an extremely important principle to maintain for any country with extensive maritime interests throughout the world. For Great Britain, then, far more than Icelandic fish were in issue. If this question were submitted to the Court, as, surprisingly, the United Kingdom proposed, the Court could have decided either way, but it could not (unless specially empowered by the parties) have explored any other means of resolution, such as a subsidy to Icelandic fisherman. Its decision would have left unresolved basic problems for one party or the other, and would have been operative not to resolve the dispute but merely to change the bargaining positions of the parties.

Furthermore, for the Court to have decided this dispute would have had worldwide repercussions affecting the interests of other countries. The breadth of the territorial sea has been hotly debated by many countries; the International Law Commission failed to resolve the problem; it was not possible to find a two-thirds majority from among the eighty nations represented at the Geneva Conference on the Law of the High Seas for any specific proposal governing the width of territorial seas. Would the Court's imprimatur on one breadth or another have been the end of dispute? Indeed, could it have risked such a decision? A good guess is that it would have been forced to say that the matter was in such doubt that it could not find any rule of international law prohibiting a state from claiming as much as twelve miles. Yet, even this decision would have been, as decisions cannot avoid being, favorable to one party at the expense

318

of the other. More importantly, it could not have overtly weighed, because neither its method nor its prestige would permit, the better rule from the viewpoint of the international community.

This controversy illustrates two other shortcomings of reference to the ICJ that should be noted. First, the Court, in deciding a particular dispute must almost inevitably lay down general principles of international law that are of considerable interest and concern to states not parties to the particular dispute. The Court is, after all, the highest existing authority on international law, and any statements it makes in clarification of existing doctrine must be taken accordingly as authoritative. It is no answer to say—as does the Charter—that decisions of the Court have no precedential authority. They cannot help but have, whatever the theories of precedent may be. The Court must pay deference to its prior decisions if it is to avoid attack on grounds of partisanship among litigants. In addition, the opinions of the Court are taken most seriously, by scholars and by foreign offices alike, and treated as authoritative on the points decided and, indeed, on those merely discussed. Given this situation, we should ask whether or not it is really desirable to use the Court as the most important instrumentality for restating general principles of international law. Even if we concede the wisdom of clarifying rules (and this should not invariably be conceded), is the litigated case preferable to other alternatives? Examples of other alternatives are the International Law Commission, and various forms of multilateral treaty. It may be easier and more generally satisfactory to negotiate treaties restating and codifying general principles of international law if the rules themselves are still moot rather than after the Court has ruled on disputed points.

A second major shortcoming rests with the underdeveloped state of international law. When the Court deals with "customary" rules, it adopts the position that states are free to take unilateral action in the absence of a clear rule prohibiting the action taken. To a lesser extent, the Court takes the same view of treaty interpretation, allowing either party to interpret its obligations within the bounds of reason. Although those who profess a fear of too much interference by the Court with "sovereign" prerogatives might take comfort from this traditional judicial conservatism, we should also be aware that the basic causes of disputes remain relatively untouched. In almost every case, the complainant is seeking to formulate a rule that suggests that matters of mutual concern should be subject to joint regulation, not unilateral decision. Yet the state of international law doctrine, and the Court's jurisprudence, tends to leave the dispute where it was by declining to curb unilateral action. Indeed, those who point with pride to the fact that the Court's judgments have almost invariably been complied with should not neglect to point out that with very few exceptions the present Court has left the parties precisely where they were when they came to Court.

These observations should not be taken as criticisms of the Court. Quite the contrary, for judicial institutions must essentially preserve the status quo. Neither the methodology nor the function really permits otherwise. Courts must make new rules slowly, conservatively, and, of necessity, interstitially; a court is ill-equipped to rewrite a whole area of law within the limits of a single narrow controversy. For these reasons the ICJ cannot really contribute greatly to relieving international tensions even should its jurisdiction be expanded; it can seldom get at the basic causes of which the particular dispute is merely symptomatic. Today, for example there is considerable controversy over whether or not a state can confiscate, without compensation, foreign-owned enterprises on a non-discriminatory basis. Would a decision on this issue by the Court be helpful? Would it reduce international tensions, whichever way it was decided?

Both the geographical composition and mode of selection of judges create some problems. It is difficult to do much about giving the Communist countries and Afro-Asia more representation without offending other nations, particularly Europe and Latin America at whose expense the seats would probably shift. Furthermore, contentions that the present distribution of seats is unfair does not represent, as it might in this country when geographical areas or minority groups demand Supreme Court representation, merely a local pride and desire for status. It is founded on the notion that the Court does play a political role and is not really non-partisan. To acknowledge these demands might be to destroy the tradition of impartial role that the Court, with great difficulty, is seeking to build. That the Court, with seven members from the Western bloc, plus three Latin Americans, a Russian, a Pole, a Pakistani, and an Egyptian, is not a suitable mechanism for determining inter-bloc disputes is obvious. Shift the seven from West to East and envision the United States' attitude toward it. The tradition of impartial administration is by all evidence far stronger in the Western world, and in those areas of Afro-Asia which have preserved the British common law, than it is among the members of the Communist bloc. A major shift in its composition would greatly affect the attitude of Americans and Europeans toward the Court.

The Court is a useful and probably necessary, though not yet very important or powerful, part of the UN organizational complex. It can offer advisory opinions on the Charter. In addition, it can provide opinions on other basic UN documents to other UN agencies and help to clarify the growing area of international administrative law. These latter functions seldom raise very hot political questions, and the present composition of the Court reflects reasonably well the membership of specialized UN agencies, although slight modifications might not affect this consideration.

But the utility of the Court, by reason of its pretension to universality, to decide disputes between Member states is more questionable. Quite apart from the difficulties of any third-party adjudication in many disputes, adjudication by the highest judicial authority raises further difficulties. We have already noted that clarification of a theoretically universal "customary" law by virtue of pronouncement in two-party litigation is problematic, and that decision by this Court cannot help but freeze rules at a time when new problems require a more flexible approach. In addition, there is some doubt of the utility of an interbloc court to resolve intrabloc differences, of the need for fifteen judges and an expensive litigation process to clarify minor technical differences of interpretation, and of the wisdom of selecting to interpret a particular bilateral arrangement a Court that, because of its composition and prestige, must look to the impact of its decision on a variety of other agreements among other parties using similar language. Although any impartial decision maker would take these considerations into account, the authority of other decision makers and the impact of their decisions on non-litigating states would be less than that of the Court, and their decisions would consequently be more responsive to the problems raised by the litigating states.

Many of these difficulties could be met by having the Court sit in smaller panels (as the Charter permits) in a more convenient location. Decisions rendered by panels composed of judges whose impartiality between the litigants would be less subject to attack, and whose opinions would be less finally determinative of the general rule of international law are a feasible alternative. But even here it is difficult to envision extensive resort to the adjudicative process. Insofar as the process of adjudication also involves the restatement and clarification of rules that have future impact on the participants, the process has a "political" element, and it is by no means clear that the participants really wish to delegate this kind of authority to third parties, no matter how impartial, at least in the absence of an alternative mechanism to which appeal can be made. This is particularly true today because the classical rules and processes of international law are strongly tinted by Western jurisprudence and by rules derived from a period of laissez-faire economics. Many were in effect legislated by the great nations of yesteryear. Recognition of these difficulties is conceded by those who propose a Court of Equity and review of its decisions by the General Assembly. But again, the clarification of important rules in the context of particular disputes is a questionable device. It has the difficulties of an interstitial approach, and lacks the moderating influence that can come from more flexible institutions capable of broadening the area of negotiation and compromise, and of recommending more comprehensive solutions.

Finally, it should be added that none of what has been said above is particularly relevant to the proposal current in the United States to remove the Connally amendment to the United States reservation with regard to compulsory jurisdiction of the World Court. The reservation states that the U.S. will not submit disputes "essentially within the domestic jurisdiction of the United States of America *as determined by the United States of America.*" (The italicized words are the so-called Connally Amendment.) Obviously, this submission, as qualified above, is a fraud, and on that ground alone should be withdrawn. The United States should be the more embarrassed that this form of submission has been widely copied by others.

There is little danger to the United States in submitting to compulsory jurisdiction of the Court reciprocally with all other states who are willing to do so. The United States has infinitely more to gain than to lose from such a submission. It is consistent with the faith professed by the United States in peaceful and legal means of settlement of disputes, and with the image that the U.S. has of itself and wishes to project into the world community. The existing state of international "customary" law, and the treaties the United States is party to, seem generally favorable to the values that the United States is trying to promote in the world today and to the position of the United States in the international system, although it would require much more prevision than any of us have to know this with certainty. And, finally, the composition of the Court could not be more favorable to the American position on virtually any important issue.

THE AUTHORITY OF THE UNITED NATIONS TO ESTABLISH AND MAINTAIN A PERMANENT UNITED NATIONS FORCE

By Louis B. Sohn

Harvard Law School

The establishment of the United Nations Emergency Force (UNEF) during the Middle Eastern crisis in November, 1957, has been generally accepted as being a proper exercise of the powers of the United Nations.[1] Proposals have been made, however, to establish a more permanent force, either on a full-time or stand-by basis, for use in future emergencies.[2] It seems desirable, therefore, to investigate the legal problems involved in the establishment of such a permanent force, composed either of national contingents or volunteers.

I. POWER OF THE UNITED NATIONS TO ESTABLISH A U.N. FORCE

A. *The Power of the Security Council*

The Security Council was given by the Charter wide discretion in respect of steps to be taken to maintain or restore international peace and security. The debates at San Francisco show clearly the desire to grant to the Council all the powers necessary to enable it to take effective collective measures for the prevention and removal of threats to the peace, and for the suppression of acts of aggression or other breaches of the peace.[3] In the execution of enforcement measures, the Council may even "intervene in matters which are essentially within the domestic jurisdiction of any state."[4] The Members of the United Nations have agreed "to accept and carry out the decisions of the Security Council," provided they have been made "in accordance with" the Charter.[5]

In an emergency situation falling under Chapter VII of the Charter, the Council has a choice of three types of action: It may call upon the

---

[1] For an analysis of the problems involved in the establishment of the United Nations Emergency Force, see the Report of the Committee on Study of Legal Problems of the United Nations in 1957 Proceedings of the American Society of International Law, pp. 206–229.

[2] Pearson, "Force for U.N.," 35 Foreign Affairs 395, 401–402 (1957); Foreign Minister of Pakistan (Mr. Firaz Khan Noon), statement before the General Assembly on Nov. 29, 1957, 11th Sess., Official Records, Plenary Meetings, p. 417; Hammarskjöld, in the Introduction to the Annual Report of the Secretary-General on the Work of the Organization, 1956–1957, General Assembly, 12th Sess., Official Records, Supp. No. 1A (Doc. A/3594/Add. 1), pp. 1–2.

[3] U.N. Charter, Arts. 1, 24, 39. See United Nations Conference on International Organization, Documents, Vol. 12, pp. 502–514.

[4] U.N. Charter, Art. 2, par. 7.   [5] *Id.*, Art. 25.

parties concerned to comply with "such provisional measures as it deems necessary or desirable"; it may decide "what measures not involving the use of armed force are to be employed"; or it may take "such action by air, sea or land forces as may be necessary." [6]

It may be argued that the Security Council could establish a U.N. Force under any one of these three headings. The Council may consider that such a Force is necessary to ensure compliance with provisional measures ordered by it. For instance, having ordered a truce, the Council may establish various subsidiary organs to supervise its observance: a commission, a corps of military observers, a truce supervision organization, and even a Force of a para-military or military character. Such a Force would differ from the other supervisory institutions only in the number of people employed, as all these institutions have employed both military officers and uniformed guards for the performance of their functions.

It is also conceivable that the Council may decide that the use of a U.N. Force for such purposes as patrolling a frontier or occupying a disputed zone would not constitute a measure "involving the use of armed force" but, on the contrary, should be considered merely as a measure designed to prevent the use of armed force by others; accordingly it may use its authority under Article 41 to "decide what measures not involving the use of armed force are to be employed to give effect to its decisions." It may be noted that the measures under that article do not depend on the prior conclusion of agreements under Article 43.

Finally, and this seems to be the most likely situation, the Security Council may establish a U.N. Force under Article 42. While action under that article "may include" operations by forces of Member States, the language of that article does not preclude the use of any other forces available to the Council. Only the use of national forces depends on the prior conclusion of special agreements pursuant to Article 43; this limitation does not apply to any forces which the Council might be able to obtain by some other method.

On the other hand, a strong argument could be made for the proposition that the measures enumerated explicitly in Chapter VII are the only ones permitted and that the Security Council cannot take any other measures, not contemplated by those who drafted the Charter. The International Court of Justice has, however, recognized in the advisory opinion concerning "Reparations for Injuries Suffered in the Service of the United Nations" that the United Nations

> must be deemed to have those powers which, though not expressly provided in the Charter, are conferred upon it by necessary implication as being essential to the performance of its duties.[7]

As the forces contemplated by Articles 43 and 45 of the Charter have not been established, it might be considered essential to establish a limited substitute Force able to perform at least some of the functions assigned by the Charter to the missing forces.

---

[6] *Id.*, Arts. 40–42.   [7] [1949] I.C.J. Rep. 174, 182.

Thus it seems possible to envisage the establishment and use of a U.N. Force by the Security Council, and the only obstacle to the use of this method is the requirement of unanimity of the permanent members of the Security Council for any such action.[8]

B. *The Power of the General Assembly*

Though the Charter confers on the Security Council "primary responsibility for the maintenance of international peace and security,"[9] it does not confer on it "exclusive" jurisdiction in respect thereof. On the contrary, the Charter empowers the General Assembly to "consider the general principles of co-operation in the maintenance of international peace and security," and to "make recommendations with respect to such principles to the Members or to the Security Council or to both."[10] Under this grant of powers the General Assembly could certainly adopt a set of regulations defining the principles which should govern the establishment, training, organization, command and use of any forces put at the disposal of the United Nations. It could then recommend to Members that they take such steps as may be necessary to implement these principles. If any Member State should then agree to implement them, no other Member State could validly contend that the action of the Assembly or of the complying state constitutes a violation of the Charter.

On the other hand, it is necessary to make clear that no recommendation of the General Assembly binds a Member State and that any Member State can refuse to comply with a recommendation that it contribute personnel, arms, bases or assistance to a U.N. Force.[11]

It is necessary to distinguish, therefore, between the general, quasi-legislative recommendations of the General Assembly, stating in advance principles applicable to any Force to be used by the United Nations, and a particular recommendation that Member States make available to the United Nations specified armed forces. Only the first kind of recommendation is authorized by the express language of paragraph 1 of Article 11 of the Charter.

---

[8] Even the Soviet Delegation seems to agree that the Security Council could establish a U.N. Force; it raised objections, however, to the establishment of the U.N. Emergency Force by the General Assembly. General Assembly, 1st Emergency Spec. Sess., Official Records, Plenary Meetings, p. 127. For a broad interpretation of the powers of the Security Council to establish an international armed force for Palestine, see the working paper of the U.N. Secretariat of Feb. 9, 1948, U.N. Doc. A/AC.21/13, pp. 7–11.

[9] U.N. Charter, Art. 24.   [10] *Id.*, Art. 11, par. 1.

[11] But a state is not entitled simply to ignore a recommendation of the Assembly, and it is at least bound to explain to the Assembly why it cannot comply with the recommendation. States must give due consideration to the recommendations of the Assembly; their discretion to refuse compliance is always limited by their duty, under par. 2 of Art. 2 of the Charter, "to fulfil in good faith the obligations assumed by them in accordance with" the Charter. *Cf.* the separate opinion of Judge Lauterpacht in the case of the "Voting Procedure on Questions relating to Reports and Petitions concerning the Territory of South-West Africa," [1955] I.C.J. Rep. 67, 117–120.

Section C of the Uniting for Peace Resolution,[12] which provides ₁ method for the establishment of "armed forces which could be used collectively,"[13] falls clearly within the scope of paragraph 1 of Article 11, which authorizes the General Assembly to "consider the general principles of co-operation in the maintenance of international peace and security" and to "make recommendations with regard to such principles to the Members" of the United Nations. Section C is limited to an invitation to each Member State

> to survey its resources in order to determine the nature and scope of the assistance it may be in a position to render in support of any recommendations of the Security Council or of the General Assembly for the restoration of international peace and security.[14]

In this resolution the General Assembly seems to assume that each Member would be able to make some contribution, however small, to such assistance, and this assumption can be justified by the obligation, under paragraph 5 of Article 2 of the Charter, to "give the United Nations every assistance in any action it takes in accordance with" the Charter, i.e., in this case, in accordance with Article 11 thereof.

The Assembly further recommended that

> each Member maintain within its national armed forces elements so trained, organized and equipped that they could promptly be made available, in accordance with its constitutional processes, for service as a United Nations unit or units, upon the recommendation by the Security Council or General Assembly.

This general directive seems also entirely consistent with the language and spirit of paragraph 1 of Article 11. It is equally in harmony with the spirit of the Charter as a whole which requires all Members to make such contribution to the maintenance of peace as is within their means, thus uniting their strength "to save succeeding generations from the scourge of war" through "effective collective measures."[15]

While each Member is given complete discretion with respect to the steps to be taken to implement this provision of the resolution, it would be entirely inconsistent with its obligation under the Charter itself to refuse

---

[12] Res. 377 A (V) of Nov. 3, 1950, General Assembly, 5th Sess., Official Records, Supp. No. 20, pp. 10–12 (Doc. A/1775); 45 A.J.I.L. Supp. 1 (1951). It does not seem necessary to discuss here all the problems raised by the Uniting for Peace Resolution, as only some of its provisions are relevant to the subject of this memorandum. For a discussion of these problems see J. Andrassy, "Uniting for Peace," 50 A.J.I.L. 563–582 (1956); L. M. Goodrich and A. P. Simons, The United Nations and the Maintenance of International Peace and Security, pp. 406–423, 430–433 (Washington, 1955); H. Kelsen, Recent Trends in the Law of the United Nations, pp. 953–990 (London, 1951). It may be noted that the Soviet Union, in the Middle East crisis of 1956, acquiesced in the use by the General Assembly of its powers under the Uniting for Peace Resolution, at least in a case of an attack by one state on another. The Soviet opposition to the action of the Assembly in the Hungarian question was not related to the Uniting for Peace Resolution, but was based primarily on the ground that an issue of domestic jurisdiction was involved there.

[13] Res. 377 A (V); last par. of Preamble.

[14] Ibid., par. 7.

[15] U.N. Charter, Preamble and Art. 1. See also Arts. 43, 45.

to make any contribution whatsoever. On the other hand, it would be permissible for a Member to make its contribution subject to such conditions as it may deem necessary; for instance, a Member could limit the availability of its troops to cases in which the Security Council had ordered the use of armed forces under Article 42 of the Charter. The obligation to furnish forces under that article cannot be entirely destroyed by the lack of the special agreements required by Article 43, and it seems quite appropriate for the General Assembly to point the way for the implementation of the general obligation under Article 42 when such agreements have not been concluded. Section C of the Uniting for Peace Resolution thus removes the procedural obstacle of Article 43, the lack of special agreements between the Security Council and Members; it provides Members with an opportunity to fulfill their original obligations through unilateral declarations rather than agreements.

Once a Member, in accordance with its constitutional processes, has made a unit or units of its armed forces available for United Nations service, its consent to the use of such troops under the Uniting for Peace Resolution could be revoked only under conditions specified in its notification of the availability of such forces or in general regulations adopted by the Assembly. An unconditional promise to make them available could not be revoked, except with the consent of the United Nations.

The Uniting for Peace Resolution has thus provided a workable plan for the establishment of a U.N. Force composed of contingents, to be earmarked in advance by Member States, and to be available not only upon the recommendation of the Security Council, but also upon recommendation by the General Assembly. Unfortunately, no attempt has been made to use the favorable atmosphere which accompanied the adoption of the resolution (by 45 votes against 5, with 7 abstentions) for its prompt implementation. The replies of Member States to a request by the Collective Measures Committee (established also by the Uniting for Peace Resolution) for information as regards the action taken under Section C of the Resolution were quite disappointing.[16] But even where conditional pledges were given, no steps were taken by the United Nations to ensure their execution once the conditions had been fulfilled; for instance, after the conclusion of the armistice in Korea, no attempt was made to ascertain whether Members whose pledges were conditioned upon the termination of hostilities in Korea had earmarked the promised troops for United Nations use.

Thus, when the emergency arose in the Middle East, the United Nations seems to have proceeded on the assumption, not entirely justified, that no forces were available to it under the Uniting for Peace Resolution and that the needed U.N. Emergency Force must be established on a new basis. The decision to establish that Force was also based on the Uniting for Peace Resolution, but it seems that this decision was based on Section A

16 For a tabulation of these replies, see First Report of the Collective Measures Committee of 1951, Annex II; General Assembly, 6th Sess., Official Records, Supp. No. 13, pp. 37–48 (Doc. A/1891).

rather than on Section C of that resolution.[17]   Section A authorizes the General Assembly, "if the Security Council, because of lack of unanimity of the permanent members, fails to exercise its primary responsibility for the maintenance of international peace," to make

> appropriate recommendations to Members for collective measures, including in the case of a breach of the peace or act of aggression the use of armed forces when necessary, to maintain or restore international peace and security.[18]

Though it may be argued that the U.N. Emergency Force does not constitute an armed force of the kind envisaged in this resolution, the establishment of that Force may be considered to fall within the scope of the phrase "collective measures."   Thus, if the Security Council, in the exercise of its primary responsibility, could have created such a Force under Chapter VII of the Charter, the General Assembly could "recommend" its creation through the exercise of its secondary responsibility.

Both Sections A and C of the Uniting for Peace Resolution envisage primarily the use of armed forces against an aggressor, and assert the right of the General Assembly to recommend their use in case of a breach of the peace or act of aggression.   The U.N. Emergency Force, however, was not used for that purpose, and its validity seems to be based on the premise that the right to establish such a smaller force is implicit in the right to establish a large fighting force.   While this conclusion does not necessarily follow from the above premise, other arguments could be made in favor of the Assembly's right to establish this Force.

The Secretary General seems to have proceeded on the assumption that the U.N. Emergency Force is a "subsidiary organ of the General Assembly" and it has been "established in accordance with Article 22 of the Charter." [19]   This reliance on Article 22 is perhaps not entirely justified, as it could be argued quite persuasively that the subsidiary organs envisaged by this article should be limited to "committees" or "commissions" assisting the Assembly in the performance of its deliberative, quasi-legislative and investigatory functions.   Once, however, it has been accepted that mediators or commissions, appointed by the Assembly to supervise a truce agreement or the observance of the resolutions of the Assembly, might need additional personnel for the exercise of their functions, there seems to be no logical limit to the number of persons needed.   Similarly, if military personnel are added to United Nations missions and guards are sent to defend the personnel and the property of such missions, it is difficult to draw the line between permitted and prohibited types of personnel and

[17] No clear reference is contained in any resolution on the subject, and the Secretary General, in his final report of Nov. 6, 1956, refers only to the fact that the Force would be functioning "on the basis of a decision to be reached under the terms of the Resolution 337 (V) 'Uniting for Peace'," without specifying the relevant section of the resolution.   U.N. Doc. A/3302, par. 9.

[18] See Res. 377 A (V) (*loc. cit.* note 12 *supra*), par. 1.

[19] Introduction to the "Regulations for the United Nations Emergency Force" of Feb. 20, 1957, U.N. Doc. A/3552; Agreement between the United Nations and Egypt of Feb. 8, 1957, U.N. Doc. A/3525, pp. 2, 7.

of weapons which may be used by them. It is not surprising, therefore, that various documents relating to the U.N. Emergency Force grant to the officers of the Command of that Force privileges and immunities of Article VI of the Convention on the Privileges and Immunities of the United Nations [20] which deals with "experts on missions for the United Nations." [21]

It is also possible to establish a U.N. Force as part of the Secretariat of the United Nations. The Charter does not establish any limitations with respect to the size of the Secretariat; it does not prohibit the recruitment of persons with military training; nor does it prohibit arming them with small or large weapons. The phrase, "such staff as the Organization may require," in Article 97 of the Charter is broad enough to include any military personnel deemed by the Assembly to be required for the purpose of maintaining peace. The Secretary General has stated on several occasions that there is no doubt about his power to establish military units in the Secretariat, even "several thousand strong," provided that budgetary approval is voted by the General Assembly.[22]

This method of establishing the U.N. Force cannot be easily applied to a Force composed of national contingents. On the other hand, it is admirably suited to recruitment of volunteers for such a Force. If the General Assembly were willing to make the necessary financial appropriations, the Secretary General could recruit as many individuals as the Assembly should authorize, provide for their training as military units of the Secretariat, and send them on such missions as the Assembly might direct. It may be useful to point out that Article 17 of the Charter contains no limit on the amount of United Nations expenses to be borne by the Members, and by a two-thirds majority the Assembly could adopt a budget containing an appropriation for the maintenance of a Force of 5,000, 20,000, or even 50,000 men. It may be doubted whether the International Court of Justice, if asked for an advisory opinion, would consider such an appropriation as an abuse of the budgetary authority conferred by Article 17.

II. Power of the United Nations to Control a Force

The United Nations' power to control a Force established by it seems to be beyond doubt. In particular, the organ of the United Nations establishing the Force, i.e., the Security Council or the General Assembly, may either itself issue the regulations governing the Force or delegate the power to issue such regulations to another organ. For instance, the General Assembly authorized the Secretary General "to issue all regula-

20 General Assembly, 1st Sess., Official Records, First Pt., Resolutions, p. 25 (Doc. A/64); 43 A.J.I.L. Supp. 1 (1949).

21 See Regulations (loc. cit. note 19 supra), par. 19 (a); Agreement (loc. cit. note 19 supra), pp. 8–9.

22 See, for instance, the Report of the Secretary General on the United Nations Guard of Sept. 28, 1948. U.N. Doc. A/656, pars. 10–11, and Appendix A (Legal Basis of the Guard).

tions and instructions which may be essential to the effective functioning" of the U.N. Emergency Force and "to take all other necessary administrative and executive action." [23]   At the same time, the General Assembly established an Advisory Committee composed of representatives of seven countries "to assist the Secretary General in responsibilities falling to him" under the relevant resolutions; and the Secretary General was requested to consult the Committee prior to issuing regulations or instructions to the Force.[24]   If there arose an important and urgent disagreement on the subject between the Secretary General and the Committee, it would have to be solved by the Assembly itself, and the Assembly empowered the Committee "to request, through the usual procedures, the convening of the General Assembly" whenever the Committee should consider this necessary.[25]

Similarly, in establishing any future Force, the Assembly might delegate the power to issue regulations for the Force to the Secretary General, acting in consultation with, or subject to approval by, a special watchdog committee. All such regulations would have to comply, of course, with any basic provisions enacted by the General Assembly itself, which would always constitute "the fundamental law" of the Force.[26]

While the Secretary General was responsible for "all administrative, executive and financial matters" affecting the U.N. Emergency Force, the Chief of the U.N. Command, appointed directly by the General Assembly, was given "full command authority over the Force." He was, therefore, responsible for the "operation" of the Force, for its "deployment" and for the "assignment of troops placed at the disposal of the Force."[27] Similar arrangements might be made for any future U.N. Force.

III. Relations between the U.N. Force and the Contributing States

If the future U.N. Force should be composed of national contingents, questions might arise as to the amount of control which would be retained by each contributing Member over the troops contributed by it. A distinction must be made here between a permanent assignment of a contingent to the United Nations and an assignment limited to a particular emergency.

In the first case, a Member which has concluded an agreement or made a declaration putting a contingent at the disposal of the United Nations would lose the right to withdraw its contingent without the permission of the United Nations, except under the circumstances clearly specified in such an agreement or declaration. It is understood, however, that a Member could substitute from time to time new troops for old ones, unless

<hr>

[23] Res. 1001 of Nov. 7, 1956, General Assembly, 1st Emergency Spec. Sess., Official Records, Supp. No. 1, p. 3 (Doc. A/3354).

[24] Ibid., pars. 6–8.   [25] Ibid., par. 9.

[26] Statement by the Secretary General, Nov. 7, 1956. General Assembly, 1st Emergency Spec. Sess., Official Records, Plenary Meetings, p. 119.

[27] Regulations for the U.N. Emergency Force of Feb. 20, 1957, U.N. Doc. ST/SGB/ UNEF/1, pars. 11, 15, 16.

they should then be in action and the Chief of the U.N. Command should find such a substitution inconsistent with the military exigencies of the situation.

In the second case, the assignment would be limited to the period of emergency and the national contingents would have to be released from United Nations service as soon as possible after the end of the emergency. The basic issue here would be who would be entitled to determine authoritatively whether the emergency has ended. Unless a Member has expressly reserved to itself the right to make such a determination, it would seem consistent with the spirit of Article 39 of the Charter and of the Uniting for Peace Resolution to leave to the Security Council and the General Assembly, respectively, the determination not only that a breach of the peace has occurred, but also that it has ended.

As no state is bound, without a special agreement, to contribute a contingent for a U.N. Force, it can accompany its offer of a contribution with such reservations as to the use of its contingent as it may deem necessary; e.g., it may make reservations with respect to the length of service of its troops, the tasks for which the contingent may be used, the need for consent of the state to the territory of which the contingent may be sent, etc. If the competent organ of the United Nations should find any such reservations incompatible with the task to be performed by the Force, and if the state should not be willing to abandon the reservations with respect to which objections have been raised, the United Nations would have a choice of either refusing to accept the particular offer or accepting it on the terms dictated by the contributing state.

The only way out of this difficulty would seem to be for the General Assembly to adopt in advance general regulations specifying the minimum conditions under which troops would be accepted, and for a sufficient number of states to accept these conditions without any reservations. If that should happen, other states would be less likely to try to impose new conditions upon the United Nations and would feel obliged to follow the pattern set by the original acceptances. In such a situation, the United Nations would be less inclined to accept too limited offers and the general standard would remain high.

If the proposed U.N. Force is to be composed of directly recruited volunteers, there should be less difficulty with a state whose nationals have volunteered for the Force. An advance consent for such recruitment would be necessary only where the recruitment campaign is to be conducted on the territory of the state concerned. No such consent would be required for the recruitment of its nationals residing abroad, as long as the state of residence does not raise any objections. A state may prohibit its nationals' entry into the Force, may refuse to give them exit visas, and may punish them for joining the Force. If such punishment should involve the loss of citizenship, the state would, however, lose further control over them to the extent that such control is based on their citizenship.

While a Member's duty in good faith to assist the United Nations in any action taken by it to fulfill the purposes of the Charter might not go so far as to oblige it to contribute a national contingent to the U.N. Force, it could be argued that a Member has at least the duty to refrain from putting obstacles in the way of its nationals or residents who wish to join the U.N. Force. Any such action violating this duty could be declared by the General Assembly as inconsistent with the Charter. Any such pronouncement would be merely declaratory of existing obligations rather than an attempt to create new obligations, would thus bind all the Members, and the Member which has enacted restrictions on enlistment in the U.N. Force would be required to abolish them.[28]

IV. The Relation between the U.N. Force and the "Host" State

The establishment of a U.N. Force by the General Assembly is, of course, not subject to veto by any state, but such a Force could not be established if more than one third of the Member States present and voting should decide to oppose it. Both a resolution establishing the Force and a resolution for its financing require a two-thirds majority.[29]

The General Assembly has also complete authority to determine the organization and composition of the Force. When it comes, however, to the deployment of the Force, it has been argued that the consent of the state in the territory of which the Force is to be deployed, i.e., of the "host" state, is required. Thus the Secretary General has stated that the U.N. Emergency Force cannot "be *stationed or operate* on the territory of a given country without the consent of that country." On the other hand, he did not exclude "the possibility that the Security Council could use such a Force within the wider margins provided under Chapter VII of the United Nations Charter."[30]

As explained in Section I above, there seems to be an agreement on the binding character of decisions of the Security Council under Chapter VII of the Charter, and no consent would be necessary if the Security Council should order a Force established by the Council itself or by the General Assembly to enter the territory of a particular state in order to maintain or restore peace.

It has also been suggested that a decision of the Council that an investi-

[28] In his report of Feb. 11, 1957, the Secretary General made the distinction "between recommendations which implement a Charter principle, which in itself is binding on Member States, and recommendations which, although adopted under the Charter, do not implement any such basic provision. A recommendation of the first kind would have behind it the force of the Charter, to which collective measures recommended by the General Assembly could add emphasis, without, however, changing the legal character of the recommendation. A decision on collective measures referring to a recommendation of the second kind, although likewise formally retaining its legal character, would mean that the recommendation is recognized by the General Assembly as being of such significance to the efforts of the United Nations as to assimilate it to a recommendation expressing an obligation established by the Charter." U.N. Doc. A/3527, par. 20.

[29] U.N. Charter, Art. 18, par. 2.

[30] Second Report of the Secretary General on the Plan for the U.N. Emergency Force, Nov. 6, 1956, U.N. Doc. A/3302, par. 9. See also his statement as to the stationing of troops on the Egyptian–Israeli armistice line, of Jan. 24, 1957, U.N. Doc. A/3512, pars. 5 (b), 20.

gating committee be sent to a territory under Article 34 of the Charter, in order to determine whether the continuance of a dispute or a situation is likely to endanger peace, does not require the consent of the state concerned.[31] Once it is accepted that the decisions of the Security Council under Chapter VI may be binding in certain circumstances, it could be argued that the General Assembly, which has the same powers as the Council under Chapter VI, could also make such binding decisions. Such an interpretation seems to go too far, however, and in any case, it would be difficult to extend this interpretation from the sending of an ordinary subsidiary organ to the sending of a large, or even small, U.N. Force to a territory of a state without its consent.

Another line of approach may be more fruitful. The consent of a state need not be explicit, and often it may be implied. If the General Assembly should by an almost unanimous vote approve a general principle that the new U.N. Force should be entitled to enter the territory of any state whenever the Assembly authorizes it to do so, all states would be presumed to have accepted this principle unless they should expressly state either at the time of the vote in the Assembly or soon thereafter that they do not accept the principle. There is no doubt that the Assembly could be authorized by a general agreement to follow the practice of some specialized agencies and could adopt rules which would become binding without ratification, provided each state be given a chance to reject the new rule within a specified period of time.[32] If only a few states should exercise such an option, the rule would become immediately binding on all other states and in due course might even become a customary rule of international law which no state would be allowed to ignore.

Distinction must be made, therefore, between a general rule applicable to unknown future contingencies and an attempt to create a new rule applicable immediately to a given situation. While, in the first case, consent may be implied in certain circumstances, in the second case, consent of the state concerned would have to be given more explicitly; and if consent should not be given, the Force would not be entitled to enter the territory of that state.

The question has also arisen whether a state can withdraw its consent after a U.N. Force has, with the consent of that state, entered its territory. On the one hand, it has been argued that the U.N. Emergency Force must leave the territory of the "host" state whenever that state should so request;[33] on the other hand, as the original Egyptian acceptance contained no reservation on the subject, it could be argued that an international agreement on the entry of the Force into Egypt having been validly con-

[31] See, for instance, the statements by the U. S. representative (Mr. Johnson) in the Greek Case in July, 1947, Security Council, Official Records, 2nd Year, Nos. 61, 63 and 64, pp. 1423, 1523, 1540–1541. But the proposed U. S. resolution was vetoed by the Soviet Union.

[32] Cf. Arts. 12, 37, 38, 54 (1) and (m) 57, 90 of the Convention on International Civil Aviation of Dec. 7, 1944, 15 U.N. Treaty Series 295; and Arts. 21–22 of the Constitution of the World Health Organization of July 22, 1946, 14 ibid. 185.

[33] See the statement by the Foreign Minister of Egypt of Nov. 27, 1956, General Assembly, 11th Sess., Official Records, Plenary Meetings, p. 348.

cluded, that agreement cannot be terminated by unilateral declaration of Egypt. In the reverse situation, if the General Assembly should wish to withdraw the Force and if Egypt should object thereto, the United Nations would have to fulfill its part of the bargain. The withdrawal would be permitted only after the emergency envisaged in the original decision to send the Force to the territory of a particular state has actually ceased, and the "host" state could request such withdrawal only if the Force has fulfilled the function for which it was sent to the territory of that state. Whether the emergency envisaged in the agreement or decision which formed the basis for the Force's entry into the territory of the "host" state has ceased is a question of both fact and law, and, if need be, a decision or an advisory opinion of the International Court of Justice might be obtained on the subject.

In cases in which the consent of the "host" state is required, such consent might be conditional, and though it has been argued that the "host" state should not be allowed to dictate to the United Nations what should be the composition of the Force, in practice it may refuse its consent unless it is guaranteed that the Force will be composed of contingents or nationals of certain states, or that contingents or nationals of some states will be excluded from the Force. Of course, where consent had been given in advance by acceptance of general regulations adopted by the General Assembly, such consent could not later be made conditional on the inclusion in or exclusion from the Force of the nationals of any state or states.

Once a U.N. Force had been admitted to the territory of a state, various privileges and immunities would be necessary in order to safeguard its independence. Article 105 of the Charter guarantees to the United Nations "such privileges and immunities as are necessary for the fulfillment of its purposes"; similarly it guarantees to United Nations officials "such privileges and immunities as are necessary for the independent exercise of their functions in connection with the Organization." These provisions are broad enough to cover a U.N. Force and its members, but it might be useful to spell out in advance what special privileges and immunities are necessary for the "independent exercise of their functions." The provisions of the Convention on the Privileges and Immunities of the United Nations,[34] of the Agreement with Egypt on the Status of the U.N. Emergency Force,[35] and of the Agreement on the Status of NATO Forces [36] may serve as useful guides for a general resolution of the General Assembly on that subject.[37] Paragraph 3 of Article 105 of the Charter expressly empowers the General Assembly to make such recommendations as may be necessary to determine the details of the application of that article.

[34] See note 20 above.   [35] See note 19 above.

[36] T.I.A.S., No. 2846; 48 A.J.I.L. Supp. 83 (1954).

[37] If the U.N. Force should be composed of volunteers rather than of national contingents, it might be necessary to combine in the hands of the U.N. Command the powers which are divided in the Egyptian agreement between the Command and the states which have contributed contingents to the U.N. Emergency Force. In addition, it would be necessary to establish more detailed military regulations for the Force and appropriate procedures and tribunals for the trial of violators.

AN APPROACH
TO DEVELOPMENT OF UN PEACE-KEEPING MACHINERY BASED ON THE SIGNIFICANCE OF UNEF AND ONUC EXPERIENCE

By MARION H. McVITTY

INTRODUCTION

A number of scholarly studies of experience gained in the United Nations Emergency Force and the UN Congo Operation are in progress by universities and foundations. Such careful analyses will undoubtedly uncover many facets of these two United Nations operations which have important implications for future planning in the development of UN peace-keeping machinery. However, considerable time will be required to complete such detailed appraisals.

The purpose here is to set out in rather broad terms some of the more obvious aspects of the UN experience with UNEF and ONUC, and to suggest some avenues of approach to the development of more effective UN peace-keeping machinery which might be explored now by those seeking to formulate new United States policies in this regard.

For this purpose, it is assumed that UN peace-keeping machinery contemplated for the near future must be created under the terms of the present United Nations Charter. It is assumed, further, that while the present Charter is flexible enough to permit some evolutionary development of peace-keeping machinery, its terms define limits which cannot be exceeded without formal amendments, or supplementary treaties. While adhering to these assumptions, recent United Nations experience in the Middle East and in Congo indicate that more radical approaches will be necessary in future to meet the kind of problems that have been encountered.

SOME FUNDAMENTAL ASPECTS OF UNEF AND ONUC EXPERIENCES

United Nations experience in the Middle East and in Congo has demonstrated that at a minimum the fundamental factors outlined below must be taken into account in plans to develop further UN peace-keeping machinery.

UN Power and the Use of Force

UNEF was armed primarily by moral force derived from informed and favorable world public opinion and from confidence in this UN operation on the part of most Governments directly involved. At Suez and in Sinai and Gaza, the small, lightly armed UN Emergency Force, symbolizing the United Nations itself, was accorded respect by the parties concerned and its authority was generally recognized by the people and national armed forces in the area.

In Congo moral force of the kind enjoyed by UNEF was largely inoperative and was insufficient to protect ONUC from various hostilities including armed attack. Division of political opinion within the UN membership, ignorance of the UN inside Congo, and mistrust of UN motives among Congolese and non-Congolese alike negated the power of the UN symbol and dissipated the moral force of public opinion. As a result ONUC was at times compelled to match the physical strength arrayed against it. UN forces in Congo had to use weapons in self-defense and armed force to overcome defiance of the ONUC mandate.

Had the United Nations Police Force in Congo had preponderant power over the local armed factions, armed defiance of the UN mandate would probably have been deterred, and occasions requiring the use of weapons in self-defense would have been relatively insignificant. In Congo, however, troops could not be raised in sufficient strength to have full control over local forces involved, and local forces could not be reduced to lesser strength than that at the service of the United Nations.

Previous experience with UNEF may have led to false hopes that moral power would reinforce UN's actual strength in Congo. In any event the Congo Operation was initiated, and has been carried out, with little definition regarding the nature and degree of force to be used in meeting eventualities. Uncertainty and criticism have resulted, further confounding an already confused situation.

Control of UN Contingents

Because neither UNEF nor ONUC were established under Chapter VII of the Charter, the UN contingents in both areas can be withdrawn at will by the nations contributing them. Similarly, the host country can expel the UN Force at its pleasure.

Contingents were withdrawn from UNEF for practical reasons by certain contributing nations which did not feel they could afford this disposition of their troops for more than a short period. In the case of Congo, contingents were withdrawn because of political disaffection with the UN operation on the part of contributing States, or their withdrawal was threatened by contributing States in order to influence the political situation underlying the emergency.

Theoretically the UN did not recognize the right of the Central Government of Congo to expel the UN Force. However, it is doubtful if a host country's wishes could be ignored if, in future, a host government made a determined effort to terminate a UN operation on its territory. In any event, the United Nations was faced with a serious aspect of this very problem when the Province of Katanga declared its secession and sought to bar ONUC from that part to the Congo. The unwillingness of that Provincial Government to entertain ONUC in that area, even after the entrance of UN troops into Katanga had been carefully negotiated, has been a root cause of much of the trouble ONUC experienced in and around Elizabethville.

So long as UN contingents can be withdrawn by contributing nations, or expelled by the host country, no UN operation can be undertaken with adequate assurance that it can be carried out to a satisfactory conclusion. The best interests of the world community may be forced to yield to the political will of individual UN members in the midst of an emergency situation.

UN Operations and Intervention in Domestic Affairs

The Charter forbids the UN to intervene in matters "which are essentially within the domestic jurisdiction of any State."

Possible intervention in domestic affairs was not a very serious problem in the UNEF operation. In this case, the primary concern was to avoid UN action which might prejudice the positions of the parties in the unresolved Arab-Israeli dispute. The Secretary General made it clear at the outset that deployment of UNEF would not be permitted to influence the settlement attendant upon the Israel-Arab Armistice agreement. To this end, Hammarskjold avoided any measure on the part of UNEF which might alter for either side the political, legal or military status quo prior to the outbreak of hostilities at Suez and in Sinai.

In Congo the original UN mandate to eliminate outside intervention and to maintain law and order within the country soon threatened to embroil ONUC in domestic affairs. Disputes between national political leaders and factions, and between the national and provincial authorities, were primary causes in most disturbances of law and order with which ONUC had to contend.

Although ONUC scrupulously sought to avoid any action which could influence the internal political situation, it is doubtful if the UN could actually avoid all prejudicial action. At times inaction was as capable of affecting the volatile internal situation as action would have been. While it is difficult to assess precisely how successful ONUC has been in avoiding intervention in Congo's domestic affairs, it is pertinent to question whether this prohibition impeded fulfillment of the UN mandate and prolonged the Congo crisis. It is necessary to consider carefully if complete internal sovereignty is always compatible with the preservation of world peace during an international emergency.

UN Competence Over Recalcitrant Individuals

A UN force which is not fighting a war to stop a war as

in Korea may be opposed, or impeded, by recalcitrant individuals not under the immediate control of any national government. The UN does not have competence over such individuals, nor does it have the institutions to detain and to prosecute them.

In Gaza, UNEF is responsible for halting raids from either side across the Armistice Demarcation Line. Raiders from either side may, or may not, be acting with the knowledge and approval of their respective governments. Raiders from either side, if apprehended by UNEF must be turned over to their own national authorities who may, or may not take punitive measures. No doubt some of the raiders are left free to raid again.

Although UNEF cannot detain or prosecute individual raiders transgressing the Demarcation Line, UNEF troops may shoot such individuals if they refuse to halt on command.

In Congo, ONUC has encountered even more difficult situations with individuals who have violated, or impeded, the UN mandate. Congolese soldiers have broken away from their commands and have committed crimes for which no authority has been able to hold them accountable. Particularly during the period when there was virtually no Central Congolese Government, violence by rebellious individuals took place with impunity.

The non-Congolese political and military advisors and the mercenaries which have opposed and obstructed the UN operation in Katanga are generally beyond the reach of their national authorities, when they are not, in fact, stateless persons. ONUC has been empowered to evict such individuals, but those evicted have frequently returned in short order to continue their illegal activities. More recently ONUC has been further authorized to hold such individuals for disposition by the national Congolese Government. It is, however, questionable whether the Leopoldville authorities have adequate judicial means to ensure prompt and fair disposition of those individuals who may come into their hands.

Unrestrained individuals have been largely responsible for the personal violence and armed attacks suffered by ONUC. Again, as in the case of UNEF, the UN may kill such individuals in battle, or shoot them in self-defense, indeed it is even authorized to expel mercenaries by force if necessary, but it cannot apprehend them and subject them to due process under its own jurisdiction.

The use of UN force against individuals in both areas is, therefore, at times necessary and authorized, but the use of force is not related to UN legal measures which might prevent, or prosecute, cases of individual opposition or obstruction. Force and justice are not integrated within UN competence.

UN Ad Hoc Forces Tend to Become Permanent

The UN has demonstrated in the cases under consideration, as well as in Korea and Kashmir, a greater ability to pacify disputes than to settle them.

In the Middle East, with the cooperation of all the parties, and with the help of the Secretary General and the World Bank, the UN successfully resolved the major conflict over the Suez Canal. However, although UNEF has done much to pacify the Israeli-Arab borders, the UN has not been able to settle the fundamental territorial dispute between Israel and the Arabs. As a result, at considerable expense and inconvenience, UNEF must remain in the area indefinitely.

There seems to be a brighter prospect for the reduction and elimination of UN Police forces in Congo. However, the duration of the UN Police action in Congo will depend substantially on the termination of outside intervention which is still being covertly aided and abetted by individuals and by neighboring governments which are not reconciled to African nationalism. The original Congo crisis had more of a domestic than an external cause. Peaceful change, rather than peaceful settlement, is requisite in this instance. The UN, at best, has faulty means by which to promote peaceful change with the kind of stability that would make continued use of UN forces unnecessary.

UN means for peaceful settlement and the promotion of peaceful change are at present so weak that UN police operations tend to become pinned down for long periods in the areas they have managed to pacify.

Appropriate Contingents for UN Are Limited

The immediate circumstances at Suez, and Cold War considerations both in the Middle East and in Congo precluded the use of most NATO, SEATO and Warsaw Pact members' military contingents in UNEF or ONUC. Both experiences indicate that UN Police operations in future will probably require contingents from smaller and less committed States if they are to be appropriate to the particular emergency at hand.

Scandinavian and Asian troops have been used in UNEF and ONUC as well as Canadian communications units in both areas. Such African troops as were available have been used in Congo probably to the limit attainable. A few Latin American contingents served in UNEF, and there is some Latin American personnel in Congo. Irish forces have been used in Congo.

The duration of the commitment of these national forces to the two present engagements, as well as the difficulties they have experienced, seem likely to have largely exhausted the contingents to be expected from these Governments for some time to come.

Should a new crisis arise requiring UN Police action before UNEF and ONUC can release their contingents, it is difficult to see where adequate and appropriate additional manpower could be found to meet the emergency. As of now, it seems likely another similar crisis would force the UN to realize that present methods for obtaining trained personnel would be so over-extended that the UN would either have to find new methods, or refuse to act.

Motivation, Morale and Esprit de Corps of UN Forces

It is probably too soon to know with any accuracy the nature of the motivation or the extent of high morale and esprit de corps which exist either in UNEF or ONUC among the individual soliders. Indeed, it may be too soon even to assess how important these factors have been in the conduct of such UN police operations.

Certain factors can, however, be identified which must affect the personal performance of individual soliders and of different national units. It is, perhaps, useful to list some of them.

1) Both Forces have had to operate in difficult and unpleasant terrain.

2) In Gaza UNEF contingents have had to cooperate closely in spite of language and custom differences which have been very great and could not be entirely bridged.

3) ONUC personnel have been subjected to violence, abuse and indignities which must often have seemed quite irrational.

4) In Congo there have been virtually no recreational facilities for ONUC.

5) In both Forces each contingent is subject to its own military discipline, and to its own national authorities in the case of civilian crimes in the host country, so that these Forces do not receive uniform treatment for similar misbehavior or criminal acts.

6) The troops in both Forces have had duties which are not usually the business of armed forces, which in some respects were contrary to their military training, and which in other respects required special training which they had not received.

7) Although the UN Commands in each area must have made every effort to give these Forces an understanding of their task, it is likely that contingent officers who have a closer relationship to the troops may give somewhat different interpretations, colored according to the moral and political point of view of their own countries.

The Difficulty of Financing UN Forces

Experience both with UNEF and ONUC has demonstrated that few UN member governments consider ad hoc UN Police forces to be a good financial investment. Several member governments have used the withholding of funds for UN forces as a political tool with which to influence the particular incident or the international situation as a whole. No government can now predict how often or how much it may be called upon to pay for UN emergency operations. Uncertainty in this regard, discourages governments from assuming specific obligations lest a precedent be set for unlimited obligations of this kind in future.

Although most UN members have agreed to the need for both UNEF and ONUC as the best available means to avoid a major war in which all might be involved, once the immediate crisis was subdued nations at a distance from the arena did not apparently feel that their own security was really at stake. The creation of ad hoc UN forces did not make possible the reduction of national defense establishments, but became instead an additional financial burden with little or no sense of greater national security.

In fact, the security rewards for financing ad hoc forces are insufficient to ensure payments, and the political advantages of default are too tempting to be resisted. Hence, the UN finds itself seriously over-extended financially, and as in the case of contingents, would be in an almost impossible situation if another emergency should arise in the near future.

TEMPORARY SUPRA-NATIONAL POWERS FOR THE UNITED NATIONS IN EMERGENCIES

When the experience gained from UNEF and ONUC is reviewed, the conclusion is inescapable that the United Nations in emergencies needs more control. The UN would be more effective in dealing with a crisis if it had more control over its Police Forces and over the actual situation in which it found itself. It is possible to conceive of temporary supra-national powers for the UN in emergencies which would be adequate to carry out its mandate with efficiency, and at the same time so limited as to prevent the UN from permanently prejudicing the fundamental rights of any of the parties.

The Concept of Temporary Supra-National Powers

When a crisis arises in which the United Nations is requested to take emergency policing action, the UN should be given supra-national powers, defined to meet the particular situation, applicable to the geographical area and to the parties concerned, for an agreed period of time specified at the outset, and renewable if necessary.

The closest analogy to the suggested concept of temporary supra-national powers for UN is probably the institution of martial law in a local community when a disaster, or other emergency, has made unusual protective measures

341

necessary. In such local crises, although military forces are used, their function is primarily a large-scale police action, and the military rule is known to be temporary and without prejudice to the early restoration of normal civilian authority. The exercise of temporary supra-national powers by the United Nations should be regarded in the same way, with the same purpose, and with the same end result.

This analogy is not perfect, and it will be recognized that the United Nations would require certain machinery which it does not now have, but which is usually in being within national or local communities. The most basic difference lies in the fact that the national or local community is governed by existing laws, whereas the UN must find means to bridge the absence of defined laws in order to meet the particular situation.

The UN Charter does not give the UN supra-national powers of the kind suggested. The UN cannot take coercive measures, save by action of the Security Council under Chapter VII. This is quite a different concept, being one that is almost certain to result in going to war to stop a war. What is being suggested here is the possibility that, without violating the Charter, there may be in an emergency a "willing suspension" of national sovereignty to the extent immediately required, for the limited time necessary.

The Nature of Supra-National Powers Needed

Broadly speaking, the UNEF and ONUC experience indicate that there are three powers the UN is likely to need to expedite an emergency policing action.

1) The UN must be in control of its forces during the emergency period specified. The host nation should give up the right to expel, and contributing nations to withdraw, UN contingents during that period.

2) The UN must have competence over individuals opposing, or impeding, its mandate during the supra-national period. Recalcitrant individuals involved in the particular emergency could be apprehended, detained, and, if necessary, prosecuted by a specially created UN legal unit under the temporary supra-national authority of the UN. Individuals likely to come under UN competence in this sense would know in advance what actions would make them liable to UN apprehension and within what geographical area this could occur. Some provision should be devised to make possible access to a court of appeals to which these individuals might apply thereafter. An appropriate international tribunal might be set up in a place removed from the scene of the emergency which would deal with legitimate grievances claimed by individuals having come under temporary UN competence.

3) The UN Charter injunction against UN intervention in domestic affairs would need to be suspended in some de-

gree. As matters stand now the host country willingly permits s o m e modification of Article 2, paragraph 7 when it requests UN police assistance. The host country and countries contributing troops would have to permit some further modification of t h a t provision, if the UN is to be given the power to d e c i d e when, and if, its contingents may be removed during the supra-national period. Access to recalcitrant individuals in the sense described above would constitute a f u r t h e r modification of.Article 2, paragraph 7, for those States whose nationals might become individually involved. In certain cases the UN might be given temporary power to disarm local forces, if such forces were obstructing, or opposing, the UN mandate, or threatened to do so. Some additional intervention in domestic affairs might become necessary to the effective execution of a particular UN mandate. H o w e v e r, the partial suspension of Article 2, paragraph 7, should be c a r e f u l l y limited to prevent UN actions w h i c h were permanently prejudicial to the form of government c h o s e n by the peoples of the emergency area. The UN power s h o u l d be limited f u r t h e r to avoid to the greatest extent possible UN actions which would permanently affect the positions of political parties, leaders, or factions, or the status quo ante of n a t i o n s in d i s p u t e prior to UN judicial procedures.

Institution and Duration of UN Supra-National Powers

Prior to any f u t u r e UN policing action, UN members should agree to a general instrument which would permit the invoking of certain UN supra-national powers, under certain emergency conditions. Unless t h i s is done objectively i n the absence of any s p e c i f i c incident which might warrant such powers, many political considerations at the time would embitter or obstruct the necessary agreement. Parties to a particular dispute would feel such ad hoc innovations to be a blow at their own n a t i o n a l prestige. If the action were taken ad hoc to cope with an emergency in some new nation, the c h a r g e of i m p o s i t i o n of UN trusteeship, or "neo-colonialism," would certainly b e raised. The consent of UN members to permit t h e invocation of extraordinary UN powers that m i g h t affect each or any one of them at some future time should be c l e a r before any occasion arises for the a p p l i c a t i o n of such powers to any specific nation, or nations.

Thereafter, when an e m e r g e n c y arose w h i c h made temporary UN supra-national powers necessary, the nature of the crisis would determine the precise degree of possible UN authority appropriate to the case. The UN would have to determine at the time it agreed to act the exact duration of the supra-national p e r i o d. This might be fixed for as little as two months or as much as six months according to the will of the Assembly at the t i m e. At the e n d of the stated supra-national period, the Assembly could again consider if it was necessary to extend the period for a specified number of weeks or months.

In order to ensure that a "willing suspension" of national sovereignty was agreeable to the UN membership generally, all action, from the original instrument to the specifics of a particular instance, should be taken by the Assembly, perhaps by an extraordinary majority of three-quarters. Once the original general instrument had been agreed, all members would know in advance what terms might be imposed if the UN decided to act in a crisis. The host country, particularly, would be well aware of what was involved for it if it appealed for UN police assistance. Contributing nations would know before they offered troops that the UN would control the disposition of those troops for some period to be specified. An Assembly vote to extend the initial period of supra-national UN powers should probably include the vote of the host country. Nations contributing contingents could probably not be constrained to continue their troops for the extended period. At the time of extension, those originally loaned might be withdrawn by the contributing nations, and fresh contingents might then have to be found from other States on the same terms for the extended operation.

Incentives to Settle Disputes

The imposition of UN supra-national powers which might be extended for a number of succeeding periods, if necessary, might provide a new incentive to settle the underlying dispute. For instance had the UNEF operation involved temporary supra-national powers for the UN, it is likely that those powers would have been extended at intervals over the past five or six years. The nations involved might have become irked by such prolonged infringement of their sovereignty.

The UN should be prepared in advance to take advantage of any resultant willingness to settle the underlying dispute engendered by the imposition of UN supra-national powers. From the outset, and at any time during the supra-national period, the UN should recognize settlement of the dispute by compulsory arbitration as terminating its supra-national authority in any given case, whether or not the supra-national period had run its course. Compulsory arbitration, based on the "recommended rules for compulsory arbitration" (prepared by the International Law Commission, and put forward as "model rules" by the UN Assembly some years ago) should be acknowledged in advance as terminating UN special powers. Parties to a dispute leading to an emergency requiring UN policing action would be offered a similar option to submit the dispute to the compulsory jurisdiction of the International Court. However, compulsory arbitration is s t r e s s e d here for two reasons: the nature of the dispute may have no legal basis which would enable the International Court to adjudicate the c a s e; the nations involved m i g h t not have acceded to the compulsory jurisdiction of the Court, and the procedures necessary to do so might unnecessarily complicate an early settlement of the specific dispute.

Relief through resort to legal procedures for the settlement of the original cause of conflict should be an integral part of the original general instrument which makes possible this w h o l e concept of temporary UN supra-national powers in the event of an international emergency.

REDUCING IMPROVISATION IN MEETING UN EMERGENCY SITUATIONS

Ad Hoc Forces; Then and Now

In the years between Suez and Congo much was made of the positive value of creating UN police forces ad hoc. The late Secretary General, and others, advocated a small planning staff in the Secretariat and stand-by forces ear-marked by smaller States as sufficient to emergencies likely to arise. It was s t r e s s e d that each crisis presented unforeseeable conditions a n d that an a p p r o p r i a t e UN f o r c e, or UN "presence," could best be devised after the circumstances of an emergency were known.

By equating situations requiring a UN "presence" with those requiring a UN policing o p e r a t i o n, the n a t u r e of desirable UN forces-in-being was rendered even more imponderable. There w a s a deliberate vagueness about defining a UN "presence" for what it is: a UN negotiator, or team of negotiators, or UN technical assistance experts who might act somewhat in the role of conciliators. This vagueness obscured t h e fact that a UN "presence" is always in being or readily available, whereas UN police forces must serve a n o t h e r purpose, a r e not in e x i s t e n c e, and are cumbersome to assemble after the trouble starts.

Even at the t i m e this preference for ad hoc arrangements may simply have been making a virtue of necessity. UNEF had been in existence only a short while before difficulty arose in finding funds to c o v e r its cost. Those who hoped that UNEF m i g h t be the prototype for a small, permanent UN emergency force soon realized that if members were unwilling to pay for UNEF itself, it would be very hard indeed to r a i s e money for a more costly permanent force which would have to be paid even when idle.

There was, perhaps, some basis for the belief that UN members are more w i l l i n g to act under the stimulus of a crisis than they are to make plans and accept obligations to meet future emergencies in the abstract. Fear and immediate self-interest a r e strong goads to a c t i o n when danger threatens. Agreement to accept the lesser of two evils is more easily reached when both evils are actually present. In an emergency, improvisation can be devised step by step, so that most urgent factors, such as armed contingents, can be dealt with first and less immediate needs, such as money, can be left to take care of themselves later. This gives an illusion of simplification.

Whatever the rationalization, after Suez and prior to Congo the notion was well established that ad hoc arrangements were not merely the best that could be made, but that improvisation was preferable in meeting a UN crisis.

Against this whole thesis, several serious objections have become more apparent since Congo.

When a crisis is faced without preparation the special political interest of nations involved immediately intrudes upon the effort to meet the situation with impartial and effective measures. The wrong-doer is particularly anxious not to help in his own downfall, but others also seek to gain national advantage from international distress. Thus political passions distort ad hoc arrangements.

Nations which feel themselves removed geographically and politically from the trouble area sooner or later become apathetic to emergency measures which serve others at their expense. Indifference on the part of a substantial number of members can undermine the operation once the initial heat is off.

If there was ever any real virtue in the advocacy of ad hoc UN emergency arrangements, it seems now to be running into the law of diminishing returns. With UNEF and ONUC both continuing, the UN is at the brink of bankruptcy and over-extended from the point of view of manpower. Unplanned UN performance in Congo has raised many damaging doubts and questions. Indeed, pure improvisation in this complex case may have caused the UN to outrun the letter of its Charter to the extent that some prevalent disaffection with the UN may be at least partially justified.

Certainly it is time to consider again whether some practical degree of advance planning and permanent arrangements can now be devised and agreed so that future UN emergency needs can be served. It is possible that a sufficient number of UN members have acquired a more compelling incentive to create in advance of further emergency situations at least the framework of UN peace-keeping machinery.

Toward a Permanent UN Peace Force

The most important element in planned UN peace-keeping machinery would seem to be the actual forces that the UN can have at its disposal. Various attempts to get UN members to earmark national units for UN use have been unsuccessful, and such units might not actually be available

346

in practice even if so designated. It would, therefore, seem wise to consider the practicability of a UN force composed of volunteers, recruited and trained by the UN, and retained on a reserve basis thereafter.

In initiating a program to develop such a UN force, it would logically start with creation of the headquarters staff, and the training cadres, and with the planning of a special training program as successive first steps taken in quick succession. Once this had been done, recruitment might begin on a small scale. The first objective might be the recruitment and training of a small nucleus standing force of 100-500 permanent UN police. Thereafter reserves could be recruited and trained in larger numbers on the basis of that original pilot project.

If the UN is to have its own force, a headquarters staff would become essential. It would seem logical to have such a staff recruited by the Secretary General as international civil servants. A competent headquarters staff for the UN force might be expected to include individuals with civilian police experience, para-military experience, and military experience.

In the Middle East, and perhaps in Kashmir and Congo, training cadres could be developed from UN units in being. Such UN cadres, from personal experience, could help devise and could carry out a training program best suited to UN policing actions. This training program should not need to include the use of the most modern weapons, or highly technical modern warfare skills, so the training would not become obsolescent while trained personnel remained on reserve.

Recruitment on an individual basis and the incorporation of individual recruits in mixed units would provide UN forces appropriate to any area or circumstance, since the UN police would thus have no recognizable national identity. Although recruits should probably be drawn as much as possible from smaller, less-committed States, their incorporation into mixed units would make possible the inclusion of nationals from every country, providing the nationals from any particular State were not permitted to predominate in any single unit. As the total number of recruits required would be relatively small, the UN could set high enlistment standards for personal ability and motivation.

With the exception of a small standing force of no more, perhaps, than 500 men, UN recruits, once trained, would return to their private lives in their home countries and remain on call as UN reserves. It should not be impossible to devise a "calling up" system. Men could be notified by the UN by telegram. Advance agreement with UN members could be reached so that UN reserves could travel to staging areas expeditiously and without charge on a UN laissez-passer. It is doubtful if the numbers of reserves requiring such transport in any one country at any one time would be large enough to disrupt domestic travel facilities. Staging areas should be earmarked in advance on a stand-by basis by nations with airfields or ports at geographically strategic locations.

The UN would have to maintain a minimum of UN force vehicles, such as jeeps and trucks, which with the nucleus standing force could be accommodated in a single base. The UN should rely for other means of transport on earmarked planes and ships to be put at UN service by member nations in case of need, and upon the practice of chartering planes which has proved practical in the Congo operation.

UN recruited and trained reserves might require to be backed up by national contingents if the UN force proved insufficient to a particular emergency. However, in that case national contingents would be sought at a later stage after the nature of the operation had been determined and political decisions had largely been made. Thus more time would be allowed for mustering national contingents and political factors would play a less influential role in the decisions of governments invited to lend troops.

A UN force of the kind outlined would seem to have every advantage over the present system of ad hoc contingents, except in respect to cost. It would be readily available and not subject to the political interests of any particular UN member, or members. It would be unquestionably appropriate to any situation. Common training, including language training, would be of the most suitable kind for UN purposes and would enhance the morale and esprit de corps of the force. All UN members would have an objective and mutual interest in the force as an adjunct to the security of all. A sense of responsibility should develop toward a common asset which was devoted to the service of every member with equal impartiality and to the protection of each with equal zeal.

Financing a UN Peace Force

The reserve system would keep the cost at a minimum, since the bulk of the troops would be paid only when in training or when on active duty. Transport and heavy equipment could be leased only when actually required. Such savings as these, however, cannot disguise the fact that a UN force of the kind outlined would be more expensive than the present national contingent system.

In this regard, the only real advantage over the present system would be that the cost would be more predictable. Some of the expenses would be regular charges for the maintenance of the standing nucleus, for training reserves, and for base facilities. Such regular charges would, naturally, become a part of the regular UN Budget as they could not conceivably be called "emergency expenses." If UN

348

members were to be regularly assessed for the training of UN reserves, it should be but a small additional hurdle to make equally acceptable, a regular additional charge in the regular Budget to build up a fund to pay those reserves should they be called to active duty.

If the financing program suggested were adopted, UN members would know in advance how much they would have to pay at specified intervals for UN policing actions. This would permit the Governments to plan and to budget for their assessments. It would be difficult, perhaps, to get the initial agreement necessary to pursue such a course, but once agreed, it would obviate the unforeseen and divisive elements of financial responsibility.

Executive Responsibility for UN Policing Actions

If the UN had its own force, and if it were granted temporary supra-national powers in time of crisis, the seat of executive authority in a UN emergency may need to be broadened. In the execution of temporary national powers with a UN force available the personal responsibility of the Secretary General might be expected to be increased by the extension of actual UN authority, and to be reduced by the greater precision and clarity of his mandate. It is possible, therefore, that the area in which he, himself, would render decisions might be considerably narrowed, but that within that narrowed area his personal decisions might be more momentous.

To ensure the maximum degree of confidence, it would seem wise to consider formalizing the device of "advisory committees" with which the Secretary General has been asked to consult in carrying out the UNEF and ONUC operations. An appropriate committee set up for each future emergency action might have certain very limited powers as an executive arm of the UN Assembly.

Such a committee would not be composed as a "troika," but should as in the cases of UNEF and ONUC be representative of UN members playing a responsible role in the particular UN action. No single member of the committee should have a veto, but by a two-thirds vote the committee as a body might have the right to take decisions in certain circumstances. This would probably be no more than the right to make the final choice if a decision of real moment had to be made which was not clearly covered by the Assembly, and over which the Assembly might be divided or otherwise incapable of prompt action.

If a temporary "executive committee" in the terms described is considered desirable, then it would seem best to work out in advance of any new crisis the general concept of its rights and functions. To wait until the crisis has arisen and the appropriate committee must be named, would be to invite the intrusion of particular national political positions into the negotiation of a just and workable formula. The suggestion here is that the role of such an "executive committee" should be defined in advance, while the composition of such a temporary committee would be determined ad hoc according to the nature of the emergency requiring it.

This proposal does not seek to weaken the executive position of the Secretary General as the chief international administrator dedicated to the impartial performance of that role. Present conditions make his executive power essential. In the long run, however, should the UN gain limited, but permanent powers to maintain peace, a one-man executive is unlikely to be the most suitable. Hence, in this intermediate period when the UN might be permitted to exercise temporary authority some more broadly-based executive for emergency situations would seem to be appropriate to present needs and future developments.

CONCLUSION

It is believed that if the foregoing suggestions could be carefully formulated and negotiated most of the difficulties experienced by UNEF and ONUC could be largely overcome in future UN actions.

There are, however, two serious problems discussed which are not likely to be much improved by the new approaches suggested. These approaches put almost no new leverage on nations to submit stubborn and dangerous international disputes to prompt and decisive international settlement. No new scheme for financing UN peace-keeping operations has been introduced.

Neither of these problems seems likely to yield to evolutionary devices, or to become strictly enforceable by the UN as presently constituted. Satisfactory measures on these two aspects of UN peace-keeping machinery seem most to depend upon national willingness to undertake international obligations and to accent international restraints.

Such evolutionary developments as can be carried out under the present Charter must of necessity make slow progress toward rather uncertain results. Small steps and slight improvements cannot be expected to produce compelling incentives to major commitments. Adequate dependable revenue, and submission of conflicting national interests to peaceful international adjudication or arbitration require compelling incentives.

At the moment, these two problems may yield somewhat if the approaches suggested here are proposed as a first step "package," thus gaining as much momentum as possible from all the possible benefits potential therein. Incentive should be further heightened if these measures are constantly stressed as being steps toward a larger and more desirable goal. To this end they should be formulated and pursued in the context of the final objective of the US proposal for general and complete disarmament. If that objective were made far more explicit and were advocated with persistence, it would give stature to the more modest steps that can be taken in the near future. Directed to and guided by such an objective, primitive forms of UN peace-keeping machinery may seem to UN members worthy of new and more strenuous efforts. Nevertheless, the question does remain as to whether essential aspects of the enforcement of world peace can be successful on a piecemeal trial and error basis.

QUESTIONS FOR SEMINAR DISCUSSION

Since 1946 the International Court of Justice has rendered forty-nine decisions (twelve of which were Advisory Opinions). Why is it that states do not make more use of the Court to resolve their disputes? Is there anything that can be done within the present framework to encourage states to take their disputes to the Court?

Under present circumstances do you think that the United States should maintain or withdraw the portion of its submission to the jurisdiction of the International Court which provides that the United States will not submit matters to the Court which are essentially within the domestic jurisdiction of the United States as determined by the United States? How significant a step in the development of world law do you think a withdrawal might be?

The Clark-Sohn provisions for dealing with international disputes and for handling the threat of use of force among nations as detailed in their proposed revisions of Chapters VI and VII of the Charter are a departure from the way in which domestic legal structure operates in that they provide the legislature (General Assembly) with much of the responsibility for initiating and supervising the day-to-day administration of pacific settlement and peace-keeping. Is this aspect of the scheme to be considered merely transitional in that as we gain experience in administering the program, and nations develop trust in the efficiency and fairness of the machinery, and notions of sovereignty become less important, we will move closer to the domestic model of law? Or is this a model on which we can rely to insure peace among sovereign states over the long run? What are the potential points of instability in the proposed system?

How important do you think a compulsory court system is to the establishment and maintenance of peace? Would there be any merit to permitting the General Assembly to settle all issues and peace-keeping problems among states, unless the states wanted to take these matters to the Court? What problems would arise under this system? Which system do you think would be more efficient and fair? Which system do you think would be more acceptable to political officials now?

Are you clear on the three different kinds of dispute-resolving mechanisms--law, equity, and conciliation and mediation--which Clark-Sohn propose, and the relationships which would exist among them and with the General Assembly? Is all this fairly complicated machinery necessary? Could any part of it be left out? Would such mechanisms make the results more or less efficient, fair or acceptable to political officials now?

Can more be done within the present framework of the United Nations to develop an efficient and reliable operating peace-keeping unit? What concrete steps would you propose now? What are the chances of their being accepted?

Do you agree with Clark and Sohn that it would "not be feasible to maintain an adequate police force unless national disarmament is not only universal but complete?" What would be the problems of developing a UN police force if disarmament were not complete? Would a permanent police force under conditions of less than complete disarmament be preferable to the present ad hoc arrangement used by the United Nations? What would be the advantages and problems in such an arrangement?

How important is a police force? Suppose the states of the world agreed to general and complete disarmament, and to the establishment of the Judicial and Conciliation system proposed by Clark-Sohn, and to all the provisions in Chapter VI and Chapter VII of the revised charter but refused to set up a permanent police force. What problems would you see in this system? Would it be operative at all? On page 334 Clark and Sohn suggest that during the transition stage the states of the world should set up military units prepared to go into action on the call from the General Assembly. Would this system be viable over the long run?

Are there any aspects of the composition or structure of the command of the proposed UN Peace Force with which you would disagree? Why?

Are you satisfied with the safeguards outlined on page 311 to prevent subversion of the Peace Force? Are any more needed? Are all of them necessary?

Are you satisfied with the provisions for "civilian control" of the Peace Force suggested by Clark-Sohn? Is the force given too much or too little power under this scheme?

Do you agree that the United Nations should have a research department to develop new weapons? Why?

On the PEACE-KEEPING POWERS and activities of the General Assembly, consult:

Andrassy, Juraj. "Uniting for Peace." Am. J. Int. Law 50: 563-82 (July 1956).
Claude, Inis L., Jr. "The UN and the Use of Force." Internatl. Concil. No. 532: 325-84 (Mar. 1961). A systematic report on the UN's use of force, vindicating the Charter provisions which seem to have blocked rather than assisted the creation of a universal collective security system, by illustrating the variety of ways in which the UN has assisted peaceful settlement.
Goodrich, Leland M., and Ann P. Simons. The United Nations and the Maintenance of International Peace and Security. Washington: Brookings Inst., 1955, 709p.
Petersen, Keith S. "The Uses of the Uniting for Peace Resolution Since 1950." Internatl. Org. 13: 219-32 (Spring 1959).
Stone, Julius. Legal Controls of International Conflict; a treatise on the dynamics of disputes- and war-law. NY: Rinehart, 1954, 851p.; with supplement: London: Stevens, 1959, 903p.
Tammes, A. J. P. "Decisions of International Organs as Sources of International Law." Recueil des Cours 94: 265-363 (1958).
Vallat, F. A. "The Competence of the UN General Assembly." Recueil des Cours 97: 203-91 (1959).

For more information on the UN POLICE FORCES, consult:

Armstrong, Hamilton Fish. "The UN Experience in Gaza." Foreign Affairs 35: 600-20 (July 1959). A close look at the steps taken to create the UNEF and some useful lessons for the organization of future forces.
Claude, Inis L., Jr. "The UN and the Use of Force." Internatl. Concil. No. 532: 325-84 (Mar. 1961).
Frye, William R. A United Nations Police Force. NY: Oceana, 1957, 227p.
Goodrich, Leland M., and Gabriella E. Rosner. "The United Nations Emergency Force." Internatl. Org. 11: 413-30 (Summer 1957). A comprehensive survey of UNEF, its creation, role and implications.
Kay, Zachariah. "The UN Forces in Korea and Sinai." Internatl. Relations 2: 169-83 (April 1961).
Munro, Sir Leslie. "Can the UN Enforce Peace?" Foreign Affairs 38: 209-18 (Jan. 1960). Urges the creation of and marshalls the statements that support a "permanent mechanism" by which units of the armed forces of member nations could be quickly endowed with UN authority and dispatched to the scene of trouble.
——————. "The Case for a UN Standing Army." The New York Times Magazine. July 27, 1958, p. 27.
Pearson, Sir Lester. "Force for UN." Foreign Affairs 35: 295-304. (Apr. 1957).

On the INTERNATIONAL COURT OF JUSTICE, see:

Bishop, W. W., Jr., and B. P. Myers. "Unwarranted Extension of Connally-Amendment Thinking." Am. J. Int. Law 55: 135-45 (Jan. 1961).
Briggs, Herbert W. "Reservations to the Acceptance of Compulsory Jurisdiction of the International Court of Justice." Recueil des Cours 93: 223-367 (1958).

_____. "The United States and the International Court of Justice: A Re-examination." Am. J. Int. Law 53: 301-318 (Apr. 1959). A discussion of the Connally Amendment reservation and its reception by the ICJ, other types of alternative reservations, and a suggested form for a new U.S. declaration concerning acceptance of jurisdiction by the ICJ.

_____. "Confidence, Apprehension and the ICJ." Proc. Am. Soc. Int. Law 54: 25-37 (1960).

Daub, George Cochran. "The Unused Potential of the World Court." Foreign Affairs 40: 463-70 (Apr. 1962). One of a vast number of scholarly polemics urging more power for the ICJ.

Fuller, L., A. Larson, and C. Morris. "Peace Through Law: The Role and Limits of Adjudication: A Panel." Proc. Am. Soc. Int. Law 54: 1ff. (1960).

Gross, Leo. "Some Observations on the International Court of Justice." Am. J. Int. Law 56: 33-62 (Jan. 1962).

Honig, F. "The Diminishing Role of the World Court." Internatl. Affairs (London) 34: 184-94 (Apr. 1958). The author views the court's future pessimistically, as so large as to be unwieldly, its reasoning too indefinite, its internal divisions too profound.

Larson, A. "Facts, the Law and the Connally Amendment." Duke Law J. 1961: 74-85 (Winter 1961).

Lauterpacht, Sir Hersh. The Development of International Law by the World Court. London: Stevens, 1958, 408p.

Schwartz, William. "The International Court's Role as an Advisor to the UN." Boston U. Law R. 37: 404-29 (Fall 1957).

Sorenson, Max. "The International Court of Justice: Its Role in Contemporary International Relations." Internatl. Org. 14: 261-76 (Spring 1960). Views the two sets of ICJ's problems--its institutional aspects and the place and scope of its juridical function in international relations.

Stone, Julius. "The International Court and World Crisis." Internatl. Concil. No. 536: 3-64 (Jan. 1962).

"World Court and UN Charter: The Principle of Effectiveness in interpretation." Duke Law J. 1962: 85ff. (Winter 1962).

Also note that until 1960, Manley O. Hudson wrote an annual review of the Court's activities, appearing in the Am. J. Int. Law.

On the problems of AGGRESSION and CONFLICT, viewed theoretically and in relation to American foreign policy, see:

Boulding, Kenneth E. Conflict and Defense; a general theory. NY: Harper, 1962.

Kissinger, Henry A. The Necessity for Choice: Prospects of American Foreign Policy. NY: Harper, 1961.

_____. Nuclear Weapons and Foreign Policy. NY: Harper, 1957.

Schelling, Thomas C. The Strategy of Conflict. Cambridge, Mass.: Harvard U. Press, 1960, 309p.

Sohn, Louis B. "The Role of International Institutions as Conflict-Adjusting Agencies." U. of Chicago Law R. 28: 205-57 (Winter 1961).

Stone, Julius. Aggression and World Order; a critique of United Nations theories of aggression. Berkeley: U. of Calif. Press, 1958, 226p.

SESSION VI

FINANCING PEACE:
A) REVENUE AND BUDGET PROBLEMS OF THE UNITED NATIONS;
B) PROBLEMS OF AIDING UNDER-DEVELOPED AREAS

This session is concerned with the economics of peace. It raises the question of how much money, raised in what fashion and used in what ways is necessary to create and maintain a world legal structure capable of eliminating the threat or use of force among states. How you answer the many facets of these questions will of course depend on the range of functions and kinds of organization which you deem required. In addition, the problem of the political acceptability for any scheme is also highly relevant. Since we have been dealing with these latter matters throughout the seminar many of you will undoubtedly have some tentative answers. However, it is unlikely that you have given any systematic attention to the actual budget itself, and it is to that we now turn our attention. For this purpose it will be instructive to look at the scheme proposed by Clark and Sohn, find out where the UN stands now on these matters, and then ask whether it is necessary and feasible to achieve and implement their scheme.

Broadly speaking Clark and Sohn are proposing that by 1980 the United Nations be given taxing and borrowing power to raise about $36,000,000,000 annually from individuals within the member states. While $9,000,000,000 would be used to support the United Nations Peace Force which we discussed in the last session, some $25,000,000,000 would be used for aid to underdeveloped areas of the world. Here the authors are articulating another major principle for the establishment of world peace. They believe that unless some broad, massive aid is provided in an organized and rational fashion to the states with underdeveloped economies these states will be a source of considerable international tension which might lead to the use of force. To achieve this immense budget the authors propose a detailed formula for raising the revenue and the creation of a World Development Authority to allocate expenditures. We shall want to look at both sides of their proposal carefully. We shall want especially to examine the figures through which Clark and Sohn demonstrate that this immense budget would cost the ordinary taxpayer and the world at large less than the present arms race.

If we turn now to the present scene we are met with the dismal fact that the entire cost of all programs of the United Nations in 1961 was but $450,000,000. As Stoessinger points out in his article "Financing the United Nations," the problems of developing more revenue, of establishing criteria of who should provide for it, and of determining how it should be spent is primarily a political rather than a financial problem. Of particular importance in this regard has been the problem concerning assessment of member states to finance the UNEF and ONUC forces. As this book goes to press the International Court of Justice has just handed down an advisory Opinion (with the Judges split 9 to 5) stating that these assessments are legally binding upon all member states. What effect this opinion will have and whether it will be necessary or expenditious to invoke Article 19 is a matter which we shall want to discuss.

The United Nations Decade of Development put out by the Secretary General's office is much more encouraging, albeit general and programmatic. Whether the programs it suggests are fair and feasible shall concern us. Finally the excerpt from "Framing a Development Program" by Gustav A. Papanek points to a series of complicated and subtle problems involved in deciding who, using what criteria, ought to decide on and administer various development programs.

Readings from World Peace Through World Law:
Raising Revenue, xxxvii-xxxix, 349-358.
World Development, xxxvi-xxxvii, 132-136, 345-348.

FINANCING THE UNITED NATIONS

by
JOHN G. STOESSINGER

The Financial Crisis

My credit now stands on such slippery ground . . .

—SHAKESPEARE,
Julius Caesar, III, 1.

THERE HAS NEVER been a shortage of Cassandras predicting that the United Nations would end with a bang. There now exists a real possibility that it may end in a whimper. A fiscal crisis has been in the making over the past few years which has become a threat to the very life of the Organization.

The cost for 1961 of the entire United Nations system is approximately $450,000,000. This figure includes the regular budget of over $60,000,000 net and at least $90,000,000 for the specialized agencies; roughly $150,000,000 for the two peace-keeping operations in the Middle East and in the Congo; and another $150,000,000 for the voluntary programs. The immediate cause of the present crisis is the cost of the two United Nations peace forces. Defaults and arrears are threatening the Organization with a deficit of $150,000,-000 by the end of 1961. Secretary-General Hammarskjold was forced to borrow extensively from other funds and to juggle accounts in order to keep UNEF and the Congo Force in the field. But this sort of temporizing can only postpone, not prevent, the moment of truth.

If one applies the standards of national defense budgets, the amount involved is a pittance. Seldom have so many important people argued so tenaciously about so little money. The reason for this seeming paradox is that fiscal problems in the United Nations cannot be divorced from their political context. Indeed, they are but another dimension of the political struggle for power and order that is being waged in the world organization.

The Role of Assessment

THE CORE of United Nations revenue for the continuing operations of the Organization is raised by assessment of member states according to an agreed scale of contributions. For the first ten years, member states were assessed for only the regular budget of the United Nations and the budgets of the specialized agencies. More than one-half of the costs of all United Nations programs had to depend on voluntary contributions for their support. In 1956 this picture changed dramatically. The General Assembly, after a heated debate, decided to assess members for the sum of $10,000,000 to defray the costs of the establishment and initial operations of a United Nations Emergency Force (UNEF) in the Middle East.

This action set an important precedent. Since UNEF had to be retained as an important stabilizing influence in the area, the General Assembly found it necessary to assess member states about $20,000,000 in each succeeding year. And when the United Nations was confronted with a grave political crisis in 1960 in the Congo, the General Assembly again resolved to rely primarily on assessment for financing a United Nations Force in the Congo (ONUC). By assessing the member states $100,000,000 to cover ONUC's costs for the first ten months of 1961, the Assembly in effect decided that voluntary contributions would no longer suffice as the most important single source of United Nations revenue. The combined UNEF and ONUC assessment now amounted to more than twice the regular United Nations budget and exceeded the combined costs of the voluntary United Nations programs. Indeed, assessment has now become the most important source of revenue for the United Nations.

The Basis of Assessment

The regular budget for the past ten years has been between $48,000,000 and $63,000,000 net. This assessed budget comprises three broad categories. First, administrative expenses, accounting for about 60 per cent of the total, include the costs of providing the services essential for the work of the Organization, such as personnel, conference servicing, public information, and over-all "housekeeping" activities. Second, basic non-operational programs comprising the work of the Departments of Political and Security Council Affairs, Economic and Social Affairs, Trusteeship, and Legal Affairs, account for roughly 20 per cent of the total. The final 20 per cent is earmarked for operational activities in member states, such as the regular technical assistance program, and for special missions, such as the United Nations Truce Supervision Organization in Palestine and the Committee on South West Africa.

The Charter provisions with regard to the budget are embodied in Articles 17, 18, and 19. Article 17 reads as follows:

1. The General Assembly shall consider and approve the budget of the Organization.

2. The expenses of the Organization shall be borne by the Members as apportioned by the General Assembly.

3. The General Assembly shall consider and approve any financial and budgetary arrangements with specialized agencies referred to in Article 57 and shall examine the administrative budgets of such specialized agencies with a view to making recommendations to the agencies concerned.

Several observations are pertinent. In the first place, the

358

Charter makes it quite clear that ultimate budgetary authority lies with the General Assembly. The League of Nations Covenant omitted this stipulation and thus precipitated a tug of war of several years' duration between the League Council and Assembly before the latter finally gained fiscal control.[1] In the United Nations system, this power of the purse placed the General Assembly in a strategic position. Second, the General Assembly was to apportion the budget among the member states. In this connection, the framers at San Francisco decided to give the Assembly as much flexibility as possible, refusing to tie it down to any detailed method of budgetary procedure.

Finally, Article 17 recognizes the autonomous character of the specialized agencies within the United Nations system. Whereas in the League all technical programs were subsumed under the League budget, the United Nations system includes twelve specialized agencies and the International Atomic Energy Agency, each with a budget and financial system of its own. Based on the powers written into Article 17, the United Nations has signed agreements with specialized agencies and IAEA which vary somewhat but in most cases provide for consultation by the agencies with the United Nations in preparing their budgets, and for examination of the administrative budgets and possible recommendations by the General Assembly; the agencies in general agree to "conform as far as may be practicable to standard forms and practices recommended by the United Nations." Two important exceptions are the agreements with the International Bank for Reconstruction and Development and the International Monetary Fund: these agencies, which finance their own operations from earnings and merely furnish annual reports to the Assembly, are exempt even from this perfunctory degree of supervision. In practice, the budgetary processes of most of the specialized agencies follow the United Nations pattern, with fiscal power vested in the deliberative body. This means that the United Nations system comprises a multiplicity of assessed budgets, with the General Assembly in clear control of the United Nations budget but with little more than a foot in the door of the specialized agencies.

Article 18, which deals with voting procedure in the General Assembly, is relevant to finance in the sense that it specifically provides that budgetary questions are to be decided by a two-thirds majority. The League of Nations required unanimity on budgetary matters and was often almost paralyzed as a result.

Article 19 incorporates one more lesson that the framers learned from precedent. Nothing in the League Covenant had provided for action in case of failure by a member state to pay its assessed contributions. As a result, League members had accumulated arrears without inhibitions. The San Francisco Conference, after weighing several possible penalties, decided on the loss of voting privileges in the General Assembly. As stated in Article 19:

A Member of the United Nations which is in arrears in the payment of its financial contributions to the Organization shall have no vote in the General Assembly if the amount of its arrears equals or exceeds the amount of the contributions due from it for the preceding two full years. The General Assembly may, nevertheless, permit such a Member to vote if it is satisfied that the failure to pay is due to conditions beyond the control of the Member.

Article 19 has never been invoked. With one minor exception,[2] no nation has ever fallen in arrears for more than two years on its assessment of the *regular* budget, although the same cannot be said regarding the special assessments for UNEF and ONUC.

The assessment principle was implied but not spelled out in detail in Article 17. The Committee on Financial Arrangements recommended in late 1945 that the task of preparing a detailed scheme be entrusted by the General Assembly to an expert Committee on Contributions whose members were to serve for "relatively long terms," be selected on the basis of "broad geographical representation and experience," and be nationals of different states. This Committee, in preparing the assessment scale, was to take into account member states' capacity to pay as determined by four criteria: total national income, per-capita income, war-caused economic dislocation, and ability to acquire foreign currency.

The ten-member Committee on Contributions has a broad mandate and hence a very delicate job. Its history has been quite stormy. When first confronted in 1946 with its important task—the preparation of a scale of assessments—its difficulties were compounded by the absence of complete and reliable statistical information with regard to the four criteria that were to serve as guidelines. To help the Committee's evaluation of "capacity to pay," the United Nations Statistical Office was instructed to gather the relevant information as quickly as possible. Although the Committee found "some lacunae" in the figures submitted by governments to the

Statistical Office, it nevertheless proposed a scale for the first three years of United Nations operations.

The proposed United States assessment—almost half the total budget—was most controversial. That country's delegation objected strenuously on two grounds. Senator Arthur H. Vandenberg pointed out that the 49.89 per-cent figure was not an accurate reflection of the United States' capacity to pay. Moreover, even if the figures were accurate, it would be unwise to make the Organization so dependent upon the financial contribution of one member. Instead, he proposed that no state should be assessed more than one-third of the total budget. Nevertheless, the United States agreed to a temporary assessment of 39.89 per cent for 1946.

During the next ten years the United States gradually succeeded in having its assessment reduced to the one-third ceiling. At the same time it waged a vigorous campaign to raise the Soviet share, which then amounted to 6.34 per cent. A 1954 Senate Foreign Relations Committee study noted:

Senator Alexander Wiley reports that on one day in 1952, for example, he listened to a member of the Ukrainian delegation in one committee of the General Assembly speak with great pride of the remarkable economic progress his country had made since the war. The Senator then went to another committee where he heard a second member of the Ukrainian delegation explain with equal fervor why his Government was unable to increase its contribution to the U.N. budget.[3]

During the ten-year battle in the Committee on Contributions, statistical information gradually improved, war damages were repaired, the European economies recovered, and momentous changes occurred in the international balance of payments. All these developments were reflected in the annual alterations made by the Committee in the assessment scale. By 1956 a formula could for the first time be codified for a three-year period. The United States assessment was reduced to the one-third limit, the Soviet share increased to nearly 14 per cent, and the United Kingdom assessment lowered to less than 10 per cent.

The battle in the Contributions Committee, however, was not merely a reflection of the East-West struggle. The one-third ceiling suggested by the United States elicited in 1954 a Canadian demand for a ceiling on any member state's per-capita assessment, in addition to the ceiling on its total assessment. The net effect would have been that countries with high national incomes and small populations would not be assessed more per capita than the United States. The Canadian plan was vigorously opposed by the delegates from the small developing nations on the ground that it would lead to a greater financial burden for the poorer countries. As a result, a compromise resolution was adopted in which those countries whose per-capita assessment exceeded that of the United States (Canada, New Zealand, Sweden, and Iceland) were promised that the difference between their per-capita assessment and that of the United States would not increase.[4]

Since 1956 the Committee on Contributions has had little more than routine responsibilities. The basic pattern of assessment has been set and the changes in each subsequent evaluation have been minor. Contrary to expectations, the admission of new states has made little difference in total revenues. Most of the new African nations have been assessed the minimum of 0.04 per cent. Not only has the increase in membership not resulted in an appreciable reduction in the share of member states already in the Organization, but the cost of alterations at United Nations Headquarters to accommodate the increased membership has required an increase in the older members' contributions.

Surveying the present pattern of assessment, one conclusion is striking: a large portion of the United Nations regular budget is dependent upon a very small minority of the membership. Fifty countries constituting 50 per cent of the membership are assessed only a little over 3 per cent of the budget. Twenty countries constituting 20 per cent of the membership contribute almost 90 per cent of the total. The Big Five are responsible for almost two-thirds, the United States for almost one-third.

The Regular Budget

In the case of the regular budget the collection of contributions has not posed a serious problem. Every year a number of states lag behind, but the total of arrears has never exceeded 15 per cent of the entire budget. Some members fall almost two years behind but always manage to complete their contributions before the question of invoking Article 19 arises. China has been the largest single debtor and has usually been responsible for over three-quarters of the total arrears. This is not surprising, since that country continues to pay the fifth largest assessment, calculated on the basis of mainland China although its resources are limited to the island of Formosa. But even China manages to pay before

Table I

SCALE OF ASSESSMENTS FOR THE REGULAR UNITED NATIONS BUDGET

Member[1]	1962-64 (%)	1959-61[2] (%)	1961 Assessment[3] ($US in thous.)	Member[1]	1962-64 (%)	1959-61[2] (%)	1961 Assessment[3] ($US in thous.)
Afghanistan	0.05	0.06	41.2	Italy	2.24	2.23	1,545.6
Argentina	1.01	1.10	762.5	Ivory Coast	0.04	0.06	41.2
Australia	1.66	1.77	1,229.6	Japan	2.27	2.17	1,504.4
Austria	0.45	0.42	295.4	Lebanon	0.05	0.05	34.3
Belgium	1.20	1.29	893.0	Luxembourg	0.05	0.06	41.2
Brazil	1.03	1.01	700.7	Madagascar	0.04	0.06	41.2
Bulgaria	0.20	0.16	109.9	Mexico	0.74	0.70	487.7
Burma	0.07	0.08	55.0	Morocco	0.14	0.14	96.2
Byelorussia	0.52	0.46	322.9	Netherlands	1.01	1.00	693.8
Canada	3.12	3.08	2,136.4	New Zealand	0.41	0.41	288.5
Ceylon	0.09	0.10	68.7	Nigeria	0.21	0.21	144.3
Chile	0.26	0.27	185.5	Norway	0.45	0.48	336.6
China	4.57	4.96	3,441.6	Pakistan	0.42	0.39	274.8
Colombia	0.26	0.31	213.0	Peru	0.10	0.11	75.6
Congo (Leo.)	0.07	0.04	27.5	Philippines	0.40	0.42	295.4
Cuba	0.22	0.25	171.7	Poland	1.28	1.36	941.1
Czechoslovakia	1.17	0.86	597.6	Portugal	0.16	0.20	137.4
Denmark	0.58	0.59	412.2	Romania	0.32	0.34	233.6
Dominican Republic	0.05	0.05	34.3	Saudi Arabia	0.07	0.06	41.2

Country	Per cent	Amount
Ecuador	0.06	41.2
El Salvador	0.04	34.3
Ethiopia	0.05	41.2
Fed. of Malaya	0.13	116.8
Finland	0.37	247.3
France	5.94	4,396.5
Ghana	0.09	48.1
Greece	0.23	158.0
Guatemala	0.05	34.3
Hungary	0.56	288.5
India	2.03	1,689.9
Indonesia	0.45	322.9
Iran	0.20	144.3
Iraq	0.09	61.8
Ireland	0.14	109.9
Israel	0.15	96.2

Country	Per cent [2]	Per cent	Amount
Senegal	0.05	0.06	41.2
South Africa	0.53	0.55	384.7
Spain	0.86	0.92	638.9
Sudan	0.07	0.06	41.2
Sweden	1.30	1.38	954.9
Thailand	0.16	0.16	109.9
Tunisia	0.05	0.05	34.3
Turkey	0.40	0.58	405.3
Ukraine	1.98	1.78	1,236.5
USSR	14.97	13.50	9,356.3
UAR	0.30	0.32	219.8
United Kingdom	7.58	7.71	5,344.5
United States	32.02	32.20	22,332.8
Uruguay	0.11	0.12	82.4
Venezuela	0.52	0.49	343.5
Yugoslavia	0.38	0.35	240.4
TOTAL	100.0	100.0	69,347.8

1 The following states are assessed the minimum 0.04 per cent:

Albania
Bolivia
Cambodia
Cameroun
Cent. Afr. Rep.
Chad
Congo (Brazza.)
Costa Rica
Cyprus
Dahomey

Gabon
Guinea
Haiti
Honduras
Iceland
Jordan
Laos
Liberia
Libya
Mali

Nepal
Nicaragua
Niger
Panama
Paraguay
Somalia
Togo
Upper Volta
Yemen

2 After integrating assessments for members admitted in 1960.

3 The assessment of 0.04 per cent amounted to $27,478 in 1961.

SOURCES: GAOR: 16th Sess., 1961, Suppl. No. 10, and United Nations Doc. ST/ADM/Ser.B/150, 4 Oct. 1961.

Article 19 can be invoked.

Conscious of the potential problem of arrears, the General Assembly in 1946 established a Working Capital Fund from which the Secretary-General is authorized to advance "such funds as may be necessary to finance budgetary appropriations pending receipt of contributions." The Fund has fluctuated between $20,000,000 and $25,000,000. Until the Congo crisis of 1960 threatened the entire financial structure of the United Nations, the Working Capital Fund was a fairly successful device for meeting emergencies.

In its attempts to close the gap between assessment and actual payment, the General Assembly has also empowered the Secretary-General to accept funds in currencies other than United States dollars. Although originally contributions were to be assessed and paid in the currency of the host country, in practice the Secretary-General has found it possible each year to accept a certain sum in other currencies. The total thus payable has fluctuated over the years between 5 per cent and 35 per cent of the total budget. On several occasions it has resulted in prompt payment by states which otherwise might have accumulated arrears.

In the search for revenue, the size and nature of the appropriations must always be kept in mind. As the Organization's revenue problems have grown, so, too, have demands for economy in expenditures. Authorizing and approving expenditures under the United Nations regular budget is a lengthy and cumbersome process. In the words of the Senate Foreign Relations Committee study:

The U.N. budget probably is given as careful a scrutiny as any budget of a similar size anywhere in the world. Representatives from member states in the General Assembly often spend days debating relatively modest sums which would be considered by some national legislative bodies in a matter of hours or even minutes.[5]

The United Nations budget process somewhat resembles that of the federal government of the United States. Budget estimates for each fiscal year are prepared by the Secretariat and approved by the Secretary-General. These estimates are then studied by a specially constituted body, the General Assembly's Advisory Committee on Administrative and Budgetary Questions. This nine-member committee is supposed to be a body of individual experts, but in fact it has become a political body, little more than a Fifth Committee in microcosm.[6] Its comments and recommendations are submitted to the Fifth Committee along with the original budget estimates of the Secretary-General. In practice, this very often gives the Advisory Committee members, now wearing different hats as Assembly delegates, the chance to recommend further cuts in appropriations. Although the Secretary-General usually participates in the debates of the Fifth Committee to defend his figures, the General Assembly in most cases adopts the Advisory Committee's recommendations as modified by the Fifth Committee. The entire process is characterized by such a strong emphasis on economy that one expert sees "national miserliness" showing through everywhere, and wistfully suggests that delegates "give at least as much attention to the *policy* implications of *financial* decisions as they do to *financial* implications of *policy* decisions."[7]

The United Nations regular budget has risen over the years in a gentle upward curve. This has also been true of the assessed budgets of the specialized agencies, whose combined total is a third more than that of the United Nations. The pattern of raising revenue and appropriating expenditures in the agencies resembles the budgetary process of the parent organization, although there are two minor variations worthy of note. First, the wide variations in membership (from 45 in the case of the Inter-Governmental Maritime Consultative Organization to 102 in the Universal Postal Union) has resulted in different scales of assessment; and second, the Soviet bloc's erratic membership pattern has skewed assessments in some agencies.

UNEF

It is generally accepted today that the United Nations Emergency Force was a political and military milestone for the United Nations. For the first time an international force was constituted, one not dominated by any single power. What is less well known is the fact that it also represented a fiscal milestone in the life of the world organization. For the first time an international body decided that the costs of such an international force should be shared by the nations of the world community. This decision was to have far-reaching consequences.

The father of UNEF was Lester B. Pearson of Canada. When, on 2 November 1956, the General Assembly was locked in acrimonious debate over the British-French-Israeli action in Suez, Mr. Pearson proposed that peace and security be restored through a United Nations Force. The Canadian resolution passed without a negative vote and the Secretary-General set about improvising the Force. After a great deal of delicate maneuvering, 6,000 troops—contingents from ten countries (Brazil, Canada, Colombia, Denmark, Finland, India, Indonesia, Norway, Sweden, and Yugoslavia)—were ready for action.[8] But it was clear that unless the question of financing was solved, the Force would not get beyond the paper stage. And unless it was solved reasonably well, UNEF would be short-lived indeed. Hence the Secretary-General, in his proposals to the General Assembly, gave the matter of financing the Force his most careful attention.

On 21 November 1956, the Secretary-General recommended that a Special Account outside the regular budget be set up for UNEF and that the costs of the Force be shared by the member states on the basis of the scale of assessments to be adopted for the 1957 budget. In addition, he suggested an initial assessment of $10,000,000 to meet the immediate cash needs of the Force. As will be seen, the Special Account device was a crucial decision. The Secretary-General preferred it to inclusion of UNEF expenditures in the regular budget because he wanted funds for the Force immediately, while the latter course would almost certainly have resulted in serious delay. This technique was successful and the General Assembly established the Special Account of $10,000,000 on 26 November as an interim measure.

On 3 December the Secretary-General faced the central problem—that of allocating the balance of the expenses of the Force—and indicated to the Assembly that the only equitable way of meeting the costs henceforth was to share them in accordance with the 1957 scale of assessments. Although financed under a Special Account, the Secretary-General nevertheless considered UNEF costs as "United Nations expenditures within the general scope and intent of Article 17 of the Charter."[9] This proposal touched off a storm of controversy and profoundly divided the Fifth Committee of the Assembly.

The United States delegate agreed with the Secretary-General and pointed out that the Committee's decision would be of crucial importance for the future of the Organization. He was supported by most of the Western nations. The statement of the delegate from New Zealand was typical: "Such responsibilities must be borne not by a fifth or a quarter of the Members or by one or two countries, but by all."[10] This view was sharply challenged by the delegates from the Soviet bloc, who insisted that the entire cost of the operation should be borne by those countries which had precipitated the crisis —Britain, France, and Israel. The New Zealand delegation retorted that not even in the case of Korea had it been considered that the country named as aggressor by the Assembly should pay the costs of the Korean action. The Arab states supported the Soviet view and suggested that it was "morally and logically unfounded" to expect Egypt, a victim of aggression, to contribute to the costs of the Force.

Several delegations expressed points of view which fell along a fairly wide spectrum between the two extremes of the Western and Soviet positions. The Brazilian delegate suggested that countries contributing troops should have their assessments reduced accordingly. The Spanish representative proposed a formula whereby the major part of the cost would be borne by the Big Five, and the remaining portion by all member states including the Big Five. The Latin American countries, in a joint statement, disputed the Secretary-General's position. The suggestion that the costs of UNEF should be considered under Article 17 was, they asserted, "at the very least, open to question" and offered the added disadvantage that Article 19 might thereby by invoked:

It would be regrettable if, by reason of the apportionment of fresh burdens which could not at present be assessed, but which might very well come close to the amount of the annual United Nations budget, certain Member States were to find themselves in the situation envisaged in Article 19.[11]

Pointing out the primary responsibility of the Big Five for keeping the peace, the joint statement proposed that only 10 per cent of the costs be assessed according to the regular scale and that the major part be raised through voluntary contributions from member states.

After an exhaustive debate, almost all of the Secretary-General's proposal was included in the Fifth Committee's draft resolution, adopted by the General Assembly by a vote of 62 in favor, 8 against, and 7 abstentions. By this resolution, the Assembly decided

that the expenses of the United Nations Emergency Force, other than for such pay, equipment, supplies and services as may be furnished without charge by Governments of Member States, shall be borne by the United Nations and shall be apportioned among the Member States, to the extent of $10 million, in accordance with the scale of assessments adopted by the General Assembly for contributions to the annual budget of the Organization for the financial year 1957; . . . that this decision shall be without prejudice to the subsequent apportionment of any expenses in excess of $10 million which may be incurred in connexion with the Force.[12]

Since the principle of collective responsibility was established, the United States delegation declared itself willing to meet up to half the amount in excess of $10,000,000 through a voluntary contribution provided other governments contributed the remaining half.

The assessment pattern was now set. In each succeeding year the General Assembly assessed the lion's share of UNEF expenditures in a similar manner: $15,000,000 in 1957, $25,000,000 in 1958, and $15,000,000 in 1959. Each year the General Assembly went through agonizing debate before arriving at this decision. In 1960, because of pressure from the Latin American and newly admitted nations, the pattern was changed somewhat. The Assembly considered it desirable to reduce the financial burden of those governments having the least capacity to pay and decided accordingly that voluntary contributions pledged prior to 31 December 1959 should be applied as a credit to reduce by 50 per cent the contributions of as many governments as possible, commencing with those assessed at the minimum of 0.04 per cent. The net result of this change was that the United States and the United Kingdom, the two largest voluntary contributors, assumed some of the burden of the smaller nations. The 1960 assessment under the new rule was $20,000,000, that of 1961 somewhat more than $19,000,000. The amounts varied from year to year because some governments, notably the United States and Canada, decided to forgo their right to reimbursement for special services such as airlifts and other means of transportation. All in all, since the inception of UNEF the General Assembly has assessed member states about $100,000,000 for the costs of the Force—almost twice the cost of the regular annual budget for the United Nations.

The decision to assess the member states has not solved the problem of financing UNEF. The heart of this problem has been to close the gap between assessment and collection. Each year arrears and defaults have amounted to roughly one-third of the total assessment. Since voluntary contributions have rarely exceeded 20 per cent of the annual cost of operations, UNEF has been running a serious annual deficit and has had to draw heavily on the Working Capital Fund. The arrears now exceed $35,000,000.

Over one-third of the member states of the United Nations

have defaulted in part or in full on their assessment. Some of the members in arrears, notably the newly admitted nations, have conceded their legal responsibility to pay but have claimed financial hardship. Theirs is primarily a practical problem and poses the least difficulty. Others, however, such as most of the Latin American countries, have regarded each Assembly resolution solely as a recommendation, not as a legal obligation. They pose the problem of legal principle. Finally, and most radically, the Soviet bloc and the Arab countries, by stressing that "the aggressors must pay," have raised the problem of legal obligation under the Charter in its starkest form.

The Secretary-General's position was clear: all member states have a legal obligation to pay under Article 17 of the Charter. This view has been supported by a majority of the membership. It is a view that may be buttressed by several arguments. First, UNEF's status is that of a subsidiary organ of the General Assembly under Article 22 of the Charter. Such an organ comes within the meaning of Article 17. Second, the language of Articles 17, 18, and 19 is imperative and clearly implies that even those voting against a financial resolution are bound by the principle expressed in the statement that "the expenses of the Organization shall be borne by the Members as apportioned by the General Assembly." Indeed, several times in the history of the United Nations the creation of subsidiary bodies was protested by some states, but such protests never extended to the question of legal obligation to contribute to the expenses of these bodies.

On the other hand, the majority position is open to reasonable doubt. The finances of all United Nations organs are subsumed under the regular budget. UNEF, however, is financed through a Special Account separate from the regular budget. While the Secretary-General preferred this technique because at a time of acute emergency it probably would not have been possible to persuade the Assembly to include UNEF in the regular budget, this procedure opened the door to a good deal of ambiguity and may well have set an unfortunate precedent for the future financing of United Nations peace and security operations.[13] By thus isolating the finances of the Force, the Secretary-General implied that the costs of UNEF were of an extraordinary nature. Thus the question may be raised whether Articles 17 and 19 are indeed applicable in this case.

At any rate, although the numerous arrears and defaults

Table 2

ASSESSMENTS FOR UNITED NATIONS FORCES IN 1961
($US in thousands)

Member	UNEF (1 Jan.-31 Dec.)			ONUC (1 Jan.-31 Oct.)		
	Gross Assessment	Net Assessment[1]	Payments	Gross Assessment	Net Assessment[2]	Payments
Afghanistan	11.3	5.6	—*	59.4	11.9	—*
Albania	7.5	7.5	—*	39.6	7.9	—*
Argentina	208.8	103.3	—*	1,099.6	219.9	—*
Australia	336.7	334.9	in full	1,773.2	1,773.2	1,422.0
Austria	80.9	80.5		426.0	426.0	—*
Belgium	244.5	243.2	200.0	1,287.8	1,287.8	—*
Bolivia	7.5	7.5	—*	39.6	7.9	—*
Brazil	191.9	94.9	—	1,010.4	202.1	—*
Bulgaria	30.1	29.9	—*	158.5	31.7	—*
Burma	15.0	7.4	in full	79.2	15.8	—
Byelorussia	88.4	87.9	—*	465.6	465.6	—*
Cambodia	7.5	3.7	—	39.6	7.9	—*
Cameroun	7.5	7.5	—	39.6	7.9	5.8
Canada	585.0	581.9	in full	3,080.7	3,080.7	2,650.0
Cent. Afr. Rep.	7.5	3.8	in full	39.6	7.9	—
Ceylon	18.8	9.3	in full	99.1	19.8	—
Chad	7.5	3.8	—	39.6	7.9	—*
Chile	50.8	25.1	—†	267.5	53.5	—*
China	942.4	466.2	—*	4,962.9	2,481.4	—*
Colombia	58.3	28.8	—†	307.1	61.4	—*
Congo (Brazza.)	7.5	7.5	—	39.6	7.9	—*
Congo (Leo.)	7.5	3.8	—	39.6	7.9	—*
Costa Rica	7.5	3.7	—†	39.6	7.9	—*
Cuba	47.0	46.8	—*	247.6	49.5	—*
Cyprus	7.5	3.8	—	39.6	7.9	—*
Czechoslovakia	163.7	162.8	—*	861.8	861.8	—*
Dahomey	7.5	3.8	3.4	39.6	7.9	7.0
Denmark	112.9	112.3	in full	594.4	594.4	in full
Dominican Rep.	9.4	9.4	—	49.5	9.9	—*
Ecuador	11.3	5.6	in full	59.4	11.9	—*
El Salvador	9.4	4.7	—*	49.5	9.9	—*
Ethiopia	11.3	5.6	—*	59.4	11.9	—*
Fed. of Malaya	32.0	15.8	in full	168.4	33.7	—

*In full arrears after 1957.	*In full arrears, 1960 net assessment.
†In partial arrears after 1957.	†In partial arrears, 1960 assessmenst.

1 After reductions requested and received under General Assembly Res. 1575 (XV).
2 After reductions pursuant to General Assembly Res. 1619 (XV).

371

Table 2 (cont'd)

Member	UNEF (1 Jan.-31 Dec.) Gross Assessment	Net Assessment[1]	Payments	ONUC (1 Jan.-31 Oct.) Gross Assessment	Net Assessment[2]	Payments
Finland	67.7	67.4	in full	356.6	356.6	—
France	1,203.9	1,197.5	in full	6,339.8	6,339.8	—*
Gabon	7.5	3.8	in full	39.6	7.9	—
Ghana	13.2	6.5	—	69.3	13.9	—*
Greece	43.3	21.4	—*	227.8	45.6	—*
Guatemala	9.4	4.7	—†	49.5	9.9	—*
Guinea	7.5	7.5	—	39.6	7.9	—*
Haiti	7.5	3.7	—†	39.6	7.9	—*
Honduras	7.5	3.7	—†	39.6	7.9	—*
Hungary	79.0	78.6	—*	416.0	83.2	—*
Iceland	7.5	3.7	—	39.6	7.9	—
India	462.8	228.9	—†	2,436.9	1,218.4	in full
Indonesia	88.4	43.7	—	465.6	93.1	—*
Iran	39.5	19.5	—	208.0	41.6	—*
Iraq	16.9	16.8	—*	89.2	17.8	—*
Ireland	30.1	29.9	in full	158.5	31.7	in full
Israel	26.3	26.2	—	138.7	27.7	—*
Italy	423.3	421.0	—	2,228.8	2,228.8	—*
Ivory Coast	11.3	5.6	—	59.4	11.9	10.3
Japan	412.0	203.7	in full	2,169.4	1,084.7	—
Jordan	7.5	7.5	—*	39.6	7.9	—*
Laos	7.5	3.7	—	39.6	7.9	—*
Lebanon	9.4	4.7	—†	49.5	9.9	—*
Liberia	7.5	3.7	—†	39.6	7.9	in full
Libya	7.5	7.5	—*	39.6	7.9	—*
Luxembourg	11.3	11.2	in full	59.4	11.9	—†
Madagascar	11.3	5.6	2.5	59.4	11.9	—†
Mali	7.5	7.5	—*	39.6	7.9	—*
Mexico	133.6	132.8	—*	703.3	140.7	—*
Morocco	26.3	13.0	—†	138.7	27.7	—*
Nepal	7.5	3.7	—*	39.6	7.9	—*
Netherlands	190.0	189.0	in full	1,000.5	1,000.5	in full
New Zealand	79.0	78.6	in full	416.0	416.0	in full
Nicaragua	7.5	3.7	—†	39.6	7.9	—*
Niger	7.5	3.8	—	39.6	7.9	—*
Nigeria	39.5	19.8	—	208.0	41.6	—

*In full arrears after 1957.
†In partial arrears after 1957.

*In full arrears, 1960 net assessment.
†In partial arrears, 1960 assessmenst.

1 After reductions requested and received under General Assembly Res. 1575 (XV).
2 After reductions pursuant to General Assembly Res. 1619 (XV).

Table 2 (concl'd)

Member	UNEF (1 Jan.-31 Dec.)			ONUC (1 Jan.-31 Oct.)		
	Gross Assessment	Net Assessment[1]	Payments	Gross Assessment	Net Assessment[2]	Payments
Norway	92.2	91.7	in full	485.4	485.4	in full
Pakistan	75.2	37.2	—	396.2	79.2	—
Panama	7.5	3.7	—*	39.6	7.9	—*
Paraguay	7.5	3.7	—*	39.6	7.9	—*
Peru	20.7	20.6	—*	109.0	21.8	—*
Philippines	80.9	40.0	—†	426.0	85.2	—*
Poland	257.7	256.3	—*	1,357.1	678.6	—*
Portugal	37.6	37.4	in full	198.1	39.6	—*
Romania	64.0	63.6	—*	336.8	336.8	—*
Saudi Arabia	11.3	11.2	—*	59.4	11.9	—*
Senegal	11.3	5.6	—	59.4	11.9	—*
Somalia	7.5	7.5	—	39.6	7.9	—*
South Africa	105.3	104.8	in full	554.7	554.7	—*
Spain	174.9	174.0	—*	921.2	184.3	—*
Sudan	11.3	11.2	—*	59.4	11.9	—*
Sweden	261.5	260.1	—	1,376.9	1,376.9	—*
Thailand	30.1	14.9	in full	158.5	31.7	—
Togo	7.5	3.8	—	39.6	7.9	—*
Tunisia	9.4	4.7	in full	49.5	9.9	—
Turkey	111.0	54.9	in full	584.4	116.9	in full
Ukraine	338.6	336.8	—*	1,783.1	1,783.1	—*
USSR	2,562.1	2,548.5	—*	13,491.8	13,491.8	—*
UAR	60.2	59.9	—*	317.0	63.4	—*
United Kingdom	1,462.5	1,453.9	in full	7,706.8	7,706.8	5,780.1
United States	6,115.5	6,115.5	in full	32,204.1	32,204.1	in full
Upper Volta	7.5	7.5	—	39.6	7.9	—*
Uruguay	22.6	11.2	—†	118.9	23.8	—*
Venezuela	94.1	46.5	—	495.3	99.1	—*
Yemen	7.5	7.5	—*	39.6	7.9	—*
Yugoslavia	65.8	32.6	in full	346.7	69.3	—*
TOTAL	$18,989.9	$17,234.9	$4,852.7	$100,000.0	$84,694.4	$45,950.4

*In full arrears after 1957.
†In partial arrears after 1957.

*In full arrears, 1960 net assessment.
†In partial arrears, 1960 assessmenst.

1 After reductions requested and received under General Assembly Res. 1575 (XV).
2 After reductions pursuant to General Assembly Res. 1619 (XV).

SOURCES: United Nations Docs. ST/ADM/Ser. B/150, 4 Oct. 1961, and A/C.5/879, 28 Sept. 1961.

had put the United Nations into serious financial straits by 1960, UNEF never threatened the financial structure of the Organization itself. It was the operation in the Congo which was to shake this structure to its very foundations.

ONUC

Historians may differ with Mr. Hammarskjold's view that the United Nations' task in the Congo was the most important responsibility that the world organization had to shoulder in the first fifteen years of its lifetime. Few, however, will disagree that the Congo problem required every diplomatic and military resource that the United Nations could possibly muster.

The United Nations was first called into the infant African republic to ensure both withdrawal of Belgian troops and maintenance of order in the existing vacuum that had reduced the Congo to a state of political unrest verging on anarchy and civil war. At a stormy meeting on the night of 13-14 July 1960, the Security Council authorized the Secretary-General

to take the necessary steps, in consultation with the Government of the Republic of the Congo, to provide the Government with such military assistance as may be necessary until, through the efforts of the Congolese Government with the technical assistance of the United Nations, the national security forces may be able, in the opinion of the Government, to meet fully their tasks.[14]

The Secretary-General's problems in putting together a United Nations Force for the Congo resembled those that had been faced in the Middle East, but the complications were vastly magnified. Again the Force had to be improvised at a moment's notice. The Secretary-General had to race against time in order to forestall great-power intervention. Within thirty hours, troops from eight African states as well as contingents from Sweden and Ireland arrived in the Congolese capital. In the next few days, it became clear that the new Congo Force would greatly exceed UNEF in magnitude. ONUC, Mr. Hammarskjold predicted, would be "far bigger and far more complicated," with "many more nations being involved, a multilingual basis to be used, military units with very different traditions to co-operate, and a vast area to be covered."[15]

As more nations offered troops, the Force was gradually built up from an average of 10,000 men in July, 15,000 during August, 16,500 during September, to an average of 20,000 men from twenty-nine nations for the last three months of 1960. But if the Force was not to be doomed to extinction, the fifteenth General Assembly had to consider the question of financing as a matter of first priority.

On 24 October 1960, the Secretary-General estimated the cost of the Congo Force for 1960 at $66,625,000. This estimate was considered by the Advisory Committee on Administrative and Budgetary Questions, which recommended that the total costs of ONUC for 1960 be held to $60,000,000, and echoed a hope expressed by the Secretary-General that nations would forgo reimbursement for troop transport. Both the United States and the Soviet governments informed the Committee that they would waive their claims of $10,-000,000 and $1,500,000 respectively. Hence, the crucial question to be decided by the Fifth Committee was how to apportion the remaining $48,500,000 among the member states.

The debate in the Fifth Committee began in a relatively mild tone. Ireland, Liberia, and Sweden suggested that ONUC's 1960 expenses be included in the regular budget and apportioned in accordance with the 1960 scale of assessments. This, the three powers maintained, would be the simplest solution and would avoid the ambiguity of the UNEF precedent. It would clearly bring ONUC within the scope of Articles 17 and 19 of the Charter.

Pakistan, Senegal, and Tunisia instead proposed a resolution creating an *ad hoc* account for financing ONUC operations, but clearly stipulating that the 1960 costs of the Congo Force were to "constitute 'expenses of the Organization' within the meaning of Article 17" and that assessments for it were to create "binding legal obligations."[16] This procedure, too, would make the enterprise a collective responsibility but would keep it separate from the regular budget for accounting purposes. In addition, the three powers suggested the solicitation of voluntary contributions to be applied to reduce assessments of member states with the least capacity to pay. This view was supported by the United States and most of the newly admitted nations.

The Communist nations stated their intention not to contribute to any part of ONUC's expenses since, in their opinion, "the main burden . . . should be borne by the chief culprits—the Belgian colonizers."[17] The rest of the money should be raised through voluntary contributions. The Latin

American countries again suggested that the expenses be paid largely by the permanent members of the Security Council.

The debate increased in intensity when the Polish delegate suggested that the proviso in the Pakistan-Senegal-Tunisia draft describing the ONUC assessments as binding legal obligations be deleted. This amendment, which would have removed ONUC from the scope of Article 19, was supported by India and Mexico in debate but was defeated by a vote of 40 to 27, with 17 abstentions. At this point, the Secretary-General offered his view to the Committee. After strongly endorsing the principle of collective responsibility, Mr. Hammarskjold deplored the tendency of the delegates to approve courses of action for the United Nations without following through financially:

Will this organization face the economic consequences of its own actions and how will it be done? Further, if it is not willing to face the financial consequences of its own decisions, is it then prepared to change its substantive policies? There is no third alternative.

He then pointed up the resulting dilemma:

The Secretariat finds itself in a difficult position. On the one hand, it has to pursue "vigorously" the policy decided upon by the General Assembly and the Security Council. On the other hand, it is continuously fighting against the financial difficulties with which these decisions under present circumstances face the Organization. Of course, the Organization cannot have it both ways.[18]

Finally the Fifth Committee, by a vote of 45 to 15, with 25 abstentions, approved the draft resolution proposed by Pakistan, Tunisia, and Senegal. It recommended an *ad hoc* account for the expenses of ONUC in the amount of $48,500,-000, to be assessed on the basis of the 1960 scale. It stressed that these assessments would be "binding legal obligations" on member states within the meaning of Article 17 of the Charter. It called on the government of Belgium to make a substantial contribution and recommended that voluntary contributions be applied to reduce by up to 50 per cent the assessment of those states with the least capacity to pay. On 20 December, this recommendation was adopted by the General Assembly by 46 to 17, with 24 abstentions. In addition, as an interim measure the Assembly authorized the Secretary-General to incur commitments up to a total of $24,000,000 for ONUC's expenses for the first quarter of 1961[19]—without, however, specifying how this amount was to be raised. It did say that at its resumed session it would give "urgent consideration" to financing the costs of the Congo Force in 1961 and requested the Secretary-General to submit cost estimates by 1 March.

The Secretary-General, in a detailed report, estimated the 1961 costs of ONUC at $135,000,000. This amount included $107,000,000 for operating costs to be incurred directly by the United Nations, and $28,000,000 for reimbursements to governments for airlifts and other extraordinary expenses. The Advisory Committee on Administrative and Budgetary Questions, on reviewing the estimates, voiced the hope that reimbursement waivers by governments and a policy of economy for the entire operation might reduce the total to $120,000,000.[20] Subsequently, the Fifth Committee settled down to the difficult job of deciding on the method of apportionment.

The Fifth Committee was deeply divided. Since the sum under consideration was the largest ever to be assessed by the United Nations for a single operation and since the decision would obviously have far-reaching consequences, more fundamental and elaborate arguments were raised than over the 1960 assessment. Moreover, the very solvency of the Organization depended on the outcome of the discussion. The United States once again favored the principle of collective responsibility on the basis of the 1960 assessment, although it offered to waive its reimbursement rights amounting to over $10,000,000 and to make a voluntary cash contribution of up to $4,000,000 to be used to reduce the assessments of governments with a limited capacity to pay.

The Soviet Union insisted that since ONUC was a Security Council "action" in the sense of Article 48 of the Charter, the General Assembly had no right to reach a decision on the matter. Article 11 of the Charter provides that "action" on any question involving peace and security shall be referred by the Assembly to the Security Council. Hence, in the Soviet view, ONUC financing should not fall under Article 17 but should be governed by the unanimity principle in the Security Council. The Secretary-General stated in rebuttal that once the Security Council had taken a decision, the implementation costs fell clearly within the meaning of Article 17 and therefore within the bailiwick of the Assembly. The Soviet position, he argued, would have the effect of extending the unanimity principle of the Big Five to matters of finance; this would clearly lead to the paralysis of the entire operation in the Congo.[21]

The Communist countries were not alone in attacking the Secretary-General's position. The Latin American nations, under the leadership of Mexico, proposed that the ONUC costs not be apportioned under Article 17 but be considered special or emergency expenses. In an elaborate defense of this view, the Mexican delegate quoted Article 43 of the Charter with regard to enforcement action and stated that expenses resulting from operations involving the use of armed forces, as in the Congo operation, were deliberately and intentionally excluded by the San Francisco Conference from the application of the penalty provided for in Article 19.

Hence, he continued, the Secretary-General's position would lead to sanctions not provided for in the Charter. Instead, 70 per cent of the ONUC costs should be borne by the Big Five, 25 per cent by those states whose investments in the Congo exceeded $1,000,000, and only 5 per cent should be apportioned on the basis of the regular assessment scale. The Indian delegation, while not agreeing with the Mexican position in all its details, also favored the financing of the Congo Force outside Article 17.[22]

The Secretary-General, in a special statement before the Fifth Committee, countered the Mexican argument by pointing out that ONUC was not an enforcement action within the meaning of Article 43, but a military operation for essentially internal security functions in the territory of a member state at the invitation of the government of that state. Hence, the Mexican argument, since it was based on Article 43 which had never been invoked in the Congo, was in essence irrelevant. Mr. Hammarskjold, while appreciating the concern of many delegations about the size of ONUC costs, went on to ask the Committee:

But how, from a legal and constitutional point of view, can these factors lead to a conclusion that they are not expenses of the Organization? The fact that these expenses have been substantial and unusual—indeed unforeseeable at the time of the San Francisco Conference—cannot mean that the Charter provision must now be disregarded.[23]

France, which had already voiced misgivings regarding ONUC, refused to associate itself with this view. The Secretary-General's position was, however, supported by the United States and many Asian and African states.

Finally, the Fifth Committee adopted a draft resolution, originally sponsored by Ghana, Liberia, Pakistan, and Tunisia, which apportioned $100,000,000 for the period 1 January to 31 October 1961 according to the 1960 assessment scale, "pending the establishment of a different scale of assessment" to defray ONUC's expenses.[23a] Reductions were again granted to states with a limited capacity to pay. This resolution, however, failed to obtain the necessary two-thirds majority in the plenary Assembly until the upper limit of the reductions had been raised to 80 per cent for states paying 0.25 per cent or less of the regular budget; and 50 to 80 per cent for those paying more than 0.25 per cent but benefiting from the Expanded Programme of Technical Assistance. Voluntary contributions were to be applied to offset the resulting deficits. The Big Five and Belgium were called upon to make substantial voluntary contributions. The final vote, taken at dawn on the last day of the session, was 54 in favor, 15 against, with 23 abstentions. The Soviet bloc, Mexico, and Belgium cast negative votes, while France and South Africa abstained and have subsequently refused to contribute.

Within four months, the mood of the General Assembly had changed considerably. The resolution of 21 April was far weaker than its predecessor and in essence represented a regression to the UNEF pattern. The acute stage of the crisis, it seemed, had passed and the Assembly once again found refuge in ambiguity.

Resolution 1619 (XV) of 21 April 1961 differed from that of the previous December in three important respects. First, while it did apportion the $100,000,000 as "expenses of the Organization," it made no specific reference to Article 17 nor did it define the cost as a "binding legal obligation." Second, the costs were described several times as "extraordinary expenses." And finally, the resolution emphasized the special responsibility of the permanent powers of the Security Council for the financing of peace and security operations.

Conscious of the necessity of devising a more adequate method of financing peace-keeping operations in the future, the fifteenth Assembly, at its final plenary meeting, decided to place on the agenda of the sixteenth session "as a matter of prime importance and urgency" an examination of methods for covering the cost of "peace-keeping operations" and the relationship between such methods and existing administrative and budgetary procedure. This resolution had grown out of a Canadian draft in the Fifth Committee which envisaged the creation of a United Nations Peace and Security Fund that could be used to finance operations like UNEF and the Congo Force.[24]

The Problem of Arrears

Several concluding remarks are now in order with regard to the role of assessment in United Nations financing. Four different aspects of United Nations activities are being financed in this manner: the regular budget, the administrative budgets of the specialized agencies, UNEF, and ONUC. This means, in effect, that since 1956 the total assessed to member states has more than doubled. For a decade, only the regular budget, hovering around $50,000,000, and administrative budgets of the specialized agencies were raised through assessment. In 1961, over $200,000,000 was assessed by the General Assembly to the member states. In the case of the regular budget, as shown earlier, almost two-thirds of the cost is borne by the Big Five, with almost one-third by the United States alone. In the case of UNEF and ONUC, this pattern is even more apparent. Although the United States was assessed less than one-third of the 1961 UNEF budget, in effect, since its voluntary contribution is used to offset the reductions granted to fifty-one countries with a limited capacity to pay, it is paying 43 per cent of the total. Regarding ONUC these reductions are somewhat greater and the United States has assumed responsibility for a portion of the assessment of seventy-nine member states. This has brought its share of the total cost to 48 per cent.

As assessments have mounted, so have arrears and defaults. In the regular budget, as we have seen, these have not been considerable. The problem has been far more serious in UNEF. Forty-three members owe all or part of their assessments for the 1960 budget, bringing arrears to over 30 per cent of the total. With ONUC, arrears and defaults have brought the Organization to the brink of bankruptcy. Seventy-two member states have accumulated a combined shortage of 45 per cent of the 1960 ONUC budget. Indeed, only twenty-seven states had paid their 1960 assessments by late September 1961.[25] Two of the five permanent powers of the Security Council—the Soviet Union and France—have declared their intention not to meet their obligations, and a third—China—has defaulted.

In view of this sorry record, one is brought to wonder

about the effectiveness of assessment as a means of raising revenue for the United Nations. The only recourse for the General Assembly is Article 19 of the Charter. In the case of the regular budget, Article 19 appears to have successfully prevented states from accumulating arrears for more than two years. In the UNEF case, in view of the ambiguous status of the initial assessment and all the subsequent ones, it is not certain that Article 19 is legally applicable. In the case of the Congo Force, only the resolution of 20 December 1960 explicitly defined the ONUC assessment as a "binding legal obligation" within the meaning of Article 17. Four months later this stipulation was once again omitted. It is doubtful whether the Assembly, in its subsequent decisions on ONUC financing, will ever again be willing to avoid ambiguity. Thus, the legal applicability of Article 19 to United Nations peace-keeping operations is clear beyond a doubt only in a single instance. Even in this case the Soviet Union and its allies, and France, have refused to be bound. Hence, the additional question is posed, in the concluding chapter of this study, as to whether the application of the sanctions of Article 19 in cases of failure to meet financial obligations for United Nations peace and security operations is politically sound and feasible.

Financing the Voluntary Programs

A NUMBER of vital United Nations operations subsist solely on the generosity of governments and private citizens' groups throughout the world. While these programs have grown less rapidly than those for which costs are assessed, their combined annual cost amounts to more than twice the regular budget. The most important of these voluntary programs are the United Nations Children's Fund (UNICEF), the United Nations High Commissioner for Refugees (UNHCR), the United Nations Relief and Works Agency for Palestine Refugees in the Near East (UNRWA), the Expanded Programme of Technical Assistance (EPTA), the Special Fund, and most recently, the Congo Fund. Two voluntary operations, the International Refugee Organization (IRO) and the United Nations Korean Reconstruction Agency (UNKRA), were terminated in 1952 and 1958 respectively. Government contributions have provided most of the support for these voluntary programs. Only the Children's Fund and the High Commissioner for Refugees have received substantial private donations.[26]

There is little logic in the distinction between the regular budget and the voluntary programs. It would be inaccurate to refer to the former as a purely administrative budget and to the latter as exclusively operational. The regular budget includes operational items and the voluntary programs must make allowances for administrative expenses. The simple reason for the independent financing of the special programs lies in the fact that voluntary contributions offered the only practical basis on which these programs could get started. To include them in the regular budget would have aroused the opposition of most member states, not only on grounds of excessive expense but also because some of the programs, such as UNRWA and UNKRA, had a fairly limited impact and were to benefit only a relatively small number of states. Thus the United Nations was equipped with several "drawers" of money.

This pattern has given each member state the freedom to contribute to each particular program in accordance with its ability—or its willingness—to pay. This has often been a disadvantage since it has made the programs dependent on the arbitrary decision of states to grant or to withhold funds. But at times the independent financing of the special programs has resulted in a larger allocation of funds. In the case of the United States, for example, Congress was willing to contribute more than one-third of the budgets of some of the programs because they were not conceived as permanent obligations. Moreover, several states which are not members of the United Nations, notably the Federal Republic of Germany and Switzerland, have made some substantial contributions.

As can be expected, the base of support has been very uneven. Only forty governments, for example, chose to contribute to UNKRA, but UNICEF is being supported by ninety-eight, including almost the entire membership of the United Nations. Contributions are announced at annual pledging conferences, but many of these pledges are subject to parliamentary approval in the member states. To encourage governments to make their pledges as generous as possible, a special body was created by the General Assembly in 1952—the Negotiating Committee for Extra-Budgetary Funds. This ten-member body stimulates contributions by appealing to governments and private sources. It also attempts to close the gap between pledges and actual payments and constantly searches for untapped resources.[27] Aside from this Committee, there is little fiscal coordination among the voluntary programs. In essence, each must assure its own livelihood.

UNICEF

The oldest of the voluntary programs is the United Nations Children's Fund. Until 1950 UNICEF focused on emergency relief to children of war-devastated countries. After that its mandate was broadened to emphasize continuing child-care programs, particularly in underdeveloped countries. While most forms of technical assistance concentrate primarily on advisory services, UNICEF has been a major supplier of such basic goods as powdered milk, anti-malaria insecticides and BCG vaccine, and factory equipment for the production of fish flour, soya milk, or antibiotics.

Financing throughout the emergency period was haphazard and depended primarily on contributions from the United States. UNICEF made its first allocations in 1947 on the basis of a $15,000,000 United States grant, and until 1952 United States contributions accounted for more than 70 per cent of the entire budget. The United States contribution proved to be the keystone of UNICEF, not only because of its size but because of a matching formula conceived by the United States government in order to stimulate contributions from other countries. This device worked quite successfully and brought government contributions between 1946 and 1953 to a total of more than $125,000,000. An average of thirty countries contributed, with Australia, Canada, France, New Zealand, and Switzerland as the next largest contributors.

The year 1953 was a watershed in the financial history of UNICEF. The Fund was put on a permanent basis and as a result its support broadened considerably. Fifty-five governments made contributions in 1953 and by 1960 there were ninety-eight donors. In 1960 these were responsible for $21,-500,000, which amounted to almost 85 per cent of the entire

UNICEF budget. The rest was raised through donations from private sources and the sale of UNICEF greeting cards.

Several observations are in order about the present financial pattern of UNICEF. In the first place, the United States has gradually reduced its matching percentage over the past eight years. In 1960 it stipulated that its contribution of $12,000,000 must not exceed 56 per cent of the total. In 1961 this ratio was further reduced to 46 per cent. Since the list of donors has grown each year, however, and most individual contributions have also increased, the actual United States donation has risen as well.[28]

Secondly, many of the developing nations have made unusually high pledges to the Fund. In 1960 twenty-eight nations contributed a higher percentage of the annual UNICEF budget than their proportionate assessment for the regular United Nations budget. In spite of their low per-capita income, many of these governments make contributions to the Fund which compare favorably with the relative support from a number of wealthier countries. The reason for this is, of course, the fact that UNICEF is primarily a supply agency to the poorer countries, which are on the receiving end. In 1960, for example, countries assisted by the Fund were contributing over 20 per cent of the government grants to UNICEF; of the twenty largest donors, nine were receiving aid from UNICEF.[29]

The members of the Soviet bloc ignored UNICEF until 1953, but since then have been regular contributors. The annual Soviet contribution for the past three years has been $500,000. This contribution, and those of the other East European countries, add up to a little over 3 per cent of the total.

In sum, government contributions to UNICEF have grown steadily since 1953, when they amounted to $14,266,000, and now approach $22,000,000. Further growth, however, will largely depend on higher contributions from governments other than the United States. This is so because the United States hopes gradually to lower its matching percentage to 40 per cent. Now that virtually all the states of the world are contributors to UNICEF, greater financial support from other governments will be needed to make fully available to the Fund the amounts pledged by the United States. Such a trend seems indeed to be in the making. Some of the largest contributors pledged sizable increases for 1961: the Federal

Republic of Germany increased its support by 120 per cent over 1960; France by 48 per cent; the Soviet Union by 41 per cent; and Australia, Canada, India, Sweden, Switzerland, and the United Kingdom—the other main contributors—all raised their support considerably.

Finally, UNICEF, like EPTA and the Special Fund, has utilized a device whereby the value of its effective resources exceeds by far that of the contributions received from donor governments. By a system of "matching" on the part of countries assisted, UNICEF generates further funds. The government of each assisted country provides an average of $2 to $2.50 for every $1 from UNICEF. Thus, in addition to the almost $26,000,000 for programs allocated by the Fund in 1960, this system of "local matching" committed governments receiving aid from the Fund to spending the equivalent of $78,440,000 over and above the allocations from UNICEF. These matching funds not only enable UNICEF's resources to go further, but assure that a project is firmly rooted in the country as a basic responsibility of its government.

Arrears have never been a serious problem in UNICEF. The Latin American countries have been somewhat tardy in paying their pledges, but few countries are more than two years behind on their payments. All things considered, the financial picture of the Children's Fund has been steadily improving.

*   *   *   *

Development Programs

Voluntary contributions from governments support three United Nations programs dealing with economic development. The first of these, the Expanded Programme of Technical Assistance, was launched in 1950; the second, the Special Fund, began operations in 1959; and a Fund for the economic development of the Congo was set up in 1960. Financing follows a similar pattern in all three programs.

Although the United Nations and various specialized agencies had carried on a modest technical assistance program almost from the beginning, the impetus for EPTA came out of Point Four of President Truman's inaugural speceh of January 1949. Subsequently, the United States proposed to the United Nations Economic and Social Council that a concrete program be elaborated for enlarging technical assistance activities. Since 1950, when EPTA began operations with $20,000,000 provided by fifty-four nations, contributions have steadily increased. In 1955 seventy nations pledged over $27,000,000. And by 1961 pledges from eight-four governments stood at $41,000,000.

Like the other voluntary programs, EPTA was launched with a sizable United States contribution, which amounted to 60 per cent of all government contributions. Since then the United States has gradually reduced its "matching" percentage and during the past few years has insisted that its contribution not exceed 40 per cent of the total. But as in UNICEF, the number of donors and the size of contributions have gone up so that the United States has also pledged increasingly larger amounts.[36] The United Kingdom contributes 8 per cent and France and Canada over 5 per cent each. The underdeveloped countries themselves contribute 10 per cent. The Soviet Union and other East European countries began to contribute in 1953 and have been responsible for slightly more than 4 per cent of the budget.

Again as in UNICEF, the actual outreach of EPTA is larger than its own financial resources would indicate. Recipient governments are obligated to pay for the local costs of EPTA projects, which amount to more than twice the annual budget of EPTA itself. On the other hand, EPTA annually runs into several financial problems. Some of the recipient countries do not fully meet their "local cost" obligations; several governments, notably those in Latin America, are chronically in arrears on their contributions; and finally, a number of governments, including the East European countries, contribute part or even all of their share in non-convertible currencies. While these practices create difficulties for EPTA, they are never serious enough to jeopardize its operations.

The Special Fund was set up in 1959 for the purpose of financing preparatory and "pre-investment" projects which would make it possible for technical assistance and development to yield optimum results. In keeping with its mandate, the Fund has concentrated on relatively large projects. Financing has been virtually a carbon copy of EPTA. The sum total of government contributions has been slightly above that for EPTA—$38,500,000 in 1960 and almost $47,-000,000 in pledges for 1961. Again, the United States limits its contribution to 40 per cent of the total. Governments increasingly regard the financing of EPTA and the Special Fund as a joint operation. Several, in fact, make a single pledge to both programs. Some, like India and Japan, make their pledges contingent on the attainment of a given minimum of total government contributions to the two programs. The Technical Assistance Committee and the Managing Director of the Special Fund have both expressed the hope that the combined annual resources of the two programs would soon reach $150,000,000. While government pledges for 1962 did not reach that figure, they did total a record $97,685,000.

The United Nations Fund for the Congo was established by the General Assembly at its fourth emergency special session on 20 September 1960. It was decided to aim at a figure of $100,000,000 for financial assistance to the fledgling republic. Responses to date have been meager. By mid-1961 a total of $18,000,000 had been contributed by eighteen nations. The United States contributed $10,000,000 and the United Kingdom, Sweden, Canada, Australia, Denmark, Norway, New Zealand, and Liberia pledged the next largest contributions. At this writing the outlook for the Congo Fund is bleak.

Private Donations

No United Nations organ is permitted to accept private donations unless specifically authorized to do so by the General Assembly. So far, while there have been some private gifts to the United Nations—most notably its new library building financed by the Ford Foundation—the amounts raised in this manner have never been great and have either come from foundations or stemmed from organized fund-raising campaigns by non-governmental organizations such as churches, schools, and citizens' groups. Both UNICEF and the High Commissioner, however, have come to depend on some regular income from private sources.

The first experiment was launched by the Secretary-General in 1946. It was the United Nations Appeal for Children, a world-wide campaign for non-governmental contributions to meet emergency needs of children, adolescents, and expectant mothers. Private groups in forty-five countries and thirty non-self-governing territories contributed $11,000,000 to UNICEF by the end of 1948. The drive was so successful that the United States Senate Committee on Expenditures suggested in 1951 that the United Nations should exert greater efforts to obtain funds from private sources:

Independent sources of income must be found for the United Nations and the specialized agencies in order to relieve member governments of their present heavy financial burdens. These sources might be developed by the performance of services for private business and educational concerns, or by obtaining private grants in support of some portions of their work.[37]

Yet the success of this first drive was never repeated. It had hinged upon a unique humanitarian appeal at the end of the war when the condition of millions of children was especially desperate in many countries. From 1950 to 1956, annual private contributions to UNICEF never exceeded $1,000,000. Since 1956, the figure has risen slowly, largely because of organized Halloween projects in the United States and Canada. The total for 1960 was $1,900,000, most of which came from the United States. A similar amount is realized annually from the sale of UNICEF greeting cards throughout the world. But all told, private contributions and income from greeting cards amount to only 15 per cent of the annual UNICEF budget.

In the life of the Office of the High Commissioner, income from private sources has played an important role on at least two occasions. The first was a $2,900,000 grant from the Ford Foundation in 1952 which enabled the High Commissioner to rehabilitate a considerable number of "hard-core" refugees living in European camps. Indeed, it was this private grant that made it possible for the Office to embark on operational work for the refugees. In that sense, it served as a pump-primer to the General Assembly, which later reluctantly endorsed the operational aspects of UNHCR's program. The second occasion arose in connection with World Refugee Year. In 1959 private contributions to UNHCR exceeded $1,000,000, constituting 20 per cent of total income. In 1960, for the first time in the history of any United Nations program, contributions from private sources exceeded those from governments. A determined world-wide fundraising campaign netted over $9,000,000, one-third more than the amount contributed by governments. This may stand as a unique example, however.

Pattern of Contributions

If we compare the pattern of voluntary contributions by governments with that of the assessed budget, several significant factors emerge. In the first place, the role of the United States is even more dominant in the voluntary programs.

While its contribution varies from 70 per cent of the total in UNRWA and UNICEF to 40 per cent in EPTA and the Special Fund, it is quite clear that the United States contribution is financially controlling over all the voluntary programs. The demises of IRO and UNKRA are cases in point. All told, the United States has paid well over half of the aggregate amount spent on all voluntary programs since their inception.

The Soviet Union and other East European countries ignored the voluntary programs completely until 1953. After the death of Stalin, they not only joined some of the specialized agencies but began to make contributions to UNICEF, EPTA, and, in 1959, to the Special Fund. Not only was the new Soviet leadership willing to experiment with new ideas, but it was apparently impressed with the evidence by mid-1953 that UNICEF and EPTA were not going to fail, that their popularity would increase, and that "more harm to the Soviet Union would result from remaining outside than from participating."[38] The annual East European contributions to the three programs have amounted to less than 5 per cent of the total—roughly one-third of the percentage these nations are assessed in the regular budget. No Soviet-bloc contribution has ever been made to the refugee programs or to the Congo Fund.

The United Kingdom has paid for about 8 per cent of the voluntary programs, approximately the same ratio as its share of the regular budget. France has pledged 3 per cent, roughly half its proportionate share of the assessed budgets. And China's contribution has been an infinitesimal 0.05 per cent. As a rule, the developing nations of Africa, Asia, the Middle East, and Latin America contribute in slightly higher proportion to the voluntary programs than to the regular budget.

Since some of the voluntary programs—UNICEF, EPTA, and now the Special Fund—are supported by virtually the entire United Nations membership, it has been suggested that, "with relatively minor adjustments, [these] could be absorbed into the regular budget."[39] Actually, this is quite unlikely because most of the member states do not contribute to the special programs in the same ratio as they are assessed for the regular budget. The Soviet Union, France, and China contribute much less, and the bulk of the deficiency is made up by the United States, which contributes a portion well in excess of its assessment under the regular budget. Furthermore, several non-member states are relatively important contributors.

The disturbing tendency of many states to vote in favor of programs and then not to pay for them is also manifest in the voluntary programs, although to a lesser degree than for UNEF and ONUC. Arrears on pledges seldom reach 15 per cent and, as in the case of the regular budget, constitute more of an irritation than a serious threat.

Except in two isolated instances, private donations have not played an important role in United Nations financing. It is clear that the "doorbell approach" is no solution in the long run. As a general rule, private groups will not launch projects that are not approved by governments; moreover, they can seldom muster the massive resources that go into the making of a long-range international program. It seems that, for better or for worse, the United Nations special programs will have to depend primarily upon the continued voluntary support of governments.

The Search for Revenue

BY NOW IT IS CLEAR that there is ample room for improvement in the financing of the United Nations. A variety of proposals for strengthening its financial structure remains to be explored. This analysis proceeds on the assumption that any meaningful evaluation of fiscal-policy proposals must take into account the political context of the Organization. Indeed, the "politicization" of United Nations financing is so all-pervasive that one may almost say that there is no such thing as an exclusively fiscal question. The truth is that virtually all questions of finance are discussed and voted on as political questions only thinly disguised as fiscal. Hence, our analysis must concern itself not only with what is fiscally desirable but also with what is politically possible.

Strengthening the Present System

It is appropriate to examine, first of all, a group of relatively modest proposals that look for improvement within the present framework of the Charter and do not envisage any drastic changes in the relationship between the world organization and its member states. Most of these suggestions are concerned with the assessed budgets of the United Nations rather than with its voluntary programs.

There has been a mounting concern in United Nations circles in recent years over growing budgets. This has been motivated sometimes by considerations of economy and sometimes by political considerations. Thus, the Soviet member of the Committee of Experts to Review the Activities and Organization of the Secretariat proposed that three budgets be established: the regular budget with a net ceiling of $50,000,000, which should include only administrative expenses; a separate account for "extraordinary expenses and all other expenses directly connected with the maintenance of international peace and security"; and an operational budget for technical assistance and the "implementation of various types of economic, social, scientific and other programmes, projects and measures." Separate agreements would be drawn up with interested member states for each of these categories.[40] The Soviet argument, which was directed particularly to peace and security operations, was that any decision by the Assembly was a clear violation of the Charter's provisions in that area and an abrogation of the authority of the Security Council.

This idea was examined and rejected by the Committee of Experts, which had been appointed by the Secretary-General at the request of the General Assembly in 1960. This eight-man Committee submitted a detailed report in June 1961 in which it expressed the opinion that the validity of removing operational costs from the regular budget was dubious. The Committee admitted that such a separation of operational costs would reduce the 1961 budget by over $13,500,000 by taking out the costs of the regular technical assistance program, special missions, the Office of the High Commissioner for Refugees, and even a part of the staff costs. While such a course would be "technically possible," the Committee noted that the trend in recent years had been toward integration of all administrative costs regardless of whether they pertained to administrative functions or to operational programs. The exclusion of such costs from the regular budget would reverse a policy that had received the approval of the Assembly. The Secretary-General agreed with the Committee's view and added that the decision to continue to include a small amount for technical assistance in the regular budget of the United Nations was a conscious policy decision of the General Assembly, as a recognition of a minimum amount of responsibility to finance technical assistance on the part of all Member States.[41]

On balance, it seems that the elimination of minimal operational costs from the regular budget would be a case of "unscrambling scrambled eggs." The same people in the Secretariat often service both administrative and operational functions. In the words of the Committee, such a separation would have to be "approximate at best." In the light of all the difficulties and relatively small returns its prospects are most unlikely.

The proposal to fix a budget ceiling had already been considered at San Francisco. Senator Vandenberg had suggested that "the United Nations must never become a rich man's club; the dues must be kept low enough so that the smallest and poorest states can afford to belong."[42] In 1950 the General Assembly's Fifth Committee warned that "if costs continued to increase, there would be a grave danger that essential activities might be severely limited by lagging contributions."[43]

The Committee of Experts again paid close attention to this proposal in 1961. The Soviet expert took the strongest stand and recommended that the level of the regular budget not exceed $50,000,000 net: any increase should require the special permission of the General Assembly. The majority of the Committee did not favor the fixing of a rigid ceiling. It did suggest, however, that the Fifth Committee, after approving the budget estimates for the approaching year, make known to the Secretary-General the limit within which the budgetary estimates for the year after that should be prepared. The majority further recommended that the Fifth Committee should each year examine in detail one or two of the main areas of expenditure following a prior review by the Advisory Committee on Administrative and Budgetary Questions. Such a procedure, the majority felt, would bring to light any lack of prudence in the normal day-to-day administration of appropriations. Finally, the majority of the Committee emphasized the importance of self-imposed control in United Nations policy organs and in the Office of the Controller in the Secretariat. In his response to the Committee's recommendations, the Secretary-General also rejected the imposition of a rigid ceiling but found himself in essential agreement with the Committee's more moderate proposals.

A ceiling for the United Nations regular budget is most improbable, but in view of the growing emphasis on economy in United Nations circles it is very likely that some or all of the Committee's recommendations will be put into effect. The Secretariat will probably try its utmost to stabilize the budget at the present level. If it succeeds, the budget-ceiling proposal will seem increasingly unnecessary and the pressure for it may gradually subside. What is certain is that the United Nations regular budget—probably the most carefully pruned in the world—will get even closer attention.

Proposals dealing with the regular budget have not focused only on the problem of greater economy. There have also been several that aim to improve the administrative and budgetary procedure.

Further administrative improvements, if adopted, might put the United Nations in a better cash position. One looks toward coordinating the various fiscal years of member states with the United Nations fiscal period, which follows the calendar year. Under United Nations fiscal regulations, assessments should be paid within one month after notification by the Secretary-General. These notifications are usually sent each January. But under the present arrangement, the United States Congress does not appropriate the funds for the United Nations budget until June or July and actual payment is made only in the second half of the year. Several other member states including the Soviet Union pay even later. Indeed, most member states pay at irregular intervals during the two-year grace period. This practice has necessitated a constant heavy drawing on the Working Capital Fund. One observer has suggested that the United States Congress appropriate money each spring, covering both the current year and the succeeding year. The second part of this double appropriation would then be available in the following January.[44] It is widely believed that if the United States were to take the initiative in such a plan, other governments would follow suit.

A second suggestion, made in the Assembly by Austria, would, if adopted, inject a greater degree of regularity into the revenue picture and might stimulate more prompt payment. This proposal would give each member state the option of making payments in regular monthly installments.[45] Still another device was suggested by the Swedish delegate to the fourteenth Assembly: he recommended that the United Nations charge interest on outstanding contributions.[46] The International Telecommunication Union already follows this practice.

Finally, there have been a number of suggestions for enhancing the size or flexibility of the Working Capital Fund. The Fund has grown steadily over the past few years, and there are indications that it will grow beyond the present $25,000,000 mark. At its fourteenth session the Assembly authorized the Secretary-General to seek short-term loans from governments as a way of shoring up the Fund. Although the Assembly rejected, as beneath the "dignity" of the United Nations, the use of commercial loans, the question is bound to arise again. As the United Nations Controller put it, it was to be "wondered whether the dignity of the Organization would be hurt more by recourse to borrowing or by failure to meet its legal and commercial obligations."[47] However, while having a large Fund may be very desirable in a crisis situation, it does not get at the real difficulties of United Nations financing; in fact it may even postpone more thorough-going remedies.

Before leaving the regular budget, a word should be said about coordinating the budgets of the specialized agencies. As pointed out earlier, each specialized agency has its own budget. This multiplicity of budgets has frequently led to embarrassing fiscal competition within the United Nations system as well as to breakdowns of coordination. The absence of central planning for the specialized agencies led the United States Senate Committee on Expenditures in the Executive Branch to suggest as early as 1951 that control over the budgets and programs of the specialized agencies be given to the General Assembly. This would entail integrating the various budgets into the regular United Nations budget, with over-all control vested in the Assembly. In 1954 the Senate took the position that

member states would . . . thus be in a much better position to give overall guidance and direction to United Nations activities. Effective control over programs and projects could be established, duplication and overlapping avoided, and substantial savings brought about.[48]

It is unlikely that such a budget consolidation will take place. It would require amendments to the constitutions of the specialized agencies in order to transfer control powers to the Assembly. A serious problem of membership coordi-

394

nation would arise, since some United Nations members do not belong to all the specialized agencies, and conversely, some agencies have members which are not represented in the United Nations. Most important has been the opposition of the specialized agencies themselves and of their "client" ministries within member governments. The tradition of autonomy has become strongly ingrained and it is doubtful whether the agencies would accept any measure of control beyond "being brought into relationship with the United Nations" under the present system. Most likely, budget coordination will have to continue along informal lines. Besides, the importance of coordinating machinery may be overestimated. As the Senate Foreign Relations Committee also pointed out:

Much of the difficulty arises from internal schizophrenia of governments; and if the governments of sovereign states insist on following conflicting policies in the U.N. and in the specialized agencies, reorganization of the U.N. will not cure them.[49]

In the United Nations, as in other political bodies, gadgetry cannot substitute for policy.

Use of Article 19

The heart of the financial crisis in the United Nations stems from the peace-keeping operations in the Middle East and in the Congo which the Organization voted into existence in 1956 and 1960 respectively. As we have seen, UNEF and ONUC arrears have brought the Organization to the brink of bankruptcy. Can anything be done within the framework of the existing situation to narrow the margin between commitments made and those fulfilled?

The defaulting nations may be grouped into two broad categories. First, there are those, like the Soviet Union and France, which simply refuse to recognize their obligation to pay under an Assembly resolution. Most of the Latin American nations, arguing that peace-keeping operations should be viewed as "extraordinary expenses" and should not be apportioned within the meaning of Article 17 of the Charter, adopt a milder variant of this position. Second, a number of nations, like China, recognize their legal obligation but, owing to the large expense involved, have fallen seriously in arrears.

The only legal sanction provided by the Charter is Article 19, the relevance of which is clear beyond a doubt only in a single instance—the initial $48,500,000 assessed for ONUC in 1960. It is likely that half the membership of the United Nations will be in arrears on its ONUC obligations when the two-year limit of Article 19 takes effect. A degree of pressure may bring forth some payments before that time. If the program costs show signs of diminishing or coming to an end, some nations may be more willing to clear their accounts. But probably the Soviet Union, France, and a large number of others will continue to withhold their contributions. If they do, the question of invoking the sanctions of Article 19 will undoubtedly arise.

Although the Charter makes the suspension of voting privileges automatic unless there is formal action to the contrary by the Assembly, no procedures have been elaborated for implementating the rather vague wording of the Article. The Committee on Contributions reports each year on the countries that may be in danger of losing their vote by the time the Assembly convenes, but there the matter rests. The one instance when a state (Bolivia) missed the two-year deadline for payments, its delegation was not present when the first voting took place; thus the question of depriving it of voting privileges did not arise. By the time of the next vote, Bolivia had discharged its debts.

Most of the specialized agencies have equivalents of Article 19 in their Charters, and precedents for their invocation exist. For example, the ILO Director-General has standing orders to inform the General Conference of those states which have lost their voting privileges under Article 13 of the Statute, which extends to all organs of the ILO rather than only to the plenary body. Voting privileges can be temporarily restored, pending receipt of the arrears, by a two-thirds vote of the General Conference. With rare exceptions, countries have *not* been given permission to retain voting privileges so long as they are in arrears. The first time IAEA's Article 13a was tested, the Fourth (1960) General Conference voted (27 to none with 27 abstentions) to allow Cuba to retain its privileges for that session. However, when the delegation of Honduras appeared the following year, its Conference votes were not counted even though Honduras had paid a token $1 on its 1958 account.

Assuming it is politically feasible, there are strong arguments in favor of invoking Article 19. First, the Assembly assessed part of the costs of the Congo Force as "binding legal obligations." Not to invoke any sanction would be to make a mockery of the Charter. Second, if confronted with the threat of Article 19, defaulting states might pay their assessments in order to avoid adverse publicity. Even the Soviet Union might decide that its vote in the Assembly was of greater value than its intransigent attitude on the Congo Force. Finally, enlightened self-interest might prompt the African, Latin American, Asian and Middle Eastern nations to honor their obligations.

On the other hand, there is a powerful case to be made against the use of Article 19. The heart of the Soviet contention is that the Assembly simply does not have the power to impose binding legal obligations as regards matters affecting peace and security. Many of the small nations have argued that an Assembly majority cannot impose its will on the minority, even in financial matters. Since a great number of the nations that have taken this position will be in arrears when the time comes to apply Article 19, it may be that this interpretation will prevail. It is even doubtful whether a majority could be mustered in the Assembly to request the International Court for an advisory opinion on this question. If it could, the Court might well uphold the Secretary- General and advise that payment was mandatory, but its opinion would not, of course, have any binding effect. Second, and more important, the Soviet Union and other defaulting nations might simply decide to withdraw from the Organization. Indeed, the use of Article 19 might wreck the United Nations by depleting its membership. This danger makes the literal application of the Charter a formidable problem.

On balance, a resort to Article 19 would probably create more problems than it would solve. In all likelihood, the shortfalls of UNEF and the Congo Force may have to be made good through a long-term loan from the United States to the Working Capital Fund. The negotiation of such a loan would be a highly sensitive issue since the impression must be avoided that the United States intends to dominate the Organization by "bailing out" its peace-keeping operations. The initiative would have to come from the General Assembly, not from the United States.

Very similar problems have been plaguing the fifteen-member working group appointed under Assembly Resolution 1620 (XV) to construct a special assessment scale for United Nations peace-keeping operations.[50] Most of the small nations have insisted that the major financial burden be borne by the great powers. Of these, France and the

Soviet Union have evinced absolutely no interest; China has claimed incapacity to pay. Only the United States, the United Kingdom, and a few other Western nations have expressed willingness to contribute to some sort of Peace and Security Fund.

In the light of these obstacles, can anything be done at all to strengthen the financial basis of the United Nations' peace-keeping responsibilities?

To return once more to UNEF and ONUC: The establishment of the former was authorized by the General Assembly without a single dissenting vote, but the vote on the initial financing resolution was 57 in favor, 8 opposed, and 9 abstaining. The latter was set up by the Security Council without a negative vote, but the Assembly votes on financing the 1960 and 1961 costs were 46-17-24 and 54-15-23 respectively. Furthermore, 43 nations are in arrears on their UNEF assessments and 75 on their ONUC assessments for 1960; the respective figures for 1961 are 79 and 92. This indicates that a large number of even those nations which voted *for* the financial resolutions cannot be counted upon to make actual payment.

As a result of this situation, several Asian countries have proposed that in cases in which emergency action of one of the principal United Nations organs has major financial implications, the initial resolution should contain a section clearly setting forth the terms under which the program would be financed. A vote for the resolution would thus carry with it a more direct commitment to help pay the bill.

To link a peace-keeping operation to a payment plan is well worth exploring, but there are some problems to be kept in mind. The commitment to pay would still be unenforceable. More important, it would probably be more difficult under such conditions to get a peace-keeping resolution through the Assembly in the first place. In the meantime, the crisis might get out of hand. The question must therefore be asked whether it is better to rush troops to a trouble spot and worry about payment later, or to make sure at the outset that the United Nations can pay its bills.

All things considered, the prospects for strengthening the financial basis of United Nations peace-keeping operations are not auspicious in the present setting. The member states may well have to decide whether they want the Organization to engage in activities of the UNEF or ONUC type in the future. A sizable United States loan and a drastic cutback in the two Forces might alleviate the immediate financial crisis, but such stop-gap measures do not augur well for the long-term financial health and stability of the United Nations.

Voluntary Contributions

As regards the voluntary programs, there has been some discussion, noted earlier, concerning the possibility of integrating those with a broad membership base into the regular United Nations budget. For example, the Commission to Study the Organization of Peace (a private United States group) proposed in 1957 that the voluntary programs be consolidated under a "programmatic budget" and be made a part of the assessed responsibilities of member states.[51] Despite the logic of this argument, any such consolidation is highly unlikely. As our previous analysis has shown, many states contribute to the assessed budgets and the voluntary programs in different ratios and would insist that the budgets be kept separate. Moreover, voluntary programs with only a local or regional impact, like UNRWA and the Congo Fund, would be even more difficult to consolidate. In all probability, the voluntary programs will continue their independent financing indefinitely.

The basic problem confronting the voluntary programs is to increase the funds available to them. Is there any way of increasing government contributions within the existing framework? The only instrument devised so far has been the General Assembly's Negotiating Committee for Extra-Budgetary Funds. The *raison d'être* of this Committee is to persuade governments to pledge more generous contributions to the voluntary programs. The major technique it has employed is the device of publicity.

The Assembly at its twelfth session introduced the procedure of convening an *ad hoc* Committee of the Whole Assembly for the announcement of pledges of voluntary contributions to the two United Nations refugee programs. This procedure, repeated annually, was first adopted at the suggestion of the Negotiating Committee in an attempt, through the increased publicity, to focus attention on the problem of refugees and thus to bring about an improvement in the financial support of these programs. The Negotiating Committee has also recommended each year that, in order to ensure maximum attendance, as much advance publicity as possible be given to the pledging conferences and that they be scheduled at times when no other meetings are being held.[52]

It is difficult to assess the effectiveness of the Negotiating Committee. While it is true that pledges have risen in recent years, it is not likely that the Committee has exerted a major influence on the decisions of member states. In the last analysis, voluntary contributions are precisely what the term connotes—voluntary.

New Sources of Funds

A brief word should be said at this juncture about a group of proposals that aim to strengthen the financial structure of the United Nations by providing the Organization with an income independent of the contributions of member states. All these recommendations have two things in common: their feasibility has not been carefully explored, and their adoption, in most instances, would require amendments to the Charter or major changes in the structure of the United Nations. Yet some of these proposals have been in the air for several years and in the light of the continuing financial crisis merit renewed consideration.

Before proceeding to the proposals themselves, we must recall that the United Nations already engages in several revenue-producing activities. These are the sale of stamps by the United Nations Postal Administration, the sale of United Nations publications and television services, the operation of the Gift Shop, guided tours for visitors, and income from investments. To be sure, the net income derived from these activities amounts to little more than $2,000,000—less than 4 per cent of the regular budget. This is not questioned by governments, since the activities would not exist as sources of revenue were it not for the existence of the United Nations itself. Nevertheless, these activities have established the principle that the United Nations can have independent sources of revenue. All the following proposals are based on the assumption that this principle can be greatly extended.

First and least complicated, there is a group of suggestions envisaging modest increments in the existing independent income. For example, charges might be made for special services, such as the preparation, on request, of a paper on a given subject based on data in United Nations files, or the issuance of international health certificates through WHO, or even international radio licenses through ITU. At the present time, under the "Funds in Trust" arrangement, governments turn over funds to the Technical Assistance Board to recruit experts for purposes which cannot be encompassed in the Expanded Programme. A service charge might well be made for such activities, just as the International Bank charges interest rates on its funds.

A somewhat more ambitious proposal was advanced in 1957 by the Commission to Study the Organization of Peace, which noted that there were a number of public services now provided by national governments that were international in character. The Commission suggested that

it might be feasible to allow the United Nations to share a small part of the fees or excises for international mail or passports or visas—on the rationale that the United Nations helps to maintain a world of peaceful communication, trade, and travel. A fraction of the tolls levied upon an international waterway would be another possible source of revenue for the United Nations in this category.[53]

Only in one instance has the United Nations come close to this type of activity. It raised the funds for clearing the Suez Canal by levying a tax on shipping through the Canal. This was an emergency operation, however, and one unlikely to be soon repeated. Moreover, any tax imposed on private international carriers would run into vigorous opposition. There is also the question of whether such a toll would be fair. It may be argued that, after all, the United Nations helps to maintain a peaceful world just as much for those people who choose not to engage in international communication, commerce, or travel as for those who do. Hence, they too ought to be taxed. Alternatively, one might advocate that governments allocate in advance a proportion of their tax collections to the United Nations; although probably unfeasible politically, and difficult to work out in practice, this could bring considerably larger sums to the international organization. All proposals that envision working through established governmental collection machinery have the virtue that, if put into effect, they could be administered almost automatically.

Turning over to the United Nations licensing rights in certain as yet unexploited areas is an even bolder proposal. Antarctica, outer space, and the sea-beds beneath international waters have been suggested as being appropriately international. Even if governments were willing to forgo any existing or potential claims in these areas, however, the United Nations would be faced with many problems, for it would be required to make politically charged decisions almost daily vis-à-vis both governments and private interests.

Perhaps most ambitious of all are such suggestions as that of the Commission to Study the Organization of Peace that the United Nations itself be permitted to exploit the potentialities of the sea-bed and Antarctica. This would involve unprecedented grants of property rights and would certainly require considerable capital investment from sources which are not made clear and on which there might be only marginal returns. Before such a proposal could be evaluated in any meaningful fashion, there would certainly have to be a careful exploratory study of the resources themselves. In any event, the self-limitations by governments that would be required to effect such a proposal may be so great as to make it almost as visionary as proposals that the United Nations be allowed to establish taxes without the intervention of governments.

The best-known proposal of this last sort has been advanced by Grenville Clark and Louis B. Sohn,[54] whose scheme is predicated on successful disarmament and consequent savings in domestic budgets. The authors propose a system under which the United Nations would assign annual revenue quotas, not to exceed a total of 2 per cent of estimated gross world product, to the "people of each member state." These quotas would be collected and enforced through regular governmental machinery to avoid creating an elaborate new bureaucracy, but they would be kept distinct from and would, in fact, replace some national taxes. Which specific national taxes were to be replaced would be left to the choice of governments, provided the totals involved were large enough to fill the assigned quota. The monies collected would be turned over to a United Nations fiscal office established in each member state. The authors also proposed United Nations borrowing powers up to 5 per cent of gross world product.

It is readily apparent that the Clark-Sohn proposal and others hoping to invest the United Nations with taxing or borrowing powers, even indirectly, are premature. Quite apart from the fact that nations have regarded the area of taxation as exclusively within their national jurisdiction, there are other questions which must be raised. Would not a United Nations tax cause resentment among people and lose support for the world organization? Could agreement be found on equitable criteria of taxation for the people of countries in varying circumstances? What, if anything, can be done about states which refuse to cooperate?

On surveying the proposals for strengthening the United Nations financial structure, one is impressed by the number and tenacity of the obstacles. In the words of one scholar, "the critical weakness of existing proposals is that they require for adoption conditions within the United Nations which do not prevail at this stage of the Organization's development."[55] The common denominator of all these obstacles is, of course, the issue of national sovereignty. Nations are most reluctant to supply the United Nations with greater revenues, let alone an independent income. They want to be in a position to withhold their financial support in the event that they disapprove of what the Organization is doing. To relinquish a measure of control over United Nations purse strings would be to relinquish a measure of control over United Nations programs. Some member states do not yield an inch on this point, others are willing to take a first step, and a few have already made a beginning. These differing conceptions of what constitutes the national interest may well hold the key to the financial future of the Organization.

The politics of United Nations financing confronts each nation with its own peculiar dilemma which it must attempt to resolve in accordance with the dictates of its national interest.

The fiscal policy of the United States has vacillated between two different views as to what constitutes the meaning of the United Nations to the United States national interest. At times the United States has viewed the Organization as a vehicle for the furtherance of its own interests, in very much the same manner as it has tended to view its alliances. But at other times—and this has been no less prominent—the United States has perceived the United Nations as a neutral mediator in the East-West and in the colonial and anti-colonial struggles.

As the richest nation and the largest donor country, the United States could dominate the finances of the United Nations without much difficulty. Indeed, it does this already to a considerable extent. The complete dependence of UNKRA upon United States support was a case in point. Here the United Nations clearly became a vehicle for United States interests. On the other hand, the United States tends to be inhibited by its conception of the world organization as neutral ground. Take, for instance, its reluctance to "bail out" the Congo operation or the insistence that its contribution to EPTA and the Special Fund must not exceed 40 per cent of the total. Such a course seems to be dictated not only by fears of being made the financial goat, but by a genuine conviction that the United States national interest would not be furthered by a policy of fiscal domination.

The United States had no problem in reconciling these two conceptions in the case of the two peace-keeping activities in the Middle East and the Congo. Both these activities coincided with United States interest in preventing any unilateral intervention by a great power; both UNEF and ONUC were operations that specifically excluded the great powers. Thus, the ideal of a neutral international organization, too, was fulfilled. The United States has never been tested in a situation in which it might be called upon to take a stand on a United Nations peace-keeping operation that it might define as inimical to its national interest. Would the United States, for example, be willing to pay its assessed share of a Peace Force dispatched by the General Assembly to shore up the revolutionary government of Fidel Castro in Cuba?

In only one instance did the United States government face a direct fiscal conflict between its two views of the United Nations. In June 1961 the Governing Council of the Special Fund debated the merits of forty-two projects in thirty-six countries. One of these was a five-year development program in Cuba for which over $1,000,000 was to be allocated. Washington was deeply divided on this issue. Many members of the executive branch favored the "neutral ground" concept and were ready to vote for the Cuban project, hoping to keep the cold war out of economic development programs. But heavy pressure on the Congress finally resulted in a negative attitude. The United States found itself in the embarrassing situation of being the sole opponent of the Cuban project. The United States delegate justified his opposition by declaring that the unstable economic conditions in Cuba made the project a bad risk. But the fact that the United States had voted for a comparable project in the Republic of Korea in the wake of a military *coup d'état* was not lost upon the other delegates on the Fund's Governing Council.

This story should not be construed as a criticism of United States fiscal policy. It does point out, however, an extreme ambivalence in the United States view of the United Nations. And when the chips are down, the pressure to employ the United Nations as a vehicle of United States interest becomes very difficult to resist.

The Soviet attitude has the virtue of consistency, but little else. Its minority position in the United Nations had led it to view with growing uneasiness the shift from the Security Council, where it has a veto, to the General Assembly. Recent events, particularly United Nations action in the Congo, have confirmed its fears that the Organization can and will act on occasion despite violent Soviet opposition. Participation in economic development programs, however, presents the USSR with a different kind of problem since abstention would leave an appealing field to the Western powers. Thus the Soviet Union has seen its national interest in the making of small contributions to the economic development programs. The amounts contributed are too small to constitute a drain, but large enough to give the Soviet Union a voice in the administration of most of the voluntary programs. And since these are aimed largely at the uncommitted countries, the Soviet Union considers its participation of great importance.

The new nations face their own unique dilemma in the determination of fiscal policy. As far as the peace-keeping operations are concerned, they are ambivalent. On the one hand, they consider UNEF and ONUC of great value since, after all, "it could happen here." Many regard the sealing off of their countries from the East-West struggle as central to their national interest. But, on the other hand, they can ill afford the relatively large expense of such sealing-off operations. No such ambivalence exists in their view of the voluntary programs. These are clearly intended for their benefit and the policy of many of the new nations to pay a larger proportion of funds to the economic development programs than to the assessed regular budget is merely a recognition of this fact.

The above analysis demonstrates that the national interest of all member states dictates a policy of fiscal caution. This caution is manifest in varying degrees: relatively mild in the case of the United States and the Western nations; far more pronounced in the policies of the new and uncommitted nations; and so intense in the case of the Soviet Union and other East European countries as to result in an attitude of downright miserliness.

These varying degrees of national penury toward the world

organization stem from the fact that nations are reluctant to make the United Nations the primary vehicle of their national policies. Thus they are unwilling to invest heavily in it and this lack of financial support, of course, tends to relegate the Organization to even greater neglect. It may be difficult to break out of this circular predicament.

There may also be another, more unconscious reason for the attitude of national miserliness that shows through everywhere. If the Organization were to become too effective, popular loyalties might in the long run tend to be transferred to the United Nations, perhaps at the expense of national loyalties.[56] In a way, then, asking nations to finance a major expansion of United Nations activities might be asking them to finance their own obsolescence.

In the last analysis, the problem of financing the United Nations is not a problem of financing at all, but a problem of building world community. The difficulties which plague the financial structure of the Organization are only symptoms of the great ideological and political rifts which divide the contemporary international scene. The quest for technical formulae and fiscal remedies will probably not succeed unless it is preceded by more fundamental political accommodation. Such accommodation must await a greater degree of harmony among the differing conceptions of what member states want the United Nations to be: a conference forum with no executive or legislative powers—which is the goal of those wishing to "walk backwards into the future"; an organization with very limited and carefully circumscribed executive powers—which, with variations, is the view of most member states; or an organization of increasing independence and authority—more than the mere sum total of its parts—which was the aim of the late Secretary-General.

[1] See J. David Singer, "The Finances of the League of Nations," *International Organization*, Vol. 13, No. 2 (Spring 1959).

[2] See p. 60.

[3] *Budgetary and Financial Problems of the United Nations*, Staff Study No. 6, Dec. 1954, in *Review of the United Nations Charter: Compilation of Studies Prepared . . . Pursuant to S. Res. 126*, Subcommittee on the United Nations Charter, Cmtte. on For. Rel., U.S. Senate, 83rd Cong., 2nd Sess. (Washington, GPO, 1955), p. 160. Hereinafter cited as Senate Staff Study No. 6.

[4] By 1961 the U.S. per-capita assessment was exceeded only by Canada's.

[5] Senate Staff Study No. 6, p. 161.

6 J. David Singer, *Financing International Organization: The United Nations Budget Process* (The Hague, Martinus Nijhoff, 1961), chap. 8, *passim*. Not unexpectedly, in view of the Committee's political significance, a proposal has been submitted this year that it be enlarged to take account of the doubling in United Nations membership. See United Nations Doc. A/4916, 10 Oct. 1961. The Fifth Committee has since recommended that the Advisory Committee's membership be increased to twelve.

7 Singer, *Financing International Organization, op. cit.*, pp. 176-177.

8 For a complete analysis of the political and military implications of UNEF, see William R. Frye, *A United Nations Peace Force* (New York, Oceana for the Carnegie Endowment for International Peace, 1957).

9 United Nations General Assembly, *Official Records* (GAOR); 11th Sess., 5th Cmtte., 541st Mtg., 3 Dec. 1956, para. 79.

10 *Ibid.*, 545th Mtg., 6 Dec. 1956, para. 3.

11 *Ibid.*, 547th Mtg., 10 Dec. 1956, para. 4.

12 General Assembly Res. 1089 (XI), 21 Dec. 1956.

13 For a detailed study of UNEF financing, see Gabriella Rosner, *The United Nations Emergency Force*, Chap. 7 (unpub. doctoral dissertation, Columbia Univ., New York, 1961).

14 United Nations Security Council, *Official Records* (SCOR): 15th Year, Suppl. for July-Sept. 1960 (Doc. S/4387), p. 16.

15 SCOR: 15th Year, 877th Mtg., 20/21 July 1960, para. 9.

16 See GAOR: 15th Sess., Annexes, Agenda items 49/50 (A/4676, paras. 7, 10). Adopted as General Assembly Res. 1583 (XV), 20 Dec. 1960.

17 GAOR: 15th Sess., 5th Cmtte., 775th Mtg., 26 Oct. 1960, para. 8.

18 United Nations Doc. A/C.5/843, 21 Nov. 1960, pp. 1, 8.

19 General Assembly Res. 1590 (XV), 20 Dec. 1960.

20 See United Nations Docs. A/4703, 1 Mar. 1961, pp. 5-6, and A/4713, 4 Mar. 1961, p. 11.

21 See GAOR: 15th Sess., Annexes, Agenda items 49/50 (A/C.5/860, 27 Mar. 1961), and United Nations Doc. A/PV.977, 5 Apr. 1961, p. 11.

22 GAOR: 15th Sess., Annexes, Agenda items 49/50 (A/C.5/862, para. 42; and A/C.5/863).

23 *Ibid.* (A/C.5/864, para. 17).

23a On 30 Oct. the Assembly authorized the Secretariat to commit up to $10,000,000 a month for the remainder of 1961. However, it left the mode of financing for "later deliberations."

24 See *ibid.* (A/4740, para. 11). Amended and adopted as General Assembly Res. 1620 (XV), 21 Apr. 1961.

25 These were: Australia, Canada, Central African Republic, Ceylon, Dahomey, Denmark, Finland, Gabon, Iceland, India, Ireland, Ivory Coast, Japan, Liberia, Malaya, Netherlands, New Zealand, Nigeria, Norway, Pakistan, Tunisia, Turkey, United Kingdom, United States. See Table 2, pp. 20-21.

26 Some specialized agencies also make use of the voluntary-contribution device. WHO's Special Account for malaria eradication, for example, amounted to almost $5,000,000 in 1960, and IAEA's annual pledging conference in 1960 produced over $1,000,000 for programs under its Voluntary Fund in addition to special offers to finance specified projects.

27 The 1960-61 members of the Negotiating Committee are: Brazil, Canada, France, Ghana, Ireland, Norway, Pakistan, Senegal, United Kingdom, and United States.

28 For a review of UNICEF financing, see Ellen Frey-Wouters, *The United Nations Children's Fund* (unpub. doctoral dissertation, Columbia Univ., New York, 1958), chap. 4.

29 Brazil, India, Iran, Italy, Japan, Mexico, Philippines, Turkey, and Yugoslavia.

*　　　　*　　　　*

36 Part of the increase is due to a decision by the United States to include in its pledge the matching of local-cost contributions of recipient countries.

37 Report No. 90, 82nd Cong., 1st Sess., pp. 69-70, cited in Senate Staff Study No. 6, p. 170.

38 Robert Loring Allen, "United Nations Technical Assistance: Soviet and East European Participation," *International Organization*, Vol. 11, No. 4 (Autumn 1957).

39 Senate Staff Study No. 6, p. 169.

40 United Nations Doc. A/4776, 14 June 1961, para. 151.

41 United Nations Doc. A/4794, 30 June 1961, p. 17.

42 Quoted in Senate Staff Study No. 6, p. 165.

43 GAOR: 5th Sess., Annexes, Agenda item 39 (A/1734), p. 62.

44 Elmore Jackson, among others, suggested this in a speech before the Eleventh Annual Conference of National Organizations, Washington, D.C., in Mar. 1961.

45 GAOR: 15th Sess., 5th Cmtte., 769th Mtg., 18 Oct. 1960, para. 22.

46 *Ibid.*, 14th Sess., 5th Cmtte., 758th Mtg., 3 Dec. 1959, para. 14.

47 *Ibid.*, 15th Sess., 5th Cmtte., 823rd Mtg., 19 Dec. 1960, para. 54.

48 See Senate Staff Study No. 6, pp. 174-175.

49 *Ibid.*, p. 176.

50 See p. 30.

51 *Strengthening the United Nations* (New York, Harper, 1957), pp. 258-259, 262.

52 See GAOR: 15th Sess., Annexes, Agenda item 55 (A/4623).

53 *Strengthening the United Nations, op. cit.*, pp. 260-261.

54 *World Peace Through World Law*, 2nd ed., rev. (Cambridge, Harvard Univ. Press, 1960).

55 Calvin J. Nichols, "Financing the United Nations: Problems and Prospects" (Cambridge, M.I.T. Center for International Studies, 1961), p. 28.

56 For discussion of this point, see Singer, *Financing International Organization, op. cit.*, p. 178.

THE UNITED NATIONS DEVELOPMENT DECADE

Proposals for action

Report of the Secretary-General

UNITED NATIONS

New York, 1962

FOREWORD

The basic problem in the present situation is to find ways in which the express desire of the advanced countries to help the developing countries can be translated into effective action. New methods of technical co-operation, added to those already well tried, will have to be found to take full advantage of the new economic and technological possibilities which have emerged in recent years.

The main economic objective for the decade is to create conditions in which the national incomes of the developing countries not only will be increasing by 5 per cent yearly by 1970, but will also continue to expand at this annual rate thereafter. If this can be done, and if the population of the developing countries continues to rise at its present rate of 2 to 2½ per cent yearly, personal living standards can be doubled within twenty-five to thirty years. If, however, the growth of population should be even more rapid by the end of the decade than it is now—and there are indications that in a number of countries the annual rate of increase is already 3 per cent or higher—it will take correspondingly longer to double living standards.

This objective for 1970 is within our reach, given a greater willingness among both the developing and the advanced countries to make the efforts and sacrifices required. And yet it is ambitious, for if achieved it would open up for a significant number of under-developed countries the prospect of a real improvement in their conditions of life. In particular, it offers hope for the younger generation of today.

A better understanding of the nature of development has resulted in the clarification of a number of issues as being irrelevant to the fundamental problems of development; for example, the demarcation of the public and private sectors in economic life, agricultural development *versus* industrial development, and education *versus* vocational training. There has perhaps been less progress in recognizing the nature of the relationship between aid policies and trade policies, but even here there are signs that a more enlightened view may be making headway.

Meanwhile, there has been increasing appreciation of the need for a number of new approaches. These include:

1. The concept of national planning—for social as well as for economic development. This is central to all the proposals for intensified action by the United Nations system during the development decade outlined in this report. Former objections to planning, based largely on a misunderstanding of the role envisaged for the private sector in most development plans, have died away. It is now generally appreciated that the purpose of a development plan is to provide a programme of action for the achievement of targets based on realistic studies of the resources available. Planning is proving to be a potent tool for the mobilization of existing and latent resources—human and material, public and private, domestic and external—available to countries for the achievement of their development aims. It has been shown that vigorous efforts are more likely to result if national and sectoral objectives are defined and translated into action programmes.

2. There is now greater insight into the importance of the human factor in development, and the urgent need to mobilize human resources. Economic growth in the advanced countries appears to be attributable in larger part than was previously supposed to human skills rather than to capital. Moreover, the widening of man's horizons through education and training, and the lifting of his vitality through better health, are not only essential pre-conditions for development, they are also among its major objectives. It is estimated that the total number of trained people in the developing countries must be increased by at least 10 per cent a year if the other objectives of the decade are to be achieved.

3. One of the most serious problems facing the developing countries is increasing under-employment and unemployment. This increase is not confined to countries already experiencing population pressures, although rapidly rising population is undoubtedly a major aggravating factor. Far-reaching action will be required if the fruits of economic progress are to benefit all the inhabitants of the world.

4. The disappointing foreign trade record of the developing countries is due in part to obstacles hindering the entry of their products into industrial markets, and in part to the fact that production of many primary commodities has grown more rapidly than demand for them. It is appreciated that "disruptive competition" from low-income coun-

tries may be felt by established industries in high-income countries. Yet, precisely because they are so advanced, the high-income countries should be able to alleviate any hardships without shifting the burden of adjustment to the developing countries by restricting the latter's export markets. A related problem to be solved is that of stabilizing the international commodity markets on which developing countries depend so heavily. Progress could certainly be made if the main industrial countries were to devote as much attention to promoting trade as to dispensing aid.

5. The acceptance of the principle of capital assistance to developing countries is one of the most striking expressions of international solidarity as well as enlightened self-interest. If such assistance increases to, and maintains, a level of 1 per cent of the national incomes of the advanced countries during the development decade, as suggested by the General Assembly, this will represent yet another essential contribution to the success of the decade. At the same time, there is a need for pragmatism and flexibility in determining the forms of capital flows and aid, in relation both to the needs of the developing countries and to the shifting balance of payments position of assisting countries.

6. Towards the end of the fifties the importance of laying an adequate groundwork for large-scale investment programmes came to be widely recognized. Many developing countries lack any detailed knowledge of their resources. However, even where potential investment opportunities can be identified, it may be impossible to implement them in the absence of one or more of the necessary factors of production—labour, capital, and entrepreneurial and technical skills. Within the United Nations, the Special Fund has concentrated on pre-investment work, paying special attention to surveys and feasibility studies of natural resources, technical and vocational training and the establishment of institutions for applied research. It is estimated that total expenditure on pre-investment work must rise to a level of about $1 billion a year by 1970, if the objectives of the decade are to be reached. This is about double the present rate of expenditure.

7. A crucial area for intensified pre-investment activity is the surveying and development of natural resources, including water, minerals and power. In the development of water resources, in particular, the United Nations system may have a significant part to play. Nearly all the world's great rivers flow through several countries, and their development is a problem requiring regional and international cooperation.

8. The potentialities of modern technology and new methods of research and development for attacking the problems of the developing countries are as yet only dimly perceived. Since the Second World War it has become clear that new techniques permit the solution of most scientific and technical problems once they are correctly posed. However, too little effort has been directed towards posing or solving the problems of the developing countries, although many of them would

appear to present no insuperable difficulties; for example, the problems involved in developing a sturdy piece of mechanical equipment which can be kept running with very little maintenance should be less than those involved in designing and launching a permanently operating space satellite. It also seems desirable to stimulate research on the social problems of developing countries entering upon a period of rapid social change.

9.   If the skills of the advanced countries are to be successfully adapted to the problems and conditions of the developing countries, the former must be willing and able to make available the necessary resources of skilled personnel. Indeed, it may be that the shortage of such highly skilled personnel, rather than a shortage of material resources or finance, will be the greatest obstacle to action in the development decade unless new steps are taken. Technical co-operation field workers or field-teams should no longer be isolated but work in close contact with those institutions in the advanced countries which have most knowledge of the problems they will encounter. Ways must also be found for the foreign experts to participate in setting up institutions which will take over and carry forward their work when they leave.

The success of the United Nations development decade in achieving its objectives will depend in large part on the application of such new approaches. Precisely because they are new, all their implications cannot yet be fully seen. They may be expected to change many existing attitudes and approaches.

The report which follows contains a number of suggestions for the intensification of the existing activities of the United Nations system, together with proposals for new deparures. These range over a wide area of development problems. But an attempt has been made, in every case, to identify those areas in which action by the United Nations system might be expected to have the maximum leverage effect on development as a whole, and the maximum linkage effect in promoting advances in other sectors.

U THANT
Acting Secretary-General

I. SETTING AND PROBLEMS FOR THE DEVELOPMENT DECADE

A. The preceding decade—achievements and remaining problems

During the previous decade there was valuable progress in various directions clearing the way for intensified action during the present decade. It came to be generally recognized that the progress of under-developed countries in solving this problem was accepted. This principle economy, and the principle of partnership of the developed and under-developed countries in solving this problem was accepted. This principle of international solidarity was not previously applied beyond national boundaries. The resolution adopted by the General Assembly at the beginning of the development decade on "Concerted action for economic development of economically less-developed countries"[1] signifies the acceptance of this principle. A number of other points won general acceptance.

(i) The developing countries came more and more to realize that their share of the joint responsibility would include not only great efforts and sacrifices, but also departures from traditions and the making of economic and social reforms as the price of goals which they might set themselves for more rapid improvement of their standard of living. Consequently, their efforts came to be expressed more and more in national plans for economic and social development.

(ii) The newly accepted principle of solidarity expressed itself in greater willingness to give assistance to developing countries. Actual aid rendered increased steadily year by year and constituted a slowly rising proportion of the national incomes of the wealthier as well as the poorer countries. This is also reflected in the increased rate of lending by the International Bank and the doubling of its capital. Moreover, a recognition has been growing that part of the assistance would have to be in forms adjusted to the repayment capacity of developing countries, if it were to be consistent with its primary purpose of promoting development. The creation of the IDA expresses this recognition most clearly, as do also the unanimously agreed principles of financing development formulated within the General Assembly Committee on a United Nations Capital Development Fund.[2] There is also growing evidence of a desire to co-ordinate assistance in its various forms and sources, including plans for the mobilization of the domestic resources of the developing countries.

---

[1] General Assembly resolution 1515 (XV).
[2] Document E/3514, paragraph 23.

(iii) The need for and techniques of development planning have been greatly clarified. They are no longer confused with unrelated extraneous issues, such as the demarcation of the public and private sectors in economic life, or the policies of a country in relation to its natural resources and foreign investors. Other irrelevant issues, such as agricultural development *versus* industrialization or infrastructure *versus* the production of goods, have also largely been disposed of. The purpose of development was also clarified as including "proper regard for its human and social aspects".[3] Thus, the ground has been cleared for a non-doctrinaire consideration of the real problems of development, namely saving, training and planning, and for action on them. In particular, the advantages of dealing with the various problems not piecemeal, but by a comprehensive approach through sound development planning, became more fully apparent.

(iv) The need for international action to solve problems arising from the structural weakness and instability of the terms of trade, and the consequent effect on export markets of developing countries, came to be recognized and some useful experiences and proposals were gathered during the 1950's.

(v) The decade also saw the growth of the idea of international technical co-operation and pre-investment activity, and towards the end of the decade there was spreading awareness of the great potential of latent resources and latent investment opportunities. The creation of the United Nations Special Fund[4] is an expression of this tendency.

(vi) Recently there has also been much more widespread realization of the importance of the human factor in economic development. Research and experience have indicated that the contribution of physical capital alone is by no means as dominant as had at one time been imagined. This realization opened up new approaches—through education, training, community development, use of idle manpower and eradication of disease—to using the vast latent human resources of the developing countries. While at the beginning of the last decade the problem of developing countries was viewed essentially as a problem of producing wealth, by the end of the decade it became widely acknowledged that the crucial factor was not production but rather the *capacity* to produce, which is inherent in people.

(vii) It was also increasingly recognized that social reform and economic strategy are two sides of the same coin, the single strategy of development. This realization came about through several intermediate stages in which an original opposition of these two ideas was replaced by a parallelism expressed in such terms as "balanced economic and social development". This ultimate identity can be best expressed by saying that the problem of the under-developed countries is not just growth, but development. Development is growth *plus* change; change,

---

[3] General Assembly resolution 1515 (XV), paragraph 3 (*e*).
[4] General Assembly resolution 1240 (XIII).

in turn, is social and cultural as well as economic, and qualitative as well as quantitative. It should no longer be necessary to speak of "economic and social development", since development—as distinct from growth—should automatically include both. A direct corollary of this new approach to development was that the purely economic indicators of progress were seen to provide only limited insight and might conceal as much as they indicated.

(viii) Trends toward regional co-operation of developing countries became apparent and developed strongly towards the end of the decade. In this, the United Nations system played an important role.

(ix) The decade saw the building up of international administrations as instruments for international action.

(x) There was also great progress in specific directions, of which perhaps control of certain diseases was particularly striking. As a result, the gap between poor and wealthier countries has been closing in terms of life expectancy—as distinct from incomes. There was also substantial gain in education.

These are indispensable foundations on which to build for a decade of development. The achievement has been described by the Committee on Programme Appraisals in its *Five-Year Perspective, 1960-1964,*[5] in the following words: "Great headway has been made in fact-finding and the establishment of internationally comparable statistics and other data. More than a start has been made in ascertaining needs and defining problems which call for action, private and public, national and international. Objectives have been formulated and standards set. Above all, through technical assistance a world-wide transfer and interchange of knowledge and technology has been organized, which lies at the very basis of economic and social development. As a result of all this, international organizations have become a potent factor in stimulating action by national governments and in assisting them in their efforts to improve economic conditions and raise levels of living."

The clarification of issues and problems and the broad agreement on many approaches are reflected in the decisions on economic and social development reached by the General Assembly, the Economic and Social Council and other United Nations bodies. The most recent sessions of various United Nations bodies have witnessed wide agreement on certain key approaches which would help the developing countries to cross the threshold of development. Accordingly, the decisions and recommendations made specifically during the first two years of the development decade provide a valuable framework for intensified United Nations and international action in the years to come. Their value is further enhanced by the fact that they usually embody the concurrence or agreement of a large number of countries at various stages of development and with different social or political systems.

---

[5] United Nations publication. Sales No.: 60.IV.14, page 95.

The Secretary-General has carefully taken into account the views of governments and the agreement reached as expressed in these decisions. He believes that his proposals are in accord with them.

But cnanges have occurred which have led to the development of new types of problems, demanding new techniques and approaches and new thinking. In this, all agencies have contributions to make in ideas, policies and execution. Together with the greater emphasis on planning by Governments, there should be an improvement of the existing mechanisms for co-ordination of policies and execution, not only amongst the various parts of the United Nations system but between it and the non-United Nations agencies now active in the field and the substantial bilateral programmes.

A number of unsolved problems of the last decade seem to call for the most urgent treatment during the development decade. They constitute a great challenge to the United Nations organizations, as they do primarily to the people and Governments of the developing countries and those wishing to assist them. Among them are the following:

(i) In spite of the progress made in reaching agreement on principles in the field of development planning, in clarification of concepts and development techniques, and in spite of some conspicuous examples of successful and purposeful planning, the general picture was still one in which the majority of countries had either no development plans, or at best had elements of development plans in the form of general projections, or public investment programmes, or plans lacking in implementation. In most cases, the factual information required to draw up such action programmes is still lacking, as are also the planning skills to use and interpret the information. A true development plan, which is an action programme for the public and private sectors of the economy alike, takes full account of the necessary sacrifices and mobilizes the necessary resources, and offers opportunities for the development of the latent resources of the country. This kind of plan is still the exception rather than the rule.

(ii) Primary commodity prices were at a high level in the early part of the last decade, but as it went on they tended to grow progressively weaker. The proceeds which under-developed countries derived from export sales of primary commodities or of manufactured goods clearly failed to develop the dynamic growth which would be necessary to finance their economic development at acceptable growth rates. This was all the more disappointing since international trade, as a whole, showed sufficient dynamism to serve as a basis for financing economic development, if only the share of under-developed countries in the trade total could have been maintained. The well maintained stable growth in the main industrial countries was seen to be insufficient by itself to give greater stability to commodity prices. There were a number of reasons for this, including a failure to treat the exports of developing countries in a manner in keeping with the recognized primary importance of the development of these exports for the balanced growth of the world economy.

(iii) As regards long-term capital flows and assistance, the total net flow to low-income countries increased considerably during the later part of the decade (more rapidly than the national incomes of the wealthier countries or of the receiving countries), but remained considerably less than 1 per cent of the combined national incomes of the wealthier countries. In spite of some progress, much of it was still made available on a basis offering no real assurance of its continuity to individual countries; it remained split up amongst a multiplicity of sources, forms and purposes; the share of multilateral aid through the United Nations system remained small. There was no clear evidence that a satisfactory basis had been found for a sustained, assured and more widely distributed flow of private capital to developing countries, nor indeed was it certain that such a flow could be expected until development had gathered more momentum. In any case, the mounting pressure of commitments for repayment of principal and interest or profits on previous investments, combined with the uncertainty and lack of dynamism of export earnings in many under-developed countries, underscored the importance of increasing the proportion of assistance in forms that would bear less heavily on the balance of payments than conventional loans. Furthermore, the fall in commodity prices in recent years has nullified much of the net increase in the assistance given to the developing countries.

(iv) Agricultural output in the developing countries increased only a little faster during the past decade than their populations. In Asia and the Far East, calorie and animal protein supplies per person are only just back to pre-war levels. In the other under-developed regions calorie supplies per person are above pre-war levels, but animal protein supplies per person are still below pre-war levels. The disparity in standards of nutrition is now greater than ever, and the number of human beings living in conditions of hunger and malnutrition is now larger than ever before in the history of the world. The rise in agricultural productivity is not sufficient at the present rate to provide the surpluses which are essential if the industrialization of the under-developed countries and accelerated growth of national incomes are to be achieved.

(v) Industrial output *per caput* increased in the developing countries during the 1950's at a rate equal to or even slightly higher than that achieved in the more advanced countries. Welcome as this fact is, only limited comfort can be derived from it, in view of the extremely small base which makes comparisons less than meaningful. While industrialization is gradually developing, manufacturing industry still accounts for less than one-fifth of the low output of the under-developed countries, and the volume of employment thus far provided by industrialization has been insufficient to prevent growing unemployment and under-employment in the developing countries.

(vi) There has been too little effort to bring science and technology to bear upon the special problems of the under-developed countries. In part, this is due to the continuing and increasing burden of armaments which makes it more difficult to direct scientific and technological attention to the problems of the developing countries. Heavy financial resources and skilled personnel, part of which might otherwise be devoted to the problems of the developing countries, are pre-empted by the armaments race. Even allowing for the continuing claims of armaments, however, it should be possible, when allocating the resources available for research and development, to allot a more reasonable priority to those problems which are of particular importance to developing countries. In the past, countries starting economic development have historically shown faster growth rates than the older industrial countries, since they were able to benefit from the accumulated stock of knowledge and technology. This historical sequence provided an element of equalization and balanced growth in the world economy until 1914, or perhaps 1929, but it has since ceased to do so. In fact, some of the older developed countries are among those with the highest growth rates. Thus, the accumulating stock of knowledge may no longer become increasingly useful to the under-developed countries, certainly not in proportion to its accumulation. Apart from the crucial lack of trained people capable of using advances in technology, the heavy capital requirements of new processes, the large scale on which they operate and their orientation towards advanced sectors make advanced technology less and less directly applicable—without deliberate direction and heavy adaptation—to the specific needs of the developing countries.

(vii) Although there has been increasing recognition that the ultimate objective of economic development is social progress, and that social reform is a necessary condition of economic improvement, these principles have not yet come to guide practical policies everywhere. Continued neglect of the social aspects of economic development might result either in stagnation in economic progress or violent reversal of the existing social order.

Thus the picture at the opening of the development decade is mixed. The under-developed countries have been making progress. Some of them developed quite rapidly—enough to demonstrate the potential of sustained growth of under-developed economies. These developing countries have usually been in an intermediate position already approaching the income levels of the more developed countries. Taken as a group, the rate of progress of the under-developed countries measured by income *per caput* has been painfully slow, more of the order of 1 per cent per annum than 2 per cent. Most indices of social progress show similar slow and spotty improvement. Moreover, the progress actually achieved in under-developed countries has often been uneven, limited to certain sectors of their economy or to certain regions or groups of countries. As a result, the disparities in levels of living within

418

under-developed countries are often as pronounced as those between developed and developing countries taken as a whole.

Progress toward a higher average level of living in the world as a whole is held back also by the shifting balance of population distribution which results from higher rates of population growth in developing countries than in wealthier countries. As the developing countries account for a larger and larger proportion of world population increases, they tend to offset the improvement of conditions in the world as a whole which would otherwise be brought about by the gains in individual countries. At any rate, the actual number of human beings living in distress and unacceptable poverty has almost certainly increased rather than diminished. This is the combined result of the rapid growth of population in the poorer countries and their failure to join fully in the general march of progress. Even in education, a field in which many under-developed countries have made important achievements during the last decade, the progress has not been enough to justify any complacency. In spite of the efforts to stamp out illiteracy, the number of illiterate people may increase, rather than diminish, as a result of the relentless growth of population. In India, for example, although the census figures for 1951 and 1961 show an increase of more than 40 million during the decade in the number of persons able to. read and write, even this accomplishment was not enough to prevent the number of illiterates from increasing by more than 11 million in the age group 5 years and over.[6]

B. Objectives of the Development Decade

Given the will to succeed, the first task is to define the objective. In this matter guidance is provided by the basic General Assembly resolution 1710 (XVI). The objective is to:

> "... accelerate progress towards self-sustaining growth of the economy of the individual nations and their social advancement so as to attain in each under-developed country a substantial increase in the rate of growth, with each country setting its own target, taking as the objective a minimum rate of growth of aggregate national income of 5 par cent at the end of the Decade;"

The emphasis on the "individual nations" and on "each country setting its own target" is significant. The proposals of the Secretary-General are based on the same assumption, namely that the key to the problem of accelerating development can only be found in each individual country. Each country has to determine its specific objectives, conditions and

---

[6] For the purpose of this comparison, the census figures have been adjusted to take account of differences in geographical coverage of the 1951 and 1961 enumerations. The uncorrected figures show an even larger increase in the number of illiterates.

development potential, preferably embodied in a comprehensive development plan. In line therefore with the emphasis of the resolution, any global requirements for fulfilling these objectives can only be assessed during the second stage, as a result of examination and mutual agreement on the basis of national development plans. The collective will to succeed must be directed towards partnership in the implementation of national plans. It need hardly be said that this does not preclude—in fact, it necessitates—regional or even wider co-operation of under-developed countries with each other, nor does it in any way preclude global action where required, particularly in such matters as trade.

In so far as the resolution does provide a quantitative objective, it is to achieve a minimum annual rate of growth of aggregate national income of 5 per cent in all—or at the very least, the great majority—of the under-developed countries by 1970. It may perhaps be assumed that to achieve this minimum position at the end of the decade, the average rate of increase of the aggregate incomes of all under-developed countries during the remainder of the decade should not be less than 5 per cent and it would be desirable if towards the end of the decade it could be as high as 6 per cent or more. The magnitude of the global efforts required might be envisaged on the basis of these assumption.

The present best estimate is that the growth rate of national incomes of all under-developed countries, together, is about 3½ per cent per year. The immediate task, therefore, will be to raise this growth rate during the coming few years by perhaps 1½ per cent to at least 5 per cent and to increase this rate by a further 1½ per cent to over 6 per cent per annum at the end of the decade. It must be emphasized, however, that the real objective of the development decade cannot be formulated in global terms, but must be decided country by country, with minimum country targets in view.

A growth rate of aggregate real incomes of 5 per cent per annum —assuming a continuation of the present rate of population increase— would permit a doubling of the personal standard of living (even given the necessary rates of savings and re-investment of incremental incomes) within a period of twenty-five to thirty years; this would mean a real improvement within the working lifetime of individual citizens. It should be emphasized, however, that a 5 per cent annual increase in aggregate national income would not be enough to bring a very rapid rise in *per caput* income in the countries where population is growing most rapidly. Rates of population growth in a number of African, Asian, and Latin American countries have recently risen into the range of 3 to 3½ per cent per annum and a projection of recent mortality trends implies that population growth at such rates is likely to become more and more prevalent in these parts of the world during the next decade, unless the birth rates drop sharply. Under these conditions, a 5 per cent increase in aggregate income would correspond to an annual increase of only 1½ to 2 per cent in *per caput* income and 35 to 50 years would be required to double *per caput* income.

It is useful to realize that a special premium or bonus is attached to any intensification of progress in under-developed countries. If the rate of growth of aggregate incomes is 3 per cent, while population increases by 2 per cent, the improvement of the average standard of living would only be 1 per cent and two-thirds of the increase is required to provide for the increase in population. But if the increase in aggregate income is doubled to 6 per cent, the improvement is raised from 1 per cent to 4 per cent; i.e., it is not doubled but quadrupled. This consideration should act as a special spur to intensify efforts, both within and outside the under-developed countries, to gain an early momentum and save in the long run on the resources needed for a task which all agree will have to be achieved sooner or later.

A related consideration is that if the acceleration of the rate of growth of incomes goes hand in hand with improvements in internal income distribution, and if the social benefits of the improvements are widespread, the number of people living below an acceptable minimum standard can be reduced at an even faster rate than the mere increase in aggregate income would suggest. It is true that the General Assembly resolution lays down a precise quantitative target only for the increase in aggregate incomes, and that there is no similar quantitative target for changes in income distribution. We can, however, take it for granted that the 5 per cent growth target established by the resolution also implies that the increment in income thus achieved should be wisely used for the benefit of the poorer sections of the population and should result in a degree of social progress which is at least in "balance" with the rise in aggregate national income. Normally, this would mean that the rise in aggregate incomes must be associated with an income distribution more equal, or at least not more unequal, than at present. The General Assembly in its resolution refers specifically to social advancement, social development, land reform, the elimination of illiteracy, hunger and disease, improvements in education and similar measures of social progress.

If a higher proportion of the increased incomes can be saved and productively invested or spent on training, education, research, discovery of natural resources and similar current developmental expenditures, the need for external assistance can be reduced.[7]

The above considerations should be an additional incentive to accelerating the growth of incomes in under-developed countries towards the target stipulated by the General Assembly. They also indicate the directions in which initial efforts should be primarily directed: the reduction of internal disparities within under-developed countries, the achievement of a high rate of savings and investment and the achieve-

---

[7] For instance, if one-fifth of the increased income generated were ploughed back into investment of reasonable productivity, external investment resources could be replaced by domestic investment within twelve to thirteen years. This statement refers to aggregate resources—the cessation of external investment resources might still create balance of payments difficulties for the developing country.

ment of a high level of training and current developmental expenditures. As will be seen, these guideposts determine the action programme for the development decade here proposed. The target can be achieved. The experience gained in the last decade, and specifically the experience of the United Nations system in its pre-investment as well as in the financing of activities enables us to say with virtual certainty that nearly all the under-developed countries have in their physical and human resources the potential means for achieving decent standards of living for their people. The problem is to mobilize these latent physical and human resources and get them into production.

We further know that careful development planning can be a potent means of mobilizing these latent resources by a rational solution of the problems involved.

A "real" development plan should cover at least the following elements:

(i) Objectives and aggregate targets, primarily in terms of national income and employment;

(ii) A public investment programme with distribution of development expenditures amongst major sectors, chiefly for building up the economic and social infrastructure;

(iii) A projection of private investment among various major sectors;

(iv) Policy measures (especially in the fiscal, financial, foreign trade, foreign exchange and foreign investment fields) to stimulate, direct and influence private investment;

(v) A programme, co-ordinated with (ii), for financing public and private investment from domestic and foreign sources, including particularly the government budget and foreign exchange budget;

(vi) Sectoral programmes containing individual projects; and

(vii) Policies aiming at basic institutional changes, including land reform, labour policy, etc.[8]

Real development planning involves a combination of all these elements in systematic relationship with one another. Provided that such a combination can be achieved—or even a reasonable approximation to such an ideal combination—experience shows that this in itself can serve to speed up present rates of progress significantly.

We may add that development planning is real only if it enrols the co-operation of people by basing development on their aspirations and using the results of development as a basis for social as well as economic progress. In the words of the Economic and Social Council's Committee on Programme Appraisals: "One of the greatest dangers in development policy lies in the tendency to give the more material

---

[8] This list is taken from "A Decade of Development Planning and Implementation in the ECAFE Region", ECAFE Conference of Asian Economic Planners, New Delhi, 1961.

aspects of growth an overriding and disproportionate emphasis. The end may be forgotten in preoccupation with the means. Human rights may be submerged and human beings seen only as instruments of production rather than as free entities for whose welfare and cultural advance the increased production is intended. The recognition of this issue has a profound bearing upon the formulation of the objectives of economic development and the methods employed in attaining them."[9]

The private inducement to invest and produce will also be greatly strengthened if the individual, planning his investment or activities, can see a picture of what is likely to happen in the rest of the economy. Uncertainty in regard to this picture will in itself reduce investment and thus contribute to stagnation. If the picture formed is one of balanced expansion, and if the Government's record inspires confidence that this expansion will be carried out, the effect may be to release powerful incentives to invest, and also to bring to light sources of finance for the additional investment thus motivated. Thus, if targets are reasonably set and consistently related, and if there is a will and an ability to implement them, they are more likely to be achieved than if they had never been set.

Another factor which will facilitate the achievement of the basic objective of the decade is the tremendous progress of modern science in developing techniques capable of expanding productivity enormously. It is true that this progress has so far been of limited value to the under-developed countries, for lack of specific direction towards their problems. This very neglect, however, implies the existence of a large potential of physical and human resources and of development planning.

The conclusion that these objectives, when considered as the objectives of a joint task, are within the means at the world's disposal, is also reached in relation to the external assistance which may be required during the decade. The national incomes of the wealthier countries are now a high multiple of the aggregate incomes of the developing countries, of the order of 10:1. This means that the diversion of comparatively small proportions of the national incomes of wealthier countries represents a major addition to the national incomes of the developing countries and an even greater addition to their possible volume of investment. A flow of capital representing 1 per cent of the incomes of the developed countries adds about 10 per cent to the national incomes of the under-developed countries, and about 100 per cent to their present net capital formation. If invested at a normal productivity ratio—which is based on the assumption of reasonable absorptive capacity and ability to mobilize the complementary domestic resources in the developing countries—this would result in an increase in their national incomes of about 3 per cent. As pointed out before, this process, if combined with a sufficiently high rate of savings and productive re-investment, could be self-terminating and growth could be-

[9] *Five-Year Perspective, 1960-1964,* United Nations publication, Sales No.: 60.IV.14, page 25.

come self-sustained, within a reasonable time. If the net flow of capital on suitable terms could be raised now to 1 per cent of the combined national incomes of the wealthier countries, and effectively used, this alone should raise the growth rate of aggregate incomes of developing countries at least half way from the present 3½ per cent to the initial target of 5 per cent each year.

The external foreign exchange resources required for increasing the growth rate of aggregate incomes from 3½ per cent to 5 per cent and later to 6 per cent and more, could also come from an improvement in the trade position of the developing countries. If their terms of trade could be improved by 10 per cent over the present level and kept at this level during the development decade this would go a long way to providing the additional resources required for the initial acceleration of growth. If, in addition, under-developed countries were also enabled to improve their present share in total world trade from 26 per cent to 28 per cent and maintain this share throughout the decade, within a total world trade expanding at recent rates, the foreign exchange requirements for the accelerated rate of growth would be covered. The startling thing about these hypothetical improvements is that they would do no more than restore the relative position of the under-developed countries during the mid-1950's. This, of course, should not be taken as implying that it will be easy to reverse the unfavourable trends in the trade of under-developed countries, some reasons for which are deep-rooted. Nor would the restored trade necessarily be the same kind of trade by commodities, direction or organization as in the 1950's. However, even with such qualifications, the above speculations as to the orders of magnitude involved should help us to see the task in its proper perspective.

Finally, reference should be made to the heavy expenditures on armaments which many countries now incur. The previous discussion has shown that the external means towards fulfilling the objectives of the development decade are within our grasp. This would be even more so if some measure of disarmament could be achieved during the decade.

The present expenditures on armaments alone are about equal to the aggregate of national incomes of all under-developed countries and about ten times their net capital formation. By the unanimous and since repeated General Assembly declaration, contained in resolution 724 (VIII), governments agreed to devote a portion of the savings achieved through internationally supervised world-wide disarmament to an international fund, within the framework of the United Nations, to assist development and reconstruction in under-developed countries. The implementation of this pledge would in itself go a long way towards providing the external resources required for the goals of the development decade. It can be estimated that the acceleration of growth of aggregate incomes in under-developed countries from perhaps 3½ per cent now to 5 per cent would require no more than the diversion of about 10 per cent of the savings resulting from a reduction in armament expenditures by one-half. The recent report, *The Economic and Social Consequences of Disarmament*,[10] pointed out that since

"the competing claims in developing countries are also urgent, there is a serious possibility that the financial resources released by disarmament might be rapidly absorbed by purely national aims. It is therefore desirable that an appropriate proportion of these resources should be allocated to international aid in its various forms simultaneously with their use for domestic purposes."

To state all these grounds for a cautious confidence that the basic objective of the development decade is feasible is in reality to state *tasks* which have to be completed to make our hopes come true. The very fact that these tasks have not yet been fully accomplished despite the progress made in the last few years is an indication that they are formidable. They are:

(i) The more systematic survey, development and utilization of physical and human resources in under-developed countries;

(ii) The formulation of true development plans providing for maximum mobilization of domestic resources and the effective utilization of external assistance;

(iii) An improvement in the machinery of administration, in institutions and in production incentives in order to meet the new and increased demands arising from these development plans;

(iv) A redirection of science and technology to increase the attention given to specific problems of low-income countries;

(v) An increase, and subsequent more vigorous growth, of the export earnings of under-developed countries;

(vi) An increased and a more assured flow of capital on suitable terms to the under-developed countries, to be further added to if the declaration adopted in General Assembly resolution 724 (VIII) is put into effect.

These six major tasks have to be performed in a specific setting which cannot be disregarded. Prominent features of this setting are the trend towards regional organizations of countries; the fact that many countries are newly independent or will be so during the development decade, with the consequence that African problems have come strongly to the foreground in the world picture; and the greatly heightened consciousness of social as well as economic objectives and of social as well as economic policies. Some elements of these new developments could help and some may hinder the achievement of the objectives of the development decade. It will therefore also be necessary to ensure that the potential affirmative contribution of these new developments is fully realized. The following proposals for intensified action in the fields of economic and social development by the United Nations system of organizations are submitted to Governments, with confidence that the task is feasible.

---

[10] United Nations publication, Sales No.: 62.IX.1.

II. THE APPROACH TO DEVELOPMENT PLANNING

In its *Five-Year Perspective, 1690-1964,* the Committee on Programme Appraisals of the Economic and Social Council reported two years ago that "National development plans are now an established pattern in many countries throughout the less developed regions of the world and their formulation and execution are a matter of profound concern to those countries.... These trends provide an opportunity that needs to be further developed for concerted action within the United Nations family".[1] As the previous chapter has explained, impressive unanimity has been achieved regarding the potential value of development planning, and progress has been made regarding methods. All the members of the United Nations system emphasize the enhanced effectiveness of their work if it can be linked with plans and policies reflecting firm and known priorities of the government, derived from a development plan. This applies both to planning in general and to plans for specific sectors such as education, agriculture, health, etc. The opportunity for concerted action, mentioned by the Committee on Programme Appraisals remains a major task of the development decade.

It is proposed that during the decade a high priority item for intensified action by the United Nations system should be assistance to each under-developed country which desires it in working out sound development plans, and assistance in carrying them out by the mobilization of its own resources and by securing supplementary external assistance and co-operation. The elements of a sound general plan have been previously described. The United Nations system itself should be willing and able to offer, or help any country to obtain, the full range of services required to prepare or revise such a development plan and action programme best suited to each country's resources and needs. It should also be able to offer services to increase the available information on these needs, resources and development potential as far as possible, in preparation for current or subsequent development plans.

It is far simpler to state these aims than it will be to achieve them, for they imply the availability of substantial resources, not only of funds but also of staff. To put into practice any substantial portion of the specific proposals made in this report would require the enlistment of a large number of economists, financial experts, engineers, sociologists, community planners and the like, that is to say staff possessing kinds of professional competence and skill which are already in short supply. Experience on both the international and national levels points to the practical difficulties of building up cadres of professional

---

[1] United Nations publication, Sales No.: 60.IV.14, page 91.

talent over a long term; to do so within the compass of a few years, as will be essential if the substantive objectives outlined in this report are to be realized within the next decade, will be that much harder.

In what follows in this chapter—as indeed in the rest of the report—references are made to the types of action the United Nations system has taken in the past and proposes to take in the future. The proposals made in this report do not in any way pre-judge the question as to which particular branch of the United Nations system would take the leadership in the action proposed. Normally, the action proposed in this report for the United Nations system refers to action by the Organization and/or one or several of the related agencies working in concert.

The area for action taken by the United Nations system can be conceived in three stages: first, help in obtaining information for planning, in the establishment of planning machinery and in methods of planning; second, help in the formulation of the plan; and third, assistance in implementing the plan. To achieve these objectives will require a number of steps, many of them in the nature of intensifying action already taken or possible now, while others would open up new fields of activity for the United Nations system.

The role here proposed for the United Nations system in helping countries to work out development plans may not by any means apply uniformly to all developing countries in all regions. In fact, the exact role and scope of United Nations support is likely to be different in each country. For instance, some countries may perhaps prefer to work out their strategy directly with regional or bilateral development assistance agencies.

Some developing countries have attained by themselves satisfactory methods of planning, and may need limited or no assistance. It is believed, however, that a number of countries would find it difficult to work out a proper development plan by themselves and would prefer to receive major assistance in this area from within the United Nations system. Particular reference may be made in this connexion to Africa generally and to the newly independent countries specifically, as well as to smaller countries in other regions.

The United Nations system is well placed to undertake this task. It can draw on a world-wide pool of experience and technical knowledge in many diverse fields, and a range of contacts which are unparalleled, if they can be brought to bear upon the problems of each country in a unified and swift manner. The services offered by it are impartial and without political strings or implications. It has no vested interest in specific sectors as against others, or in specific types of development or in specific projects for financing. Yet, while being outside local rivalries and disputes, the United Nations system is not an outside body; it embodies the idea of partnership and the assisted country is itself a Member. By their constitutional procedures, the United Nations organizations act only on the request of Governments, although their advice and suggestions are independent of Governments.

The United Nations organizations would assist the Government in formulating its development plan, give it what technical assistance it needs to execute the plan and make plain their faith in the soundness of the plan and in the capacity of the country to carry it out; at the same time they would make their expert knowledge and other resources available to all those willing to assist. The latter action in itself could go a long way towards enabling assisting countries and institutions to fit their aid into a framework of priorities and give them greater confidence that their help would be effectively used. A great number of time-consuming, individual discussions and studies would be avoided. Moreover, some countries wishing to give aid, but not having the necessary machinery or contacts for local assessment or negotiations, might make contributions which would not otherwise materialize. In the case of technical assistance and pre-investment specifically, if the necessary local (counterpart) expenditures were included in development plans and annual budgets based on them, much of the assistance could be given with less detailed negotiations about local counterpart expenditures and in respect of individual projects. The action proposed is, of course, not new. The United Nations system has been offering precisely this kind of service for years. What is in view is rather an intensification of this type of activity and an expansion of its scope over the next decade.

The suggested intensified action includes action at United Nations Headquarters and at the headquarters of the specialized agencies, as well as action at the regional and national level. This is the order in which the proposals are presented.

A. ACTION BY UNITED NATIONS STAFF IN NEW YORK AND GENEVA

It was in response to the needs of under-developed countries for assistance in drawing up development plans and formulating national development policies that the General Assembly proposed the establishment of an Economic Projections and Programming Centre, with sub-centres in the regions. One of the principal functions of the Centre and other units of the Secretariat would be to carry out, in co-operation with the regional economic commissions and regional development institutes as well as with the specialized agencies concerned, a programme of long-term projections of world economic and industrial trends. A primary aim of these projections would be to facilitate the drawing up of national development plans. If development policies are to be successful they must be formulated in the light of expected international economic trends. In part this is necessary to ensure that growth targets are consistent with foreign exchange availabilities. Knowledge of these trends is also an essential element in determining policies affecting the allocation of resources among various economic sectors, and especially in the export sector. The Secretariat would give similar support in the provision of vital industrial planning data.

Along with the need for projections as a basis for development planning there is an urgent need to improve techniques of planning and to provide technicians and administrators trained in these techniques. The Economic Projections and Programming Centre would contribute to filling these requirements through periodic meetings of experts and training seminars dealing with problems of projections and planning. The Centre, based on the staff work in New York and Geneva, would also co-operate with the other regional commissions and regional development institutes in rendering substantive support where required under United Nations Technical Assistance programmes in response to requests from Member Governments for aid in development planning. It would serve as a focal point for consultation and co-operation between the United Nations and the specialized agencies in the areas of economic projections and planning, and it would promote and maintain contacts with inter-governmental agencies outside the United Nations family, with national agencies, and with other institutions active in these fields. The need for a sound technical basis for development planning might also be met in part through a programme of studies which would deal with problems and techniques of planning under various economic and social systems.

B. ACTIVITIES OF THE AGENCIES IN THE FIELD OF DEVELOPMENT PLANNING

The International Bank's assistance in the field of development programming takes a variety of forms, a number of which will be stressed in the development decade. One will be the provision, by members of the Bank's newly established Development Advisory Service, of economic and financial advice, frequently on a long term basis, and particularly in the preparation and execution of development programmes. The Bank also expects to give still greater attention to the support of project and sector studies, designed to help its members in identifying and preparing development projects where there appears to be a possibility of ultimate Bank or IDA financing. The Bank not only helps the member concerned to find qualified consultants to carry out the work but may, in appropriate cases, organize the studies and meet part of their cost. The programme of courses of the Bank's Development Institute, where senior officials consider the practical problems that arise in the preparation and execution of development projects and programmes, is being expanded to make possible a wider variety of special courses in addition to the regular course. The consortium or consultative group approach to development financing, under which assistance is pledged and co-ordinated for support of a long-range development programme, is a recent initiative of the Bank. It has been applied in India and Pakistan and its application to a number of other countries is being considered.

The Bank expects to continue to increase the scope and variety of its technical assistance in development programming and to evolve new techniques appropriate to new situations which may arise during the decade.

In co-operation with other agencies, notably the regional economic commissions, and the regional economic development institutes as these are established, the ILO expects to intensify its research, training and advice to governments in connexion with the development of programmes of balanced economic and social development, particularly regarding the place of employment objectives in development plans and programmes and the methods of reaching these objectives. Among the aspects of development planning to which the ILO intends to give increasing emphasis in the coming years, special reference should be made to the assessment and forecasting of manpower needs and to social programmes related to development planning, e.g. the introduction and extension of social security and the development of industrial relations institutions. The ILO and FAO are co-operating closely in planning a special long-term programme of research and operational activities designed to assist Governments to raise incomes and improve living conditions in rural communities in developing countries.

During the development decade, FAO expects to intensify its activities related to the development of agriculture as an integral part of over-all national and economic planning; it will also endeavour to see that agriculture is given its proper place in national development plans so that it can meet projected increases in the output of food and agricultural products for home consumption, internal capital formation, and to provide export surpluses for financing needed imports. Studies and projections of world market trends for agricultural commodities will be continued, and countries assisted, where desired, in applying this information in their planning. FAO hopes to assist Governments in the preparation of well-conceived and realistic agricultural development plans, in the building up of their planning machinery, and also in the training of the necessary national staff through national and regional seminars and training centres, as well as through an expanded fellowship programme. At the same time it will, in consultation with governments, work on the longer term objectives of agricultural development; that is, objectives which are consistent with the population increases projected for the next and subsequent decades. During the decade, a high priority in FAO's work will be assigned to institutional and organizational problems of agricultural development, to pre-investment surveys and to providing assistance to developing countries to operate their agricultural development agencies. FAO is not only actively associated with the various regional economic commissions, through their joint agricultural divisions, in matters of agricultural development planning, but also has its own regional and subregional offices dealing especially with the technical problems of agricultural development. Their staff plays an important part in securing intra-regional co-operation through the organization of regional meetings in specific technical fields and through the transmittal of information from country to country on new approaches to problems and new techniques. The Forestry and Fisheries Commissions, the International Rice Commission and other specialized commissions are active in securing regional co-operation.

The main contribution of UNESCO will be to help to mobilize and to promote a fuller use of human resources required for accelerated economic growth during the decade, through the development of education and science and the spread of information. For this purpose, in association with the regional economic commissions and the specialized agencies, it will intensify its efforts initiated at the start of the decade in aiding countries to plan this development within the framework of general and balanced economic and social development, to expand their educational systems in accordance with agreed quantitative targets, to improve the efficiency of their educational systems, and to establish the teaching and research institutions and create the cadres of higher level manpower required both for their technological and their social progress.

The Executive Board of WHO adopted in January 1962 a resolution which recommended to Governments that they undertake, with the assistance of WHO if they so wish, ten-year public health programmes for the development decade, in co-ordination with other related plans in the social and economic fields. The WHO envisages team surveys in which it would participate, if so requested by governments, and it expects to continue to take the necessary steps to strengthen its services for meeting requests for assistance in national health planning.

The adoption of a resolution recommending to governments the preparation of national plans for the development of meteorological services, with specific objectives directly relating to an increase in the standard of living of the people, has been proposed to the Executive Committee of WMO for consideration in May-June 1962. It is intended that the proposed national plans should be based on the application of meteorology to agriculture and food production, water resource development, fisheries, shipping and aviation, and should be co-ordinated with the other related plans in the economic field. They should also take into consideration the need for training of scientific and technical personnel.

In drawing up the long-term programme of work which its General Conference has recommended, IAEA will give special attention to assisting developing countries in planning the phased introduction or expansion of nuclear science and technology, as a basis for planning their power and other investments.

C. Role of the regional economic commissions of the United Nations

While planning must be on a country-by-country basis, close regional co-operation will be increasingly necessary in coming years.

This is true for many reasons. In the first place, for many smaller countries the present markets in terms of cash buying power are simply too small to serve as a basis for national planning, and many industries may have to serve the markets of several countries if they are to be viable at all. Secondly, many essential development projects may be regional, cutting across national boundaries which are often administrative lines rather than the boundaries of true economic regions. Thirdly, if countries' plans for export promotion and import substitution are not harmonized with each other, they may become inconsistent and attempts to carry them out may do as much harm as would result from a failure to plan. Action by the United Nations system to promote the necessary co-operative action by the various countries at an early stage may be of great value. Fourthly, the promotion of intra-regional trade might help developing countries to solve the balance of payment difficulties of accelerated growth. Fifthly, some of the necessary services and institutions will be uneconomic if established on a national basis, and had best be provided for several countries together or on a regional basis. This applies specifically to more specialized training and research institutes and also to the essential advisory services for development planning.

For these reasons, regional machinery can play a most constructive role in development planning. The United Nations has the advantage of already possessing a framework for planning assistance on a regional basis, in the economic commissions it has created, three of which cover the major under-developed areas of the world. The commissions have established close links with the Governments of the region, with the specialized agencies, and, where appropriate, with their regional bodies. They enjoy the confidence of the Governments of the regions in which they are located. At the same time, they have the resources of a global organization behind them. Thus they offer a sound basis on which to build. The resources placed at the disposal of these commissions have in the past frequently been inadequate to enable them to realize their full potential in this field. The Secretary-General is reporting to the Economic and Social Council, simultaneously with the submission of this report, on steps already taken or contemplated to strengthen the work of the regional commissions.

The functions of the regional commissions have been described as follows in the Economic Commission for Africa (ECA): "To work out in concert economic targets and review them periodically in the light of the progress made; to study together the policies and methods needed to attain them; constantly to compare the results obtained and to seek out the reasons for mistakes and shortcomings; to expose oneself voluntarily to reciprocal influences, or even to restraints or obligations collectively worked out; and to do all this within the framework of a community which, however, varied in composition, is bound together by important historical characteristics and by the greatness of its aspirations—these are contemporary methods and disciplines which have proved their worth elsewhere, and of which advantage must be taken here, in working methodically for economic progress".[2]

The Economic Commission for Latin America (ECLA) has been particularly active over a number of years in the development planning field. Its experience suggests that greater emphasis might be placed in the coming years on the technique of the advisory group, particularly in countries with only a rudimentary planning staff.

In other areas, depending on the extent to which planning and administrative machinery have already been established, and trained counterpart personnel may be found, other approaches may be desirable. It is the virtue of the regional commissions that they are able to tailor their working methods and technical activities to the needs and conditions of the countries in the regions they serve.

In Asia and the Far East, where some countries made an earlier start in the establishment of comprehensive development plans, United Nations action, through the Economic Commission for Asia and the Far East (ECAFE), in accordance with the requests received from Governments, has been directed more towards the programming of specific projects, particularly in the development of industry and natural resources. However, other activities of a planning advisory nature have also been undertaken. The Conference of Asian Planners has recently suggested the formation of planning advisory groups similar to those in Latin America.

In Africa, where a large number of States have only recently obtained independence, the assembling of the statistical data needed for planning, and the establishment of administrative machinery to implement the plans, require concentrated effort during the first years of the decade. As a result, activities have related particularly to country surveys, training, technical assistance and advisory statistical services. The preparation of over-all development plans that can actually be carried out will depend in large part on the successes achieved in this initial phase. Meanwhile, planning support will depend greatly on the application of pragmatic methods based on experience and whatever knowledge of resources and conditions is available. Other African countries are already in an advanced stage of planning.

A most important development in this entire scheme of things is the "institute" concept, which was formulated a little over a year ago. According to this, economic development institutes will be established in each region to provide assistance in economic development planning which the secretariats of the regional economic commissions cannot provide on a sufficiently large scale without stopping work on virtually all other items on their work programmes. The institutes, according to the recommendation of the General Assembly, are to be closely linked to their respective regional economic commissions and to the relevant work of the specialized agencies in the region. The co-operation and

---

[2] From the opening statement by the Under-Secretary for Economic and Social Affairs to the recent session of ECA.

co-ordination built up over the years within the United Nations system, with reference to the regional economic commissions, should be extended to the new institutions so that they can enjoy the benefit of the accumulated experience of the specialized agencies and of the contributions the latter can make to development planning. To deal adequately with the interdependent problems of general and sectoral planning for economic and social development, the institutes must provide adequate staffing for both. This has already been a factor in the plans for the Latin American Institute approved by the Special Fund, and will similarly be a factor in establishing institutes for Africa and Asia. The next few years should see the formation and growth of these new institutes, which should add substantially to the success of the development decade. It is envisaged that these institutes might become the centres of training for development planning in their regions. This can only be accomplished, however, if the developed countries make both experts and funds available. It is hoped that this support will not be lacking.

D. Action on the Country Level

The Resident Representative, who is also the director of Special Fund operations, has an important role to play as the co-ordinator of action at the national level by all the United Nations agencies participating in the Expanded Programme of Technical Assistance. He will not normally be a planning expert or economic adviser, and even where he may be so qualified his many other duties would not normally permit him to act in that capacity. Nevertheless, his role in intensified United Nations action will be highly important. It is his responsibility to call to the attention of a government which has not yet established development plans the importance of doing so, and to endeavour to obtain priority for assistance in this field, where appropriate, in the EPTA country programming process and in Special Fund projects. When joint planning teams are envisaged, the Resident Representative lends his efforts to ensure that all important economic sectors are adequately covered. While not responsible for technical matters he reminds the government of the need for sound projects and draws its attention to ways of utilizing the experience gained from completed or continuing projects.

The Resident Representative, to be effective in this work, must be familiar with the plans and priorities of the Government for his own work, and must maintain contacts with those responsible for non-United Nations activities complementary to United Nations programmes. He should also be able to suggest critical areas for attention which have been overlooked. Without being a planning adviser himself, he must be able to advise the government of where and how within the United Nations system planning support can best be obtained. Where planning advisers or advisory groups are at work in the country he must be familiar with their work and assist them with their difficulties. Added to all this, he should be a man of wide experience who enjoys the confidence of the government.

These matters do not normally lend themselves to formal proposals. The role of the Resident Representative should develop gradually, the different conditions of the country, the wishes of the government and the nature of planning assistance required being determining factors. However, one specific area for action can be suggested.

Both recipient and donor countries have recognized the need for adequate information on the work and plans of the many assistance programmes operating in less developed countries. The conservation of time, effort and funds of the ministries of the recipient countries and of the aid missions requires that information be readily available on past and current projects and, to the extent possible, on future plans. To this end, the Economic and Social Council, in resolution 781 (XXX), asked the Secretary-General to report to the Council on the possibility of establishing and maintaining "a full and up-to-date record of specific technical and pre-investment assistance relating to the social and economic development of the under-developed countries, in easily accessible form." Co-ordination is not a matter requiring onerous operational procedures, but mainly a question of having the necessary information available for decision making. Neither donors nor recipients would knowingly duplicate projects adequately served by other aid programmes. Surveys and programming studies would be more effective if the results of past surveys and studies were more readily available.

The United Nations system could help all Governments to produce a central national register of development activities and assistance projects. Such a register would be available with the approval of the Government to all those giving assistance to the country concerned or contemplating such assistance. At present there is no systematic information available as to the many development activities undertaken by the various agencies and organizations in individual under-developed countries. Should it prove feasible to collect and collate it, such information could be of great value to Governments and organizations as well as to private entities and perhaps even to the Government of the country itself.

An information office for development activities could well be established under United Nations auspices on an individual country basis in the office of the Resident Representative, or on a regional basis in the regional commissions. The full co-operation of the Resident Representative who is already a repository of much of the needed data, and of the regional commissions, should be provided to Governments should they themselves seek to establish such information offices.

The task of developing a central clearing house of such information on a world basis would be formidable, perhaps too formidable for the present, although the development of information retrieval techniques combined with electronic computers puts it already within the realm of the possible. Moreover, periodic summaries and analyses of national information might be made centrally available if such a central clearing house became desirable.

This "registry" of activities and various forms of aid could be gradually expanded. It would provide the factual basis for the organized consultations at the national level mentioned elsewhere in this chapter. Beyond this, it would be the basis for rationally intensified assistance to developing countries.

E. ASSISTANCE FOR IMPLEMENTING DEVELOPMENT PLANS

Mention is made above of the new consortium or consultative group approach to development financing and to the initiatives of the International Bank in this respect. There may be room for extending this approach to non-financial assistance, by organizing international consultation at the country level so as to make most effective use of the non-financial aid potentially available from the industrialized. countries. For example, such consultations might be concerned with trade problems. Within the framework of liberalized and non-discriminatory trade policies toward developing countries suggested elsewhere in the report a consultative group might examine relevant export and import plans and elicit commitments for the necessary action by the countries concerned. The consultative approach might also provide a means of exploring the possibilities of supplementary aid programmes, increasing food aid, and aid in the form of other physical supplies. A recent example of this type of action by the United Nations itself is the Mekong project, which is described in some detail in annex II. The partnership or consultative approach to external assistance is based on the assumption that individual sources of aid will more readily play their part if they see others do their share. It is to be hoped that this approach may be further developed and made more systematic during the development decade.

*   *   *   *   *

Annex II

The Mekong River Project

The Mekong River Project is probably the most important experience to date of the mobilization, under United Nations auspices, of external assistance for a major regional project. Similar projects may emerge during the development decade. At the same time, as the Mekong project emerges from the pre-investment to the investment stage, the question arises whether the United Nations system may be able to continue to play its initiating, co-ordinating and participating role also in the financing of the project or of parts of it. In line with the thoughts and proposals expressed in chapters II and VI of the report, therefore, the following annex discusses the lessons and possible future of this project which may be of interest in considering various approaches for the development decade.

The various levels at which the United Nations system might participate in national and regional development planning have been discussed in chapter II of this report. At the most intense level of active participation in addition to a co-ordinating and advisory role the United Nations is already a partner in one major regional project, the development of the basin of the Lower Mekong River in South-East Asia. The Mekong scheme is a multipurpose project for the development of the water resources of the Lower Mekong and its major tributaries in respect of hydroelectric power generation, irrigation and water supplies, flood control, navigation and, looking further, the general economic improvement of the whole watershed area. It involves the Governments and people of Cambodia, Laos, Thailand and the Republic of Viet-Nam; a dozen other countries outside the region; eleven United Nations agencies; two private foundations; and a number of business organizations. In view of the importance of the scheme as an illustration of regional development planning under United Nations auspices, a brief account of the history of the Lower Mekong project is given in this annex, together with some general considerations suggested by it.

1. THE BACKGROUND

In terms of the volume of water discharged, the Mekong is the third largest river in Asia, after the Yangtze and the Ganges. The Lower Mekong—the stretch of river from the Burma border to the sea—is over 1,500 miles long, and flows through or forms the border between four countries: Laos, Thailand, Cambodia and the Republic of Viet-Nam. As yet, the potential resources of the river are almost completely untapped. Of the total area under cultivation in the basin of the Lower Mekong, only 2.7 per cent is irrigated, although the rainfall in the basin is at best barely adequate for rice production; there are no hydroelectric works; navigational facilities developed by the French from 1905 onwards (including a system of markers and transhipment facilities round one major fall) have been allowed to deteriorate; flooding is uncontrolled; and there is not a single bridge across the river.

Prior to the establishment of the Committee for Co-ordination of Investigations of the Lower Mekong Basin in 1957 political co-operation between the riparian countries was limited to an agreement signed in 1954, to harmonize action on matters affecting navigation and policing of the river. The three parties to this agreement, Cambodia, Laos and the Republic of Viet-Nam, undertook to observe an earlier (1926) Franco-Thai agreement relating to navigation.

2. Preliminary studies

The beginnings of the Lower Mekong project date from 1952, when the ECAFE secretariat published a preliminary study of the problems of controlling and utilizing the Mekong. This study originated in a request by the Commission to the ECAFE Bureau of Flood Control to study the technical problems of international rivers in the ECAFE area. Thus the emphasis on a multilateral approach was there right from the start.

The ECAFE study indicated that the river had a tremendous potential for hydroelectric, irrigational and navigational development, but found that its resources were quite unexplored, and that further detailed investigations would be required before any projects could be formulated. Unstable political conditions made further field work impossible for several years, however, and it was not until after the signing of the Geneva accords in 1954 that any further action could be taken.

In 1955 the three newly independent riparian states—Cambodia, Laos and the Republic of Viet-Nam—joined with Thailand in applying to the United States International Co-operation Administration for assistance in evaluating the developmental possibilities of the Lower Mekong. Early in 1956, after a short field mission, the United States Bureau of Reclamation published a study which examined the existing data relating to the river and its basin and listed the additional data which would be required. The study pointed to the need for data on a very large number of subjects, ranging from hydrological, meteorological and geological information to surveys of the potential power market within the basin, and public health requirements. It did not discuss possible projects in any detail.

Meanwhile, the ECAFE secretariat, with the assistance of consultants from India, Japan and France, had embarked on a survey of the water resources of the Lower Mekong and their development potential. This survey examined the power, navigation, irrigation and flood control possibilities of the river. It identified five possible project sites on the mainstream of the river, where multipurpose dams (power plus irrigation plus flood control plus navigation improvement) might be built, and estimated that the construction of these five projects would:

(*a*) Through irrigation, increase single crop yields, permit double cropping, and make crop diversification possible;

(*b*) Generate 32,000 million kWh of electric power annually at low cost; and that the combined effect of these gains might be to raise the area's exports by about $300 million annually.

The survey also pointed out that each of these five projects, even if situated entirely within one country, would benefit two or more of the four countries concerned, and re-emphasized the importance of an international approach and international control of the scheme throughout, beginning with data collection.

3. Organizational developments

In May 1957, on the basis of the favourable reception accorded the ECAFE report at the thirteenth session of the Commission, the four riparian Governments decided to establish a Committee for the Co-ordination of Investigations of the Lower Mekong Basin. They were assisted by the Legal Department of the United Nations and by the ECAFE secretariat in framing the statutes of this Committee, a problem of great delicacy and difficulty in view of the need to reconcile the requirements of a committee with powers to act—a Board of Directors—with those of its responsibility to the four riparian Governments. The statute provides for a committee of plenipotentiaries with sweeping functions to promote, co-ordinate, supervise and control the planning and investigation of water resources development projects in the Lower Mekong basin. Each Government has the right to appoint its own member for an indefinite term, all meetings of the Committee must be attended by all participants and its decisions are required to be unanimous. The servicing of the Committee by the ECAFE secretariat is also provided for, and under the rules of procedure, the Executive Secretary of the Commission, in addition to any one of the four members of the Committee, may convene a special meeting of the Committee.

In 1958, following a recommendation by a United Nations technical assistance mission, ,the Committee appointed a technical advisory board of engineers. Later an economist joined this board, and in 1961 a specialist in the planning and financing of development projects also joined it.

The Committee also decided, in 1959, to appoint an executive agent and ancillary staff to advise it, and through it the riparian Governments, on the administrative and technical co-ordination of plans, and to assist it in carrying out day-to-day co-ordination of the engineering, economic, agricultural and other studies undertaken at the Committee's request by the United Nations and the specialized agencies and under bilateral programmes.

4. ACTION BEGINS

The first action taken by the Committee, in November 1957, was to request the United Nations Technical Assistance Administration to review the studies made to date and to submit detailed proposals for further action. The United Nations mission's report published in January 1958, reaffirmed the existence of great potentialities in the Mekong basin, and, *inter alia,* made the following specific proposals for action:

(*a*) That the collection of data, on the basis of uniform standards to be adopted by the four countries, should begin immediately, as some of the data would not have validity until they covered a period of at least five years;

(*b*) Concurrently, special studies of fisheries, agriculture, mineral resources, transportation, the power market, etc., should be begun;

(*c*) Preliminary planning for important and promising reaches should begin as soon as essential data were available;

(*d*) Studies and investigations for the preparation of a comprehensive plan of the Lower Mekong River Basin, including major tributaries, should follow;

(*e*) Qualified, responsible firms of engineers should be employed to plan and execute the proposed operations.

The mission also drew up a timetable for action, based on the five-year period required for the recording of certain hydrologic observations. This timetable indicated that preliminary planning of priority mainstream projects might begin in the third year of the data collection programme, and work on the comprehensive basin plan and tributary projects might begin in the last year of the data collection programme.

The cost of the proposed five-year data collection programme was estimated at $9.2 million, including $1.8 million for preliminary planning work.

Besides agreeing to press forward with the implementation of the five-year data collection programme proposed in the United Nations TAA mission's report, the Mekong Committee has taken a number of other decisions regarding the approach to and implementation of various projects, including, *inter alia:*

(*a*) Recognition of the technical and economic interdependence of the mainstream projects, and thus the need for co-operative and co-ordinated action on them;

(*b*) A series of decisions to proceed with ancillary economic and fiscal, social, administrative, etc., inquiries, and industrial and agricultural investigations;

(c) An assignment of top priority to three mainstream projects and four tributary projects;

(d) A decision to seek, for each of these seven first priority projects, the preparation of a comprehensive feasibility report in a form which could subsequently be used in loan negotiations;

(e) Adoption of a navigation improvement programme.

5. FINANCING THE ACTION PROGRAMME

The finance required for the implementation of the United Nations TAA mission's proposals and for the implementation of decisions (b), (d) and (e) above is being accumulated from a large number of countries and multilateral agencies. By January 1962, just over $14 million had been pledged or collected, including $3.4 million by the United Nations through ECAFE, the Technical Assistance Board, the specialized agencies and the Special Fund, $8.9 million bilaterally by twelve countries, including contributions from seven countries made through the Colombo Plan, and the equivalent of $1.8 million for local costs pledged by the four riparian countries. These figures do not include the cost of training fellowships made available by TAB, UNESCO, the Special Fund, and seven countries.

Among United Nations agencies, the Special Fund has been the main contributor so far. Following a request by the Mekong Committee in June 1959, the Special Fund has undertaken to supervise and finance the preparation by well established engineering firms of comprehensive project feasibility reports for the four first priority tributary projects, in a form ready for use in subsequent loan negotiations. $1.3 million has been allotted for these four reports, and a further $1.4 million for three other Special Fund projects—a hydrographic survey for the improvement of navigation, a survey of the basin's mineral resources, and a delta mathematical model.

The finance for planning and developmental work on the three priority mainstream projects is being provided mainly from bilateral resources.

6. PROGRESS TO DATE

The progress made in the implementation of the various projects included in the general plan for the development of the Lower Mekong Basin may be summarized as follows:

(a) *Data collection programme.* This is proceeding on schedule and is expected to be completed by the end of 1964—i.e., within the five-year period originally scheduled;

(b) *Basin plan.* The ECAFE Bureau of Flood Control and Water Resources Development has been authorized by the Committee to prepare a greatly amplified version of the 1957 skeleton plan, in the light of the technical and engineering data becoming available and the results of concurrent economic studies;

(c) *Priority mainstream projects.* A great deal of preliminary work, such as geological surveys, soil sampling, sedimentation studies, etc., has been done. Work on one comprehensive project was begun in 1961, and preliminary investigations for another comprehensive project report were launched;

(d) *Tributary projects.* Of the four comprehensive project feasibility studies for the first priority projects, being prepared under the supervision of the United Nations Special Fund, the first is expected to be completed early in 1962, the second by the end of the year and the others in the course of 1963. It is hoped that the first of these projects will be at the construction stage by the end of 1963, and the other three by the end of 1964. Meanwhile, work has begun on the development of a fifth tributary project, which may be at the financing and construction stage by the end of 1963, and initial investigations of two further projects have started;

(e) *Navigation improvement.* A hydrographic survey of the reaches of the river important for navigation has begun, and some navigational equipment has been provided;

(f) *Ancillary projects and investigations.* Studies under way include a survey of mineral deposits; the establishment of an experimental agricultural farm with a view to developing better crop management practices, crop diversification, etc., concurrently with the development of irrigation facilities; surveys of the incidence of bilharziasis and malaria—diseases liable to spread with the development of irrigation; and a preliminary survey of the manpower resources of the Basin.

7. FUTURE DEVELOPMENTS

The 1959 Annual Report of the Mekong Committee to ECAFE estimated that, starting in 1959, the first phase of development might be completed by 1973. The preliminary work of data collection was expected to take five years (to 1964); the planning and design of specific projects two years (to 1966); arranging finance one year (1967); and construction of the first three mainstream projects six years (to 1973). It was anticipated that the construction of at least some of the tributary projects, notably the Nam Pong project in Thailand, might be completed considerably earlier, by 1966.

At the present time, work on the mainstream projects, the tributary projects and ancillary studies is proceeding on schedule. But as the time for moving on to the financing and construction stage of the first group of tributary projects draws near, the problems of finance will arise. However, the problems vary from country to country. In Thailand there should be little problem because several countries and international institutions are ready to provide assistance for any well-conceived project. In the Republic of Viet-Nam and Laos, the problem is affected by the security situation, but when the situation improves, the needed finance is likely to be made available on a bilateral basis or from international institutions. In Cambodia, reliance will presumably have to be placed on bilateral aid, since the country is not yet a member of the international financing agencies (IMF, IBRD, IDA).

A great deal of additional studies will be required before any one of these projects can be adequately justified for construction, and the important thing during the next decade will be to continue these studies in an organized way. It is not certain that initial construction can in fact begin during the development decade.

A recent rough estimate puts the cost of building the first five mainstream projects, including tributary developments roughly equivalent in cost and results to three times the totals involved in the four United Nations Special Fund tributary projects and some navigational improvement, at about $2,000 million. This estimate includes the costs of construction of dams and locks, power houses and equipment, irrigation canals and pumping stations, etc., but not such ancillary investments as factories to utilize the newly available power, electrical equipment for farms, etc., which might be three to four times as great as the initial investment of $2,000 million.

8. SOME GENERAL CONSIDERATIONS

The Lower Mekong River project is the first large multi-national, multi-purpose development project to be initiated under the auspices of the United Nations. In the belief that there is scope for further projects of this kind in Asia and in other under-developed areas, it is useful to try to identify some salient features which may be applicable to future international development projects.

(a) *The dimensions of the project.* In its essentials, the first phase of the Lower Mekong basin plan consists of a proposal to build five mainstream and about ten tributary multiple-purpose dams (hydroelectric power, irrigation, flood control) and to improve the navigational facilities on the river. But throughout the formulation of even this first phase there has been a consciousness of the ramifying nature of such a scheme, reflected in the emphasis on the need for concurrent studies of general economic conditions, agricultural problems, social and manpower problems, etc. Already the scheme includes some forty component sub-projects, and this number is constantly growing. It is also recognized that secondary investments in projects designed to utilize the additional resources created by the Mekong scheme are likely to be several times as large as the original investment, and of very great variety. The sense of a growth-initiating project, reaching out and affecting nearly every sector of the economy of the whole area, is very strong.

(b) *International aspects.* From the 1952 ECAFE study onwards the emphasis has been on the advisability of an international approach to the project, with the United Nations regional economic commission providing the initial forum for co-operation between the countries concerned, and subsequently acting in an advisory and, to some extent, in an administrative capacity, and in consequence of the fact that all the main countries contributing assistance are represented on it, as an organ for the co-ordination of their efforts. The Mekong scheme is significant for the four riparian countries politically as well as economically. It is proving to be a co-operative, constructive and stabilizing influence of considerable importance at the present time, when relations among some of the riparian countries have been difficult.

(c) *Administrative complexities.* The history of the scheme to date provides plenty of examples of the great complexity of the undertaking. The appointment of an Executive Agent—analogous to the general manager of a business—and administrative staff at an early stage was essential to ensure the proper co-ordination of the widely diversified preliminary studies already under way, and to facilitate arrangements for the execution of the preparatory work, much of which is being financed by grants in kind. Thus, for example, India has supplied 366 rain gauges to aid in the collection of essential data; Canada has commissioned a private Canadian firm to undertake aerial survey work, and Iran has supplied petroleum products.

(d) *The problem of control.* The statute establishing the Co-ordinating Committee reflects the desire of the participating countries to create an authority that would have power to act and yet would be ultimately responsible to the four Governments concerned. So far, the Committee has operated successfully as an executive body, but it is clear that its continued success depends on the continuing will of the governments to support the Committee and the scheme wholeheartedly, even in the face of local political difficulties. The Committee, in turn, reflected the need to ensure efficient day-to-day management of the whole scheme by appointing an Executive Agent.

(e) *The practical approach.* Since the adoption of the UNTAA mission's report as basis for action, the emphasis has been on identifying and performing specific studies, surveys, planning, etc., within a given time. Among the most significant of the Committee's actions was the request to the Special Fund to commission engineering firms, not *ad hoc* groups of experts, to prepare general feasibility studies of the four priority tributary projects in a form which could subsequently be used in loan negotiations, thereby eliminating a stage of the project development process.

(f) *Financing.* Most of the external assistance made available so far has been in kind rather than in cash. As yet this has not seriously hampered work on the various sub-projects, but it is becoming increasingly apparent that an operational cash account will be a necessity if development is to proceed at the maximum feasible pace. It is not always possible to find a donor to provide exactly the equipment or services needed to complete a study or project: for example, the establishment of a hydraulic budget, in connexion with one mainstream project, requires some $10,000 worth of hydrologic equipment and vehicles which it has not yet been possible to obtain. "Shopping" for donors of individual items is a wasteful and time-consuming process which could be eliminated by the establishment of a cash budget on even a quite modest scale.

(g) *The time scale.* Perhaps the most significant feature of the Mekong River project for the development decade is the time scale on which it is conceived. Already ten years have passed since the idea was first conceived, and as yet no actual construction work has begun. As early as 1959, the Committee envisaged that the completion of the first phase of the project might take twenty-five years, and outlined fairly detailed plans for the progress of development on a number of related projects during the first fourteen years, starting with five years of work on data collection. The full utilization of the economic potential created by the scheme will take very much longer—and if it contributes to the initiation of self-sustaining growth in the area affected by it, may be said never to reach an end.

In addition to these general considerations, it may also be useful to summarize the organizational and institutional framework within which the Lower Mekong project has developed. It may hold lessons for the establishment of regional projects on a similar scale elsewhere.

(a) The project must be directed by the countries in which the project is located—as the Mekong Project is directed by Cambodia, Laos, Thailand, and the Republic of Viet-Nam;

(b) The project countries must establish an international instrument to deal with the work—as Cambodia, Laos, Thailand, and the Republic of Viet-Nam have established the Mekong Committee;

(c) The international instrument thus established must have clearly specified and adequate powers—as the Mekong Committee has under its statute the authority "to promote, co-ordinate, supervise and control the planning and investigation of water resources development projects"; and the power "to receive and administer separately such financial and technical assistance...";

(d) The international instrument may be effectively serviced by an international secretariat—as the Mekong Committee is serviced by the ECAFE secretariat, and uses a United Nations staff member as its executive agent or general manager;

(e) A way must be found to attract substantial support from a number of countries, United Nations agencies, and foundations—as the Mekong scheme has attracted the support of twelve countries, eleven United Nations agencies, and two foundations;

(f) Administrative flexibility should be achieved through combining (i) permanent secretariat staff, giving continuity; (ii) major non-permanent component project teams, such as the Mekong Canadian aerial survey team, Australian Mekong Damsite geology team, Indian Mekong Tonle Sap design team, U.S. Mekong hydrologic team, and the four Special Fund Mekong project teams; and (iii) short-term technical assistance consultants and teams, for example the Wheeler mission and the Committee's advisory board;

(g) The project must seek the welfare of all populations involved and rigorously eschew consideration of differences based on politics;

(h) The project will gain from adherence to the three administrative principles of candour, anticipation, and economy.

CRITERIA FOR INTERNATIONAL PROGRAMS

by
GUSTAV F. PAPANEK

So far the discussion has been in national terms - what criteria can be applied in determining the composition of development and technical assistance programs in one country. Various aid-giving agencies, and sometimes recipient countries as well, face the problem of how to allocate resources for programs covering more than one country. It is difficult enough to apply criteria to one country, but even harder to decide on the relative size of assistance to a number of countries - to decide, for instance, whether to reduce technical or capital assistance to India in order to increase that for West Africa, or whether to drop assistance to a railroad in Brazil in order to help mineral exploration in Burma.

Some Relevant Considerations

Decisions in this field, particularly as far as bilateral programs are concerned, are made to a considerable extent on the basis of the political, economic, military, or moral interests of the donor, but these have previously been excluded from examination and, though important, will not be considered here.

Ignoring these aspects, there are at least three considerations that could influence the relative size of assistance, both technical and capital, for different countries:

1) Their relative need for assistance: Presumably the greater the need, the greater should be outside help.

2) The extent of each country's own effort with respect to development: Presumably outside assistance should not substitute for, but encourage, a country's own effort.

3) Their relative ability to use the assistance: If it is in the interest of both outside agencies and underdeveloped countries to use scarce resources efficiently, outside resources should go in larger amounts to those able to use them more efficiently.

A number of simple criteria have been used in practice to compare and evaluate the desirable extent of outside assistance to different countries. These include size of population and national income, amount of assistance provided in the past, and size of a country's own effort. When measured against the considerations discussed above, one can see both the advantages and shortcomings of such yardsticks.

The major advantage is their simplicity and measurability. The criterion of assistance per capita is easy to apply, and such a comparison does have some meaning. It

444

ignores, however, the relative ability to use assistance and the relative effort of different countries, as well as all factors of need other than numbers of people. There would probably be little disagreement with the proposition that India's much larger population is likely to need, be able to use, and contribute to more aid than Nepal, but this does not help in deciding whether both should get the same amounts per capita, or how resource-rich Iran and resource-poor Jordan should be treated.

A country's national income does indicate to some extent its ability to use assistance - the greater the size of the economy, the more likely it will be able to absorb aid effectively - but it is not a very good indicator even of this and is a poor indicator of a country's need or own effort. Outside aid related to the national income of Kuwait, Saudi Arabia, Sudan, and Libya would help those who need it least.

Relating allocation of outside resources to a country's own development effort largely ignores differences in need and ability to use assistance. Again the resource-rich countries, especially if their resources are in an easily exploitable form (for example, exports), can have a higher rate of development with less need for outside help. It is also possible that they are already exploiting the best opportunities for development, so that outside assistance yields lower returns than in other countries with a smaller development effort.

Finally, there is the possibility of allocating outside assistance on the basis of historical patterns. The soundness of this criterion obviously depends on the soundness with which allocations were made originally and the extent to which circumstances have changed. Historical patterns are often accidental: situations change and the fact that a country needed, or was able to use, or for other reasons obtained assistance of a certain amount in the past soon becomes a very poor indication of its need or ability to use it in the present.

That these various simple criteria for the allocation of outside assistance have serious defects should be obvious. Yet they do possess some usefulness, and in the absence of anything better they have been used. The question is whether some more satisfactory guidelines can be suggested. The next section examines this question with respect to each of the three considerations previously suggested as relevant.

Possible Guidelines

The need for outside assistance depends on the rate of development considered desirable and the extent to which a country can reach that rate using its own resources.

A desirable rate of development can be established in several ways. It can be related to an absolute goal (for example, underdeveloped countries need to be helped until they have a per-capita income equivalent to $200); or to a rate of growth considered desirable (for example, underdeveloped countries should increase their national income by 3 per cent a year); or to different goals for different countries (for example, each country should be helped to meet the goals it set for itself). The measure chosen makes a great deal of difference to one's conclusion about the relative need of different countries. If need is measured in terms of an absolute goal, countries with low per-capita income like Burma, India, Pakistan, and Uganda would top the list; if measured in terms of desirable rates of growth, a number of countries showing little growth (Ceylon, Chile, and Indonesia) would rank ahead of them; and if measured in terms of each country's aspirations, one would get yet another picture. In the last case one also faces the problem that the desire of most countries for development is practically limitless, and if outside assistance is known to be based on stated aspirations countries may progressively inflate their goals in order to increase outside help. (This is probably already happening to some extent.)

No single universal measure of a desirable rate of development exists, and the most appropriate one will depend on what an agency is trying to achieve. One can argue, however, that it is usually best defined in terms of a desirable rate of increase in per-capita income which is similar for all countries. This can mean, for instance, that in all countries per-capita income should increase by a significant percentage per year (say, 1 or 2 per cent) and should be maintained at a higher rate (say 2 to 4 per cent) if such a rate was achieved in the past. This approach can be justified on the assumption that the improvement experienced by people is more important than their absolute income or other factors. That is, although India's per-capita income is around $60, Ceylon's around $100, and that of some Latin American countries around $250, this level is less significant for development policy than the desire and need for an economy to grow at a rate that will outstrip the population increase and that will not be less than the rate of growth in the past.

The need for outside assistance depends not only on the desirable rate of development, but also on the ability of each country to achieve that rate on its own. Since one is concerned here with a potential, with what a country could do, ability is difficult to determine. (If one measures ability in terms of what a country actually does, "need" would lose all meaning. The less a country does, the greater its "need" in that case and the more help it should get.) Ability to achieve a desirable rate of development depends on a number of factors, including per-capita income and the ease with which part of this income can be diverted to development. The higher the per-capita income, the greater the margin above subsistence and the easier it is to save. These factors are difficult or impossible to measure, and it is even more difficult to evaluate their relative importance. For instance, Burma has a low per-capita national income, but a large international trade sector, easily taxed. The Philippines and the United Arab Republic have higher per-capita incomes but smaller international trade sectors. It is hard to say which of these countries should be better able to meet its own development needs and by how much.

In addition, the ability to raise resources for development depends very much on a country's social structure, administrative competence, political system, values, motivations, and past history. If it is politically possible and desired, most countries can obtain greater resources than they now do from the consumption of high-income groups and from the semi-luxury and luxury expenditures of the mass of the population, and can make additional resources available by mobilizing labor - all without physically unbearable hardship. But if a country can achieve a desirable rate of development without starving anyone, is it "able" to do this even if the government is convinced that it will be overthrown as a consequence?

A quantitative and simple indication of a country's potential ability to contribute the resources to achieve a desirable rate of growth can be derived from its absolute income per head and its past performance. Neither indicator is very satisfactory. Past performance is an especially poor measure of the limits imposed by political, social, and economic circumstances upon a country's ability to raise resources. However, both measures may be the best ones available. When it is possible to compare the resource endowments of different countries with somewhat greater accuracy than seems possible now, this would be a third useful measure of a country's ability to contribute to development.

The need for outside assistance is therefore difficult to judge. While a criterion can be established for a desirable rate of development, the ability to achieve it from indigenous resources is impossible to measure with any accuracy. Closely related is the second consideration suggested as relevant to the international allocation of resources - how to use outside assistance to increase, not to substitute for, a country's own development effort. If it is difficult to establish how large an effort can be expected from a country, it is even more difficult to establish whether outside assistance substitutes for or adds to the effort a country can and ought to make itself.

However, the adequacy of a country's effort in terms of

its potential may often be less important to an outside a-
gency than the effect of assistance on the actual development effort the country makes. If, as the result of outside
assistance, a country undertakes to increase its own effort,
a major purpose of such help is achieved. Changes in the
magnitude of a country's development effort cannot be the
only guide to the adequacy of this effort, since countries
whose resource endowment is favorable and whose initial
development effort was small can readily increase it, while
others may be so resource - poor or their initial effort may
have been so large that any increase is virtually impossible.
Thus, although purely historical comparisons seem to be
the only ones now readily quantifiable and though they do indicate whether a major purpose of assistance has been a-
chieved, they need to be used with caution. As a criterion
in the allocation of international resources they need to be
qualified by a judgment on differences in the resource endowment and the adequacy of past efforts of different countries.

The final consideration suggested above was the relative
ability of different countries to use outside assistance. This
is often conceived in terms of physical ability to make effective use of resources from the outside: does a country
have a government that will know how to use extension a-
gents or a fertilizer plant provided from outside, or will
such help be largely wasted? There is also a broader question. Even if outside resources can be put to good use by
two countries, there is likely to be a difference in their relative returns. A fertilizer plant in Iran may give a higher
return than if the same plant is built in Kuwait or if the
same resources are used to build a dam elsewhere. Similarly with technical assistance - a group of engineers sent
to either of two countries may be put to good use, but their
relative effectiveness, the returns from their work, almost
inevitably will differ.

Allocating resources to countries where they will yield
the greatest return has some obvious advantages. The
greater the returns from an initial effort, the greater the
resources available subsequently to develop other countries. On the other hand, allocating resources according
to results is likely to mean an increasing gap between the
relatively prosperous and relatively backward. As outside
assistance flows to countries better endowed in human or
material resources or to those where a substantial development effort has created the necessary environment for
further development, they can become still better able to
use further assistance, and thus become even better claim-
ants on further help. The gap would not widen if people
moved from one country to another to follow better opportunities, but this they cannot and often do not want to do.
The gap could also be prevented from widening if, as soon

as countries with more productive projects are launched on development, all international resources could go to those countries previously neglected. Such a policy could yield a maximum rate of growth for underdeveloped countries as a whole, but few, if any, countries would be willing to accept a slower initial rate of growth because this is best for all countries or on the understanding that this will be to their benefit some time in the future. This dilemma in the international allocation of resources is very similar to, but more serious than, the problems encountered in allocating resources to regions within a country.

Furthermore, there is a problem of measuring or estimating likely returns or ability to use assistance. Administrative and technical ability to carry out a particular project can be judged with experience, but not measured. The limits and difficulties in measuring economic returns are great when projects in a single country are considered and are aggravated in international comparisons - by problems of exchange rates, incomparability of prices, and difficulties in obtaining comparable data - to such an extent that for most projects such calculations would serve little practical purpose at present. For technical assistance, such measurements would be subject to all the uncertainties discussed earlier for a single country, but with a greater margin of error when several countries were involved.

Thus, the three considerations mentioned at the beginning of this section do appear to be relevant to allocations of resources among countries. However, they are not unambiguous guides to policy and are likely to be in conflict with one another. Need cannot be measured clearly and is likely to be greatest in those countries least able to show high returns from outside assistance. Usually neither returns nor the third consideration - the extent of a country's own effort - are measurable in a reasonably precise way or against any clear standards. No wonder international allocations of resources are often influenced by some simple "common sense" criteria where they are not entirely determined by political and related considerations.

Possible Criteria

Perhaps one can suggest somewhat less ambiguous practical guidelines. Those outlined below are subject to a number of qualifications and criticisms and they do not take account of all relevant factors. They may be useful, however, as an attempt to express in a systematic and quantifiable form some of these factors. They cannot be used without modification, but perhaps they can be used to provide a basis from which modification can start.

It was argued earlier that the need for outside aid depends partly on the size of a desirable development program and that this can best be defined in relation to a particular rate of growth in per-capita income, which would be identical for all countries. The extent to which a country can achieve the desired program from its own resources can be estimated. Suggestions for doing so were made above and such estimates have been made in practice. Outside agencies could then provide the missing resources, but only to the extent that the country is making a commensurate effort. To take an example, the desirable rate of growth can be defined as a 2 per-cent per-annum increase in per-capita income for all countries. If the population in a particular country is growing at 2 per cent per year, it should have a 4 per-cent increase in national income. If it is estimated that this country can achieve a 3 per-cent increase from its own resources, outside technical and financial assistance would be equal to one-third of any effort the country actually makes itself, up to the absolute amount required to achieve a 4 per-cent increase in national income. That is, if the country needs to devote $400,000,000 to development in order to achieve the desired 4 per-cent increase, and if it raised $300,000,000 from its own resources, outside assistance would be equal to $100,000,000. If the country devoted only $200,000,000 to development from its own resources, outside assistance would be reduced to $66,000,000 to preserve the three-to-one ratio. Outside assistance would not exceed $100,000,000 in any case. As the country's ability to raise resources increased over time, the share of aid would decline.

This approach would take account of need and would stimulate a maximum effort on the part of the country. It does not take account of differences among countries in the ability to use outside assistance and in the returns to be expected from it. Although it is difficult to estimate such differences with a reasonable degree of accuracy, it would be possible to apply some of the criteria and concepts discussed earlier to a few major projects. If the difference in returns is large enough, this is likely to be significant and cannot be explained merely by crudeness and possible error in estimating returns. In that case, the allocations of outside resources suggested above, which were related to need and to a country's effort, could be modified so that projects with a high rate of return are assisted in one country rather than others with a low rate elsewhere. The procedure outlined would need to be modified further, since it leaves out a number of factors and is not nearly so precise as the figures in the example suggest. However, it could provide a useful first approximation and approach to the problem of international allocation of resources.

Regional Projects

In addition to allocating assistance to individual countries, outside agencies occasionally provide resources to projects covering more than one country. The same considerations are relevant in both cases, but they are even more difficult to apply and need to be somewhat modified in the case of regional projects.

Regional projects can have some clear advantages over those restricted to a single country. The major one is obviously the possibility of dealing with a problem or taking advantage of a resource that encompasses more than one country. Problems like malaria and resources like river basins often do not stop at political boundaries. In these cases projects limited to a particular country usually involve greater costs or lesser benefits than if they are tackled on a regional basis. Regional projects may also have political and social advantages, since they can increase the opportunities for joint constructive work by nationals and governments of different countries.

There are concomitant disadvantages. The administrative burdens of regional projects are usually greater, since the involvement of more than one government means differences in outlook, policy, and perhaps language and procedure. In addition, while joint efforts can improve relations, they can also exacerbate them, depending on how they are handled and who is concerned.

Conclusions and Future Work

If one excludes the political, military, and other objectives of the donor agencies and countries, three considerations have been suggested here as being relevant for the international allocation of resources:

1) The need for outside assistance. This involves (a) establishing a desirable or appropriate rate of development, which can be stated in terms of a specific percentage increase in per-capita income, and (b) the potential ability of a country to contribute to the achievement of this rate, which is reflected to some extent in its absolute level of per-capita income and its past performance in supporting development.

2) A country's own effort with respect to development. This consideration may generally be best satisfied by an examination of whether and to what extent a country increases its development effort with outside assistance.

3) A country's ability to use outside assistance, both in terms of physical capacity and maximum returns for outside resources. The measures discussed earlier for returns on investment and the usefulness of technical assistance can be applied in some cases, but they are less valid in international than in intra-country comparisons.

451

These three considerations may be in conflict. Need may
be greatest in the case of some countries which make the
least effort and are likely to show the least return from
outside assistance. Allocations to countries making the
largest effort and with the highest rate of return will yield
the greatest over-all increase in growth, but will often
widen the gap between the richest and the poorest countries. The choice between "efficiency" and "equality of income" on a global basis is not likely to be subject to any
but value judgments.

It was, however, suggested that the most generally applicable set of guidelines for the international allocation of
technical and financial resources might put primary emphasis on need and a country's own effort. The outside a-
gency would stand ready to supply assistance to the extent
that the country cannot achieve a uniform desirable rate of
growth from its own resources, but only to the degree that
the country itself actually provides the resources it is
thought capable of raising. Ability to use the assistance,
differences in returns, and other factors would in some cases modify the conclusions reached on this basis.

Future progress on the question of the international allocation of resources would require first of all further
general and theoretical work. What is needed is some consideration of the problem, of the possible approaches suggested above, and of other criteria that might be used, rather than the application of existing criteria or the gathering of experience, which were suggested respectively as
the first priority in the previous discussions on selecting
national development and technical assistance programs.

WHO APPLIES CRITERIA

In principle, responsibility for decisions on a development program rests almost exclusively with the country
concerned. If suitable indigenous personnel are available
they are likely to have more extensive knowledge of the
country than foreign technicians have, and an indigenous institution would be more responsive to the wishes of
the society. And morally, the responsibility must always
be with the indigenous government, regardless of whether
or not it uses foreign technicians.

As long as outside resources play a significant role in a
development effort, outside agencies will be concerned with
the composition of that effort and will have independent
views on it. However, if a recipient country has the personnel and institutions to make sound decisions on the composition of a development program, there is no reason why
it should not itself determine that composition. The attitude of outside agencies would be a facotr to be taken into

account, but these agencies need not be brought into basic decision-making. For instance, if a country believes that it can get more assistance for an atomic reactor than for residential housing, this is a fact to be reckoned with in deciding which of the two to include in a development program, but it does not make it necessary to consult outside agencies before deciding.

In actual practice and under current circumstances, however, the answer is not quite so simple. Most countries are not engaged in a carefully thought-out development effort, and many do not have a consistent development program even for the government's part in this effort. Often, the development effort consists of a number of projects and proposals conceived and carried out by different bodies, with little attention to their relative priority and relationship. Countries which do prepare a development "Plan" frequently do not have the necessary staff and institutions to do as good a job as would be desirable. Under these circumstances technical assistance and more general cooperation with outside agencies can be extremely useful in assisting in decisions on the composition of a development program.

The opportunity to obtain or provide such assistance has often been neglected. Sometimes, the governments concerned have not seen the need for technical assistance in preparing their development programs. In other cases, they have been reluctant to use technical assistance even where they saw a need, since the relevant decisions call for considerable regard for political, social, and personal factors, and many governments prefer not to have foreigners involved in such decisions. In addition, outside agencies have not always seen the importance of assistance in programing or have not been anxious to face the problems involved in this kind of technical assistance.

A third factor also stems from the sensitive nature of some of the decisions involved. Most recipient governments would be reluctant to accept technical assistance on programing or planning problems from another government, and sometimes even from international agencies. A government is justifiably chary of providing an outsider with all the information and opportunity for participation in internal discussion that is necessary if that person is to advise on, say, the priority of a steel mill as compared with an agricultural extension service. This is especially true if the government may then want to approach the donor of the technical assistance, whether government or international agency, for help in carrying out one of the projects discussed. This problem can be avoided, in part, if advisors come from a non-governmental agency that does not provide other assistance, such as private firms, universities, foundations, and some international agencies. These

453

agencies may have other handicaps, however, arising from suspicion of a private firm with fees at stake, from an unduly academic approach, or from an inability to recruit and provide sufficiently able personnel.

For all these reasons, technical assistance has been applied less often than might be desirable to the problems of programing and planning. Yet an improvement here can yield very substantial returns. If a development program is poorly conceived, outside agencies can do relatively little to correct for this by adjusting the composition of their assistance program. In the first place, an outside agency usually finds it difficult to tell much about the soundness of decisions on the composition of a development program. Even if it has doubts on this score, it generally lacks the time, staff, and information to prepare a suggested alternative development program. Secondly, even where the outside agency has sound reasons for believing that the composition of a country's development program should be changed, it usually lacks the means to bring about much change. It can withhold assistance, although this is very difficult for some agencies and for most others leads to undesirable strains in relations with recipient governments. Even where it can be done, it is usually limited to an attempt to change a few decisions. It is quite rare for a country to change a development program significantly because some outside body presses it to do so. Finally, even where an outside agency can exert sufficient pressure to force a modification in a poorly planned program, it would have been more desirable and efficient to have assisted the country concerned in preparing a better one in the first place.

Cooperation at the preparatory stage can take several forms. First, more assistance to over-all planning bodies is desirable. Substantial improvement in the composition of development programs can take place if such bodies are helped to become more effective. At the same time, technical assistance faces special problems in this field due to reluctance on the part of recipient countries to use it, and the difficulty of outside agencies in providing suitable personnel. Second, both recipient countries and outside agencies have an interest in improving programing techniques. Outside agencies are in a good position to promote research on programing, and to work with recipient governments on rational standards of programing. Third, outside agencies now provide technical assistance to many bodies concerned with programing at various levels, and the foreign technicians involved should recognize it as their explicit function to cooperate in this programing. Foreign technicians requested for other work may not always be welcome in the role of advisors or helpers on programing problems. But to the extent that outside agencies have any influence on recipient countries, they will usually achieve more by pressing for better preparation of programs than by pressing for changes in these programs once they have been decided on.

While cooperation between the country concerned and outside agencies is highly desirable in determining the composition of a development program, especially at present when most countries lack the necessary national staff to do this work on their own, such cooperation is always essential for a technical assistance program. Outside agencies and recipient countries each have, and will continue to have, special competence with respect to different factors affecting the usefulness of technical assistance. The recipient country should be best able to judge the applicability of technical assistance to various aspects of its development program and its own need for outside assistance. The donor agency is the best judge of its own ability to provide the required assistance. However, none of these issues is the exclusive concern of either recipient or donor, and combinded analysis and decision are called for.

As in the case of cooperation on the composition of a development program, a joint effort in programing technical assistance can and should take several forms: cooperation at the national planning level; cooperation in research on and in devising machinery for effective application of programing techniques; and cooperation with ministries and other bodies at all levels in improving programing by fields, parts of fields, and on individual projects. Here again, programing for a particular field should not result primarily in strengthening its claims on technical assistance resources, but programs in other fields and in the nation as a whole should be kept in mind.

Criteria to help determine the composition of development and technical assistance programs are as yet poorly developed. There is no general agreement on the objectives and strategy of development, which would set the general gramework. In addition, much of the information required to frame or apply criteria is lacking. Despite these shortcomings, there are quite sophisticated and detailed criteria for some decisions on the composition of a development program and more general guidelines for others. Their use has lagged substantially behind their conception. In the case of technical assistance programs the criteria are a good deal less refined, but even here some general guidelines can be suggested and some relevant factors pointed out. Yet in many cases, decisions are made on a project - by - project basis and based largely on individual judgment. Criteria are probably least developed for the allocation of resources among countries, partly because inter-country comparisons are especially difficult, partly because political and other factors with a different set of guidelines are more important. Here too, however, criteria or guidelines could help make the evaluation of some of these factors more rational.

The existence of criteria and guidelines, and their limited use in practice, emphasize the importance of increased technical assistance and international cooperation in their application. Future progress in improving cooperation between recipient countries and donor agencies is not primarily a question of research, but a matter of policy decisions and administrative arrangements. Progress in this respect is becoming ever more important and can be more productive as we improve criteria for determining the composition of development and technical assistance programs, and as decisions focus more and more on integrated programs rather than on individual projects.

Since, relatively speaking, the amount of money the United States spends on the United Nations is very small in terms of its own annual budget, would it make sense for the United States unilaterally to give a good deal more money to strengthen its operations? If so, are there any particular areas in which money should not be given? If not, why not?

Stoessinger argues that the Clark-Sohn proposal for taxing and borrowing is premature. He asks these questions about the scheme: Would not a United Nations tax cause resentment among people and lose support for the world organization? Could agreement be found on equitable criteria of taxation for the people of countries in varying circumstances? What about the formula suggested by Clark-Sohn? What, if anything, can be done about states which refuse to cooperate? How would you answer his questions?

Stoessinger enumerates a number of potential sources of revenue for the United Nations which have been suggested by various groups (final chapter under heading "New Sources of Funds"). Is there any greater likelihood of getting any of these schemes accepted as over against the Clark-Sohn scheme? Would they provide a significant amount of revenue for the United Nations? Are there any special problems in them vis-à-vis establishment of world order?

The International Court of Justice in a very recent Advisory Opinion stated (by a 9-5 vote) that the assessments made by the General Assembly for UNEF and ONUC were legally binding upon member states. Since the opinion is merely advisory there is some question as to what its impact will be on the states who have refused to pay these assessments. Assuming that many of these states will still refuse to pay, do you believe that Article 19 of the Charter should be invoked by the General Assembly to deny these states their voting privileges? On what do you base your judgment? Assuming that they will pay, does this mean that the UN has been strengthened? Could it mean that the General Assembly would be less willing to authorize expensive peacekeeping operations?

Clark-Sohn would revise present Article 17 requiring two-thirds majority of members present and voting in order to establish their budget. Do you think their proposed revisions are fair and would they be acceptable now?

At present the specialized agencies of the United Nations have a good deal of autonomy in raising revenue and allocating expenditures. Clark-Sohn want the General Assembly to have this authority. Under present circumstances would you be in favor of granting this authority? Is there any merit to permitting these agencies to act as independent agencies or "authorities?"

Do the new approaches to aiding economic development of underdeveloped areas enumerated by U Thant in his Foreword to the UN Decade of Development provide any reasonable framework with which to look at the problem. Are there any of the nine which he mentions which you feel are unacceptable or would cause special problems? Which of the nine do you consider to be most important? Why?

The case-history of the Meking project in the United Nations Development Decade declares that after ten years there has been no construction begun. In light of this, doesn't it seem somewhat pointless to hope that the United Nations would be able to develop an effective aid program to underdeveloped areas? Has anything been accomplished? Would it make more sense to work with projects that would take less time to complete than this one? What are the criteria we should use for deciding amongst these projects? Who should make these decisions?

Clark-Sohn propose a $36 billion UN budget for 1980, assuming that disarmament process has been completed by then. Work carefully through their figures and evaluate whether their proposal is reasonable. Is it too small or too large in any areas? (Note that in the Addendum xiii-xiv Clark-Sohn raise the maximum annual budget of the revised UN from two per cent of the estimated gross world product annually to three per cent.)

BIBLIOGRAPHY

For more information on REVENUE and BUDGET PROBLEMS of the
UN, see:

Jackson, Commander Sir Robert. "An International Development Author-
ity." Foreign Affairs 37: 54-68 (Oct. 1958).
Nichols, Calvin J. Financing the UN; Problems and Prospects. Cam-
bridge, Mass.: MIT Center for International Studies, 1961. 36p.
Singer, Joel D. Financing International Organization; The UN Budget
Process. The Hague: Nijhoff, 1961.
U.S. Senate Committee on Foreign Relations, 87th Congress, 2nd Session.
Purchase of UN Bonds. Washington, 1962. 325p. Hearings before
the Committee, dated Feb. 1962, which include testimony from the
leaders of every internationally minded organization of size in the
U.S.
(Wilcox, Francis O.) U.S. Senate Subcommittee on the UN Charter,
Committee on Foreign Relations, 83rd Congress, 2nd Session."Bud-
getary and Financial Problems of the UN." Staff Study No. 6. Wash-
ington, 1955.

For more information on problems of AIDING UNDERDEVELOPED
AREAS, see:

Agarwala, A. N., and S. P. Singh (eds.). The Economics of Under-
development. Bombay: Oxford U. Press, 1958, 510p.
Asher, Robert E. "Economic Cooperation Under UN Auspices." Inter-
natl. Org. 12: 288-302 (Summer 1958). Arguing that there is little
sense of direction to the UN's international economic assistance pro-
grams, the author reviews their history and accomplishments to see
what can be done to provide purpose and direction.
Bauer, P. T., and B. S. Yamey. The Economics of Under-developed
Countries. Cambridge: Cambridge U. Press, 1957, 271p.
Boulding, Kenneth E. Principles of Economic Policy. Englewood Cliffs,
N. J.: Prentice-Hall, 1958, 440p.
Galbraith, John Kenneth. Economic Development in Perspective. Cam-
bridge, Mass.: Harvard U. Press, 1962, 76p.
_____. "A Positive Approach to Economic Aid." Foreign Affairs
39: 444-57 (Apr. 1961).
Gilchrist, Huntington. "Technical Assistance from the UN--As Seen from
Pakistan." Internatl. Org. 13:505-19 (Autumn 1959). Because of the
"Latent emotionalism" concerning the ways in which foreign aid is giv-
en, the author feels that multilateral aid has many advantages over
bilateral aid.
Kajitani, Yoshihisa. "Multi-Nation Approach to Aid Underdeveloped
Countries." Asian Affairs 5: 22-35 (Oct. 1960).
Millikan, Max F., and W. W. Rowtow. A Proposal; Key to an Effective
Foreign Policy. NY: Harpers, 1957, 170p.
Neal, Alfred C. "New Economic Policies for the West." Foreign Af-
fairs 39: 247-58 (Jan. 1961).
Reedman, J. N. "The United Nations and Economic Development."
Internatl. Relations 2: 125-34 (Apr. 1961).
Rosenstein-Rodan, P. N. "International Aid for Underdeveloped Coun-
tries." R. Economic Statistics 43: 107-38 (May 1961).
Rostow, W. W. The Process of Economic Growth. 2nd ed. Oxford:
Clarendon Press, 1960, 372p.
_____. Stages of Economic Growth--A Non-Communist Manifesto.
Cambridge: Cambridge U. Press, 1960, 178p.

SESSION VII

A) EVALUATING THE UNITED NATIONS
B) WHAT CAN WE EXPECT FROM THE SOVIET-SINO BLOCK

The past four sessions have been concerned with the present United Nations structure, especially as it focuses on controlling the use of armed force by member states, with an evaluation of the Clark-Sohn scheme for strengthening the organization and with some of the problems involved in attempting to implement the revisions they suggest. The one major aspect of the Clark-Sohn model for world legal structure which we have still to study is their detailed proposal for complete and general disarmament. Since this aspect of their scheme calls for major changes in the structure and functions of the United Nations and since the problems raised by the process of disarmament is so intimately related with the basic political conflicts existing in the world community, it might be useful to look at two general questions.

The first question is by way of review and deals with an over-all evaluation of the United Nations. What impact has the United Nations had on the development of an international community without war, and what are the possibilities and limitation of further contribution from the organization? The article by Hoffmann is an over-view of United Nations activities with a theoretical sweep which ties the UN to the international political system. While Hoffmann believes that the United Nations has had a stabilizing effect on international political conduct, he does not believe that the organization has been or will be crucial in the peace-keeping area. However, he does not expect the enactment of the kind of model proposed by Clark-Sohn.

Dag Hammarskjold's writing is the Introduction to his last Annual Report as Secretary General before his tragic death. It is an eloquent and moving analysis of two views of the United Nations with trenchant observation of present political conditions and suggested steps for moving toward an international organization based on effective cooperation of member states.

The second general question also looks back to our previous sessions but is germane to our study of disarmament. It is the broad political question, what can we realistically expect in dealing with the Soviet-Sino bloc on matters such as strengthening the United Nations and achieving complete and general disarmament? The readings by Dallin, and Triska and Slusser deal with the Soviet view and practice towards the United Nations and international law. Both make the point that Soviet policy is presently opposed to creation of world legal structures. The Taylor article presents a view of the Soviet Union which is that of a relentless, aggressive, devious, highly skilled and implacable advocate for the achievement of international Communism. The discussion between Fromm and Salisbury suggests another view of the matter.   It provides a provocative analysis of the domestic dynamics of both the Soviet Union and China and their implication for international relations.   It touches somewhat on what the United States as a people can expect of themselves and therefore raises a point to which we shall have to attend in the sessions on disarmament; namely, to what extent should the Soviet-Sino bloc be willing to trust the United States Government and expect it to work sincerely and seriously for the development of a peaceful world?   The excerpt from Steiner deals with the attitude of the Chinese Communists toward war and disarmament and provides a bridge to our remaining sessions which will deal with disarmament.

Readings from World Peace Through World Law:
    None

AN EVALUATION OF THE UNITED NATIONS

Stanley Hoffmann*

Sixteen years have passed since the Charter of the United Nations was drafted at the San Francisco Conference. Sixteen years after the Versailles treaty, the League of Nations was on the verge of facing, and failing to meet, its biggest challenge: an evaluation written in the summer of 1935 would have been, on the whole, a positive one. Thus, any assessment of the United Nations' contribution to contemporary world order has to be cautious and provisional.

At any given time, the kind of order which exists in the world depends on the nature of the international system; the methods and the rules by which a minimum of security, assent and flexibility is insured depend on the structure of the world, on the domestic political systems, on the trans-national forces and on the scope and means which characterize the relations between the actors on the international scene.[1] Before 1919, world order consisted of two main elements: on the one hand, the legal norms which tried to delimit the rights and duties of the states and to regulate their competition or their cooperation in various areas; on the other hand, the empirical rules of behavior which resulted from the distribution of forces, from the calculations and strategies of the states, for instance, the "laws" of the balance of power system of the eighteenth and nineteenth centuries. The creation of an international organization was supposed to bring a drastic change into world politics and world order. It was intended to close the gap which had so often appeared between the legal order and the empirical one. At the same time, the legal order was becoming far more ambitious: international law would stop being the reflection of power relations which left sovereignty intact or submitted the sovereignty of a given state merely to those restrictions which were imposed by the greater force of its combined enemies. International law would become instead a body of rules determining the conduct of states independently from power relations and curbing the essential attribute of sovereignty, the right to resort freely to violence. International organization would be the motor of this new law. The world was assumed to be capable, so to speak, of leaping from Hume to Kant.

The drama of both the League and the United Nations has resided in one basic ambiguity and in one deep abyss. The ambiguity is that of the very concept of international organization.[2] It is a

---

* Associate Professor of Government, Harvard University.

[1] For further elaboration, see the author's "International Systems and International Law," to be published in World Politics (October 1961).

[2] See Walter Schiffer, The Legal Community of Mankind (New York, 1954).

fictitious community; it represents no revolution in the structure of the world. The basic unit remains the state, but in order to be able to play an effective role in discharging such functions as the maintenance of peace, the settlement of disputes, the emancipation of non-self-governing territories, the protection of human rights or the promotion of economic cooperation, the organization should dispose of some real political power *over* the states, *i.e.*, enjoy a modicum of autonomy and supremacy. In reality, however, decisions within the organization are made *by* the states. Hence a contradiction: the basis of action and obligation is supposed to be an emergent community spirit, *as if* the states were no more than agents of this international community, *as if* the organization expressed a general will no longer divided into separate and antagonistic wills, no longer confiscated by governments. But the reality of action is precisely one of governmental interests, which remain most frequently divergent and which, even when they converge on the organization, tend to use it as an instrument, and to exploit the community fiction for their own purposes. Consequently, the efficiency and authority of the organization depend ultimately, not on its Charter, but on the state of the world outside. But it is here that we find an abyss opening under the organization. After 1919 and after 1945 there has been a tremendous difference between the kind of world which was supposed to be the starting point, the condition and the milieu of the organization's functioning, and the world which had emerged from a global war. Versailles did not create a world of satisfied nation-states and of safe democracies, in which public opinion operating freely across borders, and statesmen who recognize as a new international legitimacy the dogmas of open diplomacy and world parliamentarism would serve as trans-national forces. Now, the organization is unable to create through its own power the reality which the founders of the Organization had failed to deliver.

In the case of the League, it proved to be impossible to overcome the ambiguity and to bridge the abyss. Obviously, the deeper the latter, the stronger the former. But the paradox of the United Nations until now is that despite that abyss, the organization has been able to survive. Although totally different from the world envisaged at San Francisco, the post-war international system has, so to speak, found various uses for the United Nations; consequently, the role the United Nations plays has little in common with the role an international organization was supposed to play, in the grandiose Wilsonian design for a new world order: it is a more modest but far less utopian task and therefore the basic ambiguity, which, as we will see, is of course still there, is less destructive. I would like to examine first how and to what extent the United Nations has been able to adapt to the post-war world despite the abyss I mentioned, and secondly, what are the uses of the organization in the present international system.

II

1. In the case of the League of Nations, it became clear only gradually that the main authors of the Covenant did not agree on what they expected from the organization, and that the post-war world fitted the expectations of none of them. It took just a few months to make it clear that the world in which the United Nations was operating had no resemblance with the world envisaged by the men who made the Charter.

The world envisaged by them was full of complexities and contradictions. It was assumed, in the first place, that the Big Five would remain responsible for the maintenance of peace and act as a new Concert (but no longer restricted to Europe) in charge of security; hence, the well-known provisions of Chapter VII and the theory of the chain of events, the extension of the principle of unanimity to admissions and amendments. In the second place, the Charter embodied also another inheritance from the nineteenth century, but this one was a product of that very liberal utopia of international relations which had *opposed* the practices of the European Concert, and whose victory over those practices Wilson had tried to insure in the Covenant of the League. It was the expectation that major disputes between states would, on the whole, be few and limited. The solemn assertion of a very broad "domestic jurisdiction" principle showed that one still believed that domestic affairs and international ones could be kept separate. Another distinction was made between breaches of peace or threats to peace, and less explosive disputes. It was assumed that a hierarchy could be maintained, and that the lesser disputes could ordinarily be solved by traditional diplomatic techniques. In the third place, the Charter provisions on economic and social matters and the statutes of the World Bank and International Monetary Fund postulated a world which, after a brief period of reconstruction, would no longer be plagued by permanent financial difficulties (balance of payment troubles being primarily solved by domestic efforts), in which economic development would be assured mainly by private investors at ordinary conditions of security and profit, and in which quantitative restrictions and discriminatory measures would be gradually removed from world trade.

One can defend those postulates by saying that they were not at all utopian, but realistic in the sense of defining the only conditions in which an international organization can properly function.[3] Whereas the egalitarianism of the League had a utopian flavor, the Charter at least recognized that the success of an organization which is not a super-state depends on the existence of a concert of great powers which will be the driving force within and the mechanism thanks to which the world outside will be made such that an international organization has some chance of playing a useful role. As for the liberal conception of international relations which coexisted with the new Concert, did it not simply express the idea that an organization which is not a super-state can be effective only as long as not every dispute which it handles is a matter of life and death for some of its members? When such a matter arises, it is the Concert of the Big Five which must deal with it (and the Security Council was indeed made capable of overcoming the domestic jurisdiction clause in the case of Chapter VII). But one must assume that the organization will not have to live in the climate of tragedy all the time, for, indeed, the more often such a climate takes over, the smaller are the chances of great power solidarity. However, if this was realism, it belonged to the category which Raymond Aron has called "wrong realism"—the mistake which results from a misinterpretation of reality rather than from idealistic illusions.[4] The United Nations was launched in a world torn by the conflict between East and West, by the storm of decolonization, and by the quest for development.

2.   The history of the Organization, and especially the history of what happened to its Charter, is that of a race, the race of the United Nations to escape from the consequences of the contrast between the world postulated by the Charter and the real world. Because of this contrast, the Organization was faced with the risk of a triple paralysis. First, the conflict between East and West was threatening not only to destroy the collective security function and apparatus, but also to cripple the procedure for the peaceful settlement of disputes by the Security Council. The race away from deadlock took the well-known form of a transfer of power to the General Assembly: on the one hand, more and more ordinary disputes and situations were brought before it, under art. 11, par. 2; on the other hand, the Uniting-for-Peace revolution of 1950, voted during the Korean crisis, constituted a daring attempt at shifting responsibility for collective security from the Security Council to the General Assembly, unburdened by the veto. Secondly, the violence of most of the disputes which broke out in the

---

3 See I.L. Claude, Swords into Plowshares (2d ed., New York, 1959), Chapters 4 and 8.

4 Raymond Aron, "En quête d'une philosophie de la politique étrangère," III Revue Française de Science Politique, 69-91.

post-war world, particularly between colonial powers and their colonies and protectorates or between the new states, was such that too faithful an observance of the careful tags with which the Charter tried to define a hierarchy of conflicts, and too persistent a respect of the prohibition against intervention in domestic affairs, would have condemned the organization to permanent frustration. The race, here, led on the one hand to an implicit or explicit rejection of the exception of domestic jurisdiction whenever a state invoked it in a case where its domestic troubles had serious international repercussions, and on the other hand to a discarding of the labels of the Charter by the Security Council and by the General Assembly. Ad hoc procedures were substituted for explicit references to such and such an article. Consequently, instead of the cautious and gradual diplomatic methods of Chapter VI, the Organization has resorted to a far more energetic "policy of presence" and to collective intervention. Thirdly, the kind of massive irrelevance to post-war economic problems other than the reconstruction of western Europe, which seemed to be the fate of the United Nations and of its agencies, was avoided by a determined switch of attention to problems of technical assistance and economic development.

This triple race away from paralysis presents two aspects which are worth noting. First, in order to justify practices which were so thoroughly at variance with its original Charter, the Organization had to accentuate, rather than overcome, the fundamental ambiguity I have described: it has interpreted its Charter as if this document were the equivalent of a national constitution, whose provisions frequently lose their old meaning or receive a new interpretation, without any formal amendment, but through the practices of governmental organs and thanks to the underlying political consensus. The trouble is, of course, that the international milieu is not a community yet, but the trend toward behaving as if it had, in Mr. Hammerskjöld's vocabulary, passed from the stage of an "institutional pattern of coexistence" to that of a "constitutional system of international cooperation,"[5] is nowhere more clear than in the role played by the Secretary General. Both Mr. Lie and Mr. Hammerskjöld—the former with excessive gusto, and the latter despite his initial reluctance—have acted not merely as administrators in charge of a secretariat, nor even as trustees discharging the functions which heavy and clumsy political organs cannot perform efficiently, but as leaders speaking for that international interest or community whose "existence" justifies the twisting of the Charter. It is precisely when the normal interplay of states' clashing

---

[5] Address by Mr. Hammerskjöld at the University of Chicago Law School, 6 United Nations Review No. 12 (June 1960), 26-30.

policies threatens to reduce the Organization to impotence, that the Secretary General becomes the organ of continuity and "fills the vacuum" by taking an initiative.[6]

Secondly, the postulates on which the re-interpretation of the Charter is based describe a world which is the exact opposite of the world assumed by the original postulates, but whose "realism" is just as questionable. On the one hand, it is now assumed that the conflict between the big powers should not prevent the exercise of collective security even against one of them, and indeed, in the practice of the United Nations, collective security has been set in motion only in the Korean case, and the only nations condemned as aggressors have been Red China and the Soviet Union! Breaches of peace which do not pit East against West have been handled with methods stronger than those envisaged by Chapter VI, but far less drastic than those of Chapter VII. On the other hand, it is also assumed that the very scope of the disputes between old and new states, or between the new ones—disputes in which the old barrier between domestic and international affairs collapses, and in which force is almost always used—makes collective intervention by the Organization not only desirable but likely to succeed.

3. Precisely because those new assumptions are of dubious validity, the outcome of the race has been most ambiguous. It is easy to point out that the Organization has been unable to eliminate all those factors of present-day world politics which resisted its attempts at asserting its role; but it is also easy to show that the Organization has nevertheless survived and played a remarkable part.

In many ways, the race looks like a circular circuit rather than a straight run away from the pitfalls of the Charter. The postulate of the need for big-power unity seems largely vindicated; whenever there has been a direct clash between East and West, the role of the Organization has been limited. The fact of "bipolarity" has been stronger than the machinery of "Uniting for Peace," collective security has been tacitly abandoned as a function of the United Nations,[7] and the procedure of resorting to an emergency session of the General Assembly when the Security Council is paralyzed has been used, not in order to organize collective security against a large or even a small power (ex-

---

[6] See for instance the Secretary General's statement at the opening meeting of the General Assembly's third emergency special session on August 8, 1958, his initiatives in the Congo crisis in July 1960 and again in February 1961. Throughout the summer of 1960, the resolutions submitted by Tunisia and Ceylon to the Security Council on the Congo followed the suggestions spelled out by the Secretary General in his statements or reports.

[7] See I.L. Claude, "The United Nations and the Use of Force," 532 International Conciliation (March 1961).

cept during the Korean war), but as a way of restoring peace or solving disputes without resort to coercion, after a failure of the Security Council. Even when the issue at stake was not a direct clash between East and West, one major condition of United Nations' success in restoring peace or in reaching a settlement has been at least a tacit concert of the Big Two. The postulate according to which the Organization would be most effective if the majority of disputes were not too violent or too deep has also been largely vindicated: the United Nations has dealt with countless conflicts in which the international status or the domestic regime of nations was involved, but it has repeatedly failed to reach a substantive settlement. The expansion of the technical assistance program, the switch in the lending policies of the World Bank—from Europe to the rest of the world—the creation of the International Finance Corporation and the International Development Association do not amount to a massive transfer of aid from bilateral to United Nations channels. The "haves" remain reluctant to abandon control of their funds. Various short-circuits such as the fiasco of the International Trade Organization or the failure to stabilize the price of primary products or the resistance to SUNFED have marked the limits of United Nations action in this area.

The lesson is clear: *legal* impotence has been overcome, *political* limitations have not been removed. The failure to influence the Soviet Union or China in cases such as Hungary and Tibet, not to mention disarmament; the inability to solve the issues of Kashmir or the Arab-Israeli conflict, as well as the difficulties of the United Nations operation in the Congo; the slowness of the process of erosion by which the underdeveloped countries try to squeeze more money for capital development from the richer nations: all those facts show how deep an abyss there remains between the world as it is and the world as it ought to be in order to allow the United Nations to play the major role which both its founders and their successors wanted. Consequently, the basic ambiguity of international organization cannot fail to appear as a persistent obstacle; the world community has rarely looked more fictitious. In an area such as Laos, in which East and West clash directly, the "United Nations presence" established by the Secretary General was bound to evaporate; in the Congo crisis, there have been moments when the deadlock between conflicting camps—East and West, moderates and radicals among the new nations—was such that any attempt at pursuing a "United Nations policy" became both an exercise in fiction and a peril for the Secretary General. Indeed, in so far as this ambiguity is both summed up in, and revealed by, the Secretary General's role and fate, nothing is more discouraging for the believers in an international community than the destruction of one Secretary by the brutal attacks from the Soviet Union (which followed degrading pressures of United States witchhunters) and the threats to the position of the other Secretary which come both from the Eastern bloc and from certain new nations whose policies conflict with the "international interest" as defined by Mr. Hammerskjöld.

However, despite such unfavorable circumstances, the Organization has done far more than survive. The contrast with the League in this respect is most remarkable. The Covenant was gradually emasculated, and when the "time of troubles" came, the nations' reactions were centrifugal. On the contrary, the United Nations has emerged as one of the most interesting aspects of contemporary international relations. The Organization has become indispensable as a result of a double process. On the one hand, each camp needs the United Nations as a field of manoeuvre; in this respect, the United Nations is neither a substitute for traditional diplomacy nor the beginning of a world community, but the form of multilateral diplomacy which corresponds to the extension of the international system to the whole world. The cold war involves not only an attempt by each bloc to preserve its own forces and, if possible, to weaken the adversary. One of its main stakes is the allegiance of the new and underdeveloped nations; consequently, it becomes necessary for both East and West to be present in the United Nations, which provides them with unprecedented possibilities of influence and mobilization. Even if the Organization cannot directly affect the "core area" held by each superpower, it can exert a more subtle action on the balance of power in the area of the "third world." The revolution against colonialism operates with a similar dialectic; here, the very divisions among the major powers (and not only between East and West) give an advantage to the smaller nations and incite them to exploit to the hilt an organization which those divisions put under their numerical control. Similarly, in the battle for economic development, the needy nations use the Organization as a lever against the richer ones and the latter dare not protest too much because it is precisely for the support of those poorer nations that they compete. Thus, there is a convergence of conflicting interests on the Organization as an arena of major importance. On the other hand, there are areas in which the Organization is useful not merely as an instrument to be used *by each group* in the international competition but as an institution necessary *to all members* because of identical or convergent interests in joint action. In such cases the United Nations is more than an arena, it is a force. Thus, the United Nations contributes to the establishment of a new world order in two distinct ways. First, it is the framework in which the nations hammer out many (although, as we have noticed and shall see again, by no means *all*) of the empirical rules of behavior and of the legal norms which are supposed to prevent the present international system from resembling the war of all against all. Secondly, it is one (and only one) of the elements of stability and order in the present world.

III

Thus, the role of the United Nations in the present international system is double. The Organization reflects the system; but it also affects it—both negatively and positively.

1. Precisely because the United Nations, since 1955, has opened its doors to almost all states, the Organization is a very faithful mirror of post-war world politics. It shows both the disastrous and the hopeful sides. Let us examine the disastrous aspects first. The present international system is a revolutionary one. As such, it presents two characteristics which account for many of the United Nations' own features. In the first place, it is a heterogeneous system. The diplomatic field embraces the whole world for the first time, but there are huge differences: (1) between states, both from the viewpoint of power (contrast between the states that dispose of a capacity of general destruction, and the others) and from the viewpoint of authority (difference between well-established states, and new nations, sometimes in search of their proper borders); (2) between political regimes, both from the viewpoint of the domestic formula of legitimacy and from that of economic policy; (3) between levels of economic development; (4) between ideological camps. Those factors of heterogeneity are felt in United Nations debates on practically any subject, whether the Organization discusses the future of colonialism or tries to draft covenants on human rights or attempts to intervene in the endlessly complicated disarmament dialogue which has been going on among the superpowers. The United Nations mirrors both the universal but superficial adherence of all states to the principles of conduct expressed in the Charter, and the reality of negative solidarities which link members of blocs or groups and divide the world into contending factions.

In the second place, a revolutionary system is one in which the relations between states are no longer marked by any moderation in scope or means. The end of moderation in scope entails the following developments. On the one hand, the violence of the competition between states brings about the collapse of the zone of domestic affairs and of the principle of non-intervention; the choice of a regime determines the international conduct of a state and each major contender tries to influence the choices of lesser ones. United Nations' discussions on the French Cameroons in 1959, and even more the debates on the Congo, have reflected this aspect: not only is the United Nations' operation in the Congo caught in the contests between Congolese leaders, but various groups of states fight for the recognition of antagonistic leaders. On the other hand, in a revolutionary period, "functional" sectors previously removed from the political struggle and left to the free activities of private citizens become once again stakes in the struggles of the states: consequently, not only has the sphere of international economic affairs become one of the main battlefields, but even more technical subjects have been affected with a political interest. United Nations' discussions on economic development or on the right to nationalize natural resources have reflected this extension of world politics, while many of the specialized agencies were faced with the dilemma of eliminating from their agenda controversial issues in order to stay out of politics—but at the cost of irrelevance—or else facing the storm, but at the risk of possible deadlock. As for the end of moderation in means, it entails in particular the unlimited resort to techniques of propaganda and subversion against the enemy camp or in order to obtain the allegiance of third parties; it also entails the willingness to use force in order to wrest local gains and the determination to exploit fully the temporary advantages one may enjoy in the technological race. A list of the problems discussed by the United Nations shows that this is indeed what has kept the organization so busy, despite all the restraints which the principles of the Charter were supposed to impose on the behavior of the members. But this is also what makes agreement on the international control of atomic energy, or on reserving outer space for peaceful uses, impossible to obtain.

By definition, a revolutionary system is one in which world order is almost non-existent; and to the extent to which the United Nations has been a mirror of the system, it has been permanently threatened with paralysis. The United Nations translates into parliamentary terms the fundamental divisions of the world. The danger of paralysis has even augmented over time. Thus, the more membership has increased, the more difficult it has become to obtain a two-thirds majority in the General Assembly; the outcome of debate is often either no resolution at all, or a compromise version which verges on the meaningless.[8] Similarly, the United Nations has suffered not only from the fact of the cold war between East and West, but also from its evolution. Soviet tactics have switched, after Stalin's death, from an essentially defensive attitude, reflected in Russian behavior and arguments in

---

[8] See for instance, during the 14th session of the General Assembly, the failure to adopt a resolution on Algeria; during the 15th session, the failure of the resolution proposing sanctions against the Union of South Africa because of apartheid, and the compromise resolution on Algeria.

471

the United Nations, to a much more daring strategy which adds to the continued defense of the integrity of the Soviet bloc a determined effort to win over uncommitted nations, or at least to exasperate their antagonism toward the West. The fifteenth session of the General Assembly has been particularly spectacular in this respect. The effect of this change on the United Nations has been a faithful reflection of the effect in the world. It has meant not so much a net addition to the strength of the Soviet bloc, as a loss of influence for the United States (which finds it far more difficult to get its own viewpoint adopted by two thirds of the members, must more and more frequently leave the initiative to the uncommitted nations, and merely tries to soften or weaken their suggestions) and an increasingly deep split between moderates and radicals among the uncommitted nations.

This shift in Soviet tactics poses a very serious problem for the United Nations. Until recently, the organization's efficiency in political matters was limited by two main obstacles: the "impenetrability" of the Soviet bloc, which became sufficiently recognized so that issues like Tibet or Berlin were either barely discussed or avoided altogether, and the rockbottom obstacle which stops any international organization, *i.e.*, the unwillingness of any state to accept a substantive settlement of a dispute which goes against its interests. Here, the United Nations merely reflected the contradiction between the extension of the diplomatic field and the maintenance (and mushrooming) of separate sovereignties. Those obstacles were serious enough, for they contributed to the reluctance of UN members to allow the establishment of a permanent non-fighting force. Many states feared that it might be used either in an East-West dispute, thus endangering world peace, or against their own interests, should a conflict involving them arise. However, in between those limits there remained the area described by the Secretary General in his report to the fifteenth Assembly: "Keeping newly arising conflicts outside the sphere of bloc differences,"[9] filling the power vacuum between those blocs whenever a conflict breaks out there, so as to prevent them from rushing in. This was feasible as long as both superpowers tacitly agreed on the need for "decolonization" or on the way of handling the crises which this process provoked. But if each superpower tries to affect the process in such a way that the outcome will be a "friendly" new state, the dream of the UN filling the gap becomes the nightmare of the UN turned into a battlefield. The contrast between the Suez and Congo crises indicates the extent of the deterioration. In the Suez crisis, the UN was able to act without too many difficulties because of a joint pressure

---

[9] 7 United Nations Review No. 4 (Oct. 1960) 24.

from the U.S. and the U.S.S.R. toward a restoration of the status quo, and because of the support of most "uncommitted" nations for such a policy. Consequently, the Secretary-General was able to act as the "executive" of the Assembly, which gave him massive political backing. In the case of the Congo, the superpowers agreed only on one thing, the need for Belgian withdrawal,[10] but each one chose his own favorite among the contending leaders, and the Afro-Asian nations split and chose sides as well; consequently, from October 1960 to February 1961, the Secretary General, far from filling any vacuum, was left on his tightrope walking above a political vacuum, as was shown in most spectacular fashion by the failure of both the Security Council and the General Assembly to adopt any resolution at all in December. The long race from the Security Council to the General Assembly, from the Assembly to the Secretary, seemed to have ended in fiasco. The lesson is clear—the UN can escape from total paralysis only to the extent to which, in the sphere considered to be *the* proper UN sphere of action by the Secretary General, the states that belong to neither bloc are able to reconcile their differences and to resist the pulls and pushes of both blocs.

Is this possible? The answer is yes. Here we must turn to a far more positive side of the picture. The present revolutionary system contains one fundamental element of stability—the fear of total war. The very uncertainty which marks the danger of "escalation" has acted as a dampener on limited wars as well. Consequently the contest between the two blocs, including the competition for allegiance of the other nations, is primarily a non-military one and each superpower tries to seduce or subvert, but not to conquer or coerce. Two chances open therefore for the United Nations. First, the amount of arm-twisting which each superpower can do at the expense of the smaller nations is limited, and the United Nations reflects the desire of the latter to preserve their independence from outside encroachments, wherever they may come from, just as much as it reflects the blocs' efforts to penetrate this independence. Whatever their ambiguity, the resolutions adopted by the Security Council in February 1961 and by the General Assembly two months later, concerning the Congo, as well as the resolution adopted by the Assembly's emergency session on August 21, 1958, concerning the Middle Eastern crisis, show the restraints which the need to gain consent imposes on the superpowers. The failure of the Soviet plan to "reorganize" the Secretariat indicates the same thing. Secondly, the fear of general war re-enforces the desire of all states, and particularly of those which have the weapons of gen-

---

10 Even on this point the two states have disagreed about the speed with which it should take place and the scope it should have.

eral destruction, to "keep talking." Negotiations may be fruitless, but the dialogue must be maintained and the UN provides an ideal forum for such a dialogue. But we are here at the limit between the United Nations' role as a mirror and its role as an actor.

2. Every contemporary development toward world order has two faces; one which threatens chaos, one which promises order. There is a negative contribution by the United Nations which tends too often to be submerged behind pious expressions of faith or gallant efforts at presenting what may well be inevitable as being actually beneficial. It results from the fundamental ambiguity which was mentioned in the beginning. It expresses itself in three ways.

There is, first, a contradiction between the realities of international politics and the fictions which the UN seeks to preserve in order to be able to operate. Now, any resort to fictions conceals a weakness and multiplies difficulties. One such fiction is the principle of equality, according to which each member has one vote. Equality symbolizes the idea of homogeneity, but as we know, the members represented in the UN are neither equal in power nor homogeneous from any point of view. The idea of homogeneity and the dream of community combine in producing "majoritarianism"—the belief that the resolutions adopted by two thirds of the members really represent the opinion of mankind. Another fiction, which has gotten the Organization into all kinds of trouble, is that of non-intervention. We have seen that the UN has actually reversed the hierarchy established by the Charter, and rejected the exception of domestic jurisdiction invoked by a member whenever there was an international interest attached to the matter. But the principle of non-intervention is one to which each member clings for himself, and which the UN must proclaim in its own operations; it was supposed to be the guideline of its action in the Congo. Unfortunately, the revolutionary character of world politics has played havoc with the principle. In a situation of quasi-civil war, non-intervention can only mean staying out completely; once one goes in, it becomes almost meaningless. Indeed, in the Congo crisis, the myth of non-intervention has had three effects: it has managed to infuriate in turn each of the Congolese factions, which interpreted the "neutrality" of UNOC as an act of hostility. It has obliged the Secretary General and the members to resort to highly debatable devices in order to justify intervention while preserving the dogma of non-interference in domestic affairs: thus, the idea that what makes UN intervention necessary, and what explains the crisis, is the persistence of Belgian intervention, or—at the time when Mr. Hammerskjöld's antagonism with Mr. Lumumba was at its most heated—the distinction between internal political conflicts, which were "off-limits," and "flagrant violations of elementary human rights," which had to be stopped.[11] Finally, the myth of non-intervention itself collapsed, when the Security Council adopted a resolution asking for reorganization of the Congolese army. The main trouble with the resort to fictions is that they increase the resistance of minorities; a state or a faction which objects to a UN resolution finds in the lack of realism of the organization a good reason to stick to its guns. In a world where states are not equal, where they have no obligation to obey, and no way of being obliged to obey resolutions adopted by UN majorities, and where domestic and international problems are intertwined, the UN exposes itself to failure either when it tries to bully a reluctant state (be it a Communist state like Russia, a colonial power like Portugal, a racist country like South Africa, or the industrial nations which have been resisting SUNFED) or when it pretends to respect a principle which will merely give to the pygmies some rope with which they can bind Gulliver.

Secondly, there is a contradiction between the nature of the problems submitted to the Organization and the way in which they are handled by it. On the one hand, there is an excessive fixation on procedure: the emphasis is put less on the methods by which the issue could be solved, even less on the substance of a solution, than on the measurement of "international public opinion" as represented by the delegates. In other words, the UN tends to indulge in "barometrics" rather than in diplomacy. This is a by-product of the transfer of power to the General Assembly, but the practice of inviting "interested" states which are not members of the Security Council to come and present their views generalizes this development. Hence huge amounts of time are spent on finding the right words or the right sponsors. It is a search for the degree of indignation, concern or exhortation which will make the machine tilt—I mean, obtain the necessary two-thirds majority. Much of the criticism of parliamentary diplomacy is unfair; the length and heaviness of debate and its inevitable propaganda aspects should not make one forget that there is as much negotiation going on behind the scenes as there is posturing on the rostrum. What is seriously disturbing, however, is that so many of the secret discussions and deals in the lobbies are concerned not with action, but with wording—with symbols rather than substance. On the other hand, when the Organization in emergencies resolves to act, there is another kind of fixation. The extinction of fires, I mean the end of the use of force, seems to be the ideal and the goal; it is, of course, a fine and noble task, especially in a world in which "escalation" and general embroilment are permanent threats. But there is a formalism in this

---

[11] Statement by the Secretary General to the Security Council, 7 United Nations Review No. 4, 47 (Oct. 1960).

approach, which is not without its own peril.[12] Groups or nations often resort to force because it is the last avenue which remains open to them for the redress of a grievance or because underlying problems have received no solution. The United Nations, by putting so much more energy into the admittedly more spectacular act of rushing to smother the flames than into the difficult task of rebuilding the charred house, tends to leave too many cinders smoldering in the ashes. This was the weakness of UN action during the Suez crisis. The handling of the Congo emergency has shown a tendency to concentrate once more on the avoidance of "military solutions"; it was made inevitable both by the danger of foreign military intervention at the request of the various contending factions, and by the difficulty of recognizing openly that the cause of the drama was the lack of preparation of the Congolese for independence and the absence of any Congo-wide nationalism. However, as long as the source of the trouble remains hidden, the Organization has no choice but to see the domestic political struggles continue, the peril or the reality of outside military help resume, the lack of competent Congolese administrators and technicians persist, and its own forces treated as a party to the conflicts without disposing of all the means a party ordinarily can use. A policy of presence with limited authority may bring about the worst of all worlds. This contradiction between the nature of the problems and the UN approach tends to aggravate matters, to the extent to which attention is diverted from what is fundamental to what is merely an effect, and often from what is relevant to what is not. In particular, the concentration on the evil of force incites nations either to shift their strategy from outright violence to subtler forms of intervention (which may go unnoticed or be handled far less energetically by the UN) or else to provoke new explosions after the problems which led to previous ones have remained unsolved long enough.

There is a third contradiction, this time between the stakes of political conflicts in the world and the means at the disposal of the Organization. Those means are extremely limited: small sums of money, either for the regular budget, or for economic programs, or for special operations such as UNEF and UNOC, sums which are obtained only after painful debates, and at the cost of heavy arrears or defections; then, there are mechanisms such as emergency forces, observers, committees of conciliation or investigation, mediators and special representatives; finally, there are resolutions, pure and simple. As we have seen, there is no collective security machinery, the organs which the Uniting-for-Peace resolution was supposed to establish have faded

---

12 See Père R. Bosc, "Ideologies et Institutions de l'O.N.U. depuis 1945," *Revue de l'Action Populaire* No. 147 (April 1961), 403-14.

away, and the emergency forces themselves are doubly limited by the principle of consent of the host and by the freedom of withdrawal of the participants. The result is that the UN impact on world affairs remains necessarily limited. The UN does not reach domestic opinion, does not affect the choice of a regime, the selection of alliances, the military policies of the main powers. Attempts to handle vital problems with insufficient means may aggravate international troubles in two ways. On the one hand, whenever the UN hits (deliberately or accidentally) a vital interest of a state, and in particular whenever the UN seems to threaten what a nation considers to be its very fabric or its essential values—in other words, the image the citizens have of their nation—the reaction is bound to be violent and bitter: French attitudes toward the UN because of Algeria, South African refusals to cooperate with UN Committees, Portugal's walk-out over Angola are only the more extreme examples. The total fiasco of UN action in the field of human rights, *i.e.,* the most sensitive area of governments' relations with their citizens, points to the same moral. On the other hand, the contrast between stakes and means tends to weaken the UN as an instrument for the solution of disputes and thus to reduce the effectiveness of one of the few elements of order available in the present international system. Thus, the presence of 20,000 men in the Congo looks at times like the attempt of a few shipwrecked passengers on a raft trying to stop a storm. Coping with interventions from abroad, and with civil war and political turmoil within, is simply too much for an expeditionary force which far from being able to seal off hermetically the Congo from the outside world, must suffer the consequences of decisions taken elsewhere—for instance in Casablanca—or in the Congo itself—for instance in Matadi. The force which was supposed to act as a buffer is too weak to be effective; and the other two contradictions—the myth of non-intervention, the fixation on force—added to the present one tend to perpetuate the crisis, even if only in softened form. One may well ask if an endless, if muted, terror, is better than a terrible end—or will prevent it ultimately.

3.   The more positive effects of the UN on the international system are, however, far from negligible. The organization contributes to a transformation of three aspects of the system.

In the first place, the Organization has a double impact on the structure of the world. On the one hand, there is a subtle action on the international hierarchy, one might almost call it a gradual subversion. The effect of "bipolarity" on the hierarchy is in many ways neutralized, i.e., the super-powers, far from possessing an influence proportional to their potential (specially their military potential) are obliged to let smaller powers enjoy greater freedom of action than in many periods of history. Two qualifying remarks must be made. First, the UN does not "destroy" the international hierarchy, not only because it does not have the means to do so, but also because it has shown, in its treatment of states on which the Organization wanted to put pressure, a healthy respect for differences in power, i.e., small states have been dealt with far less cautiously than either the Soviet Union (even in the Hungarian case), or the United States (see the resolution of April 22, 1961 on Cuba), or even the United Kingdom and France. Secondly, what prevents the superpowers from playing toward the small nations a role corresponding to their overwhelming might is primarily the double factor I have singled out before, the desire to avoid general war, and the resulting reliance on persuasion or subversion rather than violence for the recruitment of clients and friends. This is the fundamental cause which explains why, in the international hierarchy of today, sheer military strength is less decisive than it has been in the past. The very destructiveness of the nuclear arsenal, which gives to the superpowers a superiority great powers never had before, also tends to neutralize this advantage as long as a war has not started.

However, the UN has not only benefited from this singularity, it has exploited and enlarged it. The transfer of power to the General Assembly has given to the weaker states a splendid opportunity to push their advantage to the hilt, and they have used it. In the UN, because of their number, they can even thwart the designs of the superpowers. The debate on the Congo has shown for instance that the very violence of Soviet attacks on the UN operation has brought the African and Asian nations close enough together to allow them to compromise for the preservation of UNOC, and both the Soviet Union and the United States, despite their objections to various provisions, had to follow. As Mr. Hammerskjöld put it recently, "the United Nations has increasingly become the main platform—and the main protector of the interests—of those many nations who feel themselves strong as members of the international family but who are weak in isolation. Thus, an increasing number of nations have come to look to the UN for leadership and support in ways somewhat different from those natural in the light of traditional diplomacy. They look to the Organization as a spokesman and as an agent for principles which give them strength in an international concert in which other voices can mobilize all the weight of armed force, wealth, an historical role and that influence which is the other side of a special responsibility for peace and security."[13] It is precisely this role of the UN as a counter-

---

[13] 7 United Nations Review No. 4, 27 (Oct. 1960).

vailing force that corrects the effects of the traditional hierarchy, to which a statesman like General de Gaulle objects so strongly, for he is attached to the classical formula of a directory of the great powers. Paradoxically, such a directory was more powerful in the League, despite a very egalitarian Covenant, than in the UN, despite a hierarchical Charter. Thus, each small state sees in the UN the one forum in which it not only "is somebody," but in which it is able to make its presence felt. Furthermore, in so far as the processes of parliamentary diplomacy resemble those of any parliamentary system marked by a multiplicity of factions and consequently by great difficulty at reaching compromises, certain small states gain considerable prestige and influence by playing a key role as brokers and conciliators, due not to their own strength but to their political position. They are the "friends of all parties," the truly non-aligned states, which play the role which isolated but centrally located and skillful personalities played in the Parliament of France's Third Republic, for instance, Ireland, Sweden, Tunisia, and often Canada and Yugoslavia.[14]

On the other hand, the UN influences the structure of the world by accelerating the increase in the number of states. The very prestige conferred by membership in the UN, and the opportunities for influence which are thus opened, are factors which confirm many nationalist leaders in their desire to press not only for full-fledged independence rather than mere internal autonomy within a crumbling empire, but also against mergers between newly independent nations. Furthermore, the Organization's own interpretation of its powers under Chapter XI, its very strict supervision of political developments in trusteeship territories, its attacks on colonialism both in separate instances of trouble and as a matter of principle, have made of the UN a matrix of new states.

Both aspects of this action on the structure of the world tend to strengthen the basic ambiguity of international organization, for there is a sharp contrast between the "community" symbolized by the UN (with its predominance of the smaller nations and its collective drive for independence from colonial rule) and the outside world, in which the superpowers remain the leaders and in which the increase in the number of states only multiplies the prospects for disputes and crises, consequently undermining whatever community there may be. What matters here, however, is that the UN does more than reflect this ambiguity, which may well condemn it to impotence at frequent intervals, it is one of its chief architects.

In the second place, the Organization affects the means at the disposal of the states in their relations. The role of the UN in this

---

14 See Sidney D. Bailey, The General Assembly, Ch. 2 (London, 1960).

respect consists of fostering at least a partial return to moderation. It has been felt in three areas. First, there is the area of the one identical aim of all states, the avoidance of general war and the desire to see even limited conflicts purged of violence because of the danger of extension. There, the UN has not been able to affect the superpowers directly, despite pleas for the suspension of nuclear tests and for disarmament, but it has skillfully handled the "limited war" in Korea—except for the blunder of crossing the 38th parallel in Oct. 1950 without sufficient awareness of the consequences—and it has developed numerous techniques, put up various kinds of alarm bells to prevent clashes between smaller nations or within a smaller nation from becoming trial grounds for a direct East-West clash. The tacit consent of both superpowers in this respect—a negative concert which does not prevent either from trying to affect the outcome of the dispute as long as resort to force is avoided or maintained at a low level— has been continuous. French and British evacuation of Egypt in 1956, U.S. withdrawal from Lebanon in 1958, and the Soviet retreat from the Congo after the fall of Lumumba have been possible not only because of the fear of war but also because the UN provided both a guarantee against excessive loss of face and a fairly impartial mechanism for removing the element of violence—without prejudging the result of the contest. This is the area in which the Secretary General has played a vital role, and acted as the representative of the one identical purpose of all segments of mankind.

A second aspect of this action of the UN corresponds to convergent interests of the various members, *i.e.*, the setting up of instruments for technical and administrative assistance as well as the expansion of channels for multilateral economic aid. The logic of the competition has forced not only the West to retreat from its hostility and to concede that a sizable portion of its aid should be granted through the UN (although the risk of giving too much control to the recipients is an unpleasant one) but also the East to abandon its initial refusal to participate at all. The desire of the underdeveloped countries for aid devoid of the political strings or implications of bilateral agreements has conversely forced them to accept, in the case of loans from the World Bank, more of a check on their own plans than they often might have wished. The results remain limited, but the partial convergence of competing interests on common channels is definitely an element of stability, whereas the separate channels of bilateral and regional agreements perpetuate the centrifugal elements of the present international system. In this area, it is the Secretariat whose role must be underlined.

A third aspect of the stabilizing role of the UN is more controversial: in the parts of the world which are not under the control of the Soviet Union, the United Nations has made it almost impossible for the stronger states to employ toward the lesser ones the more brutal means of coercion traditionally used; this is a result of, both, the fear of general war and the increased role of small powers within the United Nations. The best example was the Suez affair. It is a doubly controversial "improvement" of world politics. The Soviet bloc feels under no compulsion to observe similar restraints, and the outcry against a "double standard" of UN action arises quite legitimately. This abandonment of gunboat diplomacy also has its hypocritical aspects, since it does not prevent bigger powers from trying to impose their will on lesser ones by methods of subversion. Nevertheless there is here a partial contribution to a partial world order, and it must be taken into account as one of the consequences of the existence of the Organization.

In the third place, the UN has an impact on the trans-national forces that cut across borders. The action of the UN in this respect is twofold. On the one hand, the Organization reenforces those "separatist" solidarities which bind various nations into groups or blocs. Those entities are usually created outside the UN, but once again the world organization is more than just a mirror, it is a catalyst and an accelerator. It is easier to meet in the lobbies of the UN than in Accra or Bandung. The blocs or groups are, with the exception of the Soviet one, anything but united. Recent votes on Algeria or on the Congo reveal for instance a three-way split among the Afro-Asians.[15] But the fact is that the basic negotiating unit tends to become the bloc, that drafts are discussed first by each caucus, and that deals between groups take place only at a later stage, after a common stand has been thrashed out within each of the principal groups, or after attempts at achieving unity within them have failed.[16] The very fact that most of the major issues of international politics are brought before the UN and to a vote obliges groups which would otherwise remain vague associations of states with ideological affinities, to react in a way which either consolidates their solidarity, or decisively shows that it was fictitious.

---

[15] The Pakistani resolution on the Congo, adopted by the General Assembly on April 15, 1961, received the support of 12 African and 12 Asian states (in addition to Turkey); 7 African states voted against it; 6 African and 8 Asian states abstained. The paragraph of the resolution on Algeria which decided the organization of a referendum by the United Nations was supported by 27 African and Asian states, rejected by 11 African ones, while 5 Asian ones abstained. The resolution as a whole was supported by 31 African and Asian states and opposed by 6 African states, while 7 abstained. The resolution asking for sanctions against South Africa was supported by 23 African and 7 Asian nations and opposed by one Asian state; 13 Asian and 1 African state abstained.

[16] See Thomas Hovet, Bloc Politics in the United Nations (Cambridge, 1958).

It will be interesting to see, in this respect, to what extent a sub-group of the Afro-Asian group such as the French-speaking African one is just a transition from the former Community to totally different alignments, or to what extent on the contrary it is a genuine bloc. The UN, in which such groups rub against one another, puts them to a kind of test of truth which would probably operate much more slowly if the Organization did not exist.

Partial and often divisive solidarities are however not the only ones which the UN consolidates. The Organization also strengthens the germs of universalist tendencies which can be detected in the present world. Thus, the UN crystallizes elements of a new international legitimacy which are still weak and questionable but which might otherwise get lost altogether in the turmoil of separate interpretations and calculations. The origin of those elements is double. There is first of all the internationalization of European principles—those of the old Liberal ethos of international relations—as was shown, for instance, by the Bandung provisions on coexistence. They simply reflect the fact that the vision of a world of harmonious nation-states uncoerced by superior power is a kind of common denominator in a universe where nationalism still spreads. Secondly, there is this fear of war and the resulting restraint on the competition for allegiance which I have mentioned. What results is a kind of consensus on principles such as the avoidance of force, the need for an international presence in emergencies, the right to self-determination and the right to economic development. Needless to say, the balance sheet is mixed; not only does the Soviet bloc have its peculiar interpretation of each of those principles, but, as we have seen, there is not any of them which does not have its own limitations, drawbacks or dangers. However, there has never been any international legitimacy without inequities or flaws, and the role of the UN consists precisely of trying to put some flesh on those bones—for there can be no international legitimacy without a minimum of performance.

The United Nations tries to strengthen these principles not only by promoting common actions, but also by fostering a process of what I have elsewhere called "political mobilization," or a gradual leveling of concern.[17] The UN accelerates the effects of the extension of the diplomatic field to the whole world, by obliging all its members to take stands on all questions, thus bringing home to an unprecedented degree the idea that what concerns one part of the planet may affect all the others. The UN is unable to achieve "one world" in the sense of an orderly and unified system for collective security, the settlement

---

[17] "National Attitudes and International Order: the National Studies on International Organization," XIII International Organization 202.

of disputes, etc.; such a system requires a unity, or an overwhelming convergence, of national attitudes and responses. But at least the UN tries to bring about the prerequisite, "one world," in the sense of universality of concerns. This is precisely the area in which the League of Nations, with its de facto predominance of the Council, its essentially European aspect, and even more its link with the status quo of the peace treaties, had failed most dismally.

IV

Ambiguity has been the key of our assessment of UN history and of UN action. It remains at the center of any projection one may try to make into the future.

If we look at the general trend of UN action in the world, it becomes almost too easy to denounce the Organization as the second most powerful force of disruption of the status quo, next to Communism. The break-up of Empires, approval of measures of economic nationalism which hit mainly Western interests, a majority of anti-status quo nations which obliges the West to choose between ineffective and unpopular opposition, and giving its blessing to resolutions which weaken its positions further—all those aspects of the role of the UN may give serious worry to statesmen who fear that the only beneficiaries of disruption will ultimately be the Communists. On the other hand, we must not forget that the assault on the status quo which is thus being waged is in many ways a conservative revolution, inspired by slogans and principles which belong to the Western, and particularly to the Liberal heritage. If the cry for political and economic self-determination and the desire for welfare and development provide Communism with admirable opportunities and turn more often than not against the West in the present phase, they may at a future date provide in reverse the West with opportunities and serve as barriers against Communist imperialism. The UN merely accelerates a liquidation of the status quo which would proceed anyhow; the degree to which this should mean a liquidation of the West depends on the West's reactions far more than on UN actions.[18]

If we look at potential UN contributions to a new world order, we must realize first that such an order will still be based on the state as the main unit, and consequently that order will be possible only if conditions of stability are resolved in the international system. Now, for such a restoration we cannot count on material developments (for they may tend to accentuate the competition), on general common

---

18 On this point see Lincoln P. Bloomfield, The United Nations and U.S. Foreign Policy (Boston, 1960) and the author's "Sisyphus and the avalanche: the United Nations, Egypt and Hungary," XI International Organization, 464-9.

principles (for they may be interpreted in conflicting ways), or even on what Raymond Aron calls the dawn of universal history (for there are violently divergent manners of living the same history).[19] We cannot count on legal prescriptions, for international law loses much of its authority in revolutionary systems. We cannot count on the UN to maintain or establish such conditions of stability as an equilibrium of power between the major states (for the Organization has no responsibility in preserving the balance of terror and no way of checking nuclear diffusion) or a return to the limited state in domestic regimes, or an end of the ideological clash between East and West. But a restoration of stability presupposes also a return to moderation in the scope and means of international relations and it is here that the UN becomes important. Moderation in scope would necessitate both the end of the cold war, and improved political and economic relations between the western powers and the newly independent states. Moderation in means would require a strengthening of the measures taken to prevent the outbreak of general war or of wars which could degenerate into global conflicts. The end of the cold war is beyond the possibilities of anyone at this time; but on the other two issues, despite the persistence of the cold war which interferes with a reconciliation of "North" and "South" and makes agreements on disarmament or even arms control unlikely, the United Nations has a major role to play. It is not an exclusive role, but it is a crucial one precisely because the Organization is the only agency which includes almost all states and symbolizes, in its weaknesses as well as in its strengths, the idea of a universal world order. Nothing is more important therefore than to avoid wasting United Nations' efforts on areas where failure is guaranteed; nothing is more important than to exert leadership so that in the two areas where constructive action is possible, the United Nations do indeed contribute to world order, rather than fail to act altogether, or even act to increase tensions further.[20]

---

[19] Dimensions de la Conscience historique, Ch. VIII (Paris, 1961).

[20] For recent evaluations of the UN, see Erich Hula, "The UN in crisis 27 Social Research, 387-420, and Hamilton Fish Armstrong, "UN on trial," 39 Foreign Affairs, 388-415.

TWO DIFFERING CONCEPTS OF UNITED NATIONS ASSAYED: INTRODUCTION TO THE ANNUAL REPORT OF THE SECRETARY-GENERAL ON THE WORK OF THE ORGANIZATION, 16 JUNE 1960—15 JUNE 1961[2]

Dag Hammarskjöld

I.

Debates and events during the year since the publication of the last report to the General Assembly have brought to the fore different concepts of the United Nations, the character of the Organization, its authority and its structure.

On the one side, it has in various ways become clear that certain Members conceive of the Organization as a static conference machinery for resolving conflicts of interests and ideologies with a view to peaceful coexistence, within the Charter, to be served by a Secretariat which is to be regarded not as fully internationalized but as representing within its ranks those very interests and ideologies.

Other Members have made it clear that they conceive of the Organization primarily as a dynamic instrument of governments through which they, jointly and for the same purpose, should seek such reconciliation but through which they should also try to develop forms of executive action, undertaken on behalf of all Members, and aiming at forestalling conflicts and resolving them, once they have arisen, by appropriate diplomatic or political means, in a spirit of objectivity and in implementation of the principles and purposes of the Charter.

Naturally, the latter concept takes as its starting point the conference concept, but it regards it only as a starting point, envisaging the possibility of continued growth to increasingly effective forms of active international cooperation, adapted to experience, and served by a Secretariat of which it is required that, whatever the background and the views of its individual members, their actions be guided solely by the principles of the Charter, the decisions of the main organs, and the interests of the Organization itself.

The first concept can refer to history and to the traditions of national policies of the past. The second can point to the needs of the present and of the future in a world of ever-closer international interdependence where nations have at their disposal armaments of hitherto unknown destructive strength. The first one is firmly anchored in the time-honored philosophy of sovereign national states in armed competition of which the most that may be expected in the international field is that they achieve a peaceful coexistence. The second one envisages possibilities of intergovernmental action overriding such a philosophy, and opens the road toward more developed and increasingly effective forms of constructive international cooperation.

It is clearly for the governments, Members of the Organization, and for these

---

[2] General Assembly *Official Records* (16th session), Supplement 1A. Title cited from *United Nations Review*, September 1961 (Vol. 8, No. 9), p. 12.

governments only, to make their choice and decide on the direction in which they wish the Organization to develop. However, it may be appropriate to study these two concepts in terms of the purposes of the Organization as laid down in the Charter and, in this context, also to consider the character and the significance of the decisions of the Organization as well as its structure.

II.

The purposes and principles of the Charter are set out in its Preamble and further developed in a series of articles, including some which may seem to be primarily of a procedural or administrative nature. Together, these parts of the Charter lay down some basic rules of international ethics by which all Member States have committed themselves to be guided. To a large extent, the rules reflect standards accepted as binding for life within states. Thus, they appear, in the main, as a projection into the international arena and the international community of purposes and principles already accepted as being of national validity. In this sense, the Charter takes a first step in the direction of an organized international community, and this independently of the organs set up for international cooperation. Due to different traditions, the state of social development and the character of national institutions, wide variations naturally exist as to the application in national life of the principles reflected in the Charter, but it is not too difficult to recognize the common elements behind those differences. It is therefore not surprising that such principles of national application could be transposed into an agreed basis also for international behavior and cooperation.

In the Preamble to the Charter, Member nations have reaffirmed their faith "in the equal rights of men and women and of nations large and small," a principle which also has found many other expressions in the Charter.

Thus, it restates the basic democratic principle of equal political rights, independently of the position of the individual or of the Member country in respect of its strength, as determined by territory, population, or wealth. The words just quoted must, however, be considered as going further and imply an endorsement as well of a right to equal economic opportunities.

It is in the light of the first principle that the Charter has established a system of equal votes, expressing "the sovereign equality of all its Members," and has committed the Organization to the furtherance of self-determination, self-government, and independence. On the same basis, the Charter requires universal respect for and observance of human rights and fundamental freedoms for all "without distinction as to race, sex, language or religion."

It is in the light of the latter principle— or, perhaps, the latter aspect of the same basic principle—that the Charter, in Article 55, has committed the Members to the promotion of higher standards of living, full employment, and conditions of economic and social progress and development, as well as to solutions of international economic and related problems. The pledge of all Members to take joint and separate action, in cooperation with the Organization, for the achievement of these purposes has been the basis for the far-reaching economic and technical assistance channelled through or administered by the Organization, and may rightly be considered as the basic obligation reflected also in such economic and technical assistance as Member governments have been giving, on a bi-

486

lateral basis, outside the framework of the Organization.

It would seem that those who regard the Organization as a conference machinery, "neutral" in relation to the direction of policies on a national or international basis and serving solely as an instrument for the solution of conflicts by reconciliation, do not pay adequate attention to those essential principles of the Charter to which reference has just been made. The terms of the Charter are explicit as regards the equal political rights of nations as well as of individuals and, although this second principle may be considered only as implicit in the terms of the Charter, they are clear also as regards the demand for equal economic opportunities for all individuals and nations. So as to avoid any misunderstanding, the Charter directly states that the basic democratic principles are applicable to nations "large and small" and to individuals without distinction "as to race, sex, language and religion," qualifications that obviously could be extended to cover also other criteria such as, for example, those of an ideological character which have been used or may be used as a basis for political or economic discrimination.

In the practical work of the Organization these basic principles have been of special significance in relation to countries under colonial rule or in other ways under foreign domination. The General Assembly has translated the principles into action intended to establish through self-determination a free and independent life as sovereign states for peoples who have expressed in democratic forms their wish for such a status. Decisive action has in many cases been taken by Member governments, and then the United Nations has had only to lend its support to their efforts. In other cases, the main responsibility has fallen on the Organization itself. The resolution on colonialism, adopted by the General Assembly at its fifteenth session, may be regarded as a comprehensive restatement in elaborated form of the principle laid down in the Charter. Results of developments so far have been reflected in the birth of a great number of new national states and a revolutionary widening of the membership of the Organization.

The demand for equal economic opportunities has, likewise, been—and remains—of special significance in relation to those very countries which have more recently entered the international arena as new states. This is natural in view of the fact that, mostly, they have been in an unfavorable economic position, which is reflected in a much lower per capita income, rate of capital supply, and degree of technical development, while their political independence and sovereignty require a fair measure of economic stability and economic possibilities in order to gain substance and full viability.

In working for the translation into practical realities in international life of the democratic principles which are basic to the Charter, the Organization has thus assumed a most active role and it has done so with success, demonstrating both the need and the possibilities for such action.

Further, in the Preamble to the Charter it is stated to be a principle and purpose of the Organization "to establish conditions under which justice and respect for the obligations arising from treaties and other sources of international law can be maintained." In these words—to which, naturally, counterparts may be found in other parts of the Charter—it gives expression to another basic democratic principle, that of the rule of law. In order to promote this principle, the Charter established the International Court of Justice, but the principle permeates the approach of the Charter to international problems far beyond the sphere of competence of the

Court. As in national life, the principle of justice—which obviously implies also the principle of objectivity and equity in the consideration of all matters before the General Assembly or the Security Council —must be considered as applicable without distinction or discrimination, with one measure and one standard valid for the strong as well as for the weak. Thus, the demand of the Charter for a rule of law aims at the substitution of right for might and makes of the Organization the natural protector of rights which countries, without it, might find it more difficult to assert and to get respected.

The principle of justice can be regarded as flowing naturally from the principles of equal political rights and equal economic opportunities, but it has an independent life and carries, of itself, the world community as far in the direction of an organized international system as the two first-mentioned principles. It has deep roots in the history of the efforts of man to eliminate from international life the anarchy which he had already much earlier overcome on the national level, deeper indeed than the political and economic principles which, as is well known, were much later to get full acceptance also in national life. Long before the United Nations and long before even the League of Nations, governments were working toward a rule of justice in international life through which they hoped to establish an international community based on law, without parliamentary or executive organs, but with a judicial procedure through which law and justice could be made to apply.

The Charter states and develops the three principles mentioned here as a means to an end: "to save succeeding generations from the scourge of war." This adds emphasis to the concept, clearly implied in the Charter, of an international community for which the Organization is an instrument and an expression and in which anarchic tendencies in international life are to be curbed by the introduction of a system of equal political rights, equal economic opportunities, and the rule of law. However, the Charter goes one step further, drawing a logical conclusion both from the ultimate aim of the Organization and from the three principles. Thus, it outlaws the use of armed force "save in the common interest." Obviously, the Charter cannot, on the one side, establish a rule of law and the principle of equal rights for "nations large and small," and, on the other hand, permit the use of armed force for national ends, contrary to those principles and, therefore, not "in the common interest." Were nations, under the Charter, to be allowed, by the use of their military strength, to achieve ends contrary to the principle of the equality of Members and the principle of justice, it would obviously deprive those very principles of all substance and significance. One practical expression of this approach, which may be mentioned here, is that the organs of the United Nations have consistently maintained that the use of force, contrary to the Charter as interpreted by those organs, cannot be permitted to yield results which can be accepted as valid by the Organization and as establishing new rights.

In the Charter, the right to the use of force is somewhat more extensive than may seem to be the case from a superficial reading of the phrase "save in the common interest." Thus, apart from military action undertaken pursuant to a decision of the Security Council for repression of aggression—that is, for upholding the basic Charter principles—the Charter opens the door to the use of armed force by a nation in exercise of its inherent right to resist armed attack. This is a point on which, both in theory and in practice, the development of international law is still at a very early stage. As is well known, no agreement has been reached on a definition of aggression, beyond that found in Article 2, paragraph 4, of the Charter, and the Organization has several times had to face situations in which, therefore, the rights and wrongs in a specific case of conflict have not been clarified. It would be a vitally important step forward if wider agreement could be reached regarding the criteria to be applied in order to distinguish between legitimate and illegitimate use of force. History is only too rich in examples of armed aggression claimed as action in self-defense. How could it be otherwise, when most cases of armed conflict are so deeply rooted in a history of clashes of interests and rights, even if, up to the fatal moment of the first shot, those clashes have not involved recourse to the use of armed force?

In recognition of this situation and in the light of historical experience, the Charter makes yet another projection into international life of solutions to conflicts tested in national life, and establishes the final principle that the Organization shall "bring about by peaceful means and in conformity with the principles of justice and international law, adjustment or settlement of international disputes or situations which might lead to a breach of the peace." This principle, as quoted here from Article 1 of the Charter, is further developed specifically in Article 33, which requires parties to any dispute, the consequence of which is likely to endanger the maintenance of international peace and security, to "seek a solution by negotiation, enquiry, mediation, conciliation, arbitration, judicial settlement, resort to regional agencies or arrangements, or other peaceful means of their own choice." It is in this sphere that the Security Council has had, and is likely to continue to have, its main significance, both directly as a forum before which any dispute threatening peace and security can

be brought up for debate and as an organ which directly, or through appropriate agents, may assist the parties in finding a way out and, by preventive diplomacy, may forestall the outbreak of an armed conflict. It seems appropriate here to draw attention especially to the right of the Security Council under Article 40 to "call upon the parties concerned to comply with such provisional measures as it deems necessary or desirable" for the prevention of any aggravation of a situation threatening peace and security, and to the obligation of Members to comply with a decision on such measures.

It is in the light of the approach to international coexistence in our world today, which is thus to be found in the Charter, that judgment has to be passed on the validity of the different conceptions of the Organization which in recent times have become increasingly apparent. As already pointed out, the basic principles regarding the political equality of nations and their right to equal economic opportunities are difficult to reconcile with the view that the Organization is to be regarded only as a conference machinery for the solution, by debate and joint decisions, of conflicts of interest or ideology. It seems even more difficult to reconcile these principles with a view according to which equality among Members should be reflected in the establishment of a balance between power blocs or other groupings of nations. The same difficulty is apparent as regards the principle of justice and the principle prohibiting the use of armed force. It is easier to apply the conference concept to the principle of prevention of conflict through negotiation, but also on this point the difficulties become considerable if it is recognized that such solutions as may be sought by the Organization should be solutions based on the rules of equality and justice.

489

III.

The General Assembly, the Security Council, and other collective organs of the United Nations have features in common with a standing international diplomatic conference, but their procedures go beyond the forms of such a conference and show aspects of a parliamentary or quasi-parliamentary character.

While decisions of a conference, in order to commit its participants, must be based on their subsequent acceptance of the decisions, the organs of the United Nations act on the basis of voting, with the decisions being adopted if supported by a majority. However, the decisions of the Assembly have, as regards Member States, only the character of recommendations (except for financial assessments and certain other types of organizational action) so that obligations like those arising out of an agreement, coming into force after a conference, do not normally flow from them. But although the decisions, legally, are only recommendations, they introduce an important element by expressing a majority consensus on the issue under consideration.

Naturally, such a formula leaves scope for a gradual development in practice of the weight of the decisions. To the extent that more respect, in fact, is shown to General Assembly recommendations by the Member States, they may come more and more close to being recognized as decisions having a binding effect on those concerned, particularly when they involve the application of the binding principles of the Charter and of international law.

Both those who regard a gradual increase in the weight of decisions of the General Assembly as necessary, if progress is to be registered in the direction of organized peaceful coexistence within the Charter, and those who oppose such a development,

have to recognize that, with certain variations in individual cases, the practice still is very close to the restrictive Charter formula. Experience shows that even countries which have voted for a certain decision may, later on, basing themselves on its character of merely being a recommendation, refuse to follow it or fail to support its implementation, financially or in other respects.

What has been said applies generally to the collective organs of the Organization, but, as is well known, the Charter has gone one step further beyond the conference concept, in the direction of the parliamentary concept, in the case of the Security Council. In Article 25, Member States of the United Nations have agreed to "accept and carry out the decisions of the Security Council in accordance with the present Charter," thus, by agreement, making the decisions of the Council mandatory, except, of course, when such decisions take the form of "recommendations" within the terms of Chapter VI or certain other articles of the Charter. They have further, in Article 49, undertaken to "join in affording mutual assistance in carrying out the measures decided upon by the Security Council."

This agreed mandatory nature of certain Security Council decisions might have led to a demand for unanimity in the Council, a unanimity which was the rule for the Council of the League of Nations. Even so, however, the arrangement would have gone beyond the conference principle with its requirement that no decision reached in an international organ should be binding on an individual Member short of his agreement. With the present arrangements, requiring a majority of seven and the concurring votes of the permanent members, a bridge between the traditional conference approach and a parliamentary approach is provided by the commitment in Article 25 to agree to the carrying out of the decisions in the Council which should be considered as giving the Council its authority by general delegation as indeed stated in Article 24, paragraph 1.

What clearly remains within the Council of the traditional conference and agreement pattern is the condition that its decisions of a nonprocedural character must be supported by the unanimous vote of the five permanent members, thus avoiding for those members the risk of being bound by a decision of the Council which has not met with their agreement. It may be observed that this special position for the permanent members, apart from other reasons, has the justification that, without such a rule, the other Members of the Organization, in complying with a Security Council decision, might find themselves unwillingly drawn into a big power conflict.

In spite of the delegated authority which the Council may be considered as exercising, and the condition that decisions must be agreed to by the permanent members, the experience of the Organization, as regards the implementation of Council decisions, is uneven and does not indicate full acceptance in practice of Article 25. In this case also, examples can be given of a tendency to regard decisions, even when taken under Chapter VII, as recommendations binding only to the extent that the party concerned has freely committed itself to carry them out; there is here a clear dichotomy between the aims of the Charter and the general political practice at its present stage of development. Such cases refer not only to Members outside the Council, or, perhaps, Members inside the Council, who have not supported a specific decision, but also to Members within the Council who have cast their votes in favor of a decision but who later on are found to reserve for themselves at least a right to interpret the decision in ways which seem to be at variance with the intentions of the Council. The ambiguity of this situation emerges with special force in cases where such attitudes have been taken by permanent members of the Council, who are considered to shoulder the responsibility for the maintenance of peace and security which is reflected in the special position they hold within the Council. Obviously, the problem whether the intended legal weight is given to decisions of the Security Council arises in practice not only in cases of noncompliance but also in cases of a refusal to shoulder the financial consequences of a decision of the Council.

These observations—which have been limited to a reminder of the Charter rules and a factual reminder also of the experiences in practice—point to a situation which in any evaluation of the United Nations must be given the most serious consideration by Members. For the judgment on the various concepts of the United Nations which are put forward, it is one thing to note what the Charter stipulates; it is an entirely different but ultimately more important question as to what the situation is in practice and what, in fact, is the weight given to decisions of the Organization when they go beyond the conference pattern of agreement.

For those who maintain the conference concept of the Organization, it is natural to side-step the mandatory nature of decisions by the Security Council. For those who take a different view, it is equally natural and essential to work for a full and general acceptance of the Charter rules. Were those to be right who hold that the Charter on the points discussed here, and, maybe, also as regards the five basic principles discussed in the first part of this Introduction, is ahead of our time and the political possibilities which it offers, such a view still would not seem to justify the conclusion that the clear approach of the Charter should be abandoned. Rather, it would indicate that Member nations jointly should increase their efforts to make political realities gradually come closer to the pattern established by the Charter.

In the light of such considerations, the significance of the outcome of every single conflict on which the Organization has to take a stand, and the weight given to its decisions in such a conflict stand out very clearly. A failure to gain respect for decisions or actions of the Organization within the terms of the Charter is often called a failure for the Organization. It would seem more correct to regard it as a failure of the world community, through its Member nations and in particular those most directly concerned, to cooperate in order, step by step, to make the Charter a living reality in practical political action as it is already in law.

Were such cooperation, for which the responsibility naturally rests with each single Member as well as with all Members collectively, not to come about, and were the respect for the obligations flowing from Article 25 of the Charter to be allowed to diminish, this would spell the end of the possibilities of the Organization to grow into what the Charter indicates as the clear intention of the founders, as also of all hopes to see the Organization grow into an increasingly effective instrument, with increasing respect for recommendations of the General Assembly as well.

What this would mean for the value of the Organization as protector of the aims, principles and rights it was set up to further and safeguard, is obvious. The effort through the Organization to find a way by which the world community might, step by step, grow into organized international cooperation within the Charter, must either progress or recede. Those whose reactions to the work of the Organization hamper its development or reduce its possibilities of effective action may have to shoulder the responsibility for a return to a state of affairs which governments had already found too dangerous after the First World War.

IV.

The growth of the United Nations out of the historic conference pattern—which, as observed earlier in this Introduction, at all events naturally remains the starting point in all efforts of the Organization—is clearly reflected in what, in the light of experience, may seem to be a lack of balance in the Charter. While great attention is given to the principles and purposes, and considerable space is devoted to an elaboration of what may be called the parliamentary aspects of the Organization, little is said about executive arrangements. This does not mean that the Charter in any way closes the door to such arrangements or to executive action, but only that, at the stage of international thinking crystallized in the Charter, the conference approach still was predominant, and that the needs for executive action, if the new Organization was to live up to expectations and to its obligations under the Charter, had not yet attracted the attention they were to receive in response to later developments.

The key clause on the executive side may be considered to be Article 24 in which it is said that "in order to assure prompt and effective action by the United Nations, its Members confer on the Security Council primary responsibility for the maintenance of international peace and security." On that basis the Security Council is given the right, under Article 29, to establish such subsidiary organs as it deems necessary for the performance of its functions, the right under Article 40 to decide on so-called provisional measures, the right to use, for the purposes of the Charter, under certain conditions, armed forces made available to the Council, the right under Article 48 to request from governments action on the Council's behalf, as well as the right to request of the Secretary-General to "perform such . . . functions as are entrusted to him" by the Council.

The various clauses here briefly enumerated open a wide range of possibilities for executive action undertaken by, and under the aegis of, the Security Council. However, no specific machinery is set up for such action by the Council, apart from the Military Staff Committee, with planning responsibilities in the field of the possible use of armed force by the Security Council under Chapter VII of the Charter. In fact, therefore, the executive functions and their form have been left largely to practice, and it is in the field of the practices of the Organization that cases may be found in the light of which it is now possible to evaluate the ways in which the Organization may develop its possibilities for diplomatic, political, or military intervention of an executive nature in the field.

The forms used for executive action by the Security Council—or when the Council has not been able to reach decisions, in some cases, by the General Assembly—are varied and are to be explained by an effort to adjust the measures to the needs of each single situation. However, some main types are recurrent. Subcommittees have been set up for fact-finding or negotiation on the spot. Missions have been placed in areas of conflict for the purpose of observation and local negotiation. Observer groups of a temporary nature have been sent out. And, finally, police forces under the aegis

of the United Nations have been organized for the assistance of the governments concerned with a view to upholding the principles of the Charter. As these, or many of these, arrangements require centralized administrative measures, which cannot be performed by the Council or the General Assembly, Members have to a large extent used the possibility to request the Secretary-General to perform special functions by instructing him to take the necessary executive steps for implementation of the action decided upon. This has been done under Article 98, as quoted above, and has represented a development in practice of the duties of the Secretary-General under Article 97. The character of the mandates has, in many cases, been such that in carrying out his functions the Secretary-General has found himself forced also to interpret the decisions in the light of the Charter, United Nations precedents, and the aims and intentions expressed by the Members. When that has been the case, the Secretary-General has been under the obligation to seek guidance, to all possible extent, from the main organs; but when such guidance has not been forthcoming, developments have sometimes led to situations in which he has had to shoulder responsibility for certain limited political functions, which may be considered to be in line with the spirit of Article 99 but which legally have been based on decisions of the main organs themselves, under Article 98, and thus the exclusive responsibility of Member States acting through these organs. Naturally, in carrying out such functions the Secretariat has remained fully subject to the decisions of the political bodies.

This whole development has lately become a matter of controversy, natural and, indeed, unavoidable in the light of differences of approach to the role of the Organization to which attention has been drawn earlier in this Introduction. While the development is welcomed by Member nations which feel a need of growth as regards the possibilities of the Organization to engage in executive action in protection of the Charter principles, it is rejected by those who maintain the conference concept of the Organization. The different opinions expressed on the development are only superficially related to this or that specific action and the way in which it is considered to have been carried through. They are also only superficially related to the choice of means used for translating decisions into action. The discussion regarding the development of executive functions is basically one confronting the same fundamentally different concepts of the Organization and its place in international politics, which could be seen also in the different attitudes toward the legal weight of decisions of the Organization.

It is in this context that the principle embodied in Article 100 of the Charter is of decisive significance. This principle, which has a long history, establishes the international and independent character of the Secretariat. Thus, it is said that the Secretary-General and the staff of the Secretariat "shall not seek or receive instructions from any Government or from any other authority external to the Organization," and that they "shall refrain from any action which might reflect on their position as international officials responsible only to the Organization." In the same Article, the Members of the United Nations undertake to respect "the exclusively international character of the responsibilities of the Secretary-General and the staff and not to seek to influence them in the discharge of their responsibilities."

The significance of the principle stated in Article 100 is a dual one. It envisages a Secretariat so organized and developed as to be able to serve as a neutral instrument for the Organization, were its main organs

to wish to use the Secretariat in the way which has been mentioned above and for which Article 98 has opened possibilities. But in doing so, the principle also indicates an intention to use the Secretariat for such functions as would require that it have an exclusively international character.

In the traditional conference pattern, participants in a meeting are mostly serviced by a secretariat drawn from the same countries as the participants themselves, and constituting a mixed group regarding which there is no need to demand or maintain an exclusively international character. It is therefore natural that those who favor the conference approach to the United Nations tend to give to Article 100 another interpretation than the one which the text calls for, especially in the light of its historical background and its background also in other clauses of the Charter.

There is no reason to go more deeply into this special problem here. Suffice it to say that, while the Organization, if regarded as a standing diplomatic conference, might well be serviced by a fully international Secretariat but does not need it, the other approach to the Organization and its role cannot be satisfied with anything less than a secretariat of an exclusively international character, and thus cannot be reconciled with a secretariat composed on party-lines and on the assumption that the interests represented in the main organs in this manner should be represented and advocated also within the Secretariat. Thus, again, the choice between conflicting views on the United Nations Secretariat is basically a choice between conflicting views on the Organization, its functions, and its future.

In order to avoid possible misunderstandings, it should be pointed out here that there is no contradiction at all between a demand for a truly international Secretariat and a demand, found in the Charter itself, for as wide a "geographical" distribution of posts within the Secretariat as possible. It is, indeed, necessary precisely in order to maintain the exclusively international character of the Secretariat, that it be so composed as to achieve a balanced distribution of posts on all levels among all regions. This, however, is clearly something entirely different from a balanced representation of trends or ideologies. In fact if a realistic representation of such trends is considered desirable, it can and should be achieved without any assumption of political representation within the ranks of the Secretariat, by a satisfactory distribution of posts based on geographical criteria.

The exclusively international character of the Secretariat is not tied to its composition, but to the spirit in which it works and to its insulation from outside influences as stated in Article 100. While it may be said that no man is neutral in the sense that he is without opinions or ideals, it is just as true that, in spite of this, a neutral Secretariat is possible. Anyone of integrity, not subjected to undue pressures, can, regardless of his own views, readily act in an "exclusively international" spirit and can be guided in his actions on behalf of the Organization solely by its interests and principles, and by the instructions of its organs.

V.

After this brief review of the principles of the Organization, of the character of its decisions, and of its structure, especially as regards arrangements for executive action, presented only as a background for the consideration of what basic concepts and approaches should guide the development of the Organization, it may be appropriate, in conclusion, to give attention to the activities of the Organization and their relevance to the current international situation.

For years the Organization has been a focal point for efforts to achieve disarmament. This may still be considered as the main standing item on the agenda of the General Assembly. However, in recent years these efforts of the Organization have been running parallel to other efforts which are either outside of it or only loosely tied to the work of the United Nations. This may be justified on the basis that a very limited number of countries hold key positions in the field of armaments, so that any effort on a universal basis and by voting, to reach a decision having practical force, would be ineffective, unless founded on a basic agreement between those few parties mostly concerned. Therefore, direct negotiations between those countries are an essential first step to the solution, through the United Nations, of the disarmament problem, and do not in any way derogate from the responsibilities or rights of the Organization.

The situation may serve as an example of a problem which has become increasingly important in the life of the Organization: the right way in which to balance the weight of the big powers and their security interests against the rights of the majority of Member nations. Such a majority naturally cannot expect the big powers, in questions of vital concern to them, with their superior military and economic strength, automatically to accept a majority verdict. On the other hand, the big powers cannot, as Members of the world community, and with their dependence on all other nations, set themselves above, or disregard the views of, the majority of nations. An effort to balance the big power element and the majority element is found in the Charter rules regarding the respective competence of the

General Assembly and the Security Council and regarding the special position of the big powers within the Council. Other efforts to solve the same problem are reflected in the way in which the disarmament problem has been attacked in recent years. No fully satisfactory or definitive formula has been found, but it must be sought, and it is to be hoped that when the time comes for a Charter revision, agreement may be reached on a satisfactory solution.

What is true of the disarmament problem is, of course, true also of those more specific questions in which security interests of big powers are or may be directly involved, as for example the Berlin problem. The community of nations, represented in the United Nations, has a vital interest in a peaceful solution, based on justice, of any question which—like this one—unless brought to a satisfactory solution, might come to represent a threat to peace and security. However, the problem of the balance to be struck between the rights and obligations of the big powers and the rights and obligations of all other nations applies, in a very direct way, also to this problem which is now so seriously preoccupying the minds of all peoples and their leaders. The United Nations, with its wide membership, is not, and can, perhaps, not aspire to be a focal point in the debate on an issue such as the Berlin question, or in the efforts to solve it, but the Organization cannot, for that reason, be considered as an outside party which has no right to make its voice heard should a situation develop which would threaten those very interests which the United Nations is to safeguard and for the defense of which it was intended to provide all Member nations with an instrument and a forum.

Reference has already been made in this Introduction to the work of the Organiza-

tion devoted to furthering self-determination, self-government, and independence for all peoples. In that context it was recalled that the General Assembly, at its last session, adopted a resolution regarding the colonial problem which elaborates the basic principles of the Charter in their application to this problem.

This is, likewise, a question which for years has been before the General Assembly and it is likely to remain a major item until a final result is achieved which reflects full implementation of the basic principles in the direction indicated by last year's resolution. Experience has shown that peaceful progress in that direction cannot be guaranteed solely by decisions of the General Assembly or the Security Council, within the framework of a conference pattern. Executive action is necessary, and neither the General Assembly nor the Security Council—which has had to deal with situations in which the liquidation of the colonial system has led to acute conflict—has abstained from such action in support of the lines upheld. As in the past, executive action by the Organization in the future will undoubtedly also be found necessary if it is to render the service expected from it under the terms of the Charter.

It is in conflicts relating to the development toward full self-government and independence that the Organization has faced its most complicated tasks in the executive field. It is also in the case of executive action in this context that different concepts of the Organization and of its decisions and structure have their most pointed expressions. As regards this specific aspect of the work of the United Nations, the front line has not been the usual one between different bloc interests, but more one between a great number of nations with aims natural especially for those which recently have been under colonial rule or under other forms of foreign domination, and a limited number of powers with other aims and predominant interests. This seems understandable if one takes into account that a majority of nations wishes to stand aside from the big power conflicts, while power blocs or big powers tend to safeguard their positions and security by efforts to maintain or extend an influence over newly emerging areas. The United Nations easily becomes a focal point for such conflicting interests as the majority looks to the Organization for support in its policy of independence also in relation to such efforts, while power blocs or countries with other aims may see in the United Nations an obstacle in the way of their policies to the extent that the Organization provides the desired support. How this is reflected in the attitude toward the development of the executive functions of the United Nations can be illustrated by numerous examples. It may be appropriate in this context to say in passing a word about the problem of the Congo and the activities of the United Nations in that country.

Different interests and powers outside Africa have seen in the Congo situation a possibility of developments with strong impact on their international position. They have therefore, naturally, held strong views on the direction in which they would like to see developments in the Congo turn and—with the lack of political traditions in the country and without the stability which political institutions can get only by being tested through experience— the doors have been opened for efforts to influence developments by supporting this or that faction or this or that personality. True to its principles, the United Nations has had to be guided in its operation solely by the interest of the Congolese people and by their right to decide freely for themselves, without any outside influences and

with full knowledge of facts. Therefore, the Organization, throughout the first year of its work in the Congo, up to the point when parliament reassembled and invested a new national government, has refused— what many may have wished—to permit the weight of its resources to be used in support of any faction so as thereby to prejudge in any way the outcome of a choice which belonged solely to the Congolese people. It has also had to pursue a line which, by safeguarding the free choice of the people, implied resistance against all efforts from outside to influence the outcome. In doing so, the Organization has been put in a position in which those within the country who felt disappointed in not getting the support of the Organization were led to suspect that others were in a more favored position and, therefore, accused the Organization of partiality, and in which, further, such outside elements as tried to get or protect a foothold within the country, when meeting an obstacle in the United Nations, made similar accusations. If, as it is sincerely to be hoped, the recent national reconciliation, achieved by parliament and its elected representatives of the people, provides a stable basis for a peaceful future in a fully independent and unified Congo, this would definitely confirm the correctness of the line pursued by the United Nations in the Congo. In fact, what was achieved by parliament early in August may be said to have done so with sufficient clarity. It is a thankless and easily misunderstood role for the Organization to remain neutral in relation to a situation of domestic conflict and to provide active assistance only by protecting the rights and possibilities of the people to find their own way, but it remains the only manner in which the Organization can serve its proclaimed purpose of furthering the full independence of the people in the true and unqualified sense of the word.

497

The United Nations may be called upon again to assist in similar ways. Whatever mistakes in detail and on specific points critics may ascribe to the Organization in the highly complicated situation in the Congo, it is to be hoped that they do not lead Members to revise the basic rules which guide the United Nations activities in such situations, as laid down in the first report of the Secretary-General to the Security Council on the Congo question,[3] which the Council, a year ago, found reason, unanimously, to commend.

Closely related to a policy aiming at self-government and independence for all is the question of economic and technical assistance, especially during the first years of independence of a new Member State. The United Nations and its agencies and affiliated organs have at their disposal only very modest means for the purpose, but a rich experience has been gathered and the personnel resources are not inconsiderable.

Last year the Economic and Social Council and the General Assembly had to consider proposals designed to open up new possibilities for the Organization to respond to the demands of Member governments facing all the problems of newly achieved independence. Naturally, the problems which are of special importance for such countries are basically the same as those which face all countries which have been left behind in economic development. Therefore, the urgent attention required by newly independent countries in this respect can in no way justify a discrimination in their favor against other countries with similar difficulties.

This year the General Assembly will have before it proposals initiated by the Scientific Advisory Committee and endorsed by the Economic and Social Council for a conference under United Nations aegis, intended to provide possibilities for a break-through in the application of the technical achievements of present times to the problems of the economically less developed countries. It is sincerely to be hoped that, in the interest of international cooperation and the acceleration of the economic progress of those countries, this proposal will meet with the approval of the General Assembly.

So far, the economic and technical activities of the United Nations have been less influenced by the conflict between different concepts of the role of the Organization than its activities in other fields. However, it is impossible to isolate the economic and technical problems from the general question discussed in this Introduction. While receiving countries should have full freedom to take assistance from whatever source they find appropriate, they should not be barred, if they so wish, from getting all the assistance they need through United Nations channels or under United Nations aegis. The Organization is far from being able to meet all such demands, as donor nations continue to show a strong preference for bilateral approaches on a national or a group basis. Again, the problem arises of the basic concept of the United Nations. With the conference approach to the work of the Organization a choice is made also in favor of bilateral assistance, while the alternative approach opens the door to a development under which international assistance, in implementation of the principle of equal economic opportunities for all, would be channelled through the Organization or its related agencies to the extent that this is desired by the recipient countries and is within the capacity of the Organization.

Basic to the United Nations approach to economic and technical assistance is the principle, under all circumstances, that, although the Organization has to follow its

[3] Document S/4389 and Adds.1–6.

own rules and maintain its own independence, its services are exclusively designed to meet the wishes of the recipient government, without the possibility of any ulterior motives and free from the risk of any possible influence on the national or international policies of that government. Whatever development the executive activities of the Organization may show in the field, there should never be any suspicion that the world community would wish or, indeed, could ever wish to maintain for itself, through the United Nations, a position of power or control in a Member country. Were political groups in a country really to believe in such a risk, the explanation would seem to be that, as has indeed happened in the case of governments of Member countries with long established independence, they may find it difficult to accept the judgment of the majority of the nations of the world as to what in a specific situation is necessary in order to safeguard international peace and security, when such a judgment appears to be in conflict with the immediate aims of the group. With growing respect for the decisions of the Organization and growing understanding of its principles, the risks for such misinterpretations should be eliminated.

. . . the Organization has now reached a stage in its development where Member nations may find it timely to clarify their views on the direction in which they would like to see the future work of the Organization develop.

THE SOVIET VIEW OF THE UNITED NATIONS

Alexander Dallin

The United Nations has patently not fulfilled the high hopes which some of its sponsors had for it. A major share of responsibility for this failure has commonly been assigned to the Soviet Union, and not without reason. Yet the Soviet view and Soviet conduct have not been products of perversity or malice. They follow logically, first, from the world view held by the communist leadership, which sees the United Nations as another arena in the struggle between the two "world systems" of our age, and, second, from the Soviet experience as a minority power seeking to frustrate the efforts of the hostile majority "in control" of the UN.

One World, Two Camps, Three Blocs

The Soviet leadership sees world affairs as a secular conflict between irreconcilable opposites. "Forces" and therefore attitudes have an organic tendency to polarize around the two antagonistic camps. Deviations from this law tend to be viewed as temporary aberrations which cannot alter or affect the basic dichotomy.

The presence of a super-power with a deeply engrained "two-camp" view in a "one-world" Organization presents a challenging problem, for how can that agency function if one of its principal Members fails to subscribe to its assumptions and rules? One must inquire then whether Soviet participation in, and praise for, the principles of, the United Nations heralds the acceptance of a "one-world" view. A further element in this picture has been the emergence of the new nations as a result of the collapse of colonial empires. Does Soviet recognition of the "emerging states" as objects of particular attention and as presumptive allies—indeed, under the proposals for tripartite reorganization, their inflation into a coequal third bloc in the UN—mark a retreat from the Soviet commitment to dichotomic perception?

The evidence points overwhelmingly to the continued acceptance of the "two-camp" view. Whatever its appeals to universal goals and values, Moscow does not see the world as one international community. And, however vigorous its assertions of solidarity with the Afro-Asian world, the USSR does not in fact recognize the permanent fissure of the globe into three mutually antagonistic segments. As the 1961 Program of the Communist Party of the Soviet Union declares, "The basic contradiction of the contemporary world [is] the contradiction between socialism and imperialism." Events of recent years have no doubt reinforced Soviet belief in the correctness of its bifocal vision and in the inevitability of the shift in the balance of power in favor of the "socialist camp."

Premier Khrushchev's frequent and facile comments bear this out. They abound in such images as the balance, the see-saw, and communicating vessels where the emptying of one (the capitalist) is tantamount to the filling of the other (the communist). The United Nations itself, he

ALEXANDER DALLIN is Professor of International Relations at the Russian Institute, Columbia University. This article is based on a chapter in his forthcoming book entitled *The Soviet Union at the United Nations,* to be published by Frederick A. Praeger in the spring of 1962.

reasserted upon his return home from New York in October 1960, was the stage for "a struggle of the new and progressive against the old and the moribund." Identifying the Soviet Union, as usual, with the fight for "peace," he continued: "Lining up the forces for peace and war is a process that will quicken and develop, and will augment the forces that stand for peace. The peoples of the neutral countries face a historic choice." Neutrality, in other words, must ultimately yield to alignment. As Khrushchev told the World Federation of Trade Unions congress in Moscow on December 9, 1961, "If today you are against communism, tomorrow you will have nowhere else to go, tomorrow you will come to communism."

It has become standard practice for Soviet writers on foreign affairs—and particularly on the UN—to juxtapose "the two lines" or "two opposite approaches" to world affairs, not three.[1] Bracketing the "objective" interests of the communist and unaligned states, the Communist Party's official organ, Kommunist, commented on the fifteenth Assembly session:

The historic struggle taking place on the world stage in our days finds expression within the walls of that Organization [the UN], where the world is represented in all its manifold and of course contradictory complexity. Here a polarization is taking place in the course of which the forces of peace, freedom and social progress unite, while the advocates of aggression and colonial slavery doom themselves to isolation.[2]

Allowing for the contrived optimism of the prognosis, the approach is clear: it permits of no lasting neutrality. Leading communists have from time to time spelled out the purely tactical and manipulative nature of their present support of the neutral states.[3] Indeed, in the Soviet definition neutrality no longer means what it did: an active struggle against "imperialism" is a "necessary condition" of Soviet recognition of a state's neutrality.[4]

The typical Soviet policy in the United Nations has been to keep the UN alive but weak. While it has sometimes advocated UN action in defiance of other nations' claims to domestic jurisdiction or of regional doctrines elsewhere in the world, Moscow's normal aim has been to safeguard its own freedom of action, to keep the United Nations out of the communist bloc, and generally to minimize the Organization's power. The Soviet Union and its allies have never brought a single dispute among themselves before the United Nations. When other states have raised issues relating to the "socialist camp,"

---

[1] For instance, Grigorii Morozov, *Organizatsiia Ob'edinennykh Natsii* (Moscow, 1960), p. 9ff.; *New Times* (Moscow, 1961), no. 3, p. 3; D. Kraminov, "Ubeditel'nyi pereves sil mira," *Kommunist* (Moscow, 1960), no. 18, p. 87.

[2] Editorial, "Za mir, za razoruzhenie, za svobodu narodov," *Kommunist*, 1960, no. 14, p. 5.

[3] Paul de Groot wrote in the Moscow *Kommunist* (1957, no. 2, p. 63): "For a state over which America rules at present, neutrality guaranteed by both world camps would constitute a step forward, toward national independence. For a socialist state neutrality constitutes a step backward, toward the subjugation to American imperialism and its sphere of influence." Similarly Hungarian Foreign Minister Imre Horvath declared (June 2, 1957): "We approve of the neutrality of certain capitalist countries since it signifies that they do not join the imperialist military blocs . . . [But] neutrality for a socialist country represents an underhanded attack on peace and socialism and their betrayal." For a systematic exposition of the Soviet view, see E. A. Korovin, "Neitralitet v. proshlom i nastoiashchem," in his *Osnovnye problemy sovremennykh mezhdunarodnykh otnoshenii* (Moscow, 1959), and Boris Ganiushkin, *Sovremennyi neitralitet* (Moscow, 1958). See also George Ginsburgs, "Neutrality and Neutralism and the Tactics of Soviet Diplomacy," *American Slavic and East European Review* (New York, December 1960).

[4] N. Inozemtsev, "Razvitie mirovogo sotsializma i mezhdunarodnye otnosheniia," *Kommunist*, 1961, no. 9, p. 101.

Moscow has labeled them illegitimate interference. Khrushchev in April 1958 reiterated Stalin's old warning to the "imperialists" "not to try to put their pig snouts into our socialist garden." Undiplomatic in form, the attitude itself follows inexorably from the hypothesis that the rest of the world—including the United Nations—is controlled by the enemy camp.[5]

The Soviet efforts to restrict the UN's jurisdiction go back to the days prior to the adoption of the Charter. Ever since then, the USSR has favored a strict and literal construction of its terms and has invariably objected to attempts to broaden the prerogatives of the Assembly and the Secretariat. Subsumed under the obsessive emphasis on "sovereignty," the Soviet attitude springs from a determination not to be bound by the desires or decisions of others.

This has led Moscow to minimize the achievements of the United Nations. It has denied the UN's role even where it is manifest. The Soviet press insists that the Iran affair of 1946 was settled, not thanks to the United Nations but by direct negotiation. The UN had nothing to do with the easing of international tensions after Stalin's death: the Geneva spirit of 1955 was a product of the Great Powers' own pursuits. The Suez crisis of 1956, Khrushchev asserted, was settled not by the UN but by the Soviet Union's threat of intervention. More often than not, the United Nations has in the past acted either "under pressure from the USA" (as in Korea) or as "nothing more than a passive registrar of world events."

The special interpretation given to the term, status quo, has been peculiarly well suited to take advantage of the Soviet approach. It gives the Soviet Union sanction to ignore the outside world when it comes to relations within its own bloc, and it permits the Soviet Union also to make the problems of other nations, in and out of the UN, its own concern. For, as Khrushchev has repeatedly suggested, the essence of the status quo is revolution itself. Ultimately, this means acquiescence in the process of change whose culmination is the world-wide drift to communism.

What to the outsider might appear to be a double standard turns out to be natural and consequent, once Soviet assumptions are spelled out. The seeming ambiguity or conceptual contradiction in such cases, for instance, the Soviet view of just and unjust wars, stems from the clash of two distinct categories of analysis—of iron "laws of history," as Moscow sees them, with man-made "international law in the epoch of coexistence." In its internal analysis of the world scene, Moscow is bound to opt for the organic, fundamental laws which inform the historical process rather than the "formal, technical" and transient "bourgeois" rules.

It remains true that the Soviet approach is by no means free of unreconciled ambiguities and unresolved problems of analysis. As can be shown with numerous examples, there have been conflicting priorities of revolution and diplomacy, of exclusiveness and universality, of sovereignty and "proletarian solidarity," of esoteric class analysis and tactics of compromise. Any of these may at times confront the Soviet leadership with genuine dilemmas. Thus, to accept the world as it is means to betray

---

[5] The first time the UN plan was raised by President Roosevelt (Bohlen Minutes of November 29, 1943, meeting at Tehran), Stalin's immediate question was "whether this body would have the right to make decisions binding the nations of the world." (*Foreign Relations of the United States:* *The Conferences at Cairo and Tehran 1943,* Washington, D. C., 1961, p. 570.) On the containment of conflicts within the communist orbit, see George Modelski, *The Communist International System* (Princeton University: Center of International Studies, 1960), p. 66–68.

its long-range goals and visions; but to oppose it frankly and explicitly is to sacrifice all the advantages of propaganda, negotiations, and alliances—and, in this case, effective participation in international organizations.

Despite the fundamental constancy of the Soviet view of the world—and of the United Nations—Moscow has had its share of disagreements over strategy and tactics at home and abroad. Communist assessments of the United Nations have ranged from total rejection as an "imperialist tool" to total support as an imminent communist "front." While in the minds of some Soviet leaders such expectations regarding the UN have vacillated with changing conditions abroad, others have adhered to the same positions more or less rigidly impervious to new experiences and opportunities.

As recently as October 1961, at the 22d Congress of the Soviet Communist Party, the major protagonists of the current "moderate" line went out of their way to deny that they had "excessive faith in personal contacts and conversations" abroad; no doubt the United Nations was part of this skein of relations. Viacheslav Molotov was identified as "opposed to contacts between our statesmen and party leaders with foreign politicians, to visits abroad. . . . He warns us: look out and beware of contacts!" The problem of disarmament was now added to the issues over

which spokesmen for different communist policies ostensibly disagreed.[6] Undoubtedly we do not know the full range of disagreements relating to the UN. Yet the experience of recent years is likely to have reduced the differences in the Soviet assessment of the United Nations: neither total withdrawal nor total reliance on the UN is likely to find many advocates among the leaders of the Soviet camp.

International organizations are after all expected to be but a passing stage. Both the strategy of the "zone of peace" and pursuit of "peaceful coexistence" are deemed appropriate for the "given historical epoch"—the transitional era in which "capitalist" and "socialist" states exist side by side. Moscow has been frank in stating not only that the principle of "proletarian internationalism" among communists is a law superior to "bourgeois" codes and mores, but also that it is intended "for a longer period of time" than "peaceful coexistence."[7] Unlike the more "pragmatic" responses of other states, in the Soviet case such a long-range perspective is by no means irrelevant to the conduct of actual policy.

UN—For What?

It is commonplace to argue that Soviet "conflict strategy" encompasses a practical, if somewhat condescending, willingness to use any individual or group, institution or symbol to advance its aims. In Moscow's

---

[6] In the course of defending the Khrushchev record against what may be assumed to be charges of naiveté and failure at the UN, A. I. Adzhubei made a revealing comment about Soviet performance at the 1960 session: Soviet behavior there, far from amounting to collaboration with the class enemy (as some comrades alleged), furthered the class struggle, for the Soviet delegation "organized obstructions when mendacious, provocative speeches were made from the UN rostrum," in order to show up "the attitude of the gentlemen who engage in the deceit of the peoples." Soviet fist-banging and shoe-waving, Adzhubei continued,

were intended to "curb the pharisees and liars." These are no junkets, he argued: "Comrades, behind personal contacts and visits, there is hard work, work until you are covered with sweat, often not leaving you time for sleep or rest, work which demands constant concentration and resourcefulness, and the ability to use all the forces of argument." (Speech of October 26, 1961.)

[7] M. Airapetian and P. Kabanov, *Leninskie printsipy vneshnei politiki sovetskogo gosudarstva* (Moscow, 1957), p. 65. See also Khrushchev's interview with the editor of the Tokyo *Asahi Shimbun* on June 18, 1957.

estimation the United Nations is—or can be—one such tool. Until about 1954, it was considered an instrument of subordinate importance; since then, its potential in Soviet eyes has substantially increased.

This statement is not in conflict with the underlying skepticism about what the United Nations can do and what the Soviet Union can expect to gain from it. Fundamentally, Moscow continues to hold, an international body of diverse and antagonistic sovereign states cannot solve the problems of our days.

The Soviet Union has participated in the United Nations for limited purposes and with limited expectations. If, some observers have found, there is in the United States an acute contrast between hopes and results in the UN,[8] no such hiatus exists on the Soviet side—simply because Moscow had no such naive expectations to begin with. It sees membership as a contract based on the mutuality of certain interests. The United Nations, it maintains, has no rights or powers of its own—only those derived from its Member States. It is at all times an organ subordinate to these states, not the independent voice of a world conscience or of a common will.

Many Western observers found it hard to predict in what direction the United Nations would evolve. On a number of points, the Charter is inevitably and perhaps intentionally vague. If, in a widespread view, the UN may be considered either a locus for the exercise of national policy or else a nucleus of international government, for Moscow there has been no such choice: the UN must serve only the former, never the latter goal. Soviet writings continue to assail all projects giving the United Nations greater power and to "expose" all advocates of "the reactionary idea of 'world law.'"[9]

By the same token, the Soviet Union has not indulged in any optimism with regard to "functionalism" or "welfare internationalism" through the UN. Neither the faith that international "togetherness" will overcome basic rifts, nor the belief that the UN could or should attempt to resolve the economic and social ills of the modern world has characterized the Soviet view. This is not at all surprising. Indeed, in its predominantly political approach to the International Organization, the Soviet Union has differed fundamentally from the spokesmen of underdeveloped countries whom it has sought to court—countries for whom the health, education, and welfare activities often loom as among the most constructive tasks of the UN.

Internal Soviet estimates of the United Nations' utility appear to have changed in the course of time. The initial Soviet commitment to participate in the League of Nations and then in the United Nations was due in large measure to a desire to buttress Russian security. Since 1950 this has been a receding consideration. Experience showed that both the League and the UN were at best dubious guarantors of peace. And with the growth of Soviet military and economic power, with crucial breakthroughs in weapons technology, and with a deep reluctance to trust the mechanics of a "non-power" club, the Soviet Union has not relied and need not rely on the United Nations for its defense. One of the most bothersome of Khrushchev's arguments since 1959 has been that of Soviet reliance on its own forces—without the UN and even against the UN.[10]

---

[8] See, e.g., Lincoln P. Bloomfield, *The United Nations and U.S. Foreign Policy* (Boston: Little, Brown, 1960), p. 5.

[9] The latter reference is to the Clark and Sohn proposals. (Morozov, p. 145.)

[10] This has permitted Moscow to assume a pose of unselfishness: "In reaffirming its proposals for reorganization of the United Nations structure, the Soviet government is primarily concerned for the interests of independent Asian, African and Latin

In case of crisis, Soviet resort to the UN is of course considered infinitely less promising than its own armed might, its alliance system, and other instruments which it controls.[11]

The subordinate place of the United Nations in the Soviet scheme is also reflected in Moscow's disinclination to have the UN handle issues requiring sensitive dosage or urgent action. For such purposes, it prefers "summits" and bilateral negotiations.[12]

A similar power-conscious realism is revealed in the omission of the United Nations from the most authoritative and detailed communist analyses of contemporary affairs. The official handbook of the Communist Party of the Soviet Union, used for political training throughout the USSR and translated into various languages, in its 890 pages (including a lengthy section on world affairs, the Korean war, and the Suez crisis) does not contain a single reference to the United Nations![13] Likewise, the Declaration of 81 Communist Parties meeting in Moscow in November–December 1960, perhaps the most significant theoretical and strategic document produced by the communist universe in recent years, fails to make a single reference to the United Nations, as does the Program of the CPSU adopted in October 1961.

This does not mean that Moscow lacks theoretical criteria by which to judge the UN:

Under conditions when there are in the world states with differing social systems, international political organizations—constituting phenomena which belong to the superstructure—have the right to exist only so long as they correspond to the actual relationship of forces which constitute their base.

If the Organization fails to change in accordance with these "basic" forces, it tends to become "essentially a separate bloc, hardly distinguishable from aggressive military alliances."[14] This is the rationale of the Soviet proposals of 1960–61: the demand that the Organization be brought in line with the "realities" of international power.

What then does Moscow expect to gain from its efforts in the United Nations? Membership, even at times of considerable adversity, has given the Soviet Union valuable opportunities:

for the settlement of relatively minor disputes;

for international contacts, both to exchange views and to initiate and pursue negotiations, often informally rather than at official sessions;

for gathering information, political in-

American countries. The Soviet Union is, of course, in a position to defend itself against any aggression, but what would be the fate of weak ex-colonial nations if the imperialists, having tried out their strength in the Congo, launch an all-out offensive against the Afro-Asian movement for national liberation?" (Editorial, *New Times*, 1961, no. 10, p. 2.)

[11] See William Welch, "Soviet Commitments to Collective Action," in Arnold Wolfers, ed., *Alliance Policy in the Cold War* (Baltimore: Johns Hopkins University Press, 1959), p. 294–300.

[12] In New York Khrushchev commented that "the question of Germany is outside the limits of the United Nations." (*Pravda*, October 11, 1960.) Indeed, during the tensest phase of the Berlin crisis

in the summer of 1961, the Soviet Union made no move to involve the UN in its "resolution." To Senator Hubert Humphrey Khrushchev intimated that "the United States should be discussing questions of outer space directly with the Soviet Union instead of raising them in the UN. 'So now,' Khrushchev said, 'the United States discusses outer space with Guatemala—but Guatemala does not seem to be too advanced in outer-space science.'" (Hubert H. Humphrey, "My Marathon Talk with Russia's Boss," *Life*, January 12, 1959.)

[13] Otto Kuusinen *et al.*, *Fundamentals of Marxism-Leninism* (Moscow, 1960).

[14] Editorial, " 'Reshit' problemu reorganizatsii OON," *Kommunist*, 1961, no. 4, p. 14.

telligence, technical know-how, scientific data, and securing economic and other goods and services, as a matter of self-interest;

for gaining prestige and respectability as a major power in the family of nations; and

for engaging in propaganda, in the broadest sense of the term, and attempting to influence the views, attitudes, and political alignments of other states.

Soviet analysts have frequently stressed the value of the United Nations as a "broad forum"; as a gathering point for the different blocs, including the young nations of Africa and Asia; and as a vehicle for the dissemination of Soviet declarative proposals (such as the draft declarations on peaceful coexistence, stopping nuclear tests, and pledges not to employ nuclear weapons; the total disarmament scheme; and the anticolonialist declaration). Upon returning from the UN in the fall of 1960 Khrushchev declared that his trip had been "useful in that we had many meetings and exchanged views with the statesmen of various countries on a whole range of important international issues." With all its vagueness, this comment no doubt corresponded to his view.

In the pursuit of these objectives, Soviet policy-makers have had the choice between several models of behavior in international organizations:

(1) *Non-participation.* This course commended itself until 1934 with regard to the League and has been consistently rejected for the UN.

(2) *Minimum participation.* Basically an isolationist strategy, it is restrictive in its interpretation of UN authority, stressing Soviet prerogatives of sovereignty and strict interpretation of agreements, and minimizing outside jurisdiction in communist affairs. Adopted at a time when the

Soviet bloc was in the position of a perennial minority, it has been the predominant policy ever since 1945, though in the 1950's Moscow began to shed some of its features as it felt a distinct improvement in its "position of strength" and opportunities abroad.

(3) *Selective cooperation* against a specific foe. This strategy—seeing the UN as the equivalent of a military ally—is practiced when the Soviet Union needs international support in some form of collective action or assurance against a third power. In this fashion it sought to strengthen its position vis-à-vis Germany and Japan in the 1930's. An analogous situation has not occurred since the Second World War. While no one will admit it, Communist China may theoretically present such a problem at some future date.

(4) A broad, expansive strategy of *maximizing United Nations authority.* This is the normal Soviet policy for a communist-controlled organization. No doubt, Moscow would welcome a situation in which its "camp"—together with assorted camp followers—would emerge in control of the UN. But, after a brief interlude of extravagant hope, Khrushchev seems to have convinced himself that the day is not at hand. This policy therefore has seen and in the foreseeable future will see no systematic application.

Perplexingly Soviet policy in 1960–62 fits none of the above prescriptions precisely. The Soviet role is no longer minimal in many fields: it has increased in economic and social work; there has been greater Soviet use of the Assembly; in Soviet propaganda, the UN "principle"— but not its practice—has unmistakably become a positive symbol. Yet precisely the threats and demands voiced by the Soviet Union underscore the continuing gap between the "United Nations mentality" and that of the USSR.

Beyond the immediate opportunities that Moscow sees available for itself, is there a longer-range objective of Soviet policy in the UN? At one time it was conceivable that Moscow would merely maintain nominal membership, seeking neither to win control nor to withdraw. No longer is this a reasonable prospect; given the growth of Soviet might, activity, and ambition, such a retreat to silent partnership is difficult to conceive. Nor is the Soviet bloc likely to pull out, in spite of all its threats. If it stuck it out during the isolation of the Korean War, it is sure to feel that the present advantages of membership are infinitely greater and the prospects more encouraging still. Its threats of withdrawal, moreover, would obviously lose their bargaining value—without netting the Soviet Union any commensurate gain —were it indeed to leave the Organization.

The question remains whether (in President Eisenhower's words) the Soviet leaders "in alternating moods look upon the United Nations as an instrument for use or abuse," whether (as others have put it) Moscow seeks "the power to manipulate the United Nations for its own designs," or whether Khrushchev strives to render the Organization impotent.[15] One may suggest that the two objectives—to neutralize and to control—can coexist in Soviet minds: they may be most usefully thought of as maximum and minimum aims. The simultaneous identification of such divergent goals has a long history in Bolshevik experience and has often been characteristic of Soviet foreign affairs.[16]

No doubt the most extreme and optimistic Soviet vision is the transformation of the United Nations into a communist "front" organization, in the manner of world peace congresses, "solidarity" meetings, and labor federations which, behind a non-Soviet façade, communists seek to control (but not overtly to direct, so as not to drive noncommunists out). But obviously Moscow cannot bank on the UN's conforming to this scheme. In practice, the Soviet bloc has never even been close to controlling a majority of votes. Moreover, the Western Big Three still possess their veto power. Thus, of necessity, the Soviet Union has had to turn to more immediate and more modest goals—especially since, by 1960, Khrushchev saw it as a matter of considerable urgency to stop the Organization from being "used" by the enemy camp.

Even if Moscow prefers to have two strings to its United Nations bow, choices must sometimes be made which preclude a return to an alternative policy. In general Moscow has sought to avoid such irreversible commitments, and from the Soviet point of view a major shortcoming of the tripartite proposals is precisely the fact that their adoption would make it difficult at some future point to return to a veto-free pursuit of majority control of the General Assembly and the Secretariat. As it now stands, the Soviet plan would guarantee the veto to both the West and the collective voice of the unaligned. At present Moscow would not seriously expect to "sell" its proposal without giving such "equality" to the American-led "imperialist camp."

Thus Moscow finds itself prepared for the time being to freeze the tripartite relationship and accept a far more limited goal than its control of the UN. The most immediate Soviet task is to make

[15] Hamilton Fish Armstrong, "UN on Trial," *Foreign Affairs*, April 1961 (Vol. 39, No. 3), p. 388.
[16] See, for instance, George F. Kennan, *Russia and the West Under Lenin and Stalin* (Boston: Little, Brown, 1961), and Henry L. Roberts, *Russia and America* (New York: Harper, 1956).

sure that the United Nations will not be used against it and its friends.

But this does not exhaust what Moscow expects to achieve in or through the UN. The Soviet bloc can hope to use it in a variety of ways until such a time as, hopefully, the Charter may again be altered to bring it in conformity with what Moscow expects will then be the reality of even greater Soviet might.

Continuity and Change

A substantially constant ideological framework has permitted significant variations in Soviet strategy and tactics at the United Nations. The contrast between Moscow's policy in Stalin's days and in the Khrushchev era measures both the extent and the limits of variation.

But what has determined shifts in Moscow's policy? The primary determinant is to be found outside the UN system: this has been the Soviet perception of changes in the "real world"—above all, changes of power and of opportunity. It was precisely the contrast between the glorious sense of growing Soviet world power and the lack of commensurate success or influence in the United Nations that permitted Moscow to argue for "realistic" adjustments in the Organization's system of staffing and representation.

Another determinant is the structure of ideological preconceptions. True, certain fundamental axioms—conflict, dichotomy, optimism—have shown remarkable tenacity; and certain generalities in the Soviet world view—the call for "realism," the approach to "sovereignty," the verdict that the United Nations is "useful" but not "important"—have remained virtually unchanged. Yet the doctrinal revisions of the Khrushchev era have been important in rationalizing the Soviet policy of nonviolent competition and widening the framework of permissible techniques.

This is not to suggest that the doctrinal reformulations preceded the new perception of a changing world. It should be clear, moreover, that the specifics of Soviet policy, in or out of the United Nations, are not explicable in ideological terms alone. Like the demand for parity, the troika proposition exemplifies a Soviet effort to gain as much as the other powers might concede— a demand fully consistent with, but not predictable in terms of, its world view alone. Political realism, as Moscow sees it, is thus superimposed on ideological commitments. Only the combination of the two can explain the nature and the timing of the Soviet reorganization proposals.

Soviet policy has been capable of crude and unprincipled practicality when the rewards have seemed to warrant it. The traditional commitment to the tenet of *pacta sunt servanda* is not allowed to stand in the way of demands for greater rights due to greater power. The most "principled" insistence on the reality of three power blocs easily yields to a plethora of Soviet formulae for four, five, six, or seven Under-Secretaries when Hammarskjöld's successors are being discussed. Soviet opposition to the existing order in the United Nations, Moscow admits at times, is due not to the belief that a *single* group of powers controls the UN but that the *wrong* group does—"reactionaries" and "monopolists." Soviet insistence on unanimity as a *sine qua non* in the United Nations, which Moscow does not control, contrasts dramatically with its efforts to promote majority rule within the conclave of international communism, where it does have most member-parties on its side against Chinese Communist advocacy of unanimity. Even the sacred principle of sovereignty can be suspended when political utility demands it. "Principles," too, in other words, can be weapons in the struggle of systems, in and out of the UN.

Among the strands of Soviet experience which contribute to the reassessment of strategy is the record of the United Nations itself. The UN action in the Congo is a case in point. While on the whole events inside the UN have played a subordinate part in the crystallization of Soviet policies, the Soviet Union's own experience of being a "loser" for over a decade has surely reinforced Moscow's inclination to keep the United Nations' power at a low level. The minority position of the Soviet bloc during the early years intensified its members' resentment and sense of isolation. Then their collective nonparticipation for a time set them apart even more. While some of this gap was bridged in the post-Stalin era, the suspicion that the United Nations was part of the hostile camp remained.

It was of course true that the majority of the United Nations—and of the Great Powers—was anticommunist. With some exertion, the Western powers could usually command a majority of votes, something the USSR could not do. At every step, from San Francisco to Korea and Suez, it must have seemed to Moscow that the United States had won out. And in 1960–61 the UN was perhaps more indulgent toward the United States, over the U-2 flight and the attempted landing in Cuba, than it might have been toward other nations. All this of course did not make the UN a "tool of the State Department," as Moscow alleged, but it provided an objective basis for the Soviet claims.

Finally, the Soviet world view contains a strong self-fulfilling element. George F. Kennan, among others, has suggested that Soviet expectation and behavior are bound to engender precisely the sort of response abroad and create just such a dichotomy as Moscow professes to see. In practice, too, many United Nations agencies became "Western" during the formative years when the USSR refused to take an active part in their work. The realization that this was the case was probably among the reasons for the later change in Soviet tactics—from absence to participation in many, though not all, activities of the UN.

Nothing would be further from the truth than to suggest that the Soviet Union has been the only culprit at the UN. In fact, most powers have violated the spirit of the Charter, and many have ignored its letter time and again. Most Members have failed to rely on the United Nations as a primary instrument of national policy. Most states have valued it for what they can get out of it. All have loyalties higher than those to the UN. All the Great Powers would refuse to surrender the veto. Others, too, have insisted on keeping the domestic jurisdiction clause. Rather than entrusting their security to the United Nations, most states have bolstered their defenses or moved to regional alliance systems. Other countries, too, have resisted UN regulation of their commerce and tariffs, and have preferred to put their own label on economic aid and exercise direct control over its destination.

Moscow is right in arguing that, if universality is an objective, the absence from the UN of Communist China and Germany is difficult to defend. It is correct in stressing that "Great Power unanimity" *was* the original presupposition of the United Nations; if it implies the essentiality of agreement, it also spells the impotence of the UN when such consensus is not achieved. Many, outside the Soviet bloc, have also found the formula of "one state, one vote" in the Assembly highly unrealistic. Many new nations have felt their interests inadequately reflected on the United Nations staff and in the Security Council. Just as the Soviet Union came to look askance at a plain majority principle after its experience in the Assembly, so the United States appears to have lost some of its enthusiasm for that body since the accretion of Afro-Asian votes and the loosening of the Latin American bloc has made the Western powers a minority group too. The United Kingdom has been frankly pessimistic about the future of the UN. In its insistence on the imperative of change, the Soviet Union finds a considerable echo among other states, for there are many who, in H. G. Nicholas' words,

have joined the UN less to preserve, by mechanisms of law and order, an existing state of affairs, than to effect, by the pressure of their votes and their voices, a change not only in their own circumstances but often in their relation with the rest of the world.[17]

Even in its refusal to think and act in terms of a world community the Soviet Union is by no means alone. Indeed, a series of studies of national attitudes toward the UN prompted the conclusion that the idea of universal solidarity of man has not yet penetrated deeply. To use Maurice Bourquin's expression, the world over "People don't *feel* the unity of humankind."[18]

And yet, when all is said and done, the Soviet outlook on the United Nations remains unique in some essential ways. This unique feature is not even Soviet defiance of the UN, including its asserted willingness to use force to resist it, as illustrated by the Hungarian episode in 1956, when it ignored the body's verdict—at the same time that other violators of the Charter's spirit obeyed the UN's call to stop action at Suez. Other states—notably France—have been known likewise to challenge and ignore the UN.

The area of uniqueness lies above all in the Soviet view of the historical process and its translation into action. The profound conviction that in the long run neutrality and impartiality are impossible or nonexistent vitiates the fundamental assumption on which international organizations such as the United Nations are built. The communist image of the United Nations as an arena of struggle is not a reluctant recognition of a tragic fact but an exhilarating ride on the wave of the future.

The Soviet view, in sum, combines a revolutionary outlook with a conservative pursuit of its security and a pragmatic effort to make the most of the complex and shifting United Nations scene.

The hardheadedness of the Soviet approach contrasts strikingly with the fuzzy thinking about the UN that has often characterized others abroad. Yet—on this point the record should be convincing—Moscow has made its full share of errors and miscalculations. Soviet policy, Stalin told Anthony Eden in 1945, was "neither as simple as some thought nor as skillful as others believed."[19] Indeed, we have too often mistaken absence of information for absence of conflict or doubt on the Soviet side. We have been too much inclined to endow the masters of the Kremlin with infallible cleverness—and they to an even greater extent have seen a pattern, a design, a purpose, a conspiracy in every move and gesture of the outside world: "There are no accidents."

Soviet analysis and expectations have, in the Khrushchev era, tended to be fairly realistic about power relations, capabilities and vulnerabilities of states. They have

[17] Herbert G. Nicholas, *The United Nations as a Political Institution* (New York: Oxford University Press, 1959), p. 145.

[18] Maurice Bourquin, *L'état souverain et l'organi-sation internationale* (New York: Manhattan, 1959), p. 17.

[19] Anthony Eden, *Full Circle* (London: Deutsch, 1960), p. 7.

permitted Moscow to ignore the United Nations as a decisive obstacle on its path. Indeed, what *could* the UN do in the face of overt Soviet hostility? But a substantial lack of realism intervenes when Soviet analysis concerns a pluralistic world. As bipolarity is the natural shape to which, Moscow imagines, the universe tends, the standard Soviet image of the United Nations, too, has been one of two opposites. So long as the facts can be made to fit such formulae, Soviet analysis is simple and often shrewd even if its view of capitalism and democracy remains hopelessly out of date. But they don't always fit.

It is precisely with regard to neutralism and nonalignment that the Soviet view is apt to go awry. Which way the uncommitted will go when forced by the logic of international strife and Soviet (and American) prodding remains in doubt. But it is clear that the assumption that the ultimate interest of the neutral bloc is on the Soviet side is unwarranted and naive. Moscow has ignored the fact that the United Nations occupied a far more important place in the thinking and expectations of the developing nations than in those of the USSR, with regard to their own security and progress; their view of the UN's welfare and economic activities is far more positive; and their perspective on UN finances differs drastically from that of the Soviet Union. While on issues such as anticolonialism the Soviet bloc has naturally identified itself with the new nations, Moscow may in fact have begun to realize that the "third" bloc is not necessarily—and surely not yet—to be counted on the communist side. And it is no doubt at least a subsidiary purpose of the Soviet reorganization plan to deprive the

United Nations of its ability to compete with the communists for leadership of the "national liberation" movement. In the last analysis, the Soviet assumption that the nonaligned world—any more than the Western grouping—constitutes a cohesive, homogeneous, lasting bloc is plainly wrong. Whether or not the communist orbit is any more cohesive or lasting only the future will tell.

The Limits of Logic

The Soviet stand, enunciated in the fall of 1960 and reiterated since, is logical within the framework of Soviet assumptions and objectives. It is, to be sure, more extreme than the view Moscow had previously propounded about the United Nations. Allowing for some improvisations in the actual proposals, it has the virtue that the assumptions in back of the troika plan remove an area of suppressed ambiguity which has inhered in the Soviet compromise between inward communist hostility toward and outward identification with the UN. The view that there exists no just arbiter or administrator above the two major camps revives, almost verbatim, positions voiced in days of greater Soviet candor.

The Soviet formula made little constitutional sense: it would have frozen the balance of three blocs by institutionalizing a haphazard and transient political alignment from which the sovereign Member States might choose to withdraw at some future time. Many borderline states could not easily be put into any of the three categories. The assumption that each of the blocs had unity and permanence was obviously open to serious challenge.[20] Indeed, Soviet insistence on sovereign equal-

---

[20] Not long ago a leading Soviet scholar wrote plainly: "It is entirely self-evident that the inclusion of this or that country within one of the types characteristic for the period of the disintegra-tion of the colonial system is not immutable and given for all time." (A. A. Guber, cited in Wladyslaw W. Kulski, *Peaceful Coexistence*, Chicago, Regnery, 1959, p. 209.)

ity of states seemed to be violated by its plan to give equal weight to nine communist states, some fifty neutrals, and the forty-odd Western powers and their allies.

Administratively, objections no less weighty were voiced by the United Nations staff itself. The troika would have stymied the Secretariat's work and made the use of the UN in another Korean or Congolese crisis impossible. But this was at least part of Moscow's purpose.

No elaborate evidence is required to show that Khrushchev has not been willing to tolerate an analogous *ménage à trois* either within the leadership in the Kremlin, or in Soviet industrial management, or in relations among communist parties. Soviet insistence on tripartite equality and veto in the executive organs conflicts directly with the time-honored Bolshevik administrative principle of *edinonachalie*—unity of authority—which has been reaffirmed on innumerable occasions as "the basic method of operating the Soviet economy and the Soviet state."[21] Since the objective of *edinonachalie* is above all maximum efficiency, one may conclude that the Soviet purpose in opposing it in the United Nations is its reverse.

The political incongruity of the troika is well illustrated by Adlai Stevenson's remark that the application of the Soviet plan in the sixteenth century would have produced an organization "in which the administration of international affairs was entrusted to a triumvirate consisting of the Pope, the Sultan, and Martin Luther."[22]

If adopted, the proposals would reduce the United Nations to the highest common denominator of its Members' views. Moscow has gone so far as to insist that "the main goal of this organization consists in finding solutions acceptable to *all* its members."[23] That this is no slip of the pen is shown by the recurrence of the theme on a number of occasions since Khrushchev, in his UN speech of September 19, 1959, declared that "only such decisions should be taken in the United Nations which everyone would vote for." When asked, the following year, whether he would let a two-thirds majority of the Member States decide whether or not Hammarskjöld should stay, Khrushchev replied: "This is not a parliament. It is a forum in which the questions should be resolved in such a way as not to endanger the interests of even a single state. . . ."[24]

There is ground to question whether Moscow means quite what it says. While the extension of the unanimity rule to all Members of the United Nations is consonant with that strain of Soviet thinking which emphasizes sovereign prerogatives, the *liberum veto* would permit a single Member—say, the Union of South Africa —to prevent the adoption of a decision favored by all other states. This clearly would not be welcome to the USSR. It would be impossible, under the circumstances, to "isolate" any state or bloc of states; yet this is precisely what Soviet spokesmen have time and again called for at the UN.

What Moscow means, one may surmise, is that its own concurrence—as the leading power of the world, or so it likes to think —should be required at all times and in all organs of the United Nations. But this it cannot say openly, any more than it can afford to ask for a selective extension of the veto to a few favored nations, at a time when it courts precisely those coun-

---

[21] *Bol'shaia sovetskaia entsiklopediia*, 2d ed. (Moscow, 1952), XV, p. 475–76.

[22] Adlai Stevenson, address at the Princeton Club, Washington, D. C., May 17, 1961.

[23] Editorial, *Kommunist*, 1961, no. 4, p. 15. Italics mine.

[24] *The New York Times*, October 8, 1960.

tries of whom virtually none would be the beneficiaries of such a move.

That the operation of a United Nations in which all of its hundred-odd Members would possess a *liberum veto* would be destructive not only of the United Nations but of Soviet interests as well, is nowhere better put than in a Soviet critique of the League of Nations. As Grigorii Morozov writes in his volume on the UN, a recent and authoritative Soviet account,

This impotence of the League flowed, in particular, from the fact that the Covenant required unanimity of all its members for the adoption of all political decisions taken by its Council and Assembly. This harmful pseudo-democratism vitiated the role and responsibility of the several states in the cause of supporting international peace and practically rendered impossible the effective operation of an organization for the maintenance of peace and the prevention of aggression.[25]

An extreme expression of the Soviet view is the contention that the sovereign Member States need not be bound by what the United Nations says and does. This has been implicit in the series of Khrushchev's references, since mid-1960, to the use of force. Speaking initially about the failure of the Security Council to support the Soviet demands stemming from the U-2 incident, he remarked (on June 3, 1960) that under such circumstances in the future "we have no other way out but to rely on our own strength." At the UN that fall, he went further: the Soviet Union would ignore United Nations decisions which it deemed incompatible with its own interests. If it did not get its way, it would "uphold our interests outside this international body, outside the United Nations, by relying on our own strength."[26] The final step in this progression came in Khrushchev's speech welcoming President Nkrumah of Ghana to Moscow in July 1961:

Even if all the countries of the world adopted a decision which did not accord with the interests of the Soviet Union and threatened its security, the Soviet Union would not recognize such a decision and would uphold its rights, relying on force. And we have what [it takes] to rely on.[27]

What constitutes a threat to its security is, of course, at all times up to Moscow to decide.

Such strident formulations reveal the extent of Soviet determination to maintain its full freedom of action. Once again Soviet insistence on "unanimity" and "sovereignty" turns the clock backwards. The unanimity rule, Nicolas Politis said in 1928, amounts to an admission that "among nations no real organization is possible, for the rule of unanimity may lead to paralysis and anarchy. . . ."[28]

Moscow watched with unmitigated enmity the tragic—or pathetic—search for an international authority to deal effectively with forces greater than itself. The United Nations had not been expected to cope with disagreements among the Great Powers, and Moscow vigorously protested Western attempts to shape the UN into a serviceable tool in the conflicts between the "two camps." To its mind, what has taken place amounts to an illegal "triple play" from Security Council to General Assembly to Secretariat, as the United States and its allies tried to use one organ

[25] Morozov, p. 12.

[26] *The New York Times*, October 4 and 8, 1960. He added that the socialist states would "not recognize [inimical] decisions and will rely on their own strength to defend the interests of their state"; and "if anyone tries to interfere in our affairs, if you will excuse the rather indelicate phrase, we will just give him a punch in the nose."

[27] Khrushchev, speech of July 11, 1961 (USSR Mission to the UN, Press Release 44/61).

[28] See Inis L. Claude, *Swords into Plowshares* (New York: Random House, 1959), p. 128–29.

after another for their ends. The Council, stymied by the veto, declined in importance and use, and was widely recognized to be unable to do its job.[29] The General Assembly, even under the Uniting for Peace Resolution, could not compel compliance with its recommendations; and there were political and constitutional limits to what it could do. Even prior to its recent inflation, disappointment was widespread—in the Soviet judgment as well as in that of the West.[30] Both its inherent weakness and the growth of numbers in the General Assembly finally encouraged an expansion of executive power in the UN Secretariat—a process likewise promoted by the delegation of authority by the Security Council, as in the Laotian and Congolese crises.

Experience suggests that there are inherent flaws in the way the Secretariat was conceived. The Charter granted its Secretary-General explicitly far more authority than his inconspicuous predecessor in the League had possessed. His office has been not merely administrative but also political, both in intent and in practice.[31] As a consequence both Trygve Lie and Dag Hammarskjöld were bound to antagonize the Soviet bloc. To have avoided acting so as to clash with it would have meant failing in the fulfillment of their duties.

Yet the necessity to perform political tasks does not make "disinterested" or "objective" service impossible, as Dag Hammarskjöld argued trenchantly in his Oxford speech in May 1961.[32] It has been a matter of honorable tradition and established policy, reiterated over many years, that an international staff, to be fair and effective, must not be imbued with the

values and special interests of any one state. Yet this is precisely what Moscow has challenged. As Walter Lippmann reported on the basis of his interview with Khrushchev,

> the Soviet government has now come to the conclusion that there can be no such thing as an impartial civil servant in this deeply divided world, and that the kind of political celibacy which the British theory of the civil servant calls for is in international affairs a fiction.[33]

Beyond a doubt, the troika does radical violence to the entire UN approach, seeking to substitute for a distinguished civil service the crude arithmetic of political patronage.

It may well be that, from the Soviet viewpoint, the Secretary-General had gone beyond the original purview of his tasks. Once more, Moscow stuck to the minimal construction of the UN's role, while the Secretary-General found support for his initiatives in the broad view (expressed, for instance, in the Report of the Preparatory Commission for the United Nations) that he, more than anyone else, "must embody the principles and ideals of the Charter."

Moscow objected not only to his arrogation of authority (at the behest of the "imperialists," it would maintain) but also to his philosophy under which the United Nations must be interposed between the major camps and fill the power vacuums wherever it can. In Moscow's reading this is a pernicious doctrine incompatible with its view of the inevitable course of history. It is this attempt, more than anything else, which identified the Secretary-Gen-

---

[29] See Norman J. Padelford, "Politics and Change in the Security Council," *International Organization*, Summer 1960 (Vol. 14, No. 3), p. 381–401.

[30] See Vernon Aspaturian, "The Metamorphosis of the United Nations," *Yale Review*, Summer 1957.

[31] Dag Hammarskjöld, "The Development of a Constitutional Framework for International Co-

operation," April 29, 1960 (UN Press Release SG/910). See also Stephen M. Schwebel, *The Secretary-General of the United Nations* (Cambridge, Mass.: Harvard University Press, 1952), and Nicholas, Chapter VII.

[32] UN Press Release SG/1035 (May 29, 1961).

[33] *New York Herald-Tribune*, April 17, 1961.

eral, for the communists, with reaction, and which prompted the vigorous expression of Soviet determination not to tolerate efforts which would frustrate potential communist gains in fluid areas around the globe.

The Road Ahead

The Soviet Union may at times keep silent its belief that ultimately "one or the other must prevail." It has never abandoned the either-or approach.

The choice of when to mute and when to trumpet the extreme formulation of incompatibility is up to Moscow. Even if the outside world can help fortify or provoke a given Soviet response, it can never expect to control it. The Soviet Union may alter at will its readiness to compromise on the organization of the United Nations or its resolve to cooperate on a given task. It cannot be compelled or effectively induced to do so. With some oversimplification, one may then conclude that the United Nations is only as much as its least cooperative Members want it to be.

The question was raised earlier whether a state committed to objectives at variance with those of the United Nations can and should operate in international bodies such as the UN. Sheer logic might well lead one to answer in the negative. In the long run the contending forces as now defined and inspired may well be unable to coexist. Theoretically, or ultimately, one may indeed maintain that "international organization is hardly compatible with rampant imperialism by one state which seeks hegemony over the world."[34] Yet in the short run the essence of power politics—even on the brink of the thermonuclear precipice—remains restraint from recourse to extremes and retreat from the

logical to the political, from incompatibility to coexistence, and from the inexorable to the possible. So long as this is true, there is continuing and important room for the United Nations in the duel of our age, and for the Soviet Union in the World Organization.

This would be true even if the Soviet long-range objective of controlling the UN had greater chances of success than now seems likely. Once its efforts succeeded, of course, the need for the UN would promptly disappear, for in a future commonwealth of communist nations, the United Nations with its present complexion and philosophy can have no place.

The Soviet Union can be expected to pursue its own ends with all the vigor and determination which its "active, aggressive struggle demands."[35] Soviet policymakers realize no doubt that their reorganization proposals are not likely to be adopted in their present form. On at least one occasion—the crisis enduced by Dag Hammarskjöld's death—Moscow has demonstrated that its demands need not always amount to ultimata. In March 1961 no one would have dared predict that within six months agreement on a successor to the Secretary-General was possible—even as an "interim" solution—without fundamentally modifying the structure and operation of the UN. The deadlock likely to obtain when U Thant's term expires in April 1963 may be fraught with even graver dangers, at a time when the Soviet position promises to be considerably less flexible—unless, once more, broader considerations of policy produce a propitious climate for Soviet moderation unforeseeable today. While various compromise formulae have been suggested in response to the troika plan, Moscow has actually allowed itself little room for negotiation

---

[34] Gerard J. Mangone, *A Short History of International Organization* (New York: McGraw-Hill, 1954), p. 14.

[35] V. Matveev and M. Mikhailov, "Bor'ba za mir, za svobodu narodov i Organizatsiia Ob'edinennykh Natsii," *Kommunist* 1960, no. 15, p. 102.

or retreat without sacrificing the heart of its proposals—a veto over the activities of the Secretariat. It remains to be seen whether anything short of this will satisfy the USSR; nothing like it will be acceptable to the major noncommunist states.

To this extent, the future of the United Nations is in Soviet hands. Moscow can wreck it or build it up: in the UN's present state, Moscow is unlikely to do either. It is, however, certain to keep the United Nations from taking that giant step which Dag Hammarskjöld, in his final months, spoke of as the transition from "institutional systems of international coexistence" to "constitutional systems of international cooperation." That bridge between standing international conference and organized international community, which he saw envisaged in the UN Charter,[36] is certain to remain unspanned (among other reasons) so long as Moscow has the right and the might to interpose its veto.

The Soviet bloc cannot be expected to adopt the philosophy of the UN and pursue the objectives of the UN. As Adlai Stevenson put it to the Senate Foreign Relations Committee on January 18, 1961,

the United Nations—as an idea and as an institution—is an extension of Western ideas; of Western belief in the worth and dignity of the individual; of Western ideology. It is based on a Western parliamentary tradition. Its roots are in the Western idea of representative government. In short, it is thoroughly anti-totalitarian.

Indeed, the United Nations is founded on the belief in at least some perfectability, gradualism, and consensus. In many respects its outlook is analogous in interna-tional affairs to that of liberal democracy at home. We have been reminded that

international organization rests upon the belief that man is at liberty, not only to surrender to the operation of the iron laws of the system, or to attempt an apocalyptic leap from an era of determinism into an era of freedom, but to shape his collective destiny in the here and now.[37]

The non-Western nations may and perhaps will overwhelmingly come to share these assumptions. The communist states, as we know them, cannot.

But too much must not be anticipated or asked of the United Nations. It was never intended to clash with a Great Power or to resolve conflicts among them. The UN can be expected to alter neither the fundamental power relations among states nor the motives of their rulers. This is not an argument against the United Nations: with all its inherent limitations, its uses and values for all mankind are many. Moscow, on its part, does not expect any major impact on its world policy to come from or through the UN. The roots of conflict lie outside the Organization and extend far beyond it. In this regard, "their" and "our" view is likely to coincide, for, in the words of George F. Kennan,

it is not fair to the Organization today to ask it to resolve the predicaments of the past as well as of the present. No international organization can be stronger than the structure of relationships among the Great Powers that underlies it; and to look to such an organization to resolve deep-seated conflicts of interest among the Great Powers is to ignore its limitations and to jeopardize its usefulness in other fields.[38]

---

[36] "Introduction to the Annual Report of the Secretary-General on the Work of the Organization 16 June 1960—15 June 1961," General Assembly *Official Records* (16th session), Supplement No. 1A.

[37] Claude, p. 15.

[38] George F. Kennan, *Russia, the Atom and the West* (New York: Harper, 1958), p. 27.

TREATIES AND OTHER SOURCES OF ORDER IN INTERNATIONAL RELATIONS: THE SOVIET VIEW*

by

JAN F. TRISKA
and
ROBERT M. SLUSSER

Speaking before the American Society of International Law, Aleksandr Troianovski, the first Soviet Ambassador to the United States, summed up his views on the basic sources of order in international relations.[1] He began by rejecting the idea of a "supernational support" for international law, since the source of the rules regulating the relations among nations "lies in the nations, and not in a superforce acting from above the nations." Thus the tribunal at The Hague, he argued, is in practice nothing more than "a court of arbitration." Practical experience with the League of Nations, he felt, "goes far to prove that at the present time at least supernational bodies are not effective in binding the nations to cooperate under established rules of international law," especially since "some nations have assumed the role of supernations with the idea, not of cooperating with other nations, but of dominating and conquering them." "Moral laws and the laws of human conscience," he continued, could hardly be taken seriously as bases of international order, since "the guidance from this source is too subtle" and lacking in precision. It was necessary to find "something more positive, more concrete and definitive." The solution, he urged, was to be found in treaties-- "very precise international treaties duly signed," based on "exact formulas and determined obligations."

Mr. Troianovski emphasized that he was presenting his

---

*This study was written in connection with the Soviet Treaty Project being conducted at the Hoover Institution on War, Revolution and Peace, Stanford University, under the direction of the authors. The findings of the project are to be published in three volumes, tentatively entitled Calendar of Soviet Treaties, Analysis of Soviet Treaties, and Bibliography on Soviet Foreign Policy (all 1917-1957), by the Stanford University Press in the Hoover Institution Documentary Series. Portions of the study have been omitted here.

personal opinions, speaking "not as the Ambassador of the U.S.S.R., but as an individual who has some interest in international law and to some extent is familiar with its problems." His views, nevertheless, reflected fairly closely those of the Soviet Government. The unequivocal Soviet preference for treaties as the prima facie source of international order has been one of the few precepts in this field which have remained fundamentally unchanged throughout the existence of the Soviet State.

There has, however, been a substantial alteration in the context within which this view has been held by Soviet officials and scholars. At times treaties have been viewed as the sole source of international order; at others they have been supplemented by a wide range of additional factors, including international custom, judicial decisions, general principles of international law, the codification of international organizations, and "basic concepts" of international law.

These changes have been related, more or less directly to the requirements of Soviet foreign policy and to its treaty practice, as well as to the need to elaborate a Soviet doctrine of international law capable of challenging the doctrine of the non-Soviet world.

** ** ** **

III

To sum up:

1. International treaties and agreements, ever since the first Soviet entry into foreign relations, have remained the fundamental source and prima facie foundation of relations between Soviet Russia and other governments. The practice of the Soviet Government abundantly confirms this fact: In the forty years of its existence, the Soviet Government has concluded over 2000 treaties, agreements and conventions (more than 1800 bilateral and nearly 300 multilateral) with some 85 partners. [2]

All of the Soviet leaders, from Lenin to Khruschev, have relied more on international treaties than on all other foundations of international order combined. Both by words and deeds they have made clear their view that treaties constitute the ideal vehicle for relations between the Soviet state and the outside world. [3] This reliance on treaties has not tended to slacken as the power of the Soviet state has increased; quite the contrary. Under Khrushchev, the Soviet state has stepped up the pace of its treaty policy. During the first two years of Khrushchev's economic and cultural offensive, the Soviet Government concluded more than 3000 treaties with some forty partners, especially the leading

Afro-Asian nations: 143 in 1955 (of which 135 were bilateral agreements) and 167 in 1956 (of which 142 were bilateral), the highest number of treaties ever concluded by the Soviet Government in a two-year period. [4]

The absolute dependence of Soviet theory on the practice of the Soviet state is a well-known fact. Such distinguished students of Soviet law and Soviet international law as Calvez, De Visscher, Hazard, Kelsen, Kulski, Lissitzyn, and Meissner, agree that Soviet international law doctrine was elaborated according to Soviet state practice, in agreement with that practice, and to fortify and justify that practice. In our study of the forty-year period of Soviet treaty-making, we have found many changes and disagreements, much heresy and ideological tightrope-dancing in Soviet treaty theories in the several sharply delineated stages of development of the Soviet state. But we have also found that it was Soviet treaty practice which always preceded and determined the line of theory on treaties. Ever since the first phase of the Soviet state, when sheer necessity forced the Soviet Government to enter into relations with other states, the ideal instrument of such relations was international treaties and agreements, the great majority of which were bilateral (between 1917 and December 31, 1922, the Soviet Government concluded more than 250 treaties and agreements, of which approximately 225 were bilateral).

At first, these treaties were couched in the semantical stereotypes of traditional treaty practice and were based on principles of traditional international law. A minority of Soviet treaties contained Marxist ideological provisions, but these stipulations were isolated, far from systematic and lacked any uniting principle. If there was any underlying principle at all, it was the Soviet expectation of the benefits or at least the removal of danger a given treaty might bring about, and a given treaty partner was therefore to a high degree the determinant of both the language and the principles emphasizes. As Korovin pointed out in 1924, this obvious mixture of principles and motivations in Soviet treaty practice in the early period, which "drew arguments in articles and paragraphs [both] from extracts of treaties concluded by the [Russian] Imperial Government" and from Marxist-Leninist ideology, "resulted in an entirely ambiguous situation."[5] Consequently, there was in the earliest period no Soviet theory on treaties.

Once formal diplomatic relations with foreign Powers had been established and the Soviet Government had been recognized by the leading foreign Powers, the Soviet theory on international treaties began to take form. Lagging behind Soviet practice in time, theorists now had certain governmental practices to follow, to systematize, to analyze in terms of official ideology, and to justify and defend. Just as Soviet treaty practice during the period 1917-1922 can be characterized as a mixture of traditional and revolutionary principles, so Soviet scholars in the period 1923-1926 selected elements from this mixture in order to elaborate a systematic Soviet doctrine of treaties.

For the Soviet theorists of this period, just as for those who have followed them up to the present time, international treaties retained the crucial significance they had in Soviet practice from the beginning. As has been pointed out above, Kovovin saw in treaties signed by the Soviet government a bridge between the traditional and revolutionary systems recognized by both.[6] This was a reflection of the Soviet practice. Relations between the U.S.S.R. and the rest of the world were to be built on solid, businesslike foundations; utility, expediency, and the exaggerated Soviet criteria of security have always been best served by the instrumentality of international treaties. And, given the limitations superimposed by Soviet ideological objectives, the Soviet passion for sovereignty and explicit consent, the essential adaptability of treaties to fit particular, concrete situations, the Soviet preference for treaties as instruments of relations with other countries is understandable. Khrushchev, flexible, pragmatic, adaptable, and with all the rich experience of the Soviet past to learn from, has plunged into treaty relations--bilateral, plurilateral, and multilateral; with all kinds of partners--capitalists, socialists, Communists, and satellites; and on all kinds of subjects--political, military, economic, communications, legal, cultural and health.

2. Ever since Pashukanis' unequivocal exposition, international custom has been accepted by nearly all Soviet scholars as a second but still fundamental source of international order. Kozhevnikov's assessment of the value of international custom--

Regardless of the uncertainty, instability and relativity of international custom, it would be incorrect to underestimate, let alone to ignore its significance as a source of law for international relations--[7]

became classic. And again, this was so entirely because of Soviet needs in international relations: Why should "the Soviet Government be deprived of those rights which require no treaty formulation and derive from the very fact that normal diplomatic relations exist?"[8] Soviet practice found international custom most useful; theory reversed itself and produced international custom as the second basic foundation of order in relations between the Soviet Union and the rest of the world.

3. Soviet scholarship after World War II began to stress as another fundamental source of international law, basic "concepts and principles" of international law. These could be viewed as the Soviet interpretation of the general principles of law of Article 38, paragraph 1(c), of the Statute of the International Court of Justice. Variously understood as "legal analogies, natural law, general principles of justice" et cetera, in the West, [9] the general principles of law became for most Soviet theorists a series of "basic laws, norms, and concepts" of legal, political, ideological and ethical content. The great majority of these principles have their origins, in one way or another, either in traditional international law or in treaty law and thus have been accepted, or are acceptable, universally. The fact must never be lost sight of, however, that while the terms in which the principles are formulated by Soviet writers may be similar to or identical with those employed in the West, the content and significance of the principles are often given a completely different interpretation in the Soviet and non-Soviet worlds.

4. Decisions of international organizations such as the League of Nations, the United Nations, international courts such as the Permanent Court of International Justice and the International Court of Justice, and other "permanent and temporary" international organizations, conferences and agencies have been, more often than not, viewed by Soviet writers as "an important source of international law" for the member states, "provided that they were [so] recognized and applied in practice."[10] Such decisions "do not always receive proper attention, in spite of [their] great significance and the importance of the role which [they] play," complained Krylov, out of his extensive judicial experience. This is true: Soviet scholarship, just as Soviet and Western practice, has viewed such decisions as subsidiary sources of international law; nor does Krylov's complaint appear to have had any practical effect in altering this situation.

Similarly, (5) decisions of national courts, (6) domestic legislation, (7) doctrine, (8) the codification of international law, and (9) collision norms have been, when recognized, considered auxiliary and secondary sources; however, the pronounced over-all tendency has been gradually towards more and more recognition of these factors. International morality and international comity have been generally, though not exclusively, rejected by Soviet practice and theory.

IV

In the forty-year period of the existence of the Soviet

521

state the metamorphosis of Soviet practice and theory on sources of world order has been profound. Theory evolved from the original position--international treaties and very little else--to the present point of view--international treaties and international custom, general principles (concepts and norms) of international law, decisions of international organizations, decisions of national courts, domestic legislation, et cetera. As a consequence, the Soviet hierarchy of sources has come to resemble quite closely the generally accepted Western pattern. There are differences, to be sure:

(a) International conventions, both general and particular, still tower over other sources for Soviet theorists.

(b) The difference in "motivations" leading to conclusion of international treaties has always been solemnly pointed out. Ever since Lenin, Soviet writers claim,

The Soviet state viewed international treaties as a serious means in the struggle for peace, for the victory of communism [sic]. On the other hand, the imperialist states exploit international treaties to mask their aggressive goals and legally to secure the dependence of small states. International treaties in the hands of the imperialists become new legal forms of colonialism (Baghdad Pact and SEATO) and a cover-up for aggression (North Atlantic Pact). V. I. Lenin used to characterize such international treaties as "treaty-conspiracies.11

(c) Selectivity and eclecticism are applied to all sources under the criterion of "democratic principles," to be read "consent of the Soviet Union." In other words, the U.S.S.R. accepts those norms as foundations of international order which it recognizes itself or which it views at least as not in opposition to the goals of Soviet foreign policy; such norms are made binding by the acceptance of the Soviet state. Hence the "cornerstone" of absolute sovereignty and the Soviet advocacy of primacy of national over international law.

(d) There is an old distinction which is still preserved between substantive and formal sources of international order in the Soviet doctrine: Substantive (or material) sources of order are the "real foundations" which, in Marxist theory, condition the origin and the development of all order, namely, the productive relations characteristic for each society. That class which controls the means of production in a society is the class which forms and determines order and its concrete content. In relations among states the substantive sources, because of the presence of both

522

socialist and capitalist systems, are and must be struggle, co-existence and competition.[12] And struggle, co-existence and competition among states are the material basis of international order which is manifested in the formal, external, legal sources: international treaties, international custom, general principles of international law, decisions of international organizations, et cetera.

(e) What the Soviet authors call basic "principles," "laws," or "norms" of international law are

> the basic foundations which rule international relations in a definite historical epoch and which possess binding force for all states irrespective of whether or not they become valid through international custom or international treaty. They possess special significance for the establishment of legality in international relations. That is why the Soviet doctrine not only recognizes but especially stresses the existence of basic principles of international law.[13]

However, these and similar differences are primarily doctrinal and in fact have little to do with actual Soviet treaty practice; they do matter, but play a role which is far from decisive even in Soviet scholarship. It is significant that a recent volume of selected documents on international law published in Moscow in 1957[14] carries under the heading "Sources of International Law" these items: 1. Article 38 of the statute of the International Court of Justice; 2. Resolutions of the General Assembly of the U.N. on progressive development of international law and its codification (accepted by the General Assembly in the second part of the Second Session in New York on Dec. 11, 1946); 3. Decision concerning establishment of the International Law Commission of the U.N., Nov. 21, 1947; 4a. Organization of the International Law Commission as accepted on Dec. 18, 1946; 4b. Functions of the International Law Commission; and 4c. Co-operation of the International Law Commission with other organs. No other documents are included in the section on sources.

On the other hand, the Western view on sources of international law has not stood still in the last forty years either. International custom used to be universally viewed as "the most important source of international law" forty years ago.[15] Today it is regarded as only one of the two most important sources, and in general as the second one on the scale. This fact, at least partly, owes its origin to the presence of the Soviet Union in the world community; as Charles De Visscher aptly put it,

> Acceleration of history, and above all diminishing

homogeneity in the moral and legal ideas that have long governed the formation of law--such, in their essential elements, are the causes that today curtail the development of customary international law.[16]

International custom "is not adequate to the needs of a world that changes with unprecedented speed";[17] international treaties--flexible, decentralized, rational, specific, adaptable, innovating and stabilizing--were bound to take over where international custom, surer but slower, was proved wanting.[18]

We may conclude, then, that after forty years of "struggle," "co-existence," and "competition," there is a fairly close similarity between Soviet and Western views on the sources of order in international relations, and that in both, international treaties are of primary importance.[19]

[1] Address delivered on April 28, 1934, 1934 Proc. Am. Soc. Int. Law 195-196.

[2] Not counting Monaco, Liechtenstein and Andorra, the U.S.S.R. has had some treaty relations with all the countries of the world except the Republic of Korea, South Vietnam, and the Vatican City. (In the Soviet usage, the term "treaty" covers all agreements between governments founding relationships in international law, whatever their name, but excluding oral agreements).

[3] [Footnote omitted.]

[4] These figures are provisional and subject to revision, but may be taken as established minima.

[5] Ye. A. Korovin, Mezhdunarodnoe pravo perekhodnogo vremeni (International Law of the Transitional Period) 5 (Moscow, 1924).

[6] Ibid. 75; ....

[7] F. I. Kozhevnikov, "K voprosu o poniatii mezhdunarodnogo prava" (On the Question of the Concept of International Law), Sovetskoe gosudarstvo i provo, No. 2 (1940), p. 101.

[8] Ye. Pashukanis, Ocherki po mezhdunarodnomu provu (Essays on International Law), Ch. 2 (Moscow, 1935).

[9] Herbert W. Briggs, The Law of Nations: Cases, Documents and Notes 48 (London, 2nd ed. 1953).

[10] S. B. Krylov in V. N. Durdenevski and S. B. Krylov (eds.), Mezhdunarodnoe pravo 25 (Moscow, 1947).

[11] A. N. Talalaev, "V. I. Lenin o mezhdunarodnykh dogovorakh" (V. I. Lenin on International Treaties), Sovetskoe gosudarstvo i pravo, No. 4 (1958), p. 24. The reference is to Lenin, Sochineniia, Vol. 23, p. 116.

[12] [Footnote omitted.]

[13] "Mezhdunarodnoe pravo" in A. Ya. Vyshinski (ed.), Diplomaticheskii slovar', Vol. 2, cols. 124-125 (Moscow, 1950).

[14] [Footnote omitted.]   [15] [Footnote omitted.]

[16] Charles De Visscher, Theory and Reality in Public International Law 156 (Princeton, 1957). Italics added.

[17] Ibid. 268.

[18] [Footnote omitted.]   [19] [Footnote omitted.]

HOW THE RUSSIANS WAGE POLITICAL WARFARE

by

EDMOND TAYLOR

PARIS

"Yes, the moment has come to carry out general, universal, and controlled disarmament," Maurice Thorez declared on March 17 at a banquet for one hundred young Frenchmen about to be called up for military service organized by the city fathers of Ivry, the Paris industrial suburb that he represents in the National Assembly. The semi-invalid but still tough leader of French Communism was alluding to the latest Soviet disarmament proposal unveiled at Geneva a few days earlier. "All weapons on the junk-heap," he continued. "No more general staffs! No more generals! No more barracks! No more military service!"

The exhortations were free-hand translations of some remarks addressed by Nikita Khrushchev to the U.N. General Assembly in 1960. They contrasted sharply with the truculent tone of the speech the Soviet leader had delivered in Moscow on March 16—just twenty-four hours before the feast of love and propaganda at Ivry—boasting of the Soviet Union's so-called global nuclear missile. They were equally at variance with the cold warning of Soviet Foreign Minister Andrei A. Gromyko, delivered a short time before at the foreign ministers' meeting in Geneva, that the Soviets would never accept an effective international inspection system to police a ban on nuclear testing. And the pacifism of Khrushchev's 1960 eloquence sounded less

convincing than ever when echoed by Thorez, who is notoriously one of the least de-Stalinized Communist leaders west of Albania.

Considering that the difference between the Khrushchevian and the Stalinist concepts of peaceful coexistence is not as great as some people think, it came as no surprise when the young conscripts-to-be voted a hard-line resolution at Ivry demanding that the government reduce at once the term of military service from twenty-seven to eighteen months (the reduction has already been officially decided but cannot be carried out for a year without raising havoc in the French army), or when they asked for the immediate release of all conscripts who have already served more than eighteen months and for a crackdown on the OAS and other "fascists." (The youths apparently failed to note the contradiction between stamping out the OAS and demobilizing the forces needed for the job.) A delegation was then sent off to the Elysée Palace to lay the demands before President de Gaulle.

This little incident is indicative of a most important trend in Communist political warfare: a constantly increasing stress on the peace theme so eloquently voiced by Thorez. "Peace offensives" have been an intermittent feature of Communist propaganda for many years; now the peace offensive—synchronized in the underdeveloped countries with the struggle against imperialism—has turned into a relentless attack against the cohesion of the free world. "The banner of peace enables us to rally the masses around us," Khrushchev told an audience of party workers on January 6, 1961. "By holding aloft this banner we will be even more successful."

The peace offensive is an unceasing campaign to identify that universally-wished for commodity, peace, with the party's brand-name. In the underdeveloped countries the peace offensive is chiefly used to foment and sustain civil war, or as Khrushchev more delicately puts it, for contributing to "the success of the national liberation movement." In the West it is a multi-purpose subversive weapon for undermining public confidence in government, for driving wedges between groups, and for recruiting sympathizers and auxiliaries by involving them in oppositional—often illegal—agitation.

The Ivry togetherness banquet that Thorez addressed provided almost a textbook illustration of these tactics—at least on the plane of what may be termed open conspiracy. While it was subversive in the sense that its ultimate aim was undoubtedly to contribute to undermining the loyalty of the French Army—long a high-priority objective for the French Communist Party—not one overtly subversive word was spoken by any participant. There were no incitements to overthrow the government by force, none of the old Marxist clichés about the inevitability of revolution, the need for intensifying the class struggle, or wiping out the evils of capitalism. Communist propaganda today rarely stresses old-fashioned treason. The permanent peace offensive—and in the Third World the anticolonialist or national-liberation theme—largely obviate the need for such a crude approach.

A Refinement of Lying

There is general agreement among intelligence experts that the stress on the peace theme in Soviet political warfare and the current tendency of Communist propagandists to soft-pedal the cruder forms of revolutionary agitation (at least in the western countries) in no way reflect a genuine softening of the Soviet attitude toward the free societies. Not much importance is ascribed to the split between Moscow and Peking, or the difficulties of Soviet agriculture, or the deep changes that may actually be taking place in Soviet society. In fact there is a strong suspicion that many of the alluring reports on such developments and the policy conclusions naïvely drawn from them in the West are an evidence of the new, refined techniques of indirect penetration.

The very scale, along with the continued viciousness and the increasing deviousness of Communist propaganda, demonstrates the fundamentally aggressive intent underlying the Soviet peace offensive. Communist broadcasting activity intended to weaken and confuse the non-Communist world reached a new peak last year. According to an official study prepared by the U.S. Information Agency, Communist-bloc broadcasts increased greatly in Latin America and almost doubled in Africa, without falling off elsewhere. "We have evidence," an authorized USIA spokesman told me, "that in Uruguay, for example, the Communist bloc spends several times more money on postage to mail their magazines, pamphlets, etc., than the USIA spends on its entire country program."

Camouflaged or unattributed radio campaigns against friends or allies of the United States in various parts of the world illustrate the incendiary nature of the clandestine programs to which the USIA report refers. "Liberal students!" exhorted a recent Persian-language broadcast beamed from Soviet territory to Iran, "The opening of the university will create for us a chance to unite our forces against the shah and his despotic rule. We must cut the throats of these traitors!"

Similar incitements to murder, insurrection, and treason are broadcast by "black" Soviet transmitters to Greece and Turkey at times, and some of the overt programs are only slightly more restrained in their efforts to promote strife between groups and peoples: e.g., a recent Arabic broadcast from East Berlin declaring that "The German Democratic Republic regards Israel as a base and a tool for use by the imperialists against the Arab countries."

The same divisive shafts of Communist propaganda, though sometimes more cunningly disguised, are constantly aimed against the western alliance as well. "Moscow continued during 1961 to try to weaken the will of the people in the West to band together against Communism," the USIA report notes. "To do this, it warned of the political and economic liabilities inherent in the western pacts, and it was not reluctant to use occasional nuclear threats to make its point. It also tried to separate the U.S. from its key allies in repeated propaganda sallies, just as it tried to drive separate wedges into the western alliance whenever it was feasible by playing off the U.K. and France against the U.S. or the U.S. and Germany against the rest of Europe."

"IN MY VIEW, the big change in Soviet strategy took place in 1955," I was told by a senior U.S. Foreign Service officer concerned with NATO. "In that year Khrushchev finally realized the Soviet Union would have to give up the hope of some day conquering the West by arms because such a program would inevitably lead to a nuclear war in which both East and West would be destroyed. But he did not give up the goal of world power. He merely decided to attain it by other means. The means include diplomacy, propaganda, and other forms of psychological warfare, economic pressures, mass subversion, and above all the support of what he calls 'just wars of national liberation' in the undeveloped countries. All these forms of attack and several others are being beautifully meshed and integrated so that they support each other. Since Khrushchev made his decision, both the scale and the technical quality of Communist political warfare have been steadily rising. The Communist offensive is more dangerous today than it ever has been because it is being pushed harder and more intelligently than ever before."

A somewhat similar opinion was expressed not long ago by Desmond Donnelly, a British Labour M.P. and a long-time student of political warfare. "[The] concept of political liberty," Mr. Donnelly wrote in the monthly *Nato Letter* of April, 1961, "now faces an attack in which the emphasis is not on the brash, sometimes stupid frontal approach of Stalin or Hitler. It is the more subtle because it comes from within . . ."

The New Fronts

All eastern experts agree that in the last year or two Communist political warfare has become increasingly sophisticated, subtle, and imaginative. "There is no trick of the trade that is not known to the Communist propagandist," Edward R. Murrow, the head of the U.S. Information Agency, acknowledged recently. Many of the newest tricks seem to be in the areas of semi-covert or "gray" propaganda and in the penetration or manipulation of non-Communist groups. The stress is above all on new forms of camouflage. Hitherto little-known "transmission belts" of Communist propaganda are taking over an increased share of the burden from some of the notorious individuals and groups who have played this role in the past but who have been so compromised that their effectiveness is much diminished. Completely new ad hoc organizations of various types are replacing for many purposes the well-known old "front" outfits. The major international fronts such as the World Peace Council, the World Federation of Trade Unions, the World Federation of Democratic Youth, and the International Democratic Women's Organization are still functioning, but an effort is being made to make them look more independent and respectable while still remaining largely responsive to Communist control.

According to one of the specialists on the civilian staff at NATO headquarters here, several members of the alliance have reported greatly increased covert Communist efforts to infiltrate and control non-Communist organizations. This was most eminently the case in the recent British report on the subject.

In AN INSTANCE that has come to light in Paris recently, Communist undercover operators appear to have succeeded in exploiting the fear of German rearmament that is still keen among many French intellectuals to manipulate for their purposes a seemingly respectable local organization. The organization, which calls itself *Les Echanges Franco-Allemandes,* is headed by Professor Henri Laugier, one-time assistant-secretary-general of the U.N., and most of its leading members are reputable French intellectuals, though one of them, Professor Jacques Denis, is known as the French Communist Party's authority on German affairs. Last November the body organized a two-day seminar here that attracted a number of well-known and sometimes conservative public figures, along with the usual turnout of notorious fellow-travellers and drawing-room Communists. Many of the speeches, including one or two delivered by right-of-center political leaders supposed to be supporters of General de Gaulle, parroted familiar themes of Communist propaganda for a solution of the Berlin problem. More recently the organization dispatched a delegation headed by Professor Denis to East Berlin to attend the launching of a new friendship society under the official sponsorship of the East German government—which France does not recognize. As explained in the Communist organ *l'Humanité* by Professor Denis, the immediate aim of the friendship society is "to explain to French public opinion that the German Peoples' Republic is the first German state in history to break categorically with the fatal German past, and to respect and uphold the legitimate demands of the French nation for security against any attack." The friendship society has now opened an office in Paris which serves as an unofficial front for the East German propaganda ministry.

At Bryn Mawr

A somewhat similar—but seemingly less successful—attempt to penetrate peace organizations in the United States and tie them to the Communist-controlled international peace front was made by a Soviet political-warfare agent attached to an otherwise unobjectionable delegation of Soviet women who visited America last November. The delegation consisted of nine Soviet women attending an informal seminar organized at Bryn Mawr college by the Women's International League for Peace and Freedom, a militantly pacifist non-Communist organization of U.S. social workers and social scientists founded by Jane Addams. The Soviet party was nominally headed by Mme. Yekaterina Kolcheneva but its real leader was a strong-faced, intelligent-looking woman in her early fifties named Olga Chechetkina. A journalist on the staff of *Pravda,* Mme. Chechetkina—according to an authoritative government source in Washington—is also known as an agitprop specialist.

As early as 1940, Mme. Chechetkina held a post of major responsibility in the international Communist youth organization—a particularly vital link in the worldwide chain of subversion. In 1953, her articles in *Pravda* contributed to popular excitement about the famous "plot" of the Jewish doctors; in her own words she "helped to tear the mask from the American hirelings and monsters who used the white coat of doctors to kill." The previous June she had managed to get herself expelled from Italy—no easy feat for a foreign correspondent—because of what the Italian Government termed her "defamatory, poisonous, and untruthful reports." In 1954, as *Pravda* correspondent in Indonesia, she worked up a lurid series of poison-pen dispatches accusing the United States of plotting the assassination of President Sukarno. In a way, her appointment on the delegation to the United States was a tribute to the standing of the Bryn Mawr ladies, and so was the unusual pressure the Soviet government exerted on Washington to have the State Department override the objections of our embassy in Moscow to giving her a visa.

Under Mme. Chechetkina's authoritative guidance, the Soviet delegation tried to persuade the American women to accept an organizational link with the Soviet peace group to which they belonged, thereby becoming part of the Communist international peace front. An attempt was also made to pass a joint resolution expressing concern about West German "militarism." Enough politically sophisticated American women attended the seminar to spot these classic ploys and and block them, and the Soviet women accepted the setback with more or less good grace. In the end the Soviet delegation scored a much less important propaganda point by arranging to have the fairly innocuous joint resolution of the two groups released at a press conference in the Soviet Embassy in Washington. To date the only certain conclusion that can be drawn from the affair is that it demonstrates the extraordinary importance that Communist political warfare attaches to any possibility of infiltrating or influencing the peace movement in America.

Be Kind to Nikita

Nothing illustrates better both the deviousness and the adroitness of Communist political warfare than its black or indirect propaganda campaigns to disarm the vigilance of the western nations. Aided by a good deal of wishful thinking on the part of pundits and politicians this side of the Iron Curtain, the Soviet bloc political-warfare apparatus keeps injecting a steady stream of soporific propaganda, more or less disguised as news, into the main channels of western information. Much of the time this propaganda is disseminated in good faith by western journalists —more often than not with the blessing of equally gullible officials. A particularly interesting example of a recurrent theme of Soviet propaganda cropping up as diplomatic "news" from Moscow appeared in a recent dispatch sent out to its clients by *Agence France Presse*, a French news agency of international repute. On March 12, the Moscow bureau of AFP sent a dispatch (printed the following day in the Paris *Figaro*) based on the opinion of unidentified observers in the Soviet capital to the effect that the Soviet farm problem and various other internal difficulties might be influencing the Soviet leaders to seek a relaxation of East-West tensions. While admitting that Khrushchev had publicly manifested his decision to continue giving guns priority over butter, the dispatch said that he had no illusions about the domestic problems this policy would create if kept in force too long.

"Hence," the AFP message concluded, "we are entitled to ask ourselves whether the Soviet Union does not have even more imperious reasons than the West to wish for disarmament. And perhaps at this moment we are witnessing a deep evolution in M. Khrushchev's thinking in accordance with which peaceful coexistence is being transformed from the ideal strategy for achieving victory without war that it seemed a year ago into an ineluctable neces-

sity for the U.S.S.R. itself."

The only interesting thing about this little think-piece is its dateline. Most recent reports about the beneficent impact on Soviet foreign policy of the Sino-Soviet camp's internal difficulties have originated abroad in non-Communist circles. Some western intelligence experts believe that the difficulties, while real enough, are being deliberately played up by Soviet political warfare to mislead the West as to Khrushchev's real objectives. The AFP report had the distinction of coming straight from Moscow.

IN CERTAIN respects the AFP telegram recalls the spate of articles in the western press over the last three years suggesting that we should do business with Khrushchev rather than risk—in the words of Harrison E. Salisbury (the New York *Times*, April 3, 1959)—"the peril of a return to the harsh era of Stalin, backed this time by an intransigent Communist China and a notable nuclear armory." It has now been established that Khrushchev himself last year gave encouragement to the argument that if the West is unkind to him it will bring the Stalinists back to power. In a message to President Tito of Yugoslavia during the congress of unaligned nations in Belgrade last summer, Khrushchev claimed to be under heavy pressure from the Stalinist "anti-party" opposition at home and implicitly asked for patience and understanding on the part of the outside world —particularly in respect to the renewal of Soviet nuclear tests which he hinted was being forced on him against his will. Tito—whose closeness to the Kremlin line has been celebrated during Gromyko's visit to Belgrade—obligingly transmitted Khrushchev's plea to western diplomats in Belgrade, and was kind enough to communicate the substance of it as unattributable but usable "background" to the foreign correspondents there. Irrespective of the degree of accuracy there may be in this notion, the manner in which it keeps popping up should suffice to induce a good deal of skepticism. For instance, according to a dispatch from Washington in the London *Times,* a number of people in our capital thought that the deadlock at the Geneva conference could not really be blamed on Khrushchev since he is no longer a "free agent": he has become, so it seems, the puppet of Walter Ulbricht, who cannot be dropped until the Sino-Soviet crisis is resolved.

THE MECHANISMS by which such campaigns are launched and sustained in the non-Communist press are rather well known to western intelligence specialists. The directive indicating the theme to be stressed stems from some overall and long-range Communist campaign, like the peace offensive or the struggle against colonialism. The directive is then sent by diplomatic pouch or by code to all the Soviet and Satellite diplomatic missions in the target area. In many cases it is simultaneously transmitted by the secret police (KGB) through its own channels to its stations abroad. Depending upon how "black" or tricky the directive is, the theme will be disseminated by word of mouth through the normal press-attaché and diplomatic-cocktail-set channels, or its implementation will be turned over to a "black" specialist on the staff, who may or may not be the press attaché.

Alexander Kosnacheyev, a former attaché of the Soviet embassy in Rangoon who came over to the West in 1959 has explained that he used

to get quite satisfactory results by simply writing an article that embodied the desired slant and sending it to friends on the staffs of local papers who then adapted it to the style of their respective publications. Such services were sometimes paid for, sometimes voluntary.

According to United States and NATO intelligence specialists, the Soviet and the affiliated Satellite secret services are closely synchronized under the machinery of the Warsaw pact—and have a common code. In Paris alone, according to *Le Monde,* it is estimated that there are at least one hundred principal operatives of the Soviet-bloc secret services, mostly under diplomatic or para-diplomatic cover. Each operative has his own network of locally recruited under-cover agents, along with his circle of "honorary correspondents" (French police jargon for unpaid informants or auxilliaries).

The Gavin 'Report'

One aspect of Communist political warfare that illustrates the role of the KGB and of its sister services is the systematic poisoning of inter-Allied relations by means of forgeries and false or distorted information planted both in public media and in the intelligence channels of the Atlantic Alliance. Testifying last summer before the U.S. Senate's subcommittee on investigation of the administration of the internal-security laws, Richard Helms, at that time assistant director of the Central Intelligence Agency, gave the following pithy resumé of this form of Communist political warfare:

"The campaign of subversion which the Communists wage persistently against the free world extends to its news outlets. Their purpose is not to find news but to pervert it. . . . Because their own controlled outlets are suspect in the West, they often press the war of words through free world publications that have no evident connection with the U.S.S.R., international or national communism, or even with its multiple fronts . . . . Through hidden financial subsidies and other methods the bloc gains sufficient influence to assure the publication of false stories about western conspiracies, atrocities and military aggressions . . . .

"Inventing reports for insertion into western intelligence channels—reports designed to influence the policies of free world governments—is another minor bloc industry . . . .

"The pre-fabricated reports slipped into foreign intelligence channels are labeled as secret information about American or other western plans or policies hostile to the government of the recipient service. Some of the planned reports are designed to make the receiver distrust and fear friendly or neighboring countries."

ONE particularly vicious example of Communist inspired propaganda aimed at splitting the western alliance turned up last Spring, according to Mr. Helms, in an article of the well-known French political columnist, Mme. Geneviève Tabouis. (How it reached her was not explained.)

"In the middle of April [1961]," Mr. Helms told the senators, "Madame Tabouis planted on a Parisian newspaper two articles which alleged that Ambassador Gavin, in Paris, had reported to President Kennedy his proposals for the policy of the new administration toward the so-called European sector. The Tabouis articles also alleged that the report recommended that NATO be 'downgraded to a simple means for technical liaison.' Next, the report—which of course never existed—was alleged to have recommended that the United States undertake direct bilateral negotiations with European countries for new, conventional military arrangements. The fourth prong of the lie had the ambassador urging the President to withhold strategic nuclear protection from Western Europe and to negotiate with the Soviet for the 'retirement of all strategic U. S. bases.' "

Though, as Mr. Helms testified, the Gavin report never existed, the last "prong" of it was sufficiently like the actual policy noisily advocated by some Washington circles reputed to be close to the administration to seem plausible to many European readers. That is what made it effective propaganda.

What seems on the face of it to be a more subtle example of questionable trends in current American policy being exploited to divide us from our allies cropped up last November in *Combat,* a Paris daily which usually expresses the viewpoint of French ultra-nationalists but which has proved hospitable to certain types of pro-Soviet propaganda. (There has been intermittent collusion between the Communists and certain right-wing French nationalists since the successful campaign to scuttle the European Defense Community in 1954. The anti-EDC drive was spearheaded by a covert action group financed in part by the Soviet Embassy and jointly directed by two newspapermen, one the editor of a fellow-travelling weekly, the other the publisher of a right-wing newsletter subsidized by a section of French heavy industry. The methods employed by the group included one that Birchites and other amateur witch hunters in the United States would surely admire: attempts to frame pro-EDC French Government officials by making it appear that they had Communist sympathies.)

The article in *Combat* last November attributed to President Kennedy the belief that the two Germanies will eventually draw together "if given a chance to talk to each other." Even more astonishing was a clairvoyant paragraph revealing the administration's intimate feelings about Chancellor Adenauer on the eve of his impending visit to the United States. Alluding to the President's alleged belief that economic interests are more durable than political alliances, the *Combat* article said, "That is why Washington was not displeased to see the defeat of Chancellor Adenauer [in the German elections]. A year ago the American capital would have been wringing its hands."

Early in March *Combat* published a series of articles on East Germany by a staff writer named George Andersen, whose enthusiasm for the woebegone puppet state behind the Berlin wall is unusual even among fellow travelers. Reporting on the "success" of the Leipzig trade fair, despite a NATO recommendation to boycott it, Andersen managed to dig up an alleged British businessman, a Mr. Sternberg, who said to him, "We want the Federal Republic of Germany to know that if normal exchanges with Pankow really seem as impossible as the experts in Bonn claim, we British businessmen will undertake to take the place of West German business and fill all the orders offered by the German People's Republic."

Besides interviewing various Communist officials, including Walter Ulbricht—who assured him that the GPR's only ambition was to contribute to world peace—Andersen noted that he found everywhere in the GPR a strong desire for a "compromise" solution of the Berlin · question based, among other things, on a U.N. guarantee for West Berlin and for completely free access to the city, provided all traffic, including air traffic, between West Berlin and West Germany, were checked by the East German security services. The proposed "compromise" "merited reflection," Andersen thought. (This was basically the "compromise" Gromyko later presented in Geneva.)

"By way of conclusion," Andersen reported, "my hosts thought that the proposed solution for the Berlin crisis would contribute to an international thaw, would close a chapter in the cold war, and would constitute a decisive proof of the efficacy of peaceful coexistence."

O**N THIS LAST** point, at least, the suggestible French correspondent was probably not misled.

"The policy of peaceful coexistence," Khrushchev himself has said, "promotes the growth of the forces of progress . . . In the capitalist countries it facilitates the work of the Communist parties and the other progressive organizations of the working class, makes it easier for the peoples to combat the aggressive war blocs and foreign military bases, and contributes to the success of the national-liberation movement."

In other words, peaceful coexistence may not be so peaceful after all.

THE NEW WORLD OF COMMUNISM

The transcribed recording
from the program "The Open Mind"
NBC Television, New York City
April 1, 1962

HARRISON E. SALISBURY and ERICH FROMM

ANNOUNCER: 'The Open Mind,' free to examine, to question, to disagree. Our subject today: "The New World of Communism." Your
host on The Open Mind is Eric F. Goldman, Professor of History at
Princeton University and author of Rendezvous with Destiny and The
Crucial Decade.

MR. GOLDMAN: Hello, ladies and gentlemen. The Cold War has been
with us now some fifteen years and during that time of course America
has changed vastly. So, too, have the other side. Clearly, the 1947
American picture of a monolithic world Communism, trudging down
some pre-ordained Marxist road, is no longer true, if indeed it ever
was.

Today The Open Mind proposed to explore the new world of Communism, the world itself, the relationships between its parts, the relationship between the world and us. To do this we have invited to The
Open Mind two guests. They are not engaged in debate; they are not
engaged in a discussion in any formal sense. They are here as two
deeply informed, deeply concerned men, to talk about an important
theme in the manner of civilized conversation.

Our guest: Here to my right, Mr. Harrison E. Salisbury who won
a Pulitzer Prize for his correspondence from Russia, at present director
of national correspondence of the New York Times, and the author of a
forthcoming novel about the Leningrad of Stalin's days, a novel entitled
The Northern Palmyra Affair.

Our other guest, Dr. Erich Fromm, needless to say, a psychoanalyst of world-wide reputation. Dr. Fromm is perhaps best known to
us for his brilliant book, Escape from Freedom. He has recently
published May Man Prevail?, a fresh and exciting commentary on the
world today, including very much the Communist world today.

Mr. Salisbury, in a group of articles you wrote for the Times a
while ago, I was particularly struck by one in which you describe a new
and bitter struggle going on in the Soviet Union. You wrote this: "A
bitter struggle is emerging in the Soviet Union between a powerful neo-
Stalinist faction and a broadly based group of liberals for the dominant
role in the country's future. The outcome of the struggle will profoundly affect Moscow's relations with the West and the nature of internal evolution in that nation." Would you begin us by expanding a bit on
that?

MR. SALISBURY: Yes, I think this is perhaps the most interesting
thing that I found in my recent trip to the Soviet Union. What was most
interesting to me was not the emergence of a group of neo-Stalinists.
After all, we have known that there were bound to be many men in Russia
still in positions of influence and power who would be basically motivated

by the ideas of Stalin regardless of the lip service they might give to the repudiation of Stalin that is c a r r i e d out by Khrushchev and implicit in many of Khrushchev's policies. What startled me was the broadening out of the liberal movement. When I speak of the liberal movement in Russia, I think an explanation is warranted. These people are largely motivated by what we would call "liberal" ideals. They're the same as our ideals of liberalism but they cast them within the framework of Soviet system, that is to say, these are not men who are going to the barricades against the present dictatorship of the proletariat as they understand it. But they are men who wish to see a rule of law established in Russia, a rule of justice. They wish to see free discussion in the realm of ideas. They wish to see the artist permitted to exercise his creative talents as much as he would be in our own Western world. In other words, in the realm of ideas and things of that kind they're akin to our way of thinking. But so far as their governmental thought is concerned, they don't really propose to change the system, at least not in the present context. Later on, perhaps.

These people are mostly persons of some stature in the Soviet society, the intelligentsia--by this term the Russians mean the scientists, the writers, the men who use their minds. It's rather a broad term and includes many people in the white collar class--this is where you find that movement. They are powerful in Russia today and you can see the extent of their power in some of the things the government is doing. You see it in the discussions that are being carried on quite openly--open debate of many issues. These are not debates over foreign policy, not debates over international policy but debates over very important internal questions.

MR. GOLDMAN: Dr. Fromm, I was struck in your book, May Man Prevail?, by your description of present day Russia in which you said, "The Soviet Union under Khrushchev's leadership is a conservative, state controlled, industrial managerialism, not a revolutionary system." Does this go along with the trends that Mr. Salisbury's been describing?

DR. FROMM: Yes, in fact I think it does. Actually I would say that since about 1923 or '24, since the death of Lenin, the Soviet Union has ceased to be a revolutionary system. Under Stalin it was a fierce, reactionary, terroristic system, while, as Mr. Salisbury says, in the last few years the liberal element is increasing and makes the society in some ways more similar to our own. But coming back to the quote, I believe our great mistake in the West, that is to say, that of most people, is that they confuse Lenin and Trotsky with Stalin and Khrushchev. Stalin from 1933 on had no interest which could be in any way compared to the revolutionary interest, if you please, a messianic interest or passion which revolutionaries like Lenin and Trotsky had. He wanted to build up state capitalism or state socialism, if you want to call it that, with a strict hierarchy, with a profit motive as a main incentive for workers, for peasants and for the managers, and after he had reached a certain level of industry, Russia was capable of liberalizing. The great misunderstanding is that we take their Communist ideology seriously in a way which they don't take seriously themselves. In fact, we in the West are the only ones who take the incantations of Communist leaders very seriously. Long live the world revolution! Or Communism in the whole world! That sounds to us like a very frightening formula or a very impressive formula. But they are just old stuff. They are conventions which are said in this kind of ideology system for years, and they don't mean a thing. I would be very much interested in what Mr. Salisbury thinks of this because I know it only from reading the literature. The Russians have a problem with their young generation which is very similar to our own. I think our problem is to a large extent that our Western tradition, the religious and philosophical humanist

535

tradition, has very little weight any more. We also have our own incantations and rituals. But actually a new Jaguar is more important than anything which could be called religious or spiritual. And I think the Russians have a similar problem with their young generation, that new gadgets, more production and all that, is really what matters. And all the idealism which officially is connected with Communist ideology has actually gone out of the picture. It is just an empty ritual and yet the Russians need it because any system needs a structuralizing and unifying ideology. Since the Russians have not a religious one, since a nationalistic one isn't complete, they still stick to the old Communist ideology and throw in a piece of Marx here and a piece of Lenin there. But actually I think things have become rather ineffective as far as ideology is concerned.

MR. SALISBURY: That certainly is true, Dr. Fromm. You can see that every day in Moscow. I had the feeling at the time of Stalin's death, when the new group began to take over, that their most serious problem was in some way to recapture the interest and the enthusiasms and the fervor of their younger generation. And I think that this is one of the problems with which Khrushchev is most concerned. He's tried to cope with this problem. They tried to reinculcate some revolutionary enthusiasm or even patriotic enthusiasm in their young Communist organization. They've put young people in. As a matter of fact, the leader of the young Communists under Stalin was a man over 50, so he was not really a youth leader. They've tried to at least get some younger people in there and to arouse some enthusiasm of the type that existed in the early days, to get some enthusiasm about going out to Siberia, which is something you can get enthusiastic about.

It's really like our West; it's a place where you can go far and do big things in a big way. But they've sent hundreds of thousands of youngsters out there and I saw just the other day some figures on the number of young people who had returned from a given project in Western Siberia, not Eastern Siberia. It was 95 per cent returns within two years. Now you don't have very much enthusiasm indicated in that. If you go around the cafes in Moscow, you find enthusiasm. It's enthusiasm for the West, that's what you find among these youngsters. They're wearing Western clothes, they're dancing to Western songs, and they want to know how to do the twist. They love to have a Western newspaper, Western literature, anything of that kind. They find very little in their own society. They say again and again, it's so boring in Russia. When youth says it's so boring, I think it's lost to the leadership.

DR. FROMM: Incidentally if I may make a footnote, they are lucky that they are where people know they are being bored; most people are bored and don't know it. I think there's nothing that's more oppressive than boredom, much more so than the Oedipus complex.

MR. SALISBURY: I don't know about that. But it certainly is true in Russia, this boredom of the youth. And as far as the business of cars is concerned, you can see that also walking around the streets in Moscow. Wherever there's a new foreign car, it tends to be surrounded by young people, fifteen to twenty, looking at it. This is the most interesting thing in the world to them, cars. They don't have them there; they'd love to have them.

MR. GOLDMAN: I notice that both of you gentlemen, in various of your writings and in your comments so far, have stressed that what goes on in a country like Russia is something which we see only through some kind of distortion. This is important and I wish we would talk a little bit about it. You use the phrase, Dr. Fromm, that we and the Russians, if I remember correctly, have a "pathological" view of each other.

DR. FROMM: Yes. I mean by that the same thing that happens which happens so frequently in a war. You refer, I gather, to a part in which I wrote about what I call the paranoid way of looking at things. Well, the paranoid person is a person who is convinced, let us say, that his wife, his relatives, his friends are all ganging up against him and want to kill him or something. Now if he tells you the story (the paranoid person), then you cannot usually tell him, "Now look here, this is not possible." But you can tell him, "It is very unlikely."

Now I think a good deal of our reasoning about the Russians is not in realistic terms of what is likely to happen or likely to be the case but of what is possible. For instance, when the Russians had the astronaut there were many people in the United States who thought that was a lie-- it wasn't true--while when we had one up, they felt convinced, "Now it is true!" It could be possible, for example, that the whole struggle between the Chinese and the Russians is all a prearranged game to deceive us into believing the Russians are peaceful. Logically that's possible but it's very unlikely for anyone who analyzes the facts. Another pathological mechanism is the mechanism of projection which you find among married couples when they fight, among people in general, among nations in a war. The mechanism is very simple. I project all the evil in me on you. Then you are the devil and I'm pure and then I can deal with my evil by attacking you. I have a clear picture, a black and white, in which I'm all good. The interesting thing is what a fine sense of conscience they have because they know this and the Bible says that already. They notice the wrong things in the other person or the other nation with great clarity. They have a fine appreciation of what is wrong but they start out with a feeling that this cannot be me, hence it's over there, hence I am completely guiltless. And in the last analysis this has something to do with the very important problem of humanism. In the last analysis it goes back to one thing, to the incapacity to experience one's own humanity in one's self. By which I mean to say, if one experiences one's own humanity fully in one's self, then one experiences one's self as a criminal and as a saint, as a good and as a bad person. But if one projects, then one does not do that.

MR. GOLDMAN: Now you're stating that both sides have this pathological view of each other at the present time?

DR. FROMM: Yes.

MR. GOLDMAN: Would you, Mr. Salisbury, agree with that, specifically with respect to the Russian view of us?

MR. SALISBURY: Well, I think that you can find many manifestations of exactly the same sort of false image that they have of American conduct. For example, let's take a proposition which seems very simple to us. We say frequently, "Why, it's impossible for anyone to believe that the United States would attack Russia." Now this does not seem impossible to Russians. Russians feel that it is quite possible that the United States might attack Russia. This is a fairly simple example. The Russians also suffer from something else--although perhaps Khrushchev has some different ideas now as a result of being in this country. But they have a great tendency to see us in terms of past images. The images of the past persist in people's minds long after real changes occur. When they think of the United States, the first thing that they may very well think of is a picture of capitalism as they saw it described by Marx, who was describing capitalist conditions in England in 1840 or 1850. And when they think of a capitalist factory they think of the description that Marx gave, a very vivid one, of what life was like in the textile towns of England at that time and it was pretty terrible. And if you tell them, "But this is 120 years later and we have in our country evolved extraordinarily and our system is something quite different, they say, "Oh no, that's just a facade. You're trying to deceive us with words. We know very well what capitalism is." I've heard Khrushchev say this himself even though he had just been through a tour of this country, seeing that capitalism was something quite different from this cartoon image.

MR. GOLDMAN: Dr. Fromm, applying this to America, would you give us an instance or so which you consider important forms of this pathological view that America has of Russia?

DR. FROMM: I would just parallel what Mr. Salisbury says. The Russians see capitalism as British capitalism of 1850 and we see Russian Communism as the Communism of 1917-18, instead of seeing that since 1933 this whole system has completely changed from a revolutionary to an exceedingly anti-revolutionary conservative system. Incidentally, I don't know what your own opinion is about this but I think if we follow up what Stalin did in the directions he gave to the German Communist Party before Hitler and the direction he gave in Spain, my impression is this: Stalin, while he didn't want Hitler or Franco to win, preferred their victory to what could have been a popular revolution either in Germany or in Spain.

MR. SALISBURY: I felt that all along, Dr. Fromm, and I think you can cite other instances in which Stalin felt much more comfortable in dealing with the enemy that he didn't trust to dealing with an ally that he might be supposed to trust--that is to say, a Communist movement. I think he did the same thing in China.

DR. FROMM: Yes, exactly. Now to come back to your question. I think we have today--and this is in fact the general political line--the idea that the Communists are out either by subversion or by force to enslave us. I believe this is an unrealistic picture. The Communists are not out to do that and in fact there's no reason why they should because, as I would say, even the word "communism" is wrongly applied. This is a system which is new in the world but I think which is much more similar, let us say, to American capitalism in its essence than it is, for instance, to present-day Chinese Communism and then it is to anything which could be called Marxism.

MR. GOLDMAN: This is the nub of the matter as I see it. American opinion, I think, is certainly based on the assumption that the Soviet Union or, more generally, world Communism is out to dominate the world and specifically to enslave the U.S. And I notice you say flatly, Dr. Fromm, "Khrushchev seeks an understanding with the United States, the ending of the Cold War, and world disarmament." This is, of course, in flat contradiction, as I think you would agree, with the general opinion of the West. Or as a matter of fact with the statements of recent and present Presidents of the United States.

DR. FROMM: Yes, indeed.

MR. GOLDMAN: Mr. Salisbury, would you comment on this important point?

MR. SALISBURY: I would put a small caveat. I would say it is true Khrushchev seeks an agreement with the United States. Khrushchev has been seeking this agreement ever since he really came into power and probably this is one of the platforms that he stood on when he was fighting for power within the Soviet Union. He wants the agreement, he wants the detente with the West. He can make a very good argument about why he needs it and why it's important to have it. At the same time that he is seeking that agreement, he is not willing to pay a very high price for it. Now this may be fair or it may be wrong, but it is literally true. And when he comes close to an agreement on a given

538

point, he generally tends to pull back and try to broaden the area of bargaining so he will get an agreement on two points rather than one. Then the whole thing extends itself to the point at which one cannot help but feel that Khrushchev himself, while wanting this, has many fears and many concerns and many suspicions concerning it, which I think is fairly normal and natural for him to have these things. But nonetheless he often is his own worse enemy in trying to arrive at this sort of an agreement. Now, on the second point, I believe the second point is that he does not want a war. Is that right?

MR. GOLDMAN: And he wants world disarmament?

MR. SALISBURY: He wants world disarmament.

MR. GOLDMAN: I take it you mean real world disarmament?

DR. FROMM: Yes, real disarmament. I'm not entirely sure but I would say I think most likely he really wants world disarmament and I am convinced that this likelihood is so great that we should go on the assumption that he wants it and see whether we can get it.

MR. GOLDMAN: Mr. Salisbury, I cut you off.

MR. SALISBURY: I think that, on the question of not wanting war, this is literally true. Khrushchev does not want war. This does not mean he's not willing to go to the brink of war, as he would say, to attain his objective of peace. Now he is a participant in brinksmanship. He does it. He does want peace certainly. Why does he want peace? There may be many different reasons why he wants peace but he probably expressed one of the reasons most effectively--not to us but in an argument which is running with the Chinese because this happens to be one of the basic differences between himself and Mao Tse Tung, the Chinese-- the reason for wanting peace he puts very simply. It is this: The alternative to it is not, let's say, a war in which Communism would conquer. It's not a war which would be limited in character which the Russians might win or which might be a stalemate. It is destruction of the world. It is destruction of Russia, destruction of her opponents, destruction of the whole fabric of society as we now know it. This argument has been made in most simple plain, blunt terms in the context of the argument between the Russians and the Chinese--not to us, which is one reason why I think it may be more believable to us. He's not telling us that. This is what he's telling the Chinese.

It follows from that if you really feel that war means destruction of the world and destruction of your country that you are bound to put a great deal of effort into disarmament. And Mr. Khrushchev does do that. He puts a great deal of effort into disarmament. Here again, I don't feel that Mr. Khrushchev is terribly realistic in the way he goes about trying to produce disarmament or trying to win advocates for it. I think, for example, when he came over here in 1960 and presented his case for disarmament to the United States that his strategy and his tactics were self-defeating since he built up a great deal of antagonism in this country toward himself by the way he conducted himself. But I don't think that we should underestimate his sincerity on this question of disarmament. I think he wants it because he thinks it's the way in which Russia can survive. I think he also believes that in a disarmed world that the Soviet system is better able to compete than the American system, and would come out on top.

DR. FROMM: I think that's very true. There's a peculiar dialectical problem. We say, in general, Khrushchev wants world revolution. He wants the victory of world Communism in the world and that's why he wants to undermine us or to defeat us either by force or by subversion. I think the fact is very much more in the direction of what you said. Khrushchev is convinced that the world goes more or less in his direction, just as the West was convinced without any doubts until recently, maybe until 1914 when the first cracks showed in our Western culture, that this is the development of the world. Hence he is not panicking. He does not have to be afraid that if things go their normal course that maybe he's confronted with a catastrophe. And I would like to raise a question whether unconsciously we in the West are not panicking and have lost somewhat the faith in the future of our society, in our aims, in our visions and our goals, and hence feel much more easily open to attack then is actually the case.

MR. SALISBURY: I don't know. I don't know the answer to that question myself. I can only say that from the observation that I have been able to make in reality, I see no reason for any lack of confidence on the part of the United States or the Western system. It seems to me, if we compare the two societies, if we compare our society, let's say, on the standpoint of the ability to create a better life for its people, that we are better able to do that than the Russians are and that our society, for all its imperfections in its economic or in its social phase, is overall a more healthy organism than is their society. I'm not terribly impressed by the supposed efficiency of the Russian system. I'm not terribly impressed by the material progress they have made. It is impressive but I don't think that it is anything which needs make us feel that we can't match it or exceed it, because we do match and exceed it every day. There's just no question about that. I'm not impressed by arguments that we cannot help less well developed countries to develop in our way by utilizing our capacities more effectively than the Russians. The truth of the matter is we do just that in many countries. We don't recognize many of the things that we do.

MR. GOLDMAN: Dr. Fromm, if this be the picture, which I take it you were agreeing with, of what the actual facts are, what would be your analysis as to how American opinion got itself into the state of mind where it is, as you say, panicky?

DR. FROMM: I agree with Mr. Salisbury in his description but I would make one or two qualifications. One would be that I think the Western world has lost its spiritual roots. That is to say, we speak still in the name of religion, in the name of the humanistic philosophy on which this Republic was founded and our whole Western culture rests, while in practice, we have fallen into a spirit of materialism in which the individual becomes more and more a thing and is transformed more and more into a small cog called the organization man. Now I think this saps our vitality. We have reached our material aims but at this point the human aims have become thin. I would like to cite Goethe, who said that the most basic difference that exists between different cultures and societies is the difference between those who have belief and those who do not have belief. Those that have belief flourish and grow and those who do not have belief decay. Now it's quite clear historically that the great ages of belief were the 13th century, the Renaissance, the 18th century and to some extent still the 19th century. But I think that now in the West we are at a point where belief, not in economic productiveness, but in vision and aim of life has become very weak. I think the Russians very soon will be in a similar position. When they have reached some more of their own material aims I think they will be precisely in the position which we are in, namely, a lack of belief beyond that in more gadgets and more things.

MR. GOLDMAN: Mr. Salisbury, if I read your articles right, you say that the Russians are getting there very quickly and if they are, then we have a really supreme historical irony. Two nations, neither of which particularly believe in their ideologies anymore, marching into combat against each other in the name of the ideologies.

MR. SALISBURY: I couldn't help but think exactly that, as Dr. Fromm was talking, because his description of our society--which I don't quite accept--I think we have more belief than he does--but his description of our society fits the Russian society. Certainly in great areas of Russia, the belief in the Communist idea--and it was an ideal at one time--has vanished and it's been replaced by a desire for more creature comforts and limited goals and things of that kind. Among the youths it's been replaced by a simple looking for sensation, looking for experience, and anything that will put a little color into their life. This sort of thing, it seems to me, is two faces of the same coin. Maybe if belief is what will do it, maybe the Chinese will inherit the world.

MR. GOLDMAN: A brief interruption here to re-introduce you gentlemen. Here, just speaking, Mr. Harrison E. Salisbury, a former Moscow correspondent of the New York Times and now the New York Times director of national correspondence. Our other guest, the distinguished psychoanalyst, Dr. Erich Fromm, whose most recent volume is May Man Prevail?
Dr. Fromm, I think you were about to comment.

DR. FROMM: Well, I prefer whatever exists in aliveness in the United States to the Soviet Union. But I'm speaking of trends. And I think we must not forget that the common trend is explained by a basic common situation of Western countries--they are highly industrialized. Russia is a late comer, the United States at a more advanced industrialization, with a similar method of production which is in fact more important than the question of nationalization or not. The 19th century was very much concerned with the question of legal property because the owner was still the owner of a factory. The manager of the factory and the owner were pretty much the same. All this is today not so much of a problem. What matters today is the powers of a general bureaucracy to direct the economy and they are in charge in Russia completely. In the United States and the West this has not developed to the same point. But what the two systems have in common is the same method of production, basically the same detailed aims of more consumption and more production. And they are the two great have-states of the world confronted today with the rest of the world, aside from Western Europe, which is in the state of the have-nots. I think actually the real reason for the change in Russia is that since 1923 Russia has gone through the process which the rest of the world and the United States went through in the 19th century. It has not yet reached but is close to reaching the industrial development of Western countries. Khrushchev finds himself in a situation in which he feels--and I believe this is the real nucleus of his policy--that the two great have-states, if they have an entente, if they have modus vivendi, can control the world and prevent the have-not states, particularly China, from attacking them in such a way that the whole stability goes to pieces, including the possibility of war. The tragic misunderstanding is that we do not see that he's a representative of a conservative system. We only listen to his ideology. He cannot see it himself because he doesn't even know that his Communist ideology is one of the things which one might call a gray area where certain ideas are believed because one has to believe in something but really they are not effective. They are not potent ideas. They are, if you please, impotent ideologies.

MR. GOLDMAN: May I push this matter of Khrushchev's aim just a little bit here because it seems to me crucial in terms of American policy and the kind of public opinion that backs it. Dr. Fromm, as I read your chapter called "Is World Domination the Aim of the Soviet Union?" I take it your answer is "No."

DR. FROMM: Yes.

541

MR. GOLDMAN: Now American public policy, that of the U.S. Government, as I understand, is based on a Yes answer to that question, i.e., that is, that one way or another, peaceful or not, Khrushchev expects and seeks world domination for Communism. This is a matter of such importance that I would like to get Mr. Salisbury to comment on it again because I'm not sure I understand his position. Do you agree with Dr. Fromm's answer on this?

MR. SALISBURY: I would agree with qualification, that is to say, I think the phrase world domination is a misleading phrase in that it implies to most people world conquest which in turn implies a military offensive and when we mention that we immediately think of Hitler. In other words, we adopt a Hitlarian analogy to the Russian situation. I don't think that is fair.

MR. GOLDMAN: Suppose it means that one way or another he expects and intends to work toward a Communist world.

MR. SALISBURY: Let me put it this way: He hopes that this will occur. This is not his immediate objective nor does he expect it to happen in his lifetime. He hopes that it will happen in his grandchildren's lifetime but he has no particular plan for bringing it about. He has a great many other things which get higher priority than that. Number 1 would be, as Dr. Fromm says, preservation of the status quo, preservation of what Russia has today. Any prudent statesman wants to preserve what his country has. Number 2 is to improve that situation so far as Russia is concerned and particularly internally so far as their standard of living is concerned. Number 3, perhaps then we get into the question of expanding the Communist system around the world. I don't think he's got any plans for doing it. I think, if we take what he says in this particular context as being likely to be true, and I suspect it is, he says: "If we give people a better life in Russia, if there is more jam on our bread in Russia and more butter and shorter working hours and a car for everybody then there is in the capitalist countries, they're going to try our system because ours is superior to theirs." This is what Khrushchev says, and he says it to the Chinese who keep saying, "We want revolutions. Get out there and man the barricades."

DR. FROMM: I think that is very true. You see there is a difference between saying, he expects the world to go Communist, and he wants to produce this state of affairs. For if we put our--

MR. GOLDMAN: I think the dominant American opinion and American policy is based on the assumption that he expects to produce it if it doesn't happen.

MIXED VOICES: You're quite right. But I think this assumption is wrong. For Khrushchev, Communism is the logical thing to happen in the rest of the world. He thinks this is the most practical, most logical and most efficient method, just as we believed twenty years ago or forty years ago that capitalism was the only logical method for a state. When I was a student, the professors told their students that the idea of a national plan and directed economy was just plain nonsense; it was impossible. We were convinced that it couldn't be done; and Khrushchev is convinced that his way is a better one. But the great difference lies in whether somebody expects this will slowly get around and prove to be better or whether something has a kind of religious fervor, a fanatical fervor, in which he feels this system must win because this is the only human system. The rest is inhuman and so on and so on. And I don't think Khrushchev has any of this.

DR. FROMM: I should like, if I may, to come back to one point here, namely, the world domination of the Russians. In the form of political passion for Communism or revolution, I don't think they have that passion. Now then, it is often said, "Yes, but as an imperialist state, as the successor of the Tsars, they want to conquer the world." Here a mistake is made, too because if you study, let us say, imperialism in the 19th century, the aims of Russia, Germany, France, and England were always limited aims. None of these countries aimed at domination of the world. They tried to get a piece here and a piece there. For instance in 1907 the British and the Russians made a treaty that divided Persia. They didn't divide it after all but this is the same policy which Churchill had when he offered Stalin that Churchill take Greece and Stalin take Bulgaria. The aims were always limited and, very interestingly, until 1914 these various attempts of the big powers were always restrained by the wish to avoid a major war. They were pretty successful in it and, in fact, if it hadn't been for the stupidity of the German Kaiser and his statesmen in 1914, I think the war of 1914 might not have happened. The Kaiser was very surprised when the British suddenly declared war because in spite of the fact that his ambassador had sent him cables all the time about it he thought they wouldn't--just as Hitler didn't think the English would fight in '39. I would say even Hitler's aims were not of world domination. Hitler's aims were the domination of the Western European continent and good pieces of land in the East. I would say, 'Yes,' the traditional aim of Russia is a warm water harbor and all that, but there is one great change in comparison with the 19th century. War is so much more destructive, as you have pointed out at the beginning, that nothing really justifies a war from any rational standpoint. Then, too, there is the tremendous change in our technology. While 50 years ago one might have wanted to conquer a piece of land for raw materials for this, that, or the other, today improvement in technology creates a greater growth in the national product than 50 years ago one could have expected. Therefore, the economic rationale for war or for new conquest is today much smaller than it was in the 19th century.

MR. GOLDMAN: Gentlemen, our time is rushing on. May I move you men over into another important part of the Communist world--China-- by asking Mr. Salisbury if he would comment on these comments of Dr. Fromm's. He says, "Khrushchev wants the things that we discussed before, world disarmament and so forth. He cannot however give up his Communist revolutionary ideology nor can he turn against China without undermining his own system. Hence he has to maneuver carefully to preserve his ideological hold on the Russian people and to defend himself against both his opponents within Russia and against China and her potential allies outside." And he concludes: "If Khrushchev fails in his attempt to end the Cold War with the West, he or his successor will be forced into a close alliance with China and into a policy which would leave little hope for peace."

MR. SALISBURY: I'm glad we got on to that question because this is precisely the issue that I wanted to present. When we're talking about Khrushchev, that is one thing. I think we know Khrushchev quite well. I think we understand his policies. I don't agree it so happens, Mr. Goldman, that our policy is entirely based on the theory that Khrushchev is out to dominate the world. I think that our policy is more subtle than that and there is a pretty good understanding in highest quarters in this country of Khrushchev's limitations and the nature of his policy.

But there is this factor we have not mentioned: It isn't just Khrushchev. There is China and China follows a different policy. China follows a more classic revolutionary policy. China is not afraid of war and has said she is not afraid of nuclear war. This is not only a viewpoint of the Chinese Communists; it is a viewpoint of other Communists within Mr. Khrushchev's own Presidium. We don't know how many of the members of that Presidium support the Chinese policy or would support it in a showdown. We are pretty sure that for the time being Mr. Khrushchev has that situation well in control. But this alternative does exist. And Khrushchev is not eternal and he may not be with us too long. Who will replace him? Will it be a man who agrees with the policies of Khrushchev, who wants to preserve what he has, or will it be a person who believes, as the Chinese do, that Khrushchev's policy leads to a dead end? That Khrushchev's policy leads not to a detente while the West improves its position, who believes like the Chinese do, that the moment is ripe for revolutions and wars throughout the world? That these will bring about the collapse of the capitalist world, and that even if Communism loses, as Mao Tse Tung said, three hundred million people in China, the survivors will all be Communists? We don't know but what this is the kind of policy we will be confronted with if Khrushchev's efforts fail or if Khrushchev is replaced by another man. This, I think, is the great danger in the situation.

DR. FROMM: I would like to add something to this. The same situation you describe for Russia exists within the Western world too. The Western world also is not governed by people who want to preserve peace. From Mr. Khrushchev's standpoint or from the standpoint of his Chinese-oriented people, there's no guarantee either that there couldn't be a development here in which people would feel there's no more hope for peace, let's attack, we have to secure our position. Considering the possibilities of destruction which both blocs have, the considerations of peace or war are to a large extent considerations which exist in the tension of big powers in their foreign policy and only to some extent have anything to do with the question of revolution or not. Naturally, the Chinese Communists try to improve their position by gaining influence in Communist parties all over the world, just as Khrushchev tries to gain in the big struggle going on between the two groups. But, I believe that all this has certainly not much to do with the question of world revolution but with the question, 'How can they secure their system against the possibility of being destroyed by the opponent?'

MR. GOLDMAN: There's no disagreement, I take it, on this.

MR. SALISBURY: I don't believe so. No. I think that's fairly true all over. I cannot help but believe that the Chinese are really 100 per cent old fashioned Communists.

DR. FROMM: I'm glad you say that because I neglected in what I said to emphasize it. The Chinese, I think, have a spirit of crusading and passion and fanaticism. The Chinese have discovered, I believe, something which the Russians never discovered to that extent, namely, that if you are a country with six hundred million people without capital, if you succeed in manipulating six hundred million people in such a way that you control their brains, their passion and their arms, then you have the substitute for the capital that is lacking. That, of course, requires complete thought control, a complete destruction of individualism, and think something quite different from what happened in Russia even under Stalin. Under Stalin we had plain terror while in China you have really a quasi-religious kind of movement where the person is really brainwashed and where you really make him feel guilty when he doesn't or if he doesn't obey the main pattern, where you really unify, try to unify, the population at the expense of that which to us in the West is a most valuable quality, namely, the freedom of the individual. Not just in the political sense but in his freedom to be himself, to think, and so on.

MR. GOLDMAN: Dr. Fromm, am I stating your view of things fairly, again getting back to what fascinates me very much in your analysis-- the "distortions" in American thinking--that we are, in your view, much more "pathological" in our view of the Russians than we are in

544

our view of the Chinese; that is, our picture of the Chinese is one closer to reality?

DR. FROMM: Yes, I think that is true. I think if we would say the Chinese believe in crusading, that they believe that by wars or by great upheavals the world will be ready for their brand of Communism, I think we are much closer to the truth. However--and I wonder what Mr. Salisbury thinks about this--I wonder if the Cold War ended and therefore the power of the Chinese politically would be weakened and if at the same time a great deal of economic help could be given to them to solve their own economic problems, whether this crusading spirit and fanaticism might not be reduced in China, too. I think the Chinese flourish by the power which the Cold War gives them.

MR. SALISBURY: I think so, too. I think this is the key to the power.

DR. FROMM: And the fanaticism increases with the fact that they are so poor and have these great ambitions.

MR. SALISBURY: I think without the Cold War they would have to invent it really to maintain the momentum of their movement, the spirit of the people and all that sort of thing. I've long thought that if it were possible to reduce the general level of world tension that the most dramatic results would probably be had in China. I know many people --and some very shrewd scholars of the Russian situation who have felt that if we could reduce world tension the Russians could be depended upon to change their own society internally in directions very favorable to a maintenance of peace with the West and to developments in the direction of Western society rather than Eastern society. I think that the same thing might very well occur in China if we were ever able to arrive at that point.

DR. FROMM: Could I add to this just one short remark? One of the difficulties the West has in reaching an objective judgement about the Russian situation is our complete misunderstanding of what we call Marxism or what is Marxism, namely, we do not see that the Marxist system was precisely the opposite of the Russian system and essentially the opposite of the Chinese system. The Marxist system, as Marx wrote it very clearly--he is like the Bible the most quoted and least known author or book--was based on precisely the Western development of humanism. He had a concept of the essence of human nature, of the aim of life being the unfolding and fulfillment of this human potential, of freeing man from the shackles of the economy and making him into a person who is free enough to make his own development the aim of this life and who is precisely the opposite of the materialism which we ascribe to Marx. Now unless one has some idea of what Marxist philosophy was, one cannot possibly understand the Russians because one cannot understand what their formula means and in what way. What they are doing, the way they are developing, has nothing to do with the substance of the system which they pay lip service to.

MR. GOLDMAN: I was struck on this point, Mr. Salisbury, by one of your articles in which you talked of the search by a number of leading Soviet scientists for some spiritual meaning in life, if I don't misquote you. Is this perhaps a search to find that humanism which was originally in the Marxist tradition? Is this a new element in this upsurge of liberalism, so to speak, in Russia?

MR. SALISBURY: It's an element in the upsurge in liberalism. I don't think I would relate it to Marx and Marxist philosophy because in Russia, generally speaking, the interpretation of Marx, as Dr. Fromm has just stated it, is almost unknown. At least I must say that in all the years I was in Russia I never heard anything like that described as Marxism. I was quite struck when I encountered it in Dr. Fromm's book. I think that this movement as far as these scientists are concerned, is much more closely related to what has happened to many Western astronomers and physicists who have been confronted with these profound problems. The more they study them, the deeper they get into them, the more convinced they are that they have been confronted with things which are beyond human powers to relate. In other words, that there must be some superior force, some mystical force, some spiritual force. None of them are identical in the way they state this but it's a feeling, perhaps more than it is a philosophy, that there must be this power. It struck me as being most interesting that in Russia, where these men were brought up in that sort of society, they arrived at very much the same position as our Western scientists do in the end.

DR. FROMM: And actually, it's very interesting, the fact is that Russia is the only country in which you have practically no creative theory about Marx. You have it in England, in France, in Yugoslavia, in the United States, in Germany. There are volumes which deal with the philosophy of Marx and the humanist background. In Russia you have absolutely nothing.

MR. SALISBURY: That's for certain.

MR. GOLDMAN: Gentlemen, we only have about two minutes and may I get in here something which interests me. As I listen to you men, I wonder whether we are indulging in a form of Western optimism, if you will pardon me, that the world of Communism as you see it, is a fairly hopeful world, at least in some senses. Is this the traditional Western assumption that really the world sooner or later is going to go our way?

DR. FROMM: No, sir. For me, the Communist world is not hopeful and I would make a great difference between Russia and China in this respect. I think it is developing an organization world and developing the organization man and I'm afraid we do it, too. I'm not optimistic. I think the danger of war is tremendously great. But I also think that at the moment the important thing is to look at things sanely and with reason and not by mistaking ideologies for facts to start a war which is not necessary.

MR. GOLDMAN: Pardon me, sir, we have about 40 seconds. Mr. Salisbury?

MR. SALISBURY: I would say much the same as Dr. Fromm. I think that the essence of this situation is that it is dangerous. The more the danger, the more necessary it is for us to understand the real nature of that danger and not be mislead by superstition or propaganda.

MR. GOLDMAN: Pardon me, gentlemen, our time is up.

546

Attitudes Toward War and Disarmament

by

H. ARTHUR STEINER

IN PURSUING THE POLICY of "peaceful coexistence," authoritative Chinese Communist spokesmen declare: "The socialist countries adhere consistently and faithfully to a policy of peace. They will never invade other countries." Their current line is that the imperialist powers, "aggressive by nature," are "bound to undermine peaceful coexistence when the opportunity arises," and "the keenest vigilance with regard to the danger of war" must be maintained during a period when "U.S. imperialism still surrounds us with a network of military bases and guided missiles."[40] The policies of "peace" and "peaceful coexistence" are conceived as dynamic rather than passive, as affirmative aspects of the continuing class struggle, and the Chinese Communists can fully accept the formula of the November 1960 meeting of representatives of the world Communist movement in Moscow:

The policy of peaceful coexistence is a policy of mobilizing the masses and launching vigorous action against the enemies of peace. Peaceful coexistence of states does not imply the renunciation of the class struggle as the revisionists claim. The coexistence of states with different social systems is a form of class struggle between socialism and capitalism. . . . It implies intensification of the struggle of the working class, of all the Communist Parties, for the triumph of socialist ideas. But ideological and political disputes between states must not be settled through war.[41]

Views on "Just" Wars

Earlier, in its April 1960 analysis of imperialism as the source of modern wars, the Editorial Department of Red

---

[40] "Yü Chao-li," "Imperialism . . . ," *loc. cit.* in note 21 *ante.*
[41] *Loc. cit.* in note 26 *ante.*

Flag had warned: "Marxist-Leninists absolutely must not sink into the mire of bourgeois pacifism."[42] In this analysis, *Red Flag*, arguing the "absolute correctness" of Lenin's views of imperialism and war, anticipated the possibility of four different kinds of war under modern conditions:

War is an inevitable outcome of systems of exploitation and the source of modern wars is the imperialist system. Until the imperialist system and the exploiting classes come to an end, wars of one kind or another will always occur. There may be [1] wars among the imperialists for redivision of the world, or [2] wars of aggression and anti-aggression between the imperialists and the oppressed nations, or [3] civil wars of revolution and counter-revolution between the exploited and exploiting classes in the imperialist countries, or, of course, [4] wars in which the imperialists attack the socialist countries and the socialist countries are forced to defend themselves. All these kinds of wars represent the continuation of the policies of definite classes. Marxist-Leninists ... can only ... draw conclusions for proletarian policy by adopting the method of concrete class analysis. As Lenin put it: "Theoretically it would be quite wrong to forget that every war is but the continuation of politics by other means."

On this basis, *Red Flag* developed a series of concepts concerning "just" wars—which would consequently justify the maintenance of military establishments, exclude the possibility of unilateral disarmament, and give political coloration to any CPR disarmament policy.

Defensive wars, the fourth category, are, of course, easily justified and need not, in the view of *Red Flag,* be confined to the territory of the invaded country. Indeed, an offensive counterattack is "completely justified, absolutely necessary and entirely just" and may have useful revolutionary results.

Since the armed forces of the socialist countries fight for justice, when these forces have to go beyond their borders to counterattack a foreign enemy, it is only natural that they should exert an influence and have an effect wherever they go; but even then, the emergence of people's revolutions and the establishment of the socialist system in those places and countries where they go will still depend on the will of the masses of the people there.

Mao Tse-tung had spoken of the problem of defensive war and its political consequence on 27 February 1957:

We stand resolutely for peace and oppose war. But if the imperialists insist on unleashing another war, we should not be afraid of it. Our attitude on this question is the same as our attitude towards all disturbances; firstly, we are against it; secondly, we are not afraid of it.

The First World War was followed by the birth of the Soviet

---

42 "Long Live Leninism!" *loc. cit.* in note 21 *ante,* for this and subsequent quotations unless otherwise noted.

Union with a population of 200,000,000. The Second World War was followed by the emergence of the socialist camp with a combined population of 900,000,000. If the imperialists still insist on launching a third world war, it is certain that several hundred million more will turn to socialism; then there will not be much room left in the world for the imperialists, while it is quite likely that the whole structure of imperialism will utterly collapse.[43]

In a similar vein, the *Red Flag* article predicted the outcome of an atomic and nuclear war launched by the imperialists: "The result will certainly not be the annihilation of mankind. . . . On the debris of a dead imperialism, the victorious people would create very swiftly a civilization thousands of times higher than the capitalist system and a truly beautiful future for themselves." This passage is probably the basis for the widely circulated rumor that the Chinese Communists intended to initiate a world war for which they were willing to sacrifice 300,000,000 of their own people in order for the survivors to construct a socialist paradise.

Wars of the second category gave *Red Flag* little difficulty: "We support the revolutionary wars of the oppressed nations against imperialism [and] for their own liberation and social progress because all these . . . are just wars."

As to the third category, "No one can hold back a revolution in any country if there is a desire for that revolution and when the revolutionary crisis there has matured." "In the end," *Red Flag* continued, "the socialist system will replace the capitalist system. This is an objective law independent of human will." Because the imperialists "are armed to the teeth as never before in order to protect their savage man-eating system," the proletariat "is compelled to have resort to the means of armed revolution." *Red Flag* suggests that "Marxists have always wanted to follow the peaceful way in the transition to socialism. As long as the peaceful way is there to adopt, Marxist-Leninists will never give it up." But "the question of possible peaceful transition to socialism can be raised only in the light of the specific conditions of each country at a particular time." The morality and "justness" of the revolutionary civil war are derived from a logic of bourgeois suppression of peaceful transition to socialism, rendering the application of force by the national proletariat a form of self-defense:

Whether the transition will be carried out through armed uprising or by peaceful means is a question that is fundamentally separate from that of peaceful coexistence between the socialist

43 *Loc. cit.* in note 12 *ante*, pp. 63-64.

and capitalist countries; it is an internal affair of each country, one to be determined only by the relation of classes in that country in a given period, a matter to be decided only by the Communists of that country themselves.

"Yü Chao-li" had been more explicit in his *Red Flag* article of 1 April 1960, where he declared:

In the event of a revolution, no one can guarantee that the counter-revolutionaries will not use violence to suppress it. The Marxist-Leninist parties do not reject peaceful means for carrying out socialist revolution, but when the exploiting class uses violence against the people, the possibility of employing other means has to be considered, namely, the transition to socialism by non-peaceful means. The historical experience of mankind shows that the ruling class will not give up state power of its own accord.[44]

The several passages just quoted were contained in the major Chinese salvos against "revisionism" and brought the ideological argument with the Soviet Union in focus. They apparently reflected the Chinese belief—never explicitly stated—that Premier Khrushchev's flirtations with President Eisenhower and the then impending summit conference might produce a Soviet-United States accord on peaceful coexistence that might inhibit the possibility of waging "just" wars at the three levels of anti-colonial war, domestic revolutionary war, and wars fought in self-defense. At every point, however, the Chinese ruled out, by definition, wars at the international level to be initiated by themselves.

Position on Disarmament

Through the years, the CPR has regularly pronounced upon the need for disarmament, relaxation of international tensions, prohibition of atomic and nuclear weapons, abandonment of nuclear weapons tests, an end to military blocs and alliances, dismantling of United States overseas bases, peaceful coexistence, mass mobilization of "peace-loving peoples," and so on. It has strongly supported such unofficial conferences as the "Peace Conference of the Asian-Pacific Regions" (1952), various meetings of the World Peace Council, and the series of annual conferences against atomic and nuclear weapons held in Tokyo since 1955. Chinese representatives have also participated in the various disarmament-type resolutions adopted at meetings of the World Federation of Trade Unions and the International Students Union, among others. The record appears consistent and imposing,

---

[44] "Imperialism . . . ," *loc. cit.*

but the action has been almost entirely verbal.

The People's Republic has yet to participate in an official disarmament conference or to be brought into direct negotiations concerning its own levels of armament. Yet the Chinese views on the problem in general have contributed to the present world-wide political situation, which has thus far frustrated all efforts to achieve a significant international disarmament agreement. At the level of official public policy, the activity of the CPR has expressed itself along three lines: first, to support Soviet arms proposals; second, to originate proposals for a "nuclear weapon-free area" in Asia and the Pacific region; and third, to assert China's own freedom of action with respect to agreements reached by others without its concurrence.

Support of Soviet Arms Proposals: Chou En-lai's note of 13 April 1958 to Premier Khrushchev commended him on his proposal for a unilateral Soviet suspension of nuclear tests. The Standing Committee of the National People's Congress adopted a resolution on 14 October 1959 in support of the Soviet arms proposal of the previous September, and another similar resolution of 21 January 1960 commended an announced reduction in Soviet manpower. An official CPR statement of 6 June 1960 endorsed the Soviet arms proposal of 2 June (and was followed by a tendentious editorial in *Jen-min jih-pao* the next day). Chinese official circles applauded the references to Soviet disarmament proposals in the November 1960 Moscow Statement of the Communist and workers parties. This list could be greatly expanded. Such statements and declarations follow the principle of bloc solidarity, but none of them commits the CPR to substantive action on its part and all seem calculated to heap further abuse on "American imperialism."

Nuclear Weapon-free Zone: At various times between 1958 and 1960 Chinese official spokesmen have urged a Pacific regional settlement that would abolish the use of nuclear weapons in that area. The first such proposal came in March 1958, timed to coincide with the Manila meeting of the SEATO Council.[45] Premier Chou restated the proposal in April: "We advocate the establishment of an area free of atomic weapons, an area of peace, throughout the whole of East Asia and the Pacific region."[46] Two years later, at the Swiss National Day celebration in Peking, 1 August 1960,

45 *Peking Review,* Vol. 1, No. 3 (18 Mar. 1958), p. 22.
46 *Report on the Work of Government* (Peking, For. Lang. Press, 1958), p. 70.

the Premier specifically extended the proposal to include the United States: "We advocate that the countries in Asia and around the Pacific, including the United States, conclude a peace pact of mutual non-aggression, and make this a nuclear weapon-free area."[47] He told the United States journalist Edgar Snow that the proposal was "not a new one," but he had thought it useful to repeat it because "Western opinion has been spreading rumors to the effect that China has given up the policy of peaceful coexistence."[48] Such rumors were "all groundless slanders," he told the British correspondent Felix Greene on 5 September 1960, declaring that "the Chinese people will work tirelessly over a long period of time, together with the people of these [Asian and Pacific] countries, to bring this proposal to fruition."[49]

The United States has refused to take the proposal seriously, which led Foreign Minister Ch'en Yi to say on 13 August 1960: "Those who deliberately undermine world peace will inevitably suffer the consequences."[50]

Assertion of Chinese Freedom of Action: After Premier Khrushchev left Washington following talks with President Eisenhower in September 1959, leading spokesmen for the Department of State issued statements suggesting that Khrushchev and the Soviet Union were at least partly responsible for Chinese Communist actions at the international level. One obvious intention of the "doctrine of partial responsibility" was to test Khrushchev's professed desire to bring about a relaxation of tensions by obliging him to exercise restraint over his Asian partner. Carried to a logical conclusion, the "doctrine" would have left to Khrushchev the responsibility of obtaining Chinese concurrence for any agreement on disarmament or nuclear weapons he might have reached with President Eisenhower. Had the doctrine been capable of working, it would have presented the CPR with an accomplished agreement which could then have been ignored only at great political cost. From the viewpoint of United States policy, a means would have been found for resolving the difficult problem of bringing the CPR into an arms settlement indirectly, thereby enabling the United States to continue its relations with Taiwan and avoid the issue of diplomatic relations with Peking.

The Chinese government soon produced a definitive state-

[47] *Peking Review*, Vol. 3, No. 32 (9 Aug. 1960), p. 14.
[48] "Red China's Leaders Talk Peace on Their Terms," *Look*, 31 Jan. 1961.
[49] *Peking Review*, Vol. 3, No. 45 (8 Nov. 1960), p. 22.
[50] *Ibid.*, Vol. 3, No. 33 (16 Aug. 1960), p. 11.

ment of its own position, however. The 21 January 1960 resolution of the Standing Committee of the National People's Congress welcomed "a speedy agreement by all concerned on . . . universal disarmament," and concluded:

China has always favored universal disarmament and will unhesitatingly commit herself to international obligations *to which she agrees.* However, it must be pointed out that any international agreement concerning disarmament, without the *formal participation* of [the CPR] and the *signature of her delegate,* cannot, of course, have any binding force on China.[51]

The same insistence on formal participation of the CPR, and the signature of its representative to any agreement, was restated in the *Jen-min jih-pao* editorial of 7 June 1960 acknowledging the Soviet arms proposal of 2 June.

The assertion of CPR freedom of action, when considered along with the "nuclear weapon-free zone" proposal, has important implications for the future of armament negotiations. No general agreement can be significant or valid if it fails to curb the growing military and prospective nuclear power of the People's Republic or does not include Chinese territory in a system of arms inspection. So long as the CPR is not represented in the United Nations, it can be expected to ignore any agreement concluded under United Nations auspices. Direct negotiation outside the United Nations might well oblige the United States to face the recognition problem. Premier Chou has put his views on record:

If China [were] invited to take part in the big power conference while the C.P.R. was not recognized, we, of course, cannot consider the matter. How can one who is not recognized go to a conference with those who do not recognize him?[52]

The "nuclear weapon-free area" proposal bears upon the problem to the extent that it provides the United States with the possibility of separate negotiations with the CPR on arms questions, to supplement any separate agreement that might be reached with the Soviet Union. Given the political importance of even such a negotiation as this, however, it is difficult to see how the recognition problem could be bypassed.

---

51 Text in *ibid.,* Vol. 3, No. 4 (26 Jan. 1960), pp. 19-20. Emphasis added.
52 *Ibid.,* Vol. 3, No. 20 (17 May 1960), pp. 31-33.

SUGGESTED QUESTIONS FOR SEMINAR DISCUSSION

In line with his thesis that there is a disparity between the kind of world postulated by the Charter and the real world, Hoffmann states (Section II, paragraph 2) that the United Nations has engaged in three kinds of races or procedures to avoid paralysis of the organization. Do you disagree with any portion of his analysis on these matters? Why? Do you think that much more progress can be made under existing United Nations organization by continuing to support these procedures? What "next steps" might be taken in all three areas? Would these lead in the direction of a world legal structure of the sort suggested by Clark-Sohn?

According to Hoffmann the presence, operations and efforts of the United Nations have made "negative contributions" to world order. (Section III beginning with paragraph marked 2 and ending with paragraph marked 3.) Would you agree with his analysis of these matters? What can be done to minimize these problems? Do the Clark-Sohn proposals offer realistic proposals to cope with them?

Do you disagree with any portion of Hoffmann's analysis of the contribution to world order made by the United Nations (Section III, paragraph numbered 3, ending with Section IV.) Are there particular steps which might be taken now to maximize these contributions? Are the contributions he suggests sufficient to provide the conditions for keeping the peace in the international community? If not, what more must be done?

The Introduction to the Annual Report of the Secretary General by Dag Hammerskjold has a number of suggestions concerning next steps which might be taken to bridge the present international conference status of the United Nations to move effective international organization. Which of these steps would you consider to be most significant and how would they be implemented?

Does the Soviet view that it is impossible to find neutral and impartial international civil servants place an insurmountable obstacle in the further development of the United Nations or are there procedures and areas where this view can be accommodated and still permit progressive development? How?

Dallin believes that the past policies and practices of the Soviet Union with regard to the United Nations are such that the Soviet Union "is certain to keep the United Nations from taking the giant step . . . " to "constitutional systems of international cooperation." On the other hand he indicates that they have not always had their way in the United Nations. Is there some way of using some factors by which they have been forced to give ground for the purpose of developing these "constitutionsl systems of cooperation?"

Assuming everything which Edmond Taylor reports about the dissembling and invidious manner in which the Soviet Union has been carrying on political "warfare" throughout the world, is there any hope of coming to agreement with them on major world legal structure? Could a world legal structure operate if these activities by the Soviet Union and other states were to continue? Would any legal limitations have to be placed on these activities or could we leave that to the political structure to control?

If Fromm and Salisbury are accurate in their observations, the Soviet Union is developing a social class which is less interested in world domination than in maintaining and enhancing its position within the Soviet Union. In addition, they report that many of the youth are bored by their own system and intensely curious and drawn to western culture. Assuming that this is true, what impact do you think these groups are likely to have on U.S.S.R. foreign policy and particularly on their attitude towards strengthening and increasing the authority of international organization?

Are there any portions of the Fromm or Salisbury analysis which point to matters indicating that agreement with the Soviet Union to organize a viable international system for maintaining peace is possible? What kind of peace would it be?

It is now generally believed that the Government of Communist China is more inclined to the use of armed force than the Soviet Union or the United States. Do you believe this is so? What are the facts on which you base this judgment? Is there any set of hard-stands, concessions, or other political maneuvers which would tend to diminish this inclination? Is it possible to effectuate them?

Some pertinent questions for which no reading has been given:

Does the Soviet Union and Communist China have, in your judgment, any good reasons for distrusting the United States' conduct of foreign policy? Is there anything we can do about decreasing this distrust without appreciably diminishing our security?

What influence, if any, can the medium and small powers have on the super-powers to bring about a significant relaxation in Cold-War tensions?

Additional EVALUATIONS of the United Nations include:

Armstrong, Hamilton Fish. "U.N. on Trial." Foreign Affairs 39:388-415 (Apr. 1961). A review of the present state of the UN and its chances of surviving the crises of the period.

Bloomfield, Lincoln P. "The UN and National Security." Foreign Affairs 36:597-610 (July 1958). Should we still view the UN as another way to protect our national security, or must we see it in a new light now that its membership has changed?

Castern, Erik. "Some Aspects of the Future Activity of the UN." J. Indian Internatl. Law 1:178-83 (Oct. 1960-Jan. 1961).

Claude, Inis L., Jr. Swords Into Plowshares: The Problems and Progress of International Organization. NY: Random House, 1956, 497p.

Commission to Study the Organization of Peace. See the annual reports of the Commission, which survey topical problems facing the United Nations.

Hoffmann, Stanley. "The Role of International Organization: Limits and Possibilities." Internatl. Org. 10:357-72 (Aug. 1956). A theoretical study of what international organizations can and should do to promote the objectives laid out in the UN Charter, given the present structure of world society.

_____. "Sisyphus and the Avalanche: The United Nations, Egypt and Hungary." Internatl. Org. 11:446-69 (Summer 1957). Weaknesses in the structure of the UN and of the Western Alliance revealed by the crises of Suez and Hungary in 1956.

Jordan, William M. "Concepts and Realities in International Political Organization." Internatl. Org. 11:587-96 (Autumn 1957). Some general and rather acute observations on the approach to the problem of maintaining peace, with some historical perspective.

Mangone, Gerard J. A Short History of International Organization. NY: McGraw-Hill, 1954, 326p. The author has "attempted to portray the development of international organization along constitutional lines with attention to procedures and law, hoping to indicate a potential, though by no means inevitable, growth toward world order."

The general problem of U.S. Sino-Soviet relations cannot be handled in this seminar, nor have we attempted to include it in this Bibliography. On SOVIET ATTITUDES toward the United Nations and international law, see:

Dallin, Alexander. The Soviet Union at the United Nations. NY: Praeger, 1962. An inquiry into Soviet motives and objectives.

_____. The Soviet View of the United Nations. Cambridge, Mass.: MIT Center for International Studies, 1959, 104p.

Goodman, E. R. The Soviet Design for a World State. NY: Columbia U. Press, 1960, 512p.

Kulski, W. W. "The Soviet Interpretation of International Law." Am. J. Int. Law 49: 518-34 (Oct. 1955).

Lapenna, Ivo. "International Law Viewed Through Soviet Eyes." Yearbook of World Affairs 1961:204-32.

Triska, Jan F., and Robert M. Slusser. Theory, Law and Policy of Soviet Treaties. Stanford: Stanford U. Press, 1962. The article used in the reader will be one chapter of this book which will cover the whole field from historical, political and legal viewpoints.

SESSION VIII
PROBLEMS OF ACHIEVING AND MAINTAINING DISARMAMENT

This session initiates our study of the many problems involved in the attempt to use disarmament or some form of arms control in order to help solve our general problem, the elimination of force among states. Assuming that general agreement exists throughout the world on the desirability of preventing war (and it should be noted that within the bipolar blocs there is constant accusation that the other bloc intends to use force for aggressive purposes, that smaller powers have policies which might easily involve the use of conventional weapons, and that civil wars and wars of colonial liberation may still be considered justified by large numbers of people), disarmament is an extremely perplexing subject. Responsible, intelligent people who have studied the problem are in basic disagreement on what to do now if we wish to maintain peace. There are those who believe primarily in military strength, and although they may grant that some sort of world authority with world peace-keeping machinery is the eventual goal, they regard it as being so far in the future and the risks of attaining it so great that our only present course is to maintain our armaments system and very possibly to increase it. There are many shades of opinion within this group. There are also those who believe primarily that unless we establish a system for achieving and maintaining complete and general disarmament, major thermo-nuclear war is a certainty, and that the risks of taking steps at once toward creating some such system are less than the risks of the present arms race. This group includes those who believe that we must maintain armaments as a necessary stop-gap until the system is in being and those who, like Fromm, see advantages even in unilateral disarmament. The complexity of the problems involved has been such that the subject-matter is rapidly becoming a subject-matter for experts. There may be some merit in turning these problems over to experts, but the experts who have thought about this question are of a different mind; thus, for example, the comments of Dr. Jerome Wiesner on this matter:

> "To a distressing degree American citizens who normally insist on free and open discussion of important issues facing their country, have turned away from the problems of arms control as being of such complexity as (supposedly) to be beyond the comprehension of the ordinary citizen. But, without widespread understanding of the options available to the nation and without some ability on the part of the general public to judge the relative

557

security of various alternatives, it will not be
possible for the United States to find acceptable
arms-limitation agreements or to accept the constraints such agreements will impose on the military activities of the country."

This session will be devoted to exploring the question of
disarmament as a military-security problem, a discussion
of the relative merits of the proposals (complete and general
disarmament, arms control based on mutual deterrence, and
unilateral disarmament) and a study of a portion of the detailed proposals by Clark and Sohn for a system of complete
and general disarmament.

The article by P. M. S. Blackett is used here to state
the disarmament problem from the security-military viewpoints of the super powers. You may find that you disagree
with him about facts, conjectures or the conclusions he presents; if so, you should be clear as to what are the bases
for your disagreements. At the same time, his framework
of analysis, including notions like counterforce or first
strike potential, second strike, maximal deterrence and
minimal deterrence, are useful in answering the question--
which states, with what intentions, have what kind of weapons
and delivery systems, capable of knocking out what kinds of
targets? His thesis that the Soviet Union has been relying
on a minimal deterrence strategy with relatively soft weapons
(i.e., the Soviet Union is poised with nuclear weapons
capable of knocking out major civilian centers in Western
Europe and the United States in case of attack by the West,
weapons which are insufficient in number or not widely
enough distributed so that they, from the Soviet point of
view, cannot be considered safely protected from attack from
a power which knew their locations) is an arresting one and
has many implications for the design of a disarmament
system which the Soviet Union is likely to accept.

The materials from Clark-Sohn present rather persuasively the argument for a comprehensive system of complete and general disarmament along with a judicial and
quasi judicial system and the establishment of a United
Nations Peace Force to insure peace and security. A more
detailed analysis and argument for the theoretical position is
to be found in essay form in "Comprehensive Arms-
Limitation Systems" by Wiesner in the book Arms Control,
Disarmament, and National Security, edited by Donald
Brennan. The article by Schelling presents a provocative
and in some ways startling series of suggestions for using
the present "stable" deterrence system which might lead to
significant arms control. It should be observed that Schelling does have a preference for a disarmed world over an
armed world; however, he questions the feasibility and, as
we shall see in Session X, the stability of peace in a dis-

armed world. The article by Fromm asks how much can be done to disarm unilaterally granting that we do not want to jeopardize completely o u r security. Perhaps it would be fair to say that the unilateralists see more risk to security in the p r e s e n t arms race than a significant unilateral step which would ease tensions and stop or even reverse the race.

Since the problem of inspection has proven to be one of the major obstacles in achieving agreement between the U. S. and the U. S. S. R. you should study carefully the Clark and Sohn proposals for the establishment of an inspection system. The excerpt from Wiesner's article is helpful in that it outlines inspection objectives, range of techniques and explains in a succinct fashion the major facets of the relationship of inspection to control.

Steps toward Disarmament

by P. M. S. Blackett

The representatives of 17 nations— the two main nuclear powers, seven nations allied with one or the other of them, and eight uncommitted nations—have convened at Geneva for the third formal, full-dress attempt since the end of World War II to negotiate disarmament. It must be conceded that the circumstances are not entirely favorable to agreement. During 1961 the U.S. and the U.S.S.R. reversed the trend of nearly a decade and increased their military expenditures by something on the order of 25 per cent. The three-year moratorium on the test-

ing of nuclear weapons was terminated by the series of Soviet tests in the fall; on the eve of the Geneva meeting the U.S. announced its intention to move its present series of underground tests into the atmosphere if the U.S.S.R. did not immediately agree to a test ban.

On the other hand, both the Soviet and the Western bloc are committed by categorical public statements to the objective of complete and general disarmament under strict inspection and control. What is more, practical military considerations, arising from the nature of nuclear weapons, commend substantial reduction in armaments to the great powers as a measure that will increase their security in the first step toward disarmament.

In considering possible first steps that would lead to increased security for both sides, partisans of each side should try to understand how the present military situation must look to the other. A military commander, in planning a campaign or a battle, attempts to do this as a matter of course. He has first to find out all he can about the material facts of his opponent's military deployment and secondly to assess the probable intentions of his opponent for its use. This is the process that has been described as "guessing what is happening on the other side of the hill." A similar obligation rests on those who plan a disarmament negotiation. A military planner, it is true, can much more easily put himself mentally in the position of his military opponent than a statesman can think himself into the position of his opposite number, because a statesman must enter imaginatively into the political as well as the military thought processes of his opponent. This is hard to do at a time of acute ideological struggle. It is nonetheless essential that the military and political leaders of both sides do just this. No small part of the present crisis, concerning armaments in general and nuclear weapons in particular, has been due to a tendency in the West to attribute to ideological motives actions by the U.S.S.R. that seem to have been motivated mainly by military considerations. Conversely, much of the West's defense policy appears to have been influenced by political and economic factors.

It may be useful to start by describing the most important elements in the military capabilities of the Soviet bloc and the Western alliance. In recent months there have been significant disclosures about the nuclear weapons and their means of delivery possessed by both sides. On November 12 of last year Robert S. McNamara, Secretary of Defense of the U.S., said that the U.S. nuclear-strike force consists of 1,700 intercontinental bombers, including 630 B-52's, 55 B-58's and 1,000 B-47's. He said that the U.S. possesses in addition several dozen operational intercontinental ballistic missiles (ICBM's), some 80 Polaris missiles in nuclear-powered submarines, about the same number of Thor and Jupiter intermediate-range missiles, some 300 carrier-borne aircraft armed with megaton war heads and nearly 1,000 supersonic land-based fighters with nuclear war heads. According to his deputy, Roswell L. Gilpatric, "the total number of our nuclear delivery vehicles, tactical as well as strategic, is in the tens of thousands, and of course we have more than one war head for each vehicle.... We have a second-strike capability that is at least as extensive as what the Soviets can deliver by striking first, therefore we can be confident that the Soviets will not provoke a major conflict." The U.S. stockpile of nuclear weapons is most often estimated as around 30,000 megatons, that is, enough for some 30,000 one-megaton bombs.

Naturally no such precise figures for Soviet strength are available. I have seen no reliable estimates of the U.S.S.R.'s nuclear stockpile, nor of its possible nuclear-armed submarine strength, nor of its nuclear-armed fighter-bomber strength (the last, of course, would not have sufficient range to contribute to the Soviet strike power against the U.S.). But recent semiofficial estimates from Washington give the U.S.S.R. some 50 ICBM's, some 150 intercontinental bombers and some 400 medium-range missiles (the last able to cover Europe but not the U.S.). The same sources indicate that the U.S. may have a small lead over the U.S.S.R. in the number of ICBM's. That such estimates should issue from Washington may seem surprising in view of the role that an alleged "missile gap" played in the 1960 presidential election campaign. That the estimates

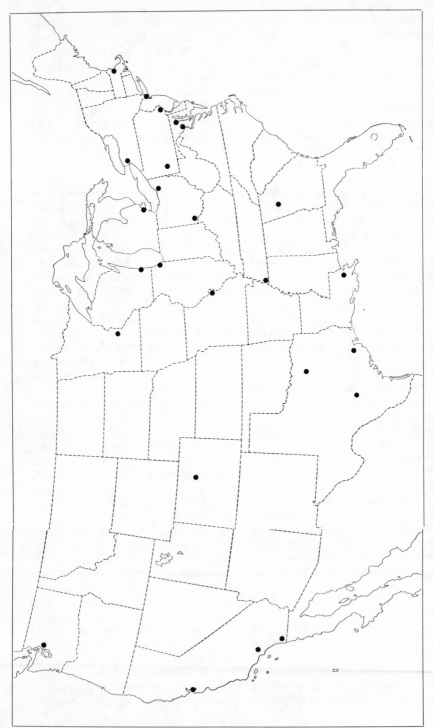

Minimum deterrent strategy of a nuclear opponent of the U.S. could logically be based on an attack on the U.S. population rather than on U.S. airfields and missile bases. The colored dots on this map represent the 25 largest U.S. cities. In the 1960 census the combined population of the metropolitan areas of these cities was 60.8 million.

are realistic, however, is indicated by the statement of Senator Stuart Symington that the U.S. intelligence estimate of the missile force available to the U.S.S.R. at the middle of 1961 was only 3.5 per cent of the number predicted a few years ago. The corresponding estimate of Soviet bomber strength, he revealed, was 19 per cent of the number predicted in 1956 [see illustrations on page 10]. Mr. Symington explained that the new figures are predicated on intelligence about Soviet "intentions" as well as "capability" and expressed his own disquiet at "the tentativeness at best of our intelligence estimates." It is one of the purposes of this article to attempt to elucidate some of these Soviet intentions.

At first sight there appears to be a contradiction between Washington's claim of a marked over-all nuclear superiority and the recent statement by Marshal Rodion Y. Malinovsky, the Soviet Minister of Defense, that the U.S.S.R. has the power to destroy all the important industrial, administrative and political centers of the U.S. and "whole countries that have provided their territories for the siting of American war bases." The explanation may be as follows. To carry out such destruction would require not more than 1,000 megatons of nuclear destructive power, say five megatons for each of 100 key targets in the U.S. and another 500 megatons for Western Europe and U.S. bases overseas. At only 100,000 dead per megaton such an attack would kill 100 million people. The U.S. stockpile, estimated at 30,000 megatons, is 30 times greater than the U.S.S.R. would need to carry out the retaliatory blow described by Malinovsky.

There is, of course, the possibility that the new U.S. estimates of Soviet nuclear strength are too low. After all, firm information about Soviet military preparations is notoriously hard to come by. It seems certain, however, that the U.S. Department of Defense must believe the

estimates to be roughly correct. It would be politically disastrous for the Administration to be found guilty of underestimating Soviet nuclear strength. But even assuming that the estimates of the relative strength of the two sides are only approximately correct, they show that the possibility of a rationally planned surprise nuclear attack by the U.S.S.R. on the nuclear delivery system of the West must be quite negligible. The question of why the U.S.S.R. has built such a small nuclear delivery system should perhaps be replaced by the question of why the U.S. has built such an enormous striking capacity.

In order to understand the possible motives behind Soviet defense policy, it is necessary to consider the history of the growth of nuclear-weapon power. During the period of U.S. atomic monopoly or overwhelming numerical superiority, say from 1947 to 1954, the role of the U.S. Strategic Air Command was to attack and destroy Soviet cities in case of war. This countercity policy, like most traditional military doctrines, had both an offensive and a defensive aspect. From the Western viewpoint, under the doctrine of "massive retaliation," this nuclear striking power was seen to be both a deterrent to the possibility of attack by Soviet land forces and, in the extreme "roll back," or "liberation," statement of the doctrine, an offensive weapon to obtain political concessions by threat of its use. By 1954 the threat was implemented by more than 1,000 intercontinental B-47 bombers, plus larger numbers of shorter range vehicles deployed around the U.S.S.R.

From the U.S.S.R.'s point of view, its land forces were the only available counter to the Western nuclear monopoly during this period. The answer to the threat of nuclear attack was the threat of taking over Europe on the ground. In retrospect the military reaction of the U.S.S.R. seems understandable. It started a crash program to produce its own nuclear weapons. It also embarked on a huge air defense program; by 1953 it was credited with an operational fighter strength of some 10,000 aircraft. As Western nuclear strength grew, the U.S.S.R. gradually built up its land forces so as to be able to invade Europe, even after a U.S. nuclear attack. At the political level the U.S.S.R. consolidated its forward military line by the political coup in 1948 in Czechoslovakia and integrated the other satellite countries more closely into the Soviet defense system. Since the main military threat then to the U.S.S.R. was from manned nuclear bombers, the greatest possible depth for air defense was vital. During World War II it was found that the efficacy of a fighter defense system increased steeply with the depth of the defense zone. Finally, the U.S.S.R. maintained strict geographical secrecy over its land area so as to deny target information to the U.S. Strategic Air Command.

The doctrine of massive retaliation became less and less plausible as the Soviet nuclear stockpile grew. It had to be abandoned after 1954, when hydrogen bombs became available to both East and West. When the U.S.S.R. proceeded to build up a fleet of long-range bombers to deliver its hydrogen bombs, the U.S. became vulnerable to nuclear counterattack. Some form of nuclear stalemate by balance of terror seemed to have arrived.

This balance seemed still further strengthened about 1957, when rapid progress in the technology of nuclear weapons and missiles made it possible to carry multimegaton hydrogen bombs in ICBM's. Because such missiles are most difficult, if not impossible, to destroy in flight, a nuclear aggressor would have to leave no enemy missiles undestroyed if it wanted to keep its own major cities from being wiped out by a retaliatory attack. The advent of long-range missiles therefore made the balance of terror more stable.

Two contrasting systems of military theory evolved in response to this new situation. The first led off from the premise that a rather stable kind of military balance had been reached, in which neither side could make use of its strategic nuclear power without ensuring its own destruction. In other words, the balance of terror was likely to be rather stable against rational action, even though the actual nuclear strengths of the two sides were markedly different, as indeed they were in the middle 1950's, when the U.S. was already vastly stronger in over-all deployed nuclear strength. This view rested on the assumption that neither side could hope to knock out the other's nuclear system entirely. Since some power to retaliate would survive attack, a rational government would be nearly as much, if not just as much, deterred from a first strike by the expectation that it would suffer, say, 10 million deaths as it would be if the expectation were 100 million.

This view led to the practical conclusion that "enough is enough." In today's jargon this is the policy of the minimum deterrent—that is, the possession of a nuclear force adequate only for a retaliatory attack on enemy cities but incapable of successful attack on the enemy's nuclear delivery system. It is clear that only a small nuclear delivery system is necessary for a minimum deterrent. One big hydrogen bomb dropped on a big city could kill several millions. The small delivery system must, however, be highly invulnerable. Otherwise the enemy might think it possible to bring off a successful "counterforce" first strike, aimed at the destruction of the system. Little operational intelligence is needed for such a minimum deterrent policy because this involves attack on cities, whose locations are known, and does not involve surprise attack on nuclear bases, whose locations therefore do not need to be known.

On the political plane, it was thought, the resulting period of relative stability would be favorable for a serious attempt to negotiate a substantial measure of disarmament, both nuclear and conventional. Far-reaching disarmament was seen to be highly desirable, if only because such a balance of terror is stable solely against rational acts of responsible governments. It is not stable against irresponsible actions of individuals or dissident groups or technical accidents. A few suitably placed individuals—a missile crew or the crew of a nuclear bomber on a routine flight—could kill a few million enemy city dwellers on their own initiative. The best way to reduce this danger·is to reduce drastically the number of nuclear weapons on both sides.

The second and quite different doctrine was that the balance of terror was not even stable against rational acts of responsible governments. This was based on the view that a determined nuclear power might be able to launch a surprise counterforce attack on the enemy's nuclear delivery system of such strength that the enemy would not be able to retaliate. The aggressor, without suffering unacceptable casualties, would then have the enemy at its mercy. The practical consequence of this doctrine is to strive for maximum superiority in number of weapons, maximum invulnerability of one's own nuclear delivery system and maximum intelligence about the enemy's nuclear system.

Plainly a successful counterforce attack would require knowledge of the location of all the enemy's nuclear missile and air bases and the power to dispatch several weapons against each, so as to ensure that at least one reached its target. A counterforce strategy thus implies the necessity for a many-fold nuclear

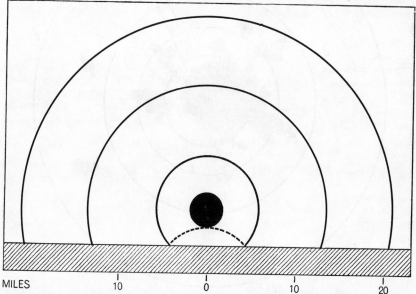

MILES   10   0   10   20

AIR BURST of a nuclear bomb would maximize its effects on a city, the most widespread of which would be due to heat. This drawing outlines the effects of a 10-megaton bomb set off at 20,000 feet. At 12 miles (*inner colored circle*) from "ground zero" the fireball, 3.4 miles in diameter, would deliver 30 calories per square centimeter at a rate sufficient to ignite virtually all flammable building materials. At 20 miles (*outer colored circle*) from ground zero the heat would be 12 calories per square centimeter, enough to cause third-degree burns and start many fires. Arc extending upward from ground below the burst is a reflected shock wave that would amplify blast effects of the explosion (*see drawing below*).

superiority over the enemy. Moreover, to have the slightest chance of success such an attack must come as a complete surprise to the enemy: it must be a first strike. This policy has various pseudonyms: maximum deterrent posture, first-counterforce-strike capability, or, in plain English, preparation for nuclear aggression.

Since the possession of nuclear armament raises the possibility that either side could adopt either one of these strategies, both of them must have been discussed in military circles in Moscow and

Washington during the years after the explosion of the first hydrogen bombs in 1954. Let us try to find out how the discussions went by studying what shape the nuclear-defense policies of the U.S.S.R. and the U.S. took in the subsequent years.

If the Washington figures for Soviet nuclear strength are valid, it is clear that the U.S.S.R. has planned for a purely retaliatory nuclear role and has definitely not planned for a surprise attack on the U.S. delivery system. As long ago as 1956 the U.S.S.R. was believed to have

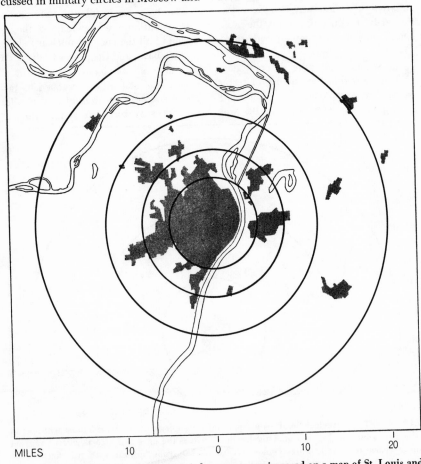

RADII OF EFFECTS of a 10-megaton air burst are superimposed on a map of St. Louis and the surrounding area. The two colored circles correspond to the colored circles in the drawing at the top of the page. The black circles concern effects due to blast. At a distance of five miles (*inner black circle*) from ground zero virtually all buildings would be destroyed. At eight miles (*outer black circle*) virtually all wooden buildings would be destroyed.

the capability of making 25 long-range bombers a month. It appears today to have only some 150, compared with the 1,700 U.S. long-range bombers able to reach the U.S.S.R. Even though Soviet medium-range bombers could reach the U.S. on a one-way flight, this is much more than counterbalanced by the 1,500 or so Western fighter bombers, carrier-borne aircraft and medium-range missiles able to reach the U.S.S.R. It is also probable that the U.S.S.R. could have made many more than the 50 or so ICBM's with which it is now credited, since its space program indicates substantial industrial resources for making missiles. The evidence is that the U.S.S.R. has based its safety on the retaliatory power of a small number of missiles and aircraft operating from bases whose exact locations are kept as secret as possible. The deterrent value of its missiles is certainly enhanced by the prestige of its space program.

That the U.S.S.R. believed the danger of a major war, intentionally initiated, had been reduced by the advent of hydrogen bombs seems indicated by the fact that it reduced the total number of men in its armed forces from 5.8 million in 1955 to 3.6 million in 1959. In January, 1960, Premier Khrushchev announced the U.S.S.R.'s intention to reduce this to 2.4 million by the end of 1961. The U.S.S.R. needed fewer troops because it no longer had to rely on a retaliatory land blow in Europe to counter a Western nuclear attack. Its concern about the danger of accidental, irresponsible or escalated war is probably one of the reasons for its strong espousal in 1955 of a drastic measure of comprehensive and general disarmament.

Turning to the history of U.S. defense policy over this period, it is to be noted that the total service manpower fell slowly from 2.9 million in 1955 to 2.6 million in 1960. The development of improved nuclear weapons, missiles and aircraft continued, but not at a great rate, even after the Soviet launching of an artificial satellite in 1957 and much boasting by the U.S.S.R. of its missile prowess. Although subjected to considerable public pressure to engage in a crash program to close the alleged missile gap, President Eisenhower maintained that the existing program was adequate for the safety of the nation. In his last State of the Union Message in January, 1961, he declared: "The 'bomber gap' of several years ago was always a fiction and the 'missile gap' shows every sign of being the same."

As 1954 was the year of the hydrogen bomb, so 1961 was for both sides in the cold war the year of the Great Rearmament. In the U.S.S.R. the decrease of total armed forces to 2.4 million projected for 1961 was deferred and the arms budget was markedly increased. In July the Soviet Government went on the diplomatic offensive to bring about changes in the status of Berlin and to get the division of Germany recognized. In August it began testing nuclear weapons again, in spite of a promise in January, 1960, by Premier Khrushchev that the U.S.S.R. would not be the first to do so. No doubt there were some political motives behind these drastic moves. Possibly heavy pressure was put on Khrushchev from China and from the opposition elements in the U.S.S.R. to admit that his policy of coexistence had not produced political gains commensurate with its possible military risks. But such drastic changes, with the inevitable adverse reaction of much of world opinion, would hardly have been made unless there were strong military reasons for them. To get at these reasons it is necessary to recall in more detail the circumstances in which the changes took place.

In the first place the flights of the U.S. reconnaissance U-2 aircraft must have had decisive importance in shaping the attitudes of Soviet military leaders. Although the over-all nuclear strength of the U.S. is now, and was then, much greater than that of the U.S.S.R., Soviet leaders could reckon that one vital factor would make a U.S. nuclear attack on the U.S.S.R. exceedingly risky: the secrecy as to the location of the Soviet nuclear bases. Obviously one of the main objectives of the U-2 flights was to locate those nuclear bases. The Soviet command knew that the U-2 flights had been going on for some years before the first aircraft was shot down in the spring of 1960; presumably they reacted by greater dispersal and camouflage. What must have disturbed the Soviet military staff was President Eisenhower's justification of the flights as essential for U.S. security. This implied that U.S. security could only be maintained if the U.S. had sufficient information as to the location of Soviet nuclear sites to make possible a successful surprise attack on the Soviet retaliatory force.

If these were the Soviet fears, the rejection by the U.S.S.R. early in 1961 of the British-American draft of a treaty to ban the testing of nuclear weapons finds explanation in the same jealous military concern to protect the country's geographical security. A detailed study of this document makes it clear that the elaborate international inspection system proposed for the prevention of underground tests could conceivably have served to reveal the location of at least some of the Soviet missile sites. It would be hard to convince a military staff officer of any nationality that this possibility was negligible. If the West had been content to monitor only the atmosphere against test violations, a much less comprehensive inspection system would have sufficed and a test-ban treaty might well have been signed. The Soviet fear of inspection may have been the more acute because there was so little in the U.S.S.R. to inspect.

The resumption of testing by the U.S.S.R. in September, 1961, would seem to fall into the same pattern of motivation. Although its timing may have been influenced by the Berlin crisis, which Khrushchev himself brought to a head, the testing of war heads with an explosive force of up to 60 megatons and the simultaneous well-publicized success of putting seven ICBM's on their target in the Pacific at a range of some 7,000 miles was an effective way of reestablishing the U.S.S.R.'s confidence in the few deployed ICBM's that formed its main retaliatory force. Soviet spokesmen were at pains to promote the credibility of the U.S.S.R.'s deterrent by emphasizing to the U.S. the accuracy of its missiles and the possible power of the war heads demonstrated in these tests.

In the redirection of Soviet military policy considerable weight must also have been carried by the fear that if the NATO rearmament continued, the time could not be far distant when West Germany would get de facto control of its own nuclear weapons. In Soviet eyes the refusal of the West to take disarmament seriously at the "Committee of Ten" conference in 1960 was evidently decisive. As early as November, 1960, the Russians stated that if the West continued to temporize on disarmament, the U.S.S.R. would be forced into massive rearmament.

Sometime in the latter half of 1960 or early in 1961 it seems probable that the Soviet military staff began to have doubts as to the adequacy of the minimum deterrent posture in relation to the near-maximum deterrent posture of the U.S. It must have been later than January of 1960, for in that month Khrushchev announced a drastic cutback of both long-range bombers and conventional forces. Since the effectiveness of the Soviet minimum deterrent rested so heavily on geographical secrecy, the U.S.S.R. command may have feared that the U.S., by further air or satellite reconnaissance, or by espionage or defections, would ultimately acquire the intelligence necessary to make a successful nuclear attack on Soviet nuclear bases. Probably the main fear of the Soviet Government was that circumstances might arise in which the U.S. Government would be pushed by irresponsible or fanatical groups into reckless action. The Russians certainly noted the doctrine of some civilian analysts that it would be quite rational to make a "pre-emptive first strike" even at the cost of 10 million deaths to the attacking side, and the doctrine of others that the U.S. should prepare itself mentally and materially to suffer such casualties.

In the U.S. the program for the Great Rearmament was projected as early as 1959 by the Democratic National Committee. In preparation for the impending presidential election the party leadership published a detailed study of defense problems and recommended a $7 billion increase (16 per cent) in the $43 billion defense budget proposed by President Eisenhower. The funds were to go partly for increased conventional forces and partly to increase the strength and reduce the vulnerability of the U.S. nuclear striking power. In January, 1961, almost immediately after taking office, the Administration authorized an increase of $3 billion and later in the year another $4 billion, thus carrying out the program in full. The present plans include the provision of up to 800 ICBM's of the solid-fuel Minuteman type in underground "hardened" bases by 1965.

The Democratic Party's campaign for increased nuclear armaments was closely linked with the theoretical doctrine of the instability of the balance of terror, derived from the alleged overwhelming advantage accruing to the nuclear aggressor. This was ably argued by civilian analysts closely associated with the U.S. Air Force. The U.S.S.R. was said to have both the capability and the intention to launch a surprise nuclear attack on the U.S. In retrospect, it would seem that these "looking-glass strategists" endowed the U.S.S.R. with a capability that it did not have and that the U.S. had once had and had now lost.

That the Soviet military staff had reason to take this element in U.S. opinion seriously may be judged by the fact that President Kennedy himself found it necessary to launch in the fall of 1961 a vigorous campaign against all those in the U.S. who urge "total war and total victory over communism... who seek to find an American solution for all problems"—against those who were living in the long-past era of the U.S. nuclear monopoly. In this campaign President Kennedy has been vigorously supported by ex-President Eisenhower. Very possibly the U.S.S.R. may have overestimated the potential influence of the proponents of aggressive nuclear strategy and the ultra-right-wing groups that yearn "to get it over with." Nonetheless, the fact that both Kennedy and Eisenhower have felt it necessary to combat them must also imply that the Soviet military planners could not afford to ignore their existence.

The Kennedy Administration's recent vigorous emphasis on the overwhelming nuclear superiority of the U.S. over the U.S.S.R., and the assertion that the U.S. possesses a second strike that is as strong as the Soviet first strike might perhaps be held in the U.S.S.R. to suggest a move by the U.S. Administration toward a preventive war posture. Undoubtedly the exact reverse is the case. The Administration's statements are designed to bury officially the fear of a Soviet first strike, sedulously propagated by those who believe that the U.S.S.R. has planned for, and in fact now has, a first-counterforce capability, and so at a time of crisis might use it. If this were in truth the situation, the argument that the U.S. must forestall the Soviet blow might seem strong. The Kennedy Administration evidently foresaw this danger arising and effectively removed it by denying that the U.S.S.R. has ever had an effective first-strike capacity; thus there would be no reason for a forestalling blow in a crisis. The President, by emphasizing U.S. nuclear superiority over the U.S.S.R., has forestalled the potential forestallers, or, in the current jargon, has pre-empted the potential pre-empters. At the same time he has refuted many of the arguments on which the Democratic Party based much of its election campaign, and indeed many of the arguments for his own present rearmament program.

It is, for instance, hard to see the military justification for the program of up to 800 Minuteman ICBM's in the next few years. If these are, as claimed, reasonably invulnerable, this number is at least 10 times larger than is necessary for an effective retaliatory force to attack Soviet cities.

The only military circumstance that could justify such a continuous build-up of nuclear striking force would be that the other party could adequately protect its cities or succeed in perfecting an anti-missile defense system. Recently Soviet generals have boasted that "the complex and important problems of destroying enemy rockets in flight have been solved." This must refer to the scientific and technical problems; these have also been solved in the U.S. A complete anti-missile defense system that is of any operational significance certainly does not exist today and, in my view, will not exist in the foreseeable future. Suppose, however, that I am wrong and that a system can eventually be constructed capable of destroying, say, 50 per cent of a retaliatory missile attack by 50 ICBM's, so reducing the number reaching the target to 25. Even this reduced blow would kill tens of millions of people. Moreover, it would only be necessary to increase the strength of the retaliatory force from 50 to 100 missiles to cancel out the antimissile missile. This illustrates the general conclusion that since a purely retaliatory nuclear force can be quite small, any possible defense system, either active or passive, can be canceled out by a small number of additional missiles. The fact that a purely retaliatory posture is little affected by

technological innovation, whereas a counterforce posture is very much affected, may prove a vital factor in disarmament negotiations.

It cannot be seriously believed now that the U.S.S.R. has either the capability or the intention of making an all-out attack on U.S. missile sites and bomber bases. Much genuine alarm in the West might have been allayed if the U.S.S.R. had been more successful. in making clearer its disbelief in the military possibility of a successful first-counterforce strike and its intention not to plan for such a possibility. After the brutality of Soviet action in Hungary in 1956 and the technological triumph of the artificial satellite the following year, there may have been legitimate grounds in the West for fearing that the U.S.S.R. might adopt the Western policy of massive retaliation, which, against a nuclear power, requires a counterforce capability. In January, 1960, however, Khrushchev explicitly declared the Soviet commitment to a purely retaliatory strategy. The Soviet second-strike force was strong enough, he said, "to wipe the country or countries which attack us off the face of the earth." To his own rhetorical question, "Will they not, possibly, show perfidy and attack us first...and thus have an advantage to achieve victory?" he replied: "No. Contemporary means of waging war do not give any country such advantages." In addition to freeing resources for capital development, the Soviet minimum-deterrent strategy has avoided the greatest military danger: that the U.S. might attack the U.S.S.R. because of a belief that the U.S.S.R. was about to attack the U.S.

If the analysis given here is approximately correct, what are the prospects of progress toward disarmament at the present meeting in Geneva? Both blocs are fully committed by official pronouncements to the goal of complete and general disarmament under strict control and inspection—notably by the British Commonwealth Prime Ministers' statement in the spring of 1961, by President Kennedy's speech to the General Assembly of the United Nations and by the Soviet-American Joint Statement of Principles, both in September of 1961. Moreover, both sides are committed to attempting to work out first steps of the disarmament process that do not impair the present strategic balance.

Clearly, conventional and nuclear disarmament must go in parallel. The fear of the West of Soviet superiority in trained and deployed land forces must be met by a drastic reduction during the first stage to low levels such as those suggested by the Anglo-French memorandum of 1954: one million or at most 1.5 million men each for the U.S., the U.S.S.R. and China. When the correspondingly limited contributions to the land forces of NATO from Great Britain, France and West Germany are taken into account, the armies of the Soviet bloc would not have the capability of overrunning Europe in a surprise land attack.

The number of nuclear weapons in existence on both sides, their explosive power and the diversity of the delivery systems are so overwhelming that no small step in nuclear disarmament can have much significance. In a situation in which the U.S. has 10,000 delivery vehicles and a stockpile of 30,000 megatons of explosive (which is said to be increasing at the fastest rate in its history), a first disarmament step involving only a small percentage reduction is not worth negotiating. To justify the labor of negotiating any agreed reduction, and to offset the undoubted strains and disputes that will inevitably arise from the operation of any inspection and control sys-

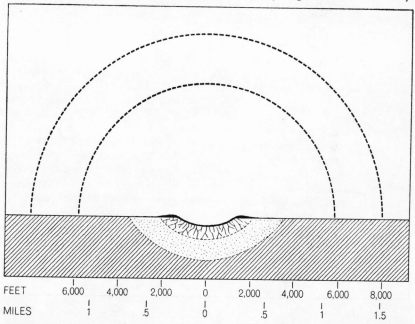

FEET 6,000 4,000 2,000 0 2,000 4,000 6,000 8,000

MILES 1 .5 0 .5 1 1.5

GROUND BURST of a nuclear bomb would be required to neutralize a "hardened" (i.e., buried) missile site. Diameter of the crater dug by a 10-megaton ground burst in dry soil would be 2,600 feet; the depth of the crater would be 250 feet. Radius of the underground "plastic zone" (*outer line below ground*) would be 3,250 feet; the radius of the "rupture zone" (*inner line below ground*) would be 2,000 feet. At a distance of 1.1 miles from ground zero the blast would exert an air pressure of some 300 pounds per square inch (*inner circle above ground*); at a distance of 1.5 miles (*outer circle above ground*), 100 pounds per square inch.

tem, the negotiated reduction must be a major one; in fact, of such magnitude as to change qualitatively the nature of the relative nuclear postures of the two giant powers.

The simplest big first step, and the one most consistent with realistic military considerations, is that both giant powers should reduce their nuclear forces to a very low and purely retaliatory role. That is, each should retain only enough invulnerable long-range vehicles to attack the other's cities if it is itself attacked, say less than 100 ICBM's with one-megaton war heads. This is still an enormous force, capable of killing tens of millions of people. A reduction to a level of 20 ICBM's or less would be much preferable. Such a reduction would at once prevent nuclear weapons from being used by sane governments as weapons of aggression or coercion. It would not, of course, prevent them from being used by irresponsible groups who do not calculate the cost. It is only at a later stage in disarmament, when nuclear weapons are completely destroyed, that this danger will be excluded. It has always been clear that the ever present danger of accidental or irresponsible war is a cogent reason for big and rapid steps in the disarmament process.

Detailed studies are needed of possible ways in which both the U.S.S.R.

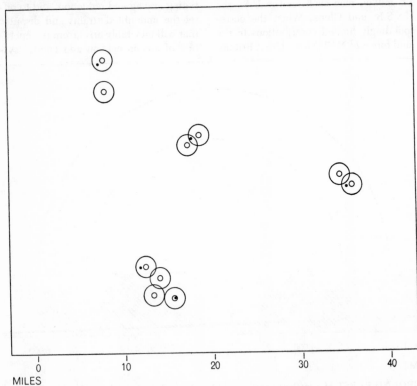

MILES

PATTERN OF GROUND BURSTS would be required to neutralize a dispersed group of hardened missile sites. In this schematic drawing a "circle of probable error" of one mile is assumed for each of the attacking missiles; this implies that at least two missiles would be directed at each of the sites. There are five sites, represented by dots. The smaller of each of the 10 pairs of concentric circles represents the 2,600-foot diameter of a 10-megaton bomb crater; the larger of the circles, the 1.1-mile radius at which the air pressure is 300 pounds per square inch. The total weight of the attack on the five bases is 100 megatons. The scale of the drawing is the same as that of the map of St. Louis at the bottom of page 6.

and the U.S. could take such an important first step without upsetting the present strategic balance. A major problem is how to phase the building up of a system of general inspection while at the same time making a drastic reduction in nuclear delivery systems by their actual destruction under international verification. Taking military considerations only into account, I believe that a procedure acceptable to both blocs could be devised.

The difference hitherto between the proposed Western and Soviet first steps in relation to nuclear weapons has been often simplified to the statement that the U.S.S.R. wants disarmament without control and the West wants control without disarmament. It would be more accurate to say that the clash is on the phasing of the stages of disarmament and the stages of control.

In its 1960 proposals the U.S.S.R. suggested that, in the first step, international teams should be dispatched to inspect the destruction of all rocket weapons, military aircraft and other carriers of nuclear weapons. It did not propose the inspection or control of those that remain waiting to be destroyed. Full inspection of a country was to be undertaken only when all weapons had been destroyed. It is clear that the U.S.S.R.'s first steps of disarmament are consistent with its presumed military policy of relying for its safety from nuclear attack on a relatively small force of purely retaliatory nuclear weapons in

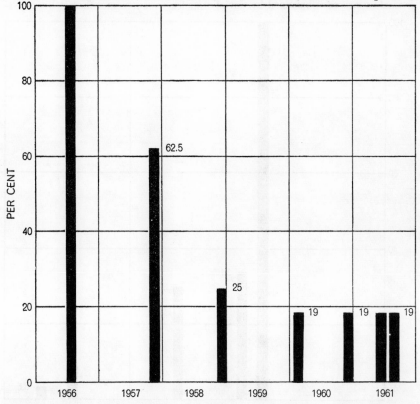

U.S. ESTIMATE OF SOVIET HEAVY-BOMBER STRENGTH by the middle of 1961, according to an article by Senator Stuart Symington in *The Reporter,* decreased by 81 per cent between August, 1956 (*bar at left*), and August, 1961 (*right*). Senator Symington's figures were given in percentages, rather than absolute numbers, for security reasons.

secret sites.

On the other hand, the U.S. proposals in 1960 envisaged widespread inspection in the first stages and no actual disarmament until the second stage. This proposal might make military sense if put by a weak nuclear power to a much stronger one. But when put by a strong power to a weaker one, rejection must have been expected. If the U.S.S.R. had accepted the proposal, the geographical secrecy of its nuclear sites would have been lost and it would have been vulnerable to nuclear attack from the much stronger West.

Any realistic first stage must start from the fact that the present nuclear balance, such as it is, has a highly asymmetric character: the West's much greater nuclear power is balanced by Soviet geographical secrecy. Since the military balance is asymmetric, so must be any mutually acceptable first step. Concessions must be made by both sides and these must be based on the realities of the military postures of the two blocs.

The U.S.S.R. should accept general inspection not, as in their proposals hitherto, when disarmament is complete but at some intermediate stage on the road to disarmament. Reciprocally, the West should not demand widespread inspection before any disarmament has taken place, as it has done hitherto, but only after substantial destruction of nuclear armaments has taken place under international verification.

In the first stage, therefore, all parties might supply to one another a list of nuclear weapons and their delivery sys-

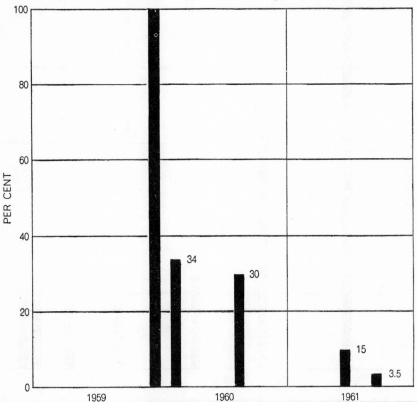

U.S. ESTIMATE OF SOVIET OPERATIONAL ICBM STRENGTH similarly decreased, according to Senator Symington, by 96.5 per cent between December, 1959, and September, 1961.

tems, together with research and production facilities. The exact location of sites would not be included at this stage. An agreed number of weapons would then be destroyed and their destruction would be verified by on-site inspection by the international control organization. When this destruction has been verified, a general inspection, using some sampling technique, would begin. The object would then be to verify the correctness of the original declared inventories by checking the numbers remaining after the agreed reductions had been verified, and to proceed to the elimination of the armament remaining.

A word must be said about the place of a test-ban agreement in the stages of a disarmament plan. If this agreement did not involve a type of inspection that might reveal the Soviet nuclear sites, it would be advantageous for it to be included in the first stage, or preferably agreed to at once. If, however, it involved widespread inspection that might reveal these sites, Soviet military planners would certainly advise its rejection. It would then have to wait for the second stage of disarmament, when general inspection starts after the destruction of agreed numbers of nuclear weapons in the first stage.

Some such compromise between Western and Soviet proposals would seem to meet many of the reciprocal criticisms made by the two parties of their respective 1960 proposals without compromising the military security of either. The problem becomes more difficult, however, when nonmilitary considerations are taken into account. Since nonmilitary considerations have played a major role in shaping the defense policies of the great powers, they must inevitably also affect their disarmament policies. For example, if it is difficult to find legitimate military reasons for the vast number of U.S. nuclear weapons and delivery vehicles, it is clear that military arguments alone are not likely to be dominant in U.S. discussion of a possible drastic first step toward nuclear disarmament. This is widely admitted in

the U.S., where the impediments to disarmament are being seen more and more as economic, political and emotional in origin rather than as based on operational military considerations. A vital aspect of the problem for the U.S. is the effect that drastic disarmament steps would have not only on the economy as a whole but also on those special sections of high-grade, science-based and highly localized industries that are now so overwhelmingly involved in defense work. A valuable step would be for both the U.S. and Soviet governments to produce and publish detailed and politically realistic economic plans for the transition to a purely retaliatory capacity.

It is fair to conclude that a realistic military basis for an agreed drastic first step in disarmament may not be impossible to find. The urgency of the situation was declared with eloquence by President Kennedy in his speech to the United Nations in September:

"Today, every inhabitant of this planet must contemplate the day when this planet may no longer be habitable. Every man, woman and child lives under a nuclear sword of Damocles, hanging by the slenderest of threads, capable of being cut at any moment by accident or miscalculation or by madness.... The risks inherent in disarmament pale in comparison to the risks inherent in an unlimited arms race."

This great goal of disarmament will be achieved only if the real nature of the arguments against disarmament are clearly identified and frankly faced. The problems of disarmament must not be obscured, as they sometimes have been in the past, by ingenious but fallacious military doctrine applied to false intelligence estimates.

The growing power of China, and the evidence of an ideological rift between it and Russia, provide an added reason for urgency in the drive for disarmament. The U.S.S.R. and the U.S. will be wise to limit drastically their nuclear arms before China becomes a major nuclear power. It is to be observed that whatever influence China may now be exerting on the U.S.S.R. to adopt a harder policy with the West certainly arises in part from the failure of Premier Khrushchev's campaign for disarmament. This failure greatly weakens Khrushchev's argument for the feasibility of peaceful coexistence of the Soviet and the Western worlds. It would seem urgently necessary to attempt to bring China into the disarmament negotiations as soon as possible.

Reciprocal Measures for
Arms Stabilization

THOMAS C. SCHELLING

THERE HAS BEEN A WIDESPREAD CHANGE IN THE THINKING ON ARMS control in the last year or so. Much of it is due to the focus of attention on "measures to safeguard against surprise attack" (to use the official terminology). Although this subject is still listed anachronistically under "disarmament," it is differently oriented. It assumes deterrence as the keystone of our security policy, and tries to improve it. It accepts a retaliatory capability as something to be enhanced, not degraded—something to be made more secure, less accident-prone, less in need of striking quickly to avoid its own destruction, less capable of gaining advantage from a sudden attack of its own. An anomaly of this approach to arms control is that it does not necessarily involve "disarmament" in the literal sense.

Another anomaly, which rather shakes the disarmament tradition, is that weapons may be more stabilizing and less aggressive if they are capable of civilian reprisal rather than of military engagement. A standoff between two retaliatory forces is in some ways equivalent to an exchange of hostages; and "inhumane" weapons, capable of inflicting damage but not able to go after the enemy's strategic forces, acquire virtue because of their clearly deterrent function and the lack of temptation they give either side to strike first.

More important, though, is the fact that schemes to avert surprise attack are manifestly compatible with a national military policy, not a renunciation of it. They emphasize the possibility that one can simultaneously think seriously and sympathetically about our military posture and about collaborating with our enemies to improve it. To propose, as does the notion of "measures to safeguard against surprise attack," that military cooperation with potential enemies may offer opportunities to improve our military posture, opens a new field for imaginative scientific and military thinking, and may eventually enlist the support of the military services themselves.

Most of this progress is still ahead of us; the revolution in thinking about arms control is barely started. Officially we have taken only the most hesitant steps in defining arms control in a way that does not contradict our national security policies. We still talk officially as though "disarmament" can only save money, without noticing that under the new philosophy it could cost more. We still work officially with an image of disarmament that makes it solely a peacetime (cold-wartime) process of negotiating explicit detailed agreements in a multinational context for the reduction or elimination of weapons, without adequately recognizing that, as in limiting war, limiting the arms race can be a more tacit and less formal process than the "treaty" idea implies. More important, the prevalent image of disarmament is still one that gives the process a uniquely defined end point—the point of no arms at all, or virtually none except in the hands of some international authority or synthetic state that would have the power to police the world against international violence but against nothing else.

The cautious and the skeptical, the pessimists and the realists, have doubts about how rapidly that end point can be approached, whether it will be approached at all, and whether the process once started may not be reversed. But the goal itself is rarely challenged except by those who have no interest in arms control. And by far the most frequent argument raised in favor of particular limited measures of arms control, perhaps the most widely persuasive, is that these limited measures are at least "steps toward" the goal of ultimate disarmament. We have not faced up to the implications of the anomaly that "measures to safeguard against surprise attack" are designed to preserve a nuclear striking power, and are not easily construed as just another "step toward" ultimate disarmament.*

We still talk about "levels" of armament or disarmament, as though there were only two directions in which to go, up and down, the arms race going in one direction and arms control in the other. We have not yet admitted that, even in the framework of arms control, it could be an open question whether we ought to be negotiating with our enemies for more arms, less arms, different kinds of arms, or arrangements superimposed on

* It should be noted here that the term, "measures to safeguard against surprise attack," has become extremely ambiguous. Some use it to refer only to schemes to avert surprise by provision of last-minute tactical warning. Others enlarge the term to include reciprocal intelligence measures to provide strategic warning or to provide reassurance of the absence of intent or capability. Some use the term more broadly to include limitations on forces, their kinds, numbers, or deployment, to make the achievement of surprise more difficult. (In an extreme interpretation, any disarmament scheme that requires visible rearmament for the initiation of general war can be viewed as a "warning system.") Others use the term to include measures not aimed at surprise itself but at vulnerability to surprise, i.e., to weapon programs or limitations that make the initial attack less potent even when surprise is achieved. All these, and many other, interpretations and usages of the term have one thing in common, however; they are all concerned with the advantage that attaches to "going first" in a major war and are concerned to reduce it or to allay the false alarms and crises that it gives rise to. Additionally, there may be measures aimed at preventing surprise or reducing its consequences in local rather than general war; these have received comparatively little attention in the last few years, but some of the Europe-oriented surprise-attack proposals of 1955-1957 were of that character.[1]

existing armaments. We have given little thought even to the weapon system that would be required by that ultimate international authority that might police the world against armed violence, and to whether it, too, would be embarrassed by a "massive retaliation" doctrine that would lack credibility; whether it, too, might be subject to surprise attack; whether it, too, would lack resolution (as some think NATO might lack resolution) to reach an awful collective decision in response to nibbling aggression or bland violation.

The point of this chapter is that there is a vast new area to be explored once we break out of the traditional confinement of "disarmament"—the entire area of military collaboration with potential enemies to reduce the likelihood of war or to reduce its scope and violence. It is an area worth exploring because our present military policies and prospects, however we feel about the adequacy of current programs, cannot promise security from a major thermonuclear war; and even modest improvements achieved through cooperation with the Soviets should be welcome.

It is not true that in the modern world a gain for the Russians is necessarily a loss for us, and vice versa. We can both suffer losses, and this fact provides scope for cooperation. We both have—unless the Russians have already determined to launch an attack and are preparing for it—a common interest in reducing the advantage of striking first, simply because that very advantage, even if common to both sides, increases the likelihood of war. If at the expense of some capability for launching surprise attack one can deny that capability to the other, it may be a good bargain. We both have a common interest in avoiding the kind of false alarm, panic, misunderstanding, or loss of control, that may lead to an unpremeditated war, in a situation aggravated by the recognition on both sides that it is better to go first than to go second. We have a common interest in not getting drawn or provoked or panicked into war by the actions of a third party (whether that party intends the result or not). And we may have an interest in saving some money by not doing on both sides the things that, if we both do them, tend to cancel out.

This common interest does not depend on trust and good faith. In fact it seems likely that unless thoroughgoing distrust can be acknowledged on both sides, it may be hard to reach any real understanding on the subject. The intellectual clarity required to recognize the nature of the common interest may be incompatible with the pretense that we trust each other, or that there is any sequence of activities in the short run by which either side could demonstrate its good faith to the other.

Ancient despotisms may have understood better than we do how to tranquilize relations between them while hating and distrusting. They exchanged hostages, drank wine from the same glass, met in public to inhibit the massacre of one by the other, and even deliberately exchanged spies to facilitate transmittal of authentic information. And perhaps, having exchanged a son for a daughter in the cold-blooded interest of contract enforcement, they may have reduced tension sufficiently to permit a little affection to grow up in later generations.

ARMS CONTROL AND MILITARY TECHNOLOGY

The premise underlying my point of view is that a main determinant of the likelihood of war is the nature of present military technology. We and the Russians are trapped by our military technology. Weapon developments of the last fifteen years, especially of the last seven or eight, have themselves been responsible for the most alarming aspects of the present strategic situation. They have enhanced the advantage, in the event war should come, of being the one to start it. They have inhumanly compressed the time available to make the most terrible decisions. They have almost eliminated any belief that a really big war either could be or should be limited in scope or brought to a close by any process other than the sheer exhaustion of weapons. They have greatly reduced the confidence of either side that it can predict the weapons its enemy has or will have in the future. In these and other ways the evolution of military technology has exacerbated whatever propensities toward war are inherent in the political conflict between us and our enemies. It might be naïve to say that this is an unmixed evil for both us and the Soviets, since it powerfully affects the bilateral contest between us; nevertheless, it is hard to escape the judgment that nature might have been kinder in the way she let our military technology unfold itself over the last decade and a half.

It is interesting—more than that, it is useful—to ask what technological achievements (available both to us and to our enemies) we wish had never occurred, and what technological failures we wish had turned out otherwise. Do we wish the hydrogen bomb had never come along to make intercontinental missiles economical? Do we wish that nuclear-powered aircraft had made airborne alert so cheap that retaliatory aircraft could stay aloft rather than be vulnerable on the ground to a missile attack? Do we hope that no one ever discovers an economical means of nullifying ballistic-missile submarines, so that neither side can hope to preclude retaliation by sudden attack? Do we wish that warning systems were so nearly perfect that "false alarm" were virtually impossible, or so poor that we could never be tempted to rely on them? Do we wish that missiles had never become so accurate that they could be used to destroy an enemy's missiles in an effort to negate an enemy's retaliatory threat? Do we wish that radioactive fallout could not occur, or do we welcome it as a peculiarly retaliatory (and hence deterrent) weapon effect that is of little use in a pre-emptive attack? Do we wish that secrecy about weapons and weapon production were much more difficult to maintain than it is, or welcome certain kinds of secrecy as a form of mutually appreciated security against surprise attack?

The reason why it is productive to speculate on these questions, rather than merely fanciful, is that arms control can usefully be thought of as a way of changing some of the answers. In addition to what we can do unilaterally to improve our warning systems, to maintain close control over our forces, to make our forces more secure against attack, to avoid the need for precipitate decisions, and to avoid accidents or the mistaken decisions that they might cause, there may be opportunities to exchange facilities or understandings with our enemies, or to design and deploy our forces differently by agreement with our enemies who do likewise, in a way that enhances those aspects of technology we like and that helps to nullify those that we do not.

If we wish that radar were better and cheaper and less limited by the Earth's curvature, we might make it so by exchanging real estate with the Russians for the construction by each of us of observation posts on each other's soil. If we hope that no one can ever predict with confidence how his own missiles would do, in a surprise attack, against the hardened missile sites of his opponent, we might deny each other the necessary knowledge by banning tests of large weapons in the era in which anyone actually has a missile in a hard underground site that he could use a weapon-effects test. If instead we wish that each side might preserve the privacy of its railroad lines for mobile missiles, we might jointly eschew certain surveillance techniques; and if we thought that anti-missile defenses of missile sites might be more feasible, and retaliatory forces correspondingly less vulnerable, with the further testing of nuclear weapons and their effects, we might look with more favor on continued weapon testing. These considerations are by no means the whole story in arms control, but they do remind us that we and our enemies can both jointly welcome, or jointly deplore, certain technological developments (like the improved accuracy of long-range missiles) and may possibly find ways, jointly, to enhance them or to offset them, over and above the things that we can do unilaterally.

NEED FOR STRATEGIC ANALYSIS

These examples suggest some of the criteria that can be applied to limited arms-control schemes, and some of the difficulties in implementing them. As to criteria, the first thing to emphasize is that it takes a good deal of strategic analysis to decide whether a particular limitation or augmentation of weapons or facilities is a good one or a bad one. Viewing limited measures on their individual merits, and not as steps in a comprehensive program that can be justified only by a long sequence of steps to follow, one has to ask whether the technological and economic consequences of a particular scheme are or are not conducive to military stability; and the answer is very unlikely to be closely correlated with whether more weapons or fewer weapons are involved, bigger weapons or smaller ones, or even whether notions of "more" and "less," "bigger" and "smaller," can be applied. Whether we would like to see reconnaissance satellites banned or encouraged may depend, for example, on whether we think they will mainly provide targeting information to the initiator of war or mainly provide warning to a potential defender so that a potential attacker is the more deterred. Whether we like big missiles or not may depend on whether we believe, as so many believed a few years ago, that missiles would be simple and sturdy and hard to destroy in their underground sites or believe as so many fear now that increased accuracies and yields make the present generation of missiles better for a first strike than for a second strike. Whether we wish missile technology to be advanced or retarded may depend on whether or not we believe, as many do, that the next generation of missiles will be easier to protect, easier to hide, or easier to keep moving, and therefore less insecure. Whether one welcomes nuclear-powered ballistic-missile submarines on both sides or deplores them depends on whether they seem to be peculiarly good at surviving and retaliating, and hence "deterrent," or peculiarly good at getting up close for a no-warning strike on an enemy's retaliatory power. And if it were somehow possible to enforce a ban on "dirty" bombs, there would still be a genuine strategic question of whether or not we wish deterrent capabilities to be enhanced by the greater punitive power of dirty bombs, recognizing that comparatively slow-acting fallout may be of much less utility to a potential attacker, whose main interest is to minimize retaliation on himself.

IMPLICATIONS FOR ARMS AGREEMENT

The fact that developments such as these require strategic analysis before it can be decided whether they are good or bad is, aside from being true, discouraging. It means that even among the experts there will be disagreement about the consequences of any particular prohibition or exchange of military facilities; it may be next to impossible to get widespread understanding of the relevant arguments, even within governments. And if fairly detailed analysis is required, and careful distinctions have to be made, prohibitions might have to be specified in equally careful detail and with equally fine distinctions. This is certainly an obstacle to negotiation. Furthermore, any analysis—and any prohibition or agreement or exchange of facilities that is justified on the basis of such analysis—is subject to rapid obsolescence. The friendly warning satellite appears, a year later, as a vicious targeting aid to the surprise attacker; the network of warning systems originally designed for mutual reassurance proves in operation to have too high a false-alarm rate; the missile-guidance systems that we deplored because of their extreme accuracy and the advantage they would give the attacker may prove, after we outlaw them, to have been the main hope for mobile missile systems desired for their invulnerability and hence for their stability. By the time we reach agreement on precisely what to allow in our satellites, where to place our radar, or what missiles to ban, new evidence or new analysis comes along to suggest that the justification of the particular scheme we are about to subscribe to is all wrong.

Finally, by the time we look at individual schemes in sufficient detail to judge whether their strategic implications are "good" for both us and our enemies, we may have narrowed them down to the point where they are intolerably biased. It is probably a mathematically sound principle that the more measures we put in a package, the more their bilateral biases will cancel out, and hence the greater will be the joint gain relative to the competitive advantage. This may mean that once a potential arms-control system is dissected into sufficiently small pieces to apply the right kind of analysis, we shall have more individual bargaining counters too small and too biased for the negotiating process.

The recent negotiations on weapon tests may prove to be typical. First, there has been almost no public discussion of whether the further testing of weapons and weapon effects would really be conducive to the development of greater bilateral military stability or instability over the coming years.* Even if the public could be got interested in this crucial question, it would be unlikely to have the information it would need to judge the answer. (There has been a good deal of public discussion of the merits and possible demerits of preventing the further spread of nuclear weapons to small countries, but remarkably little discussion of just how a test ban would obstruct the spread.) Second, while it may seem a mischievous stroke of fortune that somebody discovered, between the two conferences, facts or ideas that made the policing of a test ban appear more difficult than it had appeared the year before, this may be exactly what we have to expect in every case. If today we had "completely solved" the new technical problems introduced by the "decoupling" technique, we should still have to be prepared for somebody's discovering next year a new possibility that had been overlooked, one that contemporary detection technology could not yet cope with.

The test-ban discussions also illustrate that, when an issue has been narrowed down, the bias in the advantages may seem to outweigh the joint advantages. There is more controversy, and understandably so, over whether a prohibition on small-weapon tests is in the American interest, than on whether a prohibition covering the whole spectrum is.

But of all the characteristics of the present test-ban negotiations, the most significant may be that we have had a moratorium for some time without a formal agreement. (We do not, of course, have rights of inspection; so we cannot be sure that the moratorium has been kept; but it

---

* That is, whether further testing would mainly facilitate the development of more secure retaliatory weapon systems with better communication and control, less subject to accident and false alarm, or instead would mainly enhance the potency of weapons for pre-emptive attack and aggravate the urge, when in doubt, to strike quickly and without restraint. The answer is by no means obvious for the period immediately ahead. It should be noted that tests involve not only new-weapon performance but weapon *effects* on previously untested targets, and the latter may be especially relevant to such things as anti-ICBM defense, civil defense, and the vulnerability of fixed or mobile weapons, warning systems, and communication and control systems.

likely has been, except possibly for the most easily disguised tests.) And this moratorium resulted from no detailed negotiations, no careful specifications, and no written documents to be initialed and ratified. I do not think this result can be wholly explained by the pressure of public opinion. Part of the motivation must be that, whatever one side is sacrificing in improved technology, the other side is also foregoing tests, and each would probably resume them if the other did. Thus the main sanction of an arms-control agreement—the expectation that each will abstain only if the other does—is probably present in this case. It is therefore a genuine instance of "arms control." If it suffers from being tentative, temporary, qualified, and conditional, so might any arms-control agreement, even if duly negotiated and signed; furthermore, who can say yet that the present "agreement," if such we may call it, will not be of some duration?

INFORMAL ARMS UNDERSTANDINGS

Here, I think we have an important clue to a process by which arms control may be reached, and the kinds of arms control that can be reached by that process. Maybe arms control is destined to be something more informal than is suggested by the great diplomatic deployments in Geneva. Maybe limited measures of arms control can be arrived at by quite indirect and incomplete communication; maybe they will take the form of a proposal embodied in unilateral action (or abstention from action) which continues if matched by corresponding action on the other side and only for so long as it is. Maybe instead of *arguing* about what we should do, we will simply do it and dare the other side to do likewise, or do it and quietly suggest that we would like to keep it up, but only if they find it in their interest to do something comparable.

But if arms control is to be arrived at by a more tacit and informal process, and if we are going to call "arms control" any of the military things that we and the Russians abstain from because of an awareness that as long as each abstains the other probably will too, we should look around and see whether we do not already have a good deal of arms control. If we have, we should look at it closely to see what lessons we can draw.

Offhand, it appears (but a more imaginative examination might prove otherwise) that the tacit understandings we have with the Russians concern what we do with our weapons more than what we possess.* We seem to have some understandings about traffic rules for patrolling bombers;

---

* A possible exception is civil defense. The extraordinary aversion to civil defense in the United States Government must be complex in its explanation; but an element is very likely a belief that a genuine civil defense program might open up a new dimension of the arms race, leading either to a "civil-defense race" with the USSR or just to an aggravation of the arms competition. The same may be true in the USSR. An interesting question is how much "clandestine" civil defense the Russians are undertaking, and their reasons for keeping it private. (In pointing this out, the author is not trying to justify the aversion to civil defense.)

there are apparently certain lines we stay on this side of, lines the Russians presumably can recognize, the crossing of which they can probably monitor to some extent. This is certainly a restraint that we unilaterally observe in the interest of reducing misunderstandings and alarms. As far as I know, the traffic rules are communicated, not explicitly, but simply by behaving in accordance with them (perhaps *conspicuously* in accordance with them) and possibly by having chosen the dividing lines in such a way that their significance is recognizable. We both abstain from harassing actions on each other's strategic forces; we do not jam each other's military communications, scare each other with fallout from weapons tests, or wage surreptitious peacetime undersea wars of attrition.* We may yet develop tacit understandings about zones and traffic rules for submarines, and may (or may not) develop a tradition for leaving each other's reconnaissance satellites alone. We both very obviously abstain from assassination. The Russians recently "negotiated" (by a process of nudging) a sharper understanding about sharing the Pacific for target practice. It remains to be seen whether the U-2 incident causes certain tacit or latent understandings to come unstuck.†

In all likelihood we may abstain from the use of nuclear weapons in some limited war, though both sides often seem to denounce officially the notion that a serious limited war should be, or could be, fought without nuclear weapons. Here is an interesting case of an arms limitation that may be tacitly recognized by both sides, and recognized only because each thinks the other may observe it too, yet one that is not only not formally agreed on but even denounced and denied by both sides. It seems doubtful whether this tacit understanding could be made much stronger by a written document.‡ A restraint on the use of nuclear weapons may be more persuasive if it seems to rest on the enemy's own self-interest—on his understanding that if he abstains we may too, but only if he does—than if it pretends to rest on the power of a written agreement or on a fiction of "good faith."

LIMITED WAR AS "ARMS CONTROL"

In fact, all of the tacitly agreed limits that do apply, or may apply, in limited war can be construed as a kind of informal arms control tacitly

* Not yet, that is, or not very much. Preserving some of the mutual restraints we now enjoy may be as important an "arms-control" objective as creating more.

† It seems a correct interpretation that there is still some element of implicit understanding about not transferring nuclear weapons to other countries. Its status is presently a great deal more ambiguous than the author expected a couple of years ago; nevertheless there must be a general awareness on both sides that the restraint of either will be weakened or dissolved by promiscuousness on the other's part.

‡ It could be made much stronger by various unilateral actions. One would be to increase our *capability* to get along without nuclears in limited war. Another would be to add symbolic support to the understanding; the test-ban negotiations—especially if a formal agreement is reached—almost certainly do this, whether they are intended to or not.

arrived at. My impression is that we and the Russians will go to some length to avoid having American and Russian troops directly engage each other in a limited war, simply because such an engagement might create extremely unstable expectations about whether the war could remain limited. We and the Russians both recognize many legalistic limitations in war, such as the distinction between North Koreans and Chinese, between volunteers and regulars, between the provision of materials to an ally and the provision of manpower, between doing an ally's reconnaissance for him and doing his bombing, perhaps even the distinction between local airfields that are fair game because they are on the ground within a disputed country and the decks of carriers offshore that might for some reason be construed as "sanctuary."

Most of these limits are arbitrary, conventional, and casuistic—purely matters of tradition and precedent. For that reason they are uncertain and insecure; nobody is even nominally committed to honor them. But they demonstrate that it is possible for potential enemies to arrive tacitly, or by indirect communication, at a meeting of minds about some rules, and about how to interpret intentions through the way one operates and deploys his resources. Most important, the limits that can be observed in limited war are a powerful demonstration that sheer self-interest—the recognition of a need to collaborate with an enemy in wartime, to reach understandings that transcend the formalities of explicit communications; the recognition of a mutual interest in avoiding accidents, incidents, misunderstandings, and unnecessary alarms, and in holding to any constraints that can be found—can provide potent sanctions that need not rest on explicit negotiation and formal agreements.

We may, then, increase our understanding of the nature of arms control, what it rests on and how it may come about, by recognizing limited war as a kind of arms control in itself. And perhaps it differs from peacetime (i.e., cold-war) arms control less than we customarily think. Perhaps the psychology and the sanctions and the mode of communication, the kinds of reasoning involved, the lack of formal agreement or even acknowledgment, that typify limited war, represent a more central and typical process of international negotiation than we usually give it credit for.

There is another aspect of limited war that deserves emphasis in this connection. The limits in limited war are arrived at not by verbal bargaining, but by maneuver, by actions, and by statements and declarations that are not direct communication to the enemy. Each side tends to act in some kind of recognizable pattern, so that any limits that it is actually observing can be appreciated by the enemy; and each tries to perceive what restraints the other is observing. For that reason the limits themselves must be clear-cut, must be of an "obvious" character, must be based on qualitative distinctions rather than matters of degree. They must not be too selective, too gerrymandered in discriminating between what is inside and what is outside the limit. They must attach themselves to benchmarks, demarcation lines, and distinctions that come naturally. They must have simplicity. They must take advantage of conventions and traditions and precedents that exist, even if the precedents and traditions are biased between the two sides or a nuisance to both sides. Often they must involve all-or-none distinctions, or across-the-board distinctions like that between land and water, between material and manpower, between two sides of a border, or even some arbitrary but potent and highly suggestive feature like a parallel of latitude.[2]

This is certainly true in the case of the use of nuclear weapons in limited war. It is enormously more likely that a limit against any use of nuclear weapons could be recognized, sensed, and adhered to by both sides on condition that each other observe it, than that any particular quantitative limitation, target limitation, fission vs. fusion limitation, or limitation based on who is the "aggressor," could be jointly and tacitly converged on by the participants.

But the same is certainly true of a test suspension. A tacitly reached moratorium on testing nuclear weapons—mutual and reciprocal but essentially unilateral on both sides—is much more likely to be stable and durable, much less likely to be eroded by ambiguous behavior, than a selective moratorium. If we and the Russians are very selective in our unilateral restraints, each choosing the particular yields, altitudes, fission-fusion combinations, and localities for tests, it seems unlikely either that both sides will hit on the same limitations and maintain them with confidence, or that both will hit on "equivalent" though different restraints.

To some extent, then, the gains and losses of a particular agreement, i.e., the way any particular understanding that is reached may discriminate between the two parties (or among more than two parties), are likely to be dictated somewhat by the elements of the problem, and not altogether by the detailed preferences of the parties to the understanding or their bargaining skill. An absolute ban on weapon tests, for example, or any other across-the-board prohibition, is somewhat arbitrary in the way it distributes the advantages; but perhaps some of its appeal is precisely in the fact that it is somewhat arbitrary, somewhat determined by chance or by the very structure of the problem, dictated by circumstances rather than by either side to the other.

COMMUNICATION AND UNDERSTANDING

If an important part of our arms control—or let us call it "mutual arms accommodation"—with our enemies is going to be tacit and informal, a matter of reciprocated unilateral actions and abstentions, we need to take seriously the problem of communicating with our enemies about what we are doing, and of reaching understandings with them. In some respects informal communication is easier, in some ways harder; the process is different from that of formal, explicit, detailed negotiation, and imposes different requirements. Informal communication is usually ambiguous; a government speaks by hint as well as by overt statement and proposal, it speaks indirectly through the medium of press conferences, leaks of information, and remarks to third parties. It speaks with many voices, in the executive branch, in the congress, and even in private articles and news stories that are "inspired" or are inferred to be so. And it speaks through the actions it takes.*

The differences should not be exaggerated; even when large teams of professional diplomats and technical experts are assembled in Geneva, much of the communication takes these other forms. Nevertheless, the strategy of communication is different, particularly because of the greater need in informal negotiations to reach a real understanding. In formal and explicit negotiation, what eventually matters is to a large extent what gets written down and agreed to; even if there was not a meeting of minds, there may have been a meeting of words that provides a record of the expectations of both sides and the obligations perceived. In informal negotiation the ultimate sanction depends less on a piece of paper than on the clarity of the understanding reached. If one behaves in a particular way, in anticipation of the other's reciprocation, there is a need to make clear precisely how one is behaving, with what mutual purpose in mind, so that the other can read the proposal in it, infer what would constitute reciprocation, and design its own behavior accordingly.

There is furthermore a greater need to be persuasive. In explicit negotiation, it may be possible to reach an agreement whose terms are reasonably well understood without agreement on principles or any reciprocal understanding of each other's motives. If the letter of the agreement is clear, the spirit can remain somewhat in doubt. In informal negotiation, the spirit bears most of the burden; and if the *idea* behind what we think we are doing is not perceived by our partner (enemy), what we expect of him—or what we may reasonably be expected to expect of him—may be too dimly perceived to be the basis for genuine reciprocation.

Suppose we decide to put more emphasis on ballistic-missile submarines, for example, in the belief that they are peculiarly "stable" weapons because of their lesser susceptibility to destruction in case of a surprise attack and because they are not so much under obligation to strike quickly in the event of an ambiguous warning (or war itself), or else because their smaller warheads, with possibly a lesser degree of accuracy as compared with ground-based missiles, make them less of a threat to the enemy's retaliatory forces and more of a genuine deterrent. Suppose we decide that we could afford to do this only if the enemy himself oriented his own strategic program toward similarly "stable" weapon systems. It might not be at all clear to the Russians what our motives are, or what the conditions were for our going through with the program. Or suppose we have

---

* In a sense, the abortive summit conference of May 1960 did not involve less "negotiation" just because the meeting never took place.

a crash program for the development of a more secure ground-based missile force, this program to be financed by a sharp increase in the defense budget, with a good deal of expenditure on command, control, and communication arrangements so as to reduce both the vulnerability of our weapons and their sensitivity to accident or false alarm. In particular, suppose that our budget rises because of increased outlays associated with our desire for a *slow* reacting force, rather than one that must react rapidly. In such circumstances, our actions may be stabilizing or destabilizing, depending on whether the enemy can perceive that we are making the world safer for him rather than increasing his need (and ours) to jump the gun in a crisis. If we institute an airborne alert, it may be important to do so in a way that enhances the apparent as well as the real security and stability of our retaliatory weapon systems. This might mean that we would have to choose deliberately, say, flight patterns that manifestly enhance the security of our forces rather than the speed with which they could initiate a surprise attack of their own.

By far the most important prerequisite is that we understand our own motives well enough to take actions that are consistent with a deterrent philosophy, and well enough so that we can articulate it to ourselves. If we have such a philosophy, and if our actions are consistent with it, and if for our own purposes we articulate that philosophy in explaining our budget decisions here at home, we are probably well on the way to conveying that philosophy persuasively to our enemy, if he is at all receptive. A special problem here is that our overt position on disarmament must not be too inconsistent with the philosophy that we are trying to display and get across to our enemy. If, for example, we really believed in a policy of collaborating with the Russians to develop a stable situation of mutual deterrence, and if we determined to make important changes, to this end, in the configuration of our weapons but these changes were not in the direction of general disarmament, we would put a double burden on our communication if the front we presented on arms-control questions bore no relation to that philosophy. This does not necessarily mean that we have to speak in our formal disarmament diplomacy in a manner that is sincere and consistent with what we are fundamentally trying to get across to the Russians. It may just mean that our insincerity should be as manifest as the inconsistency, so that when we do contradict ourselves the Russians know that this is for show and that they should look for the real message elsewhere. Still, it would help if we could find the diplomatic courage to shift even the formal discussions of arms control more into accord with our basic military policy, at the same time as we try to adapt that military policy in directions that the Russians can appreciate and reciprocate, so that disarmament negotiations can help a little, or at least hinder as little as possible, the development of a genuine understanding.

Even so, it is still an unanswered question whether the Russians are at all disposed to participate in any "mutual arms accommodation" with us, beyond what we already do in a tacit way. And it is a difficult technical question whether, even if they are disposed to cooperate with us and appreciate the principle of stable retaliatory systems with minimum proclivity toward false alarm and minimum temptation toward surprise attack, there are any promising actions to be undertaken. Weapon systems can rarely be classified indisputably as first-strike or second-strike weapons, as "accident-prone" or "accident-proof"; a good deal of technical analysis has to lie behind a judgment, many of the technical judgments may not be made equally by us and our enemies, the judgment has to be made in the context of an evolving weapon system for which facts are really only forecasts, and what is known today may no longer be true tomorrow. It is, furthermore, too much to expect the massive bureaucracy of our defense establishment and our foreign service, and the partisan conflicts in Congress, to produce and maintain a coherent philosophy and transmit it with high fidelity to a suspicious enemy whose receptivity and reasoning processes we can only poorly evaluate. But it is worth trying.

RECIPROCATED DEVELOPMENT OF STABLE ARMAMENTS

One possibility, already adverted to, is to design our military forces conspicuously and deliberately in the direction of deterrence, stability, and slow reaction. That is, to articulate as a policy the design of a strategic force that is peculiarly good at waiting out crises, at surviving a surprise attack, and at punishing an attacker *ex post facto,* and not particularly good at initiating a preventive attack, not in need of responding rapidly to warning.

This may not be a bad policy to follow unilaterally; but the advantage of pursuing it is greater if the enemy pursues it too. The more each side perceives the other as designing his force for a sudden pre-emptive attack in a crisis, or for a premeditated surprise attack, the more one is tempted himself to develop a quick-reacting system, one that is peculiarly suited to catching the enemy's military forces before they have left the ground. Thus to some extent such a policy is a conditional policy; the motive is greater if the principle is reciprocated by the enemy.

It would be extraordinarily difficult, perhaps impossible, to negotiate a detailed understanding of precisely what kinds of weapons in what configurations, and how deployed, would meet the "stability" criterion. For that reason the idea may not be one that lends itself to explicit detailed negotiated agreements. But that does not rule out the possibility that both sides may perceive value in pursuing such policies in a general way, and may recognize that their own behavior not only helps the other side pursue a similar policy but helps to induce it by the tacit promise of reciprocation. As mentioned above, we already do this in such matters as the traffic rules we both unilaterally observe and reciprocate; there may be a good deal of room for gradually extending this kind of reciprocal unilateral action, even though the subject may never appear on the agenda of a diplomatic negotiation.

Compared with a *peaceful* world disarmed, schemes to stabilize mutual deterrence are a poor second best; judged against the prospect of war, measures to make it less likely may be attractive. This point of view will not appeal to any who believe that war results from the sheer existence of arms and the temptation to use them, or from the influence of militarists in modern society whose prestige increases in proportion to the arms budget, and who believe that distrust is only aggravated by people's acting as though distrust exists. History shows, it is said, that man cannot live in a world with arms without using them. History rarely shows anything quite that universal; but even granting it, the question is not whether it is asking much of man to learn to live in a world with arms and not to use them excessively. The question is whether it takes more skill and wisdom for man to learn to live in a world with arms and not to use them than it does for man to disarm himself so totally that he can't have war even if he wants it (or can't want it any longer). If modern social institutions are capable of achieving disarmament in the first place, and of avoiding arms races in perpetuity thereafter, perhaps they are capable of supporting a world with arms without war. Those who argue that peace with arms is impossible but act as though peace and disarmament are not, may be using a double standard.

And it must be remembered that total disarmament, even if achieved, does not by itself preclude subsequent arms races; nor does a good start toward total disarmament preclude a violent reversal. To the extent that an arms advantage is more easily obtained when the level of armaments on both sides is low—to the extent that the consequences of cheating are greater in a world with few arms—arms races might become more violent, the lower the level of armament from which they start. Particularly in a world in which the pace of scientific progress is rapid but jerky, uneven as between countries, and full of opportunities and uncertainties for weapons development, it is not at all clear that the world would be less uneasy about arms advantages if each side continually thought of itself as nearly naked. What can explain the complacency of the American response to the first Soviet sputnik except a feeling (superbly rationalized) that the existing level of arms provided so much security that no single new achievement, or even a revision of the comparative time schedules by a year or two, could quite upset the balance.

EXCHANGE OF STABILIZING INFORMATION

Another area of possible cooperation is in damping the arms race through the exchange of information. I am not much impressed with the budgetary fury of our participation in the arms race, but it is not hard to imagine that the budgetary arms race might get into much higher gear. If it does, part of the motivation (at least in this country) may be due to uncertainty about the level of armament on the other side. The "missile gap" that one estimates, or feels obliged to assume to exist in the absence of information, may exceed the actual missile gap, causing a more frantic increase in armaments than would be undertaken with better information. And it may induce reciprocal action on the other side, which also wishes to avoid an intolerably unfavorable imbalance.

To illustrate: suppose that either side felt reasonably secure against sudden attack as long as its enemy's numerical superiority in missiles never reached, say, 2:1. In this case, just knowing what the other possesses and is producing could make possible a stable equilibrium at a modest level of strategic armaments, while ignorance of the enemy's strength might seem to require an unlimited effort to avoid falling too far behind. With actual weapons such simple calculations are of course impossible; but the principle is valid.

An important difficulty of applying it, though, is that the ways by which one can get authentic information about the other's present and projected strength may provide more strategic information than the other side can tolerate.* A special difficulty is that the Soviets may already know most of what they need to know for this purpose; it is mainly we who do not.

But it is interesting that they might possibly prefer that we know the truth. If in fact we are on the verge of a crash program based on an exaggerated estimate of what they have already done, it could cost them money (and perhaps an increase in the risk of war) to keep up with us. It is also interesting that the truth is probably not something that they could readily reveal on their own. They have to find some way of giving us evidence for believing the truth (or a less exaggerated estimate of the truth) and give it in a way that does not yield targeting and other information that they would find intolerable. The fact that this intelligence gap is mainly on our side does not preclude Soviet interest in some means of conveying the information to us, and it does not obviate the need for cooperative techniques for receiving it.

MEASURES FOR REASSURANCE ON THE BRINK OF WAR

Measures to prevent "accidental war," war by misunderstanding, war by false alarm, are another possibility. One aspect of this has been mentioned: the reciprocal development of the kinds of forces and modes of behavior that minimize accidents or their consequences, minimize alarms and misunderstandings, minimize the need to react quickly in the face of ambiguous evidence. But there is another type of joint or reciprocal activity that could

---

* Also, one side yields a bluffing or bargaining advantage if it reveals that its weaponry is less impressive than may have been thought. It loses, too, the possibility of surreptitiously achieving a dominant superiority. But losses of this kind are the price of arms control in the first place.

help. It would be to arrange in advance, even if crudely and informally, communication procedures, exchange of information, and inspection facilities, for use in the event of an accident, alarm, or misunderstanding that created a crisis. Part of this is just procedural—making sure that we and the Russians have the same idea about who gets in touch with whom when communication or bargaining is suddenly required. Part of it is intellectual—thinking ahead of time about how one would go about reassuring the Russians in the event they had a false alarm, and what we could demand of them for our own reassurance if we ever got ambiguous evidence. Part of it is physical—making sure that, if we should need inspectors on a particular scene within a few hours to verify that something was an accident, or to verify that the Russians were calm, or to verify that the Russians were not taking actions we thought they were taking, the necessary inspectors and equipment would be available within a few hours' travel time from where we would need them. Just having some Russians available at strategic points around the United States, able to see things with their own eyes if we suddenly wanted them to and able to report home instantly through authentic channels, might be useful someday. And if we ever want them, we may want them in a hurry; there may not be time to identify them, brief them, ship them over there, and train them for their job, once the accident occurs or the crisis is on or the misinformation filters through the Russian warning system.[3]

"CRASH" ARMS CONTROL

There is a more ambitious possibility. Neither we nor the Russians at the present time take arms control terribly seriously; we do not view it as an alternative to a war that is imminent. But it is not difficult to imagine crises in which the likelihood of immediate war would become a grave preoccupation. Once the threat of imminent war rises above some threshold, the mere consciousness that each side is preoccupied with it—and with the importance of being the one to start it, if it should come—will aggravate the propensities that already exist. It is perfectly conceivable that in a real crisis there would be a sudden and drastic change in the attitudes of both sides toward arms control. "Preventive arms control" might begin to look like a risky but attractive alternative to a possibly inevitable pre-emptive war. Sudden and drastic "measures to safeguard against surprise attack" might have to be negotiated on an acutely demanding time schedule.

If so, success may depend on whether one or both sides is intellectually prepared for the contingency, whether some understandings have been reached in advance, and whether certain facilities can be improvised to monitor whatever arrangements might be forthcoming. One of the important "limited" arms-control measures that we might take in advance of such a crisis, either by ourselves or with our enemies, either informally or explicitly, is a development of understandings, procedures, personnel, and equipment, of an imaginative and adaptable sort, capable of going into action at such time as we and the Russians both decide that now is the time for arms control and we can't wait.

ARMS CONTROL IN GENERAL WAR

A final possibility, a pessimistic but a serious one and one suggested by the analogy between arms control and limited war, is the role of arms control in general war if general war occurs. We usually think of arms control or deterrence as having failed if war breaks out; and so it has, but it can fail worse if we give up at that point. It is not entirely clear that a general war—a war between the USA and the USSR, involving their strategic forces on a large scale—would necessarily be unlimited either in the way it would be fought or in the way it would be concluded. Particularly as we come to think about an inadvertent war—one that results by some kind of accident or misunderstanding, or one that is reluctantly initiated by the Russians or by us in the belief that it is urgent to pre-empt at once —it is worthwhile to consider whether fury is the only guide we need in conducting the war, and whether the exhaustion of weapons on both sides is the only condition for terminating it.

It is commonly taken for granted that if the Russians initiate a general war it would be in a vicious effort to exterminate us both as a nation and as a people, and that they would be so impatient to do this as to spend valuable weapons to create civil damage at the outset. But it is not obvious that a coldly calculating enemy would afford himself the luxury of going after cities and people when there are more urgent targets that he has to destroy in order to reduce the scale of our retaliation. Nor is it obvious that an impetuous attacker, one whose motivation is partly the fear that if he does not strike first he will be second, would be immune to the thought that he might want to surrender if the thing went badly, to accept our surrender if it went well, or to negotiate a truce between those extremes. If there is no immediate strategic need to kill our people, it may occur to him that they are worth more alive than dead; the threat of killing them gives him something to bargain with in the course of the war or at its termination. Similarly for us: if the war was a mistake we might be more interested in minimizing the consequences of the error, whosever error it was, and in maintaining the possibility of a negotiated outcome that limited damage on both sides. For this bargaining purpose, live Russians and our unspent weapons are assets, and about the only ones we'd have.

The subject is a complicated one and cannot be decided here. It has to be acknowledged that there are dangers in suggesting to the Russians that we are even aware of the possibility that an attack on us might not be cataclysmic for us both. But the possibility is so universally unmentioned and so terribly important that it deserves to be brought into the open for study. Its relation to arms control is that the mere possibility of limiting a general war between us and our principal enemy may depend on some understanding, tacit and informal as it may be, that we share ahead of time. There may be little national advantage in abstaining from certain targets in the event of war, or in attempting to communicate, unless the enemy can be alert to what is going on.

TERMINATING WAR BY ARMS CONTROL

Terminating a war through anything other than the sheer exhaustion of weapons on both sides would require some form of arms control. It is a noteworthy characteristic of a possible World War III that even unconditional surrender may be physically impossible. How do the Russians persuade us that they have destroyed (or are prepared to destroy or deliver us) some or all of their significant weapons and are prepared to submit to our political demands? We cannot even trust them not to test weapons under a test-suspension agreement; in circumstances infinitely more desperate, when a one-hour pause in the war may be of strategic benefit to somebody, if they send us an urgent message acknowledging their guilt in the war and proposing that we preserve our world by letting them surrender to us, are we likely to be able to do anything? If they are fooling, and if we are fooled, the cost will be tremendous; if they are not fooling and we choose to ignore them, the cost will be tremendous. Can we think of what they might do to prove that they mean it? Have we got the facilities to monitor them and to police them? Have we incorporated in our strategic forces, and in the operating doctrine of those forces, recognition of their potential role in policing the disarmament by which the war might be brought to a close?

Actually "surrender" is a poor word here. Anywhere between the two extremes of unconditional surrender by one side or the other, the truce or understanding or scheme for bringing the war to a close might better be described as "disarmament" or "arms control." Historically one might have allowed an enemy, when he "conditionally" surrendered, to keep some purely defensive weapons as a hedge against the victor's violating his promise. This is a kind of asymmetrical disarmament scheme. In the future, at the close of a general war, one might have to allow the conditionally surrendering enemy to retain some retaliatory weapons, these being the only kind that two major powers can use to enforce promises from each other. In effect, "measures to safeguard against surprise attack," possibly one-sided, possibly bilateral, and certainly more drastic than any that have yet been considered, might be the minimum requirement of a conditionally surrendering enemy.

Thus anywhere between the two extremes of total surrender, the outcome should be viewed as a disarmament process, with the asymmetry presumably reflecting the degree of victory or defeat. But as remarked above, even the extremes of unconditional surrender require much the same kind of procedure for mutual relaxation, cessation of hostilities, inspection, enforcement, and so forth. Any general war that is terminated by a bilateral understanding, by anything other than the independent exhaustion of weapons on both sides, requires something in the nature of an enormous, complex, and dynamic scheme for arms control.

If this possibility is to be left open, we need to anticipate it in the design of our strategic forces and in our plans for their use. It may require special facilities and equipment to bring a war to a close, of a kind not necessarily provided for in a plan that considers only the contingency of an all-out war to the finish. But it also requires some mutual awareness ahead of time, on the part of both our enemy and ourselves, and perhaps some crude and tacit, if not careful and explicit, understanding about the modes and techniques of negotiation in the event of war.

References

1. See T. C. Schelling, "Surprise Attack and Disarmament," in Klaus Knorr (ed.), *NATO and American Security* (Princeton: Princeton University Press, 1959), or the shorter version in T. C. Schelling, *The Strategy of Conflict* (Cambridge: Harvard University Press, 1960), chap. 10.

2. For an extensive study of tacit bargaining, with special reference to limited war, see T. C. Schelling, *The Strategy of Conflict* (Cambridge: Harvard University Press, 1960), chaps. 3 and 4 and Appendix A.

3. A more extensive discussion of this point appears in T. C. Schelling, "Arms Control: Proposal for a Special Surveillance Force," *World Politics*, October 1960.

The Case for Unilateral Disarmament

ERICH FROMM

THERE IS LITTLE DOUBT THAT THE PROPOSAL FOR A UNILATERAL DISARMA-
ment—in the broad sense of the unconditional dismantling of a country's
military establishment—will be acceptable neither to the United States nor
to the Soviet Union in the immediate future. Hence, inasmuch as this
chapter is concerned with *practical* suggestions for arms control, it proposes another and very limited concept of unilateral disarmament, one
which has been called by Charles Osgood *"graduated unilateral action (or
disengagement)"* or which might be called *unilateral initiative in taking
practical steps toward disarmament.* The basic idea underlying this concept is that of a radical change of our method of negotiating multilateral
disarmament. This change implies that we give up the present method of
bargaining in which every concession we make is dependent on a corresponding and guaranteed concession on the part of the Russians; that, instead, we take, unilaterally, gradual steps toward disarmament in the
expectation that the Russians will reciprocate and that, thus, the present
deadlock in the negotiations for universal disarmament can be broken
through.

In order to describe the nature of this policy of unilateral steps, I cannot improve on the following description by Osgood, who, as far as I know,
was the first one to express this idea in two brilliant and profound articles.[1]
"To be maximally effective," he writes, "in inducing the enemy to reciprocate, a unilateral act (1) should, in terms of *military aggression,* be clearly
disadvantageous to the side making it, yet not cripplingly so; (2) should be
such as to be clearly perceived by the enemy as reducing his external
threat; (3) should not increase the enemy's threat to our heartland;[2] (4)
should be such that reciprocal action by the enemy is clearly available and
clearly indicated; (5) should be announced in advance and widely publicized to ally, neutral, and enemy countries—as regards the nature of the
act, its purpose as part of a consistent policy, and the expected reciprocation; but (6) should not demand prior commitment to reciprocation by
the enemy as a condition for its commission."[3]

As to the specific steps which should be taken in this fashion, it would
require a great deal of further thought, aided by competent specialists. But

in order to give at least an idea of the concrete steps this policy would envisage, I want to mention the following (some of them in agreement with Osgood): sharing of scientific information; stopping of atomic tests; troop reductions; evacuation of one or more military bases; discontinuation of German rearmament; etc. The expectation is that the Russians are as willing as we are to avoid war, hence that they will begin to reciprocate and that once the course of mutual suspicion has been reversed, bigger steps can be taken which may lead to complete bilateral disarmament. Furthermore, I believe that disarmament negotiations should be paralleled by *political* negotiations, which aim essentially at mutual noninterference on the basis of the recognition of the *status quo*. Here, too (and again in essential agreement with Osgood's position), unilateral steps such as the recognition of the Oder-Neisse line and admission of China to the United Nations would be taken in the expectation of reciprocation by the Russians (i.e., curbing of Chinese aggression, noninterference in the Middle and Far East).

What are the premises underlying the proposition for unilateral steps toward disarmament? (At this point I shall mention only some fundamental ones, while others will be discussed in the second part of this chapter which presents the argument for total unilateral disarmament.) They are briefly: (1) that, as indicated before, the present method of negotiations does not seem to lead to the goal of bilateral disarmament because of the deeply ingrained mutual suspicions and fears; (2) that without achieving *complete* disarmament, the armament race will continue and lead to the destruction of our civilization as well as that of the Russians or, even without the outbreak of a war, will slowly undermine and eventually destroy the values in defense of which we are risking our physical existence; (3) that while unilateral steps constitute a definite risk (and must do so by the very nature of the idea), the risk at every step is not a crippling one and is infinitely smaller than the danger we run by the continuation of the arms race.

Even though the broader concept of complete—rather than graduated —unilateral disarmament is, as stated before, not a practical possibility in the near future, as far as the United States and the USSR are concerned, I believe it worthwhile to present the arguments for this position, not primarily because the editor of this volume asked me to present this position nor even because I share it with a small minority of others who believe that the risks in the continuation of the armament race are far greater than the very serious risks of unilateral disarmament. While both reasons might not be sufficient to justify the following presentation, I do believe that it is not only justified but important for another reason: thinking through the arguments for a radical—even though practically unacceptable— position contributes to breaking through the thought barrier which prevents us now from getting out of the dangerous circle of seeking peace by means of threat and counterthreat. Taking seriously the reasoning which supports the unpopular position of complete unilateral disarmament can open up new approaches and viewpoints which are important even if our practical aim is that of graduated unilateral action or even only that of negotiated bilateral disarmament. I believe that the difficulty of arriving at complete disarmament lies to a large extent in the frozen stereotypes of feelings and thought habits on both sides and that any attempt at unfreezing these patterns and of rethinking the whole problem can be of importance in finding a way out of the present dangerous impasse.

The proposal for complete unilateral disarmament has been advocated from a religious, moral, or pacifist position by such men as Victor Gollancz, Lewis Mumford, and some Quakers. It has also been supported by men like Bertrand Russell, Stephen King-Hall, and C. W. Mills, who are not opposed to the use of force under all or any circumstances, yet who are uncompromisingly opposed both to thermonuclear war and to all and any preparation for it. This writer finds himself somewhat between the position of the strict pacifists and men like Bertrand Russell and Stephen King-Hall.[4]

The difference between these two groups, however, is not as fundamental as it may seem. They are united by their critical attitude toward the irrational aspects of international politics and by their deep reverence for life. They share the conviction of the oneness of the human race and faith in the spiritual and intellectual potentialities of man. They follow the dictates of their conscience in refusing to have any "part in making millions of women and children and noncombatants hostages for the behavior of their own governments."[5] Whether they think in theistic terms or in those of nontheistic humanism (in the sense of the philosophic continuum from Stoic to eighteenth-century Enlightenment philosophy), they all are rooted in the same spiritual tradition and are unwilling to compromise with its principles. They are united by their uncompromising opposition to any kind of idolatry, including the idolatry of the state. While their opposition to the Soviet system is rooted precisely in this attitude against idolatry, they are critical of idolatry whenever it appears in the Western world whether it is in the name of God or of democracy.

While there is no proponent of unilateral disarmament who does not believe that the individual must be willing to give his life for the sake of his supreme values, if such an ultimate necessity arises, they are all equally convinced that to risk the life of the human race, or even the results of its best efforts in the last five thousand years, is immoral and irresponsible. As warfare becomes at once more senseless and more devastating, the convergence between religious pacifist, humanist, and pragmatic opponents to nuclear armament grows.

From the standpoint of the proponents of unilateral disarmament, to continue the armament race is catastrophic, *whether the deterrent works or not.* In the first place, they have little faith that the deterrent will prevent the outbreak of a thermonuclear war.[6] They believe that the results of a thermonuclear war would be such that in the very "best" case they completely belie the idea that we ought to fight such a war in order to save our democratic way of life. There is no need to enter the guessing game as to whether one-third or two-thirds of the population of the two opponents and what proportion of the neutral world (depending on how the wind blows) will be destroyed. This is a guessing game that verges on madness; for to consider the possibility of the destruction of 30%, 60%, or 90% of one's own and the enemy's population as an acceptable (although, of course, most undesirable) result of one's policy is indeed approaching pathology. The increasing split between intellect and affect, which is so characteristic of our Western development in the last centuries, has reached its dangerous, schizoid peak in the calm and allegedly rational way in which we can discuss possible world destruction as a result of our own action. It does not take much imagination to visualize that sudden destruction and the threat of slow death to a large part of the American population, or the Russian population, or large parts of the world, will create such a panic, fury, and despair as could only be compared with the mass psychosis resulting from the Black Death in the Middle Ages. The traumatic effects of such a catastrophe would lead to a new form of primitive barbarism, to the resurgence of the most archaic elements, which are still potentialities in every man and of which we have had ample evidence in the terror systems of Hitler and Stalin. It would sound most unlikely to many students of human nature and psychopathology that human beings could cherish freedom, respect for life, or love after having witnessed and participated in the unlimited cruelty of man against man which thermonuclear war would mean. It is a psychological fact that acts of brutality have a brutalizing effect on the participants and lead to more brutality.[7]

BUT WHAT IF THE DETERRENT WORKS?

What is the likely future of the social character of man in a bilateral or multilateral armed world, where, no matter how complex the problems or how full the satisfactions of any particular society, the biggest and most pervasive reality in any man's life is the poised missile, the humming data processor connected to it, the waiting radiation counters and seismographs, the over-all technocratic perfection (overlying the nagging but impotent fear of its imperfection) of the mechanism of holocaust? To live for any length of time under the constant threat of destruction creates certain psychological effects in most human beings—fright, hostility, callousness, a hardening of the heart, and a resulting indifference to all the values we cherish. Such conditions will transform us into barbarians—though barbarians equipped with the most complicated machines. If we are serious in claiming that our aim is to preserve freedom (that is, to prevent the subordination of the individual under an all-powerful state), we must admit that this freedom will be lost, whether the deterrent works or does not work.

Aside from these psychological facts, the continuation of the arms race constitutes a particular threat to Western culture. In the process of conquering nature, producing and consuming have become Western man's main preoccupation—the goal of his life. We have transformed means into ends. We manufacture machines which are like men, and we produce men who are like machines. In his work, the individual is managed as a part of a production team. During his leisure time, he is manipulated as a consumer who likes what he is told to like and yet has the illusion that he follows his own taste. In centering his life around the production of things, man himself is in danger of becoming a thing, worshiping the idols of the production machine and the state while he is under the illusion of worshiping God. "Things are in the saddle and ride mankind," as Emerson has put it. Circumstances which we created have consolidated themselves into powers which rule over us. The technical and bureaucratic system we have built tells us what to do, it decides for us. We may not be in danger of becoming slaves, but we are in danger of becoming robots, and the human values of our tradition are threatened—integrity, individuality, responsibility, reason, and love. Talking about these values more and more becomes an empty ritual.

This trend toward a world of impotent men directed by virile machines (both in the United States and in the Soviet Union)—brought about by technological and demographic factors, and by the increasing centralization and bureaucracy in big corporations and government—will reach the point of no return if we continue the arms race. Dangerous as our present situation is, we still have a chance to put man back into the saddle, to effect a renaissance of the spiritual values of the great humanistic tradition. Unless such a renaissance occurs, unless we can achieve a radical revitalization of the spirit on which our culture is founded, we shall lose the vitality necessary for survival and we shall decay, just as many other great powers have decayed in history. The real threat to our existence is not Communist ideology, it is not even the Communist military power—it is the hollowness of our beliefs, the fact that freedom, individuality, and faith have become empty formulas, that God has become an idol, that our vitality is sapped because we have no vision except that of having more of the same. It seems that a great deal of the hatred of Communism is, in the last analysis, based on a deep disbelief in the spiritual values of democracy. Hence, instead of experiencing love of what we are *for,* we experience hate of what we are *against.* If we continue to live in fear of extinction and to plan mass destruction of others, the last chance for a revival of our humanist-spiritual tradition will be lost.

BENEFITS AND DANGERS OF UNILATERAL DISARMAMENT

If these are the dangers of the policy of the deterrent, what do the proponents of unilateral disarmament consider to be the benefits—and the dangers—of their policy?

The most likely result of unilateral disarmament—whether it be undertaken by the United States or by the Soviet Union—is that it would prevent war. The main reason which could impel either the Soviet Union or the United States to atomic war is the constant fear of being attacked and pulverized by the opponent. This position is succinctly expressed by Herman Kahn, who is in no way a proponent of unilateral disarmament. Kahn states that, "aside from the ideological differences and the problem of security itself, there does not seem to be any objective quarrel between the United States and Russia that justifies the risks and costs that we subject each other to. The big thing that the Soviet Union and the United States have to fear from each other is fear itself."[8] If, indeed, the main cause of war lies in mutual fear, then the disarmament of either the Soviet Union or the United States would most likely do away with this major cause and, thus, with the probability of war.

But are there motives other than fear which could prompt the Soviet Union to try for world conquest? One such motive could be economic interest in expansion, which was a basic motivation for the initiation of war in the nineteenth century and also for the first two World Wars. Exactly here we see the difference between the nature of the conflicts in 1914 or 1939 and the present situation. In World War I, Germany threatened British markets and the French sources of coal and iron; in 1939, Hitler needed territorial conquest for the economic expansion he wanted. Today, neither the Soviet Union nor the United States has overriding economic interests in the conquest of markets and supplies, since a 2 or 3 percent rise in the level of national productivity would bring a greater advantage than would any military conquest, and, moreover, each has the capital, raw material, supplies, and population for a constant increase in its general productivity.[9]

The more serious possible motive is found in the fear, widely held in the United States, that the Soviet Union is out to conquer the world for Communism and that, if the United States disarmed, Russia would be all the more eager to achieve her wish for world domination. This idea of Russian intentions is based on an erroneous appreciation of the nature of the present-day Soviet Union. It is true that under Lenin and Trotzky the Russian Revolution was aimed at conquering the capitalistic world (or at least, Europe) for Communism, partly because the Communist leaders were convinced that there was no possibility of success for Communist Russia unless the highly industrialized states of Europe (or at least Germany) joined their system, and partly because they were prompted by the belief that the victory of the Communist revolution in the world would bring about the fulfillment of their secular-messianic hopes.

The failure of these hopes and the ensuing victory of Stalin brought about a complete change in the nature of Soviet Communism. The annihilation of almost all the old Bolsheviks was only a symbolic act for the destruction of the old revolutionary idea. Stalin's slogan of "socialism in one country" covered one simple aim—the rapid industrialization of Russia, which the Czarist system had not accomplished. Russia repeated the same process of accumulating capital which Western capitalism had gone through in the eighteenth and nineteenth centuries. The essential difference is that, while in these centuries in the West the sanctions were purely economic, the Stalinist system now developed political sanctions of direct terror; in addition, it employed socialist ideology to sugar-coat the exploitation of the masses. The Stalinist system was neither a socialist nor a revolutionary system, but a state-capitalism based on ruthless methods of planning and economic centralization.

The period of Khrushchevism is characterized by the fact that capital accumulation has succeeded to a point where the population can enjoy a great deal more consumption and is less forced to make sacrifices; as a result, the political terror can be greatly reduced.

But Khrushchevism has by no means changed the basic character of Soviet society in one essential respect: it is not a revolutionary nor a socialist regime, but one of the most conservative, class-ridden regimes anywhere in the Western world, humanly coercive, economically effective. While the aim of democratic socialism was the emancipation of man, the overcoming of his alienation, and the eventual abolition of the state, the "socialist" slogans used in Soviet Russia reflect empty ideologies, and the social reality is the very opposite of true socialism. The ruling class of the Soviet Union is no more revolutionary than the Renaissance popes were followers of the teachings of Christ. To try to explain Khrushchev by quoting Marx, Lenin, or Trotzky shows an utter failure to understand the historical development which has taken place in the Soviet Union and an incapacity to appreciate the difference between facts and ideologies. It should be added that our attitude is the best propaganda service the Russians could wish for. Against the facts, they try to convince the workers of Western Europe and the peasants in Asia that they represent the ideas of socialism, of a classless society, etc. The Western attitude, of falling for this propaganda, does exactly what the Russians want: to confirm these claims. (Unfortunately very few people except democratic socialists have sufficient knowledge of the difference between socialism and its distorted and corrupt form which calls itself Soviet socialism.)

The role of Russia is still more emphasized by the fact that Russia feels threatened by a potentially expansionist China. Russia one day might be in the same position with regard to China as we believe we are in relation to Russia. If the threat to Russia from the United States were to disappear, Russia could devote her energy to coping with the threat from China, unless by universal disarmament this threat would cease to exist.

The above-mentioned considerations indicate that the dangers which might arise if the Soviet Union were not to give up its armaments are more remote than they seem to many. Would the Soviet Union use her military superiority to try to occupy the United States or Western Europe? Aside from the fact that it would be exceedingly difficult, to say the least, for the Soviet Union's agents to run the economic and political machines of the United States or Western Europe, and aside from the fact that there is no vital need for Russia to conquer these territories, it would be most inconvenient to try to do so—and for a reason which is generally not sufficiently appreciated. Even the pro-Communist workers in the West have no idea of the degree of coercion to which they would have to submit under a Soviet system. They, as well as non-Communist workers, would oppose the new authorities, who would be forced to use tanks and machine guns against the protesting workers. This would encourage revolutionary tendencies in the satellite states, or even within the Soviet Union, and be most undesirable to the Soviet rulers; it would especially endanger Khrushchev's policy of liberalization, and hence his whole political position.

Eventually the Soviet Union might try to exploit its military superiority for the penetration of Asia and Africa. This is possible, but, with our present policy of the deterrent, it is doubtful whether the United States would really be willing to start a thermonuclear war in order to prevent the Russians from gaining certain advantages in the world outside of Europe and the Americas.

All these assumptions may be wrong. The position of the proponents of unilateral disarmament is that the chance that they are wrong is much smaller than the chance that the continuation of the arms race will finish civilization as we cherish it.

SOME PSYCHOLOGICAL CONSIDERATIONS

One cannot discuss the question of what might happen as a result of unilateral disarmament—or, for that matter, of any mutual disarmament—without examining some psychological arguments. The most popular one is that "the Russians cannot be trusted." If "trust" is meant in a moral sense, it is unfortunately true that political leaders can rarely be trusted. The reason lies in the split between private and public morals: the state, having become an idol, justifies any immorality if committed in its interest, while the very same political leaders would not commit the same acts if they were acting in behalf of their own private interests. However, there is another meaning to "trust in people," a meaning which is much more relevant to the problem of politics: the trust that they are sane and rational beings, and that they will act accordingly. If I deal with an opponent in whose sanity I trust, I can appreciate his motivations and to some extent predict them, because there are certain rules and aims, like that of survival or that of commensurateness between aims and means, which are common to all sane people. Hitler could not be trusted because he was lacking in sanity, and this very lack destroyed both him and his regime. It seems quite clear that the Russian leaders of today are sane and rational people; therefore, it is important not only to know what they are capable of, but also to predict what they might be motivated to do.[10]

This question of the leaders' and the people's sanity leads to another consideration which affects us as much as it does the Russians. In the current discussion on armament control, many arguments are based on the question of what is *possible,* rather than on what is *probable.* The difference between these two modes of thinking is precisely the difference between *paranoid* and *sane* thinking. The paranoiac's unshakable conviction in the validity of his delusion rests upon the fact that it is logically possible, and, so, unassailable. It is logically possible that his wife, children, and colleagues hate him and are conspiring to kill him. The patient cannot be convinced that his delusion is *impossible;* he can only be told that it is exceedingly *unlikely.* While the latter position requires an examination and evaluation of the facts and also a certain amount of faith in life, the paranoid position can satisfy itself with the possibility alone. I submit that our political thinking suffers from such paranoid trends. We should be concerned, not with the possibilities, but rather with the probabilities. This is the only sane and realistic way of conducting the affairs of national as well as of individual life.

Again on the psychological plane, there are certain misunderstandings of the radical disarmament position which occur in many of the discussions. First of all, the position of unilateral disarmament has been understood as one of submission and resignation. On the contrary, the pacifists as well as the humanist pragmatists believe that unilateral disarmament is possible only as an expression of a deep spiritual and moral change within ourselves: it is an act of courage and resistance—not one of cowardice or surrender. Forms of resistance differ in accordance with the respective viewpoints. On the other hand, Gandhists and men like King-Hall advocate nonviolent resistance, which undoubtedly requires the maximum of courage and faith; they refer to the example of Indian resistance against Britain or Norwegian resistance against the Nazis. This point of view is succinctly expressed in *Speak Truth to Power* (see reference 4):

Thus, we dissociate ourselves from the basically selfish attitude that has been miscalled pacifism, but that might be more accurately described as a kind of irresponsible antimilitarism. We dissociate ourselves also from utopianism. Though the choice of nonviolence involves a radical change in men, it does not require perfection. . . . We have tried to make it clear that readiness to accept suffering—rather than inflict it on others—is the essence of the nonviolent life, and that we must be prepared if called upon to pay the ultimate price. Obviously, if men are willing to spend billions of treasure and countless lives in war, they cannot dismiss the case for nonviolence by saying that in a nonviolent struggle people might be killed! It is equally clear that where commitment and the readiness to sacrifice are lacking, nonviolent resistance cannot be effective. On the contrary, it demands greater discipline, more arduous training, and more courage than its violent counterpart.[11]

Some think of armed resistance, of men and women defending their lives and their freedom with rifles, pistols, or knives. It is not unrealistic to think that both forms of resistance, nonviolent or violent, might deter an aggressor from attacking. At least, it is more realistic than to think that the use of thermonuclear weapons could lead to a "victory for democracy."

The proponents of "security by armament" sometimes accuse us of having an unrealistic, flatly optimistic picture of the nature of man. They remind us that this "perverse human being has a dark, illogical, irrational side." [12] They even go so far as to say that "the paradox of nuclear deterrence is a variant of the fundamental Christian paradox. In order to *live*, we must express our willingness to kill and to die." [13] Apart from this crude falsification of Christian teaching, we are by no means oblivious of the potential evil within man and of the tragic aspect of life. Indeed, there are situations in which man must be willing to die in order to live. In the sacrifices necessary for violent or nonviolent resistance, I can see an expression of the acceptance of tragedy and sacrifice. But, there is no tragedy or sacrifice in irresponsibility and carelessness: there is no meaning or dignity in the idea of the destruction of mankind and of civilization. Man has in himself a potential for evil; his whole existence is beset by dichotomies rooted in the very conditions of his existence. But these truly tragic aspects must not be confused with the results of stupidity and lack of imagination, with the willingness to stake the future of mankind on a gamble.

Finally, to take up one last criticism, directed against the position of unilateral disarmament: that it is "soft" on Communism. Our position is precisely based on the negation of the Soviet principle of the omnipotence of the state. Just because the spokesmen for unilateral disarmament are drastically opposed to the supremacy of the state, they do not want to grant the state the ever-increasing power which is unavoidable in the arms race, and they deny the right of the state to make decisions which can lead to the destruction of a great part of humanity and can doom future generations. If the basic conflict between the Soviet system and the democratic world is the question of the defense of the individual against the encroachment of an omnipotent state, then, indeed, the position for unilateral disarmament is the one which is most radically opposed to the Soviet principle.

After having discussed the case for unilateral disarmament (in the broad sense), I want to return to the practical proposition of unilateral steps toward disarmament. I do not deny that there are risks involved in this limited form of unilateral action but considering the fact that the present method of negotiations has produced no results and that the chances that they will in the future are rather slim, considering furthermore the grave risk involved in the continuation of the arms race, I believe that it is practically and morally justified to take this risk. At present we are caught in a position with little chance for survival, unless we want to take refuge in hopes. *If* we have enough shelters, *if* there is enough time for a warning and strategic evacuation of cities, *if* the "United States' active offenses and active defenses can gain control of the military situation after only a few exchanges," [14] we might have only five, or twenty-five, or seventy million killed. However, if these conditions do not materialize, "an enemy could, by repeated strikes, reach almost any level of death and destruction he wished." [15] (And, I assume, the same threat exists for the Soviet Union.) In such a situation, "when nations are poised at the last moment when an agreement appears possible to end the risk of horrifying war, unleashed by fanatics, lunatics or men of ambition," [16] it is imperative to shake off the inertia of our accustomed thinking, to seek for new approaches to the problem, and above all, to see new alternatives to the present choices that confront us.

References

1. Charles E. Osgood, "Suggestions for Winning the Real War with Communism," *Conflict Resolution* (December 1959) *3*: 131, and also "A Case for Graduated Unilateral Disarmament," *Bulletin of Atomic Scientists* (1960), *16:* 127 ff.

2. This condition is in my opinion to be taken only as an optimal *desideratum,* since any weakening of one power's aggressive potential means strategically some increase in the opponent's aggressive potential.

3. Charles E. Osgood, *op. cit.,* p. 316.

4. Bertrand Russell, *Common Sense and Nuclear Warfare* (London: G. Allen & Unwin, 1959). Stephen King-Hall, *Defense in the Nuclear Age* (Nyack, N.Y.: Fellowship Publications, 1959). Jerome Davis and General H. B. Hester, *On the Brink* (New York: Lyle Stuart, 1959). Lewis Mumford, *The Human Way Out* (Pendell Hill Pamphlet No. 97, 1958). C. W. Mills, *The Causes of World War Three* (New York: Simon & Schuster, 1959). George F. Kennan, "Foreign Policy and Christian Conscience," *Atlantic Monthly,* May 1959. Richard B. Gregg, *The Power of Nonviolence* (Nyack, N.Y.: Fellowship Publications, 1959). American Friends Service Committee, *Speak Truth to Power, Quaker Search for an Alternative to Balance* (1955).

5. George F. Kennan, *op. cit.,* pp. 44 ff.

6. This premise is shared by the report of the National Planning Association of America: *1970 without Arms Control; Implications of Modern Weapons Technology* (by NPA Special Project Committee on Security through Arms Control, Planning Pamphlet No. 104, May 1958, Washington, D.C.), which states: "Not only does the danger of war remain a possibility, but the probability totalled over time increases, becoming a certainty if sufficient time elapses without succeeding in finding alternatives." Or, E. Finley Carter, President of the Stanford Research Institute, writes: "In the search for security through the application of technology to weapons for destruction, the Soviet bloc and the Western allies have created a mortal common enemy—the threat of accidental nuclear war" (*SRI Journal,* Stanford Research Institute, Fourth Quarter 1959, *3*: 198). Herman Kahn also concludes, "It is most unlikely that the world can live with an uncontrolled arms race lasting for several decades" (*ibid.,* p. 139).

He emphasizes that it is unrealistic to believe that war has become impossible because of its extremely destructive character.

The advisor on Science and Technology of the Democratic Advisory Council of December 27, 1959 declared: "All-out nuclear war seems not only possible but probable as long as we pursue our present military policies and fail to achieve international agreements of broad scope designed to alleviate this unstable situation. The triggering of a nuclear war by mistake, by misadventure or by miscalculation is a constant danger." It must be stressed that the danger lies not only in technical errors, but equally in the blundering decision-making by political and military leaders. If one remembers the political and military blunders committed by many of the leaders in the conduct of wars of 1914 and 1939, it is not difficult to visualize that, given present-day weapons, the same type of leaders will blow the world to pieces, in spite of good intentions.

7. For a detailed analysis of modern society cf. my *The Sane Society* (New York: Rinehart and Co., 1955).

8. *SRI Journal* (1959), *3*: 140.

9. For the very same reasons, there is a real chance for the future abolition of war, a chance which never existed in the past. In most of man's history, the improvement of his material situation required an increase in human energy (slaves), additional land for cattle raising or agriculture, or new sources of raw materials. The techniques of the present and of the future will permit an increase in material wealth by an increased industrial and—indirectly—agricultural productivity, without the need of enslaving or robbing others. At present and in the future, war would have as its only "rationale" the irrationality of human desire for power and conquest.

10. Whether or not political leaders are sane is not a matter of historical accident. Any government which has set out to do the impossible—for instance, to achieve equality and justice when the requisite material conditions are lacking—will produce fanatical and irrational leaders. This was the case with Robespierre, as it was with Stalin. Or, a government which tries to reconcile the interests of the most backward social class (the lower middle class) with those of the economically progressive classes (workers and businessmen) as the Nazi government did, again will produce fanatical and irrational leaders. The Soviet Union today is on the road toward solving its economic problems successfully; hence it is not surprising that her leaders are realistic men of common sense.

11. *Op. cit.*, pp. 52, 65.

12. Peter B. Young, "The Renunciationists," *Airpower*, the Air Force Historical Foundation, *7*, 1: 33.

13. *Ibid.*

14. Herman Kahn, *Report on a Study of Non-Military Defense* (RAND Corporation Report R-322-RC, July 1, 1958), p. 13.

15. *Ibid.*

16. General de Gaulle, in a speech in April 1960.

Comprehensive Arms-Limitation Systems

JEROME B. WIESNER

*   *   *   *   *

V. COMPONENTS OF ARMS-LIMITATION SYSTEMS— INSPECTION AND CONTROL

An essential part of any realistic comprehensive arms-reduction proposal will be the inspection and control system. The effectiveness of the inspection system in providing assurance thaat agreements are really being respected will not only govern the security provided by the specific arrangement, but will obviously greatly influence the willingness of nations to participate in it. It is also clear that the more extensive, complicated, and costly a proposed inspection system is, the more difficult will be its acceptance and implementation. It is not necessarily true that the more elaborate the inspection system, the greater the confidence it will engender, for this is governed as much by the nature of the specific arms-limitation agreement being monitored as by the actual inspection system. Two examples will illustrate this point.

RELATIONSHIP BETWEEN SPECIFIC ARMS-LIMITATION MEASURES AND INSPECTION REQUIREMENTS

During the 1958 Geneva Conference on Means of Preventing Surprise Attack, the Western delegates proposed a very elaborate and costly system designed to detect and warn of the build-up or actual occurrence of a surprise attack. For a number of reasons the Western proposals did not include any limitation on the number or deployment of the various weapons of mass destruction the system was to control. Though in certain situations this system would provide some additional security against surprise attack, it was very costly for what it would accomplish. In addition, it was possible to imagine situations where it could be exploited by an aggressor. The difficulty with such a system is the necessity of providing continuous observation at many separate places as well as extremely rapid communication and data-processing capability between each of the observation points and national or international decision-making centers. The need for ultra-rapid, extremely reliable communication and data processing is created by the very short time of flight of ballistic missiles. In contrast to these severe requirements, an inspection system designed to monitor complete disarmament, or even the stable deterrent system to be examined later, will have no need for ultra-fast or perfectly reliable electrical communication since nearly all required responses will be measured in days, weeks, or months. In addition, to the best of my present ability to estimate, a total disarmament agreement would probably not require a larger inspection force to monitor it than would be required by the proposed system to warn of a surprise attack. These remarks are not meant to imply that there are no useful limited measures which could be undertaken to reduce the dangers of surprise attack, which there certainly are, but rather to indicate the difficulty of going very far along this path.

The problems encountered in agreeing upon a system for detecting violations of a nuclear test ban are another illustration of the difficulty of implementing partial measures. At the time of this writing, the extensiveness of an adequate system is the subject of disagreement not only between the United States–United Kingdom delegation and the Soviet Union delegation at Geneva, but between various scientific groups within the United States. The system agreed upon clearly does not have a high probability of detecting small explosions. A considerable increase in the number of stations in the network would be required to improve this situation. The Soviet Union obviously fears such an increase in the number of seismic stations and the concomitant increase in the inspection force, while many people in the United States are equally fearful of clandestine testing within the Soviet Union. Two critical years have been spent attempting to negotiate this issue. Ironically, an inspection system for monitoring a truly comprehensive disarmament agreement would probably have no need at all for a system to detect underground nuclear tests.

With properly planned stable deterrent systems, the more extensive the inspection system is, the lower will be the levels to which forces can be reduced with safety. In an initial phase of disarmament, therefore, it may be easier to reconcile the two fears (the Soviet fear of widespread inspection while weapons remain, and the Western fear of clandestine USSR forces) by starting with a stable deterrent system than by attempting to implement one of the total disarmament plans.

Different weapons will pose different inspection requirements. Ships will be easier to control than aircraft, aircraft easier than missiles, etc., and the degree of assurance required in the information concerning different weapons will vary as well. For example, much more precise information will doubtless be needed regarding the number of ballistic missiles (if any) remaining in a country than will be needed concerning the number of fighter aircraft or short-range air defense missiles. All comprehensive arms-limitation systems that are to be examined require some inspection system, but the inspection requirements will differ greatly between the systems.

The *feasibility* of the systems to be studied will depend upon the feasibility of adequate inspection; the relative *desirability* of the different plans will be affected in part by the complexity of the inspection system. Though inspection techniques of arms control are examined in more detail in Bernard T. Feld's chapter in this book, a review of pertinent information regarding the inspection systems for use in controlling nuclear weapons and for controlling the principal means of delivering them will be presented here.

SPECIFIC TECHNIQUES OF CONTROL AND INSPECTION

The negotiability of any arms-limitation proposal will be determined, to a considerable degree, by the inspection and control measures it requires. The extent to which the production or deployment of any weapon can be restricted by agreement will be established by the ability of an inspection system to verify the agreement. Furthermore, the difficulty of implementation will be determined by the inspection techniques chosen to monitor the agreements. A highly technical system, requiring the development and production of specialized new equipment such as better seismic detectors for detecting underground explosions or special large radar instruments for detecting missile firings, will take longer to install and have operating than one that depends primarily upon the use of available devices, such as existing photo reconnaissance equipment, or just upon physical inspection by observers. Since a wide variety of inspection systems appears to be possible, it is likely that some of them will be more acceptable than others. Unfortunately, they have not been studied adequately, and are not well understood, so that meaningful comparisons cannot be made between them. The planning of comprehensive arms systems should only be undertaken after the control and inspection problems associated with the individual weapons are understood reasonably well.

Objectives of Inspection. An inspection system must serve two different functions. When the arms-limitation agreements are being implemented it will be necessary to verify military forces. Verification will consist of establishing the veracity of the actual disclosures by on-site inspection, and establishing that all existing military units and equipment were included in the initial disclosure. After the verification of the initial disclosures is completed, it will be necessary to continue search for possible clandestine activities, such as the secret production of nuclear material or the construction of missiles.

The degree of assurance required of the inspection system will depend very much on the nature of the arms-limitation agreement being monitored. For example, a stable deterrent agreement which permits relatively large missile forces to remain in national hands requires less assurance regarding the existence of a small clandestine missile force than an agreement completely outlawing missiles.

Inspection and Observation Techniques. In planning arms-limitation systems, it is desirable to limit the inspection and observation components to those of a strategic nature, i.e., to those depending on information regarding location, number, etc., and to avoid the use of tactical information requiring rapid transmission and quick reaction.

The techniques available fall into two basic categories: aerial (or satellite) inspection and observation; and ground inspection using resident or mobile inspectors.

Aerial Reconnaissance for Search and Verification. Photographic reconnaissance provides one of the most effective means of checking the accuracy of facility disclosures and searching for clandestine military or production installations. With modern photographic equipment, it is possible to identify small objects on the ground even though the camera is at high altitude. Because of its great effectiveness and relatively modest cost, photographic reconnaissance is often proposed as the basic means of verification and search in arms-control systems.

Two quite different capabilities are required for the most effective use of aerial photography for search and verification purposes in an arms-control system. There is need for general high-altitude coverage and for a modest amount of very-high-resolution low-altitude reconnaissance capability to be used for investigating suspicious objects which cannot be identified from the high-altitude films. Though the high-resolution capability is not absolutely required, its existence will greatly reduce the ground inspection effort.

A quite modest flying and photo-interpreter effort appears to be adequate to verify or repudiate the disclosures regarding present-day missile-launching sites; factory and camp locations, etc.

Ground Inspection Techniques. The ground inspection system will be used to fulfill a number of quite separate functions. Principal among these are:

1. to assist in the effort to detect or verify the existence and location of all significant military weapons, military test facilities, military research establishments, and manufacturing facilities with emphasis upon those not amenable to aerial and space techniques,

2. to investigate areas of suspected military activity uncovered by aerial inspection or by other means,

3. to maintain surveillance of known facilities capable of developing, testing, or producing military weapons to insure that no illegal activities exist. This could include extensive and continuing inspection of records, raw materials, output, surveillance of personnel, etc., and

4. to operate technical systems such as surveillance radars, seismic systems, and data processing centers, used in conjunction with the inspection operation.

While the functions listed are separate, the inspectorate would no doubt be an integrated system making use of common facilities and staff wherever possible and using the information gained by each of the operations to create as reliable a picture as possible of the military state of affairs. An inspection system adequate to monitor any degree of disarmament appears to be possible, though its acceptability is by no means certain. Detailed discussions of the individual inspection problems are given elsewhere in this volume.

Psychological Inspection. The preceding sections have dealt with the inspection of things. It is also possible to "inspect" people. A variety of means has been proposed for doing this, including newspaper campaigns to familiarize people with the nature of arms-control agreements, offers of rewards, interrogation of key personnel, and the use of lie detectors. Though psychological inspection has not been examined carefully, it does appear to be an important inspection technique.

PHASING TO PROVIDE EQUITABLE IMPLEMENTATION WHILE RETAINING ADEQUATE SECURITY

One of the most difficult problems encountered in the planning of an arms-control system is that of balancing the level of disarmament and the completeness of the inspection system during the period of transition to the final conditions. One means of resolving this difficulty is by combining time-phased arms reductions with an inspection system based upon the concept of territorial disarmament proposed by Louis B. Sohn.[2] In this plan, thorough search for clandestine activities would be permitted in only a fraction of the territory of any one country at the beginning of the implementation period, and the search would progress to the point of complete coverage at the end of the period. The choice of the area to be searched at each stage is selected unpredictably by the inspecting authority and the information gained is combined with the information provided by the initial declarations and by the other inspection techniques. By the proper choice of conditions, it appears that the conflicting interests of the two sides may be made compatible.

INTERNATIONAL SECURITY FORCE

A serious point of difference between Western and Eastern proposals for comprehensive arms-control systems is the attitude taken toward the inclu-

2. Louis B. Sohn, "Territorial Disarmament," a private memorandum, November 2, 1959.

sion of some form of international "police force." In recent discussions the Western allies have insisted upon the creation of a modest military force for the international control authority before eliminating national forces, while the Soviet Union and its allies have, until recently, objected to it.

The Western view has been that, in the absence of an international force, a world disarmed down to the level required for internal security would not be stable because one of the participating nations could decide to violate the agreements and build up a dangerous nuclear force before the others could react and rebuild a nuclear deterrent. The Soviet view has been that it would not be possible to build up a very large clandestine force before the effort would be detected and counter-actions taken. It is also their view that arms-limitation agreements can only work if the large nations believe them to be preferable to an arms race, in which case they will observe the agreements. It is certainly hard to believe that a nation would deliberately eliminate a large share of the military force it has worked hard to create and then take an action that would start a new arms contest.

There are many way to create an international security force. An attractive way would be to have the smaller nations of the world take on this responsibility with financial and material support from the larger powers. It has even been suggested that France might be willing to join such a group and supply it with a nuclear capability, if it proved desirable to include a nuclear component.

SOME IMPORTANT INSPECTION PROBLEMS

The specific inspection techniques discussed in the preceding sections can be employed singly or in combination to monitor compliance of arms agreements. As already indicated, the intensity of the inspection activities will obviously be controlled by the risk involved if violations are undetected. The most serious inspection problems are posed by the limitation of nuclear weapons and ballistic missiles, and by the need for surveillance of research and development.

The nuclear-weapon and missile-control problems are interrelated. If one could be absolutely certain of the size of any controlled nuclear stockpile, the need to carry out careful control of missiles would be reduced. Likewise, if very good control could be established over missiles, aircraft, and other carriers of nuclear weapons, less adequate control over the warheads could be accepted. In fact, it will probably be necessary to accept some uncertainty in each and take advantage of the reassurance provided by the overlapping control.

Inspection and Control of Ballistic Missiles. The control and inspection system visualized here is based upon the assumption that at appropriate times, specified in the Arms Control Agreements, complete and accurate information considered necessary for the monitoring of missile limitation agreements will be provided to the control authority by the participants in the agreements. The associated inspection system will have two distinct tasks: it must first verify, within tolerable error, the initial disclosures; and thereafter it must continue to ascertain that existing missile forces are not being augmented clandestinely. Furthermore, it must be so designed that the inspection system need expand only at a rate compatible with the progress being made toward the final armament levels.

The initial verification of missile force level and facilities disclosures can be achieved by direct examination of production facilities and records, and by interrogation of personnel involved in missile production, development, and operation. The initial verification would be reinforced by the phased disclosure and verification of missile locations. This step would be accomplished by physical search, using aerial reconnaissance and other techniques in the areas opened to complete inspection. The important property of a good search system for use in verifying missile force disclosures is that it have a high probability of detecting the existence of one, or at most a few, clandestine missiles if a substantial number exist and not that it be able to find all that may exist. This fact has two consequences; it makes possible the use of random sampling techniques and it makes the possession of a sizeable clandestine force very risky.

After the agreed-upon disclosures have been made, the control authority will have the task of authenticating the information disclosed and of insuring its completeness. A variety of complementary techniques are available to verify the completeness of the disclosed data and the continued compliance with the agreements. For these techniques to be effectively employed, the inspection authority must have the right to employ at will those inspection techniques previously agreed upon.

Detailed examination of this problem leads me to believe that it is feasible to create an inspection system in the near future to verify or repudiate good faith with regard to the production and deployment of missiles.

Nuclear Stockpile Control. At the present time the principal technical difficulty encountered in making safe disarmament arrangements stems from the existence of large stockpiles of nuclear materials and the impossibility of determining for sure how large they actually are. This uncertainty in the measurement has been estimated to fall in the range of from 50 to 500 large nuclear weapons if physical means only were employed to estimate past production. It is probable that an intensive study of the physical means of estimating past nuclear production could greatly reduce this uncertainty. There is also reason to hope that psychological inspection could reduce this number considerably, but it is premature to count on this.

A somewhat easier problem is the limitation of the production of new nuclear material. While it is probable that enough material to make a very few bombs per year could be produced clandestinely or diverted from peaceful uses, I do not believe that this problem is nearly as serious as that of establishing confidence in the location of previously produced material.

Because it is obviously possible for clandestine stockpiles to exist, I feel strongly the need to retain a small nuclear deterrent force at least until considerable confidence has been developed in the inspection system.

Technological Surprise. One of the most difficult military eventualities to prepare for is the technological surprise. In the kind of world we live in, the most effective safeguards from technological surprise are a very broad and intensive research program, as much exchange of scientific and technical information as the cold war permits, and an effective intelligence system.

In a disarmed world there will be no need for secret research and development and it should be strictly forbidden. If all legitimate scientific and technical work is open and observable, the danger of the sudden appearance of unexpected weapons resulting from secret research will be greatly reduced. The techniques of psychological inspection should be particularly useful in dealing with this problem.

It should be noted that after a weapon has been invented, it must not only be developed and tested, but it must also be produced, usually in substantial quantity, before it can be regarded as a serious threat. In an open world large-scale clandestine production and deployment will also be difficult.

One interesting characteristic of highly technical inventions is that such new ideas spring up in many places around the world at more or less the same time, being more dependent upon the sudden development of new scientific knowledge than any other single factor. Because this is so, the danger from technological surprise would be less in a world in which research was conducted openly and results published freely than in the present one.

QUESTIONS FOR SEMINAR DISCUSSION

Do you understand fully what Blackett means by a minimum deterrence strategy? Do you disagree with any part of his analysis which leads him to conclude that present U.S.S.R. security and military policy with regard to a major war between the United States and the U.S.S.R. is based on a minimum deterrence strategy? If so, what are the facts on which you base your disagreement? Where did you get these facts? Where did Blackett get his facts?

Assuming that Blackett is correct about the posture of U.S. and U.S.S.R. capacity and striking power in both nuclear and conventional weapons, and after stating your view on what you believe to be the relevant political forces with regard to the problem of disarmament, which of the three general approaches suggested by our reading--general and complete disarmament as outlined in Annex I of World Peace Through World Law, arms control based on a continuing deterrence system as presented by Schelling, or unilateral disarmament argued by Fromm--have any change of providing a significant amount of disarmament within the next decade? Are they mutually exclusive approaches or can they be accommodated to one another? Explain your answer.

Is it necessary to have complete disarmament? Doesn't Blackett's suggestion that we begin with significant disarmament in nuclear weapons suggest a middle ground? Would it be easier to get agreement on this proposal than on general and complete disarmament? Why or why not?

The Clark-Sohn proposal even as amended in the Addendum (xiv) calls for a ten-year period (which could be shortened by the General Assembly) in which disarmament would be carried out. To what extent would that phase of disarmament be based on notions of mutual deterrence?

Looking at the Clark-Sohn scheme, is there any aspect of the structure of the UN Inspection Service and the way it would be related to the other organs of the United Nations with which you disagree? Why?

Is there any aspect of their phases for the disarmament process with which you disagree? Why? Do you believe that all three phases--enumeration, verification, and disarmament--are essential to an effective disarmament scheme? Need they be in that order? Which phase is likely to cause the most difficulty? Why? What can be done to minimize the difficulties?

Do you feel that the Inspection Service is given sufficient, too little, or too much authority in carrying out its functions? What changes if any would you introduce?

Given Blackett's analysis of the present posture of the U.S.S.R. deterrence machinery it is highly unlikely that they will be willing to accept all the inspection demanded by the Clark-Sohn scheme, at least, initially. What compromises could be made here? Does the Sohn proposal of randomized territorial inspection, Addendum (xiii), and Wiesner help with this problem? Do you see any difficulty with his proposals?

Wiesner lists a number of methods of inspection to achieve various objectives. So do Clark and Sohn. Of these, which are likely to be least offensive or most acceptable to the Soviet Union and still provide for a real beginning in disarmament?

BIBLIOGRAPHY

In the past there has been a good deal of literature on DISARMAMENT and ARMS CONTROL. For the most comprehensive bibliography on these matters, see Ernest W. Lefever (ed.), Arms and Arms Control. NY: Praeger, 1962, pp. 313-331.
Listed below are nine of the more basic and well-known works through which you may readily gain access to the whole field:

Barnet, Richard J. Who Wants Disarmament? Boston: Beacon Press, 1960, 141p.
Brennan, Donald G. (ed.). Arms Control, Disarmament and National Security. NY: Braziller, 1961. In addition to the readings reprinted in the Reader, the Brennan book contains an extensive group of articles by most of the foremost authorities in the field. Most of these articles appeared originally in Daedalus, the journal of the American Academy of Arts and Sciences.
Bull, Hedley. The Control of the Arms Race. NY: Praeger, 1961, 229p.
Frisch, David H. (ed.). Arms Reduction: Program and Issues. NY: Twentieth Century Fund, 1961.
Hadley, Arthur T. The Nation's Safety and Arms Control. NY: Viking, 1961.
Henckin, Louis (ed.). Arms Control: Issues for the Public, published for the American Assembly, Columbia University. Englewood Cliffs, N.J.: Prentice-Hall, 1961, 207p.
McClelland, Charles A. (ed.). Nuclear Weapons, Missiles and Future War. San Francisco: Chandler, 1960, 235p.
Schelling, Thomas C., and Morton H. Halperin. Strategy and Arms Control. NY: The Twentieth Century Fund, 1961.
Warburg, James P. Disarmament: The Challenge of the Sixties. NY: Doubleday, 1961, 288p.

SESSION IX

PROBLEMS OF ACHIEVING AND MAINTAINING DISARMAMENT

In the previous session we looked at the problem of disarmament posed as a security-military matter to the super powers, and explored three approaches--complete and general disarmament, arms control based on a system of mutual deterrence, unilateral disarmament--as possible solutions to this problem within the general problem of preventing war. In addition we began our analysis of the detailed proposals for complete and general disarmament made by Clark and Sohn. We dealt with the establishment, membership and structure of a Disarmament Commission which would be given administrative authority to handle the necessary phases of disarming over a period of years, and we were concerned with the troublesome question of inspection and the proposal by Clark and Sohn for a comprehensive Inspection Service.

In this session we shall take up the proposals by Clark and Sohn for the establishment of a United Nations Nuclear Authority, the establishment of a United Nations Outer Space Agency, the question of what kind of penalties can and should be used for violations of the disarmament agreement (both during the process of disarming and after complete and general disarmament has been completed), and the Clark-Sohn proposals for regulation, control and elimination by the United Nations of certain activities and facilities within states in order to maintain complete and general disarmament. All of these matters should be discussed within the framework established in our previous session and should be used to test the feasibility and advisability of proposals and suggestions made during that session.

The central questions concerning the two new agencies proposed by Clark and Sohn are whether they are necessary, acceptable, and set up to operate efficiently. The articles by Iklé and Schelling are concerned with the problem of what is a proper response to a violation of the disarmament agreement. They differ with Clark-Sohn on this matter since they believe that a centrally organized deterrence system is not likely to be active during the process of disarmament, and they make a number of suggestions for other techniques and devices which might be used. In addition, Schelling raises the question of what is meant by "total disarmament" and suggests that we have not dealt with all the problems involved once we have reached complete and general disarmament. You will want to evaluate to what extent Chapters III and VIII of the Clark-Sohn disarmament proposals in conjunction with the rest of their scheme, meet his objections.

Readings from World Peace Through World Law:
Disarmament: UN Nuclear Energy Authority, Outer Space Agency, Financial Provisions, Enforcement Measures, xxvii-xxix, xxxvi, 281-313; General Provisions, 246-262.

AFTER DETECTION—WHAT?

By Fred Charles Iklé

THE current debate on arms control and disarmament puts great stress on the problem of how to detect violations of whatever agreements may be reached. To this end inspection schemes and instruments for detection are developed, their capabilities and limitations discussed, and efforts made to test and improve them. Indeed, the technical question of detection dominates not only the domestic debate but also the international disarmament negotiations.

Yet detecting violations is not enough. What counts are the political and military consequences of a violation once it has been detected, since these alone will determine whether or not the violator stands to gain in the end. In entering into an arms-control agreement, we must know not only that we are technically capable of detecting a violation but also that we or the rest of the world will be politically, legally and militarily in a position to react effectively if a violation is discovered. If we focus all our attention on the technicalities of how to detect a violation, we are in danger of assuming that our reactions and sanctions will be adequate.

A potential violator of an arms-control agreement will not be deterred simply by the risk that his action may be discovered. What will deter him will be the fear that what he gains from the violation will be outweighed by the loss he may suffer from the victim's reaction to it. In other words, even if we can develop an inspection system that makes the probability of detection very high, a nation contemplating a violation will not be deterred if it thinks it can discourage, circumvent or absorb our reaction.

We have learned (almost too late, in the case of the nuclear test ban) that an opponent may thwart our detection techniques by evasive techniques of his own. We should also realize that he may thwart the consequences of detection—which we count on to deter violations—by military or political stratagems. We must study, therefore, not only what our opponent may do to avoid detection, but also what he may do to escape the penalty of being detected.

Let us discuss the question of what may happen when an evasion is detected under four general headings: (1) the reaction of world opinion; (2) the political reaction by the injured country; (3) various military measures that the injured country could undertake in an effort to restore the situation that would have existed without an arms-control agreement; and (4) military and political measures that would go beyond this "restoration."

II

World opinion, it is sometimes argued, will help to enforce disarmament agreements. World opinion supposedly will turn against the violator, provided he is discovered and "convicted" in an internationally accepted forum. He will lose prestige and influence in the uncommitted countries. In addition, various world-wide political reactions are expected to work to his disadvantage.

"World opinion" is such an amorphous concept that one finds it difficult to determine just how it can injure a violator of arms-control agreements. Speeches or resolutions in the United Nations, or critical editorials in the world press, are not likely to hurt him very much. One reason world opinion is so impotent is that its memory is so short. If the world's reaction cannot be translated immediately into substantive political or military changes damaging to the violator, it will lose all force.

The Soviet suppression of the Hungarian revolution illustrates the point. This gave an exceptionally violent shock to world opinion—in fact, more violent than many possible violations of arms-control agreements are likely to be. This is particularly true since evidence of a violation might often be equivocal and involve technicalities hard for the public to understand. Some of the most cherished beliefs of the West and also of the uncommitted countries were flouted in Hungary: a popular revolt against a dictatorial régime in a small nation was crushed from outside by a large power. Agreements were broken in the most flagrant fashion. One was the promise given by the Soviet-installed Kadar Government to the Jugoslav Government not to take punitive action against Imré Nagy when he left sanctuary in the Jugoslav Embassy. Another was the invitation extended to General Maléter and other delegates of the legal Hungarian Government to negotiate the withdrawal of Soviet forces—a trap to catch and execute them. Yet if one tries to list the penalties that world opinion imposed on the Soviet

Union and the Kadar Government for these violations of its most sacred norms and of several important articles of the United Nations Charter, there is very little to record. There was a slight loss in the strength of Communist Parties in Western Europe (confined mostly to intellectuals on the fringe of the Party), but the loss is no longer noticeable. The strain on President Tito's relations with Moscow and the strengthening of NATO ties (particularly with Iceland) were largely ephemeral. Kadar has not been officially recognized as Hungary's legal representative in the United Nations; but he has been sitting in the General Assembly.

Other recent events have aroused world opinion, such as the Peking régime's violent repressions in Tibet and its violations of the Indian border. Yet in February 1960, only a few months after indignation in India had reached its peak, the Communists increased their vote in Kerala from 35 to 43 percent. And many of Communist China's neighbors continued to favor her admission to the United Nations.

Perhaps significantly, when Khrushchev discussed the nuclear test ban before the Supreme Soviet in January 1960, he chose to emphasize the reaction of world opinion as a deterrent to disarmament violations. By arguing that it was a sufficient deterrent, he tried, in effect, to brush aside the problems of inspection and control. But even if one assumed that the reaction of world opinion constituted an adequate sanction—an assumption challenged above—inspection would still be essential. A violator who does not risk being detected obviously does not need to fear world opinion. In any case, the West has paid insufficient attention to the stratagems which a detected violator can pursue to avoid or mitigate whatever action an aroused world opinion might take.

Many devices are available for this purpose. Thus the violator can frustrate the international inspection system and prevent it from reaching an official finding (study of Communist obstruction of inspection in North Korea reveals a large bag of such tricks). Or he can blame the other side for having violated the agreement first, and thus confuse the issue, or even generate an adverse political reaction against the injured party. Or he can accuse the other side of fabricating the evidence as a pretext for breaking the agreement or for covering up some other misdeed. Or he can assert that the agreement is

620

obsolete in view of what he claims are changed political or military conditions and denounce it unilaterally prior to the intended violation (this would be analogous to the Soviet declaration that the Four-Power Agreements on Berlin were no longer valid). Finally, if some unfavorable reaction in world opinion is unavoidable, it may turn out that the violators "will cover themselves with shame"—as Khrushchev argued when he spoke about the nuclear test ban: "If some side violates the assumed commitments, the initiators of this violation will cover themselves with shame, they will be branded by all the peoples of the world." Yet, six weeks before making this assertion that a nuclear test ban would be enforced by world opinion, Khrushchev had this to recommend: "International reactionary circles are still trying to discuss the so-called 'Hungarian question' in the United Nations. Let them keep it as a souvenir if this consoles them."

Not only may the violator be contemptuous of world opinion, but he also may justify his acts on the grounds that they are demanded by the welfare of "the people" or by History—History being his conception of a superior morality that takes precedence over world opinion. "Had we not helped you," Khrushchev told the Hungarian Communists, "we would have been called stupid, and History would not have forgiven us this stupidity."

III

To be effective, a sanction must be applied as a result of governmental decisions by the injured countries. In democratic countries, government decisions are influenced by active public opinion, or, more precisely, by the conception of public opinion held by the government leaders. In these circumstances, democratic governments might experience serious political difficulties in reacting effectively to a detected evasion:

(1) The injured government must acknowledge the fact that there has been a violation. If the violation is open and well-publicized, no difficulty exists. But if evidence of the violation is equivocal or based on secret intelligence, the government may be reluctant to acknowledge the evasion or feel unsure of its ability to convince public opinion. For example, an admission that the control agreement had failed might be ex-

ploited at home by the political opposition, particularly if the agreement had been made originally by the party in power. In such a situation some decision-makers may favor an interpretation which casts doubt on the intelligence data relating to evasion or which belittles the importance of the evasion. Responsible decision-makers seldom distort evidence deliberately.[1] But the interpretation of complicated information is often a matter of judgment and discretion; hence subtle biases may decide the issue. Responsible officials would be particularly disinclined to accept equivocal evidence about an evasion of a disarmament agreement if they had previously been forced to defend the agreement against partisan charges that it might be violated. Yet a democratic government could institute only minor penalties against an evasion without informing legislative bodies and the public about the exact situation and explaining the need for drastic retaliatory or corrective measures.

(2) The injured government must be willing to increase military expenditures and to offend pacifist feelings. Now the reaction to a localized or minor violation need not disturb the defense budget appreciably (the new military equipment needed to counteract the North Korean violations of the rearmament clause was not a heavy burden); but the breaking of a major disarmament agreement will almost certainly require new military measures, perhaps a full-scale program of rearmament. The decision to react firmly and regardless of expense will be a hard one. Public opinion may not approve, especially if the evasion occurred gradually or if it merely consists of a resumption of some activity that had been discontinued—such as testing. If knowledge of the evasion is based exclusively on clandestine intelligence sources that cannot be revealed, the opponent's denial may find receptive ears among domestic opposition groups.

We have already questioned the effectiveness of world opinion as a sanction against arms-control evasions. It is ironic that it may be domestic public opinion—or rather the government's conception of it—that actually prevents effective sanctions being taken. The classic instance of this, and one that may have been a con-

---

[1] When Germany violated rearmament restrictions in the 1930s, Winston Churchill suspected that "somewhere between the Intelligence Service and the ministerial chief there has been some watering down or whittling down of the facts." (Speech of May 22, 1935, in "While England Slept." New York: Putnam, 1938, p. 190.) Prime Minister Baldwin's later admission suggested that there might have been something deliberate about this "watering down," and perhaps at the highest level.

tributing cause of World War II, was England's reluctance to rearm in response to Hitler's violations of the Versailles rearmament restrictions. With what he called "an appalling frankness," Prime Minister Baldwin explained in 1936 why his own government had been unable to react:

You will remember at that time [1932–33] the Disarmament Conference was sitting in Geneva. You will remember at that time there was probably a stronger pacifist feeling running through this country than at any time since the war. You will remember the election at Fulham in the autumn of 1933, when a seat which the National Government held was lost by about 7,000 votes on no issue but the pacifist. . . . I asked myself what chance was there . . . within the next year or two of that feeling being so changed that the country would give a mandate for rearmament? Supposing I had gone to the country and said that Germany was rearming and that we must rearm, does anybody think that this pacific democracy would have rallied to that cry at that moment? I cannot think of anything that would have made the loss of the election from my point of view more certain.[2]

(3) The injured government must accept the new risks created by its reaction to the violation. It may see more than the domestic difficulties involved. For example, it may have embarked on long-range policies which seem more promising and important than counteracting an accomplished evasion, and it may hesitate to jeopardize them.[3]

It has been argued that all countries will be deterred from violating a major arms-control agreement in present circumstances because to do so would set off an unrestricted arms race that would eventually lead to disaster for the guilty as well as the innocent.[4] But this is an assumption which may not be shared by a country set on violating the agreement. Its leaders may reason that the very prospect of an unrestricted arms race might itself inhibit the injured party from reacting to the violation. And in fact the injured party might feel it safer to write off the violation as a loss rather than risk new dangers by a policy of rearmament

[2] Baldwin's reply to Churchill as quoted in Churchill, "While England Slept." New York: Putnam, 1938, p. 333.
[3] Churchill was aware of this when he was pleading for a more effective response to Hitler's treaty violations: "Then it is said—and I must give this explanation of the extraordinary fact—that 'we were laboring for disarmament,' and it would have spoiled the disarmament hopes if any overt steps to raise our Air Force had been taken." Speech of May 22, 1935, op. cit., p. 190.
[4] For example, the Committee on Science and Technology of the Democratic Advisory Council wrote on March 14, 1960, about the nuclear test ban: "A nation which violates such an agreement automatically sets into motion an arms race from which there may never be an end."

—especially if it now finds itself in a weaker military position as a result of having complied with the agreement.

This dilemma is most serious. For example, the nuclear test-ban conference adopted an article on March 19, 1959, upon the insistence of the United States and the United Kingdom, affirming a country's "inherent right" to withdraw from the treaty if its provisions, "including those providing for the timely installation and effective operation of the control system," are not being fulfilled. This article might be of cardinal importance in connection with China's accession to the test-ban treaty, because part of the control system would have to be installed in China. But would it give the Western powers much leverage against Chinese obstructionism? In the absence of a known instance of illegal testing, would the West be willing to withdraw from a test-ban treaty with the Soviet Union, resume testing and risk accelerating the arms race merely because the "timely installation" of the control system was being prevented by China?

(4) The injured government may have to reach agreement with allies before it can react. All disarmament agreements of current interest involve the United States with one or more of its allies. It is usually a difficult task to prepare a joint negotiating position vis-à-vis a Communist opponent. Agreeing on a Western response to a violation will raise anew the problem of allied coördination. The stronger and more explicit the reaction proposed, the more difficult it will be to achieve agreement. And all the problems of domestic public opinion and partisan politics discussed above will be evident in the allied nations whose coöperation is required.

IV

The military sanctions against evasion of an arms-control agreement can either be confined to measures that restore the situation that would have existed without the agreement or they can go further. Let us call the former "restorative measures." If the violator resumes testing, the injured country will do likewise; if the violator reoccupies his part of a neutralized zone, the other will move back into his; and if the violator rearms, his opponent will rearm to the same extent.

The problem of deterring violations has often been oversimplified by assuming that a detected evasion would automatically be taken care of by the cancellation of the agreement and the application of such "restorative measures." But three conditions have to be met if "restorative measures" by themselves are to be an adequate deterrent:

(1) The potential violator must fear the risk of being detected.

(2) He must also fear that a detected violation will cause an unwanted response by the injured country.

(3) He must not expect a violation to bring him an irrevocable advantage that would outweigh whatever gain he derives from abiding by the agreement.

The importance of the first condition is fully recognized. The second condition depends on the political factors we have just discussed. Both these conditions are needed for deterring an evasion by any type of sanctions, whether "restorative" or "punitive." Here we are interested in the third condition, because if it is not met, "restorative measures" alone are inadequate.

This third condition is not met, for example, if an agreement comprises several arms-control measures in such a way that the separate measures, taken individually, favor either one side or the other. The agreement remains in the interest of both parties only if all measures are observed. Violation of a part of it cannot be deterred by the threat of "restorative measures" confined only to this particular part. Additional sanctions are required. Otherwise the violator can break just those control measures that are not to his advantage. He will stand to gain if his violation remains undiscovered or ignored; and he will also gain if the violated part of the agreement is cancelled, because the residual agreement will then be more to his advantage.

This is precisely what happened with the Korean armistice. The clause prohibiting the introduction of new military equipment was violated by the Communists from the first day, but cancellation of this clause by the United Nations Command did not come until four years later. So the Communists gained on the first count. They also gained on the second count (after the United Nations eventually instituted "restorative measures"), because the residual armistice agreement was more favorable to them than the original agreement. (It was they who had been primarily constrained by the cancelled rearmament clause.)

It might be argued that an arms-control measure can survive only if all its separable components are equally in the interest of both parties. If this argument is true, the future for disarmament agreements is bleak. It is hard enough to arrive at over-all agreements that will not, over time, seem disadvantageous to one side or the other. But individual components of an agreement are inevitably of unequal value to opposing nations. For example, in addition to the Korean armistice, several of the current proposals for disengagement zones are composed of very unequal provisions.

There are other situations where the threat of "restorative measures" would be insufficient to deter an evasion. The violator may gain an irrevocable technological lead or an irreversible strategic advantage. As has often been pointed out, if American and Soviet troops were withdrawn from Western and Eastern Europe, the United States might find it difficult or impossible to return in the event that Soviet troops moved back in. Western alliance arrangements might have lapsed, the American troops might have been demobilized, and in any case they would have to be transported a greater distance—not to mention the American public's unwillingness to send "the boys" back overseas, particularly under a threat of nuclear war.

To sum up, "restorative measures" will not deter a nation contemplating a violation of a disarmament agreement in those situations where our third condition is not met, namely, when the violator expects to gain less from abiding by the agreement than from abandoning it. Indeed, a potential violator might enter into agreements solely in order to seek gains by violating them. He would calculate that there would always be a chance of his escaping detection or that "restorative measures" might be delayed or frustrated for political reasons. And if he lost out on these chances, a mere return to the status quo would leave him no worse off than before he entered into the agreement. The violator, in fact, would be playing a profitable game: "Heads you lose, tails we're even."

v

Where the threat of "restorative measures" is not enough to deter evasions, additional penalties are required. But to deter a would-be violator effectively they must be credible.

By far the most important and practical penalty would be a general increase in the military effort, going beyond what would be required to restore the pre-agreement situation. (A threat to start a war would not be equally credible and would therefore be less effective.) Suppose the aggrieved nation increases its defense budget by $20 billion. (As a result of the North Korean aggression, the United States increased its national security expenditures from $13 billion to $52 billion.) If the violator does not follow suit, he will become relatively weaker than he was before breaking the disarmament agreement. If he does follow suit, he would, in effect, be "fined" the equivalent of $20 billion, though of course both sides would bear this burden.

The injured country may be able to step up its defense effort in ways that do not require a large increase in the budget and still impose significant penalties on the violator: for example, by changing the deployment and readiness of weapons, or by resuming military activities that were voluntarily limited beforehand. However, in doing this the injured party must be prepared to run the risk that such a "punitive" increase in its defense effort will renew or accelerate the arms race. Actually, the violator may wish to avoid an arms race with so determined an opponent; he may be unwilling or unable to pay his full "fine" and have to accept a loss in relative military strength.

Those who wish to prevent the violation of arms-control agreements must deter potential violators by their evident determination to make a double sacrifice. In the event a violation occurs they must be ready to assume a greater economic burden for defense, and they must risk a step-up in military competition. The willingness to make such sacrifices involves less, however, than would be required to deter limited aggression. To do that successfully a country must be willing not only to accept increased defense costs if deterrence fails, but also to suffer casualties and face the risk that the limited conflict may expand.

Political sanctions are likely to be less effective than an increased defense effort, although they may play an important complementary role. What they might be is difficult to predict in the abstract. If the potential violator is cautious, this uncertainty may help to deter him; if he is adventurous, like Hitler, he will gamble on his ability to meet and overcome the political reaction.

The remaining question is how to make the penalties of evasion seem more inevitable and severe and the gains more dubious. Parliamentary governments are more likely to take strong action against a violation if they are supported by public opinion. The evidence of violation must therefore be such as to impress the public as authoritative and impartial. A finding by an international organization will be influential in this regard, especially with public opinion outside the countries directly affected. An international body, however, has many weaknesses that can be exploited by a violator. Ideally, one would want the best of both worlds: the greater authenticity and dramatic impact that an international inspectorate provides, and the flexibility and versatility of national intelligence systems. One should at any rate avoid entering into arms-control arrangements that are administratively closed to intelligence information. The current draft treaty for the nuclear test ban sets up a rigidly confined scheme from which intelligence information is essentially excluded.[5] The Antarctica treaty, on the other hand, provides for complete freedom of inspection by anyone without any international mechanism (except suggestions for arbitration in the event of "disputes").

The deterrence of evasions could also be strengthened if parliamentary governments took steps to simplify and speed up their decision-making procedures. The United States Government, for example, has sometimes adopted enabling legislation to facilitate quick Presidential action, in order to disabuse a potential aggressor of the idea that partisan conflict or public quarreling about constitutional limitations or the issue at hand might inhibit an effective response. The Formosa resolution of 1955 is an example of Congressional authorization for the President to take action on the basis of his finding alone. The United Nations Participation Act of 1945 authorizes the President to act upon a decision by an international body, the United Nations Security Council. To strengthen a disarmament agreement both types of authorizations might be useful, and a good time to enact the appropriate enabling legislation would be when Congress ratifies an arms-control treaty.

The power and influence of the legislative branch of the government might be brought to bear in other ways so as to increase the likelihood that the reaction to an evasion would be prompt and strong. Special parliamentary committees might

[5] Both the Soviet and the Western drafts allow the parties to select their annual quota of on-site inspections freely from among seismic disturbances that meet certain criteria. However, should a violation be unaccompanied by such a disturbance (e.g. a muffled underground test), the violator would not have to permit an inspection and the international control system would remain closed to all other evidence.

assume an explicit responsibility for all arms-control agreements, and stand ready to mobilize legislative support for any necessary response to some breach of a treaty. The Joint Committee on Atomic Energy, which has privileged access to classified information and is on intimate terms with the executive, offers appropriate administrative precedents. Thus Congress might create a "Joint Committee on the Observance of Arms Controls" to demonstrate its determination to make arms-control agreements succeed.

An effective response will often require coördination and agreement among allies. The difficulties which this involves might be lessened by making arrangements in advance for joint action. First, in order to ensure agreement as to the fact of evasion, all evidence could be evaluated by an inter-allied agency permanently set up for this purpose. To minimize considerations of domestic politics, it should not have the responsibility for recommending any action. The next step by the allied governments might be a relatively minor one, on which agreement could easily be reached, namely to give publicity to the committee's findings; for example, they might forward a report on the evasion to the United Nations or to an international control system provided by the disarmament treaty. From this point on, the allied governments having jointly held and publicized their interpretation of the violation would feel under more compulsion to reach agreement on the effective sanctions needed.

It may be argued that allied governments cannot be "tricked" into such a procedure, because if they are opposed to or afraid of vigorous action they will avoid taking the first step: the evaluation of evidence. This argument would have force if the procedure were to be determined *after* the violation had been charged. But it is proposed here that by a preparatory agreement the Allies shall firmly establish the procedure at the time they conclude the arms-control treaty, when they are still fairly confident that the other side will adhere to it, hence are less opposed to a firm commitment for joint action against what seems a remote contingency.

All these political measures must be planned to the accompaniment of whatever military preparations will be necessary to deal with violations of the agreement. For instance, under an agreement that prohibits only the testing of certain weapons, both sides will remain free to continue research and development. The country that is determined to abide by the agreement cannot afford to neglect this research without opening the way for a potential violator to gain and then exploit a technological lead. Unless the public understands this fact, parliamentary governments will be handicapped in maintaining a research effort for weapons whose testing has been prohibited. The same problem would also arise under an agreement which does not prohibit the development of a weapon but does prevent the deployment of it—for example, a ban on placing weapons of mass destruction in orbit.

A program to deter evasion of arms-control agreements, like the one suggested here, does raise some additional problems for which an analogy can be found in the strategy of deterrence against nuclear attack. First, there is the problem of carrying out a threat if deterrence fails, that is, of imposing sanctions in the event of evasion or of retaliating in the event of attack. An advance commitment to carry out the threat is rational and necessary for a policy aimed at deterrence; but carrying out the threat after deterrence has failed may be undesirable or even irrational. Second, a policy of deterrence has to cope with accidental violations of the agreement, just as a policy of deterrence against nuclear attack has to control the risk of accidental war. In the former case, both sides will wish to correct the unintended violation and preserve the agreement; in the latter, both will want to avoid or correct an "accident" before it leads to full exchanges of violence. Third, there is some resemblance between the advantage of a first strike in mutual deterrence against nuclear attack and the advantage of gaining time through an evasion in certain arms-control agreements. None of these analogies is exact, of course. But they do suggest that ideas in the literature on deterrence can be as relevant to the prevention of violations in arms-control agreements as they are to the prevention of war.

THE ROLE OF DETERRENCE IN
TOTAL DISARMAMENT

By Thomas C. Schelling

A SHARP distinction is often drawn between arms control and disarmament. The former seeks to reshape military incentives and capabilities; the latter, it is alleged, eliminates them. But the success of either depends on mutual deterrence. Short of universal brain surgery, nothing can erase the memory of weapons and how to build them. If "total disarmament" is to make war unlikely, it must reduce the incentives. It cannot eliminate the potential for destruction; the most primitive war can be modernized by rearmament as it goes along.

To determine whether and how disarmament might make war less likely we have to look at what the military opportunities, risks, dangers, fears and potential capabilities would be in a disarmed world. If nations now suspect each other of contemplating war, we have to suppose that they might suspect each other of contemplating rearmament. If nations are willing to risk war, or to threaten it, they certainly might risk rearming or threatening to rearm. Nations thought capable now of being panicked into war might be panicked into rearmament. To suppose the contrary is to assume away the problem that disarmament is intended to help solve.

An international military authority is commonly proposed as a part of plans for total disarmament. It does make a difference whether or not we assume the existence of such an authority to police the otherwise disarmed world. But for the visible future it is a little extreme to suppose that an international force could contain or deter the United States and the Soviet Union; more than that, the concept poses problems of deterrence not wholly unlike those that would confront the major powers in a fully disarmed world. So we shall first consider universal disarmament without any international security force. And we shall assume a world disarmed to the levels proposed by those who favor the most drastic "total disarmament."

There are good reasons why this phrase should be set off in quotation marks. An obvious one is that there can be no absolute assurance that some nuclear weapons have not been kept. But, cheating aside, war can be waged with even the most primitive weapons, especially with the help of commercial aircraft, ships, trucks, radios and the other paraphernalia of industrial society. More important, if war breaks out a nation can rearm unless its capacity is destroyed at the outset and kept destroyed. By the standards of 1944, the United States was fairly near to total disarmament when World War II broke out. Virtually all munitions later expended by United States forces were nonexistent in September 1939. "Disarmament" did not preclude U.S. participation; it just slowed it down.

As we eliminate weapons, warning systems, vehicles and bases, we change the criteria of military effectiveness. Airplanes are more important if missiles are banned; complex airplanes are needed less if complex defenses are banned. Since weapons themselves are the most urgent targets in war, to eliminate a weapon eliminates a target and changes the requirements for attack. At some stage in disarmament a donkey becomes a means of delivery, though we assume that "total" disarmament stops short of that.

The difficulty cannot be avoided by banning weapons of attack and keeping those of defense. If nations were large, self-sufficient islands, coast artillery might seem useless for aggression and valuable safeguards against war and the fear of war. But they are not; and in the present era, "defensive" weapons often embody equipment or technology that is superbly useful in attack and invasion. Moreover, a prerequisite of successful attack is some ability to defend against retaliation or counterattack. In a disarmed world, whatever lessens the scale of retaliation reduces the risk a nation runs in starting war. Defenses against retaliation thus are close substitutes for offensive power.

II. GENERAL WAR IN A DISARMED WORLD

Disarmament would not preclude the eruption of a crisis; war and rearmament could seem imminent. Even without possessing complex weapons, a nation might consider initiating war with whatever resources it had, on grounds that delay would allow an enemy to strike or mobilize first. If a nation believed its opponent might rush to rearm to achieve military preponderance, it might consider "preventive war" to forestall its opponent's dominance. Or, if confidence in the maintenance of disarmament were low and if war later under worse conditions seemed at all likely, there could be motives for "preventive ultimatums," or for winning a short war through coercion with illicitly retained nuclear weapons, or for using force to impose a more durable disarmament arrangement.

The decision to attack might be made reluctantly, motivated not by the prospective gains of victory but by the disadvantages of not seizing the initiative. Motives to undertake preventive or preëmptive war might be as powerful under disarmament as with today's weapons—perhaps more powerful.

In a disarmed world, as now, the objective would probably be to destroy the enemy's ability to bring war into one's homeland, and to "win" sufficiently to prevent his subsequent build-up as a military menace. The urgent targets would be the enemy's available weapons of mass destruction (if any), his means of delivery, his equipment that could be quickly converted for strategic use, and the components, stand-by facilities and cadres from which he could assemble a capability for strategic warfare.

Suppose both sides have violated the agreement and possess nuclear bombs at least in the scores or hundreds (or suppose the attacker has, and must anticipate that his opponent has). The attacker's first objective is to forestall the delivery of bombs in return. Compared with the present, the disarmed world would offer the attacker both advantages and disadvantages.

An advantage is that the time scale of attack may be more lenient. The victim may have a secret nuclear stockpile; but if he is unprepared it will take time to bring together, say, commercial aircraft, crews and the hidden nuclear weapons, and to improvise fueling arrangements and target plans. To do this in the hostile environment of even small-scale nuclear attack might be difficult. But the attacker would be coördinated rather than surprised and could make effective use of evacuation procedures or of any air defenses he could improvise.

If, instead, each side has plans for the contingency and maintains a "reserve force"—some part, say, of its commercial air fleet and crews—the victim of attack may react quickly. The attacker's own air defenses have been banned by agreement (and air defenses may be hard to conceal); in these conditions a retaliatory force of even low efficiency may be effective if it is large and dispersed.

If the aggressor has nuclear weapons and the victim does not, the latter's response will depend on how rapidly production can be resumed. Standby capacity may be available, or there may be nuclear facilities that can be converted to produce weapons. If

633

these facilities have not been destroyed, the lag may be short, but a matter of days at least. Critically important would be the defenses, the dispersal or the secrecy of the facilities for producing nuclear materials or for assembling nuclear weapons. If the sites are few in number, of known location, above ground and without air defense, they would be destroyed before operations could be resumed. If the production facilities are in secret locations, we may as well assume that nuclear weapons also exist.

III. A WAR OF NUCLEAR MOBILIZATION

In the event that neither side had nuclear weapons, asymmetrical lead-times in nuclear rearmament could be decisive. Whether it took days or months, the side that believed it could be first to acquire a few dozen megatons through a crash rearmament program would expect to dominate its opponent. This advantage would be greatest if nuclear facilities themselves were vulnerable to nuclear bombardment: the first few weapons produced would be used to spoil the opponent's nuclear rearmament. Even if facilities are deep under the ground, well disguised or highly dispersed, a small difference in the time needed to acquire a few score megatons might make the war unendurable for the side that is behind. If one side appears likely to gain the decisive advantage, it might find "preventive rearmament" coupled with a surrender ultimatum an irresistibly attractive move.

It would not necessarily be essential to possess nuclear weapons in order to destroy nuclear facilities. High explosives, commandos or saboteurs could be effective. "Strategic warfare" might reach a purity not known in this century: like the king in chess, nuclear facilities would be the overriding objective. Their protection would have absolute claim on defense.

In such a war the object would be to preserve one's mobilization base and to destroy the enemy's. To win a war would not require overcoming the enemy's defenses—just winning the rearmament race. If commandos can bypass home defenses and paralyze the adversary's nuclear mobilization base, the jig is up—unless all participants can do this to each other. If they can, the prospect is for a bizarre kind of "broken-backed" war, bizarre because no back is broken, and the struggle to acquire nuclear weapons goes on—hopefully not too fast and too furiously to allow parallel negotiations for an agreed stalemate or a second try at "disarmament."

Another kind of warfare may emerge—"nuclear coercion." If an attacker possesses illicit nuclear weapons that can be dropped on a country that is unable to retaliate promptly, it might force a surrender through the destruction of cities and the threat of destroying more. Or the coercive campaign could combine preclusive destruction of the mobilization base with the demoralizing effects of concurrent civil damage. The expectation would be that, if significant rearmament could be retarded, capitulation would be forthcoming.

Such a war might be less destructive than war under present conditions, not primarily because disarmament had reduced the attacker's capability but because, with the victim unable to respond, the attacker could adopt a more measured pace that allowed time to negotiate a cease-fire before he had reduced his victim to rubble. Victory, of course, might be achieved without violence. If one side appears to have an advantage so convincingly decisive as to make the outcome of the war seem inevitable, it could then deliver an ultimatum instead of weapons.[1]

Disarmament might also cause nuclear weapons to be a greater equalizer among nations than they are now. A future Castro might be in a better position to plague or coerce the great powers by secreting nuclear weapons on his territory. In a world in which such forms of nuclear mischief have replaced the space-age machinery of war and in which the push-button has given way to improvised aerial ferries, the military environment may become less predictable and possibly more unstable.

To sum up: a stable military environment will not result automatically from a ban on weapons and the facilities to make them. The timing of war and rearmament, and the role of speed and initiative, will remain critically important in a world in which the pace of war is initially slowed. War may become more calculable and less fearsome. And there would remain, even in the design of "total disarmament," the difficult choice between minimizing war's destructiveness and minimizing its likelihood. If disarmament is to discourage the initiation of war and to remove the incentives toward preëmptive and preventive war, it has to be *designed* to do that. Disarmament does not eliminate military potential; it changes it.

[1] Deterrence being largely a matter of credibility, it might not always be an advantage to have it believed that one is complying with the prohibition on nuclear weapons. At the slightest suspicion that others might be initiating preparations, a government might prefer to hint that it was already prepared. A small nuclear capability might be used to demonstrate a larger professed capability.

While disarmament would eliminate the guns, it would not eliminate the trucks, aircraft, ships, communication equipment and canned food that are required for limited military campaigns. Nations could be expected to have plans for limited-war mobilization, including limited departures from the arms agreement itself.[2]

As important as the direct consequences that disarmament would have for limited war would be the indirect consequences. If disarmament reduces fears of general war—if explosion or escalation into general war seems a less likely prospect, or less disastrous if it should occur—the result may be fewer inhibitions on limited war. There could also be new restraints. If it is perceived that the outbreak of local wars may destroy the agreement itself —either through a sudden breakdown or steady erosion—this may create a determination to preserve what has been achieved and a recognition that to abandon restraints would signal "open season" on military competition. Of course, the more all parties value the climate of disarmament, the more can be gained by threatening to disturb it.

As "limited war" is possible, so is "limited violation" of disarmament. Since limits on hostilities can evidently be observed during war itself, limits on rearmament might be arrived at in similar fashion, even in the course of limited hostilities. The responses of countries not participating in the war would be important—perhaps an important brake, possibly a stimulus, on the resumed armament.

In limited war as in general war under conditions of "total disarmament," timing would be important. Offensive strategy in a limited war is often designed to achieve a *fait accompli*. Defense against this strategy in a disarmed world would depend on the ability of the defender (or protector) to rearm in time to repel or to stalemate the aggression. If we reflect on the critical timing of the North Korean invasion and the shortage of ammunition that plagued us throughout the whole Korean campaign, or the problems of the preëmptive landing of Marines in Lebanon or the progress of the Suez campaign, it is evident that logistical considerations can be decisive. The likelihood that limited aggression

[2] The Chinese civil war of 1948–49 may illustrate how extensive a war can be fought with poor weaponry and primitive logistical support. Or the American Civil War.

will be deterred by the threat of limited rearmament may therefore depend on the mobilization speed that can be achieved from a standing start.

V. THE DETERRENCE OF REARMAMENT IN A DISARMED WORLD

Many concepts that apply to the deterrence of war apply to deterrence of rearmament: "preventive" rearmament, "preëmptive" rearmament, "escalation" of rearmament, "catalytic" rearmament, and rearmament stimulated by misinformation, misinterpretation, accident, false alarm, unauthorized conspiracy and other processes analogous to those that might trigger "inadvertent war" in an armed world. In addition, there are the possibilities of rearmament bubbling up out of a crisis, occurring in the course of a limited war or being undertaken by cool premeditation.

But despite the parallel, rearmament is not war. The fears, motives and moral attitudes that make initiation of war an opprobrious act do not apply with the same force to rearmament. The question whether to remain disarmed or to initiate limited rearmament could become a legitimate political issue. If the disarmament is so delicately balanced that there is great advantage in being the first to rearm, the mere existence of a political party pledged to abandon the disarmament treaty might disturb the arrangement. And to the extent that the treaty explicitly allows certain weapons or a mobilization base, continuing developments in technology will make armament, as well as disarmament, a proper topic of discussion and continuing negotiation.

The essential requirement is for some stable situation of "rearmament parity." If disarmament is to be durable, it must be apparent that the disadvantages of being behind in case an arms race should resume are not too great and that, in the face of ambiguous evidence of clandestine rearmament or overt evidence of imminent rearmament, nations can react without haste. The straightforward elimination of so-called "military production facilities" might, by sheer coincidence, provide the stability; but stability is more likely if there is a deliberately designed system of "stable equal readiness for rearmament." It is impossible to eliminate the ability to rearm; one can only hope to stretch the time required to reach, from the word "go," any specified level of rearmament. The problem is not *whether* to leave a mobilization base for rearmament, but what kind.

It is not certain that maximizing the time required to rearm is a way to deter it. Lengthening the racecourse does not necessarily lessen the incentive to be first under the wire. But it may reduce the advantage of a small head-start; it may allow time to renegotiate before the race has too much momentum; and it may reduce the confidence of a fast starter that he could win if he called for a race.

If rearmament is undertaken to improve mutual deterrence, not to achieve offensive superiority, it may not matter whether some nations fall behind. The leader will not necessarily race as fast as he can; for if he does, other nations may have to regard his behavior as a declaration of war and to respond accordingly. If a low-grade war of nuclear reprisal is within the capability of some laggard in the rearmament race, he may feel obliged to initiate such a war to disrupt another's rearmament; thus rearmament could lead to preëmptive action and trigger a war. On the other hand, this prospect may help deter rearmament itself.

The likelihood of war, then, depends on the character of the disarmament. If mobilization potentials are such that a head-start is not decisive and the racecourse is long, preëmptive action may be delayed until motives are clear. This, however, presents a dilemma analogous to that of deterring limited war today: the smaller the fear that rearmament will precipitate general war, the smaller the inhibition on rearmament.

Important elements for stability in a disarmed world would be the dispersal and duplication of standby facilities for rearmament and of reserve personnel or cadres around which rearmament can be mobilized. Dispersal is important because of the interaction between rearmament and war itself. If a nation can achieve just enough production of weapons to disrupt its opponent's rearmament, it may gain a decisive advantage. Once the race is on, a few easily-located facilities for producing nuclear weapons might invite a "preventive" and very limited war. If instead there were, say, scores or hundreds of laboratories able to produce unconventional weapons and if their destruction would require substantial military capabilities, there might be less incentive on one side to acquire and exploit a small advantage and less fear on the other of falling a little behind and being taken advantage of.

Nations are now willing to threaten war; in a disarmed world they certainly might threaten rearmament. The agreement itself would certainly have to be renegotiated from time to time, or continuously; and, just as a threat of "no sale" hangs over the head of commercial traders, so will the threat of rearmament hang over the heads of negotiators. The main sanction on the negotiations will be that, in the absence of a satisfactory agreement, nations may take unilateral steps for their own security or take steps to put pressure on others.

VI. ATTITUDES TOWARD REARMAMENT

The terms of an agreement must take into account what the attitude toward rearmament would be in the disarmed world. One approach would be that any overt rearmament would be a mortal sin, a total failure of the disarmament process, a contingency that can neither be planned for nor discussed coolly within countries or between governments. Alternatively, rearmament might be viewed as we view war now—as a tragedy and a failure of policy, but a tragedy that can occur, that can even occur from motives of self-defense, that can perhaps be limited and contained, and that need not signal the termination of all efforts at settlement and reconciliation.

The first attitude, which would try to insulate rearmament from the cold war and deprecate any planning for the contingency of rearmament, might be preferable if it could promise to create sufficiently strong inhibitions. If, instead, we have to expect—as surely we do—lapses under even the most ideal disarmament scheme, it is better to plan for such contingencies and to create the expectation that occasional lapses need not trigger a real arms race or the full fury of war itself. We cannot have it both ways. For if we recognize "limited rearmament" as a possibility and prepare for "limited responses" against it, we take some of the curse off rearmament, just as plans for limited war seem to legitimize war. This is a genuine dilemma.

Rearmament has other dimensions than speed and volume. We should distinguish between rearmament aimed at stable deterrence and rearmament aimed at brinkmanship or war. In this country we would certainly want to have careful rearmament plans so that, in the event we found ourselves unavoidably drawn into a renewed arms race, our actions would be consistent with deterrence of war and with an effort to slow down the pace of rearmament. The further rearmament goes and the more unstable the environment which it creates, the harder it will be to get back to the business of disarmament if we wish to.

It will also make a difference whether military and strategic

639

planning is permitted and expected or frowned on. The dilemma is that stability will require careful planning of a kind inconsistent with the philosophy that military planning is illegal, immoral and a sign of evil intent. If nations suddenly awoke to rearmament dangers of which they had not been aware, their response might be more undisciplined and more unstable in the absence of military planning than if vigilance had been deliberately maintained.

It should not be expected that reduced tensions will be the natural consequence of a disarmament agreement. Not everyone will be confident that disarmament provides a viable military environment or promises the political atmosphere most conducive to peace and good relations. It is hard to believe that any sober person under any conceivable world arrangement could come to believe with confidence that war had at last been banished from human affairs until there had been at the very least some decades of experience. There will be surprises, rumors and sharp misunderstandings. Even if something that looks like "general and complete disarmament" is achieved, it is not out of the question that responsible governments might decide that international apprehensions would be reduced if they possessed more secure, more diversified and more professionally organized mobilization bases or weapon systems, with more freedom to improve them, drill them and discuss the strategy of their use.

It is even conceivable that a "rearmament agreement" would be negotiated in the interest of reducing tensions, the likelihood of war, the scope for "rearmament blackmail," the Nth-country problem, and perhaps even the economic costs of preparedness. It might be that moderate though expensive modern weapon systems, professionally organized and segregated from the main population centers, would provide less—not more—military interference in everyday life than a "total" disarmament agreement under which every commercial pilot carried emergency mobilization instructions in his briefcase. In any event, a decision on total disarmament, taken jointly by the major powers, would not bring an end to arguments about arms control.

VII. AN INTERNATIONAL MILITARY AUTHORITY

Some kind of international authority is generally proposed as part of an agreement on total disarmament. If militarily superior to any combination of national forces, an international force implies (or is) some form of world government. To call such an ar-

640

rangement "disarmament" is about as oblique as to call the Constitution of the United States "a Treaty for Uniform Currency and Interstate Commerce." The authors of the Federalist Papers were under no illusion as to the far-reaching character of the institution they were discussing, and we should not be either. Here, however, we can focus only on those aspects of an International Force that directly affect the military environment.

One concept deserves mention in passing: that the projected police force should aim to control persons rather than nations. Its weapons would be squad cars, tear gas and pistols; its intelligence system would be phone taps, lie detectors and detectives; its mission would be to arrest people, not to threaten war on governments. Here, however, we shall concentrate on the concept of an International Force to police nations—and all nations, not just small ones. The most intriguing questions are those that relate to the Force's technique or strategy for deterring and containing the former nuclear powers.

The mission of the Force would be to police the world against war and rearmament. It might be authorized only to stop war; but some kinds of rearmament would be clear signals of war, obliging the Force to take action. There might be, explicitly or implicitly, a distinction between the kinds of rearmament that call for intervention and the kinds that are not hostile.

The operations of the Force raise a number of questions. Should it try to contain aggression locally, or to invade the aggressor countries (or all parties to the conflict) and to disable them militarily? Should it use long-range strategic weapons to disable the country militarily? Should it rely on the threat of massive punitive retaliation? Should it use the threat or, if necessary, the practice of limited nuclear reprisal as a coercive technique? In the case of rearmament, the choices would include invasion or threats of invasion, strategic warfare, reprisal or the threat of reprisal; "containment" could not forestall rearmament unless the country were vulnerable to blockade.

Is the Force intended to do the job itself or to head a worldwide alliance against transgressors? In case of aggression, is the victim to participate in his own defense? If the Indians take Tibet, or the Chinese encourage armed homesteading in Siberia, the Force would have to possess great manpower unless it was prepared to rely on nuclear weapons. A Force could not be maintained on a scale sufficient to "contain" such excursions by a

641

nation with a large population unless it relied on the sudden mobilization of the rest of the world or on superior weaponry—nuclear weapons if the defense is to be confined to the area of incursion. But the use of such weapons to defend, for example, South Viet Nam against Chinese infiltrators, Western Europe against the Soviet bloc, East Germany against West Germany or Cuba against the United States, would be subject to the ordinary difficulties of employing nuclear weapons in populated areas. A country threatened by invasion might rather capitulate than be defended in that fashion. Moreover, the Force might require logistical facilities, infrastructure and occasional large-scale manœuvres in areas where it expects to be called upon. Keeping large forces stationed permanently along the Iron Curtain is a possibility, but not one that brings with it all the psychological benefits hoped for from disarmament.

A sizeable intervention of the Force between major powers is not, of course, something to be expected often in a disarmed world. Nevertheless, if the Force is conceived of as superseding Soviet and American reliance on their own nuclear capabilities, it needs to have some plausible capability to meet large-scale aggression; if it hasn't, the major powers may still be deterred, but it is not the Force that deters them.

A capability for massive or measured nuclear punishment is probably the easiest attribute with which to equip the Force. But it is not evident that the Force could solve the problems of "credibility" or of collective decision any better than can the United States alone or NATO collectively at the present time. This does not mean that it could not solve them—just that they are not automatically solved when a treaty is signed. If the Force is itself stateless, it may have no "homeland" against which counter-reprisal could be threatened by a transgressor nation; but if it is at all civilized, it will not be wholly immune to the counter-deterrent threats of a transgressor to create civil damage in other countries. These could be either explicit threats of reprisal or implicit threats of civil destruction collateral to the bombardment of the Force's own mobilization base. (The Force presumably produces or procures its weaponry in the industrial nations, and cannot be entirely housed in Antarctica, on the high seas or in outer space.)

If it should appear technically impossible to police the complete elimination of nuclear weapons, then we should have to assume that at least minimal stockpiles had been retained by the major powers. In that case, the Force might not be a great deal more than one additional deterrent force; it would not enjoy the military monopoly generally envisaged.

One concept needs to be disposed of—that the Force should be strong enough to defeat a coalition of aggressors but not so strong as to impose its will against universal opposition. Even if the world had only the weapons of Napoleon, the attempt to calculate such a delicate power balance would seem impossible. With concepts like preëmption, retaliation and nuclear blackmail, any arithmetical solution is out of the question.

The knottiest strategic problem for an International Force would be to halt the unilateral rearmament of a major country. The credibility of its threat to employ nuclear weapons whenever some country renounces the agreement and begins to rearm itself would seem to be very low indeed.

The kind of rearmament would make a difference. If a major country openly arrived at a political decision to abandon the agreement and to recover the security it felt it had lost by starting to build a merely retaliatory capability and sizeable home-defense forces, it is hard to envisage a civilized International Force using weapons of mass destruction on a large scale to stop it. Limited nuclear reprisals might be undertaken in an effort to discourage the transgressor from his purpose. But unless the rearmament program is accompanied by some overt aggressive moves, perhaps in limited war, the cool and restrained introduction of nuclear or other unconventional weapons into the country's population centers does not seem plausible, unless non-lethal chemical or biological weapons could be used.

Invasion might offer a more plausible sanction, perhaps with paratroops armed with small nuclear weapons for their own defense; their objective would be to paralyze the transgressor's government and mobilization. But if this should be considered the most feasible technique for preventing rearmament, we have to consider two implications. We have provided the Force a bloodless way of taking over national governments. And a preëmptive invasion of this kind might require the Force to act with a speed and secrecy inconsistent with political safeguards.

There is also the question of what kinds of rearmament or political activity leading to rearmament should precipitate occupation by the Force. In our country, could the Republicans or Democrats campaign on a rearmament platform, go to the polls and win, wait to be inaugurated, denounce the agreement, and begin orderly rearmament? If the Force intervenes, should it do so after rearmament is begun, or after a party has introduced a rearmament resolution in Congress? The illustration suggests that one function of the Force, or the political body behind it, would be to attempt first to negotiate with a potential rearming country rather than to intervene abruptly at some point in these developments.

Again, the character of rearmament would make a difference. Suppose the President presented a well-designed plan to build an obviously second-strike retaliatory force of poor preëmptive capability against either the International Force or other countries, but relatively secure from attack. If he justified it on the grounds that the current military environment was susceptible to sudden overturn by technological developments, political upheavals, irrepressible international antagonisms, the impotence of the Force for decisive intervention, the corruption or subversion of the Force, or other such reasons, then the authorization of a drastic intervention by the Force in the United States would be less likely than if the President ordered a crash program to assemble nuclear weapons, trained crews and long-range aircraft. It would make a considerable difference, too, whether rearmament occurred at a time of crisis, perhaps with a war going on, or in calmer times.

The point of all this is simply that even an International Military Authority with an acknowledged sole right in the possession of major weapons will have strategic problems that are not easy. This is, of course, aside from the even more severe problems of political control of the "executive branch" and "military establishment" of the world governing body. If we hope to turn all our international disputes over to a formal procedure of adjudication and to rely on an international military bureaucracy to enforce decisions, we are simply longing for government without politics. We are hoping for the luxury, which most of us enjoy municipally, of turning over our dirtiest jobs—especially those that require strong nerves—to some specialized employees. That works fairly well for burglary, but not so well for school integration, general strikes or Algerian independence. We may achieve it if we create a sufficiently potent and despotic ruling force; but then some of us would have to turn around and start plotting civil war, and the Force's strategic problems would be only beginning.

644

This is not an essay against disarmament, even "total disarmament." It is simply a warning against the notion that there is any once-for-all solution to the problems of world peace and government. It is against the notion that if only disarmament is "total" enough, we can forget about deterrence and all that. It is against the notion that under "total" disarmament there is no military potential to be controlled, balanced or stabilized.

There should be no divorce between deterrence and disarmament. If disarmament is to work, it has got to improve deterrence and to stabilize deterrence. Until a much greater community of interest exists in the world than is likely in this generation, war will have to be made unprofitable. It cannot be made impossible.

It is sometimes argued that to perpetuate military deterrence is to settle for a peace based on fear. But the implied contrast between arms control and total disarmament is not persuasive. What would deter rearmament in a disarmed world, or small wars that may escalate into large ones, must be the apprehension of a resumed arms race and war. The extent of the "fear" involved in any arrangement—total disarmament, negotiated mutual deterrence, or anything else—is a function of confidence. If the consequences of transgression are plainly bad—bad for all parties, and little dependent on who transgresses first—we can take the consequences for granted and call it a "balance of prudence." What keeps us from stepping off a train before it stops is not "fear"; we just know better.

QUESTIONS FOR SEMINAR DISCUSSION

Would you agree with Clark and Sohn that a separate United Nations Nuclear Authority should be established to deal with nuclear energy? Do you think that it would be necessary to set up an Agency to deal exclusively with objects and organisms that might be used in biological warfare? Would it jeopardize the plan if the Inspection Service performed the functions outlined for the Agency? Do you think that the presence or absence of the Agency would make any difference in the acceptability of the rest of the disarmament scheme?

Do you agree with all the provisions for membership and structure of the Nuclear Authority and also with its relationship to the other organs proposed by Clark and Sohn?

Do you see any particular problems of achieving acceptance for a Nuclear Energy Authority? Do you see particular problems in administering the functions of the Nuclear Energy Authority which they propose?

Would you agree with Clark and Sohn that an Outer Space Agency to handle the functions outlined on pages 296-297 of World Peace Through World Law is necessary to achieve effective disarmament? What problems would arise if there were only an inspection service concerned with weapons and delivery systems but no Outer Space Agency? Is it possible that it might be easier to get agreement on the establishment of the Outer Space Agency than on other parts of their proposal?

Iklé and a good deal of Schelling's article can be usefully viewed as dealing with the problems of violation during the process of disarming. They see the problems here being solved within a framework of a related balance-of-power deterrent system and a more centralized system of deterrence. Clark and Sohn rely almost solely on a centralized system of deterrence to inhibit violations. Which approach is likely to be most acceptable to the states today? Which system is likely to break down during the disarmament process.

Are there any facets of the Clark-Sohn proposals for dealing with violations with which you disagree? Why? Are there any matters which you would add to these proposals?

Assuming that the disarmament process is completed, do the provisions in Chapter III of the Disarmament Annex (page 246) regulate, control, and abolish all those matters and activities of states which would be necessary to maintain disarmament? Are there any of these provisions which might be dropped because they would be unacceptable to major states but would not pose a serious problem to the viability of the system?

Schelling makes the point that "total" disarmament is impossible since human beings can always organize to develop and use some objects as weapons. How significant a point is this? Isn't it true that in domestic societies men can (and a few do) organize to use weapons, but the presence of police, who have the job of seeing to it that this activity is prohibited, prevents this from breaking out into widespread violence? Or is there more to his point?

CURRENT PROSPECTS FOR DISARMAMENT

In the previous two sessions we looked at the problem of using disarmament and arms control from the relatively narrow viewpoint of security-military problems, although it has been obvious that major political problems were related to them. We will be unable to focus direct attention on these relationships, but their significance will become even more apparent as we move to an investigation of disarmament negotiations.

Our central concern in this session will be an analysis and evaluation of the most current proposals on disarmament made by the USSR and the US in the spring of 1962 at the eighteen nation Disarmament Conference in Geneva. Both proposals call for complete and general disarmament supervised by a new international organization working closely with the United Nations. We shall want to compare these plans along three dimensions: amount, kind and phasing of disarmament; amount and type of verification of the disarmament; the structure and function of peace-keeping machinery. We shall also want to assess to what extent each plan offers an acceptable and effective system for achieving and maintaining disarmament.

Three additional readings for this session are provided: two to give us historical background, and one as a comparative measure. The Bechhoefer and McVitty articles remind us that these negotiations have been going on since 1945, and both authors are inclined to believe that for a good many of the negotiations the participants were not adequately prepared nor seriously involved. Whether the 1962 proposals are evidence of progress is something we shall want to discuss. The McVitty piece also contains a brief but helpful analysis of the two disarmament proposals.

The "Brief Summary of a World Disarmament and World Development Organization within the framework of the United Nations" by Clark and Sohn represents a model for a new world organization based on the same principles and containing much of the same detail we studied in World Peace Through World Law. As the most detailed and comprehensive scheme for complete and general disarmament it offers us a common standard with which to view each of these proposals as a system. And again it raises the question as to which is more realistic and effective -- a series of small steps, a limited system moving slowly to a more comprehensive organization, or agreement to the creation of that organization in one step with implementation to follow on an agreed time schedule.

Readings from World Peace Through World Law:
    None

The Disarmament Deadlock: 1946-1955

By Bernhard G. Bechhoefer

ON JUNE 14, 1946, Bernard Baruch, America's elder statesman, addressed a solemn warning to the first meeting of the United Nations Atomic Energy Commission:

My Fellow Members of the United Nations Atomic Energy Commission, and my Fellow Citizens of the World, We are here to make a choice between the quick and the dead. That is our business. Behind the black portent of the new atomic age lies a hope which, seized upon with faith, can work our salvation. Let us not deceive ourselves. We must elect World Peace or World Destruction.[1]

This address opened the years of discussions of disarmament in the United Nations and in the commissions and committees created by or affiliated with the United Nations, discussions which still continue.

When the charter of the United Nations was signed in June, 1945, it was never contemplated that the subject of disarmament would assume such a dominant role in the United Nations during the early years of its existence. The charter, like the covenant of the League of Nations, rested on the premise

that the scourge of war had become so terrible that steps had to be taken to control and ultimately to reduce national armaments. The League covenant, however, had looked to disarmament as one of the first principal steps toward peace. In contrast, the United Nations uses the word disarmament only twice.[2]

The principal powers engaged in the struggle against Germany deliberately sought to avoid the fruitless negotiations for disarmament which had taken place under the auspices of the League of Nations during almost the entire period between the first and second World Wars. The United Nations Charter, therefore, placed emphasis upon the establishment first of an effective system of collective security as a prelude to any attempt to limit the armaments of the great powers. In fact, Churchill, Stalin and Roosevelt had contemplated disarming all countries except the "Big Three" and with some reservations, France.

Almost immediately after the signing of

649

the Charter in San Francisco in August, 1945, the explosion of the atomic bomb over Hiroshima introduced a new element into international relations which altered the thinking of all countries. The frightening magnification of destructive capability immediately brought to the fore the entire problem of the regulation of armaments. The United States took the initiative in urging immediate action in the direction of international control of atomic energy. Within a few days after Hiroshima, President Truman devoted an entire speech to the international consequences of nuclear weapons.

> The atomic bomb is too dangerous to be loose in a lawless world. That is why Great Britain and the United States, who have the secret of its production, do not intend to reveal the secret until means have been found to control the bomb so as to protect ourselves and the rest of the world from the danger of total destruction. . . . We must constitute ourselves trustees of this new force to prevent its misuse, and to turn it into the channels of service to mankind.[3]

President Truman proceeded to consult with the British and Canadian Prime Ministers and Stalin and on December 27, 1945, a Soviet-Anglo-American communiqué, popularly known as the Moscow Declaration, revealed that the three powers "agreed to recommend, for the consideration of the General Assembly of the United Nations, the establishment by the United Nations of a commission to consider problems arising from the discovery of atomic energy and related matters."[4] The Security Council and General Assembly in January, 1946, unanimously established the United Nations Atomic Energy Commission consisting of the members of the Security Council and, in addition, Canada when that state was not a member of the Security Council. Bernard Baruch was appointed United States representative on this Commission in March, 1946, and at its first meeting introduced into the Commission an outline of the United States plan for the control of atomic energy which from that date on became known as the Baruch Plan. In October, 1946, when the General Assembly reconvened, the Soviet Union, without any consultation and as a complete surprise to the Western powers, took the initiative in putting before the United Nations the problem of the reduction of conventional armaments.[5] Whether the Soviet initiative can be regarded merely as a propaganda effort or as a broader approach to the entire armaments problem, the effect was to place before the United Nations at this early date the entire problem of control and reduction of all types of armed forces and armaments.

The problem has remained before the United Nations ever since.

Even at this early stage, another event transpired which vitally affected all of the negotiations, the rapid demobilization of all of the Western armed forces immediately after World War II. This ran completely contrary to the dictum of President Roosevelt that in the post-war period "the real decisions should be made by the United States, Great Britain, Russia and China, who would be the powers for many years to come that would have to police the world."[6] Thus, the concept of the "Four Policemen" which was so related to the plans for dealing with regulation of armaments had vanished within a short time after the armistice. We now know as a matter of hindsight the direct relationship between the military weakness of the West in the years immediately following the armistice and the intransigence of the Soviet Union.

For the purposes of this article, it is convenient to divide the ten years of negotiations commencing in 1946 into three periods. The first period may be described as the period of the Baruch Atomic Energy Plan beginning with the first General Assembly of the United Nations in January, 1946, and lasting through the final Soviet rejection of this plan in the fall of 1948. The second period which may be described as the period of complete futility lasted from the fall of 1948 until the creation of the United Nations Disarmament Commission in the fall of 1951. The third period which may be described as the period of the comprehensive disarmament approach extended from the creation of the United Nations Disarmament Commission until United States "reservation" of all previous positions in August 1955,[7] the terminal point of this article.

The First Three Years

From 1946 until the fall of 1948 the disarmament negotiations in the United Nations proceeded simultaneously in two separate commissions: the Atomic Energy Commission and the Commission for Conventional Armaments.

The discussions in the Atomic Energy Commission were based upon the Baruch Plan and the Soviet counter proposals. The central thought of the Baruch Plan was its provision for international control of the entire process of producing atomic weapons from the uranium and plutonium mines to the completed weapons.[8] This depended upon complete accountability for all materials capable of nuclear fission from mines to weapons. In 1946, complete accountability appeared to be a realizable objective. Only the United States and the United Kingdom had a knowledge of the technique of producing fission materials and weapons. It was recognized, however, that this monopoly would not last and the Soviet Union in five years or less would probably likewise be able to produce weapons. This to a certain extent accounted for the urgency and speed of the original negotiations.

In 1946, the United States believed that uranium was a scarce material and that the United States itself could purchase all uranium that might be produced anywhere in the world. Gigantic plants and tremendous expenditure were deemed essential to separate the fissionable U-235 from natural uranium as at Oak Ridge, Tennessee, or to produce plutonium as at Hanford, Washington. Indeed, a scientific committee of the United Nations Atomic Energy Commission after a study unanimously agreed that affective control through complete accountability was technically feasible. For the first and almost last time during these discussions the Soviet Union reached the same conclusion as the United States.

The second basic feature of the Baruch Plan was to promote the use of atomic energy "for peaceful and humanitarian ends."[9] Obviously, there would be no divergence between the Soviet Union and the West on this objective. The Soviet Union had much more to gain than the West from a policy of making available to the entire world the possible benefits of the technologies of nuclear fission.

At the second meeting of the Atomic Energy Commission on June 19, 1946, only five days after the first presentation of the Baruch Plan, Andrei Gromyko presented the Soviet Plan which called for an international convention to prohibit immediately "the production and employment of weapons based on the use of atomic energy."[10] Even this early, the basic difference between the Soviet and the Western approach made its appearance. Gromyko was calling for immediate prohibition of weapons and destruction of stockpiles with no international control machinery to insure the observance of commitments. Baruch was calling for the immediate establishment of complete control machinery with the prohibition of nuclear weapons and elimination of nuclear stockpiles taking place only at a later date after the establishment of the international control system.

Initially, Gromyko rejected all controls, contending that they were not reconcilable with the principle of sovereignty of states. In October, however, the Soviet Foreign Minister, Vyacheslav Molotov, modified the initial position to recognize in theory the need for international controls, and in June, 1947, after a year of negotiations, the Soviet Union finally presented its proposal for controls,[11] which proved entirely inadequate.

During 1946 and 1947, the discussions of the Baruch and Soviet proposals were precise and detailed and might easily have led to an impasse on the sole ground that the Soviet Union refused to permit sufficient penetration of its Iron Curtain to permit the West to be reasonably certain that the Soviet Union was observing its commitments. Indeed, this issue was squarely joined in a discussion on August 11, 1947. The Chinese representative asked what would happen if after the prohibition of nuclear weapons, no agreement was reached on the control system. Gromyko replied, "If there is found to be no basis for agreement, then naturally the convention [on controls] cannot be concluded."[12]

This argumentation might readily have convinced world opinion that the impasse in the atomic energy negotiations arose entirely from Soviet unwillingness to breach its Iron Curtain. Unfortunately, other issues intervened which muddied the waters and permitted the Soviet Union to reject the Baruch Plan for the wrong reasons. The most important of these issues related to the great power veto in the international control organ responsible for regulation of atomic energy. Baruch had originally asserted with vehemence that no state should have the right of a veto in the control organ. Ultimately the Soviet Union accepted this idea but insisted that the control organ could go little farther than to determine a violation and notify the United Nations Security Council. Any steps to punish the violator would have to be taken in the Security Council where the Soviet Union had a veto.

Baruch, however, insisted that all of the great powers by treaty give up their veto on atomic matters in the Security Council. The United States had always recognized that a major violation of the Atomic Energy Convention by a great power such as the Soviet Union would mean world war. Under such circumstances it would make little difference whether the United Nations Security Council acted or failed to act since the United Nations lacked the military strength to wage a major war. The United States emphasis on the veto tended to obscure the main and fundamental divergence between the Soviet position and that of the West.

A second factor muddying the waters was the United States absence of a position on the phasing and timing of the elimination of nuclear weapons. The United States' statements were sufficiently vague so that the Soviet Union could logically conclude that the elimination of nuclear weapons would not take place in whole or in part until complete establishment of the control organ in all areas of the world and the transfer to the control organ of all installations dealing with nuclear energy. The Soviet Union could contend that at that late date, when it was no longer possible for nations to re-establish their sovereignty, the United States might refuse to go ahead with its commitment to eliminate nuclear weapons.

As a result of these and other issues tending to obscure the basic difference, many individuals like Henry Wallace in the United States sought to find a middle position between the Baruch and Soviet proposals. For many years, they believed that a compromise position giving security to both East and West might have been achieved. In retrospect, it seems clear that in these latter years of Stalin it would have been impossible for the Soviet Union to agree to any substantial breach of its Iron Curtain. It had been impossible for the Soviet Union to respond favorably to the Marshall Plan which offered economic aid without any strings attached to it to rehabilitate all of Europe, including the Soviet Union. If the minimum amount of cooperation required for an agreement on Marshall Plan aid was impossible, the vast cooperation required for successful implementation of the Baruch Plan would have been out of the question.

During this period, the Soviet Union was moving as rapidly as possible to develop its own nuclear weapons. It had no intention of serious negotiations at least until it could improve its negotiating position through developing its own nuclear capability. However, the negotiations on the Baruch Plan were detailed and precise and could easily have resulted in a treaty if any substantive agreement had been reached. This situation did not reappear in the disarmament negotiations for more than 10 years.

In contrast, the discussions in the Commission for Conventional Armaments never went beyond the stage of pure propaganda. The Soviet Union in all of its discussions concentrated on a demand for a one-third reduction of all armaments and armed forces. At the same time the Soviet Union resisted any efforts to establish the figures from which the one-third reduction would take place. Furthermore, in view of the admitted superiority of the Soviet bloc in conventional armaments, the effect of any such reduction even if faithfully observed would have widened the strategic imbalance already favoring the Soviet Union.

While the Western Powers pointed out effectively both in the Commission for Conventional Armaments and in the United Nations General Assembly the inadequacy of the Soviet proposals, their own proposals were of little consequence. The West was taking the position that proposals for reductions in conventional armaments could be put into effect only in an atmosphere of international confidence and security; and that the international control of atomic energy (i.e., acceptance of the Baruch Plan) together with other conditions, such as possible settlements with Germany and Japan, were essential to the establishment of such an atmosphere of confidence and security. This created the strange result that under the United States proposals atomic energy could be controlled and atomic weapons eliminated without an improvement in the international atmosphere but that reduction of conventional weapons and armed forces had to wait for an improvement in international affairs. Thus, the West would give up the one weapon where it had superiority before it would even discuss reduction of the weapons where the Soviet Union had superiority.

The illogical and anomalous position stemmed basically from confusion in the higher echelons of the United States government. Such thinking, however, as in the case of the atomic energy negotiations, prevented the emergence of the one clear-cut issue of all the negotiations: whether the Soviet Union would permit sufficient breach of its Iron Curtain to give a reasonable assurance to the world that it was observing its own commitments.

Serious negotiations to control atomic energy came to an end in the fall of 1948 when the United Nations General Assembly, despite the opposition of the Soviet Union, approved a part of the Baruch Plan which thus became the "United Nations Plan" and thereafter was so described by the Western Powers but not by the Soviet bloc.

The final report of the United Nations Atomic Energy Commission had also recommended suspension of the negotiations. The General Assembly, however, did not go along with this portion of the recommendations, and suggested further negotiations. This was the first but not the last occasion when the smaller states declined to accept the verdict of the Great Powers that negotiations had reached an impasse and should be abandoned; it showed the universal concern that channels of negotiation remain open.

The United Nations approval by an overwhelming vote of the Baruch Plan over Soviet opposition was a futile act with importance only in the field of propaganda. In the existing state of world power, it is basic that any arms control agreement in order to be effective must have the approval both of the Soviet Union and the United States.

Complete Futility

The period from the fall of 1948 until the fall of 1951 can best be characterized by the term "complete futility." Each year the United Nations General Assembly and subsidiary groups debated the subject of disarmament, but there was no progress toward agreement. After 1949, the few meetings on atomic energy were purely pro forma. In the field of conventional armaments, the only substantive action in 1949 was the approval of a French paper calling for a census and verification of armed forces and armaments.

In the spring of 1950, the Soviet Union withdrew both from the Atomic Energy Commission and from the Conventional Arms Commission because of the failure of these Commissions to seat a representative of Communist China. In the summer of 1950, the United States perhaps taking advantage of the absence of the Soviet Union from these meetings, introduced into the Commission for Conventional Armaments preliminary studies made within the United States government on certain phases of disarmament. These studies as well as the French proposal for census and verification represented an extremely preliminary and tentative approach. The census and verification proposal provided merely for a one-time operation. One of the United States papers —on industrial safeguards—was only a half page in length.

In effect, from 1948 to 1951 there was a complete stalemate in all United Nations negotiations on arms control. The important developments took place outside the United Nations where the Soviet Union embarked on two intense campaigns of propaganda. The first was the so-called Stockholm appeal[13] a petition circulated all over the world with millions of signatures—the message of which can be summarized by the phrase "Ban the Bomb." The second, which reached its climax in 1952, was the campaign to prove that the United States troops had used bacteriological warfare in Korea. The relation of this second campaign to arms control was logically somewhat remote. The Soviet Union called for a General Assembly recommendation for a convention prohibiting bacteriological and chemical warfare without safeguards to ensure the observance of the convention. This would furnish a precedent for a similar recommendation in connection with atomic warfare.

As these campaigns developed in intensity, it became increasingly clear that the object of the Soviet Union in all the negotiations was to secure, if possible, the unilateral disarmament of the West. The United Nations discussions would merely be one propaganda vehicle to effectuate that objective. Both of the major Soviet propaganda campaigns called for disarmament without safeguards —which could be the equivalent of the unilateral disarmament of the West. The propaganda slogans were linked to other features of the Communist party line: such as, liquidating overseas bases and bringing the boys home. Simultaneously the Soviet Union was extending the Iron Curtain to Hungary and Czechoslovakia and trying to bring Greece, Berlin and South Korea within the Communist orbit.

This blatant propaganda approach boomeranged against the Soviet Union in the United Nations. All members of the United Nations except the Soviet bloc opposed all Soviet proposals and the delegates expressed their disgust and displeasure at the Soviet attitudes. Outside the United Nations the propaganda campaigns, while initially stirring up a certain amount of emotional sentiment, lost their appeal after the Communist attack on South Korea. Unfortunately, during this period while the Soviet Union was using disarmament negotiations solely as a propaganda vehicle, the Western powers had no program at all, except the Baruch Plan, a situation prevailing until the General Assembly of 1951.

Comprehensive Disarmament

In the United Nations General Assembly of 1950, President Truman had suggested that it might be useful to consolidate the work of the Atomic Energy Commission and the Commission for Conventional Armaments, and create a single disarmament commission. The time was ripe for such a change. It was inconceivable that the United States would eliminate nuclear weapons where it had superiority without some action to correct the strategic imbalance favoring the Soviet Union in conventional weapons. Any agreement for arms control would involve both nuclear and conventional weapons and therefore it was appropriate for a single body to treat both problems.

In addition to combining the Atomic Energy and Conventional Armaments negotiations, the Western proposals in 1951 signalled several major changes in substantive position. The West had abandoned its earlier insistence that disarmament negotiations (excepting in the field of atomic energy) could not go forward until an improvement in the general political situation. It was recognized that agreement on disarmament would lead to reduction of tension and therefore that discussion of disarmament could go forward simultaneously with attempts to solve other international political problems.

The General Assembly Resolution which resulted from the Western proposals set forth as the aim of the newly constituted Disarmament Commission a draft treaty calling for: 1, regulation and balanced reduction of all armed forces and all armaments; 2, elimination of weapons of mass destruction; 3, effective international control of atomic energy; 4, safeguards. This became the framework for all of the Western proposals until 1956. The new Disarmament Commission held its first meeting dealing with substance on March 14, 1952. The United States Representative, Benjamin V. Cohen, after introducing a short draft plan, made a plea with almost religious fervor for rapid progress toward the goal of a world where national armaments would be reduced drastically and where mass destruction would be eliminated so that no state need fear aggression from another state. In reply, the Soviet Representative, Y. A. Malik, accused the United States of waging bacteriological warfare in North Korea and Communist China, a completely irrelevant issue brought forward solely for purposes of propaganda.

Despite the discouraging start, the Western Powers during the next four months brought forward a series of proposals for comprehensive disarmament which covered many, if not all, of the chief segments of the problem. In presenting his proposals, Ambassador Cohen had stressed, "These proposals are intended only to provide a basis for discussion; they are not intended to express definitive or inflexible positions of my Government."

In 1952, the most important Western proposals dealt with three main topics: the objectives of a disarmament program, safeguards, and limitation of armed forces and armaments. A paper submitted by the United States entitled "Essential Principles for a Disarmament Program"[14] suggested that the goal of disarmament was not to regulate but to prevent war. To achieve this goal, all states must cooperate to establish an open and substantially disarmed world in which armed forces and armaments would be so reduced that no state would be in a condition to start a war and "in which no State will be in a position to undertake preparations for war without other States having knowledge of such preparation long before an offending State could start a war."

The United States made a fresh approach to the problem of safeguards in a paper entitled "Disclosure and Verification of Armed Forces and Armaments."[15] This was the first paper introduced into this set of meetings and the first United States proposal of consequence since the Baruch Plan. In this paper, the United States recognized that in the existing state of international tension it was impossible to suggest immediate disclosure by all states of their military secrets. Therefore, disclosure and verification would take place in stages proceeding from the less secret areas to the more secret areas. Disclosure of atomic weapons must accompany disclosure of arms, armed forces and conventional weapons. The United States for the first time recognized that it was desirable to arrange the inspection system in such a manner that "verification can take place with a minimum of interference in the internal life of the respective countries."

A paper introduced by France, the United Kingdom and the United States on May 28, called for the numerical limitation of all armed forces. This paper was supplemented by a further paper introduced on August 12, suggesting the approach toward limiting armaments as well as armed forces. These papers, which were the answer of the West to the Soviet proposals for one-third reduction of armed forces and armaments, in essence proposed ceilings for the armed forces of the Soviet Union, the United States, China, the United Kingdom and France. Ceilings would be worked out for other states having substantial forces. Arms would be limited to such as were necessary and appropriate to maintain the ceilings proposed for the armed forces.

The Soviet reaction to the Western proposals was completely negative. The Soviet Union itself made no proposals to the Disarmament Commission. The only Soviet-written paper was a plan of work which would have pre-determined the outcome of the discussions. Its first item was "Adoption of a Decision on the unconditional prohibition of atomic weapons and all other kinds of weapons of mass destruction and on the establishment of strict international control over the observance of such prohibition, it being understood that the prohibition of atomic weapons and international control shall be put into effect simultaneously."[16]

This was typical of all of the items in the Plan of Work. They did not state the subject for discussion but the conclusion which must result from the discussion. The Soviet speeches were only rarely addressed to the issues before the Disarmament Commission, and consisted almost entirely of propaganda invective appropriate for republication in *Pravda* and *Izvestia* and for international broadcast.

By August, 1952, it had become apparent that no progress was possible. The Session of the General Assembly in the fall of 1952 took place during the presidential campaign in the United States. It would have been difficult for the United States representative to express any official view on disarmament until after the election and until there was some indication of the attitude of the new Administration. President Eisenhower, in his inaugural address and in a much more detailed statement made on April 8, 1953, stated clearly his support of the approach of the previous Administration to the problems of disarmament. However, partly because of the death of Stalin and the obvious inability of the Soviet representatives to reach new decisions, the next serious discussions of disarmament did not take place until the General Assembly Session in the fall of 1953. At that time representatives of some of the smaller powers proposed and both the Soviet Union and Western powers agreed that "the Representatives of the Principal Powers involved should seek in private an acceptable solution and report to the Disarmament Commission."

The Disarmament Commission in April, 1954, established a Subcommittee consisting of representatives of Canada, France, the Soviet Union, the United Kingdom and the United States to discuss in private the entire problem of disarmament. This Subcommittee continued as the negotiating group until September, 1957. Morehead Patterson, a prominent industrial leader, was appointed to represent the United States on this Subcommittee which met in its first session in May and June.

In substance the meetings of the Subcommittee were a continuation of the 1952 discussions of the Disarmament Commission. The Western Powers filled in the two important gaps in the previous Western proposals. The United States introduced a paper outlining the type of international control authority required to ensure the implementation of a program of comprehensive disarmament.

The United Kingdom and France towards the end of the discussions on June 11, 1954, introduced a Memorandum on phasing and timing the elements of a disarmament program.[17] On this subject the Soviet Union had always maintained a consistent position: reductions and prohibitions must precede the installation of controls. While the West had proposed that the installation of controls and likewise the prohibitions and limitations should take place by stages, there were no Western proposals indicating the time relationship between the installation of controls and the effective date of the prohibitions and reductions. The Anglo-French Memorandum sought to remedy this difficulty and thus to find a middle ground between the Soviet position and the previous Western positions.

The United States gave general support to the British-French Memorandum, explaining that support did not necessarily include endorsement of every detail. The United States anticipated that when the states got down to drawing up a treaty, the matter of carrying out the treaty would be more complicated than was indicated in the Anglo-French Memorandum. This foreshadowed the reappraisal of all positions as a result of the development of thermonuclear weapons.

The Soviet delegate emphatically rejected the Western proposals, but his speeches were less blatantly propagandistic and at least dealt with the subjects under discussion.

Policy Reappraisals

At the very end of the first session of the Subcommittee, in June, 1954, members of the Soviet delegation at the official level gave some intimations to their opposite numbers in the United States and United Kingdom delegations of an impending change in Soviet policy. This change would be linked to a new Soviet policy of increasing cultural and economic contacts with the West. The changed policy became official when Soviet Delegate Andrei Vyshinsky at the opening of the General Assembly in September, 1954, suggested that the Anglo-French memorandum be used as the basis for an international treaty.

Vyshinsky sought to create the impression that the Soviet Union had accepted practically the entire Western position and that agreement on a disarmament treaty would be fairly simple and quick. The extended discussions in the General Assembly showed some change in Soviet positions but there were tremendous areas where the Soviet and Western positions remained far apart. It was unanimously agreed that additional private sessions of the Subcommittee were essential and might be helpful in bridging the gap. Accordingly the Subcommittee reconvened in February, 1955. In March of the same year, President Eisenhower appointed Governor Harold Stassen to the newly created position of Special Adviser on Disarmament with Cabinet rank. Stassen assumed responsibility for the negotiations at the third session of the Subcommittee in August, 1955.

During March and April, 1955, the Soviet Union in its negotiating reverted to its pre-1954 intransigent positions. Suddenly without warning on May 10, 1955, the Soviet Union submitted new and vastly changed proposals.[18] In essence these proposals suggested three separate means for reducing tensions and eliminating the arms race. The first section called for political settlements to end the cold war and was only remotely related to disarmament. The second section followed the format of the Western proposals in calling for comprehensive disarmament in stages, and was far closer to the Western position than previous Soviet proposals.

The really startling changes in Soviet position were contained in the third part which had a long preamble pointing out that the production of fissionable materials had now reached a point where "there are possibilities beyond the reach of international control for evading this control and for organizing the clandestine manufacture of hydrogen and atomic weapons." Therefore, in lieu of a program for comprehensive disarmament, the Soviet Union was willing to proceed with partial measures that would improve world confidence and permit more extensive agreements when confidence became greater.

Even more startling was the Soviet suggestion of an international control organ including the power "to exercise control, including inspection on a continuing basis to the extent necessary to insure implementation of the above mentioned convention by all States."

The eminent statesman and scholar, Philip Noel-Baker, speaks of May 10, 1955, as "the moment of hope."[19] Jules Moch, the French Representative and the Dean of all Western disarmament negotiators immediately responded: "I would almost say the whole thing looks too good to be true." The Soviet Union had certainly gone a long distance in accepting in principle the main Western positions. This is of course far removed from agreement on a detailed and practical program to implement the principles.

The new Soviet position unquestionably was a part of the vast change in the Soviet Union that followed the death of Stalin. Closely related to this changed viewpoint

were statements of Soviet leaders bringing home to their populations the consequences of thermonuclear warfare—mutual devastation, if not mutual destruction. The Soviet proposals of May 10, 1955, at a minimum established a framework for future negotiations taking account of the thermonuclear revolution.

The United States planning, as evidenced by President Eisenhower's memorable address to the United Nations on December 8, 1953, on the peaceful uses of the atom, had been following parallel lines. The indicated next step would be a negotiation to transform the apparent agreement in principle into a convention.

Since a Summit Meeting was scheduled in Geneva in July, it was logical for the Disarmament Subcommittee to adjourn until after the Summit Meeting. At the Summit Meeting, Eisenhower suggested as a first and separable confidence building measure his proposal for "open skies"—complete aerial reconnaissance to lessen the danger of surprise attack. The Soviet Union then made suggestions for ground control posts to prevent large military formations in tinder-box areas. Both of these proposals played a large role in later negotiations. However, the United States proposal was far too limited in its scope to be a full response to the Soviet program of May 10.

The United States response came on August 29, 1955, when the Subcommittee reconvened with Stassen sitting for the first time as the United States negotiator. Stassen referred to the new international situation under which it was no longer possible to determine through inspection compliance with any agreements involving past nuclear production. Accordingly he said:

The United States does now place a reservation upon all of its pre-Geneva substantive positions taken in this Subcommittee or in the Disarmament Commission or in the United Nations on these questions in relationship to levels of armaments pending the outcome of our study jointly or separately of inspection methods and control arrangements and of review of this important problem.[20]

This statement in effect withdrew all past United States positions regardless of their relation to the problem of nuclear materials accountability, including proposals which had contributed greatly to the prestige of the United States such as the 1952 paper on "Essential Principles for a Disarmament Programme." This latter paper made its next appearance when Khrushchev quoted it almost literally but without attribution in his address to the United Nations in September, 1959, and received great acclaim for his position. The new broom was sweeping clean.

After the destruction of the old framework, the negotiations floundered for two years until the construction of a new framework containing many elements that had been swept away in August, 1955.

Lost Opportunities

In perspective it is apparent that no genuine accord was possible between the Soviet Union and the West during the period of this study (1946–1955).

The Baruch proposals were good proposals: the best that could have been anticipated in the light of the revolution in international thinking that had to accompany the nuclear revolution. The rigidity of the Soviet position during the last days of Stalin would have prevented any East-West agreement in the field of disarmament short of a complete surrender by the West. Therefore, the failure to reach an accord which would lessen the menace of nuclear warfare during the years when the United States alone had nuclear weapons cannot be termed a lost opportunity.

The United States, however, during the negotiations on the Baruch Plan did have the opportunity of demonstrating convincingly to the world that the one overwhelming obstacle to East-West agreement in the field of disarmament was the Soviet insistence on maintaining its secrecy. The United States emphasis on less important issues such as the extent of the veto in the Security Council, and the failure of the United States to develop a logical position on reduction of conventional armaments tended to obscure the one main issue, the Soviet Iron Curtain. To this extent, the course of negotiations in the period from 1946 through 1948 represented a lost opportunity.

From 1952 through 1954 the Western Powers pursued an approach directed toward the objective of comprehensive disarmament which had great political appeal throughout the world and which remedied most of the shortcomings of the earlier approach. The thermonuclear revolution required basic changes in that approach. The reaction of Soviet leaders to the thermonuclear revolution, however, to a large degree paralleled the reaction of the West. With the relaxation of Soviet rigidity after the death of Stalin, a genuine negotiation now became possible within the framework of the previous Western approach modified to meet the novel situation created by thermonuclear weapons. Yet after May 10, 1955, the United States destroyed the framework of the negotiations by withdrawing the previous proposals. Two years later the negotiations did take place with many of the Western positions paralleling their earlier proposals.

In two respects this delay in the negotiations can be deemed a wasted opportunity. First, the spectacle of a wavering position in the United States created world-wide doubts as to the sincerity of United States advocacy of arms control and disarmament. Second, in 1955, the climate for an East-West negotiation was much better than in 1957 after the Hungarian and the Suez episodes.

It would not be possible within the scope of this article to analyze in detail the reasons underlying the wasted opportunities. It should merely be noted that at no time during the 10 years of negotiations did the United States or any of its Western Allies have an adequate organization to work out a sound and detailed program of arms control and to carry on the extensive negotiation essential to implement such a program. At no time during these 10 years was there sufficient continuity in Western and, in particular, in the United States leadership in this field to produce a consistent policy. Finally, and even more important, at no time during this ten-year period was there any apparent over-all plan which placed disarmament and arms control within a broad framework comprehending our entire foreign relations. When on May 10, 1955, the Soviet Union at least ostensibly reversed its previous positions, the United States was unprepared and had no immediate answer.

657

[1] U.N. Atomic Energy Commission, The International Control of Atomic Energy, The First Report to the Security Council, Dept. of State Publication 2737 (December 31. 1946), Appendix 1, p. 81.

[2] Article 11, 47. U.S. Dept. of State, Charter of the United Nations and Statute of the International Court of Justice, Publication 2368 (1945).

[3] U.S. Department of State, The International Control of Atomic Energy: Growth of a Policy, Publications 2702 (1946), p. 108. Cited hereafter as Growth of a Policy.

[4] Ibid., p. 120.

[5] United Nations Document A/Bur/42, USSR: Draft Proposal (October 29, 1946).

[6] Robert E. Sherwood, Roosevelt and Hopkins (1948), p. 717.

[7] U.N. Disarmament Commission Subcommittee of the Disarmament Commission, Third Report, Annex 5, Doc. DC/SC.1/41 (March 27, 1956), pp. 26-27.

[8] Growth of a Policy, op. cit., pp. 49-50.

[9] "The Three-Nation Agreed Declaration on Atomic Energy...November 15, 1945," Ibid., p. 118.

[10] Ibid., p. 213.

[11] U.N. Atomic Energy Commission, The International Control of Atomic Energy, The Second Report to the Security Council, Dept. of State Publication 2932 (December, 1947), p. 88.

[12] U.S. Department of State, The International Control of Atomic Energy: Policy at the Crossroads, Publication 3161 (1948), p. 154. Cited hereafter as Policy at the Crossroads.

[13] "Stockholm Appeal of the World Peace Council, March 19, 1950," in U.S. Dept. of State, Documents on Disarmament, Vol. I (1945-56), Publication 7008 (August, 1960), p. 252.

[14] U.S. Department of State, United States Efforts Toward Disarmament, Report to the President by the Deputy U.S. Representative on the United Nations Disarmament Commission, Publication 4902 (February, 1953), pp. 5-6.

[15] U.N. Disarmament Commission, Official Records, Special Supplement No. 1, pp. 22-30.

[16] U.N. document DC/4/Rev.1 (March 19, 1952), text in DC/20, pp. 6-7.

[17] U.N. Document DC/SC.1/10 (June 11, 1954), pp. 21-22.

[18] Annex U.N. Document DC/SC/26/Rev.2., May 10, 1955.

[19] Philip Noel-Baker, The Arms Race (1958), Chapter 2.

[20] U.N. Document DC/SC.1/PV54, September 1, 1955, pp. 26, 27.

DISARMAMENT NEGOTIATIONS--1956-1962

By MARION H. McVITTY

Six weeks after the Soviet Union accepted so much of the Western disarmament plan that the U.S. put a "moratorium" on all its earlier disarmament policies, negotiations on the whole issue took a new turn. The emphasis was abruptly shifted by the U.S. from "comprehensive" disarmament plans to "first step" proposals.

At the Summit meeting in Geneva, June 1955, President Eisenhower inaugurated the new approach with his "Open Skies" plan against surprise attack. This was a system of East-West reciprocal observation designed to create mutual confidence by taking the important element of surprise out of any attack either side could make upon the other. The U.S. plan was originally limited to air reconnaissance, but a Soviet proposal for strategic "ground posts" was soon added to the general concept.

The United States Government made a strenuous effort, both at home and abroad, to enlist public support for this mutual inspection system which required no immediate cut in armaments. The American people had not been very well informed about disarmament for some time, but it was evidently hoped that this plan had a chance of becoming popular because the U.S. could feel safer while still staying militarily as strong as ever.

Whatever Americans thought of this plan (and few of them thought about it at all), the Soviet Union did not like it. The 1955 UN Assembly sent the Disarmament Sub-Committee back to work on this and certain other "first steps" which included a proposal by India "regarding the suspension of experimental explosions of nuclear weapons." The Soviet Union finally indicated during Sub-Committee meetings in the early summer of 1956 that it might accept a regional "Open Skies" plan as a part of some program for "disengagement" in Central Europe. When the U.S. negotiator, Harold Stassen, sought to probe this possibility in informal, bilateral talks he was recalled to Washington and rebuked. The United States and its NATO allies were totally unprepared for serious negotiations which involved the most potentially dangerous trouble area in the world.

The 1956 UN Assembly showed a general desire for some actual arms reductions, so that early in 1957 the United States added some first steps in disarmament to the "Open Skies" plan. These included an internationally controlled ban on nuclear weapons tests, a token cut in conventional arms and armed forces, an inspected halt of nuclear weapons production and a small transfer of atomic materials from weapons to the International Atomic Energy Agency, which

659

had been established a few months earlier.

The U.S.S.R., however, following the "first step" approach to its finest point, demanded a nuclear weapons test suspension as the most essential first requirement for control. The Soviets rejected the U.S. "package" of "first steps" and insisted that only a nuclear test suspension should be negotiated. France being unwilling thus to forego becoming an atomic power, and the U.S. Government departments being in disagreement, the West refused to explore the Soviet proposal save as one item in the West's own "package."

The West won a rather reluctant UN majority for its first steps "package" in the Assembly in 1957, but the UN Disarmament Sub-Committee was dead. The Soviet Union refused to negotiate further in a group in which it was one against four.

Thereafter, the issue of an "appropriate" UN disarmament negotiating body went through a number of faintly ludicrous reversals. The U.S.S.R. wanted a UN Disarmament Commission composed of all members. The West refused to consider that proposal on the grounds that nothing could be accomplished by so large and unwieldy a body. The neutrals sought a compromise which would enlarge and make more representative the old UN Disarmament Commission of Twelve. The U.S. took up the neutralist suggestion and forced through adoption of a 25 nation commission, the composition of which was so unacceptable to the U.S.S.R. that it never met. In 1958 the U.S.S.R. urged creation of a Disarmament Commission composed of an equal number of representatives from each side. The U.S. rejected this concept of "parity," since the U.S. insisted that the UN was not equally divided in its support for the two sides, a majority always having supported the West. However, in order to avoid this Soviet solution to the problem, the U.S. accepted "for one year only" creation of a UN Disarmament Commission of all members. Although the Commission of all members was made permament the next year, it had not been able to function as a negotiating forum. In 1959, therefore, the U.S. and its allies agreed to a Disarmament Committee made up of five Eastern and five Western nations. Earlier Western objections to the "parity" formula were rather lightly obviated by the device of establishing the new Committee of Ten "outside the UN framework."

During this two year period from 1957 to 1959, in spite of these procedural gyrations, and in spite of the West having won Assembly approval for its 1957 "package" proposal, it was on nuclear test suspension that serious substantive negotiations went forward. Alarmed by nuclear fall-out and encouraged by the prospect of one quick and easy step in disarmament which might then lead to others, public opinion all over the world had begun to clamor for a nuclear test suspension. In the United Nations, where "new" and "neutral" members had begun to multiply, great pressure was put upon the West to concentrate negotiations on a nuclear test mora-torium.

In 1958, technical experts of the U.S., the U.S.S.R. and the U.K. met and agreed that effective methods for international inspection of a ban on nuclear tests was feasible. By degrees the U.S. yielded to the growing pressure for the suspension of nuclear testing. It was finally decided by the U.S., Britain and the Soviet Union that they would negotiate a nuclear test-ban treaty, and that during those negotiations, there would be a voluntary moratorium on nuclear tests. France refused to be bound by the moratori-um and actually began testing in the Sahara.

A nuclear test-ban treaty, although providing no actual disarmament, promised several advantages. It could slow down the arms race between East and West, halt the spread of nuclear weapons, and make possible a first experiment in international inspection.

For a year and a half those negotiations made progress in spite of many difficulties. Public hope built up in many quarters. Success for the nuclear test-ban treaty often seemed within reach. Mass movements in many parts of the world grew to sizeable proportions in favor of a "peace" and "disarmament" cause which seemed both attainable and comprehensible to people tired of complexity and fear.

Khrushchev made his first visit to the United Nations in 1959. In September of that year, he made an impassioned plea for a new concept--general and complete disarmament. Having got news in advance of what the Soviet leader was about to do, the United Kingdom one day earlier, unveiled a comprehensive plan of its own, more cautious, but no less complete in its final stage than Khrushchev's plan. For the first time since World War II, the nations were asked to address themselves to the proposition of total, universal disarmament, disarmament of all nations down to the lightly armed police forces, or militia, that each might require to maintain internal order.

The Soviet Chief of State in his UN speech on September 19, 1959 explained why total disarmament would be more satisfactory, and even easier of attainment than any partial disarmament scheme. Khrushchev said realization of total disarmament would "completely exclude any inequality and would rule out the possibility that military advantages of any kind would be created for any state." "Furthermore," he said, "with the destruction of armaments and the abolition of armed forces, no physical possibility whatsoever would remain that states could pursue any policy but that of peace." "General and complete disarmament," he stated, "will re-move also the difficulties connected with control. In such circumstances states will have nothing to hide from each

661

other."

While the press denounced the proposal as "Utopian" and as "mere propaganda," the UN Assembly debated the new disarmament concept at length. As the delegations expressed their views on the nature of a warless world, many new aspects of the concept emerged. The following quotations indicate the scope of that discussion:

United States: "If all nations lay down their arms, there must be institutions to preserve international peace and security and promote the rule of law."

Yugoslavia: "Progress in the field of disarmament should open new prospects for strengthening the authority . . . of the United Nations in this sphere."

Italy: "It appears quite clear that the rules at present contained in our Charter, which have been conceived in view of partial and not total disarmament, should be revised in order to furnish the Security Council and the Assembly with an international military instrument to guarantee peace effectively."

Japan: "No nation in the world could be expected to renounce force, and therefore, to disarm, unless adequate and effective means are provided for peaceful settlement of disputes."

Liberia: "It would mean some revision of the Charter which would change the voting in the Security Council or a new and separate body where the veto would not be applicable in any disarmament agreement."

Pakistan: "Pakistan has always been a staunch supporter of the concept of an international police force to preserve world peace and security. We have also on several occasions urged that the Charter machinery for the peaceful settlement of disputes should be strengthened and the scope of compulsory jurisdiction of the International Court enlarged."

Haiti: "At the same time, and it would be an error to believe otherwise, and wrong not to take this matter up immediately, we will inevitably have to deal with another important and delicate problem, that of economic and social stability in the world of tomorrow."

Burma: "If we expect to achieve any real and enduring system of disarmament among the Powers, big and small, some settlement of the China issue must take place."

India: "If, as in the case of Nuremberg, punishment hangs over people who violate the laws of men, as set forth in a treaty and sanctioned by this organization, that may well serve as a deterrent."

As a result of this debate, the 1959 UN Assembly adopted unanimously a resolution which considered "that the question of general and complete disarmament is the most important one facing the world today" and expressed the hope "that measures leading towards the goal of general and complete disarmament under effective international control will be worked out in detail and agreed upon in the shortest possible time."

With those instructions, the Committee of Ten began to meet in Geneva in the spring of 1960. However, general and complete disarmament negotiations drew little public interest that year. Western governments were ill-prepared to discuss an elaborate program for which little or no governmental planning had been done. Thus, for example, Mr. Frederick Eaton, representative to the ten nation disarmament Conference in 1960 for the Eisenhower administration, testified at a hearing of the Senate Foreign Relations Committee in connection with setting up a disarmament Agency for the United States to the following:

> Although in every disarmament plan advanced over the past ten years we have proposed a gradual reduction of arms, we have never had an acceptable program as to what weapons should be scrapped, let alone agreement with our allies.

The nuclear test-ban treaty talks were continuing also in Geneva, and a ban on nuclear testing still seemed to most people the most promising approach to arms control. In fact, a suspension of nuclear tests had become in the public mind almost an end in itself. In these circumstances, general and complete disarmament did not seem so much a more desirable goal as an unwarranted distraction. Neither the governments nor the peoples seemed to realize that the U.S.S.R. was losing interest in this partial disarmament step, as it had lost interest in all partial measures--that nothing short of general and complete disarmament was likely to make inspection acceptable to the Soviets.

The Western nations agreed in broad terms to the goal of general and complete disarmament, but when they got down to cases, they had detailed proposals for Stage I and only verbal generalities for Stages II and III. Stage I in effect was really the Western 1957 "package" of first steps with little arms reduction and much inspection. When the Soviets learned that the West wanted this Stage I implemented through a separate treaty before agreements on Stages II and III were to be negotiated, the five Communist states walked out of the Committee of Ten. The Committee of Ten never met again after June 1960.

General and complete disarmament remained at a standstill for a year and a half thereafter. Meanwhile the nuclear test-ban talks were beginning to bog down. The United States suspected that the U.S.S.R. was prolonging those negotiations in order to keep the West bound to the voluntary moratorium on testing. Thus the Soviets could have a test ban without international controls. The United States warned that it would have to resume nuclear testing if more rapid progress were not made.

Perhaps as part of its disaffection with world organization in general and the UN in particular because of the Congo situation, the U.S.S.R. took back its agreement to certain articles in the draft test-ban treaty. Most serious was their sudden insistence that the control organ should be headed by the same kind of "troika" they were urging to head the UN Secretariat. This was bad enough, but worse was to come. The Soviets announced they were going to resume testing, and they did.

The test-ban negotiations were broken off, and in September 1961 the U.S.S.R. exploded atmospheric tests of unprecedented magnitude. The United States resumed underground nuclear tests shortly thereafter. World public opinion received almost as traumatic a shock as the American people experienced when the Soviet Union rejected the Baruch Plan in 1946.

New activity on general and complete disarmament was lost in the din of Soviet atomic explosions and of public clamor against this Soviet perfidy, with which the less dangerous U.S. testing was equated in the UN Assembly. Four significant moves on the larger issue hardly made a mark of any kind on public attention!

1) In the last week of September, the U.S.S.R. and the U.S. issued a joint statement of principles which they agreed should direct general and complete disarmament negotiations. There was much substance in that statement covering both the goal and means to its attainment.

2) In the same week, the United States Congress approved a new statutory Disarmament and Arms Control Agency for the United States Administration. By sizeable majorities both Houses of Congress had apparently recognized that this government must take disarmament and the enforcement of peace seriously, and that much expert preparation must be undertaken by a competent body.

3) On September 25th President Kennedy addressed the UN Assembly in a forceful speech in which he outlined the United States approach to general and complete disarmament with security and justice under law in the following terms: "To destroy arms, however, is not enough. We must create even as we destroy--creating world-wide law and law enforcement as we outlaw world-wide war and weapons . . .

"The United States recommends that all member nations earmark special peace keeping units in their armed forces, to be on call of the United Nations, to be specially trained and quickly available, and with advance provision for financial and logistic support. . .

"In addition, the American delegation will suggest a series of steps to improve the United Nations machinery for the peaceful settlement of disputes, for on-the-spot factfinding, mediation and adjudication, for extending the rule of international law."

4) That afternoon a new U.S. proposal was released which elaborated a U.S. disarmament plan in the terms explained by the President.

If the nuclear test-ban treaty had failed, the larger goal of general and complete disarmament was at once more real and more promising.

But the public would not have it so. The United Nations Assembly would not have it so. The United States Government would not have it so. The people could think of nothing but their lost cause. The UN majority was bent on getting the nuclear testing stopped again, with or without international control. The United States Government could not forego the golden opportunity to make cold war capital out of the Soviets indefensible behavior.

For six months "banning the bomb" held stage center. Suspension of tests with controls, suspension without controls, U.S. atmospheric testing as a need and as a threat, bilateral and multilateral talks, to be held, or not to be held --all were discussed at much length, and to little purpose. Even after a new disarmament committee (composed of the old Committee of Ten plus eight less committed nations) had been set up by UN and had begun to meet, nuclear testing remained the prime topic.

The 18 nation Disarmament Committee started its work on March 14, 1962 and was instructed to report back to the UN by June 1, 1962. France refused to take part in the negotiations, largely because the nuclear test-ban treaty had been included in the terms of reference of the committee, but the problem of Algeria and deGaulle's disaffection with UN also played a significant part in this French decision.

In the first few weeks, the 18 nation committee established a sub-committee, comprised of the U.S., the U.S.S.R. and Britain, to continue efforts to control nuclear tests. Plenary meetings of the committee were devoted to general and complete disarmament, while partial measures to reduce tension and improve prospects for the goal were taken up in meetings of the committee sitting as a committee of the whole. Thus various approaches to disarmament could receive due consideration without giving any one a priority or diluting the importance of the full objective.

The U.S.S.R. had put its program for total disarmament into the form of a draft treaty. The U.S. plan was still a general proposal with some detail about Stage I, and rather vague and somewhat ambiguous suggestions for Stages II and III. The Soviets insisted since their treaty was the only complete plan, it alone should be the basis for discussion in the Committee. The less committed members were somewhat embarrassed by the logic of this claim, since the U.S. plan was so sketchy in its final phases. The U.S.

was urged to submit its own plan in the form of a draft treaty. Within three to four weeks the U.S. submitted a treaty outline. This was far more complete and detailed than its September proposal. However, it is doubtful if the Administration could have secured the agreement of all its relevant departments to a blueprint so hastily devised.

Whatever the degree of seriousness on the part of the major powers regarding general and complete disarmament, both sides submitted proposals more comprehensive than anything either had put forward in the past. There is evidence also in these plans that each sought to overcome some of the obstacles which had created deadlocks in earlier discussions.

Both draft proposals address themselves to the agreed goal of disarmament of all nations to those levels required for maintaining internal order within each State; each envisages accomplishing that goal in three stages.

The Soviet plan and the United States plan provide for international inspection to a roughly comparable degree. The dispute over whether or not inspection should be applied to armaments retained at any stage, as well as to armaments reduced or abolished, has lost much of its significance. The U.S.S.R. proposal would abolish every means for the delivery of nuclear weapons (including tactical weapons), and every factory making such carriers, or parts thereof, in Stage I. What would remain to any nation which was not then open to inspection, under the Soviet treaty would be relatively unimportant in the balance of military power. With such far-reaching international inspection in being, it is doubtful if hidden arsenals could be kept entirely secret, or be of any use with no means left to deliver them to the target. At the same time, the new U.S. proposal offers the new method of "zonal" inspection which should reduce Soviet fears about inspection being a form of "espionage." What has been "uninspectable" in Soviet terms heretofore may thus become less vital both to the West and to the U.S.S.R.

The two plans integrate nuclear and conventional disarmament in all three stages. Each contains very similar proposals for insuring national use of outer space for peaceful purposes only.

Both plans call for a Disarmament Organization to be established at the outset to implement disarmament controls. The composition of that organization as well as its functions are almost identical in the two programs. In both plans the primary function of the Disarmament Organization would be the routine inspection process. The Soviet proposal makes it clear that no nation would have a veto in the Disarmament. Organization itself, whereas the U.S. plan omits any reference to voting procedures in the control organ.

Where the two sides are now in most disagreement is on

the means to enforce peace in a disarmed world. In recent months the United States has made great progress in its thinking in this field. It has emphasized the need for new and quite radical provisions for a UN Peace Force and effective means to settle international differences within a framework of law and law enforcement. The Soviets meanwhile continue to emphasize disarmament as the essential attribute of a warless world, and have been content to include in their plan half-hearted and ineffective measures for international security with justice.

The result is that the Soviet draft treaty has no enforcement provisions of any kind that cannot be frustrated by a major power. The proposed Disarmament Organization could not deal with violations according to the U.S.S.R. plan. Violations of the disarmament agreements would be referred to the Security Council, where a major power could veto any remedial action against itself. During the disarmament process, the Soviets stipulate that Article 43 of the Charter (providing that armed contingents of the Big Five be made available to UN) should be implemented, although it has been impossible for the major powers to agree at any time in the past sixteen years on the size and the nature of forces that the Big Five should place at the disposal of the UN. When disarmament has been achieved, the U.S.S.R. suggests that nations should make available to the Security Council, in the event of aggression, contingents of their national police or militia retained for their own internal security. Even this provision becomes meaningless since the Soviet draft insists that such contingents must be commanded by a "troika" operating under the unanimity rule. The whole matter of peaceful settlement of international disputes is taken care of with a few pious declarations about nations agreeing to "base relations" on "the principles of peaceful and friendly coexistence and cooperation."

In contrast the U.S. treaty outline provides in Stage I that within the United Nations an agreement be concluded "for the establishment of a United Nations Peace Force in Stage II, including definitions of its purpose, mission, composition and strength, disposition, command and control, training, logistical support, financing, equipment and armament." In this way an international deterrent would begin to replace national deterrents before disarmament reached its most crucial period. By the time the disarmament process is completed, according to the U.S. plan, the UN Peace Force would have been strengthened "until it has sufficient armed forces and armaments so that no State could challenge it." On the matter of peaceful settlement of international disputes the U.S. outline provides among other things that at the beginning of Stage II, parties to the treaty shall accept without reservations the compulsory jurisdiction of the International Court of Justice. Recognizing that a UN

Peace Force and greater use of the International Court will make real changes in international relations and organization, the U.S. plan provides at the outset that "parties to the treaty would agree to support measures strengthening the structure, authority, and operation of the United Nations so as to improve its capability to maintain international peace and security." This may mean that the United States would be prepared to go so far as to revise the UN Charter, if necessary, for the enforcement of peace with justice in a disarmed world. However, the U.S. plan is presently ambiguous as to whether the final enforcement authority shall be a revised United Nations, or the new International Disarmament Organization to be established by a disarmament treaty. As it is unlikely that such authority can be shared between the UN as it is and some related agency, a choice between the two would seem to be necessary before the disarmament process is actually initiated.

The old differences regarding timing remain in the new positions. The U.S.S.R. still proposed that the whole process be completed in four years. The U.S. now suggests that Stages I and II each be completed in a period of three years, if all goes well. No timetable is suggested by the U.S. for Stage III.

There is a real philosophical difference involved in this question of timing. The U.S.S.R. apparently believes that the whole period during which disarmament will be in process will be a time of great anxiety and high tension. Their idea of how to make this transition most safely is by taking very large steps very rapidly in a total program fully agreed in advance by the parties. The West, on the other hand, has long felt that confidence can be engendered if very small steps are tried out in practice before nations are committed to the whole program. The United States has urged in the past that ample time be allowed for the verification of each small step and for the parties to negotiate later stages on the basis of experience.

These two diverse approaches are brought somewhat closer together in the two drafts now being considered. The United States has put forward a treaty outline covering the whole disarmament process which presumably this country is willing to negotiate as a whole. Furthermore, the U.S. in Stage I proposed much more substantial reductions than it has been willing to consider in the recent past. If the West would stand by comprehensive negotiations and a considerable measure of real disarmament at the start, the U.S.S.R. is not likely to insist on its four-year schedule.

The narrowing of some old differences, and the greater elaboration and improvements which are visible in these two plans, are but words on paper unless governments on both sides are animated by a sincere intent to carry them out. Perhaps formulation must precede any determination to act.

If so, formulation has progressed, but is not yet complete in either plan. The sincerity of the Russians can only be tested against a U.S. plan that is, itself, sincerely offered, not for public relations purposes, but for governmental action.

When the United States is fully prepared to seek an effective agreement there will be outward, visible signs not now present. Among them, look for the following:

1) The Arms Control and Disarmament Agency will receive financial appropriations commensurate with its task; 2) Plans for economic adjustment from a defense to a consumer economy will be in the forefront of official concern; 3) Communist China will be approached to take part in disarmament negotiations; 4) The Administration will seek the support of the American people by making sure that they thoroughly understand a total program which is specific and unambiguous; 5) The people and the press will give the time and the space to an issue that will take precedence over all other national concerns, foreign or domestic.

T R E A T Y

ON GENERAL AND COMPLETE DISARMAMENT
UNDER STRICT INTERNATIONAL CONTROL

Draft Submitted by Union of Soviet Socialist Republics
March 22, 1962

PREAMBLE

THE states of the world,

Acting in accordance with the aspirations and will of the peoples,

Convinced that war cannot and must not serve as a method for settling international disputes, the more so under the present conditions of the headlong development of means of mass annihilation, such as nuclear weapons and rocket devices for their delivery, but must forever be banished from the life of human society,

Discharging the historic mission of saving all the nations from the scourge of war,

Proceeding from the fact that general and complete disarmament under strict international control is a sure and feasible way to fulfil mankind's age-old dream of assuring eternal and inviolable peace on earth,

Desirous of putting an end to the senseless waste of human labour on the creation of the means of annihilation and of destruction of material values,

Seeking to direct all resources towards the assurance of the further growth of wellbeing and social and economic progress in all countries of the world,

Conscious of the need to build relations among states on the basis of the principles of peace, neighbourliness, equality of states and peoples, non-interference, and respect for the independence and sovereignty of all countries,

And reaffirming their dedication to the aims and principles of the United Nations Charter,

Have resolved to conclude the present Treaty, and to implement forthwith general and complete disarmament under strict and effective international control.

ARTICLE 1

Disarmament Obligations

The states parties to the present Treaty undertake :

1. To carry out, over a period of four years, general and complete disarmament entailing :

The disbanding of all armed forces and the prohibition of their re-establishment in any form whatsoever;

The prohibition, and the destruction of all stockpiles and the cessation of the manufacture, of weapons of mass destruction of all kinds, including atomic, hydrogen, chemical, biological and radiological weapons;

The destruction and discontinuance of the manufacture of all means of delivering weapons of mass destruction to their targets;

The dismantling of foreign military bases of all kinds, and the withdrawal and disbanding of all foreign troops stationed on the territory of any state;

The abolition of any kind of military conscription for citizens;

The termination of military training of the population and the closing of all military educational institutions;

The abolition of War Ministries, of general staffs and their local agencies, and of all other military and paramilitary establishments and organisations;

The elimination of all types of conventional armaments and military equipment, and the termination of their manufacture, except for the manufacture of strictly limited amounts of agreed types of light firearms for the equipment of the police (militia) contingents to be retained by states after the accomplishment of general and complete disarmament;

The discontinuance of the appropriation of funds for military purposes, whether from state budgets or from organisations or private individuals.

2. To have at their disposal, upon the completion of general and complete disarmament, only strictly limited contingents of police (militia) equipped with small firearms, and intended for the maintainence of internal order and for the discharge of their obligations with regard to the maintenance of international peace and security, under the United Nations Charter and under the provisions of Article 37 of the present Treaty.

3. To carry out general and complete disarmament simultaneously, in three consecutive stages, as is set forth in Parts II, III, and IV of the present Treaty. Transition to a subsequent stage of disarmament shall take place upon a decision by the International Disarmament Organisation that all disarmament measures of the preceding stage have been carried out and verified, and that any additional verification arrangements, recognised to be necessary for the next stage, have been prepared and can, when appropriate, be put into operation.

4. To carry out all measures of general and complete disarmament in a manner that will ensure that at no stage of disarmament could any state or group of states gain a military advantage and that security is ensured equally for all states parties to the Treaty.

ARTICLE 2

Control Obligations

1. The states parties to the Treaty solemnly undertake to carry out all disarmament measures, from beginning to end, under strict international control, and to assure the implementation on their territories of all control measures set forth in Parts II, III and IV of the present Treaty.

2. Each disarmament measure shall be accompanied by such control measures as are necessary for verification of that measure.

3. To implement control over disarmament, an International Disarmament Organisation including all states parties to the Treaty shall be established within the framework of the United Nations. It shall begin operating as soon as the disarmament

measures are initiated. The structure and functions of the International Disarmament Organisation and its bodies are laid down in Part V of the present Treaty.

4. In all countries parties to the Treaty the International Disarmament Organisation shall have its own staff, recruited internationally and in such a way as to assure the adequate representation on it of all three existing groups of states.

This staff shall exercise control, on a temporary or permanent basis depending on the nature of the measure being carried out, over the compliance by states with their obligations to reduce or eliminate armaments and their manufacture, and to reduce or disband their armed forces.

5. The states parties to the Treaty shall in good time submit to the International Disarmament Organisation such information about their armed forces, armaments, military production and military appropriations as are necessary to carry out the measures of the corresponding stage.

6. Upon completion of the programme of general and complete disarmament, the International Disarmament Organisation shall be kept in being to maintain supervision over the implementation by states of the obligations they have assumed, so as to prevent the re-establishment of the military potential of states in any form whatsoever.

ARTICLE 3
Obligations to Maintain International Peace and Security

1. The states parties to the Treaty have solemnly resolved in the course of, and after general and complete disarmament :

(a) To base relations with each other on the principles of peaceful and friendly co-existence and co-operation;

(b) Not to resort to the threat or use of force to settle any international disputes that may arise, but to use for this purpose the procedures provided for in the United Nations Charter ;

(c) To strengthen the United Nations as the principal institution for the maintenance of peace and for the settlement of international disputes by peaceful means.

2. The states parties to the Treaty undertake to refrain from using the contingents of police (militia) remaining at their disposal upon completion of general and complete disarmament, in any manner other than for the assurance of the internal security of states or for the discharge of their obligations to maintain international peace and security under the United Nations Charter.

PART II.   FIRST STAGE OF GENERAL AND COMPLETE DISARMAMENT

ARTICLE 4
First-Stage Tasks

The states parties to the Treaty undertake, in the course of the first stage of general and complete disarmament, to effect the simultaneous elimination of all means of delivering nuclear weapons and of all foreign military bases on alien territories, to withdraw all foreign troops from these territories, and to reduce their armed forces, conventional armaments and the manufacture of these armaments, and military expenditures.

CHAPTER   I.

Elimination of the Means of Delivering Nuclear Weapons and Foreign Military Bases on Alien Territories, and

A. Means of Delivery

ARTICLE 5

Elimination of Rockets Capable of Delivering Nuclear Weapons

1. There shall be eliminated from the armed forces, and destroyed, all rockets capable of delivering nuclear weapons, of any calibre and range, whether strategic, operational or tactical (except for strictly limited numbers of rockets to be converted to peaceful uses), as well as pilotless aircraft of all types. There shall be completely demolished all launching pads, ramps and platforms for the launching of rockets and pilotless aircraft, other than those pads that will be retained for peaceful launchings under the provisions of Article 15 of the present Treaty. All instruments for the equipment, launching and guidance of the aforementioned rockets and pilotless aircraft shall be destroyed. All underground depots for such rockets, pilotless aircraft and subsidiary facilities s h a l l b e demolished.

2. The manufacture of all kinds of rockets and pilotless aircraft, and of the materials and instruments for their equipment, launching and guidance referred to in Paragraph 1 of this Article, shall be completely discontinued.

All enterprises, or workshops thereof, engaged in their manufacture shall be dismantled; machine tools and equipment specially and exclusively designed for the manufacture of such items shall be destroyed, and the premises of such enterprises, as well as general-purpose machine tools and equipment, shall be converted to peaceful uses. All proving grounds for tests of such rockets and pilotless aircraft shall be demolished.

3. Inspectors of the International Disarmament Organisation shall control the execution of the measures referred to in Paragraphs 1 and 2.

4. For the peaceful exploration of space there shall be allowed the manufacture and testing of appropriate rockets, provided that the plants manufacturing such rockets, as well as the rockets themselves, are subject to supervision by the inspectors of t h e International Disarmament Organisation.

ARTICLE 6

Elimination of Military Aircraft Capable of Delivering Nuclear Weapons

1. There shall be eliminated from the armed forces, and destroyed, all military aircraft capable of delivering nuclear weapons. Military airfields serving as bases for such aircraft, repair and maintenance facilities, and storage places at these airfields shall be rendered inoperative or converted to peaceful uses. Training establishments for crews of such aircraft shall be closed.

2. The manufacture of all military aircraft referred to in Paragraph 1 of this Article shall be completely discontinued. Enterprises, or workshops thereof, designed for the manufacture of such military aircraft shall be either dismantled or converted to the manufacture of civil aircraft or other peaceful items.

3. Inspectors of the International Disarmament Organisation shall control the execution of the measures referred to in Paragraphs 1 and 2.

ARTICLE 7

Elimination of All Surface Warships Capable of Being Used as Vehicles for Nuclear Weapons, and Submarines

1. There shall be eliminated from the armed forces, and destroyed, all surface warships capable of being used as vehicles for nuclear weapons, and submarines of any class or type. Naval bases and other installations for the maintenance of these warships and submarines shall be demo-

lished or dismantled and converted to peaceful uses by the merchant marine.

2. The building of warships and submarines referred to in Paragraph 1 of this Article shall be completely discontinued. Shipyards and plants, wholly or in part designed for the building of such warships and submarines, shall be dismantled or converted to peaceful production.

3. Inspectors of the International Disarmament Organisation shall control the execution of the measures referred to in Paragraphs 1 and 2.

ARTICLE 8

Elimination of All Artillery Systems Capable of Serving as Means of Delivering Nuclear Weapons

1. There shall be eliminated from the armed forces, and destroyed, all artillery systems capable of serving as means of delivery for nuclear weapons. All subsidiary instruments and technical facilities designed for controlling the fire of such artillery systems shall be destroyed. Surface storage places and transport facilities for such systems shall be destroyed or converted to peaceful uses. The entire non-nuclear stock of munitions for such artillery systems, whether at the gun site or in depots, shall be completely destroyed. Underground depots for such artillery systems, and for the non-nuclear munitions thereof, shall be destroyed.

2. The manufacture of artillery systems referred to in Paragraph 1 of this Article shall be completely discontinued. To this end all plants, or workships thereof, engaged in the manufacture of such systems shall be closed or dismantled. All specialised equipment and machine tools at these plants and workshops shall be destroyed, the remainder being converted to peaceful uses. The manufacture of non-nuclear munitions for these artillery systems shall be discontinued. Plants and workshops engaged in the manufacture of such munitions shall be completely dismantled and their specialised equipment destroyed.

3. Inspectors of the International Disarmament Organisation shall control the execution of the measures referred to in Paragraphs 1 and 2.

B.   Foreign Military Bases and Troops on Alien Territories

ARTICLE 9

Dismantling of Foreign Military Bases

1. Simultaneously with the destruction of the means of delivering nuclear weapons under Articles 5 to 8 inclusive of the present Treaty, the states parties to the Treaty which have army, air force or naval bases on foreign territories shall dismantle all such bases, whether principal or stand-by, as well as all depot bases of any designation. All personnel of such bases shall be evacuated to their national territory. All installations and armaments at such bases for which provision is made in Articles 5 to 8 inclusive of the present Treaty, shall be destroyed on the spot. Other armaments shall be destroyed on the spot in accordance with Article 11 of the present Treaty or evacuated to the territory of the state which owned the base.

All installations of a military nature at such bases shall be destroyed. Living quarters and subsidiary installations of foreign bases shall be transferred for peaceful uses to the states on whose territory they are located.

2. The measures referred to in Paragraph 1 of this Article shall be fully applicable to those military bases that are used by foreign troops, even though legally they may belong to the state on whose territory they are located. The said measures shall also be implemented with regard to those army, air force and naval bases that have been set up under military treaties and agreements for use by other states or groups of states, regardless of whether any foreign troops are present at these bases at the time of the conclusion of the present Treaty.

All previous treaty obligations,

decisions of the bodies of military blocs and any rights or privileges pertaining to the establishment and use of military bases on foreign territories, shall become invalid and not subject to renewal. The granting henceforth of military bases for use by foreign troops and the concluding for this purpose of any bilateral or multilateral treaties and agreements shall be prohibited.

3. The legislatures and governments of the states parties to the present Treaty, shall enact legislation and promulgate decrees to ensure that no military bases for use by foreign troops are established on their territory. Inspectors of the International Disarmament Organisation shall control the execution of the measures referred to in Paragraphs 1 and 2 of this Article.

ARTICLE 10
Withdrawal of Foreign Troops from Alien Territories

1. Simultaneously with the destruction of the means of delivering nuclear weapons under Articles 5 to 8 inclusive of the present Treaty, the states parties to the Treaty which have troops, or military personnel of any nature, on foreign territories, shall withdraw all such troops and personnel therefrom. All armaments, and all installations of a military nature, which are located at points where foreign troops are stationed and for which provision is made in Articles 5 to 8 inclusive of the present Treaty, shall be destroyed on the spot. Other armaments shall be destroyed on the spot under Article 11 of the present Treaty or evacuated to the territory of the state withdrawing the troops. Living quarters and subsidiary installations formerly held by such troops or personnel shall be transferred for peaceful uses to the states on whose territory such troops have been stationed.

2. The measures set forth in Paragraph 1 of this Article shall be fully applicable to foreign civilians employed in the armed forces, or engaged in the manufacture of armaments or any other activities serving military purposes on foreign territory. The said persons shall be recalled to the territory of the state whose citizenship they hold, and all previous treaty obligations, decisions by bodies of military blocs, and any rights or privileges pertaining to their activities shall be invalidated and made not subject to renewal. The future dispatching of foreign troops, military personnel or the said civilians to foreign territories shall be prohibited.

3. Inspectors of the International Disarmament Organisation shall control the withdrawal of troops, the destruction of installations and the transfer of the premises referred to in Paragraph 1 of this Article. The International Disarmament Organisation shall have the right to exercise control over the recall of civilians referred to in Paragraph 2 of this Article. The legislation and decrees referred to in Paragraph 3 of Article 9 of the present Treaty, shall include provisions prohibiting the citizens of states parties to the Treaty from serving in the armed forces or from engaging in any other activities for military purposes in foreign states.

CHAPTER II

Reduction of Armed Forces, Conventional Armaments and Military Expenditures; Control Over Such Measures

ARTICLE 11
Reduction of Armed Forces and Conventional Armaments

1. In the first stage of general and complete disarmament the armed forces of the states parties to the Treaty shall be reduced to the following levels:

The United States of America — 1,700,000 enlisted officers and men and civilian employees;

The Union of Soviet Socialist Republics—1,700,000 enlisted officers and men and civilian employees.

....

[agreed levels of armed forces for

other states parties to the Treaty shall be included in this Article].

2. The reduction of the armed forces shall be carried out primarily through the demobilisation of personnel released due to the elimination of the means of delivering nuclear weapons, the dismantling of foreign bases and the withdrawal of foreign troops from alien territories, as provided for in Articles 5 to 10 inclusive of the present Treaty, and primarily by way of the complete disbandment of units and ships' crews, their officers and enlisted men being demobilised.

3. All released conventional armaments, military equipment and munitions of the disbanded units shall be destroyed, and the means of transportation and subsidiary equipment shall be either destroyed or converted to peaceful uses. Conventional armaments and equipment intended for reserve forces shall also be destroyed.

All living quarters, depots and special premises previously occupied by units being disbanded, as well as the territories of all proving grounds, firing ranges and drill grounds, shall be transferred for peaceful uses to the civilian authorities.

4. Inspectors of the International Disarmament Organisation shall exercise control at places where troops are disbanded and released and where conventional armaments and military equipment are destroyed, and shall also control the conversion to peaceful uses of means of transportation and other non-combat equipment, premises, proving grounds, etc

ARTICLE 12
Curtailment of Manufacture of Conventional Armaments

1. Proportionately to the reduction of armed forces, as provided for in Article 11 of the present Treaty, the manufacture of conventional armaments and munitions not referred to in Articles 5 to 8 inclusive of the present Treaty shall be curtailed. Such curtailment shall be carried out primarily through the elimination of enterprises engaged exclusively in the manufacture of such armaments and munitions. These enterprises shall be dismantled, their specialised machine tools and equipment shall be destroyed, and their premises, and general-purpose machine tools and equipment shall be converted to peaceful uses.

2. Inspectors of the International Disarmament Organisation shall exercise control over the measures referred to in Paragraph 1 of this Article.

ARTICLE 13
Reduction of Military Expenditures

1. The states parties to the present Treaty shall reduce their military budgets and appropriations for military purposes proportionately to the destruction of the means of delivering nuclear weapons and the discontinuance of their manufacture, to the dismantling of foreign military bases and withdrawals of foreign troops from alien territories, as well as to the reduction of armed forces and conventional armaments and to the curtailment of the manufacture of such armaments as are provided for in Articles 5 to 12 inclusive of the present Treaty.

The funds released through the implementation of the first-stage measures shall be used for peaceful purposes, including the reduction of taxes on the population and the subsidising of the national economy. At the same time a certain share of the funds thus released shall be diverted to economic and technical assistance to underdeveloped countries. The size of this share shall be subject to agreement between the parties to the Treaty.

2. The International Disarmament Organisation shall control the execution of the measures referred to in Paragraph 1 of this Article through its financial inspectors, whom the states parties to the Treaty shall undertake to assure unhindered access to the records of central financial offices pertaining to the reduction of budgetary allocations of states due to the destruction of the means of delivering nuclear weapons, to the dismantling of foreign military bases and to the reduction of conventional armaments, including the relevant acts of their legislative and executive bodies.

CHAPTER III.

Measures to Ensure the Security of States

ARTICLE 14

Restriction of Displacement of the Means of Delivering Nuclear Weapons

1. From the very beginning of the first stage and until the final destruction of all means of delivering nuclear weapons under Articles 5 to 8 inclusive of the present Treaty, the placing in orbit or stationing in outer space of any special devices capable of delivering weapons of mass destruction, the leaving of their territorial waters by warships, and the flying beyond the limits of their national territory by military aircraft capable of carrying weapons of mass destruction, shall be prohibited.

2. The International Disarmament Organisation shall control the compliance by the states parties to the Treaty with the provisions of Paragraph 1 of this Article. The states parties to the Treaty shall provide advance information to the International Disarmament Organisation about all launchings of rockets for peaceful purposes, as provided for in Article 15 of the present Treaty, as well as about all flights of military aircraft within their national frontiers and movements of warships within their territorial waters.

ARTICLE 15

Control over Launchings of Rockets for Peaceful Purposes

1. The launching of rockets and space devices shall be carried out exclusively for peaceful purposes.

2. The International Disarmament Organisation shall exercise control over the implementation of the provisions of Paragraph 1 of this Article through the establishment of inspection teams at the sites for peaceful rocket launchings and these teams shall be present at the launchings and shall thoroughly examine every rocket or satellite before it is launched.

ARTICLE 16

Prevention of the Further Spread of Nuclear Weapons

The states parties to the Treaty owning nuclear weapons shall undertake to refrain from transferring control over nuclear weapons and from transmitting information necessary for their manufacture to states not owning them.

The states parties to the Treaty not owning nuclear weapons shall undertake to refrain from manufacturing or otherwise obtaining nuclear weapons and shall refuse to admit the nuclear weapons of any other state into their territories.

ARTICLE 17

Prohibition of Nuclear Tests

The holding of nuclear tests of any kind shall be prohibited. [If such a prohibition is not implemented under other international agreements by the time this Treaty is signed].

ARTICLE 18

Measures to Improve the Capacity of the United Nations to Assure International Peace and Security

1. To ensure that the United Nations is capable of effectively protecting the states against threats to, or breaches of the peace, all states parties to the Treaty shall, between the signing of the Treaty and its entry into force, conclude agreements with the Security Council on making available to the latter armed forces, assistance and appropriate facilities, the right of passage included, as provided for in Article 43 of the United Nations Charter.

2. The armed forces provided under the said agreements shall form part of the national armed forces of the corresponding states and shall be stationed within their territories. They shall be fully

manned, equipped and prepared for combat. When used under Article 42 of the United Nations Charter, these forces, commanded by the military authorities of the corresponding states, shall be placed at the disposal of the Security Council.

CHAPTER IV.

Time Limits for Measures of the First Stage; Transition from First to Second Stage

ARTICLE 19
Time-Limits for Measures of the First Stage

1. The first stage of general and complete disarmament shall be initiated six months after the Treaty comes into force (under Article 46 of the present Treaty), within which period the International Disarmament Organisation shall be set up.

2. The duration of the first stage of general and complete disarmament shall be 15 months.

ARTICLE 20
Transition from First to Second Stage

In the course of the last three months of the first stage, the International Disarmament Organisation shall review the results of the implementation of the first-stage measures of general and complete disarmament with a view to reporting on them to the states parties to the Treaty, as well as to the Security Council and the General Assembly of the United Nations.

PART III. SECOND STAGE OF GENERAL AND COMPLETE DISARMAMENT

ARTICLE 21
Second-Stage Tasks

The states parties to the Treaty undertake, in the course of the second stage of general and complete disarmament, to effect the complete elimination of nuclear and other weapons of mass destruction, as well as the further reduction of their armed forces, conventional armaments and the manufacture of these armaments, and military expenditures.

CHAPTER V.

Elimination of Nuclear, Chemical, Biological and Radiological Weapons; Control Over Such Measures

ARTICLE 22
Elimination of Nuclear Weapons

1. (a) There shall be eliminated from the armed forces, and destroyed, nuclear weapons of all kinds, types and capacities. Fissionable materials extracted from such weapons, whether directly attached to the troops or stored in various depots, shall be appropriately processed to render them unfit for the immediate re-establishment of weapons, and they shall form a special fund for peaceful uses, belonging to the state which previously owned the nuclear weapons. Non-nuclear components of such weapons shall be completely destroyed.

All depots and special storage spaces for nuclear weapons shall be demolished.

(b) All stockpiles of nuclear materials for nuclear weapons purposes shall be appropriately processed to render them unfit for immediate use in nuclear weapons, and shall be transferred to the aforementioned special funds.

(c) Inspectors of the International Disarmament Organisation shall control the execution of the measures to eliminate nuclear weapons referred to in sub-paragraphs (a) and (b) of this paragraph.

2. (a) The manufacture of nuclear weapons, and of fissionable materials for weapons purposes shall be completely discontinued. All plants, installations and laboratories specially designed for the manufacture of nuclear weapons or their components shall be eliminated or converted to peaceful production. All workshops, installations and laboratories for the manufacture of the components of nuclear weapons at plants that are partially engaged in the manufacture of such weapons, shall be destroyed or converted to peaceful production.

(b) The measures for the discontinuance of the manufacture of nuclear weapons and of fissionable materials for weapons purposes referred to in sub-paragraph (a), shall be executed under the control of inspectors of the International Disarmament Organisation.

The International Disarmament Organisation shall have the right to inspect all enterprises which extract raw materials for atomic production or which produce or use fissionable materials or atomic energy.

The states parties to the Treaty shall make available to the International Disarmament Organisation documents pertaining to the extraction of nuclear raw materials, to their processing and to their utilisation for military or peaceful purposes.

3. Each state party to the Treaty shall, in accordance with its constitutional procedure, enact legislation on the complete prohibition of nuclear weapons and on liability under the criminal law for any attempt at their re-establishment by individuals or organisations.

ARTICLE 23
Elimination of Chemical, Biological and Radiological Weapons

1. There shall be eliminated from the arsenals of states, and destroyed (neutralised), all kinds of chemical, biological and radiological weapons, whether directly attached to the troops or stored in various depots and storage places. Simultaneously, all instruments and facilities for the combat use of such weapons, as well as all special devices and facilities for their storage and conservation, shall be destroyed.

2. The manufacture of all kinds of chemical, biological and radiological weapons and of all means and devices for their combat use, transportation and storage shall be completely discontinued. All plants, installations and laboratories that are wholly or in part engaged in the manufacture of such weapons shall be destroyed or converted to peaceful production.

3. The measures referred to in Paragraphs 1 and 2 shall be executed under the control of inspectors of the International Disarmament Organisation.

CHAPTER VI.

Further Reduction of Armed Forces, Conventional Armaments and Military Expenditures; Control Over Such Measures

ARTICLE 24
Further Reduction of Armed Forces and Conventional Armaments

1. In the second stage of general and complete disarmament, the armed forces of the states parties to the Treaty shall be further reduced to the following levels:

The United States of America— one million enlisted officers and men and civilian employees;

The Union of Soviet Socialist Republics—one million enlisted officers and men and civilian employees.

....

[Agreed levels of armed forces for other states parties to the Treaty shall be included in this Article].

The reduction of the armed forces

shall be carried out primarily through the demobilisation of personnel previously attached to the nuclear or other weapons subject to elimination under Articles 22 and 23 of the present Treaty, and mainly by way of the complete disbandment of units and ships' crews, their officers and enlisted men being demobilised.

2. All released conventional armaments, military equipment and munitions of the units being disbanded shall be destroyed, and the means of transportation and subsidiary equipment shall be either destroyed or converted to peaceful uses.

All living quarters, depots and special premises previously occupied by units being disbanded, as well as the territories of all proving grounds, firing ranges and drill grounds, shall be transferred for peaceful uses to the civilian authorities.

3. As in the implementation of such measures in the first stage of general and complete disarmament, inspectors of the International Disarmament Organisation shall exercise control at places where troops are disbanded and released and conventional armaments and military equipment destroyed, and shall also control the conversion to peaceful uses of means of transportation and other non-combat equipment, premises, proving grounds, etc.

ARTICLE 25
Further Curtailment of Conventional Armaments Manufacture

1. Proportionately to the reduction of armed forces, as provided for in Article 24 of the present Treaty, the manufacture of conventional armaments and munitions shall be curtailed. Such curtailment shall, as in the first stage of general and complete disarmament, be carried out primarily through the elimination of enterprises engaged exclusively in the manufacture of such armaments and munitions. These enterprises shall be dismantled, their specialised machine tools and equipment shall be destroyed, and their premises and general-purpose machine tools and equipment shall be converted to peaceful uses.

2. The measures referred to in Paragraph 1 of this Article shall be carried out under the control of inspectors of the International Disarmament Organisation.

ARTICLE 26
Further Reduction of Military Expenditures

1. The states parties to the Treaty shall further reduce their military budgets and appropriations for military purposes proportionately to the destruction of nuclear, chemical, biological and radiological weapons and the discontinuance of their manufacture, as well as to the further reduction of armed forces and conventional armaments and to the curtailment of the manufacture of such armaments as provided for in Articles 22 to 25 inclusive of the Treaty.

The funds released through the implementation of the second-stage measures shall be used for peaceful purposes, including the reduction of taxes on the population and the subsidising of the national economy. At the same time a certain share of the funds thus released shall be diverted to economic and technical assistance to underdeveloped countries. The size of this shall be subject to agreement between the parties to the Treaty.

2. Control over the measures referred to in Paragraph 1 of this Article shall be exercised in accordance with the provisions of Paragraph 2 of Article 13 of the Treaty. Financial inspectors of the International Disarmament Organisation shall also be assured unhindered access to materials pertaining to the reduction of budgetary allocations of states due to the elimination of nuclear, chemical, biological and radiological weapons.

CHAPTER VII.

Measures to Ensure the Security of States

ARTICLE 27

Continued Improvement of the Capacity of the United Nations to Assure International Peace and Security

The states parties to the Treaty shall continue to implement the measures, referred to in Article 18 of the present treaty, regarding the placing of armed forces at the disposal of the Security Council for use under Article 42 of the United Nations Charter.

CHAPTER VIII.

Time Limits for Measures of the Second Stage; Transition from Second to Third Stage

ARTICLE 28

Time-Limits for Measures of the Second Stage

The duration of the second stage of general and complete disarmament shall be 15 months.

ARTICLE 29

Transition from Second to Third Stage

In the course of the last three months of the second stage, the International Disarmament Organisation shall review the results of the implementation of the stage.

Measures pertaining to the transition from the second to the third stage of general and complete disarmament shall be similar to those provided for the first stage under Article 20 of the present Treaty.

PART IV. THIRD STAGE OF GENERAL AND COMPLETE DISARMAMENT

ARTICLE 30
Third-Stage Tasks

The states parties to the Treaty undertake, in the course of the third stage of general and complete disarmament, to disband fully all their armed forces and thereby to complete the elimination of the military establishment of states.

CHAPTER IX.

Completion of the Elimination of the Military Establishment of States; Control Over Such Measures

ARTICLE 31

Completion of the Elimination of Armed Forces and Conventional Armaments

1. With a view to completing the process of the elimination of armed forces, the states parties to the Treaty shall disband the entire personnel of the armed forces which remain at their disposal after the accomplishment of the first two stages of disarmament. The system of military reserves of each state party to the Treaty shall be fully abolished.

2. The states parties to the Treaty shall destroy all armaments, military equipment and munitions, whether held by the troops or in depots, that remain at their disposal after the accomplishment of the first two stages of the Treaty. All military equipment which cannot be converted to peaceful uses shall be destroyed.

3. Inspectors of the International Disarmament Organisation shall exercise control over the disbanding of troops and over the destruction of armaments and military equipment, and shall control the conversion of

transport and other non-combat equipment, premises, proving grounds, etc., to peaceful uses.

The International Disarmament Organisation shall have access to documents pertaining to the disbanding of all personnel of the armed forces of the states parties to the Treaty.

ARTICLE 32

Complete Termination of Military Production

1. Military production at factories and plants shall be terminated, with the exception of the production of agreed types and quantities of light firearms for purposes referred to in Paragraph 2 of Article 36 of the present Treaty. The factories and plants subject to elimination shall be dismantled, their specialised machine tools and equipment shall be destroyed, and the premises, general-purpose machine tools and equipment shall be converted to peaceful uses. All scientific research in the military field at all scientific and research institutions and at designing offices shall be discontinued. All blueprints and other documents necessary for the manufacture of the weapons and military equipment subject to elimination shall be destroyed.

All orders placed by military departments for the manufacture of armaments, military equipment, munitions and matériel with national or foreign government-owned enterprises and private firms shall be annulled.

2. Inspectors of the International Disarmament Organisation shall exercise control over the measures referred to in Paragraph 1 of this Article.

ARTICLE 33

Abolition of Military Establishments

1. There shall be abolished War Ministries, general staffs and all other military and paramilitary organisations and institutions designed to organise the military effort of states parties to the Treaty. The states parties to the Treaty shall:

(a) Demobilise all personnel of these institutions and organisations;

(b) Abrogate all legislative acts, rules and regulations governing the organisation of the military effort and status, structure and activities of such institutions and organisations;

(c) Destroy all documents pertaining to the planning of the mobilisation and the operational deployment of the armed forces in time of war.

2. The entire process of the abolition of military and paramilitary institutions and organisations shall be carried out under the control of inspectors of the International Disarmament Organisation.

ARTICLE 34

Abolition of Military Conscription and Military Training

In accordance with their respective constitutional procedures, the states parties to the Treaty shall enact legislation prohibiting all military training, abolishing military conscription and all other forms of recruiting armed forces, and discontinuing all military courses for reservists. Simultaneously there shall be disbanded all establishments and organisations dealing with military training as provided for in Article 33 of the present Treaty. The disbanding of all military training institutions and organisations shall be carried out under the control of inspectors of the International Disarmament Organisation.

ARTICLE 35

Prohibition of the Appropriation of Funds for Military Purposes

1. There shall be discontinued the appropriation of funds for military purposes in any form, whether from government bodies or private individuals and public organisations.

The funds released through the implementation of general and complete disarmament shall be used for peaceful purposes, including the reduction or complete abolition of taxes on the population and the subsidising of the national economy. At the same time, a certain share of the funds thus released shall be diverted to economic and technical assistance to underdeveloped countries. The size of this share shall be subject to agreement between the parties to the Treaty.

2. To organise control over the implementation of the provisions of this Article, the International Disarmament Organisation shall have the right of access to legislative acts and budgetary documents of the states parties to the present Treaty.

CHAPTER X.

Measures to Ensure the Security of States and to Maintain International Peace

ARTICLE 36
Contingents of Police (Militia)

1. To maintain internal order, including the safeguarding of the frontiers and the personal security of citizens, and to ensure compliance with their obligations pertaining to the maintenance of international peace and security under the United Nations Charter, the states parties to the Treaty shall be entitled to have, after the complete abolition of armed forces, strictly limited contingents of police (militia), equipped with small firearms.

The strength of these contingents of police (militia) for each state party to the treaty shall be as follows :

....

2. The states parties to the Treaty shall be allowed to manufacture strictly limited quantities of light firearms intended for such contingents of police (militia). The list of plants producing such arms, and their quotas and types for each party to the Treaty shall be specified in a special agreement.

3. Inspectors of the International Disarmament Organisation shall exercise control over the compliance by the states parties to the Treaty with their obligations with regard to the restricted production of the said small firearms.

ARTICLE 37
Provision of Police (Militia) Units to the Security Council

1. The states parties to the Treaty undertake to place at the disposal of the Security Council, on its request, units from the contingents of police (militia) retained by them, as well as to provide assistance and appropriate facilities, including the right of passage. The placing of such units at the disposal of the Security Council is carried out under the provisions of Article 43 of the United Nations Charter. To ensure that urgent military measures may be undertaken, the states parties to the Treaty shall maintain in a state of immediate readiness that part of the police (militia) contingents which is intended for joint international enforcement action. The size of the units which the states parties to the Treaty undertake to place at the disposal of the Security Council, as well as the areas where they are stationed, shall be specified in agreements to be concluded by the states parties to the Treaty with the Security Council.

2. The command of the units referred to in Paragraph 1 shall be made up of representatives of the three principal groups of states existing in the world on the basis of equal representation. The commanding body shall decide on all questions by agreement among its members representing the three groups of states.

ARTICLE 38
Control over the Prevention of the Re-establishment of Armed Forces

1. The police (militia) contingents retained by the states parties to the Treaty after the completion of general and complete disarmament shall be under the control of the Inter-

national Disarmament Organisation, which shall verify the reports by states about the areas where such contingents are stationed and their strength and armaments in each such area, and about all movements of substantial contingents of police (militia).

2. For purposes of control over the prevention of the re-establishment of armed forces and armaments abolished as a result of general and complete disarmament, the International Disarmament Organisation shall have the right of access at any time to any point within the territory of each state party to the Treaty.

3. The International Disarmament Organisation shall have the right to institute a system of aerial inspection and aerial photography over the territories of the states parties to the Treaty.

CHAPTER XI.

Time Limits for Measures of the Third Stage

ARTICLE 39

The third stage of general and complete disarmament shall be completed over a period of one year. During the last three months of this stage, the International Disarmament Organisation shall review the results of the implementation of the third-stage measures of general and complete disarmament, with a view to reporting on them to the states parties to the Treaty, as well as to the Security Council and the General Assembly of the United Nations.

PART V.   STRUCTURE AND FUNCTIONS OF THE INTERNATIONAL DISARMAMENT ORGANIZATION

ARTICLE 40
Functions and Main Bodies

The International Disarmament Organisation, to be set up under Paragraph 3 of Article 2 of the present Treaty, hereinafter referred to as the "Organisation", shall have a conference of all states parties to the Treaty, hereinafter referred to as the "Conference", and a control council, hereinafter referred to as the "Council".

The Organisation shall deal with questions pertaining to supervision over the compliance by states with their obligations under the present Treaty. All questions related to the assurance of international peace and security, which may arise in the course of the implementation of the present Treaty, including preventive and enforcement measures, shall be decided on by the Security Council in conformity with its powers under the United Nations Charter.

ARTICLE 41
The Conference

1. The Conference shall comprise all states parties to the Treaty. It shall hold regular sessions at least once a year, and special sessions which may be summoned by decision of the Council or on the request of a majority of the states parties to the Treaty with a view to considering matters pertaining to the implementation of effective control over disarmament. The sessions shall be held at the headquarters of the Organisation, unless otherwise decided by the Conference.

2. Each state party to the Treaty shall have one vote. Decisions on questions of procedure shall be taken by a simple majority, and on all other matters by a two-thirds majority. In accordance with the provisions of the present Treaty, the Conference shall adopt its own rules of procedure.

3. The Conference may discuss any matters pertaining to the measures of control over the implementation of general and complete disarmament, and may make recommendations to the states parties to the Treaty and to the Council on any such matters or

measures.

4. The Conference shall:

(a) Elect non-permanent members of the Council;

(b) Consider the annual, and any special, reports of the Council;

(c) Approve the budget recommended by the Council;

(d) Approve reports to be submitted to the Security Council and the General Assembly of the United Nations;

(e) Approve amendments to the present Treaty in accordance with Article 47 of the present Treaty;

(f) Take decisions on any matter specifically referred to the Conference for this purpose by the Council;

(g) Propose matters for consideration by the Council and request from the Council reports on any matter relating to the functions of the Council.

ARTICLE 42
The Control Council

1. The Council shall consist of:

(a) The five permanent member-states of the United Nations Security Council;

(b) . . . [number] other states parties to the Treaty elected by the Conference for a period of two years.

The composition of the Council must ensure proper representation of the three principal groups of states existing in the world.

2. The Council shall:

(a) Direct in practice the measures of control over the implementation of general and complete disarmament; set up such bodies at the headquarters of the Organisation as it deems necessary for the discharge of its functions; establish procedures for their operation, and devise the necessary rules and regulations in accordance with the present Treaty;

(b) Submit to the Conference annual reports and such special reports as it considers it necessary to prepare;

(c) Be in constant touch with the United Nations Security Council as the organ bearing the main responsibility for the maintenance of international peace and security; periodically inform it of the progress achieved in the implementation of general and complete disarmament, and promptly notify it of any infringements by the states parties to the Treaty of their disarmament obligations under the present Treaty;

(d) Review the results of the implementation of the measures included in each stage of general and complete disarmament with a view to reporting on them to the states parties to the Treaty, and to the Security Council and the General Assembly of the United Nations;

(e) Recruit the staff of the Organisation on an international basis, so as to ensure that the three principal groups of states existing in the world are adequately represented. The personnel of the Organisation shall be recruited from among those persons who are recommended by the governments and who may or may not be citizens of the country of the recommending government;

(f) Prepare and submit to the Conference the annual budget estimates for the expenses of the Organisation;

(g) Elaborate instructions to direct the operations of the various control elements;

(h) Make timely analyses of incoming reports;

(i) Request from states such information on their armed forces and armaments as may be necessary to control the implementation of the disarmament measures provided for by the present Treaty;

(j) Perform such other functions as are envisaged in the present Treaty.

3. Each member of the Council shall have one vote. Decisions of the Council on procedural matters shall be taken by a simple majority, and on other matters by a two-thirds majority.

4. The Council shall be so organised as to be able to function continuously. The Council shall adopt its own rules of procedure and shall

be authorised to establish such subsidiary organs as it deems necessary for the performance of its functions.

ARTICLE 43

Privileges and Immunities

The Organisation, its personnel and representatives of the states parties to the Treaty shall enjoy on the territory of each state party to the Treaty such privileges and immunities as are necessary for the exercise of independent and unrestricted control over the implementation of the present Treaty.

ARTICLE 44

Finances

1. All the expenses of the Organisation shall be met by the states parties to the Treaty. The budget of the Organisation shall be drawn up by the Council and approved by the Conference in accordance with Paragraph 4(c) of Article 41 and Paragraph 2(f) of Article 42 of the present Treaty.

2. The states parties to the Treaty shall contribute funds to cover the expenditures of the Organisation according to the following scale : ......
....
[the agreed scale of contributions shall be included in the present Article].

ARTICLE 45

Preparatory Commission

Immediately after the signing of the present Treaty the states represented on the 18-power Disarmament Committee shall set up a preparatory commission with the task of taking practical steps to establish the International Disarmament Organisation.

PART VI. FINAL CLAUSES

ARTICLE 46

Ratification and Entry into Force

The present Treaty shall be subject to ratification by the signatory states in accordance with their constitutional processes, within a period of six months from the date of the signing of the Treaty, and shall come into force upon the deposit of instruments of ratification with the United Nations secretariat by all the permanent members of the Security Council, as well as by those states that are their allies in bilateral and multilateral military alliances, and by . . . [number] non-aligned states.

ARTICLE 47

Amendments

Any proposal to amend the text of the present Treaty shall come into force after it has been adopted by a two-thirds majority at a conference of all states parties to the Treaty, and ratified in accordance with their constitutional procedures by the states referred to in Article 46 of the present Treaty.

ARTICLE 48

Authentic Texts

The present Treaty, done in the Russian, English, French, Chinese and Spanish languages, each being equally authentic,

Shall be deposited with the United Nations secretariat, which shall transmit certified copies thereof to all the signatory states.

In witness whereof, the undersigned, duly authorised, have signed the present Treaty.

Done at . . . . .

Outline of Basic Provisions

of a Treaty on

General and Complete Disarmament in a Peaceful World

UNITED STATES ARMS CONTROL AND DISARMAMENT AGENCY

Statement by President Kennedy

Press Conference, April 18, 1962

The United States has today tabled at Geneva an outline of every basic provision of a treaty on general and complete disarmament in a peaceful world. It provides a blueprint of our position on general and complete disarmament as well as elaboration of the nature, sequence, and timing of specific disarmament measures.

This outline of a treaty represents the most comprehensive and specific series of proposals the United States or any other country has ever made on disarmament. In addition to stating the objectives and principles which should govern agreements for disarmament, the document calls for the grouping of individual measures in three balanced and safe-guarded stages. We are hopeful through the give-and-take of the conference table this plan will have a constructive influence upon the negotiations now in progress.

I want to stress that with this plan the United States is making a major effort to achieve a breakthrough on disarmament negotiations. We believe that the nations represented at Geneva have a heavy responsibility to lay the foundations for a genuinely secure and peaceful world starting through a reduction in arms.

Foreword

An ultimate goal of the United States is a world which is free from the scourge of war and the dangers and burdens of armaments, in which the use of force has been subordinated to the rule of law, and in which international adjustments to a changing world are achieved peacefully. Today, in a world riven by dangerous tensions and mistrust, the attainment of this goal necessitates continuing and patient efforts to achieve the progressive reduction of national warmaking capabilities in such a manner as to increase the security of all nations. Thus, responsible arms control and disarmament proposals cannot be directed toward the attainment of unilateral political or military advantage. They must be fully responsive to the legitimate security interests of all nations.

On the basis of these considerations, President Kennedy on September 25, 1961, presented to the General Assembly of the United Nations the "United States Program for General and Complete Disarmament in a Peaceful World." To provide a more precise statement of the United States approach to disarmament and the manner in which that approach should be implemented, the United States on April 18, 1962, presented to the conference of the 18-nation Committee on Disarmament, meeting in Geneva, an "Outline of Basic Provisions of a Treaty on General and Complete Disarmament in a Peaceful World." Although not a draft treaty, the "Outline" elaborates and extends the proposals of September 25 and provides in specific terms a substantial basis for the negotiation of arms control and disarmament treaty obligations.

The principal provisions of the United States Outline are described in the summary that follows. The complete text of the Outline begins on page 5.

Outline of Basic Provisions of a Treaty on General and Complete Disarmament in a Peaceful World

SUMMARY

Principles and Process of Disarmament

Disarmament would be implemented progressively and in a balanced manner so that at no stage could any state or group of states obtain military advantage. Compliance with obligations would be effectively verified. As national armaments were reduced, the United Nations would be progressively strengthened.

Disarmament would be accomplished in three stages—the first to be carried out in 3 years; the second, also in 3 years; and the third, as promptly as possible within an agreed period of time. Stage I would be initiated by the United States, the Soviet Union, and other agreed states. All militarily significant states would participate in Stage II; and all states possessing armaments and armed forces, in Stage III.

Transition from one stage of disarmament to the next would take place upon a determination that all undertakings in the preceding stage had been carried out and that all preparations for the next stage had been made.

Disarmament Measures

A. ARMAMENTS. During Stage I, inventories of major categories of both nuclear delivery vehicles and conventional armaments would be reduced by 30 percent. Fixed launching pads would be reduced with associated missiles. Half of the remaining inventories would be eliminated during Stage II, and final reductions would be made in Stage III. Upon the completion of Stage III, states would have at their disposal only agreed types of nonnuclear armaments for forces required to maintain internal order and protect the personal security of citizens.

Production of armaments during Stage I would be limited to agreed allowances and would be compensated for by the destruction of additional armaments to the end that reductions would not be impaired. In Stage II, production of armaments would be halted except for parts for maintenance of retained armaments. Any further production of national armaments would be ended in Stage III except for production of agreed types of nonnuclear armaments for internal forces.

Military research, development, and testing would be subject to increasing limitations during the disarmament process. During Stage III, appropriate action would be taken to insure that new scientific discoveries and technological inventions of military significance were not used for military purposes.

B. ARMED FORCES. Force levels of the United States and Soviet Union would be reduced to 2.1 million at the end of Stage I. Half of the remaining forces of these two states would be disbanded during Stage II, and final reductions would be made in Stage III. Other states would also progressively reduce their force levels. By the end of Stage III, states would have at their disposal only those agreed forces and related organizational arrangements required to maintain internal order and protect the personal security of citizens.

C. NUCLEAR WEAPONS. Production of fissionable materials for use in nuclear weapons would be halted in Stage I, and limitations would be imposed on the production of fissionable materials for other purposes. The availability of fissionable materials for use in nuclear weapons would be reduced during Stage I and subsequent stages by safeguarded transfers to nonnuclear weapons purposes.

If nuclear weapons tests had not already been halted under effective international control, arrangements to this end would be undertaken in Stage I. States which had manufactured nuclear weapons would agree in Stage I not to transfer control over nuclear weapons to states which had not manufactured them or to assist such states in their manufacture. States which had not manufactured nuclear weapons would refrain from seeking them. Transfers of fissionable materials between states would be limited to peaceful purposes and would be safeguarded.

Beginning in Stage II, nonnuclear components and assemblies of nuclear weapons would be destroyed and limitations would be imposed on further production or refabrication of nuclear weapons. At the end of Stage II, remaining nuclear weapons would be registered internationally to assist in verifying the fact that by the end of Stage III states would not have such weapons at their disposal.

D. OUTER SPACE. The placing of weapons of mass destruction in orbit would be prohibited in Stage I, and limitations would be imposed on the production, stockpiling, and testing of boosters for space vehicles. States would support increased cooperation in peaceful uses of outer space.

E. MILITARY BASES. Reduction of military bases, wherever they might be located, would be initiated in Stage II, and final reductions would be made in Stage III.

F. MILITARY EXPENDITURES. Military expenditures would be reported throughout the disarmament process.

Verification

The verification of disarmament would be the responsibility of an International Disarmament Organization, which would be established within the framework of the United Nations. Reductions of armaments and armed forces would be verified at agreed locations; and limitations on production, testing, and other specified activities, at declared locations. Assurance that agreed levels of armaments and armed forces were not exceeded and that activities subject to limitation or prohibition were not being conducted clandestinely would be provided through arrangements which would relate the extent of inspection at any time to the amount of disarmament being undertaken and to the risk to the disarming states of possible violations.

Such assurance might, for example, be accomplished through arrangements under which states would divide themselves into a number of zones through which inspection would be progressively extended. By the end of Stage III, when disarmament had been completed, all parts of the territory of states would have been inspected.

Reduction of the Risk of War

To promote confidence and reduce the risk of war during the disarmament process, states would, beginning in Stage I, give advance notification of major military movements and maneuvers, establish observation posts to report on concentrations and movements of military forces, and insure rapid and reliable communications among heads of governments and with the Secretary-General of the United Nations.

An International Commission on Reduction of the Risk of War would examine possible extensions and improvements of such measures as well as additional measures to reduce the risk of war through accident, miscalculation, failure of communications, or surprise attack.

Arrangements for Keeping the Peace

In Stage I, states would undertake obligations to refrain from the threat or use of force of any type contrary to the United Nations Charter. Throughout the three stages of disarmament, states would use all available means for the peaceful settlement of disputes, would seek to improve processes for this purpose, and would support measures to improve the capability of the United Nations to maintain international peace and security.

A United Nations Peace Observation Corps would be established in Stage I, and a United Nations Peace Force, in Stage II. The United Nations Peace Force, which would be equipped with agreed types of armaments and would be supplied agreed manpower by states, would be progressively strengthened until, in Stage III, it would be fully capable of insuring international security in a disarmed world.

Outline of Basic Provisions of a Treaty on General and Complete Disarmament in a Peaceful World

COMPLETE TEXT

In order to assist in the preparation of a treaty on general and complete disarmament in a peaceful world, the United States submits the following outline of basic provisions of such a treaty.

A. OBJECTIVES

1. To ensure that (a) disarmament is general and complete and war is no longer an instrument for settling international problems, and (b) general and complete disarmament is accompanied by the establishment of reliable procedures for the settlement of disputes and by effective arrangements for the maintenance of peace in accordance with the principles of the Charter of the United Nations.

2. Taking into account paragraphs 3 and 4 below, to provide, with with respect to the military establishment of every nation, for:

(a) Disbanding of armed forces, dismantling of military establishments, including bases, cessation of the production of armaments as well as their liquidation or conversion to peaceful uses;

(b) Elimination of all stockpiles of nuclear, chemical, biological, and other weapons of mass destruction and cessation of the production of such weapons;

(c) Elimination of all means of delivery of weapons of mass destruction;

(d) Abolition of the organizations and institutions designed to organize the military efforts of states, cessation of military training, and closing of all military training institutions;

(e) Discontinuance of military expenditures.

3. To ensure that, at the completion of the program for general and complete disarmament, states would have at their disposal only those non-nuclear armaments, forces, facilities and establishments as are agreed to be necessary to maintain internal order and protect the personal security of citizens.

4. To ensure that during and after implementation of general and complete disarmament, states also would support and provide agreed manpower for a United Nations Peace Force to be equipped with

agreed types of armaments necessary to ensure that the United Nations can effectively deter or suppress any threat or use of arms.

5. To establish and provide for the effective operation of an International Disarmament Organization within the framework of the United Nations for the purpose of ensuring that all obligations under the disarmament program would be honored and observed during and after implementation of general and complete disarmament; and to this end to ensure that the International Disarmament Organization and its inspectors would have unrestricted access without veto to all places as necessary for the purpose of effective verification.

B. PRINCIPLES

The guiding principles during the achievement of these objectives are:

1. Disarmament would be implemented until it is completed by stages to be carried out within specified time limits.

2. Disarmament would be balanced so that at no stage of the implementation of the treaty could any state or group of states gain military advantage, and so that security would be ensured equally for all.

3. Compliance with all disarmament obligations would be effectively verified during and after their entry into force. Verification arrangements would be instituted progressively as necessary to ensure throughout the disarmament process that agreed levels of armaments and armed forces were not exceeded.

4. As national armaments are reduced, the United Nations would be progressively strengthened in order to improve its capacity to ensure international security and the peaceful settlement of differences as well as to facilitate the development of international cooperation in common tasks for the benefit of mankind.

5. Transition from one stage of disarmament to the next would take place upon decision that all measures in the preceding stage had been implemented and verified and that any additional arrangements required for measures in the next stage were ready to operate.

Introduction

The Treaty would contain three stages designed to achieve a permanent state of general and complete disarmament in a peaceful world. The Treaty would enter into force upon the signature and ratification of the United States of America, the Union of Soviet Socialist Republics and such other states as might be agreed. Stage II would begin when all militarily significant states had become Parties to the Treaty and other transition requirements had been satisfied. Stage III would begin when all states possessing armed forces and armaments had become Parties to the Treaty and other transition requirements had been satisfied. Disarmament, verification, and measures for keeping the peace would proceed progressively and proportionately beginning with the entry into force of the Treaty.

Stage I

Stage I would begin upon the entry into force of the Treaty and would be completed within three years from that date.

During Stage I the Parties to the Treaty would undertake:

1. To reduce their armaments and armed forces and to carry out other agreed measures in the manner outlined below;

2. To establish the International Disarmament Organization upon the entry into force of the Treaty in order to ensure the verification in the agreed manner of the obligations undertaken; and

3. To strengthen arrangements for keeping the peace through the measures outlined below.

A. ARMAMENTS

1. Reduction of Armaments

a. Specified Parties to the Treaty, as a first stage toward general and complete disarmament in a peaceful world, would reduce by thirty percent the armaments in each category listed in subparagraph b below. Except as adjustments for production would be permitted in Stage I in accordance with paragraph 3 below, each type of armament in the categories listed in subparagraph b would be reduced by thirty percent of the inventory existing at an agreed date.

b. All types of armaments within agreed categories would be subject to reduction in Stage I (the following list of categories, and of types within categories, is illustrative):

(1) Armed combat aircraft having an empty weight of 40,000 kilograms or greater; missiles having a range of 5,000 kilometers or greater, together with their related fixed launching pads; and submarine-launched missiles and air-to-surface missiles having a range of 300 kilometers or greater.

(Within this category, the United States, for example, would declare as types of armaments: the B–52 aircraft; Atlas missiles together with their related fixed launching pads; Titan missiles together with their related fixed launching pads; Polaris missiles; Hound

Dog missiles; and each new type of armament, such as Minuteman missiles, which came within the category description, together with, where applicable, their related fixed launching pads. The declared inventory of types within the category by other Parties to the Treaty would be similarly detailed).

(2) Armed combat aircraft having an empty weight of between 15,000 kilograms and 40,000 kilograms and those missiles not included in category (1) having a range between 300 kilometers and 5,000 kilometers, together with any related fixed launching pads. (The Parties would declare their armaments by types within the category).

(3) Armed combat aircraft having an empty weight of between 2,500 and 15,000 kilograms. (The Parties would declare their armaments by types within the category).

(4) Surface-to-surface (including submarine-launched missiles) and air-to-surface aerodynamic and ballistic missiles and free rockets having a range of between 10 kilometers and 300 kilometers, together with any related fixed launching pads. (The Parties would declare their armaments by types within the category).

(5) Anti-missile missile systems, together with related fixed launching pads. (The Parties would declare their armaments by types within the category).

(6) Surface-to-air missiles other than anti-missile missile systems, together with any related fixed launching pads. (The Parties would declare their armaments by types within the category).

(7) Tanks. (The Parties would declare their armaments by types within the category).

(8) Armored cars and armored personnel carriers. (The Parties would declare their armaments by types within the category).

(9) All artillery, and mortars and rocket launchers having a caliber of 100 mm. or greater. (The Parties would declare their armaments by types within the category).

(10) Combatant ships with standard displacement of 400 tons or greater of the following classes: Aircraft carriers, battleships, cruisers, destroyer types and submarines. (The Parties would declare their armaments by types within the category).

2. Method of Reduction

a. Those Parties to the Treaty which were subject to the reduction of armaments would submit to the International Disarmament Organization an appropriate declaration respecting inventories of their armaments existing at the agreed date.

b. The reduction would be accomplished in three steps, each consisting of one year. One-third of the reduction to be made during Stage I would be carried out during each step.

c. During the first part of each step, one-third of the armaments to be eliminated during Stage I would be placed in depots under supervision of the International Disarmament Organization. During the second part of each step, the deposited armaments would be destroyed or, where appropriate, converted to peaceful uses. The number and location of such depots and arrangements respecting their establishment and operation would be set forth in an annex to the Treaty.

d. In accordance with arrangements which would be set forth in a Treaty annex on verification, the International Disarmament Organization would verify the foregoing reduction and would provide assurance that retained armaments did not exceed agreed levels.

3. Limitation on Production of Armaments and on Related Activities

a. Production of all armaments listed in subparagraph b of paragraph 1 above would be limited to agreed allowances during Stage I and, by the beginning of Stage II, would be halted except for production within agreed limits of parts for maintenance of the agreed retained armaments.

b. The allowances would permit limited production in each of the categories of armaments listed in subparagraph b of paragraph 1 above. In all instances during the process of eliminating production of armaments:

(1) any armament produced within a category would be compensated for by an additional armament destroyed within that category to the end that the ten percent reduction in numbers in each category in each step, and the resulting thirty percent reduction in Stage I, would be achieved; and furthermore

(2) in the case of armed combat aircraft having an empty weight of 15,000 kilograms or greater and of missiles having a range of 300 kilometers or greater, the destructive capability of any such armaments produced within a category would be compensated for by the destruction of sufficient armaments within that category to the end that the ten percent reduction in destructive capability as well as numbers in each of these categories in each step, and the resulting thirty percent reduction in Stage I, would be achieved.

c. Should a Party to the Treaty elect to reduce its production in any category at a more rapid rate than required by the allowances provided in subparagraph b above, that Party would be entitled to retain existing armaments to the extent of the unused portion of its production allowance. In any such instance, any armament so retained would be compensated for in the manner set forth in subparagraph b (1) and, where applicable, b (2) above to the end that the ten percent reduction in numbers and, where applicable, destructive capability in each category in each step, and the resulting thirty percent reduction in Stage I, would be achieved.

d. The flight testing of missiles would be limited to agreed annual quotas.

e. In accordance with arrangements which would be set forth in the annex on verification, the International Disarmament Organization would verify the foregoing measures at declared locations and would provide assurance that activities subject to the foregoing measures were not conducted at undeclared locations.

4. Additional Measures

The Parties to the Treaty would agree to examine unresolved questions relating to means of accomplishing in Stages II and III the reduction and eventual elimination of production and stockpiles of chemical and biological weapons of mass destruction. In light of this examination, the Parties to the Treaty would agree to arrangements concerning chemical and biological weapons of mass destruction.

B. ARMED FORCES

1. Reduction of Armed Forces

Force levels for the United States of America and the Union of Soviet Socialist Republics would be reduced to 2.1 million each and for other specified Parties to the Treaty to agreed levels not exceeding 2.1 million each. All other Parties to the Treaty would, with agreed exceptions, reduce their force levels to 100,000 or one percent of their population, whichever were higher, provided that in no case would the force levels of such other Parties to the Treaty exceed levels in existence upon the entry into force of the Treaty.

2. Armed Forces Subject to Reduction

Agreed force levels would include all full-time, uniformed personnel maintained by national governments in the following categories:

a. Career personnel of active armed forces and other personnel serving in the active armed forces on fixed engagements or contracts.

b. Conscripts performing their required period of full-time active duty as fixed by national law.

c. Personnel of militarily organized security forces and of other forces or organizations equipped and organized to perform a military mission.

3. Method of Reduction of Armed Forces

The reduction of force levels would be carried out in the following manner:

a. Those Parties to the Treaty which were subject to the foregoing reductions would submit to the International Disarmament Organization a declaration stating their force levels at the agreed date.

b. Force level reductions would be accomplished in three steps, each having a duration of one year. During each step force levels would be reduced by one-third of the difference between force levels existing at the agreed date and the levels to be reached at the end of Stage I.

c. In accordance with arrangements that would be set forth in the annex on verification, the International Disarmament Organization would verify the reduction of force levels and provide assurance that retained forces did not exceed agreed levels.

4. Additional Measures

The Parties to the Treaty which were subject to the foregoing reductions would agree upon appropriate arrangements, including procedures for consultation, in order to ensure that civilian employment by military establishments would be in accordance with the objectives of the obligations respecting force levels.

C. NUCLEAR WEAPONS

1. Production of Fissionable Materials for Nuclear Weapons

a. The Parties to the Treaty would halt the production of fissionable materials for use in nuclear weapons.

b. This measure would be carried out in the following manner:

(1) The Parties to the Treaty would submit to the International Disarmament Organization a declaration listing by name, location and production capacity every facility under their jurisdiction capable of producing and processing fissionable materials at the agreed date.

(2) Production of fissionable materials for purposes other than use in nuclear weapons would be limited to agreed levels. The Parties to the Treaty would submit to the International Disarmament Organization periodic declarations stating the amounts and types of fissionable materials which were still being produced at each facility.

(3) In accordance with arrangements which would be set forth in the annex on verification, the International Disarmament Organization would verify the foregoing measures at declared facilities and would provide assurance that activities subject to the foregoing limitations were not conducted at undeclared facilities.

2. Transfer of Fissionable Material to Purposes Other Than Use in Nuclear Weapons

a. Upon the cessation of production of fissionable materials for use in nuclear weapons, the United States of America and the Union of Soviet Socialist Republics would each transfer to purposes other than use in nuclear weapons an agreed quantity of weapons-grade U-235 from past production. The purposes for which such materials would be used would be determined by the state to which the material belonged, provided that such materials were not used in nuclear weapons.

b. To ensure that the transferred materials were not used in nuclear weapons, such materials would be placed under safeguards and inspection by the International Disarmament Organization either in stockpiles or at the facilities in which they would be utilized for purposes other than use in nuclear weapons. Arrangements for such safeguards and inspection would be set forth in the annex on verification.

3. *Transfer of Fissionable Materials Between States for Peaceful Uses of Nuclear Energy*

a. Any transfer of fissionable materials between states would be for purposes other than for use in nuclear weapons and would be subject to a system of safeguards to ensure that such materials were not used in nuclear weapons.

b. The system of safeguards to be applied for this purpose would be developed in agreement with the International Atomic Energy Agency and would be set forth in an annex to the Treaty.

4. *Non-Transfer of Nuclear Weapons*

The Parties to the Treaty would agree to seek to prevent the creation of further national nuclear forces. To this end the Parties would agree that:

a. Any Party to the Treaty which had manufactured, or which at any time manufactures, a nuclear weapon would:

(1) Not transfer control over any nuclear weapons to a state which had not manufactured a nuclear weapon before an agreed date;

(2) Not assist any such state in manufacturing any nuclear weapons.

b. Any Party to the Treaty which had not manufactured a nuclear weapon before the agreed date would:

(1) Not acquire, or attempt to acquire, control over any nuclear weapons;

(2) Not manufacture, or attempt to manufacture, any nuclear weapons.

5. *Nuclear Weapons Test Explosions*

a. If an agreement prohibiting nuclear weapons test explosions and providing for effective international control had come into force prior to the entry into force of the Treaty, such agreement would become an annex to the Treaty, and all the Parties to the Treaty would be bound by the obligations specified in the agreement.

b. If, however, no such agreement had come into force prior to the entry into force of the Treaty, all nuclear weapons test explosions would be prohibited, and the procedures for effective international control would be set forth in an annex to the Treaty.

6. *Additional Measures*

The Parties to the Treaty would agree to examine remaining unresolved questions relating to the means of accomplishing in Stages II and III the reduction and eventual elimination of nuclear weapons stockpiles. In the light of this examination, the Parties to the Treaty would agree to arrangements concerning nuclear weapons stockpiles.

D. OUTER SPACE

1. *Prohibition of Weapons of Mass Destruction in Orbit*

The Parties to the Treaty would agree not to place in orbit weapons capable of producing mass destruction.

2. *Peaceful Cooperation in Space*

The Parties to the Treaty would agree to support increased international cooperation in peaceful uses of outer space in the United Nations or through other appropriate arrangements.

3. *Notification and Pre-launch Inspection*

With respect to the launching of space vehicles and missiles:

a. Those Parties to the Treaty which conducted launchings of space vehicles or missiles would provide advance notification of such launchings to other Parties to the Treaty and to the International Disarmament Organization together with the track of the space vehicle or missile. Such advance notification would be provided on a timely basis to permit pre-launch inspection of the space vehicle or missile to be launched.

b. In accordance with arrangements which would be set forth in the annex on verification, the International Disarmament Organization would conduct pre-launch inspection of space vehicles and missiles and would establish and operate any arrangements necessary for detecting unreported launchings.

4. *Limitations on Production and on Related Activities*

The production, stockpiling and testing of boosters for space vehicles would be subject to agreed limitations. Such activities would be monitored by the International Disarmament Organization in accordance with arrangements which would be set forth in the annex on verification.

E. MILITARY EXPENDITURES

1. Report on Expenditures

The Parties to the Treaty would submit to the International Disarmament Organization at the end of each step of each stage a report on their military expenditures. Such reports would include an itemization of military expenditures.

2. Verifiable Reduction of Expenditures

The Parties to the Treaty would agree to examine questions related to the verifiable reduction of military expenditures. In the light of this examination, the Parties to the Treaty would consider appropriate arrangements respecting military expenditures.

F. REDUCTION OF THE RISK OF WAR

In order to promote confidence and reduce the risk of war, the Parties to the Treaty would agree to the following measures:

1. Advance Notification of Military Movements and Maneuvers

Specified Parties to the Treaty would give advance notification of major military movements and maneuvers to other Parties to the Treaty and to the International Disarmament Organization. Specific arrangements relating to this commitment, including the scale of movements and maneuvers to be reported and the information to be transmitted, would be agreed.

2. Observation Posts

Specified Parties to the Treaty would permit observation posts to be established at agreed locations, including major ports, railway centers, motor highways, river crossings, and air bases to report on concentrations and movements of military forces. The number of such posts could be progressively expanded in each successive step of Stage I. Specific arrangements relating to such observation posts, including the location and staffing of posts, the method of receiving and reporting information, and the schedule for installation of posts would be agreed.

3. Additional Observation Arrangements

The Parties to the Treaty would establish such additional observation arrangements as might be agreed. Such arrangements could be extended in an agreed manner during each step of Stage I.

4. Exchange of Military Missions

Specified Parties to the Treaty would undertake the exchange of military missions between states or groups of states in order to improve communications and understanding between them. Specific arrangements respecting such exchanges would be agreed.

5. Communications Between Heads of Government

Specified Parties to the Treaty would agree to the establishment of rapid and reliable communications among their heads of government and with the Secretary General of the United Nations. Specific arrangements in this regard would be subject to agreement among the Parties concerned and between such Parties and the Secretary General.

6. International Commission on Reduction of the Risk of War

The Parties to the Treaty would establish an International Commission on Reduction of the Risk of War as a subsidiary body of the International Disarmament Organization to examine and make recommendations regarding further measures that might be undertaken during Stage I or subsequent stages of disarmament to reduce the risk of war by accident, miscalculation, failure of communications, or surprise attack. Specific arrangements for such measures as might be agreed to by all or some of the Parties to the Treaty would be subject to agreement among the Parties concerned.

G. THE INTERNATIONAL DISARMAMENT ORGANIZATION

1. Establishment of the International Disarmament Organization

The International Disarmament Organization would be established upon the entry into force of the Treaty and would function within the framework of the United Nations and in accordance with the terms and conditions of the Treaty.

2. Cooperation of the Parties to the Treaty

The Parties to the Treaty would agree to cooperate promptly and fully with the International Disarmament Organization and to assist the International Disarmament Organization in the performance of its functions and in the execution of the decisions made by it in accordance with the provisions of the Treaty.

3. Verification Functions of the International Disarmament Organization

The International Disarmament Organization would verify disarmament measures in accordance with the following principles which would be implemented through specific arrangements set forth in the annex on verification:

a. Measures providing for reduction of armaments would be verified by the International Disarmament Organization at agreed depots and would include verification of the destruction of armaments and, where appropriate, verification of the conversion of armaments to peaceful uses. Measures providing for reduction of armed forces would be verified by the International Disarmament Organization either at the agreed depots or other agreed locations.

b. Measures halting or limiting production, testing, and other specified activities would be verified by the International Disarmament Organization. Parties to the Treaty would declare the nature and location of all production and testing facilities and other specified activities. The International Disarmament Organization would have access to relevant facilities and activities wherever located in the territory of such Parties.

c. Assurance that agreed levels of armaments and armed forces were not exceeded and that activities limited or prohibited by the Treaty were not being conducted clandestinely would be provided by the International Disarmament Organization through agreed arrangements which would have the effect of providing that the extent of inspection during any step or stage would be related to the amount of disarmament being undertaken and to the degree of risk to the Parties to the Treaty of possible violations. This might be accomplished, for example, by an arrangement embodying such features as the following:

(1) All parts of the territory of those Parties to the Treaty to which this form of verification was applicable would be subject to selection for inspection from the beginning of Stage I as provided below.

(2) Parties to the Treaty would divide their territory into an agreed number of appropriate zones and at the beginning of each step of disarmament would submit to the International Disarmament Organization a declaration stating the total level of armaments, forces, and specified types of activities subject to verification within each zone. The exact location of armaments and forces within a zone would not be revealed prior to its selection for inspection.

(3) An agreed number of these zones would be progressively inspected by the International Disarmament Organization during Stage I according to an agreed time schedule. The zones to be inspected would be selected by procedures which would ensure their selection by Parties to the Treaty other than the Party whose territory was to be inspected or any Party associated with it. Upon selection of each zone, the Party to the Treaty whose territory was to be inspected would declare the exact location of armaments, forces and

other agreed activities within the selected zone. During the verification process, arrangements would be made to provide assurance against undeclared movements of the objects of verification to or from the zone or zones being inspected. Both aerial and mobile ground inspection would be employed within the zone being inspected. In so far as agreed measures being verified were concerned, access within the zone would be free and unimpeded, and verification would be carried out with the full cooperation of the state being inspected.

(4) Once a zone had been inspected it would remain open for further inspection while verification was being extended to additional zones.

(5) By the end of Stage III, when all disarmament measures had been completed, inspection would have been extended to all parts of the territory of Parties to the Treaty.

4. Composition of the International Disarmament Organization

a. The International Disarmament Organization would have:

(1) A General Conference of all the Parties to the Treaty;

(2) A Control Council consisting of representatives of all the major signatory powers as permanent members and certain other Parties to the Treaty on a rotating basis; and

(3) An Administrator who would administer the International Disarmament Organization under the direction of the Control Council and who would have the authority, staff, and finances adequate to ensure effective and impartial implementation of the functions of the International Disarmament Organization.

b. The General Conference and the Control Council would have power to establish such subsidiary bodies, including expert study groups, as either of them might deem necessary.

5. Functions of the General Conference

The General Conference would have the following functions, among others which might be agreed:

a. Electing non-permanent members to the Control Council;

b. Approving certain accessions to the Treaty;

c. Appointing the Administrator upon recommendation of the Control Council;

d. Approving agreements between the International Disarmament Organization and the United Nations and other international organizations;

e. Approving the budget of the International Disarmament Organization;

f. Requesting and receiving reports from the Control Council and deciding upon matters referred to it by the Control Council;

g. Approving reports to be submitted to bodies of the United Nations;

h. Proposing matters for consideration by the Control Council;

i. Requesting the International Court of Justice to give advisory opinions on legal questions concerning the interpretation or application of the Treaty, subject to a general authorization of this power by the General Assembly of the United Nations;

j. Approving amendments to the Treaty for possible ratification by the Parties to the Treaty;

k. Considering matters of mutual interest pertaining to the Treaty or disarmament in general.

6. *Functions of the Control Council*

The Control Council would have the following functions, among others which might be agreed:

a. Recommending appointment of the Administrator;

b. Adopting rules for implementing the terms of the Treaty;

c. Establishing procedures and standards for the installation and operation of the verification arrangements, and maintaining supervision over such arrangements and the Administrator;

d. Establishing procedures for making available to the Parties to the Treaty data produced by verification arrangements;

e. Considering reports of the Administrator on the progress of disarmament measures and of their verification, and on the installation and operation of the verification arrangements;

f. Recommending to the Conference approval of the budget of the International Disarmament Organization;

g. Requesting the International Court of Justice to give advisory opinions on legal questions concerning the interpretation or application of the Treaty, subject to a general authorization of this power by the General Assembly of the United Nations;

h. Recommending to the Conference approval of certain accessions to the Treaty;

i. Considering matters of mutual interest pertaining to the Treaty or to disarmament in general.

7. *Functions of the Administrator*

The Administrator would have the following functions, among others which might be agreed:

a. Administering the installation and operation of the verification arrangements, and serving as Chief Executive Officer of the International Disarmament Organization;

b. Making available to the Parties to the Treaty data produced by the verification arrangements;

c. Preparing the budget of the International Disarmament Organization;

d. Making reports to the Control Council on the progress of disarmament measures and of their verification, and on the installation and operation of the verification arrangements.

8. Privileges and Immunities

The privileges and immunities which the Parties to the Treaty would grant to the International Disarmament Organization and its staff and to the representatives of the Parties to the International Disarmament Organization, and the legal capacity which the International Disarmament Organization should enjoy in the territory of each of the Parties to the Treaty would be specified in an annex to the Treaty.

9. Relations with the United Nations and Other International Organizations

a. The International Disarmament Organization, being established within the framework of the United Nations, would conduct its activities in accordance with the purposes and principles of the United Nations. It would maintain close working arrangements with the United Nations, and the Administrator of the International Disarmament Organization would consult with the Secretary General of the United Nations on matters of mutual interest.

b. The Control Council of the International Disarmament Organization would transmit to the United Nations annual and other reports on the activities of the International Disarmament Organization.

c. Principal organs of the United Nations could make recommendations to the International Disarmament Organization, which would consider them and report to the United Nations on action taken.

NOTE: The above outline does not cover all the possible details or aspects of relationships between the International Disarmament Organization and the United Nations.

H. MEASURES TO STRENGTHEN ARRANGEMENTS FOR KEEPING THE PEACE

1. Obligations Concerning the Threat or Use of Force

The Parties to the Treaty would undertake obligations to refrain, in their international relations, from the threat or use of force of any type—including nuclear, conventional, chemical or biological means of warfare—contrary to the purposes and principles of the United Nations Charter.

2. Rules of International Conduct

a. The Parties to the Treaty would agree to support a study by a subsidiary body of the International Disarmament Organization of the codification and progressive development of rules of international conduct related to disarmament.

b. The Parties to the Treaty would refrain from indirect aggression and subversion. The subsidiary body provided for in subparagraph a would also study methods of assuring states against indirect aggression or subversion.

3. Peaceful Settlement of Disputes

a. The Parties to the Treaty would utilize all appropriate processes for the peaceful settlement of all disputes which might arise between them and any other state, whether or not a Party to the Treaty, including negotiation, inquiry, mediation, conciliation, arbitration, judicial settlement, resort to regional agencies or arrangements, submission to the Security Council or the General Assembly of the United Nations, or other peaceful means of their choice.

b. The Parties to the Treaty would agree that disputes concerning the interpretation or application of the Treaty which were not settled by negotiation or by the International Disarmament Organization would be subject to referral by any party to the dispute to the International Court of Justice, unless the parties concerned agreed on another mode of settlement.

c. The Parties to the Treaty would agree to support a study under the General Assembly of the United Nations of measures which should be undertaken to make existing arrangements for the peaceful settlement of international disputes, whether legal or political in nature, more effective; and to institute new procedures and arrangements where needed.

4. Maintenance of International Peace and Security

The Parties to the Treaty would agree to support measures strengthening the structure, authority, and operation of the United Nations so as to improve its capability to maintain international peace and security.

5. United Nations Peace Force

The Parties to the Treaty would undertake to develop arrangements during Stage I for the establishment in Stage II of a United Nations Peace Force. To this end, the Parties to the Treaty would agree on the following measures within the United Nations:

a. Examination of the experience of the United Nations leading to a further strengthening of United Nations forces for keeping the peace;

b. Examination of the feasibility of concluding promptly the agreements envisaged in Article 43 of the United Nations Charter;

c. Conclusion of an agreement for the establishment of a United Nations Peace Force in Stage II, including definitions of its purpose, mission, composition and strength, disposition, command and control, training, logistical support, financing, equipment and armaments.

6. *United Nations Peace Observation Corps*

The Parties to the Treaty would agree to support the establishment within the United Nations of a Peace Observation Corps, staffed with a standing cadre of observers who could be despatched promptly to investigate any situation which might constitute a threat to or a breach of the peace. Elements of the Peace Observation Corps could also be stationed as appropriate in selected areas throughout the world.

I. TRANSITION

1. Transition from Stage I to Stage II would take place at the end of Stage I, upon a determination that the following circumstances existed:

a. All undertakings to be carried out in Stage I had been carried out.

b. All preparations required for Stage II had been made; and

c. All militarily significant states had become Parties to the Treaty.

2. During the last three months of Stage I, the Control Council would review the situation respecting these circumstances with a view to determining whether these circumstances existed at the end of Stage I.

3. If, at the end of Stage I, one or more permanent members of the Control Council should declare that the foregoing circumstances did not exist, the agreed period of Stage I would, upon the request of such permanent member or members, be extended by a period or periods totalling no more than three months for the purpose of bringing about the foregoing circumstances.

4. If, upon the expiration of such period or periods, one or more of the permanent members of the Control Council should declare that the foregoing circumstances still did not exist, the question would be placed before a special session of the Security Council; transition to Stage II would take place upon a determination by the Security Council that the foregoing circumstances did in fact exist.

Stage II

Stage II would begin upon the transition from Stage I and would be completed within three years from that date.

During Stage II, the Parties to the Treaty would undertake:

1. To continue all obligations undertaken during Stage I;

2. To reduce further the armaments and armed forces reduced during Stage I and to carry out additional measures of disarmament in the manner outlined below;

3. To ensure that the International Disarmament Organization would have the capacity to verify in the agreed manner the obligations undertaken during Stage II; and

4. To strengthen further the arrangements for keeping the peace through the establishment of a United Nations Peace Force and through the additional measures outlined below.

A. ARMAMENTS

1. Reduction of Armaments

a. Those Parties to the Treaty which had during Stage I reduced their armaments in agreed categories by thirty percent would during Stage II further reduce each type of armaments in the categories listed in Section A, subparagraph 1.b of Stage I by fifty percent of the inventory existing at the end of Stage I.

b. Those Parties to the Treaty which had not been subject to measures for the reduction of armaments during Stage I would submit to the International Disarmament Organization an appropriate declaration respecting the inventories by types, within the categories listed in Stage I, of their armaments existing at the beginning of Stage II. Such Parties to the Treaty would during Stage II reduce the inventory of each type of such armaments by sixty-five percent in order that such Parties would accomplish the same total percentage of reduction by the end of Stage II as would be accomplished by those Parties to the Treaty which had reduced their armaments by thirty percent in Stage I.

2. Additional Armaments Subject to Reduction

a. The Parties to the Treaty would submit to the International Disarmament Organization a declaration respecting their inventories existing at the beginning of Stage II of the additional types of armaments in the categories listed in subparagraph b below, and would during Stage II reduce the inventory of each type of such armaments by fifty percent.

b. All types of armaments within further agreed categories would be subject to reduction in Stage II (the following list of categories is illustrative):

(1) Armed combat aircraft having an empty weight of up to 2,500 kilograms (declarations by types).

709

(2) Specified types of unarmed military aircraft (declarations by types).

(3) Missiles and free rockets having a range of less than 10 kilometers (declarations by types).

(4) Mortars and rocket launchers having a caliber of less than 100 mm. (declarations by types).

(5) Specified types of unarmored personnel carriers and transport vehicles (declarations by types).

(6) Combatant ships with standard displacement of 400 tons or greater which had not been included among the armaments listed in Stage I, and combatant ships with standard displacement of less than 400 tons (declarations by types).

(7) Specified types of non-combatant naval vessels (declarations by types).

(8) Specified types of small arms (declarations by types).

c. Specified categories of ammunition for armaments listed in Stage I, Section A, subparagraph 1.b and in subparagraph b above would be reduced to levels consistent with the levels of armaments agreed for the end of Stage II.

3. Method of Reduction

The foregoing measures would be carried out and would be verified by the International Disarmament Organization in a manner corresponding to that provided for in Stage I, Section A, paragraph 2.

4. Limitation on Production of Armaments and on Related Activities

a. The Parties to the Treaty would halt the production of armaments in the specified categories except for production, within agreed limits, of parts required for maintenance of the agreed retained armaments.

b. The production of ammunition in specified categories would be reduced to agreed levels consistent with the levels of armaments agreed for the end of Stage II.

c. The Parties to the Treaty would halt development and testing of new types of armaments. The flight testing of existing types of missiles would be limited to agreed annual quotas.

d. In accordance with arrangements which would be set forth in the annex on verification, the International Disarmament Organization would verify the foregoing measures at declared locations and would provide assurance that activities subject to the foregoing measures were not conducted at undeclared locations.

5. Additional Measures

a. In the light of their examination during Stage I of the means of accomplishing the reduction and eventual elimination of production and stockpiles of chemical and biological weapons of mass destruction, the Parties to the Treaty would undertake the following measures respecting such weapons:

(1) The cessation of all production and field testing of chemical and biological weapons of mass destruction.

(2) The reduction, by agreed categories, of stockpiles of chemical and biological weapons of mass destruction to levels fifty percent below those existing at the beginning of Stage II.

(3) The dismantling or conversion to peaceful uses of all facilities engaged in the production or field testing of chemical and biological weapons of mass destruction.

b. The foregoing measures would be carried out in an agreed sequence and through arrangements which would be set forth in an annex to the Treaty.

c. In accordance with arrangements which would be set forth in the annex on verification the International Disarmament Organization would verify the foregoing measures and would provide assurance that retained levels of chemical and biological weapons did not exceed agreed levels and that activities subject to the foregoing limitations were not conducted at undeclared locations.

B. ARMED FORCES

1. Reduction of Armed Forces

a. Those Parties to the Treaty which had been subject to measures providing for reduction of force levels during Stage I would further reduce their force levels on the following basis:

(1) Force levels of the United States of America and the Union of Soviet Socialist Republics would be reduced to levels fifty percent below the levels agreed for the end of Stage I.

(2) Force levels of other Parties to the Treaty which had been subject to measures providing for the reduction of force levels during Stage I would be further reduced, on the basis of an agreed percentage, below the levels agreed for the end of Stage I to levels which would not in any case exceed the agreed level for the United States of America and the Union of Soviet Socialist Republics at the end of Stage II.

b. Those Parties to the Treaty which had not been subject to measures providing for the reduction of armed forces during Stage I would reduce their force levels to agreed levels consistent with those to be reached by other Parties which had reduced their force levels during Stage I as well as Stage II. In no case would such agreed levels exceed the agreed level for the United States of America and the Union of Soviet Socialist Republics at the end of Stage II.

c. Agreed levels of armed forces would include all personnel in the categories set forth in Section B, paragraph 2 of Stage I.

2. *Method of Reduction*

The further reduction of force levels would be carried out and would be verified by the International Disarmament Organization in a manner corresponding to that provided for in Section B, paragraph 3 of Stage I.

3. *Additional Measures*

Agreed limitations consistent with retained force levels would be placed on compulsory military training, and on refresher training for reserve forces of the Parties to the Treaty.

C. NUCLEAR WEAPONS

1. *Reduction of Nuclear Weapons*

In the light of their examination during Stage I of the means of accomplishing the reduction and eventual elimination of nuclear weapons stockpiles, the Parties to the Treaty would undertake to reduce in the following manner remaining nuclear weapons and fissionable materials for use in nuclear weapons:

a. The Parties to the Treaty would submit to the International Disarmament Organization a declaration stating the amounts, types and nature of utilization of all their fissionable materials.

b. The Parties to the Treaty would reduce the amounts and types of fissionable materials declared for use in nuclear weapons to minimum levels on the basis of agreed percentages. The foregoing reduction would be accomplished through the transfer of such materials to purposes other than use in nuclear weapons. The purposes for which such materials would be used would be determined by the state to which the materials belonged, provided that such materials were not used in nuclear weapons.

c. The Parties to the Treaty would destroy the non-nuclear components and assemblies of nuclear weapons from which fissionable materials had been removed to effect the foregoing reduction of fissionable materials for use in nuclear weapons.

d. Production or refabrication of nuclear weapons from any remaining fissionable materials would be subject to agreed limitations.

e. The foregoing measures would be carried out in an agreed sequence and through arrangements which would be set forth in an annex to the Treaty.

f. In accordance with arrangements that would be set forth in the verification annex to the Treaty, the International Disarmament

Organization would verify the foregoing measures at declared locations and would provide assurance that activities subject to the foregoing limitations were not conducted at undeclared locations.

2. *Registration of Nuclear Weapons for Verification Purposes*

To facilitate verification during Stage III that no nuclear weapons remained at the disposal of the Parties to the Treaty, those Parties to the Treaty which possessed nuclear weapons would, during the last six months of Stage II, register and serialize their remaining nuclear weapons and would register remaining fissionable materials for use in such weapons. Such registration and serialization would be carried out with the International Disarmament Organization in accordance with procedures which would be set forth in the annex on verification.

D. MILITARY BASES AND FACILITIES

1. *Reduction of Military Bases and Facilities*

The Parties to the Treaty would dismantle or convert to peaceful uses agreed military bases and facilities, wherever they might be located.

2. *Method of Reduction*

a. The list of military bases and facilities subject to the foregoing measures and the sequence and arrangements for dismantling or converting them to peaceful uses would be set forth in an annex to the Treaty.

b. In accordance with arrangements which would be set forth in the annex on verification, the International Disarmament Organization would verify the foregoing measures.

E. REDUCTION OF THE RISK OF WAR

In the light of the examination by the International Commission on Reduction of the Risk of War during Stage I the Parties to the Treaty would undertake such additional arrangements as appeared desirable to promote confidence and reduce the risk of war. The Parties to the Treaty would also consider extending and improving the measures undertaken in Stage I for this purpose. The Commission would remain in existence to examine extensions, improvements or additional measures which might be undertaken during and after Stage II.

F. THE INTERNATIONAL DISARMAMENT ORGANIZATION

The International Disarmament Organization would be strengthened in the manner necessary to ensure its capacity to verify the measures undertaken in Stage II through an extension of the arrangements based upon the principles set forth in Section G, paragraph 3 of Stage I.

G. MEASURES TO STRENGTHEN ARRANGEMENTS FOR KEEPING THE PEACE

1. Peaceful Settlement of Disputes

a. In light of the study of peaceful settlement of disputes conducted during Stage I, the Parties to the Treaty would agree to such additional steps and arrangements as were necessary to assure the just and peaceful settlement of international disputes, whether legal or political in nature.

b. The Parties to the Treaty would undertake to accept without reservation, pursuant to Article 36, paragraph 1 of the Statute of the International Court of Justice, the compulsory jurisdiction of that Court to decide international legal disputes.

2. Rules of International Conduct

a. The Parties to the Treaty would continue their support of the study by the subsidiary body of the International Disarmament Organization initiated in Stage I to study the codification and progressive development of rules of international conduct related to disarmament. The Parties to the Treaty would agree to the establishment of procedures whereby rules recommended by the subsidiary body and approved by the Control Council would be circulated to all Parties to the Treaty and would become effective three months thereafter unless a majority of the Parties to the Treaty signified their disapproval, and whereby the Parties to the Treaty would be bound by rules which had become effective in this way unless, within a period of one year from the effective date, they formally notified the International Disarmament Organization that they did not consider themselves so bound. Using such procedures, the Parties to the Treaty would adopt such rules of international conduct related to disarmament as might be necessary to begin Stage III.

b. In the light of the study of indirect aggression and subversion conducted in Stage I, the Parties to the Treaty would agree to arrangements necessary to assure states against indirect aggression and subversion.

3. United Nations Peace Force

The United Nations Peace Force to be established as the result of the agreement reached during Stage I would come into being within the first year of Stage II and would be progressively strengthened during Stage II.

4. United Nations Peace Observation Corps

The Parties to the Treaty would conclude arrangements for the expansion of the activities of the United Nations Peace Observation Corps.

5. National Legislation

Those Parties to the Treaty which had not already done so would, in accordance with their constitutional processes, enact national legislation in support of the Treaty imposing legal obligations on individuals and organizations under their jurisdiction and providing appropriate penalties for noncompliance.

H. TRANSITION

1. *Transition from Stage II to Stage III would take place at the end of Stage II, upon a determination that the following circumstances existed:*

 a. All undertakings to be carried out in Stage II had been carried out;

 b. All preparations required for Stage III had been made; and

 c. All states possessing armed forces and armaments had become Parties to the Treaty.

2. *During the last three months of Stage II, the Control Council would review the situation respecting these circumstances with a view to determining at the end of Stage II whether they existed.*

3. *If, at the end of Stage II, one or more permanent members of the Control Council should declare that the foregoing circumstances did not exist, the agreed period of Stage II would, upon the request of such permanent member or members, be extended by a period or periods totalling no more than three months for the purpose of bringing about the foregoing circumstances.*

4. *If, upon the expiration of such period or periods, one or more of the permanent members of the Control Council should declare that the foregoing circumstances still did not exist, the question would be placed before a special session of the Security Council; transition to Stage III would take place upon a determination by the Security Council that the foregoing circumstances did in fact exist.*

Stage III

Stage III would begin upon the transition from Stage II and would be completed within an agreed period of time as promptly as possible.

During Stage III, the Parties to the Treaty would undertake:

1. To continue all obligations undertaken during Stages I and II;

2. To complete the process of general and complete disarmament in the manner outlined below;

3. To ensure that the International Disarmament Organization would have the capacity to verify in the agreed manner the obligations undertaken during Stage III and of continuing verification subsequent to the completion of Stage III; and

4. To strengthen further the arrangements for keeping the peace during and following the achievement of general and complete disarmament through the additional measures outlined below.

A. ARMAMENTS

1. *Reduction of Armaments*

Subject to agreed requirements for non-nuclear armaments of agreed types for national forces required to maintain internal order and protect the personal security of citizens, the Parties to the Treaty would eliminate all armaments remaining at their disposal at the end of Stage II.

2. *Method of Reduction*

a. The foregoing measure would be carried out in an agreed sequence and through arrangements that would be set forth in an annex to the Treaty.

b. In accordance with arrangements that would be set forth in the annex on verification, the International Disarmament Organization would verify the foregoing measures and would provide assurance that retained armaments were of the agreed types and did not exceed agreed levels.

3. *Limitations on Production of Armaments and on Related Activities*

a. Subject to agreed arrangements in support of national forces required to maintain internal order and protect the personal security of citizens and subject to agreed arrangements in support of the United Nations Peace Force, the Parties to the Treaty would halt all applied research, development, production, and testing of armaments and

716

would cause to be dismantled or converted to peaceful uses all facilities for such purposes.

b. The foregoing measures would be carried out in an agreed sequence and through arrangements which would be set forth in an annex to the Treaty.

c. In accordance with arrangements which would be set forth in the annex on verification, the International Disarmament Organization would verify the foregoing measures at declared locations and would provide assurance that activities subject to the foregoing measures were not conducted at undeclared locations.

B. ARMED FORCES

1. Reduction of Armed Forces

To the end that upon completion of Stage III they would have at their disposal only those forces and organizational arrangements necessary for agreed forces to maintain internal order and protect the personal security of citizens and that they would be capable of providing agreed manpower for the United Nations Peace Force, the Parties to the Treaty would complete the reduction of their force levels, disband systems of reserve forces, cause to be disbanded organizational arrangements comprising and supporting their national military establishment, and terminate the employment of civilian personnel associated with the foregoing.

2. Method of Reduction

a. The foregoing measures would be carried out in an agreed sequence through arrangements which would be set forth in an annex to the Treaty.

b. In accordance with arrangements which would be set forth in the annex on verification, the International Disarmament Organization would verify the foregoing measures and would provide assurance that the only forces and organizational arrangements retained or subsequently established were those necessary for agreed forces required to maintain internal order and to protect the personal security of citizens and those for providing agreed manpower for the United Nations Peace Force.

3. Other Limitations

The Parties to the Treaty would halt all military conscription and would undertake to annul legislation concerning national military establishments or military service inconsistent with the foregoing measures.

C. NUCLEAR WEAPONS

1. Reduction of Nuclear Weapons

In light of the steps taken in Stages I and II to halt the production of fissionable material for use in nuclear weapons and to reduce nuclear weapons stockpiles, the Parties to the Treaty would eliminate all nuclear weapons remaining at their disposal, would cause to be dismantled or converted to peaceful use all facilities for production of such weapons, and would transfer all materials remaining at their disposal for use in such weapons to purposes other than use in such weapons.

2. Method of Reduction

a. The foregoing measures would be carried out in an agreed sequence and through arrangements which would be set forth in an annex to the Treaty.

b. In accordance with arrangements which would be set forth in the annex on verification, the International Disarmament Organization would verify the foregoing measures and would provide assurance that no nuclear weapons or materials for use in such weapons remained at the disposal of the Parties to the Treaty and that no such weapons or materials were produced at undeclared facilities.

D. MILITARY BASES AND FACILITIES

1. Reduction of Military Bases and Facilities

The Parties to the Treaty would dismantle or convert to peaceful uses the military bases and facilities remaining at their disposal, wherever they might be located, in an agreed sequence except for such agreed bases or facilities within the territory of the Parties to the Treaty for agreed forces required to maintain internal order and protect the personal security of citizens.

2. Method of Reduction

a. The list of military bases and facilities subject to the foregoing measure and the sequence and arrangements for dismantling or converting them to peaceful uses during Stage III would be set forth in an annex to the Treaty.

b. In accordance with arrangements which would be set forth in the annex on verification, the International Disarmament Organization would verify the foregoing measure at declared locations and provide assurance that there were no undeclared military bases and facilities.

E. RESEARCH AND DEVELOPMENT OF MILITARY SIGNIFICANCE

1. Reporting Requirement

The Parties to the Treaty would undertake the following measures respecting research and development of military significance subsequent to Stage III:

a. The Parties to the Treaty would report to the International Disarmament Organization any basic scientific discovery and any technological invention having potential military significance.

b. The Control Council would establish such expert study groups as might be required to examine the potential military significance of such discoveries and inventions and, if necessary, to recommend appropriate measures for their control. In the light of such expert study, the Parties to the Treaty would, where necessary, establish agreed arrangements providing for verification by the International Disarmament Organization that such discoveries and inventions were not utilized for military purposes. Such arrangements would become an annex to the Treaty.

c. The Parties to the Treaty would agree to appropriate arrangements for protection of the ownership rights of all discoveries and inventions reported to the International Disarmament Organization in accordance with subparagraph a above.

2. International Cooperation

The Parties to the Treaty would agree to support full international cooperation in all fields of scientific research and development, and to engage in free exchange of scientific and technical information and free interchange of views among scientific and technical personnel.

F. REDUCTION OF THE RISK OF WAR

1. Improved Measures

In the light of the Stage II examination by the International Commission on Reduction of the Risk of War, the Parties to the Treaty would undertake such extensions and improvements of existing arrangements and such additional arrangements as appeared desirable to promote confidence and reduce the risk of war. The Commission would remain in existence to examine extensions, improvements or additional measures which might be taken during and after Stage III.

2. Application of Measures to Continuing Forces

The Parties to the Treaty would apply to national forces required to maintain internal order and protect the personal security of citizens those applicable measures concerning the reduction of the risk of war that had been applied to national armed forces in Stages I and II.

G. INTERNATIONAL DISARMAMENT ORGANIZATION

The International Disarmament Organization would be strengthened in the manner necessary to ensure its capacity (1) to verify the measures undertaken in Stage III through an extension of arrangements based upon the principles set forth in Section G, paragraph 3 of Stage I so that by the end of Stage III, when all disarmament measures had been completed, inspection would have been extended to all parts of the territory of Parties to the Treaty; and (2) to provide continuing verification of disarmament after the completion of Stage III.

H. MEASURES TO STRENGTHEN ARRANGEMENTS FOR KEEPING THE PEACE

1. Peaceful Change and Settlement of Disputes

The Parties to the Treaty would undertake such additional steps and arrangements as were necessary to provide a basis for peaceful change in a disarmed world and to continue the just and peaceful settlement of all international disputes, whether legal or political in nature.

2. Rules of International Conduct

The Parties to the Treaty would continue the codification and progressive development of rules of international conduct related to disarmament in the manner provided in Stage II and by any other agreed procedure.

3. United Nations Peace Force

The Parties to the Treaty would progressively strengthen the United Nations Peace Force established in Stage II until it had sufficient armed forces and armaments so that no state could challenge it.

I. COMPLETION OF STAGE III

1. *At the end of the time period agreed for Stage III, the Control Council would review the situation with a view to determining whether all undertakings to be carried out in Stage III had been carried out.*

2. *In the event that one or more of the permanent members of the Control Council should declare that such undertakings had not been carried out,*

the agreed period of Stage III would, upon the request of such permanent member or members, be extended for a period or periods totalling no more than three months for the purpose of completing any uncompleted undertakings. If, upon the expiration of such period or periods, one or more of the permanent members of the Control Council should declare that such undertakings still had not been carried out, the question would be placed before a special session of the Security Council, which would determine whether Stage III had been completed.

3. After the completion of Stage III, the obligations undertaken in Stages I, II and III would continue.

General Provisions Applicable to All Stages

1. Subsequent Modifications or Amendments of the Treaty

The Parties to the Treaty would agree to specific procedures for considering amendments or modifications of the Treaty which were believed desirable by any Party to the Treaty in the light of experience in the early period of implementation of the Treaty. Such procedures would include provision for a conference on revision of the Treaty after a specified period of time.

2. Interim Agreement

The Parties to the Treaty would undertake such specific arrangements, including the establishment of a Preparatory Commission, as were necessary between the signing and entry into force of the Treaty to ensure the initiation of Stage I immediately upon the entry into force of the Treaty, and to provide an interim forum for the exchange of views and information on topics relating to the Treaty and to the achievement of a permanent state of general and complete disarmament in a peaceful world.

3. Parties to the Treaty, Ratification, Accession, and Entry into Force of the Treaty

a. The Treaty would be open to signature and ratification, or accession, by all members of the United Nations or its specialized agencies.

b. Any other state which desired to become a Party to the Treaty could accede to the Treaty with the approval of the Conference on recommendation of the Control Council.

c. The Treaty would come into force when it had been ratified by _____ states, including the United States of America, the Union of Soviet Socialist Republics, and an agreed number of the following states:

_____

d. In order to assure the achievement of the fundamental purpose of a permanent state of general and complete disarmament in a peaceful world, the Treaty would specify that the accession of certain militarily significant states would be essential for the continued effectiveness of the Treaty or for the coming into force of particular measures or stages.

e. The Parties to the Treaty would undertake to exert every effort to induce other states or authorities to accede to the Treaty.

f. The Treaty would be subject to ratification or acceptance in accordance with constitutional processes.

g. A Depository Government would be agreed upon which would have all of the duties normally incumbent upon a Depository. Alternatively, the United Nations would be the Depository.

4. *Finance*

a. In order to meet the financial obligations of the International Disarmament Organization, the Parties to the Treaty would bear the International Disarmament Organization's expenses as provided in the budget approved by the General Conference and in accordance with a scale of apportionment approved by the General Conference.

b. The General Conference would exercise borrowing powers on behalf of the International Disarmament Organization.

5. *Authentic Texts*

The text of the Treaty would consist of equally authentic versions in English, French, Russian, Chinese and Spanish.

A BRIEF SUMMARY

of a

*Proposed Treaty for the Establishment of a World Disarmament and World Development Organization within the framework of the United Nations

GRENVILLE CLARK

LOUIS B. SOHN

———————◆◆———————

Under pressure of the ever-increasing power of modern weapons and the economic burdens of the arms race, the time draws near when all the nations of the world must make a *serious* and *persistent* effort to achieve total disarmament and the abolition of war.

It is greatly to be hoped that this effort will be made in 1962-63. But, if not, it is reasonably certain that, as a matter of sheer necessity, the effort will be made during the 1960s.

Whenever this serious and persistent discussion at last begins, the negotiators will find themselves faced with the question: What form shall our effort take? Shall we seek an agreement for the thorough and detailed revision of the present United Nations Charter which will be essential if the United Nations is to be the agency to implement general and complete disarmament and thereafter to police the peace? Or shall we leave the United Nations without change and seek agreement upon a treaty creating a wholly new peace-keeping organization, closely affiliated with the United Nations and yet equipped with adequate powers and resources of its own?

In accordance with the former alternative, the undersigned authors have proposed a detailed plan for U. N. Charter revision in their book "World Peace through World Law". (Harvard University Press, 1958; Second Edition (Revised), 1960)

And now (May 1962), having in mind that the second alternative of a new world organization affiliated with the U. N. may prove to be more practicable than a radical revision of the U. N. Charter itself, the authors have cast their proposals in the form of a comprehensive draft Treaty, creating a new organization to be called the "World Disarmament and World Development Organization."*

---

* Translations of the book "World Peace through World Law", or of the Introduction thereto summarizing its main features, have been made into Arabic, Chinese, Dutch, French, German, Italian, Japanese, Norwegian, Polish, Russian, Spanish and Swedish; and it is hoped that this alternative Treaty plan will also be translated into a number of languages. Meanwhile this brief Summary may be translated into several of the major languages.

The following is a highly condensed summary of the main features of this alternative plan.

The stated purpose of the proposed Treaty is to supplement the existing machinery of the United Nations available for the maintenance of international peace and security and the advancement of the social and economic welfare of all peoples,—through the creation, within the framework of the United Nations, of a new Organization the membership of which would be open to all nations without exception.

The World Disarmament and World Development Organization would be closely affiliated in various ways with the present United Nations, the Charter and functions of which would remain undisturbed. But the new Organization would have fully adequate powers and resources of its own to maintain peace and effectively to mitigate the immense gap in standards of living between the industrialized nations and the low-income areas of the world.

To these ends the new Organization would have the following purpose, structure and powers:

I. **Purpose.** The World Disarmament and World Development Organization would have a single great purpose, namely, to act as a strong auxiliary of the United Nations for the maintenance of peace. This objective would be accomplished: (1) by carrying out an agreed plan for total national disarmament under an adequate inspection system, and through a strong world police force, together with an effective judicial and conciliation system for the settlement of all international disputes; and (2) through a World Development Authority equipped with sufficient resources effectively to bring about a revolutionary improvement of living standards in all the low-income areas of the world.

II. **Membership.** Any nation in the world having the legal status of an independent state would be entitled to become a member of the Organization. Under this provision, such nations as mainland China, West Germany and East Germany, North Korea and South Korea, North Viet-Nam and South Viet-Nam (none of which are now Members of the United Nations) would be eligible to join the new Organization and would presumably do so. Once having joined, no member nation could either resign or be expelled, although every member nation would be subject to suspension for nonobservance of the obligations of membership as defined in the Treaty.

III. **A World Representative Assembly and a World Executive.**

(1) *The General Conference.* The most important powers of the Organization and the limitations thereon would be set forth in considerable detail in the Treaty itself. But, since it is impossible to foresee all contingencies and since certain matters, such as the adoption of the budgets of the Organization and of various binding regulations, would require action by a

724

body fairly representative of all the member nations, a unicameral assembly is proposed to be called the General Conference and to be composed of Representatives from each and every member nation. The apportionment of Representatives would be related to the populations of the respective member nations, but with a maximum of 30 Representatives for even the largest (*i.e.,* the most populous) nation and with the provision that even the smallest nation shall have one Representative.

In order to keep the General Conference within workable limits as to size and also to give due recognition both to relative populations and to the element of separate nationhood, Representatives would be allotted in accordance with seven categories. The four largest (most populous) nations would have 30 Representatives each, the eight next largest 15 each, the twelve next largest 10 each, the twenty next largest 6 each, the thirty next largest 4 each, and the thirty next largest 2 each, while a final category composed of the smallest nations would have one each. Representation would also be provided for all the non-self-governing territories of the world on a proportional population basis. Assuming that every independent state in the world would join the Organization, the number of Representatives in the General Conference in 1965 on the basis of estimated populations in that year would be about 700 (including 8 from the non-self-governing territories).

The Representatives would be chosen for four-year terms. They would vote as individuals rather than as delegates representing their governments. For most votes a majority of all the Representatives, whether or not present and voting, would be sufficient; but larger special majorities would be required in respect of several important matters.

The Representatives would receive adequate compensation from the Organization itself and would be expected to devote the major part of their time to their duties as Representatives. They would at first be chosen by their national legislatures, but provision would be made whereby they would all be chosen by popular vote in their respective countries within not more than 40 years.

The proposed Treaty provides that the General Conference shall have the primary and general responsibility for the maintenance of peace. The below mentioned Executive Council would, however, have temporary and emergency powers as the agent of the General Conference in case the Conference is not in session, in which event it is provided that the Conference shall be forthwith convened to review any such emergency action. The Conference would choose the Executive Council and could remove that Council, provided that a new Council were forthwith appointed. The General Conference would also appoint, or approve the appointment of, various other important officials of the Organization.

Another all-important power of the General Conference would be the authority to approve the yearly budgets of the Organization, which could amount to as much as 3 per cent of the estimated gross world product in any year.

Additional powers would include authority to fix the strength, within certain limits defined in the Treaty, of a world police force (to be called the United Nations Peace Force) and to adopt regulations concerning that Force; to provide penalties for violation of the Treaty or of any regulations adopted thereunder; to receive and consider recommendations from the General Assembly or Security Council of the United Nations; to supervise and support the World Development Authority (described below) in its effort to mitigate the vast difference in standards of living between the "have" and "have not" areas of the world; and to exercise a general supervision over all the other organs and agencies of the Organization.

(2) *The Executive Council.* Although, as above mentioned, the General Conference would have the primary and general responsibility for the maintenance of peace, there would be constant need for an effective executive organ responsible for the *carrying out* of the disarmament plan to be set forth in the Treaty and for the enforcement of the regulations adopted by the General Conference; and also for exercising executive supervision over all the non-judicial organs and agencies of the Organization.

For these functions an Executive Council is provided for, to be composed of 17 members chosen by the General Conference from among the Representatives in the Conference and to be responsible to and removable by the Conference. Careful provision is made for a well-balanced Council in which each of the four largest nations would have one of its Representatives on the Council at all times and the eight next largest in alternate four-year periods, while the other nine members would be Representatives from the smaller nations, selected under a plan ensuring fair representation to all of the principal regions of the world.

Decisions of the Executive Council, in contrast to the Security Council of the United Nations, would not be subject to the veto of any one nation; but the voting system would ensure that all important decisions would require a vote reflecting a strong preponderance of world opinion.

This executive body would have much the same relation to the General Conference as that of the British Cabinet to the House of Commons. Its composition and authority should enable it to function effectively as the executive arm of the General Conference which would always have the final responsibility for the fulfillment of the basic aims of the Organization.

IV. **The Disarmament Plan.** The proposed Treaty includes a highly developed and detailed plan for general and complete disarmament, to be carried out under adequate inspection by every nation in the world without exception step by step over an eleven-year period.

During the first year after the coming into force of the Treaty, an Inspection Service would be organized and would conduct an arms census whereby every nation would supply a complete list of its armed forces, armaments and armament production facilities, but without being required to disclose the location of certain secret installations. In each year thereafter 10 per cent of any and all military organizations and of all armaments and armament-making facilities would be disbanded, destroyed or converted to other uses. The result would be that at the end of the 10-year period (11 years after the taking effect of the Treaty) no nation would possess any *military* forces whatever and the only military force in the world would be the United Nations Peace Force.

This complete elimination of all national *military* forces would, however, be without prejudice to the retention by every nation of such very lightly armed internal police forces as are needed for internal order only—subject to careful restrictions as to the maximum size of such police forces relative to population and as to the character of the weapons permitted to them.

After completion of the arms census an arms truce would take effect, under which all nations would be legally bound not to increase their existing armed strength. Then would follow the above-mentioned ten annual disarmament stages, each consisting of a 10 per cent across-the-board arms reduction, applying equally to all categories of military units, armaments and armament production facilities.

During each of the ten years, every nation would give the Inspection Service advance notice of the specific military units, armaments, armament facilities and excess internal police forces which it proposes to eliminate in that year, in order to comply with the 10 per cent reduction requirement. When these proposals have been checked and found adequate, the proposed reductions would take place under the direct supervision of the Inspection Service. During that year the Inspection Service would also conduct a thorough inspection of a region, chosen by a decision of the Inspection Service, comprising one tenth of the territory of each nation, in order to verify the accuracy of the initial arms census (which, for each nation, would contain a separate inventory for each of ten substantially equal regions into which the nation would be divided). The purpose and effect would be, therefore, that after ten years all national military strength (and all internal police forces in excess of the prescribed limits) would have been eliminated, and the original arms census would have been completely verified.

This step-by-step reduction would provide every nation with an effective safeguard against cheating by others, since each stage would have to be completed by *all* nations before *any* nation could be called upon to begin the next stage. Provision would be made for delaying the whole process (by one or more six-month postponements) until any noncomplying nation was brought into line. On the other hand, there would be provision for accelerating the process after the third year if this appeared to the General Conference to be safe and feasible.

A portion of the eliminated national armaments would be turned over to the United Nations Peace Force, which would be built up to its full strength during the same period as that of the disarmament process. Another portion, consisting of all nuclear weapons and all nuclear materials from which they could be made, would be turned over to a civilian agency, to be known as the United Nations Nuclear Energy Authority. In both cases, fair compensation would be paid. All the rest of the eliminated national armaments would simply be destroyed.

The United Nations Nuclear Energy Authority would see to it that nuclear materials were used only for power production and other peaceful purposes, except that it would hold some nuclear weapons for delivery to the Peace Force if (and only if) the General Conference deemed the use or possible use of such weapons to be absolutely necessary. The Nuclear Energy Authority would also assist the Inspection Service by providing special technical skills needed for inspecting nuclear facilities and devices. Similar regulatory and inspection functions in the field of rockets, satellites and spacecraft would be performed by another civilian agency, to be known as the United Nations Outer Space Agency.

After completion of the disarmament and census-verification period, effective safeguards against rearmament of any kind would come into effect.

V. **The World Police Force.** Just as in any local community the maintenance of law and order requires an efficient police force in addition to definite laws against violence and courts to interpret and apply those laws, an effective world police force is essential to any adequate plan for peace.

The proposed Treaty, therefore, provides for such a world police, which would be called the United Nations Peace Force. Its standing full-time component would have a strength of not less than 200,000 or more than 400,000 (as determined from time to time by the General Conference), and there would be a partially trained Peace Force Reserve with a strength of between 300,000 and 600,000 (as also determined by the General Conference.)

This Peace Force would be built step by step in proportion to the above described process of total national disarmament. And, since no nation could have any *military* forces whatever after the completion of the disarmament process, both components of the Peace Force would necessarily be made up of individual volunteers rather than of national contingents.

There would be careful safeguards to limit the number of nationals of any nation or group of nations, and all major command positions would be restricted to nationals of the smaller nations.

The standing component would be highly mobile, strongly armed and well-paid. It would not, however, possess nuclear weapons or other weapons of mass destruction, although, as above mentioned, some nuclear weapons would be held in reserve in the custody of civil authority, to be released for possible use only in case of the actual or imminently threatened use of similar weapons clandestinely concealed.

The United Nations Peace Force would be under the direction of the Executive Council (subject to the over-all control of the General Conference) and could be used to impose sanctions only in carefully defined circumstances where clearly necessary to prevent or suppress international violence.

The recruitment, training, discipline, pay, and disposition of the Peace Force would be governed by regulations adopted by the General Conference, and there would be a special committee of the Conference, to be called the Standing Committee on the Peace Enforcement Agencies, to act as a watchdog over all activities of the Peace Force.

In general, every possible safeguard would be provided against any abuse of power by this world police force which, while indispensable to any adequate plan for world peace, must at all times be under the strictest supervision and control by the civil elements of the world peace-keeping authority.

VI. **The Judicial and Conciliation System.** The nations cannot be expected wholly to disband their armed forces, destroy all their armaments and remain permanently disarmed unless, in addition to an effective inspection system and an adequate world police force, reliable means are provided for the peaceful settlement of all international disputes.

With this in mind the proposed Treaty calls for: (1) the compulsory submission to the existing International Court of Justice of all international disputes which are in any way dangerous to peace and are susceptible of decision upon established legal principles; and (2) the compulsory reference to a World Equity Tribunal of all dangerous international disputes which are not of a legal nature.

In respect of legal disputes, the nations concerned would be obligated to abide by the decisions of the International Court under penalty of sanctions for non-compliance, including action in extreme cases by the United Nations Peace Force.

In respect of dangerous non-legal disputes referred to the World Equity Tribunal, the Treaty would provide that if the Tribunal's recommendations, arrived at after careful hearings, were not heeded by the parties, the General Conference could, by a large special majority, require that such recommendations be complied with under penalty of sanctions similar to those provided for non-compliance with judgments of the International Court.

By a further provision the International Court of Justice would be given authority to rule upon the validity of regulations adopted by the General Conference and upon the validity of any action taken by that body or other organs and agencies of the World Disarmament and World Development Organization, if claim were made that the Conference or any such organ or agency had exceeded its authority.

In addition to the International Court of Justice and the World Equity Tribunal, the Treaty would provide for a World Conciliation Board, available for the conciliation of any international dispute in which diplomacy had failed but where an agreed settlement might still be possible.

Through these several agencies, means would be available for the settlement, in the manner most appropriate to the particular case, of *all* disputes between nations. And thus any excuse that force must be employed because of the lack of alternative peaceful means to deal with a dispute would be entirely inadmissible.

Apart from these provisions for the settlement of all serious disputes between nations, there would be a system of United Nations Regional Courts to deal with violations of the Treaty or of regulations adopted thereunder, and to exercise certain functions in connection with the inspection process under the disarmament plan.

There would also be an Attorney General and a small civil police force under his direction, to aid in the enforcement of the Treaty and of all regulations adopted thereunder.

VII. **The World Development Authority.** In 1962 the estimated world population is about 3 billion. Of these some 2 billion persons are living in dire poverty, i.e., with an average per capita income of less that $150 per annum, in comparison with about $2,300 per capita, or over fifteen times as much, in the United States, and about $1,200 per capita in Western Europe, or eight times as much. Moreover, in some areas, containing at least one billion people, the average per capita annual income is less than $100.

This vast gap between the economic condition of the industrialized and the low-income countries tends to widen rather than to contract; and this tendency is aggravated by the fact that population growth tends to be highest in the poorest and least literate areas.

Thus, the great and growing discrepancy between the "haves" and the "have nots" of the world is a constant cause of unrest and instability and is, therefore, an underlying cause of international conflict and potential war.

The efforts to deal with this situation as of 1962 are, however praiseworthy, totally inadequate to the problem. For, although what is plainly required even in 1962 is an annual flow of capital and technical assistance from the industrialized areas to the low-income countries of the order of $50 billion per annum in aid of the 2 billion poverty-stricken people of these countries (or $25 per capita), the current flow in 1962 does not exceed $8.5 billion, or only about one-sixth of what is required to make any real impression on the problem.

In view of this situation, and as an essential part of any *sufficient* and *effective* plan for peace, the proposed Treaty calls for a World Development Authority adequately staffed and financed.

This Authority would be under the general direction of a World Development Council of 24 members appointed by the General Conference and so constituted as to provide fair representation both for those countries which would supply most of the funds and for those most needing assistance.

The budget of the World Development Authority would be part of the annual budget of the World Disarmament and World Development Organization annually voted by the General Conference. As already mentioned, the General Conference could adopt an annual budget up to 3 per cent of the estimated gross world product in that year. And since, looking ahead to 1980, the gross world product is likely to be $2,500 billion, the budget could then be $75 billion. Of this amount, perhaps $15 billion would be needed for the United Nations Peace Force, the Inspection Service and all the other organs and agencies of the Organization, leaving some $60 billion potentially available for the World Development Authority.

If this amount seems large, let it be remembered that it would represent less than $25 per capita per annum for the approximately 2.5 billion people who will, in all probability, be living in dire poverty in 1980,—a per capita amount which is barely enough to achieve any appreciable improvement in their standards of living. Let it be remembered also that this expenditure on behalf of the poverty-stricken areas of the world would come to pass only when the process of universal and complete disarmament had been completed, thereby eliminating a world tax burden for armaments which in 1962 already exceeds $120 billion and, in the absence of disarmament, is likely to grow to an amount more than double the assumed $75 billion budget of the proposed new Organization.

It cannot be too strongly emphasized that even with a new revenue need of, say, $75 billion per annum for the new Organization, the tax burden of the world would be far less than under the conditions of the arms race.

The rationale of the proposed World Development Authority is that world development, in the sense of bringing about a really significant change in the economic and social welfare of the "have not" peoples of the world, is an absolutely essential part of the plan for peace embodied in the proposed Treaty—no less so than the other great essential of total national disarmament under adequate inspection and enforceable world law.

This is also the reason for linking together the two concepts in the proposed name—"World Disarmament and World Development Organization."

VIII. **The Revenue System.** Nothing could be more futile than the adoption of a plan purporting to establish the world institutions essential for genuine peace without making provision for reliable revenues to maintain those institutions.

Accordingly, the draft Treaty includes a revenue system designed to provide with all reasonable assurance sufficient revenues to maintain all the organs and agencies of the World Disarmament and World Development Organization, including an adequately financed World Development Authority.

The main features of this system would be: (1) conferring upon the General Conference of the Organization authority to adopt annual budgets not exceeding 3 per cent of the estimated gross world product in each year; (2) apportionment of the annual budgets as between the member nations of the Organization (which would necessarily include all the major nations and all or nearly all of the smaller nations) upon the principle of ability to pay; (3) assignment to the Organization by each of the member nations of all or part of certain specified national taxes (for example, income taxes or liquor, tobacco and gasoline taxes), payment to be made directly into the treasury of the Organization, but national fiscal machinery to be used for the verification and, if necessary, the collection of the assigned taxes; (4) the annual estimates of gross world product, the making up of the annual budgets, and their apportionment, to be in charge of a Standing Committee on Budget and Finance of the General Conference, its recommendations to be subject to approval by the General Conference itself.

Under this system, there would be reliable machinery for the collection of sums really adequate to the great responsibilities of the World Disarmament and World Development Organization.

IX. **Privileges and Immunities.** It would obviously be necessary to prevent any interference by national or local authorities with the performance of the official functions of the Organization. Its agencies, officials, employees, communications and property (including documents) must therefore be protected by the Treaty from interference or harassment—whether by national or local regulation, taxation, legal process, censorship, travel restrictions or otherwise. These protections would be embodied in a detailed statement of privileges and immunities, which the General Conference would be authorized to implement by any necessary regulations.

The Treaty would also, however, contain safeguards against abuse of these privileges and immunities, and against unnecessary interference with national or local law enforcement.

X. **Limitations and Guarantees.** As a protection against unwarranted expansion of the powers of the Organization, its carefully limited authority would be defined with great precision. However, as an additional safeguard, the Treaty would contain explicit prohibitions against the usurpation by the Organization of any *additional* powers, and also specific guarantees against violation by the Organization of certain individual rights which are or ought to be universally recognized as fundamental to human dignity and security. These rights would include the right to fair trial; the privileges against double jeopardy, *ex post facto* laws, excessive bail, cruel and unusual punishments, unlawful detention, and unreasonable searches and seizures; and freedom of religion, communication, assembly and petition.

XI. **Relationship between the United Nations and the World Disarmament and World Development Organization.** As set forth in the preamble of the proposed Treaty, its basic purpose would be "to supplement the machinery of the United Nations now available to maintain international peace and security and to promote the economic and social advancement of all peoples." And it is to *accomplish* this purpose that the Treaty provides for the establishment of the World Disarmament and World Development Organization "within the framework of the United Nations."

Since the proposal is that the present United Nations and its Charter shall remain wholly intact and that the new Organization shall "supplement" the existing and continuing machinery of the United Nations, it is necessary to define the relationship between them.

In order that the two organizations shall function in maximum harmony for the accomplishment of their joint purpose to maintain peace and to promote the economic and social advancement of all the people of the world, the draft Treaty contains the following provisions:

(1) All the organs and agencies of the new Organization shall

consult with the organs and agencies of the United Nations on all matters of mutual interest or concern.

(2) Annual and special reports shall be made to the United Nations as to the activities of the Organization.

(3) Persons duly authorized by the General Assembly of the United Nations shall have the right to take part, but without vote, in the deliberations of the General Conference of the Organization; and persons duly authorized by the Security Council and the Economic and Social Council of the United Nations shall correspondingly have the right to participate, but without vote, in the deliberations of the Executive Council and the World Development Authority.

(4) The General Assembly and other principal organs of the United Nations may make any recommendations which they desire to the Organization, the appropriate organs of which would be obligated to give due consideration thereto.

(5) In the all-important matter of sanctions to maintain peace, careful provisions are proposed whereby the initiative for such sanctions could be taken either by the United Nations, through its General Assembly or Security Council, or by the General Conference of the Organization. If the Security Council has decided under Chapter VII of the United Nations Charter that sanctions are necessary or the General Assembly by a large special majority has recommended sanctions, the Organization would be bound to "support the United Nations in such measures to the extent and in such manner as the General Conference of the Organization shall determine". On the other hand, the General Conference of the Organization could direct sanctions, subject only to the revocation or modification thereof by a large special majority of the General Assembly. These provisions are intended to ensure that sanctions, when clearly needed to maintain peace, shall be effective and not subject to frustration by the veto of any single nation, while also giving assurance that no sanctions shall be applied unnecessarily or with undue harshness.

Apart from the above specific provisions designed to harmonize and coordinate the work of the two organizations, the interrelationship would be symbolized by attaching the name of the United Nations to various of the most important organs and agencies of the new Organization. This would be done by calling the world police force the "United Nations Peace Force" and by using the names "United Nations Disarmament Authority", "United Nations Inspection Service", "United Nations Inspection Commission", "United Nations Nuclear Energy Authority", "United Nations Outer Space Agency", "United Nations Regional Courts", and so forth, for certain organs and agencies of the Organization.

The United Nations would remain as a great world forum in which all questions affecting the peace of the world and the economic and social welfare of its people could be constantly reviewed, with each and every member nation having an equal right to be heard and an equal vote, irrespective of population, wealth or any other factor. On the other hand, the World Disarmament and World Development Organization, in close affiliation and cooperation with the United Nations, would have the financial, judicial and military power which the United Nations now lacks to fulfill its declared purposes.

XII. **Ratification and Amendment.** The proposed Treaty, in providing for total national disarmament and for enforceable world law against international violence or the threat of it, together with the world institutions essential to these ends, would call for a truly revolutionary change in world affairs. It is, therefore, essential that the Treaty be accepted not only by all the major powers, but also by a great majority of all the nations and of the world's population.

Accordingly, the draft Treaty provides that it shall come into force only when ratified, in accordance with their respective constitutional processes, by five sixths of all the independent states of the world, with the provisos: (a) that the ratifying nations shall include *all* of the twelve nations with the largest populations; and (b) that the population of the ratifying nations shall be at least five sixths of the estimated world population.

These exacting requirements, together with the previously noted provision that no member nation, once having joined, may resign or be expelled, should give maximum assurance of the stability and permanence of the peace-keeping machinery embodied in the new Organization.

Conclusion.

The United Nations was not given by the framers of its Charter adequate powers to fulfill the main purpose for which it was organized, namely, the prevention of war.

The United Nations lacks a standing world police force; it lacks a judicial system with compulsory jurisdiction over international disputes; it lacks a reliable revenue system; and in other respects it is not adequately equipped to fulfill its fundamental purpose.

Nevertheless, the United Nations has often rendered most useful service, and is also an important symbol of the world's aspiration for genuine peace. Accordingly, there must be no question of abolishing the United Nations, but only of how best to supplement its existing machinery so that its basic purpose—the maintenance of peace—can be effectively fulfilled.

Such is the purpose of the proposed Treaty establishing the World Disarmament and World Development Organization which, *working with the United Nations,* would supply the indispensable elements which are now lacking. If the world really wants general and complete disarmament and genuine peace, it must face the fact that the present machinery of the United Nations must be radically reinforced. To accomplish this, there are two alternative methods: (1) a drastic and detailed revision of the U. N. Charter itself; and (2) the method embodied in this proposed Treaty, whereby the United Nations would be left intact but its machinery would be effectively *supplemented* by the new Organization.

For purposes of discussion, an illustrative model of a revised United Nations Charter is set forth in detail in the authors' book "World Peace through World Law." With the same purpose, this draft Treaty is submitted as illustrative of the second alternative method and in the hope that it will promote constructive discussion of the paramount problem of our time.

SUGGESTED QUESTIONS FOR SEMINAR DISCUSSION

Looking at 1) the methods of disarmament proposed (timing and phasing of what kinds of weapons in what amounts), 2) the inspection or verification of disarmament and 3) the peace-keeping machinery and the control of units to police the disarmament proposals, and bearing in mind the Blackett analysis, what risks do you see to the security of the USSR in the US proposal? Do the Clark-Sohn proposals handle all these risks?

Do you agree with McVitty that in these proposals the US and the USSR are not far apart on inspection? What difference, if any, remains between them? To what extent are the differences on inspection due to difference on approaches to establishment of a police force to handle violations and as to how this police force should be controlled?

Under the Soviet view command of police force contingents would be made up of representatives of the three groups (east, west, uncommitted) of states in the world and decisions of the command would be made only by unanimity. The US is silent on the subject; assuming they would be opposed to the plan, what do you think would be an acceptable and workable alternative? Would one person from a small, uncommitted state offer a reasonable basis for coming to an agreement? How about the Clark-Sohn scheme for five persons from the smaller states comprising a command by majority vote with review by the Security Council and ultimately by the General Assembly?

The Clark-Sohn proposals call for admission of "mainland China, West and East Germany, North Korea and South Korea, North Viet-Nam and South Viet-Nam" to the World

Disarmament and World Development Organization. Doesn't this indicate that unitl a good number of international political issues are r e s o l v e d, it is impossible to think in terms of general and complete disarmament? Or are i n i t i a l steps toward disarmament a w a y of achieving settlements here? How about Berlin, the Arab-I s r a e l i tensions, the conflict between India and Kashmir? Would these need to be settled before we could achieve disarmament?

Some persons are concerned that the establishment of a new international organization in the field of disarmament would, despite the best of intentions and attempts to set up a working relationship with t h e United Nations, ultimately lead to the tail wagging the dog with the United Nations becoming a subsidiary o r ganization of the disarmament organization. Do any of the three proposals handle this problem adequately? Supposing that were to o c c u r, what harm, if a n y, w o u l d this new development cause?
Neither t h e Soviet Union nor the United States plan suggest in the slightest t h a t the disarmament problem must be related to a world development authority, y e t Clark and Sohn in their s c h e m e would make that agency of c o m p a r a b l e d i g n i t y to the disarmament agency. Do you think that the effort to establish a development authority at the same time as a disarmament organization is helpful or harmful to t h e effort to establish the latter? Why?

Both Bechhoefer and McVitty feel t h a t negotiations on disarmament have frequently been meaningless because neither side was adequately p r e p a r e d to deal seriously with t h e problems. In light of their description of substantive proposals put forward in the past, bearing in mind the security problems suggested by Blackett, and l o o k i n g at the major international political problems leading to tensions, do you consider these proposals to show serious intents to achiev e general and complete disarmament? On w h a t do you base your judgment?

Here is a list of some proposals which are l e s s than comprehensive in their approach to disarmament and arms control: reduction of conventional weapons (men and arms), atomfree zones, disengaged zones, ban on bomb t e s t i n g, open skies inspection, c ontrol of· nuclear energy. Do these raise f e w e r problems than comprehensive approaches? Do you think there is any likelihood of getting agreement on a n y o f these proposals?

Using the criteria of acceptability, fairness and effectiveness, and looking a t everything which we have studied to this point, which of the three proposals, the USSR, the US or the Clark-Sohn, would you favor?

736

SESSION XI

SOME ECONOMIC AND SOCIAL PROBLEMS OF DISARMAMENT

For the past three sessions we have been discussing the security-military-political context of disarmament. In this session we turn to another major facet of disarmament which lies outside this field but is likely to have an important bearing upon whether and in what fashion the primary problems of disarmament are resolved. Our concern will be how to avoid or ameliorate potentially troublesome and harmful economic consequences if a major disarmament agreement were to be implemented.

Our discussion centers on two documents, both entitled "Economic and Social Consequences of Disarmament." These reports represent expert analysis and opinion, having been produced by panels of distinguished economists engaged respectively by the U.S. Arms Control and Disarmament Agency and the UN Department of Economic and Social Affairs in response to a General Assembly resolution endorsing and requesting study of the problems consequent to disarmament. Both reports have been written so as to be understood by the intelligent lay person. This point is important since any major downward revisions in the development and production of armaments will have serious repercussions in the areas where armament production is now concentrated, and could have serious nation-wide repercussions. And furthermore, unless we inform ourselves and prepare to meet the economic dislocations resulting from the disarmament process, the actual process of disarmament may be jeopardized by serious political squabbles resulting from the fears and uncertainties of large numbers now employed directly or indirectly in the development and production of armaments.

Many of the seminar participants may have had little experience with formal economic thinking. We have therefore prepared the following analytical outline of the problems treated in the reports. This outline is not a summary of the reports, but rather a guide to understanding them.

Disarmament, if completed rapidly, will create three major domestic economic problems which may be summarized as "conversion," "stabilization" and "economic growth."

Conversion. Disarmament will engender a major problem of adjustment in the production structure of the economy; more specifically, the composition of total output will necessarily shift in relation to the composition of total demand. Certain other adjustments will be necessary. Both reports stress that armament production is highly concentrated in a few industries and unevenly distributed over various regions in a country. Under these conditions dis-

737

armament is likely to cause imbalances in industrial structure and regional economies which will have to be corrected.
Together these problems have been called the "structural
problems of disarmament" and are frequently said to form
the crux of the economic problems of disarmament.

Stabilization.   Disarmament will lead to unemployment
of certain resources and perhaps depression in over-all
economic activity.   It might at the same time also lead to
"specific inflation" as a result of the shifts in total demand.
Disarmament will thus require "stabilization" of the economy in the face of these dynamics.   These are problems
which domestic societies in the Western world have been
meeting with increasing success since World War II although
there are still many problems to be solved.   The reports
shed light on these problems.

Economic Growth.   Disarmament could prove harmful
to "economic growth."   Shifts in the composition of total
demand may affect the "optimum" rate of economic growth,
the latter being defined as the maximum possible rate of
growth given the constraints of resources and basic value
systems.

Besides these three internal domestic problems, disarmament will affect the composition and direction of foreign
trade and in turn might affect the pattern of world trade relations.   By enlarging the scope of foreign assistance to
underdeveloped countries and by creating a more favorable
climate for the development of trade relations with centrally-
planned countries, disarmament might also bring the world
closer to the ideal of "one world community."

In summary, both reports agree that major cutbacks in
the production of armaments will create new problems in
those areas where arms production are now concentrated
and may create serious dislocations in other areas.   Both
reports strongly support the view, however, that rational
solutions are available for any problems created by disarmament if we will only do the necessary planning.

In our outline thus far we have been talking about the
U.S. and UN reports simultaneously, because by and large
both have used the same analytical tools.   There are, however, two basic respects in which they differ, and you will
want to examine the implications of these differences.

Firstly, they differ in their assumptions.   Whereas the
UN report assumes "that disarmament, once agreed upon,
would be general and complete," so that there will be no
need for any defense expenditures, the U.S. reports assumes
the "even in a disarmed or disarming world resources .. .
must be devoted to the maintenance of security."   Accordingly, some defense expenditures shall have to be incurred
perhaps in the form of an "international police force."   The
off-shoot of this latter assumption is that the intensity and
scope of the over-all conversion problem could be reduced,

perhaps significantly. The UN and U.S. reports also differ on the question of timing. While the UN report assumes that disarmament, once agreed upon, shall be "rapid," the U.S. report appears to assume that the disarmament process might take quite some time. In fact, the U.S. report is uncertain as to the "timing, phasing, and duration of disarmament."

Secondly, the two reports differ in their approach. The U.S. report looks at economic problems of disarmament, both national and international, understandably enough from a national viewpoint. The UN report, on the other hand, makes a genuine attempt to treat this aspect of disarmament from the point of view of an international system.

Readings from World Peace Through World Law:
Introduction, xxxvi-xxxix.

THE ECONOMIC AND SOCIAL CONSEQUENCES OF DISARMAMENT

The United States of America

Table of Contents

9. Estimated Direct and Indirect Employment by Broad Occupational Group for the Production of Defense Goods and Services by Industry, Excluding Government, and in Nonagricultural Industries for the U.S. Economy, 1960

10. U.S. Government Grants and Credits to Other Countries and International Organizations, Military and Non-Military, 1956-1960

11. Relation of U.S. Military Expenditures Abroad, and Military and Economic Assistance, to Total Recorded U.S. Transactions by Areas, 1960

---

*These tables have not been reproduced here.

Introduction

The motivating force behind the efforts of the United States to achieve general and complete disarmament under effective international control is to save present and future generations from the scourge of war, and to attain for them a more certain and beneficent security.

This basic and vital objective completely overshadows any economic calculations of gain or loss connected with disarmament. Actually, the United States can maintain as high or as low a level of defense expenditures as is deemed necessary for its security. At the same time it is clear that a basic change in our methods of achieving security will have distinct effects on our economy. Any examination of the question of disarmament therefore requires study of its economic impact in order to enlarge our understanding of the policies, programs, and actions required to derive the maximum economic and social benefit from it for ourselves and the rest of mankind.

It must be stressed that the allocation of resources to purely military purposes is not an economically creative process, except in an incidental way. It yields relatively few goods or services which contribute to the enrichment of individual lives or to the growth of the national economy. It prevents or retards the satisfaction of many civilian needs. By the same token, if the world should be fortunate enough to be able to rid itself of the burden of national defense efforts, resources would then be released everywhere which could be devoted to the production of those goods and services which advance man's material, cultural, and spiritual state. This is the basic economic interest of the United States in disarmament, and it is an entirely positive one.

This study of the extent to which the defense effort affects the American economy, and of the economic problems and opportunities which would be encountered under a program of general and complete disarmament is in no sense definitive. This is because there are important gaps in our basic knowledge of detailed facts, and because there is as yet no indication as to the timing, phasing, and duration of the disarmament p r o g r a m which may eventually emerge from international negotiations.

Despite these l i m i t a t i o n s, it is possible to arrive at several significant conclusions.

(1) The current national defense effort of the United States takes about one tenth of our gross national product and employs somewhat less than that portion of our employed labor force. This a l l o c a t i o n of human and m a t e r i a l resources must be seen against the background of the vast and costly changes which have been taking place in the technology of arms, and of the tremendous enlargement, geographically and otherwise, in the security requirements of the United States as the leading Power in the Free World. As a component of total economic demand defense expenditures are not of such magnitude that the economy is vitally dependent on them. In fact, the American economy proved itself after World War II, to be very resilient to a considerably greater and more rapid reduction in defense expenditures than w o u l d be i n v o l v e d u n d e r any disarmament program starting at the present level of armaments.

(2) The currently recognized needs of Americans individually and collectively are so extensive that, if translated into economic demand, they would more than offset the loss of demand resulting from an agreed disarmament program. The factors required to effect this t r a n s l a t i o n of civilian needs into economic demand are well understood. Moreover, there are increasingly r e f i n e d tools available with which to observe, analyze and influence the development of the economy. Advance planning and sensible policies at all levels of government will be essential to the maintenance of over-all economic activity in the face of progressive elimination of defense demand.

(3) Unquestionably, any program of disarmament will in the short and intermediate run give rise to problems of adjustment in all f a c t o r s of production. However, these adjustment problems--of varying intensity depending on the timing, phasing, and duration of any agreed disarmament program--are not n o v e l to the American economy; quite apart from p r e v i o u s successful a d j u s t m e n t s to major changes in defense expenditures, the economy is constantly undergoing a d j u s t m e n t in a wide range of industries as a result of changes in technology and economic demand. Concerted effort on the part of government at all levels and of business and labor, to bring to bear n u m e r o u s available instruments and, if necessary, to create additional ones, can reduce to a m i n i m u m any hardship and waste in the adjustment process under a program for general and complete disarmament.

(4) The United States has long recognized that general and complete disarmament would present opportunities for

enlarged assistance to less developed countries and has sponsored United Nations resolutions in this sense. However, the United States has not waited for disarmament; it has extended foreign economic aid over the past twenty years on a scale unequalled by any other country. The United Nations, recognizing that added impetus needs to be given in the current decade to economic cooperation for development in under-developed countries, has designated the 1960's as the International Decade of Development. The United States, as one of the sponsors of this resolution, will do its part. When and as disarmament is achieved, the American people can be expected to face imaginatively the added challenges and opportunities which this development would hold for the welfare of mankind.

(5) In the area of international economic relations, the elimination, as a result of disarmament, of U.S. Government defense-related expenditures abroad, and of defense-related imports of raw materials and other commodities, would have a corrective effect on the U.S. balance of payments deficit. There would probably be a noticeably adverse effect in only a few countries; these effects could be overcome with increased external economic assistance and growth and diversification in the respective economies. The elimination of military-oriented production and trade controls under disarmament would permit more international trade to flow on the basis of comparative advantage.

I.   The Impact of Defense on the National Economy

Size and composition of defense expenditures. Annual expenditures for goods and services for national defense* in

---

*Included in the term "national defense" in this study are those items which the Department of Commerce includes in the National Defense component of Gross National Product, except when otherwise indicated. Specifically included under this heading are: Department of Defense military functions and military assistance, stockpiling, expansion of defense production, and purchases by the Atomic Energy Commission (AEC), National Aeronautics and Space Administration (NASA), Selective Service System, and Federal Civil Defense Administration. Excluded are such items as economic assistance for defense support under the mutual defense assistance program, and the civilian functions of the Army Corps of Engineers. It should be noted that the Department of Commerce classification is not identical with the National Defense category in the Federal budget document. Furthermore, the AEC and NASA components include substantial expenditures for purely civilian purposes which cannot be separated out of the total because of the non-availability of relevant data.

742

the 1955-60 period have consistently accounted for about 9-10 per cent of gross national product in current dollars and have constituted about 86 per cent of total Federal purchases of goods and services.

Of total defense spending in 1960 approximately 35 per cent ($16.0 billion) was for purchases of military equipment, somewhat less than that (15.6 billion) was for military and civilian personnel, about 20 per cent ($9.5 billion) was for purchases of non-military goods and services (such as food for the armed services, office equipment, etc.), about 5 per cent ($2.3 billion) was in the atomic energy field, and less than 5 per cent ($2.1 billion) was devoted to all other purposes, among which construction was the principal item. Research and development are included in various of the above categories.

In the period 1955 to 1960 total defense purchases increased from $39 billion to $45.5 billion in current prices, while declining slightly as a per cent of GNP. Within the total, the shares of expenditures for military equipment, "other goods and services," and atomic energy activities have increased, whereas all other items (personnel expenditures, construction, stockpiling and defense facilities, and miscellaneous) have declined relatively.

In the expenditures for military equipment during the same period, there were major increases for missiles and a considerable decline for aircraft, ordnance and vehicles. Procurement expenditures for electronics and communications also increased.

Impact on employment. Corresponding to the expenditures on defense, more than 6 million persons were employed in all Federal and industrial defense-related activities in 1960. They represent about 9 per cent of all U.S. employment.

a. Federal defense-related employment. Active duty military personnel totaled approximately 2.5 million. Slightly more than 1 million civilians were employed in 1960, in Federal defense-related agencies, principally the Department of Defense, but also including the Atomic Energy Commission, the National Aeronautics and Space Administration, and several smaller organizations. Together these employees represented 47 per cent of all Federal civilian employment. It is important to note, however, that employment in defense-related activities in the U.S. government has represented a constantly decreasing share of all U.S. employment, both civilian and military, since 1953, when the Korean hostilities ended.

During the Korean War period, a rapid build-up took place. The number of U.S. military personnel increased from less than 1.5 million in 1950 to 3.6 million in 1952, and employment in Federal civilian defense-related activi-

743

ties also expanded sharply. At the peak in 1952 these two groups combined formed 7.7 per cent of total U.S. employment, public and private.

In every year from 1953 to 1960 a decline occurred both in numbers engaged in defense activities of the Federal Government and in their proportion of total employment. The number of military personnel was less than 2.5 million in 1960, down by more than over 1 million, and the number of civilian personnel in Federal defense-related agencies was down from over 1.3 million in 1952 to about 1 million in 1960. Together they represented only slightly more than 5 per cent of total U.S. employment in 1960. In the summer and autumn of 1961, the size of the Armed Forces increased slightly to a total of 2.7 million in October.

b. Industrial defense-related employment. It has been estimated that in 1960 approximately 2.6 million persons--5 per cent of all nonagricultural employment-- were employed directly and indirectly in supplying goods and services, principally (but not exclusively) military equipment, to the Federal defense-related agencies. This includes employment in industries providing materials, supplies and services such as transportation.

Distrubution of defense geographically and by industry. A principal characteristic of defense spending in the U.S. is its uneven distribution, geographically and by industry. While no detailed nationwide information is available on the geographic impact of national security programs combined, sufficient evidence is at hand to indicate the areas of greatest concentration. For this purpose, good indicators are employment in the four leading defense-related manufacturing industries in relation to over-all employment, and the disbursement of payrolls in these defense-related industries and in Federal defense-related agencies, in relation to total personal incomes in the areas concerned.

All of the employment in the ordnance industry, over 93 per cent of employment in aircraft and missiles construction, 60 per cent of employment in ship and boat building, and 21 per cent of employment in the electrical machinery industry (38 per cent in radio and communications equipment) was attributable to defense procurement.

Employment in these four manufacturing industries which are most dependent upon defense totaled 1,233,000 in the year 1960. At that time the total, which, of course, includes employment on production not related to defense, represented only about 7 1/2 per cent of all manufacturing employment and less than 2 1/2 per cent of total nonagricultural employment.

These major defense manufacturing industries have a high degree of concentration in certain States and cities. The military establishments and civilian government employment connected with defense are also concentrated to a considerable degree. Not infrequently both are located in the same general area.

Among the areas most affected are Alaska and Hawaii; California, and the State of Washington; the Maryland, Virginia, and District of Columbia complex; certain New England States, notably Connecticut and Massachusetts; some of the less populous mountain States like New Mexico and Utah where the government's defense operations loom large, and some of the Southern States where there are growing military installations, such as Oklahoma, Kansas, Alabama, Georgia and South Carolina.

A summary of wages and salaries in the four defense-related industries and in the Federal defense-related agencies in the year 1960 shows that their impact is greatest, relatively, in Alaska and Hawaii, where 29 and 22 per cent of these States' personal income, respectively, is from these sources.* Next in order is the State of Virginia, with 15 per cent; and then Washington, Maryland, the District of Columbia, and New Mexico, with 11-12 per cent; and California, Kansas, South Carolina, Georgia and Utah, each with 9-10 per cent.

In actual dollars, the payrolls in the above defense-related activities (including pay of military personnel) are greatest in California, where in 1960 they exceeded $4,250 million; in Texas with almost $1,350 million and in Virginia with over $1 billion. Payments were also very substantial in some of the other larger States, such as New York and Pennsylvania, but industries, the impact of defense expenditures is relatively much smaller than in many of the smaller States listed above.

Excluding the Armed Services, which are deployed in many parts of the world, and considering only employment in the four principal defense-related industries and civilian employment in the Federal defense agencies, a similarly concentrated geographic pattern prevails. About 10 per cent of all nonagricultural employment in five States is provided by these civilian activities, namely in Washington, Alaska, Utah, Virginia, and Connecticut.
In another eight States 6 to 9 per cent is provided: California, Maryland, Kansas, New Mexico, Alabama, the District of Columbia, Colorado, and Maine. In Oklahoma, Arizona and Massachusetts the ratio is 5 per cent.

The four defense-related industries are especially important in the less populous States where new installations have developed in what were originally agricultural and trading areas. Kansas, New Mexico, Utah and Arizona are good examples.

---

*For the Armed Services the allocation is to their place of residence.

Within these States, certain communities have a notably high concentration of defense-connected activities. Examples are the Los Angeles-Long Beach and San Diego areas in California; the Seattle-Takoma area in Washington; Greater Washington, D.C.; Wichita, Kansas; the Boston-Cambridge area in Massachusetts; Huntsville, Alabama, etc. Smaller areas in which military installations and other defense activities are concentrated include such cities as Newport, Rhode Island; Portsmouth, New Hampshire; Norfolk, Virginia; and New London, Connecticut. In certain small communities the economy is built almost entirely around specialized plants producing defense materiel or around military bases. Some of them are areas with high and persistent unemployment.

Impact on research and development, (R&D). In fiscal year 1960/61 46 per cent of the national R&D effort was financed by the Department of Defense alone, and when the contributions of NASA and the AEC are counted, the R&D spending of defense-related agencies was 56 per cent of the estimated national total of $14 billion. In addition to work done in government laboratories, the defense agencies paid for better than half of the research undertaken in industry-run laboratories, and about 60 per cent of the work performed by universities and other non-profit institutions. In the industries producing aircraft and parts and communications and other electrical equipment, which account for more than 75 per cent of government research funds spent in industries, R&D spending exceeds 10 per cent of sales, while for all other industries together R&D spending does not exceed 3 per cent.

Another significant characteristic of defense R&D is that it employs more equipment, materials and overhead per scientific personnel than does civilian R&D. Finally, it is clear that defense needs have, in recent years, significantly restricted the availability of R&D scientists and engineers for the civilian sector.

Impact on civilian expenditures. Any analysis of the economic impact of defense spending cannot leave out of account the fact that the allocation of substantial financial resources to this sector inevitably involves individual and collective self-denial in others. The large national defense budget has decreased the Federal Government's ability to finance many worthwhile and important non-military programs because of pressures against increasing an already large tax burden. High Federal taxes have tended to limit the ability of State and local governments to pay for basic services and public facilities and have retarded local solutions to such problems as urban blight, inadequate educational facilities, and overburdened mass transportation systems. Finally, the current tax burden has prevented individuals and firms from giving freer rein to the satisfaction of their needs for s e r v i c e s, consumer goods, and new capital equipment.

With due regard for the incidental benefits which flow from the defense program to the civilian sector (peaceful uses of military t e c h n o l o g i c a l development, training of personnel, etc.), this continuous self-denial is substantial, and its implications for our current and future economic and social well-being are incalculable. It is here that the real cost of the defense program is expressed.

II. The Problems of Adjustment to Disarmament

In considering the problems which must be dealt with if, as, and when an agreed disarmament program permits the American people to reallocate the human and material resources now d e v o t e d to defense, two important factors must be taken into account.

<u>Continuing expenditures for s e c u r i t y.</u>   In the first place, it is clear that even in a disarmed or disarming world resources--possibly substantial ones--must be devoted to the maintenance of security.   In this connection it is useful to recall the Joint U.S.-USSR Statement of Agreed Principles for Disarmament Negotiations, of September 20, 1961:

"The program for general and complete disarmament shall ensure that States will have at their disposal only those non-nuclear armaments, forces, facilities, and establishments as are a g r e e d to be necessary to maintain internal order and protect the personal security of citizens; a n d that States shall support and provide agreed manpower for a UN peace force." (Item Two)

"All disarmament m e a s u r e s should be implemented f r o m beginning to end under such strict and effective international control as would provide firm assurance that all parties are h o n o r i n g their obligations. D u r i n g and a f t e r the implementation of general and complete disarmament, the most thorough control should be exercised, the nature and extent of such control depending on the requirements for verification and disarmament measures being carried out." (Item Six)

"..... during and after the implementation of the program of general and complete disarmament, there should be taken, in accordance with the principles of the United Nations Charter, the necessary measures to maintain international peace and security, including the obligation of States to place at the disposal of the United Nations agreed m a n p o w e r necessary for an international peace force to be equipped with agreed types of armaments. Arrangements for the use of this force should ensure that the United Nations can effectively deter or suppress any threat or use of arms in violation of the purposes and principles of the United Nations." (Item Seven)

It is upon these types of measures that security and world peace will depend under a disarmament program. The United States Disarmament Program of September 25, 1961, expands upon these measures. It foresees the establishment, in Stage I, of an International Disarmament Organization and sets forth its duties. The program also provides for arrangements for the establishment, in Stage II, of a UN Peace Force and foresees in Stage I the creation of a UN peace observation group. In later stages the International Disarmament Organization, the Peace Force and the machinery for the settlement of disputes would all be expanded. In Stage III of the U.S. program national forces are to be limited, the UN Peace Force fully functioning, and arms manufacturing prohibited except for agreed types to supply the UN Force.

The logical conclusion from the foregoing is that the achievement of "general and complete disarmament," while setting a new framework for security and resulting in changes in the instruments and methods for safeguarding security, will not relieve the United States and other nations of the necessity to continue to allocate funds and resources for purposes of international peacekeeping. Indeed, the new forms and instruments of security will have first call on human and material resources which would be released by the elimination of our national military program. To the-- at this time unknown--extent that this occurs, it would naturally reduce somewhat the scope of the over-all conversion problem.

Timing, phasing, and duration of disarmament. The second consideration affecting examination of the economic effects of disarmament is that at this time there is no indication when a disarmament agreement might go into effect, how its incidence on particular defense expenditures would be phased, and how long it would be before the entire process has been concluded. Yet these variable factors have profound effect on the problems of economic adjustment. Thus, a disarmament program phased over a considerable number of years and having no sudden and major impact on any one group of defense expenditures would present different problems of adjustment than would, for example, greatly accelerated or concentrated programs. Likewise, the commencement of a disarmament program at a peak in a business cycle would influence the problem of maintaining over-all demand differently than if significant disarmament began in a cyclical trough.

In the absence of specific details on the timing, phasing, and duration of a disarmament program it is therefore not possible to discuss the problems of adjustment except in general terms.

Two basic problems of adjustment. It is important to distinguish between two basic problems of adjustment. The first is to maintain aggregate economic demand in the nation despite more or less substantial and progressive declines in demand from the defense sector. The second is to minimize hardships and waste as the human and material resources now devoted to defense find new uses.

These two problems, while different in nature and in the policy instruments suited to deal with them, are inter-connected. Thus, if there is general inadequacy of aggregate demand, it will be more difficult, if not impossible, to overcome the structural problems of transition. On the other hand, if the transition from national defense efforts to general and complete disarmament should be characterized by persistent structural maladjustment, the effect of measures to maintain aggregate demand on output and employment would tend to be dissipated in inflation. With advance planning and sensible policies at all levels of government and on the part of business and labor, it should be possible to master both of these problems satisfactorily.

A.   Maintaining Aggregate Demand

The Problem.   It is clear that, if not offset, significant and progressive declines in defense spending would re-duce the growth rate of economic activity and quite possibly bring about an absolute decline. In the absence of compen-sating factors, total demand would be reduced by signifi-cent more than the reduction in defense spending. Declining defense spending would be reflected in reduced income for employees of the defense industries and of the industries supplying, directly and indirectly, the defense contractors. Decreases in personal income would be moderated, to some extent automatically, by reduced taxes and increased transfer payments, but, with existing legis-lation, a dollar reduction in defense spending would cause, directly and indirectly, about a dollar reduction in personal consumption. In addition, the decline in aggregate demand would lead to a reduction in capacity and inventory require-ments and thus to some fall in the rate of investment.

In the event of disarmament it would be necessary to encourage, stimulate, or create those offsets which would counteract these negative factors to the maximum extent and absorb the slack in the economy. The nature of the required policies is well understood, and historical experience testi-fies to the ability of the American economy to respond in a healthy way to major reductions in defense expenditures.

[A discussion of the post-World War II and the post-Korean War experience has been omitted. A good deal of

749

this material is to be found in the United Nations document, "The Economic and Social Consequences of Disarmament," Chapter 3, under the heading, "The post-war conversion."]

Meeting the problem of aggregate demand.   The most important factor to bear in mind in meeting the problem of aggregate demand in the event of a sizeable disarmament program getting under way within the decade is that today and in the foreseeable future there are in the United States as well as in other countries very substantial unmet needs and opportunities which could work as a powerful factor on the economy given the necessary conditions.   Some of these needs and opportunities will be described in greater detail in the next chapter.   Many of them will be increasingly met as the decade progresses, whether there is a program for general and complete disarmament or not, but they will not be eliminated; moreover, new needs will become apparent with the passage of time.

Reference has been made to the role of dynamic optimism in our society after World War II as a positive influence on economic development.   It would be hard to imagine that the American people would not respond very positively to an agreed and safeguarded program to substitute an international rule of law and order for the present national security efforts, once the full implications of such a change were understood.   The beneficent effect of such a development on the economic plans and actions of the American people, acting individually and through their institutions, would be incalculable.

Even without the psychological stimulus that could be expected from the type of disarmament program which it is the object of our policy to obtain, the American economy does not lack dynamism.   It is the strength of the free enterprise system that it not only affords large opportunities for the exercise of inventive genius and economic initiative but in fact inspires them on a large scale.   These are among the principal forces which have provided the motive power for the growth of the American economy, and they will certainly contribute significantly to maintaining the momentum of the economy in the event of disarmament.

Government policy will have a vital role in dealing with the problem of aggregate demand. Sensitive response to the particular economic facts and forces prevailing prior to and at the commencement of disarmament, and far-sighted action can contribute strongly to the creation of the conditions which will allow the unmet needs of society to be translated into the kind of economic demand that will-- potentially--more than take up the slack caused by the progressive decline in national defense spending.   Several powerful tools and instruments are available to the Federal Government and, to a more limited extent, to State and local governments, for this purpose.

An important and obvious tool for action to translate civilian needs into economic demand is reduction in Federal tax schedules. Such reductions would, of course, make more funds available to individuals and businesses. Some of these funds would go into investment, others would go into consumption. Federal tax reductions would also leave additional room for State and local taxes to finance new or enlarged public programs and investments in such areas as education, social services, recreational facilities, water supply, waste disposal, and so forth, which, in the aggregate, could go far in helping to offset the decline in defense spending. In any case, Federal tax reductions would stimulate total economic demand, though, depending on the precise measures adopted, in different ways and with different time impacts.

Another significant possibility is to expand public civilian expenditures, which, as noted, have tended to be confined within relatively narrow limits as a result of the major need for funds for the defense effort, to the detriment of numerous areas where our growing population and other factors have intensified the need for increased governmental activity.

The fields of resource development and conservation, civil aviation, education, public health and public works afford numerous possibilities for the Federal Government in this regard. Federal expenditures for civilian atomic energy development and space exploration could also be readily expanded to the benefit of present and future generations.

State and local governments could expand their programs in such fields as urban development, public housing, school and hospital construction, roads and other public works; in-- creased Federal loans and grants to State and local governments for these purposes could have significant beneficial effect.

Undoubtedly there would also be expanded transfer payments by the Federal Government, some of which would occur automatically under existing laws. By supporting income levels, they would have a stabilizing effect on total demand. Included among possibilities under this heading are such measures as unemployment compensation, various types of retirement benefits, mustering-out pay to military personnel, education and training grants and other similar programs discussed in Chapter III, in some cases requiring new lesislation in order to provide new or improved coverage.

The Federal Government also has direct control of a series of loan programs to individuals and business firms which would be beneficially employed in an integrated economic program to provide offsets to declining military expenditures.

Aid to less developed countries, which is discussed in Chapter IV, would afford another meaningful opportunity for expansion of Federal civilian expenditures.

In this connection it is pertinent to note that in the post-World War II years the total purchases of non-defense goods and services by government at all levels actually were lower, on a per capita basis and also as a per cent of gross national product, than in 1939.

A third tool is monetary policy. Measures to lower interest rates, to reduce reserve requirements, to increase liquidity could act as a stimulant to the economy which would be felt particularly in such areas as industrial investment and housing. They would, of course, be taken in the context of our international balance of payments and other factors.

All of these tools were used successfully after World War II and some after the Korean War. There is no reason why they should not be used, with maximum impact, again. In this connection it is of interest to note the President's recent request to Congress for standby authority to accelerate public improvement programs, to implement income tax reductions, and to provide extended unemployment compensation payments in the event of threatening recession. Adoption of this proposal would, of course, be most helpful in dealing with substantial declines in defense spending under a disarmament program.

Determination of the precise combination of measures to support aggregate demand under a disarmament program is in itself a complex process requiring advance planning, continuing evaluation of economic developments and likely economic impacts, and political decision. As noted at the beginning of this chapter, the success of any program of maintaining demand will also be dependent on the success of parallel measures to deal with any structural problems such as regional or local concentration of defense activities, and industry and manpower specialization.

At every step there will be the problem of making choices, of striking the most appropriate balance as between numerous possible courses of action, each of which will have a different impact on the economy. Thus, either an increase in government expenditures for goods and services or a decrease in taxes increases aggregate demand and brings additional resources into employment. Either action has a multiplier effect which is greater than its initial impact. The initial expenditures--increased private consumption or investment in the case of a tax cut, increased school or road construction, for example, in the case of a rise in government outlays--create additional income which, in turn, is spent and re-spent. Thus either tax reduction or increased government spending indirectly stimulates almost all categories of private demand, and, in particular, private consumption. But the direct effect of a tax reduction is to employ resources for private consumption or investment, while the direct effect of government spending is to employ resources on production of public goods and services.

The proper balance between tax reduction and increased public civilian expenditures will involve an economic and political evaluation of the relative priorities of the goods and services which would be purchased by households and businesses if their incomes were greater--food, houses, automobiles, medical services, college education, machine tools--as against those of public goods--school construction, highways, resource conservation and development, public health, urban renewal. Similarly, the proper balance between reduced personal and excise taxes on the one hand and reduced profits taxes and a policy of easy money on the other will be governed, generally, by the relative importance accorded respectively to consumption and investment.

An element of uncertainty in a situation involving the systematic elimination of the current pattern of military expenditures over a period of time would be the precise reaction of private consumption, and of private investment in plant and equipment and inventories, to the decline in defense orders and to the compensating policies. What fraction of tax reductions on personal incomes would in fact go into consumption? What lags would be involved? How would inventories and investment develop in different industries? These are some of the imponderables to which the answers will not be readily available. However, the very fact that the timing, phasing and likely duration of a disarmament program would be known well in advance to policymakers places the whole problem of providing for adequate demand offsets on a considerably more certain and favorable basis than is normally available for the development of countercyclical policy. Utilization of this favorable circumstance by the Federal Government and, as appropriate, by State and local governments to prepare in advance the desirable offsetting measures in the fields of taxation, public expenditures, and monetary policy, would have a most beneficial effect on public confidence that the economic and social benefits of disarmament would be realized. This in itself would be a potent factor making for success in the adjustment process.

B. Overcoming Structural Problems

The Problem. Any considerable change in the composition of final demand is bound to require some degree of structural adjustment as regards both manpower and physical facilities, and it may entail geographic redistribution of production and related activities. Actually the economy is constantly experiencing structural changes as a result of technological developments, the introduction of new products

753

and services, population developments, and other factors. Taken together these changes over a period of time are substantial, and while it cannot be said that they have always proceeded with a minimum of hardship and waste, nevertheless it is clear that they have not prevented the attainment of substantial growth in the economy.

Disarmament could, and probably would, seriously add to the problems of structural adjustment. The likely quantitative effect of disarmament is difficult to predict with any precision at this time. Certainly the timing, phasing, and duration of a disarmament program would be important factors--the more gradual the process, the easier the required shift in resources to civilian demand. Another factor is the nature and composition of the civilian demand that will emerge as the financial burden of the national defense program is lifted; if it is such as to be readily satisfied to a large extent by the kinds of resources being released from the defense effort, the problem of adjustment will be minimal.

Although more information is required on the precise composition and distribution of resources now serving defense effort, directly and indirectly, and on the other factors noted above, it is evident that disarmament would require considerable adjustment, geographically, occupationally, and as regards actual production. As noted in Chapter I, one of the principal characteristics of the current defense effort is the relatively high concentration of its economic impact geographically and by industry. Moreover, a large share of defense work is in the hands of specialized defense contractors whose product and expertise may not be readily adaptable to production for a civilian market. After World War II many firms which had stressed military production during the conflict had little difficulty in reconverting. It is not clear whether the same easy shift would be possible under present conditions on as wide a scale.

Under the circumstances disarmament will require some shifting of manpower to new industries, occupations, and possibly even to new locations. Many plants will have to convert to new lines of production, and to the extent that such conversion on existing sites is not possible or desirable, relocations and in some cases liquidations may in order; also, it is to be expected that new industries will have to be encouraged to establish themselves in many areas where defense production is now concentrated.

These structural adjustments would be faced in the context of the sizeable increase in the labor force and in automation which is expected to develop over the coming years.

It will be desirable to bend every effort to reduce the friction in the process of adjustment to a minimum, in order to minimize hardship and waste, and as another means of maximizing the benefits of disarmament. There are several significant instruments and factors as well as a growing body of experience which will be helpful in this connection.

Area Redevelopment.   Increasing attention has been given by government, labor, and business to the problem of depressed areas which is directly relevant to the problem of adjusting to disarmament because of the heavy geographic concentration of the defense effort.   Thousands of local communities have over the years established development and promotional agencies to attract business, apart from the State development commissions in virtually every State. Many have organized development loan funds to buy land and erect buildings and to assist potential newcomers in other ways.   Increasing awareness of the need for coordinated action to meet specific local problems is evident.   Furthermore, in dealing with this problem, as with others, the initiative of American entrepreneurs in our free enterprise system is an invaluable asset.

Recognition that redevelopment of "depressed areas" which already exist in our country was a matter transcending local interest led to the adoption of the Federal Area Redevelopment Act under which the Federal Government seeks to assist local and State groups in the economic development of areas with high and persistent unemployment. In addition to the support of retraining programs which will be discussed below, this aid takes the form of technical assistance for planning economic redevelopment and Federal participation, if needed, in low-rate loans for land and buildings for industrial or commercial enterprises and for needed public facilities.   One of the principal achievements of this new legislation has been the encouragement of hundreds of communities to develop Overall Economic Development Plans.   These communities are thus better able to cope with any kind of economic adjustment that may be necessary--whether it be due to armament cutbacks, trade impacts, automation, depletion of natural resources, or other causes.

The deactivation of defense installations in the course of a disarmament program will create specific redevelopment situations, which will be of major proportions where the installations are the economic mainstay of particular communities.   It will no doubt be found that many of these facilities can be adapted to civilian uses in such fields as education, health, research, recreation and industry.   Such adaptation will benefit from adequate and coordinated advance planning by the local communities, the Federal Government, and other interested elements; it could make a real contribution not only to the life of the affected communities, but also in filling some of the over-all needs for plant and equipment which are discussed in Chapter III.

In this connection it is pertinent to note that since the beginning of 1961 the Federal Government has concerned itself specifically with the economic adjustment problems attendant upon the deactivation of defense installations-- whether in the so-called depressed areas or not--in con- nection with the changing requirements of our defense programs. Thus, there was established in the Department of Defense a high level position of Economic Adjustment Adviser whose responsibility it is to assist the affected local communities with adjustment measures. Subsequently the President directed the establishment of an inter-agency committee to advise the Secretary of Defense in this field and bring to bear the experience and instruments available in other parts of the Federal Government. The scope of these arrangements has since been expanded to include eco- nomic adjustment to shifts in defense programs.

Experience with area redevelopment to date suggests that solutions are not quick or easy and emphasizes the need for careful appraisal of potential difficulties and for advance planning, as well as coordinated and united action by all ele- ments involved. The practical lessons under the Area Redevelopment Act and the numerous other measures and programs having the same general objective will be invalu- able in dealing with such significant local or regional dis- locations as may be caused by disarmament.

Industrial conversion. In our free enterprise system the task of converting industrial production from defense to civilian uses will in the main rest on the affected firms, responding to the actual and anticipated demands in the market at home and abroad. Here, too, advance planning will go a long way in smoothing and expediting the adjust- ment process. The problems will not be basically different from those which continually arise in a changing economy. The increasing emphasis which many American firms place on careful analysis of trends and prospects not only in their own markets but in the economy generally, as a basis for their production programs, will be most helpful in meeting the conversion problem in the industrial sector. Many firms will no doubt find it profitable to accelerate their civilian activities in scientific and technical research and development, in some cases readily reallocating facilities and manpower now devoted by them to military work.

Policies and measures which the Federal Government will apply to the termination or cancellation of defense con- tracts under a progressive disarmament program could be designed with a view to facilitating the adjustment process in the affected firms. There is a considerable body of successful experience in this area in connection with the demobilization at the end of World War II.

The Federal Government could also aid the adjustment process by extending loans and technical assistance to those firms which have a particular need for such support. If the proposed Trade Expansion Act of 1962 is adopted, its provision for loans and technical assistance to businesses adversely affected by imports would provide valuable experience which would be relevant to adjustment problems in industry under disarmament.

Adaptability of American labor.   The mobility of the American labor force is one of the nation's assets in adjusting to economic change.   This is true whether the need for change arises out of the development of new industrial technology and shifts in civilian demand or whether it is induced by mobilization or disarmament.

Geographically there has been continuous movement from one area to another in the United States.   Many of these moves are to nearby areas, but others are long moves, between States.   The increase in population of the three Pacific Coast States from 1940 to 1960 is ample evidence of this shift.   California's population rose from 6.9 million to 15.7 million or 128 per cent; and Washington's from 1.7 million to 2.9 million or 64 per cent.

Many American workers also move into and out of the labor force by choice.   During the course of a single year, the size of the labor force varies by several million from the seasonal peak in the autumn to the low of employment in the late winter.   Most adult men over 25 and under 65, who are able to work are permanently attached to the labor force. However, millions of adult women, young people, and older people who have retired or can retire from work either do not work or seek work for part of the year.   During the course of the year 1960, for example, there were 4,800,000 more people in the labor force in June than in January.

There has also long been substantial movement of workers to higher levels of skill and responsibility, both in the nonagricultural and in the agricultural sector.

Although there are indications that willingness to move has diminished in recent years with the accumulation of a variety of financial assets attached to the community, such as more general homeownership and increased rights to pensions and other benefits associated with seniority in employment in a particular firm, there is still a great deal of shifting both geographically and, to a more limited extent occupationally.   Young people, in particular, are willing to make changes; and the more education they have, the more readily they move.

Analysis of the occupations of the people now engaged directly in the defense effort in the United States--in the armed services, the Federal civilian agencies engaged in national security activities, and the industries producing weapons and other defense material--indicates a relatively high proportion in the professions, and in the skilled occupations.   As a group, they are relatively well educated. Moreover, they are generally younger (the median age of male military personnel on active duty was 24.5 years in mid-1960), but still with some experience to count in their favor in finding a job. These characteristics of younger age, higher education, skill and training are assets in re-adjustment. They should offset to some extent the problems attendant on the high degree of specialization in much of today's defense effort.

The educational level of military personnel is higher than that of the general population. The Department of Defense has estimated that about two-thirds of the enlisted personnel and more than 99 per cent of the commissioned officers on active duty as of 1960 had a high school education or better. In contrast, only about 60 per cent of the new young workers entering the labor force in the 1950's had completed their high school education. A considerable number of the military personnel receive comprehensive vocational training while in the armed forces. Many enlisted men are trained for occupations for which there is a growing demand in the civilian economy, such as electronics main-tenance and repairmen, automotive and aircraft mechanics, construction craftsmen, medical and technical assistants, and draftsmen.

The occupational distribution of employees in defense-related governmental agencies indicates that a considerable number of personnel employed by these agencies is in white-collar occupations, for which the demand is increasing in our economy.

Of the estimated 2.6 million persons employed directly and indirectly in all private industries providing defense goods and services in 1960, it is estimated that over 380,000 were professional and technical workers. Another 545,000 were skilled craftsmen. (See Table.)* These proportions are very high relative to the national average, and employ-ment prospects in these occupational fields are expected to expand rapidly over the next decade. On the other hand, over 30 per cent were semi-skilled workers ("operative"), as compared to under 20 per cent for all nonagricultural employment. For this group unemployment rates have been higher than average. Clerical workers, for whom demand is quite good, are in about the same proportion in defense as in all industries, while service workers and laborers--with an even higher rate of unemployment--are relatively less numerous.

Opportunities for training and retraining. Opportuni-ties for training and retraining arise in a variety of ways and from a variety of sources, including industry, local institutions and State and Federal programs. In large part the initiative rests with private individuals and business firms. Individuals voluntarily learn new skills and increase their knowledge by a variety of means; attending school formally or going to special classes in off hours or the eve-ning, taking correspondence courses, learning the job.

---

*Table omitted.

Private industry has extensive on-the-job training and re-training programs. In fact, most training in the skilled crafts and in many technical occupations is effectively done on the job through apprenticeship and other forms of train-ing. The extent of training programs in industry and the number of people who benefit by them is not known, but some form of induction training is almost universal in large private enterprises, and many have extensive training programs for experienced workers. Thus, a large pro-portion of the persons now engaged in defense-related activi-ties could expect to be trained or retrained by their new employers.

It has long been a policy of the government of the United States to encourage and help support certain types of vo-cational education and occupational training. Important among these is the vocational education system in the public high schools largely financed by local and State educational authorities, with assistance from the Federal government. Once directed primarily to young people already in school attention has turned more recently to vocational training and and retraining of out-of-school youth and adults. In-creasingly this type of class has been used for training the unemployed. In fiscal year 1960, 43, 900 unemployed or underemployed adults and out-of-school youths enrolled in these short-term classes to prepare for entering into em-ployment in new occupational pursuits. Training programs were offered for 62 different occupations, including welding, machine operators, automotive repair, draftsmen, electrical workers and electronics technicians, nursing aides, beauty operators, and food trades workers.

In addition, several States have established their own special programs for retraining the adult unemployed. The State of Pennsylvania, for example, has had such a program for ten years. In 1960-61 it had over 20 local programs in operation teaching a variety of skills, with an enrollment of approximately 500 unemployed persons. The placement record of those enrolled has been particularly high--between 70 and 80 per cent.

The passage of the Area Redevelopment Act in 1961 established additional Federal aid for the training of unem-ployed workers in areas with long standing unemployment. The Act provided for financial assistance by the Federal government in qualified "redevelopment areas" in the pro-vision of educational facilities and services, and for benefits for up to 16 weeks at the level of State unemployment com-pensation to unemployed persons while retraining. The program under present financial limitations in the Act is relatively small, permitting training of less than 20, 000 persons per year.

A much broader program, embodied in the Manpower Development and Training Act of 1962, was adopted in

March 1962. It provides a nationwide opportunity for occupational training, with priority given to experienced unemployed persons who are heads of families. Training will also be given to employed persons to improve their skills.

This is a 3-year program, with total authorization of $435 million, many times larger than that in the Area Redevelopment Act. It should make possible the training of as many as a million people in 3 years. Its benefits are not confined to areas in which unemployment has been persistent, as is the Area Redevelopment Act, but are available to any area. The Act provides a program of Federal financial assistance for vocational education and on-the-job training, to be carried out primarily through the existing State vocational education agencies under the general supervision of the Department of Health, Education and Welfare. Training allowances roughly equal to unemployment compensation in each State may be paid to persons in training, for a period of up to 52 weeks. Many courses in skilled and technical occupations can now be provided because of the longer duration of available retraining allowances.

Special provision is made for training of unemployed persons 19-21 years old. The Act also provides for an annual Manpower Report by the Secretary of Labor to the Congress on skill requirements, occupational outlook, job opportunities, labor supply in various skills, and employment trends.

Enactment of the proposed Trade Expansion Act of 1962 would be of further relevance in this context. In addition to the possibility of assistance to industries adversely affected by imports it also foresees the institution, where appropriate, of worker training programs after vocational counselling and testing.

Also before the Congress in 1962 is the Youth Employment Opportunities Bill, which should provide work experience and further occupational training for a limited number of out-of-school youth through a Youth Conservation Corps to work on Federal conservation and recreational facilities, through employment on local public works programs, combined with further education, and through on-the-job training,

Since these measures are directed toward the relief of localized problems of unemployment, they should greatly strengthen the capabilities of the United States to help members of the civilian work force presently engaged in defense-related work to equip themselves for new jobs in the event of disarmament.

At the close of World War II and again at the close of the Korean War the Government undertook massive programs for the education, training and job placement of men and women discharged from the Armed Services. These programs, for which approximately $20 billion was spent, were exceedingly effective not only in restoring millions of individuals fairly promptly to a useful role in the economy of the country but also in providing extensive educational and technical training.

Among the veterans of World War II, 7.8 million had entered training under Public Law 346 through June 1955. Of these 28 per cent attended colleges and universities, 45 per cent schools below college level and approximately 18 per cent engaged in on-the-job training. Following the Korean War more than 2 million Korean veterans--about one-third of those eligible--had entered training under Public Law 550 by June 1958. It is anticipated that before this program is concluded about half of those eligible will have taken advantage of these training opportunities as in the case of World War II veterans.

Both of these programs were on a very large scale, dealing with millions of men--far more than are at present in the armed services. Both were effective. Both have been appraised, and recommendations for their improvement have been made. Experience in their administration provides a basis for planning similar programs to meet future needs.

Other means of easing the adjustment process in the labor force. Programs of training and retraining would need to be complemented by a nationwide system for collecting information on employment opportunities and available manpower to facilitate the matching of men with jobs. Extended unemployment compensation for workers released by defense industries and for veterans, and relocation grants or loans to help workers move to areas where the employment opportunities are greatest are other possibilities. Here, again, the proposed Trade Expansion Act of 1962, with its provision for financing reasonable costs of relocating families in cases where the head of the household is made unemployed by imports and has a definite job offer elsewhere, could provide valuable practical experience in dealing with disarmament adjustment problems.

The special case of research and development. Employment of scientists and engineers is growing at a faster rate than employment of almost any other occupational group. In recent years non-military R&D has grown rapidly and in all likelihood would have grown even faster had more resources been available. The release of scientists and engineers by defense industries should facilitate an acceleration of civilian R&D. Such an increase in R&D manpower could be used with great benefit to society and yield high returns in many industries where presently very little R&D is directed toward improving products or processes. The civilian economy would benefit especially from increased long-range research and experimentation with advanced technological possibilities of the sort that the research teams presently employed by defense industries have conducted so successfully.

It is, however, impossible to predict how much private research support would increase in the event of disarmament. Certainly the increase would be substantial. It is likely, however, that in order to absorb the released R&D resources smoothly and to help guide them to the highest priority uses a positive government program would be required. It could operate with effectiveness in matching personnel becoming available with employment opportunities. A particular problem--possibly more severe than would be encountered in other occupations--might arise in switching scientists and engineers who have spent their careers in one field to other new specializations, and appropriate government assistance to facilitate the adjustment might be in order and yield large benefits.

A disarmament program would provide an unmatched opportunity to review public policies toward non-military R&D. There are in fact urgent needs for more research and development in areas where private incentives and financial capabilities are inadequate or non-existent. Some of the R&D resources freed by disarmament would no doubt be transferred to more substantial civilian atomic energy and space programs. But there are also urgent needs or desirable goals for research and development in such fields as urban transportation, housing, health, education, and exploration and exploitation of the ocean resources.

Released R&D resources could also be used to great advantage to complement as expanded foreign aid program. Efforts here might well focus on such problems as the development of simple teaching machines and related communications equipment, techniques for overcoming aridity, efficient and low cost transportation systems, cheap and reliable power sources, and other equipment and processes specially tailored to the resources and labor availabilities of the less developed countries. Research and engineering personnel released by disarmament might serve as technical consultants on development and planning and in helping to establish new industries on a sound technical basis.

The freeing of R&D resources could be one of the most important economic benefits of disarmament. But here, as in other aspects, advanced planning and coordinated action will minimize the transitional problems and make it possible to profit more extensively from the large opportunities which disarmament affords.

III. Disarmament and Domestic Needs

The United States enjoys at this time a high level of economic well being which is unprecedented and unparalleled, and the fruits of American prosperity are widely shared. This is the product of an economic system which has been the foundation of our political and social democracy.

Yet, our very accomplishments in developing a high standard of living, in providing higher levels of education for a larger proportion of the population than has been achieved by any other country, in equipping our nation with vast, complex and technologically advanced transportation and communications systems and production and service facilities, call to our attention the economic, social, and cultural needs which remain unmet; for in the United States there are still pockets of poverty and inequity, and the nation as a whole has not fully realized the potential inherent in our society and available national resources. It is also clear that the sizeable increase which our population is undergoing is providing progressively larger dimensions for our domestic civilian needs.

A significant part of the economic and social "shortfall" in the United States is, as pointed out in Chapter I, due to the substantial requirements for national defense. As these demands are progressively eliminated by an adequate and effective disarmament agreement we can look for more rapid progress towards the economic and social goals which Americans set for themselves individually and collectively. However, even general and complete disarmament could not provide more than a part of the resources that would be needed to satisfy our unmet civilian needs--these needs are far greater than the defense effort. The basic problem for the United States in the event of disarmament is not one of an excess of human and physical resources but of how we can most quickly and efficiently shift the released resources to serving our numerous and extensive civilian require-ments. Even without disarmament we will cope more ade-quately with many of these civilian needs, but it is clear that progress could be much faster, if the resources now devoted to defense could be freed for such uses as are dis-cussed below.

It is impossible to predict with any certainty how the American people will in fact employ the resources which would be released by general and complete disarmament. In a free society such as ours the individual values and preferences of each member will have a vital impact both on his own decisions and actions and on the decisions of his representatives in government on such matters as taxation and public expenditures which have been referred to in Chapter II. The following discussion of some of the areas of civilian needs which are apparent today is intended to be illustrative of the opportunities which disarmament would present or enhance. It cannot be exhaustive, nor can it in any way prejudge the choices and decisions regarding these and other areas of potential expenditure which will eventually be made by the American people and their elected govern-ments.

Both individual and collective needs can be met by private or by governmental activity. In the United States the pattern which has been evolving through history includes a very large reliance on private initiative and a growing role for public programs; in some matters there is a close combination of the two. The discussion that follows is concerned primarily with suggesting the dimensions of certain needs which are of broad significance; the methods of satisfying them, whether by private effort, governmental programs, or a combination of the two, are incidental to this purpose.

Growth in Population and National Product

The Bureau of the Census projects an increase in the population of the United States from 180.6 million in 1960 to 244 million by 1980 and to 329 million by the year 2000. Concurrent increases in total available manpower will facilitate the growth in Gross National Product which is essential to our well-being. Thus, during the 1960's the American labor force is expected to increase at roughly half again its rate of growth during the 1950's, a reflection of the sharp increase in the birth rate which occurred during the middle and later 1940's. The economy will require progressively higher levels of education and skills in the working population; some of the implication of this trend are discussed under the heading of educational needs below. It is also clear that new capital equipment will be required to complement the expanding labor force. Just to keep pace with the rate of increase in manpower will require capital investment of at least 7 per cent of GNP; if capital stock per employed persons is to grow at a pace sufficient to permit productivity increases at the rate achieved during the 1950's investment will have to be significantly higher than the 8.6 per cent of GNP used in this way in recent years.

The special requirements and opportunities for civilian research and development have already been touched upon in Chapter II. If satisfied, they also would require significant investment in plant and equipment.

[Omitted here are projections which were made for the following civilian needs between 1970 and 1980: residential construction; urban needs: urban growth, urban renewal and future metropolitan development, urban mass transit, urban water and sewage disposal facilities, and other community facilities; the natural resources field: water resources development, other renewable resources (forestry, soil and watershed conservation, range land conservation, park and recreational conservation, fish and wildlife conservation). These projections are based on technical economic models. Those persons seriously interested in this topic would have to evaluate the sufficiency of the models.]

In identifying educational n e e d s, 1970 is only the day after tomorrow; all of the children who will then be enrolled in the f o u r t h grade or higher have already been born, and those who will then be above the sixth grade are already in earlier stages of the educational process.

Minimum needs.   A t r e n d projection for 1970 indicates that the number of s t u d e n t s in elementary and high school grades will rise from 42.5 m i l l i o n in 1960 to 53.0 million in 1970 and the number of students in institutions of higher learning will double to reach about 7 million.   This assumes no change in the causal factors which determined attendance rates in the 1950's and no educational improvements as r e g a r d s dropouts, staff-pupil ratio or kindergarten enrollment.

Assuming present levels of the teaching art and t e c h nology and also present composition of educational c o s t s, school enrollments in kindergarten through 12th g r a d e b y 1970 will require an annual expenditure of about 50 per cent more than the 1960-61 expenditures which are e s t i m a t e d at about $20 billion.   This estimate i n c l u d e s a major increase in investment for additional capital f a c i l i t i e s, increased expenditures for the training and employment of additional teachers, and an increase in salaries of a b o u t   40 per cent over 1957-58 levels in order to c o m p e t e f o r the required number of teachers in the r a n k s o f intellectually able.   Public and private school operating and capital costs are assumed to be essentially identical for this purpose.

To accommodate the number of students anticipated in institutions of higher learning which give degrees, with no change in present staff-student instructional and residential space ratios, would r e q u i r e total annual expenditures by 1970 of more than 2 1/2 times present estimated expenditures of $6.7 billion.   This, again, allows f o r major increases in annual outlay for capital facilities, and includes a salary increase of 50 per cent over 1957-58 levels, without which it would not be possible to compete for the necessary additional staff.   Here, too, it is assumed that there are no cost differentials between public and private institutions .

Improvement beyond trend projections.   The foregoing projections constitute pressing minimum educational needs for 1970 which will presumably be met whether there is disarmament by then or not.   However, the s o c i e t y and the economy of the 1970's will actually make greater demands on education.

The accelerating r a t e of technological innovation and additions to knowledge in various fields will call for more extended study by more people.   Evolving social values and educational thinking will place new emphasis on programs for students with both higher and lower levels of talent, on the reduction of dropouts of the less talented and provision for a significantly higher proportion of the more talented to obtain the benefits of higher education. Furthermore, the labor market will increasingly favor those who offer better educational and training qualifications. Most important however, would be the major changes that would transpire if the deliberate decision were made, in response to these and other factors to invest heavily in education and to devise the new kinds of education called for by the needs and the capacities of those portions of the population not now considered as part of the post-secondary school clientele, and by the rising demands for highly skilled and educated people that could be expected in the economy and society of 1970.

Translation of these factors into estimates of educational needs at the elementary school level would involve an extension of kindergarten opportunity to one million more 5 year olds. At the secondary level it would call for the retention of about 400,000 students who would otherwise fail to complete the 12th grade. Retention of this group would be beneficial not only from the educational point of view but also in terms of social welfare; it will require that schools develop special programs adapted to the needs of significant numbers in this group who, for various reasons, do not readily fit into standard ecucational programs. Dealing with pupil exceptionality, whether at higher or lower ends of the endowment scale, means smaller classes, more, and more varied, equipment and teaching materials, and better trained teachers with increased back-up in the way of psychological and psychiatric services, and other resources.

General application to elementary and secondary schools of such qualitative improvements as the lowering of staff-pupil and classroom-pupil ratios would, in conjunction with enrollment increases indicated above, require massive investments in capital facilities, perhaps almost doubling capital outlays and increasing annual operating costs by one-third above those indicated for the estimates of minimum needs.

There will also be a strong case for a sharp increase over trend estimates for minimum needs in expenditures for post-high school education. It is likely that the demand for education at the college and university levels will tend to increase at a rate greater than the rate of increase in the 1950's. The need for post-doctoral study and mid-career updating in the learned professional fields will also increase at greater than trend rate.

With decreasing demand for the semiskilled in an increasingly automated technology, older forms of vocational education are likely to be absorbed in a variety of more educationally extensive, non-degree, liberal and vocational, post-high school programs of from six months to three years' duration. Such programs would train sub-professional

766

technologists and those entering sub-professional and personal service occupations. They would serve not only the high school leavers, but also those already in the work force who are in need of additional skills and insights required for transfer or upgrading in relation to individual development and technological change. It is likely that within a few years the post-high school category will constitute a major educational challenge. The Panel of Consultants on vocational education, which was appointed at the request of the President, is now undertaking an intensive study of this area. It will make recommendations on the content and institutional framework which will be required for vocational educational institutions under the changing technological and socio-economic conditions of the future.

Health Services

In 1959-60, the U.S. devoted 5.4 per cent of GNP, or $26.5 billion, to public health, personal health services, construction of medical facilities, and medical research. The level of use of medical facilities and health personnel obviously reflects a high degree of effective demand. But significant groups in the population, particularly among the aged, in rural areas, and in low income groups generally, receive less than optimum medical care and would use additional medical services were they able to obtain them. There are also significant regional differences in the level of use of medical services.

Progress towards a more completely available high level of medical care in the United States calls for a concerted attack on many fronts. It will depend on a larger supply of health personnel, a greater investment in health facilities, achievement of a greater degree of coordination among health services, and generation of more purchasing power through improved systems of financing personal health services.

The material that follows is illustrative of significant expansions which would be desirable in this field.

Health personnel. Basic to any expansion in health services is the availability of an adequate supply of well-trained health personnel.

In 1960 there were some 250,000 physicians in the United States, a ratio of 140 physicians per 100,000 population. The present rate of graduation of physicians is such that the supply of physicians in the coming years will fall short of maintaining even the present ratio. Even the current supply of physicians does not meet the present needs of medical care in mental and other long-term hospitals.

In 1960 there were about 102,300 dentists in the United States, or 56 dentists per 100,000 population, a ratio which has been declining steadily since 1940. Although at currently projected levels of graduation of students from existing and planned schools the total number of dentists will grow to 112,800 in 1970, the ratio of dentists to population will continue to decline, falling to 53 per 100,000 persons.

In order even to maintain the existing ratios of physicians and dentists to the population, it is estimated that by 1970 it will be necessary not only to strengthen and expand existing medical and dental schools but to establish, equip and staff 20 to 24 new medical schools and 20 new dental schools. The cost of building these teaching facilities is estimated at $1 billion at present prices.

Health facilities. At present, the United States has 7.7 acceptable hospital beds of all types per 1,000 persons in the population. Merely to maintain the same ratio as population expands will require the provision of more than 23,000 additional hospital beds each year throughout the next decade.

Beyond this, there is a need to increase present ratios and to replace obsolete plant and equipment. Scientific and technological changes have created new services and new methods of therapy requiring costly changes in physical plant. Much renovation and modernization is needed in order to adapt older hospital facilities to their changing functions and to modern practice.

Increasing urbanization and the growth of the suburbs will require new construction and metropolitan planning for hospital and medical facilities. In addition there is a need for many new types of community facilities. The development of nursing homes providing skilled nursing care outside of a hospital setting is a relatively recent phenomenon. An increase in these and other facilities for chronic care is needed today and will be increasingly important as the proportion of aged persons in the population rises.

In the field of mental health a variety of community resources needs to be developed to reduce the need for institutionalization. Such resources include mental health centers and psychiatric treatment units in the larger community general hospitals and the development of organized home care programs.

It is estimated that in order to increase slightly the number of hospital beds per person, to replace obsolete hospital plants (defined as more than 50 years old), to carry out the most necessary renovation and modernization, and to construct additional outpatient care facilities at the same general rate of net gain achieved in the past decade for public health centers and diagnostic and treatment centers, but with an increase in rehabilitation facilities, would require that the expenditure over the next decade be at least $6 billion higher than the present level of $9 billion.

Community health services. Public health services traditionally provided in the U.S. have included services

768

related to communicable diseases and to maternal and child health and special services for crippled children. The programs of modern health departments include also services necessary to prevent or control chronic diseases and to improve the medical care of the entire community. However, one-fifth of the counties in the United States, with 6 per cent of the total population, still have no organized, local, tax-supported health service. Many areas have services which are only fragmentary because of limitations in staff and financial resources.

It has been estimated that an expenditure of at least $4 per capita is required for the provision of a minimum level of adequate public health services by official State and local health agencies. To attain this level of expenditure would require an increase in annual expenditures of $383 million (about 90 per cent more than the current expenditures of State and local health departments).

Environmental health. Recognized as a problem largely since World War II, air pollution control will require an intensified program of biological and engineering research to identify and measure harmful contaminants and determine their effects. At present the total national expenditure for air pollution control is about $300-400 million per year. It is estimated that by 1970 the total expenditures should more than double.

The needs and opportunities as regards adequate water supplies and pollution control have already been noted. With more people, more industry, more processing, and more waste, the problem of solid waste disposal is becoming more critical. Current total national expenditures for urban solid waste collection and disposal are approximately $2 billion annually. This rate will have to be raised by about 50 per cent to correct present unsatisfactory practices and to meet increasing needs.

Medical research. The reports of two expert groups[*] suggest that on the basis of capacity, long-range trends in support of research and other relevant factors, a national health research program of $3.0 billion in 1970 is feasible. If research facilities and personnel now devoted to defense-

---

[*]Secretary's Consultants on Medical Research and Education. The Advancement of Medical Research and Education Through the Department of Health, Education, and Welfare. Washington, D.C., Government Printing Office, 1958.

Committee of Consultants on Medical Research to the Subcommittee on Departments of Labor and Health, Education and Welfare of the Senate Appropriations Committee. Federal Support of Medical Research. Washington, D.C., Government Printing Office, 1960.

related r e s e a r c h activities were to become available as a result of disarmament, it would be possible to step up research in the f i e l d of health and medical care much more rapidly than would otherwise be possible.

Social Security and Social Welfare

Income maintenance programs.   The United States has, today, an extensive s y s t e m of public income maintenance m e a s u r e s.   Public income maintenance payments under social insurance, v e t e r a n s; and public assistance programs in 1960 amounted to $27 billion, or 5. 3 per cent of GNP and 7.6 per cent of total disposable personal income.

Aggregate benefit payments under these programs have been rising as a per cent of the total national output, largely as a result of the expanding coverage and gradual maturing of the Old Age, Survivors and Disability Insurance (OASDI) system.   This trend will continue, though at a slower pace, for some time without any changes in existing laws.

Important a n d extensive as are t h e social insurance protections now available, both the coverage and the level of b e n e f i t s in many of the programs are less adequate than would be desirable.   The g e n e r a l magnitude of desirable improvement in the expenditures involved can be illustrated by reference to some of the major programs.

Old-Age, Survivors, and Disability Insurance.   The national old-age, s u r v i v o r s, and d i s a b i l i t y insurance program now c o v e r s about 90 per cent of the active labor force.   The number of beneficiaries will continue to increase f a i r l y rapidly over the next few decades as an increasing proportion of those reaching retirement age have insured status.

Since 1950 the Congress has increased benefits under this program almost every two years.   The changes since 1940, when benefits first began, have been more than sufficient to match i n c r e a s e s in the general price level.   They have been less than a third as large as increases in general wage levels during the period.   If defense needs should continue to require tax revenues of the order of magnitude now prevailing, one might a n t i c i p a t e a similar trend in the future.   In the event of disarmament, however, the Nation may well decide that the aged, the disabled, and widows and children should share more nearly equally in the increasing output of the economy.   It has been estimated that if the law were amended to increase benefit outlays in relation to increases in productivity, aggregate benefit payments in 1970 (in constant dollars) w o u l d be more than double the 1960 figure of $11. 2 billion; without such a c h a n g e it would be 60 per cent greater.

Private pension plans.   In 1960 private pension plans paid about $1. 7 billion in p e n s i o n s for retired workers. These payments also will increase in the future as more of the workers covered by relatively new plans retire. Very few private plans at present attempt to adjust benefits to changing price or wage levels. Furthermore, many of the workers now under private pension plans will not actually stay with the same employer long enough to acquire pension rights. Additional resources might well be directed toward the improvement of private pension benefits.

Cash sickness benefits. At present railroad workers and employees in four States are covered by compulsory cash sickness insurance programs usually providing benefits of 26 weeks duration. In addition a considerable number of workers have some protection against wage loss in case of temporary illness through private employee benefit plans.

A nationwide system of sickness insurance covering all wage and salary workers in private industry and providing benefits equal to two-thirds of weekly wage loss after a one-week waiting period would increase the amount of benefits into dollars, this increase would have resulted in benefits paid by at least 2 1/2 times over present levels. Translated into dollars, this increase would have resulted in benefits of $2.2 billion in 1960, instead of the $0.8 billion actually paid under public and private plans. Population increases and increases in real wage levels would bring the dollar amounts for similar protection in 1970 to a figure more than 50 per cent higher in 1960 prices.

Workmen's compensation. Total payments for wage loss and medical benefits under State and Federal workmen's compensation laws in 1960 were the equivalent of 60 cents for every $100 of covered payroll.

These benefits reflect current laws which have incomplete coverage, medical care limited in duration and amount in many States, and cash benefits that probably replace less than two-fifths of the wage loss in the average temporary disability case and an even smaller proportion in fatalities or permanent injuries.

If current laws were amended to provide (1) unlimited medical care, (2) cash benefits for all days lost because of temporary or permanent disability (after a one-week waiting period) at a rate of 2/3 of average fulltime wages, and (3) survivors benefits to widows for life and to children to age 18, it is estimated that benefit payments and premium costs would increase by more than 50 per cent. Such an increase would have resulted in benefits of $2 billion in 1960 instead of $1.3 billion.

Public assistance. In any society, no matter how extensive its social insurance program or other social measures, there will be some persons who are currently unable to meet from their own income and resources all of their basic living requirements. In the United States there are several public assistance programs designed to provide a minimum income to needy individuals and families.

An expanding economy will reduce to some extent the need for public assistance but there will presumably always remain older persons, marginal workers, broken families, and individuals with special needs who do not have the current income necessary for a socially acceptable level of living.

It is impossible to estimate with any degree of precision how many people in the United States are likely to need public assistance a decade from now. This will depend in considerable part on how need is then defined and on the extent to which the contribution of OASDI and other programs to meet the need may have been enlarged. Currently some seven million persons are receiving public assistance. Assuming that, concurrent with the population increase, the standards of assistance will be raised as they have been in the past when general levels of living move upward, it could reasonably be expected that seven million persons might also receive assistance in 1970.

A 1958 study, Unmet Needs in Public Assistance,* which measured assistance payments against a standard which provided only twice the amount needed for a low cost food budget, a not very high standard, found that assistance expenditures for old age recipients then on the rolls would have to increase by six per cent, and for dependent children by 72 per cent. Extending such estimates to other categories of assistance, this analysis implies that an additional $1 billion could be spent today for public assistance, excluding the costs of medical care, to assure reasonable levels of living for dependent groups throughout the nation.

No ready basis exists for estimating the total amounts of medical care required by assistance recipients. Such care, however, is an important item of need among recipients of public aid, whose poverty results in health neglect that both causes and aggravates illness and disabilities. An estimate is available of the increase in expenditures for medical care under old-age assistance and aid to dependent children that would have occurred in 1958 if all States had provided care similar in scope and cost to the care provided through these programs in the 24 State with costs above the national median. The annual increase would have amounted to $322 million or almost 120 per cent. Taking into account the other assistance programs, including the program of medical assistance for the aged, total medical care expenditures through public assistance may need to undergo further substantial expansion. What amounts of medical care should be provided through public assistance will depend on the extent to which other public programs are available.

Social services. Community services in the U.S. have developed in a number of ways and been organized

---

*Social Security Bulletin, April 1960, pp. 3-11.

through both public and private agencies. The schools provide guidance and placement in addition to direct educational services. In many communities the public school is a center for a variety of recreational, cultural and civic activities for young people and adults. The health agencies have increasingly been concerned with the availability of homemaker services, skilled nursing homes and other chronic care institutions, and with mental health programs. The public welfare agencies provide casework and supportive services not only to public assistance families but increasingly to persons who are not in economic need. Child welfare services, in particular, are generally provided without regard to economic need. Private social agencies are active in the fields of child care and family counseling services. The courts, particularly those dealing with children, are increasingly developing social services to help rehabilitate those who come within their jurisdiction. Community centers and special services are increasingly being developed in connection with public housing and urban renewal projects. Vocational rehabilitation agencies provide both medical and occupational guidance and training services. The U.S. has a wide network of employment services, and much attention is being given to their further development.

It is not possible to estimate either the total current expenditures on community and social services or the additional amounts that might be so used, but that a substantial expansion of many of these services is needed to meet the needs of a complex and growing urban economy is clear. Such expansion would require both increased expenditures of money and large increases in trained manpower.

A few illustrative figures can indicate some of the potentialities. At present, about half of the counties in the U.S. lack the services of a public child welfare worker. Public expenditures for child welfare services amounted in 1950 to $211 million of which almost $150 million was used to pay for foster care for children removed from their own families. If such services were to be extended to all counties and to more of the children in need of them, total expenditures might more than double by 1970, with perhaps $250 million going for foster care and $200 million for counseling, adoptive, protective and other services.

Caseloads in many public assistance agencies today are too large to allow time and attention for services that might help families to become self-supporting or able better to handle their own affairs. An expansion of the counseling services provided to a limited number of families not in financial need might require expenditures of approximately as much again as the $345 million presently spent for administration of public assistance.

Adequate day care services for children would require public expenditures of possibly $60 million or about 12 times the amounts spent for this purpose at present. If home-maker services were available throughout the Nation in the same ratio to population as now prevails in certain European countries, expenditures for such services would be at least $40 million, almost ten times what they are today.

The number of persons needing rehabilitation services to enable them to lead active productive lives is growing as the population increases and as an increasing number of our people live longer. The number of persons disabled annually who need vocational rehabilitation services in order to work is estimated at 275,000, and this number can be expected to increase. We are rehabilitating vocationally today about 100,000 disabled people. With greater resources we could meet substantially more of the present and future needs for rehabilitation. Among other things, the training of professional personnel and research could be stepped up.

We shall undoubtedly spend increasing amounts for social services in any event but the needed expansion will be greatly expedited if additional resources become available as a result of disarmament.

Social research. In order to solve or mitigate the problems resulting from rapid social and economic change and to direct social policy more effectively towards our general welfare objectives, we need to step up both the scope and intensity of social research. A relatively small proportion of the total research expenditures of the Federal Government or of the academic institutions of the country goes for social research as compared with research in the natural sciences and in medicine. The amounts available for support of the social sciences and for research and demonstration projects in the social field have, however, increased in recent years.

There is a serious lack of trained research workers in the social sciences and in social research generally. The increasing availability of funds for social research should help somewhat to encourage more competent people to enter these fields. The trend toward greater encouragement and support of social research could be speeded up by the proper direction of the research funds, facilities and potential that would be released by disarmament.

* * * * * * * *

Most of the above examples of domestic civilian needs to which the savings achieved under disarmament might be applied would call for increased allocation of public funds. Many of them would, however, also require substantial private expenditure. Quite generally it is, in fact, to be anticipated that increased private consumption and investment would employ a substantial portion of the resources which will be released by disarmament.

It should also be observed that while disarmament could contribute significantly to progress in the satisfaction of the civilian needs outlined in this Chapter, the effect on aggregate demand and on employment, of new or larger expenditures to meet these needs will differ from case to case. These differences in economic effect will, of course, have a bearing on the choice of measures which must be adopted to offset the decline in defense demand discussed in Chapter II.

IV.   Disarmament and External Aid

The historical record of U.S. external aid.   The United States has a long tradition of constructive leadership in rendering assistance to other nations.   Our aid has flowed through a variety of channels, governmental and private.   The U.S. Government has not waited for disarmament to undertake or to increase its economic aid to other peoples on a scale which has not been equalled by any other country.

The most recent public statement of the government's policy, contained in President Kennedy's address to the General Assembly of the United Nations on September 25, 1961, reflects the very broad framework in which our official aid programs and policies are conceived and expressed:

"... Political sovereignty is but a mockery, without the means of meeting poverty, illiteracy and disease.   Self-determination is but a slogan if the future holds no hope.

"That is why my nation--which has freely shared its capital and its technology to help others help themselves--now proposed officially designating this decade of the 1960's as the United Nations Decade of Development.   Under the framework of that resolution, the United Nations' existing efforts in promoting economic growth can be expanded and coordinated."

The President's proposal was accepted by the General Assembly of the United Nations on December 19, 1961 when it adopted the United Nations Decade of Development Resolution setting forth a program of international economic cooperation.

The roots of American external aid are to be found first of all in numerous private efforts in various parts of the globe beginning in the 19th century.   The government itself began broad programs of assistance in 1940 under the impact of wartime military and civilian needs in many foreign areas where military aggression was threatening the freedom of nations.   During the war years 1941-1945 the government devoted more than $51 billion to aid to other countries including $49 billion in the form of lend-lease; repayment on such aid was limited to a fraction of the original assistance.

Since World War II the United States has made available around $62 billion in loans and grants in every continent on the globe. At first largely directed toward post-war recovery and rehabilitation in Europe and elsewhere, assistance is now largely geared to economic development plans. Of the total of $62 billion, approximately $13 billion were grants of agricultural foodstuffs and other relief supplies, $13 billion Marshall Plan aid, and $18 billion Mutual Security support for economic stability, developmental projects, and technical aid. Over a billion dollars has been contributed to the United Nations and other international organizations.

U.S. Foreign Assistance - Fiscal Years 1946 - 1961

(Billions of Dollars)

A. By Purpose

	Amount
Total	$62[1]
Relief (Including PL 480, Titles II & III)	12
Marshall Plan	13
Other Mutual Security Programs	18
Export-Import Bank Long-term Loans	7
British Loan (1947)	4
PL 480 (Title I) Local Currency Sales	4
Surplus Property Credits	2
Contributions to International Organizations	1
Other	1

B. By Region and Period

	1946-48	1949-53	1954-61
Europe and Japan	12	16	4
Other	3	6	21

---

[1]In addition, the U.S. has invested almost $11 billion in capital of the International Bank for Reconstruction and Development (IBRD), International Monetary Fund (IMF), International Development Association (IDA), and Inter-American Development Bank (IDB).

[An historical review of United States economic and military aid programs during each of the post-war years has been omitted here, as has a discussion of U.S. indirect economic assistance through United Nations agencies.]

New perspective.   Past experience has helped to shape our present concepts and programs in the field of external aid and given us a new perspective for the future. It is clear that U.S. and other external aid can be truly effective only as it goes hand in hand with other measures, measures of international cooperation and coordination, measures in the recipient countries to create the most favorable conditions for effectiveness of external assistance programs, measures to promote constantly expanding and healthy international trade and investment for development.   These concepts are reflected in President Kennedy's Special Message on Foreign Aid which he sent to the Congress on March 22, 1961:

"In short we have not only obligations to fulfill, we have great opportunities to realize.   We are, I am convinced, on the threshold of a truly united and major effort by the free industrialized nations to assist the less-developed nations on a long-term basis.   Many of these less-developed nations are on the threshold of achieving sufficient economic, social and political strength and self-sustained growth to stand permanently on their feet.   The 1960's can be --and must be--the crucial 'Decade of Development' --the period when many less-developed nations make the transition into self-sustained growth--the period in which an enlarged community of free, stable and self-reliant nations can reduce world tensions and insecurity.   This goal is in our grasp if, and only if, the other industrialized nations join us in developing with the recipients a set of commonly agreed criteria, a set of long-range goals and a common undertaking to meet these goals, in which each nation's contribution is related to the contributions of others and to the precise needs of each less-developed nation.   Our job, in its largest sense, is to create a new partnership between the northern and southern halves of the world, to which all free nations can contribute, in which each free nation must assume a responsibility proportional to its means."

And in the Preamble of the new U.S. foreign aid law enacted by Congress:

"Assistance shall be based upon sound plans and programs; be directed toward the social as well as economic aspects of economic development; be responsive to the efforts of the recipient countries to mobilize their own resources and help themselves; be cognizant of the external and internal pressures which hamper their growth; and should emphasize long-range development assistance as the primary instrument of such growth."

777

These ideas also underlie the decisions of the American nations meeting in Bogota and Punta del Este in 1961 in connection with the development of the Alliance for Progress Specifically, the inter-American program for social and economic development deals with improvement of conditions of rural living and land use, including farm credits and land tenure institutions; the improvement of educational systems and training facilities; the improvement of public health; the strengthening of democratic institutions; the establishment of greater social justice; the reform of tax laws and tax administration; the mobilization of their own financial resources; sound monetary policies, and continental economic integration.

Thus, economic aid and development is a many-sided problem which cannot be solved simply by mathematical estimates of foreign capital requirements. The dimensions are considerably larger and require a broad range of internal and external approaches.

Improving the ability of the less-developed countries to utilize their own resources, to plan competently for the systematic growth of their economies, and to absorb and utilize external resources to the best advantage at varying stages of development, as well as the development of suitable trading patterns and practices to support the nation's development plan, are of much more significance over the long term.

Increasing the use of multilateral institutions. It is commonplace to hear the suggestion that the U.S. should channel more of its assistance through UN agencies. What is frequently overlooked by those making this suggestion is that the ability of the U.S. to increase its utilization of UN agencies is limited by the recognition, both within the U.S. and among other member nations, of the wisdom of restricting the U.S. contribution so that it does not exceed a reasonable proportion of the total. The basic fact, therefore, is that the ability and willingness of other nations to channel more of their foreign aid contributions through such UN agencies provides the primary and operative limit upon what the U.S. is able to do through such agencies.

Several courses of action are open to the world community. The first and most obvious course of action is for other nations to put a greater share of their own resources at the disposal of the UN for these purposes. The U.S. would be happy to increase its contribution to UN aid activities as other countries increase theirs.

A second course would be to increase the amount of bilateral or multilateral assistance from all potential donors extended under the "umbrella" of the UN, as of other multilateral groups, for sound plans and projects drawn up under international auspices.

While the U.S. takes no position at present on specific

proposals which may be made in the event of disarmament, consideration might also be given to other possible courses of action, such as creating for the UN some independent continuing source of funds for its use.

By whichever route the role of the UN and the specialized agencies in development is enhanced, it is likely that increasing the total volume of UN activity may have a beneficial effect beyond the monetary amounts, for through the UN improvements in societies may be achieved which otherwise might not be possible.

As noted above, the U.S. found it necessary and desirable from time to time to join in other multilateral groupings, regional or otherwise, to help accomplish its objectives of effective support to development. That the various types of institutions can be fitted together for the common goal of development is proven by the cooperative relationships now being developed among UN, regional, and national institutions in this area.

As the volume of aid activity rise, we foresee an increasingly urgent need for development of more integrated and better coordinated organizational and financial machinery for handling and expediting the flow of international aid among the nations of the world. The U.S. does not perceive a need for new UN institutions in this field.

Resources to be released by disarmament. On numerour occasions the United States government has taken the position that the achievement of disarmament would present opportunities for enlarged assistance to less-developed countries.

Thus, on October 24, 1950, speaking to the General Assembly of the United Nations, President Truman said:

"If real disarmament were achieved, the nations of the world, acting through the United Nations, could join in a greatly enlarged programme of mutual aid. As the cost of maintaining armaments decreased, every nation could greatly increase its contributions to advancing human welfare. All of us could then pool even greater resources to support the United Nations in its war against want.

"In this way, our armaments would be transformed into food, medicine, tools for use in under-developed areas, and into other aids for human advancement. The latest discoveries of science could be made available to men all over the globe. Thus we could give real meaning to the old promise that swords shall be beaten into ploughshares, and that the nations shall not learn war any more."

The policy remained the same, though administrations changed. Thus, on April 16, 1953, speaking before the American Society of Newspaper Editors, President

779

Eisenhower said:

"We are prepared to reaffirm, with the most concrete evidence, our readiness to help build a world in
which all peoples can be productive and prosperous.

"This Government is ready to ask its people to
join with all nations in devoting a substantial percentage of the savings achieved by disarmament to a fund
for world aid and reconstruction. The purposes of
this great work would be to help other peoples to
develop the under-developed areas of the world, to
stimulate profitable and fair world trade, to assist
all peoples to know the blessings of productive freedom.

"The monuments to this new kind of war would be
these: roads, and schools, hospitals and homes,
food and health.

"We are ready, in short, to dedicate our strength
to serving the needs, rather than the fears, of the
world.

"We are ready, by these and all such actions, to
make of the United Nations an institution that can
effectively guard the peace and security of all
peoples."

And in April 1956, President Eisenhower reiterated that
pledge.

*　　*　　*　　*　　*

While the U.S. has thus clearly recognized the further
impetus which disarmament would provide for economic
development, it is not possible at this time, in the absence
of international agreement, to anticipate when disarmament
would enable the U.S. Government to realize the savings
which could be used for additional U.S. aid to other peoples
struggling to attain minimum standards of existence and
economic growth. Nor is it possible to commit Congressional action. However, the historical record of
official U.S. leadership in aiding the development of other
countries provides valuable guidance in this regard.
Further, elimination of official U.S. expenditures abroad for
military purposes would provide a more favorable balance of
payments framework for enlarged external aid.

Apart from these general considerations it is pertinent
to note, as discussed elsewhere in this study, that disarmament would release in the U.S. valuable human and material
resources which would be ideally suited for expanded
development assistance and which would undoubtedly tend to
be directed, through various channels, to those ends. The
release of manpower and facilities from the current military

780

research and development effort could directly and substantially aid less-developed countries in providing needed skills and in facilitating research and development geared to the more rapid and effective solution of specific economic and social problems. The American capital goods industries could readily shift some of the production facilities now devoted to military requirements, to production for economic development abroad. The improved climate to be expected from disarmament would encourage development capital to move in greater volume to less-developed countries.

The U.S. believes, however, that the nations should not wait for disarmament to enlarge both the participation in and the volume of aid for development. Every nation could now, by its own action, make the 1960's an International Decade of Development. It will be the U.S. aim to do so. When and as disarmament is achieved the American people can be expected to face imaginatively the added challenges and opportunities which this development would hold for the welfare of mankind.

V.   Impact of Disarmament on U.S. International Economic Relations

Disarmament would entail the progressive reduction of all defense outlays abroad by the U.S. Government, including both dollar expenditures (for troop pay, services, military construction and supplies), and direct grants of military equipment and supplies to foreign countries. Furthermore, the composition of U.S. imports would change, at least temporarily, as the result of a shift from defense to civilian production. On the export side, the U.S. would ship more machinery and equipment for development, and there might be some addition to usual supplies of a number of commodities in world markets as the result of the orderly disposal of U.S. inventories of strategic commodities. Also, the improved international climate resulting from the initiation of a total disarmament program would influence the movement of U.S. trade and capital and would affect allocations of aid for economic development.

A.   U.S. Defense Outlays Abroad

Global impact.   U.S. Government military and non-military outlays abroad totalled $6.8 billion in 1960. Military outlays accounted for $4.3 billion or almost three quarters of this total, the remainder being economic aid.

The elimination of U.S. defense expenditures abroad would in itself result in a corresponding reduction of dollar earnings by other countries and an improvement in the U.S. balance of payments if there were no other offsetting transactions or forces. The U.S. payments deficit of $3.9

billion in 1960 compared with $2.7 billion for defense expenditures abroad affecting the U.S. balance of payments.* The elimination of the latter would thus have contributed substantially to wiping out the 1960 deficit.

For the recipient countries U.S. defense expenditures abroad constituted a major source of dollar exchange, equally about one-sixth of total U.S. civilian imports of goods and services. Lower U.S. foreign defense expenditures would adversely affect some countries, but there could be little adverse impact in many areas, especially where a major portion of our military expenditures occurs, i.e., Europe.

Regional impact. Table 11** shows the importance of military expenditures to U.S. recorded balance of payments transactions with four regions of the world. U.S. military expenditures are important in the U.S. payments balance in the case of Canada, Western Europe, and Asia, Africa and Oceania but are relatively small in Latin America.

The total Canadian payments deficit with the world was $1.2 billion in 1960, due largely to capital transfers. Total Canadian receipts from U.S. defense transactions amounted to $343 million, and the elimination of these expenditures would tend to increase the Canadian payments deficit; some reductions in these expenditures is already taking place because of reduced imports of uranium.

The effects in Western Europe would be quite different. Continental Europe is prospering and could undoubtedly adjust without much difficulty to the loss of income from U.S. military purchases. U.S. military expenditures in Europe accounted for about half of U.S. foreign military outlays, and their elimination would be of net beneficial economic effect to the U.S. by more than wiping out our payments deficit with the region, thereby easing the current payments disequilibrium. The U.S. payments deficit was $870 million with Western Europe in 1960, while net military expenditures there were $1.4 billion.

In Asia, Africa and Oceania, U.S. defense expenditures of $914 million in 1960 contributed to the $1.6 billion U.S. payments deficit with the region. In addition, $780 million was provided in the form of military grants. Several Asian and African countries would be adversely affected by the

_____

*Military outlays include some assistance in the form of equipment obtained in the U.S. under military assistance grants. These grants appear in balance of payments data exactly balanced by U.S. exports, and have no direct effect on the payments position of other countries with the U.S. This accounts for the difference between $4.3 billion of total military outlays and the $2.7 billion which affect the U.S. payments balance.

**Table omitted.

cessation of military expenditures, but more economic assistance could be used to good advantage in these areas which require considerable capital for development.

Latin America received a net income of only $40 million from U.S. defense expenditures as such in 1960--chiefly for petroleum--and would be little affected by the loss of these funds, although other more important, indirect effects would be felt from disarmament, i.e., on commodity trade. These might be offset by greater economic assistance and internal development under the Alliance for Progress.

In conclusion, no serious problems should result in Western Europe and Latin America, taken as a whole, from the elimination of U.S. Government military outlays. In Canada and in certain countries of Asia and Africa, the initial effects could be depressing to their economies. In Asia and Africa these could be alleviated by compensatory programs such as increased economic aid. In Canada and other countries economic growth could in time be expected to create new economic demand to replace U.S. military purchases.

B. Effects on Commodity Trade

Shift of expenditures from defense to other segments of the economy. Until detailed studies have been completed it is difficult to estimate with any accuracy the extent to which U.S. foreign trade in individual commodities would be affected if the current expenditures for defense items were shifted to other parts of the economy.* However, there are indications of some of the possible direct and indirect effects which would be of importance in certain cases. It is known that, by weight, only a small part, approximately 2 per cent, of total U.S. steel production is used for direct (and some indirect) military programs. A much larger proportion of special steel is so used. Under conditions of disarmament requirements for these steels would probably decline despite increased uses in other segments of the economy. However, it is not clear to what extent this might affect imports of individual ferroalloy raw materials, since alloy steels are widely used in other segments of the economy.

Some decrease in U.S. demand for other broadly used metals, such as copper and aluminum, would probably also be experienced. The impact on imports of copper, and of bauxite for aluminum, would be minor because of defense needs for these commodities have been declining due to the

---

*See, however, the estimates contained in Table 3-3 of the UN Report on the Economic and Social Consequences of Disarmament (E/3593, 28 February 1962) which were not available at the time of preparation of this study.

shift away from conventional defense armaments.

Currently military purchases of petroleum account for approximately 7.5 per cent of total U.S. petroleum consumption. Under conditions of disarmament off-shore procurement of petroleum, at least initially, would decline, although the effect on the world market would be mitigated by continued growth of civilian demand.

While requirements for certain commodities would be reduced for military purposes, demand could be expected to be augmented by higher production in other segments of the economy. For example, in an expanded foreign aid program U.S. exports of machinery and other development goods would increase, creating additional requirements for commodities used to produce this equipment. In any event the over-all impact on most primary producing countries that could result from a U.S. shift from defense to other expenditures is not expected to be serious. U.S. military purchases represent only part and, in many cases, a small part, of total requirements for a commodity. Such difficulties as may be encountered by these countries would be similar to those which arise from technological advances, although they might be more rapid, unless shifts in demand were minimized by careful economic planning. In any event, the need for diversifying the economies of some countries now dependent on the exports of a few primary commodities would be intensified.

Reductions in U.S. strategic inventories. The U.S. Government owns large inventories of strategic and critical materials which were valued at $7.8 billion in 1961. Procurement for these inventories has had considerable effect on commodity markets in some instances.

However, purchases for the strategic stockpile have virtually ceased. The 76 materials currently on the stockpile list represent items for which the United States has been or is dependent, at least in part, on foreign sources of supply. Materials include 13 non-metallic minerals, 16 fibers and chemicals and rubber. These commodities have come from virtually all of the world's principal commodity exporting countries, as well as from smaller producing countries. In the event of total disarmament, it seems reasonable to expect that the strategic stockpile objective would be sharply reduced or altogether eliminated, that procurement would cease and that the bulk of the strategic stockpile, or possibly the whole of it, would be declared surplus.

Disposals from the strategic stockpile, as established by law,* provide for "the protection of the United States against avoidable loss on the sale or transfer of the material

---

*P. L. 520, 78th Congress, 1946, as amended.

to be released and the protection of producers, processors, and consumers against avoidable disruption of their usual markets..."

In addition, it is the declared policy[*] of the U.S. that disposals will avoid "adverse effects on international interests of the United States..." In practice, the U.S. has given evidence of its attention to the concern of foreign countries as, for example, in the 9-year disposal plan for natural rubber announced in 1959. Under conditions of total disarmament, U.S. policy on orderly disposals from its inventories would remain substantially the same. Further, the U.S. is supporting a large and continuing program of foreign aid to less-developed countries, many of which are important suppliers of primary commodities. It is not reasonable to expect that disposals would be made in a manner that would substantially reduce or nullify the aid which the U.S. is extending to these countries.

U.S.--Soviet Trade. Some expansion of U.S. trade with the Soviet Bloc would in all probability occur under disarmament as strategic and other trade inhibitions were removed and Bloc needs for many types of capital and consumer goods were met in the West. However, the extent to which trade actually increased would in turn depend on the extent to which the autarchic economic policies of the Soviet Bloc were modified. It is problematical whether the Soviet Bloc could or would revise its basic economic policies to permit a full expansion of trade with the U.S., but under disarmament some increase of trade might occur in special categories of goods.

Thus, in conclusion, the short run effects of disarmament are likely to be relatively small on U.S. foreign trade, although particular commodities and countries may be adversely affected, at least for a time. In the long run, export competition will increase as the Common Market and other industrial countries also transfer resources from military to civilian production and as more and a wider variety of goods become available for export to world markets.

C.   More Efficient Resource Use

With reduced political tension and the elimination of military expenditures, a greater portion of U.S., and indeed the world's resources would be put to more efficient and beneficial use. Production and trade would be based on a more rational division of labor. For example, special measures to encourage defense-related production of certain materials such as uranium and nickel would be terminated. The strategic or defense justifications for trade controls, as

[*]Defense Mobilization Order V-7, 1959.

on petroleum, or controls on Soviet Bloc trade, would be lessened. Similarly, controls over shipping could be reduced and the size of the U.S. merchant fleet and shipping subsidies would no longer be affected by military considerations; the merchant fleets of some countries would benefit. As U.S. private investment were shifted from defense-oriented industries, other outlets would be sought, including investment in the less-developed countries. A more favorable investment climate would prevail with the elimination of war threats; this would be a factor encouraging more private foreign investment.

In short, because military-oriented production and trade controls would be removed by disarmament, more trade would tend to flow on the basis of comparative advantage.

Economic and Social Consequences of Disarmament

REPORT OF THE SECRETARY-GENERAL
TRANSMITTING THE STUDY
OF HIS CONSULTATIVE GROUP

ACTING SECRETARY-GENERAL'S PREFACE

This report was prepared by a group of experts appointed by the late Secretary-General, Mr. Dag Hammarskjold, under General Assembly resolution 1516 (XV) to assist him in conducting a study of the economic and social consequences of disarmament in countries with different economic systems and at different stages of economic development.

The members of the group acted in their personal capacities and their observations and recommendations were put forward to me on their own responsibility. I am convinced that their report represents a major step forward in the consideration of the economic and social consequences of disarmament and I am pleased to endorse their general findings. It is now my privilege to submit the report to the Economic and Social Council for its consideration and transmittal, along with its comments, to the General Assembly.

The members of the group were: V. Y. Aboltin, Deputy Director, Institute of World Economics and International Relations, Academy of Sciences of the Union of Soviet Socialist Republics; Mamoun Beheiry, Governor, Bank of Sudan; Arthur J. Brown, Head, Department of Economics, University of Leeds, England; B. N. Ganguli, Head, The Delhi School of Economics, India; Aftab Ahmad Khan, Chief Economist, Planning Commission, Government of Pakistan; Oskar Lange, Chairman, Economic Council, Council of Ministers of the Government of the People's Republic of Poland; W. W. Leontief, Professor of Economics, Harvard University, United States; José Antonio Mayobre, Ambassador of Venezuela to the United States; Alfred Sauvy, Director, National Institute of Demographic Studies, Government of France; and Ludek Urban, Economic Institute, Czechoslovakian Academy of Sciences. Mr. Sauvy was represented at the meetings of the second session of the group by Paul Paillat, also of the National Institute of Demographic Studies. Mr. Jacob L. Mosak, Director of the Division of General Economic Research and Policies of the United Nations Secretariat, served as Chairman.

In preparing the report the experts had available replies of Governments to a *note verbale* of the Secretary-General on the economic and social consequences of disarmament, which was sent in accordance with the unanimous recommendation of the group. Communications on the subject were also received from a number of the specialized agencies of the United Nations. The replies of Governments, together with the relevant information from the specialized agencies, are reproduced in part II of the report.

The group was assisted in its work by members of the Secretariat from the Department of Economic and Social Affairs at United Nations Headquarters and from the Economic Commission for Europe, collaborating in accordance with that Commission's resolution 1 (XVI).

It is everywhere recognized that the problems of disarmament considered in the present report are among the most vital before the United Nations today. In dealing with its economic and social consequences the experts have adopted the assumption that disarmament, once agreed upon, would proceed rapidly and would be general and complete. They have reviewed the resources devoted to military purposes and the peaceful uses to which these resources might be put when released. They have examined the conversion problems that might arise and the impact of disarmament on international economic relations and on aid for economic development, and they have called attention to some social consequences of disarmament.

It is a source of profound gratification to me, as I am sure it will be to all Governments, that, on a subject that has until recently been so beset by ideological differences, it has now proved possible for a group of experts drawn from countries with different economic systems and at different stages of economic development to reach unanimous agreement. It is particularly encouraging that the Consultative Group should have reached the unanimous conclusion that "all the problems and difficulties of transition connected with disarmament could be met by appropriate national and international measures", and that "there should thus be no doubt that the diversion to peaceful purposes of the resources now in military use could be accomplished to the benefit of all countries and lead to the improvement of world economic and social conditions".

On behalf of the United Nations, I wish to thank the members of the group for their valuable contribution and to express my appreciation to the institutions with which the experts are associated for their willingness to release them from their normal duties so that they might undertake this extremely important task.

U THANT
Acting Secretary-General

INTRODUCTION

1. Realization that the disarmament issue is important—as important as the survival of humanity itself—is world-wide. This is exemplified by a resolution adopted in 1959 by the General Assembly in which the question is called "the most important one facing the world today", and in which hope is expressed that "measures leading towards the goal of general and complete disarmament under effective international control will be worked out in detail and agreed upon in the shortest possible time".[1] This sense of urgency springs mainly from the existence of a threat to mankind that has grown into one of mass destruction. But in part, also, it comes from the consciousness that the resources that make this threat possible, and many more resources devoted to less spectacularly destructive military uses, are being diverted from the tasks of lightening the burdens and enriching the lives of individuals and of society.

2. At the same time, it is seen that disarmament would affect individuals, countries and the entire world economy in many different ways. A substantial part of the world's labour force now earns its living, directly or indirectly, in meeting military demands. To redeploy this force for non-military purposes is an operation large enough to give rise to important problems of economic and social adjustment. Careful advance study is required for full advantage to be taken of the potential benefits disarmament could make possible. The following chapters attempt a survey of the magnitude of both the benefits it would bring and the difficulties that would have to be overcome in the economic and social fields.

3. In many respects the available data fall short of what is needed for a comprehensive and quantitative analysis. Nevertheless, the broad nature and magnitude of the economic and social benefits and the problems of conversion arising from disarmament, and the general lines on which the main problems can be solved, emerge sufficiently clearly from what is already known.

4. This Consultative Group on the economic and social consequences of disarmament has dealt with the subject on the assumption that disarmament, once agreed upon, would be general and complete and also rapid. It has done so in the belief that this was the intention of the General Assembly resolution under which it was appointed,[2] and also because this interpretation gives the clearest form to both the benefits and the difficulties, thereby minimizing the risk that the latter will be under-estimated.

---

[1] See *Official Records of the General Assembly, Fourteenth Session, Supplement No. 16,* resolution 1378 (XIV).

[2] The text of General Assembly resolution 1516 (XV), under which the group was appointed, is given in annex 1.

5. The report represents the unanimous findings of the Consultative Group. It deals with the volume of resources devoted to military purposes and the peaceful uses to which these resources might be put when released, and with the transitional or conversion problems that would arise, both at the aggregate level of national production and employment and in particular sectors of the economy. The impact of disarmament on international economic relations is studied as well as the effects of disarmament on the volume and framework of aid for economic development. Finally, some social consequences of disarmament are considered.

CHAPTER 1

RESOURCES DEVOTED TO MILITARY PURPOSES

6. The most fundamental way in which disarmament affects economic life is through the liberation of the resources devoted to military use and their re-employment for peaceful purposes. This shift in the composition of the aggregate demand for goods and services is simply a large-scale manifestation of a phenomenon that is constantly taking place in all economies as the demand for certain goods and services shrinks while the demand for other goods and services expands; thus disarmament in its economic aspects should not be considered as a unique phenomenon. Short-term shifts in demand on an even larger scale than that which would accompany any agreed disarmament programme have occurred when economies have been converted to war production, or when they have undergone conversion to peacetime patterns of production at the end of the war.

7. It is important, however, that countries, in preparing to disarm, should take stock of the various resources that disarmament would release for peaceful uses. Such a survey would facilitate economic planning and adjustment at all levels, public and private, national and international.

8. To assess the transitional problems that may arise and to determine the peaceful uses to which the resources released may be put, it is necessary to ascertain in some detail the volume and composition of resources so released. An approximation to the volume of resources that would be liberated by disarmament is provided by the published official estimates of military expenditure.[1] On the basis of available data there appears to be general agreement that the world is spending roughly $120 billion annually on military account at the present time. This figure is equivalent to about 8-9 per cent of the world's annual output of all goods and services; it is at least two-thirds of—and according to some estimates may be of the same order of magnitude as—the entire national income of all the under-developed countries. It is close

---

[1] Available data on military expenditures in the national budgets of countries are given in annex 2, tables 2-1, 2-2 and 2-3.

to the value of the world's annual exports of all commodities and it corresponds to about one-half of the total resources set aside each year for gross capital formation throughout the world.

9. The world's armed forces now number about 20 million persons. This figure does not include all those currently employed in supplying military goods or services directly to the armed forces or in producing the raw materials, equipment and other goods that are needed indirectly in the production of military supplies and services. The total of all persons in the armed forces and in all productive activities resulting from military expenditure may amount to well over 50 million.

10. These figures demonstrate that the total volume of manpower and of other productive resources devoted to military use at the present time is very large indeed. The available data do not, however, make it possible to assess with the desired degree of accuracy the volume of resources that disarmament would actually release. For one thing, the existing estimates may not be comprehensive: some categories of military expenditure may be excluded. Further, there may be considerable inconsistency in the pricing of military output compared with the pricing of other production, as also in the relationship between the pay of the armed forces and civilian wages and salaries. For these and other reasons it would be wrong to interpret the share of military expenditure in total output as a precise measure of the real share of national resources allocated to military purposes, unless appropriate adjustments could be made for coverage, price differentials and other elements of incomparability.

11. Although the data provide an inadequate basis for precise comparisons of the military burdens among countries, it can be safely asserted that within most countries military expenditure accounts for a very significant proportion of total output. In many countries the estimates of military expenditure range between 1 and 5 per cent of gross domestic product, while in others, particularly in some of the larger countries, the corresponding ratio ranges between 5 and 10 per cent.

12. While the burden of armaments is wide-spread, the great bulk of the world's military expenditure is highly concentrated in a handful of countries. Available indications are that about 85 per cent of the world's military outlays is accounted for by seven countries—Canada, the Federal Republic of Germany, France, the People's Republic of China, the Union of Soviet Socialist Republics, the United Kingdom of Great Britain and Northern Ireland and the United States of America. Total military expenditure in all the under-developed countries amounts to about one-tenth of that of the industrial private enterprise economies. This means that although many under-developed countries devote significant proportions of their resources to military purposes, the great bulk of the resources released by disarmament would be concentrated in a very few countries.[2]

---

[2] This is less true of manpower than of other resources, since the under-developed countries rely much more on numbers of men than on advanced and expensive armaments and equipment.

13. It should be noted that an agreed disarmament programme would involve alternate security arrangements. Thus, the recent joint statement of the United States and the Soviet Union on agreed principles for disarmament negotiations provided that "During and after the implementation of the programme of general and complete disarmament there should be taken, in accordance with the principles of the United Nations Charter, the necessary measures to maintain international peace and security, including the obligation of States to place at the disposal of the United Nations agreed manpower necessary for an international peace force to be equipped with agreed types of armaments".[3] While these arrangements would necessitate the continued allocation of funds and resources to military purposes, it may be assumed that these would be small in relation to current expenditure.

14. In order to formulate economic and social policies so as to take full advantage of the opportunities afforded by disarmament, it is necessary for the countries concerned to know in detail the possible alternative uses for the resources released. In general it can be said that the ease and effectiveness with which the various resources liberated by disarmament might be employed for peaceful purposes would depend on the extent to which the composition of the demand for additional civilian uses approximated that of the resources now devoted to armaments. Because of the relative immobility of some resources in the short run, systematic advance study is needed so as to minimize wastage in the transitional stage, though in the long run any country's industrial capacity can be adapted to meet the changing pattern of demand.

15. To prepare a list of the resources absorbed by armaments, it is desirable that each country should, at the appropriate time, determine the composition of military expenditure and estimate the productive resources that it absorbs. The latter calculation is straightforward with respect to certain components of military expenditure. The members of the armed forces, for example, constitute a labour supply that would otherwise be available for peaceful purposes. Similarly, those research facilities employed for military purposes which are adaptable to civilian research are readily identified. Other productive resources, however, are devoted to military use only in an indirect manner which may not be apparent at first glance. While it is clear, for example, that the labour and capacity in ordnance production are employed solely for military purposes, it is impossible to state, without careful analysis, what proportion of the manpower and other resources devoted to, say, coal mining are so employed. If ordnance factories use any coal, some portion of the productive resources of the coal mining industry are engaged, indirectly, in the production of armaments. But to take into account all the inter-industry relationships in a national economy in order to provide a complete picture of the resources absorbed for military purposes requires con-

[3] See General Assembly document A/4879, *Joint Statement on Agreed Principles for Disarmament Negotiations,* submitted by the Soviet Union and the United States.

siderable statistical information and a thorough economic analysis of an economy's productive structure. The degree of elaboration with which statistics should be compiled and economic analysis performed for this purpose varies from country to country according to the complexity and size of the national economy. Analogous considerations apply to the determination of the amount of resources required directly and indirectly to satisfy alternative peacetime needs.

16. Data made available by a number of countries show that military production is highly concentrated in a few industry groups, notably munitions, electrical machinery, instruments and related products, and transportation equipment, including airplanes and missiles. There is a similar concentration in the same industries of the employment resulting from military expenditure.[4] In most other industries military outlays account for a relatively small proportion of total demand. Industries dependent on military expenditure also have a high degree of concentration in certain regions and cities. While this pattern of concentration of output and employment is not necessarily characteristic of all countries, it appears to apply generally to the major military powers.

17. The situation is rather different in those countries that rely upon imports for their supplies of military goods or in which the major part of military expenditure is for the pay and subsistence of the armed forces, rather than for their equipment. In such cases, the resources devoted to military purposes consist essentially of manpower and foreign exchange. This is especially true of the under-developed countries. While disarmament would require all countries to make significant adjustments, the realization of the great potential gains from disarmament in under-developed countries would depend on a major intensification of efforts to promote economic development. Such efforts would be facilitated in so far as military spending were channelled to development expenditure and as scarce foreign exchange resources hitherto directly or indirectly utilized for military objectives were freed for development purposes; and still more to the extent that aid were forthcoming from the industrially advanced countries in the form of both capital equipment and technical assistance.

---

[4] See, for example, the reply of the Government of the United States of America.

CHAPTER 2

THE PEACEFUL USE OF RELEASED RESOURCES

18. There are so many competing claims for usefully employing the resources released by disarmament that the real problem is to establish a scale of priorities. The most urgent of these claims would undoubtedly already have been largely satisfied were it not for the armaments race.

19. The resources liberated by disarmament within any country could be employed in part to promote economic and social progress at home in part to expand foreign aid. The question of aid to under-developed countries is sufficiently important to warrant treatment in a separate chapter (chapter 6). The main civilian purposes for which the freed resources, whether domestic or foreign in origin, could be applied, may be classified as follows:

Raising standards of personal consumption of goods and services;

Expanding or modernizing productive capacity through investment in new plant and equipment;

Promoting housing construction, urban renewal, including slum clearance, and rural development;

Improving and expanding facilities for education, health, welfare, social security, cultural development, scientific research, etc.

Part of the gain from disarmament could also take the form of an increase in leisure as, for example, through a reduction in average working hours without a corresponding reduction in real income, or through an increase in paid vacations.

20. The various claims upon resources listed above are, of course, closely interlinked. A rise in personal consumption may necessitate new investment in industry or agriculture or both. Enlarged aid from the industrial to the under-developed countries may involve expanding capacity for the production of the goods that the latter countries need, notably capital equipment. As regards the under-developed countries themselves, if additional aid is to bring the greatest benefits, a larger volume of investment out of domestic resources is likely to be required; this would be facilitated by the release of internal resources through disarmament.

21. Since it can be assumed that the economy as a whole is highly flexible in the long run, the resources freed by disarmament could ultimately be used for any one or more of the purposes listed above, and in any combination. Labour can be retrained and, where necessary, can move to other areas. As old equipment becomes obsolete it can be replaced by new equipment oriented to new patterns of

demand. In the long run, there should be little difficulty in adapting resources to needs.

22. In the very short run, by contrast, the range of choice may be somewhat more limited. It takes time to turn swords into plough-shares or to make an office clerk or factory worker out of a soldier. Studies in some industrial countries have shown that the productive capacities released from military use would be much more immediately adaptable to the increased output of consumer durables and industrial equipment than to the production of houses, food, clothing or educational facilities. Thus, in the transition period, countries may wish to take into account not merely the unsatisfied needs for higher consumption, investment and foreign aid, but also the extent to which alternative patterns of new expenditure would take full advantage of the particular resources that disarmament would make available. It should, however, be borne in mind that some of the major military powers now have fairly comfortable margins of productive capacity available to them. In these cases it is unlikely that disarmament would generate many new demands that could not fairly readily be satisfied from available resources.[1]

23. In the centrally planned economies, even though they have generally been operating approximately at capacity, the transfer of industrial capacity and labour force to the production of goods for peaceful uses could be achieved in a relatively short time. This transfer could be readily achieved by measures formulated within the framework of the general economic plans which can ensure a desirable balance between demand and resources.

24. In the under-developed countries the principal resource released, apart from the purely financial, would be manpower, both skilled and unskilled. In some cases a significant proportion of industrial and transport capacity would also become available for other uses. In many there would also be considerable savings in foreign exchange. The effective utilization of released resources would depend upon the soundness and vigour of development programmes and the volume and character of aid received.

PERSONAL CONSUMPTION AND PRODUCTIVE INVESTMENT

25. Among the alternative uses of resources released by disarmament, increased personal consumption might well absorb a large share. It is fair to suppose that even in the developed countries there would be strong pressure on Governments to raise the level of living. Disarmament would, in particular, offer an important opportunity to

---

[1] See, for example, W. Leontief and M. Hoffenberg, "The Economics of Disarmament", *Scientific American* (New York), vol. 204, No. 4, April 1961, pp. 47-55. An unpublished study made at the Department of Applied Economics, Cambridge, England, suggests that, if military expenditure in the United Kingdom ceased and were replaced in equal parts by increased private consumption, increased domestic fixed capital formation, and increased foreign aid, output would be reduced in only two out of nineteen sectors of the economy (military services, and ship, aircraft and railway vehicle construction) and would be required to expand in most others by between 3 and 6 per cent—the main exceptions being textiles (9 per cent increase) and motor vehicles (14 per cent increase).

raise incomes of low income sections of the population and to facilitate equalizing the rates of pay for men and women.

26. In most countries, however, not all the resources freed by disarmament would be allocated directly to consumption, no matter what the level of income might be. In the first place, a substantial portion of the released resources would be used for expansion of productive capacities because only such expansion can provide a firm basis for further increases in consumption. Ministers representing the countries of western Europe and North America recently set as a collective target the attainment during the decade from 1960 to 1970 of a growth in real gross national product of 50 per cent for all the countries taken together.[2] In the Soviet Union, according to existing plans for economic development, industrial production should reach, in the course of the present decade, a level two and one half times the present volume. A more rapid rate of growth would also enable countries with a higher degree of industrialization to contribute more effectively—through greater financial and technical assistance and through the widening of markets for exports—to the development of countries that are less advanced industrially.

27. Recent experience in both private enterprise and socialist economies provides a rough guide in judging how much additional investment a specific growth target requires. Among the industrialized private enterprise economies, it appears that during the nineteen fifties a country experiencing a 4 per cent annual rate of growth needed, on the average, to devote about 2 per cent more of gross national product to investment than did a country having a 3 per cent rate of growth.[3] In most of these countries, 2 per cent would constitute a very significant proportion of the resources disarmament would release. In the less developed countries which have low levels of income and saving, the utilization of released resources for capital formation must be considered vitally important.

SOCIAL INVESTMENT

28. Social investment is an important alternative both to private consumption and to industrial and agricultural investment. Its claims rest partly upon the clear urgency of the direct need for improved social amenities, and partly upon the fact that growth of industrial and agricultural productivity is dependent upon developments in education, housing, health, and other fields. Since social investment has had to compete with military claims for state funds, it (like aid to underdeveloped countries) has probably been particularly affected by the armaments race. Recognition of the necessity to remedy the resulting deficiencies in the stock of social capital is wide-spread among countries at different stages of economic development and with different economic systems. There is no common measure of need according to which it is possible to add up, or to compare, the deficiencies in different fields of social investment or different countries. Nevertheless, the

---

[2] Organisation for Economic Co-operation and Development, Press Communiqué, OECD/PRESS/A(61)10 (Paris) 17 November 1961.

[3] For further details, see United Nations, *World Economic Survey, 1959* (Sales No.: 60.II.C.1), chap. 1.

importance of the subject warrants an attempt to set out the main relevant pieces of evidence.

29. In the United States the National Planning Association estimated at the end of 1959 the cumulative expenditure requirements for selected government programmes over the next five years.[4] These estimates were not intended to be precise but simply represented a summary of the existing programmes of development and improvement in various fields over the next five years. The significance of these estimates, which imply annual average expenditures of $66 billion, may be judged from the fact that the present spending of the Federal, State and local governments on all these programmes amounts to about $30 billion per year. It is therefore apparent that these programmes could absorb much or most of any resources released by disarmament.

30. In the Soviet Union the task has been set of achieving a sharp improvement in living standards within the next twenty years by raising the income of the population and also by expanding social benefits (education, health protection, social insurance, housing construction, etc.). As stated in an official document, "general and complete disarmament on the basis of an appropriate agreement between States would make it considerably easier to overfulfil the planned improvement in the living standards of the working people".[5]

31. It will be noted that the highest single figure among the programmes for the United States mentioned above is that for *urban renewal and development,* including slum clearance, low-cost housing and community redevelopment. The problem of urban renewal is worldwide. In 1950 about 80 per cent of the world's population was still living in rural areas. Between 50 and 60 million people are being added to the world's total population every year, mainly to its urban areas. In Asia as many as 500 million persons may be added between 1950 and 1975 to the population of cities with over 20,000 inhabitants. In Latin America, sixty-two cities with over 100,000 people accounted in 1960 for some 40 per cent of the region's total. In Africa a considerably higher rate of growth is taking place in urban areas than in rural areas. Rapid urbanization is characteristic of Europe and North America.

32. The rural and urban environments in many countries are both deteriorating, mainly under the impact of this rapid growth. The social

---

[4] National Planning Association, *Looking Ahead,* March 1960. The estimates covering the next five years were as follows:

		($ billion)
Education		30
Classroom construction	16	
Current operation	14	
Highways and skyways		75
Urban renewal		100
(Slum clearance, low-cost housing and community redevelopment)		
Water supply and conservation		60
Health and hospitals		35
Other programmes		30
(Air pollution, research and development, etc.)		
	TOTAL	330

[5] *Programme of the Communist Party,* adopted at the 22nd Party Congress.

and physical symptoms of this deterioration are bad housing, poor community services and delinquency, the paralysis of city traffic, and in many of the less developed countries an absence of sanitation accompanied by a high incidence of communicable disease. In many metropolitan cities of such less developed countries "squatters' settlements" already contain a considerable part of the population.

33. The magnitude of the resources required for dealing with the problem of urbanization is very large. In India alone, for example, approximately $1 billion a year will be required to house the new inhabitants of cities with over 100,000 people. The provision of city-wide services, utilities and transportation would at least double the needed investment. In Latin America it was estimated by the Organization of American States in 1954 that an annual investment of $1.4 billion was required over a period of thirty years to wipe out the housing backlog, to replace obsolescent dwellings and to provide homes for new households. According to rough estimates by the United Nations Bureau of Social Affairs, as many as 150 million families in the less developed countries are in need of adequate homes. These immense requirements are contributing in many under-developed countries to the maintenance of a level of spending on housing and urban development such that the pressing claims of directly productive sectors have to be curtailed.

34. In the Soviet Union a housing shortage still exists despite the building of dwellings for nearly 50 million people in the last five years. "The housing problem remains acute. The growth of the urban population in the Soviet Union during the past few years is considerably in excess of the estimates."[6] In order to overcome the shortage and house every family in "a separate, comfortable apartment", an increase in twenty years of about 200 per cent would be required in the existing housing facilities. To reach this goal it is required that average annual housing construction be raised from the target of 135 million square metres in 1961-65 to 400 million square metres in 1976-80.[7]

35. Another field in which the supply of social capital is deficient in many countries is *road and air transportation*.[8] The rapid increase in the stock of automobiles and the lag in road facilities in these countries during the post-war years have been accompanied by extraordinary congestion and numbers of accidents. Airports and other air facilities are also deficient in many under-developed areas as well as in some more advanced economies, and investment in civil aviation will claim a share of the resources freed by disarmament.

36. The *development and conservation of natural resources* provides another important field for increased outlays in the event of disarmament. In the United States it has been estimated that Federal

---

[6] N. Khrushchev, *Report to the 22nd Congress of the Communist Party* (Cross Currents Press, New York, 1961), p. 118.

[7] *Report on the Programme of the Communist Party,* delivered to the 22nd Party Congress; Soviet Booklet, No. 81 (London, 1961), p. 47.

[8] Even countries as industrially advanced as the United States may have such a deficiency. For example, the second largest figure in the National Planning Association estimates cited in the footnote to paragraph 29 is for highways and skyways.

expenditure requirements up to 1980 in the field of water resource development alone total almost $55 billion, while $173 billion will be needed for non-Federal programmes.[9] The Soviet Union could advance the preparation and implementation of a number of important nature-transforming projects in various parts of the country in order to improve living and working conditions for the people. There is, for example, a plan to divert part of the waters of the Pechora, Vychegda and Ob Rivers into the basins of the Volga and the Caspian and Aral Seas. This would bring about a considerable change in the climate and in living conditions in Central Asia and in the southern European part of the Soviet Union. In under-developed countries there are also many important multipurpose schemes for the conservation and the utilization of water resources.

37. The world's demand for water is growing much more rapidly than the supply, and a continuation of present trends implies a growing deterioration in the balance of demand and supply. Increasing supplies of water are needed not merely in order to keep pace with the rapid rise in population, but also in order to meet the still faster growing needs for irrigation and industry. In many countries most of the cheapest source of supply for water have already been tapped, so that further expansion of supplies necessitates increasingly heavy investment in obtaining access to other sources, including the purification of sea water.

38. Other urgent requirements for natural resource development and conservation exist in the fields of forestry, soil and watershed conservation, rangeland conservation, park and recreational development and fish and wildlife conservation. In the United States the total Federal cost of proposed programmes in these areas over a period of ten years implies an annual rate of almost $4 billion, or almost twice the current rate of expenditure. In addition, scientific research and investigation in the field of natural resources will have to be expanded at considerable cost. In western Pakistan a master plan has been prepared for soil reclamation and conservation in order to combat the twin menaces of water-logging and salinity. The cost during the next ten years is estimated at $1.2 billion.

INVESTMENT IN HEALTH, EDUCATION AND SOCIAL SERVICES

39. Another major use of the resources released from disarmament is investment to raise standards of health, education and social services. There is an urgent need for improvement in *health services* throughout the world. In many countries the ratio of doctors, dentists and other medical personnel to the population is inadequate and even falling, and there are also great deficiencies in the supply of hospitals and hospital beds as well as of other basic health facilities. The backlog that many countries have to make up in order to attain the best current levels of hospital facilities is very large. In some of the poorer countries of Europe, for example, the medical facilities available to each doctor have been estimated to be as little as one-fiftieth of those prevailing in the better equipped countries. Yet even in the richest countries there is great need to improve standards of medical services. In Canada and

---

[9] See the reply of the Government of the United States of America.

the United States, for instance, the deficit in hospital beds has been estimated at from a quarter to a half of the existing number.[10] In under-developed countries the need for improved medical care is obviously greater. This is indicated, for example, by infant mortality rates in excess of 100 per 1,000 in many of these countries as opposed to rates of 20 to 30 per 1,000 in economically advanced countries.

40. An indication of the magnitude of investment requirements for medical care may be gained from projections for the United States. The present rate of construction, plus a limited programme of renovation, modernization and increase in rehabilitation facilities, would require at least $15 billion over the next decade instead of the $9 billion that would be needed if such changes were not carried out.[11] In the Soviet Union it has been officially suggested that hospital accommodation might be increased by 40 per cent (that is, by several hundred thousand beds) at low cost by converting into hospitals part of the buildings now in military use.[12]

41. In most developed countries *educational needs* are rising and are bound to expand even more rapidly; with the ever wider spread of technical progress there will be a rising premium on a higher educational background, on better scientific and technological skills and on a broader range of knowledge. At the same time greater efforts will be directed towards reducing the drop-out rate of the less talented and towards ensuring that an increasing proportion of the highly talented reach upper levels. The realization of all these purposes would imply the devising of new kinds of education and provision of adequate means so that people keep abreast of the latest developments in knowledge.

42. In the United States, existing standards currently require an expenditure level of $20 billion for school enrolments in kindergarten through twelfth grade, and of $6.7 billion for institutions of higher education. Projections on this basis alone indicate for 1970 a rise of 50 per cent in the first case and of more than 250 per cent in the second case. In a disarmed economy it would also be easier to meet the demands for better standards of education.

43. According to recent estimates, western Europe's expenditure on education may rise from $9 billion in 1958 (including both current and capital outlays) to over $18 billion, on a high estimate, in 1970— an increase of over 100 per cent.[13] As a result, outlays for education may rise from 3.2 per cent of gross national product to 4.0 per cent. Western Europe would also face important problems at the university level if a target were set for raising the European enrolment in the 20-24 year age group from 5 per cent as at present to the United States ratio of over 20 per cent.[14]

---

[10] Royal Commission on Canada's Economic Prospects, *Housing and Social Capital* (Ottawa, 1957), and annual reports of the United States Department of Health, Education and Welfare (Washington, D.C.).

[11] See the reply of the Government of the United States of America.

[12] Embassy of the Union of Soviet Socialist Republics, Washington, D.C., Press Department Release No. 66, 2 February 1960.

[13] Organization for European Economic Co-operation, *Targets for Education in Europe,* by Svennilson, Edding and Elvin, p. 105.

[14] Dewhurst, Coppock, Yates and Associates, *Europe's Needs and Resources,* (New York, 1961) p. 343.

44. In the Soviet Union general and polytechnical secondary (eleven-year course) education for all children of school-going age is to be introduced in the next ten years. It is planned that the number of students resident in boarding schools and extended day-care schools should increase from 1.5 million at present to 2.5 million in 1965. The shortage of space in schools has led to using the building facilities in shifts; but teaching on a shift basis is expected to stop completely in the near future. Besides the extension of secondary school facilities, it is estimated that the present enrolment of 2.6 million students in higher educational establishments will triple by 1980.[15] All these developments will require construction of many more schools and training of a large body of teachers, both of which would be facilitated by disarmament.

45. In the under-developed countries, the magnitude of the educational problem may be seen from the fact that most of them still have illiteracy rates of well over 50 per cent of the population aged fifteen years and over. The cost of educational requirements in under-developed countries for education is exemplified by a recently adopted African programme.[16] On the basis of inventories of educational needs of the countries covered by the African plan[17] the total cost of the programme is expected to increase from $590 million in the first year to $1,150 million in 1965, $1,880 million in 1970 and $2,600 million in 1980. It is assumed that the share of national income devoted to education will rise from 3 to 4 per cent between 1961 and 1965, and thereafter will increase further, reaching 6 per cent of national income by 1980. This means that the difference, amounting in the same years to $140 million, $450 million, $1,010 million and $400 million, respectively, would need to be covered by foreign aid.

46. Apart from needs in the fields of health and education, there are urgent requirements for expansion in *social services*. Even in the most advanced countries, there are pronounced shortcomings in the provision of child welfare services, vocational rehabilitation agencies, community centres and other special services.

47. It is thus clear that, so far as social investment is concerned, there is already a heavy backlog of urgent need, and the recent acceleration of population growth and of technical change make it certain that the need, and the demand, will grow. Social investment therefore is likely to claim an increasing volume of resources, to which disarmament would make a welcome contribution.

SCIENTIFIC RESEARCH FOR PEACEFUL PURPOSES

48. The release of scientific and technical manpower would be one of the important consequences of disarmament. Amongst the major

---

[15] Based on information in *Report on the Programme,* op. cit., p. 66, and N. Khrushchev's *Report,* op. cit., p. 122.

[16] United Nations Economic Commission for Africa and United Nations Educational, Scientific and Cultural Organization, *Outline of a Plan for African Educational Development* (UNESCO/ED/180) ; and *Final Report* (UNESCO/ED/181).

[17] The plan covers only thirty-five States and territories of Africa. It excludes, in particular, the countries bordering on the Mediterranean and the Union of South Africa.

powers a significant part of the national research and development effort currently serves military purposes. The total elimination of military spending would bring about a sizable release of resources for civilian research and development. With disarmament it would thus become possible to encourage programmes of basic scientific research in fields which have hitherto been neglected, and to mobilize great scientific potential for the solution of some of the world's greatest problems in such areas as medicine, urban development and reorganization, and the technical problems associated with the economic development of under-developed countries. If human ingenuity, in the space of a very few years, has so vastly increased man's powers for destruction, it should be able to make an equally massive contribution to peaceful and constructive achievement.

49.   Not all of the needs described above can be satisfied by single nations acting alone. In some instances their satisfaction will require international co-operation.[18] Serious gaps exist in the permanent world-wide network of meteorological observing stations and in the corresponding telecommunication facilities, and a marked increase is required in the funds available for basic research on improving meteorological services. Furthermore, the funds currently available for assisting meteorological development in the less developed countries are far less than needed to satisfy current demands, not to mention prospective demands. Telecommunications are important to developing economies and there is need to pursue a number of objectives in this field, including the development of networks. There is also considerable scope for international co-operation in developing the world's air transport facilities.

50.   Disarmament would also open up possibilities for joint international ventures of an even more ambitious kind, including the utilization of atomic energy for peaceful purposes, space research, the exploration of the Arctic and Antarctic for the benefit of mankind and projects to change the climates of large areas of the world. Joint research into the earth's interior may lead to discoveries that would be of real value to the who'e world. In addition, joint projects to assist the development of under-developed countries as well as programmes of co-operation in the social and economic fields could be undertaken. These international projects could have a major impact on world living standards and civilization.

51.   It is evident from the foregoing illustrative discussion of the magnitude of current and impending needs that the resources freed by disarmament wou'd not be large enough for the many claims upon them. Though it would take active decisions by Governments in the light of national and international needs to set in motion the necessary programmes for employing the released resources, it seems abundantly clear that no country need fear a lack of useful employment opportunities for the resources that would become available to it through disarmament.

---

[18] For communications received from specialized agencies of the United Nations on matters discussed in these paragraphs, see volume II of this report (E/3593/Rev.1/Add.1).

CHAPTER 3

THE IMPACT OF DISARMAMENT ON NATIONAL PRODUCTION AND EMPLOYMENT

52. Disarmament would raise both general problems of maintaining the over-all level of economic activity and employment and specific problems in so far as manpower or productive capacity might require adaptation to non-military needs. Structural problems of conversion of the latter type will be discussed in chapter 4. Successful maintenance of the level of aggregate demand, production and employment would facilitate the solution of specific structural or frictional problems. Conversely, economic policies which dealt smoothly and effectively with the structural or frictional problems would help to promote the solution of the general problems. In both cases, careful preparation would be required to ensure that the various stages of the disarmament process were accompanied by as little disturbance of economic life as possible.

53. In the economic life of all countries, shifts in the pattern of demand and in the allocation of productive resources are continually occurring in response to changes in technology, foreign trade, consumer tastes, per capita income, the age distribution of the population, migration, and many other factors. Some industries grow more rapidly than others, while the output of certain industries may even decline in absolute terms. Such shifts involve a transfer of manpower and capital between occupations, industries and regions. The reallocation of productive resources which would accompany disarmament is in many respects merely a special case of the phenomenon of economic growth.

54. There are, however, some aspects of the process of disarmament which would raise problems significantly different from those that have been experienced in the usual process of economic growth. While many of the continuous changes in the composition of demand work themselves out only over a long period of time, it seems reasonable to assume that disarmament, once decided upon, would occur more rapidly—over a period of only a few years. For some components of military demand, the whole of the shift might occur within a very short period of time such as a single year. The reallocation of resources attendant upon disarmament would therefore pose some special problems. The more rapid the rate of growth of an economy, however, the easier it would be to bring about the economic changes disarmament might require.

55. The conversion of resources that would be required as a result of disarmament at the present time would be far smaller, in the aggregate, than that which took place at the end of the Second World War. Thus an examination of the early post-war conversion may help to give perspective to the present problem. The experience of the

smaller-scale conversion that followed the end of the hostilities in Korea also deserves consideration.

56. The post-war conversion was a much larger one and involved a more rapid transfer of resources than total disarmament would require at present. During the last years of the war, the world devoted about one half of its resources to destruction. The real military expenditure and the number of people in uniform were about four times as high as today. The extent of devastation in the areas overrun by armies or bombed from the air was immense. The usual network of trade both within and between countries was thoroughly disrupted. Despite these difficulties, huge armies were quickly demobilized without a significant rise in unemployment in most countries, and the pace of recovery, particularly of industrial output, was impressively rapid.

57. During the post-war conversion, the major concern of economic policy was to restrain, rather than to maintain, over-all demand. This period was characterized by intense pressure of excess demand for both consumption and investment. Most commodities were in short supply. Their distribution was carried out nearly everywhere with the aid of rationing or at least under a system of price controls. The wartime accumulation of liquid savings in the hands of the population guaranteed a high level of continued effective demand. As plant and equipment were released from war production and repaired or replaced, they were immediately turned to producing goods for which demand had remained unsatisfied or deferred in some countries during nearly fifteen years of the Great Depression and the war. Most of the demobilized manpower found employment in civilian occupations, while the total labour force declined, reflecting a voluntary withdrawal of some women, minors and veterans from the labour market. As supply conditions improved, price and distribution controls were progressively eased.

58. There were large arrears not only of consumption but also of investment. The capital stock had in many countries been run down by destruction, obsolescence and lack of maintenance. Technological progress had continued and in fact sharply accelerated in some fields during the war years. But much of it had remained unincorporated in plant and equipment—during the depression because of lack of effective demand, and during the war because of diversion of resources to wartime needs. Residential construction had undergone successive postponement in some countries. These factors led to an upsurge in business and residential investment after the war, financed in part by the accumulated liquid resources of corporations and of consumers and in part by various forms of public assistance.

59. In the *United States*, by the end of the Second World War, the military budget had accounted for over 40 per cent of the gross national product. Between 1945 and 1946, expenditure on national security was reduced by 80 per cent. The decline in military expenditure was equal to one-third of the gross national product and nearly two-thirds of personal consumption in 1944. By way of comparison it may be said that the military budget in the United States in recent years

has been somewhat less than 10 per cent of the gross national product and about 15 per cent of personal consumption.

60. The decline in total real demand was less than half the drop in military spending because of the advance in all other sectors of demand. The small decline in national output was perhaps no more than could have been expected as a result of voluntary withdrawals from the labour force and from the shortening of working hours.

61. The sharpest increase took place in gross private domestic investment which rose from $21 billion to $51 billion—or from less than 6 per cent of gross national product to about 15 per cent. The rise in consumption also contributed in absolute terms nearly as much as investment, although its relative contribution was not so large. There were also increases in public expenditure for civilian purposes and in net foreign investment. Assistance through UNRRA, other grants and credits to various countries for relief and rehabilitation helped toward a substantial expansion of United States exports. Thus the economy showed a high degree of flexibility even in the relatively short run.

62. Between August 1945 and June 1946, the size of the United States armed forces was reduced by over 9 million men. There was a small reduction in the labour force as women and minors returned to home and school, and veterans continued their interrupted education. As a result of this, and of the cutting back of overtime, unemployment in 1946 remained below 4 per cent of the labour force, despite the very extensive and rapid demobilization.

63. While the large backlog of demand of private business and consumers was responsible for much of the ease with which the post-war adjustment was made, effective government policies also helped. Taxes were reduced. There was a very great increase in transfer payments, principally veterans' cash benefits and payments related to the veterans' training and education programme. As a result, despite the massive decline in military spending, disposable income fell hardly at all. As regards investment, a large veterans' loan programme helped to finance the purchase of homes and farms, quick settlements were made to business on termination of war contracts, and an easy credit policy was maintained. The Government of the United States of America notes that:

"Tried measures such as these would be under active consideration again in the event of the acceptance of a disarmament program."[1]

64. In *western Europe* the conversion process took somewhat longer than in the United States because of the damage or destruction to productive facilities and the fact that the total output had in many cases fallen below pre-war levels. Inflationary pressures were severe. Confidence in currencies was shaken. Many key products, notably coal, steel, certain imported materials, and foodstuffs were in short supply.

65. Despite these difficulties the conversion was relatively rapid. Eighteen months after the cessation of hostilities, industrial output had recovered its pre-war level nearly everywhere except in the Federal Republic of Germany and in Italy. The demobilized armed forces were

---

[1] See the reply of the Government of the United States of America.

rather quickly absorbed in employment in civilian occupations. Except in the two countries just mentioned, unemployment declined well below pre-war levels. The recovery of western Europe was assisted by a considerable amount of external aid.

66.   In the United Kingdom, it is estimated that at the end of the war, 9 million persons, or 42 per cent of the total working population, were either in the armed forces or engaged in the manufacture of equipment and supplies for them. Sixteen months later, the total number in these two categories had fallen by almost 7 million. Of this total about 1.2 million corresponded to a voluntary decline in the labour force, while involuntary unemployment rose by about 0.7 million. Thus over 5 million people were absorbed into civilian employment in the short space of sixteen months, whereas the corresponding number that would have to be absorbed in the event of disarmament now is just over 1 million. It is noteworthy that the number unemployed at any one time never greatly exceeded six or seven weeks' release at the maximum rate reached, and that it stood at this level only so long as releases continued at a substantial rate. Even so, unemployment remained below 4 per cent of the labour force.

67.   In some of the *under-developed countries,* the post-war recovery presented special problems. This was partly because agriculture, which formed a much larger proportion of the output of the under-developed than of the developed countries, was generally slower to recover than was industry. The long years of war had led in many cases to heavy exhaustion of farms and livestock and to disturbance of trading patterns. There was a world shortage of fertilizers, and recovery was also delayed in many cases because initially inadequate industrial, transport and mining equipment had been strained beyond its rated capacity during the war. For some time after the war, too, delivery of equipment was delayed by conversion and re-equipment needs in the industrial countries.

68.   There is, however, no reason to believe that any future disarmament would be attended, in the under-developed countries, by the same types of problem as prevailed after the Second World War. As indicated previously, the main question in these countries would be whether development programmes could be enlarged and stepped up significantly—and in sufficiently good time—to permit the absorption of the demobilized armed forces and other resources into productive employment.

69.   In the *Soviet Union,* experience of conversion immediately following the Second World War was significantly different from that in other countries, because of the much greater destruction and devastation which had taken place during the war. Much equipment had been damaged or was in a bad state of repair. Plant and equipment constructed during the war had been designed entirely for military purposes, and was therefore somewhat less "convertible" than facilities constructed in peace-time. Superimposed on all this was the problem of transferring workers in the eastern territories—who had been evacuated from areas occupied by the Germans—back to their home districts in the western part of the country. For all these reasons there was a decline in industrial production from 1945 to 1946, concentrated in the producer goods

sector. Since some manpower had to be employed in tasks for which it was untrained there was a decline in output per man. These developments, however, were the result of the devastation and dislocation referred to above. The subsequent recovery was very rapid and by 1948 industrial production was already nearly one-fifth above the 1940 level. The circumstances of any future disarmament would be much more favourable to a smooth conversion process than those at the end of the Second World War.

70. In other *eastern European* countries the conversion process had also to overcome heavy human and material losses caused by the Second World War. In Poland alone, over 6 million people perished during the war and Nazi occupation. The respective Governments had to face the great damage caused to productive capacity, transport and housing, apart from dislocation of populations, monetary disturbances and other difficulties. Recovery was facilitated by the planned direction of the process of reconstruction and readjustment which was made possible by the gradual nationalization of banking, of most industry and of transportation. The recovery proceeded relatively quickly, so that in 1948 in most countries the pre-war level of production was surpassed.

CONVERSION AFTER THE KOREAN WAR

71. In the United States at the end of the Korean hostilities many of the special features associated with demobilization after the Second World War were no longer present. Military spending fell from $62 billion (in 1960 prices) in 1953 to $51 billion in 1954. This was accompanied by a liquidation of inventories that in part was associated directly with the fall in military expenditure itself, and in part reflected some business uncertainty regarding the immediate outlook for demand. The total decline in the national product, however, was less than half the reduction in military spending, largely because of increases in consumption and domestic investment. The latter, in turn, were made possible by a reduction in taxes and a policy of monetary ease which was particularly important in stimulating expenditure on housing. Unemployment, after rising to 5.6 per cent of the labour force in 1954, declined to less than 4.4 per cent in 1955 in the face of further cutbacks in military spending.

72. Characterizing the effectiveness of policies during this period, the Government of the United States of America observes that:

"Despite the mildness of the 1954 recession it now is clear that fiscal and monetary policies might have been applied with more vigor. The reason they were not is that the decline in defence spending following the Korean War was not treated by the policy makers as a major demobilization requiring strong compensatory action. For this reason the 1953-1954 period does not provide a significant guide to the behavior of the American economy in a disarmament program during the 1960's."[2]

73. In other countries, for which information is available, the degree of involvement in the Korean war was not such that its end provided experience of comparable relevance for the purpose of this study. With the cessation of hostilities in Korea, however, there was

[2] *Ibid.*

a diminution of international tensions which brought about reductions in military expenditure and releases from armed forces in various countries. No significant problems of reabsorption of the demobilized personnel arose in these countries.

EXPERIENCE IN THE CENTRALLY PLANNED ECONOMIES

74.   The experience of the centrally planned economies in reducing the armed forces is also of interest. In the Soviet Union, the armed forces were reduced from 5.8 million men in 1955 to 3.6 million men in 1958.[3] There were also reductions in military forces in other centrally planned economies during that period. No significant problems were created by the demobilization in these countries since the demand for labour was continually increasing. Discharged officers were absorbed in administrative posts in industry or agriculture and were provided with opportunities for retraining at government expense. In a number of countries in eastern Europe, expansion in output of durable consumer goods was greatly facilitated after 1954 by utilizing the equipment which had earlier been devoted to producing armaments.

IMPACT ON NATIONAL PRODUCTION AND EMPLOYMENT

75.   National experience with general economic policies during previous conversion periods will unquestionably be valuable for policy makers in the future. In adopting a programme of general and complete disarmament, Governments would certainly wish to assess very carefully the probable impact of disarmament on national production and employment, and to examine their economic policies to ensure that these were as well thought out as possible. It would be important to maintain a high general level of domestic demand for goods and services and thereby to support satisfactory levels of output and employment. This is already a well-established objective of national policy, but it would have additional urgency both during the conversion period and also in the long run, after general and complete disarmament had been achieved.

76.   The economic measures needed to maintain over-all effective demand are different in the private enterprise economies from those in the centrally planned economies. In the latter, economic decision-making is centralized. Most of the productive capacity is government-owned. The national economic plans are directed toward the achievement of a set rate of growth and higher levels of living. In the private enterprise economies, on the other hand, where the private sectors are much larger than the government sectors, the power to make economic decisions is diffused. Governments must therefore rely heavily, in influencing economic decision-making in the private consumption and investment sectors, on relatively indirect means such as fiscal and monetary policies. In general, the governments of under-developed countries cannot count as readily as those of the more developed countries on an expansion of private investment. Greater attention needs

---

[3] There was a government decision for a further reduction to 2.4 million men in 1960. Statement by Prime Minister Khrushchev reported in *Pravda*, 15 January 1960.

therefore to be given to undertaking whatever volume of expenditure may prove necessary in the government-owned sector in the under-developed countries.

77. Much attention has already been given in the *industrialized private enterprise economies* to the methods by which total effective demand can be maintained. Member countries are pledged under the United Nations Charter to maintain full employment. A number of Governments have further undertaken in national statements of policy to adopt measures toward that objective. The instruments available for the prevention of any substantial shortfall of demand are well known. Their relative merits, however, vary widely from one country to another and from one time to another because of differences in institutions and attitudes.

78. The nature and magnitude of the task of maintaining total demand at an adequate level to assure the fullest possible employment would depend to some extent upon the purpose to which the resources released from military use were applied. In some cases, it might be decided to use the released resources by reducing taxes on income, particularly of lower income groups. In others, it might be decided to reduce the burden of indirect taxes on mass consumption goods borne mainly by the lower income groups in the community. It might, also, be seen fit to adopt fiscal measures designed to stimulate investment expenditure. In yet other cases importance might be attached to reduction of the public debt. Alternatively, a decision might also be taken to replace military expenditure by other kinds of government expenditure. These different policies would have different impacts upon the level of effective demand. In practice, different combinations of them would be likely to be used in different countries.

79. Disarmament would lead to an immediate reduction of effective demand only in so far as total expenditure of the government-owned sector were reduced. It might seem at first sight that this result would be avoided if tax revenue were reduced by the same amount as government expenditure, but this is not, in general, the case, since some of the increased disposable income would be saved rather than spent. The effect on consumption would depend on which type of tax were reduced, whether direct or indirect, and on which income group were affected. Generally, reduction in taxes diminishing the burdens on low income groups are the most effective. Even so, however, some fall in income would result under these assumptions. A setback of this kind, unless counteracted by other measures, might also discourage private investment and thus lead to a further fall in income.

80. It should, perhaps, be observed that in so far as it is desired to raise private consumption, the appropriate means cannot lie exclusively in reductions in direct taxation because those benefited by such a measure do not include the poorest sectors of the population whose incomes are too low to be taxed. Supplementary measures of various types would be required to ensure that all parts of the community benefited to some extent from the higher consumption levels made possible by disarmament.

81. The effect of using the money saved by a reduction of military expenditure for repaying public debt would be twofold. On the one

hand government expenditure on goods and services would be lower, since debt repayment does not in itself constitute a direct offset to the reduction in military spending. On the other hand, by substituting holdings of money for holdings of public debt some private spending on goods and services would probably be stimulated. The extent of this stimulation is difficult to assess, and would vary with the kind of debt redeemed, but it would be unlikely to offset the deflationary impact of the original reduction in government expenditure.

82. Monetary and fiscal policy could be used to offset the effect of a shortfall in total demand that might result from a decline in government expenditure. Monetary policy, whether operated mainly through interest rates or mainly through a more direct control of credit, gives some scope for the encouragement of both capital formation by business and purchases of durable goods by consumers. Changes in taxation, or transfers, in addition to their immediate effects on purchasing power, to which some reference has already been made, may also be expected to exert some influence on the formation of business capital; tax concessions may be designed to encourage private investment in general or to give special encouragement to investment in particular industries or localities where it will most effectively employ resources formerly in military use. Moreover, although in some countries there are severe limits to the extent to which it is practicable to use unbalanced budgets as a means of adjusting the level of effective demand, such measures, where they are acceptable, are powerful instruments for this purpose. Tax revenue might be deliberately reduced by more than the net reduction in government expenditure brought about by disarmament. In some countries, the changes that have already taken place in the net budget balance of the government sector within small numbers of years appear to have been of the same order of magnitude as those that might be required to offset a shortfall of demand consequent upon disarmament.

83. If a shortfall of effective demand cannot be fully dealt with by the foregoing methods, there always remains the possibility of an increase in civilian government expenditure designed at least in part to help in solving this problem. Expenditure on goods and services is, in general, likely to be more effective for this purpose than transfer expenditure—the increase of grants and subsidies to various sections of the community—but in the not unlikely event of the recipients being disposed to spend nearly all the cash benefits they receive, the difference would be small.

84. The instruments of adjustment referred to above are more highly developed, easier to bring into operation, and may be expected to work more effectively in some countries than in others. Bearing in mind, however, that a substantial part of military expenditure would probably be replaced by other government expenditure in most countries, it may be concluded from the foregoing paragraphs that the maintenance of effective demand in the face of disarmament should not prove difficult. Indeed, it should be practicable not merely to maintain the level of demand during the transition period, but to move forward to the more rapid growth in total real income that a transfer of resources from military use to productive investment would render physically possible.

85. It has been argued that in so far as disarmament might lead to a reduction in the relative size of the government sector, the stabilizing effect that the existence of a substantial public sector exercises upon the general level of activity might be diminished. Military expenditure, however, has itself been notoriously subject to variations which, being unconnected with the requirements of stabilization policy, have disturbed the level of activity in the economies in question and in the world as a whole. Disarmament need not therefore increase the difficulty of economic stabilization, even if it should lead to a fall in the relative size of the government sector.

86. For many *under-developed countries,* the effect of disarmament upon the industrial countries' demands for primary products, and thus on the export earnings of the primary producing countries, would be of great importance. So would the methods of dealing with the liquidation of strategic stockpiles. These problems are discussed in chapter 5. It is necessary to add here that the industrial countries' success in maintaining effective demand during the immediate period of disarmament would be of great concern to all primary producing countries. The significance of disarmament for an expansion of aid to under-developed countries is dealt with in chapter 6.

87. The effects of disarmament within the under-developed countries themselves would vary from one to another. In some cases, the ratio of the military budget to the gross domestic product is of the same order of magnitude as in the major military powers (4-10 per cent). In the majority of cases (including most of the larger under-developed countries), it is less than 4 per cent. So far as growth rates are concerned, however, the effects of the release for non-military purposes of these proportions of the national resources, whether high or low, might be greater than the figures would by themselves suggest. Both total capital formation and government expenditure are generally smaller in relation to gross domestic product in the under-developed countries than in the richer ones. The ratio of military expenditure to gross domestic capital formation in the majority of under-developed countries for which the data exist lies in the same range (10 per cent and upward) as in the majority of other countries. Thus the contribution of disarmament to their economic growth would be very substantial.

88. Under-developed countries usually obtain their supplies of munitions from abroad either as direct purchases or as grants under military agreements or both. To the extent that these imports are received without payment, their cessation would have little economic impact on under-developed countries. On the other hand, to the extent that these imports have required the expenditure of foreign exchange, disarmament would make it possible to reallocate foreign exchange to imports of capital goods and of other equipment needed for economic growth. There are, however, a few countries which have been receiving considerable foreign exchange from foreign military aid and military expenditure including the outlays of foreign personnel. In consequence, it is important that any disarmament programme should include measures to relieve the strain on the external balances of such countries.

89. Reductions in the military budgets of most under-developed countries would have their main effects through the reduction of man-

power in the armed forces and the associated decrease in local expenditure on the products used by the armed forces. The release of unskilled military personnel would to some extent aggravate the already difficult problems of unemployment and under-employment. On the other hand, the members of the armed forces in the under-developed countries are frequently better provided with potentially useful skills than the rest of the population. The more skilled men should be easier to absorb into productive employment and their absorption should contribute substantially to the development of the economy.

90. As was pointed out above with respect to the industrialized private enterprise economies, the maintenance of the level of effective demand may require sustaining the level of government expenditure. This consideration appears to apply with greater force to the under-developed countries, where tax reduction may be less effective in stimulating private expenditure than it is in the more developed economies. The need to plan alternative government expenditure would therefore be particularly great.

91. In the *centrally planned economies,* the maintenance of effective demand while reducing military expenditure would be simply a matter of efficiency of planning techniques. Since decisions concerning the production of military output as well as of investment and consumer goods are co-ordinated through the national economic plan, the substitution of one type of expenditure for another does not raise any basic problems for the maintenance of effective demand. The reply from the Government of the Czechoslovak Socialist Republic indicates that this can be accomplished by certain adjustments in the current economic plans without necessitating the establishment of any special economic institutions. The effect of the decline in armaments expenditure could be largely offset by corresponding increases in investment in plant and equipment and for other purposes such as housing as well as by increases in personal consumption. A rise in personal consumption could be brought about by a reduction in taxation corresponding in magnitude to that part of armament expenditure which was not replaced by investment.

92. In consequence, effective demand could be readily maintained, and the principal problems of conversion would concern the physical adaptation of plants producing armaments to the production of goods for civilian use. The problems of reallocation of resources are discussed in some detail in the reply from the Government of the Polish People's Republic.[4] It is indicated that the period of short-term transition may be divided into three major stages. In the first stage, the main concern would be to utilize the existing military fixed assets and skilled manpower for facilitating an increase in the output of civilian goods and services. The role of new investment and development of additional supplies of raw materials would be relatively minor. It is suggested that the warehouses, transport and communications equipment, repair shops and other capital equipment and raw materials used for military purposes would be converted as far as technically possible to the production of civilian goods. Military personnel with specialized

---

[4] See the reply of the Government of the Polish People's Republic.

higher education would be transferred to civilian functions in the departments of health, education and social services.

93. The second stage involves an expansion of plant and equipment, in which there is relatively limited or no excess capacity at present, for the absorption of the manpower released from military use. Particular attention would have to be paid to overcoming the shortages of raw materials that might develop. For this purpose, an increase in the domestic output of these commodities as well as in exports to pay for imports would be called for. With an adequate expansion of productive capacities and of the raw materials base, it would then be possible in the third stage to reap the full benefits of conversion—in the form of a higher rate of growth of the economy and of levels of living than is currently envisaged.

CHAPTER 4

STRUCTURAL PROBLEMS OF CONVERSION

94. Even with the successful maintenance of total effective demand during a period of disarmament, significant problems of adjustment would remain in specific sectors and areas of the economy. Part of the personnel released by the armed forces and the armaments industry would have to be trained or retrained so as to permit absorption into peacetime occupations. Some plant and equipment would have to be converted. Productive capacity might contract in some industries, and might have to be expanded in others. Where the manufacture of armaments has been concentrated in particular regions, it would be necessary either to shift resources out of those regions to other areas of growing demand, or alternatively to undertake schemes of redevelopment. The necessary steps would have to be taken to modify the direction of research and of technological development.

95. It has already been suggested that the broad problem of re-adaptation of industry and manpower resulting from disarmament is not basically dissimilar from that experienced in the normal process of economic growth. For example, a decline in demand for coal in western Europe and North America has created special problems in the coal mining communities. The position in some of the textile towns is similar. In the centrally planned economies, problems of this type can be handled by planning. In private enterprise economies, where adjustments may be delayed because of such circumstances as immobility of some labour or capital and rigidity of prices, they can be dealt with by special government measures.

96. The higher the rate of growth of the economy, the easier the process of adaptation. In the longer run, disarmament would allow each country to raise the rate of investment and to adapt productive capacity more adequately to the needs of the population and to the requirements of economic growth, both in the private enterprise and the centrally planned economies.

97. In the shorter run, the smoothness of the transition would largely depend on the ability of Governments to anticipate the types of problem that might arise, and on the adequacy of preparations. This calls for an adequate assessment of the direct and indirect demands of military expenditure on each industrial sector and region, and of the extent to which a replacement of military by other expenditure would involve a modification of the structure of demand. Such a confrontation of military demands and of civilian alternatives can be carried out in detail only by national Governments. The present discussion sets out only some of the more important considerations involved.

98. The resources now supplying military requirements could be adapted to peacetime needs partly by shifts within industries and plants, and partly by shifts between industries.

(a) *Shifts within industries and plants.* In a large number of cases, it may be possible for a given plant to shift the nature of the end-product from military equipment to durable consumer goods and investment goods while using the same productive equipment and man-power. For instance, there might be a shift from tanks to tractors, from military to civilian aircraft, from naval vessels to merchant ships, or from electronic equipment for military purposes to television sets. This might be a relatively easy procedure, in many cases involving little more than changes in designs, retooling, and minor adaptations of skills, particularly in plants and enterprises which already produce both military and civilian goods.

(b) *Shifts between industries.* Other cases, however, might call for a more complex form of conversion requiring the output of some industries to be completely stopped or sharply curtailed and that of others to be correspondingly expanded. Many ordnance factories might cease to produce altogether. In some countries, the total output of aircraft, ships and boats would have to be reduced since civilian demand for such products would not fully offset the fall in military demand. On the other hand, a considerable expansion of output in the cement, brick, glass and building industries might be required should there be a shift in expenditure in favour of civilian construction. Shifts of this type cannot be accommodated within the same plant but require instead a movement of resources from one industry to another.

99. Shifts between industries would necessitate acquisition of different types of skill by the working force as well as new investment in plant and equipment. They would take a somewhat longer time to accomplish than shifts within industries, the length of time depending on how major or far-removed were the shifts. If the two industries were to have a similar resource content—as do the aircraft industry and the general engineering industry, for instance—the adaptation would be easier and would take a shorter time than if the two industries were to differ significantly in resource content—as do the aircraft industry and the building materials industry, for example. The extent to which the conversion would involve shifts within industries and plants as opposed to shifts between industries can be judged from studies made in a number of countries.

THE PROBLEM OF INTER-INDUSTRY SHIFTS

100. In the *United States,* owing to the concentration of military expenditure in a limited number of industries, only a few industries would be affected sharply by reductions in military demand. Professor Leontief has prepared a hypothetical study of the inter-industrial ramifications of conversion in the United States on the assumption that military expenditure is replaced wholly by increases in expenditure on other kinds of goods and services in proportion to their shares in total demand in 1958.[1] Such a reallocation of military expenditure would

---

[1] W. Leontief and M. Hoffenberg, "The Economic Effects of Disarmament", *Scientific American* (New York), vol. 204, No. 4, April 1961, pp. 47-55.

release 1,320,000 employees from the contracting industries for employment elsewhere. Over four-fifths of the decline in employment would be in four industries—aircraft and parts (which includes missiles), radio, ordnance, and ships and boats (see annex 3, table 3-1). Employment would be totally eliminated in the ordnance industry and would fall by more than 90 per cent in the aircraft and parts industry; expansion of demand for civilian aircraft would have only a minor influence on output in the latter industry.

101. In addition to the 1,320,000 employees released from contracting industries, the 2,530,000 members of the armed forces and about 790,000 civilian employees of military agencies would become available for alternative employment. Thus, about 4.5 million persons —some 6 or 7 per cent of the total labour force in employment in 1958 —would, on these assumptions, have to change their employment from one industry group to another or find civilian instead of military employment.

102. Professor Leontief estimates the number absorbed into expanding sectors to be some 600,000 less than that released from the military establishment and the contracting industries. This difference, taken literally, would imply that an increase of about 1 per cent in total government and private expenditure, spread over the duration of the disarmament process, would be required to preserve the general level of employment. It is, however, a residual figure which should be treated with reserve, since it is less than the margin of error of this hypothetical calculation.

103. A similar calculation, though with less narrowly defined industry groups, has been made for the *United Kingdom* by Professor J. R. N. Stone and his colleagues of the University of Cambridge, Department of Applied Economics. The assumption in this case is that military expenditure is replaced as to one-third by increased private consumption expenditure, one-third by fixed capital formation at home, and one-third by increased foreign aid. The only industrial group in which output (and hence employment) is estimated to decline is that including the manufacture of ships and aircraft, in which the fall is about 20 per cent (see annex 3, table 3-2). Including the members of the armed forces themselves, and civilian employees of the military establishment, the number of persons required to change their "industry group" would be about 900,000, or between $3\frac{1}{2}$ and 4 per cent of the labour force.

104. In both cases, these calculations indicate the numbers who would have to move from one industry to another (or out of direct military employment) in the event of very rapid disarmament. If the operation were to extend over a number of years, the change per annum would be only a fraction of the total. Moreover, a substantial proportion of the shrinkage in the armed forces and in the contracting industries might take place through the normal process of turnover, thereby diminishing the number of persons actually required to move from one kind of employment to another.

105. The replies received from a number of *other countries of western Europe* indicate that the problem of shifts from one industry

to another would be a relatively small one.[2] According to these replies, the rate of economic growth is now limited by labour shortages and it could be accelerated if manpower were released from military uses.

106.   *Under-developed countries* generally have been meeting their requirements for military goods and services by imports, so that their disarmament would release foreign exchange rather than industrial workers. As indicated in chapter 3, it would also free members of the forces with many useful skills and training. Some of these would be absorbed by the growing labour market; others could be usefully employed in the development of social capital by construction of minor irrigation works, feeder-roads and other community development projects, which would help to mitigate the already acute problem of under-development.

107.   In some of the *semi-industrialized countries,* however, the newly started basic industries which manufacture, for example, chemical fertilizers, heavy machine tools, heavy vehicles, aircraft and electronic equipment, have been serving both military and civilian needs. In the event of disarmament these industries could concentrate, without any transitional difficulty, on the manufacture of capital goods so urgently needed for both consumer goods industries and capital goods industries. Transport capacity, particularly vehicles, released from military uses, would supp'ement the inadequate transport facilities available in the present stage of their development.

108.   In the *centrally planned economies,* as indicated previously, productive capacity is usually fully utilized. Thus it would be necessary to convert plants producing military equipment to production of durable consumer goods and of such investment goods as can be produced in them with only minor retooling. Such conversion could be achieved rapidly. Many plants producing military equipment produce also certain goods for civilian purposes. In Poland, for instance, plants which manufacture military equipment also account for about 50 per cent of the national output of motor cycles and scooters, 80 per cent of the sewing machines, 70 per cent of the washing machines and 30 per cent of the refrigerators produced in the country.[3] The reply of the Government of the Czechoslovak Socialist Republic mentions experience with conversion of a number of plants from military production to production of medium-sized trucks, tractors and television sets, in all of which no more than 3 to 4 per cent of the productive equipment was found to be unutilizable after conversion.[4]

109.   In the longer run, disarmament would make possible substantial increases of investment, so that the more adequate adaptation of productive capacity to the needs of the population and to the requirements of economic growth could proceed fairly rapidly. In Poland, for instance, it is estimated that total disarmament would allow the total amount of capital investment to rise by over 9 per cent as compared with the level of 1962.[5] In Bulgaria an increase of investment by 10

[2] See volume II of this report (E/3593/Rev.1/Add.1).
[3] See the reply of the Government of the Polish People's Republic.
[4] See the reply of the Government of the Czechoslovak Socialist Republic.
[5] See the reply of the Government of the Polish People's Republic, Addendum.

to 12 per cent would be possible in consequence of disarmament.[6] A considerable increase in investment would also take place in Hungary.[7]

110. The replies of the Governments of the centrally planned economies state that there will be no difficulty in absorbing released manpower. In countries such as Czechoslovakia, the German Democratic Republic and Hungary, the supply of labour in recent years has not kept pace with growing labour requirements. In Poland it is estimated that in the next few years the increase of the industrial labour force will be drawn mainly from the natural increase of the urban population with relatively little influx of workers from agriculture to industry. In these circumstances it would appear that demobilization of manpower might slow down the transfer of labour from agriculture to industry. But the increase of investment following disarmament would raise considerably the requirement of labour for industry and construction. The final effect, therefore, would be to stimulate rather than to slow down the transfer of labour from agriculture to industry. In the Soviet Union the absorption of demobilized personnel would be greatly facilitated by the growing demand for manpower in the rapidly expanding eastern territories. The construction of new industrial centres and the expansion of cultivation of land in the less populated Asian parts of the Soviet Union, particularly in Siberia, has generated a demand for labour which cannot be fully met by local resources. Migration to these territories is being encouraged and disarmament would provide a welcome source for addition to the manpower required.

SPECIAL PROBLEMS

111. The preceding analysis of the changes resulting from the process of reallocation of military expenditure to other purposes suggests that the net shifts in employment and output would be relatively small. As already indicated, however, special problems would arise from a concentration of the military effort in certain industries or areas. These problems may be broadly classified as follows:

(i) Adaptation of skills to peace-time requirements.

(ii) Problems of assistance to particular enterprises, industries and localities, heavily oriented to military use.

(iii) Reorientation of research and technological development.

(i) *Adaptation of skills*

112. In some instances, the skills that are essential for service in the armed forces or in some of the major industries producing military goods may not be readily adaptable to the requirements of civilian employment. Consequently, there would arise a necessity to retrain part of the skilled manpower and to train some of the unskilled.

113. (a) *Armed personnel and employees in the Ministry of Defence.* Most of the officers in modern armed forces have received

---

[6] See the reply of the People's Republic of Bulgaria.

[7] According to the reply of the Government of the Hungarian People's Republic, military expenditure in 1959 was 2.5 thousand million forints while total investment was 19.5 thousand million forints. If only half of the military expenditure were turned to investment, the latter would increase by about 6.5 per cent.

training that would fit them easily for technical, engineering, medical and similar posts in civilian life. As the reply of the Government of the United States of America indicates, 85 per cent of the commissioned officers in that country have completed some form of college training. However, some of the senior officers in the armed forces have been trained for purposes significantly different from those that are needed in civilian life. A special effort would have to be made to find suitab!e employment for them. Some of them might be called on to serve in various capacities in the international organs to be set up for control of disarmament. Some would find useful occupations in civilian activities where their organizational abilities may be a special requirement. Since the number of officers is usually not very large, it should not be hard to absorb them into civilian life.

114. The demobilization of the non-professional members of the armed forces would involve a much larger number of persons. But most of these men have been drawn from civilian life where they were previously engaged in non-military occupations. They are usually young and relatively mobile. Military service has often interrupted their education. In many cases, however, they have acquired new technical skills while in military service. In most of the under-developed countries, the regular armed forces possess a much higher level of industrial and technical skills than the civilian population; this would tend to give them a relatively greater chance of being absorbed into civilian employment, particularly in an expanding economy.

115. The release of the armed forces, over some years, would imply only that the number of new entrants for that period would be augmented by this special factor. In some countries, particularly in Europe, which are faced with shortages of manpower, the availability of a larger labour force could indeed contribute to an acceleration of the rate of economic growth. Moreover, the financial resources released by disarmament should make it possible to arrange for termination pay and special allowances for various types of training. For instance, the Government of the United States carried out, after the Second World War, a large programme for education, training and job placement for demobilized army personnel. Nearly 8 million veterans took advantage of the training programme. Similarly, 2 million, or one-third of the eligible veterans of the Korean war have benefited from such training facilities.[8]

116. The reply of the Government of the Polish People's Republic indicates the magnitudes involved in re-employing the non-professional members of the armed forces. It is anticipated that a majority of the draftees from rural areas would return to the countryside to help in the projected intensification of agriculture. Some 20 to 30 per cent are expected to be employed in plants which now produce military equipment but could immediately be converted to produce investment goods, export commodities and raw materials. This would further facilitate the productive employment of the remainder.

117. (b) *Industries producing military goods.* As pointed out above, the problem of conversion in the industrial countries[9] is likely

---

[8] See the reply of the Government of the United States of America.

[9] Owing to virtual absence of major military goods industries in the under-developed countries, this question has relatively limited relevance for them.

to be a short-term one for most industries. In industries depending heavily on military orders, many of the employees possess a level of skill that should find gainful employment in other branches of production,[10] so long as over-all effective demand is rising. Moreover, where some form of retraining or additional training would be needed for employment, it could be acquired through the facilities for apprenticeship and on-the-job training often provided by individual firms or plants for their new labour force. Even so, there might be some special cases which would require special assistance to encourage the adaptation of skills to new jobs. Such help could be provided through opportunities for vocational training financed by such means as termination pay or other special measures.

118. In this age of automation the demand for highly skilled labour is rising faster than the demand for semi-skilled and unskilled. Therefore a significant number of those who would be released in the latter categories might be faced with difficult problems, particularly if they were of an advanced age. While the experience of a much more extensive demobilization and conversion at the end of the Second World War suggests that the problems thus arising are by no means insuperable, governments should stand ready to assist the reabsorption of such workers into productive employment.

(ii) *Particular enterprises and localities*

119. Owing to the concentration of military output in a few industries, termination of military contracts would bear specially upon the activities of particular enterprises. These would have a choice of three courses of action: complete shut-down, the adaptation of existing plant and equipment to the production of other goods through major retooling, and investment in entirely new plants. Similar problems on a much larger scale were faced at the end of the last war and tackled with a considerable degree of success.

120. The geographical distribution of the activity based on military expenditure is very uneven in many countries. The readjustments necessitated by disarmament would therefore impinge particularly heavily on certain areas and localities. Various forms of public and other assistance would thus prove necessary to facilitate readjustment. Measures of three types would be required. First, attempts should be made to diversify the structure of employment by developing new industries where possible. Secondly, adequate relocation allowances should be provided to facilitate the movement of those who are mobile to areas where the labour market is expanding. Thirdly, adequate relief should be granted to those whose attachment to the locality is too deep or whose age is too advanced to contemplate moving to other areas. The costs of the necessary measures would be very small in relation to the resources that disarmament would release.

---

[10] Of the 2.5 million persons employed directly or indirectly in producing military goods and services in the private sector in the United States in 1960, nearly 1.5 million, or 60 per cent of the total, possessed various types of skills such as professional, technical, managerial, clerical or skilled craftsmanship. See the reply of the Government of the United States of America.

(iii) *Reorientation of research and technological development*

121.   In the centrally planned economies Governments have always played a major role in promoting research and development. In the private enterprise economies also, this role has expanded everywhere in recent years, particularly through the growth of research for military purposes. In the United Kingdom, direct military expenditure is responsible for nearly two-fifths of the total spent on research and development. Approximately half of the research and development effort in the United States is financed out of the military budget; this part of research is highly concentrated in a few industries.

122.   The magnitude of the task of shifting scientific and technical personnel to non-military fields of research would differ from country to country, but the estimates that have been made for the United States may have some relevance elsewhere. In that country, expenditure on research and development is six to seven times higher per dollar of military demand than per dollar of final civilian demand.[11] Therefore, on the hypothetical assumption of an unchanged proportional allocation of funds to science by the civilian sector, the reply of the Government of the United States of America estimates that a reallocation of total military expenditure to civilian purposes would lead to a reduction of about 40 per cent in spending for research and development. The corresponding decline in the employment of scientific personnel would amount to only half the decline in research and development spending, or about 20 per cent.[12]

123.   No reduction in the actual employment of scientific and technical personnel need be feared, however, because the demand for civilian research would increase rapidly. Indeed, one of the main reasons why scientific research is still far from adequately applied in many civilian fields is the fact that highly qualified personnel have been scarce, and have been pre-empted by military demands. A more adequate supply of specialists would make it possible to open up new fields of inquiry, hitherto virtually neglected, as well as to devote larger resources to existing lines of scientific investigation in both the developed and under-developed countries. The scope for peaceful research in the physical, chemical, biological and human sciences is unlimited, and the potential benefits to the whole of humanity incalculable.

---

[11] See the reply of the Government of the United States of America.
[12] The smaller decline in employment is due in part to the fact that the materials and equipment content of research expenditures is much higher for military than for civilian research and in part to the fact that more scientists and engineers are required in posts not directly connected with research and development in the non-military industries than in the military.

CHAPTER 5

THE IMPACT OF DISARMAMENT ON INTERNATIONAL ECONOMIC RELATIONS

124. Disarmament would be bound to have favourable effects on the development of international economic relations. The political *détente* that would accompany an international disarmament programme would in itself imply that nations were willing to reconsider their economic relations with one another. The consequent relaxation of international tensions would provide a sound basis for reduction of trade barriers and for modification of existing trade agreements and trading practices. In the long run this would encourage an expansion of international trade, a more rational international division of labour and a more effective use of the world's resources. In the short term it might help conversion by generating new demand for exports from existing sources of supply that could be satisfied fairly easily from existing capacities.

125. The relaxation of international tension would benefit trade through the elimination of the concern with national defence as a factor affecting national trade policies. The needs of national defence have long been accepted as a legitimate reason for the pursuit of discriminatory and protectionist policies.[1] Among the justifications advanced for the protection of agriculture and mining in many industrial countries has been the need to guarantee an adequate national supply of food and raw materials. In many instances, the domestic production of manufactured goods, as well, has been promoted on security grounds, to the detriment of international trade. Security is not the only consideration in such cases, and may not even be the decisive one; nevertheless, it carries considerable weight with Governments at the present time. After disarmament, however, its force would be lost, and an opportunity would be afforded to re-examine and improve the framework of world trade.

126. An important aspect of this matter is trade between the centrally planned economies and the rest of the world. Although this trade has been rising in relation to world trade in recent years, its share is still low in comparison with the levels prevailing before the Second World War and, especially, in comparison with the share of these economies in world output and with the levels that could be achieved under favourable conditions in the future. The centrally planned economies are expanding rapidly and form a growing market, particularly for durable producers' goods and raw materials. At the

---

[1] It is true that at certain times national security considerations have led to higher trade flows in particular directions than might otherwise have taken place; strategic stockpiling, for example, has stimulated purchases of some commodities. However, this stimulus has not been an unmixed blessing, and in any case stockpiling is no longer significant in world trade.

same time, they are capable of serving as a source of supply to the rest of the world for certain primary products and manufactures. The obstacles that stand in the way of closer economic relations between state trading and private enterprise economies are not basically of a technical character. To a considerable extent they reflect mutual lack of confidence. A lessening of international tensions and a rebuilding of confidence would help to remove them.

127. Disarmament would bring about a change in the composition and rate of growth of output and thus affect the structure and rate of expansion of world trade. While the composition of the non-military production that would replace military output cannot be precisely foreseen, it appears to be a safe assumption that all the main categories of civilian output would increase their share in national product. In so far as increased investment and greater economic aid would accelerate the rate of economic growth in developed and under-developed countries, a more rapid expansion of world trade could be anticipated. However, there are more immediate effects that might follow the shift in demand; these hinge on the difference between the import content of military expenditure and the import content of the increments to consumption, investment and foreign aid that disarmament would facilitate.

128. It is possible in principle to estimate the import content of any country's military expenditure, as well as of the civilian expenditure that would replace it, by means of an analysis of an economy's inter-industry structure. Such an analysis would indicate whether a shift from military expenditure to, say, housing construction would result in a net increase or a net decrease in the demand for imports both in the aggregate and for specific commodities.

129. Some exports of primary products, such as petroleum, rubber and most metallic ores depend significantly at present on direct and indirect demand generated by military purchases. An estimate of this dependence with respect to the United States economy is summarized in annex 3, table 3-3. These figures show, for instance, that the direct and indirect demand for copper generated by United States military expenditure in 1958 amounted to 7.8 per cent of that year's total world supply and to 7.4 per cent of the supply in 1959. On the assumption that the demand generated by the combined military outlays of all industrialized countries may be about twice as 'large as that computed for the United States alone, the table indicates that some 15-16 per cent of world copper output has served, directly and indirectly, military purposes (see columns 3 and 4). For tin, nickel, lead and zinc the corresponding figure is over 9 per cent; for petroleum, between 8 and 9 per cent. In view of the well-known sensitivity of the prices of these products to changes in demand, the elimination of all armament expenditure, if there were no offsetting rise in civilian demand, could have a seriously adverse effect on the income of those under-developed countries whose exports consist largely of such raw materials.

130. Table 3-4 (in annex 3) shows, however, that the demand of the United States and of the world for these raw materials would be reduced only fractionally—by less than 2 per cent—if the elimination of military expenditure were accompanied by a corresponding increase in private and public non-military expenditure. These hypothetical

estimates, it should be noted, are based on the assumption that private consumption, investment, non-military government purchases and other categories of non-military demand would all increase in the same proportion. However, since the content of these raw materials in military production does not differ significantly from that of the most important categories of non-military production, the impact on over-all demand for the items listed in the table would appear to be only marginal for any likely change in the composition of civilian demand.

131.   Since the importance of military expenditure for most other primary commodities is smaller than for those discussed above, its cessation, even if not offset by an equal increase in non-military expenditure, would produce a smaller percentage of reduction in demand for them. The reallocation of military expenditure to non-military purposes would probably bring about a net increase in this demand. The hypothetical calculations made for the United States and the United Kingdom, for instance, suggest that this reallocation would increase the demand for both food and clothing and thus for foodstuffs and textile materials in general.

132.   Since disarmament may be expected to result in an acceleration of economic growth, it should stimulate the growth of demand for primary production in general. Coupled with the fact that disarmament should be associated with a tendency for the advanced countries to open their markets more widely to foodstuffs, for instance, this would make for a substantial growth of primary commodity trade. Accelerated economic growth would be still more powerful in increasing total demand for manufactures. In the past, an increased world demand for manufactures has normally been associated with increased international trade in them. The tendency to reduce trade barriers should be particularly important in enabling developing countries to increase their exports of manufactures to the more highly developed.

133.   The over-all impact of disarmament on the trade of underdeveloped countries is likely to be favourable, not only because of the acceleration of economic growth but also because of the greatly expanded aid to be expected from the more advanced countries. Both private enterprise and centrally planned economies should also be prepared to open their markets more widely to under-developed countries once the trade restrictions imposed for security reasons are lifted. There might, however, be instances in which declines in demand for particular commodities would cause appreciable difficulties. In these cases consideration should be given to special aid for the countries concerned, in the same way as for particular industries or areas within the principal disarming countries.

134.   The immediate impact of disarmament on international economic relations during the conversion period is a matter that needs to be given careful study along with the other conversion problems already discussed in chapters 3 and 4. Changes in the level of aggregate economic activity associated with disarmament in the major industrial countries would be a major determinant of the level of international trade during the conversion period. In the international field, as in the domestic, nations need to be prepared to take whatever measures may prove appropriate to facilitate the reallocation of resources and to

ensure that any temporary dislocations of economic life that might occur are minimized. The degree to which special policies might be called for would depend partly on the speed of the disarmament process.

135.   If appropriate steps are taken it should be possible even in the short run to avoid any significant reductions in the general level of primary product prices, but it needs nevertheless to be realized that any failure to achieve this goal could have serious consequences. For many of the countries mainly dependent on the export of primary commodities, a percentage decline in their export earnings which might appear small arithmetically could cause grave damage. For example, a 6 per cent drop in their average export prices, were it to take place, would imply for the under-developed countries a decline in their foreign exchange earnings equivalent to something like one-half of all official economic grants and loans currently received from abroad in a year.[2] Recessions in activity in the industrial countries have caused declines of this order of magnitude in the recent past. Concerted international action would, therefore, be required to prevent any such decline in the prices and incomes of primary producing countries as a result of disarmament.

136.   Even with favourable prospects for total trade, however, special problems might arise during the conversion period for particular countries or for trade in particular commodities. One such problem stems from the fact that a few countries have been receiving considerable foreign exchange from military aid and military expenditure, including the outlays of foreign personnel. In these cases, special attention should be given to the possibility of arranging future programmes of developmental assistance, and especially their timing, so as to avoid adverse effects on their balances of payments.

137.   A more wide-spread problem relates to particular countries that are largely dependent on the export of those commodities for which world demand might suffer a temporary decline. In conjunction with the formulation of any disarmament programme, therefore, it is highly desirable that a detailed study be undertaken on the changes in demand for the various primary commodities which would result from disarmament. The reduction of strategic stockpiles of primary commodities should be planned in such a way as to cause a minimum of disturbance to international markets, and consideration should be given to the adequacy of already existing compensatory measures and the possibility that additional measures might be required during the conversion period. Regardless of the technique employed, no country should be allowed to suffer a disruption to its economic life, even temporarily, as a result of disarmament.

---

[2] In 1956-1959 the sum of net official donations and official net long-term lending to under-developed countries averaged $3.2 billion annually, or about 12.6 per cent of the $25.2 billion annual average value of these countries' exports during the same period. (See, respectively, United Nations, *International Flow of Long-term Capital and Official Donations, 1951-1959* (Sales No.: 62.II.D.1), table 3 and United Nations, *Monthly Bulletin of Statistics*, February 1962, table 43. The two sets of statistics differ somewhat in country coverage.)

THE EFFECTS OF DISARMAMENT ON THE VOLUME AND FRAMEWORK OF AID FOR ECONOMIC DEVELOPMENT

138. The promotion of economic and social development in under-developed countries is one of the most important ways in which the resources released by disarmament could be put to use. Two-thirds of the world's population lives in countries that obtain only a modest part of the benefits which modern technology and science are capable of providing. The peoples of the under-developed areas are determined to raise their levels of living, and the peoples of the more industrialized countries have undertaken to help them do so. Progress has been made since the Second World War in raising real incomes per capita in many under-developed countries. The planning of economic and social development has been intensified in some and initiated in others, and the mobilization of domestic resources for national development has become a major policy objective. In many instances, domestic resources have been supplemented by foreign loans, grants, private capital flows and technical assistance.

139. National efforts and international co-operation in the development of the under-developed countries have so far not brought about the desired acceleration of economic growth. The average rate of growth in per capita income over the past decade was still less than 2 per cent per annum, and possibly as little as 1 per cent.[1] The absolute gap between per capita incomes of rich and poor countries has been progressively widening.[2] Even if future growth in the developed areas is left out of account and the present levels of income in the developed areas are taken as a target, the recent experience of under-developed areas still appears disappointing. In under-developed areas the average level of real income per capita is now less than one-sixth—and in many of them less than one-tenth—of that enjoyed in such countries as Belgium, Denmark, Norway and the United Kingdom. Consequently, a future growth rate no higher than 2 per cent per annum could be expected to raise the level of living in poor countries to that now prevailing in the countries just mentioned only after a very long time.

140. An acceleration of the rate of growth of under-developed countries depends upon many factors, including the adoption of appropriate national development programmes and, in many cases, social and institutional reforms. Among these programmes an important role must be assigned to encouragement of productive investment both from domestic and foreign resources. To this end world disarmament could make a major contribution. Despite the inadequacies of the available statistics, it appears that the world's military expenditures far exceed the combined gross investment expenditures of the less developed areas; they are probably at least five times as large and may be much greater.

---

[1] Owing to the margin of error in the population estimates of many under-developed countries (especially the inter-censal estimates), estimates of real income in these areas, which are rather crude in any case, are subject to an even wider margin of error when expressed in per capita terms.

[2] To narrow the gap, under-developed areas must experience a substantially higher growth rate than the more advanced areas, since in the higher-income areas a given rate of growth implies much larger absolute increments to income.

A much larger volume of resources could thus be allocated to investment for productive development in these countries even if only a fraction of the resources currently devoted to military purposes were used in this way.

141. Assuming that the necessary national development programmes and social and institutional reforms were effectively realized, under-developed countries would be able to absorb a considerably larger flow of productive investment. The consequent effect upon the rate of growth may be illustrated by a hypothetical example in which it is assumed that these countries devoted half of the resources liberated by disarmament to investment in productive capacity and that at the same time the rate of total capital flow from more advanced countries (both private enterprise and centrally planned) rose to around $15 billion annually, or somewhat more than 1 per cent of their aggregate national product. This is a modest increase in view of the 8 or 9 per cent they now devote to military purposes. Under these conditions, the less advanced countries might be expected to increase their annual rate of growth of national product from, say, 3 per cent to 5 per cent. Assuming an annual rate of population growth of around 2 per cent, this could mean a trebling of the rate of increase in per capita income from 1 per cent to 3 per cent.

142. The hypothetical example just given is based on certain assumptions concerning income and investment and their interrelationship in under-developed areas. Although different sets of assumptions would inevitably lead to somewhat different estimates of acceleration in the rate of growth in under-developed areas, there clearly emerges the general conclusion that disarmament could bring about a marked increase in the rate of growth of real income in the poorer parts of the world.

143. These conclusions are reinforced by a comparison of the volume of resources now being devoted to military use with the various estimates made in recent years of the external financial needs of the under-developed countries. Four relatively comprehensive estimates of global aid requirements are available,[3] apart from a number of estimates of aid needed for specific purposes. In these calculations, the total amount of foreign capital required by the under-developed areas, over and above their domestic resources devoted to investment, is estimated to range from $6 billion to $10 billion annually. These figures are based on conservative assumptions: the target rates of growth are based on per capita real income are about 2 per cent, and the computation, on the one assumed ratios between increments to real income ... the one

[3] These estimates of financial needs are based on ... been compared in a United Nations document prepa... United Nations Capital Development Fund: *The ...or the Economic Develop-the Less Developed Countries* (A/AC.102/5). T... II.B.2). Its estimates con-a report prepared for the United Nations: ...a for 1949 and earlier years. *ment of Under-Developed Countries* (Sal...Millikan and W. W. Rostow, cerned the nineteen-fifties, and were ba...ate, contained in Paul G. Hoffman, The second estimate is contained in...uarter...1959, Billion People (Washington, *A Proposal, Key to an Effective For 1959* ... and concerns the decade of the data for 1953 and earlier years. T... in P. N. Rosenstein-Rodan, "Interna-*One Hundred Countries, One...ies", Review of Economics and Statistics* 1960), is based on informatio...1) and covers the years 1962-1976. nineteen-sixties. The fourth... tional Aid for Under-de... (Cambridge, Mass.) X...

hand, increments to employment, or, on the other hand, increments to the stock of capital, which past experience suggests are reasonable but which could conceivably turn out to have underestimated the capital needs should conditions prove to be less favourable than anticipated. After allowing for the present flow of foreign capital through existing institutions and arrangements, the authors cited believe that there is a deficiency of about $3 billion a year that needs to be made good in order to achieve the modest annual rate of growth in income of 2 per cent per capita.[4]

144.   Two further questions arise. First, would disarmament release in sufficient quantity the particular resources required for economic development? Secondly, is the present institutional framework of aid to under-developed countries likely to be affected by disarmament?

145.   In the longer run, productive capacities can be adapted to any changed patterns of demand, and provided that the needs of under-developed countries are known in sufficient detail, no serious problems should arise in matching resources to uses. Even in the short run, how-ever, it seems probable that a significantly large proportion of the resources absorbed for military use would indeed prove to be of a type useful for investment in under-developed countries. An important pro-portion of military expenditure absorbs the output of heavy industry and of the engineering and construction industries. The output of these industrial sectors could undoubtedly make a valuable contribution to the industrialization of the less developed areas and to their accumula-tion of social capital. Transportation and communication equipment, for example, is an important component of military expenditure and is urgently required by under-developed countries. When a disarmament programme is adopted it would be desirable for Governments to estimate what resources would become available for peaceful purposes in the various stages of the programme. In the light of these data and detailed information concerning the resources which under-developed countries could usefully employ in their developmental programmes, it would be possible for Governments to assess the share of the released resources to be allocated to the investment needs of the less industrialized parts of the world.

146.   Disarmament would also release personnel, such as scientific research workers and engineers, who could be utilized for other purposes. In the event of disarmament, it should prove possible for the industrial-ized countries to provide greater technical assistance and thereby help remove one of the serious limitations to development efforts in these countries. Furthermore, disarmament would free from military service in both the more and the less developed countries large groups of young people. and countries large groups thusiasm in a numb experience in utilizing their good will and en-from military preocc countries indicates that when completely freed contribution to econo many of them could make an important areas. social development in under-developed

147.   With respect to ct of disarmament on the frame-

• *Ibid.*

work and structure of aid to under-developed countries several points need to be made. If we leave out of account—as seems proper in the present context—short-term finance of all kinds, private grants, and military and defence-support aid, the principal international flows of capital to under-developed countries consist of (1) official grants, (2) official loans and credits on non-commercial terms, (3) long-term loans and credits on commercial terms made by national governments and by international authorities, and (4) private long-term loans or direct investment. Unlike capital flows of the last three types, official grants do not, of course, burden the recipient country's balance of payments. Official loans and credits on non-commercial terms are less burdensome than public or private lending on commercial terms: hence the distinction between the second and third categories.

148. Comprehensive statistics of loans and grants to under-developed countries are not available according to the fourfold classification just mentioned. However, an impression of the over-all magnitude and composition of loans and grants to under-developed countries can be obtained from various sources.[5] During the past few years the total net flow of capital, as just defined, from private enterprise developed countries to under-developed countries averaged between $3.5 billion and $4 billion annually. About half represented official grants. The remainder consisted mostly of private lending.

149. In the fifteen years from 1945 to 1960 the sum total of credits granted by the centrally planned countries to under-developed countries and of mutual assistance among the centrally planned countries themselves amounted to about 52 billion old roubles. In the earlier years the greater part of the credits was granted to other centrally planned economies; in more recent years the emphasis has shifted to credits to under-developed countries.

150. The increased international flow of capital to under-developed countries that is certain to result from disarmament could take any one or more of the forms referred to above. Their relative importance would be likely to change, however, since each of them would be affected somewhat differently by the implementation of a disarmament programme.

151. As regards the flow of private capital, it may be ___sumed that this would continue to respond to commercial c__led with ___ations. Diminished world tension resulting from disarmamen_ in under- additional means of encouraging private foreign inv__r movement developed countries, might be expected to lead to_ official grants of private capital into these countries. ___ateral and multi-

152. At the present time, nine-tenths ___ticular advantages and loans are given under bilateral pro__which now prompt lateral programmes of aid each have ___n the other hand, in so and disadvantages, and many of th__eight in determining the Governments to favour bilateral __al and Official Donations, 1951- tinue to hold good even in a ___d Economic Survey, 1960 (Sales far as political circumstan__

[5] See *International ___
1959 (Sales No.: 62 ___
No.: 61.II.C.1), pp.

direction and form of aid, effective disarmament and the related lessening of international tensions should improve the prospects for more co-operative international action.

153. The discussions that have been held in the Economic and Social Council and the General Assembly during the past eight years concerning the need for an increased flow of aid through an international fund within the framework of the United Nations have frequently emphasized the importance of the savings to be derived from general disarmament. The basic position of the General Assembly on this matter remains resolution 724 (VIII), adopted unanimously in 1953. Under this resolution the General Assembly made the following declaration:

> "We, the Governments of the States Members of the United Nations, in order to promote higher standards of living and conditions of economic and social progress and development, stand ready to ask our peoples, when sufficient progress has been made in internationally supervised world-wide disarmament, to devote a portion of the savings achieved through such disarmament to an international fund, within the framework of the United Nations, to assist development and reconstruction in under-developed countries."

154. It should be realized that the repayment of loans granted on commercial terms may impose heavy burdens on the balances of payments of these countries. Concern has already been expressed in recent years regarding the heavy accumulated indebtedness of a number of countries and the growing difficulties they have been experiencing in servicing outstanding loans. It seems urgent that as large a proportion of economic aid as possible should take the form of grants or "soft" loans. Disarmament would likely facilitate the increased flow of such aid. This is so because the savings afforded by disarmament would provide the aid-giving countries with a favourable opportunity to increase their assistance without imposing an additional burden on civilian expenditure. This should also lead to a desirable broadening of the existing basis of aid to include types of projects not adequately covered under existing policies, and should therefore facilitate a balanced execution of development plans. Increased aid in the fields of social investment should also become possible, as it is now generally recognized that substantial investment in health facilities and particularly in education is a prerequisite for obtaining the maximum benefits from other development efforts.

155. [...] also urg[...]cause the competing claims in developed countries are released [...]ere is a serious possibility that the financial resources aims. It is [...]nament might be rapidly absorbed by purely national resources s[...]se desirable that an appropriate proportion of these simultaneou[...]llocated to international aid in its various forms

156. It [...]ir use for domestic purposes. supplementary fo[...] responsibility [...]phasized that foreign aid can play only a would continue [...]velopment of these countries and that the cerned. There are [...] intensification of development efforts are by no means th[...] with the governments and peoples con- economic growth. S[...]th in which foreign exchange resources [...]he main limitation on the rate of [...]ot likely to be in a position to

utilize larger amounts of aid effectively unless they take the domestic measures necessary to encourage such growth. There is reason to look to the major powers to be generous in allocating resources freed by disarmament to the development of under-developed countries. But there is also every reason to look to the under-developed countries themselves to create the conditions favourable to their economic growth. In this as in other fields discussed in this report, advance planning and preparation are likely to enhance greatly the favourable impact of general disarmament.

CHAPTER 7

SOME SOCIAL CONSEQUENCES OF DISARMAMENT

157.   The economic and social consequences of disarmament are inextricably intertwined. As already discussed, it would be possible to bring about a significant improvement in many aspects of social life, provided that some of the resources released by disarmament were earmarked for fields such as education and scientific research, health, housing and urban development. An idea of the magnitude of the needs in these fields has been given in chapter 2. There are, however, some aspects of social life which elude measurement, but which none the less greatly affect individual and family life and on which smoother human relations within and between nations largely depend.

158.   In a disarmed world, a general improvement could be expected in the *level of living* and in the conditions of under-privileged and low-income groups such as the old and retired people whose share in the social well-being is often meagre, even in the more developed countries. With the end of the armaments race, Governments would accord these social objectives a higher priority than in the past. The implementation of measures discussed in chapter 2 would lead to a cumulative diffusion of social benefits.

159.   The more rapid rate of economic growth and the increase in productivity that may be expected to result from disarmament might well permit a reduction in working hours, an improvement in the conditions of work and a lengthening of paid vacations. To take full advantage of the resultant longer leisure and the higher level of living, wider cultural facilities would be required. In this context, education acquires special significance as a means for disseminating culture.

160.   In the domain of *personal and family life,* disarmament and recession of the threat of war would decrease tensions which often bring about psychosomatic illnesses. Human life would acquire a new meaning, once war and preparations for war were eliminated. The whole prospect of life would be brightened, especially for young people about to enter a profession or found a family. There would no longer be any separation from the family for compulsory military service, so that the psychological, moral and material evils which this creates would be avoided. A greater stability in the family nucleus would be likely to exert a favourable influence on morality.

831

161.   The very fact of disarmament would lead to a diminution of tensions between nations and races. The tendency to divert individual and national frustrations into national and racial hatreds would be lessened significantly.

162.   In a disarmed world, the danger that security considerations and armed forces might play an excessive role in forming the values of the community would be eliminated. It is important to note, however, that attention would need to be paid to constructive outlets for individual and collective aspirations.

163.   If confidence is one of the necessary conditions for concluding a disarmament agreement, an increase of confidence would also be one of its happiest consequences. A decrease in tensions and in the influence of groups interested in armaments would bring about a profound change in the form and content of *international relations*. Political and economic. conflict between nations, with its attendant risk of war, would more rapidly be replaced by constructive emulation. Scientific co-operation between nations would advance more rapidly, and the peaceful utilization of science and technology would be accelerated. The arts, too, would greatly benefit from an extension of international exchanges. All the great civilizations in the past have gained from such cultural contacts and have exerted their influence beyond their own frontiers. Disarmament would remove the main barriers to the far greater exchanges that are now technically possible. Humanity would thus be able to carry out co-operatively the projects which lie beyond the resources of a single country or a group of countries.

164.   In short, disarmament would release resources from uses in which they are not only wasted but also in many ways make the remainder of mankind's wealth less effective in promoting welfare than it would otherwise be. In reckoning the gains from it, one must take into account a general easing of tension and frustration and an enhanced possibility of co-operation that would reinforce the direct economic contribution of the resources released.

165.   In view of this, as well as the conclusions reached in previous chapters, there should be no doubt that the diversion to peaceful purposes of the resources now devoted to military expenditure could and should be of benefit to all countries and would lead to improvement of world social conditions.

CHAPTER 8

SUMMARY AND CONCLUSIONS

166.   The present level of military expenditure not only represents a grave political danger but also imposes a heavy economic and social burden on most countries. It absorbs a large volume of human and material resources of all kinds, which could be used to increase economic and social welfare throughout the world—both in the highly in-

dustrialized countries, which at the present time incur the bulk of the world's military expenditures, and in the less developed areas.

RESOURCES DEVOTED TO MILITARY PURPOSES

167.   There appears to be general agreement that the world is spending roughly $120 billion annually on military account at the present time. This corresponds to about one-half of the total gross capital formation throughout the world. It is at least two-thirds of— and according to some estimates, of the same order of magnitude as —the entire national income of all the under-developed countries.

168.   It is important that countries, in preparing to disarm, should take stock of the various resources that disarmament would release for peaceful uses. In the major military powers, military production is highly concentrated in a few industry groups. In those countries that rely upon imports for their supplies of military goods or in which the major part of military expenditure is for the pay and subsistence of the armed forces, rather than for their equipment, the resources devoted to military purposes consist essentially of manpower and foreign exchange.

THE PEACEFUL USE OF RELEASED RESOURCES

169.   There are so many competing claims for usefully employing the resources released by disarmament that the real problem is to establish a scale of priorities. The most urgent of these claims would undoubtedly already have been largely satisfied were it not for the armaments race.

170.   Increased personal consumption might well absorb a large share of the released resources. A substantial portion of them, however, would be used for expansion of productive capacities because only such expansion can provide a firm basis for further increases in consumption. In the less developed countries, the utilization of released resources for capital formation must be considered vitally important.

171.   Social investment is an important alternative both to private consumption and to industrial and agricultural investment. Its claims rest partly upon the clear urgency of the direct need for improved social amenities, and partly upon the fact that growth of industrial and agricultural productivity is dependent upon developments in education, housing, health, and other fields.

172.   The release of scientific and technical manpower would make it possible to encourage programmes of basic scientific research in fields which have hitherto been neglected. Disarmament would also open up possibilities for joint international ventures of an ambitious kind, such as the utilization of atomic energy for peaceful purposes, space research, the exploration of the Arctic and Antarctic for the benefit of mankind and projects to change the climates of large areas of the world.

173.   Thus, though it would take active decisions by Governments in the light of national and international needs to set in motion the necessary programmes for employing the released resources, it seems

abundantly clear that no country need fear a lack of useful employment opportunities for the resources that would become available to it through disarmament.

IMPACT ON NATIONAL PRODUCTION AND EMPLOYMENT

174. Disarmament would raise both general problems of maintaining the over-all level of economic activity and employment and specific problems in so far as manpower or productive capacity might require adaptation to non-military needs. In the economic life of all countries, shifts in the pattern of demand and in the allocation of productive resources are continually occurring. The reallocation of productive resources which would accompany disarmament is in many respects merely a special case of the phenomenon of economic growth.

175. The post-war conversion was a much larger one and involved a more rapid transfer of resources than total disarmament would require at present. Nevertheless, huge armies were quickly demobilized without a significant rise in unemployment in most countries. The pace of recovery, particularly of industrial output, was impressively rapid. During the post-war conversion, however, the major concern of economic policy was to restrain, rather than to maintain, over-all demand.

176. Much attention has already been given in the industrialized private enterprise economies to the methods by which total effective demand can be maintained. Monetary and fiscal policy could be used to offset the effect of a shortfall in total demand that might result from a decline in military expenditure to the extent that it were not offset by a rise in civil government expenditure. Bearing in mind that a substantial part of military expenditure would probably be replaced by other government expenditure in most countries, it may be concluded that the maintenance of effective demand in the face of disarmament should not prove difficult.

177. For many under-developed countries, the effect of disarmament upon the industrial countries' demands for primary products, and thus on the export earnings of the primary producing countries, would be of great importance. So would the methods of dealing with the liquidation of strategic stockpiles.

178. In the centrally planned economies, the maintenance of effective demand while reducing military expenditure would be simply a matter of the efficiency of planning techniques. In consequence, effective demand could be readily maintained, and the principal problems of conversion would concern the physical adaptation of plants producing armaments to the production of goods for civilian use.

STRUCTURAL PROBLEMS OF CONVERSION

179. Even with the successful maintenance of total effective demand during a period of disarmament, significant problems of adjustment would remain in specific sectors and areas of the economy. The resources now supplying military requirements could be adapted to peace-time needs partly by shifts within industries and plants. This might be a relatively easy procedure, in many cases involving little more than

changes in designs, retooling, and minor adaptations of skills, particularly in plants and enterprises which already produce both military and civilian goods. Shifts between industries would necessitate new investment and acquisition of different types of skill by the working force. In the longer run disarmament would allow each country to raise the rate of investment and to adapt productive capacity more adequately to the needs of the population and to the requirements of economic growth, both in the private enterprise and the centrally planned economies.

180. Hypothetical studies on the assumption that military expenditure is replaced wholly by increases in expenditure on other kinds of goods and services suggest that in the event of very rapid disarmament some 6 or 7 per cent (including the armed forces) of the total labour force in the United States and 3½ to 4 per cent in the United Kingdom would have to find civilian instead of military employment or change their employment from one industry group to another. These shifts would be small if spread out over a number of years and would be greatly facilitated by the normal process of turnover. The higher the rate of growth of the economy, the easier the process of adaptation.

181. Under-developed countries generally have been meeting their requirements for military goods and services by imports, so that their disarmament would release foreign exchange rather than industrial workers. It would also free members of the forces, many with useful skills and training. Some of these could be usefully employed in the development of social capital. In some of the semi-industrialized countries, newly started basic industries could concentrate, without any transitional difficulty, on the manufacture of capital goods.

182. In the centrally planned economies, where productive capacity is usually fully utilized, it would be necessary to convert plants producing military equipment to production of durable consumer goods and of such investment goods as can be produced in them with only minor retooling. This could be done rapidly.

183. Some special problems would arise with regard to re-employment and training of manpower and reorientation of scientific research. While most members of the armed forces have received training that would fit them easily for civilian life, a special effort would have to be made to find suitable employment for the rest. The demobilization of the non-professional members of the armed forces would imply only that the number of new entrants for that period would be augmented by this special factor.

184. In industries depending heavily on military orders, many of the employees possess a level of skill that should find gainful employment in other branches of production, so long as over-all effective demand is rising. Even so, there might be some special cases which would require special assistance to encourage the adaptation of skills to new jobs. The uneven geographical distribution of the activity based on military expenditure would give rise to a need for various forms of public and other assistance to facilitate readjustment.

185. The task of shifting scientific and technical personnel to non-

military fields of research in some countries would be considerable. No reduction in the actual employment of scientific and technical personnel need be feared, however, because the demand for civilian research would increase rapidly.

IMPACT ON INTERNATIONAL ECONOMIC RELATIONS

186. Disarmament would be bound to have favourable effects on the development of international relations. The political *détente* that would accompany an international disarmament programme would in itself imply that nations were willing to reconsider their economic relations with one another. The relaxation of international tensions would provide a sound basis for reduction of trade barriers and for modification of existing trade agreements and trading practices. An important consequence of this would be a substantial increase in trade between the centrally planned economies and the rest of the world.

187. Since disarmament may be expected to result in an acceleration of economic growth, it should stimulate the growth of demand for primary production in general. Accelerated economic growth would be still more powerful in increasing total demand for manufactures. The over-all impact of disarmament on the trade of under-developed countries is likely to be favourable, not only because of the acceleration of economic growth but also because of the greatly expanded aid to be expected from the more advanced countries.

188. Some exports of primary products, such as petroleum, rubber and most metallic ores, depend significantly at present on direct and indirect demand generated by military purchases. Provided, however, that military expenditure were fully replaced by public and private non-military spending, the impact on over-all demand for these commodities would be only minor. There might, however, be instances in which declines in demand for particular commodities would cause appreciable difficulties. In these cases consideration should be given to special aid for the countries concerned, in the same way as for particular industries or areas within the principal disarming countries. For most other primary commodities, the reallocation of military expenditure to civilian use would probably bring about a net increase in demand.

189. During the conversion period changes in the level of aggregate economic activity associated with disarmament in the major industrial countries would be a major determinant of the level of international trade. It is believed that significant fluctuations in the general level of international trade could be avoided, but it should nevertheless be realized that any failure to achieve this goal could have serious consequences. Regardless of the technique employed, no country should be allowed to suffer a disruption to its economic life, even temporarily, as a result of disarmament.

EFFECTS ON THE VOLUME AND FRAMEWORK OF AID FOR ECONOMIC DEVELOPMENT

190. National efforts and international co-operation in the de-

velopment of the under-developed countries have so far not brought about the desired acceleration of economic growth. A much larger volume of resources could be allocated to investment for productive development in these countries even if only a fraction of the resources currently devoted to military purposes were used in this way. Disarmament could thus bring about a marked increase in the rate of growth of real income in the poorer parts of the world.

191.   Bilateral and multilateral programmes of aid each have their own particular advantages and disadvantages, but in so far as political circumstances have had any weight in determining the direction and form of aid, effective disarmament and the related lessening of international tensions should improve the prospects for more co-operative international action. Since repayment of loans granted on commercial terms may impose heavy burdens on the balances of payments of the under-developed countries, as large a proportion of economic aid as possible should take the form of grants or "soft" loans.

192.   Because the competing claims in developed countries are also urgent there is a serious possibility that the financial resources released by disarmament might be rapidly absorbed by purely national aims. It is therefore desirable that an appropriate proportion of these resources should be allocated to international aid in its various forms simultaneously with their use for domestic purposes.

193.   Foreign aid, however, can play only a supplementary role in the development of these countries and the responsibility for initiation and intensification of development efforts would continue to lie entirely with the Governments and peoples concerned.

Some social consequences

194.   In a disarmed world, a general improvement could be expected in the level of living, including an increase in leisure. With the end of the armaments race, Governments would accord social objectives a higher priority. The psychological, moral and material evils of compulsory military service and of stationing troops away from their homes would be avoided; so would the danger that security considerations and the armed forces might play an extensive role in forming the values of the community. Scientific co-operation and the arts would benefit from an extension of international exchanges.

Conclusion

195.   The Consultative Group is unanimously of the opinion that all the problems and difficulties of transition connected with disarmament could be met by appropriate national and international measures. There should thus be no doubt that the diversion to peaceful purposes of the resources now in military use could be accomplished to the benefit of all countries and lead to the improvement of world economic and social conditions. The achievement of general and complete disarmament would be an unqualified blessing to all mankind.

ANNEXES

Annex 1

TERMS OF REFERENCE

RESOLUTION 1516 (XV), ADOPTED BY THE GENERAL ASSEMBLY
Economic and social consequences of disarmament

The General Assembly,

Recalling its resolution 1378 (XIV) of 20 November 1959,

Conscious that the impact of disarmament is likely to set in motion great changes in the domestic economies of States and in international economic relations, as a result of the progressive diversion of human and material resources from military to peaceful purposes,

Recognizing that effective action at the national and international levels will need to be taken to make use of material and human resources becoming available as a consequence of disarmament, in order to promote social progress and better standards of living in the world,

Bearing in mind the importance of comprehensive and systematic studies in this field to enable Member States, especially those which are under-developed, to make the necessary economic and social adjustments in the event of disarmament,

Convinced that it is both timely and desirable to undertake such studies,

1. *Requests* the Secretary-General to examine:

(*a*) The national economic and social consequences of disarmament in countries with different economic systems and at different stages of economic development, including, in particular, the problems of replacing military expenditures with alternative private and public civil expenditures so as to maintain effective demand and to absorb the human and material resources released from military uses;

(*b*) The possible development of structural imbalances in national economies as a result of the cessation of capital investment in armaments industries, and the adoption of possible corrective measures to prevent such imbalances, including expanded capital assistance to the under-developed countries;

(*c*) The impact of disarmament on international economic relations, including its effect on world trade and especially on the trade of under-developed countries;

(*d*) The utilization of resources released by disarmament for the purpose of economic and social development, in particular of the under-developed countries;

2. *Recommends* that the Secretary-General should conduct the proposed examination with the assistance of expert consultants to be appointed by him with due regard to their qualifications and to the need of geographical representation and intimate knowledge of countries with different economic systems and at different stages of economic development;

3. *Appeals* to Governments of Member States to give full co-operation to the Secretary-General in the fulfilment of the task entrusted to him;

4. *Requests* the Secretary-General to submit a preliminary report on the results of the examination to the Economic and Social Council at its thirty-third session;[a]

5. *Requests* the Economic and Social Council to transmit the report with its views to the General Assembly at its seventeenth session.

948th plenary meeting,
15 December 1960.

Annex 2

OFFICIAL MILITARY EXPENDITURE STATISTICS

1. Information concerning military expenditure is contained in the official public accounts of central Governments and the national accounts dealing with gross national or material product and related data. Countries differ, however, in their definitions of military expenditure, and information concerning their methods of classification is commonly not available. It is therefore impossible in many instances to determine the content of the official statistics from an economic and social point of view. Some expenditures that would be considered as military from this viewpoint may be excluded from the official data, while others that would be considered as non-military may be included. In addition, there are commonly differences within countries in the basis of pricing of military output as compared with that of the output of the rest of the economy. These differences alone, even if the coverage of the expenditure statistics were appropriate, would make it impossible to indicate with any precision the proportion of resources devoted to military purposes. Furthermore, different countries have different economic structures and patterns of prices, so that in comparing countries one would obtain different ratios of military expenditure to national product and its components merely from using the different price patterns. For all these reasons, official statistics of military expenditure have only limited value as a basis for measuring the economic burden imposed by the armaments race.

2. The following tables include the most readily available official statistics on military expenditure and compare these with domestic product and fixed capital formation. These three tables cover industrial private enterprise, under-developed and centrally planned countries respectively. In accordance with usual statistical practice, the concept of domestic product in the first two tables is different from that in the third table. In tables 2-1 and 2-2, domestic product includes output originating in both "material production" and services. In table 2-3, domestic product includes output originating in material production only. A further difference is that domestic product in tables 2-1 and 2-2 is gross, depreciation not having been deducted from gross investment or income, while domestic product in table 2-3 is net of depreciation. Accordingly, military expenditure is compared with a more broadly defined measure of product in tables 2-1 and 2-2 than in table 2-3.

---

[a] In response to a suggestion by the Group of Experts, made at their first session, the Economic and Social Council agreed to defer consideration of this item to its thirty-fourth session.

Table 2-1

INDUSTRIAL PRIVATE PNTERPRISE COUNTRIES: MILITARY EXPENDITURE AS STATED IN
BUDGET ACCOUNTS, COMPARED WITH OTHER STATISTICS, 1957-1959[a]

Country, period and currency unit	Military budget expenditure	Gross domestic product[a]	Gross domestic fixed capital formation	Military budget expenditure as percentage of	
				Gross domestic product	Gross domestic fixed capital formation
AMERICA, NORTH					
Canada (million dollars) :					
1957	1,668.5[b]	32,347.0	8,590.0		
1958	1,424.7[b]	33,186.0	8,292.0		
1959	1,506.1[b]	35,110.0	8,456.0		
Average 1957-1959..	1,533.1[b]	33,548.0	8,446.0	4.6	18.4
United States (million dollars) :					
1957	43,270.0[d]	441,764.0	76,981.0[e]		
1958	44,142.0[d]	443,869.0	72,270.0[e]		
1959	46,426.0[d]	481,253.0	80,374.0[e]		
Average 1957-1959..	44,613.0[d]	455,628.0	76,542.0[e]	9.8	58.3[e]
ASIA					
Japan[b] (billion yen) :					
1957	176.0	10,135.8	2,727.0[e]		
1958	178.0	10,414.8	2,772.8[e]		
1959	189.0	12,561.4	3,509.6[e]		
Average 1957-1959..	181.0	11,037.3	3,003.1[e]	1.6	6.0[e]
EUROPE					
Austria (million schillings) :					
1957	1,714.0	121,800.0[f]	27,000.0		
1958	1,986.0	126,700.0[f]	28,400.0		
1959	1,989.0	134,600.0[f]	30,700.0		
Average 1957-1959..	1,896.0	127,700.0[f]	28,700.0	1.5[f]	6.6
Belgium (million francs) :					
1957	16,638.0	550,100.0	95,900.0		
1958	16,433.0	547,600.0	91,600.0		
1959	18,047.0	565,700.0	95,400.0		
Average 1957-1959..	17,039.0	554,467.0	94,300.0	3.1	18.1
Denmark (million kroner) :					
1957	941.0[b]	32,939.0	5,705.0		
1958	973.0[b]	34,374.0	6,020.0		
1959	1,015.0[b]	38,100.0	7,025.0		
Average 1957-1959..	976.0[b]	35,138.0	6,250.0	2.8	15.6

Table 2-1 (continued)

Country, period and currency unit	Military budget expenditure	Gross domestic product[a]	Gross domestic fixed capital formation	Military budget expenditure as percentage of	
				Gross domestic product	Gross domestic fixed capital formation
EUROPE (*continued*)					
Finland (billion markkaa) :					
1957	18.4	1,112.0	294.5		
1958	20.6	1,186.3	303.0		
1959	22.4	1,259.6	331.2		
Average 1957-1959..	20.5	1,186.0	309.6	1.7	6.6
France (million new francs) :					
1957	14,120.0	211,200.0	39,100.0		
1958	14,190.0	239,100.0	43,100.0		
1959	15,830.0	258,400.0	45,100.0		
Average 1957-1959..	14,713.0	236,200.0	42,433.0	6.2	34.7
Germany (*Federal Republic*) (million Deutche mark) :					
1957	7,547.0[b]	214,200.0	46,650.0		
1958	8,824.0[b]	228,510.0	50,350.0		
1959	9,403.0[b]	247,520.0	57,200.0		
Average 1957-1959..	8,591.0[b]	230,077.0	51,400.0	3.7	16.7
Ireland (million pounds):					
1957	8.1[b]	545.0	77.2	1.5	10.5
Italy (billion lire) :					
1957	496.1[d]	15,638.0	3,434.0		
1958	543.6[d]	16,656.0	3,481.0		
1959	548.9[d]	17,656.0	3,730.0		
Average 1957-1959..	529.5[d]	16,650.0	3,548.0	3.2	14.9
Netherlands (million guilders) :					
1957	1,725.0	35,120.0	9,044.0		
1958	1,546.0	35,830.0	8,210.0		
1959	1,438.0	38,170.0	9,120.0		
Average 1957-1959..	1,570.0	36,373.0	8,791.0	4.3	17.9
Norway (million kroner) :					
1957	986.6[d]	28,826.0	8,187.0		
1958	967.8[d]	28,645.0	9,067.0		
1959	1,058.7[d]	30,294.0	8,799.0		
Average 1957-1959..	1,004.4[d]	29,255.0	8,684.0	3.4	11.6

Table 2-1 (continued)

Country, period and currency unit	Military budget expenditure	Gross domestic product[a]	Gross domestic fixed capital formation	Military budget expenditure as percentage of	
				Gross domestic product	Gross domestic fixed capital formation
EUROPE (*continued*)					
Sweden (million kronor) :					
1957	2,450.0[d]	52,558.0	10,605.0		
1958	2,663.0[d]	54,825.0	11,615.0		
1959	2,748.0[d]	58,386.0	12,926.0		
Average 1957-1959..	2,620.0[d]	55,256.0	11,715.0	4.7	22.4
Switzerland (million francs) :					
1957	930.1	30,800.0	7,700.0[f]		
1958	1,019.1	32,000.0	7,300.0[f]		
1959	972.4	33,400.0	8,000.0[f]		
Average 1957-1959..	973.9	32,067.0	7,667.0[f]	3.0	12.7[f]
United Kingdom (million pounds) :					
1957	1,429.7[b]	21,719.0	3,340.0		
1958	1,467.7[b]	22,623.0	3,476.0		
1959	1,504.0[b]	23,741.0	3,631.0		
Average 1957-1959..	1,467.1[b]	22,694.0	3,482.0	6.5	42.1
OCEANIA					
Australia[d] (million pounds) :					
1957	183.4	5,751.0	1,408.0[h]		
1958	172.0	5,829.0	1,522.0[h]		
1959	181.9	6,250.0	1,613.0[h]		
Average 1957-1959..	179.1	5,943.0	1,514.0[h]	3.0	11.8[h]
New Zealand[b] (million pounds) :					
1957	24.2	1,096.0	245.0		
1958	25.5	1,154.0	242.0		
1959	27.3	1,247.0	251.0		
Average 1957-1959..	25.7	1,166.0	246.0	2.2	10.4

SOURCE: United Nations, *Statistical Yearbook* and *Yearbook of National Accounts Statistics,* various issues.

[a] For differences between the concept of domestic product used in tables 2-1 and 2-2, as compared with table 2-3, see para. 2 of this annex.

[b] Fiscal years beginning 1 April.

[c] Including increase in stocks of local government enterprises.

[d] Fiscal year ending 30 June.

[e] Excluding government expenditure on equipment.

[f] Gross national product.

[g] Including increase in stocks.

[h] Including expenditure on maintenance of roads and expenditure on motor vehicles for personal use.

Table 2-2

UNDER-DEVELOPED PRIVATE ENTERPRISE COUNTRIES: MILITARY EXPENDITURE, AS
STATED IN BUDGET ACCOUNTS, COMPARED WITH OTHER STATISTICS, 1957-1959[a]

Country, period and currency unit	Military budget expenditure	Gross domestic product[a]	Gross domestic fixed capital formation	Military budget expenditure as percentage of	
				Gross domestic product	Gross domestic fixed capital formation
AFRICA					
Sudan[b] (million pounds):					
1957	3.4	...	26.2		
1958	4.9	...	42.8		
1959	5.0	...	38.2		
Average 1957-1959..	4.4	...	35.7	...	12.3
Union of South Africa (million pounds):					
1957	18.1[e]	2,345.0	485.0		
1958	19.6[e]	2,411.0	544.0		
1959	21.8[e]	2,518.0	525.0		
Average 1957-1959..	19.8[e]	2,425.0	518.0	0.8	3.8
AMERICA, LATIN					
Argentina (million pesos):					
1958	6,924.8[d]	318,400.0	65,610.0		
1959	15,589.4[d]	604,547.0	107,985.0		
Average 1958-1959..	11,257.1[d]	461,474.0	86,798.0	2.4	13.0
Brazil (billion cruzeiros):					
1957	34.6	1,063.1	124.5		
1958	40.8	1,299.3	165.6		
1959	41.1	1,837.4	228.5		
Average 1957-1959..	38.8	1,399.9	172.9	2.8	22.4
Chile (million escudos):					
1957	73.1	2,252.7[e]	247.0		
1958	82.2	2,971.8[e]	309.9		
1959	91.1	4,163.0[e]	405.0		
Average 1957-1959..	82.1	3,129.2[e]	320.6	2.6[e]	25.6
Colombia (million pesos):					
1957	288.6	17,651.0	2,630.0		
1958	306.4	20,477.0	3,350.0		
1959	274.7	22,995.0	3,919.0		
Average 1957-1959..	289.9	20,374.0	3,300.0	1.4	8.8
Costa Rica (million colones):					
1957	13.4	2,302.7[f]	434.8		
1958	12.8	2,465.0[f]	404.0		
1959	13.1	2,529.8[f]	451.4		
Average 1957-1959..	13.1	2,432.5[f]	430.1	0.5[f]	3.0

Table 2-2 (continued)

Country, period and currency unit	Military budget expenditure	Gross domestic product[a]	Gross domestic fixed capital formation	Military budget expenditure as percentage of	
				Gross domestic product	Gross domestic fixed capital formation
AMERICA, LATIN *(continued)*					
Ecuador (million sucres):					
1957	289.0	12,007.0	1,561.0		
1958	282.0	12,355.0	1,586.0		
1959	273.0	12,424.0	1,553.0	2.2	17.6
El Salvador (million colones):					
1957	19.2	1,218.2[g]	...		
1958	19.0	1,249.9[g]	...		
1959	17.0	1,226.7[g]	...		
Average 1957-1959..	18.4	1,231.6[g]	...	1.5[g]	...
Guatemala (million quetzales):					
1957	8.9[b]	652.5	97.5[h]		
1958	9.7[b]	647.0	97.4[h]		
1959	9.9[b]	659.1	84.1[h]		
Average 1957-1959..	9.5[b]	652.9	93.0[h]	1.5	10.2[h]
Honduras (million lempiras):					
1957	8.9	688.3	94.1	1.3	9.5
Mexico (million pesos):					
1957	791.7	103,000.0[i]	15,544.0		
1958	861.5	114,000.0[i]	16,282.0		
1959	971.0	122,000.0[i]	18,066.0		
Average 1957-1959..	874.7	113,000.0[i]	16,631.0	0.8[i]	5.3
Peru (million soles):					
1957	1,083.8	34,342.0[e]	9,149.0		
1958	1,265.4	37,691.0[e]	8,643.0		
Average 1957-1958..	1,174.6	36,016.0[e]	8,896.0	3.3[e]	13.2
Venezuela (million bolivares):					
1957	419.3[b]	23,847.0	5,950.0[j]		
1958	572.0[b]	24,585.0	5,964.0[j]		
1959	630.2[b]	24,904.0	6,721.0[j]		
Average 1957-1959..	540.5[b]	24,445.0	6,212.0[j]	2.2	8.7[j]
ASIA					
Burma[k] (million kyats):					
1957	368.5	5,429.0	1,018.0		
1958	407.6	5,299.0	1,135.0		
1959	403.3	5,493.0	1,015.0		
Average 1957-1959..	393.1	5,407.0	1,056.0	7.3	37.2
Cambodia:					
1957	...	...	...	4.0	...

Table 2-2 (continued)

Country, period and currency unit	Military budget expenditure	Gross domestic product[a]	Gross domestic fixed capital formation	Military budget expenditure as percentage of	
				Gross domestic product	Gross domestic fixed capital formation
ASIA (*continued*)					
Ceylon (million rupees) :					
1957	39.9[k]	5,382.0	660.6		
1958	64.1[k]	5,662.6	682.6		
1959	72.4[k]	6,032.9	805.5		
Average 1957-1959..	58.8[k]	5,692.5	716.2	1.0	8.2
China (Taiwan) :					
Average 1957-1959..	...	...	...	10.8[l]	...
Federation of Malaya (million dollars) :					
1957	160.6	5,310.0	610.0	3.0	26.3
India[e] (million rupees) :					
1957	2,828.0	114,100.0[m]	...		
1958	2,787.0	124,800.0[m]	...		
Average 1957-1958..	2,808.0	119,450.0[m]	...	2.4[m]	...
Indonesia (million rupiah) :					
1957	6,052.0	171,000.0[n]	7,600.0		
1958	11,085.0	180,200.0[n]	8,299.0		
1959	8,788.0	210,000.0[n]	8,895.0		
Average 1957-1959..	8,642.0	187,100.0[n]	8,265.0	4.6[n]	104.6
Israel (million pounds) :					
1957	197.1[e]	3,054.0[o]	829.0[j]		
1958	217.1[e]	3,501.0[o]	897.0[j]		
1959	251.1[e]	4,022.0[o]	961.0[j]		
Average 1957-1959..	221.8[e]	3,526.0[o]	896.0[j]	6.3[o]	24.8[j]
Korea (Republic of) (billion hwan) :					
1957	112.9	1,615.7	200.9		
1958	127.8	1,706.8	219.4		
1959	141.1	1,840.0	265.0		
Average 1957-1959..	127.3	1,720.8	228.4	7.4	57.8
Lebanon (million pounds) :					
1957	39.1	1,503.0[m]	...		
1958	45.6	1,325.0[m]	...		
Average 1957-1958..	42.4	1,414.0[m]	...	3.0[m]	...
Pakistan :					
Average 1957-1958..	...	...	...	3.0[l]	...
Philippines (million pesos) :					
1957	157.0[b]	10,119.0	890.0		
1958	181.1[b]	10,666.0	851.0		
1959	183.6[b]	11,161.0	901.0		
Average 1957-1959..	173.9[b]	10,649.0	881.0	1.6	19.7

Table 2-2 (continued)

Country, period and currency unit	Military budget expenditure	Gross domestic product[a]	Gross domestic fixed capital formation	Military budget expenditure as percentage of Gross domestic product	Gross domestic fixed capital formation
ASIA (*continued*)					
Syrian Arab Republic (million pounds) :					
1957	140.0	2,514.0[p]	266.0	5.6	52.6
Thailand (million baht) :					
1957	1,566.7	44,670.0	6,434.0	3.8	24.4
1958	1,389.7	45,458.0	6,669.0		
1959	1,439.0	49,010.0	7,334.0		
Average 1957-1959..	1,465.1	46,379.0	6,812.0	3.2	21.5
Turkey (million lires) :					
1957	959.1[q]	30,668.0	4,033.0		
1958	956.2[q]	38,652.0	5,278.0		
1959	1,146.1[q]	46,640.0	7,463.0		
Average 1957-1959..	1,020.5[q]	38,653.0	5,591.0	2.6	18.3
EUROPE					
Greece (million drachmas) :					
1957	4,500.0	80,772.0	12,531.0		
1958	4,560.0	85,750.0	15,320.0		
1959	4,590.0	88,515.0	18,470.0		
Average 1957-1959..	4,550.0	85,012.0	15.440.0	5.4	29.5
Portugal (million escudos) :					
1957	1,754.0	57,396.0	8,808.0		
1958	1,845.6	59,017.0	9,625.0		
Average 1957-1958..	1,799.8	58,206.0	9,216.0	3.1	19.5
Spain (million pesetas) :					
1957	10,881.0	437,200.0[l]	...	2.5[l]	...

SOURCE: United Nations, *Statistical Yearbook* and *Yearbook of National Accounts Statistics,* various issues, except for Cambodia, China (Taiwan) and Pakistan, the source for which is United Nations, *Economic Survey of Asia and the Far East,* 1960 (Sales No.: 61.II.F.1), table 32, p. 83.

[a] For differences between the concept of domestic product used in tables 2-1 and 2-2, as compared with table 2-3, see para. 2 of this annex.
[b] Fiscal year ending 30 June.
[c] Fiscal year beginning 1 April.
[d] Fiscal year ending 31 October.
[e] Including a statistical discrepancy.
[f] Including current international transfers.
[g] At market prices of 1950.
[h] Including increase in stocks.
[i] Gross national product.
[j] Including change in stock of livestock held on farms.
[k] Fiscal year ending 30 September.
[l] Ratio to net national product.
[m] Net domestic product at factor cost.
[n] Gross domestic product at factor cost.
[o] Including interest on public debt.
[p] Net domestic product at factor cost of 1956.
[q] Year beginning 1 March.

Table 2-3

CENTRALLY PLANNED COUNTRIES: MILITARY EXPENDITURE AS STATED IN BUDGET
ACCOUNTS, COMPARED WITH OTHER STATISTICS, 1957-1959[a]

Country, period and currency unit	Military budget expenditure	Net domestic product[a]	Gross fixed investment[b]	Military budget expenditure as percentage of	
				Net domestic product	Gross fixed investment
Bulgaria (million leva):					
1957	1,540	32,089	5,172		
1958	1,729	34,863	6,321		
1959	1,628	42,198	10,103		
Average 1957-1959.....	1,632	36,383	7,199	4.5	22.7
China (mainland) (million yuan):					
1957	5,510	93,500[e]	12,400[e]		
1958	5,000	125,400[e]	21,400[e]		
1959	5,800	152,500[e]	24,800[e]		
Average 1957-1959.....	5,437	123,800[e]	19,533[e]	4.4[e]	27.8[e]
Czechoslovakia (million korun):					
1957	9,319	...	29,090		
1958	8,933	...	31,470		
1959	8,789	...	36,094		
Average 1957-1959.....	9,014	...	32,218	...	28.0
Eastern Germany (million marks):					
1958	1,650	64,899	9,798	2.5	16.8
Hungary (million forints):					
1957	1,912	107,310	11,100		
1959	2,500	126,500	30,500		
Average 1957 and 1959.	2,206	116,905	20,800	1.9	10.6
Poland (million zloty):					
1957	10,136	301,400	47,356		
1958	11,220	321,300	52,106		
1959	14,259	345,800	61,653		
Average 1957-1959.....	11,872	322,833	53,705	3.7	22.1
Romania (million lei):					
1957	3,817	...	13,966[d]		
1958	3,597	...	15,234[d]		
1959	3,446	...	17,803[d]		
Average 1957-1959.....	3,620	...	15,668[d]	...	23.1[d]
Soviet Union (million roubles):[e]					
1957	95,000	1,258,000[f]	237,800		
1958	93,600	1,357,000[f]	273,580		
1959	93,700	1,466,000[f]	309,330		
Average 1957-1959.....	94,100	1,360,333[f]	273,570	6.9[f]	34.4

Table 2-3 (continued)

Country, period and currency unit	Military budget expenditure	Net domestic product[a]	Gross fixed investment[b]	Military budget expenditure as percentage of	
				Net domestic product	Gross fixed investment
Yugoslavia (million dinars):					
1957	158,300	1,829,400	550,000		
1958	178,500	1,833,600	587,000		
1959	195,600	2,269,000	750,000		
Average 1957-1959.....	177,500	1,977,300	639,000	9.0	27.8

SOURCE: Division of General Economic Research and Policies of the United Nations Secretariat, based on official sources.

[a] For differences between the concept of domestic product used in tables 2-1 and 2-2, as compared with table 2-3, see para. 2 of this annex.

[b] In state and co-operative sector, excluding capital repairs. Figures for China (mainland) pertain only to budgetary fixed investment; figures for Eastern Germany exclude co-operative investment from own resources.

[c] Product and investment in 1952 prices.

[d] Investment in 1959 prices.

[e] Before exchange of 1961.

[f] Product in 1960 prices.

Annex 3

ANALYTICAL TABLES ILLUSTRATING CERTAIN HYPOTHETICAL ECONOMIC CHANGES DURING DISARMAMENT

TABLES FOR CHAPTERS 4 AND 5

Table 3-1
CHANGES IN EMPLOYMENT IN THE UNITED STATES FOLLOWING A REALLOCATION[a]
OF MILITARY EXPENDITURE, 1958

Production sectors	Change in employment in man years (thousands)	As percentage of employment in the production sector
(a) *Showing decline*		
Armed forces	−2,532	100.0
Civilian employment of military agencies........	−791	100.0
Aircraft and parts............................	−705	93.1
Radio	−172	31.6
Ordnance	−142	100.0
Ships and boats..............................	−137	57.1
Instruments	−31	12.6
All others	−133	...
TOTAL DECLINE	*−4,642*	...
(b) *Showing increase*		
Non-military government service and domestic service	1,196	
Trade	752	7.9
Professional and service......................	565	7.6
Restaurants, hotels, amusements................	244	9.4
Banking, finance	204	8.6
Business services	136	5.2
Railroads, trucking	64	3.5
Automobile and other repairs..................	28	7.9
Other transportation	16	3.1
Construction	188	7.1
Food products	77	8.0
Textile mill	58	6.4
Lumber, wood products........................	50	5.1
Motor vehicles	34	5.3
Livestock, poultry	31	7.3
Non-metallic minerals	27	4.2
All others	344	...
TOTAL INCREASE	*4,014*	...

SOURCE: Based on data in W. Leontief and M. Hoffenberg, "The Economic Effects of Disarmament", *Scientific American*, April 1961.
[a] The estimates relate to reallocation of total military purchases to each demand category proportionally to its 1958 share.

Table 3-2
INFLUENCE OF DISARMAMENT[a] ON VARIOUS INDUSTRIAL SECTORS
IN THE UNITED KINGDOM, 1959

Industrial sector	Changes in net output		
		As percentage of	
	£ million 1959	Gross national product	Net output of sector
I. *Showing declines*			
Military services	−547	−2.7	−100.0
Ships, aircraft, etc.	−124	−0.6	−19.8
TOTAL	−671		

Table 3-2 (continued)

		Changes in net output		
			As percentage of	
Industrial sector		£ million 1959	Gross national product	Net output of sector

II. *Showing expansion*

Industrial sector	£ million 1959	Gross national product	Net output of sector
Distribution	126	0.3	4.9
Transport	42	0.2	2.6
Other services	24	0.3	0.5
Engineering	96	0.5	4.6
Building	84	0.4	7.1
Motors	59	0.3	13.9
Textiles	47	0.3	8.7
Metals	43	0.2	6.4
Coal, etc.	38	0.2	4.1
Chemicals	33	0.1	5.2
Food	33	0.2	4.0
Agriculture	30	0.2	3.5
Other manufactures	27	0.2	3.5
Clothing	20	0.1	6.0
Gas, water, electricity	19	0.1	3.5
Wood	11	0.1	5.6
TOTAL	732		

SOURCE: Unpublished study by the University of Cambridge, Department of Applied Economics.
ᵃ Assuming that armament expenditure is distributed equally among personal consumption, capital formation and foreign aid.

Table 3-3

DIRECT AND INDIRECT MILITARY DEMAND FOR SELECTED RAW MATERIALS
(*As percentage of their total world supply 1958 and 1959*)

	1958 U.S. military demandᵃ		Estimated aggregate military demand of industrial countriesᵇ	
	1958	1959	1958	1959
	Column 1	Column 2	Column 3	Column 4
Crude Petroleum	4.5	4.1	8.9	8.3
Natural rubber (crude)	1.5	1.4	3.0	2.9
Metallic ores:				
Copper	7.8	7.4	15.7	14.7
Nickel	6.0	4.8	12.0	9.5
Tin	4.9	4.7	9.8	9.3
Lead and zinc	4.7	4.7	9.4	9.4
Molybdenum	4.2	3.4	8.3	6.8
Bauxite	3.5	3.3	7.1	6.6
Iron ore	2.6	2.5	5.3	4.9
Manganese	1.3	1.3	2.7	2.6
Chromite	1.1	1.1	2.3	2.2

SOURCES AND METHODS: Direct and indirect military demand for raw material was computed from the worksheets for "The Economic Effects of Disarmament"

Continued

Table 3-3 (footnotes, continued)

(by W. W. Leontief and Marvin Hoffenberg, *Scientific American,* April, 1961) obtained from the Harvard Economics Research Project. World supplies of natural rubber are from *Rubber Statistical Bulletin,* 16:2 (November 1961), p. 2. World supplies of mineral are from U.S. Department of the Interior, *Minerals Yearbook,* 1959, vol. I, pp. 124, 125.

[a] Generated by $41,585 million of goods and services purchased under the U.S. military budget of 1958.

[b] As a rough approximation, assumed to be equal to twice the U.S. military expenditure.

Table 3-4

CHANGE IN WORLD DEMAND FOR SELECTED RAW MATERIALS AFTER PROPORTIONAL
REALLOCATION OF MILITARY PURCHASES TO OTHER DEMAND CATEGORIES

(As percentage of world supply, 1958 and 1959)

Item	After reallocating 1958 United States military purchases[a]		After reallocating 1958 military purchases of industrial countries[b]	
	1958	*1959*	*1958*	*1959*
Crude petroleum	−0.09	−0.08	−0.18	−0.16
Natural rubber (crude)..................	0.05	0.05	0.10	0.09
Metallic ores:				
Copper	−0.96	−0.90	−1.92	−1.81
Nickel	−0.76	−0.60	−1.51	−1.21
Tin	−0.33	−0.32	−0.67	−0.63
Lead and zinc.......................	−0.32	−0.32	−0.64	−0.64
Molybdenum	−0.06	−0.05	−0.11	−0.09
Bauxite	−0.52	−0.48	−1.04	−0.96
Iron ore	−0.04	−0.03	−0.07	−0.07
Manganese	−0.02	−0.02	−0.04	−0.04
Chromite	−0.02	−0.02	−0.03	−0.03

SOURCE: See table 3-3. The figures in this table were derived by multiplying the appropriate entries in table 3-3 by those in column 2 of W. Leontief and M. Hoffenberg, op. cit., table 8.

[a] Equal to $41,585,000,000.

[b] Assumed equal to twice the United States military expenditure.

SUGGESTED QUESTIONS FOR SEMINAR DISCUSSION

The UN Report is based on the assumption "that disarmament once agreed upon, would be general and complete and also rapid." Do you think it is an accurate assumption to make? What prerequisites must exist for this assumption to hold good?

As a result of disarmament, the heavily arming countries' defense related expenditures abroad and defense related imports of raw materials and other commodities will completely stop and this will have several consequences for certain other countries. The UN Report expects the disarmament planning by every country to give due considerations to these problems of the world at large. In fact, the UN Report mainly focuses its attention on the resource-absorption after disarmament on the world level and tries to convince the reader that there exists a complete harmony between the two. Their conception might be said to be various "world economies armed" and one "world economy disarmed." It thus expects quite a high degree of co-operation and coordination between the countries of the world. Do you think that it is achievable? To what extent can this task be entrusted to the UN? Review the Clark-Sohn discussion of a World Development Authority and the readings in Session VI.

Although "in the long run, there should be little difficulty in adapting resources to needs," the real problems arise in the short run when it "takes time to turn swords into plough-shares or to make an office clerk or factory worker out of a soldier." In your opinion does the UN Report give enough attention to these transitional problems of disarmament or problems of "rapid disarmament shock" to the economy?

Total disarmament of the U.S. in a short time period would bring about various economic imbalances--imbalances in the industrial structure, imbalances in the regional economies and imbalances in the resource-capabilities and demand-patterns. What other structural imbalances and problems do you foresee and what efforts would be needed to resolve all of these structural problems?

Disarmament means complete cessation of military expenditures and hence release of equipment, manpower and other resources. In order to keep them employed, the community's consumption expenditures shall have to be raised. What methods do the reports suggest to do this? Do you regard these methods as adequate?

Government expenditures can be varied in quantities, timing and phasing. This characteristic of government expenditures endows it with the advantages of an instrument for combating depressions and booms. It thus makes it a good stabilizer tool. Total disarmament will mean cessation of military expenditures which presently form a large proportion of government expenditures. Do you think that disarmament places a definite limit on our abilities towards stabilization policy? What "other" forms of government expenditures can act as a substitute (perhaps better) for military expenditures? What will be the effect of this substitution on stabilization policy? Will they lead to more government interference into the free working of the economy? Are they politically feasible programs for the United States?

Defense expenditures in advanced countries have been regarded by some economists as a way of keeping the resources busy which otherwise would be idle and which might thus become a cause for the stagnation of the free enterprise system. What other factors might keep up the growth rate of the advanced capitalist economy without any additional encroachment of government into the sphere of private enterprise?

Both reports recommend that foreign aid to underdeveloped countries be substantially increased as resources are released from armaments. Even a small amount (relatively) of present foreign aid is creating some economic problems --especially outflow of gold, adverse balance of payments, etc. What problems will arise with larger foreign aid? To what extent can we make use of the present organizational and financial machinery of the UN and other international organizations to solve these problems? Or will new organizations predicated on greater integration and cooperation among states be needed?

Defense expenditures at present support a great proportion of scientific research and technological developments. Will the cessation of these expenditures affect the pace of these in any way--either by affecting the necessity and zeal to work for them or by affecting the amount of support for them? What can be done to smooth the transition in this sector of the economy?

The conversion from war-uses to peace-uses of the resources hardly poses any serious economic problems in view of our experiences of the post-war and post-Korean War conversions. Do you accept this statement? What special factors would you consider in projecting these past experiences into the total disarmament conversion in the context of the 1960's?

Try to enumerate the full range of groups in the U.S. that might be opposed to disarmament on grounds of the social and economic consequences resulting therefrom. Try listing the full range of reasons which these groups will offer. Is it possible to develop a program that will meet all these objections? Is it necessary to meet these objections? What groups are in a good position to benefit immediately from the social and economic consequences of disarmament? *

BIBLIOGRAPHY

See the basic works listed at the end of Sessions VIII and IX for some articles on the ECONOMIC CONSEQUENCES OF DISARMAMENT. In addition there are the following:

Benoit, Emile. Economic Adjustments to Disarmament. NY: Institute for International Order, 1961, 24 p. While disarmament is basically a political issue, economic analysis can help us carry out the decisions made on non-economic grounds.
_____. "The Propensity to Reduce the National Debt out of Defense Savings." Am. Econ. Review LI: 455-59 (May 1961).
Boulding, Kenneth E. "Economic Implications of Arms Control," in Arms Control, Disarmament and National Security, ed. by Donald Brennan. NY: Braziller, 1961, pp. 153-164.
Chase, Stuart. "Peace, It's Terrible! Economic Consequences of Peace," "Peace, It Could Be Wonderful." Progressive 24: 17-19 (Jan. 1960), 15-17 (Feb. 1960).
Colm, Gerhard. "Economic Implications of Disarmament." Illinois Business Review 14: 6-8 (July 1957).
Fishman, Leslie. "A Note on Disarmament and Effective Demand." J. Political Economy LXX: 183-6 (Apr. 1962).
Harris, Seymour E. "The Economics of Disarmament." Current History 33: 216-20 (Oct. 1957).
Leontif, W. and M. Hoffenberg. "The Economic Effects of Disarmament." Scientific American 204: 47-55 (April 1961).
Lombardi, Ricardo. "Disarmament and the American Economy." Review International Affairs 11: 10-12 (Mar. 1960).
Piel, Gerard. "The Economics of Disarmament." Bul. Atomic Scientists 16: 117-22 (Apr. 1960).
Schelling, T. C. "Arms Control Will Not Cut Defense Costs." Harvard Business Review 39: 6-15 (Mar. -Apr. 1961).
Seligman, Ben R. "Can the U.S. Reconvert to Peace?" Dissent 7: 12-16 (Winter 1960).

*The editor wishes to acknowledge the help of Vedt Gandhi in preparing this session. Mr. Gandhi, formerly of Hans Raj College, Delhi, is at present in the economics department at Harvard University.

REVIEW AND SUGGESTIONS FOR FURTHER STUDY

The purpose of this seminar has been to bring responsible and thoughtful persons together to study what might be done now to establish a s t a b l e system of peace for the evolving world community. Our perspective has been that of evaluating how law might be u s e d to achieve and maintain world order. We looked at a wide range of legal devices, compared t h e present United Nations structure with a comprehensive and detailed model for world legal structure which included a program a n d organization for complete a n d general disarmament, and we asked whether it was necessary and feasible to move, and how rapidly, from the present operation of the U n i t e d N a t i o n s to that model. While it is unlikely that seminar members will have arrived at complete agreement on all m a t t e r s discussed, it is hoped that this joint study and discussion buttresses attitudes which recognize the immensely formidable task of organizing for a peaceful world but b e l i e v e that it is within our capacity to accomplish it. As such, this seminar should be viewed as a foundation both for further study and for rational action.

In dealing with the problem of war prevention in a limited number of s e s s i o n s as we did, it was necessary to slight and o m i t certain matters relevant to the discussion. This session is intended to provide an opportunity for members of the seminar to cover some of these topics. Listed below are a number of subjects from which you might choose. The list is by no means exhaustive a n d it is strongly urged that seminar groups select their own topics in light of their own inclinations and previous discussion.

1) There have been t w o omissions from Clark and Sohn which some of you may wish to discuss. The first is Annex VI d e a l i n g with Privileges and Immunities. The other is Annex VII which is e n t i t l e d Bill of Rights. A word about this latter Annex may be appropriate. The entire thrust of this course has been in the direction of setting up rules and structures which would c o n t r o l and regulate the activitie s of states and individuals. To be sure, the activity to be regulated is violence and therefore its regulation is a l m o s t non-controversial as a goal; in addition, the Clark and Sohn m o d e l placed a constant emphasis upon express limitation of any organization to control or r e g u l a t e behavior which did not lead to t h r e a t or use of force by states. How important these ideas and values are to i n d i v i d u a l s in their societies and to the e s t a b l i s h m e n t of world peace needs investigation; however, for many of us in Western societies, an important aspect of law has been its use in protecting the individual from the misuse of power from politically organized society.

2) Regionalism; see the remarks in the Foreword in regard to this topic.

3) There are a number of problem areas which might be said to bear upon a good deal of the matter we have talked about but which have entered our discussion only tangentially. What major forces are at work which have significant but diffuse impact upon the problem of preventing war and establishing peace? Here is a partial listing: Population explosion including potential breakthrough in biology on the problem of aging and significant increase in longevity; the scientific revolution, including potentialities for inexpensive energy, instantaneous world-wide communication, and inexpensive and rapid world-wide transportation; uses of outer space.

4) A final and important omission has been a systematic investigation of the major contemporary international political issues. A study of the problem of world order from that perspective could be quite rewarding. This is especially true in connection with the problems of disarmament and it would be useful to discuss the following set of questions: What problems must be solved prior to disarmament? What political issues can we solve as we move through disarmament? And what problems may we permit to remain between nations without diminishing the acceptability or administration of disarmament?

A Final Word

Throughout this course we have been dealing with the general problem of acceptability of proposals to political officials and peoples of the world. In one sense the entire problem of transition from a world in which force and violence are used by nations to a peaceful world may be viewed as a problem of acceptability. Listed below are three general questions which might be useful in initiating discussion from this perspective.

What is the relationship in different societies of the individuals to the official solution of these problems? To what extent must they work through their existing officials, and to what extent may they go beyond them?

To what extent are the officials and people of the US willing to accept an effective world structure for a disarmed world under law of the type proposed by Clark and Sohn?

Readings from World Peace Through World Law:
 Privileges and Immunities, Bill of Rights, xxxix-xl,
 359-370.

THE UNITED NATIONS AT PRESENT

As of January 1961

INTER-NATIONAL ATOMIC ENERGY AGENCY

OPERATION IN CONGO

GENERAL ASSEMBLY

SECURITY COUNCIL

TRUSTEESHIP COUNCIL

ECONOMIC AND SOCIAL COUNCIL

INTERNATIONAL COURT OF JUSTICE

SECRETARIAT

MILITARY STAFF COMMITTEE
DISARMAMENT COMMISSION

UNITED NATIONS ADMINISTRATIVE TRIBUNAL

UNITED NATIONS SCIENTIFIC ADVISORY COMMITTEE
SCIENTIFIC COMMITTEE ON EFFECTS OF ATOMIC RADIATION
COMMITTEE ON THE PEACEFUL USES OF OUTER SPACE
COMMITTEE ON INFORMATION FROM NON-SELF-GOVERNING TERRITORIES
INTERNATIONAL LAW COMMISSION
ADVISORY COMMITTEE ON ADMINISTRATIVE AND BUDGETARY QUESTIONS
COMMITTEE ON CONTRIBUTIONS
OTHER SUBSIDIARY BODIES OF GENERAL ASSEMBLY

UNITED NATIONS EMERGENCY FORCE
UNITED NATIONS RELIEF AND WORKS AGENCY FOR PALESTINE REFUGEES
UNITED NATIONS SPECIAL FUND
UNITED NATIONS CHILDREN'S FUND (UNICEF)
OFFICE OF UNITED NATIONS HIGH COMMISSIONER FOR REFUGEES
REGIONAL ECONOMIC COMMISSIONS
FUNCTIONAL COMMISSIONS

ADMINISTRATIVE COMMITTEE ON COORDINATION
TECHNICAL ASSISTANCE BOARD

THE SPECIALIZED AGENCIES

INTERNATIONAL LABOUR ORGANISATION
FOOD AND AGRICULTURE ORGANIZATION OF THE UNITED NATIONS
INTERNATIONAL CIVIL AVIATION ORGANIZATION
UNITED NATIONS EDUCATIONAL, SCIENTIFIC AND CULTURAL ORGANIZATION
UNIVERSAL POSTAL UNION
WORLD HEALTH ORGANIZATION
INTERNATIONAL TELECOMMUNICATION UNION
INTERNATIONAL MONETARY FUND
WORLD METEOROLOGICAL ORGANIZATION
INTERNATIONAL BANK FOR RECONSTRUCTION AND DEVELOPMENT
INTER-GOVERNMENTAL MARITIME CONSULTATIVE ORGANIZATION
INTERNATIONAL FINANCE CORPORATION
INTERNATIONAL TRADE ORGANIZATION General Agreement on Tariffs and Trade

Adapted from *Yearbook of the United Nations 1959*, with permission of the UN

857

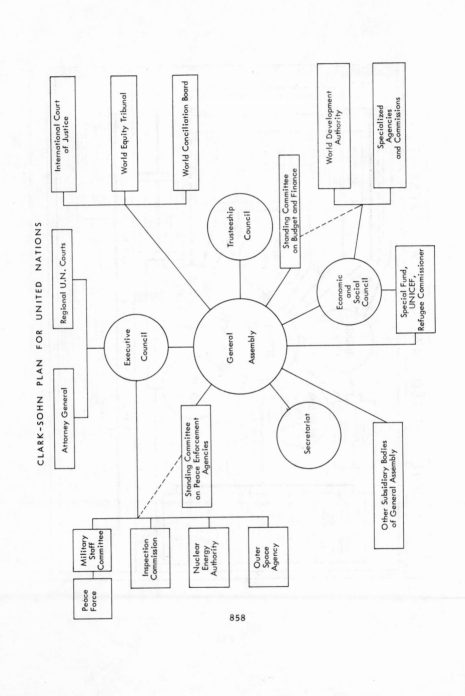

CLARK-SOHN PLAN FOR UNITED NATIONS

International Court of Justice

World Equity Tribunal

World Conciliation Board

Regional U.N. Courts

Attorney General

Executive Council

Trusteeship Council

Standing Committee on Budget and Finance

World Development Authority

Specialized Agencies and Commissions

General Assembly

Economic and Social Council

Special Fund, UNICEF, Refugee Commissioner

Secretariat

Standing Committee on Peace Enforcement Agencies

Peace Force

Military Staff Committee

Inspection Commission

Nuclear Energy Authority

Outer Space Agency

Other Subsidiary Bodies of General Assembly